CITIES AND CHURCHES

an international bibliography

Volume III, 1980–1991
& Indexes

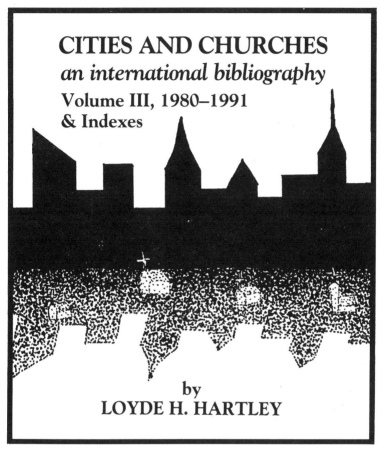

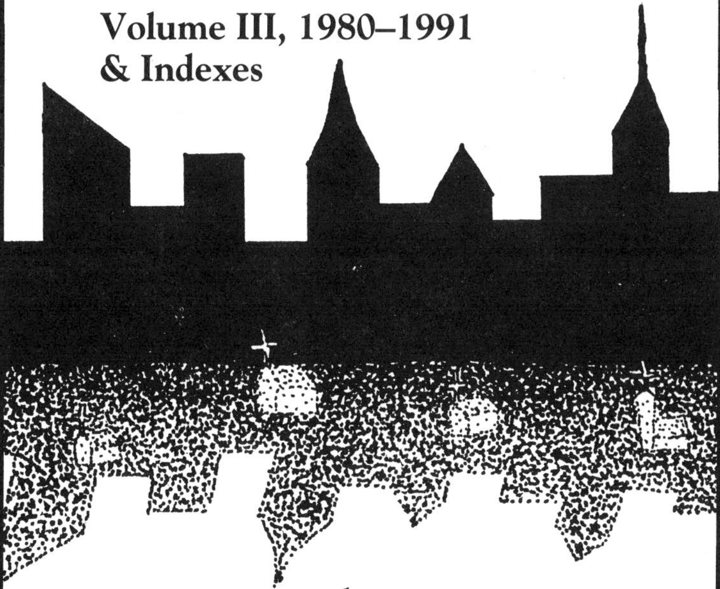

by
LOYDE H. HARTLEY

foreword by Martin E. Marty

ATLA Bibliography Series, No. 31

American Theological
Library Association
and
The Scarecrow Press, Inc.
Metuchen, N.J., & London
1992

Title page/cover illustration by
Catherine A. Hartley

Manufactured in the United States of America
Printed on acid-free paper

8. Urban Ethnic Church Predominance: 1980-1991

An Overview of Trends

The trend toward increased Black political and social influence in cities accelerated during the 1980s. The proportion of urban Black churches also increased. Riverside Church, New York City, called its first Black pastor in 1990.

Other ethnic churches also grew rapidly in US cities during the 1980s, but the proportion of the total USA population living in large cities decreased. Some urban church buildings housed several different ethnic congregations. One congregation in Queens, New York City, accommodated Haitian, Korean, Indian, and White congregations in its building. The original White congregation, which continued to own the property and rent to the other groups, had only six remaining members. Whites had completely abandoned many parts of the large cities, but remained in some of the central districts of smaller metropolitan areas.

Homelessness reemerged and became an urban commonplace, the homeless having nowhere else but cities to turn for food and shelter. Some of the homeless had been discharged from mental health institutions when government funding was shut off. Some came from middle class backgrounds, their financial woes being traceable to changing economic trends over which they had no control. Others became homeless because of domestic or health problems. The number of church sponsored shelters increased dramatically, but not rapidly enough to meet the need.

Mainline White churches continued to withdraw from the central cities, although a few remained and even prospered by adopting a pioneering spirit or by attracting a "gentrified" membership. The number of evangelical Protestant urban missions increased. Evangelicals continued also to increase their numbers of suburban congregations, while Mainline church extension virtually stopped in both cities and suburbs. Renewed interest in urban ministry was stimulated in Britain by the Archbishop of Canterbury's Commission on Urban Priority Areas (1985). Excessively rapid urbanization in Africa, Asia, and Latin America stimulated new church strategies in those regions.

A Chronology of Key Events and Publications

1980 Lausanne Consultation on World Evangelism held, with "mini-consultations" on urban issues
1980 Crystal Cathedral, Garden Grove, CA, erected
1980 Antonio Stevens-Arroyo published Prophets Denied Honor: An Anthology on the Hispano Church in the United States
1980 James H. Davis and Woodie White published Racial Transition in the Church
1981 John J. Vincent published Starting All Over Again, Hints of Jesus in the City
1981 Michael Paget-Wilkes,published Poverty, Revolution and the Church
1981 Cities Magazine commenced publication
1982 Donald L. Benedict (b. 1917) published Born Again Radical
1982 Claude S. Fisher published To Dwell Among Friends: Personal Networks in Town and City
1982 Ronald D. Pasquariello, et al, published Redeeming the City: Theology, Politics, and Urban Policy
1982 Benjamin Tonna published A Gospel for the City
1982 Larry L. Rose and C. Kirk Hadaway published The Urban Challenge
1982 John J. Vincent published Into the City
1982 Homelessness became a newly noticed and important issue in the USA
1983 Urban Mission, a periodical sponsored by Westminster Theological Seminary, commenced publication
1983 G. Willis Bennett published Guidelines for Effective Urban Church Ministry
1983 John P. Egan and Paul D. Colford published Baptism of Resistance, Blood and Celebration
1983 David Sheppard published Bias to the Poor

1983 Gordon J. Melton published Encyclopedic Handbook of Cults in America
1983 City Cries, journal of the Evangelical Coalition for Urban Mission (London), commenced publication
1983 Wayne A. Meeks published The First Urban Christians
1983 Austin Smith published Passion for the Inner City
1983 David Claerbaut published Urban Ministry
1984 Harvie M. Conn published A Clarified Vision for Urban Mission
1984 David Roozen, et al., published Varieties of Religious Presence: Mission in Public Life
1984 World Council of Churches began publishing a periodical on the theme of Urban Rural Mission
1984 Tex Sample published Blue-collar Ministry
1984 Second Urban Congress, sponsored by Seminary Consortium for Urban Pastoral Education (SCUPE)
1984 Harvey Cox published Religion in the Secular City: Towards a Post-Modern Theology
1985 Brother Leonard of Taizé published Listening to the People of Hope
1985 Faith in the City, a report published by the Archbishop of Canterbury's Commission on Urban Priority Areas
1985 Robert Bellah published Habits of the Heart
1986 David B. Barrett published World Class Cities and World Evangelization
1986 Peter Hawkins, et al, published a collection of essays titled Civitas: Religious Interpretations of the City
1987 Raymond Bakke published The Urban Christian
1987 James F. Hopewell's Congregation: Stories and Structures published posthumously
1987 George D. Younger published From New Creation to Urban Crisis, a reflection on the rise and decline of urban action-training centers
1987 Earl E. Shep published AIDS and the Church
1988 David Sheppard and Derek Worlock published Better Together, the story of two bishops, one Anglican and one Roman Catholic, finding a basis for cooperation in Liverpool
1988 Jesse Jackson (b. 1941) ran as a Democraticatic candidate for US President
1988 Philip Amerson publishes Tell Me City Stories as a resources for the Fourth Urban Congress, sponsored by SCUPE
1989 John J. Vincent elected President of the Methodist Church in Great Britain
1989 Cardinal Edmund Szoka published his justification for closing many Detroit, MI, Catholic churches; Catholic and mainline

	Protestant urban church closings were commonplace elsewhere
1990	United Methodist Bishop Felton May spent a sabbatical year in Washington, DC, to work with communities afflicted with the drug problem
1990	Berlin wall torn down
1991	Economic recession deepens in the USA, affecting greatly the middle classes as well as the poor and homeless
1991	USSR dissolved

15331-15332. Abatso, George and Yvonne Abatso. (1980s?) The Black Christian Family. Chicago, IL: Urban Ministries. While preferring the family form with the father as the head, the Abatsos recognize that this ideal often is not the case with Black families. They suggest, in situations where the father abdicates this role, that the wife need not submit to the husband. Chapters deal with communications, problem children, financial management, single parenthood, abuse, and marital stress.

15333. Adams, Kenneth. (1980s) Faith, Wealth and Industry. London: Industrial Christian Fellowship. A pamphlet.

15334. Allen, Jere and George Bullard. (1980) Hope for the Church in the Changing Community. Atlanta, GA: Home Mission Board, Southern Baptist Convention. Allen and Bullard define characteristics of churches in changing communities, list types of community change, offer church typologies, and suggest how to evaluate the stages of a congregation's life cycle. Illustrative surveys are included along with suggestions for constructing a congregation's profile. The SBC produced many similar specialized ministry studies during the 1980s.

15335. Altheimer, Rosenwald Delano. (1980) The Social Implications of the Afro-American Experience in the Roman Catholic Church: An Examination of Attitudes and Habits of Parishioners in Two Inner-city Detroit Churches. Thesis (Ed. D.). Detroit, MI: Wayne State University.

15336. Amberson, Talmadge R. (1980) Reaching Out to People. Nashville, TN: Broadman Press. Written by an urban pastor, this book offers suggestions and strategies, often in the form of anecdotes of success, for ministry among persons living in apartment buildings and in mobile home parks. Bibliography.

15337. Ambler, Rex and David Haslam, eds. (1980) Agenda for Prophets: Towards a Political Theology for Britain. London: Bowerdean Press.

15338. Amerson, Philip A. (1980s) "A Resource Packet for the Urban Congregation," Evansville, IN: Occasional Papers of the Patchwork Community. Amerson provides resources for cooperative urban ministries such as yoked parishes.

15339. Ammerman, Nancy T. (1980) "The Civil Rights Movement and the Clergy in a Southern Community," Sociological Analysis. Vol. 41, No. 4 (Winter), pp. 339-350. In a study of clergy in Tuscaloosa, AL, Ammerman finds that their participation in the civil rights movement correlates with having had a childhood in the city, higher educational attainment, and belonging to a mainline denomination.

15340. Amorim Pimentel, Belardin de. (1980) An Introduction to the Study of the Problem of Urban Evangelism. Rio de Janeiro, Brazil: the author. [Location: Fuller Theological Seminary, Pasadena, CA]. A pamphlet.

15341. Anderson, Clyde. (1980s) Missional Strategy for Black New Church Development. New York: [National Division, Board of Global Ministries, United Methodist Church]. [See note 3]. A privately distributed paper.

15342. Anderson, Lorna. (1980) You and Your Refugee Neighbor. Pasadena, CA: William Carey Library. Anderson calls for greater emphasis on church work with foreigners, immigrants, and refugees.

15343. Anderson, T. Lee. (1980) Church Property/Building Guidebook. Nashville, TN: Convention Press.

15344. Angus, David L. (1980) "Detroit's Great School Wars: Religion and Politics in a Frontier City, 1842-1853," Michigan Academician. Vol. 12, No. 3, pp. 261-280.

15345. Arias, Esther and Mortimer Arias. (1980) The Cry of My People. New York: Friendship Press. Written by Bolivian Methodist leaders. Re: poverty and suffering in Latin America viewed from the perspective of liberation theology. Protestants, evangelicals and Catholics cooperate for the sake of social change.

15346. Askew, Rebecca Ann. (1980) A Study of Catholic Education in a Selected Metropolitan Area. Thesis (Ph. D.). Hattiesburg, MS: University of Southern Mississippi.

15347. Askin, Steve. (1980) "Southern Labor's New Religious Allies," The Christian Century. Vol. 97, No. 35 (November 5), pp. 1068-1071. Southern church involvement in labor concerns is one of the consequences of the J. P. Stevens labor dispute.

15348. Baer, Hans A. (1980) "An Anthropological View of Black Spiritual Churches in Nashville, Tennessee," Central Issues in Anthropology. Vol. 2, No. 2, pp. 53-68.

15349. Bagdon, Philip. (1980) "An Exile in Gotham ... George 'Bill' Webber: Examining Mission Field Mentality for New York," Alternatives. Vol. 8 (April-May), pp. 5+.

15350. Bakke, Raymond J. (1980) "Return to the City," Christian Life. Vol. 42, No. 1 (May), pp. 32-33+.

15351. Barreiro, Alvaro. (1980) "Grass Roots Ecclesial Communities and the Evangelization of the Poor," Foundations. Vol. 23, No. 4 (October), pp. 294-331.

15352. Bauen mit Geschichte: [Dokumentation über den 17. Evangelischen Kirchbautag Lübeck 1979]. (1980) Gütersloh, West Germany: G. Mohn. Re: church extension in Germany.

15353. Baum, Gregory, ed. (1980) Work and Religion. New York: Seabury. Edinburgh, Scotland: Clark. This volume contains articles on the nature of work, the relationship of work to identity, social theory on religion and work (Hegel, Marx, Max Weber), church-labor relations, and the persistence of poverty.

15354. Bavarei, Michael. (1980) Chrétiens du bout du monde. Paris: Cana. English translation: New Communities, New Ministries: The Church Resurgent in Asia, Africa, and Latin America. Maryknoll, NY: Orbis Books, 1983. Reviewed: Missionalia, Vol. 13, No. 1 (April,1985), p. 36.

15355. Beal, John David. (1980) The Urban Church Seeking to Meet Needs of Multifamily Housing Residents. Thesis (D. Min.). Decatur, GA: Columbia Presbyterian Seminary.

15356. Bean, Kevin. (1980s?) A Connecticut Budget for Jobs and Peace. Hartford, CT: Peace Education, Inc. Bean, an Episcopal clergyman who is director of the Naugatuck Valley Project, develops an alternative to the state budget for Connecticut.

15357. Bellah, Robert N. (1980) Varieties of Civil Religion. New

York: Harper and Row. Bellah's discussion of civil religion, while not precisely urban in orientation, has important insights for urban church studies.

15358. Benedict, Donald L. (1980) The Gospel in an Overdeveloped Society. [Sound Recording]. Stahlstown, PA: Thompson Media.

15359. Berckman, Edward M. (1980) "Episcopal Caucus Focuses on Parish," Christian Century. Vol. 97, No. 3 (March 19), p. 312. This brief article on the Episcopal Urban Caucus mentions Youngstown, Ohio, and the bishops' efforts to keep blue collar jobs there.

15360. Beukema, George G. (1980) "What's 'Right' about Urban Churches?" Church Herald. Vol. 37, No. 14 (July 11), pp. 13+.

15361. Borchard, Toti. (n.d., 1980?) Our Experiment in Cinisello. s.l.: A presentation at the WSCF European Education Conference. [Location: ICUIS 4455, see note 2]. Description of the worker's school at Cinisello commune, Milan, Italy.

15362. Borchert, James. (1980) Alley Life in Washington: Family, Community, Religion, and Folklife in the City, 1850-1980. Urbana, IL: University of Illinois Press.

15363. Bosi, Alessandro. (1980) "Mythe et action sociale en Allemagne--Note sur le "Mouvement pour la radio des travailleurs" au temps de la République de Weimar," Social Compass [Thematic issue: The Religion of the Working Class]. Vol. 27, Nos. 2-3, pp. 231-242. Re: the mythic aspects of technology during the time of the Wiemar Republic.

15364. Bowman, James S. (1980) "Whistleblowing in the Public Service: An Overview of the Issues," Review of Public Administration. Vol. 1 (Fall), pp. 15-28.

15365. Boyte, Harry C. (1980) The Backyard Revolution: Understanding the New Citizen Movement. Philadelphia, PA: Temple University Press. Populist citizens' movements are advanced as strategies for addressing urban problems, with some attention given to the church's role in cooperatives, community organizing, and social action. Such movements are urged to root themselves in populist culture. Bibliography and a list of networks for community organizations. See further related works by the same author: Commonwealth: A Return to Citizen Politics. New York: Free Press, 1989; and Moving into Power: Reinvigorating Public Life for the 1990s. Chicago, IL:

Community Renewal Press, Occasional Papers, 1989.

15366. Bracamonte, Jose A. (1980) "Undocumented Workers: Myth, Reality and Responsibility," The City of God. Vol. 2, No. 2 (Fall), pp. 22-34. Re: illegal aliens and their impact on the workforce in the USA.

15367. Brandão, Carlos. (1980) Os deues do povo. São Paulo, Brazil: Brasilense. Gods of the people--religious life in Brazil. Bibliography.

15368. Brewer, Richard L. (1980) Faith-Hope-Love in Christ, Inc. [Miscellaneous materials]. Peoria IL: Faith-Hope-Love in Christ, Inc. [Location: ICUIS 4462, see note 2]. Materials produced by a Christian group in Peoria, IL, concerned with men and women in jails and prisons. The organization grew out of predecessor groups in the United Methodist and Roman Catholic Churches. They operate a half-way house for parolees, counseling services, letter writing services, retreats, Bible studies, devotional materials distribution services, daily jail visits by clergy, ministries with inmates' friends and family, job development programs, and financial counseling services. Their materials offer models for local churches with similar interests. Bibliography.

15369. Bridge Street African Wesleyan Methodist Episcopal Church. (1980) The African Wesleyan Methodist Episcopal Church (Known as Bridge Street AWME Church). New York: the Church.

15370. Britt, David Tillman. (1980) Concepts of Church Growth in the Southern Baptist Convention. Atlanta, GA: Research Division, Home Mission Board, Southern Baptist Convention.

15371. Brown, Sydney T. and Anne McGlinchey. (1980) "East Harlem Interfaith's Boiler Repair Business," Church and Society. Vol. 70, No. 4 (May). [Location: ICUIS collection, see note 2]. East Harlem Interfaith, an ecumenical group of churches in New York City, sponsors projects related to housing rehabilitation, a school of faith, employment programs, and even a boiler repair shop. The repair shop was initiated to show that a small, non-profit, community based business could competently and competitively repair boilers in old tenement houses, thereby providing jobs and serve as an example for others to start similar businesses.

15372. Buckley, Anne. (1980) "The Church and Newark's Inner-City," Our Sunday Visitor Magazine. Vol. 69 (August 10), pp. 4-5+. [See Note 3].

15373. Bullard, George W. (1980) The Development, Use and Evaluation of Processes for Consultation with Churches in Transition in Metropolitan Settings. Thesis (D. Min.). Lousiville, KY: Southern Baptist Theological Seminary.

15374. Bürgel, Rainer. (1980) Bauen mit Geschichte. Gütersloh, West Germany: Gütersloher Verlagshaus, G. Mohn. Re: church development in cities.

15375. Burrows, William R. (1980) New Ministries: The Global Context. Maryknoll, NY: Orbis Books. Burrows, a Divine Word Priest who lived in Papua, New Guinea, observes that the present organization of the church is ill-suited for ministering to urban masses. He advocates a base Christian community approach in rural as well as urban areas.

15376. Calcutta Urban Service. (1980) [Annual Report--1979, and miscellaneous materials]. Calcutta, India: Calcutta Urban Service. [Location: partial file, ICUIS 4508, see note 2]. A report of the serving arm of the church in Calcutta on the occasion of its tenth anniversary reaffirms its goal of bringing hope to the lives of people in the urban slums who suffer silently and indifferently, expecting nothing from the future. Programs include: education, crafts, community service, agricultural development, along with cooperative efforts with other agencies. In addition, eight medical programs are supported: general health education, mother and child health, school health, mobile community health care, nutrition, leprosy control, training for health workers, and health referrals.

15377. Campling, Andrew. (1980) "Calcutta's Fools for Christ," Coracle. No. 80 (February), pp. 9-11. Re: Mother Teresa and others.

15378. "Can Four Women Ministers Start a Co-Op Taxicab Company?" (1980) Christian Century. Vol. 97, No. 2 (January 16), pp. 45-47. Innovations by a church related Community Development Program in New Haven, CT.

15379. Caplan, Lionel. (1980) "Class and Christianity in South India: Indigenous Responses to Western Denominationalism," Modern Asian Studies. Vol. 14, Part 4 (October), pp. 645-671.

15380. Carroll, Jackson W. and Robert Wilson. (1980) Too Many Pastors? Understanding the Clergy Job Market. New York: Pilgrim Press. Written at a time of clergy oversupply to identify options available to clergy and church officials.

15381. Castro, Emilio, ed. (1980-1981) "Melbourne Reports and Reflections," International Review of Mission [Thematic issue]. Vol. 69, Nos. 276-277 (October-January), pp. 377-596.

15382. Childs, John Brown. (1980) The Political Black Minister: A Study in Afro-American Politics and Religion. Boston, MA: G. K. Hall. A case study of three politically active Black clergy in Buffalo, NY. Bibliography.

15383. Chilton, Charles A. (1980s?) Planting the House Church. Baltimore, MD: Prince George's Baptist Association.

15384. Christian Conference of Asia, Urban Rural Mission Office. (1980) Christian Response to Race and Minority Issues in Asia: Proceedings and Findings of a Regional Consultation ... March 24-29, 1980, New Delhi. Hong Kong: Urban Rural Mission, Christian Conference of Asia. [Location: ICUIS 4460, see note 2]. A report dealing with questions of land use, civil rights and cultural identity of racial and minority groups in Asia. Bibliography.

15385. Chung, Si Woo. (1980) Bilingual Needs of the Korean Immigrant Churches in Los Angeles. Thesis (D. Min). Claremont, CA: School of Theology at Claremont.

15386. Church of Scotland. (1980) Into the Eighties: Report of the Joint Working Party on a Programme for Action. Edinburgh, Scotland: Church of Scotland.

15387. "A Church under Fire: Taiwan National Report." (1980) Asian Issues [Tokyo: International Affairs Desk, Christian Conference of Asia]. Series 2, No. 2 (September). [Location: ICUIS 4496, see note 2]. A thematic edition of Asian Issues focuses on the crisis of the Presbyterian Church in Taiwan. Rev. Kao Chun-Ming and others were on trial in military court for harboring a fugitive accused of plotting the overthrow of the government. Asian Issues depicts the crisis as a circumstance in which the church must choose whether to be faithfully obedient to the government or to adopt the servant role in God's efforts to redeem human society.

15388. The Church's Growing Edge, Single Adults: A Planning Guide. (1980) New York: United Church Press.

15389. The Cinisello Community [Milan, Italy]. (n. d., 1980?) s.l.: Christian Communes. [Location: ICUIS 4454, see note 2]. A British observer comments on the Cinisello commune and its educational program for young workers in Milan, Italy. Emphasis is placed on the ministry of Protestant churches in Italy.

15390. Cipriani, Roberto. (1980) "Tendances récentes dans les recherches sur la thème 'Religion et classe ourvrière,'" Social Compass [Thematic issue: The Religion of the Working Class]. Vol. 27, Nos. 2-3, pp. 297-306. A comparison of case studies on working class attitudes toward religion and the church.

15391. City Lutherans in Action. (beginning in the 1980s) Just Cities: City Lutherans in Action. Detroit, MI: City Lutherans in Action. An independent periodical published by a groups of urban-minded Lutherans lists conferences and news of Lutheran urban ministry.

15392. Clarebaut, David. (1980) "A Theology for Ministry to the Urban Poor," Covenant Quarterly. Vol. 38, No. 2 (May), pp. 29-37.

15393. Clark, Tony. (1980) Communities for Justice: A Look at New Principles and Forms of Ecclesiology Emerging in the Canadian Experience. Toronto, Canada: Proceedings of the 1979 Conference, Institute for Christian Life in Canada. [Location: ICUIS 4456, see note 2]. Small Christian communities have organized in Canada around assorted justice issues, e.g., poverty, unemployment, workers' rights, native peoples' issues, immigration, hunger, prison reform, disarmament, housing problems, nuclear energy, development of the northlands, regional disparities, etc. Clark describes the communities and gives examples. Bibliography.

15394. Clarke, Tina. (1980s) Concern into Action: An Advocacy Guide for People of Faith. Washington, DC: National Impact. Suggestions for developing advocacy ministries on local and national levels.

15395. Clarkson, Kathy. (1980) "Unconventional Evictions," The Catholic Worker. Vol. 46, No. 7 (September). Over 36,000 people, including children, live in New York City's parks, subways, and abandoned buildings. Holy Name Society, a ministry run by Archdiocesan priests, buried 74 homeless men in the Bowery section alone. On the evening of the Democratic National Convention, the homeless were thrown out of Penn Station, a gathering point for many, in order to give the city a more pleasant appearance for the visiting politicians. As a response, a vigil was begun at a nearby Catholic church to commemorate the homeless who die in the streets.

15396. Cleveland Covenant. (1980) The Cleveland Covenant

Concept [Papers, materials]. Cleveland Heights, OH: Cleveland Covenant. [Location: ICUIS 4730, see note 2]. Henry Anderson, pastor of the Fairmount Presbyterian Church in Cleveland Heights, OH, convenes a groups of business leaders for bible study, prayer, and discussion of their visions for Cleveland.

15397. Cochran, John R. (1980) "Church Renewal in the Eucharist," Center City Lutheran Parish News. Vol. 16 (March), p. 1.

15398. Cohn, J. (1980) "Demographic Studies of Jewish Communities in the United States: A Bibliographic Introduction and Survey," American Jewish Archives. Vol. 32, No. 1 (April), pp. 35-50. [See note 3].

15399. Collins, Sheila. (1980) "Faith in the People," Response: United Methodist Women. Vol. 12, No. 8 (September), pp. 17-19. Background and philosophy of the People's Advocacy Service of Schenectady, NY, a United Methodist and Roman Catholic supported advocacy and organizing center.

15400. Conwill, Giles A. (1980) "Development of Black Religious Vocations," The City of God. Vol. 2, No. 1 (Summer), pp. 47-60.

15401. Cooper, Howard and Dan Wooding. (1980) Miracles in Sin City. Orange, CA: Christian Resource Associates. Evangelistic work and city missions produce results in Reno, Nevada.

15402. Cork, Delores Freeman. (1980) Farming the Inner City for Christ, The Gladys Farmer Story. Nashville, TN: Broadman. A recounting of the life of Gladys Farmer describes the mission of the Baptist Center in Montgomery, AL.

15403. Corneck, Graham, Tim Foreman, Maureen Vitler, and Paul Felton. (1980) "When Words Fail," pp. 154-158 in Jeanne Hinton, ed. Renewal: An Emerging Pattern. Poole, England: Celebration Press.

15404. Cortese, Anthony Joseph Paul. (1980) Ethnic Ethics: Subjective Choice and Inference in Chicano and Black Children. Thesis (Ph. D.). Notre Dame, IN: University of Notre Dame.

15405. "Covenant House Always Overwhelmed." (1980) World Vision. Vol. 24, No. 9 (September), p. 20.

15406. Crecelius, Daniel. (1980) "The Course of Secularization in

Modern Egypt," pp. 49-70 in John L. Esposito, ed. Islam and Development: Religion and Sociopolitical Change. Syracuse, NY: Syracuse University Press.

15407. Crowder, Roy B. and John J. Vincent. (1980) Inner City Issues [LISS Occasional Papers]. Liverpool, England: Liverpool Institute of Socio-Religious Studies. A critical assessment of the different explanations of urban problems and their accompanying methods of change, for use by Christian groups who want to make some sense out of the myriad competing groups trying to do something about the inner city. Bibliography.

15408. Cunningham, W. J. (1980) Agony with Social Change: One Church's Struggle with Social Change. Jackson, MS: University Press of Mississippi. A Methodist church in Jackson, MS, struggles with race relations and community changes.

15409. Curran, Thomas J. (1980) The Irish Family in Nineteenth Century Urban America: The Role of the Catholic Church. Working Paper Series. Notre Dame, IN: Center for the Study of American Catholicism, University of Notre Dame.

15410. Dale, Robert D. (1980) The Urban Pastor as Leader: Occasional Paper of the Metropolitan Missions Board. Atlanta, GA: Home Mission Board, The Southern Baptist Convention. Dale lists "coach" as the most effective leadership style for city clergy and speaks positively about such often rejected leadership styles as joker, dictator, workaholic, and hermit.

15411. Daly, Gabriel. (1980) Transcendence and Immanence: A Study in Catholic Modernism. New York: Clarendon.

15412. Davis, Dewitt. (1980) "A Geographic Perspective of Jewish Attitudes towards Neighborhood Transition: A Core Study," Geographical Perspectives. Vol. 45 (Spring), pp. 35-48.

15413. Davis, James Hill and Woodie W. White. (1980) Racial Transition in the Church. Nashville, TN: Abingdon. This volume reports research in 20 cities and 100 congregations over a period of six years, and shows churches to be uneasy with racial transitions. The authors list a developmental set of stages for community and church change and relate how racial transition impacts a church's program, role in the community, self image, membership, and dynamic patterns. They identify practical consequences for church finances and property. Local churches that assume, erroneously, they are immune from changes in their neighborhood run risk of closing. A chapter on gentrification is included. Bibliography.

15414. Davis, John. (1980s) A Good Worker, a Good Christian Worker--What's the Difference? London: Industrial Christian Fellowship. A pamphlet.

15415. Davis, Winston. (1980) "The Secularization of Japanese Religion: Measuring the Myth and the Reality," pp. 261-285 in Frank E. Reynolds, ed. Transitions and Transformations. Lieden, The Netherlands: E. J. Brill.

15416. Dawes, Gil. (1980) "Raising Our Sights in the Class War: A Speech to the United Auto Workers," Radical Religion. Vol. 5, No. 2, pp. 24-29.

15417. Dayton, Edward R. and David A. Fraser. (1980) Planning Strategies for World Evangelization. Grand Rapids, MI: Eerdmans.

15418. DeBoer, John C. (1980) Energy Conservation Manual for Congregations. New York: Joint Strategy and Action Committee, [National Council of Churches]. A manual for congregations not familiar with the language and hardware of energy conservation.

15419. Dempsey, Jan. (1980) "Breakthrough in a Transitional Community: First Congregational Church of Revere, MA," New England Journal of Ministry. Vol. 1, No. 1 (December), pp. 44-51.

15420. Denk, Hans Dieter. (1980) Die christliche Arbeiterbewegung in Bayern bis zum Weltkrieg. Mainz, West Germany: Matthias-Grünewald-Verlag. Re: the Christian worker's movement in Bavaria before the World War.

15421. Deroo, André. (1980) Un missionnaire du travail: le Père Stéphane-Joseph Piat, Franciscain. Paris: Editions Franciscaines. Re: church and labor.

15422. DeSilva, Ranjit Nihal. (1980) Discipling the Cities in Sri Lanka: A Challenge to the Church Today. Thesis (MA). Pasadena, CA: Fuller Theological Seminary, School of World Mission.

15423. Doig, Desmond. (1980) "Mother Teresa's Universe," World Press Review. Vol. 27, No. 2 (February), pp. 36-37.

15424. Donnison, David Vernon and Paul Soto. (1980) The Good

City: A Study of Urban Development and Policy in Britain. London: Heinemann Educational.

15425. Dougherty, James. (1980) The Fivesquare City: The City in the Religious Imagination. Notre Dame, IN: Notre Dame Press. Bibliography.

15426. Driedger, Leo. (1980) "Jewish Identity: The Maintenance of Urban Religious and Ethnic Boundaries," Ethnic and Racial Studies [England]. Vol. 3, No. 1 (January), pp. 67-88. Re: Jews in Canada.

15427. Duchrow, Ulrich. (1980) "L'église entre l'adaptation à la société et l'imitation du Christ," Revue de Théologie et de Philosophie. Vol. 112 (3rd Series: 30), No. 3, pp. 253-270.

15428. Dumas, Lloyd J., Cliff Aron, Peter Fisher, and William Winpisinger. (1980) "Economic Conversion from Military to Civilian Industry," JSAC Grapevine. Vol. 11, No. 7 (November), pp. [1-5]. The arms race not only threatens human life but also contributes to economic decline in cities.

15429. Durham, James Edward. (1980) The Place of Preaching in the Delaware Street Baptist Church as a Means of Changing Congregational Attitudes toward Ministry in the Community. Thesis (D. Min.). Madison, NJ: Drew University.

15430. du Toit, Brian M. (1980) "Religion, Ritual, and Healing among Urban Black South Africans," Urban Anthropology. Vol. 9, No. 1 (Spring), pp. 21-50.

15431. Dwan, Peter. (1980) Mother Teresa: Apostle of the Unwanted. London: Catholic Truth Society. A pamphlet.

15432. Egan, Eileen. (1980) "Mother Teresa, the Myth and the Person," America. Vol. 142, No. 11 (March 22), pp. 239-243. Reply: Vol. 143, No. 4 (August 16-23), pp. 74-75.

15433. Ehara, Jun. (1980) Ministry to the Japanese Ethnic Community in the United States of America. Thesis (D. Min.). Claremont, CA: School of Theology at Claremont.

15434. Eller, Vernard. (1980) The Outward Bound: Caravaning as the Style of the Church. Grand Rapids, MI: Eerdmans.

15435. Elliott, John Y. (1980) Our Pastor Has an Outside Job.

Valley Forge, PA: Judson Press.

15436. Ellis, Bryan. (1980) "Corporate Witness in the Inner-City," pp. 71-76 in Jeanne Hinton, ed. Renewal: An Emerging Pattern. Poole, Dorset, England: Celebration Publishing.

15437. Ellis, Norman. (1980s?) The Church Is Dead! Long Live the Church! Don Mills, Ontario, Canada: N. Ellis.

15438. Ellison, Craig W. (1980) "The Concrete Mission Field," HIS. Vol. 40, No. 6 (March), pp. 16-18.

15439. Elwood, Douglas J. (1980) Asian Christian Theology: Emerging Themes. Philadelphia, PA: Westminster.

15440. Elwyn, Thornton. (1980) Theological Training for Industrial Ministry. London: Churches' Consortium on Industrial Mission. [Location: ICUIS 4802, see note 2]. Elwyn surveys the training available in Britain for industrial ministries and stresses the need for better preordination in-service training for social mission. Illustrations of training programs are included.

15441. Episcopal City Mission Society, St. Barnabas Multi-Service Senior Center. (1980?) A Directory of Housing Options for Senior Citizens. Los Angeles, CA: Episcopal City Mission Society.

15442. "Episcopalians Recently Established a Church Structure for Ministry to the Cities." (1980) Christianity Today. Vol. 24, No. 7 (April 4), p. 49.

15443. Estivill, Jordi and Gustav Barbat. (1980) "L'anticléricalisme populaire en Catalogne au début du siècle," Social Compass [Thematic issue: The Religion of the Working Class]. Vol. 27, Nos. 2-3, pp. 215-230. Re: working class conditions in Barcelona, Spain, and the anticlerical attitudes of oppressed classes of Catalonia.

15444. Faber, Heije. (1980) "The Ministry in a Changing Society," Perkins Journal. Vol. 34, No. 1 (Fall), pp. 1-27.

15445. Fanning, Charles, Ellen Skerrett and John Corrigan. (1980) Nineteenth Century Chicago Irish: A Social and Political Portrait. Chicago, IL: Loyola University of Chicago, Center for Urban Policy, Urban Insight Series. A pamphlet.

15446. Felton, Carroll M, Jr. (1980) The Care of Souls in the

Black Church: A Liberation Perspective. New York: Martin Luther King Press.

15447. Ferguson, Gene M. (1980) Renewal in the Church: From Survival to Mission, A Local Church Consultation. Thesis (D. Min.). Boston, MA: Boston University.

15448. File, Edgar. (1980) The Ministry of the Church in the 80's: A Paper Delivered to the Downtown Churchworkers Association Annual Meeting. Toronto, Canada: Canadian Urban Training Project for Christian Mission. [Location: ICUIS 4492, see note 2].

15449. Fischer, Claude S. (1980) "The Spread of Violent Crime from City to the Countryside, 1955-1975," Rural Sociology. Vol. 45, No. 3 (Fall), pp. 416-434.

15450. Folsom, Harry G. (1980) "Urban Indians: The Struggle to Survive," New World Outlook. n.s. Vol. 41, No. 1 (September), pp. 37-38. Re: the plight of Native Americans in the city.

15451. Forell, George W. and William H. Lazareth, eds. (1980) Corporation Ethics: The Quest for Moral Authority. Philadelphia, PA: Fortress Press, Justice Books.

15452. Freeman, James M. and James Preston. (1980) "Two Urbanized Orissan Temples," pp. 97-117 in S. Seymore, ed. The Transformation of a Sacred Town: Bhubaneshwar, India. Boulder, CO: Westview Press.

15453. Fresno Metropolitan Ministry. (1980) Fresno Metro Ministry Newsletter [and related materials]. Fresno, CA: the Ministry. [Location: incomplete file, ICUIS collection, see note 2]. A periodical.

15454. Frindte, Matthias. (1980) Verkehrungen wirklichen Lebens: eine Studie über soziale Bedingungen und Inhalte der Kommunikation von Arbeiterfamilien und deren volkskirchlicher Metakommunikation. Frankfurt am Main, Germany: Bern. Re: the church and communication patterns in working class families in Germany. Originally a doctoral thesis. Bibliography.

15455. Fuller, Millard and Diane Scott. (1980) Love in the Mortar Joints. Piscataway, NJ: New Century. Fuller, a wealthy businessman turned promoter of housing for the poor, relates experiences of home building in Africa and Central America with the poor.

15456. Gallup, George, Jr. and David Poling. (1980) The Search for America's Faith. Nashville, TN: Abingdon Press.

15457. Gaston, Maria Luisa. (1980) "Hispanic Catholics and Church Development," The City of God. Vol. 2, No. 2 (Fall), pp. 3-8.

15458. Geertz, Clifford. (1980) Negara: The Theatre State in Nineteenth Century Bali. Princeton, NJ: Princeton University Press. Geertz's work discusses the relationships between political power and religious symbolism and is important for comparative studies of the relationship between religion and urbanization. Geertz has written several works on cities of Indonesia.

15459. Genska, Depaul A. (1980) A Course on Street Ministries: With Emphasis on Female Prostitution--A Course Given at Catholic Theological Union, April 2-June 4, 1980. Thesis (MTS). Catholic Theological Union.

15460. Gettman, Seymour. (1980) "Adjustment of Work Schedules for Religious Observances," pp. 296-304 in US Commission on Civil Rights. Religious Discrimination: A Neglected Issue. Washington, DC: the Commission, Government Printing Office. Bibliography.

15461. Giese, Vincent J. (1980) You Got It All: A Personal Account of a White Priest in a Chicago Ghetto. Huntington, IN: Our Sunday Visitor. Re: Catholic Church work with ghetto youth.

15462. Gilbert, Alan D. (1980) The Making of Post-Christian Britain, A History of the Secularization of Modern Society. London: Longman. Bibliography.

15463. Gillett, Richard W. (1980) "Hispanics and Latin America: Moving Center Stage," The Witness [Ambler, PA]. Vol. 63, No. 9 (September), pp. 4-8+.

15464. Gomes, David. (1980?) Winning the Cities: The Preoccupation of Evangelism. Rio de Janeiro, Brazil: the author. [Location: Fuller Theological Seminary, Pasadena, CA]. A pamphlet.

15465. González-Balado, José Luis. (1980) Mother Teresa: Always the Poor. Liguori, MO: Ligouri Publications. Adapted from the Spanish.

15466. Good News to the Poor: The Church and City Problems.

(1980) Albingdon, Oxon, England: [Roman Catholic] Commission for Social Welfare. Re: church work with the poor.

15467. Goode, James E. (1980) "The Black Catholic Church: Its Purpose and Mission," The City of God. Vol. 2, No. 3 (Summer), pp. 17-24.

15468. Graham, W. Fred. (1980) "Declining Church Membership: Can Anything Be Done?" Reformed Journal. Vol. 30, No. 1 (January), pp. 7-13.

15469. Green, Mark and Robert Massie, Jr., eds. (1980) The Big Business Reader. New York: Pilgrim.

15470. Greer, Scott, ed. (1980) Ethnics, Machines, and the American Urban Future. Cambridge, MA: Schenkman.

15471. Gregg, Howard D. (1980) History of the African Methodist Episcopal Church. Nashville, TN: the Church.

15472. Grimes, Seamus. (1980) "Irish Immigrant Friendship Patterns in Australia," Social Studies: Irish Journal of Sociology (Christus Rex Society). Vol. 6, No. 4 (Winter), pp. 374-380. Re: a small Irish immigrant population in Sydney, Australia.

15473. Grizzard, Nigel and Paula Raisman. (1980) "Inner City Jews in Leeds," Jewish Journal of Sociology. Vol. 22, No. 1 (June), pp. 21-34.

15474. Gross, Bertram. (1980) Friendly Fascism: The New Face of Power in America. New York: M. Evans.

15475. Hadden, Jeffrey K. (1980) "Religion and the Construction of Social Problems," Sociological Analysis. Vol. 41, No. 2 (Summer), pp. 99-108.

15476. Hadden, Jeffrey K. (1980) "H. Paul Douglass: His Perspective and His Work," Review of Religious Research. Vol. 22, No. 1 (September), pp. 66-88. An appreciative biography. Bibliography.

15477. Hale, Russell. (1980) The Unchurched: Who They Are and Why They Stay Away. San Francisco, CA: Harper and Row. Hale studies the six counties in the USA with the lowest church membership and interviews 165 people. The result is a kind of market research for evangelism. He provides taxonomy of unchurched people with ten categories and concludes the unchurched phenomena may be primarily rural rather than urban. Questionnaire.

15478. Hall, Douglas John. (1980) Has the Church a Future? Philadelphia, PA: Westminster.

15479. Hallett, Stanley J. (1980) "To Build a City: A Chicagoan's View," Sojourners. Vol. 9, No. 9 (September), pp. 15-18.

15480. Hallett, Stanley J. (1980) "Lamentations or Transformations," Justice Ministries. Nos. 7-8 (Winter-Spring), pp. 35-38. Hallett's article is followed by descriptions of councils, agencies and church groups working to create employment.

15481. Hallett, Stanley J. (1980) "Low Cost Options: Explorations in Alternative Urban Constitutions, Policies, and Practices," in Edward W. Hanten, Mark J. Kasoff, and F. Stevens Redburn. New Directions for the Mature Metropolis: Policies and Strategies for Change. New York: Schenkman.

15482. Hamilton, C. M. (1980) "The Salt Lake Temple: A Symbolic Statement of Mormon Doctrine," pp. 103-127 in Thomas G. Alexander, ed. The Mormon People. Provo, UT: Brigham Young University Press.

15483. Hammer, Don E. (1980s?) Self Study Guide for Churches. Atlanta, GA: Home Mission Board, Southern Baptist Convention.

15484. Hannerz, Ulf. (1980) Exploring the City: Inquiries toward an Urban Anthropology. New York: Columbia University Press. Addressed to incipient urban anthropologists, this book encourages the new discipline of urban anthropology to borrow theoretical heritages from other disciplines of urban study. Recommended are the Chicago School (Parks, et. al.), the studies of urban Central Africa produced by the Rhodes-Livingston Institute in 1937ff, Erving Goffman's dramaturgy, certain geographers, as well as the traditional social theorist (Marx, Weber, etc.). Hannerz does not draw much from the traditional rural anthropological studies or spell out what they contribute, except for emphasis on network analysis (see esp. p. 200f). The book does not directly mention religion or churches. Interesting references include: the Greek poet Archilochus' fox and hedgehog analogy related to Redfield's (1954) orthogenetic vs. heterogenetic cities, p. 280. [Can churches also be described this way?] See also the discussion of "mau-mauing" and "flack catching" as network models or types, p. 189f.

15485. Hargleroad, Bobbi Wells. (1980) "The Ministry of the Early Church in the Context of the Urban Roman Empire," Justice Ministries: Resources for Urban Mission. No. 9 (Summer), pp. 16-19. Followed by an annotated bibliography on the church's social ministry, including denominational statements, descriptive models of social ministry, and resources about social ministry in the area of employment.

15486. Hazard, David M. (1980) "Standing in the Urban Gap," Christian Herald. Vol. 103, No. 8 (September), pp. 40-44+. Re: ministry at the National Presbyterian Church, Washington, DC.

15487. Hengsbach, Friedhelm, ed. (1980) Aussperrung und Streik: ungleiche Mittel. Mainz, Germany: Matthias-Gruenwald-Verlag. Re: the church in regard to strikes, lockouts, and industrial arbitration in West Germany.

15488. Henriot, Peter and Joe Holland. (1980) Social Analysis: Linking Faith and Justice. Maryknoll, NY: Orbis. A second edition: Holland, Joe and Peter Henriot. Social Analysis: Linking Faith and Justice. Washington, DC: Dove Communications and Orbis Book, 1983. Three philosophies of social analysis -- traditional, liberal and radical -- are assessed from theological and pastoral perspectives. Reviewed: AFER: African Ecclesial Review, Vol. 26, August, 1984, p. 255. International Bulletin of Missionary Research, Vol. 8 (July, 1984), p. 140. Sociological Analysis, Vol. 45 (Fall, 1984), p. 259.

15489. Hessel, Dieter T., ed. (1980) Rethinking Social Ministry. New York: Office for Church Education Services--Social Education, United Presbyterian Program Agency. At the time of writing, Hessel was Associate for Social Education in the Program Agency of the United Presbyterian Church USA.

15490. Hesselgrave, David J. (1980) Planting Churches Cross-Culturally: A Guide for Home and Foreign Missions. Grand Rapids, MI: Baker Book House.

15491. Hill, Clifford S. (1980) Towards the Dawn: What Is Happening to Britain Today. London: Fount Paperbacks. Re: church renewal in Britain.

15492. Hines, Samuel George. (1980) "How Can Christian Stations Help?" Religious Broadcasting [Thematic issue: Reaching cities]. Vol. 12, No. 3 (April), pp. 17-18f. Accompanied by additional related articles.

15493. Hoehl, Lockwood. (1980) "10 More Years of Ambiguity, Part 1," The Witness [Ambler, PA]. Vol. 63, No. 6 (June), pp. 4-6; "Ministry in the Shadow of TMI's Towers, Part 2," Vol. 63, No. 7 (July), pp. 14-17. Consequences for ministry of the Three Mile Island nuclear disaster.

15494. Hollyday, Joyce. (1980) "Church of the Messiah [Episcopal]: New Life from a Dying Parish on Detroit's East Side," Sojourners. Vol. 9, No.4 (April), pp. 20-22. Re: Church of the Messiah (Episcopal).

15495. Hougland, James G. and James R. Wood. (1980) "Correlates of Social Participation in Local Churches," Sociological Focus. Vol. 13, No. 4 (October), pp. 343-358.

15496. Howell, Leon. (1980) People Are the Subject: Stories of Rural-Urban Mission. Geneva: Commission on World Mission and Evangelism, the World Council of Churches. Howell recounts stories of fishermen in Puerto Rico, women textile workers in Korea, and slum dwellers in South Africa, India, and Argentina, showing how they attempt to move beyond being objects of oppression and exploitation.

15497. Hudson, Norman S. (1980) "Dallas Church Runs Bilingual Program: La Puerta Abierta," New World Outlook. n.s. Vol. 40, No. 7 (March), pp. 37-38. Re: a preschool program with Anglo and Mexican American children.

15498. Industrial Mission Association, Theology Development Group. (1980) The End of Work? Papers on Theology and Technological Change. Manchester, England: the Association.

15499. Interfaith Action for Economic Justice. (1980s) People Working for Justice: An Interfaith Action for Economic Justice Survey and Study. Washington, DC: Interfaith Action for Economic Justice. A description of a coalition of religious bodies and its work on the issues of housing, homelessness, employment, health care and voter registration. A list of resources and tools is appended.

15500. Johnson, Douglas W. (1980) "Program Dissensus between Denominational Grass Roots and Leadership and Its Consequences," pp. 330-3345 in Ross Scherer, ed. American Denominational Organization. Pasadena, CA: William Carey Library.

15501. Johnston, Earl W. (1980) Toward a Cooperative Southern Baptist Ministry in the Inner City of San Antonio, Texas. Thesis (D.

Min.). San Anselmo, CA: San Francisco Theological Seminary.

15502. Jones, Marcus E. (1980) Black Migration in the United States with Emphasis on Selected Cities. Saratoga, CA: Century Twenty One Publishing.

15503. Jones, Nathan. (1980) "Evangelization in the Black Community," The City of God. Vol. 2, No. 3 (Winter), pp. 19-24.

15504. Joseph, M. Vincentia, Sr. and Ann Patrick Conrad, Sr. (1980) "A Parish Neighborhood Model of Social Work Practice," Social Casework. Vol. 61, No. 7 (September), pp. 423-432. Parishes provide networks and mediating structures to link people to the large service providing systems.

15505. Joyce, Patrick. (1980) Work, Society and Politics: the Culture of the Factory in Later Victorian England. New Brunswick, NJ: Rutgers University Press. Re: industrialization and popular Protestantism in England.

15506. Kamstra, J. H. (1980) "Urbanisatie en de dood van de voorouders in Japan," Nederlands Theologisch Tijdschrift. Vol. 34, No. 1 (January), pp. 1-14. Urbanization has effects on ancestor worship in Japan.

15507. Kane, Margaret. (1980) Gospel in Industrial Society. London: SCM Press. Kane seeks ways to make Christianity a hope for individuals who live outside the influence of academic theological debates, specifically working class people in England. She finds hopeful signs in the urban, industrial, and technical society, but is critical of it when it generates threats to the humanity of people whose lives are inexorably caught up in it. Moreover, she is critical of private pietism, humanistic psychology and Marxist ideology for their inability to deal with the problems of industrialism. She seeks pastoral ways to help people believe that God is involved in their lives. Bibliography.

15508. Kantowicz, Edward R. (1980) "Church and Neighborhood," Ethnicity. Vol. 7, No. 4 (December), pp. 349-366. Reprinted: Brian Mitchell, ed. Building the American Catholic City. New York: Garland, 1988. Kantowicz describes the ethnicity of Roman Catholics in Chicago, IL.

15509. Kao, Chun-Ming. (1980) "A Letter from Prison," Asian Issues [Tokyo: International Affairs Desk, Christian Conference of Asia]. Series 2, No. 2 (September). [Location: ICUIS 4497, see note 2].

Rev. Kao was arrested, tried, and sentenced to five years imprisonment. See further: "A Church under Fire: Taiwan National Report" (1980).

15510. Kasdorf, Hans. (1980) Christian Conversion in Context. Scottdale: Herald Press.

15511. Kazemi, Farhad. (1980) "Urban Migrants and the Revolution," Iranian Studies: Journal for the Society of Iranian Studies. Vol. 13, Nos. 1-4, pp. 257-278. A summary of Kazemi's book on rural migrants in Iranian cities, and on their living conditions in shanty towns and squatter villages.

15512. Kim, Byong-suh and Sang Hyun Lee, eds. (1980) The Korean Immigrant in America. Montclair, NJ: Association of Korean Christian Scholars in North America.

15513. Kim, Paul Shu. (1980) A Study of Ministry to Second Generation Korean Immigrants in the Church. Thesis (D. Min.) Madison, NJ: Drew University.

15514. King, David S. (1980) No Church Is an Island. New York: Pilgrim. King seeks encourage mission to provide a network for various congregations with specialized ministries in the United Church of Christ. A directory of ministries is appended which lists congregations specializing in, among other emphases: advocacy, arts, bilingual outreach, blood donor drives, bookstores, children's work (arts, bookmobile, day programs, community homes), city redevelopment, community centers, community forums, community organization, community resources directory, community services, counseling (divorce, drug, family), disaster response, ecology, ecumenical relation, outreach to the elderly (day care, home repairs, housing), farmers markets, ministries to the handicapped, ministries to homosexuals, health care, Hispanic ministries, hospitality and guest rooms, housing, hunger and food banks (cooperative, pantry, funding), Native American ministries, local mission funding, mass media, mental health clinic, minority empowerment, night ministry, parish education regarding community issues, public education, refugee resettlement, rural poverty, scholarships, sewing instruction, sick room equipment loan, tourism, transients, urban ministry, women's issues, world peace, and youth (education, homes, tutorial).

15515. King, Martin Luther, Sr. with Clayton Riley. (1980) Daddy King: An Autobiography. New York: William Morrow. Attention is given to Martin Luther King, Sr.'s years at Ebenezer Baptist Church, Atlanta, although the main emphasis of the book is his persistence in supporting nonviolence in spite of repeated family tragedies.

15516. Kirkeby, Oliver Murle. (1980) The Salem Story: A Case Study. Thesis (D. Min.). Columbus, OH: Trinity Lutheran Seminary.

15517. Klein, James H. and John W. Patton. (1980) Organizing for Neighborhood Justice: The Formation and Implementation of the Uptown-Edgewater Neighborhood Justice Center in Chicago. Chicago, IL: Loyola University of Chicago, Center for Urban Policy, Urban Insight Series. A pamphlet.

15518. Knoxville United Ministries. (1980-1985) Cities Magazine. Knoxville, TN: Knoxville United Ministries. A publication designed to provide a forum for the urban ministry projects and groups in the USA.

15519. Kolbe, Edward H. (1980) "Let's Affirm the City," Christian Ministry. Vol. 11, No. 6 (November), pp. 15-16.

15520. Kraus, Norman C., ed. (1980) Missions, Evangelism, and Church Growth. Scottdale, PA: Herald. Kraus raises questions about methods of evangelism, e. g ., "homogeneous unit" principle, that result in a truncated gospel. Miller's article titled "Evangelizing the Central City" is included.

15521. Kromer, Helen. (1980) "South Side Settlement Knows Its Neighborhood," New World Outlook. n.s. Vol. 41, No. 1 (September), pp. 20-23. A settlement located in a poor blue collar neighborhood in Columbus, OH, began its work with Eurpoean ethnics, but now relates mainly to Appalachian outmigrants, Native Americans, and a large number of Hmong Laotian refugees. The settlement has new quarters, provides summer camps, advocates area planning, offers health services, has resources for utility assistance, and houses many groups meeting for many purposes. Religion is no longer the defining factor at South Side Settlement, and charity is no longer given.

15522. Laska, Shirley Bradway and Daphne Spain. (1980) Back to the City: Issues in Neighborhood Renovation. New York: Pergamon Press. An analysis of gentrification and urban renewal.

15523. Lausanne Commitee for World Evangelization. (1980) Christian Witness to Secularized People. Wheaton, IL: the Commitee, Lausanne Occasional Paper, No. 8.

15524. Lausanne Commitee for World Evangelization, Consultation on World Evangelization, Mini-Consultation on Reaching the Urban Poor, Pattaya, Thailand. (1980) The Thailand Report on the Urban Poor: Report of the ... Mini-Consultation on Reaching the Urban Poor. Wheaton, IL: the Committee, Thailand Report, No. 22. [Cover title: Christian Witness to the Urban Poor]. Edited by Colin Marchant, this report on urban poverty includes a description of poor people, an interpretation of Biblical views on the poor, a variety of perspectives on the purposes of urban evangelism, and some strategic recommendations. The Mini-Consultation that produced the report was chaired by Jim Putton, a British evangelical. An appendix on Hebrew words for the poor is included.

15525. Lausanne Commitee for World Evangelization, Consultation on World Evangelization, Mini-Consultation on Reaching Large Cities. (1980) The Thailand Report on Large Cities: Report of a Consultation on World Evangelization, Mini-Consultation on Reaching Large Cities. Wheaton, IL: the Committee, Lausanne Occasional Papers, No. 9. A consideration of the church's evangelization program in light of an increasingly urban world population addresses such questions as: What are the primary functions of cities? How do cites affect the hopes and values of residents? What are the subgroups of the city and what are the best ways to evangelize them? A list of hindrances to evangelism is included.

15526. Lee, Eun Soo. (1980) A Ministry to the Second Generation of a Korean Immigrant Church: The Korean Dong San Church of the Bronx. Thesis (D. Min.). New York: New York Theological Seminary.

15527. Lee, Raymond L. M. and S. E. Ackerman. (1980) "Conflict and Solidarity in a Pentecostal Group in Urban Malaysia," Sociological Review (England). Vol. 28, No. 4, pp. 809-828.

15528. Leech, Kenneth. (1980) Brick Lane 1978: The Events and Their Significance. Birmingham, England: AFFOR. [Location: ICUIS 4670, see note 2]. Leech explains circumstances surrounding the 1978 racial violence and anti-racist demonstrations in London's East End where he was serving as a parish priest. See further additional materials by Leech in the ICUIS collection, Nos. 4688-4691.

15529. Leech, Kenneth, ed. (1980) Thatcherism: The Jubilee Lent Lectures, 1980. London: Jubilee Group. [Location: ICUIS 4678, see note 2]. Leech comments on the positions of the Tory Party and the ideology of Thatcherism in regard to race, defense, law and order, and poverty.

15530. Lefeber, Larry A. (1980) Building a Young Adult Ministry. Valley Forge, PA: Judson.

15531. Lefebvre, Pierre. (1980) "Structures et agents de l'évangelisation en milieu urbain," in Ntedika Konde, et al. L'évangelisation dans l'Afrique. Kinshasa, Zaire: Faculté du théologique Catholique. Re: Catholic urban evangelization in the Diocese of Kinshasa, Zaire.

15532. Lesbaupin, Ivo. (1980) "A Igreja Católica e os movimentos populares urbanos," Religiâo e Sociedade [Brazil]. No. 5, pp. 189-198. Re: the Catholic church and popular urban movements.

15533. Lincoln, C. Eric and Lawrence H. Mamiya. (1980) "Daddy Jones and Father Divine: The Cults as Political Religion," Religion in Life. Vol. 49, No. 1 (Spring), pp. 6-23.

15534. Lingeman, Richard. (1980) Small Town America: A Narrative History, 1620--the Present. Boston, MA: Houghton Mifflin. Includes treatment of religion and values of small towns encountering industrialization and urbanization. Bibliography.

15535. Linz, Juan J. (1980) "Religion and Politics in Spain: From Conflict to Consensus above Cleavage," Social Compass [Thematic issue: The Religion of the Working Class]. Vol. 27, Nos. 2-3, pp. 255-277. Re: religiosity, anticlericalism, and the working class in Spain.

15536. Linzer, Norman. (1980) "The Modern Jew and the Human Condition: The Impact of Tradition and Secularism," Journal of Jewish Communal Service. Vol. 56, No. 3 (Spring), pp. 238-245. Implications of privatization and secularization for the Jewish community.

15537. [Lovell, George]. (1980) Diagrammatic Modelling: An Aid to Theological Reflection in the Church and Community. Manchester, England: William Temple Foundation. A paper on theology written by an exponent of non-directive community development.

15538. Luecke, Richard Henry, ed. (1980) Reclaiming Work for Community. Chicago, IL: Community Renewal Society. A pamphlet.

15539. Luecke, Richard Henry. (1980) "Looking Beyond Economics," Justice Ministries, Resources for Urban Mission. Nos. 7-8 (Winter-Spring), pp. 14-19. Followed by an annotated bibliography on economic conditions in the United States.

15540. Lutheran Center for Church Renewal. (beginning in 1980) Renewal. St. Paul, MN: the Center. A periodical.

15541. Lyke, James. (1980) "When the Poor Evangelize the Church," Origins: NC Documentary Service. Vol. 10, No. 3 (June 5), pp. 33-38. Lyke illustrates changes made possible through grants of the Roman Catholic Campaign for Human Development which has given $78 million to poor people since its founding in 1970. Grants are aimed at self-help projects.

15542. Machor, James L. (1980) The Pastoral City: Urbanism and the Garden Idea of America. Thesis (Ph. D.). Urbana, IL: University of Illinois at Urbana-Champaign.

15543. Mader, Donald. (1980) "Neighborhoods in Transition," Church Herald. Vol. 37, No. 10 (May 16), pp. 4-7. Part 2: "After the Transition," No. 11 (May 30), pp. 10-12.

15544. Madigan, Kathleen E. and William J. Sullivan. (1980) Crime and Community in Biblical Perspective: Plans and Resources for 14 Sessions. Valley Forge, PA: Judson. A study guide prepared by the ecumenical Judicial Processes Commission of Rochester, NY, is designed for local church use in: 1) analyzing criminal justice institutions, 2) evaluating the criminal justice system in light of religious ethics, 3) searching for greater justice, and 4) discovering personal responsibility for justice ministry.

15545. Maher, Tom. (1980?) A Study on Unemployment and Underdevelopment in Boston. Jamaica Plains, MA: Episcopal City Mission.

15546. Mancini, Janet K. (1980) Strategic Styles: Coping in the Inner City. Hanover, NH: University Press of New England.

15547. Mann, Gail L. (1980) "Contact Baltimore--A Hotline Ministry," New World Outlook. n.s. Vol. 41, No. 4 (December), pp. 35-36. Re: teleministry in Baltimore, MD, and its methods for suicide prevention.

15548. Marchant, Colin, comp. (1980) The Urban Poor. London: Nationwide Initiative in Evangelism. A pamphlet.

15549. Marsden, George. (1980) Fundamentalism and American

Culture: The Shaping of Twentieth Century Evangelism, 1870-1925. New York: Oxford. Reviewed: Review of Religious Research, Vol. 24 (March, 1983), p. 278. Journal of Ecumenical Studies, Vol. 19 (Fall, 1982), p. 814. Churchman: Journal of Anglican Theology, Vol. 97, No. 2, (1983), p. 170.

15550. Martino, Cesare. (1980) "Comportamenti religiosi nell'area urbana," pp. 277-290 in Tullio Tentori, et al. Religione e morale popolare cristiana ricera interdisciplinare. Bologna, Italy: Edisioni Dehoniane. Re: secularization and urbanization.

15551. Marty, Martin E., Vernon Schmid and Walter E. Ziegenhals. (1980) "Secular City Revisited," Christian Ministry. Vol. 11. No. 6 (November), pp. 5-14.

15552. McClain, George D. (1980) "Pioneering Social Gospel Radicalism: An Overview of the History of the Methodist Federation for Social Action," Radical Religion [Thematic issue: History of the MFSA]. Vol. 5, No. 1, pp. 10-23. A history of the MFSA's accomplishments from its inception in 1907.

15553. McFadden, Dwight J. (1980) "The Plight of the Burned-Out Pastor," pp. 409-417 in Wilbert Shenk, ed. Mission Focus. Scottdale, PA: Herald Press.

15554. McGaw, Douglas. (1980) A Tale of Two Congregations: A Comparative Study of Religious Meaning and Belonging. Hartford, CT: Hartford Seminary.

15555. McGohon, Buddy Clay. (1980) The Basis for a Ministry to Apartment Dwellers in the South Avondale Baptist Church Community. Thesis (D. Min.). Louisville, KY: Southern Baptist Theological Seminary.

15556. McLeod, Hugh. (1980) "The Dechristianization of the Working Class in Western Europe, 1850-1900," Social Compass [Thematic issue: The Religion of the Working Class]. Vol. 27, Nos. 2-3, pp. 191-214. McLeod outlines the history of working class disaffection with religion.

15557. McMath, Neil C., et al. (1980) Seeds of a People's Church: Challenge and Promise from the Underside of History: Presentations from the Neil C. McMath Lectureship of the Episcopal Diocese of Michigan, Detroit, August 1-4, 1980. s.l.: s.n. [Location: Chicago Theological Sreminary].

15558. Meeks, Wayne A. (1980) "Toward a Social Description of Pauline Christianity," pp. 27-41 in W. Green, ed. Approaches to Ancient Judaism. Chico, CA: Scholars Press.

15559. Meen, Sharon P. (1980) "Holy Day or Holiday? The Giddy Trolly and the Canadian Sunday, 1890-1914," Urban Historical Review [Canada]. Vol. 9, No. 1, pp. 49-63.

15560. Melwick, Ralph. (1980) "Billy Simons: The Black Jew of Charleston," American Jewish Archives. Vol. 32 (April), pp. 3-8.

15561. Metro United Church. (1980) Directions: A Mission Strategy for the Metro United Church, 1980-1985. Toronto, Canada: Mission Strategy Toronto, Metro United Church. [Location: ICUIS 4541, see note 2]. A report to two presbyteries in the Toronto metropolitan area of a joint committee on mission strategy. The report anticipates issues that will arise in urban ministry over the five year period and suggests ways of addressing them.

15562. Migliore, Daniel L. (1980) Called to Freedom: Liberation Theology and the Future of Christian Doctrine. Philadelphia, PA: Westminster.

15563. Mikhailova, L. V. (1980) "Katolicheskaia tserkov" i rabochii klass FGR. Moskow, Russia: Nauka. Re: the Catholic Church and labor in West Germany. Romanized title, text in Russian.

15564. Miller, Vern. (1980) "Evangelizing the Central City: Problems and Possibilities," pp. 123-139 in C. Norman Kraus, ed. Missions, Evangelism, and Church Growth. Scottdale, PA: Herald Press.

15565. A Ministry to International Seamen. (1980) Atlanta, GA: Home Mission Board, Southern Baptist Convention.

15566. Mitterling, Philip I. (1980) US Cultural History: A Guide to Information Sources. Detroit, MI: Gale Research. An annotated general bibliography of the cultural history of the USA since colonial times.

15567. "Money Management in Black Families." (1980s) New York: Committee on Ministries with Black Families. Because many Black congregations and families have poor money management practices, this guide booklet was prepared to promote budgeting, to explain the various types of credit, and generally to encourage good money management. Special attention is given to church contributions.

15568. Monroe, Johnnie. (1980) A Descriptive Study of the Origins and Impact of Black Presbyterians United upon the Mission and Ministry of the Presbytery of Philadelphia. Thesis (D. Min.). Philadelphia, PA: Eastern Baptist Theological Seminary.

15569. Moore, David. (1980) "Urban Pilgrimage," pp. 21-25 in Rex Ambler and David Haslam, ed. Agenda for Prophets: Toward a Political Theology for Britain. London: Bowerdean. Re: city missions in London.

15570. Morrison, Henry. (1980) "Time for a New Church, Labor Alliance," The Witness. Vol. 63, No. 7 (July), pp. 4-7. Morrison sketches the history of church-labor relationships in the early 20th century, particularly in the Episcopal church, and suggests ways of strengthening the alliance between religion and labor.

15571. Mouw, Richard J. (1980) Called to Holy Worldliness. Philadelphia, PA: Fortress Press. Although this book does not expressly deal with the city, church urbanologists have regularly recommended it to laity. The author's spiritual journey begins in the isolation of conservative evangelicalism and moves toward corporate responsibility and solidarity with the poor. He does not repudiate his heritage in evangelicalism, but instead gently raises and discusses the sorts of questions that have shaped his evolving understanding of God's mission. The book addresses laity who seek to expand their vision of ministry. Reviewed: Review and Expositor, Vol. 81 (Spring, 1984), p. 342. International Review of Missions, Vol. 72 (July, 1983), p. 423.

15572. Mpayo, Owdencalm. (1980) Urban and Rural Mission, Christian Council of Tanzania--Report in Evangelism Department. Morogoro, Tanzania: Urban and Rural Mission, Christian Council of Tanzania. [Location: ICUIS 4490, see note 2]. A paper reports the inception, development and collapsing of church sponsored urban industrial projects in Tanzania. Mpayo, who at the time of writing served on the staff of the Christian Council, laments the churches' neglect of urban issues. An earlier draft of the paper may be found in ICUIS No. 4171. Bibliography.

15573. Mukenge, Ida Faye Rousseau. (1980) The Black Church in Urban America: A Case Study in Political Economy. Thesis (Ph. D.). Berkeley, CA: University of California. Republished: Lanham, MD: University Press of America, 1983. A study of the North Richmond Baptist Church using theoretical formulations developed by Mayer Zald. Militancy among Black urban churches has decreased as the prominence of secular protest organizations has grown, Mukenge argues. Urban black churches have had some of their communal functions transfered to secular politics, education, and economics.

15574. Muldoon, Maureen. (1980) Abortion: An Annotated Indexed Bibliography. New York: The Edwin Mellen Press.

15575. National Capital Semester for Seminarians [brochure, syllabus]. (1980) Washington, DC: Wesley Theological Seminary. [Location: ICUIS 4371, see note 2]. An opportunity for seminarians to study church-state relationships in Washington, DC.

15576. National Council of the Churches of Christ in the USA, Joint Commission on Mission Education. (1980) Crossroads at Cedarmont [Filmstrip: 64 frames, black and white]. New York: the Commission. Re: the church and race relations.

15577. National Office for Black Catholics. (1980) "The Crisis of Catholic Education in the Black Community," The City of God. Vol. 2, No. 1 (Summer), pp. 39-46.

15578. Neighbour, Ralph Webster, Jr., compiler. (1980) Future Church. Nashville, TN: Broadman.

15579. Nelson, Jack A. (1980) Hunger for Justice. Maryknoll, NY: Orbis.

15580. Nesti, Arnaldo. (1980) "Religion et classe ouvrière dans les sociétés industrielles--Une hypothèse de recherche," Social Compass [Thematic issue: The Religion of the Working Class]. Vol. 27, Nos. 2-3, pp. 169-190. A theoretical contribution to the interpretation of popular religion in industrial societies.

15581. Nickel, Herman. (1980) Crusade against the Corporation: Church Militants on the March. Washington, DC: Ethics and Public Policy Center. Reprited from: Fortune Magazine, June 16, 1980. Re: church opposition to the Nestle Corporation.

15582. O'Brien, Maureen R. and Donald McNeill. (1980) "A Multi-Faceted Look at the Unseen City," Horizons: The Journal of the College Theology Society. Vol. 7, No. 2 (Fall), pp. 285-296. The outline, syllabus and evaluation of an "urban plunge" type of interdisciplinary college course. Bibliography.

15583. O'Neill, Patrick Ireland. (1980) The Single Adult. New York: Paulist. Re: church work with single people.

15584. Office of Energy Policy. (1980) Energy Efficient Churches: Reducing Energy Costs in Religious Buildings. Pierre, SD: the Office. A pamphlet.

15585. Oliveira, Francisco de, et al. (1980) Pastoral urbano. São Paulo, Brazil: Edições Paulinas. Re: urban pastoral work and trends in Brazil. Bibliography.

15586. Oosterwal, Gottfried. (1980) "How Shall We Work the Cities--From Within?" Ministry [Seventh-Day Adventist]. Vol. 53, No. 6 (June), pp. 18-22+. Oosterwal is at Andrews University Theological Seminary.

15587. Orlandis, José. (1980) "La familia en la sociedad urbana e industrial," pp. 553-556 in Agusto Sarmiento, et al., eds. Cuestiones fundamentales sobre matrimonio y familia. Pamplona, Spain: Ediciones Universidad de Navarra. Re: Christian family life.

15588. Owens, Virginia Sten. (1980) The Total Image: or, Selling Jesus in the Modern Age. Grand Rapids, MI: Eerdmans.

15589. Parachin, Victor M. (1980) "How Do You Get Them Off the Farm?" Christianity Today. Vol. 24, No. 13 (July 18), pp. 52-53.

15590. Patterson, James Oglethorpe and German Ross, eds. (1980) Church of God in Christ Directory. Memphis, TN: COCIC Publishing House. Provides data on a rapidly growing urban African American denomination

15591. Paz, Denis G. (1980) "The Episcopal Church in Local History Since 1950: An Annotated Bibliography," Historical Magazine of the Protestant Episcopal Church. Vol. 49, No. 4 (December), pp. 389-409.

15592. Peachey, Urban, ed. (1980) Mennonite Statements on Peace and Social Concerns, 1900-1978. Akron, PA: Mennonite Central Committee. In addition to statements on peace, see also the sections on industrial relations, race relations and social ethics.

15593. Pennings, Johannes M. (1980) "Environmental Influences on the Creation Process," in John R. Kimberly et al., eds. The Organizational Life Cycle. San Francisco, CA: Jossey-Bass.

15594. Pepper, C. B. (1980) "I'm a Little Pencil in God's Hand," McCalls. Vol. 107 (March), pp. 73-74+. Re: Mother Teresa.

15595. Perkins, Perry. (1980) "Concrete Theology: A Response to the Urban Crisis," Sojourners. Vol. 9, No. 9 (September), pp 11-14.

15596. Perry, Everett L. (1980) "Congregational Models for Missions--Factors in Adaptation and Goal Attainment," in Ross P. Scherer, ed. American Denominational Organization: A Sociological View. Pasadena, CA: William Carey Library.

15597. Phillips, Paul T. (1980) "Religion and Society in the Cloth Region of Wiltshire, 1830-1870," Journal of Religious History. Vol. 11, No. 1 (June), pp. 95-110. Phillips discusses the effects of economic stability and stagnation on religious affairs in an industrialized section of Victorian England.

15598. Poethig, Richard P., ed. (1980) "Plant Closings: The Church's Response," Justice Ministries: Resources for Urban Mission. Vol. 10 (Fall), pp. 1-54. A bibliography.

15599. Poethig, Richard P. (1980) High Rise Ministries: Reflections and Projections. Chicago, IL: Institute on the Church in Urban-Industrial Society. [Location: ICUIS 4401, see note 2]. Poethig lists reasons why apartment ministries fail: 1) the church failed to realize the diversity of people living in apartments. 2) the church's ministry based on the family unit failed to interest the large number of singles, single parents, and elderly living in apartments. 3) the church leaders thought that, since the people lived in the same building, people should be contacted at their residence. Churches that are successful in reaching apartment dwellers don't consider apartments a special ministry at all, but reach the people in the church's regular program of pastoral care or evangelism.

15600. Poethig, Richard P. (1980) South Chicago Religious Community Responds to Steel Crisis. Chicago, IL: ICUIS. [Location: ICUIS collection, No. JM-410, see note 2]. Wisconsin Steel Company suddenly closed its doors, idling 3400 steelworkers. An interfaith committee was formed to alert the community to economic problems to encourage research, and to serve as a bridge to unify labor, industry, and government efforts. Participating groups include: Roman Catholic, Presbyterian, Methodist, Lutheran, Baptist, and Muslim bodies. A pamphlet.

15601. Poethig, Richard P., ed. (1980) Report on a Consultation on the Church, the Gospel and the Wage Earner. Chicago, IL: Institute on the Church in Urban-Industrial Society, Occasional Paper No. 9. Interpretations of Presbyterian ministries among working people.

15602. Ponce, Frank. (1980) "Enculturation and Evangelization in the US Catholic Church: A Vision and Some Pastoral Implications," The City of God. Vol. 2, No. 3 (Winter), pp. 41-51.

15603. Ponce, Frank. (1980) "Hispanic Catholics in the United States, an Overview," The City of God. Vol. 2, No. 2 (Fall), pp. 9-21.

15604. Porter, Janet W. (1980) "Evangelization and the Black Catholic Church as an Institution," The City of God. Vol. 2, No. 3 (Winter), pp. 25-40.

15605. Pottieger, Cecil P. E. (1980) Apartment House Ministry Handbook: Local Church Strategies for Ministry in Apartment Houses. New York: Educational and Cultivation Division, Board of Global Ministries, the United Methodist Church. A pamphlet.

15606. Pulker, E. A. (1980) "The Social Concern of Canon Scott," Journal of the Canadian Church Historical Society. Vol. 22 (October), pp. 1-16. Frederick George Scott (1861-1944), an Anglican chaplain in Work War I, was a noted Canadian advocate of labor who sought to improve living conditions for the working class.

15607. Pursiainen, Terho. (1980) Oma paa ja paaoma: puheenvuoroja kristinuskon ja tyovaenliikkeen valisesta suhteesta. Helsinki, Finland: Tammi. Re: social policy in Finland and the issues of communism, trade unions, and the church's relation to labor.

15608. Raby, William L., ed. (1980) "Ministries of Restoration: People Helping People Create Work Opportunities in Their Communities," Church and Society [Thematic issue]. Vol. 70, No. 4 (May-June), pp. 5-75. Re: Presbyterian community organization efforts in Youngstown, OH, and Bronx, NY. Bibliography.

15609. Ramalho, J. P., ed. (1980) Signs of Hope and Justice. Geneva: World Council of Churches.

15610. Ramsden, William E. (1980) The Church in a Changing Society. Nashville, TN: Abingdon. Describes major economic, demographic, and values orientation trends in society and their impacts on central concerns of the church--money, members, and mission. This volume is first in the series titled "Into Our Third Century" prepared as part of the 200th anniversary celebration of Methodism.

15611. Ravetz, Alison. (1980) Remaking Cities: Contradictions of the Recent Urban Environment. London: Croom Helm. Post war architects and developers are blamed for destroying the old and treasured city and for replacing it with the new and ugly. Ravetz provides a severe critique of the "sweep clean" style of urban planning and argues for a radical change of architectural style.

15612. Rayan, Samule. (1980) "Reflections on a Live-In Experience: 'Slumdwellers," pp. 50-56 in Virginia Fabella, ed. Asia's Struggle for Full Humanity. Maryknoll, NY: Orbis.

15613. Reaching Out to All People: The Catholic Church. (1980s?) [Cassette tape and filmstrip]. Philadelphia, PA: Archdiocese of Philadelphia. The story of a Black inner city Catholic parish, this filmstrip is intended to attract prospective members in the city.

15614. Read, William, Victor M. Monterroso, and Harmon A. Johnson. (1980) Brazil 1980: A Tool for the Evangelization of Brazil. Pasadena, CA: Fuller School of World Mission.

15615. Rees, David W. (1980) "Goals for the Churches in the '80s," The Christian Ministry. Vol. 11, No. 1 (January), pp. 12-14.

15616. "Refugees at Bay from Miami to Khartoum." (1980) JSAC Grapevine. Vol. 12, No. 3 (September), pp. [1-6].

15617. Remy, Jean. (1980) "Work and Self-Awareness," pp. 3-11 in Gregory Baum, ed. (1980) Work and Religion. New York: Seabury. Edinburgh, Scotland: Clark.

15618. Reus-Smit, Karel. (1980) A Statement on Urban Theology. Parkville, Victoria, Australia: Department of Education, University of Melbourne. [Location: ICUIS 4469, see note 2]. Urban theology places the Christian on the side of the poor, the powerless, and the alienated as they struggle with persons of power and privilege. A pamphlet.

15619. Roberts, J. Deotis. (1980) Roots of a Black Future: Family and Church. Philadelphia, PA: Westminster Press.

15620. Rolim, Francisco. (1980) "Religion and Poverty: Brazil," pp. 43-50 in Gregory Baum, ed. Work and Religion. New York: Seabury. Edinburgh, Scotland: Clark.

15621. Rooney, James F. (1980) "Organizational Success through Program Failure: Skid-Row Rescue Missions," Social Forces. Vol. 58, No. 3 (March), pp. 904-924. Rooney claims that city missions fail to rescue people because the missions' institutional survival depends on people continuing to need to be rescued. For a response, see Mauss (1982).

15622. Rowlingson, Donald T. (1980) "A Suburban Church under Pressure," The Christian Ministry. Vol. 11, No. 3 (May), pp. 20-23. Re: First Congregational Church, Winchester, MA.

15623. Running Shoes and Big City Blues. (1980) [Filmstrip, 124 frames, color, sound cassette, manual]. Atlanta, GA: Home Mission Board, the Southern Baptist Convention.

15624. Rutter, Michael. (1980) Changing Youth in a Changing Society: Patterns of Adolescent Development and Disorder. Cambridge, MA: Harvard University Press. Rutter examines the relative importance of heredity, childhood, family, schooling, media, peer groups, religions, and the urban environment in a model of adolescent development. The model helps explain real psycho-social disorders as well as ill-founded imagined problems that self correct with age.

15625. Rwehikiza, Felician. (1980) Parking Boys Revisited (Nairobi). Nairobi, Kenya: AMECEA Documentation Service, No. 10/80/210. A pamphlet.

15626. Sala, Ulisese Elisara. (1980) A Theology of Samoan Christian Immigrants in the United States. Thesis (D. Min.). Claremont, CA: School of Theology at Claremont.

15627. Samuel, Vinay Kumar. (1980) The Meaning and Cost of Discipleship. Bombay, India: Bombay Urban Industrial League for Development (BUILD). [Location: ICUIS 4717, see note 2]. Samuel finds that the church in India does not reflect true discipleship; it fails to display servanthood and does not enable the poor to achieve humanity.

15628. Sartori, Luís Maria Alves. (1980) O trabalho na dinâmica do evangelho: teologia, filosofia e pastoral do mundo do trabalho. São Paulo, Brazil: Edições Loyola. Re: pastoral work with laborers in Brazil.

15629. Schaller, Lyle E. (1980) The Multiple Staff and the Larger Church. Nashville, TN: Abingdon Press.

15630. Schaper, Donna. (1980s?) Streets to Dwell In: One Look at Public Ministry. Chicago, IL: Urban Academy in Chicago. A pamphlet.

15631. Schlundt, Gail. (1980) The Impact of Urbanism on the Protestant Religious Landscape of Athens County, Ohio. Thesis (MA). Athens, OH: Ohio University.

15632. Schmid, Vernon Lee. (1980) "Facing the Facts of Urban Life," Christian Ministry. Vol. 11, No. 6 (November), pp. 9-10.

15633. Schmidt, Henry J. (1980) "The Urban Ethos: Building Churches in a Pagan Environment," Mission Focus. Vol. 8, No. 2 (June), pp. 25-33.

15634. Schmieder, Arnold. (1980) "Is Religion Incidental? The Religiousness of the West German Workers," Social Compass [Thematic issue: The Religion of the Working Class]. Vol. 27, Nos. 2-3, pp. 243-253. Schmieder observes that laborers do not need the church as a social institution or as a moral example. Religion for the worker, far from being nonexistent, tends to be a private matter that does not necessarily impact everyday actions and thought.

15635. Schuller, David Simon, Merton Strommen, and Milo Brekke, eds. (1980) Ministry in America: A Complete Report and Analysis, Based on an In-Depth Survey of 47 Denominations in the United States and Canada. San Francisco, CA: Harper and Row. Reviewed: Journal of Supervision and Training, Vol. 5, 1982, p. 216.

15636. Scott, Waldron. (1980) Bring Forth Justice. Grand Rapids, MI: Eerdmans. Evangelism cannot be separated from justice and peace making. Reviewed: International Bulletin of Missionary Research, Vol. 7 (January, 1983), p. 25.

15637. Serjeant, R. B., ed. (1980) The Islamic City: Selected Papers from the Colloquium Held at the Middle East Center Faculty of Oriental Studies, Cambridge, United Kingdom, January 19 to 23, 1976. Paris: UNESCO. A Spanish translation: Barcelona, Spain: UNESCO, 1982.

15638. Sethi, S. Prakash. (1980) Interfaith Center on Corporate Responsibility (ICCR): A Sponsored-Related Movement of the National Council of Churches. Richardson, TX: University of Texas at Dallas, School of Management and Administration.

15639. Seymour, Susan, ed. (1980) The Transformation of a Sacred Town: Bhubaneshwar, India. Boulder, CO: Westview. Reports a study carried out in India over a period of twelve years, with the assistance of Harvard University, dealing with how a modern city developed on a traditional religious site. Hinduism is capable of adapting itself in unexpected ways, the study concludes.

15640. Shepherd, Samuel Claude, Jr. (1980) Churches at Work: Richmond, Virginia, White Protestant Leaders and Social Change in a Southern City, 1900-1929. Thesis (Ph. D.). Madison, WI: University of Wisconsin.

15641. Shriver, Donald W., Jr. (1980) "The Pain and Promise of Pluralism," pp. 1-22 in Joseph L. Allen, ed. Annual of the Society of Christian Ethics. Dallas, TX: Society of Christian Ethics.

15642. Sider, Ronald J., ed. (1980) Cry Justice: The Bible on Hunger and Poverty. New York: Paulist Press. A Bible study guide, arranging scriptural passages in such a way as to encourage Christians to put their Biblical faith into action in behalf of the hungry and poor. Study questions.

15643. Sigrist, Helen. (1980) The Role of the Minister in Providing Counseling Services to Employed Ex-Offenders. Thesis (D. Min.). Washington, DC: Catholic University of America.

15644. Skirrow, Paul. (1980s) Justice in Business and at Work. [London]: Industrial Christian Fellowship. A pamphlet.

15645. Snider, David J. (1980) "The News on Unemployment: A Christian Reading," Justice Ministries: Resources for Urban Mission. Nos. 7-8 (Winter-Spring), pp. 2-5. Followed by an annotated bibliography on theological and biblical reflections on employment.

15646. Snow, David A., Louis Sucherm Jr., and Sheldon Ekland-Olson. (1980) "Social Networks and Social Movements: A Microstructural Approach to Differential Recruitment," American Sociological Review. Vol. 45, No. 5 (October), pp. 787-801. A study of membership recruitment in churches and other voluntary organizations and movements shows that mere dispositional susceptibility is insufficient to recruit new adherents. Other factors include structural proximity, availability, and affective interaction with movement members. Groups that fail to take into account the importance of the latter three factors, even though potential members might agree with them, will find recruitment difficult.

15647. Snyder, Graydon F. (1980) "The Social Ministry of Jesus," Brethren Life and Thought. Vol. 25, No. 1 (Winter), pp. 14-19.

15648. Snyder, Howard A. (1980) The Radical Wesley and Patterns of Church Renewal. Downers Grove, IL: InterVarsity. Snyder recounts the ministry of John Wesley in London, especially among the poor, unemployed, and orphaned.

15649. Spann, Ron. (n. d., 1980?) The Church of the Messiah [Miscellaneous materials]. Detroit, MI: the Church. [Location: ICUIS 4428, see note 2]. Once large and powerful, an Episcopal church in Detroit's lower East Side was decimated because of White flight to suburbs. Charismatic renewal was attempted, as were a number of conserted efforts to reach to neighborhood which suffered from high unemployment rates and housing problems. Positive changes began to occcur. The congregation's program, under the promotion of the Diocese of Michigan, eventually became known in Episcopal circles as the "Michigan Plan."

15650. Sproul, Robert Charles. (1980) Stronger than Steel: the Wayne Alderson Story. San Francisco, CA: Harper and Row.

15651. Stevens-Arroyo, Antonio M., ed. (1980) Prophets Denied Honor: An Anthology on the Hispano Church of the United States. Maryknoll, NY: Orbis. Assembled as a correction to the literature about Catholic immigrants that consistently overlooks the Hispanics, these documents, speeches, poems, and articles trace many of the contributions of Spanish-speaking Americans in the Roman Catholic Church. As with most US Catholic immigrants, a large number of the Hispanics have settled in urban areas and the collected materials reflect this urban orientation.

15652. Stevens-Arroyo, Antonio M. (1980) "Puerto Rican Struggles in the Catholic Church," in Clara E. Rodriquez, Virginia Sanchez Korrol, and Jose Oscar Alers, eds. The Puerto Rican Struggle: Essays on Survival in the US. New York: Puerto Rican Migration Research Consortium, Inc.

15653. Stevenson, Foy. (1980) "Opening the Doors," New World Outlook. n.s. Vol. 40, No. 6 (February), pp. 27-30. Church efforts to settle Vietnamese refugees in Columbia, SC.

15654. Stockwell, Clinton E. (1980) A General Bibliography for Urban Ministers. Chicago, IL: Urban Church Resource Center, SCUPE.

15655. Stubley, Peter. (1980) "Churchmen in a Late Victorian Industrial Town," Theology. Vol. 83, No. 695 (September), pp. 346-354.

Failure on the part of church leaders to understand industrial culture led to poor pastoral ministry in Middlesborough.

15656. Styles, Lawrie. (1980) Industrial Mission in the 80s. Melbourne, Victoria, Australia: Interchurch Trade and Industry Mission in Australia and New Zealand. [Location: ICUIS 4545, see note 2]. The interchurch Trade and Industry Mission often publishes reports which review and reflect on church meetings and issues. Styles' comments on a recent meeting of the World Conference of Mission and Evangelism which met in Melbourne in May of 1980. For other reports by Styles or pertaining to the Interchurch Mission, see ICUIS Nos. 3887 and 3948.

15657. Stylios, Euthymios. (1980) To synchronon astikon perivallon hos poimantikon provlema: melete "poimantikes koinoniologias." Athens: Heptalophos. The urban environment as a pastoral problem for Greek Orthodox Churches in Athens. Originally published as the author's thesis at the School of Theology, University of Athens. Bibliography.

15658. Sweeting, George. (1980) "The City: Vast Laboratory of Need," Moody Monthly. Vol. 81, No. 1 (September), pp. 80+.

15659. Takayama, K. Peter. (1980) "Strains, Conflicts, and Schisms in Protestant Denominations," pp. 298-329 in Ross P. Scherer, ed. American Denominational Organization. Pasadena, CA: William Carey Library.

15660. Tamney, Joseph B. (1980) "Functional Religiosity and Modernization in Indonesia," Sociological Analysis. Vol. 41, No. 1 (Spring), pp. 55-65. Tamney finds that functional religiosity increases with education and urbanization in Indonesia, counter to the normal secularization hypotheses.

15661. Tamney, Joseph B. (1980) "Modernization and Religious Purification: Islam in Indonesia," Review of Religious Research. Vol. 22, No. 2 (December), pp. 207-218. A study of religious behavior among the Javanese shows that modernization (increased education and urbanization) does not so much lead to secularization as to a purification of religious life styles and a decline of folk religion. Bibliography.

15662. Thernstrom, Stephan, ed. (1980) Harvard Encyclopedia of American Ethnic Groups. Cambridge, Massachusetts: Harvard University Press. Basic reference information about ethnic groups.

15663. Thomson, Randall and David Knoke. (1980) "Voluntary

Associations and Voting Turnout of American Ethnoreligious Groups," Ethnicity. Vol. 7, No. 1, pp. 56-69.

15664. Toronto Area Presbytery and Toronto United Church Council. (1980) Directions: A Mission Strategy for the Metro United Church, 1980-1985. Toronto, Canada: Toronto Area Presbytery and Toronto United Church Council.

15665. Trabold, Robert. (1980) "Christian Perspectives on the City," The City of God. Vol. 2, No. 3 (Winter), pp. 3-18.

15666. Tranvouez, Yvon. (1980) "Entre Rome et le peuple, 1920-1960," pp. 413-480 in François Lebrun, ed. Histoire des Catholiques en France. Toulouse, France: Privat.

15667. Tucker, Robert. (1980) "Class and Culture in Anglo-American Religious Historiography: A Review Essay," Labour/Le Travail. (Autumn), pp. 159-169. A review of literature regarding the religious aspects of labor protest in the USA and Britain.

15668. United Methodist Church, General Board of Discipleship. (1980s?) Large Membership Church Initiative. [Video recording] Nashville, TN: the Board.

15669. Urban Church Resource Review. (beginning in the 1980s?) Boston, MA: Emmanuel Gospel Center. A newsletter.

15670. Urban Ministries, Inc. (1980s) [Miscellaneous documents, papers, curricula]. Chicago, IL: Urban Ministries, Inc. Publishes a quarterly church school curriculum for preschool, primary, junior, youth, and adult.

15671. Urban Update. (beginning in the 1980s?) Boston, MA: Emmanuel Gospel Center. A periodical.

15672. Van Hemert, M. M. J. (1980) En zij verontschuldigen sich ... De ontwikkeling van het misbezoekcijfer 1966-1979. Den Haag, Netherlands: KASKI, Memorandum No. 213. A comparison of Dutch mass attendance with attendance rates of other nations allows the author to draw conclusions about motives of Catholics for choosing to attend or not to attend. Community size is one explanatory variable, along with other demographic and social variables.

15673. Verbunt, Gilles. (1980) L'integration par l'autonomie: La CFDT, l'Eglise catholique, la FASTI face aux revendications d'autonomie des travailleurs immigrés. Paris: CIEMM. Re: the church and alien labor in France. Originally a doctoral thesis. Bibliography.

15674. Villa, James. (1980) Renewing the Faith Community: A Liturgical-Catechetical Model for the Religious Formation of Adult Members of St. Pamphilus Parish. Thesis (D. Min.). Pittsburgh, PA: Pittsburgh Theological Seminary.

15675. Vincent, John J., ed. (1980s?) Services, Agapes, Housewarmings, Services for the Home, House Group Liturgies, Community Prayers. Sheffield, England: Ashram Community, Urban Theology Unit. A pamphlet.

15676. Vishnewski, Stanley. (1980?) Wings of Dawn. New York: Catholic Worker.

15677. Vrcan, Srdjan. (1980) "Social Class and Religion in Yugoslavia," pp. 68-77 in Gregory Baum, ed. Work and Religion. New York: Seabury.

15678. Wahlstrom, Pera. (1980) "Storstadmission," Svensk Missionstiddskrift [Thematic issue: City missions]. Vol. 68, No. 3, pp. 1-77. Re: city missions in Sweden.

15679. Walker, Orris George, Jr. (1980) Developing a Program for a Culturally Inclusive Urban Episcopal Parish. Thesis (D. Min.). Madison, NJ: Drew University.

15680. Wallace, Samuel E. (1980) The Urban Environment. Homewood, IL: Dorsey Press.

15681. Walters, Thomas Paul. (1980) A Study of the Relationship between Religious Orientation and Cognitive Moral Maturity in Volunteer Religion Teachers from Selected Suburban Catholic Parishes in the Archdiocese of Detroit. Thesis (Ph. D.). Detroit, MI: Wayne State University.

15682. Washington, Preston R. (1980) A Planning Guide for City Day Camps. New York: American Baptist Churches of Metropolitan New York. A resource for local churches that operate summer day camps or all-day vacation Bible schools, this brief pamphlet outlines planning processes, activities available in urban areas, and job descriptions for staff members.

15683. Webster, Douglas D. (1980) "Social Action Begins in the Local Church," Christianity Today. Vol. 24, No. 17 (October 10), pp. 28-29+.

15684. Wesson, Anthony J. (1980) Technology, Philosophy and the Person. London: Chester House Publications. The Charles Coulson lecture delivered on October 27, 1980 at the Luton Industrial College.

15685. Weverbergh, Roger. (1980) Het Utrechts citypastoraat: een rapport. Leiden, The Netherlands: Interuniversitaire Instituut Voor Missiologie en Oecomenica. Re: city ministries in Utrecht, Netherlands.

15686. "What's Ahead for Urban Clergy?" (1980) JSAC Grapevine. Vol. 11, No. 9 (April), pp. [1-5]. Includes short articles by William R. Grace, Robert K. Hudnut, Nancy Barnhart, and T. Richard Snyder.

15687. Whitehead, Evelyn Eaton and James D. Whitehead. (1980) Method in Ministry. New York: Seabury Press.

15688. Whitehurst, James Emerson. (1980) "The Mainstreaming of the Black Muslims: Healing the Hate," Christian Century. Vol. 97, No. 2 (February 27), pp. 225-229. Whitehurst comments on the movement of Black Muslims toward being more thoroughly integrated in society: from tirades against "white devils" to patriotic slogans, from weapons to welcoming arms, and from separation to openness.

15689. Wiegers, William C. and Fred Stickney. (1980) Planning Assistance: Vocational Rehabilitation, Sekondi-Takoradi, Ghana and Oakland, CA. s.n.: Goodwill Industries International.

15690. Wilke, Harold H. (1980) Creating a Caring Congregation: Guidelines for Ministering with the Handicapped. Nashville, TN: Abingdon. Suggestions for churches about inclusiveness for handicapped persons, including resource listings.

15691. William Temple Foundation. (1980) Involvement in Community: A Christian Contribution. Manchester, England: William Temple Foundation. A working party of persons involved in community agencies and inner city ministries recommend stronger connections among their various community programs and greater inclusiveness of persons from all classes in program leadership. The authors are committed to increasing self-determination for the poor and powerless. The relationship between faith and community work is discussed.

15692. William, John. (1980) "A Ministry in Relation to the Town Hall," Crucible. [Vol. 19, No. 2] (April-June), pp. 77-82.

15693. Williams, Cecil. (1980) I Am Alive: An Autobiography. San Francisco, CA: Harper and Row. At the time of writing, Williams was the innovative and controversial pastor of Glide Memorial United Methodist Church, San Francisco, CA.

15694. Williams, Peter W. (1980) Popular Religion in America: Symbolic Change and the Modernization Process in Historical Perspective. Englewood Cliffs, NJ: Prentice-Hall.

15695. Williams, Peter W. (1980) Catholicism Militant: The Public Face of the Archdiocese of Cincinnati, 1900-1960. Notre Dame, IN: Center for the Study of American Catholicism, University of Notre Dame. A pamphlet.

15696. Williamson, Joseph C. (1980) "A Mainline Parish-Based Protestant Ministry with Students," pp. 285-302 in Robert Rankin, ed. Recovery of Spirit in Higher Education. New York: Seabury Press.

15697. Wilson, Robert Leroy. (1980) Urban Living Qualities from the Vantage Point of the Elderly. Chapel Hill, NC: Institute for Research in Social Science, University of North Carolina.

15698. Wilson, Robert Leroy, Patrick Miller and Lee M. Mandell. (1980) Dirty Rotten Kids? A Description of Children Who Are Labeled as Behavior Problems and Their Relationship to the Human Service System. Raleigh, NC: Applied Research Group, Center for Urban Affairs and Community Service.

15699. Wilson, Stephen. (1980) "Cults of Saints in the Churches of Central Paris," Comparative Studies in Society and History. Vol. 22, No. 1, pp. 548-575. Same title: pp. 233-260 in Stephen Wilson, ed. Saints and Their Cults: Studies in Religious Sociology, Folklore, and History. Cambridge, England: Cambridge University Press, 1983.

15700. Wilson, William Julius. (1980) The Declining Significance of Race: Blacks and Changing American Institutions. [2nd edition]. Chicago, IL: University of Chicago Press.

15701. Winter, Derek, ed. (1980) Putting Theology to Work.

London: Conference for World Mission, the British Council of Churches. A collection of articles, all papers from the Fircroft Conference, about the impact of Latin American theology in Europe, with particular reference to Christian basic communities. Articles by Jose Miguez Bonino and John J. Vincent are included.

15702. Wolkovich Valkavicius, William. (1980) Lithuanian Pioneer Priests of New England. Brooklyn, NY: Franciscan Press.

15703. Woodward, Kathleen, ed. (1980) Myths of Information: Technology and Postindustrial Culture. London: Routledge and Kegan Paul. Also: Madison, WI: Coda Press.

15704. World Council of Churches, Commission on World Mission. (1980) "Mission in Rotterdam: In Bits and Pieces," One World [World Council of Churches]. No. 53 (January-February), pp. 16-17.

15705. World Council of Churches, World Conference on Faith, Science, and the Future [1979, Massachusetts Institute of Technology, Cambridge, MA]. (1980) Faith and Science in an Unjust World: Report of the World Council of Churches' Conference on Faith, Science and the Future. Geneva, Switzerland: World Council of Churches. Plenary presentations and reports of the conference. Volume 1 edited by Roger L. Shinn; Volume 2 edited by Paul Abrecht. Bibliography.

15706. World Movement of Christian Workers. (beginning in the 1980s?) Infor. Brussels, Belgium: the Movement. A periodical.

15707. Wright, Elliott. (1980) "Atlantic City after Casinos," New World Outlook. n.s. Vol. 41, No. 4 (December), pp. 15-19. Legalized gambling appears not to have solved Atlantic City's economic and social problems with a large flow of new income, as was promised by developers and other supporters of gambling.

15708. Wulff, Joan. (1980) "Tale of Two City Ministries," HIS. Vol. 40, No. 6 (March), pp. 19-23.

15709. Yacoob, May Mirza. (1980) The Ahmadiyya: Urban Adaptation in the Ivory Coast. Thesis (Ph. D.). Boston, MA: University of Boston.

15710. Zehr, Howard and Earl Sears. (1980) Mediating the Victim-Offender Conflict. Akron, PA: Mennonite Central Committee. [Location: Mennonite Historical Society, Lancaster, PA]. Begun in Kitchener, Ontario, in 1974, a Mennonite program seeks to fulfill the biblical injunction to reconcile victims and offenders. Victims are allowed to resolve nagging questions about the offender's intentions. Offenders learn the true consequences of their actions and the reasons for their punishment. Bibliography. A pamphlet.

15711. Ziegenhals, Walter E. (1980) "A Perspective on Urban Ministry: 1950-1980," Christian Ministry. Vol. 11, No. 6 (November), pp. 11-14.

15712. Ziegert, Richard. (1980) Der neue Diakonat: das freie Amt für eine missionarische Kirche, Bilanz einer französischen Bewegung, 1959-1977. Göttingen, West Germany: Vandenhoeck und Ruprecht. Re: Worker priests.

15713. African Union Methodist Protestant Church. (1981) The Big Quarterly: Wilmington's Oldest Folk Festival, Sunday, August 30, 1981. Wilmington, DE: the Church. A pamphlet.

15714. Agócs, Carol. (1981) "Ethnic Settlement in a Metropolitan Area: A Typology of Communities," Ethnicity. Vol. 8, No, 2 (June), pp. 127-148.

15715. Alexander, David. (1981) "Survival in the City," Church Herald. Vol. 38, No. 3 (February 6), pp. 16-17.

15716. Allen, Jere and George Bullard. (1981) Shaping a Future for the Church in the Changing Community. Atlanta, GA: Home Mission Board, Southern Baptist Convention. A guidebook to help congregations analyze and plan for community change in racial or ethnic composition, in socio-economic level of residents, in lifestyles, and in population density. Community change is discussed in terms of developmental stages, from the newly developed to post-transition. A typology of city churches is offered: old First churches, neighborhood churches, metro/regional churches, special purpose churches, and urban fringe churches. Bibliography.

15717. Ankeny, Edwin Alonzo. (1981) Ministering to Persons Living in the Eastport Area Apartment Complexes. Thesis (D. Min.). Madison, NJ: Drew University.

15718. Appleyard, Robert B. (1981) "A Bishop Ponders His Role in Plant Closings," The Witness [Ambler, PA]. Vol. 64, No. 1 (January), pp. 4-7.

15719. Armstrong, James. (1981) From the Underside: Evangelism from a Third World Vantage Point. Maryknoll, NY: Orbis. Evangelism represents good news only when it addresses the needs of the poor and the poor understand the message. Armstrong advocates a kind of evangelism in which the evangelists identify with the poor and their concerns.

15720. Atherton, John. (1981) "Trade Unionism: Dilemmas and Challenges for Christian Thought and Practice," Theology. Vol. 84, No. 701 (September), pp. 348-356.

15721. Austin, Tom. (1981) "Can Wealthy Christians Reach the Poor?" Christianity Today. Vol. 25, No. 20 (November 20), pp. 42-43+. Ghetto workers are skeptical of the efforts mobilized by "high power" groups.

15722. Baer, Hans A. (1981) "Prophets and Advisors in Black Spiritual Churches: Therapy, Palliative, or Opiate," Culture, Medicine and Psychiatry. Vol. 5, pp. 145-170.

15723. Bakke, Raymond J. (1981) "Toward a Theology of the City," Cities. Vol. 1, No. 5 (September), pp. 7-12. Reflection on the biblical and historical resources the church brings to urban ministry.

15724. Balasuriya, Tissa. (1981) "Health as a Function of Justice," Point: Forum for Melanesian Affairs [10]. No. 2, pp. 7-13.

15725. Baldwin, Leland Dewitt. (1981) The American Quest for the City of God. Macon, GA: Mercer University Press. Baldwin traces the effects of the Christian concept of the City of God on the emergence of the American city from its English roots and colonial expression to the cold war era.

15726. Barth, Robert. (1981) Protestantismus, soziale Frage und Sozialismus im Kanton Zürich 1830-1914. Zürich, Switzerland: Theologischer Verlag. A history of Protestantism and socialism in the Canton of Zürich. Bibliography.

15727. Bastian, Hans-Dieter, ed. (1981) Kirchliches Amt im Umbruch. Munich, West Germany: Kaiser. Re: radical change in church ministry.

15728. Beal, John David. (1981) Sent Forth to Multifamily Residents. Atlanta, GA: Metropolitan Mission, Baptist Home Mission Board, Southern Baptist Convention. A pamphlet.

15729. Belknap, Charles. (1981) "The Urban Church: Choosing between Two Gods," The Witness [Ambler, PA]. Vol. 64, No. 2 (February), pp. 16-17.

15730. Belknap, Charles and David Duncan. (1981) "Short Formula for a Resourceful Parish," The Witness [Ambler, PA]. Vol. 64, No. 9 (September), pp. 8-9.

15731. Belth, Nathan C. (1981) A Promise to Keep: Narrative of the American Encounter with Anti-Semitism. New York: Schocken.

15732. Benjamin, Barbara. (1981) "Strangers in the Land: How I Learned to Minister in Christ's Name to Newly Immigrant Americans," The Other Side. Vol. 118 (July), pp. 26-38.

15733. Benjamin, Barbara. (1981) "Embracing Our New Neighbors: Immigrant Love," HIS. Vol. 42, No. 2 (November), pp. 10-11.

15734. Bethel, Elizabeth Rauh. (1981) Promiseland: A Century of Life in a Negro Community. Philadelphia, PA: Temple University Press.

15735. Blackburn, Tom. (1981) Christian Business Ethics: Doing Good while Doing Well. Chicago, IL: Fides/Claretian.

15736. Bledsaw, Jim and R. Franklin Cook. (1981) "Serving in the City Means Sacrifice--and Spiritual Rewards," Preacher's Magazine [Thematic issue: Urban ministry]. Vol. 56, No. 4 (June), pp. 12-13.

15737. Boonstra, John, ed. (1981) "Labor and Religion," Radical Religion [Thematic issue]. Vol. 5, No. 3, pp. 3-94.

15738. Bowden, Charles and Lew Kreinberg. (1981) Street Signs Chicago: Neighborhood and Other Illusions of Big City Life. Chicago, IL: Chicago Review Press. Re: economic and social conditions in Chicago neighborhoods.

15739. Boyer, John W. (1981) Political Radicalism in Late Imperial Vienna: Origins of Christian Social Movement, 1848-1897. Chicago, IL: University of Chicago Press.

15740. Bradshaw, Thornton F. and David Vogel. (1981) Corporations and Their Critics: Issues and Problems of Corporate Social Responsibility. New York: McGraw-Hill.

15741. Brakelmann, Günter. (1981) Kirche in Konflikten ihrer Zeit. Munich, West Germany: Kaiser. Re: the church's involvement with conflict in the 19th and 20th century.

15742. Branch, Harold T. (1981) "Implications of Multiple Affiliation for Black Southern Baptists," Baptist History and Heritage [Thematic issue: Black Southern Baptists]. Vol. 16, No. 3 (July), pp. 49-60.

15743. British Council of Churches. (1981) A Statement on Behalf of the Brixton Council of Churches. London: the Council. [Location: ICUIS 4756, see note 2]. Signing pastors describe the Brixton riot and suggest remedies. For additional materials on economic and social problems in Britain, see ICUIS Nos. 4750-4757.

15744. Brock, Charles. (1981) Indigenous Church Planting. Nashville, TN: Broadman Press.

15745. Brown, Robert McAfee. (1981) Making Peace in the Global Village. Philadelphia, PA: Westminster.

15746. Brown, Ronald A. (1981) Technology, Change and Christian Belief: The Charles Coulson Lecture, October 31, 1981. London: Polytechnic of North London. Although technology is not new and the alienation between technology and the church is long standing, Brown calls for renewed theological study in light of recent rapid, inexorable and often frightening technological changes. Delivered as the 1981 Charles Coulson lecture at the Luton Industrial College, Luton, England. A pamphlet. Bibliography.

15747. Bruce, Joe Wayne. (1981) Plan for Developing the Ministry of City Missionary by Formulating a Program of Urban Evangelism. Thesis (D. Min.). Fort Worth, TX: Southwestern Baptist Theological Seminary.

15748. Buckleiter, Anne. (1981) "Babes in the Urban Woods," Church Herald. Vol. 38, No. 17 (August 21), pp. 4-5. Impressions of a small town dweller upon visiting the low income section of a large city.

15749. Buenker, John D., Gerald Michael Greenfield, and William J. Murin. (1981) Urban History: A Guide to Information Sources. Detroit, MI: Gale Research. A general bibliography on cities and towns in the United States.

15750. "Built as a City." (1981) Crucible. [Vol. 20, No. 4] (October-December), pp. 145-147. An editorial on urban discontent and violence in England.

15751. Cafferty, Pastora San Juan. (1981) The Politics of Language: The Dilemma of Bilingual Education for Puerto Ricans. Boulder, CO: Westview. Introduction by James Coleman.

15752. Calthorpe, Peter. (1981) "Marin Solar Village: A Paradigm for Growth and Sustainability," Cities. Vol. 1, No. 4 (July), pp. 18-22. Plans for turning an abandoned Air Force base in California into an energy efficient community.

15753. Caplan, Arthur L. and Daniel Callahan. (1981) Ethics in Hard Times. New York: Plenum. This volume has implications regarding the ethical aspects of public policy and policy making.

15754. Caplan, Lionel. (1981) "Morality and Polyethnic Identity in Urban South India," in A. C. Mayaer, ed. Culture and Morality: Essays in Honour of Christoph von Fürer-Haimendorf. Delhi, India: OUP.

15755. Carder, Kenneth. (1981) "The Church and the Prisoner," Cities. Vol. 1, No. 4 (July), pp. 13-14. Carder describes people who clamor for severity and harshness in the treatment of prisoners as sentimentalists who refuse to face facts.

15756. Carnahan, Roy E. (1981) "Measuring Ministerial Success in Central City Ministry," Preacher's Magazine [Thematic issue: Urban ministry]. Vol. 56, No. 4 (June), pp. 14-16.

15757. "Los Católicos hispanos en los Estados Unidos." (1981) Pro Mundi Vita: Dossiers Series 'Informes' for Latin America. Re: Catholic Hispanics in the United States.

15758. Chalfant, H. Paul, Robert E. Beckley and E. Eddie Palmer. (1981) Religion in Contemporary Society. Sherman Oaks, CA: Alfred Publishing.

15759. Chastain, C. R., Jr. (1981) "An Urbana," Cities. Vol. 1, No. 6 (November), pp. 15-16.

15760. Cho, Paul Yonggi. (1981) Successful Home Cell Groups. Plainfield, NJ: Logos.

15761. Christian Conference of Asia, Urban Rural Mission.

(1981) Struggling to Survive: Women Workers in Asia. Kowloon, Hong Kong: the Conference. [Location: ICUIS 4705, see note 2]. Stories of working women in Southeast Asia reflect massive oppression. Attempts to form unions and organize protest meet with uneven success.

15762. "The Church and the City: Signs of Despair, Signs of Hope." (1981) JSAC Grapevine. Vol. 13, No. 2 (July), pp. [1-4]. Includes brief articles by Michael Harrington, Herman Badillo and Shirley Chisholm. Reprints the "Hispanic Manifesto."

15763. Cipolla, Costantino. (1981) Religione e cultura operaia. Brescia, Italy: Morcelliana. Bibliography.

15764. CISL: 1948-1957: Ispirazione cattolica, scelta de classe, nuovo sindacato. (1981) Messina, Italy: Hobelix. History of Confederazione italiana sindacati lavoratori, an Italian trade union.

15765. The Cities: Challenges and Dreams. (1981) [Filmstrip, 87 frames, color, sound cassette, manual]. Atlanta, GA: Home Mission Board, the Southern Baptist Convention.

15766. Clark, David L. (1981) "The Mythic Meaning of the City," pp. 269-290 in Clifford G. Christians, ed. Jacques Ellul: Interpretative Essays. Urbana, IL: University of Illinois Press.

15767. Clay-Tor, Francois. (1981) "Washington's New Lansburg Center," Cities. Vol. 1, No. 6 (November), pp. 26-27.

15768. Clifford, Richard Lorenzo. (1981) A Systems Approach to Parish Development among Churches Located in a Village Setting within a City. Thesis (D. Min.). Madison, NJ: Drew University.

15769. Community Analysis. (1981) Pasadena, CA: Charles E. Fuller Institute of Evangelism and Church Growth.

15770. Community Work in the Inner City. (1981) St. Albans, England: Christian Action.

15771. Cone, Roger Daniel. (1981) A Suburban Church Faces Change. Thesis (D. Min.). Claremont, CA: School of Theology at Claremont.

15772. Connell, John. (1981) "The Jewish Ghetto in Nineteenth Century Leeds: A Case of Urban Involution," Urban Anthropology.

Vol. 10, No. 1 (Spring), pp. 1-26. Jewish migration to Leeds was rapid in the 1880s, resulting in a large community developing in an inner city area. Parallels are drawn to migration in 20th century "third world" nations.

15773. Consejo Episcopal Latinoamericano. (1981?) Pastoral de la metropoli. Bogotá, Colombia: Consejo Episcopal Latinoamericano, Documentos CELAM. Re: pastoral theology in metropilitan areas.

15774. Cook, R. Franklin. (1981) "The Jonah Syndrome," Preacher's Magazine [Thematic issue: Urban ministry]. Vol. 56, No. 4 (June), pp. 1-6.

15775. Copsey, Katheryn. (1981) "The Child in Urban Industrial Mission," pp. 167-182 in John Ferguson, ed. Christianity, Society and Education: Robert Raikes, Past, Present, and Future. London: SPCK.

15776. Corwin, Charles. (1981) "Cultural Diversity as a Dynamic for Growth," Evangelical Missions Quarterly. Vol. 17, No. 1 (January), pp. 15-22.

15777. Costantino, Frank. (1981) The Crime Fighter's Handbook: Sound Suggestions for All Who Desire to Reflect the Love of the Lord Jesus Christ to Lonely, Forgotten Men and Women in Jail and Prison. Dallas, TX; Acclaimed Books.

15778. Courtes-Lapeyrat, Jean, et al. (1981) Paris, où va ton église? Paris: Le Centurion. Re: the church in Paris, France. Bibliography.

15779. Cousineau, Jacques. (1981) L'Église d'ici et le social, 1940-1960. Montréal, Canada: Editions Bellarmin. Re: church and labor relations in Quebec, Canada.

15780. Crysdale, Stewart. (1981) Conflict in Worker's Families and the Effect of Religion. Paper presented at the 1981 Meeting of the Association for the Sociology of Religion. [Location: SUNY at Buffalo, NY].

15781. Cunningham, Barry K. (1981) "Evangelizing Urban Blacks," Preacher's Magazine [Thematic issue: Urban ministry]. Vol. 56, No. 4 (June).

15782. Curry, Leonard P. (1981) The Free Black in Urban America, 1800-1850. Chicago, IL: University of Chicago Press.

15783. Dale, Robert D. (1981) To Dream Again. Nashville, TN: Broadman Press. Dale assumes churches go through a life cycle analogous to animals, with birth, growth, maturity, decline and death all being expected stages. Revitalization is possible too, the life cycle analogy notwithstanding, and several suggestions are offered on how to accomplish it.

15784. Davis, James Hill. (1981) "Dilemmas of Racial Transition," Cities. Vol. 1, No. 5 (September), pp. 18-23.

15785. Day, Dorothy. (1981) "Room for Christ," The Other Side. Vol. 17, No. 12 (December), pp. 12-15. A reprint.

15786. Deedy, John. (1981) "The Church in the World: The Unification Church and the City of Gloucester," Theology Today. Vol. 37, No. 4 (January), pp. 480-486.

15787. Dewitt, Robert L. (1981) "Episcopal Urban Caucus: A Promising 1-Year-Old," Witness [Ambler, PA]. Vol. 64, No. 1 (January), pp. 3+.

15788. DeWitt, Robert L., ed. (1981) "Bishops Ponder Urban Apocalypse," The Witness [Ambler, PA]. [2 parts] Vol. 64, No. 3 (March), pp. 4-9; No. 4 (April), pp. 14-18. Response: No. 6 (June), pp. 10-14.

15789. Dick, Malcolm. (1981) "Urban Growth and the Social Role of the Stockport Sunday School, 1784-1833," pp. 53-67 in John Ferguson, ed. Christianity, Society and Education. London: SPCK.

15790. Dietrich, Jeff. (1981) "The Kingdom of God and of the Poor," America. Vol. 145, No. 21 (December 26), pp. 422-423. Well crafted vignettes of the skid row outcasts in Los Angeles support Dietrich's call to serve Christ's Kingdom in the inner city.

15791. Dobbelaere, Karel. (1981) "Secularization: A Multi-Dimension Concept," Current Sociology. Vol. 29, No. 2 (Summer), pp. 3-213. Dobbelaere reviews the development and refinement of secularization as a sociological concept, arguing that distinctions must be made among the notions of declines in church involvement, religious change, and secularization as a process of laicization. He concludes that secularization, or laicization, is not a straight line process with society moving more or less steadily from the sacred toward to secular, but is in fact reversible depending on the configuration of influences existent in any particular society. Dobbelaere's work represents an attempt to organize secularization theory systematically. An annotated bibliography is attached.

15792. Dougherty, Mary A. (1981) "The Social Gospel According to Phoebe: Methodist Deaconesses in Metropolis, 1885-1918," pp. 200-216 in Hildah F. Thomas, ed. Women in New Worlds. Nashville, TN: Abingdon.

15793. Drescher, Tim. (1981) "The Community Mural Movement," Cities. Vol. 1, No. 6 (November), pp. 17-22.

15794. Drimmelen, Rob van. (1981) Dutch Churches, Church Organizations, and Transnational Corporations. Amsterdam, The Netherlands: Ecumenical Study and Action Centre on Investments. [Location: ICUIS 4763, see note 2]. A summary of Dutch efforts to influence the policies of transnational corporations. For additional materials on the effects of transnational corporations in Asia, see ICUIS Nos. 4276-4279, 4736-4742. For information on transnational corporations in other parts of the world, see ICUIS Nos. 4758-4774.

15795. DuBose, Francis M. (1981) "Challenge of Serving the Urban Family," Social Work and Christianity. Vol. 8, Nos. 1-2 (Spring-Fall), pp. 11-24.

15796. Duntze, Klaus. (1981) Die Berliner Wohnungspolitik: Ihre sozialen Auswirkungen und die Aufgabe der Kirche. Berlin: Dokumentation 24, 1981 des Evangelischen Bildungswerks Berlin. Comment on the social consequences of the politics of building houses, with implications for the church.

15797. Ellerman, David P. (1981) "What Is a Worker Cooperative?" Cities. Vol. 1, No. 6 (November), pp. 8-32.

15798. Elliott, John H. (1981) A Home for the Homeless. Philadelphia, PA: Fortress Press.

15799. Elliott, Ralph. (1981) "Dangers of the Church Growth Movement: Is It Possible to Maintain Our Identity as the Church and to Be a 'Successful' Institution at the Same Time?" The Christian Century. Vol. 98, No. 25 (August 12-19), pp. 799-801.

15800. Ellis, Marc H. (1981) Peter Maurin: Prophet in the Twentieth Century. New York: Paulist Press.

15801. Elmore, Ralph Monroe. (1981) Discipling Inner City

Peoples: Models for Church Growth among Ethnic Groups in Los Angeles. Thesis (Th. M.). Pasadena, CA: Fuller Theological Seminary, School of World Mission. Suggestions for revitalizing downtown churches.

15802. Elrod, John W. (1981) Kierkegaard and Christendom. Princeton, NJ: Princeton University Press. See especially Chapter 1 for a discussion of social conditions in Denmark during Kierkegaard's life (1813-1855) and their influence on his philosophical views regarding cities, centralization, and modernity.

15803. Evangelization Portraits: Hispanic Communities. (1981?) [Washington, DC]: Catholic Bishops Evangelization Committee.

15804. Figueroa, Jose E. (1981) The Cultural Dynamic of Puerto Rican Spiritism: Class, Nationality, and Religion in a Brooklyn Ghetto. Thesis (Ph. D.). New York: City University of New York.

15805. Firebaugh, Glenn. (1981) "How Effective Are City-Wide Crusades?" Christianity Today. Vol. 25, No. 6 (March 27), pp. 24-29. Firebaugh assesses the work of the Billy Graham Association in the Seattle-Tacoma, WA, crusade. Most clergy responding to Firebaugh's questions give positive evaluations of the campaign's lasting impact.

15806. Fischer, Claude S. (1981) "The Public and Private Worlds of City Life," American Sociological Review. Vol. 46, No. 3 (June), pp. 306-316.

15807. Fisher, Paul. (1981) "Not Yet Utopia: Questions about Micro-Technology," Crucible. [Vol. 20, No. 2] (April-June), pp. 70-75.

15808. Flynt, J. Wayne. (1981) "Southern Baptists: Rural to Urban Transition," Baptist History and Heritage. Vol. 16, No. 1 (January), pp. 24-34.

15809. Foster, Alice. (1981) The City. Toronto, Canada: Berkeley Studio.

15810. Fowler, Dorothy Granfield. (1981) A City Church: The First Presbyterian Church of New York, 1716-1976. [New York]: the Church. Parkhurst was pastor of this church. Bibliography.

15811. Fowler, James. (1981) Stages of Faith: The Psychology of Human Development and the Quest for Meaning. New York: Harper and Row.

15812. Fuller, Millard. (1981) "Habitat for Humanity: A New Frontier in Christian Mission," Cities. Vol. 1, No. 4 (July), pp. 15-17.

15813. Funchion, Michael M. (1981) "Irish Chicago: Church, Homeland Politics and Class, the Shaping of an Ethnic Group, 1870-1900," pp. 15-45 in Peter De A. Jones and Melvin Holli, eds. Ethnic Chicago. Grand Rapids, MI: Eerdmans. Reprinted: Dolores A. Liptak, ed. A Church of Many Cultures. New York: Garland, 1988.

15814. Gable, Dennis R., Mary Ann McClemens and Robert E. Larson, Jr., eds. (1981) Contact Training and International Norms of Federation. Harrisburg, PA: Contact Teleministries USA. Re: a training program for laity and clergy who answer calls received in a telephone ministry.

15815. Galilea, Segundo. (1981) Religiosidad popular y pastoral hispano-americana. New York: Centro Católico de Pastoral para Hispanos del Nordeste. Re: Catholic pastoral work with Hispanic Americans.

15816. Gallagher, Robert. (1981) Staying in the City. Cincinnati, OH: Forward Movement Publications. A pamphlet.

15817. Garcia, S. (1981) "Why Aim for the Cities," Wesleyan Advocate. (December 21), pp. 5+. [See note 3].

15818. Gartner, Lloyd P. (1981) "Urban History and the Pattern of Provincial Jewish Settlement in Victorian England," Jewish Journal of Sociology. Vol. 23, No. 1 (June), pp. 37-56.

15819. Genet, Harry. (1981) "Inter-Varsity Generates Soul to Reach the Heart of the City," Christianity Today. Vol. 25, No. 3 (February 6), pp. 72-80. Re: the 1980 meeting of Inter-Varsity Christian Fellowship in Washington.

15820. Gerard, Emmanuel and Eugeen de Jonghe. (1981) De Kracht can een overtuiging: 60 jaar ACW, 1921-1981. Zele, Belgium: Reinaert. A history of Algemeen Christelijk Werkersverbond, a Catholic trade union in Belgium. Bibliography.

15821. Ghirelli, Tommaso. (1981) La liberazione del lavoro nelle encicliche. Thesis (STD). Rome: Pontificia Università lateranense.

15822. Gibbs, Mark. (1981) Christians with Secular Power. Philadelphia, PA: Fortress. Reviewed: Review and Expositor, Vol. 81

(Spring, 1984), p. 351. Book Newsletter of Augsburg Publishing House, No. 493 (September-October, 1981). International Review of Missions, Vol. 72 (July, 1983), p. 423. Perkins Journal, Vol. 37 (Summer, 1984), p. 42.

15823. Gilder, George. (1981) Wealth and Poverty. New York: Basic Books. Reviewed: Concordia Journal, Vol. 9 (March, 1983), p. 79. Christian Scholar's Review, Vol. 12, No. 1 (1983), p. 72.

15824. Gillett, Richard W. (1981) "Plant Closures: Major New Issue," The Witness [Ambler, PA]. Vol. 64, No. 1 (January), pp. 4-7.

15825. Girgis, Sami Said. (1981) Plan for Developing a Christian Community Center to Serve the Needs of Immigrants from the Arab World in Jersey City, New Jersey. Thesis (D. Min.). Madison, NJ: Drew University.

15826. Gondolf, Edward. (1981) The Church and Urban Problems. Elsah, IL: Principia College. An Alton Community Training Program. Alton's religious leaders consider the role of their churches in meeting community needs.

15827. Göpfert, Michael and Christian Modehn, eds. (1981) Kirche in der Stadt: Erfahrungen, Experimente, Modelle in europäischen Großstädten. Stuttgart, West Germany: Verlag W. Kohlhammer. A collection of articles about the experiences and experiments of religious groups in major European cities, with biographical notes about the authors. Bibliographical footnotes.

15828. Gorman, Charles D. (1981) "The Downtown Priest," Homiletic and Pastoral Review. Vol. 81, Nos. 11-12 (August-September), pp. 19-23. Gorman describes how priests might cope with excessive numbers of appeals for financial and other assistance in inner city parishes.

15829. Grant, Geraldine S. (1981) New Immigrants and Ethnicity: A Preliminary Research Report on Immigrants in Queens. New York: Ethnic Studies Project, Queens College of CUNY.

15830. Gray, Henry David. (1981) "The Urban Opportunity," Congregational Journal. Vol. 6, No. 3 (April), pp. 2-22.

15831. Green, Alfred. (1981) Growing Up in Attercliffe: Honey with a Ladle...Vinegar with a Teaspoon. Sheffield, England: New City Paperbacks [Urban Theology Unit]. Green tells stories from the 1920s about ordinary people's daily life and faith in Sheffield's now demolished East End.

15832. Gremmels, Christian, et al., eds. (1981) An Ort der Arbeit: Berichte und Kommentare: überlegungen zu einer Theologie der Arbeit. Munchen, Germany: Kaiser. Re: a theology of labor and conditions of laboring classes in Germany. Bibliography.

15833. Guide for Establishing Ethnic Congregations. (1981) Atlanta, GA: Language Mission Division, Home Mission Board, Southern Baptist Convention.

15834. Guinan, Michael D. (1981) Gospel Poverty: Witness to the Risen Christ, a Study in Biblical Spirituality. New York: Paulist Press.

15835. Hadaway, C. Kirk. (1981) "The Demographic Environment and Church Membership Change," Journal for the Scientific Study of Religion. Vol. 20, No. 1 (March), pp. 77-89. Hadaway reports conclusions of a study in four cities regarding the adaptive constraints placed on White Protestant churches as the result of their city locations. Bibliography.

15836. Hadden, Jeffrey K. (1981) Prime Time Preachers: The Rising Power of Televangelism. Reading, MA: Addison-Wesley. A socio-biographical assessment of television evangelists and their growing influence in American society. Bibliography.

15837. Hall, Douglas A. (1981) "The Inner-City Family," Evangelizing Today's Child. Vol. 8, No. 3 (May-June), pp. 22-25.

15838. Hall, Peter Geoffrey, ed. (1981) The Inner City in Context. London: Heinemann. [Also a final report]. Aldershot, England: Gower, 1986.

15839. Hamblett, Beatrice. (1981) "Pedro Silva, Sculptor and Community Artist," Cities. Vol. 1, No. 6 (November), pp. 33-34.

15840. Hammersley, John. (1981) TAP Handbook for Teams and Groups. London: British Council of Churches.

15841. Hanna, William J. and Judith L. Hanna. (1981) Urban Dynamics in Black Africa. New York: Aldine.

15842. Harris, Jamie. (1981) "One Neighborhood's Hopes in the

Housing Crisis: Virginia's Dream Becomes Reality, A Story from 4th and Gill," Cities. Vol. 1, No. 6 (November), pp. 5-10.

15843. Harris, Jeffrey. (1981) "Urbanization and Industrialization," Cities. Vol. 1, No. 5 (September), pp. 13-14.

15844. Hennock, E. P. (1981) "The Anglo-Catholics and Church Extension in Victorian Brighton," pp. 173-188 in M. J. Kitch, ed. Studies in Sussex Church History. London: Leopard's Head Press.

15845. Hill, Edward V. (1981) "Inner City Evangelism," Religious Broadcasting. Vol. 13, No. 8 (October), pp. 52-53.

15846. Hoellein, Ronald R. (1981) The Effects of a Depressed Area on Church Involvement. Thesis (D. Min.). Pittsburgh, PA: Pittsburgh Theological Seminary.

15847. Holler, S. (1981) "Fear Thy Neighbor: A Student Learns to Live in the Inner City," HIS. Vol. 41, No. 2 (November), pp. 7-9.

15848. Holman, Bob. (1981) Kids at the Door. Oxford, England: Basel Blackwell. In 1976 Holman left a university professorship to start a Church of England project aimed at reducing the problems of youth in Council Estates. He lived on an estate to respond to the needs directly and in his book describes how youth work can be done through personal contacts with the youth and their parents and by establishing youth clubs. An informal evaluation of the program consists of after-the-fact interviews with 30 people in 1979. Most respondents' comments quoted are positive but not very descriptive of the program or of their feelings about it. The book does not report the research methods or provide a copy of the interview schedule.

15849. Holmes, Douglas Reginald. (1981) Contract, Work, and Status: Patterns of Livelihood in an Italian Parish. Thesis (Ph. D.). Stony Brook, NY: State University of New York at Stony Brook.

15850. Hopler, Thomas. (1981) A World of Difference: Following Christ beyond Your Cultural Walls. Downers Grove, IL: InterVarsity Press.

15851. Howe, Elizabeth and Jerome Kaufman. (1981) "The Values of Contemporary Urban Planners," Journal of the American Planning Association. Vol. 47, No. 3 (July), pp. 266-278.

15852. Howe, Elizabeth and Jerome Kaufman. (1981) "Ethics of

Professional Practice in Planning and Related Policy Professions," Policy Studies Journal. Vol. 9, No. 4, pp. 585-595.

15853. Howell, Leon. (1981) "After the Funeral, 35,000 'Vacant Posts:' Christians in Sri Lanka Take a Stand on Behalf of Thousands of Striking Workers," One World. Vol. 68 (July), pp. 9-10.

15854. Hull, Jerry. (1981) "Urban Ministry Education: The Task of the Local Church," Preacher's Magazine [Thematic issue: Urban ministry]. Vol. 56, No. 4 (June), pp. 17-18.

15855. "Immigration: Year of Decision." (1981) JSAC Grapevine. Vol. 13, No. 3 (September), pp. [1-6]. Reviews and critiques Reagan administration policy regarding immigration and recommends strategy for churches.

15856. Jackson, Dave. (1981) Dial 911: Peaceful Christians and Urban Violence. Scottdale, PA: Herald Press. A member of the Reba Place Fellowship, Evanston, IL, relates experiences with crime and violence, asking what the Christian's response to violence ought to be. Reach for a gun? Turn the other cheek? Dial 911?

15857. John Paul II, Pope [Karol Wojtyla]. (1981) Laborem exercens. Città del Vaticano: Libreria Editrice Vaticana. English edition: Washington, DC: United States Catholic Conference, 1981. An encyclical dealing with the Catholic Church's teaching on labor, just wages, trade unions, multinational corporations, handicapped workers, and other social issues. Many commentaries have been written in many languages. The Library of Congress lists these commentaries under the subject: "Catholic Church. Pope (1978- : John Paul II) Laborem exercens" or simply "Laborem exercens." For the selection of citations included herein, see further the Subject Index "Encyclicals, Papal (Laborem exercens)."

15858. Jones, Peter d'A. and Melvin G. Holli, eds. (1981) Ethnic Chicago. Grand Rapids, MI: Eerdmans. Includes chapters on various ethnic groups and their impact on Chicago's history.

15859. Joselit, Jenna Weissman. (1981) Dark Shadows: New York Jews and Crime, 1900-1940. Thesis (Ph. D.). New York: Columbia University.

15860. Jules-Rosette, Bennetta. (1981) "Faith Healers and Folk Healers: The Symbolism and Practice of Indigenous Therapy in Urban Africa," Religion: Journal of Religion and Religions. Vol. 11, No. 2

(April), pp. 127-149. Re: folk religion in Zambia.

15861. Kaiser, Jochen-Christoph. (1981) Arbeiterbewegung und organisierte Religionskritik: proletarische Freidenkerverbände in Kaiserreich und Weimarer Republik. Stuttgart, West Germany: Klett-Cotta. Re: the worker movement and the organized critique of religion by proletarian free thinker societies in the German Empire and Weimar Republic.

15862. Kaslow, Andrew J. (1981) "Saints and Spirits: The Belief System of Afro-American Spiritual Churches in New Orleans," pp. 61-68 in John Cooke and Mackie J-V Blanton, eds. Perspectives on Ethnicity in New Orleans. New Orleans, LA: Committee on Ethnicity in New Orleans.

15863. Kaslow, Andrew J. and Claude Jacobs. (1981) Prophecy, Healing, and Power: The Afro-American Spiritual Churches of New Orleans. New Orleans, LA: Archaeological and Cultural Research Program, University of New Orleans. A Cultural Management Study, Jean Lafitte National Historic Park, National Park Service by the Department of Anthropology and Geography, University of New Orleans.

15864. Katznelson, Ira. (1981) City Trenches: Urban Politics and the Patterning of Class in the United States. New York: Pantheon.

15865. Kaufman, Jerome L. (1981) "Teaching Planning Ethics," Journal of Planning Education and Research. Vol. 1, No. 1 (Summer), pp. 29-34.

15866. Kavanaugh, John. (1981) Following Christ in a Consumer Society. Maryknoll, NY: Orbis. Suggestions for Christian response to the USA economic system and its cultural foundations.

15867. Kelly, Pete. (1981) "Strategy for Labor in the 80s," pp. 33-38 in Linda Unger, ed. Seeds of a People's Church: Challenge and Promise from the Underside of History--Presentations from the Neil C. McMath Lectureship of the Episcopal Diocese of Detroit, August 1-4, 1980. Detroit, MI: Seeds of a People's Church.

15868. Kemendo, Robert B. (1981) The Urban Church: The Role of Active Churches in Urban Design. Thesis (Master of Architecture in Urban Design). Cambridge, MA: Harvard University.

15869. Kibble, David G. (1981) "The Working Classes and the

Christian Ethic," Evangelical Quarterly [Exeter]. Vol. 53 (July), pp. 165-177. Kibble lists reasons for laborers' lack of participation in church life. Churches must adapt to different social classes and stress the importance of living the Christian ethic.

15870. Kim, Woong-min. (1981) History and Ministerial Roles of Korean Churches in the Los Angeles Area. Thesis (D. Min.). Claremont, CA: School of Theology at Claremont.

15871. Kim, Young-Ir. (1981) Developing a Program of Ministry with Single Adults. Thesis (D. Min.). Madison, NJ: Drew University.

15872. King, William M. (1981) "The Emergence of Social Gospel Radicalism: The Methodist Case," Church History. Vol. 50, No. 4 (December), pp. 436-449. Harry F. Ward and the Methodist Federation for Social Service represent an example of the continuation of Social Gospel themes in the interwar period. Bibliograhical footnotes.

15873. Knight, Barry and Ruth Hayes. (1981) Self Help in the Inner City. London: London Voluntary Service Council. A study of small organizations in the inner city dealing with self help, mutual aid, community initiatives, and informal care includes illustrations of church groups, among others. One chapter lists factors that help and hinder such groups. Bibliography.

15874. Kochman, Thomas. (1981) Black and White Styles in Conflict. Chicago, IL: University of Chicago Press.

15875. Krass, Alfred C. (beginning in 1981) "Seeking the Peace of the City: A Monthly Column Focusing on Urban Discipleship," The Other Side. Vol. 17, No. 4 (April and subsequent issues), pp. 44-46.

15876. Krass, Alfred C. (1981) "Economic Development: What Kind? Working to Revitalize Urban Economies Isn't Enough--We Must also Raise Value Questions," The Other Side. Vol. 17, No. 5 (May), pp. 44-47.

15877. Krass, Alfred C. (1981) "Learning to Look at the City in Another Way: It's Not Just a Collection of Problems," The Other Side. Vol. 17, No. 9 (September), pp. 61-64.

15878. Kraus, Ingrid Marianne. (1981) The Berlin Catholic Church, 1871-1918: Its Social and Political Endeavors. Thesis (Ph. D.). Lincoln, NE: University of Nebraska.

15879. Krawczyk, Joseph. (1981) The House that Ritter Built: What Makes a Man Build a Shelter for Exploited Kids on New York City's Minnesota Strip?" The Other Side. Vol. 17, No. 12 (December), pp. 17-24. Ritter is involved with the ministry of Covenant House in New York. See further: Bruce Ritter. (1988) Sometimes God Has a Kid's Face: The Story of America's Exploited Street Kids. [New York]: Covenant House. In 1990, Ritter resigned his position in the face of accusations of improper sexual contact with Covenant House residents.

15880. Lalive d'Epinay, Christian, et al. (1981) "Popular Culture, Religion and Everyday Life: People Aged 65 and Above in the Rural and Industrial Urban Milieux," Social Compass: International Review of Sociology of Religion. Vol. 30, No. 4, pp. 405-427. Lalive d'Epinay reports results of a study of people aged 65 years or more in urban Protestant Geneva, Switzerland, and rural Catholic central Valais.

15881. Lalive d'Epinay, Christian. (1981) "Culture populaire, religion et vie quotidienne," pp. 167-190 in Roland J. Campiche, et al. Religion, valeurs et vie quotidienne. Paris: Centre National de la recherche scientifique de France. Popular culture, religion and everyday life.

15882. Lane, George A. (1981) Chicago Churches and Synagogues. Chicago, IL: Loyola University Press. A guide to places of worship.

15883. Lee, Betsy. (1981) Mother Teresa: Caring for All God's Children. Minneapolis, MN: Dillon.

15884. Leech, Kenneth. (1981) "Understanding Urban Conflict," Crucible. [Vol. 20, No. 4] (October-December), pp. 148-154.

15885. Leland, Thomas Elgon. (1981) Developing a Model of Religious Education for Black Southern Baptist Churches. Thesis. Louisville, KY: Southern Baptist Theological Seminary.

15886. Lenardi, Barbara and Jocelyn Barkevicius. (1981) "A Holistic Approach to Crime Prevention," Cities. Vol. 1, No. 4 (July), pp. 11-12. Advocates the use of neighborhood justice centers.

15887. Lenhart, Thomas Emerson. (1981) Methodist Piety in an Industrializing Society: Chicago, 1865-1914. Thesis (Ph. D.). Evanston, IL: Northwestern University.

15888. Lewis, Christopher. (1981) "From City to Community:

Christian Community in the Modern Metropolis," Epiphany: A Journal of Faith and Insight. Vol. 1, No. 4 (Summer), pp. 38-47. Lewis urges urban churches toward creating groups guided by Platonic and theological ideal forms of community, with emphasis on the church's need to reestablish the primacy of the family in social life and to promote Jesus' teachings regarding love of neighbors. Bibliography.

15889. Lewis, G. Douglass. (1981) Resolving Church Conflicts: A Case Study Approach for Local Congregations. New York: Harper and Row. Reviewed: Review and Expositor, Vol. 80 (Summer, l983), p. 462.

15890. Liddall, Marton Gloria. (1981) The St. Pancras Vestry: A Study in the Administration of a Metropolitan Parish 1760-1838. Thesis (Ph. D.). New Brunswick, NJ: Rutgers.

15891. Lindberg, Carter. (1981) "Through a Glass Darkly: A History of the Church's Vision of the Poor and Poverty," Ecumenical Review. Vol. 33, No. 1 (January), pp. 37-52.

15892. Linder, John Thomas. (1981) The Lutheran Church in Hong Kong, 1949-1980. Thesis. Ft. Wayne, IN: Concordia Theological Seminary.

15893. Lipset, Seymour Martin. (1981) Political Man: The Social Basis of Politics, expanded edition. Baltimore, MD: Johns Hopkins Press. See especially pages 97ff regarding the relationship of sectarian religious experience and political radicalism. See Christiano (1988) for further discussion.

15894. Lockwood, George Frank. (1981) Recent Developments in US Hispanic and Latin American Protestant Church Music. Thesis (D. Min.). Claremont, CA: School of Theology at Claremont.

15895. London, Herbert I. and Albert L. Weeks. (1981) Myths that Rule America. Washington, DC: University Press of America. London and Weeks combat prevailing myths of success, technology, work, poverty, American isolationism, absolute freedom, and the opinion that small is beautiful. The confusion of the 1960s created a climate in which unhealthy myths emerge. These the authors expose and hope to change by a dose of conservative polemic. Glossary.

15896. Long, Norton E. (1981) Cities without Citizens. Philadelphia, PA: Center for the Study of Federalism, Temple University.

15897. Lopez, Bernardo. (1981) Using Hispanic Evangelical Ministers as Volunteer Para-Professional Counselors to Spanish Speaking Parolees in the South Bronx. Thesis (D. Min.). New York: New York Theological Seminary.

15898. Lopez, Robert. (1981) "Capital in Crisis: Making the Workers Pay," pp. 42-48 in Linda Unger, ed. Seeds of a People's Church: Challenge and Promise from the Underside of History--Presentations from the Neil C. McMath Lectureship of the Episcopal Diocese of Detroit, August 1-4, 1980. Detroit, MI: Seeds of a People's Church.

15899. Lucas, Isidro. (1981) The Browning of America: The Hispanic Revolution in the American Church. Chicago, IL: Fides/Claretian. Lucas attempts to explain to non-Hispanics the character and aspirations of Hispanic people, calling on churches to quit neglecting them. The churches have not made adequate plans for the rapidly growing Hispanic population.

15900. Luckhardt, Ken and Brenda Wall. (1981) Working for Freedom. Geneva, Switzerland: Programme to Combat Racism, World Council of Churches. [Location: ICUIS 4803, see note 2]. Apartheid, racism, and economic exploitation predominate in South Africa and are especially evident in the nation's labor laws. Luckhardt and Wall trace the development of trade unionism among Blacks in South Africa during the 1970s. Bibliography. For additional resources on Black Trade unions, see ICUIS Nos. 4804-4808.

15901. Ludlow, John Malcolm Forbes. (1981) The Autobiography of a Christian Socialist. London: Frank Cass. Ludlow (1821-1911) was an early associate of F. D. Maurice.

15902. Ludwig, Heinrich and Heinz-Georg Ludwig, eds. (1981) Kirchen kampfen mit: die VFW-Fokker-Aktion zur Erhaltung der Arbeitsplatze. Mainz, Germany: Matthias-Grunewald-Verlag. Re: church and labor issues in Speyer, Germany, especially plant shutdowns. Bibliography.

15903. Lutheran Council in the United States of America. (1981) A Statement on Immigration Policies: Undocumented Persons. New York: the Council. A pamphlet.

15904. Lutheran School of Theology, Task Force on Banking Alternatives. (1981) Banking on Differences: A Comparison of Banking Patterns and Programs which Bear on the Economic Revitalization of

South-Side Neighborhoods in Chicago. Chicago, IL: Lutheran School of Theology. [Location: ICUIS 4794, see note 2]. In response to student concerns, the trustees of a Lutheran school of theology authorized a study to determine whether they should stop doing business with the Continental Bank of Illinois because of its connections with South Africa. Questions are raised about the extent to which banks benefit the communities of which they are a part.

15905. Luton Industrial College. (beginning in 1981) Friends of Luton Industrial College. Luton, England: the College. A periodical.

15906. Lynch, Kevin. (1981) A Theory of Good City Form. Cambridge, MA: MIT Press. Lynch hopes to revive interest in utopian theory about cities and generally in normative approaches to the city life. He raises and discusses the question, "What makes a good city?" The resulting book critiques existing urban theory, especially the functional variety that "pretends" to be value free. Lynch's personal utopia is "an urban countryside, a highly varied but humanized landscape. It is neither urban nor rural in the old sense, since houses, workplaces, and places of assembly are set among trees, farms and streams. Within this extensive countryside, there is a network of small, intensive urban centers" (p. 294). Lynch is a doodler and enlivens the margins of his book with hand drawn illustrations, some of which are purely for fun.

15907. Lyon, David. (1981) "Secularization and Sociology: The History of an Idea," Fides et Historia. Vol. 13, No. 2 (Spring), pp. 38-52.

15908. Malsch, Carl. (1981) Kirche für die Stadt: St. Petri-Gemeinde in der City von Hamburg. Hamburg, West Germany: Lutherisches Verlagshaus. A study of a parish in Hamburg, Germany.

15909. Marcum, John P. and Mary Radosh. (1981) "Religious Affiliation, Labor Force Participation and Fertility," Sociological Analysis. Vol. 42, No. 4 (Winter), pp. 353-362. Catholic and Protestant women have different fertility rates and, as the result, different patterns of employment. Data collected in 1965 are used.

15910. Marianski, Janusz. (1981) "Dynamics of Changes in Rural Religiosity under Industrialization: The Case of Poland," Social Compass. Vol. 28, No. 1, pp. 63-78. Analysis of 1967 data collected in the rapidly industrializing rural Plock region of Poland and among rural residents in Polish cities leads Marianski to conclude that industrialization and urbanization may lead to greater selectivity in religiosity, but not necessarily to atheism. Indifference to religion appears to spread more rapidly than athiesm.

15911. Mariante, Benjamin R. (1981) Pluralistic Society, Pluralistic Church. Washington, DC: University Press of America. Reviewed: 1) Sociological Analysis, Vol. 44, Fall, 1983, p. 256.

15912. Marshall, Paul and Edward Vanderkloet. (1981) Foundations of Human Rights. Rexdale, Ontario, Canada: Christian Labour Association of Canada.

15913. Martin, Keith. (1981) "Lessons from Liverpool: Public Policy and Urban Ministry," Christian Century. Vol. 98, No. 30 (September), pp. 963-966. Riots in Liverpool provide occasion for Martin to urge greater attention to American cities by religious denominations. Martin, agreeing with Andrew Greeley, claims denominations are too parochially-oriented. Urban problems must be addressed at the public policy level.

15914. Martinez, Joel, et al. (1981) "Models and Means of Hispanic Church Development," JSAC Grapevine. Vol. 13, No. 1 (June), pp. [1-6].

15915. Marty, Martin E. (1981) "If Only We Could Disagree," New World Outlook [Thematic issue: Pluralism]. n.s. Vol. 41, No. 10 (June), pp. 8-11. Re: pluralism.

15916. Marty, Martin E. (1981) The Public Church: Mainline--Evangelical--Catholic. New York: Crossroad. Marty attempts the discovery and description of an emergent ecclesiology that can address the public issues of modern urban society.

15917. Maryknoll Fathers and Brothers. (1981) Social Analysis and Research: Basic Models and Approaches. Maryknoll, NY: Maryknoll Mission Research and Planning Department. Describes models for social analysis with local groups drawn from a variety of sources.

15918. Mastruko, Lvica. (1981) Klasni mir katolicanstva: radnicko pitanje u socijalno-politickoj doktrini Katolicke crkve. Split, Yougslavia: Marksisticki centar Konferencije SKH Zajednice opcina Split. Re: Catholic teaching on labor. Written in Serbo-Croatian. Bibliography.

15919. Mattai, Giuseppe. (1981) Il Lavoro: le encicliche sociali dalla "Rerum Novarum" alla "Laborem Exercens." Padova, Italy: Edizioni Messaggero.

15920. Maust, John. (1981) "New Yorkers: Ninevites Looking for a Jonah?" Christianity Today. Vol. 25, No. 6 (March 27), pp. 32-35. Maust reviews contemporary evangelistic work, para-church organizations, and missionary work in New York City. See further an accompanying artice titled "God's Miracle in Manhattan."

15921. Maynard, Kent Arthur. (1981) Christianity and Religion: Evangelical Identity and Sociocultural Organization in Urban Ecuador. Thesis (Ph. D.). Bloomington, IN: Indiana University.

15922. McBeth, Leon. (1981) "Images of the Black Church in America," Baptist History and Heritage [Thematic issue: Black Southern Baptists]. Vol. 16, No. 3 (July), pp. 49-60.

15923. McCall, Emmanuel L. (1981) "Home Mission Board Ministry in the Black Community," Baptist History and Heritage [Thematic issue: Black Southern Baptists]. Vol. 16, No. 3 (July), pp. 49-60.

15924. McCarty, Doran. (1981) Types of Churches: The Urban Fringe. Atlanta, GA: Home Mission Board, Southern Baptist Convention, Occasional Paper No. 3. Fringe churches are located outside the metropolitan area but the members are served by the city. McCarty's paper lists strategies for such congregations.

15925. McClain, William B. (1981) Traveling Light. New York: Friendship Press. Church school curriculum for studying the oppression of ethnic groups in the USA with discussion starters, e.g., a case study of a prosperous Anglo church trying to offer a Hispanic church "financial aid," which charity is rejected as a tokenism and debasement.

15926. McClory, Robert J. (1981) Racism in America. Chicago, IL: Fides/Claretian.

15927. McIntosh, Alex and Jon P. Alston. (1981) Religion and the New Immigrants: Initial Observations Concerning Lao Refugees in Houston, Texas. Paper presented at the annual meeting of the Association for Sociology of Religion. s.l.: s.n. Bibliography.

15928. McIntyre, Dewitt Thomas. (1981) A Program for: Revitalizing an Urban Black Church Sunday School through Relational Evangelism. Thesis (D. Min.). Madison, NJ: Drew University.

15929. McKinney, George. (1981) "HIS interview with the Rev. George McKinney," HIS. Vol. 41, No. 9 (June), pp. 21-24.

15930. McLeod, Hugh. (1981) Religion and the Peoples of Western Europe, 1789-1970. Oxford, England: Oxford University Press. Reviewed: Sociological Analysis, Vol. 45 (Fall, 1984), p. 262. Archives de Sciences Sociales des Religions, Vol. 27 (April-June, 1982), p. 327.

15931. McSwain, Larry L. (1981) Principles for Effective Church Growth. Atlanta, GA: Metropolitan Missions Department, Home Mission Board, Occasional Paper Number 2. Lists eleven principles: leadership, lay commitment, ministry, new units, intimacy, community growth, realism, intentional growth, balance, conservation, and Kingdom growth.

15932. McSwain, Larry L. and William C. Treadwell, Jr. (1981) Conflict Ministry in the Church. Nashville, TN: Broadman Press.

15933. Mens, Larry W. (1981) "Responding to the Visions of the Urban Indian," Engage/Social Action. Vol. 9, No. 11 (November), pp. 16-19.

15934. Merker, Margaret. (1981) "Open Arms," Other Side. Vol. 17, No. 12 (December), pp. 38-42.

15935. Merry, Sally Engle. (1981, 1986) Urban Danger: Life in a Neighborhood of Strangers. Philadelphia, PA: Temple University Press.

15936. Metz, Johannes Baptist. (1981) The Emergent Church: The Future of Christianity in a Postbourgeois World. New York: Crossroads. Metz recommends the creation of small Christian communities.

15937. Michel, Barbara. (1981) "Le bon voisin, le mauvais voisin: Ebauche d'une sociologie de l'ethos de voisinage," Social Compass. Vol. 30, No. 4, pp. 357-380. Neighborliness in interpersonal relations provides the opportunity to experiment with value systems in play and conflicted circumstances, which points to general value-forming mechanisms.

15938. Miles, Delos. (1981) Church Growth--A Mighty River. Nashville, TN: Broadman Press.

15939. Miller, Edward M. (1981) "The Urban Church," pp. 121-136 in Mark Searle, ed. Parish: A Place for Worship. Collegeville, MN: Liturgical Press. Re: St. Bernadine's Church, Baltimore, MD.

15940. Miller, Keith. (1981) The Single Experience. Waco, TX: Word.

15941. Miller, Mike. (1981) "What Is an Organizer," Christianity and Crisis. Vol. 41, No. 6 (April 13), p. 99.

15942. Minangkabua! Stories of People vs. TNCs in Asia. (1981) Hong Kong: Urban-Rural Mission--Christian Conference of Asia. [Location: ICUIS 4640, see note 2]. Essays that attack the myth that transnational corporations (TNCs) benefit Asian people. Efforts to protest the practices of the TNCs are recounted and strategy suggestions offered. Bibliography.

15943. Mingione, Enzo. (1981) Social Conflict and the City. Oxford, England: Basil Blackwell.

15944. Monahan, Sharon. (1981) "Bread Line [St. Francis of Assisi Church, New York City]," America. Vol. 144, No. 10 (March 14), p. 206.

15945. Monsma, Timothy. (1981) "Urban Explosion and Missions Strategy," Evangelical Missions Quarterly. Vol. 17, No. 1 (January), pp. 5-12.

15946. Moore, David O. (1981) "The Withdrawal of Blacks from Southern Baptist Churches Following the Emancipation," Baptist History and Heritage [Thematic issue: Black Southern Baptists]. Vol. 16, No. 3 (July), pp. 49-60.

15947. Morauta, Louise. (1981) "Urban Youth Out of Work," Point. Vol. 10, No. 1, pp. 73-87.

15948. Mosender, Ursula. (1981) "Charismatic Renewal and the Slums of Latin America," pp. 189-192 in Arnold Bittlinger, ed. The Church is Charismatic. Geneva, Switzerland: Renewal and Congregational Life, World Council of Churches.

15949. Mowrey, George Edwin and Blaine A. Brownell. (1981) The Urban Nation: 1920-1980. New York: Hill and Wang.

15950. Mumford, Stephen. (1981) "Illegal Immigration, National Security, and the [Catholic] Church," Humanist. Vol. 41, No. 6 (November-December), pp. 24-30+.

15951. Nawyn, William E. (1981) American Protestantism's Response to Germany's Jews and Refugees, 1933-1941. Ann Arbor, MI: UMI Research Press. A revision of a thesis. Bibliography.

15952. Neighbour, Ralph Webster, Jr. (1981) Survival Kit for New Christians: A Practical Guide to Spiritual Growth. Nashville, TN: Convention Press. Special editions exist for children and youth.

15953. Newman, Aubrey, ed. (1981) The Jewish East End, 1840-1939. London: The Jewish Historical Society of England.

15954. Nichols, Frank. (1981) "A Theology from Within," Theology. Vol. 84, No. 698 (March), pp. 95-98. The church must listen to the working class and its authentic voice of culture in order to discern the presence of God in modern realities. Middle-class biases often limit the church in its theological task.

15955. Niehaus, Juliet Anne. (1981) Ethnic Formation and Transformation: The German-Catholics of Dubois County, Indiana, 1838-1979. Thesis (Ph. D.). New York: New School for Social Research.

15956. Niklaus, Robert. (1981) "Cities: Staggering Statistics," Evangelical Missions Quarterly. Vol. 17, No. 4 (October), pp. 246-247.

15957. Nkonge, Julius M. (1981) A Critical Analysis of the Church's Ministry to Urban Squatters in the Mathare Valley and a Proposed Model for Future Ministry. Thesis (D. Min.). Atlanta, GA: Interdenominational Theological Center.

15958. Novak, Michael. (1981) "A Theology of the Corporation," in Michael Novak and John W. Cooper, eds. The Corporation: A Theological Inquiry. Washington, DC: American Enterprise Institute for Public Policy Research. A paper delivered at a seminar. Bibliography.

15959. Novak, Michael. (1981) Toward a Theology of the Corporation. Washington, DC: American Enterprise Institute for Public Policy Research. Revised edition: Lanham, MD: University Press of America, 1990. Private business examined from theological perspectives.

15960. O'Connor, Anthony M. (1981) Urbanization in Tropical Africa: An Annotated Bibliography. Boston, MA: G. K. Hall.

15961. Ogle, George. (1981) "Opportunity for US Labor to

Chart a Future Course," Engage/Social Action. Vol. 9, No. 10 (November), pp. 2-6.

15962. Oppusunggu, Hotma P. (1981) A Sense of Dwelling-Praxis in the Created Order of the City and Architecture. Toronto, Ontario, Canada: Institute for Christian Studies. A pamphlet.

15963. Orens, John R. (1981) "Politics of the Kingdom: The Legacy of the Anglican Left," Anglican Theological Review. Vol. 63, No. 1 (January), pp. 21-41. A brief history of the socialist movement within Anglicanism from Maurice through the early 20th century.

15964. Ornstein, Allan C. (1981) Educating the Inner City Child: A Review of Research Findings Over Two Decades. Chicago, IL: Loyola University of Chicago, Center for Urban Policy, Urban Insight Series. A pamphlet.

15965. Orton, Lawrence D. (1981) Polish Detroit and the Kolasinski Affair. Detroit, MI: Wayne State University Press.

15966. Owen, James R. (1981) "The Church's Voice in the Marketplace," A. D. Vol. 10, No. 1 (January), pp. 24-26. Churches began to exercise their power as stockholders in 1971 when the Episcopal Church petitioned General Motors to withdraw from South Africa. Other denominations followed suit with stockholder petitions related to labor practices, human rights, toxic waste disposal, nuclear energy, plant closings, and military contracts.

15967. Paget-Wilkes, Michael. (1981) Poverty, Revolution and the Church. Exeter, Devon, England: Paternoster Press. Why doesn't the inner city church grow? Why don't people want to know about Christ? Why is there silent antagonism and fear of getting involved with the church? Why are church leaders often out of touch with the neighborhood of the church? Why isn't the church touching the teenagers, the workers, the leaders of the inner city? Paget-Wilkes, a London inner city vicar returned from missionary service in Africa, concludes that inequity and oppression are the root causes. He offers suggestions about how Christians can overcome their biases of class and wealth. Reviewed: Evangelical Quarterly, Vol. 56 (April, 1984), p. 113.

15968. Pallmeyer, Dwight. (1981) Our Neighbors in Hiding: A Resource Book for Congregations Engaging in a Ministry with Undocumented Persons. Minneapolis, MN: Augsburg.

15969. Palmer, Parker. (1981) The Company of Strangers:

Christians and the Renewal of America's Public Life. New York: Crossroad. Palmer, a Quaker in Philadelphia, writes about the richness of human life achieved in public spaces, a wealth that is denied by the private spaces which reinforce the privatization of life. He lists ten human experiences that flourish in public arenas, e.g., strangers meet on common ground, fear of strangers is overcome, conflict occurs and often is resolved, mutual responsibility becomes evident. Reviewed: Chicago Theological Seminary Register, Vol. 72, No. 3 (Fall, 1982), p. 46. TFS Bulletin, Vol. 7, No. 2 (November-December, l983), p. 24.

15970. Parot, Joseph John. (1981) Polish Catholics in Chicago, 1859-1920: A Religious History. DeKalb, IL: Northern Illinois University Press.

15971. Pasquariello, Ronald D. (1981) "Cities and Reagan Economics," Cities. Vol. 1, No. 5 (September), pp. 24-26.

15972. Pasquariello, Ronald D. (1981) "Urban Ministry Enters a New Phase," Modern Ministries. Vol. 2, No. 8 (November), pp. 17-19.

15973. Pazmiño, Robert William. (1981) The Educational Thought of George W. Webber: Theological Educator and Issues in Theological Education. Thesis (Ed. D.). New York: Columbia University, Teacher College. An abstract: Religious Education. Vol. 78 (Summer, 1983), p. 424.

15974. Peil, Margaret. (1981) "African Cities and the Church," Pro Mundi Vita's Africa Dossier. No. 17, (October, 1981), pp. 1-19. Same title: pp. 5-41 in Peil, Margaret, Simon Sirikwa, Pierre C. Lembugusala, et al. African Cities and Christian Communities. Eldoret, Kenya: Gaba Publications, 1982.

15975. Pender, Donald Wagner. (1981) An Urban Mission for the Paulist Fathers in Houston, Texas. Thesis (M. Arch.). Austin, TX: University of Texas at Austin.

15976. Perani, Cláudio. (1981) "Communidades eclesiais de base e movimento popular," Cadernos do CEAS (Brazil). No. 75, pp. 25-33. Re: Christian base communities.

15977. Peters, Victor. (1981) "The German Pietists: Spiritual Mentors of the German Communal Settlements in America," Communal Sociology. (Autumn), pp. 55-66.

15978. Phillips, E. Barbara and Richard T. LeGates. (1981) City

Lights: An Introduction to Urban Studies. New York: Oxford University Press. Bibliography.

15979. Pike, Burton. (1981) The Image of the City in Modern Literature. Princeton, NJ: Princeton University Press.

15980. Pilgrim, Walter E. (1981) Good News to the Poor: Wealth and Poverty in Luke-Acts. Minneapolis, MN: Augsburg. Reviewed: Journal of Biblical Literature, Vol. 102 (September, 1983), p. 506. Currents in Theology and Mission, Vol. 10 (February, 1983), p. 63.

15981. "Plant Closings Challenge Churches." (1981) Faith and Justice Newsletter [Dayton, OH]. Vol. 1, No. 2 (July). [Location: ICUIS 4748, see note 2]. Suggestions for pastors who counsel workers affected by plant closings. Bibliography. For additional materials on the church's response to plant closings, see ICUIS, Nos. 4743-4749.

15982. "Pluralism." (1981) The Chicago Theological Seminary Register [Thematic issue]. Vol. 71, No. 2 (Spring), pp. 1-38.

15983. Poethig, Richard P., ed. (1981?) The Church, the Gospel and the Wage Earner. ICUIS Occasional Paper, No. 9. Chicago, IL: Institute on the Church in Urban-Industrial Society (ICUIS). A report of the Spiritual Life Committee, Presbytery of Chicago.

15984. Poethig, Richard P. and Tim Anderson, eds. (1981) "The Church and Immigration," Justice Ministries: Resources for Urban Mission. Nos. 11-12 (Winter-Spring), pp. 1-76. A bibliography.

15985. Presbyterian Church in the US, United Presbyterian Church in the USA. (1981) "Urban Ministry," Church and Society. Vol. 71, No. 6 (July-August), pp. 6-15. An official denominational statement of two Presbyterian bodies.

15986. Preston, Ronald H. (1981) Winters of Discontent: Industrial Conflict, a Christian Perspective. London: Published for the General Synod Board for Social Responsibility by Church Information Office Publishing.

15987. Racine, Carl. (1981) "Don't Neglect Third World ... Suburbia," Missiology: An International Review. Vol. 9, No. 2 (April), pp. 171-180.

15988. Raines, John C. (1981) "America's Stalled Dream," The Christian Century. Vol. 98, No. 39 (December 2), pp. 1256-1259. A

Temple University professor reflects on unemployment as it affects Philadelphia's ethnic populations. He calls for new fairness in distribution of wealth.

15989. Ramirez, Christine. (1981) "An Appeal to Workers," pp. 49-50 in Linda Unger, ed. Seeds of a People's Church: Challenge and Promise from the Underside of History--Presentations from the Neil C. McMath Lectureship of the Episcopal Diocese of Detroit, August 1-4, 1980. Detroit, MI: Seeds of a People's Church.

15990. Ramsden, William E. (1981) Ministering through Non-Parish Institutions. Nashville, TN: Abingdon. A study of social change and church related service agencies--hospitals, colleges, community centers, children and youth serving agencies, hostels, neighborhood houses, etc. Part of the "Into Our Third Century" emphasis celebrating the 200th anniversary of Methodism. Bibliography.

15991. Ranck, Lee, ed. (1981) "The Ethnic Minority Local Church: In the Midst of Social and Economic Issues," Engage/Social Action [Thematic issue]. Vol. 9, No. 5 (May), pp. 9-40. Includes articles on church finances, community relations, police, youth work and street ministry.

15992. Reed, Millard. (1981) "Why We Stayed in the City," Preacher's Magazine [Thematic issue: Urban ministry]. Vol. 56, No. 4 (June), pp. 21-23.

15993. Reed, Myer S. (1981) "An Alliance for Progress: The Early Years of the Sociology of Religion in the United States," Sociological Analysis. Vol. 42, No. 1 (Spring), pp. 27-46. Using the method of content analysis, Reed traces the emergence of the sociology of religion in the United States from 1895 to 1929, concluding that the discipline was dominated by religionists who, under the influence of the Social Gospel, saw sociology as a means for achieving social and religious aims. Bibliography.

15994. Renewal House [Newsletter]. (beginning in 1981) Roxbury Crossing, MA: Renewal House. A periodical.

15995. Rhee, Amos Seung Woon. (1981) Stabilizing and Vitalizing the Church Membership of Central Korean Church of Yonkers, New York. Thesis (D. Min.). Madison, NJ: Drew University.

15996. Rice, Howard. (1981) "Toward an Urban Strategy," Cities. Vol. 1, No. 4 (July), pp. 4-9. A discussion of the mission of the church in cities, and the implications of social change.

15997. Robbins, Thomas and Dick Anthony, eds. (1981) In Gods We Trust: New Patterns of Religious Pluralism in America. New Brunswick, NJ: Transaction Books. A collection of sociological papers about change in American religion, with emphasis on new, innovative religious movements as well as on the rise of evangelicalism and the decline of liberal Protestantism. Bibliography. Reviewed: International Bulletin of Missionary Research, Vol. 7 (April, 1983), p. 86. Archives de Sciences Sociales des Religions, Vol. 27 (April - June, 1982), p. 304.

15998. Roberts, Vella-Kottarathil. (1981) The Urban Mission of the Church from an Urban Anthropological Perspective. Thesis (D. Miss.). Pasadena, CA: Fuller Theological Seminary, School of World Mission.

15999. Rodda, Alan. (1981) "The Challenge of Metropolitan Ministry," Preacher's Magazine [Thematic issue: Urban ministry]. Vol. 56, No. 4 (June), pp. 30-32.

16000. Rosell, Garth, comp. (1981) Cases in Theological Education, 1981 Bibliography. Vandalia, OH: Case Study Institute, Association of Theological Schools. Includes urban oriented cases.

16001. Rousseau, Ann Marie. (1981) "No Room in the Inn," The Other Side. Vol. 17, No. 12 (December), pp. 30-38. Re: shopping bag ladies.

16002. Roussel, Bernard. (1981) "R. W. McAll: Évangéliste auprès des prolétaires parisiens, entre la légende et l'histoire: le 18 août 1871," Revue d'Histoire et de Philosophie Religieuses. Vol. 61, No. 4, pp. 389-411. English title: "R. W. McAll: An Evangelist among Paris Workingmen, between Legend and History, August 18, 1871." This article attempts to sort fact from fiction in the hagiography of a British congregational minister, Robert Whitaker McAll, who established a city mission in Paris in the late 19th century.

16003. Russell, Michael B. (1981) "J. P. Stevens Caves In: The Fabric of a Good Labor Contract," Sojourners. Vol. 10, No. 4 (April), pp. 10-11.

16004. Rymer, J. O. (1981) "A Modern Cathedral?" St. Mark's Review. No. 105 (March), pp. 12-17.

16005. Saggau, Elise. (1981) "Shalom in the Inner City," Modern

Ministries. Vol. 2, No. 5 (May-June), pp. 13-16+.

16006. Samuel, Vinay Kumar. (1981) The Meaning of and Cost of Discipleship. Bombay, India: Bombay Urban Industrial League for Development.

16007. Saprykin, Vladimir Aleksandrovich. (1981) Urbaniza'tˋsi'iˋa, ateizm reigi'iˋa: Problemy formirovani'iˋa nauchnomaterialisticheskogo ateisticheskogo mirovozzreni'iˋa v uslovi'iˋakh so'tˋsialisticheskogo goroda. Alma-Ata, Soviet Union: Kazakhstan. Re: atheism and urbaniztion in the Soviet Union. Text in Russian.

16008. Schatz, Ronald W. (1981) "American Labor and the Catholic Church, 1919-1950," International Labor and Working Class History. No. 20 (Fall), pp. 46-53.

16009. Schillebeeckx, Edward. (1981) Ministry: A Case For Change. London: SCM Press. Schillebeeckx reviews the biblical basis for ministry and argues for change in 20th century Catholic approaches to ministry.

16010. Schobel, Paul. (1981) Dem Fliessband ausgeliefert: ein Seelsorger erfährt die Arbeitswelt. Munich, West Germany: Kaiser. Re: a pastor's experience with automobile assembly line work.

16011. Seminario sobre "iglesia y situacion socioeconomica en la España de los 80:" materiales, febrero-mayo, 1981. (1981) Madrid: Universidad Comillas de Madrid. A collection of materials for a seminar on social problems, labor issues, and unemployment in Spain.

16012. Shanabruch, Charles. (1981) Chicago's Catholics: The Evolution of an American Identity. Notre Dame, IN: University of Notre Dame Press. In a detailed history of the Archdiocese of Chicago from 1833 to 1924, Shanabruch traces the proliferation of ethnic parishes and interethnic rivalries which were subsequently welded into a single sectarian structure under the leadership of George Cardinal Mundelein. The utility of the transcending Catholic identity overrode the cohesiveness of the ethnic components. Reviewed: Church History, Vol. 52 (June, 1983), p. 244. Journal of the American Academy of Religion, Vol. 51 (March, 1983), p.154.

16013. Shaping Tomorrow. (1981) London: Home Missions Division of the Methodist Church.

16014. Shusterman, Donna. (1981) "An Alternative to Gentrification: CDC's--Local Control of Housing," Cities. Vol. 1, No. 4 (July), pp. 28-29. Reprinted from: Shelterforce. (Spring, 1979).

16015. Sider, Ronald J., ed. (1981) Evangelicals and Development: Toward a Theology of Social Change. Philadelphia, PA: Westminster. Evangelicals are mandated to serve the poor and needy, to correct injustice, and to strive for peace. Sider, at the time of writing, was professor at Eastern Baptist Theological Seminary, Philadelphia, PA.

16016. Siegel, Adrienne. (1981) The Image of the American City in Popular Literature, 1820-1870. Port Washington, NY: Kennikat.

16017. Sills, Mark R. (1981) "An Urban Christmas," Cities. Vol. 1, No. 6 (November), pp. 12-14.

16018. Sine, Thomas W., Jr. (1981) The Mustard Seed Conspiracy: You Can Make a Difference in Tomorrow's Troubled World. Waco, TX: Word. Sine, a futurist and an evangelical, interprets futurism to evangelical readers. He speculates on coming changes in the church and nation and corrects a few assumptions that some evangelicals hold about the future, particularly in regard to eschatology. Changes in Third World cities receive particular attention. Sine believes that most of the poor people who are swelling populations in these cities do not share the perspectives articulated by Western futurists in the 1970s about the limits to growth and, therefore, face great difficulty in the 1980s and 1990s. Reviewed: Christianity Today, Vol. 27, February 4, 1983, p. 91. Bibliography.

16019. Sivanandan, A. (1981) "Imperialism in the Sylvan Age," The Witness [Ambler, PA]. Vol. 64, No. 11 (November), pp. 7-9.

16020. Skipper, Debbie. (1981) "Nagasaki: The City of Suffering," America. Vol. 145, No. 18 (November 28), pp. 355-357. Catholic holocaust victims remember, forgive, and work for peace. Implications are drawn for the victims of the United States' war in Viet Nam.

16021. Smith, Cecil H. (1981) "An Outer City Challenge," Alliance Witness. Vol. 116, No. 7 (April), pp. 16-17.

16022. Smith, David Marshall. (1981) Inequality in an American City, Atlanta, Georgia, 1960-1970. London: Department of Geography, Queen Mary College, University of London.

16023. Smith, J. Alfred, Sr. (1981) For the Facing of This Hour: A Call to Action. Elgin, IL: Progressive Baptist Publishing House. A collection of speeches and sermons by the pastor of Allen Temple Baptist Church, Oakland, CA. Smith and Allen Temple have received numerous awards for urban ministry. Many of the speeches were delivered at Southern Baptist schools.

16024. Smith, Sidney. (1981) "Growth of Black Southern Baptist Churches in the Inner City," Baptist History and Heritage [Thematic issue: Black Southern Baptist Heritage]. Vol. 16, No. 3 (July), pp. 49-60. Based on conversations with 350 Black Southern Baptist pastors, Smith advances eleven models for growth in membership of these churches. The models, each of which reflects a particular strategy or type of ministry that fosters growth, are named: 1) religious education, 2) social service, 3) urban planning, 4) preaching, 5) church music, 6) multiracial merger, 7) mission congregations, 8) Black-sponsored mission congregations, 9) transitional community, 10) predominantly Black multi-ethnic, and 11) old Black first church. A list of the weaknesses Black pastors see in the Southern Baptist Convention is included.

16025. Sobrino, Jon. (1981) Oscar Romero, profeta y mártir de la liberacíon. Lima, Peru: Centro de Estudios y Publicationes. See also regarding the life and assassination of Romero: Archbishop Romero: Model of Faith. [London]: Catholic Institute for International Relations, 1984.

16026. Söderberg, Kjell. (1981) Den första massutvandringen: en studie av befolkningsrörlighet och emigration utgående från Alfta socken i Hälsingland 1846-1895. Umeå, Sweden: Universitetet; Stockholm, Sweden: Almqvist and Wiksell International. Re: Scandinavian immigrants. Summary in English.

16027. Sokol, Dolly and Jack Doherty. (1981) "The Alternative Parish," pp. 155-178 in Mark Searle, ed. Parish: A Place for Worship. Collegeville, MN: Liturgical Press.

16028. Soleri, Paolo. (1981) "Earthly Cities," Parabola: The Magazine of Myth and Tradition. Vol. 6, No. 2, pp. 61-65.

16029. Southern Baptist Convention, Home Mission Board. (beginning in 1981) Mission USA. Atlanta, GA: the Board. Succeeded a periodical titled: Home Missions.

16030. Sovik, Edward A. (1981) Accessible Church Buildings. New York: Pilgrim Press.

16031. Sowell, Thomas. (1981) Ethnic America. New York: Basic

Books. Ethnic histories with statistical data.

16032. Spring, Beth. (1981) "One Ministry: A Case Study in Urban Evangelism," Christianity Today. Vol. 25, No. 3 (February 6), p. 75. Re: the work of J. Staggers in Washington, DC.

16033. Stave, Bruce M. and Sondra A. Stave, eds. (1981) Urban Bosses, Machines and Progressive Reformers. Huntingdon, NY: Krieger Publishers.

16034. Steinberg, Stephen. (1981) The Ethnic Myth. New York: Atheneum.

16035. Stevens-Arroyo, Antonio M. (1981) The Indigenous Elements in the Popular Religion of Puerto Ricans. Thesis (Ph. D.). New York: Fordham.

16036. Stockwell, Clinton E. (1981) The Christian and the Workplace: A Selected Bibliography. Chicago, IL: Urban Church Resource Center, SCUPE.

16037. Stoggers, John. (1981) "How to Eat an Elephant: Inner-city Insights for You to Chew On--Interview with John Stoggers," HIS. Vol. 42, No. 2 (November), pp. 1+.

16038. Sugden, Christopher. (1981) Radical Discipleship. Basingstoke, England: Marshall, Morgan and Scott. Reviewed: Churchman, Vol. 96, No. 2 (1982), p. 175.

16039. Sulgit, Julian D. (1981) A Prophetic Word for Local Churches. Thesis (D. Min.). Dayton, OH: United Theological Seminary.

16040. Swearer, Donald K. (1981) Buddhism and Society in Southeast Asia. Chambersburg, PA: Anima.

16041. Takenaka, Masao. (1981) "Living Christ with People in Asian City--A Case Study of PROUD," Church Labor Letter. No. 144 (May), pp. 1-17. PROUD (People's Responsible Organization of United Dharavi), a large grass roots people's organization located in Bombay's slums, seeks better housing conditions, better sanitation, and general improvement of the quality of life for Bombay's poor. It is a democratic structure with representatives of all castes, ages, religion, and sexes. Its elected officers represent four religious groups. Takenaka interprets PROUD as as an ecumenical movement of shalom. Other materials about PROUD are found in the ICUIS collection, Nos. 4679-4680 [Location: see note 2].

16042. Taylor, John V. (1981) "Signs of Growth in the Church of England: New Shoots from an Old Tree," pp. 5-25 in A. Wedderspoon, ed. Grow or Die: Essays on Church Growth to Mark the 900th Anniversary of Winchester Cathedral. London: SPCK.

16043. Taylor, Meg. (1981) "Prostitution," Point: Forum for Melanesian Affairs [10]. No. 1, pp. 118-123.

16044. Telfer, David Alden. (1981) Red and Yellow, Black and White and Brown. Anderson, Indiana: Warner Press. Re: church work with minorities in the Church of God, Anderson, Indiana.

16045. Tergel, Alf. (1981) Kyrkan och industrialismen ungkyrkorörelsen 1912-1917. Uppsala, Sweden: Universitit, Skeab. Re: church and labor in Sweden. Part of a series titled: Svenska kyrkans Kulturinstituts dialogserie. Bibliography. Tergel covers the years 1901-1911 in an earlier volume titled: Ungkyrkomännen, arbetarirågan och nationalismen. Uppsula, Sweden: 1969.

16046. "Three Mile Island: Diaries of a Near Disaster." (1981) JSAC Grapevine. Vol. 12, No. 10 (May), pp. [1-6].

16047. Toffler, Alvin. (1981) The Third Wave. New York: Bantam.

16048. Tse, Christina. (1981) The Invisible Control: Management Control of Workers in a US Electronic Company. Kowloon, Hong Kong: Center for the Progress of Peoples. [Location: ICUIS 4739, see note 2]. US corporations in Asia exploit women and promote passivity. Bibliography. For additional materials on the effects of transnational corporations in Asia, see ICUIS Nos. 4276-4279, 4736-4742. For information on transnational corporations in other parts of the world, see ICUIS Nos. 4758-4774.

16049. Tuck, William P. (1981) "A Theology of Healthy Church Staff Relations," [Part of a thematic issue on church staffs], Review and Expositor. Vol. 78, No. 1 (Winter), pp. 15-28.

16050. Tucker, Graham. (1981) A Strategy for Ministry in the Business Community. Thesis (D. Min.). Toronto, Ontario, Canada: Toronto School of Theology.

16051. Umansky, Ellen M. (1981) Lily H. Montagu and the Development of Liberal Judaism in England. Thesis (Ph. D.). New York: Columbia University.

16052. United Methodist Church, Interagency Coordinating Committee. (1981?) Developing and Strengthening the Ethnic Minority Local Church. Evanston, IL: United Methodist Communications. Bibliographical references.

16053. United Presbyterian Church in the USA. (1981) A Joint Urban Policy for the United Presbyterian Church in the USA and the Presbyterian Church in the United States. New York: The Program Agency the United Presbyterian Church in the USA. Reprinted: Cities. Vol. 1, No. 4 (July), pp. 32-33. Provides theological basis for urban ministry and describes the two biblical attitudes toward the city.

16054. United Presbyterian Church in the USA, Advisory Committee on Housing Ministries. (1981) A Call to Renewed Ministries in Housing. New York: the Advisory Committee. [Location: ICUIS 4632, see note 2]. A report discussing the housing crisis and its causes, with suggested steps to be taken by the 193rd Assembly of the UPCUSA.

16055. Updike, John. (1981) Rabbit Is Rich. New York: Knopf. Rabbit makes his fortune in a Toyota car dealership. For other novels in the Rabbit series, see Updike (1960, 1971, 1990).

16056. Urban Mission for the United Church of Canada: A Dream that Is Not for the Drowsy--A Working Theology for Presence and Future-Building in the Metro Core across Our Country. (1981) Toronto, Canada: Task Group on the Church in the Metropolitan Core. [Location: ICUIS 4500, see note 2]. Urban churchworkers in the United Church of Canada hold divergent views about the mandate for urban ministry. A Task Group was formed to conduct inquiries about the nature and mission of urban ministry. This theological statement is one of the documents produced by that Task Group.

16057. Vandebroek, Pros. (1981) Inventaris van het archief van het Algemeen Christelijk Werkersverbond van het arrondissement Brussel: 1919-ca. 1975. Leuven, The Netherlands: KADOC. Re: 20th century history of the relations of the Catholic church with trade unions in Belgium.

16058. Vincent, John J. (1981) Starting All Over Again: Hints of Jesus in the City. Geneva: World Council of Churches, Risk Book

Series No. 13. A new beginning of Christianity in the city requires a new lifestyle and new understanding of mission. Reviewed: Missionalia, Vol. 11, August, 1983, p. 98.

16059. Vincent, John J. (1981) "Situation Analysis," in Backyard Seminary. Sheffield: Urban Theology Unit.

16060. Wagner, C. Peter. (1981) Church Growth and the Whole Gospel: A Biblical Mandate. San Francisco, CA: Harper and Row.

16061. Wallis, Jim. (1981) The Call to Conversion: Recovering the Gospel for These Times. San Francisco, CA: Harper and Row. Wallis describes social spirituality from the evangelical perspective of Sojourners magazine. Reviewed: Review and Expositor, Vol. 81 (Spring, 1984), p. 329. Christianity Today, Vol. 27 (January 21, 1983), p. 44. International Review of Missions, Vol. 72 (July, 1983), p. 423.

16062. Walsh, Jack. (1981) "Asian Industrialization and the Uprooting of Local Asian Communities," Pro Mundi Vita, Asia-Australasia Dossier. No. 19 (October), pp. 1-27. Bibliography.

16063. Warren, Donald I. (1981) Helping Networks: How People Cope with Problems in Urban Communities. Notre Dame, IN: University of Notre Dame Press.

16064. Webber, George Williams. (1981) "The Struggle for Integrity," Review of Religious Research. Vol. 23, No. 1 (September), pp. 3-21. Webber uses the occasion of the 1980 H. Paul Douglass Lecture, an annual event of the Religious Research Association, to review his 30 years' ministry in the inner city. In his typical pace, which proceeds at an urgent amble, Webber both describes the depth of his despair about city and suburban churches and reports several "clues" he has discovered. Pastoral integrity is essential to the church, he contends, and the struggle for integrity is never ending. Helpful "clues" are found, among other places, in the works of Mead (1972) and DesPortes (1973) which report the impact of Project Test Pattern, in Fletcher's (1975) writing about the Inter-Met program, and in John Westerhoff's approach to faith development. Other "clues" in the search for pastoral and congregational integrity include: combining the strengths of the Troeltschian types of church and sect; rediscovering the power of Wesley's small groups for creating accountability and discipline; recapturing the centrality of the Kingdom of God in theology.

16065. Wheeler, David. (1981) "A Vision of Hope for Mexico's Children," Christian Century. Vol. 98, No. 14 (April 22), pp. 437-438.

16066. Wheeler, Edward O. (1981) "An Overview of Black Southern Baptist Involvements," Baptist History and Heritage [Thematic issue: Black Southern Baptists]. Vol. 16, No. 3 (July), pp. 49-60.

16067. "When You Feel Lost You Come to the Bowery." (1981) Christian Herald. Vol. 104, No. 10 (November), pp. 36-38+.

16068. White, George Abbott. (1981) "Simone Weil's Work Experiences: From Wigan Pier to Chrystie Street," Cross Currents. Vol. 31, No. 2 (Summer), pp. 129-149, 162. Same title: pp. 137-179 in George Abbott White, ed. Simone Weil. Amherst, MA: University of Massachusetts Press. White compares Simone Weil, George Orwell, and Dorothy Day in their attempts to find mental stimulation in manual labor. Each sought in his or her own way to depict the gradual enslaving character of the industrial world, and each stressed the need to respect workers' dignity.

16069. Wiebe, Bernie. (1981) "Christians in the Concrete Jungle," The Mennonite. Vol. 96, No. 8 (February 24), p. 132. Editorial comment on human need in cities and the rural Mennonite heritage.

16070. Wilkinson, David R. and Paul Obregón. (1981) Urban Heartbeat: The Human Touch in Metropolitan Missions. Atlanta, GA: Home Mission Board, Southern Baptist Convention. Narration and photographs about the city.

16071. William Temple Foundation. (1981) The Poverty Debate and the Churches: Occasional Papers, No. 5. Manchester, England: William Temple Foundation. Ecumenical Christian perspectives on the persistence of poverty. This was one of the documents that led to the formation of Church Action on Poverty, an ecumenical membership organization in Great Britain.

16072. Williams, Kathy M. (1981) The Rastafarians. London: Ward Lock Educational.

16073. Wimberly, Edward P. (1981) "Developing Support Systems in an Urban Setting," Cities. Vol. 1, No. 5 (September), pp. 3-6.

16074. Winter, Gibson. (1981) Liberating Creation: Foundations of Religious Social Ethics. New York: Crossroad. Winter analyzes the social and spiritual implications of the root mechanistic metaphor in Western technology and civilization, finding it in crisis and inadequate for the future.

16075. Winters, Donald E. (1981) The Soul of Solidarity: The Relationships between the IWW[Industrial Workers of the World] and American Religion during the Progressive Era. Thesis (Ph. D.). Minneapolis, MN: University of Minnesota.

16076. Wood, James R. (1981) Leadership in Voluntary Organizations: The Controversy over Social Action in Protestant Churches. New Brunswick, NJ: Rutgers University Press. Wood uses data on the church controversy regarding social action to test hypotheses about the legitimization of leadership. Reviewed: Review of Religious Research, Vol. 24 (June, 1983), p. 362. Journal for the Scientific Study of Religion, Vol. 22 (September, 1983), p. 290. Sociological Analysis, Vol. 44 (Fall, 1983), p. 255. Bibliography. Questionnaire. Wood has written extensively regarding the effects of participation in social activism by voluntary organizations.

16077. Woods, Denis J. (1981) "Housing Discrimination: An Analysis of Social Structures," America. Vol. 145, No. 3 (August 1-8), pp. 49-53.

16078. Wright, Tennant C. (1981) "Immigration and the [Catholic] Church," America. Vol. 144, No. 5 (February 7), pp. 99-100.

16079. Yankelovich, Daniel. (1981) New Rules: Searching for Self Fulfillment in a World Turned Upside Down. New York: Random House. Yankelovich investigates data associated with the "self-fulfilment" goals of the 1970's, critiquing the excessive self-centered approach to fulfillment. Changes are needed in the '80s, he concludes. He advances some hypotheses about cities: e.g., cities have become the receptacle for persons whose self-fulfillment has been thwarted, broken, or otherwise rendered unobtainable. People before 1970 were willing to sacrifice to get ahead or for their children to get ahead. In the 70s, people demanded both personal fulfillment and material wealth at the same time. The ethic of commitment was lost, as was the realization that self fulfillment is found only in relationship to others. Recovery of both is needed. See further by Yankelovich: The New Morality. New York: McGraw-Hill, 1974; and the periodical: The Yankelovich Monitor.

16080. Yeo, Eileen. (1981) "Christianity in Chartist Struggle, 1838-1842," Past and Present. No. 91 (May), pp. 109-139.

16081. Young, Kathy. (1981) "The State of Prison Ministry," JSAC Grapevine [Thematic issue: Prison ministry]. Vol. 12, No. 9 (April), pp. [2-4].

16082. Zehr, Howard. (1981) The Christian as Victim. Akron, PA: Mennonite Central Committee A pamphlet.

16083. Zulehner, Paul Michael. (1981) Religion im Leben der Österreicher: Documentation einer Umfrage. Vienna, Austria: Herder. Since 1970, Zulehner has conducted a confidential study for the Catholic bishop regarding declining religious participation in Austria. Many people have become disaffected and uninterested in church affairs, particularly among the people with higher education. Resentment of the authoritarian leadership in the Church is a key factor. Zulehner frequently conducts empirical studies for the Austrian church. Bibliography.

16084. Adams, Jennifer A. (1982) The Solar Church. New York: Pilgrim. Adams, who regularly writes books on solar energy, offers suggestions for energy consciousness in the church.

16085. Agarwal, Anil. (1982) "Science and Technology Act as Tools of Control," Engage/Social Action. Vol. 10, No. 9 (October), pp. 35-40.

16086. Akpem, Yosev Yina. (1982) A Family Life Education for the Church's Ministry to Urban Migrants in Nigeria. Thesis (D. Miss.). Pasadena, CA: Fuller Theological Seminary, School of World Mission.

16087. Allen, Jere. (1982) "The Church in the Changing Community," Southwestern Journal of Theology [Thematic issue: Urban ministry]. Vol. 24, No. 2 (Spring), pp. 20-27. Allen, who has done most of his research in connection with the Home Mission Board of the Southern Baptist Convention, frequently writes about social change in urban neighborhoods, about churches that have reached a membership plateau and have ceased to grow, and about churches experiencing conflict.

16088. Amerson, Philip A. (1982) "On Asking a Fish to Jump into a Barrel: Reflections on Urban Evangelization," Covenant Quarterly [Thematic issue]. Vol. 40, No. 2 (May), pp. 19-30. Amerson asks why, given the Biblical mandate for evangelism, are so many urban American Christians embarrassed and confused when asked to witness to the gospel.

16089. Ammering, Josef, et al. (1982) Berichte aus der Arbeitswelt: Neue pastorale Modelle der Betriebsseelsorge. Vienna, Austria: Herder. Reports from the work-world, new pastoral models for industrial chaplaincies.

16090. Archer, Kieth. (1982) "'To the Known God': A Search for His Activity in Industry," The Modern Churchman. n.s. Vol. 25, No. 2, pp. 4-15.

16091. Bahr, Howard M. (1982) "Shifts in the Denominational Demography of Middletown, 1924-1977," Journal for the Scientific Study of Religion. Vol. 21, No. 2 (June), pp. 99-114. A study of changes in denominational preferences among Middletown residents shows a growing rift between Protestants of a Northern and Southern orientation. There is no evidence of a decline in church attendance.

16092. Baker, Vaughn Willard. (1982) Faith Sharing Groups as a Means of Inner City Evangelism. Thesis (D. Min.). Dallas, TX: Perkins School of Theology, Southern Methodist University.

16093. Banana, Canaan. (1982) The Theology of Promise: The Dynamics of Self Reliance. Harare, Zimbabwe: College Press.

16094. Barker, Michael Kenneth. (1982) Steps towards Pluralism within a Local Church. Chicago, IL: manuscript. [Location: Chicago Theological Seminary].

16095. Barreira, I. A. F. [Barreiro, Alvaro?]. (1982) "Igreja: Discurso e açào pastorale: Anali se da reflexão religiosa sobre a questaõ urbana," Revista de Ciências Sociais [Ceara]. Vol. 12, No. 3, (nn. 1-2), pp. 45-62. [See note 3].

16096. Barreiro, Alvaro. (1982) Basic Ecclesial Communities: The Evangelization of the Poor. Maryknoll, NY: Orbis.

16097. Barrett, David B. (1982) World Christian Encyclopedia. New York: Oxford University Press. Because of Barrett's interest in cities, the encyclopedia has many urban related items.

16098. Bartelt, Michael. (1982) Wertwandel der Arbeit: der Bedeutungsrückgang der Werte Arbeit, Beruf, Leistung als sozialethisches Problem. Frankfurt am Main, West Germany: Haag + Herchen. Re: the value of work and its decline as a social-ethical problem.

16099. Baum, Gregory. (1982) "The Pope's Progressive Labor Policy," Social Policy. Vol. 13 (Fall), pp. 12-13.

16100. Baum, Gregory. (1982) The Priority of Labor: A Commentary on Laborem Exercens: Encyclical Letter of Pope John Paul II. New York: Paulist Press. Commentary on Pope John Paul II's social encyclical which, Baum contends, represents an important shift to the left in Catholic social thought. Labor has clear priority over capital. Bibliography.

16101. Bavinck, J. H. (1982) The Church between the Temple and the Mosque. Grand Rapids, MI: Eerdmans.

16102. Beal, John David. (1982) "8.5 by '85 and Multifamily Housing Residents," Church Administration. Vol. 24, No. 12 (September), pp. 29-30.

16103. Beale, Robert. (1982) "Search for Faith on an Urban Trail," (Center for the Study of Religion and Education in the Inner City, Salford, England). One World [World Council of Churches]. No. 73 (January), pp. 7-8.

16104. Beeson, Trevor. (1982) "First Aid and Cure in Britain," Christian Century. Vol. 99, No. 3 (January 27), pp. 93-94. Beeson comments about the church's role as mediator between police and rioters. He gives evidence to support the practice of churches keeping property owned in the inner city even beyond the time when the congregation must close its doors. (Under what circumstances and auspices, one might ask, should the church own abandoned property)?

16105. Beijbom, Anders. (1982) "En ar Polen ej forlorat:" kyrkan och solidaritet i kamp for demokratin. Vallingby: Harrier. [Location: Library of Congress]. Re: trade unions and church-labor issues in Poland.

16106. Belknap, Charles, et al. (1982?) Discovering Church Vocations: A Report on Pilot Training Programs for Ministry in the Diocese of Los Angeles. [Los Angeles, CA: Episcopal Church in the Diocese of Los Angeles].

16107. Benedict, Donald L. (1982) Born Again Radical. New York: Pilgrim Press. Although Benedict denies that this book is, strictly speaking, an autobiography, his trail blazing career as advocate for the oppressed in New York and Chicago provides the basis for his statements on ministry and his personal reflections on the city ministry projects with which he has been associated. This memoir has historical importance because the conversations and discussions reported are otherwise unavailable. Reviewed: Sojourners, Vol. 12 (October, 1983), pp. 38-39.

16108. Benkart, Paula Kaye. (1982) "Paul Fox: Presbyterian Mission and Polish Americans," Journal of Presbyterian History. Vol. 60, No. 4 (Winter), pp. 301-313. Bibliographical footnotes on Fox and Protestant ministries among Polish immigrants.

16109. Bennett, Caroline Barker. (1982) "A Community in Christ in the Workplace?" Crucible. [Vol. 21, No. 2] (April-June), pp. 58-66.

16110. Bennett, G. Willis. (1982) Urban Church Ministry for Louisville, A Seminar for Methodist Ministers [Sound recording]. Louisville, KY: Southern Baptist Theological Seminary.

16111. Bennett, G. Willis. (1982) "Reaching America's Cities," pp. 158-167 in Larry L. Rose and C. Kirk Hadaway, eds. The Urban Challenge: Reaching America's Cities with the Gospel. Nashville, TN: Broadman Press.

16112. Bennett, G. Willis and David T. Britt. (1982) A Selected Bibliography: The City, Church and Ministry. Atlanta, GA: Metropolitan Missions Department, Home Mission Board of the Southern Baptist Convention, Occasional Paper No. 5.

16113. Berckman, Edward M. (1982) "Putting a Human Face on Urban Ministry," The Witness [Ambler, PA]. Vol. 65, No. 10 (October), pp. 12-14.

16114. Bergs, Manfred and Dieter von Kietzell. (1982) "Gemeinwesenarbeit und Kirchengemeinde: Ein Plädoyer für ein Verbundsystem sozialer Arbeit im Wohnbereich," Pastoraltheologie. Vol. 71, pp. 119-126. Berg pleads for greater church involvement in social issues, including social work and the providing of shelter.

16115. Best, Ernest E. (1982) Religion and Society in Transition: The Church and Social Change in England, 1560-1850. New York: Edwin Mellen. Some chapters deal with 19th century Christian socialism and the works of F. D. Maurice. Bibliography.

16116. Beukema, George G. (1982) The Servant's Community: A Study of the Development of a Servant Style of Ministry in the Inner City. Thesis (D. Min.). Holland, MI: Western Theological Seminary.

16117. Biéler, André. (1982) Chrétiens et socialistes avant Marx: les origines du grand malentendu entre les églises chrétiennes et le monde du travail: les efforts de chrétiens français pour le dissiper et transformer la société industrielle, avant 1848. Genève, Switzerland: Labor et Fides. Christians and socialists before Marx: the origins of the great misunderstanding between Christian churches and the world of labor: efforts on the part of French Christians to clarify the issues and transform industrial society, before 1848. Bibliography.

16118. Blackwell, James E. and Philip S. Hart. (1982) Cities, Suburbs and Blacks: A Study of Concerns, Distrust and Alienation. Bayside, NY: General Hall.

16119. Blake, Richard A. (1982) "Condominiums in the Global Village," America. Vol. 146, No. 22 (June 5), pp. 433-436. Blake comments on Marshall McLuhan's vision of a world more closely linked by communications technology, now frustrated by the newer technologies that make viewing and listening more insulated. Mere growth in accumulated information does not assure growth in the number or quality of the informed.

16120. Block, Walter, et al., eds. (1982) Morality of the Market. Vancouver, British Columbia, Canada: The Fraser Institute.

16121. Bluestone, Barry and Bennett Harrison. (1982) The Deindustrialization of America. New York: Basic Books.

16122. Bodner, John E. (1982) Worker's World: Kinship, Community and Protest in an Industrial Society, 1900-1940. Baltimore, MD: Johns Hopkins Press.

16123. Bodner, John E. (1982) Lives of Their Own: Blacks, Italians, and Poles in Pittsburgh, 1900-1960. Urbana, IL: University of Illinois Press.

16124. Bonner, Daniel E. (1982) The Renewal of the City Church. Thesis (D. Min.). Boston, MA: Boston University. Church renewal resulting from the transition of homogeneous congregations into inclusive churches in North American cities. Bibliography.

16125. Borgeault, Guy. (1982) "Church and Worker in Quebec: A Context for Political Theology," pp. 215-223 in Benjamin C. Smillie, ed. Political Theology in the Canadian Context. Waterloo, Ontario, Canada: Wilfrid Laurier University Press.

16126. Bose, Ashish. (1982) "Patterns of Urban Growth in India," Social Action [India]. Vol. 32, No. 2 (April), pp. 113-126.

16127. Boudon, Raymon. (1982) The Unintended Consequences of Social Action. New York: St. Martin's Press. In a highly theoretical work, closely argued, that presents an explanation of social change in modern industrial society based on the analysis of perverse effects, Boudon's ultimate purpose is to provide a social scientific basis for human freedom of choice. Perverse effects produce change that is often counter-intuitive and on occasion apparently disadvantageous to all involved. His examples are mostly drawn from education, but church oriented examples readily occur to the reader: e.g., a church that receives a large bequest may find that member contributions drop sharply, or a church might discover that as more people are recruited into its membership the less dedication the membership has to the historic values of that church such as ministry with the poor or commitment to a particular form of evangelism. Theory of perverse effects is one way of explaining such phenomena. Planners for city churches will find the theory presented in this book, although abstract, insightful. Bibliography.

16128. Boulter, Robert O. (1982) "Reflections on Urban Violence," Cities. Vol. 2, No. 3 (July), pp. 23-26.

16129. Bowker, Lee H. (1982) "Battered Women and the Clergy," Journal of Pastoral Care. Vol. 36, No. 4 (December), pp. 226-234. Victims of marital violence (146 women, mostly White and middle class) in Milwaukee evaluate their contact with clergy as being more positive than negative, with the middle class being more positive in their evaluations than the working class women. Protestant clergy were rated higher than Catholic priests in their effectiveness by the women, while the husbands rated the two groups of clergy opposite. Bowker advocates counseling and shelters for battered women.

16130. Brewer, Earl D. C. (1982) Continuation or Transformation? Nashville, TN: Abingdon. A review of Methodist social policy.

16131. Brewer, Kathleen and Patrick A. Taran. (1982) Manual for Refugee Sponsorship. New York: Church World Service, Immigration and Refugee Program.

16132. Britton, Margaret. (1982) The Single Woman in the Family of God. London: Epworth.

16133. Brooks, James A., ed. (1982) "Studies in the Church and the City," Southwestern Journal of Theology [Thematic issue: Urban ministry]. Vol. 24, No. 2 (Spring), pp. 5-83.

16134. Brown, Diane R. and Ronald W. Walters. (1982?) Exploring the Role of the Black Church in the Community. Washington, DC: Mental Health Research and Development Center and Institute for Urban Affairs and Research, Howard University.

16135. Brown, Hubert. (1982) "Ministering in the Urban World," Mission Focus. Vol. 10, No. 2, pp. 17-18.

16136. Brueggemann, Walter. (1982) Living toward a Vision: Biblical Reflections on Shalom. Philadelphia, PA: United Church Press. Brueggemann, a theologian and Biblical scholar in the United Church of Christ, often writes Biblical exposition related to contemporary social issues.

16137. Bucey, Harry Richard. (1982) Multiple Staff Ministry in the United Church of Christ. Thesis (D. Min.) Lancaster, PA: Lancaster Theological Seminary.

16138. Burgman, Hans. (1982-3) "Urban Apostolate in Kisumu" [in two parts] AFER: African Ecclesial Review. Vol. 24, No. 6 (December), pp. 337-342; Vol. 25, No. 1 (February), pp. 7-15.

16139. Burke, Cyril C. (1982) Venture in Mission: St. Monica's Episcopal Church--a Middle-Class, Predominantly Black Church Attempts to Minister to Its Community. Thesis (D. Min.). Hartford, CT: Hartford Seminary Foundation.

16140. Burns, Terry and Gail Burns. (1982) "Africa's Cities Beckon New Missionaries," Impact [Conservative Baptist Foreign Missions Society]. Vol. 39, No. 1 (January), pp. 12-13. Re: plans for a new mission in Abidjan, Ivory Coast.

16141. Burson-Marsteller, Public Affairs. (1982) Church, State and Corporation: A Report on the Impact of Religious Organization on Corporate Policy. New York: Burson-Marsteller.

16142. Butts, Calvin Otis, III. (1982) The Construction of a Plan for the Effective Influence of an Urban Church on Public Policy. Thesis (D. Min.). Madison, NJ: Drew University.

16143. "Call for National Emergency Coalition on Economic Crisis," (1982) Cities. Vol. 2, No. 1 (March-April), pp. 24-27. The "new poor," whose poverty is the result of plant closings, need a new national coalition to seek justice and promote humanitarian purposes.

16144. Carlson, Arthur B. (1982) "The Kansas City Disaster: July

17, 1981--The Hyatt Regency Hotel," American Protestant Hospital Association Bulletin. Vol. 46, No. 3, pp. 69-73.

16145. Carpenter, James A. (1982) Equipping the Laity for Pastoral Ministry. Thesis (D. Min.). Enid, OK: Phillips University Graduate Seminary.

16146. Carr, Alan. (1982) "Drug Abuse," Social Studies: Irish Journal of Sociology (Christus Rex Society). Vol. 7, No. 1 (Winter), pp. 20-32. Carr reviews the various literatures on drug usage. Bibliography.

16147. Carter, Michael V. and Kenneth P. Ambrose. (1982) Appalachian Serpent Handlers in the Urban Midwest: A Test of a Satisfaction Hypothesis. [Paper delivered at the 5th Annual Appalachian Studies Conference Held at the Virginia Polytechnic Institute, March, 1982].

16148. Casson, Lloyd. (1982) "EUC to Pursue Tough, Multi-Issue Platform," Witness [Ambler, PA]. Vol. 65, No. 5 (May), pp. 13+.

16149. Castillo, Metosalem Q. . (1982) "Shepherding the Urban Church," Philippines Church Growth News. Vol. 5 (April), pp. 6+.

16150. Castillo, Metosalem Q. (1982) The Church in Thy House. Manila, Philippines: Alliance. Bibliography.

16151. Catholic Church Extension Society of Canada. (beginning in 1982) Home Missions. Toronto, Ontario, Canada: the Society. A periodical.

16152. Catholic Church, Archdiocese of New York, Office of Pastoral Research. (1982) Hispanics in New York: Religious, Cultural and Social Experience: A Study of Hispanics in the Archdiocese of New York. [Two volumes]. New York: Office of Pastoral Research.

16153. Chaney, Charles L. (1982) Church Planting at the End of the Twentieth Century. Wheaton, IL: Tyndale House.

16154. Chaudhury, Rafiqul Huda. (1982) "Urbanization in Bangladesh," Social Action [India]. Vol. 32, No. 2 (April), pp. 179-213.

16155. Cheathamm, Carl Wade. (1982) Social Christianity: A Study of English Nonconformist Social Attitudes, 1800-1914, with Special Reference to Hugh Price Hughes, Samuel Edward Keeble, John Clifford, and Reginald John Campbell. Thesis (Ph. D.). Nashville, TN:

Vanderbilt University.

16156. Chesebro, Scott Elliot. (1982) The Mennonite Urban Commune: A Hermeneutic-Dialectical Understanding of Its Anabaptist Ideology and Practice. Thesis (Ph. D.). Notre Dame, IN: University of Notre Dame.

16157. Chevallier, Dominique. (1982) "Non-Muslim Communities in Arab Cities," pp. 159-165 in Benjamin Braude and Bernard Lewis, eds. Christians and Jews in the Ottoman Empire. New York: Holmes and Meier.

16158. Christensen, Michael J. (1982) "Golden Gate Community: An Urban Mission," Herald of Holiness. Vol. 71, No. 5 (March 1), pp. 6+.

16159. Clark, Dennis. (1982) A History of the Society of Friendly Sons of St. Patrick for the Relief of Emigrants from Ireland in Philadelphia, 1951-1981, with an Abridged Account of the Society from Its Founding in Philadelphia in 1771. Philadelphia, PA: [The Friendly Sons of St. Patrick].

16160. Coleman, John A. (1982) An American Strategic Theology. New York: Paulist. Re: the Catholic dialogue between religion and sociology, particularly in North America.

16161. Collins, Rebecca. (1982) "When Native Americans Move to the City," Church Herald. Vol. 39, No. 15 (August 20), pp. 16-17. Collins is director of a program for Native Americans in Denver, CO.

16162. Congresso Batista Latino Americano de evangelismo urbano e missôes. (1982) Rio de Janeiro, Brasil: Junta de Evangelismo de Convençâo Batista Brasileira. [Location: Southern Baptist Theological Seminary, Louisville, KY].

16163. Conn, Harvie M. and Clinton E. Stockwell. (1982) A Bibliography for Community Ministry in the City of Chicago. Chicago, IL: Urban Church Resource Center, SCUPE.

16164. Connolly, G. P. (1982) "Little Brother Be at Peace: The Priest as Holy Man in the Nineteenth-Century Ghetto," pp. 191-206 in W. J. Sheils, ed. The Church and Healing. Oxford, England: Published for the Ecclesiastical History Society by Basil Blackwell.

16165. Consejo Episcopal Latinoamericano. (1982) Pastoral y parroquia en la ciudad. Bogotá, Colombia: Consejo Episcopal Latinoamericano, CELAM. Pastoral work in city nieghborhoods.

16166. Consejo General de la Pontificia Comisión para América Latina. (1982) Animadores para el cambio social: Guia práctica de formación. Bogotá, Colombia: Consejo General de la Pontificia Comisión para América Latina. Re: social change and a practical guide for training social change agents.

16167. Conzemius, Victor. (1982) Adolf Kolping: der Gesellenvater aktuell: Damals und Heute. Freiburg, Switzerland. Imba Verlag. A biography of Kolping (1813-1865), a German Catholic priest and leader of laborers. Bibliography.

16168. Cook, R. Franklin and Tom Nees. (1982) Renew the Ruined Cities. Kansas City, MO: Beacon Hill Press. Re: urban ministry for the Church of the Nazarene.

16169. Cook, William [Guillermo]. (1982) "Grass Roots Communities and the 'Protestant Predicament,'" Occasional Essays [San Jose, Costa Rica: CELEP]. Vol. 9, No. 2 (December), pp. 53-86.

16170. Corcoran, Theresa. (1982) Vida Dutton Scudder. Boston, MA: Twayne. Scudder was a reformer, radical socialist, advocate of immigrants, organizezer Women's Trade Union League, daughter of a Congregationalist missionary, member of Episcopal church, and noted for harmonizing social concern with spiritual life. She wrote about English literature, especially poetry, and taught English at Wellesley. She was kicked out because of radical views, later to be readmitted. She had keen interest in spiritual masters of the middle ages.

16171. Cordes, Valorie. (1982) "People and Places: All County Church Emergency Support System," Cities. Vol. 2, No. 2 (May-June), p. 11.

16172. Costas, Orlando E. (1982) "La misión del pueblo de Dios en la ciudad," Boletín Teológico. Tomo 7, pp. 85-96.

16173. Costas, Orlando E. (1982) Christ Outside the Gate: Mission Beyond Christendom. Maryknoll, NY: Orbis. Perspectives on mission from Costas, a Hispanic evangelical who speaks to that tradition and beyond, originate in the viewpoint of the poor on the fringes of society. Reviewed: Journal for Ecumenical Studies, Vol. 21 (Fall, 1984), p. 784.

16174. Cox, Jeffrey. (1982) The English Churches in a Secular Society: Lambeth, 1870-1930. New York: Oxford University Press. Cox describes the churches' adaptation to urban society: direct and indirect poor relief, thrift societies, medical services, educational programs, church clubs, and popular recreation and entertainment. Bibliography.

16175. Cox, Kevin B. (1982) Gentrification and Urban Form: Research Report. Columbus, OH: Center for Real Estate Education and Research, Ohio State University.

16176. Craighill, Peyton G. (1982) "The Ministry of the Episcopal Church in the United States of America to Immigrants and Refugees: A Historical Outline," Historical Magazine of the Protestant Episcopal Church. Vol. 51, No. 2 (June), pp. 203-218.

16177. Cunningham, William T. (1982) "Hunger in Detroit," The Christian Century. Vol. 99, No. 12 (April), pp. 423-424. Testimony before the Senate Special Committee on Aging, February 25, 1982.

16178. Curran, Charles E. (1982) American Catholic Social Ethics, Twentieth Century Approaches. Notre Dame, IN: Notre Dame University Press. Social ethical analysis of four major 20th century schools of Catholic social thought: 1) John A. Ryan, 2) Frederick Kenkel and the German Catholic Central Verein, 3) Peter Maurin and Dorothy Day and the Catholic Worker, and 4) John Courtney Murray.

16179. Cutolo, Eugenio. (1982) Il mondo del lavoro nel pensiero di Giovanni Paolo II. The Vatican, Città del Vaticano: Libreria editrice vaticana.

16180. Dade, Malcolm G. (1982) "St. Cyprian's Looks Back and Looks Ahead," pp. 41-45 in John M. Burgess, ed. Black Gospel/White Church. New York: Seabury Press.

16181. Daniels, Bill. (1982) "Neighborhood Arts Movements," Cities. Vol. 2, No. 1 (March-April), pp. 6-7. Art contributes to the growth of self pride and is the natural ally of the church in urban ministry.

16182. Davis, James Hill. (1982) Virginia Conference [Methodist] Churches in Transitional Communities: From Bull-Dog to Platypus--Progress Report, 1977-1981. Richmond, VA: Virginia Conference Churches in Transitional Communities Task Force.

16183. Davis, King E. (1982) "The Status of Black Leadership: Implications for Black Followers in the 1980s," Journal of Applied Behavioral Sciences. Vol. 18, No. 3, pp. 309-322.

16184. Dayton, Edward and Samuel Wilson, eds. (1982) Unreached Peoples '82. Elgin IL: David C. Cook. Part of annual series.

16185. Dayton, Edward R. (1982) God s Purpose/Man's Plans: A Workbook. Monrovia, CA: MARC [Missions Advanced Research and Communication Center]. Suggestions for congregational planning, goal definition, and problem-solving.

16186. Debès, Joseph. (1982) Naissance de l'Action catholique ouvrière. Paris: Editions ouvrières. Re: Catholic labor groups in France. Originally presented as the author's doctoral thesis. Bibliography.

16187. Deck, Allan Figueroa and Joseph Armando Nunez. (1982) "Religious Enthusiasm and Hispanic Youths," America. Vol. 147, No. 12 (October 23), pp. 232-234. Deck analyzes the religious orientations of Hispanic and Chicano youth in the Los Angeles area. Revivalistic-evangelistic approaches are compared with Catholic sponsored efforts.

16188. Deniel, Raymond. (1982) Croyants dans la ville. Abidjan, Côte d'Ivoire: INADES-Edition. Re: religion and religious belief in West Africa.

16189. De Souza, Luis Alberto Gomez. (1982) "Church and Society in Brazil: The Basic Elements for an Analytical Framework," Journal of International Affairs. Vol. 36 (Fall), pp. 285-295. De Sousa critiques the views of Vallier (1970) and others who view the history of Brazil evolving toward a vague concept of modernization. He advocates more rigorous analytical methods.

16190. Deutsche Bischofskonferenz. (1982) Pastorale Anregungen zum Problem der Arbeitslosigkeit: ein Wort der deutschen Bischöfe an die Priester, Pfarrgemeinden und Verbände. Bonn, West Germany: Das Sekretariat. Re: Catholic pastoral initiatives to the problem of unemployment.

16191. Donaldson, Peter J. (1982) "A Life in the City," America. Vol. 147, No. 11 (October 16), pp. 205-208. Donaldson traces the journey of one family through New York neighborhoods, looking at population shifts from the perspective of individual initiatives rather than government policy.

16192. Donaldson, Thomas. (1982) Corporations and Morality. Englewood Cliffs, NJ: Prentice-Hall.

16193. Douglas, Mary. (1982) "The Effects of Modernization on Religious Change," Daedalus. Vol. 11, No. 1 (Winter), pp. 1-19. Same title: pp. 25-43 in Mary Douglas and Steven M. Tipton, eds. Religion and America: Religions in a Secular Age. Boston, MA: Beacon, 1983. Modernization does not necessarily precipitate the decline of religion.

16194. Driedger, Leo and J. Howard Kauffman. (1982) "Urbanization of Mennonites: Canadian and American Comparisons," Mennonite Quarterly Review. Vol. 56, No. 3 (July), pp. 269-290. Urban and rural Mennonites do not appear to have important differences in their interpretations of Anabaptist and biblical beliefs and practices. Urban Mennonites tend to be somewhat more liberal on personal moral issues such as smoking tobacco, attending movies, social dancing, use of alcohol, homosexuality and issues related to divorce.

16195. Duggan, Dan. (1982) "The Bind of Ministry: The Role of the Department of Pastoral Care in a Labor/Management Dispute," American Protestant Hospital Association Bulletin. Vol. 46, No. 3, pp. 11-17.

16196. Dulles, Avery Robert. (1982) A Church to Believe in: Discipleship and the Dynamics of Freedom. New York: Crossroad. After reviewing the types of church metaphors and images that currently exist in the literature and in the minds of parishioners, Dulles defends the notion of the church as "community of disciples" as the most helpful. Other contenders, all of which have at least some merit, include the church as institution, the church as sacrament, the church as body of Christ, and the church as proclaimer. Reviewed: Horizons, Vol. 10 (Spring, 1983), pp. 167-168. Theology Today, Vol. 4 (July, 1983), pp. 200+. Christian Century, Vol. 100 (February 2-9, 1983), pp. 125-126. Theological Studies, Vol. 44 (March, 1983), pp. 139-141.

16197. Dummett, Ann. (1982) "Across Party Lines: The British Nationality Bill, the Lobbyists and the Churches," The Modern Churchman. n.s. Vol. 25, No. 1, pp. 36-43.

16198. Eaves, James F. (1982) "An Annotated Bibliography on Evangelism and Church Growth in Urban Areas," Southwestern Journal of Theology [Thematic issue: Urban ministry]. Vol. 24, No. 2 (Spring), pp. 76-83.

16199. Eaves, James F. (1982) "Effective Church Evangelism in the City," Southwestern Journal of Theology [Thematic issue: Urban ministry]. Vol. 24, No. 2 (Spring), pp. 66-76. Eaves identifies the urgency and difficulties of urban evangelism.

16200. Edmonds, Patty. (1982) "Parish Stays Committed to a Depressed Detroit as Money and Jobs Flee," National Catholic Reporter. Vol. 18 (February 5), pp. 1+.

16201. Edwards, Dan W. and Sloan T. Letman. (1982) Alcoholism in the Urban Community: A Review of the Literature on Alcohol Abuse and Treatment Strategies. Chicago, IL: Loyola University of Chicago, Center for Urban Policy, Urban Insight Series. Deals with patterns of alcohol consumption among different ethnic groups. Bibliography.

16202. Elliott, Odessa Southern. (1982) "The Cathedral Ministry to the City," New Catholic World [Church in the City]. Vol. 225, No. 1347 (May), pp. 113-116. Elliott describes the accommodative ministries of the Episcopal Cathedral of St. John the Divine in New York City.

16203. Elsas, Christoph. (1982) Ausländerarbeit. Stuttgart, West Germany: Kohlhammer. Re: church work with foreigners and alien laborers in Germany.

16204. Emerson, Tilly Jo and Sally Bucklee. (1982) "'Where Cross the Crowded Ways of Life': The Story of St. Agnes', East Orange, New Jersey," pp. 20-25 in William A. Yon, ed. To Build the City--Too Long a Dream. Washington, DC: Alban Institute.

16205. La Encíclica Laborem Excercens y América Latina. (1982?) [Bogotá, Colombia]: Consejo Espiscopal Latinoamericano.

16206. Escobar, Samuel (1982) "Formación del pueblo de Dios in las grandes urbes," Boletín Teológico. (July/September), pp. 37-83. The formation of the people of God in large cities.

16207. Farley, Gary. (1982) "Community Typology," in Robert E. Wiley, ed. Change in Big Town/Small City. Atlanta, GA: Home Missions Board, the Southern Baptist Convention.

16208. Farley, Gary. (1982) "Typology of Churches," in Robert E. Wiley, ed. Change in Big Town/Small City. Atlanta, GA: Home Missions Board, the Southern Baptist Convention.

16209. Fasol, Al. (1982) "Using the Media to Reach the City for Christ," Southwestern Journal of Theology [Thematic issue: Urban ministry]. Vol. 24, No. 2 (Spring), pp. 55-65. Fasol reviews religious broadcasting and lists reasons for media reluctance to be involved in religious broadcasting. He describes resources and guidelines for churches interested in broadcasting.

16210. Fetsch, Cornelius and Peter H. Werhahn, eds. (1982) Laborem exercens, ein Konzept für die Deutsche Wirtschaft? Köln, West Germany: J. P. Bachem. A German analysis of the encyclical Laborem exercens. Papers presented at a conference held December 1, 1981, by Vereinigung zur Förderung der Christlichen Sozialwissenschaften.

16211. Finks, P. David. (1982) "Parish Churches and Community Organizations," New Catholic World [Church in the City]. Vol. 225, No. 1347 (May), pp. 121-123. A retrospective assessment of the community organization strategies of Saul D. Alinsky.

16212. Fischer, Claude S. (1982) To Dwell among Friends: Personal Networks in Town and City. Chicago, IL: University of Chicago Press. Fischer puts the theory first articulated in his article, "Toward a Subcultural Theory of Urbanism" (1975), to the empirical test. In doing so, he challenges the popular notion that urban life is detrimental to health, community, ethnicity, and religious faith, and that urban life contributes to the distortion of human relations, estrangement, or psychological distress and deviant behavior. He finds that urban life "supports rather than weakens" human relationships. Urbanization leads to a variety of distinct, intense social worlds, and the church is one such subculture (see pp. 208ff). Data used to test Fischer's hypotheses were gathered from 50 northern California communities in 1977-78, ranging in size from small towns to San Francisco. He found small town respondents more likely to claim religious affiliation, but city church-goers knew more members of their churches by name, a result he considers in support of his theory, as were generally the results regarding ethnicity, passtimes, occupations, and other subcultures. Questionnaire.

16213. Fisher, Neal F. (1982) "The Hope of the City," Cities. Vol. 2, No. 2 (May-June), pp. 7-10.

16214. Fisher, Neal F. (1982) "The Wholeness of the City," Cities. Vol. 2, No. 1 (March-April), pp. 28-32. Fisher writes about the pervasive influence of cities. Everyone is urban, whether they think of themselves in that way or not. The wholeness of the city promises to break boundaries that separate people.

16215. Fones-Wolf, Kenneth Alan. (1982) "Revivalism and Craft Unionism in the Progressive Era: The Syracuse and Auburn Labor Forward Movements of 1913," New York History. Vol. 63, No. 4 (October), pp. 389-416.

16216. Foote, Catherine Jeanne. (1982) A Model for Communicating the Christian Faith in the Inner City. Thesis (Ed. D.). Louisville, KY: Southern Baptist Theological Seminary.

16217. Fortunato, John. (1982) Embracing the Exile: Healing Journeys of Gay Christians. Minneapolis, MN: Winston/Seabury. Re: spirituality, homosexuality and psychological wholeness.

16218. Frost, Linda Gail. (1982) A Program to Develop Community Awareness for Walnut Street Baptist Church, Louisville, Kentucky. Thesis (D. Min.). Lousiville, KY: Southern Baptist Theological Seminary.

16219. Fuechtmann, Thomas Gerhard. (1982) Steeples and Stacks: A Case Study of the Youngstown [Ohio] Ecumenical Coalition. Thesis (Ph. D.). Chicago, IL: University of Chicago.

16220. Gagne, David W. (1982) "Christian Sharing Fund--A Diocesan Model," New Catholic World [Church in the City]. Vol. 225, No. 1347 (May), pp. 127-130. Re: self-help grants for social change projects in the low income communities of Minneapolis-St. Paul, MN.

16221. Galin, Amira. (1982) Halakhah u-ma'aseh bi-ya. hase 'avodah. Tel-Aviv, Israel: Tsrikover. Re: Judaism and labor.

16222. Gallup, George, Jr. (1982) Religion in America: The Gallup Report. Princeton, NJ: Princeton Religion Research Center. Questionnaire.

16223. Gappert, Gary and Richard V. Knight, eds. (1982) Cities in the 21st Century. Beverly Hills, CA: Sage.

16224. Gartner, Alan, Colin Greer and Frank Riessman. (1982) What Reagan Is Doing to Us. New York: Harper and Row.

16225. Garvin, Alexander. (1982-1983) "We Can Solve Urban Problems," World Order: A Baha'i Magazine. Vol. 17, No. 2 (Winter), pp. 31-42. The Baha'i Faith encounters urban issues, offering solutions for slums, poverty, economic problems, urban renewal, and other social problems.

16226. Gilbert, Alan, ed. (1982) Urbanization in Contemporary Latin America. Chichester, NY: John Wiley.

16227. Gillett, Richard W. (1982) "Case Study: California General Electric Iron Factory Sacrificed to Singapore: International Profit vs. Community Well-Being," Witness [Ambler, PA]. Vol. 65, No. 9 (September), pp. 8-11.

16228. Glide Foundation. (1982-1984) Humpty Dumpty Report. San Francisco, CA: the Foundation. An antinuclear movement periodical.

16229. Goba, Bonganjalo. (1982) "The Role of the Urban Church: A Black South African Perspective," Journal of Theology for Southern Africa. Vol. 38, No. 38 (March), pp. 26-33. Same title: Evangelical Review of Theology. Vol. 8, No. 1 (April, 1984), pp. 90-99.

16230. Goodwin, John Albert Reed. (1982) Long-Range Planning in the Face of Change. Thesis (D. Min.). Lousiville, KY: Southern Baptist Theological Seminary.

16231. Gowdy, Kenneth. (1982) "Communities and Urbanization," pp. 362-384 in Stephen A. Grunlan and Milton Reimer, eds. Christian Perspectives on Sociology. Grand Rapids, MI: Zondervan. Bibliography.

16232. Gray, Helen T. (1982) "Lack of Money, Interest, Closed Linwood Ministries," The Kansas City Times. (October 22), Section B, p. 1. Decline of White's interest in the inner city and its massive human need result in the closing of service oriented ministries in Kansas City.

16233. Gray, Richard. (1982) "Small Congregations," Justice Ministries. No. 4 (Winter-Spring), pp. 15-16.

16234. Green, Garey. (1982) The Black Church and the Criminal Justice System: A Pilot Project Designed to Train Black Clergy and Laymen in Pastoral Care and Counseling. Thesis (D. Min.). Columbia, SC: Lutheran Theological Southern Seminary.

16235. Greenleaf, Robert K. (1982) The Servant as Religious Leaders. Peterborough, NH: Windy Row Press.

16236. Griffiths, Brian. (1982) Morality and the Market Place. London: Hodder and Stoughton. Griffiths writes on economic matters from a conservative religious perspective. Bibliography.

16237. Gutiérrez, Gustavo. (1982) Sobre el trabajo humano: comentarios a la encíclica "Laborem exercens." Lima, Perú: Centro de Estudios y Publicaciones. Commentary on Laborem Exercens, John Paul II's encyclical, especially regarding the dignity of work. Bibliography.

16238. Gutiérrez-Cortés, Rolando. (1982) "Un programa urbano de evangelización," Boletín Teológico [Editorial]. Tomo 7, pp. 1-14. Re: urban evangelism.

16239. Hadaway, C. Kirk. (1982) "The Church in the Urban Setting," pp. 80-99 in L. Rose and C. K. Hadaway, eds. The Urban Challenge. Nashville, TN: Broadman.

16240. Hadaway, C. Kirk. (1982) "Church Growth (and Decline) in a Southern City," Review of Religious Research. Vol. 23, No. 4 (June), pp. 372-386. Reply: Douglas Walrath. Hadaway uses Walrath's typology (1977) to analyze membership increases and decreases for Southern Baptist churches in Memphis, TN. He finds the typology useful in explaining how environmental factors strongly affect numerical church growth potential. As presented, Hadaway's data imply the growth of the Black population in the community might be a better predictor than community type of whether a Southern Baptist church is growing or declining, although Hadaway does not draw that conclusion. Walrath comments on Hadaway's article in the same issue of The Review, adding some further refinements to his typology.

16241. Haddad, Juliette. (1982) "Sacré et vie quotidienne: Perspectives sur une société arabo-musulmane moderne," Social Compass. Vol. 29, No. 4, pp. 311-333. Haddad reports a study conducted in Jordan regarding the impact of modernity upon the traditional religious system of a primitive society with nomadic tendencies.

16242. Hammer, Don E. (1982) "Home Mission Board Resources for City Churches," Southwestern Journal of Theology [Thematic issue: Urban ministry]. Vol. 24, No. 2 (Spring), pp. 28-39. Hammer lists urban mission objectives for the Southern Baptists up to the year 2000 and summarizes published materials to help churches in urban settings. Bibliography.

16243. Hammer, Don E., Jere Allen, and George W. Bullard. (1982) "Urban Strategy through Cooperative Efforts," pp. 145-147 in Larry L. Rose and C. Kirk Hadaway, eds. The Urban Challenge: Reaching America's Cities with the Gospel. Nashville, TN: Broadman Press.

16244. Hargrove, Beverly Milton. (1982) Developing a Strategy of Ministry for a Church in a Community in Racial Transition. Thesis (D. Min.). Madison, NJ: Drew University.

16245. Harman, Jim. (1982) "City Streets Become Highways and Hedges," Fundamentalist Journal. Vol. 1, No. 4 (December), pp. 54-55.

16246. Hayes, John. (1982) The Protestant Ethic and Its Critics," Social Studies: Irish Journal of Sociology (Christus Rex Soceity). Vol. 7, No. 1 (Winter), pp. 67-91.

16247. Heacock, Jack D. (1982) "Evangelism and Social Ethics: Some Practical Implications, Reflections of a Downtown Pastor," Perkins School of Theology Journal. Vol. 35, No. 2 (Winter-Spring), pp. 23-24. Part of a panel discussion.

16248. Hengsbach, Friedhelm. (1982) Die Arbeit hat Vorrang: eine Option katholischer Soziallehre. Mainz, West Germany: Matthias-Grünewald-Verlag. Catholic social doctrine regarding work. Bibliography.

16249. Hengsbach, Friedhelm. (1982) "The Church and the Right to Work," pp. 40-49 in Jacques Pohier and Dietmar Mieth, eds. Unemployment and the Right to Work. Edinburgh, Scotland: T. and T. Clark.

16250. Hessel, Dieter T. (1982) Social Ministry. Philadelphia, PA: Westminster. Hessel contends that the central functions of parish life include not only liturgy, Bible study and pastoral care, but also social service, community organization, and public policy action. Recommendations for congregational planning are based on the author's interviews of clergy and laity. Reviewed: Anglican Theological Review, Vol. 66 (April, l984), p. 220. Christian Ministry, Vol. 14, No. 3 (May, 1983), p. 37. Sojourners, Vol. 12 (August, 1983), p. 36.

16251. Hinton, Leonard O. (1982) Census Data Manual for Church Planning. Atlanta, GA: Home Mission Board of the Southern Baptist Convention. How to draw inference from census data for church planning.

16252. Holladay, J. Douglas. (1982) "19th Century Evangelical Activism: From Private Charity to State Intervention, 1830-1850," Historical Magazine of the Protestant Episcopal Church. Vol. 5 (March), pp. 53-79.

16253. Holstead, Roland Edward. (1982) The Differential Responses of Protestant Church Polities to Racial Change in an Urban Area. Thesis (Ph. D.). Storrs, CT: University of Connecticut.

16254. Hopewell, James F. (1982) "Ghostly and Monstrous Churches," The Christian Century. Vol. 99, No. 20 (June 2), pp. 663-665. By reviewing the titles of books about local churches from 1960 forward, Hopewell discovers the literary metaphors of ghost and monster stories used more often than Christian metaphors. Hopewell takes this usage as being unintentional, but revealing of the unspoken ecclesiologies of the authors. Several books reviewed deal principally with the urban church: Gibson Winter (1961, 1963, and passim), George W. Webber (passim), James D. Glasse (1972), for example.

16255. Houghton, Graham and Ezra Sargunam. (1982) "Church Planting among the Urban Poor," Africa Pulse. Vol. 15, No. 2 (May), pp. 1-6.

16256. Houghton, Graham and Ezra Sargunam. (1982) "The Role of Theological Education in Church Planting among the Urban Poor: A Case Study from Madras," Evangelical Review of Theology. Vol. 6, No. 1 (April), pp. 141-144. Reprinted from: TRACI Journal, April, 1981. The Association for Evangelical Theological Education in India discusses how to prepared clergy for work among the poor.

16257. "Housing: Rehabilitating the Rainbow." (1982) JSAC Grapevine. Vol. 13, No. 9 (April), pp. [1-6].

16258. Howell, Barbara and Leon Howell. (1982) "Food Stamps: Stories and Statistics," The Christian Century. Vol. 99, No. 22 (June 23-30), pp. 728-730.

16259. Industrial Mission Association, Theology Development Group. (1982) Thinking in Practice: Theology and Industrial Mission. [Leeds, England: Industrial Mission Association].

16260. Interfaith Center on Corporate Responsibility [ICCR]. (1982?) Church Proxy Resolution. New York: the Center. Similar volumes were produced throughout the 1970s and 1980s by the ICCR.

16261. The Interfaith Coalition on Energy. (1982?-forward) ICEmelter Newsletter. Philadelphia, PA: the Coalition. ICE, the Interfaith Coalition on Energy, was conceived in 1980 by the religious community in the Philadelphia area to reduce energy costs in religious buildings, thereby freeing money for additional human services. ICE offers workshops, technical information, newsletters, and energy audits without bias from any outside influence, and operates strictly in the best interests of the congregations it serves.

16262. Irvine, Gordon P. (1982) "Toward A New Humanity," Cities. Vol. 2, No. 1 (March-April), pp. 18-23. A 20th century renaissance is emerging, the result of the passing of male dominated society.

16263. Iyer, R. (1982) "Industrial Strife: Workers' Paradise Lost," Madras Diocesan News and Notes. Vol. 16, pp. 9-18. [See Note 3].

16264. Jacquet, Joseph and Alfred Ancel. (1982) Un militant ouvier: dialogue avec un évêque. Paris: Editions Ouvières: Messidor/Editions Sociales. Dialogue between a militant worker and a bishop.

16265. Jaech, Richard E. (1982) "Latin American Undocumented Women in the United States," Currents in Theology and Missions. Vol. 9, No. 4 (August), pp. 196-211.

16266. Jehu-Appiah, Jerisdan. (1982) "Varieties of Expression, but the Same Spirit," Christian Action Journal. (Autumn), pp. 6-7.

16267. Jennings, James R. (1982) "Urban Ministry in Today's New Social Context," New Catholic World [Church in the City]. Vol. 225, No. 1347 (May), pp. 131-134.

16268. Johansen-Berg, John. (1982) Good News to the Poor. London: United Reformed Church.

16269. John Paul II, Pope. (1982) The Person in Work: A Programme of Enquiries into the Place of Work in Society Based on the Encyclical Letter of Pope John Paul II: "Laborem Exercens. London: World of Work. A pamphlet.

16270. John, Alexander D. (1982) "A Congregation in a Pluralistic Setting," pp. 207-220 in Richard L. Taylor, ed. Religion and Society. Madras, India: Published for the Christian Institute for the Study of Religion and Society, Bangalore, by the Christian Literature Society.

16271. Johnson, Douglas W. (1982) The Challenge of Single Adult Ministry. Valley Forge, PA: Judson.

16272. Joint Strategy and Action Committee [JSAC]. (1982) "JSAC in Action--The South Bronx Experience," New York: JSAC

Grapevine. Vol. 13, No. 7 (February), p. [7]. Describes denominational ministries in a "hopeless" area of New York City.

16273. Jones, Donald G., ed. (1982) Business, Religion and Ethics: Inquiry and Encounter. Cambridge, MA: Oelgeschlager, Gunn and Hain.

16274. Jones, Jacqueline. (1982) "To Get Out of This Land of Suffering:" Black Migrant Women, Work and the Family in Northern Cities, 1900-1930. Working Paper No. 91. Wellesley, MA: Wellesley College Center for Research for Women.

16275. Jones, Lawrence N. (1982-1983) "Urban Black Churches: Conservators of Value and Sustainers of Community," Journal of Religious Thought. Vol. 39, No. 2 (Fall-Winter), pp. 41-50.

16276. Jones, Nathan. (1982) Sharing the Old, Old Story: Educational Ministry in the Black Community. Winona, MN: St. Mary's Press, Christian Brothers Publications.

16277. Joslin, Roy. (1982) Urban Harvest. Weleyn, England: Evangelical Press. Blue collar alienation from the institutional church and structural rigidity of the churches themselves combine to complicate evangelism in the city. Joslin discusses ways of reaching industrial and inner city people, stressing the importance of Christians staying in the city. Bibliography.

16278. Kahn, Si. (1982) Organizing: A Guide for Grassroots Leaders. New York: McGraw-Hill. Deals with such concerns as meetings, strategies, research, tactics, training, media, coalitions, unions, politics, money, leadership, and constituencies as they impinge on the work of community organizers. Some attention is given to organization in churches and synagogues.

16279. Kane, Matt. (1982) "'The People Who Built the Wall': Bethel Church: Self Help Development at Work in a West Side Neighborhood," Chicago, IL: The Neighborhood Works.

16280. Kateri, sr. (1982) "Serving Newcomers," Ecumenism. No. 64 (January), pp. 27-28. [See note 3].

16281. Kawano, Roland. M. (1982) "The Ethnic Pastor in a Multicultural Society," Christian Century. Vol. 99, No. 34 (November 3), pp. 1099-1102.

16282. Keenan, Marjorie. (1982) "The Liberation and Justice Dimension of the Mission of the Local Church: A United States Experience," pp. 579-595 in Mary Motte and Joseph R. Lang, eds. Mission in Dialogue: The SEDOS Research Seminar on the Future of Mission, March 8-19, 1981, Rome Italy. Maryknoll, NY: Orbis.

16283. Kennedy, Roger C. (1982) American Churches. New York: Crossroads.

16284. Kenyon, John. (1982) "Out of the Rubble Grows a Garden," Christian Herald. Vol. 105, No. 1 (January), pp. 46-47. A Lutheran church grows vegetables in Manhattan.

16285. Kersey, Robert J. (1982) "Rebirth through Union," Christian Ministry. Vol. 13, No. 1 (January), pp. 32-33. A pastor who served three merging congregations recounts the circumstances surrounding the unions. Merger is seen as a way of restoring confidence and enthusiasm to dispirited congregations.

16286. Kim, Kyung-Suk. (1982) Urban Church, Manhattan, New York. Thesis (B. Arch.). Ithaca, NY: Cornell University.

16287. Klose, Alfred. (1982) "Konflikt und Ausgleich in der Wirtschaftsgesellschaft," pp. 53-70 in W. Weber, ed. Jahrbuch für Christliche Sozialwissenschaften. Vol. 23. Münster, West Germany: Institut für Christliche Sozialwissenschaften, Universität Münster. Conflict and reconciliation in industrial society.

16288. Knoke, David and James R. Wood. (1982) Organized for Action: Commitment in Voluntary Organizations. New Brunswick, NJ: Rutgers University.

16289. Knox, Marv. (1982) "Pragmatism in New York City," Church Administration. Vol. 24, No. 5 (February), pp. 30-33.

16290. Krass, Alfred C. (1982) Evangelizing Neo-Pagan North America. Scottdale, PA: Herald Press. Reviewed: International Bulletin of Missionary Research, Vol. 8 (April, 1984), p. 83. Perkins School of Theology Journal, Vol. 37 (Summer, 1984), p. 41. Has appendix with 11 church statements or declarations on evangelism.

16291. Krass, Alfred C. (1982) "Beyond Fighting Cutbacks: Our Society Is Going through Some Major Changes--How Will We Respond?" The Other Side. Vol. 18, No. 7 (July), pp. 28-29.

16292. Krass, Alfred C. (1982) "Letter to a June Graduate: If You Want to Be Involved in Urban Mission, Plan to Stay for a Long Time," The Other Side. Vol. 18, No. 6 (June), pp. 34-35.

16293. Kyewalyanga, Francis X. (1982) "Der Kulturwandel in Ostafrika," Zeitschrift für Missionswissenschaft und Religionswissenschaft. Vol. 66 (July), pp. 200-219. Cultural change and rural-urban migration in East Africa.

16294. Lacinak, Michael. (1982) "Religion and Labor Make Common Cause," The Christian Century. Vol. 99, No. 26 (August 18-25), pp. 845-846. Reports a meeting of the National Conference on Religion and Labor at Wilwaukee, WI.

16295. Lacinak, Michael. (1982) "New Hope in the City," Modern Ministries. Vol. 3, No. 5 (May), pp. 4-8+.

16296. Lammers, Ann Conrad. (1982) "A Woman on the Docks," Journal of Pastoral Care. Vol. 36, No. 4 (December), pp. 219-225. A record of a woman chaplain's experiences working at the Seamen's Church Institution in New York describes experiences of humiliation, rejection, and sexist stereotyping in a male dominated environment. Vignettes of shipboard encounters are included.

16297. Landgraff, John R. (1982) Creative Singlehood and Pastoral Care. Philadelphia, PA: Fortress.

16298. Lathuihamallo, Peter D. (1982) "God in a Developing Plural Society: The Indonesian Experience," The South East Asia Journal of Theology. Vol. 23, No. 2, pp. 93-102.

16299. Lau, Lawson. (1982) "Singapore: The Lion Faces Change," Evangelical Missions Quarterly. Vol. 18, No. 4 (October), pp. 226-231.

16300. Leals, Daniel J., ed. (1982) Labor History [Thematic issue: Labor archives]. Vol. 23, No. 4 (Fall), pp. 485-598. A description of the major labor libraries and archives in the USA.

16301. Lefever, Harry G. (1982) "The Value Orientation of the Religious Poor," Sociological Analysis. Vol. 43, No. 3 (Fall), pp. 219-230. Data collected in a low income neighborhood of Atlanta, GA, are used to test hypotheses related to Talcott Parsons' pattern variables.

16302. Lekachman, Robert. (1982) Greed Is Not Enough: Reaganomics. New York: Pantheon.

16303. Lewins, Frank William. (1982) "The Multicultural Challenge," pp. 89-94 in Dorothy Harris, Douglas Hynd, and David Millikan, eds. The Shape of Belief. Homebush West, Australia: Lancer.

16304. Linberg, Edwin C. (1982) "What We Yet May Be: A Sermon on the 40th Anniversary of Temple City Christian Church, California, January 10, 1982," Impact [Claremont]. No. 8, pp. 31-35.

16305. Lind, Millard C. (1982) "The Rule of God: Agenda for the City," Covenant Quarterly [Thematic issue]. Vol. 40, No. 2 (May), pp. 3-18. An assessment of views of the city in the Bible intended to inform local congregations understanding of their mission. Bibliography.

16306. Liptak, Dolores A. (1982) "The Bishops of Hartford and Polish Immigrants in Connecticut, 1880-1930," pp. 48-61 in Stanislaus Blejwas and Mieczyslaw Biskupski, eds. Pastor of the Poles. New Britain, CT: Central Connecticut State College.

16307. Long, Loran Dean. (1982) Preparing for Holistic Church Planting among Mexico's Urban Poor. Thesis (MA). Pasadena, CA: Fuller Theological Seminary, School of World Mission. Long identifies the implications of massive social inequality and injustice for church extension efforts.

16308. Lovell, George. (1982) Human and Religious Factors in Church and Community Work. Pinner, Middlesex, England: Grail. A discussion of the relation between faith and community service work.

16309. Lyles, Jean Caffey. (1982) "Reaganomics and a Dream Denied," The Christian Century. Vol. 99, No. 33 (October 27), pp. 1081-1083.

16310. Mader, Donald. (1982) "Gentrification: Challenge for Urban Churches," Church Herald. Vol. 39, No. 11 (May 28), pp. 9-11. Mader describes the effects of gentrification on churches and mentions programs especially for new people. Gentrification appears to be a mixed blessing for churches and cities.

16311. Madigen, Kevin V. (1982) "How Shall We Sing the Lord's Song in a Foreign Land?" New Catholic World [Church in the City]. Vol. 225, No. 1347 (May), pp. 104-106. Manhattan's old ethnic congregations are declining because the communities in which they are located have become filled with young, single upwardly mobile professionals.

16312. Maida, Adam J., ed. (1982) Issues in the Labor-Management Dialogue--Church Perspectives. St. Louis, MO: Catholic Health Association of the United States. Re: collective bargaining and the operation of church and union owned health care facilities. Bibliography.

16313. Mallone, George. (1982) "Public Rallies Foster Unity," Eternity. Vol. 33, No. 1 (January), pp. 52-53.

16314. Mamiya, Lawrence H. (1982) "From Black Muslim to Bilalian: The Evolution of Movement," Journal for the Scientific Study of Religion. Vol. 21, No. 2 (June), pp. 138-152. Mamiya traces developmental changes in Black Muslim groups. Bibliography.

16315. Marris, Peter. (1982) Community Planning and Conceptions of Change. London: Routledge and Kegan Paul. This brief essay raises the question of why it is that as people working in urban communities for beneficial change have come to understand their problems better, they have increasingly felt at a loss about what to do. What can be done about powerlessness and impotence underlying community organizations and struggles? Marris wants to find ways of integrating understanding with action, which he says depends not only on knowing what we're up against, but also on how that knowledge is translated by language, metaphors, paradigms, and conceptualizations. His reflections on why the connections between understanding of the problems and concrete action become increasingly hard to make stem from his analysis of two British attempts to revive deteriorating inner cities -- specifically, the Home Office Community Development Project and a scheme to redevelop London's Docklands. Peoples' articulation of what they know about city issues affects profoundly what they are able to do and actually do, according to Marris.

16316. Marshall, Paul. (1982) "Urban Schizophrenia," The Mennonite [Thematic issue: Church in the city. Vol. 97, No. 8 (April 13), pp. 173-174. A discussion of urban theological symbols, with reference to the work of Jacques Ellul.

16317. Marshall, Sandy and Sally Bucklee. (1982) "'Hoboken: The Polyglot Checkerboard'--A Story of Holy Innocents," in William A. Yon, ed. To Build the City--Too Long a Dream. Washington, DC: Alban Institute.

16318. Martin, Dan. (1982) "Churches in Miami: a Struggle with Transition," Church Administration. Vol. 24, No. 6 (March), pp. 34-35.

16319. Martini, Carlos María. (1982) El evangelio de San Juan, ejercicios espirituales sobre San Juan. Bogotá, Colombia: Ediciones Paulinas. The Gospel of St. John, spiritual exercizes.

16320. Marty, Martin E. (1982) "The Catholic Ghetto and All the Other Ghettos," Catholic Historical Review. Vol. 68, No. 2 (April), pp. 184-205.

16321. Mauss, Armand L. (1982) "Salvation and Survival on Skid-Row: A Comment on Rooney," Social Forces. Vol. 60, No. 3 (March), pp. 898-904. Reply to Rooney (1980).

16322. McDowell, John Patrick. (1982) The Social Gospel in the South: The Women's Home Mission Movement in the Methodist Episcopal Church, South, 1886-1939. Baton Rouge, LA: Lousiana State University Press. McDowell describes Southern Methodist interest in city missions and church work among immigrants. In 1893 Southern Methodist women began city mission work in St. Louis, followed shortly by similar efforts in New Orleans, Atlanta, Los Angeles, and Houston. Bibliography with citations of church press materials.

16323. McEachern, Theodore. (1982) "You Can Get There from Here," Cities. Vol. 2, No. 1 (March-April), p. 33. Reflections on the eleventh anniversary Southeastern Jurisdiction Urban Workers Network.

16324. McIlwraith, Niel, ed. (1982) Ghost Town. Birmingham, England: SCM Publications.

16325. McKinney, George D. (1982) "Professing Christ in the City," pp. 217-227 in J. Alexander, ed. Confessing Christ as Lord, Urbana '81. Downers Grove, IL: InterVarsity Press.

16326. McKinney, William J., Jr., David A. Roozen, and Jackson W. Carroll. (1982) Religion's Public Presence: Community Leaders Assess the Contribution of Churches and Synagogues. Washington, DC: Alban Institute. Although public leaders criticize churches and synagogues for retreating into their own passive, uninvolved, and essentially selfish congregations, the same leaders do have many suggestions about how congregations can become involved and express hope that the religious bodies will become more involved.

16327. McSwain, Larry L. (1982) "Understanding Life in the City: Context for Christian Ministry," Southwestern Journal of Theology [Thematic issue: Urban ministry]. Vol. 24, No. 2 (Spring), pp. 6-

19. McSwain identifies biblical mandates for urban ministry and describes such urban problems as overcrowding, pluralism, and anonymity. Lifestyles in urban, suburban and exurban areas receive attention.

16328. McSwain, Larry L. (1982) God's Agenda for the City: Metropolitian Missions Occasional Paper. Atlanta, GA: Home Mission Board, Southern Baptist Convention.

16329. McSwain, Larry L., ed. (1982) Southern Baptist Churches in Transitional Communities: A Research Report. Atlanta, GA: Department of Metropolitan Missions, Division of Associational Services, Home Mission Board, Southern Baptist Convention. Transitional communities are defined as those undergoing some form of racial, ethnic, economic, and land use change. Various patterns of transition are identified along with their implications for city churches. Annotated bibliography. Questionnaire.

16330. Menezes, Louis. (1982) "An Approach to Urban Land Policy," Social Action [India]. Vol. 32, No. 2 (April), pp. 166-178.

16331. Messer, Donald A. (1982) "When the Pastor Enters Politics," The Christian Ministry. Vol. 13, No. 3 (May), pp. 9-12.

16332. Metropolitan Lutheran Ministry of Greater Kansas City. (1982) Kansas City, MO: Metropolitan Lutheran Ministry.

16333. Meyer, Charles. (1982) "Getting Involved in Criminal-Justice Ministries," The Christian Century. Vol. 99, No. 17 (May 12), pp. 573-578.

16334. Miles, Delos. (1982) Sent Forth to Grow. Atlanta, GA: Metropolitan Missions Department, Home Mission Board, Southern Baptist Convention, Occasional Paper No. 6.

16335. Milgrom, Jacob. (1982) "The Levitic Town: An Exercise in Realistic Planning," Journal of Jewish Studies. Vol. 33 (Spring-Autumn), pp. 185-188.

16336. Miller, William D. (1982) Dorothy Day: A Biography. San Francisco, CA: Harper and Row.

16337. Ministry Opportunities in Multifamily Housing. (1982) [76 slides, color, sound cassette, manual]. Atlanta, GA: Home Mission Board, the Southern Baptist Convention.

16338. Moberg, David O. (1982) "The Salience of Religion in Everyday Life: Selected Evidence from Survey Research in Sweden and America," Sociological Analysis. Vol. 43, No. 3 (Fall), pp. 205-217.

16339. Morano, Roy William. (1982) The Challenges to American Corporation in the 1970s by Protestant Churches on the Issue of Corporate Social Responsibility. Thesis (Ph. D.). New York: New York University.

16340. Mosso, Sabastiano. (1982) La Chiesa e il lavoro: Salario, cogestione, diritto al sindacato, sciopero, disoccupazione, mobilita, lotta di classe: il pensiero sociale della Chiesa attraverso le encicliche e i messaggi pastorali: dai Vangeli alla Rerun novarum delle tematiche Laborem exercens, una panoramica delle tematiche connesse al "lavoro." Rome: EL. A history of the teaching of the Catholic Church on labor issues covering the late 19th century through the 20th, based on the encyclicals and pastoral letters of the Church. Bibliography.

16341. Murphy, Humphrey Joseph. (1982) A Qualitative Study of Work Satisfaction among Archdiocesan Associate Pastors in Team and Traditional Style Urban Parochial Ministries. Thesis (D. Min.). Boston, MA: Boston University School of Theology.

16342. Murphy, William P. (1982) "Moral and Ethical Aspects of Labor-Management Relations," pp. 157-203 in Andrew R. Cecil, et al. Conflict and Harmony. Dallas, TX: University of Texas at Dallas. A discussion of Rerum Novarum and a historical survey of labor-management relations.

16343. Murray, John Clark. (1982) The Industrial Kingdom of God. Ottawa, Canada: University of Ottawa Press. Bibliography.

16344. Neighbor, Chad. (1982) "The American Church in London," New World Outlook. n.s. Vol. 42, No. 5 (January), pp. 28-29. Re: an exported American church program in England for Americans away from home.

16345. Neitzel, Sarah C. (1982) "The Salzburg Catholic Gesellenverein: An Alternative to Socialism," Journal of Religious History. Vol. 12, No. 1 (June), pp. 62-73.

16346. Nelson, F. Burton. (1982) "Christian Faith and Public Policy: The View from Below," Covenant Quarterly [Thematic issue]. Vol. 40, No. 2 (May), pp. 3-18.

16347. Niklaus, Robert. (1982) "Brazil: Pentecostal Invasion," Evangelical Missions Quarterly. Vol. 18, No. 2 (April), pp. 117-118.

16348. Niklaus, Robert. (1982) "World First Religious Census," Evangelical Missions Quarterly. Vol. 18, No. 4 (October), pp. 256-257.

16349. Norman, Colin. (1982) ""Ecologically Safe Technologies," Engage/Social Action. Vol. 10, No. 9 (October), pp. 22-26.

16350. Norton, Will. (1982) John Perkins: The Stature of a Servant," Christianity Today. Vol. 24, No. 1 (January 1), pp. 18-27. Re: the Voice of Calvary Ministries, Jackson, MS.

16351. Novak, Michael. (1982) The Spirit of Democratic Capitalism. New York: Simon and Schuster.

16352. Novak, Michael. (1982) "God and Man in the Corporation," pp. 169-188 in Donald G. Jones, ed. Business, Religion, and Ethics: Inquiry and Encounter. Cambridge, MA: Oelgeschlager, Gunn and Hain.

16353. Nugent, Robert, ed. (1982) A Challenge to Love: Gay and Lesbian Catholics in the Church. New York: Crossroads.

16354. O'Connor, Elizabeth. (1982) Letters to Scattered Pilgrims. New York: Harper and Row. O'Connor's letters, written when the Church of the Savior, Washington, DC, was reorganizing itself into six separate faith communities, reflects the personal commitment necessary for participation in that city ministry.

16355. O'Connor, Richard Allan. (1982) Urbanism and Religion: Urban Thai Buddhist Temples. Ann Arbor, MI: University of Michigan Press. See further the author's doctoral dissertation: Urbanism and Religion: Community, Hierarchy and Sanctity in Urban Thai Buddhist Temples. Ithaca, NY: Cornell University, 1978.

16356. Oates, Stephen B. (1982) Let the Trumpet Sound: The Life of Martin Luther King, Jr. New York: Harper and Row. Stories of King's life collected and retold. Bibliography.

16357. Ohsberg, H. Oliver. (1982) The Church and Persons with Handicaps. Scottdale, PA: Herald Press. Ohsberg advances suggestions for churches about inclusiveness of handicapped persons, including resource listings.

16358. Olstad, Keith. (1982) Outreach Ministry of Our Savior's Lutheran Church. Minneapolis, MN: Our Savior's Lutheran Church.

16359. On Human Work: A Resource Book for the Study of Pope John Paul II's Third Encyclical. (1982) Washington, DC: US Catholic Conference.

16360. Palm, Irving. (1982) Frikyrkorna, arbetarfrågan och klasskampen: Frikyrkorörelsens hållning till arbetarnas facklige och politiska kampåren kring sekelskiftet. Stockholm, Sweden: Almqvist & Wiksell International. History of church and labor relations in Sweden, based on a doctoral thesis, Uppsala Universitet, 1982. Abstract and summary in English.

16361. Paris, Arthur E. (1982) Black Pentecostalism: Southern Religion in an Urban World. Amherst, MA: The University of Massachusetts Press. Reviewed: Sociological Analysis, Vol. 44 (Summer, 1983), p. 163. Journal for the Scientific Study of Religion, Vol. 22 (September, 1983), p. 295. Review of Religious Research, Vol. 25 (December, 1983), p. 178.

16362. Pasquariello, Ronald D. (1982) "Sunbelt and Frostbelt," Cities. Vol. 2, No. 1 (March-April), pp. 15-17. Questions of justice and geography emerge from reflections on the economic growth in the sunbelt and decline in the frostbelt.

16363. Pasquariello, Ronald D., Donald W. Shriver, Jr. and Alan Geyer. (1982) Redeeming the City: Theology, Politics, and Urban Policy. New York: Pilgrim Press. The authors argue that urban ministry necessarily involves challenging public policy and providing alternatives supported by city churches. Both Carter's and Reagan's urban policy are critiqued. Appendix B lists eleven denominational policy statements about the city. Reviewed: Sojourners, Vol. 12 (August, 1983), p. 36.

16364. Paz, Denis G. (1982) "The Anglican Response to Urban Social Dislocation in Omaha, 1875-1920," Historical Magazine of the Protestant Episcopal Church. Vol. 51, No. 2 (June), pp. 131-146.

16365. Peachey, Paul. (1982) "Free Cities, Free Churches, and Urbanized Societies," Brethren Life and Thought. Vol. 27, No. 4 (Autumn), pp. 199-205. Observing that three Anabaptist groups had instituted urban programs, Peachey asks, "Do cities merit special religious attention?" Cities pose a paradox for Anabaptists. Although the free church movement clearly originated as an urban movement, it has scarcely prevailed in cities.

16366. Peil, Margaret, Simon Sirikwa, Pierre C. Lembugusala, et al. (1982) African Cities and Christian Communities. Eldoret, Kenya: Gaba Publications, AMECEA Pastoral Institute, Spearhead 72. Sociological and theological perspectives on African urbanization show contrasts with the effects of urbanization on religion in Europe and North America. Peil's article is a reprint of Pro Mundi Vita's Africa Dossier, No. 17. Bibliography.

16367. Pérez, César Moreno. (1982) "México: la ciudad más grande de América Latina," Boletín Teológico. Tomo 7, pp. 15-35. Re: Mexico city.

16368. Perkins, John. (1982) With Justice for All. Ventura, CA: Regal Books. Perkins, founder of the "Voice of Calvary Ministries" in Jackson, MI, describes the ministry's efforts in behalf of Black Christian community development and reconciliation through the church. He stresses the three "Rs" of the Christian revolution: reconciliation, relocation, and redistribution. Autobiographical.

16369. Phipps, William E. (1982) "Trinity-St. Paul's United Church: Urban Ministry," International Review of Mission. Vol. 71, No. 283 (July), pp. 336-340. Re: two Toronto congregations merge with good result.

16370. Piehl, Mel. (1982) Breaking Bread: The Catholic Worker and the Origin of Catholic Radicalism in America. Philadelphia, PA: Temple University Press. A History of the Catholic Worker Movement, comparing it with other schools of Catholic thought on missions and social issues. Bibliography.

16371. Pittman, Clarence O. (1982) Enabling a Church to Plan and Act for Its Future through Organizational Development. Thesis (D. Min.). Columbia, SC: Lutheran Theological Southern Seminary. Describes ministry in a textile mill.

16372. Piven, Frances Fox. (1982) "The Transformation of City Politics: How We Got This Way," The Witness [Ambler, PA]. Vol. 65, No. 9 (September), pp. 4-7.

16373. Podojil, Catherine. (1982) Mother Teresa. Glenview, IL: Scott, Foresman.

16374. Poethig, Enice Blanchard, ed. (1982) 150 Plus Tomorrow:

Churches Plan for the Future. Chicago, IL: Presbytery of Chicago. Research on Chicago Presbyterians shows, among other things, that Presbyterians are among the first to "sniff" urban decline and abandon the city.

16375. Poethig, Richard P., ed. (1982) Economics for the City and Suburbs: Discovering the Church's Role. Chicago, IL: Institute on the Church in Urban Industrial Society, ICUIS Occasional Paper No. 10, pp. 1-48. Includes articles on the economic future of Chicago, suburban-inner city linkages, and Christian participation in the formation of economic policy.

16376. Poethig, Richard P., ed. (1982) "Redeveloping the Urban Congregation," Justice Ministries: Resources for Urban Mission. Nos. 15-16 (Winter/Spring), pp. 1-67. Bibliography.

16377. Pohier, Jacques and Dietmar Mieth, eds. (1982) Unemployment and the Right to Work. Edinburgh, Scotland: T. & T. Clark.

16378. Pollard, David A. (1982) "Toward a New City," New Catholic World [Church in the City]. Vol. 225, No. 1347 (May), pp. 117-120. Re: the work of Catholic Charities in Oakland, CA.

16379. Preston, D. S. (1982) "How to Be a Fisher of Businessmen," Christianity Today. Vol. 24, No. 1 (January 1), pp. 44-45. Re: evangelizing business executives.

16380. Price, Clay. (1982) A Study of Southern Baptist Convention Churches in Transitional Communities in Metropolitan Areas. Atlanta, GA: Home Mission Board of the Southern Baptist Convention. Price describes churches located in changing communities based on results of a questionnaire. Findings include: there are more Southern Baptist churches in transition than was thought, churches in transitions are stereotyped as being "down and out," most of the pastors serving the churches grew up in communities that differ from where they are serving, churches in transitional communities are not adjusting to the change, and most such churches do not have plans to change their approach to ministry. Resource needs for the churches are identified.

16381. Protestant Episcopal Church in the USA, Diocese of Los Angeles, Committee for Urban Studies, Charlotte Jackson, chair. (1982?) Training for Metropolitan Church Vocations: A Report to the Bishop and Council of the Episcopal Church, Diocese of Los Angeles. Los Angeles, CA: Episcopal Church in the Diocese of Los Angeles.

16382. Ptolemy, Kathleen. (1982) "Canadian Refugee Policies," International Review of Mission. Vol. 71, No. 283 (July), pp. 363-367.

16383. Pulliam, Russ. (1982) "Putting God to Work in Pittsburgh," Christianity Today. Vol. 26, No. 8 (April 23), pp. 16-19. Re: the work of Robert Lavelle in behalf of housing for the poor.

16384. Quayle, Vincent P. (1982) "The Housing Ministry in Baltimore," The New Catholic World [Church in the City]. Vol. 225, No. 1347 (May), pp. 100-103. Quayle founded the St. Ambrose Housing Aid Center.

16385. Quigley, Margaret and Michael Garvey, eds. (1982) The Dorothy Day Book. Springfield, IL: Templegate. A summary with quotations by various authors reprinted from the "On Pilgrimage" column of The Catholic Worker, a Catholic newspaper edited by Day.

16386. Quinn, Bernard, et al. (1982) Churches and Church Membership in the United States, 1980: An Enumeration by Region, State and County Based on Data Reported by 111 Church Bodies. Atlanta, GA: Glenmary Research Center. Demography of religion in the United States, a sequel to Douglas Johnson, et al. (1974).

16387. Quinn, Peter A. (1982) "City Limits," America. Vol. 147, No. 2 (July 17), pp. 29-30. Myths that pervade some of the movements directed toward the city often blind adherents to important realities. Myths of the gentrification movement are likened to those of the flower children of the 1960s who found escape from the city in idyllic beach life, the late 19th and early 20th century reform movement which found the cities "unamerican," and other such myths.

16388. Raborg, Frederick A. (1982) "The Life Bandits: A House and a Family Lie Demolished, Caught in the Depersonalizing Clutches of Poverty and Wealth," Church Herald. Vol. 39, No. 15 (August 20), pp. 12-14.

16389. Raines, John C. (1982) "Conscience and the Economic Crisis," The Christian Century. Vol. 99, No. 27 (September 1-8), pp. 883-887.

16390. Rasmussen, Larry. (1982) "Reflecting a Glory Not Our Own, but God's," Engage/Social Action. Vol. 10, No. 9 (October), pp. 27-34.

16391. Ratledge, Wilbert H. (1982) Evangelicals and Social

Change: The Social Thought of Three British Evangelical Preachers--Robert William Dale, Hugh Price Hughes, and William Connor Magee, 1850-1900. Thesis (Ph. D). Denton, TX: North Texas State University.

16392. Ray, David R. (1982) Small Churches Are the Right Size. New York: Pilgrim Press. Reviewed: Lutheran Forum, Vol. 17, No. 3 (1983), p. 41. Theology Today, Vol. 40 (July, 1983), p. 252.

16393. "Redefining the City." (1982) Impact [Conservative Baptist Foreign Missions Society]. Vol. 39, No. 1 (January), pp. 8-11.

16394. Renkiewicz, Frank. (1982) "Polish American Workers, 1880-1980," pp. 116-136 in Stanislaus A. Blejwas and Mieczyslaw B. Biskupski, eds. Pastor to the Poles: Polish American Essays. New Britain, CT: Central Connecticut State College.

16395. "Report of the Meeting of the Advisory Group on the 'Energy for My Neighborhood.'" (1982) Anticipation: Christian Social Thought in Future Perspective [World Council of Churches]. No. 29 (November), pp. 6-26.

16396. Ribeiro, E. F. N. (1982) "Planning for the Urban Poor: Basic Needs and Priorities," Social Action [India]. Vol. 32, No. 2 (April), pp. 127-150.

16397. Ring, Roger J. (1982) "The Crisis of Unemployment: Cheers or Tears," American Protestant Hospital Association Bulletin. Vol. 46, No. 3, pp. 1-7.

16398. Roache, James P. (1982) "Anglo Minister in Black-Hispanic-Ethnic Communities," New Catholic World [Church in the City]. Vol. 225, No. 1347 (May-June), pp. 124-126. Re: the urban apostolate in Chicago and its efforts to minister in changing communities.

16399. Rogers, Garth. (1982) What Churches Can Do. Sheffield: Urban Theology Unit.

16400. Rose, Larry L. and C. Kirk Hadaway, eds. (1982) The Urban Challenge: Reaching America's Cities with the Gospel. Nashville, TN: Broadman Press.

16401. Rosenthal, Steven. (1982) "Minorities and Municipal Reform in Istanbul, 1850-1870," pp. 369-385 in Benjamin Braude and

Bernard Lewis, eds. Christians and Jews in the Ottoman Empire. New York: Holmes and Meier.

16402. Rowe, Albert Prince. (1982) Developing Laity as Ministers in an Urban Church. Thesis (D. Min.). Philadelphia, PA: Eastern Baptist Theological Seminary.

16403. Rowell, Don. (1982) "Adult Runaways," America. Vol. 146, No. 4 (January 30), pp. 69-70. Deserters, dropouts, quitters, escapists -- these are terms sometimes used to describe adult dropouts who might better be called the dissatisfied, the bored and misunderstood, the harassed and over-worked. Not an exclusively male syndrome, adult women are joining the ranks of America's runaways. Rowell offers suggestions for a personality profile of the adult runaway.

16404. Salvatore, Nick. (1982) Eugene V. Debs: Citizen and Socialist. Urbana, IL: University of Illinois Press. Debs, known for his firery speeches and millennial fervor, employed popular religious imagery to support his socialist radicalism.

16405. Samuel, Vinay Kumar and Christopher Sugden. (1982) Sharing Jesus in the Two-Thirds World: Evangelical Christologies from the Contexts of Poverty, Powerlessness and Religious Pluralism. Bangalore, India: Partnership in Mission--Asia.

16406. Schaffer, Daniel. (1982) Garden Cities for America: The Radburn Experience. Philadelphia, PA: Temple University Press. Schaffer writes a history of Radburn, New Jersey, an early effort in the USA to achieve the goals of the garden city movement (on which, see E. Howard, 1898). Radburn has been much cited as an example of balance between urban and rural life styles. No attention is given in this volume to churches or religion, a persistent omission in planning of such cities. The religious reader might ask, can the pluralism of American religion fit into the planned city notion? Or, of necessity, must religion compromise, or even lose its variability if it is to be included in planned urban environments? Radburn is much smaller in size than some of such recent planned cities as Columbia, MD, and Reston, VA.

16407. Schiller, John A., ed. (1982) The American Poor. Minneapolis, MN: Augsburg. Contributors, all on the faculty of Pacific Lutheran University, interpret the nature of poverty from their disciplinary perspectives -- economics, sociology, social work, political science, and religion.

16408. Schmid, Vernon. (1982) "The Poor: American Outcasts,"

The Christian Century. Vol. 99, No. 35 (November 10), pp. 1126-1127. Reply: No. 39 (December 8), p. 1266. Schmid summarizes the history of Black church involvement as social servants from the time of the benevolent societies to contemporary urban congregations.

16409. Schneider, Michael. (1982) Die christlichen Gewerkschaften 1894-1933. Bonn, West Germany: Verlag Neue Gesellschaft. A history of Catholic German unions.

16410. Schneider, Michael. (1982) "Religion and Labour Organization: The Christian Trade Unions in the Wilhelmine Empire," European Studies Review. Vol. 12, No. 3 (July), pp. 345-369.

16411. Sebba, Anne. (1982) Mother Teresa. London: MacRae.

16412. Seccombe, David P. (1982) Possessions and the Poor in Luke-Acts. Linz, Austria: Studien zum Neuen Testament und seiner Unwelt.

16413. Seldon, Paul and Margot Jones. (1982) Moving On: Making Room for the Homeless--A Practical Guide to Shelter. New York: United Church Board for Homeland Ministries. A basic how-to guide for setting up a shelter in New York: zoning requirements, permits, city agency notification, model programs, sources of help, steps for opening a shelter, staffing, location of funding sources, rules of operation, etc.

16414. Sélim, Monique. (1982) "Rapports sociaux et représentations religieuses dans une cité HLM: Communauté Seffaradi et Témoins de Jéhovah," Ethnologie Française. Vol. 12, No. 2, pp. 203-208. [See Note 3].

16415. Shannon-Thornberry, Milo. (1982) "Technology: Lifestyle Changes and Some Hidden Costs," Engage/Social Action. Vol. 10, No. 9 (October), pp. 10-16.

16416. Shen, Philip. (1982) "Concerns with Politics and Culture in Contextual Theology: A Hong Kong Chinese Perspective," Ching Feng. Vol. 25, No. 3 (September), pp. 129-138.

16417. Shenk, Paul. (1982) "Models for Urban Witness," The Mennonite [Thematic issue: Church in the city]. Vol. 97, No. 8 (April 13), pp. 170-172.

16418. Shigeno, Nobuyuki. (1982) "Among Japan's Forgotten

People," The Japan Christian Quarterly. Vol. 48, No. 4 (Fall), pp. 200-201. Re: ministry in the slums of Tokyo and Yokohama.

16419. Simmons, James Berkley. (1982) Determining the Feasibility of Maintaining Revell Chapel as a Mission of First Baptist Church, Ashville, NC. Thesis (D. Min.). Lousiville, KY: Southern Baptist Theological Seminary.

16420. Singer, Merrill. (1982) "Life in a Defensive Society: The Black Hebrew Israelites," pp. 45-81 in Jon Wagner, ed. Sex Roles in Contemporary American Communes. Bloomington, IN: University of Indiana Press.

16421. Snyder, Herbert J. (1982) A Process for Developing a Worship Program That Is Communal and Meaningful to People of Different Cultural, Racial, Socio-Economic and Religious Backgrounds. Thesis (D. Min.). Lancaster, PA: Lancaster Theological Seminary.

16422. Sodeman, Lowell F., comp. (1982) Industrial Chaplaincy. Atlanta, GA: Home Mission Board, Southern Baptist Convention.

16423. Soto-Fontanez, Santiago. (1982) Misión a la Puerta: una historia del trabajo Bautista Hispano en Nueva York. Mission at the Door: A History of Hispanic Baptist Work in New York. Santo Domingo, Dominican Republic: Editora Educativa Dominicana. Spanish and English on opposite pages.

16424. Southern Baptist Convention, Home Mission Board. (1982?) PACT Planbook [Project: Assistance for Churches in Transitional Communities]. Atlanta, GA: the Board.

16425. Spink, Kathryn. (1982) The Miracle of Love: Mother Teresa of Calcutta, Her Missionaries of Charity and Her Co-Workers. New York: Harper and Row.

16426. Stacey, Gerald F., ed. (1982) "From Stranger to Neighbor," Church and Society [Thematic issue: Immigrants, Mexican Americans]. Vol. 72 (May-June), pp. 1-71.

16427. Stean, Robert L. (1982) "The South Bronx Pastoral Center," New Catholic World [Church in the City]. Vol. 225, No. 1347 (May), pp. 111-112.

16428. Stockwell, Clinton E. (1982) Resources for Urban Ministry--A Bibliographic Essay," Covenant Quarterly [Thematic issue].

Vol. 40, No. 2 (May), pp. 3-18.

16429. Stockwell, Clinton E. (1982) Ethnic Groups in the American City: Bibliography. Chicago, IL: Urban Church Resource Center, SCUPE.

16430. Stockwell, Clinton E. (1982) General Bibliography on Housing. Chicago, IL: Urban Church Resource Center, SCUPE.

16431. Stockwell, Clinton E. (1982) Hunger, Food, and Poverty: A Bibliography and List of Resource Organizations. Chicago, IL: Urban Church Resource Center, SCUPE.

16432. Stockwell, Clinton E. (1982?) Urban History, Policy and the History of Urban Christianity. Chicago, IL: Urban Church Resource Center, SCUPE. A bibliography.

16433. Stockwell, Clinton E. (1982) Biblical and Theological Resources for Urban Ministry. Chicago, IL: Urban Church Resource Center, SCUPE. A bibliography.

16434. Stockwell, Clinton E. (1982) A Biblical Approach to Urban Culture: A General Bibliography of Materials on Paul's Letters to the Corinthians. Chicago, IL: Urban Church Resource Center, SCUPE.

16435. Stockwell, Clinton E. (1982?) The Case Method in Community Ministry: A General Bibliography. Chicago, IL: Urban Church Resource Center, SCUPE.

16436. Strege, Merle Dennis. (1982) "Where Scandinavian Is Spoken": Ethnic Identity and Assimilation among Scandinavian Immigrants in the Church of God (Anderson, Indiana). Thesis (Th. D.). Berkeley, CA: Graduate Theological Union.

16437. Symposium from Rerum Novarum to Laborem Exercens, Towards the Year 2000. (1982?) Città del Vaticano, The Vatican: Pontificia Commissio Iustitia et Pax. In French, English, Italian, and Spanish. Bibliography.

16438. Szasz, Ferenc M. (1982) The Divided Mind of Protestant America, 1880-1930. University, Alabama: University of Alabama Press. Re: liberalism and evangelicalism.

16439. Tabb, William K. (1982) "The Crisis of the Present Economic System and Renewing the American Dream," pp. 12-32 in Cornel West, et al., eds. Theology in the Americas: Detroit Conference Papers. Maryknoll, NY: Orbis.

16440. Task Force on Gay/Lesbian Issues. (1982) Homosexuality and Social Justice: A Report of the Task Force on Gay/Lesbian Issues. San Francisco, CA: Commission on Social Justice, Archdiocese of San Francisco.

16441. Theissen, Gerd. (1982) The Social Setting of Pauline Christianity: Essays on Corinth. Philadelphia, PA: Fortress. Theissen continues his exploration of the thesis that early Christianity, after rejecting Judaism, assumed an urban character developed in Hellenistic cities. Because of this urban environment, early Christian literature was more theological, more speculative, and more reflective. See further by Theissen: The Sociology of Early Palestinian Christianity. Philadelphia, PA: Fortress, 1978.

16442. Thompson, Robert V. (1982) "Ministering to the Unemployed," The Christian Century. Vol. 99, No. 27 (September 1-8), pp. 887-890.

16443. Tillapaugh, Frank R. (1982) The Church Unleashed. Ventura, CA: Regal Books. [Retitled for the 1985 edition: Unleashing the Church: Getting People Out of the Fortress and into Ministry].

16444. Tinsley, Virginia, Bill Holt and Jeannie Hollifield. (1982) "Beyond Green Ribbons," Cities. Vol. 2, No. 1 (March-April), pp. 4-5. The killing of Black youths in Atlanta led to the emergence of several programs to ameliorate the situation that led to their deaths. The authors analyze the programs.

16445. "To Open a Door: Wanderers in Our Cities." (1982) Sojourners. Vol. 11 (December), pp. 8-9.

16446. Toffin, Gérard. (1982) "La notion de ville dans une société asiatique traditionnelle: L'exemple des Néwar de la ville de Kathmandou," L'Homme. Vol. 22, No. 4, pp. 101-111. Urban space in Katmandu corresponds to and replicates Hindu and Buddhist religious conceptions of the universe, concretizing an ideal image of the universe.

16447. Torres, Sergis and John Eagleson, eds. (1982) The Challenge of Basic Christian Communities. Maryknoll, NY: Orbis.

16448. Towell, Juli and Sally Bucklee. (1982) "'Take Up Your Bed and Walk:' A Story of Grace Van Vorst, Jersey City, New Jersey," pp. 15-18 in William A. Yon, ed. To Build the City--Too Long a Dream. Washington, DC: Alban Institute.

16449. Tradizione cristiana, industrializzazione e pluralismo culturale. (1982) Vicenza, Italy: Edizioni del Rezzara, Dossier sul seminario tenuto a Villa Cordelline-Lombardi di Montecchio Maggiore nei giorni 1-3 maggio 1981.

16450. Ulrich, Thomas. (1982) Leben im Akkord: eine christliche Deutung des Arbeiter--Alltags. Munich, West Germany: Grünewald. Christianity in the ordinary workday of the laboring classes.

16451. Umbreit, Mark S. (1982) "Victim-Offender Reconciliation Is Ultimately Practical: VORP Provides Benefits to the Victim, to the Offender, and to the Community," Christianity Today. Vol. 26, No. 7 (April 9), p. 36.

16452. Umbreit, Mark S. (1982) "Reconciling Victims and Offenders: A Practical, Christian, Justice Ministry," Engage/Social Action. Vol. 10, No. 2 (February), pp. 41-43.

16453. Valverde, Antônio José, ed. (1982) Trabalho humano em debate: Comentários à laborem exercens, conflito entro trabalho e capital. São Paulo, Brazil: EDUC, Edições Paulinas. Papers on the church and labor issues and the theology of work compiled from the presentations made at a conference held at the Pontifícia Universidade Católica of São Paulo Departamento de Teologia, on October 5-8, 1981. Valverde was the organizer.

16454. Van Gelder, Craig E. (1982) Growth Patterns of Mainline Denominations and Their Churches: A Case Study of Jackson, Mississippi, 1900-1980. Thesis (Ph. D.). Fort Worth, TX: Southwestern Baptist Theological Seminary.

16455. Velasquez, Roger. (1982) Theological Education for Hispanic Pastors in the American Baptist Churches, USA. Thesis (D. Min.). Philadelphia, PA: Eastern Baptist Theological Seminary.

16456. Villafañe, Eldin. (1982) "A Cross-Cultural Perspective on Ethnic Ministry," Cities. Vol. 2, No. 3 (July-August), pp. 32-35.

16457. Vincent, John J. (1982) Into the City. London: Epworth Press. Urban flight leaves behind emaciated city churches which, even in their greatly reduced state, Vincent believes have an important purpose and mission. Notwithstanding the encumbrance of old and often unusable buildings, these churches work alongside the underprivileged, the unemployed, the immigrants, and others who have been ignored and forgotten. Vincent's work with eight such churches (comprising the Sheffield Inner City Ecumenical Mission, Sheffield, England), some of which have only a dozen members, provide the basis for this narrative of successes and failures. Small, barely surviving churches can have important, exciting ministries. Bibliography. Reviewed: Churchman, Vol. 97, No. 2 (1983), p. 179. Modern Churchman, n.s. Vol. 26, No. 3 (1984), p. 61.

16458. Walsh, Bryan O. (1982) "The Church and the City: The Miami Experience," New Catholic World [Church in the City]. Vol. 225, No. 1347 (May), pp. 107-110. Re: ministry among refugess.

16459. Walsh, John. (1982) Evangelization and Justice. Maryknoll, NY: Orbis.

16460. Watkins, Derrel. (1982) "Crisis Ministry in Inner-City Churches," Southwestern Journal of Theology [Thematic issue: Urban ministry]. Vol. 24, No. 2 (Spring), pp. 40-54. Defines crisis ministry and identifies four types of crisis ministry in Southern Baptist Churches: needs providing, problem solving, conflict resolving, system change.

16461. Wensierski, Peter. (1982) "Unterwegs zur 'Offenen Kirche,'" in Reinhard Henkys, ed. Die evangelischen Kirchen in der DDR. Munich, West Germany: Kaiser. Re: social change and the church in East Germany.

16462. Wheeler, Edward L. (1982) "A Team That's Tough to Beat," Church Administration. Vol. 25, No. 1 (October), pp. 38-39.

16463. Whitehead, Evelyn Eaton and James D. Whitehead. (1982) Community of Faith: Models and Strategies for Developing Christian Communities. New York: Seabury Press. Reviewed: Religious Education, Vol. 78 (Fall, 1983), p. 594. Theological Studies, Vol. 44 (September, 1983), p. 544.

16464. Wiebe, Bernie. (1982) "Our Worst and Our Best," The Mennonite [Thematic issue: Church in the city]. Vol. 96, No. 8 (April 13), p. 192. An editorial on urban conditions.

16465. Wiley, Robert E., ed. (1982) Change in Big Town/Small City. Atlanta, GA: Home Missions Board, the Southern Baptist Convention. One of several SBC reports on social change and the church.

16466. Williams, June A. (1982) A Comparison of Three Models of Community Service Ministries Promoting Local Involvement of Lay Christians. Thesis (D. Min.). Boston, MA: Boston University.

16467. Williams, Oliver and John W. Houck, eds. (1982) The Judeo-Christian Vision and the Modern Corporation. Notre Dame, IN: University of Notre Dame Press.

16468. Wilson, Bryan R. (1982) Religion in Sociological Perspective. New York: Oxford University Press. Wilson's lectures, delivered in Japan, summarize the sociological approach to the study of religion. Reviewed: Journal for the Scientific Study of Religion, Vol. 22 (March, 1983), p. 87. Journal of the American Academy of Religion, Vol. 51 (December, 1983), p. 713.

16469. Wogaman, J. Philip. (1982) "Strategic Thinking for Urban Ministry," Cities. Vol. 2, No. 1 (March-April), pp. 8-11. Same title: Paper Presented to the Northeastern Urban Ministries Network Workshop, The United Methodist Church, Held at Wesley Theological Seminary, Washington, DC., May 8-10, 1979. Reprinted in: Source Book: United Methodist Urban Ministries Strategies. New York: Office of Urban Ministries, United Methodist Church, 1979. Theology contributes new hope for dealing with urban problems.

16470. Wolcott, Roger T. (1982) "The Church and Social Action: Steelworkers and Bishops in Youngstown," Journal for the Scientific Study of Religion. Vol. 21, No. 1 (March), pp. 71-79. A study of clergy led social ministries during the Youngstown, OH, industrial crisis of plant closings. Bibliography.

16471. Wong, Wayland. (1982) "Immigration and the Church--Opportunities and Dangers," About Face. Vol. 4, No. 1 (February).

16472. Wood, James L. and Maurice Jackson. (1982) Social Movements: Development, Participation, and Dynamics. Belmont, CA: Wadsworth.

16473. World Council of Churches, Commission on the Churches' Participation in Development. (1982) Transnational Corporations: A Challenge for Churches and Christians. Geneva, Switzerland: the Commission. A portfolio of documents and essays. Bibliography.

16474. Woznicki, Andrew N. (1982) Journey to the Unknown: Catholic Doctrine on Ethnicity and Migration. San Francisco, CA: Golden Phoenix Press.

16475. Wyatt, John Will. (1982) Revitalizing and Expanding the Ministry to Internationals of Central Baptist Church. Thesis (D. Min.). Louisville, KY: Southern Baptist Theological Seminary.

16476. Yon, William A., ed. (1982) To Build the City--Too Long to Dream: Studies of Urban Churches. Washington, DC: Alban Institute. A collection of stories of churches that have important ministries in the inner city, most but not all of which are Episcopalian.

16477. Yon, William A. (1982) "'This Sickness to Heal--This Bondage to Destroy:' The Struggle for Racial Inclusiveness in the Diocese of Atlanta," pp. 34-39 in William A. Yon, ed. To Build the City--Too Long a Dream. Washington, DC: Alban Institute.

16478. Zald, Mayer. (1982) "Theological Crucibles: Social Movements in and of Religion," Review of Religious Research. Vol. 23, No. 4 (June), pp. 317-336.

16479. Ziska, Patrick J. (1982) "Who Will Buy What Technology Produces if Only Technology Works?" Engage/Social Action. Vol. 10, No. 9 (October), pp. 17-21.

16480. Ackerman, Todd. (1983) "Church Coalition Helps Inner City," National Catholic Register. Vol. 59 (August 21), pp. 1+.

16481. [Addy, Tony [Anthony J.]]. (1983) Joint Action: Resourcing Community Involvement in the Inner City. Manchester, England: William Temple Foundation. A critical evaluation of the Foundantion's strategy to promote community organization in the city of Salford, England

16482. Alexander Research and Communications. (1983) "What Do Americans Think about Their Neighborhoods?" Urban Outlook. Vol. 5, No. 21, pp. 4-5.

16483. Allen, Jere. (1983) "Guiding Churches through Change," Review and Expositor. Vol. 80, No. 4 (Fall), pp. 571-581. Allen advocates the use of denominational consultants and conferences for helping local churches face disquieting change.

16484. Allen-Baley, C. (1983) "Inner-City Kids Find a New Kind of Gang," World Vision. Vol. 27, No. 9 (September), pp. 14-16.

16485. Amerson, Philip A. (1983) "Strategy and Urban Ministry," Cities. Vol. 3, No. 1 (Summer), pp. 25-31. As a starting point for strategy, urban ministers must hear the stories of urban people. When stories are heard, living relationships emerge, not lifeless strategies. Amerson recounts some urban stories that have influenced his ministry.

16486. Amerson, Philip A. (1983) "Justice Ministries and Urban Transformation: The Case of Moderate-Sized Cities." Unpublished paper delivered at the Annual Meeting of the Religious Research Association, Fall, 1983. [Location: personal files].

16487. Armendáriz, Rubén P. (1983) "The Preparation of Hispanics for the Ministry of the Church," Theological Education. Vol. 20, No. 1 (Autumn), pp. 53-57.

16488. Atherton, John. (1983) The Scandal of Poverty: Priorities for the Emerging Church. London: Mowbray. Director of the William Temple Foundation, Atherton explores the theological and ethical implications of poverty persisting in the midst of affluence, using case vignettes to depict the effects of poverty.

16489. Bailey, Wilma A. (1983) Catalogue of Resources for Black and Integrated Congregations. Elkhart, IN: Mennonite Board of Missions. A listing of resources the author has found helpful in working with local churches, this bibliography evaluates each resource in terms of its readability, targeted age group, potential uses for the local church, and its theological assumptions. Annotations are a page long each. The annotations also critique the materials from the perspective of a Black Mennonite. The author points out photographs from supposed community oriented inner city churches that show all White leadership and observes that the "mission to" bias of much that is written negates the indigenous church in the inner city. Bibliography.

16490. Baker, Benjamin S. (1983) Shepherding the Sheep: Pastoral Care in the Black Tradition. Nashville, TN: Broadman. The pastor of Main Street Baptist Church, Louisville, KY, describes Black clergy role-models: pastors, preachers, healers, teachers, priests, and prophet-servants.

16491. Baldovin, John Francis. (1983) "The City as Church, The Church as City," Liturgy. Vol. 3, No. 4 (Fall), pp. 69-73.

16492. Barrett, David B. (1983) "Silver and Gold Have I None:

Church of the Poor or Church of the Rich?" International Bulletin of Missionary Research. Vol. 7, No. 4 (October), pp. 146-151.

16493. Benjamin, Don C. (1983) Deuteronomy and City Life: A Form Criticism of Texts with the Word City. Lanham, MD: University Press of America. Benjamin concludes that Deuteronomy does reflect an urban tradition that endorses city life as a setting in which the nation of Israel met and served Yahweh. Hence, Israel as early as the 13th century BCE cannot be considered to be completely non-urban. A revision of the author's doctoral dissertation. Bibliography.

16494. Bennett, G. Willis. (1983) "The Changing Face of the Contemporary City," Review and Expositor [Thematic issue: Urban ministry]. Vol. 80, No. 4 (Fall), pp. 489-499. Same title: Urban Mission. Vol. 2, No. 2 (November, 1984), pp. 15-25. Bennett tells how the church might respond intelligently to seven kinds of changes in the city.

16495. Bennett, G. Willis. (1983) Effective Urban Church Ministry [Cover title: Guidelines for Effective Urban Church Ministry]. Nashville, TN: Broadman Press. Bennett recounts the story of Allen Temple Baptist Church in Oakland, California, using it to illustrate his understanding of effective urban ministry. Bennett's work has been instrumental in forming Southern Baptist policy regarding the city.

16496. Bicknell, Catherine. (1983) "Detroit's Capuchin Soup Kitchen," Labor History. Vol. 24, No. 1 (Winter), pp. 112-124. Verbatim interviews with two directors of a Franciscan city mission, one during the Great Depression and the other following World War II.

16497. Billington, David P. (1983) "The Acts in Technology," Anglican Theological Review. Vol. 65, No. 1 (January), pp. 31-48. Billington interprets Christian responses to technology, beginning with the book of Acts. Spirituality places technology in its proper perspective. Technology is seen as a reflection of the church in action, representing both salvation and damnation. Billington is a civil engineer.

16498. Blumberg, Janice Rothschild. (1983) "The Bomb That Healed: A Personal Memoir of the Bombing of the Temple in Atlanta [GA]," American Jewish History [Thematic issue: 250th anniversary of Jewish settlement in Georgia, 1733-1983]. Vol. 73, No. 1 (September), pp. 20-38. Re: bombing of Atlanta's Hebrew Benevolent Congregation.

16499. Boan, Rudee Devon, et al. (1983) "Annotated Bibliography on the Urban Church," Review and Expositor. Vol. 80, No. 4 (Fall), pp. 583-594.

16500. Bowman, James S., et al. (1983) Professional Ethics: Whistle-Blowing in Organizations: An Annotated Bibliography and Resource Guide. New York: Garland.

16501. Braidfoot, Larry. (1983) "Let Justice Roll Down Like Waters," Church Administration. Vol. 25, No. 9 (June), p. 30.

16502. Branner, John Ky. (1983) Chinese Leadership Patterns and Their Relationship to Pastoral Ministry among Taiwan's Urban Masses. Thesis (D. Miss.). Pasadena, CA: Fuller Theological Seminary, School of World Mission.

16503. Brown, Joseph. (1983) "Leadership in the Black Community," Fundamentalist Journal. Vol. 2, No. 9 (October), pp. 23-24.

16504. Brown, Thomas. (1983) "Seven Years in Suburban Canberra," St. Mark's Review [Thematic issue]. No. 114 (June), pp. 17-20.

16505. Browning, Neil. (1983) "Japan: Technology Opens an Ancient Door," World Christian. Vol. 2, No. 5 (November-December), pp. 14-21.

16506. Bullard, George W. (1983) "Using Consultation in Strategy Planning," Review and Expositor. Vol. 80, No. 4 (Fall), pp. 561-570.

16507. Bullard, George W. (1983) "Developing Mission Strategies for Larger Metropolitan Areas," Church Administration. Vol. 25, No. 5 (February), pp. 33-35. Acknowledging that no single urban mission strategy will work in all situations, Bullard offers guidelines for testing any particular proposed strategy for its adequacy. Strategies should come from the grassroots, deal with the Baptist associational context, take into account the entire city, related to what other denominations are doing, identify target groups, be prophetic, and involve a dream of what the Kingdom of God can mean for the city. Bullard, at the time of writing, was associated with the Metropolitan Missions Department, Home Mission Board, the Southern Baptist Convention.

16508. Bullard, George W. (1983?) Mega Focus Cities: A Plan of Megalopolitan Strategy Development. Atlanta, GA: Metropolitan Missions Department, Home Mission Board, the Southern Baptist Convention. Reprinted: Institute on the Church in Urban-Industrial Society. Handbook of Denominational Statements on Urban Mission and Ministry. Chicago, IL: the Institute, 1986. A statement of strategy for city evangelism for the Southern Baptist Convention. A pamphlet.

16509. Byford, E. C., ed. (1983) "Urban Ministry" St. Mark's Review [Thematic issue: Urban church]. No. 119 (June), pp. 1-27.

16510. Cafferty, Pastora San Juan. (1983) Backs Against the Wall: Urban-Oriented Colleges and Universities and the Urban Poor and Disadvantaged. New York: Ford Foundation.

16511. Cafferty, Pastora San Juan, et al. (1983) The Dilemma of American Immigration: Beyond the Golden Door. New Brunswick, NJ: Transaction Books.

16512. Callahan, Kennon L. (1983) Twelve Keys to an Effective Church: Strategic Planning for Mission. New York: Harper and Row.

16513. Campbell, Kathleen and Darrell L. Reeck. (1983) "Asian Refugees Since the Federal Cutoff," Christian Century. Vol. 100, No. 7 (March 9), pp. 211-214. Government cutbacks create problems for refugee resettlement in Pierce County, Washington, which has one of the highest refugee concentrations in the nation. Private charity has been generous, but insufficient.

16514. Campbell, William J. (1983) "Baptists Working Together," Church Administration. Vol. 25, No. 4 (January), pp. 36-37.

16515. Campolo, Anthony. (1983) A Reasonable Faith: Responding to Secularization. Waco, TX: Word Books. Reviewed: Review and Expositor, Vol. 82 (Winter, 1985), p. 156. Christianity Today, Vol. 28 (February 17, 1984), p. 49. TSF Bulletin, No. 8 (September, 1984), p. 40.

16516. Campolo, Anthony, Jr. (1983) The Power Delusion. Wheaton, IL: Victor.

16517. Campolo, Anthony. (1983) Ideas for Social Action: A Handbook on Mission and Service for Christian Young People. Grand Rapids, MI: Zondervan. Over 200 social action strategies recommended to evangelicals, with particular attention to urban youth. Bibliography.

16518. Caplow, Theodore, Howard M. Bahr, Bruce A. Chadwick, et al. (1983) All Faithful People: Challenge and Continuity in Middletown's Religion. Minneapolis, MN: University of Minnesota. A partial replication of the Lynd's essays on Middletown. Caplow finds the religion of Middletown resistant to secularism and virtually apolitical.

16519. Caraballo, José A. (1983) A Certificate Program for Hispanic Clergy and Lay Leaders in an Accredited Seminary: A Case Study with Projections. Thesis (D. Min.). Madison, NJ: Drew University.

16520. Cashmore, Ernest E. (1983) Rastaman: The Rastifarian Movement in England. London: Unwin. Cashmore reports his interviews and observations of participants in a millenarian movement.

16521. Casper, Dale E. (1983) Religious Groups in Urban America, a Bibliography. Monticello, IL: Vance Bibliographies. An interesting but brief bibliography of the history of the church in urban America has several entries about Jewish influences.

16522. Castells, Manuel. (1983) The City and the Grassroots: A Cross-Cultural Theory of Urban Social Movements. Berkeley, CA: University of California Press. Studies of social movements in France, Spain, the United States and Latin America are used as a basis of an analysis of urban social change and a theory of the "good city." Passing reference is made to religious support of and resistance to urban social movements. Bibliography includes French and Spanish sources.

16523. Catholic Church, Archdiocese of St. Louis [MO], Human Rights Office. (1983) Urban and Black Community Ministry Planning Process: Final Report. St. Louis, MO: Urban Ministry and Minority Concerns Division, Human Rights Office, Archdiocese of St. Louis.

16524. "Century-old Church Saved." (1983) Engineering News-Record. Vol. 211 (November 24), pp. 14+. Re: St. Peter's Roman Catholic Cathedral, Erie, PA.

16525. Cheuiche, Antônio do Carmo. (1983) "O problema da pastoral urbana," Teocomunicação [Porto Alegre]. Vol. 13, No. 1, pp. 5-10. Urban pastoral problems.

16526. Christensen, Michael J. (1983) Repair the Ruined Cities. Radix. Vol. 15, No. 3 (November), pp. 15-18.

16527. Christian, Henry A. (1983) City and Literature: An Introduction. Newark, NJ: Rutgers University Press. Bibliography.

16528. Christiano, Kevin J. (1983) Religious Diversity and Social Change in Turn-of-the-Century American Cities. Thesis (Ph. D.). Princeton, NJ: Princeton University.

16529. Chung, Tai Ki. (1983) Pastoral Care for Korean Immigrants in the United States Experiencing Cross-Cultural Stress. Thesis (D. Min.). Claremont, CA: School of Theology at Claremont.

16530. Chung, Young Kwan. (1983) A Project of the Inner-City Church Growth. Thesis (D. Min.). Pasadena, CA: Fuller Theological Seminary. A case study of Central Methodist Church, Seoul, Korea. The text is in Korean, with an abstract in English.

16531. Claerbaut, David. (1983) Urban Ministry. Grand Rapids, MI: Zondervan. Claerbaut, a professor of sociology at North Park College, Chicago, combines sociological and evangelical Christian perspectives on the city. From this vantage he analyzes urban social stratification, poverty, youth culture, ethnicity and minority concerns, and the urban church in general. Reviewed: International Review of Missions, Vol. 74 (January, 1985), p. 124. Calvin Theological Journal, Vol. 19 (November, 1984), p. 244. Bibliography.

16532. Clancey, Jack, Filo Hirota and Denis Murphy, eds. (1983) Labor and the Church in Asia. Hong Kong: Center for the Progress of Peoples. Includes presentations at a conference on labor and church held in Hong Kong March 1-9, 1983.

16533. Cogswell, James A. (1983) No Place Left Called Home. New York: Friendship Press. A Presbyterian staff member writes about the theological implications of the plight of refugees and the homeless, calling the reader to join them in their journey and struggle. Too often churches adopt a condescending posture, viewing refugees as being something less important than and different from rooted Christians. The 1980 US Refugee Act is discussed.

16534. Cohen, Steven Martin. (1983) American Modernity and Jewish Identity. New York: Tavistock Publications, 1983. Re: the importance of context in ministry. Cohen writes mostly about Jewish social characteristics.

16535. Colombo, Vittorino. (1983) Cattolicismo sociale, movimento operaio, democrazia cristiana. Milan, Italy: Massimo.

16536. Conn, Harvie M. (1983) "Christ and the City," Urban Mission. Vol. 1, No. 2 (November), pp. 25-30.

16537. Consultation on Community Ministries, October 31-November 2, 1983, Lousiville, KY. (1983) Doing the Gospel in Our Neighborhood [Two Videocassettes, color, manual]. Lousiville, KY: Southern Baptist Theological Seminary.

16538. Cook, J. Keith. (1983) The First Parish: A Pastor's Survival Manual. Philadelphia, PA: Westminster Press. A veteran Presbyterian pastor in Omaha, NE, advises seminarians on the practical business of the parish. Reviewed: Trinity Seminary Review, Vol. 7, No. 1, Spring, 1985, p. 51. Based on a D. Min. thesis of the same title at San Francisco Theological Seminary.

16539. Cook, William [Guillermo]. (1983) "Evangelical Reflections on the Church of the Poor," Missiology. Vol. 11, No. 1 (January), pp. 47-53.

16540. Courtney, Tom. (1983) "Mission to the Urban Poor," Urban Mission. Vol. 1, No. 2 (November), pp. 17-24.

16541. Cramp, A. B. (1983) Economics in Christian Perspective: A Sketch Map. Toronto, Ontario, Canada: Institute for Christian Studies. Bibliography.

16542. Crawford, James W. (1983) To a Church in the Hub. Boston, MA: s.n. A sermon regarding Old South Church, Boston, MA.

16543. Creasey, Graham. (1983) Contemporary Spirituality. Luton, England: Luton Industrial College. A paper commenting on the fact that personal devotional piety and commitment to social and political goals are rarely found in the same person.

16544. Cummings, Scott. (1983) Immigrant Minorities and Urban Working Classes. Port Washington, NY: Associated Faculty Press.

16545. Crepu, Michel, et al. (1983) Repertoire des archives centrales de la Jeunesse ouvrière chrétienne. Paris: CNRS. A brief catalog of holdings of the archive of Jeunesse ouvrière chrétienne.

16546. Davies, Graham. (1983) "Squires in the East End?" Theology. Vol. 86, No. 712 (July), pp. 249-259. Davies deals critically with the slum-priest image of some Anglo-Catholics, particularly in terms of the lack of a coherent position on social justice, which he suggests is the result of the sacramental constraints of the church. Charitable action is possible from the Anglo-Catholic orientation, but not social justice.

16547. Davies, Michael J. (1983) Peace in the City: A Report on ... Pastoral Care and Support of Ministers Working in the Inner City. London: Thames North Province of the United Reformed Church. Report of a sabbatical project regarding the pastoral care of inner city clergy.

16548. Davis, C. Anne. (1983) "The Practice of Urban Ministry: Christian Social Ministries," Review and Expositor. Vol. 80, No. 4 (Fall), pp. 523-528.

16549. Dayton, Edward and Samuel Wilson, eds. (1983) The Refugees among Us: Unreached People '83. Monrovia, CA: MARC.

16550. Dearnley, Pat and Pete Broadbent. (1983) "Jesus Christ, the Life of the City?" Churchman: Journal of Anglican Theology [London]. Vol. 97, No. 1, pp. 41-54.

16551. DeBoer, John C. (1983) "Sharing Facilities," JSAC Grapevine. Vol. 14, No. 10 (May), pp. [1-8]. Reports a study of churches that share buildings, most of which are in urban settings.

16552. Dew, Bob. (1983) "God's City?" Crucible. [Vol. 22, No. 1] (January-March), pp. 27-32. Dew, at the time of writing, was a member of the Liverpool Industrial Mission and a chaplain with special responsibility for the unemployed.

16553. Diaz Ramirez, Ana Maria. (1983) The Roman Catholic Archdiocese of New York and the Puerto Rican Migration, 1950-1973: A Sociological and Historical Analysis. Thesis (Ph. D.). New York: Fordham University.

16554. Dickinson, Richard D. N. (1983) Poor, Yet Making Many Rich: The Poor as Agent of Creative Justice. Geneva, Switzerland: Commission on the Church's Participation in Development, World Council of Churches.

16555. Directory of Congregational Studies. (1983, 1989) Atlanta, GA: Rollins Center for Church Ministries, Candler School of Theology, Emory University. The Rollins Center publishes a list of individuals involved in research related to congregations, many of whom have interest in urban congregations. Brief self-submitted statements about research interests are included for each person. The 1989 edition is completely revised. An updated file is maintained by the Center.

16556. Donaldson, Thomas and Patricia H. Werhane, eds. (1983)

Ethical Issues in Business: A Philosophical Approach. Englewood Ciffs, NJ: Prentice-Hall. Bibliography.

16557. Dorff, Nina and Fay Katlin. (1983) "The Soviet Immigrant Client: Beyond Resettlement," Journal of Jewish Communal Service. Vol. 60, No. 2 (Winter), pp. 146-154.

16558. Dorsett, Lyle W. (1983) Denver Rescue Mission: A Brief History. Denver, CO: Denver Rescue Mission.

16559. Driedger, Leo, Raymond Currie, and Rick Linden. (1983) "Dualistic and Wholistic Views of God and the World: Consequences for Social Action," Review of Religious Research. Vol. 24, No. 3 (March), pp. 225-244. The authors test Robert Wuthnow's dualist and wholist perspective with Mennonites and find it applies.

16560. Driedger, Leo, Roy Vogt and Mavis Reimer. (1983) "Mennonite Intermarriage: National Regional and Intergenerational Trends," Mennonite Quarterly Review. Vol. 57, No. 2 (April), pp. 132-144. The effects of urbanization on Mennonite endogamy.

16561. DuBose, Francis M. (1983) "The Practice of Urban Ministry: Urban Evangelism." Review and Expositor. Vol. 80, No. 4 (Fall), pp. 515-521.

16562. Dudley, Carl S., ed. (1983) Building Effective Ministry. New York: Harper and Row. Fourteen essays on local church dynamics. Reviewed: Journal of Psychology and Theology, Vol. 13 (Spring, 1985), p. 73. Perkins School of Theology Journal, Vol. 38 (Winter, 1985), p. 45. Bibliography.

16563. Duren, James. (1983) The Stranger Who Is among You: A Guide to Conservative Baptist Churches That Want to Reach Out to the Ethnic Groups in Their Communities. Pasadena, CA: William Carey Library.

16564. Durston, Rhondda. (1983) "Mission and Ministry in Canberra," St. Mark's Review [Thematic issue]. No. 114 (June), pp. 21-24.

16565. Early, Tracy. (1983) "Community Developer in Chinatown," New World Outlook. n.s. Vol. 43, No. 9 (May), pp. 17-19. United Methodist ministry among Chinese Americans.

16566. Eck, Diana L. (1983) Bararas: City of Light. London: Routledge and Kegan Paul. This volume is based on the author' 1976 doctoral dissertation at Harvard University on sacred places in India.

16567. Egan, John J. (1983) "Liturgy and Justice: An Unfinished Agenda," Origins, Vol. 13, No. 15 (September 22), pp. 245-253. Reprint: Collegeville, MN: Liturgical Press.

16568. Egan, John J. and Paul D. Colford. (1983) Baptism of Resistance, Blood, and Celebration: The Road to Wholeness in a Nuclear Age. Mystic, CT: Twenty-Third Publications.

16569. Ellison, Craig W. (1983) "Stress and Urban Ministry," Urban Mission. Vol. 1, No. 2 (November), pp. 5-16. Ellison lists symptoms and causes of psychological stress among people who work in cities. He describes stress of overload, stress of urban isolation, stress of criticism and conflict, and stress of spiritual temptation. Personal advice for coping skills is offered.

16570. Ellison, Frederick A. (1983) Conflicting Loyalties in the Workplace. Notre Dame, IN: University of Notre Dame Press. Re: whistleblowing and ethical responsibilities in the workplace.

16571. Estévez, Filipe J. (1983) "The Hispanic Search Beyond Biculturalism," Theological Education. Vol. 20, No. 1 (Autumn), pp. 58-64.

16572. Evangelical Coalition for Urban Mission. (beginning in 1983) City Cries: Journal of the Evangelical Coalition for Urban Mission. London: ECUM. A periodical.

16573. Evans, Robert A. and Thomas D. Parker. (1983) Christian Theology: A Case Study Approach. New York: Harper and Row.

16574. Everist, Norma J. (1983) Education Ministry in the Congregation: Eight Ways We Learn from One Another. Minneapolis, MN: Augsbury Publishing House.

16575. Ferm, Deane William. (1983) Alternative Lifestyles Confront the Church. New York: Seabury Press.

16576. Floristán Samones, Casiaio. (1983) "La pastoral de las grandes ciudades; la Diócesis de Madrid," Informes Pro Mundi Vita (Brussels). No. 30, pp. 1-27. Re: city churches in Madrid, Spain.

16577. Foner, Philip S., ed. (1983) Black Socialist Preacher. San Francisco, CA: Synthesis Publications. George Washington Woodbey, a clergyman in San Diego, California, and a national leader of Afro-American socialists in the early 20th century, left several essays, speeches and articles urging Blacks to adopt socialism. This edited volume comprises not only Woodbey's works, but also those of his disciple, George W. Slater.

16578. Fones-Wolf, Elizabeth and Kenneth Alan Fones-Wolf. (1983) "Trade Union Evangelism: Religion and the AFL in the Labor Forward Movement, 1912-1916," pp. 153-184 in Michael H. Frisch and Daniel J. Walkowitz, eds. Working-Class America: Essays on Labor, Community, and American Society. Urbana, IL: University of Illinois Press.

16579. Franklin, R. W. (1983) "Pusey and Worship in Industrial Society," Worship. Vol. 57, No. 5 (September), pp. 386-412. A survey of the Oxford movement and Edward B. Pusey (1800-1892) in regard to their involvement with the working classes.

16580. Fraser, Derek and Anthony Sutcliffe, eds. (1983) The Pursuit of Urban History. London: Edward Arnold. Edited essays that derive from a conference held at Leicester University in 1980. The book as a whole is seen as an effort to promote cross-disciplinary study of the city. Particularly notable are the articles by Graeme Davison and Sam Bass Warner.

16581. Freeman, Edward Barnes, Jr. (1983) Ministry in the Transitional Community Church. Atlanta, GA: Metropolitan Missions Department, Home Mission Board, Southern Baptist Convention, Occasional Paper 7. Freeman identifies three categories of advice for helping congregations deal with social change: the community situation, the strategies available, and the individual consultants working with the church in change.

16582. Frohman, Roderic Paul. (1983) Pastoral Hospitality with Worship Visitors in a Multi-Racial Setting. Thesis (D. Min). Princeton, NJ: Princeton Theological Seminary. Bibliography.

16583. Fromer, Paul. (1983) "Beyond Pity: What Churches Can Do," Christianity Today. Vol. 29, No. 9 (May 20), pp. 21-23.

16584. Gable, Dennis R. and Robert E. Larson, Jr., eds. (1983) Publicity/Public Relations Handbook: A Book of Resources for Promoting and Publicizing the Ministry of Contact. Harrisburg, PA: Contact Teleministries USA. Re: a community relations concerns in a telephone ministry.

16585. Gallagher, Sharon. (1983) "The John Perkins/Eldridge Cleaver Interview," Radix. Vol. 15, No. 3 (November), pp. 4-10. Perkins, founder of the Voice of Calvary Ministries, and Cleaver, former minister of information for the Black Panthers, comment on urban issues.

16586. Gauder, Winston. (1983) "Case Study: Temcare--Helping Children When They Hurt," Urban Mission. Vol. 1, No. 2 (November), pp. 36-37.

16587. Gillett, Richard W. (1983) "The Reshaping of Work: A Challenge to the Churches," The Christian Century. Vol. 100, No. 1 (January 5-12), pp. 10-13.

16588. Godwin, Roy E. (1983) "Area Ministries through Church Clustering," Review and Expositor. Vol. 80, No. 4 (Fall), pp. 553-560.

16589. Grant, James. (1983) "Inner Urban Comparisons," St. Mark's Review [Thematic issue]. No. 114 (June), pp. 7-10+.

16590. Greene, Carol. (1983) Mother Teresa: Friend of the Friendless. Chicago, IL: Childrens' Press. A book of pictures.

16591. Greenway, Roger S. (1983) "Editorial: Mission to an Urban World," Urban Mission. Vol. 1, No. 1 (September), pp. 1-2.

16592. Greenway, Roger S. (1983) "Editorial: The Shift of Ethnic Mission," Urban Mission. Vol. 1, No. 2 (November), pp. 3-4.

16593. Greenway, Roger S. (1983) "Don't Be an Urban Missionary Unless..." Evangelical Missions Quarterly. Vol. 19, No. 2 (April), pp. 86-94. Recommendations for aspiring urban missionaries: be mature, understand the city and the nature of mission, possess practical skills. A training program is described.

16594. Griffiths, Brian. (1983) The Moral Basis of the Market Economy. London: Conservative Political Center.

16595. Gutwirth, Jacques. (1983) "Jews among Evangelists in Los Angeles," Jewish Journal of Sociology. Vol. 24, No. 1 (June), pp. 39-56. Re: Jewish converts in the Open Door Community Church.

16596. Hadaway, C. Kirk. (1983) "Learning from Urban Church Research," Review and Expositor. Vol. 80, No. 4 (Fall), pp. 543-552. Reprinted: Urban Mission. Vol. 2, No. 3 (January), pp. 33-43. Hadaway explains how the urban church can use social scientific research.

16597. Hall, Douglas. (1983) "Emmanuel Gospel Center, Boston, MA: Contextualized Urban Ministry," Urban Mission. Vol. 1, No. 2 (November), pp. 31-36.

16598. Halsey, Peggy. (1983) "Meeting the Needs of Incarcerated Women," Engage/Social Action. Vol. 11, No. 5 (May), pp. 35-40.

16599. Hammer, Don E. (1983) "The Practice of Urban Ministry: A Postscript," Review and Expositor. Vol. 80, No. 4 (Fall), pp. 537-541.

16600. Hanson, Allen. (1983) "Prison Outreach Ministry," Theology Today. Vol. 39, No. 4 (January), pp. 395-401.

16601. Harding, Vincent. (1983) There Is a River: The Black Struggle for Freedom in America. New York: Vintage.

16602. Hargrove, Barbara Watts. (1983) "Churches as Mediating Structures," Theology Today. Vol. 39, No. 4 (January), pp. 385-394. Hargrove believes that churches can bridge the gap between public and private spheres in modern life. Churches should reclaim the public dimensions of their roles.

16603. Hargrove, Barbara Watts. (1983) "Modernity and Its Disadvantaged: The Cultural Context of Theological Education," Theological Education. Vol. 20, No. 1 (Autumn), pp. 10-19. Controversy and new possibilities in theological education are created because some people have been excluded from it.

16604. Hartley, Loyde H. (1983) After the Merger: A Study of Linwood United Church, Kansas City, Missouri. Lancaster, PA: Research Center in Religion and Society, Lancaster Theological Seminary. An inner city congregation, merged from three predecessor congregations, considers strategies for its future.

16605. Healey, Joseph G. (1983) "Let the Basic Christian Communities Speak," Missiology: An International Review. Vol. 11, No. 1 (January), pp. 15-30.

16606. Heitzer, Horstwalter. (1983) Georg Kardinal Kopp und der Gewerkschaftsstreit, 1900-1914. Köln, West Germany: Böhlau. A biography of Cardinal Kopp (1837-1914) and a history of the relationship between the church and unions. Bibliography.

16607. Hendrickse, Clarry. (1983) One Inner Urban Church and Lay Ministry. Grove Pastoral Series No. 13. Bramcote, England: Grove. Hendrickse encourages other clergy to support the ministry of the laity, giving as example his own experience as the vicar of a central city parish in Liverpool, Christ Church.

16608. Henrici, Peter. (1983) "The Church and Pluralism," Communio: International Catholic Review. Vol. 10, No. 2 (Summer), pp. 128-132.

16609. Hessel, Dieter T., ed. (1983) Social Themes of the Christian Year. Philadelphia, PA: Geneva Press. Commentary on the lectionary and church year from the perspectives of persons involved in social ministries provides insights into the theological and worship orientations of the authors.

16610. Hill, Robert A., ed. (1983, 1984) The Marcus Garvey and the Universal Negro Improvement Association Papers. Berkeley, CA: University of California Press. Three volumes.

16611. Hindman, Tom. (1983) "The Weatherization Conspiracy: How Christians for Urban Justice Are Making the Most of the Cold Winters of Boston," The Other Side. Vol. 19, No. 9 (September), pp. 16-17.

16612. Hirota, Filo, Denis Murphy and Jack Clancey. (1983) "The Situation of Industrial Workers in Asia and the Church's Response," Pro Mundi Via Dossiers: Asia and Australasia. Dossier No. 26, pp. 1-30.

16613. Hirschfield, Robert. (1983) "Street Despair," The Christian Century. Vol. 100, No. 23 (July 20), pp. 671-672.

16614. Hirschon, Renée B. (1983) "Women, the Aged, and Religious Activity: Oppositions and Complementarity in an Urban Locality," Journal of Modern Greek Studies. Vol. 1, No. 1 (May), pp. 113-129. An anthropological study of generational conflict over mourning customs in urban Greece.

16615. Hoehn, Richard A. (1983) Up from Apathy. Nashville, Abingdon Press. Hoehn raises the question of what prods people into becoming activists. His findings are drawn from interviews with 87 people with diverse characteristics and backgrounds. Questionnaire.

16616. Holifield, E. B. (1983) A History of Pastoral Care in

America. Nashville, TN: Abingdon.

16617. Hombs, Mary Ellen and Mitch Snyder. (1983) "I Was Homeless, and You Gave Me Shelter," Christianity and Crisis. Vol. 43, No. 2 (February 21), pp. 36-38.

16618. Honeycutt, Roy L., ed. (1983) "The Urban Church," Review and Expositor [Thematic issue]. Vol. 80, No. 4 (Fall), pp. 487-607.

16619. Hopewell, James F. (1983) "The Jovial Church: Narrative in Local Church Life," in Carl S. Dudley, ed. Building an Effective Ministry. New York: Harper and Row.

16620. Hostetler, Virginia. (1983) "Faith in a Favela: Why Two North Americans Chose to Live in a Brazilian Slum," The Other Side. Vol. 19, No. 5 (May), pp. 24-27.

16621. Houck, John W. and Oliver F. Williams, eds. (1983) Co-Creation and Capitalism: John Paul II, Laborem Exercens. Washington, DC: University Press of America. Bibliography.

16622. House, Jay Wesley. (1983) The Church Confronts Society. Thesis (D. Min.). Dayton, OH: United Theological Seminary. Program for a Lutheran and United Methodist yoked parish involves theological preaching, prayer, and outreach.

16623. Houston Metropolitan Ministries, Interfaith Refugee Settlement Committee. (1983) Sponsor Resource Manual. Houston, TX: Interfaith Refugee Settlement Committee.

16624. Huffman, D. L. (1983) "A Shopping Mall Church: An Interview," Herald of Holiness. Vol. 72, No. 5 (March 1), pp. 6+.

16625. Hunsicker, Ronald. (1983) "Project Grace: Gratitude, Recovery, Acceptance, Comfort and Empathy," American Protestant Hospital Association Bulletin. Vol. 47, No. 3, pp. 46-49.

16626. Huston, Sterling W. (1983) Crusade Preparation for Large Cities [Sound cassette]. Minneapolis, MN: World Wide Publications. [Location: Southern Baptist Theological Seminary, Louisville, KY].

16627. The Islamic City. (1983, 1988) [Videorecording, 38 min.]. Princeton, NJ: Films for the Humanities.

16628. Jenkins, J. Craig. (1983) "Resource Mobilization Theory and the Study of Social Movements," Annual Review of Sociology. Vol. 9, pp. 527-553. Jenkins analyzes the organization and politics of people's movements including alignments, leadership coalitions, and other structures.

16629. Jiménez Carvajal, Jorge. (1983) "Pastoral planificada: Posibilidades y exigencias en las grandes ciudades," Medellín [Medellín, Colombia]. Vol. 9, n. 33, pp. 75-88. Pastoral planning: possibilities and requirements in large cities.

16630. Jimmerson, Robin Leroy. (1983) Neighborhood Transition and Urban Church Ministry: A Case Study of Butchertown. Thesis (Th. M.). Lousiville, KY: Southern Baptist Theological Seminary.

16631. Johnson, Ben Campbell. (1983) An Evangelism Primer: Practical Principles for Congregations. Atlanta, GA: John Knox Press. Reviewed: Reformed Review, Vol. 35 (Autumn, 1984), p. 75.

16632. Johnson, Douglas W. (1983) Reaching Out to the Unchurched. Valley Forge, PA: Judson Press.

16633. Johnson, Ronald and Russell Long. (1983) Social Ministry: A Congregational Manual. Philadelphia, PA: Parish Life Press. Practical strategy for becoming involved in social ministries in the 1980s.

16634. Joselit, Jenna Weissman. (1983) "What Happened to New York's 'Jewish Jews?' Moses Rischin's The Promised City Revisited," American Jewish History. Vol. 73, No. 2 (December), pp. 173-204.

16635. Joselit, Jenna Weissman. (1983) Our Gang: Jewish Crime in the New York Jewish Community. Bloomington, IN: Indiana University Press. See further the author's dissertation (1981). Bibliography.

16636. Kantowicz, Edward R. (1983) Corporation Sole: Cardinal Mundelein and Chicago Catholicism. Notre Dame, IN: Notre Dame University Press.

16637. Kazin, Alfred. (1983) "Fear of the City, 1783-1983," American Heritage. Vol. 43, No. 2 (February), pp. 14-23.

16638. Kennedy, Michael and Maurice D. Simon. (1983) "Church and Nation in Socialist Poland," pp. 121-154 in Peter H. Merkl and Ninian Smart, eds. Religion and Politics. New York: New York University Press.

16639. Kim, Ick Won. (1983) A Study of the Korean Church Growth in Context of the Korean National Characteristics. Thesis (D. Min). Pasadena, CA: Fuller Theological Seminary.

16640. Kim, Won Kie. (1983) Evangelization of the Korean Immigrants in the United States of America. Thesis (D. Min.). Dallas, TX: Perkins School of Theology at Southern Methodist University.

16641. Kinsler, F. Ross, ed. (1983) Ministry by the People: Theological Education by Extension. Maryknoll, NY: Orbis Books. Reviewed: International Bulletin of Missionary Research, Vol. 8 (July, 1984), p. 138. Scotish Journal of Theology, Vol. 37, No. 3 (1984), p. 412. Modern Churchman, n.s. Vol. 26, No. 4 (1984), p. 55.

16642. Krass, Alfred C. (1983) "Don't Leave It to Chance: The Importance of Writing for Urban Ministry, (Seeking the Peace of the City)," The Other Side. Vol. 19, No. 11 (November), pp. 32-33.

16643. Krass, Alfred C. (1983) "Beyond the Service Syndrome: Hard Questions for Us Clergy--And for the Church," The Other Side. Vol. 19, No. 7 (July), pp. 30-31.

16644. Krauß-Siemann, Jutta. (1983) Kirchliche Stadtteilarbeit. Stuttgart, West Germany: Verlag W. Kohlhammer. City churches which respond to their neighborhood context discover not only the importance of their ministry but also the salvation and well-being of their own parishioners. A large bibliography of works on urban ministry in German, 1970-1983, is included.

16645. Krietemeyer, Ronald T. (1983) "US Bishops on Unemployment and Economic Justice," New Catholic World [Thematic issue: Religion and the Economy]. Vol. 226, No. 1354 (July), pp. 176-179.

16646. Krupavicius, Mykolas. (1983) Visuomeniniai klausimai: straipsniu rinkinys is jo palikimo. [Chicago, IL?]: Popieziaus Leono XIII fondas. Re: church, labor and politics in Lithuania, 1918-1945.

16647. Lam, Peter. (1983) The Work of the Episcopal Church among the Chinese in the Diocese of New York. Thesis (MA). New York: General Theological Seminary.

16648. Landrey, J. Paul, Director. (1983) San Francisco Networks. San Francisco, CA: US Ministry and World Vision. A compilation of ministry resources in the San Francisco Bay area and an example of network construction.

16649. Leak, A. S. (1983) "What are Cathedral Chapters for?" Theology. Vol. 86, No. 710 (March), pp. 106-113. A discussion of the role of cathedral chapters in the rapidly changing religious environment. Is diocesan control of such chapters too great?

16650. Leech, Kenneth. (1983) "Outcast London Revisited," Crucible. [Vol. 22, No. 3] (July-September), pp. 124-127.

16651. Leonard, Charles. (1983) A Study of Some Multi-Ethnic Congregations in Light of Church Growth and the Homogenous Unit Principle. Thesis (D. Min.). Philadelphia, PA: Eastern Baptist Theological Seminary.

16652. LeRoy, Michael G. (1983) Riots in Liverpool 8. [London]: Evangelical Coalition for Urban Mission.

16653. Leslie, Annie Ruth Johnson. (1983) A Study of Black Mores and the Non-Sinful Outlook Regarding Motherhood among Poor Urban Black Mothers. Thesis (Ph. D.). Chicago, IL: Northwestern University.

16654. Lincoln, C. Eric. (1983) "The American Muslim Mission in the Context of American Social History," pp. 215-233 in Earle H. Waugh, et al, eds. The Muslim Community in North America. Edmonton, Alberta, Canada: University of Alberta Press.

16655. Lindley, Susan. (1983) "Social Gospel's Messages for Today," The Witness [Ambler, PA]. Vol. 66, No. 5 (May), pp. 7-9.

16656. Link, Eugene P. (1983) Labor-Religion Prophet: The Times and Life of Harry F. Ward. Boulder, CO: Westview Press. Bibliography.

16657. Lumerman, Juan Pedro, et al. (1983) La dignidad del trabajo humano: Comentario a "Laborem Exercens" de Juan Pablo II. Buenos Aires, Argentina: Editorial Guadalupe. Commentary on Laborem Exercens, John Paul II's encyclical, especially regarding the dignity of work.

16658. Macleod, David I. (1983) Building Character in the American Boy: The Boy Scouts, YMCA, and Their Forerunners, 1870-1920. Madison, WI: University of Wisconsin Press.

16659. Mader, Donald, et al. (1983) A Witness in the City: Greenpoint Reformed Church. Brooklyn, NY: the Church.

16660. Maduro, Otto. (1983) Religion and Social Conflicts. Maryknoll, NY: Orbis.

16661. Mamiya, Lawrence H. (1983) "Minister Louis Farrakhan and the Final Call: Schism in the Muslim Movement," in Earle H. Waugh, et al, eds. The Muslim Community in North America. Edmonton, Alberta, Canada: University of Alberta Press.

16662. McBride, Esther Barnhart. (1983) Open Church: History of an Idea. Albuquerque, NM: Starline Creative Printing. McBride writes a sympathetic history of the open church movement which, at the turn of the 20th century, did away with pew rentals in churches and challenged the churches to minister to the social and human needs of people in their neighborhoods. Advocates of the open church promoted fundamental changes in urban evangelism, church architecture, church programming, and worship -- all in the direction of responding to urban human needs. This movement was one institutional expression of orthodox Social Gospel theology and represented an important stage in Protestant welfare thought. The extensive bibliography, especially on institutional churches and pew rentals, compiled by McBride and her social work students at Tulane University concludes the book.

16663. McGavran, Donald. (1983) "New Urban Faces of the Church," Urban Mission. Vol. 1, No. 1 (September), pp. 2-11.

16664. McKee, Judith and Thomas McKee. (1983) "A Time of Change--For Better Not For Worse," Lutheran Focus. Vol. 17, No. 3, pp. 28, 30-31.

16665. McKinney, William and Dean R. Hoge. (1983) "Community and Congregational Factors in the Growth and Decline of Protestant Churches," Journal for the Scientific Study of Religion. Vol. 22, No. 1 (March), pp. 51-56. A study of membership trends in the United Church of Christ shows marked decline in city churches while small town and rural churches have remained stable. Bibliography.

16666. McSwain, Larry L. (1983) "Community Forms and Urban Church Profiles," Review and Expositor. Vol. 80, No. 4 (Fall), pp. 501-514. Reviews past approaches to identifying church types: adaptive, ecological, functional, and integrative. A classification of city churches is offered: 1) the communal group (house church, storefront church, ethnic church, special purpose church); 2) the neighborhood church (current and ex-neighborhood varieties); 3) the multi-neighborhood church (old first church, regional church).

16667. Meeks, Wayne A. (1983) The First Urban Christians: The Social World of the Apostle Paul. New Haven: Yale University Press. Based on an analysis of Paul's letters, Meeks' description of the urban quality of the first Christian's experience in the church dispels any lingering notion that the Bible has an agrarian bias. (See, for example, Roger Shinn, Christianity and Crisis, Vol. 22, No. 20, p. 203, who writes "We must face the fact that the Bible was written ... in an agrarian society.") A scholarly work, this book with guidance can help contemporary urban Christians identify with their first century counterparts and spiritual ancestors. Paul's well known words analyzed sociologically yield fresh impressions of urban diversity in Corinth, Ephesus, and the other New Testament cities. Reviewed many places, including: American Historical Review, Vol. 88 (December, 1983), p. 497. Christian Century, Vol. 100 (February 16-23, 1983), p. 162. Religious Studies Review, Vol. 11, No. 4 (October, 1985), pp. 329-335.

16668. Melton, J. Gordon. (1983) A Biographical Dictionary of American Cult and Sect Leaders. New York: Garland. Biographical sketches.

16669. Melton, J. Gordon. (1983) Encyclopedic Handbook of Cults in America. New York: Garland. A reference work on 500 cults in North America.

16670. Milloy, Courtland. (1983) "Black Pastors Seen Losing Authority to Congregation," The Washington Post. (November 12).

16671. Mol, Johannis J. [Hans]. (1983) The Meaning of Place: An Introduction to the Social Scientific Study of Religion. New York: The Pilgrim Press. Reviewed: Theology Today, Vol. 40 (October, 1983), p. 386. Sociological Analysis, Vol. 45 (Spring, 1984), p. 71. Review of Religious Research, Vol. 26 (December, 1984), p. 198.

16672. Monsma, Timothy. (1983) "Case Study: The Tiv Soldiers of Nigeria," Urban Mission. Vol. 1, No. 1 (September), pp. 29-31. Re: evangelistic work with military people in Nigeria.

16673. Montêquin, François-Augusta de. (1983) "Religious, Social, and Physical Qualities of Islamic Urbanization," Hamdard Islamicus. Vol. 6, No. 1 (Spring), pp. 63-86. Montêquin concludes that the traditional ideal Muslim city is based on notions of privacy, neutrality, and religiousness.

16674. Montero García, Feliciano. (1983) El primer catolicismo social y la Rerum Novarum en España, 1889-1902. Madrid, Spain:

CSIC. Re: church and labor relations in Spain following Rerum Novarum.

16675. Morris, Orrin D. (1983) The Future of America's Large Cities. Atlanta, GA: Research Division, Home Mission Board of the Southern Baptist Convention. A statistical study.

16676. Murnion, Philip Joseph. (1983) "The Paradox of Urban Ministry Today," Origins. Vol. 12, No. 45 (April 21), pp. 741-744.

16677. Murnion, Philip Joseph. (1983) "Urban Ministry: Sacrament in the City," Christianity and Crisis. Vol. 43, No. 8 (May 16), pp. 187-191. Good urban ministry is simply good ministry anywhere. An urban church must minister both to the personal and corporate needs, just as might be expected of churches in other situations. Murnion, the Director of the National Pastoral Life Center and the Director of Clergy Continuing Education for the Archdiocese of New York, calls churches to a sacramental style of ministry that emphasizes the divine-human interrelationship and that can cope with the imperfections of social action.

16678. Murthy, B. Srinivasa. (1983) Mother Teresa and India. Long Beach, CA: Longbeach Publications.

16679. Nakamaki, Hirochika. (1983) "The 'Separate' Coexistence of Kami and Hotoke: A Look at Yorishior" [translated by N. Ablemann], Japanese Journal of Religious Studies. Vol. 10, No. 1 (March), pp. 65-86.

16680. Natale, Samuel M. (1983) "Pastoral Counseling and Psychotherapy in Industry: Differing Results?" Journal of Pastoral Counseling. Vol. 18 (Fall-Winter), pp. 23-28.

16681. Nell-Breuning, Oswald von. (1983) Arbeit vor Kapital: Kommentar zur Enzyklika Laborem exercens von Johannes Paul II. Vienna, Austria: Europaverlag. Nell-Breuning comments on the social encyclical of John Paul II.

16682. Newton, Jim. (1983) "The Challenge of Change: Home Mission Board Offers Help to Churches in Transitional Change," Missions USA. [An insert]. Reprinted: Home Missions Board, Southern Baptist Convention. An explanation of PACT (Project: Assistance in Transitional Communities), an emphasis of the Southern Baptist Convention's Home Mission Board.

16683. Norton, Thomas Joseph Aquinas. (1983) The Police Chaplaincy, a Ministry of Listening. Thesis (D. Min.). Madison, NJ: Drew University.

16684. O'Cleireacain, Carol. (1983) "Unemployment and the Economy," New Catholic World [Thematic issue: Religion and the Economy]. Vol. 226, No. 1354 (July), pp. 155-157.

16685. Oakley, Jerry. (1983) "Running on Retreads: A New Trend in Missions," Church Administration. Vol. 25, No. 12 (September), pp. 16-17.

16686. Ogle, George. (1983) "A Primer on Unemployment and Justice Action," Engage/Social Action [Thematic issue: Unemployment]. Vol. 11, No. 6 (June), pp. 27-40.

16687. Oostdyk, Harv. (1983) Step One: The Gospel and the Ghetto. Basking Ridge, NJ: SonLife International. Oostdyk offers poetry, prose, photographs, and biblical interpretation intended to portray ghetto ministry. For many years, he worked in New York City ghettos, and more recently in Dallas. His list of eight principles for ministering to the poor (see pp. 223-236) outlines a strategy for evangelical urban ministry. Reviewed: Christian Scholar's Review, Vol. 13, No. 3 (1984), p. 298. Urban Mission, Vol. 1, No. 4 (March, 1984), pp. 39-40.

16688. Parker, Tony, ed. (1983) The People of Providence. London: Hutchinson. An oral history of urban "high-rise" dwellers in an English housing estate.

16689. Pasquariello, Ronald D. (1983) "A Church Advocacy Office on Urban Policy," Cities. Vol. 3, No. 1 (Summer), pp. 35-36.

16690. A pastoral das migrações. (1983) São Paulo, Brazil: Edicões Paulinas.

16691. Peerman, Dean. (1983) "Helping the Homeless," The Christian Century. Vol. 100, No. 7 (March 9), pp. 207-208.

16692. Perkins, H. Wesley. (1983) "Organized Religion as Opiate or Prophetic Stimulant: A Study of American and English Assessment of Social Justice in Two Urban Settings," Review of Religious Research. Vol. 24, No. 3 (March), pp. 206-224. A study of residents in New Haven, CT and London, England, raises the question of the extent to which religion instills and encourages member's commitment to justice and equality or, to the contrary, suppresses them. Social conformity, a common element in religious identification, tends to lower concern for social equality, Perkins finds, while internalization of the faith tends to heighten such concern.

16693. Perkins, John. (1983) "Leadership for Justice," Urban Mission. Vol. 1, No. 1 (September), pp. 12-18.

16694. Perry, Jos. (1983) Roomsche kinine tegen roode koorts: arbeidersbeweging en katholieke kerk in Maastricht, 1880-1920. Amsterdam, The Netherlands: Van Gennep. Re: Catholic Church and trade unions in the Netherlands. Summary in French. Bibliography.

16695. Peter, Val J. (1983) "A Primer on Pluralism," Communio: International Catholic Review. Vol. 10, No. 2 (Summer), pp. 133-148.

16696. Petersen, Larry and Peter Takayama. (1983) "Local-Cosmopolitan Theory and Religiosity among Catholic Nuns and Brothers," Journal for the Scientific Study of Religion. Vol. 22, No. 4 (December), pp. 303-315. A test of Wade C. Roof's local-cosmopolitan theory (1972, 1976, 1978). Bibliography.

16697. Pickering, John. (1983) "Consumerism, Consumption and the Churches," Crucible. [Vol. 22, No. 3] (July-September), pp. 107-113.

16698. Pierce, Gregory F. Augustine. (1983) Activism That Makes Sense: Congregations and Community Organization. New York: Paulist Press. Republished: Chicago, IL: ACTA Publication, 1984. An anecdotal explanation of organizational approaches to solving personal and group problems, this book is both forceful and intensely practical. Pierce provides a theological rationale for the Alinsky approach applied to congregations, weighing pros and cons. He contends that Christians have no right to lose, and places strong emphasis on the need for ecumenical and secular alliances. His experience in organizing comes from the Industrial Areas Foundation. Bibliographical notes. See further an article with the same title in The Other Side (February, 1984).

16699. Pieterse, Hennie J. C. (1983) "Preaching in Urban Congregations," Theologia Evangelica. Vol. 16, No. 1 (March), pp. 21-28. Cities are pluralistic in faith, knowledge, occupation and social status. Clergy must be able to deal with a variety of needs, concepts and idioms. Pieterse offers an approach to hermeneutics in the city.

16700. Polen, Nehemiah. (1983) "Neo-Hasidism in Suburbia,"

The Christian Century. Vol. 100, No. 3 (January 26), pp. 68-70.

16701. Poppy, John. (1983) "Sheltering the Homeless: The Power of Futility," The Witness [Ambler, PA]. Vol. 66, No. 4 (April), pp. 6-9.

16702. Potter, Juanita Wright. (1983) "A Gospel Miracle: How a Chicago Neighborhood Is Being Transformed," The Other Side. Vol. 19, No. 7 (July), pp. 13-17.

16703. Power, David N. (1983) "Households of Faith in the Coming Church," Worship. Vol. 57, No. 3 (May), pp. 237-255. Power believes that extra ecclesial communities of faith (base communities) are the best contemporary response to the breakdown of church life. He finds similarities between these communities and the reform movements of the 12th and 13th centuries. The communities have evangelical poverty and solidarity with the oppressed. Their liturgy commemorates the suffering and the resurrection of Jesus and celebrates the freedom that comes as a gift of the spirit.

16704. Preservation League of New York State. (1983) How to Care for Religious Properties. Albany, NY: Preservation League. Maintenance and repair of old church buildings, a continuing concern of the Preservation League, may be accomplished through low cost procedures that preclude major repairs. Check lists, sources of information, suggestions on cleaning and repairs, and management of volunteers are among the topics covered in this book.

16705. Preston, Ronald H. (1983) Church and Society in the Late Twentieth Century: The Economic and Political Task [Scott Holland Lectures for 1983]. London: SCM. Preston evaluates the Christian socialist tradition from which Scott Holland and others, such as R. H. Tawney, gained inspiration. He criticizes both the radical right for its individualism and the Christian social theologies that have not dealt adequately with economic realities. Reviewed: Expository Times, Vol. 95 (August, 1984), p. 348. Baptist Quarterly [London], Vol. 30 (July, 1984), p. 336. Journal of Ecclesiastical History, Vol. 36 (January, 1985), p. 165. Theology, Vol. 88 (March, 1985), p. 159.

16706. Pury, Pascal de. (1983) People's Technologies and People's Participation. Geneva, Switzerland: World Council of Churches Commission on Churches' Participation in Development. People in developing nations cannot use new technologies, even the most rudimentary ones, unless workers are organized in groups that give them power, knowledge, and tools appropriate to their work.

16707. Raines, John C. (1983) "Capital, Community, and the Meaning of Work," Christianity and Crisis. Vol. 43, No. 16 (October 17), pp. 375-379.

16708. Ramirez, Ricardo. (1983) "Reflections on the Hispanication of the Liturgy," Worship. Vol. 57, No. 1 (January), pp. 26-34.

16709. Ranck, Lee. (1983) "'Blackjack, Roulette, Craps, Baccarat, Big Six, and Banks of Glistening Slot Machines,' Impact of Casino Gambling on Atlantic City," Engage/Social Action. Vol. 11, No. 8 (September), pp. 24-31.

16710. Ranck, Lee. (1983) "The Frustration Is: What Do We Do about It?" Engage/Social Action [Thematic issue: Unemployment]. Vol. 11, No. 6 (June), pp. 20-26.

16711. Reapsome, James W. (1983) "Cities Must Have Our Best Effort," Evangelical Missions Quarterly. Vol. 19, No. 2 (April), pp. 98-99. An editorial inquiry: "How does one attack a city?"

16712. Reid, John R. (1983) "Urban Ministry: A Sydney Experience," St. Mark's Review [Thematic issue]. No. 114 (June), pp. 11-16+.

16713. Restrepo, Luis Alberto. (1983) ¿Hacia una socialización auténtica? Manual para el estudio de la Encíclica Laborem Exercens. Bogotá, Colombia: Indo-American Press Service. Re: the papal encyclical Laborem Exerens and labor issues.

16714. Rosenberg, Stuart. (1983) "Suburban Judaism," Mainstream. (November), pp. 30-32.

16715. Rubenstein, Richard L. (1983) The Age of Triage: Fear and Hope in an Overcrowded World. Boston: Beacon.

16716. Russell, Dora Winifred Black, Countess. (1983) The Religious of the Machine Age. London: Routledge and Kegan Paul.

16717. Samore, Lee Thomas. (1983) A Sociolinguistic and Historical Survey of the Lebanese Orthodox-Christian Community in Sioux City, Iowa. Thesis (MA). Tucson, AZ: University of Arizona.

16718. Samuel, Vinay Kumar and Christopher Sugden. (1983) Evangelism and the Poor. Bangalore, India: Partnership in Mission--Asia.

16719. Sandoval, Moises, ed. (1983) The Mexican American Experience in the Church: Reflections on Identity and Mission. New York: Sadlier. Strategies for Hispanic survival in the church.

16720. Santos, Aloysio. (1983) O pensamento social da Igreja e o trabalho humano. Rio de Janeiro, Argentina: Shogun Arte. Re: Catholic social though regarding human labor.

16721. Schibilsky, Michael. (1983) Alltagswelt und Sonntagskirche: sozialethisch orientierte Gemeindearbeit im Industriegebiet. Munich, West Germany: Kaiser. Re: church and labor issues and practical theology. Bibliography.

16722. Schrock, Dan and Gary Martin. (1983) Mennonites in the City: Developing Urban Churches. [123 2x2 slides and script]. Newton, KS: Prepared for Bethlehem '83 workshops.

16723. Schultz, Joseph P. and Carla L. Klausner. (1983) "Rabbi Simon Glazer and the Quest for Jewish Community in Kansas City, 1920-1923," American Jewish Archives. Vol. 35, No. 1 (April), pp. 13-16.

16724. Schweickart, David. (1983) "Is There an Answer to Plant Closings?" New Catholic World [Thematic issue: Religion and the Economy]. Vol. 226, No. 1354 (July), pp. 180-183.

16725. Senn, Frank C. (1983) Christian Worship and Its Cultural Setting. Philadelphia, PA: Fortress. Reviewed: Currents in Theology and Mission, Vol. 11 (October, 1984), p. 314. Worship, Vol. 58 (November, 1984), p. 560. Lutheran Forum, Vol. 18, No. 3 (1984), p. 216.

16726. Serjeant, R. B. and R. Lewcock. (1983) San'Ã': An Arabian Islamic City. London: World of Islam Festival Trust.

16727. Shaffir, William. (1983) "Hassidic Jews and Quebec Politics," Jewish Journal of Sociology. Vol. 25, No. 2 (December), pp. 105-119. Jewish reactions to French being declared the official language of Quebec.

16728. Sharp, John. (1983) "Second Deliverance," Christian Herald. Vol. 106, No. 11 (December), pp. 34-35.

16729. Sheffield, Walter R. (1983) "Bring Them In," Alliance Witness. Vol. 118, No. 20 (October 12), pp. 24-25. Youth, described as "young warriors for Christ," come to New York City to spend a short time "teaching" poor children, then retreat. The article deals as much with the trips to and from the city as with what was done there.

16730. Sheppard, David, bp. (1983) Bias to the Poor. London: Hodder and Stoughton. God is biased toward the poor, yet society heaps the burden of unemployment and disadvantage unequally on the poor. The church should reflect God's bias. Reviewed: Churchman, Vol. 97, No. 2 (1984) p. 183. Modern Churchman, ns Vol. 26, No. 3 (1984), p. 61.

16731. Shoaf, Mary Eve. (1983) An Inquiry into the Relationship of Ecumenism to Church Architecture and the Ecclesiastical Arts in The United States during the Twentieth Century: A Formal Analysis and Comparison of Three Selected Works. Thesis (Ph. D.). Athens, OH: Ohio University.

16732. Shonis, Anthony. (1983) "The Hoboken Experience," Priest. Vol. 39, No. 12 (December), pp. 6-7.

16733. Shorter, Aylward. (1983) White Fathers--Urban Pastoral Project. Tabora, Tanzania: s.n. [See note 3].

16734. Shorter, Aylward. (1983) "The Interaction of Town and Country: Apostolates in East Africa. AFER: African Ecclesial Review. Vol. 25, No. 6 (December), pp. 362-368. A summary of a larger (135 page) report on missionary urban commitment. Shorter visited 13 urban parishes in two East African countries and seven specialized urban apostolates.

16735. Shriver, Donald W., Jr. (1983) "To Repair Ruined Cities," The Witness [Ambler, PA]. Vol. 66, No. 4 (April), pp. 10-14.

16736. Shumsky, Neil L. and Timothy Crimmins, eds. (1983) Urban America: A Historical Bibliography. Santa Barbara, California: ABC-Clio Information Services, Inc.

16737. Simmons, Paul D. (1983) "The Practice of Urban Ministry: Relating to Issues through Social Action," Review and Expositor. Vol. 80, No. 4 (Fall), pp. 529-536. Also, "A Postscript to the Practice of Urban Ministry," pp. 537-541.

16738. Simon, Rita J. and Melaine Brooks. (1983) "Soviet Jewish Immigrants' Adjustment in Four US Cities," Journal of Jewish Communal Service. Vol. 60, No. 1 (Fall), pp. 56-64.

16739. Sly, Julie. (1983) "Church Seeks to Heal Pain of Inner City," National Catholic Register. Vol. 59 (October 2), pp. 1+.

16740. Small, Sarah Leah. (1983) Attitudes of Professional and Lay Leaders of Congregations in a Major Metropolitan Jewish Community, Chicago, toward the Employment of Women as Administrators of Congregational Religious Schools (Illinois). Thesis (Ph. D.). Kansas City, MO: University of Missouri.

16741. Smith, Austin. (1983) Passion for the Inner City: A Personal View. London: Sheed and Ward. A Roman Catholic priest working in Liverpool writes about pastoral involvement with some of England's most needy people. The book portrays his efforts to live and suffer with the people of "Liverpool 8."

16742. Smith, Fred. (1983) "Growth through Evangelism in Lima, Peru," Urban Mission. Vol. 1, No. 1 (September), pp. 19-28.

16743. Smith, Luther E. (1983) "Community: The Partnership of Freedom and Responsibility," pp. 23-31 in Henry J. Yopung, ed. God and Human Freedom: A Festschrift in Honor of Howard Thurman. Richmond, IN: Friends United Press.

16744. Snyder, Howard A. (1983) Liberating the Church: The Ecology of Church and Kingdom. Downers Grove, IL: InterVarsity.

16745. Soukaros, George James. (1983) A Study of the Interpersonal Methods Employed by Baptist Urban Missionaries towards the Winning and Development of Spiritual Converts and the Establishment of Neighborhood Churches in the City of Boston. Thesis (Ed. D.). Boston, MA: Boston University.

16746. Statnick, Roger Andrew. (1983) Dorothy Day's Religious Conversation: A Study in Biographical Theology. Thesis (Ph. D.). Notre Dame, IN: University of Notre Dame.

16747. Steger, Gerhard. (1983) Marx kontra Christus? die Entwicklung der Katholischen Arbeiterjugend Osterreichs 1946 bis 1980. Vienna, Austria: Osterreichischer Bundesverlag. Re: a history of communism and Christianity among youth in Austria. A revision of the author's doctoral dissertation. Bibliography.

16748. Steinbruck, John F. (1983) "The Church as Hospice," Liturgy. Vol. 3, No. 4 (Fall), pp. 77-83. Luther Place Memorial Church in Washington, DC, develops a comprehensive outreach program to the neighborhood with hospitality as the principal motif, including: medicine, shelter, clothing, counseling, and food.

16749. Stockwell, Clinton E. (1983) "Sociological Interpretations of the New Testament Are Boon to Urban Pastoral Education: Part 1," Cities. Vol. 3, No. 2 (Fall), pp. 30-33.

16750. Stockwell, Clinton E. (1983, 1984) "Christian Witness in the City: An Annotated Bibliography" [in 2 parts], TSF Bulletin. Vol. 7, No. 2 (November), pp. 17-19 and Vol. 7, No. 3 (January, 1984), pp. 20-22.

16751. Stockwell, Clinton E. (1983) A Selected Annotated Bibliography for Urban Ministries. Chicago, IL: Urban Church Resource Center, SCUPE.

16752. Sweetser, Thomas P. (1983) Successful Parishes: How They Meet the Challenge of Change. Minneapolis, MN: Winston Press.

16753. Takayama, K. Peter. (1983) "The Decline of the 1960s Religious 'Justice' Movement Organizations," Unpublished, presented at annual meeting of the Society for the Study of Religion. Knoxville, Tennessee.

16754. Tamney, Joseph B. and Stephen D. Johnson. (1983) "The Moral Majority in Middletown," Journal for the Scientific Study of Religion. Vol. 22, No. 2 (June), pp. 145-157. A study in Muncie, IN, the Lynd's Middletown (1929, 1937), attributes the extent of persuasion toward the "moral majority" to the influence of religious television, to the fundamentalist stress on preserving the status-quo, and to the general influence of the Christian Right perspective. Bibliography.

16755. Tao Fong Shan Ecumenical Center. (beginning in 1983) Bridge: Church Life in China Today. Hong Kong: the Center. A periodical regarding churches in Hong Kong and in some Mainland China cities. News articles are included. The journal is intended to serve as a bridge among the Chinese peoples.

16756. Thistlethwaite, Susan Brooks. (1983) Metaphors for the Contemporary Church. New York: Pilgrim. Thistlethwaite identifies and describes the metaphors functioning in church life regarding ministry, mission and the church itself. Reviewed: Chicago Theological Seminary Register, Vol. 74 (Winter, 1984), p. 45. Christian Century, Vol. 101 (April 11, 1984), p. 376.

16757. Thomas, J. Mark. (1983) "Pillaging Winthrop's 'City upon the Hill,'" Christianity and Crisis. Vol. 43, No. 7 (May 7), pp. 154+.

16758. Thung, Mady A. (1983) "From Pillarization to New Religious Pluralism: A Social Science Congress on Religion and Politics, Amsterdam, 1983," Social Compass. Vol. 30, No. 4, pp. 503-524.

16759. Tonn, Milan. (1983) Inner City Ministry [Videorecording]. Ft. Wayne, IN: Concordia Theological Seminary.

16760. Tranvouez, Yvon. (1983) "Résistance au pouvoir dans le catholicisme: La Quinzaine face à l'ACA (1952-1954)," Archives de Sciences Sociales des Religions. Vol. 28, No. 1, pp. 5-35. Re: worker priests and laborers' views of the Catholic church.

16761. Turner, Brian. (1983) "Suburban Ministry in South London and Canberra: Some Comparisons and Reflections," St. Mark's Review [Thematic issue]. No. 114 (June), pp. 25-27.

16762. Uertz, Rudolf, ed. (1983) Kirche und Wirtschaft. [Fachkonferenz der Politischen Akademie der Konrad-Adenauer-Stiftung]. Melle, West Germany: E. Knoth. Re: the church and economics.

16763. Umansky, Ellen M. (1983) Lily Montagu and the Advancement of Liberal Judaism: From Vision to Vocation. New York: Edwin Mellen. A critical biography of the founder of the liberal Judaism movement in Great Britain and of the World Union of Progressive Judaism.

16764. "Urban Ministry." (1983) [Pp. 1295-1297 in] The Brethren Encyclopedia. Philadelphia, PA: The Brethren Encyclopedia, Inc. The bibliography lists Church of the Brethren articles about cities and rescue missions from the late 19th century forward.

16765. Urban Mission. (1983-forward) Philadelphia, PA: Westminster Theological Seminary. Published by the Westminster Theological Seminary, this journal publishes popular articles with a scholarly basis, case studies, book reviews, and news items of interest to urban ministers. Although Westminister is committed to a conservative Calvinist stance, the articles reflect a broad range of evangelical perspectives on city issues. Roger Greenway was the first editor.

16766. Vallin, Pierre. (1983) Le travail et les travailledurs dans le monde chrétien. Paris: Desclee. A history of work and workers in the

Christian world. Bibliography.

16767. Vanderstel, David G. (1983) The Dutch of Grand Rapids, Michigan, 1849-1900: Immigrant Neighborhood and Community Development in a Nineteenth Century City. Thesis (Ph. D.). Kent, OH: Kent State University.

16768. Vaught, Bonny. (1983) "A South Bronx Ministry: Symbol and Reality," Christian Century. Vol. 100, No. 20 (June 22-29), pp. 616-618. Re: St. Peter's Lutheran Church, Bronx, New York City.

16769. Villalba, Angela. (1983) "Stories from the Urban Rural Mission (URM) Room," International Review of Mission. Vol. 72, No. 288 (October), pp. 614-615.

16770. Vincent, John J. (1983) "Towards an Urban Theology," New Blackfriars. Vol. 64, No. 751 (January), pp. 4-17.

16771. Vorster, W. S., ed. (1983) Church and Industry: Proceedings of the Seventh Symposium of the Institute for Theological Research (UNISA) held at the University of South Africa, September 7-8, 1983. Pretoria, South Africa: University of South Africa. Bibliography.

16772. Vree, Dale. (1983) "A Radical Holiness: On the Catholic Worker's Fiftieth Anniversary," Commonweal. Vol. 110, No. 9 (May 6), pp. 266-269.

16773. Wald, Kenneth D. and Michael B. Lupfer. (1983) "Religion and Political Attitudes in the Urban South," pp. 84-100 in Tod A. Baker, et al., ed. Religion and Politics in the South. New York: Praeger.

16774. Walrath, Douglas A. (1983) New Possibilities for Small Churches. New York: Pilgrim Press.

16775. Wasdell, David. (1983) A Profile of Havering Road Methodist Church. London: Urban Church Project. A case study of a congregation located in the North East London District of the Methodist Church.

16776. "'Weatherization Ministry' Helps People Save." (1983) The Witness [Ambler, PA]. Vol. 66, No. 4 (April), pp. 16-17. Reprint of article in Cities Magazine, (July), 1982.

16777. Webber, George Williams. (1983) "New York Theological Seminary: Seeking the Shalom of the City," pp. 192-203 in F. Ross Kinsler, ed. The Ministry by the People: Theological Education by Extension. Geneva, Switzerland: World Council of Churches, and Maryknoll, NY: Orbis.

16778. Weber, Herbert F. (1983) The Parish Help Book: A Guide to Social Ministry in the Parish. Notre Dame, IN: Ave Maria Press. Weber offer practical suggestions for starting social ministries in local churches.

16779. Weisbrot, Robert. (1983) Father Divine and the Struggle for Racial Equality. Urbana: University of Illinois Press. Reviewed: American Historical Review, Vol. 89 (April, 1984), p. 542. Journal of Ecumenical Studies, Vol. 20 (Fall, 1983), p. 669.

16780. Welch, Kevin W. (1983) "Community Development and Metropolitan Religious Commitment: A Test of Two Competing Models," Journal for the Scientific Study of Religion. Vol. 22, No. 2 (June), pp. 167-181. Welch shows the importance of migration rates in predicting urban church participation. Cities in the Mountain and Pacific states have substantially lower membership rates than do other regions of the USA. Bibliography.

16781. Wheatley, Paul. (1983) Nagara and Commandery: Origins of Southeast Asian Urban Traditions. Chicago, IL: University of Chicago Press. Re: Southeast Asian urbanisim and Asian approaches to different varieties of urbanism. The role of religion is emphasized.

16782. White, Jerry. (1983) The Church and the Parachurch. Portland, OR: Multnomah Press. Reviewed: International Bulletin of Missionary Research, Vol. 8 (July, 1984), p. 135.

16783. Wilber, Charles K. and Kenneth P. Jameson. (1983) An Inquiry into the Poverty of Economics. Notre Dame, IN: University of Notre Dame Press.

16784. Williams, Melvin D. (1983) "The Conflict of Corporate Church and Spiritual Community," pp. 55-67 in Carl S. Dudley, ed. Building an Effective Ministry. New York: Harper and Row.

16785. Willimon, William H. (1983) "A Labor Day Reflection in the Work Ethic," The Christian Century. Vol. 100, No. 25 (August 31), pp. 776-778.

16786. Wilmore, Gayraud S. (1983) Black Religion and Black Radicalism: An Interpretation of the Religious History of Afro-American People. Revised Edition. Maryknoll, NY: Orbis Books. A history textbook on the Black church and Black religion from the religion of the slave to Black power.

16787. Wilmore, Gayraud S. (1983) Black and Presbyterian: The Heritage and the Hope. Philadelphia, PA: Published for Black Presbyterians United by Geneva Press. Reviewed: Theology Today, Vol. 41 (October, 1984), p. 372. Church History, Vol. 53 (December, 1984), p. 564.

16788. Wolterstorff, Nicholas. (1983) Until Justice and Peace Embrace: The Kuyper Lectures for 1981, Delivered at the Free University of Amsterdam. Kampen, Netherlands: Uitgiversmaatschappijj, J. H. Koh. Also: Grand Rapids, MI: Eerdmans, 1983. An orthodox Christian addresses the grievances of the world's poor, dealing with the political and social justice vision of shalom. Chapter 6 is titled "A City of Delight."

16789. Wong, Joseph. (1983) "Why Plant an Ethnic Church?" About Face. Vol. 5, No. 5.

16790. World at Your Doorstep: A Consultation on Reaching Ethnics for Christ. (1983) Wheaton, IL: National Association of Evangelicals Evangelism and Home Missions Association, Ramada Inn, Des Plains, IL, November 16-18, 1983. Several reports exist from workshops held at this meeting.

16791. World Council of Churches. (1983) Violence, Nonviolence, and Civil Conflict. Geneva, Switzerland: the Council. Also: a French edition. Two reports, one prepared in 1973 and the other in 1983, review the continuing debate about the role of violence and nonviolence in the struggle for social justice. A pamphlet.

16792. World Council of Churches, Commission on the Churches' Participation in Development. (1983) Churches and the Transnational Corporations: An Ecumenical Programme. Geneva, Switzerland: World Council of Churches.

16793. Worley, Robert C. (1983) A Gathering of Strangers: Understanding the Life of Your Church. Philadelphia, PA: Westminster Press. Worley offers suggestions on how to find unity amid the diversity of goals, gifts and expectations people bring to their church. The solution lies in a renewed appreciation for the ministry of administration and its adaptation to changing environments.

16794. The Worship Songbook: Church in the City. (1983) [Waco, TX]: Star Song, distributed by Word Books.

16795. Yacoob, May Mirza. (1983) Ahmadiyya and Urbanization: Migrant Women in Abidjan. Boston, MA: African Studies Center, Boston University. A pamphlet.

16796. Young Men's Christian Association World Communique. (beginning in 1983) Quarterly of the World Alliance of YMCAs. Geneva, Switzerland: World Alliance of YMCAs. A periodical.

16797. "Young People in African Towns: Their Pastoral Care." (1983) Spearhead. Vol. 79, pp. 1-82.

16798. Yu, Suk-Chong. (1983) An Inclusive Church: Korean Ministry at the Fern Hill United Methodist Church. Thesis (D. Min). Claremont, CA: School of Theology at Claremont.

16799. Yule, Sandy. (1983) "The City as Wilderness," St. Mark's Review [Thematic issue]. No. 114 (June), pp. 2-6.

16800. Zoppetti, Leighsa. (1983) "The Single Parent and Unemployment," New Catholic World [Thematic issue: Religion and the Economy]. Vol. 226, No. 1354 (July), pp. 166-169.

16801. Zorazim, Josef. (1983) Israeli Families in New York City: Utilization of Social Services, Unmet Needs, and Policy Implications. Thesis (Ph. D.). New York: Columbia University School of Social Work.

16802. Addy, Tony [Anthony J.] and Alan Gawith. (1984) Christian Social Concern: Two Contemporary Issues. Manchester, England: William Temple Foundation. At the time of writing, Addy was Director of the William Temple Foundation and Gawith was Secretary of the Board ofSocial Responsibility, Manchester Diocese, Church of England.

16803. Agnew, John A., John Mercer, and David E. Sopher, eds. (1984) The City in Cultural Context. Boston, MA: Allen and Unwin.

16804. Aleman, Louis T. (1984) "Vocation in a Post-Vocational Age," Word and World: Theology for Christian Ministry [Thematic issue: Vocation]. Vol. 4, No. 2 (Spring), pp. 131-140.

16805. Alexander, June Granatir. (1984) "The Laity in the Church: Slovaks and the Catholic Church in Pre-World War I Pittsburgh," Church History. Vol. 53, No. 3 (September), pp. 363-378. Reprinted: Dolores Liptak, ed. A Church of Many Cultures. New York: Garland, 1988. A historical survey, documented with bibliographic footnotes.

16806. Allgood, B. Dexter. (1984) A Study of Selected Black Gospel Choirs in the Metropolitan New York Area. Thesis (Ph. D.). New York: New York University.

16807. Amerson, Philip A. (1984) "Ministry on the Urban Frontier," pp. 83-94 in David Frenchak, et al., eds. Signs of the Kingdom in the Secular City. Chicago, IL: Covenant Press.

16808. Amerson, Philip A., Raymond J. Bakke, Howard Snyder and Clinton E. Stockwell. (1984) "Urban Evangelism and Evangelization: An Annotated Bibliography," Urban Mission. Vol. 1, No. 5 (May), pp. 26-37.

16809. Ancel, Alfred, bp. (1984) Le mouvement ouvrier. Saint-Etienne, France: Essor. Re: the Catholic Church and the labor movement in France.

16810. Anderson, Digby C., ed. (1984) The Kindness that Kills: The Churches' Simplistic Response to Complex Social Issues. London: SPCK. A critique of the Social Gospel and left-leaning economic policies advocated by many church leaders. Reviewed: Theology. Vol. 88 (July, 1985), p. 321.

16811. André-Gallego, José. (1984) Pensamiento y acción social de la Iglesia en España. Madrid, Spain: Espasa-Calpe. Re: the Catholic Church and social problems in Spain. Bibliography.

16812. Andrews, Dee. (1984) "The African Methodists of Philadelphia, 1794-1802," Pennsylvania Magazine of History and Biography. Vol. 108, No. 4 (October), pp. 471-486.

16813. Ansari, Hamied N. (1984) "The Islamic Militants on Egyptian Politics," International Journal of Middle East Studies. Vol. 16, No. 1, pp. 123-144. Ansari interprets Islamic militancy, albeit confined to the margins of urban society, as a by-product of rapid urbanization and rural-urban migration.

16814. Anthony, Everett and Cline W. Borders. (1984) "The Association: Churches Reaching All People," Church Administration. Vol. 26, No. 6 (March), pp. 6-10.

16815. Anzenbacher, Arno. (1984) "Arbeitslosigkeit und Arbeit," Internationale Katholische Zeitschrift "Communio." Vol. 13 (March), pp. 124-134. Re: unemployment and the encyclical of John Paul II.

16816. Arias, Mortimer, bp. (1984) "Simeon and Anna Sodalities: A Challenge to Churches in Transition," Missiology. Vol. 12, No. 1 (January), pp. 97-101.

16817. Arias, Mortimer, bp. (1984) Announcing the Reign of God: Evangelization and the Subversive Memory of Jesus. Philadelphia, PA: Fortress Press. Reviewed: Theology Today, Vol. 42 (July, 1985), p. 270.

16818. Armstrong, Richard Stoll. (1984) The Pastor as Evangelist. Philadelphia, PA: Westminster Press.

16819. Ashby, LeRoy. (1984) Saving the Waifs: Reformers and Dependent Children, 1890-1917. Philadelphia, PA: Temple University Press.

16820. Ata, A. W. (1984) "The Impact of Westernization and Other Factors on the Changing Status of Moslem Women," Eastern Anthropologist. Vol. 37, No. 2, pp. 95-126. Factors influencing the status of Muslim women include Westernization, industrialization and urbanization.

16821. Bachelder, Robert S. (1984) "The Gospel of Equality and the Gospel of Efficiency," The Christian Century. Vol. 101, No. 12 (April 11), pp. 368-370. Pulpit and pew differ on economic vision. Clergy want a fair distribution of wealth while laity, at least the business leaders who are laity, want the creation of new wealth. Bachelder, pastor at First Congregational UCC, Shrewsbury, MA, proposes that both production of new wealth and fairness in distribution are essential values for the economy, and neither can stand alone.

16822. Badcock, Blair. (1984) Unfairly Structured Cities. Oxford, England: Basil Blackwell. Badcock presents an analysis of the interplay of capital, state, and class interests as they affect city formation in the United Kingdom, the USA and Australia. He describes how governments use urban space with the result being inequality of income for urban dwellers and offers suggestions about how groups of residents can sometimes change the distribution of real urban income by overriding the effects of government and business decisions. He criticizes urban geographers for being trapped in the epistemology, method, and value assumptions of logical positivism, which for geographers means empirical spatial analysis. Although the book does not deal with churches or religion, many of its implications are relevant for and cited by researchers in religion. For example, Badcock observes: "The notion of education for 'life without work' will not only change the nature of schooling, but it must force educational planners radically to alter the place of school facilities in the ... urban setting" (p. 338). Why not also for churches? Extensive bibliography.

16823. Baer, Hans A. (1984) The Black Spiritual Movement: A Religious Response to Racism. Knoxville, TN: University of Tennessee Press. Reviewed: Journal for the Scientific Study of Religion, Vol. 24, June, 1985, p. 225.

16824. Bakke, Raymond J. (1984) "The City and the Scriptures," Christianity Today. Vol. 28, No. 9 (June 15), pp. 14-18. Bakke outlines an approach to biblical theology for urban ministry and identifies the role of Biblical teaching in cities.

16825. Bakke, Raymond J. (1984) "Urban Evangelization: A Lausanne Strategy Since 1980," International Bulletin of Missionary Research. Vol. 8, No. 4 (October), pp. 149-154. Same title: Journal of the Academy for Evangelism in Theological Education. Vol. 1 (1985), pp. 9-21.

16826. Bakke, Raymond J. (1984) Seminar on Latfricasian Urban Evangelism/Church Planting. Cedar Grove, NJ: SIMI International.

16827. Baldock, N. (1984) "Le ministère en milieu urbain," Pro Mundi Vita, Ministères et Communautés. Vol. 39, pp. 9-11. [See note 3]. Ministry in the urban environment.

16828. Barbour, Claude Marie. (1984) "Seeking Justice and Shalom in the City," International Review of Mission. Vol. 73, No. 291 (July), pp. 303-309. Shalom Ministries, Chicago, is interested in urban and international ministries of justice and peace. The founder of this program discusses the importance of four basic theological strategies: mission in reverse, basic Christian communities, contextualization, and bridge building.

16829. Barna, George. (1984) Vital Signs: Emerging Social Trends and the Future of American Christianity. Westchester, IL:

Crossway Books.

16830. Barthold, Stan and Mary Barthold. (1984) "Japan Apartment House Evangelism: Case Study," Urban Mission. Vol. 2, No. 1 (September), pp. 44-46.

16831. Beckford, James A. (1984) "Religious Organization: A Survey of Some Recent Publications," Archives de sciences sociales de religion. Vol. 29, No. 57/1 (January-March), pp. 83-102. Bibliography.

16832. Beecham, Noel Oscar. (1984) Developing a Program of Ministry to the Aging Members of the Metropolitan United Methodist Church, Pomonkey, Maryland. Thesis (D. Min.). Madison, NJ: Drew University.

16833. Belury, William R. (1984) Creating an Independent [Mexican] Episcopal Congregation in the Neighborhood of an Existing [Anglo] Episcopal Parish. Thesis (D. Min.). Forth Worth, TX: Brite Divinity School.

16834. Berckman, Edward M. (1984) "Ministering to the 'New Poor,'" Witness [Ambler, PA]. Vol. 67, No. 6 (June), pp. 21-23. Career consultant M. Kenney engages in church work with the unemployed.

16835. Bergsma, Paul. (1984) "Case Study: Holistic Ministry in Honduras," Urban Mission. Vol. 1, No. 3 (January), pp. 40-42.

16836. Berkowitz, Bill. (1984) Community Dreams: Ideas for Enriching Neighborhood and Community. San Luis Obispo, CA: Impact Press. Berkowitz offers suggestions about how people can envision a better community.

16837. Bestard, Joan. (1984) "Desafíos de la nueva realidad urbana a la parroquia," Sal Terrae (Santander). Vol. 72, No. 9, pp. 655-674. Challenges of the new urban reality to the parish.

16838. Bird, Warren. (1984) "Just How Urban Minded Is the Alliance?" Alliance Witness. Vol. 119, No. 25 (December 24), pp. 24-25.

16839. Bishop, Bryan. (1984) "The Fireside Paved Over: For Duncan Angami, the Village Has Disappeared," World Christian. Vol. 3, No. 1 (January), pp. 24-25.

16840. Bloomquist, Karen L. (1984) "The Unemployed: Challenge to the Church," Currents in Theology and Mission. Vol. 11, No.

1 (February), pp. 34-37. Bloomquist suggests ways to minister to the unemployed who have lost their identity, worth and power.

16841. Bodner, John E. (1984) An Ethnic Bibliography of Pennsylvania History. Harrisburg, PA: Pennsylvania Historical and Museum Commission.

16842. Boff, Leonardo and Virgil Elizondo, eds. (1984) The People of God Amidst the Poor. Edinburgh, Scotland: T. and T. Clark.

16843. Bourg, Carroll J. (1984) "Religion in the City of Man," Sociological Analysis. Vol. 45, No. 2 (Summer), pp. 99-106.

16844. Boyte, Harry C. (1984) Community Is Possible: Repairing America's Roots. New York: Harper and Row.

16845. Bradley, J. C. (1984) "An Association Is What the Churches Make It," Church Administration. Vol. 26, No. 6 (March), pp. 11-14.

16846. Bradley, J. C. (1984) A Baptist Association. Nashville, TN: Convention Press.

16847. Brakelmann, Günter, et al. (1984) Ökonomie und Ethik: Die Herausforderung der Arbeitslosigkeit. Frankfurt am Main, West Germany: Haag Herchen. Re: economics, ethics, and the challenge of unemployment.

16848. Brodsky, Harold. (1984) "Anti-Urbanism in the Bible: A Critique," Urbanism Past and Present. Vol. 9, No. 1 (Winter), pp. 36-39.

16849. Bronkema, Fred. (1984) "Corporate Responsibility and the Church," JSAC Grapevine. Vol. 16, No. 1 (June), pp. [1-5].

16850. Brown, Robert McAfee. (1984) Unexpected News: Reading the Bible with Third World Eyes. Philadelphia, PA: Westminster Press.

16851. Brumm, Anne Marie. (1984) "Death, Poetry and the City," Zeitschrift für Religions- und Geistesgeschichte. Vol. 36, No. 4, pp. 346-360. Brumm interprets the nature of the poet's encounter with the city in the 20th century. She concludes that poets (e.g., Sanburg, Rilke, Lorca) were concerned with the threat of the city to the natural life cycle. Death, often alone without the comfort of friends or religion, is a recurrent theme in 20th century poetry about the city.

16852. Burnett, Scott and Bryan Bishop. (1984) "A Home in the City: Native Christian Fellowship Fulfills Needs of Indians in Vancouver," World Christian. Vol. 3, No. 1 (January-February), pp. 20-25.

16853. Burr, Angela. (1984) "The Relationship between Muslim Peasant Religion and Urban Religion in Songkhla," Asian Folklore Studies. Vol. 43, No. 1, pp. 71-83.

16854. Byrne, Kevin. (1984) "New Patterns of Urban Ministry," Clergy Review. Vol. 69, No. 1 (January), pp. 31-33.

16855. Calian, Carnegie Samuel. (1984) "Between Recession and Recovery," Theology Today. Vol. 41, No. 1 (April), pp. 47-50.

16856. Canty, Donald. (1984) "Interview: Urban Black Churches and Foreign Missions," Urban Mission. Vol. 1, No. 3 (January), pp. 36-39.

16857. Caplan, Lionel. (1984) "Bridegroom Price in Urban India:" Class, Caste and 'Dowry Evil' among Christians in Madras," Man. n.s. No. 19, pp. 216-233.

16858. Carey, George. (1984) The Church in the Market Place. Eastbourne, England: Kingsway.

16859. Carney, Glandion. (1984) Creative Urban Youth Ministry: A Resource for Leaders of Young People. Cincinnati, OH: Standard. Motivation and practical suggestions for evangelical approaches to urban youth work, especially among the poor. Bibliography.

16860. Carney, Glandion. (1984) "Evangelistic Crusades in Inner Cities, II," pp. 451-454 in J. D. Douglas, ed. The Work of an Evangelist: International Conference for Itinerant Evangelists, Amsterdam, The Netherlands. Minneapolis, MN: World-Wide Publications.

16861. Carson, Clayborne, Jr. (1984) "Blacks and Jews in the Civil Rights Movement," pp. 113-131 in Joseph R. Washington, Jr., ed. Jews in Black Perspective. Carnbury, NJ: Associated University Presses.

16862. Casterline, Gail Farr. (1984) "St. Joseph's and St. Mary's: The Origins of Catholic Hospitals in Philadelphia," Pennsylvania Magazine of History and Biography. Vol. 108, No. 3 (July), pp. 289-314. Reprinted: Brian Mitchell, ed. Building the American Catholic

City. New York: Garland, 1988.

16863. Cavanaugh, John, et al. (1984) "Conglomerates: Where the Product is Profit," Engage/Social Action [Thematic issue]. Vol. 12, No. 10 (November), pp. 9-42.

16864. Cavenaugh, Gerald E. (1984) "Employment and Unemployment," New Catholic World [Thematic Issue: the Economy]. Vol. 227, No. 1360 (July-August), pp. 161-163.

16865. Cavenaugh, Thomas E. and Lorn S. Foster. (1984) Jesse Jackson's Campaign: The Primaries and Caucuses, Election '84. Washington, DC: Joint Center for Political Studies.

16866. Chapman, Terry S., Mary L. Lai, and Elmer L. Steinbock. (1984) Am I Covered For--? A Guide to Insurance for Nonprofit Organizations. [San Jose, CA]: [Consortium for Human Services].

16867. Charley, Julian W. (1984) Pastoral Support for the Unemployed. Bramcote, England: Grove Booklet No. 19. A pamphlet.

16868. Cho, Paul Yonggi. (1984) More Than Numbers. Waco, TX: Word.

16869. Cho, Paul Yonggi. (1984) "Reaching Cities with Home Cells," Urban Mission. Vol. 1, No. 3 (January), pp. 4-14.

16870. Cho, Sung-Whan. (1984) Personal and Spiritual Growth of a Korean-American Congregation. Thesis (D. Min.). Madison, NJ: Drew University.

16871. "The Church in Economic Affairs: The Policies of the Presbyterian Church, USA, 1930-1980." (1984) Church and Society. Vol. 74, No. 4 (March-April), pp. 82-102.

16872. Church of England, Diocese of Sheffield Social Responsibility Committee. (1984) The Church in the Mining Communities. Sheffield, England: Diocese of Sheffield. A judicatory study describes industrial disputes and recommends that the church adopt strategies of action, worship, prayer, education, and efforts to make the church "an island of peace."

16873. "Claiming Turf in Hispanic Chicago." (1984) Eternity. Vol. 35, No. 6 (June), p. 25.

16874. Clasper, Paul. (1984) "The Persistence of Religious 'Man' in an Urbanized World," Ching Feng. Vol. 27, No. 4 (December), pp. 209-216.

16875. Clayton, Paul Clark. (1984) Peter, Paul, and Mary's Son: Church, Mission and Context, Their Interrealtionship and Its Effect on Ministry. Thesis (D. Min.). Newton Center, MA: Andover Newton Theological School.

16876. Cliquet, Maurice. (1984) Sillons: 50 ans d'action pour la justice sociale. Paris: Editions Témoignage Chrétien. Fifty years of action for social justice--Jeunesse ouvrière chrétienne (Young Christian Workers).

16877. Clouse, Robert G., ed. (1984) Wealth and Poverty: Four Christian Views of Economics. Downers Grove, IL: InterVarsity.

16878. Cochran, Robert Dennis. (1984) A Study of the Development of New Congregations among Southern Baptists in Selected Metropolitan Areas Since 1970. Thesis (Ph. D.). Louisville, KY: Southern Baptist Theological Seminary.

16879. Compa, Lance. (1984) "Conglomerates: Spearheading New Anti-Labor Offensive," Engage/Social Action. Vol. 12, No. 10 (November), pp. 19-25.

16880. Cone, James H. (1984) For My People: Black Theology and the Black Church. Maryknoll, NY: Orbis Books. A description of the emergence of multifaceted Black theology in the United States. Reviewed: Journal of Theology for Southern Africa, No. 51 (June, 1985), p. 84. Encounter, Vol. 446 (Spring, 1985), p. 187. Journal of Religious Thought, Vol. 42 (Spring-Summer, 1985), p. 88. Bibliography.

16881. Conn, Harvie M. (1984) "The Kingdom of God, Its Advance, and the City," Urban Mission. Vol. 1, No. 5 (May), pp. 16-25.

16882. Conn, Harvie M. (1984) "Sin in the City: The Privatization Myth," Evangelical Journal. Vol. 2, No. 2, pp. 51-65. Conn discusses anti-urban images many North Americans have of the city and the neglect of the city by evangelicals since the influx of non-White and non-Protestant people. He lays blame on the privatization myth, with its individualist notions of sin and salvation, and suggests steps toward demythologizing privatizaton.

16883. Conn, Harvie M. (1984) "The Rural-Urban Myth and World Mission," Reformed Review. Vol. 37, No. 3 (Spring), pp. 125-136. Conn refutes all claims that the Bible supports the notion that the rural, pastoral world is the ideal and that the city is synonymous with evil. He analyzes the roots of American anti-urbanism and urges evangelicals toward urban mission.

16884. Conn, Harvie M. (1984) "The City: The New Frontier," Evangelical Missions Quarterly. Vol. 29, No. 4 (October), pp. 395-398.

16885. Conn, Harvie M. (1984) "Sin City?" Eternity. Vol. 35, No. 6 (June), pp. 16-19.

16886. Conn, Harvie M. (1984) Eternal Word and Changing Worlds: Theology, Anthropology, and Mission in Trialog. Grand Rapids, MI: Zondervan. Reviewed: Calvin Theological Journal, Vol. 20, April, 1985, p. 139.

16887. Conn, Harvie M., ed. (1984) Reaching the Unreached: The Old-New Challenge. Phillipsburg, NJ: Presbyterian and Reformed.

16888. Conn, Harvie M. (1984) Evangelism: Doing Justice and Preaching Grace. Grand Rapids, MI: Zondervan.

16889. Conn, Harvie M. and Samuel F. Rowen. (1984) Missions and Theological Education in World Perspective. Farmington, MI: Association Urbanus.

16890. Conn, Harvie M. and Clinton Stockwell. (1984) Justice and Urban Ministry: A Bibliography of Philosophical and Theological Resources. Chicago, IL: Urban Church Resource Center, Seminary Consortium for Urban Pastoral Education.

16891. Coote, Robert T., ed. (1984) The Gospel and Urbanization: A Workbook/Reader for Participants in a Seminar Held, April 22-26, 1985. Ventnor, NJ: Overseas Ministries Study Center. Photocopied articles about the church and urbanization. For discussion see individual listing of the articles as per original publication. See especially the article by Allan Boesak. Bibliography.

16892. Costas, Orlando E. (1984) "Evangelizing an Awakening Giant: Hispanics in the US," pp. 55-64 in David Frenchak, et al., eds. Signs of the Kingdom in the Secular City. Chicago, IL: Covenant Press.

16893. Costello, George. (1984) Without Fear or Favor: George Higgins on the Record. Mystic, CT: 23rd Publications. Biography of Higgins, champion against the evils of discrimination, intolerence, poverty, antisemitism, violation of human rights and workers' rights and war.

16894. Courtney, Tom, et al. (1984) The Effective Non-Profit Executive Handbook. San Francisco, CA: Public Management Institute.

16895. Cox, Harvey G. (1984) "Religion in the Secular City: A Symposium," Christianity and Crisis. Vol. 44, No. 2 (February 20), pp. 35-45.

16896. Cox, Harvey G. (1984) "Response to Commentators," Sociological Analysis. Vol. 45, No. 2 (Summer), pp. 107-114.

16897. Cox, Harvey G. (1984) Religion in the Secular City: Towards a Post-Modern Theology. New York: Simon and Schuster. Written 20 years after Cox's essay tited: The Secular City, this re-xamination of religion and politics in the postmodern world does not reject the author's earlier hypotheses about secularization, but rather interprets secularization as one important stage in 20th century religious history. Chiding those who would deny the importance of liberal thought on secularization, Cox concludes, "No one can move beyond the secular city who has not first passed through it" (p. 268). Reviewed: Journal for the Scientific Study of Religion, Vol. 24 (June, 1985), p. 222. Review of Religious Research, Vol. 27 (September, 1985), p. 92. Fundamentalist Journal, Vol. 3, No. 11 (December, 1984), p. 53. Southwestern Journal of Theology, Vol. 27, No. 2 (Spring, 1985), p. 66.

16898. Crawley, Winston. (1984) "Urbanization and Christian Ministry in World History," pp. 37-50 in Larry L Rose and C. Kirk Hadway, eds. An Urban World. Nashville, TN: Broadman Press.

16899. Crichton, Iain. (1984) "The History of the 'Black Muslim' Movement in America," Urban Mission. Vol. 1, No. 5 (May), pp. 5-15.

16900. Crunden, Robert M. (1984) Ministers of Reform: The Progressives' Achievement in American Civilization, 1889-1920. Urbana, IL: University of Illinois Press.

16901. Dale, Robert D. (1984) Ministers as Leaders. Nashville, TN: Broadman.

16902. Dale, Robert D. (1984) Surviving Difficult Church Members. Nashville, TN: Abingdon Press.

16903. Dannenbaum, Jed. (1984) Drink and Disorder: Temperance Reform in Cincinnati from the Washingtonian Revival to the WCTU. Urbana, IL: University of Illinois Press.

16904. Dannowski, H. W. (1984) "Kirche in dieser Stadt, zu einer Gesamtkonzeption kirchlicher Arbeit in der Großstadt," Theologia Practica. Vol. 19, pp. 186-192. Dannowski develops a comprehensive approach to city church work.

16905. Day, Dorothy. (1984) Little by Little, the Selected Writings of Dorothy Day. New York: Knopf.

16906. Dearnley, Pat. (1984) "Church Life in the Inner City," Shaft. Vol. 41, pp. 13-16.

16907. Dehn, Ulrich. (1984) "Kampf um volle Menschlichkeit: Theologie der Befreiung in Indien?" Zeitschrift für Mission. Vol. 10, No. 1, pp. 26-34. Re: liberation theology in India.

16908. Delooz, Pierre. (1984) "Prisons," Pro Mundi Vita Dossiers: Europe-North American Edition. Vol. 26, pp. 2-43.

16909. Delooz, Pierre. (1984) "Pastoral Care for Supercities," Pro Mundi Vita Bulletin--English Edition. Bulletin 99, No. 4, pp. 29-52. Catholic churches challenged by the rapid growth of the "super cities" must adapt to accomplish their mission. Racism and exclusivism must be overcome if the church is to cope the future. Views of thologians working in rapidly growing cities are reviewd.

16910. Deutsch, Wilhelm Otto. (1984) Ghetto and Diaspora: The Ministry of a Black Gathered Inner City Church to the Community. Thesis (D. Min.). Washington, DC: Wesley Theological Seminary.

16911. "Developing to Preserve." (1984) Engineering News-Record. Vol. 212 (May 31), pp. 34+. Re: a mixed use plan and a historic church in Stamford, CT.

16912. Digan, Parig. (1984) Churches in Contestation: Asian Christian Social Protest. Maryknoll, NY: Orbis. Reviewed: Ching Feng, Vol. 27, No. 4 (1984), p. 241. Journal of Ecumenical Studies, Vol. 21 (Fall, 1984), p. 786. Sociological Analysis, Vol. 46 (Spring, 1985), p.

77. An analysis of Asian churches' responses to social conditions.

16913. Dilling, Yvonne. (1984) In Search of Refuge. Scottdale, PA: Herald Press.

16914. Dillon, David. (1984) "The Episcopal City Mission: A Voice for the Voiceless," pp. 28-45 in Mark J. Duffy, ed. Episcopal Diocese of Massachusetts, 1784-1984. [Boston, MA]: Episcopal Diocese of Massachusetts.

16915. Dobbelaere, Karel. (1984) "Secularization Theories and Sociological Paradigms: Convergences and Divergences," Social Compass. Vol. 31, Nos. 2-3, pp. 199-219. Bibliography.

16916. Domini, May L. (1984) Ethical Investing. Reading, MA: Addison-Wesley. Bibliography.

16917. Dowley, Roger, comp. (1984) Towards the Recovery of a Lost Bequest: A Layman's Work-Notes on the Biblical Pattern for a Just Community. London: Evangelical Coalition for Urban Mission. A pamphlet.

16918. Downs, David William. (1984) The Use of the "Baptist Faith and Message," 1963-1983: A Response to Pluralism in the Southern Baptist Convention. Thesis (Ph. D.). Louisville, KY: Southern Baptist Theological Seminary.

16919. Droel, William. (1984) The Christian and the Work Place: A Selected Bibliography. Chicago, IL: Urban Church Resource Center, Seminary Consortium for Urban Pastoral Education (SCUPE).

16920. Droel, William. (1984) "Work and Faith: A Report on the National Center for the Laity," Cities. Vol. 4, No. 1 (Winter), p. 7.

16921. DuBose, Francis M. (1984) "Cities Aren't All Alike," Urban Mission. Vol. 1, No. 3 (January), pp. 15-23. Lists implications for missionary work in differing types of cities.

16922. DuBose, Francis M. (1984) "Urban Poverty as a World Challenge," pp. 51-74 in Larry L. Rose and C. Kirk Hadway, eds. An Urban World. Nashville, TN: Broadman Press.

16923. Duce, Alan R. (1984) "First Aid in Pastoral Care: Pastoral Care of Prisoners and Delinquents," Expository Times. Vol. 95, No. 9 (June), pp. 260-264.

16924. Dyson, David. (1984) "Comments from a Labor Perspective," Church and Society. Vol. 74, No. 4 (March-April), pp. 141-144.

16925. Eckbald, Eric. (1984) "Tips for Urban Church Planters," Urban Mission. Vol. 1, No. 3 (January), pp. 24-29.

16926. Eller, Jim, et al., eds. (1984) A Handbook for Urban Congregations. Boston, MA: Unitarian Universalist Association, Urban Church Coalition. In response to the decline in most and death of some Unitarian Universalist urban congregations, the Urban Church Coalition offers a loose-leaf handbook with administrative strategies for: church growth, worship and celebration, leadership and organization, research and data collection, community involvement, urban-suburban relationships, buildings and grounds, finances, and communication. Bibliography.

16927. Erdmann, Judith Klein. (1984) "The Gospel Is Alive and Well and Living in the South Bronx," The Christian Century. Vol. 101, No. 39 (December 12), pp. 1173-1175. Lutherans in the Bronx cooperate in a program called the Planning Association of Bronx Lutheran Churches for the purpose of initiating food programs for the poor, sponsoring concert choirs, supporting parish schools, and encouraging connectedness among Lutheran churches. Their cooperative planning anticipates a future in which poverty will get worse.

16928. Etling, Mark G. (1984) "The Call to Freedom: Salvation in the City," Priest. Vol. 40, No. 12 (December), pp. 36-41.

16929. Evangel Temple Inner City Pastors Conference. (1984) Evangel Temple Inner City Pastors Conference [Materials]. Washington, DC: Evangel Temple.

16930. Evangelische Kirche in Deutschland. (1984) Menschengerechte Stadt: Aufforderung zur humanen und okologischen Stadterrung. Gutersloh, Germany: G. Mohn. Re: urban renewal and urban ecology in Germany cities.

16931. Ezekiel, Raphael S. (1984) Voices from the Corner: Poverty and Racism in the Inner City. Philadelphia, PA: Temple University Press.

16932. Fahlbusch, Wilhelm. (1984) Evangelische Kirche und Arbeiterschaft. Hannover, West Germany: Lutherhaus Verlag. Protestant church work and the laboring classes.

16933. Finestead, David Ray. (1984) The United Methodist Senior Minister's Role. Thesis (D. Min.). Chicago, IL: Christ Seminary--Seminex.

16934. Finks, P. David. (1984) The Radical Vision of Saul Alinsky. New York: Paulist Press. A biographical history of Alinsky, with particular attention to his relationship with the Archdiocese of Chicago and the FIGHT organization in Rochester, NY.

16935. Finnell, David L. (1984) A Computerized Church and Community Research Model. Thesis (Ed. D.) Fort Worth, TX: Southwestern Baptist Theological Seminary.

16936. Fischer, Clare B. (1984) "Liberating Work," pp. 117-140 in Judith L. Weidman, ed. Christian Feminism: Visions of a New Humanity. San Francisco, CA: Harper and Row.

16937. Freeman, Harry. (1984) Collingwood Coke. Melbourne, Australia: Spectrum Publications. Re: a Methodist city mission in Collingwood, Australia.

16938. Frenchak, David, Clinton Stockwell and Helen Ujvarosy, comp. and ed. (1984) Signs of the Kingdom in the Secular City. Chicago, IL: Covenant Press. Articles published here were collected from those presented at the second Urban Congress sponsored by SCUPE. In addition to those reprinted here, most of the speeches delivered at the Congress are preserved on audio tapes.

16939. Friffioen, Donald J. (1984) Open Windows and Open Doors: Open to Renewal and Growth. Grand Rapids, MI: Christian Reformed Board of Evangelism of Greater Grand Rapids.

16940. Fryman, Jeleta. (1984) "Alexandria: Signs of Hope," World Christian Magazine. Vol. 3, No. 17 [i.e., No. 6] (November-December), pp. 17-23.

16941. Fuller, George C. (1984) "Guest Editorial: A Circle of Ministry" Urban Mission. Vol. 2, No. 1 (September), pp. 3-4.

16942. Fustero, Steven. (1984) "Home on the Street," Psychology Today. Vol. 18, No. 2 (February), pp. 56-63.

16943. Fütterer, Klaus. (1984) Streit um die Arbeit: Industriegesellschaft am Scheideweg. Stuttgart, West Germany: Kreuz. Church work and the problems of laborers.

16944. Gable, Dennis R. (1984) "Contact: A Telephone Ministry That Makes a Difference," New World Outlook. n.s. Vol. 44, No. 6 (February), pp. 14-17. Gable, at the time of writing, was an executive for CONTACT Teleministries.

16945. Gallup, George, Jr. (1984) Religion in America: The Gallup Report. Report No. 222. Princeton, NJ: Princeton Religion Research Center. A major resource for monitoring changes in religious attitudes and practices. Editions exist for other years. Questionnaire.

16946. Galush, William. (1984) "Both Polish and Cathoplic: Immigrant Clergy in the American Church," Catholic Historical Review. Vol. 70, pp. 407-427. Reprinted: Dolores A. Liptak, ed. A Church of Many Cultures. New York: Garland, 1988.

16947. Gartner, Lloyd P. (1984) The Great Jewish Migration, 1881-1914. Cape Town, South Africa: Kaplan Center, Jewish Studies and Research.

16948. Gerard, Karen. (1984) American Survivors. San Diego, CA: Harcourt Brace Jovanovich. The mildly acerbic personal reflections of a woman who served as Deputy Mayor for Economic Policy and Development in New York City, this book presents a perspective on such diverse urban issues as jobs, business location decisions, gentrification, graffiti, historic preservation, taxpayer revolts, the ethics of people who work for the government, technology, housing, middle-aged baby boomers, immigrants, crime, poverty, and the role of women in the city. Highly readable.

16949. Gibbs, Mark. (1984) "Vocation, Work and Work for Pay," Word and World: Theology for Christian Ministry [Thematic issue: Vocation]. Vol. 4, No. 2 (Spring), pp. 126-130.

16950. Gibson, Jo. (1984) "An Experiment at Woodberry Down," pp. 34-49 in James Barnett, ed. Theology at 16+. London: Epworth Press.

16951. Gillett, Richard W. (1984) "Revolution in the Workplace," The Witness [Ambler, PA]. Vol. 67, No. 11 (November), pp. 16-18.

16952. Glazer, Nathan. (1984) "Jews and Blacks: What Happened to the Grand Alliance?" pp. 105-112 in Joseph R. Washington, Jr., ed. Jews in Black Perspective. Cranbury, NJ: Associated University Presses.

16953. The Gods Must Be Crazy. (1984) Hollywood, CA: Twentieth Century Fox. [Also available in video cassette]. A comedy based on the presumed effects of technology on primitive people. A soda bottle drops from a passing airplane, leading its primitive discoverers to conclude that the gods must be crazy.

16954. Gonzalez Nieves, Roberto Octavio. (1984) Ecological, Ethnic and Cultural Factors of Church Practice in an Urban Roman Catholic Church. Thesis (Ph. D.). New York: Fordham University.

16955. Good, Robert W. (1984) Forty Years on Diamond Street. Philadelphia, PA: the author. [Location: Mennonite Historical Society, Lancaster, PA]. Re: the Diamond Street Mennonite Church, Philadelphia, PA.

16956. Gordon, David F. (1984) "The Role of the Social Context in Social Movement Accommodation: A Case Study of Two Jesus People Groups," Journal for the Scientific Study of Religion. Vol. 23, No. 4 (December), pp. 381-395. Gordon's study shows differences in accommodation of social movement groups in city and suburban settings (the two Jesus People groups). The city group resisted accommodation to its environment while the suburban group became relatively less aggressive toward its environment, a finding that is attributable to the local social context -- membership and leadership base, tangible resources, symbolic environment, values of members, perceptions of local needs, potential responses to various tactics, and the efficiency of various tactics in local situations. Bibliography.

16957. Goslin, Thomas S. (1984) The Church Without Walls. Pasadena, CA: Hope Publishing.

16958. Greathouse, Gordon. (1984) "Historical Turbulence of Scudder, Spofford Years," The Witness [Ambler, PA]. Vol. 67, No. 7 (July), pp. 14-18. Re: Vida Dutton Scudder (1861-1954) and William B. Spofford, both leaders in the Christian socialist movement in the Episcopal Church. Spofford was editor of The Witness from 1919 to 1967.

16959. Greene, Thomas R. (1984) "Catholic Thought and World War II Labor Legislation," Records of the American Catholic Historical Society of Philadelphia. Vol. 95, No. 1, pp. 37-55. Catholics sought to moderate the US Government's weakening support for labor during the war.

16960. Greenstein, Robert and Gordon Adams. (1984) End Results: The Impact of Federal Policies since 1980 on Low Income Americans. Washington, DC: Interfaith Action for Economic Justice, Center for Budget and Policy Priorities. Interfaith Action produced several research reports similar to this one.

16961. Greenway, Roger S. (1984) "Let These Women Go!! Prostitution and the Church," Urban Mission. Vol. 1, No. 4 (March), pp. 17-25.

16962. Greenway, Roger S. (1984) "The Homeless on Our Streets: How Can the Church Minister to Them?" Urban Mission. Vol. 2, No. 1 (September), pp. 44-46.

16963. Greenway, Roger S. (1984) "Reaching Apartment Dwellers," Urban Mission. Vol. 1, No. 4 (March), pp. 2-3.

16964. Griffiths, Brian. (1984) The Creation of Wealth. London: Hodder and Stoughton. A case for capitalism from a religious perspective.

16965. Grigg, Viv. (1984) Companion to the Poor. Sutherland, Australia: Albatross Books. Also: Sydney: Lion Publishers. Based on his experience in Asian cities, particularly Manila, Grigg develops a theology and praxis for "establishing the Kingdom in the slums." He finds that the missionary movement has largely ignored the migration of third world rural people to the "mega-cities." Grigg has lived in the shanties of Manila slums, and more recently of Calcutta, in order to identify with the condition of the poor and to minister to their spiritual and physical needs. Combining theologies of incarnation and the Kingdom, he calls Christian workers to live with the poor and to stop treating them as objects of pity and charity.

16966. Gross, Robert. (1984) "A History of Brethren Criminal Justice," Brethren Life and Thought. Vol. 29, No. 1 (Winter), pp. 32-34. Brethren Criminal Justice, an agency created in 1975, offers workshops and publishes materials intended to inform members of the Church of the Brethren about criminal justice and to encourage their informed involvement in prison ministry.

16967. Gross, Robert. (1984) "Crime Is a Peace Issue: A New Call to Justice Making," Brethren Life and Thought. Vol. 29, No. 1 (Winter), pp. 43-48. Brethren, Mennonites, and Quakers need to apply their peace stance to prisons and the criminal justice system. Peace churches need to expose the violence of the prison system and to lead the way toward reconciliation, restoration, and restitution through non-violence.

16968. Gruner, LeRoy. (1984) "Heroin, Hashish, and Hallelujah: The Search for Meaning," Review of Religious Research. Vol. 26, No. 2 (December), pp. 176-186. Gruner describes ministry with teenage drug abusers and compares the success rates of religious and secular agencies working with them. Particular attention is given to the Teen Challenge Centers which were started in Brooklyn, NY, by David Wilkerson. These centers report a particularly high success rate.

16969. Guest, Avery M. and R. S. Oropesa. (1984) "Problem Solving Strategies of Local Areas in the Metropolis," American Sociological Review, Vol. 49, No. 6 (December), pp. 828-840.

16970. Gutman, Herbert. (1984) "Parallels in Urban Experience," pp. 98-104 in Joseph R. Washington, Jr., ed. Jews in Black Perspective. Cranbury, NJ: Associated University Presses.

16971. Hadaway, C. Kirk. (1984) "Religious Involvement and Drug Use among Urban Adolescents," Journal for the Scientific Study of Religion. Vol. 23, No. 2 (June), pp. 109-128. Interviews of 600 adolescents attending public school in Atlanta, Georgia, are used to examine the relationship between religious involvement and drug/alcohol use. After controlling for other important influences, religiosity of the respondents and their parents is shown to have a significant deterring effect on alcohol and drug use as well as on attitudes opposed to drug use. The importance of religion as a predictor variable differs according to the substance involved, reflecting the degree to which the church speaks alone against drug/alcohol use or together with other sources of social control. As religiosity increases, deviance does not necessarily decrease. The respondents' friends use of drugs/alcohol is shown to be the strongest encouragement for the respondents to do the same. Bibliography.

16972. Hadaway, C. Kirk, David G. Hackett, and James Fogle Miller. (1984) "The Most Segregated Institution: Correlates of Interracial Church Participation," Review of Religious Research. Vol. 25, No. 3 (March), pp. 204-219. A secondary analysis of NORC data is employed to challenge the often repeated statement that Sunday worship is "the most segregated hour." Most urban church attenders, especially those in the northeast and far western areas of the USA, are found to attend worship with at least some people of a race different from their own.

16973. Haider, Gulzar. (1984) "Habitat and Values in Islam: A Conceptual Formulation of an Islamic City," pp. 170-208 in Ziauddin Sardar, ed. The Touch of Midas: Science, Values, and Environment in

Islam and the West. Manchester, England: Manchester University Press.

16974. Haines, John F. (1984) "Reaching Muslims in French Cities," Urban Mission. Vol. 2, No. 2 (September), pp. 20-32.

16975. Hales, Peter B. (1984) Silver Cities: The Photography of American Urbanization, 1839-1915. Philadelphia, PA: Temple University Press. Bibliography.

16976. Hall, Leda McIntyre. (1984) Urban Change Agents in the Third Sector: A Case Study of the United Methodist Church in Detroit. Thesis (Ph. D.). Detroit, MI: Wayne State University.

16977. Hallett, Stanley J. (1984) "To Build a City," pp. 3-7 in David Frenchak, et al., eds. Signs of the Kingdom in the Secular City. Chicago, IL: Covenant Press.

16978. Halper, Jeff. (1984) "On the Way: The Transition of Jerusalem from a Ritual to a Colonial City," Urban Anthropology. Vol. 13, No. 1 (Spring), pp. 1-32.

16979. Harmsel, Henrietta. (1984) "Looking to the Holy City," The Reformed Journal. Vol. 34, No. 11 (November), p. 6.

16980. Harrison, D. Tommy. (1984) Training a Task Force to Develop a Plan to Discover, Reclaim, and Minister to Inactive Church Members in an Urban Setting. Thesis (D. Min.). Fort Worth, TX: Southwestern Baptist Theological Seminary.

16981. Hartley, Loyde H. (1984) Understanding Church Finances. New York: Pilgrim Press. Using survey data and case studies, Hartley analyzes the financial condition of local churches. Most of the case studies are of urban churches. The study was funded by the Lilly Endowment. Bibliography. Questionnaire.

16982. Hegy, Pierre. (1984) "Harvey Cox and La Sociologie Engagée," Sociological Analysis. Vol. 45, No. 2 (Summer), pp. 91-98.

16983. Heifetz, Julie Ann. (1984) The Role of the Clergy at the Vietnamese Buddhist Temple in Los Angeles as Culture Brokers in Vietnamese Refugee Resettlement. Ann Arbor, MI: University Microfilms International.

16984. Heinecken, Martin J. (1984) "When Work Is Over," Word and World: Theology for Christian Ministry [Thematic issue: Vocation]. Vol. 4, No. 2 (Spring), pp. 165-172.

16985. Hendricks, Charles E. (1984) Tremont Temple Baptist Church: A Historical and Projective Study of Its Ministry of Pastoral Care. Thesis (D. Min.). Newton Center, MA: Andover Newton Theological School.

16986. Henry, David B. (1984) "The Jesus Gang: Learnings from the Encounter of a Traditional Sunday School with the Children of the City," pp. 15-30 in Perry Lefevre and W. Widick Schroeder, eds. Spiritual Nurture. Chicago, IL: Exploration Press.

16987. Herman, Nancy J. (1984) "Conflict in the Church: A Social Network Analysis of an Anglican Congregation," Journal for the Scientific Study of Religion. Vol. 23, No. 1 (March), pp. 60-74. Congregational networks are identified in a conflicted Anglican congregation of 40 members. Bibliography.

16988. Heutgren, Arland J. (1984) "Working and Ministry," Word and World: Theology for Christian Ministry [Thematic issue: Vocation]. Vol. 4, No. 2 (Spring), pp. 115-117.

16989. Hiebert, Paul G. (1984) "Barrett and Beyond," Evangelical Missions Quarterly. Vol. 12, No. 1 (January), pp. 63-68.

16990. Hirschfield, Robert. (1984) "Exploiting the Shopping-Bag Ladies," The Christian Century. Vol. 101, No. 17 (May 16), p. 508. Two workers in a Catholic shelter for the homeless are dismayed to find the likenesses of two women, both bag ladies, imprinted on T-shirts in a Minneapolis shopping mall. They act to stop production and to recall unsold shirts.

16991. Hoffmann, Ingeborg. (1984) "Gemeinde" in Gemeinde: Ein Phänomen in der Sozialstruktur des Wohnviertels. Frankfurt am Main, West Germany: Peter Lang. Hoffmann has written several works on specialized ministries, this one on church work with apartment dwellers. Other essays deal with ministry with the sick and handicapped.

16992. Holden, Tony. (1984) People, Churches and Multiracial Projects: An Account of English Methodism's Response to Plural Britain. London: The Methodist Church, Division of Social Responsibility. Re: The British Methodist Church's accommodation to ethnic, cultural and faith pluralism, with quotations for inner city people.

Holden is a minister at Bow Mission in London's West End. Bibliographical notes.

16993. Holland, Joe. (1984) "Transforming the World Economy: The Crisis of Progress and the Priority of Labor," pp. 285-315 in John W. Houck and Oliver F. Williams, eds. Catholic Social Teaching. Washington, DC: University Press of America.

16994. Hollenbach, David. (1984) "Unemployment and Jobs: A Theological and Ethical Perspective," pp. 110-138 in John W. Houck and Oliver F. Williams, eds. Catholic Social Teaching. Washington, DC: University Press of America.

16995. Holthaus, H. Lee. (1984) "The Union Rescue Mission of Los Angeles," Urban Mission. Vol. 2, No. 2 (November), pp. 5-14.

16996. Holthaus, H. Lee. (1984) "Changing Lives Since 1891: The Union Rescue Mission of Los Angeles," Urban Mission. Vol. 2, No. 2 (November), pp. 5-14.

16997. "The Homeless." (1984) JSAC Grapevine. Vol. 16, No. 5 (November), pp. [1-8].

16998. Hope, Anne, Sally Timmel, and C. Hodzi. (1984) Training for Transformation. Zimbabwe: Mambo Press. A training program based on the philosophy of Paulo Freire.

16999. Hope, Marjorie and James Young. (1984) "The Homeless: On the Street, On the Road," Christian Century. Vol. 101, No. 2 (January 18), pp. 48-52. Two sociologists identify the "new poor" and contrast their circumstances with the skid-row myth. The new homeless, unlike the derelicts, tend to be evicted families, mentally disabled, abused spouses and children, elderly single people, drug addicts, and alcoholics. Church efforts at providing shelter are described.

17000. Hopewell, James F. (1984) The Whole Church Catalog. Washington, DC: The Alban Institute. Loose leaf descriptions of instruments and devices used by consultants attempting to understand and alter corporate behavior in congregations comprise this book. Hopewell offers suggestions on how to select tools in terms of their intended objectives and expected outcomes.

17001. Hopewell, James F. (1984) "A Congregational Paradigm for Theological Education," Theological Education. Vol. 21, No. 1 (Autumn), pp. 60-70.

17002. Houck, John W. (1984) "Human Work and Employment Generation," pp. 23-35 in John W. Houck and Oliver F. Williams, eds. Catholic Social Teaching and the United States Economy: Working Papers for a Bishops' Pastoral. Washington, DC: University Press of America.

17003. Hoyt, Michael and Mary Ellen Schoonmaker. (1984) "Laborers in the Vineyard: BGM/UMC vs UAW," Christianity and Crisis. Vol. 44, No. 2 (February 20), pp. 32-34.

17004. Huston, Sterling W. (1984) "Crusade Preparation for Large Cities in North America," pp. 319-326 in J. D. Douglas, ed. The Work of an Evangelist: International Conference for Itinerant Evangelists, Amsterdam, The Netherlands. Minneapolis, MN: World-Wide Publications. Huston describes preparations for a Billy Graham crusade.

17005. Hyer, Marjorie. (1984) "The Storefront Church: Sanctuaries of Worship in Born-Again Places," Washington Post. (July 21), p. 86. Re: a photographic exhibit of the work of Perry Letson, Jr., displayed in the Martin Luther King Library.

17006. Jackson, P. (1984) "Social Disorganization and Moral Order in the City," Transactions, Institute of British Geographers. Vol. 9, pp. 168-180. [See Note 3].

17007. Jacobs, Jane. (1984) Cities and the Wealth of Nations. New York: Random House. Jacobs, in her iconoclastic diagnosis of decay in cities, dismisses virtually all economic theories of the past in the first chapter of this book: they fail to anticipate or explain stagflation. She concludes economic stability can be achieved only by cities becoming (again) the basic economic entities, replacing the economic role of nation states. Her vision is one of cities achieving wealth principally through the strategy of import substitution, i.e., replacing goods the cities once imported with goods they make for themselves. Cities with poor economies should seek to work with other backward cities rather than trying to import economic wealth from the rich cities, which she contends almost always leads to disaster. The poor are better at solving their problems than the rich are at helping them. Jacobs deals with the issue of monetary control, over which cities must have major influence if any degree of self-reliance is to be achieved, but does not treat the socio/political problem of migration control which her critics contend is equally germane to the import substitution strategy. Excerpts appeared in The Atlantic, Vol. 253, No. 3 (March, 1984), pp. 41-66.

17008. Jacquart, Joanne. (1984) End of the Line: The Story of

Chaplain Max Jones. Dallas, TX: American Evangelistic Association, International Prison Ministry.

17009. James, Eric, ed. (1984) "Urban Training: A Plea for Priority," Christian Action Journal. (Autumn), [entire Issue].

17010. James, Samuel M. (1984) "Training for Urban Evangelism," pp. 51-74 in Larry L. Rose and C. Kirk Hadway, eds. An Urban World. Nashville, TN: Broadman Press.

17011. Jenkins, Keith. (1984) The Closed Door: A Christian Critique of Britain's Immigration Policies. London: British Council of Churches.

17012. John Paul II, Pope (Karol Wojtyla). (1984) "Address to Members of the Plenary Session of the Sacred Congregation for the Clergy Stressing the Importance of Local Parishes." Rome: the Vatican.

17013. Johnson, Benton. (1984) "Continuity and Quest in the Work of Harvey Cox," Sociological Analysis. Vol. 45, No. 2 (Summer), pp. 79-84.

17014. Jones, Chris. (1984) "Racism or Xenophobia or Cultural Incompatibility? Muslim Migrant Workers in the Federal Republic of Germany and West Europe," Migration Today [World Council of Churches]. No. 33, pp. 4-6. [Excerpts from a longer article]. Re: the resurgence of racism and responses of the church, with particular reference to Muslim migrants.

17015. Kaldor, Peter. (1984) A Gulf Too Deep? The Protestant Churches and the Urban Working Class in Australia. [Sydney, Australia?]: Board of Mission, The Uniting Church in NSW. A pamphlet.

17016. Kang, Wi Jo. (1984) "The Background of the US Immigration Policy toward Asians: Implications for the Urban Church Today," pp. 75-82 in David Frenchak, et al., eds. Signs of the Kingdom in the Secular City. Chicago, IL: Covenant Press.

17017. Kelley, Allen and Jeffrey G. Williamson. (1984) What Drives Third World Cities' Growth? Princeton, NJ: Princeton University Press.

17018. Kiernan, J. P. (1984) "A Cesspool of Sorcery: How [Zulu] Zionists Visualize and Respond to the City," Urban Anthropology. Vol.

13, Nos. 2-3 (Summer-Fall), pp. 219-236. For Zulu Zionists, sorcery is the most common cause of poverty and ill health. In a township near Durban, they level the accusation of sorcery at outsiders and at the city as a whole, but not at persons within their group.

17019. King, William M. (1984) "Hugh Price Hughes and the British Social Gospel," Journal of Religious History. Vol. 13, No. 1 (June), pp. 66-82.

17020. Kinney, Terry D. (1984) Liberation Theology in a North American Urban Setting. Thesis (D. Min.). San Anselmo, CA: San Francisco Theological Seminary.

17021. Kistler, Robert C. (1984) Adventists and Labor Unions in the United States. Hagerstown, MD: Review and Herald Publishing Association. Bibliography.

17022. Klopfenstein, Gordon, et al. (1984) "A Local Church Works for Criminal Justice," Brethren Life and Thought. Vol. 29, No. 1 (Winter), pp. 55-58. Ministries of the Beacon Heights Church of the Brethren in Fort Wayne, IN, involve counseling, evangelistic work, and support ministries with offenders and ex-offenders.

17023. Knight, John E. N. (1984) Parish Revitalization through Small Groups: A Case Study of Centre United Methodist Church in Malden, Massachusetts. Thesis (D. Min.). Boston, MA: Boston University School of Theology.

17024. Korean Church Industrial Mission. (1984) The Labor Scene and Witness ... in Commemoration of the 25th Anniversary Celebration of the Korean Church Industrial Mission. Seoul, Korea: Pool-pit Publishing Company. Text in Korean.

17025. Krass, Alfred C. (1984) "The Loneliness of a Long Distance Runner: The Laity in Urban Mission," The Other Side. Vol. 20, No. 9 (September), pp. 48-49.

17026. Kritzinger, J. J. (1984) "Missiological and Ethical Aspects of Black Urbanization in South Africa: A Historical View," Theologia Evangelica. No. 1 (March), pp. 31-39.

17027. Lachmann, Werner. (1984) Die Krise der Arbeitsgesellschaft: Chancen und Grenzen christlicher Verantwortung. Wuppertal, West Germany: Brockhaus. The crisis of the laboring classes, and the opportunities and limits of Christian responsibility.

17028. Lau, Lawson. (1984) The World at Your Doorstep: A Handbook for International Student Ministry. Downers Grove, IL: InterVarsity Press. Re: church work with foreign students.

17029. Leas, Speed. (1984) The Development of Conflict in a Local Church. Atlanta, GA: Home Mission Board, Southern Baptist Convention, Occasional Paper No. 8. Leas summarizes his views on the positive and negative effects of conflict in churches, and includes suggestions for conflict management strategy. A schematic diagram helps groups decide which conflicts are insignificant and which are threatening and require management.

17030. Leas, Speed.. (1984) Discover Your Conflict Management Style. Washington, DC: Alban Institute. An instrument for use in coping with church controversies.

17031. Lee, Barrett A., R. S. Oropesa, Barbara J. Metch and Avery M. Guest. (1984) "Testing the Decline-of-Community Thesis: Neighborhood Organizations in Seattle, 1929 and 1979," American Journal of Sociology. Vol. 89, No. 5 (March), pp. 1161-1188.

17032. Leech, Kenneth and Terry Drummond, eds. (1984) Letters from Seven Churches Addressed to the Archbishop's Commission on Urban Priority Areas. London: Jubilee Group. Personal testimony of priests and lay people collected for the inquiry conducted by the Archbishop's Commission. A pamphlet.

17033. Lehmann, Paul. (1984) "Harvey Cox, Martin Luther and a Macro-Sociological Appropriation of the Decalogue," Sociological Analysis. Vol. 45, No. 2 (Summer), pp. 85-90.

17034. Lightbody, C. Stuart. (1984) "New Christian Agency in Peru Helps Small Businessmen," Pulse. Vol. 19, No. 22 (November 21), pp. 3-4.

17035. Livingston, Paul L. (1984) The Inner City Church: Its Problems and Its Potential. Thesis (D. Min.). San Anselmo, CA: San Francisco Theological Seminary.

17036. Long, Grace Cumming. (1984) "The Marketing of Health Care," The Christian Century. Vol.101, No. 7 (February 29), pp. 222-224. Spiraling health care costs threaten the financial well-being of cities and the nation as well as that of families with seriously ill people. Health care is becoming less available to the poor.

17037. Loritts, Crawford W., Jr. (1984) "Evangelistic Crusades in Inner Cities, I," pp. 449-450 in J. D. Douglas, ed. The Work of an Evangelist: International Conference for Itinerant Evangelists, Amsterdam, The Netherlands. Minneapolis, MN: World-Wide Publications.

17038. Loux, Gordon D. (1984) A Plan for the Development of a Christian, Cross-Cultural Volunteer Program in Criminal Justice. Thesis (MS). Washington, DC: National College of Education.

17039. Luck, James Russell. (1984) The Determination of Ministry Priorities through an Analysis of the Franconia Baptist Church and Its Community. Thesis (D. Min). Louisville, KY: Southern Baptist Theological Seminary.

17040. Ludwig, Heiner and Franz Segbers, eds. (1984) Handbuch der Arbeiterpastoral. Mainz, West Germany: Matthias-Grünewald-Verlag. A handbook for pastoral work with laborers.

17041. Luecke, Richard H. (1984) "Faith, Work, and Economic Structures," Word and World: Theology for Christian Ministry [Thematic issue: Vocation]. Vol. 4, No. 2 (Spring), pp. 141-150. Re: historical precedents for church engagements with economic structures applierd to contemporary issues.

17042. Lumley, John Barry. (1984) "New Sounds on English Streets," Urban Mission. Vol. 1, No. 4 (March), pp. 26-28.

17043. Lupton, Robert D. (1984) "Walking in the Street," Urban Mission. Vol. 1, No. 4 (March), pp. 38-39.

17044. Lupton, Robert D. (1984) "Urban Perspectives: Invitation to Suffering," Urban Mission. Vol. 2, No. 2 (November), pp. 44-45.

17045. Lynch, Kevin. (1984) "Reconsidering 'The Image of the City,'" pp. 151-162 in R. M. Hollister and L. Rodwin, eds. Cities of the Mind. New York: Plenum.

17046. Madany, Bassam M. (1984) "The Forgotten Christians of the Middle East," Urban Mission. Vol. 1, No. 4 (March), pp. 4-9.

17047. Mahairas, T. (1984) "An Interview with Tom Mahairas," Fundamentalist Journal. Vol. 3, No. 1 (January), pp. 42-45.

17048. "Making the Hotel My Parish." (1984) Bridges. Vol. 1,

No. 2 (Fall), pp. 4-5.

17049. Maroney, Jimmy K., Ronald Hill, and David Finnell. (1984) "Urban Ministry in Third World Cities: Three Examples," pp. 117-146 in Larry L. Rose and C. Kirk Hadaway, eds. An Urban World. Nashville, TN: Broadman Press.

17050. Marsh, Clifton E. (1984) From Black Muslims to Muslims: The Transition from Separatism to Islam, 1930-1980. Metuchen, NJ: Scarecrow.

17051. Marsot, Afaf Lutfi al-Sayyid. (1984) "Religion or Opposition? Urban Protest Movements in Egypt," International Journal of Middle East Studies. Vol. 16, No. 4, pp. 541-552. A description of radical reform movements in the Middle East which use the Muslim idiom as a basis for their demands, a practice Marsot finds well rooted in Islamic tradition.

17052. Martí, Casmiro. (1984) L'eglésia de Barcelona (1850-1857): implantatacío social i dinamisme interns. Barcelona, Spain: Curial Edicions Catalanes. Text in Catalan with excerpts in Spanish. Two volumes. Bibliography.

17053. Marty, Martin E. (1984) Pilgrims in Their Own Land: 500 Years of Religion in America. Boston, MA: Little, Brown.

17054. Marx, Leo. (1984) "The Puzzle of Antiurbanism in Classic American Literature," pp. 163-180 in Lloyd Rodwin and Robert M. Hollister, eds. Cities of the Mind. London: Plenum Press.

17055. Máspero, Emilio. (1984) Importancia y significado de la enciclica sobre el trabajo humano del papa Juan Pablo II para el movimiento obrero latinamericano. Caracas, Venezuela: Central Latinoamericana de Trabajadores. Re: Pope John Paul II's encyclical Laborem exercens and church-labor relations in Latin America. Bibliography.

17056. Maust, John. (1984) Cities of Change: Urban Growth and God's People in Ten Latin American Cities. Coral Gables, FL: Latin American Mission.

17057. Maxwell, Milton A. (1984) The Alcoholics Anonymous Experience: A Close-Up View for Professionals. New York: McGraw-Hill. Bibliography.

17058. McBrien, Richard D. (1984) "American Economy: Some Ecclesiological Considerations," New Catholic World [Thematic Issue: the Economy]. Vol. 227, No. 1360 (July-August), pp. 164-167.

17059. McClung, Lloyd Grant. (1984) Readings in the Church Growth Dynamics of the Missionary Expansion of the Pentecostal Movement. Thesis (MTM). Pasadena, CA: Fuller Theological Seminary School of World Mission.

17060. McCormack, Arthur. (1984) "Megalopolis: A Demographic Approach," Pro Mundi Vita Bulletin--English Edition. Bulletin 99, No. 4, pp. 2-28.

17061. McCoy, Charles S. (1984) Organizations as Moral Agents. [Paper delivered at the meeting of the American Academy of Religion in Chicago, December 10, 1984]. [Location: General Theological Seminary, New York].

17062. McFadden, Dwight J. (1984) "An Anabaptist Theological Perspective on Economic Growth," pp. 45-54 in David Frenchak, et al., eds. Signs of the Kingdom in the Secular City. Chicago, IL: Covenant Press.

17063. McGuire, Malcolm. (1984) The Educational Interests and Needs of Older Adult Episcopalians in Selected Urban Parishes. Thesis (Ed. D.). Philadelphia, PA: Temple University.

17064. McLeod, Hugh. (1984) Religion and the Working Class in Nineteenth-Century Britain. London: Macmillan. McLeod, a church historian in the department of theology at the University of Birmingham, looks at the subject of working class religion and irreligion in 19th Century England, Scotland, and Wales. He sorts through the different conclusions historians have proposed regarding to the role of religion among the working class, especially regarding the rise of Methodism, working class political organizations, and the growth of religious indifference. McLeod stresses the critical nature of the class variable in British religion.

17065. McSwain, Larry L. (1984) "Christian Ethics and the Business Ethic," Review and Expositor. Vol. 81, No. 2 (Spring), pp. 197-209.

17066. Medhurst, Kenneth. (1984) The Church and Labour in Columbia. Manchester, England: Manchester University Press. Bibliography.

17067. Meyers, Patricia Ann. (1984) One Strategy for Inner City Mission and Ministry. Thesis (D. Min.). Dayton, OH: United Theological Seminary.

17068. Michael, Christine. (1984) Equipping Congregations for Urban Ministry. Thesis (D. Min.) Oak Brook, IL: Bethany Theological Seminary.

17069. Micksch, Jürgen. (1984) Mit Einwanderern leben: Positionen Evangelischer Ausländerarbeit. Frankfurt am Main: Otto Lembeck. Re: church work with immigrants and alien laborers.

17070. Mikesell, Milton L. (1984) A Planning Model for a Year's Ministry in the Local Church. Thesis (D. Min.). Pittsburgh, PA: Pittsburgh Theological Seminary. Recommended processes include reflection on the nature of the church's mission in light of social changes, a Mission Sunday to help formulate a statement of mission, and a planning retreat.

17071. Mitcham, Carl and Jim Grote. (1984) Theology and Technology: Essays in Christian Analysis and Exegisis. Lanham, MD: University Press of America. An outgrowth of a symposium organized by the authors for the Society of Philosophy and Technology, augmented by several additional papers. Large annotated bibliography.

17072. Mitchell, Rudy. (1984) "Evangelism in the City," Urban Mission. Vol. 1, No. 3 (January), pp. 30-35.

17073. Mitchell, Rudy and Eldin Villafañe. (1984) "Case Study: The Center for Urban Ministerial Education: Boston's Center for Urban T. E. E.," Urban Mission. Vol. 2, No. 2 (November), pp. 31-39.

17074. Morano, Roy W. (1984) The Protestant Challenge to Corporate America: Issues of Social Responsibility. Ann Arbor, MI: UMI Research Press. Revision of a thesis at New York University, 1982. Bibliography.

17075. Morris, Aldon D. (1984) The Origins of the Civil Rights Movement: Black Communities Organizing for Change. New York: Free Press. Attention is given to the formative role of Black urban churches during the years when Martin Luther King rose to national prominence. The study is based on interviews with civil rights leaders.

17076. Mouw, Richard. (1984) "A Reformed Theological Perspective on Politics," pp. 37-44 in David Frenchak, et al., eds. Signs of the

Kingdom in the Secular City. Chicago, IL: Covenant Press.

17077. Movimiento de Trabajadores Cristianos. (1984) El mundo de la clase obrera y el compromiso Cristiano. Lima, Perú: Centro de Estudios y Publicaciones. The world of the working class and Christian commitment.

17078. [Moyes, Gordon Keith M.] (1984) Mission On! The Story of the World's Most Amazing Mission. Sydney, Australia: Wesley Central Mission.

17079. Murphy, Denis, ed. (1984) Spirituality of Social Action: Answers of Christians in Asia to the Question, "Why Do You Work with the Poor?" Manila, Philippines: Office for Human Development, Federation of Asian Bishops Conference.

17080. Myers, K. (1984) "Establishing Advocates for Inner-City Philadelphia," Eternity. Vol. 35, No. 6 (June), p. 26.

17081. Myra, Harold. (1984) "The Glamorous Prostitute: The Myth of 'Happy Hookers' Enjoying Their Trade," Christianity Today. Vol. 28, No. 14 (October 5), pp. 14-19.

17082. Nam, Moon Hee. (1984) The Role of the Korean Immigrant Church for Korean Bilingual-Bicultural Education in the Los Angeles Area. Thesis (D. Min). Claremont, CA: School of Theology at Claremont.

17083. National Conference of Catholic Bishops. (1984) The Hispanic Presence, Challenge and Commitment: A Pastoral Letter on Hispanic Ministry. Washington, DC: United States Catholic Conference. The bishops adopt a statement describing socioeconomic conditions of Hispanics and specify urgent pastoral implications for liturgy, preaching, catechesis, vocations, education, youth work, ecumenism, etc.

17084. Nees, Tom. (1984) "In the Ghetto, Where Authentic Christianity Lives: A White Minister in Inner City Finds Hope as Well as Poverty," Christianity Today. Vol. 28, No. 3 (February 17), pp. 29-31. An interview.

17085. Neighbour, Ralph Webster, Jr. (1984) The Journey Continues: Survival Kit II. Nashville, TN: Convention Press. A packet of materials.

17086. Netting, F. Ellen. (1984) "Church-Related Agencies and

Social Welfare," Social Service Review. Vol. 58 (December), pp. 404-420.

17087. Nicholls, David. (1984) "William Temple and the Welfare State," Crucible. [Vol. 23, No. 4] (October-December), pp. 161-168.

17088. Niklaus, Robert. (1984) "Hong Kong: Familiarity Factor," Evangelical Missions Quarterly. Vol. 20, No. 4 (October), pp. 410-414.

17089. Niklaus, Robert. (1984) "Korea: The Prayer Way," Evangelical Missions Quarterly. Vol. 20, No. 4 (October), pp. 408-410.

17090. Notre Dame Study of Catholic Parish Life. (1984-1988) A Comprehensive Survey of Roman Catholic Parishes in the United States. Notre Dame, IN: University of Notre Dame. This inquiry produced fifteen reports, scheduled bi-monthly and issued irregularly, December 1984--December 1988.

17091. Novak, Michael. (1984) Freedom with Justice: Catholic Social Thought and Liberal Institutions. San Francisco, CA: Harper. A second edition: New Brunswick, NJ: Transaction, 1989.

17092. O'Connor, Thomas H. (1984) Fitzpatrick's Boston: 1846-1866: John Bernard Fitzpatrick, Third Bishop of Boston. Boston, MA: Northeastern University Press.

17093. Obidinski, Eugene. (1984) "Parochial School Foundations of Buffalo's Polonia," Urban Education. Vol. 18 (January), pp. 438-451. Reprinted: Brian Mitchell, ed. Building the American Catholic City. New York: Garland, 1988.

17094. Oines, Joel H. (1984) "Ministry to the Working Church," Word and World: Theology for Christian Ministry [Thematic issue: Vocation]. Vol. 4, No. 2 (Spring), pp. 118-125.

17095. Olivarez, Graciela [Grace]. (1984) "The Poor You Shall Always," New Catholic World [Thematic Issue: the Economy]. Vol. 227, No. 1360 (July-August), pp. 183-188.

17096. Olszamovski, Leon Marion. (1984) Maintaining Religious Identity: A Study of Formal Catechesis in the Byzantine Ruthenian Catholic Church in the United States of America. Thesis (Ph. D.). Washington, DC: Catholic University of America.

17097. Ortiz, Hector. (1984) Juvenile Justice and the Church: Challenge and Response. Thesis (D. Min.). Lombard, IL: Northern

Baptist Theological Seminary.

17098. Ortiz, Isidro. (1984) "Chicano Urban Politics and the Politics of Reform in the Seventies," Western Political Quarterly. Vol. 37 (December), pp. 564-577.

17099. Ortiz, Manuel. (1984) "A Church in Missiological Tension," Urban Mission. Vol. 2, No. 1 (September), pp. 12-19. Ethnic ministries in the Spirit and Truth Fellowship on the Near North Side of Chicago are described.

17100. p'Bitek, Okot. (1984) Song of Lawino. Nairobi, Kenya: East African Publishing House.

17101. Parker, Andrew T. (1984) "1995: Urban Georgia's Future," Cities. Vol. 4, No. 1 (Winter), pp. 12-13.

17102. Patnaik, Theophilus. (1984) Urban Churches in Cross-Cultural Ministries. Thesis (D. Min.). San Anselmo, CA: San Francisco Theological Seminary.

17103. Perdue, William G. (1984) Developing Ministry to a Changing Community: With Special Focus on Churches in Ethnic Transition. Thesis (D. Min.). San Anselmo, CA: San Francisco Theological Seminary.

17104. Phipps, Joyce. (1984) "Four Ways Clergy Can Minister to the Unemployed," Christian Ministry. Vol. 15, No. 2 (March), pp. 27-28.

17105. Pichler, Joseph A. (1984) "Radical Charity and Involuntary Poverty," Communio: International Catholic Review. Vol. 11, No. 3 (Fall), pp. 227-243. Pichler summarizes Catholic perspectives on the causes, implications, and amelioration of involuntary poverty.

17106. Pichler, Joseph A. (1984) "The Pastoral Letter and Employment," New Catholic World [Thematic Issue: the Economy]. Vol. 227, No. 1360 (July-August), pp. 179-182.

17107. Pierrard, Pierre. (1984) L'Eglise et les ouvriers en France: 1840-1940. [Paris]: Hachette litérature. Re: a history of the church in relation to the working class in France. Bibliography.

17108. Platt, John Vernon. (1984) The Development of an Administrative Design for a Baptist Association that Is Changing from

Rural to Urban. Thesis (D. Min.). Madison, NJ: Drew University.

17109. Portor, John and Deborah Portor. (1984) "Case Study: Paris: Claim It for Christ," Urban Mission. Vol. 1, No. 4 (March), pp. 36-37.

17110. Protestant Episcopal Church in the USA, Office of Hispanic Ministries. (1984?) Directory, Hispanic Ministries: The Episcopal Church in the United States. New York: the Office. [Location: General Theological Seminary, New York].

17111. Rabey, Steve. (1984) "Churches' Support Falters When Their Workers Organize," Christianity Today. Vol. 28, No. 4 (March 2), pp. 54+.

17112. Radding, Michael. (1984) "Street People," America. Vol. 150, No. 6 (February 18), pp. 111-112. Street people and skid row denizens, although not considered the "beautiful poor," can give Americans an understanding of Jesus' work with the poor uncluttered by sentimentality.

17113. Ragaz, Leonhard. (1984) Signs of the Kingdom: A Ragaz Reader. Grand Rapids, MI: W. B. Berdamans.

17114. Ramseyer, Robert L. (1984) "Case Study: Church Planting in Hiroshima," Urban Mission. Vol. 1, No. 3 (January), pp. 43-47.

17115. Ravetez, Alison. (1984) "Values and the Built Environment: A Case Study of British Planning and Urban Development," pp. 134-149 in Ziauddin Sardar, ed. The Touch of Midas: Science, Values and Environment in Islam and the West. Manchester, England: Manchester University Press.

17116. Reapsome, James W. (1984) "People Groups: Beyond the Push to Reach Them Lie Some Contrary Opinions," Evangelical Missions Quarterly. Vol. 20, No. 1 (January), pp. 6-19.

17117. "A la recherche de la justice et du shalom dans la ville." (1984) Pro Mundi Vita, Ministères et Communautés. Vol. 41, pp. 13-18. Research on justice and peace in the city.

17118. "Redacción: Pastoral de barrios." (1984) SIC [Servicio de Informacíon, Caracas]. Vol. 47, No. 461, pp. 30-40. Pastoral work in neighborhoods.

17119. Reichert, Michael. (1984) Coping and Resistance in a Catholic Ghetto. Thesis (Ph. D.). Philadelphia, PA: University of Pennsylvania.

17120. Rendle, Gilbert R., Jr. (1984) "Welfare, Charity and Ministry: Postures in the Helping Relationship," Christian Century. Vol. 101, No. 15 (May 2), pp. 464-467. Getting food or money is not an insurmountable problem for a soup kitchen, but inter-church conflict is. Churches may cooperate in feeding the hungry but disagree about how the program should be run, about whether to "save" souls before feeding bellies, and about the purpose of charity itself. The author is pastor of a Reading, Pennsylvania, church that houses a soup kitchen.

17121. Reps, John W. (1984) Views and Viewmakers of Urban America: Lithographs of Towns and Cities in the United States and Canada, Notes on Artists and Publishers, and a Union Catalog of Their Works, 1825-1925. Columbia, MO: University of Missouri Press. Large lithographs of cities, usually drawn from an elevated vantage, became popular in the 19th century and continue to be sought by collectors. Church spires are prominant in these lithographs, being the tallest urban structures of their time.

17122. Richardson, David. (1984) "Crusade Preparation for Large Cities in Africa," pp. 335-341 in J. D. Douglas, ed. The Work of an Evangelist: International Conference for Itinerant Evangelists, Amsterdam, The Netherlands. Minneapolis, MN: World-Wide Publications.

17123. Richter, Klaus. (1984) Die Katholische Kirche und die ausländischen Arbeitnehmer: Die Ausländerpastoral und ihre Bedeutung für die deutsche Ortsgemeinde. Altenberg, West Germany: Akademische Bibliothek; Vertrieb und Auslieferung, CIS-Verlag. Re: the importance of Catholic church work with foreign workers for the local community. Originally presented as the author's thesis (doctoral), Universität Münster. Bibliography.

17124. Roberts, Nancy L. (1984) Dorothy Day and the Catholic Worker. Albany, NY: State University of New York Press. Roberts analyzes the themes of articles appearing in the Catholic Worker, finding them to be anti-capitalist and pro-labor, pro-peace, and anti-racism. It was also opposed to communism, and pro-papal authority, although articles on these subjects appeared less frequently. Bibliographical footnotes are comprehensive. A doctoral dissertation. Bibliography.

17125. Rodwin, Lloyd and Robert M. Hollister, eds. (1984) Cities of the Mind: Images and Themes of the City in the Social Sciences. New York: Plenum Press. Social scientists critique the images of the city currently used in the literature of geography, economics, political science, anthropology, sociology, history and city planning.

17126. Roos, Lothar. (1984) "On a Theology and Ethics of Work," Communio: International Catholic Review. Vol. 11, No. 2 (Summer), pp. 100-119. Roos traces the roots of Catholic thought on human labor.

17127. Roozen, David A., William McKinney and Jackson Carroll. (1984) Varieties of Religious Presence: Mission in Public Life. New York: Pilgrim Press. Detailed case studies of congregations in Hartford, CT, provide a typology of city churches: activist churches, civic churches, sanctuary churches and evangelistic churches. Questionnaire.

17128. Rose, Larry L. and C. Kirk Hadaway, eds. (1984) An Urban World: Churches Face the Future. Nashville, TN: Broadman Press. A symposium, the product of research stimulated by the Center for Urban Church Studies of the Southern Baptist Convention, this companion volume to Rose and Hadaway (1982) aims to inspire and challenge the church to give high priority to evangelizing cities, particularly third world cities. Notable chapters are: 1) Crawley's on the history of urban ministry which, after finding mandates in the Bible and early church history, interprets modern urban church history as a struggle of predominantly rural denominations finding their role in the city; 2) Starkes', which decries the growing influence of non-Christian religions even in western cities; and 3) Bakke's on evangelization.

17129. Rothauge, Arlin J. (1984) Sizing Up a Congregation. s.l.: Produced for the Education for Mission and Ministry Office by Seabury Professional Services.

17130. Ruether, Rosemary Radford. (1984) "Church and Family IV: The Family in Late Industrial Society," New Blackfriars. Vol. 65, No. 766 (April), pp. 170-179.

17131. Saint Thomas Episcopal Church, Philadelphia. (1984) Dedication Service of a State Historical Marker Commemorating the Reverend Absalom Jones and the Founding of St. Thomas's African Episcopal Church at the Church's Original Site Fifth Street and Saint James Place, Philadelphia, Sunday, September 30, 1984. Philadelphia, PA: the Church. A pamphlet.

17132. Sample, Tex. (1984) Blue-Collar Ministry: Facing Economic and Social Realities of Working People. Valley Forge, PA: Judson. Pastors with blue-collar members in their congregations misjudge if they believe all blue-collar people are alike in values, habits, interests, or views of religion. Sample offers a corrective to this bias by describing the dignity, achievements, and problems of three blue-collar life styles: winners, losers, and survivors. The variety of conditions that give rise to these life styles include, among others, class bias, inequality of opportunity, and work environment. Bibliography.

17133. Sangster, Verley. (1984) Every Kid. Denver, CO: Young Life Urban Ministries.

17134. Scanlon, A. Clark. (1984) "Planning a Holistic Strategy for Urban Witness," pp. 51-74 in Larry L. Rose and C. Kirk Hadway, eds. An Urban World. Nashville, TN: Broadman Press.

17135. Schatz, Ronald W. (1984) "Connecticut's Working Class in the 1950s: A Catholic Perspective," Labor History. Vol. 25, No. 1 (Winter), pp. 83-101.

17136. Schippers, K. A. (1984) Met het oog op de stad: enkele overwengingen met betrekking tot 'urban mission' in Nederland. Kampen, Nedterlands: J. H. Kok. Re: urban mission in the Netherlands. Bibliography.

17137. Schreck, Harley Carl, Jr. (1984) Helping the Needy Elderly in Urban America: An Analysis of Volunteerism in Strengthening Neighborhood Support Systems for Homebound Elderly Persons in Seattle, Washington. Thesis (Ph. D.). Seattle, WA: University of Washington. An ethnographic study of the church-based Volunteer Chore Ministry (VCM), a volunteer network which provides homebound elderly people a variety of services, seeks to explain why volunteers have supported this organization. Volunteers, Schreck found, tended to want to help those elderly persons who could be seen as being fellow community members and who were truly needy. VCM presented its clients to the volunteers as being both neighbors and in true need, consistent with the Christian tenets of the supporting organization and with the volunteers' perception of whom they wanted to help. As the result, VCM built a set of former strangers into a neighborhood support network for elderly persons in need and, consequently, altered the social organization of the city.

17138. Schreckengost, George Earl. (1984) The Effect of Latent Racial, Ethnic, and Sexual Biases on Open Itineracy in East Ohio Conference, The United Methodist Church. Thesis (D. Min.). Lancaster,

PA: Lancaster Theological Seminary.

17139. Schulte, Anton. (1984) "Crusade Preparation for Large Cities in Europe," pp. 351-356 in J. D. Douglass, ed. The Work of an Evangelist. Minneapolis, MN: World-Wide Publications.

17140. Schuurman, Egbert. (1984) "A Christian Philosophical Perspective on Technology," pp. 107-119 in Carl Mitcham and Jim Grote. Theology and Technology: Essays in Christian Analysis and Exegesis. Lanham, MD: University Press of America.

17141. Schwarz, Brian. (1984) "Urbanization," Point: Forum for Melanesian Affairs. Series No. 5, pp. 231-256.

17142. Sedgwick, Peter. (1984) "Unemployment--Priorities for a Mercyside Response," Crucible. [Vol. 23, No. 2] (April-June), pp. 53-61.

17143. Sedgwick, Peter. (1984) "Power in Industry," Crucible. [Vol. 23, No. 2] (April-June), pp. 62-67.

17144. Shapiro, Robert D. (1984) A Reform Rabbi in the Progressive Era: The Early Career of Stephen M. Wise. Thesis (Ph. D.). Cambridge, MA: Harvard. Reprinted: New York: Garland. Wise, a Zionist rabbi and progressive crusader, founded the Free Synagogue in New York City and the American Jewish Congress. A strong advocate of labor reform, he was known as a defender of minority rights. Bibliography.

17145. Sherwood, Bill. (1984) "Revitalizing Northwest Pasadena," Bridges. Vol. 1, No. 2 (Fall), pp. 10-11.

17146. Shik, Oh Jae. (1984) "Chickens Used to Fly," International Review of Mission. Vol. 73, No. 289 (January), pp. 80-85.

17147. Shopshire, James M. (1984) "The Church and Questions of Ministry in the Urban Environment," AME Zion Quarterly Review. Vol. 96, No. 1 (April), pp. 2-12. Shopshire develops a typology of assumptions about urban ministry and describes various modes of urban church work.

17148. Shriver, Donald W., Jr., et al. (1984) "Landmark Churches and the Dictates of Public Policy," New York Times. (February 6), p. 18.

17149. Sine, Thomas W., Jr. (1984) "The Future--On Earth as It Is in Heaven," pp. 31-36 in David Frenchak, et al., eds. Signs of the

Kingdom in the Secular City. Chicago, IL: Covenant Press.

17150. Sinnott, Thomas G. (1984) "Theological Reflections on Housing," Currents in Theology and Mission. Vol. 11, No. 3 (June), pp. 176-179. Sinnott relates the meanings of the word "house" in the Bible to the contemporary plight of the homeless.

17151. Smith, Alfredo C. (1984) "The Evangelist's Commitment to the Church: We Serve the Church," pp. 151-155 in J. D. Douglas, ed. The Work of an Evangelist. Minneapolis, MN: World-Wide Publications.

17152. Smith, Ebbie C. (1984) Balanced Church Growth. Nashville, TN: Broadman.

17153. Smith, J. Alfred. (1984) "Church Ministry and Economic Issues," Review and Expositor. Vol. 41, No. 2 (Spring), pp. 249-255. Re: Allen Temple Baptist Church, Oakland, CA.

17154. Smith, Luther E. (1984) "The Vital Congregation: Socio-Cultural Factors," pp. 34-43 in George E. Morris, ed. Rethinking Congregational Development. Nashville, TN: Discipleship Resources. Smith, whose background is in the Christian Methodist Episcopal Church, is a professor at Emory University's Candler School of Theology.

17155. Smith, Paul Raymond. (1984) The Development of a Purpose-Centered Program of Ministry in the Immanuel United Presbyterian Church in McKeesport, Pennsylvania. Thesis (D. Min.). Deerfield, IL: Trinity Evangelical Theological Seminary.

17156. Sobrino, Jon. (1984) The True Church and the Poor. London: SCM Press. A Salvadoran liberation theologian assesses the church in Latin America, emphasizing that the poor are the means by which God's spirit is made clear. He celebrates, along with other liberation theologians, the ascendance of the church of the poor over the church for the poor.

17157. Son, Myong Gul. (1984) "The Korean-American Church: A Stranger or an Angel?" New World Outlook. n.s. Vol. 44, No. 11 (September), pp. 33-35. Comments on the spread of Korean churches in the USA.

17158. Spielvogel, Lawrence G. and Andrew Rudin. (1984) "Religious Building Energy Use," ASHRAE Journal. (January), pp. 40-

45. Rising energy costs cause churches to look for efficient energy use.

17159. Spong, John Selby, bp. (1984) "The Urban Church: Symbol and Reality," Christian Century. Vol. 101, No. 27 (September 12), pp. 828-831. Replies: No. 31 (October 17), p. 966. No. 35 (November 14), p. 1077. Bishop Spong (Episcopal) reviews the history of growth and decline in US cities and celebrates the survival of the urban church. The church must stay in the city, not because it can solve all the city's problems or bring about requisite political, economic, and social changes, although the church needs to be involved in these concerns. The city church must survive because of the church's own need to be the church -- a community of self conscious Christians, an outpost of the Kingdom of God, a light in darkness. Spong believes that suburban Christians will someday realize this urban witness is important to them, too.

17160. Starkes, M. Thomas. (1984) "Non-Christian Religion and Culture in the Cities of the World," pp. 95-116 in Larry L. Rose and C. Kirk Hadway, eds. An Urban World. Nashville, TN: Broadman Press.

17161. Stegmann, Franz Josef, et al. (1984) Soziale Frage und Kirche im Saarrevier: Beiträge zu Sozialpolitik und Katholizismus im späten 19. und frühen 20. Jahrhundert. Saarbrücken, West Germany: Saarbrücker Druckerei und Verlag. History of Catholic involvement with social problems in the Saarland.

17162. Stewart, Ruth A. (1984) Black Churches and Brooklyn. Brooklyn, NY: Long Island Historical Society.

17163. Stockwell, Clinton E. (1984) The Church in Urban Society: A Bibliography for the Congress on Urban Ministry, 1984. Chicago, IL: Urban Church Resource Center, SCUPE.

17164. Stockwell, Clinton E. (1984) Resources for Urban Ministry: A Bibliographic Essay. Atlanta, GA: Metropolitan Missions Department, Home Missions Board, Southern Baptist Convention, Occasional Paper No. 9.

17165. Stockwell, Clinton E. (1984) "Barriers and Bridges to Evangelization in Urban Neighborhoods," pp. 95-104 in David Frenchak, et al., eds. Signs of the Kingdom in the Secular City. Chicago, IL: Covenant Press.

17166. Stringfellow, William. (1984) The Politics of Spirituality. Philadelphia, PA: Westminster.

17167. Taylor, Raymond P. (1984) "First Aid in Pastoral Care: Pastoral Care and High Unemployment," The Expository Times, Vol. 95, No. 8 (May), pp. 228-232.

17168. Taylor, William Craig. (1984) A Community Organizing Approach to Forced Tenant Relocation in the Capitol Home Public Housing Project. Thesis (D. Min.). Atlanta, GA: Emory University.

17169. Teague, Dennis Jay. (1984) An Annotated Bibliography on Christian Leadership Development for Urban Ministries Using Andragogical Methods. Thesis (MA). Pasadena, CA: Fuller Theological Seminary, School of World Mission. Teague's bibliography contains about 200 annotated entries, half of which deal with the city and urban ministries. The remaining half is related to adult Christian education and leadership training.

17170. Thomas, Lizzie M. (1984) "The Autobiography of Malcolm X: A Social Commentary on Black American Urban Society," Afro-Americans in New York Life and History. Vol. 8, No. 1 (January), pp. 41-50.

17171. Tomasi, Silvano M. (1984) The Response of the Catholic Church in the United States to Immigrants and Refugees. New York: Center for Migration Studies (Occasional Paper).

17172. Tomasi, Silvano M. (1984) The Pastoral Action of Bishop John Baptist Scalabrini and His Missionaries among Immigrants in the Americas, 1887-1987. New York: Center for Migration Studies. A pamphlet.

17173. Trigo, Pedro. (1984) "Pastoral liberadora y experiencia espiritual," SIC (Servicio de Información, Caracas). Vol. 47, No. 462, pp. 74-78.

17174. Tucker, Cynthia Grant. (1984) A Woman's Ministry: Mary Collson's Search for Reform as a Unitarian Minister, a Hull House Social Worker, and a Christian Science Practitioner. Philadelphia, PA: Temple University Press.

17175. Uittenbosch, Hans. (1984) "Case Study: Montreal Harbor Ministry," Urban Mission. Vol. 1, No. 5 (May), pp. 39-41.

17176. Urban Industrial Mission, Ch'ongju, South Korea. (1984) "Aiding Those Forgotten by Korea's Economic Miracle," One World [World Council of Churches]. No. 94 (April), pp. 14-15.

17177. Valentine, James C. (1984) An Assessment of Parish Development in Two Administratively-Related Suburban Churches for Missional Growth and Identification. Thesis (D. Min.). Madison, NJ: Drew University.

17178. Van Houten, Richard L. (1984) "Mission Options in Hong Kong," Urban Mission. Vol. 2, No. 2 (September), pp. 5-11.

17179. Vaughan, John. (1984) The World's Twenty Largest Churches. Grand Rapids, MI: Baker.

17180. Vincent, John J. (1984) "Theological Education for Urban Mission," Ministerial Formation. No. 27 (July), pp. 20-22. Reports a consultation urban theological education held at Stanwick, England, June, 1984.

17181. Vincent, John J. (1984) OK, Let's Be Methodists. London: Epworth Press.

17182. Von Sivers, Peter. (1984) "National Integration and Traditional Rural Organization in Algeria, 1970-80: Background for Islamic Traditionalism?" pp. 94-118 in Said Amir Arjomand, ed. From Nationalism to Revolutionary Islam. Albany, NY: SUNY Press. Von Sivers traces the thread of religion that has emerged powerfully in Algerian cities among rural migrants in cities and landless peasants in the countryside.

17183. Vos, Nelvin. (1984) "Laity in the World: The Church at Work," Word and World: Theology for Christian Ministry [Thematic issue: Vocation]. Vol. 4, No. 2 (Spring), pp. 151-158.

17184. Vreeman, Jerry. (1984) "Mass Media and the Local Church," Urban Mission. Vol. 1, No. 4 (March), pp. 10-16.

17185. Wagner, Oskar. (1984) Der Evangelische Handwerker-Verein von 1848 e.V. München: 1848 bis 1984: ein Beitrag zur Geschichte der evangelischen Gemeinde und der evangelischen Sozialarbeit in München. Munich, West Germany: Evangelische Handwerkstag. A history of Protestant skilled worker unions in Munich, Germany.

17186. Walker, John D. (1984) Theological Tensions in Suburbia. Luton, England: Luton Industrial College. People living in suburbs often are unaware of their strengths and opportunities.

17187. Walrath, Douglas A. (1984) Planning for Your Church. Philadelphia, PA: The Westminister Press. A guidebook on how to collect and use data in evaluation, goal setting, program revision, and long range planning.

17188. Wangerin, Walter, Jr. (1984) Ragman and Other Cries of Faith. New York: Harper and Row. Stories, some autobiographical and some fables, written by a Lutheran urban pastor.

17189. Warner, Sam Bass, Jr. (1984) "Slums and Skyscrapers: Urban Images, Symbols and Ideology," pp. 181-196 in L. Rodwin and R. M. Hollister, eds. Cities of the Mind. London: Plenum Press.

17190. Washbourn, Penelope. (1984) "Women in the Workplace," Word and World: Theology for Christian Ministry [Thematic issue: Vocation]. Vol. 4, No. 2 (Spring), pp. 159-164.

17191. Webber, George Williams. (1984) "Signs of the Kingdom, Luke 7:18-23," pp. 19-30 in David Frenchak, et al., eds. Signs of the Kingdom in the Secular City. Chicago, IL: Covenant Press.

17192. Welch, Michael R. and John Baltzell. (1984) "Geographic Mobility, Social Integration, and Church Attendance," Journal for the Scientific Study of Religion. Vol. 23, No. 1 (March), pp. 75-91. Geographic mobility inhibits church attendance because the migrants' social networks and community attachment bonds are disrupted. Bibliography.

17193. Wenke, Karl Ernst, ed. (1984) Ökonomie und Ethik: die Herausforderung der Arbeitslosigkeit. Frankfurt am Main, West Germany: Haag Herchen. The challenge of psychological and ethical aspects of unemployment.

17194. Wentholt, G. J. M. (1984) Een arbeidersbeweging en haar priesters: het einde van een relatie: theologische vooronderstellingen en pastorale bedoelingen met betrekking tot do katholieke arbeidersbeweging in Nederland (1889-1979). Nijmegen, The Netherlands: Dekker & Van de Vegt. Re: trade unions and labor issues in the Netherlands. Bibliography.

17195. Wiley, Gary D. (1984) The Responsibility of the Evangelical Church to Prisoners and the Familes in Correctional Institutions. Thesis (Th. M.). Dallas, TX: Dallas Theological Seminary.

17196. Wiley, Robert E. (1984) But Our Situation Is Different:

Churches on Mission in Their Setting. Nashville, TN: Broadman.

17197. Willems, Lisa. (1984) "From Jungle to City: Enduring yet Endangered, Tribal People Look for Hope in the Urban World," World Christian Magazine. Vol. 3, No. 1 (January-February), pp. 16-19. A description of social conditions in migratory tribes around the world.

17198. Willems, Lisa. (1984) "The Explosion, the Slumber, and the City of Light: Three South American Cities Encounter the Gospel," World Christian. Vol. 3, No. 3 (May), pp. 30-33.

17199. Williams, June A. (1984) SOS: Strategy Of Service. Grand Rapids, MI: Zondervan Publishing.

17200. Williams, Oliver. (1984) "Who Cast the First Stone?" Harvard Business Review. Vol. 84. No. 5 (September-October), pp. 151-160. Williams encourages church groups and international corporations to halt their battle, rethink their positions, and begin new conversations based on reality, not on prejudices.

17201. Willock, John. (1984) "The Bowery Mission: a New Director Shares His Outlook," Christian Herald. Vol. 107, No. 11 (December), pp. 51-54.

17202. Wilson, Samuel. (1984) "The Field Is the World and the World Is Increasingly Urban," pp. 9-18 in David Frenchak, et al., eds. Signs of the Kingdom in the Secular City. Chicago, IL: Covenant Press.

17203. Wisz, Gerald M. (1984) "Helping Inner Cities," Christian Herald. Vol. 107, No. 3 (March), p. 32.

17204. Wogaman, J. Philip. (1984) "The Church, Business and Ethical Issues," New World Outlook. n.s. Vol. 45, No. 3 (December), pp. 34-36. An interview of Wogaman.

17205. Wolensky, Robert P. (1984) Power, Policy, and Disaster: The Political-Organizational Impact of a Major Flood. Stevens Point, WI: University of Wisconsin, Center for the Small City. A study of the impact of the Agnes flood in central Pennsylvania and subsequent organizational developments, this report gives some attention to the role of church leaders when other channels of help broke down under the weight of heavy demand. See especially pp. 136-137. One role the church undertook was to insure that Federal funds actually got to the victims, there being a high level of mistrust of the government officials' capacity to do this. Lutheran and UCC pastors were interviewed regarding the interventions they jointly sponsored. Bibliography.

17206. World Council of Churches, Urban Rural Mission. (beginning in 1984) URM Newsletter. Geneva, Switzerland: the Council. A periodical newsletter.

17207. Wright, Don. (1984) Mantle of Christ: A History of the Sydney Central Methodist Mission. St. Lucia, Australia: University of Queensland Press.

17208. Wright, Jeremiah A., Jr. (1984) "A Case Study in Black Church Renewal," pp. 65-74 in David Frenchak, et al., comp. and ed. Signs of the Kingdom in the Secular City. Chicago, IL: Covenant Press.

17209. Yamamori, Tetsuano. (1984) "How to Reach Urban Ethnics," Urban Mission. Vol. 1, No. 4 (March), pp. 29-35. Yamamori lists six strategies for dealing with ethnic groups, including the WASPs who are described as having a low intensity of ethnic consciousness and are assimilative in nature. He identifies how churches respond to a variety of ethnic circumstances, for example, communities and churches changing ethnic composition.

17210. Yeo, Alfred. (1984) "Crusade Preparation for Large Cities in Asia," pp. 343-350 in J. D. Douglas, ed. The Work of an Evangelist. Minneapolis, MN: World-Wide Publications.

17211. Yinger, J. Milton. (1984) Countercultures: The Promise and Peril of a World Turned Upside Down. New York: Free Press.

17212. Yingling, L. Carroll, Jr. (1984) The Adaptation of the Church in an Urban Renewal Project with Special Focus upon the Southwest Washington [DC] Urban Renewal Area. Thesis (D. Min.). Washington, DC: Wesley Theological Seminary.

17213. Zechariah, Chelliah. (1984) "Case Study: Growth Patterns in the Assemblies of God Congregations in Tamil Nadu," Urban Mission. Vol. 2, No. 2 (November), pp. 40-43.

17214. Adam, Tom. (1985) The Jail: Mission Field for Churches. Nashville, TN: Broadman.

17215. Adams, Mathew. (1985) The Formation of a Prison Ministry for a Local Church. Thesis (D. Min.). Madison, NJ: Drew University. A Methodist church develops a ministry with Taconic State Correctional Facility, New York.

17216. Addison, Howard A. (1985) "Toward the Revitalization of an Urban Synagogue," Conservative Judaism. Vol. 38 (Fall), pp. 38-50.

17217. Aderhold J. Don. (1985) "Revitalizing an Urban Church: The Role of Pastor and Deacons," Urban Review [Southern Baptist]. Vol. 1, No. 2 (July), pp. 5-15.

17218. Aldridge, David. (1985) "Children in Distress," Crucible. [Vol. 24, No. 2] (April-June), pp. 67-76.

17219. Allen, Jere. (1985) "Stages of Transition," Urban Review [Southern Baptist]. Vol. 1, No. 3 (October), pp. 4-12.

17220. Amerson, Philip A. (1985) We've Made Unemployment a Fulltime Job! Evansville, IN: Patchwork Central. A pamphlet.

17221. Apthorp, Stephen P. (1985) Alcohol and Substance Abuse: A Clergy Handbook. Wilton, CT: Morehouse-Barlow.

17222. Araujo, Djaalma, William Boggs, and Chang Soon Lee. (1985) "A Changing City--An Adapting Church," New World Outlook. n.s. Vol. 45, No. 5 (February), pp. 12-15. Re: Los Angeles, ethnic change, Wilshire United Methodist Church, a congregation working at multi ethnic ministry.

17223. Armstrong, James. (1985) "The Maturing of Church Corporate Responsibility," Business and Society Review [Thematic Issue: Church Activism and Corporate America]. No. 54 (Summer), pp. 6-9. At the time of writing, the author was a Senior Vice President for Pagan International and a visiting professor at Iliff School of Theology.

17224. Arns, Paulo E., et al. (1985) Igreja, classe trabalhadora e democracia: IV Semana do Trabalhador, 23-27 de julho, 1984, Sao Bernardo do Campo, Brazil. Sao Paulo, Brazil: Edicoes Paulinas. Re: a conference on the church and the laboring classes in Brazil.

17225. Aronica, Michele Teresa, sr. (1985) The New York Catholic Worker Movement's Development: A Case Study of Adaptation Beyond Charismatic Leadership. Thesis (Ph. D.). Boston, MA: Boston College.

17226. Arrunategui, Herbert. (1985) Evaluation of the Development and Implementation of Hispanic Ministries Programs in the Episcopal Church and the Role of the National Hispanic Officer. Thesis (D. Min.). Madison, NJ: Drew University.

17227. Asaf, Menahem. (1985) ha-'Avodah ba-me, korot: lu . kat mi-tokh TaNa"KH, Mishnah, Talmudim, Midrashim, Zohar, RaMBa"M, Rishonim. va-A, haronim. Jerusalem, Israel: Re'uven Mas.

17228. Baer, Hans A., ed. (1985) Black Church Ritual and Aesthetics. Hattiesburg, MI: University of Southern Mississippi.

17229. Bakke, Corean. (1985) "Creative Worship and Worship Styles for the Urban Church," Urban Review [Southern Baptist]. Vol. 1, No. 2 (July), pp. 25-33.

17230. Bakke, Raymond J. (1985) "Faithful to the Cities of the World," pp. 88-98 in James McLeish, ed. Faithful Witness: The Urbana 84 Compendium. Downers Grove, IL: InterVarsity Press.

17231. Bakke, Raymond J. (1985) "Strategy for Urban Ministry," TSF Bulletin [Theological Students Fellowship]. Vol. 8, No. 4 (March-April), pp. 20-21. Bakke describes evangelical approaches to "mega-cities." He lists 18 types of churches found in most cities and expresses concern about the phenomena of world population growth and increasing "asianization." "World class" cities are defined as those with population over 1,000,000 that have also achieved some kind of world significance. There will be 500 such cities by the year 2000, Bakke predicts, whereas there were only 240 in 1982. He offers a classification of cities: industrial, administrative, cultural, commercial, ... etc.

17232. Balanoff, Elizabeth. (1985) "Norman Thomas: Socialism and the Social Gospel," The Christian Century. Vol. 102, No. 4 (January 30), pp. 101-103. Thomas, six-time candidate for the US presidency on the Socialist ticket, is interpreted by Balanoff as reflecting the leadership style of a Social Gospel minister rather than that of a modern politician. His background lends credibility to her thesis: He was the son of a Presbyterian minister, was educated at Princeton and Union Theological Seminary, worked on the staff of Spring Street Presbyterian Church in Manhattan Slums, and was heavily influenced by Rauschenbusch.

17233. Ballard, Paul. (1985) "The Work Crisis--Pointers for Ministry," Crucible. [Vol. 24, No. 3] (July-September), pp. 115-119.

17234. Ballard, Paul. (1985) "Community Skills for the Church,"

Christian Action Journal. (Summer), pp. 4-7.

17235. Bartocci, Enzo. (1985) Chiesa e società industriale: da Benedetto XIV a Leone XIII. Milan, Italy: F. Angeli. Bibliography.

17236. Bau, Ignatius. (1985) This Ground Is Holy: Church Sanctuary and Central American Refugees. New York: Paulist.

17237. Bellah, Robert N. (1985) Tokugawa Religion: The Cultural Roots of Modern Japan. New York: Free Press.

17238. Bellah, Robert N., Richard Madsen, William M. Sullivan, Ann Swidler, and Steven M. Tipton. (1985) Habits of the Heart: Individualism and Commitment in American Life. Berkeley, CA: University of California Press. Bellah, et al., criticize American society for idolizing the individual. Urbanization has heightened the dominance of the individual and diminished commitment to public welfare as characterized by the associational life of the townships. "What duties," the authors ask, "does one have toward the vast agglomeration of anonymous individuals...? Can the impersonal metropolis be a community of memory?" (p. 178). They conclude that only when we discover the poverty of our affluence and decide to rejoin the human race will the American society escape the downward spiral of self centered privatization. Reviewed: American Journal of Sociology, Vol. 97, No. 1 (July, 1986), pp. 183-186. Journal for the Scientific Study of Religion, Vol. 25, No. 3 (September, 1986), pp. 373-374. Ethics, Vol. 96, No. 2 (January, 1984), pp. 431-432. The Other Side, Vol. 22, No. 2 (March, 1986), pp. 56-57. Review of Religious Research, Vol. 27, No. 3 (March, 1986), pp. 286-287. Princeton Seminary Bulletin, ns Vol. 7, No. 1 (1986), pp. 81-84.

17239. Bennett, G. Willis. (1985) "How to Study an Urban Church," Urban Review [Southern Baptist]. Vol. 1, No. 1 (April).

17240. Benton, John W. (1985) "Can Prostitutes Be Helped?" Urban Mission. Vol. 3, No. 2 (November), pp. 37-39.

17241. Berge, Mark Vanden. (1985) "Latchkey Children: By-Products of a Changing Society," Urban Mission. Vol. 3, No. 2 (November), pp. 29-31. Latch key children are seen as a problem for the church to address.

17242. Bidegain de Uran, Ana Maria. (1985) Iglesia, pueblo y politica: en estudio de conflictos de intereses: Colombia, 1930-1955. Bogota, Colombia: Pontifica Universidad Javeriana, Facultad de Teologia.

Re: history of the Catholic Church and political conflict, especially regarding labor issues, in Colombia.

17243. Bidwai, Praful. (1985) "Social Implications of the Bhopal Catastrophe," Social Action: A Quarterly Journal of Social Trends [India]. Vol. 35, No. 4 (October), pp. 351-365. Re: the disaster at the Union Carbide Corporation factory in Bhopal, India.

17244. Birch, Bruce C. (1985) What Does the Lord Require? The Old Testament Call to Social Witness. Philadelphia, PA: Westminster Press. Re: the faith of the people of Israel and its implications for contemporary world economic problems and social witness of the church.

17245. Bird, Warren. (1985) "A Family for Singles," Alliance Witness. Vol. 120, No. 4 (February 13), pp. 24-25. A Raleigh, North Carolina ministry with single adults in a Christian and Missionary Alliance Church.

17246. Bishop, Bryan. (1985) "To Live among the Poor," World Christian. Vol. 4, No. 5 (September-October), pp. 18-25.

17247. Bjork, Don. (1985) "Foreign Missions: Next Door and Down the Street," Christianity Today. Vol. 29, No. 10 (July 12), pp. 17-21. New immigrants provide Americans missionary opportunities at home. Foreign and home missions agencies need to cooperate more fully, forming joint task forces. Local churches have responsibility in reaching their new neighbors.

17248. Blasi, Anthony J. and Michael Cuneo, compilers. (1985) Issues in the Sociology of Religion: A Bibliography. New York: Garland Press. This bibliography includes 3,582 unannotated entries with an elaborate topical heading system, covering the years before 1985.

17249. Blizzard, Samuel W. (1985) The Protestant Parish Minister: A Behavioral Science Interpretation. Storrs, CT: Society for the Scientific Study of Religion.

17250. Bloomquist, Karen L. (1985) Toward the Redemption of American White Working-Class Reality: A Liberation Theology. Thesis (Ph. D.). New York: Union Theological Seminary.

17251. Blumberg, Janice Rothschild. (1985) One Voice: Rabbi Jacob M. Rothschild and the Troubled South. Macon, GA: Mercer University Press. A biography of a rabbi who led the Atlanta, GA, congregation at the time it was bombed in 1958. The bombing incident was featured in the Oscar winning film of 1989: Driving Miss Daisy. Foreword by Coretta Scott King.

17252. Boan, Rudee Devon. (1985) Southern Baptist Church-Type Missions: Origin, Development, and Outcome, 1979-1984. Thesis (Ph. D.). Louisville, KY: Southern Baptist Theological Seminary. Analysis of various approaches to church extension.

17253. Bobick, Michael W. (1985) "New York's New Neighbors: Reaching Chinese Immigrants in the 1980's," Urban Mission. Vol. 2, No. 5 (May), pp. 20-32.

17254. Bodnar, John E. (1985) The Transplanted: A History of Immigrants in Urban America. Bloomington, IN: Indiana University Press. A description of the state of scholarly inquiry about ethnic identity. Bibliography.

17255. Bookser Feister, John. (1985) "The Struggle for Work-Place Justice," The Other Side. Vol. 21, No. 3 (April-May), pp. 46-49.

17256. Borrowdale, Anne. (1985) "Women and the Theology of Work," Crucible. [Vol. 24, No. 4] (October-December), pp. 169-174.

17257. Bosserman, Vern. (1985) An Urban Evangelism Project for the Ridgemont Community Church. Thesis (D. Min). Ashland, OH: Ashland Theological Semianry.

17258. Bowie, Vaughan. (1985) "Scaffolding: Urban Mission in Australia," Urban Mission. Vol. 2, No. 5 (May), pp. 46-51.

17259. Boyer, Richard and David Savageau. (1985) Places Rated Almanac. Chicago, IL: Rand McNally Inc. Value assumptions about cities are used to construct a rating of cities from the most desirable to the least. Reviewed negatively: American Demographics, March, 1986, pp. 8f.

17260. Bradshaw, York W. (1985) "Overdevelopment and Underdevelopment in Sub-Sahara Africa: A Cross National Study," Studies in Comparative International Development. Vol. 20, No. 3 (Fall), pp. 74-101.

17261. Brayan, Robert Lawson. (1985) Developing a Strategy for Community Ministry Using Shared Praxis Approach. Thesis (D. Min.). Atlanta, GA: Emory University.

17262. Brett, Paul. (1985) "Unemployment: The Issue and the Responses," Theology. Vol. 88, No. 723 (May), pp. 182-189. At the time of writing, Brett was director of the Chelmsford Diocesan Council for Social Responsibility.

17263. Britt, David Tillman. (1985) Local Factors in Urban American Church Growth: Two Protestant Denominations in Jefferson County, Kentucky. Thesis (Ph. D.). Louisville, KY: Southern Baptist Theological Seminary. Britt reviews the writings of church growth theory proponents and their critics, providing an empirical test of a church growth model.

17264. Brose, Eric Dorn. (1985) Christian Labor and the Politics of Frustration in Imperial Germany. Washington, DC: Catholic University of America Press.

17265. Buchanan, Susan H. (1985) Scattered Seeds: The Meaning of the Migration for Haitians in New York City. Thesis (Ph. D.). New York: New York University.

17266. Burke, Shane Robinson. (1985) Management and Labor Relations Principles in Higher Education: The Catholic Viewpoint. Thesis (Ph. D.). Cambridge, MA: Harvard University.

17267. Byers, David M., ed. (1985) Justice in the Market Place, Collected Statements of the Vatican and the US Catholic Bishops on Economic Policy, 1891-1984. Washington, DC: United States Catholic Conference. A convenient compendium of Catholic social teaching on economic matters.

17268. Caprile, G. (1985) "Problemi pastorali di Roma," Civilta Cattolica. Vol. 136, No. 3235 (April 6), pp. 62-73. [See note 3]. Re: pastoral work and religious life in Rome, Italy.

17269. Carmen, Arlene and Howard Moody. (1985) Working Women: The Subterranean World of Street Prostitution. New York: Harper and Row.

17270. Carney, Glandion. (1985) "Harvest on Concrete," Christianity Today. Vol. 29, No. 10 (July 12), p. 19.

17271. Casper, Dale E. (1985) The Community Experiences of Immigrant Minorities. Monticello, IL: Vance Bibliographies.

17272. Casper, Dale E. (1985) Urban America Examined: A Bibliography. New York: Garland. A bibliography with 2070 entries covering, generally, 1973-1983 with a section on religion.

17273. Cave, Dave. (1985) Jesus Is Your Best Mate: Evangelism in the Inner-City and Council Estate Cultures. London: Mashall Morgan and Scott. A minister in Liverpool asks why the church is retreating from the inner city where it is most desperately needed and offers suggestions for how the church can return.

17274. "The Challenge of Urban Ministry: Diocese of Oakland." (1985) Origins. Vol. 15, No. 10 (August 15), pp. 156-160.

17275. Chang, Yoon Sung. (1985) Marital Problems among Korean Immigrants with Implications for Ministry. Thesis (D. Min.). San Anselmo, CA: San Francisco Theological Seminary.

17276. Chapman, Ian. (1985) "Commitment and Tenure of the Urban Pastor," Urban Review [Southern Baptist]. Vol. 1, No. 2 (July), pp. 43+.

17277. Childs, Loyd. (1985) "Teams Multiply Churches in Malaysia/Singapore," Urban Mission. Vol. 2, No. 5 (May), pp. 33-39.

17278. Chudacoff, Howard P. (1985?) The Evolution of American Urban Society. Englewood Cliffs, NJ: Prentice-Hall. This short history of the development of the American city gives major attention to America's treatment of the poor.

17279. Chung, Hong Kwon. (1985) Generational Problems in the Korean Immigrant Churches of Philadelphia. Thesis (D. Min.) Chestnut Hill, PA: Westminster Theological Seminary.

17280. "Church Activism and Corporate America." (1985) Business and Society Review [Thematic issue]. No. 54 (Summer), pp. 4-44.

17281. Church of England, Commission on Urban Priority Areas. (1985) Faith in the City: A Call for Action by Church and Nation. London: Church House Publishing. Commissioned by the Archbishop of Canterbury, this widely acclaimed study and the elaborate preparations for it have inspired renewed interest in urban ministry in England. The Commission conducted its inquiry with the legal power to take evidence and the documents it produced include nothing for which evidence could not be obtained. As the result, the authenticity of assertions made the Commission's reports is exemplary. The final report calls church and government alike to accountability for urban policies that do not serve the people, for poverty, for abandoning the Urban Priority Areas, for housing and health problems, for crime, and for the problems of youth and the aged. Specific recommendations for the church and government are included. Criticisms of the Commission's report point to its lack of theological depth. Reviewed: Transformation, Vol. 3, No. 3 (July, 1986), pp. 30-32. Churchman, Vol. 100, No. 1 (1986), pp. 79-80. Theology, Vol. 89 (November, 1986), pp. 487-489. Baptist Quarterly, Vol. 31, No. 8 (October, 1986), pp. 401-404.

17282. "The Church, the City and the Poor: A Challenge." (1985) [Conference, St. John's Church, Bronx, NY, Lutheran Church Leadership] Lutheran Forum. Vol. 19, No. 3, pp. 9-10+.

17283. Clapp, Rodney. (1985) "Looking from the Downside Up. An Interview with Walter Wangerin, Jr. by Rodney Clapp," Christianity Today. Vol. 29, No. 4 (March 1), pp. 14-20.

17284. Cochran, Thomas Childs. (1985) Challenges to American Values: Society, Business, and Religion. New York: Oxford University Press.

17285. Cochrane, James. (1985) "The Churches and the Trade Unions," pp. 174-188 in Charles Ville-Vicensio and John W. DeGruchy. Resistance and Hope. Cape Town, South Africa: D. Philip. Also: Grand Rapids, MI: Eerdmans, 1985. Bibliography.

17286. Collins, Sheila. (1985) The Rainbow Challenge: The Jackson Campaign and the Future of US Politics. New York: Monthly Review Press.

17287. Collum, Danny. (1985) "The State of Unions," Sojourners. Vol. 14, No. 5 (May), pp. 5-6.

17288. Colson, Charles. (1985) "A Call to Rescue the Yuppies," Christianity Today. Vol. 29, No. 8 (17 May), pp. 17-20. Decries materialism among young urban professionals, and their meld of economic conservatism with social libertarianism.

17289. Conferencia--"La Enseñanza Social de la Iglesia y el mundo del trabajo en la América Latina de los 80". [between 1985 and 1987] [Caracas, Venezuela]: s.n. Findings and conclusions of a conference held in Caracas, Venezuela, in 1985, re: church and labor in Latin America. In English.

17290. Congresso Nacional de Jovens Trabalhadores. (1985) Os jovens trabalhadores conquistando trabalho e justiça. São Paulo, Brazil: Edições Paulinas. Reports of a Catholic congress regarding working class youth and labor in Brazil and their struggles for justice.

17291. Conn, Harvie M. (1985) The Depersonalization Misunderstanding. Atlanta, GA: Metropolitan Missions Department, Home Mission Board, Southern Baptist Convention, Occasional Paper No. 10. Reprinted from: Urban Mission (May, 1985). Conn corrects the erroneous assumption that rural areas are ideal havens while cities are places of depersonalization.

17292. Conn, Harvie M., comp. (1985) Urban Church Research: Methods and Models, Collected Readings. Philadelphia, PA: Urban Missions Program, Westminster Theological Seminary. These materials, consisting of reprinted articles and bibliographies, have been compiled for a theological seminary course on urban field research. The focus is on collecting data for urban church growth and mission, using primarily ethnographic methods. Some attention is given to questionnaire construction. Bibliography. Questionnaire.

17293. Conn, Harvie M. (1985) "Lucan Perspectives and the City," Missiology: An International Review. Vol. 13, No. 4 (October), pp. 409-428. Observations on the urban setting of Acts written by a professor at Westminster Theological Seminary, Philadelphia, PA. Special attention is given to the Greek words: Polis and Kome.

17294. Conn, Harvie M. (1985) "In the City, I'm a Number, Not a Person: The Depersonalization Misunderstanding," Urban Mission. Vol. 2, No. 5 (May), pp. 6-19.

17295. Conn, Harvie M. (1985) "Any Faith Dies in the City," Missiology. Vol. 13, No. 4 (October), pp. 6-19.

17296. Cornehls, James. (1985) "Urbanization in Third World Countries: The Case of Mexico City," Urban Review [Southern Baptist]. Vol. 1, No. 1 (April), pp. 24-38.

17297. Covell, Ralph, ed. (1985) [American Society of Missiology, American Professors of Mission, 1985 Conference Papers: Vatican II Missiology, Special Issue]. Missiology: An International Review. Vol. 13 (October), pp. 387-499.

17298. Cram, Ronald Hugh. (1985) Cultural Pluralism and Christian Education: Laura Thompson's Design for Anthropology and Its Use in Christian Education with Ethnic Groups. Thesis (Ph. D.).

Princeton, NJ: Princeton Theological Seminary.

17299. Croll, Marty. (1985) "Winning Them One by One," Church Administration. Vol. 27, No. 4 (January), pp. 31-33.

17300. Cruz, Rogelio El. (1985) Filipinos in Chicago: A Target of Urban Ministry. Thesis (M. Th.). Oak Brook, IL: Bethany Theological Seminary.

17301. Davidson, James D. (1985) Mobilizing Social Movement Organizations: The Formation, Institutionalization, and Effectiveness of Ecumenical Urban Ministries. Storrs, CT: Society for the Scientific Study of Religion. Davidson examines the Lafayette (IN) Urban Ministry, an example of the ecumenically sponsored inner city programs which were established in the 1960s and 1970s. He describes the organization's origins, resources, goals, and practices drawing on sociological theory. Bibliography. Questionnaire.

17302. Davis, Howard and David Gosling, eds. (1985) Will the Future Work? Values for Emerging Patterns of Work and Employment. Geneva, Switzerland: World Council of Churches.

17303. Davis, John. (1985) Engineering for God or Mammon? London: Industrial Christian Fellowship, St. Katherine Cree Church. A pamphlet.

17304. De Silva, Ranjit. (1985) "Discipling in Three Sri Lankan Cities," Urban Mission. Vol. 2, No. 4 (March), pp. 33-40.

17305. Diehl, William E. (1985) "Ministry in the Marketplace," Ministry Development Journal [An Episcopal Quarterly, USA]. No. 8, pp. 23-29. A Bethlehem Steel executive and business consultant raises the question of whether a person can be Christian and continue to work in industry. He answers affirmatively. A target of aggressive questions from church leaders about business practices, Diehl answers questions of accountability in business. He argues that because materialism, greed, and lust for power are universal characteristics. Industry should not be singled out as the only target for criticism. Justification is by faith, not by works. The author sees ministry occurring within industry: e.g., by teaching, coaching, and encouraging others to do their best; by ministry of interpersonal relations; by a ministry of stewardship (salesclerks are stewards of the goods they have for sale); by a ministry of introducing change (Diehl learns to fetch his own coffee); and by a ministry of raising values (Diehl rejects a managerial parking place when promoted).

17306. Diehl, William E. (1985) Plant Closings. New York: Division for Mission in North America, Lutheran Church in America.

17307. Diehl, William E. (1985) The Church as Shareholder: Socially Concerned Investing for Groups and Individuals. New York: Division of Mission in North America, Lutheran Church in America.

17308. Dietrich, Glenn M. (1985) Membership Growth in United Methodist Inner-City Churches. Thesis (D. Min.). Lancaster, PA: Lancaster Theological Seminary. Questionnaire.

17309. Dillingham, Manuel Lamont. (1985) The Role of the Pastor in Planning and Implementing a Program of Total Ministry for a Predominantly Black Baptist Urban Congregation. Thesis (D. Min.). Pittsburgh, PA: Pittsburgh Theological Seminary.

17310. Dimond, Jean Ann. (1985) Interview of Jean A. Dimond. [Sound recording, 2 cassettes, 150 minutes]. [Location: Presbyterian Historical Association, Philadelphia]. Part of an oral history project.

17311. Dobbelaere, Karel. (1985) "Secularization Theories and Sociological Paradigms: A Reformulation of the Private-Public Dichotomy and the Problem of Social Integration," Sociological Analysis. Vol. 46, No. 4 (Winter), pp. 377-387. Bibliography.

17312. Dolan, Jay P. (1985) The American Catholic Experience: A History from Colonial Times to the Present. Garden City, NY: Doubleday. A survey history.

17313. Domínguez, Javier. (1985) Organizaciones obreras cristianas en la oposicíon al franquismo (1951-1975): Con 65 documentos clandestinos e inéditos. Bilbao, Spain: Mensajero. Christian labor organizations in opposition to Franco.

17314. Domosh, Mona. (1985) Scrapers of the Sky: The Symbolic and Functional Structures of Lower Manhattan. Thesis (Ph. D.). Worcester, MA: Clark University.

17315. Dulles, Avery Robert and Patrick Granfield. (1985) The Church: A Bibliography. Wilmington, DE: Michael Glazier.

17316. Duncan, Graham. (1985) "Practical Theology: 'Faith Apart from Works Is Dead,'" Journal of Theology for Southern Africa. No. 53 (December), pp. 47-53. Re: the Federal Theological Seminary and theological education in South Africa.

17317. Dunnell, Terry, ed. (1985) Mission and Young People at Risk. [London]: Frontier Youth Trust. A resource book for workers with troubled city youth.

17318. Eagle, Julian. (1985) "Rebuilding and Economy for Jobs and Peace," Crucible. [Vol. 24, No. 1] (January-March), pp. 12-14.

17319. Ellison, Craig W. (1985) "Attitudes and Urban Transition," Urban Mission. Vol. 2, No. 3 (January), pp. 12-26.

17320. Etchells, D. R. (1985) God Is Boss in This Plant. London: Industrial Christian Fellowship. A pamphlet.

17321. Etzioni-Halevy, Eva. (1985) The Knowledge Elite and the Failure of Prophecy. London: George Allen and Unwin. Intellectuals have failed to offer usable knowledge and to predict the future with accuracy. The author debunks the futurologists, forecasters and social-scientific prophets.

17322. Faling, Richard. (1985) "Adapting to Transition: The State Convention," Urban Review [Southern Baptist]. Vol. 1, No. 3 (October), pp. 40+.

17323. Farrell, Carolyn. (1985) "Let the Voters Decide," pp. 236-244 in Madonna Kolbenschlag, ed. Between God as Caesar. New York: Paulist.

17324. Fish, John Hall. (1985) "Liberating Education," pp. 15-29 in C. Amjad-Ali and W. Pitcher, eds. Liberation and Ethics: Essays in Religious and Social Ethics in Honor of Gibson Winter. Chicago, IL: Center for the Scientific Study of Religion.

17325. Fogarty, Gerald P. (1985) "The Parish and Community in American Catholic History," U. S. Catholic Historian. Vol. 4, pp. 232-257. Reprinted: Brian Mitchell, ed. Building the American Catholic City. New York: Garland, 1988.

17326. Fones-Wolf, Kenneth Alan. (1985) Trade Union Gospel: Protestantism and Labor in Philadelphia, 1865-1915. Thesis (Ph. D.). Philadelphia, PA: Temple University.

17327. Fones-Wolf, Kenneth Alan. (1985) "Contention and Christianity: Protestantism and the Labor Movement in Philadelphia, 1890-1920," in Vincent Mosco and Janet Wasko, eds. Critical Communications Review, 3rd Series. New York: Ablex Press.

17328. Forest, James E. (1985) "Adapting to Transition: The Association," Urban Review [Southern Baptist]. Vol. 1, No. 3 (October), pp. 32-39.

17329. Francesconi, Mario. (1985) Giovanni Battista Scalabrini, vescovo di piacenza e degli emigrati. Roma: Città Nuova. Re: the work of Giovanni Battista Scalabrini with Italian emigrants.

17330. Frostin, Per. (1985) "Sweden: The Union of Christian Labor Members," pp. 40-44 in Virginia Fabella and Sergio Torres, eds. Doing Theology in a Divided World. Maryknoll, NY: Orbis.

17331. Fukuyama, Yoshio. (1985) Social Research and the Churches: A Report to the Lilly Endowment of the State of Research and Survey Departments in Councils of Churches, Denominations and Theological Seminaries. [Chicago, IL]: Chicago Theological Seminary. Fukuyama assesses the declined state of applied research for the church, which, since its "golden era" in the 1950s and 60s, has received too little attention from church leaders.

17332. Gallagher, Sharon. (1985) "The Feminization of Poverty," Radix. Vol. 16, No. 5 (March), pp. 4-5.

17333. Gant, Edwin P. (1985) "'Evangelism Explosion': A Tool God Is Using in Many Cities," Urban Mission. Vol. 3, No. 2 (November), pp. 32-36.

17334. Gardner, Ian, et al. (1985) "The Thrill of Delinquency," Youth in Society. No. 102 (May), pp. 22-23.

17335. Giddings, Lynn. (1985) "Faith, if It Has Not Works, Is Dead," Point: Forum for Melanesian Affairs. Series No. 7, pp. 191-218.

17336. Gillett, Richard W. (1985) The Human Enterprise: A Christian Perspective on Work. Kansas City, MO: Leaven Press.

17337. Girouard, Mark. (1985) Cities and People. New Haven: Yale University Press.

17338. Glaser, Mitch. (1985) "Urban Evangelism: Kosher Style," Urban Mission. Vol. 2, No. 4 (March), pp. 6-11.

17339. Godfrey, Wendy, ed. (1985) Down to Earth: Stories of Church Based Community Work. London: British Council of Churches. A collection of stories about churches involved in community service work in their neighborhoods includes examples of a youth and community center, a team ministry, and a community house, all sponsored by churches. The concluding chapter, by Paul Ballard, offers a theology of church based community work. Bibliography.

17340. Golzio, Karl H. (1985) "Max Weber on Japan: The Role of the Government and the Buddhist Sects," Journal of Developing Societies. Vol. 1, No. 2 (December), pp. 212-223.

17341. Gonzalez, Justo L. (1985) The Hispanic Ministry of the Episcopal Church in the Metropolitan Area of New York and Environs: A Study Undertaken for the Trinity Grants Board. New York: the Board. [Location: General Theological Seminary, New York].

17342. Goodin, Robert E. (1985) Protecting the Vulnerable: A Reanalysis of Our Social Responsibilities. Chicago, IL: University of Chicago Press. A philosophical inquiry into the nature of social justice argues that when an individual is vulnerable, those on whom that person depends are morally bound to aid and protect. If people are vulnerable, anyone with power over them must protect them and, in the final analysis, release them from their vulnerable condition. Bibliography.

17343. Gordon, Mark W. (1985) "Rediscovering Jewish Infrastructure: The Legacy of US 19th Century Synagogues," American Jewish History. Vol. 75, No. 3 (March), pp. 296-306. Reprinted: Waltham, MA: American Jewish Historical Society, 1986. Gordon identifies current uses of 19th century synagogues.

17344. Green, R. H., ed. (1985) Labour, Employment and Unemployment: An Ecumenical Reappraisal. Geneva, Switzerland: World Council of Churches, Commission on the Churches' Participation in Development, Advisory Group on Economic Matters.

17345. Greenway, Roger S. (1985) "Reaching the Unreached in the Cites," Urban Mission. Vol. 2, No. 5 (May), pp. 3-5.

17346. Greenway, Roger S. (1985) "City, Seminaries and Christian Colleges," Urban Mission. Vol. 3, No. 1 (September), pp. 3-6.

17347. Greenway, Roger S. (1985) "The 'Luz Del Mundo' Movement in Mexico," Missiology. Vol. 1, No. 2 (April), pp. 113-124.

17348. Gregory, Joel. (1985) "Effective Urban Preaching," Urban Review [Southern Baptist]. Vol. 1, No. 2 (July), pp. 16-24.

17349. Gustafsson, Goran. (1985) "De nya forortskyrkorne," Svensk Teologisk Kvartalskrift. Vol. 61, No. 4, pp. 145-153. Re: church attendance, suburban churches, church architecture, and the sociology of religion in Swedish Lutheranism.

17350. Hadaway, C. Kirk. (1985) "Types of Growing Churches in Transition," Urban Review [Southern Baptist]. Vol. 1, No. 3 (October), pp. 13-22.

17351. Hammond, Phillip E., ed. (1985) The Sacred in a Secular Age: Toward Revision of the Scientific Study of Religion. Berkeley, CA: University of California Press. A collection of sociological articles, including some regarding the church, justice, power, and social action. Bibliography.

17352. Handy, Robert T. (1985) "American Methodism and Its Historical Frontier: Methodism on the 20th Century Urban Frontier," Methodist History. Vol. 23, No. 2 (October), pp. 3-14.

17353. Hanson, Allen. (1985) "Witnessing in Jails and Prisons," Alliance Witness. Vol. 120, No. 5 (February 27), pp. 6-7.

17354. Hanson, P. J. (1985) "Austin Farrer and Jacques Ellul," Cross Currents [Thematic issue: Ellul]. Vol. 35, No. 1 (Spring), pp. 81-83.

17355. Harris, James Henry. (1985) Laity Expectations of Ministers in the Black Urban Church: A Study of Political and Social Expectations in the Context of Ministry to Community and World. Thesis (Ph. D.). Norfolk, VA: Old Dominion University.

17356. Harrison, Paul. (1985) Inside the Inner City: Life Under the Cutting Edge. Harmondsworth, England: Penguin. Re: social conditions in Hackney, London, England.

17357. Hart, Jim. (1985) "Urban Perspectives," Urban Mission. Vol. 3, No. 2 (November), p. 44.

17358. Harvey, David. (1985) Consciousness and the Urban Experience: Studies in the History and Theory of Capitalist Urbanization. Baltimore, MD: Johns Hopkins University Press. A Marxist interpretation of urbanization, with passing reference to the role of religion in urbanization.

17359. Haunca, Hilario. (1985) "Andinos en Arequipa: Reestructuración de su relación con Dios," Boletín del IDEA (Perú). Series 2, No. 21, pp. 49-69. Re: the restructuring of beliefs among Andean migrants to Arequipa, Peru.

17360. Heath, Susan. (1985) "Building a Downtown Ministry: An Interview with Susan Heath," Alban Institute Action Information. Vol. 11, No. 5 (September), pp. 13-15.

17361. Henkelman, Ervin F. and Stephen J. Carter. (1985) How to Develop a Team Ministry and Make It Work. St. Louis, MO: Concordia Publishing House. The authors offer suggestions for local church staff management based on a managerial model. Large churches with parochial schools will find the book more helpful than will small or middle-sized churches. The authors assume that working for a happy team is worth the effort and offer practical suggestions.

17362. High, David Gilbert. (1985) Towards the Liberation of the Affluent: A Curricular Model for a Suburban Congregation. Thesis (D. Min.). Philadelphia, PA: Eastern Baptist Theological Seminary.

17363. Hinton, Keith. (1985) Growing Churches Singapore Style: Ministry in an Urban Context. Singapore: Overseas Ministries Fellowship Books.

17364. Hogan, David John. (1985) Class and Reform: School and Society in Chicago, 1880-1930. Philadelphia, PA: University of Pennsylvania Press. See Chapter 3 regarding Protestant child saving agencies.

17365. Hohenberg, P. M. and L. H. Lees. (1985) The Making of Modern Europe 1000-1950. Cambridge, MA: Harvard University Press.

17366. Hoisington, R. Michael. (1985) "How You Can Start a Singles Group," Christian Life. Vol. 47, No. 5 (September), pp. 67-72.

17367. Hollingsworth, William G. (1985) "Controlling Illegal Immigration," The Christian Century. Vol. 102, No. 22 (July 1-10), pp. 648-650.

17368. Holton, Susan and David L. Jones. (1985) Spirit Aflame: Luis Palau's Mission to London. Sevenoaks, England: Hodder and Stoughton. Re: evangelistic work. Bibliography.

17369. Hope, Marjorie and James Young. (1985) "The Homeless Poor: What Is the Church Doing for America's Destitute?" Christianity Today. Vol. 29, No. 14 (October 14), pp. 30-35.

17370. Hopkins, Stephen, Bill Bosworth, and Brad Lennon. (1985) "Urban People in Poverty: Towards an Alternative Model of Ministry," pp. 153-161 in Christopher Lind and Terry Brown, eds. Justice as Mission: An Agenda for the Church: Essays in Appreciation of Marjorie and Cyril Powles. Burlington, Ontario, Canada: The Trinity Press.

17371. Houck, John W. and Oliver F. Williams, eds. (1985) Catholic Social Teaching and the United States Economy: Working Papers for a Bishops' Pastoral. Lanham, MD: University Press of America. Four themes -- the creation of jobs, income for the poor, USA trade with poorer nations, and planning the USA economy -- are recurrent in the 15 papers prepared by business people, labor leaders and theologians as background for the American Catholic Bishops' pastoral on the US economy.

17372. Hoyt, Michael. (1985) "How to Make Steel: Agitate and Organize--Stirrings along the Monongahela," Christianity and Crisis. Vol. 45, No. 3 (March 4), pp. 62-65. Re: US Steel plant closings.

17373. Hualde, A. C. (1985) "La pastoral de las grandes ciudades: Bogotá," Pro Mundi Vita, Dossier Africain. Vol. 38, pp. 2-34. Pastoral work in large cities in Africa.

17374. "Hunger in America." (1985) JSAC Grapevine. Vol. 16, No. 10 (May), pp. [1-8].

17375. I T V. (1985?) Voices from the City: [A study booklet prepared for use with the Thames Television Series "City Priest."] London: ITV. A pamphlet.

17376. Inchausti, Robert. (1985) "Interpreting Mother Teresa," The Christian Century. Vol. 102, No. 31 (October 16), pp. 919-920. The author criticizes most biographies of Mother Teresa for being unintentionally comic, degenerating into parody because of the writers need for a good story clashing with the wordless deeds of love they observe. Interviews with Mother Teresa are often disappointing to journalists. They are too simple, seemingly trite platitudes in churchly language. Some corrections are offered.

17377. Industrial Christian Fellowship. (1985) Work in Worship: An Anthology of Materials Suitable for Worship Concerned with Industry, Commerce and All Forms of Work. London: Hodder and

Stoughton. Typical of resources developed by ICF.

17378. Institute on the Church in Urban-Industrial Society. (1985-1989) Metro-Ministry News. Chicago, IL: the Institute. A periodical.

17379. Jackson, Kenneth T. (1985) Crabgrass Frontier: The Suburbanization of the United States. Oxford, UK: Oxford University Press. Bibliography.

17380. Jahn, Christoph. (1985) "Die große Stadt, der kleine Glaube: zehn Anmerkungen nach dem Buch Jona," Zeitschrift für Mission. Vol. 11, No. 4, pp. 194-197. Re: faith in the city based on a study of the book of Jonah.

17381. James, Eric, ed. (1985) "Health and the Inner City," Christian Action Journal. (Spring), [Entire issue].

17382. Janssen, Henk. (1985) "Ministries in an Urban Settlement," Point Series. No. 7, pp. 184-190.

17383. Jenkins, Shirley, Mignon Sauber, and Eva Friedlander. (1985) Ethnic Associations and Services to New Immigrants in New York City. New York: Community Council of Greater New York.

17384. Jennings, Alvin Ray. (1985) How Christianity Grows in the City. Fort Worth, TX: Star Bible Publications. Re: direct mail technology applied to evangelism, along with other methods. An expanded version of the author's book titled: 3Rs of Urban Church Growth.

17385. John, A. J. (1985) "Women and the Evangelization of Indian Cities," Urban Mission. Vol. 3, No. 1 (September), pp. 15-25.

17386. Johnson, David James. (1985) Aiding Parish Ministers in Maintaining Christian Community with Their Parishioners: At the State Correctional Institution at Pittsburgh. Thesis (D. Min.). Pittsburgh, PA: Pittsburgh Theological Seminary.

17387. Johnson, Paul L. (1985) "Clairton, USA," The Christian Century. Vol. 102, No. 23 (July 14-24), pp. 680-682. Pastors of the Trinity Lutheran Church in Clairton adopt a radical position in support of people who are losing jobs as the result of plant closings. Their confrontational methods are opposed by the Lutheran hierarchy. Johnson uses the occasion to write about the theological significance of conflict and the work ethic.

17388. Johnston, Arthur P. (1985) "Essentials for Urban Ministry," Alliance Witness. Vol. 120, No. 5 (February 27), pp. 8-10.

17389. Jonsson, John N. (1985) "Ferment in the Cities of Developing Countries: A Missions Concern," Review and Expositor. Vol. 82, No. 2 (Spring), pp. 185-197. Injustice, anger and poverty accompany the rapid urbanization occurring throughout the world. Missionary activities need to identify with the poor and their suffering.

17390. Jordan, Patrick. (1985) "Dorothy Day: Still a Radical," Commonweal. Vol. 112, No. 21 (November 29), pp. 665-669. An appraisal of Dorothy Day's influence in American Catholicism and the direction of the Catholic Worker since her death on November 19, 1980.

17391. Kaldor, Peter, Vaughan Bowie, and Glenn Farquhar-Nicol, eds. (1985) Green Shoots in the Concrete: Towards a More Sensitive Christian Presence in Our Cities. Torrens Park, Australia: Pan Print for the Board of Mission, The Uniting Church in NSW. Stories and experiences of ministry in Australian urban areas. Bibliography.

17392. Kallas, Endel. (1985) "Alexis de Tocqueville: Portrait of American Religion: An Anniversary Tribute," Dialog. Vol. 24, No. 4 (Fall), pp. 267-271. Kallas comments on Tocqueville's observations of American religion 150 years ago, finding comparable 20th century circumstances: e.g., religious pluralism, privatism, individualism, interest in personal religious piety, indifference to religion as a force shaping national life, preoccupation with prosperity, and captivity to the democratic principle.

17393. Kaslow, Andrew J. (1985) Neighbors: Soul of the City. New Orleans, LA: Arts Council of Louisiana.

17394. Kenhoe, Mary. (1985) "Union Outreach through Coalitions," Grail: An Ecumenical Journal [Thematic issue: Unions]. Vol. 1 (June), pp. 69-78.

17395. Kidd, Beth. (1985) "Interview: Inner-City Missionary Nurse," Urban Mission. Vol. 2, No. 4 (March), pp. 12-21.

17396. Kim, Dae Gee. (1985) Major Factors Conditioning the Acculturation of Korean-Americas: With Respect to the Presbyterian Church in America and Its Missionary Obedience. Thesis (D. Miss.).

Pasadena, CA: Fuller Theological Seminary.

17397. Kim, Young-suk. (1985) The Poor in the City. Seoul, Korea: Achim. Text in Korean.

17398. Klassen, Jacob P. (1985) "Quito, Ecuador, Transferable Principles of Urban Outreach," Urban Mission. Vol. 3, No. 1 (September), pp. 32-40.

17399. Kleba, Gerald J. (1985) "Rev. Gerald Kleba: Pastor for the Poor" [Interview by Carol Clark], Today's Parish. Vol. 17, No. 1 (January), pp. 8-13.

17400. Koning, Gerry. (1985) "Kid Power--An Urban Children's Program," Urban Mission. Vol. 3, No. 1 (September), pp. 40-42.

17401. Krämer, Werner. (1985) Konzepte kirchlicher Arbeiterbildung. Mainz, West Germany: Matthias-Grünewald-Verlag. A conceptualization of church educational work with laborers in Germany. Bibliography.

17402. Kraybill, J. Nelson. (1985) "The Name Does Matter," Gospel Herald. Vol. 78, No. 29 (July 16), pp. 494-495. The name "Mennonite" proves embarrassing to some congregations as they become more urbanized and secularized, but not to others. Kraybill advocates using the name.

17403. Kugelmass, Jack. (1985) "Even Solomon Would Have Trouble: Storytelling in the South Bronx," Prooftexts. Vol. 5, No. 1 (January), pp. 45-65. A spiritual leader of a small inner city synagogue conducts a weekly review of the Torah portion for his congregation. He retells biblical narratives convincingly.

17404. Kwant, Kees. (1985) "Unemployment and Young People in the Netherlands," pp. 37-47 in John Coleman and Gregory Baum, eds. Youth without a Future. Edinburgh, Scotland: T. and T. Clark. Bibliography.

17405. Lapierre, Dominique. (1985) Cité de la joie. Paris: R. Laffont. Translation: City of Joy. New York: Warner Books, 1986. Re: Mother Teresa.

17406. Larson, Robert E., Jr. (1985) A Basic Bibliography and Directory of Organizations for Contact Teleministries USA. Harrisburg, PA: Contact Teleministries USA.

17407. Leas, Speed. (1985) Moving Your Church through Conflict. Washington, DC: The Alban Institute.

17408. Lees, Andrew. (1985) Cities Perceived: Urban Society in European and American Thought, 1820-1940. New York: Columbia University Press. Also Manchester, England: Manchester University Press, 1985. Lees traces pro- and anti-urban thought in Europe and the USA from the 19th through the early 20th century, providing a suitable introduction for persons interested in moral aspects of the philosophy of urbanization. Much attention is given to the influence of the churches and clergy, whose opinions ranged from guardedly critical to excessively anti-urban for those in the Church of England and from anti-urban diatribes to exuberant pro-urban endorsements among nonconformists. Critiques of urbanization are juxtaposed with positive views of city life in this book. The promises of modernity and the record of communal accomplishments are balanced with awareness of poverty, fears about overcrowding and the resulting implications for health, and doubts about the city's moral fiber. Inexplicably, Lees omits reference to Marx and Max Weber. Bibliography.

17409. Lehmann, Hartmut. (1985) "Friedrich von Bodelschwingh," pp. 244-260 in Martin Greschat, ed. Die neueste Zeit II. Stuttgart, West Germany: Kohlhammer. Biography of Friedrich von Bodelschwingh (1831-1910), a leader in inner missions and work with children, the unemployed, the sick, and the poor.

17410. Leigh, Vanora. (1985) Mother Teresa. New York: Bookwright Press.

17411. Le Joly, Edward. (1985) Mother Teresa of Calcutta: A Biography. San Francisco, CA: Harper and Row. Part 1 was originally published under the title Servant of Love: Mother Teresa and Her Missionaries of Charity. San Fancisco, CA: Harper and Row. Part 2 was originally published under the title Messenger of God's Love. [Calcutta, India?]: St. Paul Publications.

17412. Leonard of Taizé, Brother. (1985) Belonging. New York: Pilgrim Press. Brother Leonard recounts experiences of people who find a word of love and commitment in most unlikely urban settings.

17413. Leonard of Taizé, Brother. (1985) Listening to the People of Hope. New York: Pilgrim Press. Brother Leonard, a much traveled member of the ecumenical Taizé Community in France, narrates a compassionate travelogue based on his experiences with urban people in the United States.

17414. Leonard, Henry B. (1985) "Ethnic Tensions, Episcopal Leadership and the Emergence of the Twentieth Century American Catholic Church: The Cleveland Experience," Catholic Historical Review. Vol. 71, pp. 394-412. Reprinted: Dolores A. Liptak, ed. A Church of Many Cultures. New York: Garland, 1988.

17415. Lester, Andrew D. (1985) Pastoral Care with Children in Crisis. Philadelphia, PA: Westminster. Bibliography.

17416. Lewis, Donald M. (1985) "The Evangelical Mission to the Poor in 19th Century England," Crux: A Quarterly Journal of Christian Thought and Opinion. Vol. 21, No. 3 (September), pp. 9-16. Re: Thomas Chalmers and David Nasmith -- their evangelistic work and efforts to help the poor in England and Scotland.

17417. Liptak, Dolores A. (1985) "The National Parishes: Concept and Consequences for the Diocese of Hartford, 1890-1920," Catholic Historical Review. Vol. 71 (July), pp. 52-64. Reprinted: Dolores A. Liptak, ed. A Church of Many Cultures. New York: Garland, 1988.

17418. Lively, Robert D. (1985) "Spilled Milk and Broken Promises: An Apache's Introduction to the City," Sojourners. Vol. 14, No. 1 (January), pp. 30-31.

17419. Lloyd, Anthony Frazier. (1985) The Urban Black Church's Role in Community Mental Health Care. Thesis (D. Min.). Claremont, CA: School of Theology at Claremont.

17420. Lonergan, Connie. (1985) Christianity in Irish Industry. Dublin, Ireland: Irish Messenger Publications.

17421. Long, Daniel M. (1985) "Toward Effective Ministry with Hispanics," Word and World, Theology for Christian Ministry. Vol. 5, No. 1 (Winter), pp. 33-42.

17422. Lovett, Leonard. (1985) "Aspects of the Spiritual Legacy of the Church of God in Christ," Midstream. Vol. 24 (October), pp. 389-397. Re: spirituality related to the social involvement of the Church of God in Christ, a rapidly growing urban Black denomination.

17423. Luecke, Richard Henry. (1985) "How Cities Talk," pp. 67-79 in Charles Amjad-Ali and W. Alvin Pitcher, eds. Liberation and

Ethics: Essays in Religious Social Ethics in Honor of Gibson Winter. Chicago, IL: Center for the Scientific Study of Religion.

17424. Mackey, Virginia, et al. (1985) "Police-Community Relations within the Wider Context of Violence in America," Engage/Social Action. Vol. 13, No. 3 (March), pp. 9-48.

17425. Magalis, Elaine. (1985) "Congregations in Mission: First UMC of Germantown," New World Outlook. n.s. Vol. 46, No. 2 (November-December), pp. 8-13. Issues raised by an urban ministry include: the uncertainty regarding what course of action faith demands, the inclusive language controversy, music and arts in a city church, the sanctuary movement for illegal aliens, and change and recollections of the past.

17426. Maldonado, Lionel and Joan Moore, eds. (1985) Urban Ethnicity in the United States. Urban Affairs Annual Reviews, No. 29. Newbury Park, CA: Sage Publications.

17427. Marchant, Colin. (1985) Signs in the City. London: Hodder and Stoughton.

17428. Marguardt, Werner. (1985) Arbeiterbewegung und evangelische Kirchengemeinde im wilhelminischen Deutschland: Kirchstuhlfrage und Kirchenvorstandswahlen in Gross Lengden bei Gottingen. Gottingen, Germany: Vandenhoeck and Ruprecht. Re: history of church and labor issues in Gross Lengen, Germany. Bibliography.

17429. Marianski, Janusz. (1985) "Kontinuität und Wandel der religiösen Tradition in der polnischen Gesellschaft," Collectanea Theologica. Vol. 55, pp. 89-106. [See note 3]. Continuity and change in the religious traditions of Polish society.

17430. Markiewicz, Stanslaw. (1985) Chrze'scija'nstwo a zwi«azki zawodowe. Warsaw, Poland: Instytut Wydawniczy Zwi«azków Zawodowych. Re: religion and political activity in trade unions in Poland.

17431. Martini, Carlos María. (1985) Hacia la ciudad unida: Problema de las ciudades modernas desde la perspectiva cristiana. Madrid, Spain: s.n. Towards a united city: Problems of the modern city from a Christian perspective.

17432. Martini, Carlos María. (1985) Evangelio y comunidad cristiana. Bogotá, Colombia: Ediciones Paulinas. Re: city evangelization.

17433. Marty, Martin E. (1985) "Devastating Decline in White People's City Churches Continues," Context. Vol. 17, No. 2 (January 15), p. 5.

17434. Máspero, Emilio. (1985) "El hombre y el trabajo," pp. 155-204 in F. Moreno, et al. Desafíos a la doctrina social de la Iglesia en América Latina. [Bogotá, Colombia?]: Consejo Episcopal Latinoamericano. Re: Papal encyclicals and the Church's teaching on labor.

17435. Masure, Roger. (1985) "A Reflection on Pastoral Work among Workers," Pro Mundi Vita Dossiers: Europe/North America. No. 29, pp. 2-31.

17436. Matsuda, Mizuho. (1985) "'Strangers within Our Gates:' Asian Women in Migration Situations, a Report," East Asian Journal of Theology. Vol. 3, No. 1 (April), pp. 50-55.

17437. McCandless, Richard L. (1985) "The Church and the Economy: 'Rust Bowl' Parishes Face New Challenges," Alban Institute Action Information. Vol. 11, No. 4 (July), pp. 6-7. A Sharon, PA, Episcopal church links its heritage to the turn of the century social activist tradition of St. George's Church [New York]. Its rector asks how such a church can address the economic upheaval of the 1980's for decaying industrial towns. He suggests several ministries to the economically dislocated, such as job clinics, employment counseling, direct aid, and clergy training.

17438. McClung, Lloyd Grant. (1985) The Church Growth/Church Planting Study Guide: A Two-Phase Reading and Self-Study Course. Thesis (D. Miss.). Pasadena, CA: Fuller Theological Seminary.

17439. McConnel, C. Douglas. (1985) Urban Ministries Training: Evaluating for Effectiveness. Altadena, CA: Barnabas Resources.

17440. McConnell, Doug. (1985) The Bresee Institute for Urban Training: A Study in the Analysis of Urban Training. Thesis (MA). Pasadena, CA: Fuller Theological Seminary, School of World Mission. Re: an assessment of contextual training.

17441. McCoy, John. (1985) "Downtown Churches Fight for Life," Seattle Post-Intelligencer. (February 2), Section: AB.

17442. McGavran, Donald A. and Kip McKean. (1985) "Case Study: Effective Evangelization in Modern Cities," Urban Mission.

Vol. 2, No. 4 (March), pp. 40-43.

17443. McLean, Edward B. (1985) Roman Catholicism and the Right to Work. Lanham, MD: University Press of America. Bibliography.

17444. McManus, James. (1985) "Evangelization Key to Future of Indianapolis Urban Parishes' Growth Plans," National Catholic Reporter. Vol. 21, No. 12 (January 18), pp. 1+.

17445. McNamara, Patrick H. (1985) "American Catholicism in the Mid-Eighties: Pluralism and Conflict in a Changing Church," The Annals of the American Society of Political and Social Sciences. Vol. 480 (July), pp. 63-74.

17446. McWilliam, John. (1985) "Mass Evangelism--Reaching Your City in the Eighties," Urban Mission. Vol. 3, No. 1 (September), pp. 7-14.

17447. Michael, Stanley Reginald. (1985) West Indian Immigrants in St. Croix, United States Virgin Islands, 1960-1982: A Case Study in Immigration and Changes in Religious Affiliation. Thesis (Ph. D.). Boston, MA: Boston University.

17448. Miller, Kenneth R. and Mary Elizabeth Wilson. (1985) Church that Cares: Identifying and Responding to Needs in Your Community. Valley Forge, PA: Judson Press. A manual for community oriented ministry. Questionnaire.

17449. Moritz, Hans. (1985) "Religion und Gesellschaft in der DDR," Theologische Literaturzeitung. Vol. 110, No. 7 (August), pp. 574-587. Re: religion and society in East Germany.

17450. Mulkey, James Broughton. (1985) The Networking for Church and Parachurch Ministry in a Local Area. Thesis (D. Min.). Pasadena, CA: Fuller Theological Seminary.

17451. Muraro, Valmir Francisco. (1985) Juventude operária Católica (JOC). São Paulo, Brazil: Brasiliense.

17452. Murdoch, Norman H. (1985) The Salvation Army: An Anglo-American Revivalist Social Mission. Thesis (Ph. D.). Cincinnati, OH: University of Cincinnati.

17453. Murphy, Jimmy. (1985) Christ's Transforming Power in

the Place They Called Devil's Island. Basingstoke, England: Marshalls.

17454. Murray, Eileen H. (1985) An Adaptation of the Learning Center Concept of Education to Teaching Christian Education in Urban Sunday Schools in India. Thesis (Ed. D.). New York: New York University.

17455. Mwantila, Simalike. (1985) "Case Study: Urban Missions in Tanzania, East Africa," Urban Mission. Vol. 2, No. 4 (March), pp. 44-47.

17456. Natale, Samuel M. (1985) "Assessing Ethical and Religious Dimensions of Decision Making in Industry: Pastoral Counseling," The Journal of Pastoral Counseling. Vol. 20, No. 1 (Spring-Summer), pp. 65-71.

17457. National Hispanic Consultation. (1985) The Episcopal Church and the Hispanic Challenge: A Report on the State of Hispanic Ministries, Pasadena, CA, November 28-December 1, 1984. New York: Office of Hispanic Minisrties, the Episcopal Church. [Location: General Theological Seminary, New York]. An analysis of Episcopal Hispanic ministry with recommendations.

17458. NCCB Committee on Migration and Tourism. (1985) Pastoral Care of Vietnamese Catholics in the United States: A Preliminary Report. Washington, DC: the Committee. Reprinted: Dolores A. Liptak, ed. A Church of Many Cultures. New York: Garland, 1988.

17459. Needham, Barrie. (1985) "Town Planning and Human Values," Faith Freedom: A Journal of Progressive Religion. Vol. 38, No. 112 (Spring), pp. 41-43.

17460. Newman, Aubrey. (1985) "A Note on the Recent Research on the Jewish East End of London," Jewish Journal of Sociology. Vol. 27, No. 2 (December), pp. 135-138.

17461. Ng, John Lai. (1985) Cultural Pluralism and Ministry Models in the Chinese Community [in North America]. Thesis (D. Min.). Pasadena, CA: Fuller Theological Seminary.

17462. Nichols, Bruce, ed. (1985) In Word and Deed: Evangelistic and Social Responsibility. Grand Rapids, MI: Eerdmans.

17463. Nieves, Alvaro L. (1985) "Urban Minorities and Christian

Higher Education," Urban Mission. Vol. 3, No. 2 (November), pp. 20-28.

17464. Niklaus, Robert. (1985) [Editorials] "World: Megacity Strategies," [and] "Colombia: 'Flashpoint of Growth,'" Evangelical Missions Quarterly. Vol. 21, No. 2 (April), pp. 173-176.

17465. Niklaus, Robert. (1985) "World: Massive Growth," Evangelical Missions Quarterly. Vol. 21, No. 3 (July), pp. 315-316.

17466. Norman, B. (1985) "What Single Adult Ministry Has Done for a Church," Church Administration. Vol. 27, No. 9 (June), pp. 25-27.

17467. Novak, Michael. (1985) Toward the Future: Catholic Social Thought and the US Economy. Lanham, MD: University Press of America.

17468. Nuesse, C. Joseph. (1985) "Henry George and Rerum Novarum: Evidence Is Scant that the American Economist Was a Target of Leo XII's Classic Encyclical," The American Journal of Economics and Sociology. Vol. 44 (April), pp. 241-254.

17469. O'Brien, William. (1985) "Serving Christ in the City," Other Side. Vol. 21, No. 5 (July), pp. 8-9.

17470. O'Neill, Charles. (1985) "Audio-Visual Resources for Urban Ministry," Cities. Vol. 5, No. 1, (Spring), pp. 6-8. A bibliography.

17471. Ogletree, Thomas W. (1985) Hospitality to the Stranger: Dimensions of Moral Understanding. Philadelphia, PA: Fortress. A central dynamic of moral experience is hospitality.

17472. Olson, Joan. (1985) "On the Ledge: Between the Glitter and the Slums, LaSalle Street Church Cares for the Poor and the Shunned," World Christian. Vol. 4, No. 4 (July), pp. 14-16.

17473. Olver, Paul S. (1985) A Strategy for Urban Church Planting for the Free Methodist Church of North America. Thesis (MA). Deerfield, IL: Trinity Evangelical Divinity School.

17474. Orsi, Robert Anthony. (1985) The Madonna of 115th Street: Faith and Community in Italian Harlem, 1880-1950. New Haven, CT: Yale University Press.

17475. Paris, Peter J. (1985) The Social Teaching of the Black Churches. Philadelphia, PA: Fortress Press. Paris interprets the moral ambiguities and conflicts that emerged in the independent Black churches during the 1960s and 1970s in light of the heritage of the Black Christian tradition and its biblical vision. Bibliography.

17476. Parker, Andrew T. (1985) "My Hospice Story: A Study in the Evolution of Hospice as Urban Ministry," Cities. Vol. 5, No. 1 (Spring), pp. 18-20.

17477. Partain, Eugene C. (1985) "Sheltering the Suburban Homeless," The Christian Century. Vol. 102, No. 12 (April 10), pp. 353-356. Suburban churches have a role to play in meeting the housing needs of suburban homeless people, as is shown in the case of First Baptist church in Evanston, IL.

17478. Parvin, Earl. (1985) Missions USA. Chicago, IL: Moody. Bibliogaphy.

17479. Pasquariello, Ronald D. (1985) "Taxing the Poor," The Christian Century. Vol. 102, No. 7 (February 27), pp. 215-216. Consequences of tax laws.

17480. Pasquariello, Ronald D. (1985) "The Bible, the City, and Urban Reform," Cities. Vol. 5, No. 1, (Spring), pp. 10-14.

17481. Patch, William L. (1985) The Christian Trade Unions in the Weimer Republic, 1918-1933: The Failure of "Corporate Pluralism." New Haven, MA: Yale University Press.

17482. Pennick, Paul, Jr. (1985) "An Experiment in Christian Sharing," Columbia. Vol. 6 (July), pp. 8-15.

17483. Pierce, Robert M. (1985) "Rating America's Metropolitan Areas," American Demographics. Vol. 7, No. 7 (July), pp. 21-25. Quality rating devices for metropolitan areas burgeoned during the 1980s, with the promoters of various approaches hotly defending their particular recipe for assessment. The ratings are based on a number of social indicators (number of museums, cost of housing, number of higher education institutions, etc.) presumed to reflect the quality of life in cities. Here Pierce, the developer of one such scheme, criticizes the earlier Places Rated Almanac by Richard Boyer and David Savageau, offering his own solutions to rating problems. His assessments, he claims, are based on how the public actually rates cities, while other approaches reflect merely the values of the researchers. Popular during the 1980s, such indexes usually attracted national press attention when they appeared.

17484. Pinyan, Charles. (1985) "Pressure from the Pulpit," Chemical Week. Vol. 137 (December 11), pp. 14-15. Church investor groups seek policy assurances from Union Carbide.

17485. Platte, Ardeth. (1985) "Public Office: An Option for One, a Mandate for Another," pp. 272-281 in Madonna Kolbenschlag, ed. Between God and Caesar. New York: Paulist. The author reflects on her term on the Saginaw, MI, City Council as a woman religious.

17486. Portaro, Sam A. (1985) "Is God Prejudiced in Favor of the Poor?" The Christian Century. Vol. 102, No. 14 (April 24), pp. 404-405. Portaro is uncomfortable with the notion, growing in popularity, that God is biased in favor of the poor. He opposes the canonization of poverty.

17487. Pyko, Kimberly and Rick Rosenfeld. (1985) "Unions Avoid Divestiture Talk: Churches Take Harder Line," Pensions and Investments Age. Vol. 13 (August), p. 32.

17488. Ramsden, William E., Kinmoth W. Jefferson and Rene O. Bideaux. (1985) Inner Vitality, Outward Vigor: The Missional Urban Church. New York: General Board of Global Ministries, United Methodist Church. A study of 22 Methodist churches in a variety of city settings yields eight conclusions about what constitutes effective urban ministry, e.g., "the process of congregational development and mission to community were linked," "the congregation was open to strangers/visitors ...."

17489. Ranck, Lee. (1985) "To Listen and to Care," Engage/Social Action. Vol. 13, No. 3 (March), pp. 25-27.

17490. Reilly, Lorraine. (1985) Chemical Dependency: The Family Disease: A Pastoral Counselor's Techniques in Educating and Counseling Family Members in Breaking the Addiction Cycle. Thesis (D. Min.). New York: New York Theological Seminary.

17491. Rice, Larry. (1985) "A Night on the Streets," Urban Mission. Vol. 2, No. 3 (January), pp. 27-32.

17492. Richards, Michael. (1985) "Cosmopolitan World View and Counterinsurgency in Guatemala," Anthropological Quarterly. Vol. 58, No. 3 (July), pp. 90-107.

17493. Rieder, Jonathan. (1985) Canarsie: The Jews and Italians of Brooklyn against Liberalism. Cambridge, MA: Harvard University Press.

17494. Riley, Negail Rudolph, ed. (1985) An Enduring Legacy: Black United Methodists and the National Program Division. New York: General Board of Global Ministries, the United Methodist Church. Riley was Executive Secretary of the Department of Urban Ministries of the United Methodist Church, perhaps the first Black executive of a major USA Protestant denomination's city work.

17495. Rippin, Bryan. (1985) The Christian Juggler. London: Epworth Press. Rippin, a Methodist city mission superintendent, describes life in London's East End and how it shaped his faith.

17496. Rochester, Colin. (1985) "What's It Like Down There?" Youth in Society. No. 102 (May), pp. 16-19.

17497. Rochford, E. Burke, Jr. (1985) Hare Krishna in America. New Brunswick, NJ: Rutgers University Press. Rochford describes characteristics of Hare Krishna members and traces the evolution of the group.

17498. Rockefeller, David. (1985?) Giving: America's Greatest National Resource. New York: Rockefeller Brothers Fund. A pamphlet.

17499. Root, John. (1985) "Issues for the Church in a Multi-Racial Society," Christian Action Journal. (Summer), pp. 8-14.

17500. Roseberry, P. (1985) "A Skinny White Christian Moves to the Ghetto," Social Work and Christianity. Vol. 12, No. 2 (Fall), pp. 5-13.

17501. Rosner, Victor. (1985) "Case Study: Schools for Calcutta's Pavement Children," Urban Mission. Vol. 2, No. 3 (January), pp. 44-46.

17502. Rowen, Samuel. (1985) "Doing Mission," Evangelical Missions Quarterly. Vol. 21, No. 2 (April), pp. 204-209. Reviews periodical literature on a variety of topics, including urban missionaries.

17503. Rowen, Samuel. (1985) "Is Continued Urban Growth Inevitable?" Evangelical Missions Quarterly. Vol. 21, No. 4 (October), pp. 418-420.

17504. Rubenstein, Richard L. (1985) "Civic Altruism and the Resacralization of the Political Order," pp. 3-17 in M. Darrol Bryant and Rita Mataragnon, eds. The Many Faces of Religion and Society. New York: Paragon House.

17505. Rush, James P. (1985) Changing Fate to Destiny: A Local Church Growth Group Process in a Textile Community. Thesis (D. Min.). San Anselmo, CA: San Francisco Theological Seminary.

17506. Rwoma, Desiderius. (1985) "Understanding and Solving Youth Problems," AFER: African Ecclesial Review. Vol. 27, No. 6 (December), pp. 351-356.

17507. Ryan, Michael. (1985) "Labour's Hard Choices: Some Ethical Issues Facing Organized Labour in Canada Today," Grail: An Ecumenical Journal [Thematic issue: Unions]. Vol. 1 (June), pp. 57-68.

17508. Sallnow, Theresa. (1985) "Sinai in the Inner City," British Journal of Religious Education. Vol. 8. No. 1 (Autumn), pp. 9-12. Re: spirituality in urban areas.

17509. Sartori, Luís Maria Alves. (1985) Liberação Cristã do mundo do trabalho. Petrópolis, Brazil: Vozes. Chritian liberation of the working class.

17510. Sawatsky, Ben A. (1985) "A Church Planting Strategy for World Class Cities," Urban Mission. Vol. 3, No. 2 (November), pp. 7-19.

17511. Schissel, Steve M. (1985) "City Singles," Urban Mission. Vol. 3, No. 1 (September), pp. 26-31.

17512. Schnepp, Gerald J. (1985) Province of St. Louis, 1908-1985: The First Seventy-Five Years. St. Louis, MO: Marianist Press. Bibliography.

17513. Schöpfer, Hans. (1985) Christen und Gastarbeiter: Handbuch zur Gastarbeiterpastoral. Meitingen, West Germany: Kyrios-Verlag. A handbook for working with foreign workers.

17514. Schuman, Howard, Charllotte Steeh, and Lawrence Bobo. (1985) Racial Attitudes in America: Trends and Interpretations. Cambridge, MA: Harvard University Press. While the overall attitudes about racial discrimination have generally moved in the direction of tolerance and greater rejection of discrimination, not all race-related attitudes have had a similar positive direction according to this social psychological assessment of existing indicators. Some attention is given in this volume to the impact of nationally prominent Afro-American clergy on the attitudes of Whites. Bibliography.

17515. Schwarz, Brian. (1985) "Ministry in the Urban Context," Point: Forum for Melanesian Affairs, Series No. 7, pp. 166-183. Bibliography.

17516. Sellers, I. (1985) "A New Town: The United Reformed Churches in the Warrington/Runcorn Urban Complex," Journal of the United Reformed Church History. Vol. 3, pp. 290-307. [See Note 3].

17517. Sellers, James E. (1985) "The Polis in American Imagio Dei: Neither Secular nor 'Born Again,'" pp. 173-202 in James Turner Johnson, ed. The Bible in American Law, Politics, and Political Rhetoric. Philadelphia, PA: Fortress.

17518. Sethi, S. Prakash. (1985) "The Righteous and the Powerful: Differing Paths to Social Goals," Business and Society Review [Thematic issue: Church activism and corporate America]. No. 54 (Summer), pp. 37-44.

17519. Shapiro, Edward S. (1985) "Orthodoxy in Pleasantdale," Judaism: A Quarterly Journal of Jewish Life and Thought. Vol. 34, No. 2 (Spring), pp. 163-170. Re: suburban Orthodox Judaism in West Orange, NJ.

17520. Shelp, Earl E. and Ronald H. Sunderland. (1985) "AIDS and the Church," The Christian Century. Vol. 102, No. 27 (September 11-18), pp. 797-800. Reply: No. 31 (October 16), p. 910.

17521. Siebert, Rudolf J. (1985) "Urbanization as a World Trend: A Challenge to the Churches," Missiology: An International Review. Vol. 13, No. 4 (October), pp. 429-443. Urban crisis precipitates the need for new theology. Siebert suggests a political theology with a hermeneutic of danger. Churches must seek to meet human needs and to administer justice.

17522. Silvoso, Eduardo. (1985) "Renewal from Within--The Bruno Model from South America," Urban Mission. Vol. 2, No. 5 (May), pp. 40-45.

17523. Simpson, Dick and Clinton Stockwell, eds. (1985) The

Struggle for Peace, Justice, and Sanctuary [Justice Ministries Series, Spring, 1985]. Chicago, IL: Institute on the Church in Urban Industrial Society (ICUIS). A bibliography.

17524. Simpson, Dick and Clinton Stockwell, eds. (1985) Fighting the War Against ... Hunger, Homelessness, Joblessness [Justice Ministries Series, Winter, 1985]. Chicago, IL: Institute on the Church in Urban-Industrial Society. An accumulation of clippings, statements about model programs, and resource lists.

17525. Sklar, Kathryn Kish. (1985) "Hull House in the 1890s: A Community of Women Reformers," Signs. Vol. 10 (Summer), pp. 658-677.

17526. Slack, Kenneth. (1985) "Taking Stock in the Violence," The Christian Century. Vol. 102, No. 34 (November 6), pp. 988-989.

17527. Slack, Kenneth. (1985) "Renewed Violence in the Inner City," The Christian Century. Vol. 102, No. 31 (October 16), pp. 908-909.

17528. Slusher, Steven L. (1985) "Southlawn Baptist Church: Its Death and Rebirth," Urban Review [Southern Baptist]. Vol. 1, No. 3 (October).

17529. Smith, Famous. (1985) A Man Called Famous: Elder Famous Smith. Edited by Ida Sykes. West Memphis, AR: Fifteenth Street Church of God in Christ.

17530. Smith, Geoffrey Boulton. (1985) "Dark Night of the Urban Soul," Month. n.s. Vol. 18, No. 111 (November), pp. 385-387.

17531. Smith, Joe E. (1985) The Sacred Sojourner: A Prescriptive Model for an Urban Church. Thesis (D. Min.). Berkeley, CA: Pacific Lutheran Theological Seminary. Re: St. James Lutheran Church, Portland, OR.

17532. Smith, Timothy. (1985) "Church Activists in the 1980s: The Conscience of Corporate America," Business and Society Review [Thematic issue: Church activism and corporate America]. No. 54 (Summer), pp. 15-20. Smith is the director of the Interfaith Center on Corporate Responsibility. He calls the church to confront business practices which are ethically suspect and prejudicial.

17533. Smith, Wallace Charles. (1985) The Church in the Life of the Black Family. Valley Forge, PA: Judson.

17534. Smucker, John I. (1985) Reflections and Implications of Urban Mennonite Mission in the South Bronx. Thesis (Ph. D.). Cincinnati, OH: Union for Experimenting Colleges and Universities. Re: Friendship Community Church.

17535. Southern Baptist Convention, Sunday School Board. (1985-1986) Urban Review: A Journal of Urban Church Studies. Nashville, TN: the Board. A periodical.

17536. Spain, Daphne. (1985) "Will the 'Back to the City' Movement Revive the Urban Church," Urban Review [Southern Baptist]. Vol. 1, No. 1 (April), pp. 12-24.

17537. Speight, R. Marston. (1985) "Islam in America," JSAC Grapevine. Vol. 17, No. 4 (October), pp. [1-6].

17538. Spooner, Bernard. (1985) "Developing Christian Education in the City," Urban Review [Southern Baptist]. Vol. 1, No. 2 (July), pp. 34-42.

17539. St. Pierre, Roland H. (1985) "Three Term Priest-Mayor," pp. 245-253 in Madonnna Kolbenschlad, ed. Between God and Caesar. New York: Paulist Press.

17540. Stanley, Arthur L. (1985) Out of the Past a Present, Out of the Present a Future: A Plan for the Renewal of the Christian Ministry of the Bethany Presbyterian Church, Trenton, NJ. Thesis (D. Min.). New York: New York Theological Seminary.

17541. Stark, Rodney and William Bainbridge. (1985) The Future of Religion: Secularization, Revival and Cult Formation. Berkeley: University of California Press. An analysis of cultic religions which, among other points, advances the argument that cults are more likely to form and develop in cities because of the level of anonymity afforded there and the large number of people from which to draw membership--an observation consistent with Fischer (1975). Extensive bibliography on sects and cults.

17542. Stockwell, Clinton E. (1985) Urban Research Project: A Handbook for Urban Ministry. Chicago, IL: Baptist General Conference, Midwest District. Descriptive profiles of 21 inner city Baptist churches in Chicago serve as the basis for recommendations regarding decisions the churches are facing and, more generally, for urban evangelism strategies. Bibliography. Questionnaire.

17543. Stoese, Dennis E. (1985) The Story of Home Street Mennonite Church, 1957-1982: Responses to the Urban Environment. Winnipeg, Manitoba, Canada: the Church. [Location: Mennonite Historical Society, Lancaster, PA].

17544. Stoltzfus, Gene. (1985) "Seeing the City," The Other Side. Vol. 20, No. 1 (January-February), pp. 44-46. Re: the Urban Life Center of Chicago and Chicago's social conditions.

17545. Stone, Sara Margaret. (1985) Song Composition, Transmission, and Performance Practice in an Urban Black Denomination, the Church of God and Saints of Christ. Thesis (Ph. D.). Kent, OH: Kent State University.

17546. Sugden, Christopher. (1985) Christ's Exclusive Claims and Inter-Faith Dialog. Grove Pastoral Series No. 22. Bramcote, England: Grove Books. Anglican evangelical perspectives on other religious groups.

17547. Sullivan, Patrick J. (1985) US Catholic Institutions and Labor Unions, 1960-1980. Lanham, MD: University Press of America. Bibliograpy.

17548. Sullivan, Robert E. and James O'Toole, eds. (1985) Catholic Boston. Boston, MA: s.n. A history of the development of the Catholic Church in Boston emphasizes the leadership of Cardinal O'Connell. Among topics discussed: training of priests, Catholic schools, Catholic charities.

17549. Sussman, Lance J. (1985) "The Suburbanization of Judaism as Reflected in Synagogue Building and Architecture," American Jewish History. Vol. 75, No. 1 (September), pp. 31-47. Architecture for suburban synagogues combines elements of the Jewish heritage with suburban cultural influences.

17550. Swarthout, Marjorie. (1985) "Case Study: St. Stephen's Boston: Mission to the South End," Urban Mission. Vol. 3, No. 2 (November), pp. 40-43. Re: St. Stephen's Episcopal Church, Boston, MA.

17551. Sweeting, George. (1985) "The Challenge of the City," Trinity World Forum. Vol. 10, No. 3 (Summer), pp. 1-6.

17552. Tassello, Graziano and Luigi Favero, comp. (1985) Pontificia Commissione per la pastorale delle migrazionie de turismo, Vaticano; Chiesa e mobilità umana: documenti della Seda dal 1883 al 1983. Rome: Centro studi emigrazione. Re: over 300 official Catholic and Papal documents on church work with travelers and immigrants, mostly in Latin.

17553. Tatgenhorst, David. (1985) Transforming Angels: Cooperative Ministry as an Urban Strategy. Thesis (M. Div.). New York: Union Theological Seminary.

17554. Teresa, Mother. (1985) Mother Teresa: Contemplative in the Heart of the World. Ann Arbor, MI: Servant Books.

17555. Terpenning, Peter A. (1985) Death and New Life in Urban Churches: Case study of selected C.I.T. Churches, 1977-1985. Chicago,IL: [manuscript]. [Location: Chicago Theological Seminary]. A pamphlet.

17556. Theobald, Robin. (1985) "From Rural Populism to Practical Christianity: The Modernization of the Seventh-Day Adventist Movement," Archives de sciences sociales de religions. Vol. 30, Nos. 60/1 (July), pp. 109-130.

17557. Thomas, Charles B., Jr. (1985) "Clergy in Racial Controversy: A Replication of the Campbell and Pettigrew Study," Review of Religious Research. Vol. 26, No. 4 (June), pp. 379-390. A study of 55 Bostonian clergy and their involvement in school desegreation during the mid 1970s.

17558. Thomas, Joseph, s.j. (1985) "Nouveaux lieux d'église," Etudes. Vol. 361 (April), pp. 535-544.

17559. Thompsett, Fredrica Harris. (1985) "Exploring a Corporate Theology," Ministry Development Journal. No. 8, pp. 23-29.

17560. Thompson, Phyllis. (1985) To the Heart of the City. London: Hodder and Stoughton.

17561. Thung, Mady A., et al. (1985) Exploring the New Religious Consciousness: An Investigation of Religious Change by a Dutch Group. Amsterdam, Netherlands: Free University Press.

17562. Tlhagale, Buti. (1985) "Towards a Black Theology of Labour," pp. 126-134 in Charles Ville-Vicensio and John W. DeGruchy.

Resistance and Hope. Cape Town, South Africa: D. Philip. [See Note 3].

17563. Toogood, Michael. (1985) "Stepping Back into the City," Urban Mission. Vol. 2, No. 3 (January), pp. 6-13. Evangelical strategy for the city of London.

17564. Tsai, Kuo-shan. (1985) "How to Reach the Industrial Workers in Taiwan," Chinese Around the World. Vol. 4, No. 5 (June), pp. 4-5.

17565. Tsai, Kuo-Shan. (1985) The Evangelization of the Urban Industrial Workers in Taiwan in Missiological Perspectives. Thesis (D. Miss.). Pasadena, CA: Fuller Theological Seminary, School of World Mission.

17566. Tutterow, Michael. (1985) "Reaching America's Ethnic Stew Pot," Bridges [World Vision]. Vol. 2, No. 1 (Summer), pp. 1-3.

17567. Urban Connections: Inter Mennonite Urban Newsletter. (beginning in 1985) Elkhart, IN: Mennonite Board of Missions. A periodical newsletter, published quarterly.

17568. Vail, Bruce. (1985) "Standing Up for Seafarers," American Shipper. Vol. 27 (November), pp. 50-51. Re: Seamen's Church Institute.

17569. Vanderstel, David G. (1985) "Dutch Immigrant Neighborhood Development in Grand Rapids, 1850-1900," pp. 125-155 in Robert P. Swierenga, ed. The Dutch in America: Immigration, Settlement, and Cultural Change. New Brunswick, NJ: Rutgers University Press.

17570. Vaughn, Ellen Santilli. (1985) "The Surprising Results of Prison Ministry," Moody Monthly. Vol. 85, No. 9 (May), pp. 22-26.

17571. Velichko, Olga I. (1985) Politicheskii katolitsizm i rabochee dvizhenie v Avstrii, 1918-1984. Moskow, Russia: "Nauka." Re: The Catholic Church in Austria and the conditions of laboring classses in the 20th century. Bibliography. Title Romanized.

17572. Vidyasagara, Vijaya. (1985) "Urban Rural Mission of the Church," pp. 18-47 in George Ninan, ed. Theology and Ideology in Asian People's Struggle. Hong Kong: Christian Conference of Asia, Urban Rural Mission.

17573. Vinatier, Jean. (1985) Les prêtres ouvriers, le cardinal Liénart et Rome: histoire d'une crise, 1944-1967. Paris: Editions de témoignage chrétien, Editions Ouvrières. A history of worker priests and their controversy with the Catholic Church.

17574. Volp, Rainer. (1985) "Kirche in der Stadt: Umgang mit alten Kirchen," Berliner Theologische Zeitschrift. Vol. 2, No. 2, pp. 304-316. What to do with old city churches.

17575. Von der Haar, Christine M. (1985) Organizational Commitment to the Catholic Church in America: An Empirical Study of the Factors Influencing Urban Parishioners in the Eighties. Thesis (Ph. D.). Bloomington, IN: Indiana University.

17576. Wachs, Martin, ed. (1985) Ethics in Planning. New Brunswick, NJ: Center for Public Policy Research. A collection of articles about the role of social ethics in urban planning, including sections on corruption and whistle-blowing, environmental ethics, and ethics and policy making. Bibliography.

17577. Walton, Susan. (1985) "To Preserve the Faith: Catholic Charities in Boston, 1920-1930," pp. 67-119 in Robert Sullivan and James O'Toole, eds. Catholic Boston: Studies in Religion and Community, 1870-1970. Boston, MA: Archdiocesse of Boston. Reprinted: Brian Mitchell, ed. Building the American Catholic City. New York: Garland, 1988.

17578. Waterman, Stanley. (1985) "A Note on the Migration of Jews from Dublin," Jewish Journal of Sociology. Vol. 27, No. 1 (June), pp. 23-29. Re: the decline of the small Jewish community of Dublin, Ireland.

17579. Watts, Gary. (1985) "Realism and Freedom within a Penitentiary," pp. 78-93 in Walter Freitag, ed. Festschrift: A Tribute to Fr. William Hordern. Saskatoon, Saskatchewan, Canada: University of Saskatchewan.

17580. Weidman, Robert. (1985) "Equipping the Congregation for Evangelism and Ministry," pp. B1-B17 in Clinton Stockwell, comp. Urban Research Project. A Handbook for Urban Ministry. Chicago, IL: Baptist General Conference, Midwest District.

17581. Welch, Kevin W. (1985) Church Membership in American Metropolitan Areas, 1952-1971. Thesis (Ph. D.). Seattle, WA: University of Washington.

17582. Westgate, James E. (1985) "Transition and the Urban Church," Urban Mission. Vol. 2, No. 4 (March), pp. 22-32. Committee tasks and local church structures for congregations facing ethnic and economic change in their neighborhoods.

17583. Wheale, Gerald. (1985) "The Parish and Politics," pp. 146-168 in George Moyser, ed. Church and Politics Today: Essays on the Role of the Church of England in Contemporary Politics. Edinburgh, Scotland: T. and T. Clark. Re: clergy and political activity in Manchester, England.

17584. White, Kathleen. (1985) Mother Teresa. [London]: Marshalls. Written for children.

17585. William Temple Foundation. (1985) Health and Poverty: A Christian Contribution. Manchester, England: William Temple Foundation. Reflections by an industrial chaplain on the failure of the National Health Service in England to address the needs of the disadvantaged. Policy proposals are included.

17586. William Temple Foundation. (1985) The Creation of Wealth. Manchester, England: the Foundation. Includes a paper on the theology of poverty and a paper on economic policy and poverty, among others.

17587. William Temple Foundation and Ruskin College. (1985) Communities in Crisis: A Resource Programme for Local Organizations and Leaders. Manchester, England: Ruskin College, Oxford, and the William Temple Foundation, Manchester. Description of training programs for community activists, with illustrations of projects and political action.

17588. Willock, John. (1985) "Looking Up Down at the Bowery: Interview," Christian Herald. Vol. 108, No. 11 (December), pp. 23-28. Willock is director of the Bowery Mission.

17589. Wilson, Pip. (1985) Gutter Feelings: Christian Youth Work in the Inner City. Basingstoke, England: Marshalls. Wilson relates and reflects on his personal experience as a youth in the inner city, his conversion to Christianity, and his subsequent career as an inner city youth worker. Wilson's narrative style is intended to convey the humiliation, frustration, and agitation of British inner city youth, as well as some of their triumphs. He writes for non-inner city readers.

17590. Wilson, R. Boyce. (1985) Church Growth by Church Division: A Mexican Model for Church Growth. Thesis (D. Miss.). Deerfield, IL: Trinity Evangelical Divinity School.

17591. Wilson, Robert. (1985) "Another Look at Old First Church," Urban Review [Southern Baptist]. Vol. 1, No. 1 (April), pp. 4-11.

17592. Wilson, Thomas C. (1985) "Urbanism, Misanthropy and Subcultural Processes," The Social Science Journal. Vol. 22, No. 3 (July), pp. 89-101. Wilson tests theories about the degree to which urbanism (population size) contributes to misanthropy (negative feelings toward others). The hypothesis is rejected.

17593. Winter, J. Alan and Lester I. Levin. (1985) The Cost of Jewish Affiliation and Participation: Implications for Federations, Agencies, and Councils. New York: Council of Jewish Federations. A pamphlet.

17594. Winter, Miriam Therese. (1985) "Sing if You Know Justice," Liturgy. Vol. 5, No. 1, pp. 69-73. A Hartford, CT, seminary professor comments on teaching Christian communities to pray through the use of music. The Psalms, sung as liturgical prayers, can form a basis for members' faith and can transform people's attitudes toward social justice issues.

17595. Winters, Donald E. (1985) The Soul of the Wobblies: The I. W. W., [Industrial Workers of the World] Religion, and American Culture in the Progressive Era. Westport, CT: Greenwood Press. Bibliography.

17596. Wright, Robert. (1985) "Urban Ministry," Christian Herald. Vol. 108, No. 9 (October), pp. 39-43.

17597. Yamamori, Tetsuano. (1985) "Urban Perspectives: Finding Ethnic America," Urban Mission. Vol. 2, No. 5 (May), pp. 52-53.

17598. Yardeni, Myriam. (1985) Le refuge protestant. Paris: Presses universitaires de France. Re: Protestant church work with refugees.

17599. Zanotti, Gabriel J. (1985) Economia de mercado y doctrina social de la Iglesia. Buenos Aires, Argentina: Editorial de Belgrano. An essay on religious teachings and economic theory, written from the persective of the Austrian school of economics, deals with marginal utility, value, and church-labor relations.

17600. Zorazim, Josef. (1985) "Israeli Families in New York City: Their Utilization of Social Services and Unmet Needs," Journal of Jewish Communal Service. Vol. 61, No. 3 (June), pp. 330-341.

17601. Abrecht, Paul. (1986) "Technology in Tension with Human Values," New World Outlook [Thematic issue: Technology]. n.s. Vol. 46, No. 8 (June), pp. 8-11. Churches must challenge the values underlying technological development lest humanity become crippled by its own creation.

17602. Ahn, Yoo Kwang. (1986) The Usefulness of Selected Programs in the Contemporary Christian Family Life Movement for Korean Family Life in New York City. Thesis (Ph. D.). New York: New York University.

17603. Allen, Frank W. (1986) "Toward a Biblical Urban Mission," Urban Mission. Vol. 3, No. 3 (January), pp. 6-15.

17604. Allen, Frank W. (1986) "Poem: Show Me the Throngs," Urban Mission. Vol. 3, No. 5 (May), p. 51.

17605. Allen, Jere and Truman Brown. (1986) Church and Community Diagnostic Workbook. Nashville, TN: Convention Press.

17606. Allis, Andrew P. B. (1986) Seek the Welfare of the City: An Intentional Ministry for St. Peter's Church, 1986-1991. Thesis (D. Min.). Pittsburgh, PA: Pittsburgh Theological Seminary.

17607. Alnor, William. (1986) "Hope Comes to 22nd Street," Christian Herald. Vol. 109, No. 4 (April), pp. 16-19. Church inspired urban renewal efforts in North Philadelphia, PA.

17608. American Baptist Convention, General Board. (1986) "Metropolitan Ministries" [policy, 1979]. American Baptist Quarterly. Vol. 5, Nos. 2-3 (June-September), pp. 138. The same issue contains other related policies and resolution statements: "Labor" [resolution, 1981], pp. 246-247. "Plant Closings" [resolution, 1980], pp. 275-276. "Immigration and Refugee Policy" [policy, 1982], pp. 135-138. "Housing" [policy, 1983], pp. 126-128.

17609. Amerson, Philip A. (1986) Servant Leadership. (Sound recording). Albuquerque, NM: Hosanna. Advice for urban pastors.

17610. Amirtham, Samuel and S. Wesley Ariarajah. (1986) Ministerial Formation in a Multifaith Milieu: Implications of Interfaith

Dialog for Theological Education. Geneva, Switzerland: World Council of Churches.

17611. Amirtham, Samuel and John S. Pobe. (1986) Theology by the People. Geneva, Switzerland: World Council of Churches. Reviewed: The Expository Times, Vol. 98, No. 12 (September, 1987), p. 380. Missiology, Vol. 15, No. 3 (July, 1987), p. 394.

17612. Anders, Sarah Frances. (1986) "Ministry to Single Parent Families," Urban Review [Southern Baptist]. Vol. 2, No. 1 (April), pp. 13-22.

17613. Anderson, Alan B. (1986) Confronting the Color Line: The Broken Promise of the Civil Rights Movement in Chicago. Athens, GA: University of Georgia Press. Chicago is cited for excessive racial segregation. The authors have extensive background in urban church work and clergy training. Bibliography.

17614. Anderson, James D. and Ezra Earl Jones. (1986) Ministry of the Laity. San Francisco, CA: Harper and Row.

17615. Anderton, Douglas L. (1986) "Urbanization, Secularization, and Birth Spacing: A Case Study of an Historical Fertility Transition," The Sociological Quarterly. Vol. 17, No. 1, pp. 43-62. A study of fertility transition and interbirth intervals in 19th century Utah.

17616. Archer, Anthony. (1986) The Two Catholic Churches. London: SCM Press. Archer, writing about the Catholic Church in England, finds the reforms of Vatican II not to have made the Church more accessible for all people, but rather to have been a triumph for middle-class intellectuals. The working class has be marginalized even more severely than it was before Vatican II. Traditionally, the English Catholic Church had been a working class church, but now it appears to be moving even closer to the English civil establishment and toward embracing the ambitions of middle class English society. For an extensive review and response to Archer's work, see New Blackfriars, Vol. 68, No. 802 (February, 1987), pp. 54-108.

17617. Arjomand, Saïd Amir. (1986) "Social Change and Movements of Revitalization in Contemporary Islam," pp. 87-112 in James A. Beckford, ed. New Religious Movements and Rapid Social Change. Paris: UNESCO.

17618. Armitage, Michael. (1986) Jesus Loves Brixton Too. Basingstoke, England: Marshall Pickering. Brixton, Europe's most densely populated urban area, is portrayed in vignettes of homelessness, poverty, racism, unemployment, and conflict. Armitage finds signs of God's Kingdom in the city and believes Jesus' revolutionary, liberating teaching offers hope.

17619. Armstrong, Floris Barry. (1986) Outer Edges Prison Ministries, Inc.: A Pastoral Care Model Addressing the Issue of Recidivism. Thesis (D. Min.). Pittsburgh, PA: Pittsburgh Theological Seminary.

17620. Arnal, Oscar L. (1986) Priests in Working-Class Blue: The History of the Worker Priests, 1943-1954. New York: Paulist Press.

17621. Asociacion Nacional de Jovenes Empresarios (Dominican Republic). (1986) Influencia del sector privado sobre la realidad nacional. [Santo Domingo, Dominican Republic]: ANJE. Papers presented at a seminar on capitalism, business enterprises, and industry sponsored by the ANJE in 1985 held in Santo Domingo.

17622. Bakke, Raymond J. (1986) "The Challenge of World Urbanization to Mission Thinking and Strategy: Perspective on Demographic Realities," Urban Mission. Vol. 4, No. 1 (September), pp. 6-17. Reprinted: Atlanta, GA: Metropolitan Missions Department, Home Mission Board, Southern Baptist Convention, Occasional Paper No. 12, 1987. God is urbanizing the world, believes Bakke, but the Biblical resources are sufficient to the task of evangelizing the exploding cities. Bakke comments on the shift of world power to Asia and Africa.

17623. Bakke, Raymond J. (1986) "Sociology and Demographics of World Class Cities," [A paper]. Moody Bible Institute, Trinity Evangelical Divinity School, Wheaton College and Graduate School. The Trinary Study Conference on the Evangelization of the World, March 14-17, 1986.

17624. Bakke, Raymond J. and Samuel K. Roberts. (1986) The Expanded Mission of Old First Churches. Valley Forge, PA: Judson Press. A retrospective look at older downtown churches which, although not at the peak of their influence, still hold potential for city ministry.

17625. Ballard, Monroe and JoeAnn Ballard. (1986) Serving in the City: Nurturing the Poor to Independence. Kansas City, MO: Beacon Hill. A loose leaf handbook on church administration offers suggestions for programs to help city people find work, adequate housing, medical care, education, etc.

17626. Ballard, Paul. (1986) "Community Work and Mission," The Modern Churchman. Vol. 28, No.3, pp. 35-40.

17627. Barrett, David B. (1986) "Annual Statistical Table on Global Mission: 1986," International Bulletin of Missionary Research. Vol. 10, No. 1 (January), pp. 22-23.

17628. Barrett, David B. (1986) World-Class Cities and World Evangelization. Birmingham, AL: New Hope. Commissioned by the Southern Baptist Foreign Missions Board, the first of the "AD 2000 Series," this study on urban evangelism calls for evangelization of the world by the year 2000. "Megastrategies" for "megaministries" in "megacities" characterize Barrett's perspective. Widely cited as authoritative by evangelical authors, the book is based on a survey of 2200 cities with populations of 100,000 or more. Barrett's work has contributed to the emphasis on "supercities" among evangelicals.

17629. Barrett, Lois. (1986) Building the House Church. Scottdale, PA: Herald. Practical suggestions for getting started -- worship, music, intergenerational education, discipling, decisions and conflict resolution -- in addition to descriptions of house churches around the world and considerations of the theological and biblical bases for house churches. Barrett draws on her experience in the Mennonite Church of the Servant, Wichita, KS. Bibliography.

17630. Baum, Gregory. (1986) "Recent Roman Catholic Social Teaching: A Shift to the Left," pp. 47-72 in Walter Block and Irving Hexham, eds. Religion, Economics and Social Thought. Vancouver, British Columbia, Canada: Fraser Institute.

17631. Baum, Gregory. (1986) "John Paul II's Encyclical on Labor," pp. 233-240 in Charles E. Curren and Richard A. McCormick, eds. Official Catholic Social Teaching. New York: Paulist Press.

17632. Bechler, LeRoy. (1986) The Black Mennonite Church in North America, 1886-1986. Scottdale, PA: Herald Press.

17633. Beckford, James A., ed. (1986) New Religious Movements and Rapid Social Change. London: Sage Publications.

17634. Bentham, John. (1986) Worship in the City. [Grove Worship Series, No. 25]. Bramcote, England: Grove. A pamphlet.

17635. Berger, Peter L. (1986) "Religion in Post Protestant America," Commentary. Vol. 81, No. 5 (May), pp. 41-46.

17636. Biger, Gideon. (1986) "Urban Planning and the Garden Suburbs of Jerusalem, 1918-1925," Studies in Zionism, Vol. 7, No. 1 (Spring), pp. 1-9.

17637. Biggar, Nigel, Jamie S. Scott and William Schweiker, eds. (1986) Cities of Gods: Faith, Politics and Pluralism in Judaism, Christianity, and Islam. Westport, CT: Greenwood Press.

17638. Biggins, Maria Goretti. (1986) School Climate as Perceived by Principals and Teachers in Inner City Catholic Elementary Schools (New York). Thesis (Ed. D.). New York: Columbia University Teachers College.

17639. Bilhartz, Terry D. (1986) Urban Religion and the Second Great Awakening: Church and Society in Early National Baltimore. Cranbury, NJ: Associated University Presses. History of evangelical and millennial ferment in early 19th century Baltimore. The bibliography gives special attention to primary sources, minutes, denominational materials and other fugitive sources.

17640. Blakeborough, Eric. (1986) No Quick Fix. Basingstoke, England: Marshall Pickering. An account of one church's ministry to the young, the homeless and drug addicts, this book is written as personal reflections on experiences in a London Baptist church. The self-acknowledged controversial program called Kaleidoscope is the principal focus of the ministry. Kaleidoscope has led the church toward greater emphasis on prayer, Eucharistic celebration, and a "profound" ecumenicity. One of the church's deacons is Roman Catholic.

17641. Bobo, Kimberley A. (1986) Lives Matter: A Handbook for Christian Organizing. Kansas City, MO: Sheed and Ward. Resources for mobilizing local churches on hunger issues. Bibliography on hunger action efforts.

17642. Boff, Clodovis. (1986) Como trabajar con el pueblo: Metodología del trabajo popular. Bogotá, Colombia: Indo-American Press Service. Re: Church work with laborers. A Spanish translation of the Portuguese "Como Trabalhar Com o Povo."

17643. Boff, Leonardo. (1986) Ecclesiogenesis: The Base Communities Reinvent the Church. London: Collins Press. A proponent of liberation theology interprets the philosophy underlying basic Christian Communities. The Latin American emergence of such communities is interpreted for the church in other nations in theological and ecclesiological terms. Boff is Franciscan and, at the time of writing, working in Brazil.

17644. Boltniew, George. (1986) A Functional Analysis of Ethnic/Bilingual Baptist Churches Ministering to Russian-Speaking Immigrants in the USA. Thesis (D. Min.). Philadelphia, PA: Eastern Baptist Theological Seminary.

17645. Bouman, Stephen Paul. (1986) "Your Face, Your Cloak, Your Coat, Your Shoes: Parish-Based Community Organization," Urban Mission. Vol. 3, No. 4 (March), pp. 5-18.

17646. Bowker, Lee H. (1986) Ending the Violence: A Guidebook Based on the Experience of 1000 Battered Wives. Holmes Beach, FL: Learning Publications.

17647. Boyd, Malcolm. (1986) Gay Priest: An Inner Journey. New York: St. Martin's Press.

17648. Boyte, Harry C., Heather Booth, and Steve Max. (1986) Citizen Action and the New American Populism. Philadelphia, PA: Temple University Press. The authors interpret the role of religion in urban populist action movements.

17649. Boyte, Harry C. and Frank Riessman, eds. (1986) The New Populism. Philadelphia, PA: Temple University Press. A collection of articles that discusses the future of populism -- defined as the return of power to ordinary people -- in light of the emergence of the New Right and Reaganism. Joe Holland's contribution is titled: "Populism and America's Spiritual Crisis."

17650. Brakelmann, Günter. (1986) "Evangelischer Bund und evangelische Arbeitervereinsbewegung," pp. 129-155 in Gottfried Maron, ed. Evangelisch und ökumenisch. Göttingen, West Germany: Vanderhoeck und Ruprecht. Protestant church involvement in the workers' movement.

17651. Brakelmann, Günter. (1986) Evangelische Kirche in sozialen Konflikten der Weimarer Zeit: das Beispiel des Ruhreisenstreits. Bochum, West Germany: SWI-Verlag. The Protestant church and labor conflicts during the Weimar Republic and the metal-workers' strike, 1928-1929. Bibliography.

17652. Briefs, Henry. (1986) "The Limits of Scripture: Theological Imperatives and Economic Reality," pp. 57-96 in R. Bruce Douglass, ed. The Deeper Meaning of Economic Life. Washington, DC: Georgetown University Press.

17653. Browning, Ron. (1986) Down and Under: Discipleship in an Australian Urban Setting. Melbourne, Australia: Spectrum Publications. Special characteristics of urban ministry in Australia related by an Anglican Priest in Melbourne.

17654. Bruce, Steve. (1986) "The Threatened Elect: Presbyterians in Ulster and South Africa," pp. 261-291 in Roy Wallace and Steve Bruce. Sociological Theory, Religion and Collective Action. Belfast, Northern Ireland: Queens' University of Belfast. In both Ireland and South Africa, Bruce finds that narrowly interpreted Calvinist doctrine, when combined with feelings of threat by non-Calvinist groups, result in conservative Protestant politics.

17655. Brundage, David. (1986) "Irish Land and American Workers: Class and ethnicity in Denver, Colorado," pp. 46-67 in Hoerder, Dirk, ed. Struggle a Hard Battle. DeKalb, IL: University of Northern Illinois.

17656. Buess, Eduard and Markus Mattmuller. (1986) Prophetischer Sozialismus: Blumhart, Ragaz, Barth. Freiburg, Switzerland: Edition Exodus. Re: interpretations of Swiss socialism in the writings of Christoph Blumhardt, Leonhard Ragaz and Karl Barth.

17657. Bühlmann, Walbert. (1986) The Churches of the Future: A Model for the Year 2001. Maryknoll, NY: Orbis Books.

17658. Building and Urban Strategy. (1986) [Videorecording]. New York: Produced for the Office of Metropolitan/Urban Ministry, Presbyterian Church, USA. Linda Chase, producer; Robert Chase, writer and director.

17659. Burstin, Barbara Stern. (1986) From Poland to Pittsburgh: The Experience of Jews and Christians Who Migrated to Pittsburgh after World War II. Thesis (Ph. D.). Pittsburgh, PA: University of Pittsburgh.

17660. Büttner, Manfred, et al. (1986) Religion und Siedlungsraum. Berlin: D. Reimer. Re: religious work in suburbs and new cities.

17661. Buttry, Daniel L. (1986) "One in the Body: How an Urban Church Learned to Thrive on Diversity," Christian Ministry. Vol. 17, No. 2 (March), pp. 12-15. Dorchester Baptist Temple in Boston thrives on pluralism of the community and congregation.

17662. Butz, Geneva M., with the Children of Old First UCC, Philadelphia. (1986) Color Me Well. New York: Pilgrim Press.

17663. Byars, Larry L. (1986) "Peace on Earth, Good Will in Albuquerque," Christian Herald. Vol. 109, No. 11 (November), pp. 20-24. Church conciliation efforts result in conflicts being settled out of court. A list of local chapters of Christian Conciliation Services in 33 cities is appended.

17664. Camp, Richard L. (1986) "The Rights and Duties of Labor and Capital," pp. 32-50 in Charles E. Curren and Richard A. McCormick, eds. Official Catholic Social Teaching. New York: Paulist Press.

17665. Cancik, Hubert. (1986) "Rome as Sacred Landscape: Varro and the End of Republican Religion in Rome," pp. 250-265 in H. Kippenberg et al., eds. Approaches to Iconology. Leiden: E. J. Brill.

17666. Carlson, Ronald W. (1986) Films about the City: A Selected Bibliography of Films for Sensitizing Christians to Urban Life and Its Problems," Urban Mission. Vol. 4, No. 1 (September), pp. 24-34. Films selected mostly to sensitize suburban Christians to city life and problems.

17667. Carroll, Jackson W., Carl S. Dudley, and William McKinney, eds. (1986) Handbook for Congregational Studies. Nashville, TN: Abingdon Press. A compendium of research models for local churches, this book challenges clergy and churches to use the kinds of data they can collect to formulate their goals and strategies for ministry. Several different approaches are outlined, including an operationalization of Hopewell's (1987) notion of congregational stories. Sample questionnaires offer users the opportunity to adapt instruments to their own needs. The editors want to move local church research beyond the level of information gathered for specific problem solving to the level of empirical data that inform the core notions of a local church's mission and ministry. Reviewed: Christian Century, Vol. 103 (November 26, 1986), pp. 1075-1076. Questionnaire.

17668. Carrow, David J. (1986) Bearing the Cross: Martin Luther King, Jr., and the Southern Christian Leadership Conference. New York: Vintage Books, Random House. A critical biography deals with Martin Luther King, Jr.'s life in terms of the various city campaigns he waged: e.g., Montgomery bus boycott, Birmingham, Washington, St. Augustine and the beginnings of SCLC, Selma, Chicago, and Memphis, and the Poor People's Campaign. Bibliography.

17669. Carter, Nancy A. (1986) "A Methodist Congregation in New York Finds an Epidemic on Its Doorstep," JSAC Grapevine. Vol. 17, No. 8 (March), pp. [4-6]. Re: AIDS.

17670. Carter, Robert L. (1986) New Life for the Church in a Changing Community. Thesis (D. Min.). Madison, NJ: Drew University.

17671. Cashmore, Gwen. (1986) "A Place of Incarnation," One World [World Council of Churches]. No. 121 (December), pp. 17-18.

17672. Casper, Dale E. (1986) Architecture for Spiritual Guidance: Journal Articles on Building, Maintaining, and Preserving Churches, 1980-1985. Monticello, IL: Vance Bibliographies. Bibliography.

17673. Catholic Church, Archdiocese of Detroit. (1986) Detroit City-Church Task Force Recommendations. (1986) Detroit, MI: the Archdiocese. A study cited as contributing to the decision to close 30 Catholic churches in Detroit during the late 1980s.

17674. Cesarz, Kathleen M. (1986) "Bud Brink's Truck Stop Ministry," New World Outlook. n.s. Vol. 46, No. 3 (January), pp. 14-15. Cesarz, chaplain at a truck stop, discusses a ministry of counseling truck drivers.

17675. Chambers, Mary Jane. (1986) "The Suburban Untouchables," Christianity and Crisis. Vol. 46, No. 6 (April 21), pp. 134-135. Vignettes of homeless men and women amid suburban Fairfax County, VA, affluence support Chambers' plea for clothing, shelter, and compassion. Part of a trilogy on homelessness.

17676. Chang, Peter. (1986) "Ministerial Formation for the Working Class: The Jifu Programme," Evangelical Review of Theology. Vol. 10, No. 4 (October), pp. 365-372.

17677. Changing the World. (1986) Bromley, Kent, England: MARC Europe. Bibliography.

17678. Charlton, William. (1986) The Christian Response to Industrial Capitalism. London: Sheed and Ward.

17679. Choron-Baix, Catherine. (1986) Bouddhisme et migration: La reconstitution d'une paroisse bouddhiste lao en banlieue parisienne. [Paris?]: Rapport à la Mission du Patrimoine Ethnologique, Ministére de la Culture.

17680. Chuck, James. (1986) "Patterns of Faith: Woven Together in Life and Mission," American Baptist Quarterly. Vol. 5, No. 4 (December), pp. 373-378.

17681. Church of England, General Synod. (1986) Gallup Survey of Church of England Clergymen: With Particular Reference to Comparative Differences between Urban Priority Areas and Elsewhere. London: Church House, Dean's Yard: General Synod of the Church of England. Background research for the Archbishop's report on urban priority areas (1985).

17682. Church of England, Social Policy Committee of the Board for Social Responsibility. (1986) Not Just for the Poor: Christian Perspectives on the Welfare State. London: Church House Publishing. This document points out the achievements and shortcomings of the British Welfare services and considers criticism of the system offered from feminists, Marxists, and the new right perspectives. Good social welfare services, the report concludes, should be more than a safety net for the poor, but offer a framework of support for all people throughout their lives.

17683. "Churches for the Cities." (1986) Impact [Conservative Baptist Foreign Missions Society]. Vol. 43, No. 1 (February), pp. 6-11. Reviews Conservative Baptist missions in third world cities.

17684. Cocklin, Paul. (1986) Using Small Group Process to Revitalize the Official Structure of a Small Church. Thesis (D. Min.). Dayton, OH: United Theological Seminary. Re: College Hill United Methodist Church, Cincinnati, OH.

17685. Cohn, James. (1986) "[A review of] Charles Brecher and Raymond D. Horton: Setting Municipal Priorities, 1986," Commentary. Vol. 81, No. 5 (May), pp. 74-78.

17686. Cohn-Sherbok, Dan. (1986) "Faith in the City and Jewish Spiritual Resources," Crucible. [Vol. 25, No. 4] (October-December), pp. 156-163.

17687. Coleman, Bonnie. (1986) "Rebuilding a Battered Community: Harambee Center Finds the Future in Youth," World Christian. Vol. 5, No. 2 (March), pp. 14-17.

17688. Collins, Sheila. (1986) "The New Underground Railroad," Monthly Review (New York). Vol. 38 (May), pp. 1-7. Re: the sanctuary movement and their efforts to resettle illegal aliens.

17689. Collins, Trudy B. and Ian Crichton. (1986) "Prison Ministry--Putting Humpty Dumpties Back Together Again," Urban Mission. Vol. 3, No. 3 (January), pp. 14-20.

17690. Conn, Harvie M. (1986) "Missions and Our Present Moment in History," Evangelical Missions Quarterly. Vol. 22, No. 2 (April), pp. 178-183.

17691. Conn, Harvie M. (1986) "Kagawa of Japan: Evangelist Cum Reformer," Urban Mission. Vol. 3, No. 5 (May), pp. 6-19.

17692. Conn, Harvie M. (1986) "'Any Faith Dies in the City:' The Secularization Myth," Urban Mission. Vol. 3, No. 5 (May), pp. 6-19.

17693. Conn, Harvie M. (1986?) Urban Mission: An Annotated Bibliography. [Philadelphia, PA: Westminster Theological Seminary]. Conn provides concise annotations for 136 entries plus 18 journals of interest to students of urban mission and ministry. About one third of the 136 are secular references representing books and articles in urban history, sociology, anthropology, and ethnic studies. Another 30 deal with biblical perspectives on the city. Although most of the remaining entries concern urban ministry in the United States, a selection of materials from elsewhere are included, particularly from the third world. All entries are English language titles. The bibliography is intended as an instructional aide.

17694. Connor, John Harold. (1986) A Relational Study between the Wesleyan Church and the Los Angeles Based Korean Wesleyan Church. Thesis (Th. M.). Pasadena, CA: Fuller Theological Seminary, School of World Mission.

17695. Cook, Paul and Judith Zeiler. (1986) Neighborhood Ministry Basics: A No-Nonsense Guide. Washington, DC: Pastoral Press. A Catholic parish, having undergone an urban transition from an ethnic neighborhood to an upper middle-class community with high rise apartments and a transient population of college educated professionals, discovers a sense of renewal through involving lay persons in a ministry called HOST -- Home Service Team. The book tells the story of St.

Joseph's Parish in Cockeysville, MD. HOST tries to provide a ministry of presence in the neighborhood for the sake of communication, service and ministry. The book is written as a guide for other churches that might want to begin such a program. HOST is offered as an alternative to "base communities," which are seen as besetting potential contacts with yet another meeting to attend and, therefore, prone to rejection by the persons HOST wishes to reach. The authors provide materials which can be used in lay training.

17696. Cox, Gabrielle. (1986) "Power and the Powerless," Christian Action Journal. (Winter), pp. 7-8.

17697. Cracknell, Kenneth and Christopher Lamb. (1986) Theology on Full Alert. London: British Council of Churches. The authors mount an argument for the inclusion of theology of mission and practical aspects of ministry as part of the training for clergy in the United Kingdom.

17698. Cram, Leo L. (1986) "Shared Housing," JSAC Grapevine. Vol. 17, No. 10 (May), pp. [1-4]. A suggestion for coping with housing shortages.

17699. Crichton, Iain. (1986) "Out-of-Wedlock Teenage Pregnancies in the Black Community," Urban Mission. Vol. 4, No. 2 (November), pp. 14-27.

17700. Cronin, John Francis. (1986) "Forty Years Later: Reflections and Reminiscences," pp. 69-76 in Charles E. Curren and Richard A. McCormick, eds. Official Catholic Social Teaching. New York: Paulist Press.

17701. Crouthamel, Luther A. (1986) "The Real Agenda in Pittsburgh: Who Speaks for the Unemployed?" Lutheran Forum. Vol. 20, No. 2, pp. 12-13.

17702. Dale, Robert D. (1986) Pastoral Leadership. Nashville, TN: Abingdon Press.

17703. Dale, Robert D. and Delos Miles. (1986) Evangelizing the Hard to Reach. Nashville, TN: Broadman.

17704. Darwen, Robert, S. J. (1986) "Why the Church Fails the City," Month. n.s. Vol. 19, Nos. 7-8 (July-August), pp. 267-270.

17705. Davidson, James D. (1986) "Captive Congregations: Why

Local Churches Don't Pursue Equality," pp. 239-261 in John Rouse, Stephen Johnson, and Joseph Tamney, eds. The Political Role of Religion in the United States. Boulder, CO: Westview. Davidson, a sociologist, lists reasons why churches fail in efforts to promote justice and equality, e.g., domination by the interests of the powerful elite. He urges church leaders to redouble their efforts.

17706. Davis, David. (1986) "Philadelphia's Dignity Shelter," New World Outlook. n.s. Vol. 46, No. 7 (May), pp. 8-12. United Methodists help with a grass roots shelter for the homeless.

17707. Dawson, Rosemary. (1986) And All That Is Unseen: A New Look at Women's Work. London: Church House.

17708. de la Torre, Edicio. (1986) Touching Ground, Taking Root: Theological and Political Reflections on the Philippine Struggle. London: CIIR in Association with the British Council of Churches.

17709. De'Ath, Erica. (1986) "Faith in the Children in the City," Crucible. [Vol. 25, No. 3] (July-September), pp. 100-105.

17710. Dearnley, Pat. (1986) "Urban Man," The Third Way. Vol. 9, No. 6 (June), pp. 14-16. Dearnley was, at the time of writing, the Archbishop of Canterbury's officer for Urban Priority Areas.

17711. Debès, Joseph and Emile Poulat. (1986) L'appel de la J. O. C. [Jeunesse ouvrière chrétienne], 1926-1928. Paris: Editions du Cerf. Re: church, youth and labor in France. Bibliography.

17712. Delgado, Gary. (1986) Organizing the Movement: The Roots and Growth of ACORN. [Introductions by Richard A. Cloward and Francis Fox Piven]. Philadelphia, PA: Temple University Press. ACORN (The Association of Community Organizations for Reform Now) began as an organization of welfare mothers in Little Rock, Arkansas, in 1970, spread quickly to all sorts of poor people in cities throughout the nation and formed itself as a powerful coalition. It became the largest poor people's organization since the 1930s.

17713. De Souza Martins, Helosia Helena T. (1986) "Catolicismo y clase obrera en Brasil, los años posteriores a 1964," Christianismo y Sociedad (Santo Domingo). Vol. 24, No. 90, pp. 35-64. Re: Catholicism and the working class in Brazil following 1964.

17714. Diehl, Richard Clinton. (1986) Between the No Longer and the Not Yet: The Impact of an Interim Minister on an Urban

Church in Transition. Thesis (D. Min.). Hartford, CT: Hartford Seminary. A case study on ministry opportunities available to interim clergy in transitional churches.

17715. Djait, Hichem. (1986) Al-Küfa: Naissance de la ville islamique: Islam d'hier et d'aujourd'hui. No. 29. Paris: G. -P. Maisoneuve et Larose. Re: Islamic cities and towns.

17716. Dobra, Al. (1986) "Taking the Gospel to Urban Africa," Impact [Conservative Baptist Foreign Missions Society]. Vol. 43, No. 1 (February), pp. 12-14. Re: Conservative Baptist missions in Abidjan, Ivory Coast. This journal frequently has articles on missions in Third World cities.

17717. Dollar, Truman. (1986) "Fundamentally One," Leadership: A Practical Journal for Church Leaders. Vol. 7, No. 4 (Fall), pp. 12-20.

17718. Donahue, Thomas R. (1986) "From Rerum Novarum to Laborem Exercens: A United States Labor Perspective," pp. 384-410 in Charles E. Curren and Richard A. McCormick, eds. Official Catholic Social Teaching. New York: Paulist Press.

17719. Dorn, Jacob Henry. (1986) "Religion and Reform in the City: The Re-Thinking Chicago Movement of the 1930s," Church History. Vol. 55, No. 3 (September), pp. 323-337. The Re-Thinking Chicago Movement is an example of interwar city reform efforts, a time period often neglected by historians. A major source for Dorn's inquiry was the collection of Arthur E. Holt papers at Chicago Theological Seminary.

17720. Douglas, R. Bruce, ed. (1986) The Deeper Meaning of Economic Life: Critical Essays on the US Catholic Bishops' Pastoral Letter on the Economy. Washington, DC: Georgetown University Press. Essays by eight theologians regarding the Catholic Bishops' pastoral.

17721. Doyo, Ceres. (1986) "Wounded Healer: The Diary of Peter Geremia," The Other Side. Vol. 22, No. 4 (May), pp. 41-46.

17722. Dunn, James D. G., ed. (1986) The Kingdom of God in North-East England. London: SCM. After an introductory chapter on "Kingdom theology," this book presents 12 very brief descriptions of programs said to manifest the work of the Kingdom and to respond to its presence in Northern Britain. Objectives of the programs are reported rather than the results. Only positive evidences of the Kingdom in programs and schemes are presented, omitting prophetic evidences or statements of the Kingdom in judgment of programs, schemes, and conditions. Dunn is a biblical scholar.

17723. Dye, Richard. (1986) "Case Study: Church Growth in Acapulco--Planting a Whole Presbytery," Urban Mission. Vol. 3, No. 3 (January), pp. 34-38.

17724. Eastman, A. Theodore, bp. (1986) "The Mission of Christ in Urban America," pp. 225-242 in Philip W. Turner and Frank Sugeno, eds. Crossroads Are for Meeting: Essays on the Mission and Common Life of the Church in a Global Society. Sewanee, TN: SPCK.

17725. Edwards, Nymphas R. (1986) A Christian Stewardship Ministry among Economically Deprived Families through Trinity Methodist Church, Nassau, Bahamas. Thesis (D. Min.). Madison, NJ: Drew University.

17726. Eichhorn, Garth L. (1986) The Church in the Marketplace. Thesis (D. Min.). San Anselmo, CA: San Francisco Theological Seminary.

17727. Eipper, Chris. (1986) The Ruling Trinity: A Community Study of Church, State, and Business in Ireland. Brookfield, VT: Gower.

17728. Eisenstadt, S. N. and A. Shachar. (1986) Society, Culture and Urbanization. Newbury Park, CA: Sage Publications. After critically reviewing existing theories of urbanization, the authors advance their own macrosocietal, comparative theoretical perspective. Support for their thesis is drawn from their analysis of nine urban civilizations.

17729. El Banna, Gamel. (1986) "The Crisis of Unionism between Contemporary Ideologies and Islam," The Islamic Quarterly. Vol. 30, No. 1, pp. 5-19.

17730. Elliott, W. Winston. (1986) A Biblical and Systemic Analysis of Church Growth with Emphasis on Urban Ministry. Thesis (D. Miss.). Pasadena, CA: Fuller Theological Seminary, School of World Mission.

17731. Enlow, David R. (1986) Search for Security: The Story of Oscar M. Woodall. Eustis, FL: Eternal Life Ministries.

17732. "Episcopalians Shape a Response in Ministering to AIDS Victims." (1986) JSAC Grapevine. Vol. 17, No. 8 (March), pp. [1-3]. A denominational response to a health crisis.

17733. Evangelical Coalition for Urban Mission. (1986) Urban Mission Resource List. London: the Coalition. A bibliography.

17734. Evans, Richard Philip. (1986) A Manual for Conducting Evangelistic Meetings in the Local Church in Suburban America. Thesis (D. Min.). Dallas, TX: Dallas Theological Seminary.

17735. Fagan, Ronald W. (1986) "Ministering in the Hinterland: a Survey of Rescue Mission Directors," Journal of Pastoral Counseling. Vol. 21, No. 2 (Fall/Winter), pp. 79-87.

17736. Falcón, Rafael. (1986) The Hispanic Mennonite Church in North America 1932-1986. Scottdale, PA: Herald Press.

17737. Fann, Bridget E. and Elizabeth Dodds. (1986) "Autumn Liverpool, a City Poised on the Brink of Bankruptcy," Crucible. [Vol. 25, No. 3] (July-September), pp. 112-114.

17738. Fernandez, Vivian Eloise. (1986) The Effects of Belief in Spiritism and/or Santeria on Psychiatric Diagnosis of Puerto Ricans in New York City. Thesis (Ph. D.). Garden City, NY: Adelphi University, The Institute of Advanced Psychological Studies.

17739. Fey, Thomas M. (1986) "The Unholy War," Security Management. Vol. 30, (October), pp. 114-120. Re: crimes against church property.

17740. Finnell, David. (1986) Evangelism in Singapore: A Research Analysis among Baptists. Singapore: Singapore Baptist Bookstore.

17741. Fisher, Humphrey J. (1986) "Liminality, Hijra and the City," Asian and African Studies [Thematic issue: Religion and the city]. Vol. 20, No. 1, pp. 153-177. A study of urban-rural relations in Islamic West Africa.

17742. Fleming, Kenneth C. (1986) "The Gospel to the Urban Zulu: Three Cultures in Conflict," Evangelical Missions Quarterly. Vol. 22, No. 1 (January), pp. 24-31.

17743. Fluent, Mike. (1986) "Who Ministers to the Unlovely?"

Fundamentalist Journal. Vol. 5, No. 11 (December), pp. 45-46. [See note 3].

17744. Forbes, Anne. (1986) Faith in Leeds: Searching for God in Our City. Leeds, England: Leeds Churches' Community Involvement Project. A report prepared for the Leeds Churches' Community Involvement Project on the question: "How can the Church in Leeds respond to the needs of the City's Urban Priority Areas?"

17745. Forest, James H. (1986) Love Is the Measure: A Biography of Dorothy Day. New York: Paulist Press. Bibliography.

17746. Forshaw, Eric. (1986) "Industrial Chaplaincy and Ministry in Secular Employment," pp. 67-74 in John Fuller and Patrick Vaughan, eds. Working for the Kingdom: The Story of Ministers Working in Secular Employment. London: SPCK.

17747. Forster, Greg, ed. (1986) Hope in the City: A Response to the Archbishop's Commission Report on Urban Priority Areas. Grove Booklet on Ethics No. 61. Bramcote, England: Grove Books. Four persons involved heavily in city ministries question whether or not the report of the Archbishop's Commission on Urban Priority Areas (1985) needs stronger theological underpinning than it has if the requisite transformations in cities are to be accomplished. The authors intend these essays as a supplement to the Faith in the City report. Bibliography.

17748. Franklin, Doris. (1986) "Ministry in Bombay," New World Outlook. n.s. Vol. 46, No. 9 (July-August), pp. 31-34. Methodism in India combines evangelism and social work to serve the poor in Bombay.

17749. Franzen, Janice Gosnell. (1986) "Colleen Townsend Evans: Bridging the Gap," Christian Life. Vol. 48, No. 3 (July), pp. 20-23.

17750. Freeman, Richard B. (1986) "Who Escapes? The Relation of Churchgoing and Other Background Factors to the Socioeconomic Performance of Black Male Youths from Inner City Tracts," in Richard B. Feeman and Harry J. Holzer, eds. The Black Youth Employment Crisis. Chicago, IL: University of Chicago Press. Bibliography.

17751. Fukuyama, Yoshio. (1986) "Social Research and the Churches," Review of Religious Research. Vol. 28, No. 1, pp. 71-82. Fukuyama traces the roots of social research to 19th Century Protestant clergy and their interest in social reform, noting that the first professors of sociology in the USA were clergy. The need for social information led to institutionalized social research. Comments by Jackson Carroll and Mary Mattis are included.

17752. Fuller, John and Patrick Vaughan. (1986) Working for the Kingdom: The Story of Ministers in Secular Employment. London: SPCK.

17753. Fuller, Millard. (1986) No More Shacks! Waco, TX: Word Books. Fuller, founder of Habitat for Humanity, articulates his vision of volunteers helping poor people build their homes.

17754. Gaither, Gloria. (1986) "Savior in the City," Christian Herald. Vol. 109, No. 10 (November), pp. 20-25. A photo essay on city conditions.

17755. Galli, Carlos. (1986) "El desafío pastoral de la cultura urbana," Saedio-Documentación (Buenos Aires). Vol. 12, Nos. 90-91, passim. The challenge of pastoral work in urban environment.

17756. Garcia, Ana de and George S. Johnson. (1986) Evangelism and the Poor: A Biblical Challenge for the Church. Minneapolis, MN: Augsburg.

17757. George, Alan. (1986) "Feel the Inner City," Urban Mission. Vol. 3, No. 4 (March), pp. 19-24.

17758. Gilkes, Cheryl Townsend. (1986) "The Roles of Church and Community Mothers: Ambivalent American Sexism or Fragmented African Familyhood," Journal of Feminist Studies in Religion. Vol. 2, No. 1 (Spring), pp. 41-59.

17759. Gillett, Richard W. (1986) "The Church Acts for Economic Justice," pp. 268-277 in William K. Tabb, ed. Churches in Struggle: Liberation Theologies and Social Changes in North America. New York: Monthly Review Press.

17760. Gladwin, John. (1986) "Faith in the City," Crucible. [Vol. 25, No. 1] (January-March), pp. 4-8. A defence of the report prepared by the Church of England's Commission on Urban Priority Areas (1985).

17761. Glenn, Charles L. (1986) "Beyond Liberation: An Agenda for Educational Justice," The Christian Century. Vol. 103, No. 34 (November 12), pp. 1006-1008. Public schools in multiracial society must emphasize character, justice and virtue.

17762. Golden, Renny. (1986) Sanctuary: The New Underground Railroad. Maryknoll, NY: Orbis. Bibliography.

17763. Goossen, Rachel Waltner. (1986) "An Urban Mennonite Church--the First Two Decades," Mennonite Life. Vol. 41, No. 3 (September), pp. 22-26. Re: First Mennonite Church, Normal, Illinois.

17764. Gordon, Paul. (1986) "Black People, White Laws," Christian Action Journal. (Autumn), pp. 9-11.

17765. Gornick, Mark R. (1986) "Youth Ministry Is the Urban Context," Urban Mission. Vol. 4, No. 2 (November), pp. 28-37.

17766. Gossard, John Harvey. (1986) The New York City Congregational Cluster, 1848-1871: Congregationalism and Antislavery in the Careers of Henry Ward Beecher, George B. Cheever, Richard S. Storrs and Joseph P. Thompson. Thesis (Ph. D.). Bowling Green, OH: Bowling Green State University.

17767. Green, Clifford. (1986) "Ecumenism in Metropolis," JSAC Grapevine. Vol. 18, No. 1 (June), pp. [1-18]. Re: the importance of ecumenism in a rapidly urbanizing world.

17768. Greenway, Roger S. (1986) "History of Evangelizing World Class Cities," Paper 4. [Moody Bible Institute, Trinity Evangelical Divinity School, Wheaton College and Graduate School; The Trinary Study Conference on the Evangelization of the World, March 14-17, 1986].

17769. Greenway, Roger S. (1986) Pauline Paradigms for Urban Mission. Atlanta, GA: Metropolitan Missions Department, Home Mission Board, Southern Baptist Convention, Occasional Paper No. 11.

17770. Greenway, Roger S. (1986) "Urban Prospective: Who Lives in This City?" Urban Mission. Vol. 3, No. 5 (May), pp. 57-58.

17771. Grubbs, Larry J. (1986) Formulating a Mission Statement in an Inner City Congregation. Thesis (D. Min.). Madison, NJ: Drew University.

17772. Grundy, Malcolm. (1986) "Can We Say 'Thanks to Industry?'" Crucible. [Vol. 25, No. 1] (January-March), pp. 23-27.

17773. Hadaway, C. Kirk. (1986) SBC [Southern Baptist Convention] Growth in Major Metropolitan Areas. Nashville, TN: Research Services Department, Office of Planning and Research, Sunday School Board of the Southern Baptist Convention. A series of yearly updates follow this initial report, variously titled "SBC Growth in Major Metropolitan Areas, Revised Version" (November 1986), "SBC Growth in the U. S. Metropolitan System" (January, 1987), "SBC Metropolitan Growth, 1986 Update (April, 1987), etc. Hadaway, an urban church growth specialist for the Southern Baptists, also published some results in an occasional periodical issued by the Research Services Department of the Baptist Sunday School Board titled: Research Information Report.

17774. Hall, Douglas. (1986) "The Church and Its Community," Urban Mission. Vol. 4, No. 2 (November), pp. 36-44. Reprinted: Robert C. Linthicum, ed. Urban Ministry, Vol. 2, [Pasadena, CA]: Technical Services, World Vision International. Hall recounts the ministry of Emanuel Gospel Center, Boston, and offers suggestions for new church starts in the inner city.

17775. Hamakonda, Koiki Gikoe. (1986) A Balanced Growth Model for Local Church Ministry in the Urban Context of Jakarta. Thesis (D. Miss.). Pasadena, CA: Fuller Theological Seminary, School of World Mission.

17776. Hammer, Don E. (1986) "Action Reflection Model for Urban Training," Urban Review [Southern Baptist]. Vol. 2, No. 2 (July).

17777. Hammond, Phillip E. (1986) "Religion in the Modern World," pp. 143-158 in James Davison Hunter and Stephen C. Ainlay, eds. Making Sense of Modern Times: Peter Berger and the Vision of Interpretive Sociology. London: Routledge and Kegan Paul.

17778. Harris, Barbara C. (1986) "EUC: The Sleeping Giant Stirs," Witness [Ambler, PA]. Vol. 69, No. 2 (February), p. 11.

17779. Harrison, Beverly W., Robert L. Stivers, and Ronald H. Stone, eds. (1986) The Public Vocation of Christian Ethics. New York: Pilgrim Press. Essays in honor of Roger L. Shinn, some of which raise questions regarding urban ethics, racism in the city, the meaning of work, the morality of technology, and other topics related to the city.

17780. Hauerwas, Stanley and William H. Willimon. (1986) "Embarrassed by the Church: Congregations and the Seminary," The Christian Century. Vol. 103, No. 5 (February 5-12), pp. 117-120.

Christian ethics requires an ecclesial context and cannot ignore the centrality of the church for Christian thought. Economic and political realities of the middle class church cannot be disdained by theologians and ethicists if their work is to impact the lives of people in America. Broadway United Methodist Church, South Bend, Indiana, provides the subject for a lengthy case study. The authors call seminaries to make liturgy a central curricular focus.

17781. Hawkins, Peter S., ed. (1986) Civitas: Religious Interpretations of the City. Atlanta, GA: Scholar's Press. The authors of this collection apply the discipline of socio-linguistics, broadly conceived, to the question of the religious significance of the city. A conversation, or even the most casually written words, about the city implies deep identification of the speaker with the fate of the city. Nine authors, all historians of Christianity or biblical scholars, write about views of the city extant in the Christian heritage. Hawkins writes in the introduction, "... the city remains our forum for entertaining the major questions of human existence: questions about God or God's absence; about transcendence and finitude; about the nightmares and dreams of civic life. To read the cities ... is to read the spiritual biography of our civilization" (p. xii). Chapters are given to: Old Testament, St. Paul, Jerusalem, an exploration of the idea of alien citizenship in the early church, medieval Constantinople, Dante's Commedia, a medieval commune in Siena, St. Augustine, and various literary images.

17782. Heim, David. (1986) "A Recipe for Community: Friends, Not Servants," The Christian Century. Vol. 103, No. 33 (November 5), pp. 965-966.

17783. Heim, David and Eugene C. Roehlkepartain. (1986) "Urban Ministry: Strategy and Faith for the City," Christian Century. Vol. 103, No. 17 (May 14), pp. 491-495. This article, in reporting the 1986 Congress on Urban Ministry, lists several strategies for issues related to urban ministry: e.g., the convergence of mainline and evangelical Protestantism in inner cities, the problem of wasted resources of urban congregations that close or merge. One suggestion that merits attention: "... find ways to take the throwaway resources of our society -- empty buildings, vacant lots -- and transform them into urban ministries of tomorrow's world."

17784. Herbers, John. (1986) The New Heartland: America's Flight Beyond the Suburbs and How It Is Changing Our Future. New York: Times Books. Herbers, a correspondent for the New York Times, describes changes in population and economic growth patterns he discerns as the result of his travel as a correspondent. He sees urban flight beyond the suburbs portending a new kind of urban reality -- metropolitan areas that are not metropolitan. The older industrial cities will die, for the most part, becoming havens only for the poorest people. Economic growth will occur in the smaller cities and dispersed urban areas because people who are wealthy can choose to live anywhere they want and quality of life is better in small cities than in the crowded big cities. Herbers, predicting that the next century will experience a rebirth of interest in small cities, finds present-day prototypes in the economic growth of North Carolina, in small state capitals, and in such small metropolitan areas as State College, PA, Fort Collins, CO, and Lafayette, LA.

17785. Hewitt, John H. (1986) "The Sacking of St. Philip's Church, New York," Historical Magazine of the Protestant Episcopal Church. Vol. 49, No. 1 (March), pp. 7-20.

17786. Hiemstra, John. (1986) "Strangers within Our Gates," The Church Herald. Vol. 43, No. 6 (September 19), pp. 5-6.

17787. Higgins, George G. (1986) "The Catholic Church and Labor in the United States," New Catholic World [Thematic issue: Catholic Social Teaching]. Vol. 229, No. 1373 (September-October), pp. 196-203.

17788. Higgins, George G. (1986) "The Present State of Catholic Social Teaching," pp. 169-187 in Fredrick E. Greenspahn, ed. Contemporary Ethical Issues in Jewish and Christian Traditions. Hoboken, NJ: Ktav.

17789. Hirschfield, Robert . (1986) "Hotel for the Homeless," Christianity and Crisis. Vol. 46, No. 6 (April 21), pp. 133-134. Part of a trilogy on homelessness.

17790. Hoffsis, Larry A. (1986) "Bible and Mission in the Suburban Congregation," pp. 185-194 in Wayne Stumme, ed. Bible and Mission. Minneapolis, MN: Augsburg.

17791. Homan, Roger, compiler. (1986) The Sociology of Religion: A Bibliographical Survey. Westport, CT: Greenwood Press. Homan, a Principal Lecturer in Education at Brighton Polytechnic, limits his work to 1013 entries with annotations, all of which are sociological studies of religion.

17792. Honeywell, Charles L. (1986) "Whose Agenda in Pittsburgh?" The Lutheran Forum. Vol. 22, No. 3, pp. 6-8.

17793. Hooker, Roger and Christopher Lamb. (1986) Love the Stranger: Ministry in Multi-Faith Areas. London: SPCK.

17794. Hope, Glenda. (1986) "Contemplation: Not for Mystics Only," The Witness [Ambler, PA]. Vol. 69, No. 10 (October), pp. 16-19.

17795. Houseworth-Findlay, J. (1986) "Revitalizing an Urban Parish," Other Side. Vol. 22, No. 2 (March), pp. 8-9.

17796. Housley, Kathleen. (1986) "Churches Respond to Teen Suicide," The Christian Century. Vol. 103, No. 15 (April 30), pp. 438-439. Prevention efforts in Glastonbury, CT.

17797. Huckstep, Mary. (1986-1987) "Urban Youth Evangelist," World Vision [leader's edition]. Vol. 30, No. 6 (December-January), pp. 16. Re: Buster Soaries.

17798. Hunter, Jim Ernest, Jr. (1986) A Gathering of Sects: Revivalistic Pluralism in Tulsa Oklahoma, 1945-1985. Thesis (Ph. D.). Louisville, KY: Southern Baptist Theological Seminary.

17799. Hurst, Antony. (1986) Rendering unto Caesar: Towards a Framework for Integrating Paid Employment with Christian Belief. Worthing, West Sussex, England: Churchman Publications.

17800. Hyung-Kyu, Park. (1986) "A Street Congregation," The Ecumenical Review. Vol. 38, No. 1 (January), pp. 98-100.

17801. Idle, Christopher. (1986) "Down Town by Riverside," pp. 71-87 in Gavin Reid, ed. Hope for the Church of England? Eastbourne, England: Kingsway.

17802. In, Myung-Jin. (1986) Rethinking the Work of Urban Industrial Mission in the Presbyterian Church of Korea. Thesis (D. Min.). San Anselmo, CA: San Francisco Theological Seminary.

17803. Industrial Christian Fellowship. (1986) Business for People: A Conference. London: the Fellowship.

17804. Institute of Global Urban Studies. (beginning in 1986) City Watch, A Research Bulletin of the Institute of Global Urban Studies. Pasadena, CA: the Institute. A periodical offers brief articles from an evangelical perspective dealing mainly with urban poverty in the developing nations. A computerized bibliography is maintained by the Institute.

17805. Institute on the Church in Urban-Industrial Society [ICUIS]. (1986) Handbook of Denominational Statements on Urban Mission and Ministry. Chicago, IL: ICUIS. Includes statements from the American Baptist Church, the Episcopal Church, the Presbyterian Church USA, the Unitarian Universalist Association, the United Church of Christ, the United Methodist Church. the American Lutheran Church, the Church of the Brethren, the Lutheran Church in America, and the Southern Baptist Convention.

17806. International Union of Gospel Missions. (1986) What Is a Gospel Rescue Mission? Kansas City, MO: the Union.

17807. Ishii, Kenji. (1986) "The Secularization of Religion in the City," Japanese Journal of Religious Studies. Vol. 13, Nos. 2-3 (June-September), pp. 193-209.

17808. Jacques, André. (1986) The Stranger within Your Gates, Uprooted People in the World Today. Geneva, Switzerland: World Council of Churches. Jacques challenges the church to respond to the needs of refugees.

17809. Jenner, Brian. (1986) The Coal Strike: Christian Reflections in the Miners' Struggle. Sheffield, England: New City. A book of "Christian story-telling," prepared as the result of persons seeking to bring their Christian commitment to bear on events associated with the 1984-85 coal strike in Yorkshire.

17810. Johnson, Darlington Gyeladi. (1986) A Theological Rationale for Inner-City Ministry and a Measure of the Self Concepts of Inner-City Children in Tulsa, Oklahoma. Thesis (D. Min). Enid, OK: Graduate Seminary of Phillips University.

17811. Johnson, Ray E. (1986) "The Challenge of Compassion," The Lutheran Forum. Vol. 20, No. 4, pp. 18+.

17812. Johnson, Stephen D. and Joseph B. Tamney. (1986) "The Clergy and Public Issues in Middletown," pp. 45-70 in Stephen D. Johnson and Joseph B. Tamney, eds. The Political Role of Religion in the United States. Boulder, CO: Westview Press. Clergy views in Muncie, IN, most of which are conservative.

17813. Johnson, Timothy V. (1986) Malcolm X: A Comprehensive Annotated Bibliography. New York: Garland.

17814. Jones, Phillip B. (1986) "A Metropolitan/Nonmetropolitan Reexamination of Fastest Growing Churches in The Southern Baptist Convention 1975-1980," Urban Review [Southern Baptist]. Vol. 2, No. 1 (April), pp. 22-31.

17815. Joyce, John T. (1986) "Reflections on Catholic Social Thought from a Labor Perspective," New Catholic World [Thematic issue: Catholic Social Teaching]. Vol. 229, No. 1373 (September-October), pp. 204-209.

17816. Juhl, Paulgeorg. (1986) "Erwartungen an künftige EKD-Äusserungen zur Arbeitnehmer-Partizipation," Zeitschrift für Evangelische Ethik, Vol. 30, No. 3 (July-September), pp. 316-330. Re: Lutheran church and the desired participation of workers in management in East Germany.

17817. Juliani, Richard J. (1986) "The Parish as an Urban Institution: Italian Catholics in Philadelphia," Records of the American Catholic Historical Society. Vol. 96, pp. 49-65. Reprinted: Brian Mitchell, ed. Building the American Catholic City. New York: Garland, 1988.

17818. Jurgensen, Barbara. (1986) "Bible and Mission in an Inner-City Congregation," pp. 111-119 in Wayne C. Stumme, ed. Bible and Mission: Biblical Foundations and Working Models for Congregational Ministry. Minneapolis, MN: Augsburg.

17819. Kaganoff, Nathan M. (1986) "Jewish Landmanshaftn in New York City before World War I," American Jewish History. Vol. 74, No. 1 (September), pp. 56-66. Re: Jewish documents in New York City.

17820. Kaiser, Walter C. (1986) "Biblical Theology of the City," Paper 1. Moody Bible Institute, Trinity Evangelical Divinity School, Wheaton College and Graduate School. The Trinary Study Conference on the Evangelization of the World, March 14-17, 1986. See further: Urban Mission. Vol. 7, No. 1 (September, 1989), pp. 6-18.

17821. Kelly, Tom. (1986) "No Place Like Home," Christianity and Crisis. Vol. 46, No. 6 (April 21), pp. 130-133. Living with Manhattan's homeless yields memories, insights, and lice.

17822. Kennell, Joseph Eugene. (1986) The Roles Played by an Inner City Church in the Social Support Networks and Interpersonal Problem-Solving Competence of Its Members. Thesis (Ph. D.). Bowling Green, OH: Bowling Green State University.

17823. Kleba, Gerald J. (1986) People's Parish: A Model of Church Where People Flourish. Notre Dame, IN: Ave Maria Press. Kleba describes how to conduct parish ministry in the poorest of St. Louis, MO, neighborhoods: efforts at improving housing, establishing credit unions, etc.

17824. Kleiman, Jeffery D. (1986) The Great Strike: Religion, Labor and Reform, in Grand Rapids, Michigan, 1890-1916. Thesis (Ph. D.). East Lansing, MI: Michigan State University.

17825. Klejment, Anne and Alice Klejment. (1986) Dorothy Day and the Catholic Worker: A Bibliography and Index. New York: Garland.

17826. Koetsier, C. Henk. (1986) "The Church Situation in European Cities," Urban Mission, Vol. 3, No. 3 (January), pp. 45-47.

17827. Krätzig, Guillermo. (1986) "Tent Evangelism in Argentine Cities," Urban Mission. Vol. 3, No. 5 (May), pp. 51-56.

17828. Kugelmass, Jack. (1986) Miracle of Intervale Avenue: The Story of a Jewish Congregation in the South Bronx. New York: Schocken. An anthropological study of a congregation with members mostly over the age of 80 located in an ethnically changing neighborhood. Cooperation between Jews and Puerto Ricans is described.

17829. Kunkelman, Gary A. (1986) The Religion of Ethnicity. Thesis (Ph. D.). Philadelphia, PA: University of Pennsylvania. Reprinted: New York: Garland. Kunkelman identifies reasons for the persistence of Greek Orthodox identity in America. Bibliography.

17830. McTighe, Michael J. (1986) "'True Philanthropy' and the Limits of the Female Sphere: Poor Relief and Labor Organizations in Ante-Bellum Cleveland," Labor History. Vol. 27, No. 2 (Spring), pp. 227-256. McTighe compares labor and evangelical Protestant views on charity and the employment of women.

17831. Langan, John. (1986) "The American Context of the US Bishops' Pastoral Letter on the Economy," pp. 1-19 in R. Bruce Douglass, ed. The Deeper Meaning of Economic Life. Washington, DC: Georgetown University Press. Bibliography.

17832. "Large Metros Becoming More Racially Polarized. (1986)

RD Digest [Southern Baptist]. Vol. 8, No. 5 (May), pp. 1+.

17833. Larson, Robert E., Jr. (1986) An Accreditation Manual for Contact Teleministries, USA. Thesis (D. Min.). Lancaster: Lancaster Theological Seminary. A proposed guidebook for accreditation visits to Contact Teleministry centers, plus a procedure followed in testing it.

17834. Latham, Robert and Amy Macdonald. (1986?) The Unitarian Universalist Extension Manual. [Boston, MA]: Published by the Extension Department of the Unitarian Universalist Association. Church growth theory and strategy for Unitarian Universalist Churches. Attention is given to church extension in cities.

17835. Lazerow, Jama. (1986) "Religion and Labor Reform in Antebellum America: The World of William Field Young," American Quarterly. Vol. 38, No. 2 (Summer), pp. 265-286. Young was a reformer in the 1840s who edited a journal titled: The Voice of Industry.

17836. Leech, Kenneth. (1986) "The Urban Church in Retreat: Some Lessons from Chicago," Crucible. [Vol. 25, No. 4] (October-December), pp. 146-155.

17837. Lehman, Edward C., Jr. (1986) "The Local/Cosmopolitan Dichotomy and Acceptance of Women Clergy: A Replication and Extension of Roof," Journal for the Scientific Study of Religion. Vol. 25, No. 4 (December), pp. 461-482. A test of hypotheses developed by Roof (1974, 1976, 1978). Bibliography.

17838. Leonard of Taizé, Brother. (1986) Along an Inner Shore: Echoes from the Gospel. New York: Pilgrim Press. Spiritual meditations of an urban pilgrim, these 56 brief essays are rooted not only in the author's New York experiences but also in his searchings with people of faith everywhere he travelled.

17839. Leslie, William. (1986) "Evangelizing High-Rise Dwellers," Urban Review [Southern Baptist]. Vol. 2, No. 1 (April), pp. 3-12.

17840. Levine, Daniel H. and Scott Mainwaring. (1986) Religion and Popular Protest in Latin America. Notre Dame, IN: Helen Kellogg Institute for International Studies, University of Notre Dame. A working paper. Bibliography.

17841. Levtzion, Hehemia. (1986) "Rural and Urban Islam in West Africa: An Introductory Essay," Asian and African Studies

[Thematic issue: Religion and the city]. Vol. 20, No. 1, pp. 7-26. In West Africa, urban and rural Islam appear to have few differences.

17842. Lewis, Donald M. (1986) Lighten Their Darkness: The Evangelical Mission to Working-Class London, 1828-1860. New York: Greenwood Press. City missions were, in some of the poor sections of London, as plentiful as pubs. Lewis recounts the history of such organizations as the London City Mission and the Scripture Reader's Association.

17843. Lews, James N. Jr. (1986) "Training Needs of the Urban Home Missionary," Urban Review [Southern Baptist]. Vol. 2, No. 2 (July), pp. 15-23.

17844. Light, Paul W. (1986) "Race and Ethnicity in the ABC [American Baptist Church]: Summarizing a Research Process," American Baptist Quarterly [Thematic issue: Racial justice]. Vol. 5, No. 1 (March), pp. 36-48. Related articles appear in the same issue, including a reprint of some of Martin Luther King's writings.

17845. Lightbody, C. Stuart. (1986) "New Strategies for a New Era," Urban Mission. Vol. 3, No. 3 (January), pp. 30-33.

17846. Lightbody, C. Stuart. (1986) "History in the Making in Lima," Latin America Evangelist. Vol. 66, No. 3 (July-September), pp. 4-8.

17847. Lindberg, Tod. (1986) "New York Down, Washington Up," Commentary. Vol. 81, No. 1 (January), pp. 36-42. Replies, Vol. 81, No. 4, pp. 8-9; Rejoinder.

17848. Linthicum, Robert C. (1986) Networking: Hope for the Church in the City. [Pasadena, CA]: Field Development Division, World Vision International, World Vision International Ministry Notes, No. 5. Same title: Urban Mission. Vol. 4, No. 3 (January, 1987), pp. 32-50. A pamphlet.

17849. Linton, Thomas Dwight. (1986) Planting Cross-Culture Presbyterian Churches in the United States. Thesis (D. Miss.). Pasadena, CA; Fuller Theological Seminary.

17850. Lockard, W. David. (1986) "Feeding the Urban Poor," Urban Review [Southern Baptist]. Vol. 2, No. 1 (April), pp. 40+.

17851. Loder, Ted. (1986) No One but Us: Personal Reflections on Public Sanctuary by an Offspring of Jacob. San Diego, CA: Lura Media. Spiritual implications of the Public Sanctuary Movement.

17852. Loraux, Nicole. (1986) Invention of Athens: The Funeral Oration in the Classical City. Cambridge, MA: Harvard University Press. Bibliography.

17853. Loury, Glenn C. (1986) "A Prescription for Black Progress," The Christian Century. Vol. 103, No. 15 (April 30), pp. 434-438. Loury urges Blacks to adopt a spirit of economic adventurism to lift their communities to self sufficiency and to avoid taking "guilt money."

17854. Lowder, Stella. (1986) Inside Third World Cities. London: Croom Helm. Lowder traces social characteristics of Third World cities from their origins through their colonial legacies to modern times, with some attention given to religious factors. Chapter 7 evaluates the usefulness of models of cities developed for use in Western nations for use in the study of Third World cities.

17855. Luna, David. (1986) "Patterns of Faith: Woven Together in Life and Mission," American Baptist Quarterly. Vol. 5, No. 4 (December), pp. 393-397.

17856. Lupton, Robert D. (1986) "Urban Perspectives: On Stewardship--Reflections on the Gospel and the Poor," Urban Mission. Vol. 3, No. 3 (March), p. 39.

17857. Mandeville, Kathleen. (1986) "Gentrification in Hell's Kitchen," The Witness [Ambler, PA]. Vol. 69, No. 5, p. 17.

17858. Marchant, Colin, Bruce Reed, and Austin Smith. (1986) "Faith in the City," The Modern Churchman. n.s. Vol. 28, No. 2, pp. 3-10.

17859. Maroney, Jimmy K. (1986) "Urban Training Needs for the Foreign Missionary," Urban Review [Southern Baptist]. Vol. 2, No. 2 (July), pp. 24-33.

17860. Marshall, Harvey and John Stahura. (1986) "The Theory of Ecological Expansion: The Relation between Dominance and Suburban Differentiation," Social Forces. Vol. 65, No. 2 (December), pp. 352-369.

17861. Martin, Joan. (1986) "A Day in the Life of a Shelter

Worker," Christian Herald. Vol. 109, No. 27 (November), p. 26. A suburban woman works in a shelter for the homeless.

17862. Maslow-Armand, Laura. (1986) "The Newark Tenant Rent Strike: Public Housing Policy and Black Municipal Governance," Patterns of Prejudice. Vol. 20, No. 4 (October), pp. 17-30.

17863. McCall, Emmanuel. (1986) "Reaching Blacks in Urban America," Urban Review [Southern Baptist]. Vol. 1, No. 4 (January).

17864. McClain, William B. (1986) Blacks in the United Methodist Church. Durham, NC: Black Church in the African American Experience Research Project, Department of Religion, Duke University.

17865. McCloughry, R. (1986) "Is There Faith in the City?" Grass Roots. Vol. 12, No. 2, pp. 16-17. [See Note 3].

17866. McClung, Lloyd Grant, ed. (1986) Azusa Street and Beyond. South Plainfield, NJ: Bridge Publishing, Inc.

17867. McCommon, Margaret, ed. (1986) Multifamily Housing: Ministry/Witness Resource Guide. Atlanta, GA: Home Mission Board, Southern Baptist Convention. A pamphlet.

17868. McKinley, Edward H. (1986) Somebody's Brother: A History of the Salvation Army Men's Social Service Department, 1891-1985. Lewistown, NY: Edward Mellen Press.

17869. McLean, Timothy A. (1986) Ethnicity and School Selection among Irish-American Catholics. Thesis (Ph. D.). Albany, NY: State University of New York at Albany.

17870. McRory, Peg and Lincoln Dring. (1986) How to Select and Develop Community Housing Programs. New York: Interreligious Coalition for Housing, Joint Strategy and Action Committee. A guide for community groups involved in housing advocacy.

17871. McShane, Joseph M. (1986) Sufficiently Radical: Catholicism, Progressivism, and the Bishop's Program of 1919. Washington, DC: Catholic University of America Press.

17872. McSpadden, Bruce. (1986) Manual on Shared Facilities. New York: General Board of Global Ministries, the United Methodist Church. Sharing church facilities became in the mid-1980s a major church strategy for the cooperation of multiple ethnic and foreign language congregations. This manual provides a theology for sharing church buildings and some sample documents. See further by Arthur Gafke and Bruce McSpadden an unpublished book titled: Pastor as Organizer. San Francisco, CA: Methodist Mission, 1989, 1990 (various editions).

17873. McSwain, Larry L. (1986) "Practical Approaches to Ethnic Ministry: Integrating What Is with What Should Be," Urban Review [Southern Baptist]. Vol. 1, No. 4 (January), pp. 6-14.

17874. Menezes, Carlos Alberto de. (1986) Ação social catolica no Brasil: corporativismo e sindicalismo. São Paulo, Brasil: Ediçòes Loyola, CEPEHIB. Re: Catholic social action in Brazil regarding management and labor. A reprint of articles originally published 1898-1908. Bibliography.

17875. Michael, Christine. (1986) "Urban Vision in the Third Way," pp. 103-109 in Henry J. Schmidt, ed. Witnesses of a Third Way: Materials Drawn from the Plenary Session and Workshops of Alive '85, Denver, CO, April 11-14, 1985. Elgin IL: Brethren Press.

17876. Micksch, Jürgen. (1986) Evangelische Ausländergemeinden. Frankfurt am Main: Verlag O. Lembeck. Re: church work with foreigners.

17877. Milliken, Bill. (1986) "Dropping Out: The Once and Future Crisis," Christianity Today. Vol. 30, No. 15 (October 17), pp. 32-36.

17878. Mission Advance Research and Communications [MARC]. (1986) The City for God's Sake, an Agenda for Urban Ministry. [Three videocassettes, 151 minutes]: Monrovia, CA: MARC. Features Raymond Bakke.

17879. Mitchell, Brian C. (1986) "'They Do Not Differ Greatly:' The Pattern of Community Development among the Irish in the Late Nineteenth Century Lowell, Massachusetts," pp. 53-73 in Timothy J. Meagher, ed. From Paddy to Studs: Irish American Communities in the Turn of the Century Era, 1880 to 1920. Westport, CT. Greenwood. Reprinted: Brian Mitchell, ed. Building the American Catholic City. New York: Garland, 1988.

17880. Mitchell, Henry H. and Nicholas Cooper Lewter. (1986) Soul Theology: The Heart of American Black Culture. San Francisco,

CA: Harper and Row.

17881. Mohl, Raymond A. and Neil Betten. (1986) Steel City: Urban and Ethnic Patterns in Gary Indiana, 1906-1950. New York: Holmes and Meier.

17882. Moltmann, Jürgen, ed. (1986) Versöhnung mit der Natur. Munich, West Germany: Christian Kaiser Verlag. Contains articles on ecology, technology, economic and environmental policy, church and industry, and ethics.

17883. Monsma, Timothy. (1986) "Case Study: African Cities--Choosing New Urban Fields," Urban Mission. Vol. 3, No. 5 (May), pp. 49-50.

17884. Moore, David B., comp. (1986) Minister's Guide to Community Ministry Resources and Referrals. Louisville, KY: Long Run Baptist Association.

17885. Morris, Orrin D. (1986) "The Shape of Ethnic America," Urban Review [Southern Baptist]. Vol. 1, No. 4 (January), pp. 35-46.

17886. Moss, Len. (1986) "The 'Gypsy Problem' and the Church," Crucible. [Vol. 25, No. 4] (October-December), pp. 173-175.

17887. Mumper, Sharon E. (1986) "Case Study: Taiwan's Urban Population--Time for a Spiritual Harvest," Urban Mission. Vol. 4, No. 1 (September), pp. 35-38.

17888. Murdoch, Norman H. (1986) "The Salvation Army and the Church of England, 1882-1883," Historical Magazine of the Protestant Episcopal Church. Vol. 55, No. 1 (March), pp. 31-55.

17889. National Conference of Catholic Bishops. (1986) Economic Justice for All: Pastoral Letter on Catholic Social Teaching and the US Economy. Washington, DC: National Catholic Conference. Other printings exist, e.g., Origins. Vol. 16, No. 24 (November 27, 1986), subtitled "Final Text." A widely respected consensus among church leaders, this pastoral letter on United States economic policies met with mixed praise and criticisms in secular arenas. The Bishops examine the issues of poverty, unemployment, food, US relationships with developing nations and, generally, the morality of the economic system.

17890. Neff, David. (1986) "Excellence for Artists," Christianity

Today. Vol. 30, No. 12 (September 5), p. 61. Re: the Christian witness of Greenwich Village artists affiliated with the New York Arts Group.

17891. Neighbour, Ralph Webster, Jr. (1986) "Training Needs for the Urban Pastor," Urban Review [Southern Baptist]. Vol. 2, No. 2 (July), pp. 5-14.

17892. Nelson, Douglas J. (1986) A Brief History of the Church of God in Christ. Durham, NC: Black Church in the African American Experience Research Project, Department of Religion, Duke University.

17893. Neubert, E. (1986) "Megapolis DDR und die Religion: Konsequenzen aus der Urbanisierung," Kirche im Sozialismus. Vol. 12, pp. 155-164. [See Note 3]. Church and large cities in East Germany.

17894. Newman, David, et al. (1986) Taking on Faith in the City. Grove Pastoral Series No. 26. Bramcote, England: Grove Books. Four essays offering Anglican evangelical perspectives on city ministry.

17895. Newsinger, John. (1986) "Historical Materialism and the Catholic Church: The Irish Example," Monthly Review. Vol. 37 (January), pp. 12-22.

17896. Nicholls, Bruce J., ed. (1986) The Church: God's Agent for Change. Exeter, Devon, England: Paternoster Press. Consists of 31 brief vignettes of churches and articles about evangelization taken from throughout the world.

17897. Nowell, Robert. (1986) "English Anglicans Debate Urban Priorities Report," Ecumenical Press Service. Vol. 53, No. 5 (February 16-20), p. 76.

17898. O'Brien, Richard, David Donnison, Duncan Forrester, et al. (1986) Faith in the Scottish City: The Scottish Relevance of the Report of the Archbishop's Commission on Urban Priority Areas. Edinburgh, Scotland: Edinburgh Department of Christian Ethics and Practical Theology.

17899. Ontiveros, Suzanne, ed. (1986) Corporate Social Responsibility: Contemporary Viewpoints. Santa Barbara, CA: ABC-CLIO.

17900. Oren, Martin Luther. (1986) "Aging in the City," Urban Mission. Vol. 3, No. 5 (May), pp. 36-48.

17901. Overman, J. Andrew. (1986) "The Parish as Context for Theological Education," Quarterly Review. Vol. 6, No. 2 (Summer), pp. 30-38.

17902. Ovitt, George. (1986) "The Cultural Context of Western Technology: Early Christian Attitudes toward Labor," Technology and Culture. Vol. 27 (July), pp. 477-500.

17903. Pawlikowski, John T. (1986) "Jewish Approaches to Pluralism: Reflections of a Sympathetic Observer," pp. 55-72 in Nigel Biggar, et al., eds. Cities of Gods: Faith, Politics and Pluralism in Judaism, Christianity and Islam. New York: Greenwood.

17904. Pemberton, Sherman Shipley. (1986) Why Are They White? A Study into Why White Churches Remain White in Multi-Ethnic Communities. Thesis (MA). Fullerton, CA: California State University.

17905. Phelan, Craig. (1986) "William Green and the Ideal of Christian Cooperation," pp. 141-143 in Melvin Dubofsky and Warren Van Tine, eds. Labor Leaders in America. Urbana, IL: University of Illinois press.

17906. Phillips, Brian Douglas. (1986) Doing Theology in a Working Class Church. Thesis (D. Min.). New York: New York Theological Seminary.

17907. Piwowarski, Wladyslaw and Witolda Zdaniewicza. (1986) Zbadan nad religijonsci a polska: Studia i materialy. Poznan, Poland: Pallottium.

17908. Polding, M. Fred. (1986) "Case Study: Kinshasa, Zaire--An African Strategy for Urban Church Growth," Urban Mission. Vol. 3, No. 4 (March), pp. 36-38.

17909. Porter, David. (1986) Mother Teresa, The Early Years. Grand Rapids, MI: W. B. Eerdmans.

17910. Pound, Keith. (1986) "Faith in the Offender," Christian Action Journal. (Winter), pp. 14-16.

17911. Price, Clay. (1986) Trends in Metropolitan Population 1980-2000. Atlanta, GA: Research Division, Home Mission Board of the Southern Baptist Convention. Demographic statistics arranged to facilitate denominational planning.

17912. Pulliam, Russ. (1986) "The Difference Christ Makes through Us," Christian Herald. Vol. 109, No. 2 (February), pp. 41-44. Biographical sketches of Christian heroes who have "made a difference," some of them in cities.

17913. Rader, Victoria. (1986) Signal through the Flames: Mitch Snyder and America's Homeless. Kansas City, MO: Sheed and Ward. Rader describes the Community for Creative Non-Violence in Washington, DC, and their efforts to live with the poor, retelling poor people's stories to the rest of the world. Mitch Snyder, leader of that organization, is described as a shepherd of the poor. Bibliography.

17914. Rahman, Falzur. (1986) "Islam and Poltical Action: Politics in the Service of Religion," pp. 153-166 in Nigel Biggar, et al., eds. Cities of Gods: Faith, Politics and Pluralism in Judaism, Christianity and Islam. New York: Greenwood.

17915. Raines, John C. and Donna C. Day-Lower. (1986) Modern Work and Human Meaning. Philadelphia, PA: Westminster. Deals with Johnstown, PA, at a time when it had the highest unemployment rate in the nation.

17916. Ramírez de Jara, María Clemencia and Carlos Ernesto Pinzón. (1986) "Los hijos del bejuco solar y la campana celeste: el yaje en la cultura," América Indigena. Vol. 46, No. 1 (January), pp. 163-188. [See Note 3]. Re: urbanization and the Kamsa Indians in Colombia.

17917. Recinos, Harold Joseph. (1986) The Evangelical Parish and Social Witness: Toward a Theology of Social Justice. Thesis (D. Min.). New York: New York Theological Seminary.

17918. Reed, Adolph L. (1986) The Jessie Jackson Phenomenon. New Haven: Yale University Press.

17919. Reissner, Anne Campanella. (1986) Celebrating the Urban Church as Teacher. Thesis (D. Min.). Newton Center, MA: Andover Newton Theological School.

17920. Reynolds, Keld J. (1986) "The Church under Stress: 1931-1960," pp. 170-207 in Gary Land, ed. Adventism in America: A History. Grand Rapids, MI: Eerdmans.

17921. Richter, Rainer G. (1986) Exploring the Mission of the Miami Springs United Methodist Church within a Transitional

Community. Thesis (D. Min.). Madison, NJ: Drew University.

17922. Roberts, Samuel K. (1986) "Urban Racism and Afro-American Integrity," pp. 111-120 in Beverly Wildung Harrison et al., eds. The Public Vocation of Christian Ethics. New York: Pilgrim Press.

17923. Robinson, Lila Wistrand. (1986) Handbook of Helps: Christian Ministry with Minority and Ethnic Groups: Cultural Backgrounds and Practical Suggestions. [Lynchburg, VA]: L. W. Robinson.

17924. Rodda, William H. (1986) "Underwriting Update: Curbing Church Vandalism," Best's Review (Property/Casualty Insurance Edition). Vol. 87 (December), pp. 78+.

17925. Rodda, William H. (1986) "Underwriting Update: The Price of Worship," Best's Review (Property/Casualty Insurance Edition). Vol. 87 (June), pp. 70+.

17926. Rogan, Eugene Lawrence. (1986) "Physical Islamization in Amman," The Muslim World. Vol. 76, No. 1 (January), pp. 24-42.

17927. Romo, Oscar I. (1986) "Editorial: Tomorrow Is Now," Urban Review [Southern Baptist]. Vol. 1, No. 4 (January), pp. 2-5.

17928. Rosenbaum, Larry. (1986) You Shall Be My Witnesses: How to Reach Your City for Christ. San Francisco, CA: SOS Ministries Press.

17929. Rowland, Trent. (1986) "Streets of Gold: Turkey's Villagers Seek Riches in the City," World Christian Magazine. Vol. 5, No. 4 (July-August), pp. 16-18. Re: Istanbul, Turkey.

17930. Rowland, Trent and Frank Jameson. (1986) "Istanbul: Loosed from Its Muslim Moorings," World Christian. Vol. 5, No. 6 (November-December), pp. 18-26.

17931. Rubingh, Eugene. (1986) Strategies for Evangelization in Cities. Grand Rapids, MI: Centennial Missions Scholarship Committee, Christian Reformed Church.

17932. Russell, Hilary. (1986) "Present Tense, Future Imperfect: Education and Unemployment," Crucible. [Vol. 25, No. 3] (July-September), pp. 106-111.

17933. Saarinen, Martin F. (1986) The Life Cycle of a Congregation. Washington, DC: The Alban Institute.

17934. Sanchez, Daniel. (1986) "Reaching Urban Hispanics," Urban Review [Southern Baptist]. Vol. 1, No. 4 (January), pp. 15-24.

17935. Satterwhite, John H. (1986) The Black Methodist Churches. Durham, NC: Black Church in the African American Experience Research Project, Department of Religion, Duke University.

17936. Sawyer, Mary R. (1986) Black Ecumenism: Cooperative Social Change Movements in the Black Church. Thesis (Ph. D.). Durham, NC: Duke University.

17937. Schloegel, Judith M. and Robert L. Kinast. (1986) From Cell to Society. Grand Rapids, MI: Eerdmans.

17938. Schmidt, Henry J., ed. (1986) Witnesses of a Third Way: A Fresh Look at Evangelism. Elgin, IL: Brethren Press. See especially Schmidt's article titled, "Urban Evangelism Strategies in the Third Way."

17939. Schneirov, Richard. (1986) "Free Thought and Socialism in the Czech Community in Chicago, 1875-1887," pp. 121-142 in Hoerder, Dirk, ed. "Struggle a Hard Battle:" Essays on Working Class Immigrants. DeKalb, IL: University of Northern Illinois Press.

17940. Schoonover, Melvin E. (1986) "Miami: Cycles of Fear," Christianity and Crisis. Vol. 46, No. 7 (May 19), pp. 174-175.

17941. Schreiber, Dale. (1986) "The Urban Muslims of Ivory Coast," Urban Mission. Vol. 3, No. 3 (January), pp. 39-43.

17942. Schultz, Rima Lumin. (1986) The Church and the City: A Social History of 150 Years at St. James, Chicago. Chicago, IL: Cathedral of St. James.

17943. Searle, Mark. (1986) "The Notre Dame Study of Catholic Parish Life," Worship. Vol. 60, No. 4 (July), pp. 312-333. Bibliography.

17944. Sechrist, Gail L. Schlundt. (1986) Church Buildings Enter the Urban Age: A Louisiana Example of the Church in Settlement Geography (1885-1930). Thesis (Ph. D.). Baton Rouge, LA: Louisiana State University and Agricultural and Mechanical College.

17945. Servier, Jean. (1986) "L'harmonie dans la cité," pp. 325-369 in Rudolf Ritsema, ed. Beauty of the World. Frankfurt am Main, West Germany: Insel Verlag. Re: Islam and urbanization.

17946. Sharot, Stephan [i.e, Stephen], Hannah Ayalon, and Eliezer Ben-Rafael. (1986) "Secularization and the Diminishing Decline of Religion," Review of Religious Research. Vol. 27, No. 3 (March), pp. 193-207. A study of the decline in religiosity of Jews in modernizing societies. Bibliography.

17947. Shenk, David W. (1986) "Urban Perspective: The City Is a Gift," Urban Mission. Vol. 4, No. 1 (September), p. 39.

17948. Shenk, David W. (1986) "The City as Gift," Urban Mission. Vol. 4, No. 1 (September), pp. 39-40.

17949. Shipp, Glover Harvey. (1986) Research as a Tool for Urban Evangelism in Developing Countries. Thesis (D. Miss.). Pasadena, CA: Fuller Theological Seminary, School of World Mission.

17950. Shirley, James Michael. (1986) From Congregation Town to Industrial City: Industrialization, Class, and Culture in Nineteenth Century Winston and Salem, North Carolina. Thesis (Ph. D.). Atlanta, GA: Emory University.

17951. Shriver, Donald W., Jr. (1986) "Emerging Issues in Urban Ethics," pp. 139-155 in Beverly Wildung Harrison, et al., eds. The Public Vocation of Christian Ethics. New York: Pilgrim Press. Shriver names the city as the indispensable context for modern Christian social ethics. He asks if White Protestants are contributors to the development of a humane urban pluralism or the chief opponents of such a development.

17952. Silversides, Mark. (1986) Folk Religion: Friend or Foe? Grove Pastoral Series No. 25, Bramcote, England: Grove Books. Silversides defines folk religion, not in the common anthropological usage, but in terms similar to what others have called marginal (Fichter, 1953), or implicit (Ahern and Davie, 1987), or invisible (Luckmann, 1967) -- namely, the religion of those who publicly identify with the church only at major turning points of their life such as birth, death, or marriage or on major civic occasions, such as the crowning of a monarch or prayers in courts. He raises the question of pastoral responsibility to such persons and the possibilities for encouraging their fuller understanding of and participation in the church.

17953. Simon, Deborah. (1986) "Congregations in Mission: The Des Moines Inner City Cooperative Parish," New World Outlook. n.s. Vol. 46, No. 4 (February), pp. 11-13.

17954. Sine, Thomas W., Jr. (1986) "Shifting Urban Mission into the Future Tense," in Linthicum, Robert C., ed. Urban Ministry, Vol. 2. [Pasadena, CA]: Technical Services, World Vision International. Address delivered at the Congress on Urban Ministry, April 11, 1986, Chicago, IL.

17955. Singer, Steven. (1986) "Jewish Religious Observance in Early Victorian London: 1840-1860," Jewish Journal of Sociology. Vol. 28, No. 2 (December), pp. 117-138.

17956. Slack, Kenneth. (1986) "The Church and Urban Priorities," The Christian Century. Vol. 103, No. 9 (March 12), pp. 261-262.

17957. Slack, Tim. (1986) "All Change ... or No Change?" Youth in Society. (April), pp. 16-19.

17958. Slaughter, James N. (1986) Where Grown Men Cry: An Endeavor to Free the Spirit in a Prison--A Detailed Description of a Prison Project. Chelsea, MI: Book Crafters.

17959. Smith, Brian H. (1986) "Chile: Deepening the Allegiance of Working-Class Sectors to the Church in the 1970s," pp. 156-186 in Daniel H. Levine, ed. Religion and Political Conflict in Latin America. Chapel Hill, NC: University of North Carolina.

17960. Smith, Gordon T. (1986) "The Call to the City," Alliance Witness. Vol. 121, No. 13 (June 18), p. 17.

17961. Smith, Greg. (1986) How Can We Tell if God Is at Work? Edinburgh, England: Handsel Press. [Cover title: In the Inner City]. Smith searches for theological and sociological criteria for discerning God's will in inner city ministry. He concludes that his search has been less than satisfactory, raising more questions that it answered. Further academic pursuit of the inquiry is rejected, however, in light of the pressing needs of the inner city.

17962. Smith, Sidney. (1986) 10 Super Sunday Schools in the Black Community. Nashville, TN: Broadman.

17963. Smucker, Joseph. (1986) "Religious Community and Individualism: Conceptual Adaptations by One Group of Mennonites,"

Journal for the Scientific Study of Religion. Vol. 25, No. 3 (September), pp. 273-291. Smucker describes the conceptual adaptations of Mennonite migrants to cities. His research show a loosening of individual's commitment to rural values. Often some compensating behavior emerges, such as philanthropic projects and the use of psychological terminology. These behaviors help bridge the gap between traditional understandings of what it means to be Mennonite and urban values. Bibliography.

17964. Stack, Kenneth. (1986) "The Inner City: Church and Government Clash," The Christian Century. Vol. 103, No. 3 (January 22), pp. 60-62. Margart Thatcher's urban policy results in alienation with church leaders.

17965. Steinbruck, John F. (1986) "Bible and Mission in a Center-City Congregation," pp. 173-184 in Wayne C. Stumme, ed. Bible and Mission: Biblical Foundations and Working Models for Congregational Ministry. Minneapolis, MN: Augsburg.

17966. Stewart, James B. (1986) The Black Church as a Religio-Economic Institution. Durham, NC: Black Church in the African American Experience Research Project, Department of Religion, Duke University.

17967. Stockwell, Clinton E. (1986) St. Louis City Profile. Chicago, IL: Institute on the Church in Urban Industrial Society.

17968. Stöd Till Invandrarnas Trossamfund: Rapport (1986) Från arbetsgruppen för "Oversyn av reglerna om statligt stöd till invandrarnas trossamfund m. m." Stockholm, Sweden: Liber. Re: church work with immigrants.

17969. Stone, Sonja H. (1986) The Opportunities Industrialization Centers as a Religio-Economic Institution. Durham, NC: Black Church in the African American Experience Research Project, Department of Religion, Duke University.

17970. Storkey, Alan. (1986) Transforming Economics: A Christian Way to Employment. London: SPCK. A radical Christian interpretation of capitalism, wealth, unemployment, the welfare state, and the general state of the economy, all of which are issues of faith as well as matters of economic importance. Particular attention is given to unemployment. Bibliography.

17971. Sweeting, George. (1986) "Dwight Moody and the School

He Founded in Chicago," Urban Mission. Vol. 4, No. 1 (September), pp. 18-23.

17972. Takenaka, Masao. (1986) God Is Rice: Asian Culture and Christian Faith. Geneva, Switzerland: Risk Book Series, World Council of Churches. See further: Masao Takenaka. "God's People in Asia: The Task of Christian Community in Asia of the 1980s," Church Labor Letter. No. 143 (1980).

17973. Taliaferro, Dale. (1986) "Case Study: Disciples Downtown," Urban Mission. Vol. 3, No. 4 (March), pp. 34-35.

17974. Tarro, Paul. (1986) "Families at Risk: A Personal Encounter with America's Largest City," Evangelizing Today's Child. Vol. 13, No. 5 (September-October), pp. 8-11.

17975. Taylor, Winston H. (1986) "Congregations in Mission: Washington's Asbury," New World Outlook. n.s. Vol. 42, No. 2 (November-December), pp. 21-25.

17976. Teije, Carel Wilhelm ten. (1986) De opkomst van het socalisme in Breda: actie en reactie tot 1908. Thesis (Doctorate). Tilburg, The Netherlands: Katholieke Hogeschool Tilburg. Re: the history of 19th century church involvement with trade unions and socialism.

17977. "Theology Steps into the Industrial Arena: Report on ICWIM Winter School." (1986) Journal of Theology for Southern Africa. No. 55 (June), pp. 64-71.

17978. Thomas J. V. (1986) "Baptist In London: An Historical Overview," Urban Review [Southern Baptist]. Vol. 2, No. 1 (April), pp. 32-39.

17979. Thomas, John C. (1986) Between Citizen and City. Lawrence, KS: University of Kansas Press. In his assessment of neighborhood groups as a buffer between the city and the individual, Thomas uses Cincinnati as a case study. Although he makes no mention of the church's role in creating such a buffer, churches may function as buffers in ways similar to other neighborhood groups. He includes a chapter on the future of neighborhood groups.

17980. Thomas, Maria H., ed. (1986) Sanctuary: Challenge to the Churches. Washington, DC: Institute on Religion and Democracy.

17981. Thompson, Rolland. (1986) "Renovation--The Process--The New New Old South Church," Faith and Form. Vol. 20 (Fall), pp. 30-33.

17982. Tink, Fletcher L. (1986) "An Urban Missionary Encounters Jane Jacobs," Urban Mission. Vol. 3, No. 3 (1986), pp. 21-29.

17983. Tlapa, Richard J. (1986) The Priest in the Pew. Columbus, GA: Brentwood Christian Press.

17984. Trench, William Crowell. (1986) The Social Gospel and the City: Implications for Theological Reconstruction in the Work of Washington Gladden, Josiah Strong, and Walter Rauschenbusch. Thesis (Ph. D.). Boston, MA: Boston University.

17985. Trinary Consultation, Chicago, IL. (1986) The Trinary Consultation: A Consultation on Evangelizing World Class Cities, Chicago, Illinois, March 14-17, 1986. [Location: Billy Graham Library, Wheaton, IL]. A consultation sponsored by Moody Bible Institute, Trinity Evangelical Divinity School, and Wheaton College. Bibliography.

17986. Tucker, Ruth. (1986) "African Women's Movement Finds Massive Response," Evangelical Missions Quarterly. Vol. 22, No. 3 (July), pp. 282-290.

17987. Turner, Donald E. (1986) Draft for a Position Paper on Urban Transformational Ministries. Richmond, VA: Human Needs Ministry Office, Foreign Mission Board of the Southern Baptist Convention. [Mimeographed].

17988. Turner, Richard Brent. (1986) Islam in the United States in the 1920's: The Quest for a New Vision in Afro-American Religion. Thesis (Ph. D.). Princeton, NJ: Princeton Unveristy.

17989. "Urban Church Strategies, Lutherans and American Baptists Share Their Experiences." (1986) JSAC Grapevine. Vol. 18, No. 2 (July), pp. [1-8]. Includes short articles by George Younger, Yamina Apolinaris, and Tom Sinnott.

17990. Vaughan, Patrick. (1986) "Historical Perspective in Ministers in Secular Employment," pp. 117-187 in John Fuller and Patrick Vaughan, eds. Working for the Kingdom. London: SPCK.

17991. Vincent, John J. (1986) Radical Jesus: The Way of Jesus--

Then and Now. Great Britain: Anchor Brendon. An interpretation of Mark's story of Jesus provides the occasion for Vincent to restate his Christology in light of his thinking since his earlier essay, Secular Christ (1968). Vincent believes that Jesus walks in the contemporary world doing the same things he did in Mark's Gospel story.

17992. "'Vision Quest' Highlights EUC Meet." (1986) The Witness [Ambler, PA]. Vol. 69, No. 5, pp. 16 18.

17993. Washington, Preston R. (1986) From the Pew to the Pavement: Messages on Urban Outreach. Morristown, NJ: Aaron Press.

17994. West, Cornel. (1986) "Unmasking the Black Conservatives," The Christian Century. Vol. 103, No. 22 (July 16-23), pp. 644-648. Poor people's welfare is at stake in a misguided and dangerous intellectual game between liberals and conservatives.

17995. Westgate, James E. (1986) "Emerging Church Planting Strategies for World Class Cities," Urban Mission. Vol. 4, No. 2 (November), pp. 6-13.

17996. Westmeier, Karl Wilhelm. (1986) "The Enthusiastic Protestants of Bogotá, Colombia: Reflections on the Growth of a Movement," International Review of Missions. Vol. 75, No. 297 (January), pp. 13-24.

17997. White, O. Z. (1986) "Communities within Communities," Journal of Religion and Aging. Vol. 3, Nos. 1-2 (Fall-Winter), pp. 193-205. Urban ministries with aged people.

17998. Wiberg, Sally Johnson and Stockwell, Clinton. (1986) Self-Helping Each Other: The Discovery Experience--Steps for Renewal and Outreach for Urban Churches. Chicago, IL: Central Conference of the Evangelical Covenant Church. The authors present a process intended to nurture and enliven the city church for neighborhood ministry. The planning process and recommended workshops are outlined, followed by a series of case studies. Bibliography. Questionnaire.

17999. Wilde, Margaret D. (1986) "Out of Hand in Philadelphia," The Christian Century. Vol. 103, No. 6 (February 19), pp. 166-167. White residents demonstrate against two newly arrived families in their community, one Black the other interracial. The resulting conflict led Philadelphia's mayor, Wilson Goode, to declare a six-week state of emergency and to ban outdoor gatherings.

18000. Willmer, Haddon. (1986) "Politview I: Faith in the City," The Modern Churchman. n.s. Vol. 28, No. 3, pp. 11-14.

18001. Wilmore, Gayraud S. (1986?) "Theological Education in a World of Religious and Other Diversities," Theological Education, Supplement. Vol. 23, pp. 142-164. Same title: Manuscript. [Location: General Theological Seminary Library, New York].

18002. Wilson, Samuel. (1986) "Hope for the City," Urban Mission. Vol. 3, No. 4 (March), pp. 25-33.

18003. Wogaman, J. Philip. (1986) Economics and Ethics. Philadelphia, PA: Fortress.

18004. Worlock, Derek, archbp. (1986) "Affirming Faith in the City," Christian Action Journal. (Summer), pp. 3-10.

18005. Yacoob, May Mirza. (1986) "Ahmadiyya and Urbanization: Easing the Integration of Rural Women in Abidjan," Asian and African Studies [Thematic issue: Religion and the city]. Vol. 20, No. 1, pp. 125-140. A study of the adaptation of poor women to urban life shows how the Ahmadiyya, an urban religion that is not bound by ethnicity, appears to be meeting the needs of such women. It provides not only an authority structure, but also allows ethnic intermarriage, encourages and supports education, offers a social identity, and helps converts to detach themselves from traditional obligations of Islam. Yacoob's study was conducted in Abidjan.

18006. Yancey, Philip. (1986) "The Good News, Brick by Brick," Christianity Today. Vol. 30, No. 13 (September 19), pp. 14-15.

18007. Yankelovich, Skelly, and White, Inc. (1986) The Charitable Behavior of Americans. Washington, DC: Independent Sector, Commissioned by the Rockefeller Brothers Fund.

18008. Zepp, Ira G., Jr. (1986) The New Religious Image of Urban America: Shopping Mall as Ceremonial Center. Westminster, MD: Christian Classics.

18009. Zuber, Robert. (1986) "Learning, Work and Worship: F. D. Maurice," Religious Education. Vol. 81, No. 4 (Fall), pp. 594-608.

18010. Abonyi, Malvina Hauk. (1987) The Role of Ethnic Church Schools in the History of Education in the United States: The

Detroit Experience, 1850-1920. Thesis (Ed. D.). Detroit, MI: Wayne State University.

18011. Abu-Lughod, Janet L. (1987) "The Islamic City--Historic Myth, Islamic Essence, and Contemporary Relevance," International Journal of Middle East Studies. Vol. 19, No. 2, pp. 155-176. A critique of Western orientalists' concepts of the Islamic city for use as a resource by Arab urban planners. The orientalists' notion is based on too few cases. Bibliography.

18012. Adair, James R. (1987) "Pacific Garden Mission: Shining in Darkness," Fundamentalist Journal. Vol. 6, No. 10 (November), pp. 55-57.

18013. Ahern, Geoffrey and Grace Davie. (1987) Inner City God: The Nature of Belief in the Inner City. London: Hodder and Stoughton. Two studies which identify invisible aspects of religious beliefs in British inner cities.

18014. Aldrich, Sandra P. (1987) "Forgiving the Killer," Christian Herald. Vol. 110, No. 10 (November), pp. 16-20. A mother seeks parole for her son's murderer.

18015. Alexander, June Granatir. (1987) The Immigrant Church and Community: Pittsburgh's Slovak Catholics and Lutherans, 1880-1915. Pittsburgh, PA: University of Pittsburgh Press.

18016. Alexander, Vernon P. (1987) The Plight of the Industrial Worker Entering the Information Age. Thesis (D. Min.). San Francisco, CA: San Francisco Theological Seminary.

18017. Allen, Frank W. (1987) "Urban Perspective: Partners in the City," Urban Mission. Vol. 4, No. 4 (March), pp. 54-55.

18018. Allen, Jere. (1987) Challenge for Churches in Changing Communities. Atlanta, GA: Home Mission Board, Southern Baptist Convention, Occasional Papers No. 13. Allen recommends that churches in changing communities develop strategies for ministering to the newly developing groups.

18019. Allen, Robert Raymond. (1987) Singing in the Spirit: An Ethnography of Gospel Performance in New York City's African-American Church Community. Thesis (Ph. D.). Philadelphia, PA: University of Pennsylvania.

18020. Amidei, Nancy. (1987) "Rethinking Hunger in America: Adapting the Sullivan Principles," The Christian Century. Vol. 104, No. 2 (January 21), pp. 51-54. What the 1980's lack is a sense of outrage and shock at urban poverty. Anger and commitment are essential to get things done. The principle articulated by Leon Sullivan for guiding business investments in South Africa might be adapted for use regarding American inner cities. e.g., wages ought to at least equal the poverty level, employers should provide child care for parents who require it, and health coverage should be a part of the salary package.

18021. Anderson, David E. (1987) "The Welfare Reform Bubble," Christianity and Crisis. Vol. 47, No. 15 (October 26), pp. 354-356.

18022. Anderson, Fred R. (1987) "A Case Study of Daily Prayer in a Downtown Presbyterian Church," Reformed Liturgy and Music. Vol. 21 (Fall), pp. 224-227.

18023. Arnal, Oscar L. (1987) "An Agenda for Canadian Lutherans: The Search for Prophetic Soil," Consensus: A Canadian Lutheran Journal of Theology. Vol. 13, No. 3, pp. 51-66.

18024. Aronica, Michele Teresa, sr. (1987) Beyond Charismatic Leadership: The New York Catholic Worker Movement. New Brunswick, NJ: Transaction Books. Bibliography.

18025. Asimpi, Kofi. (1987) The Third World Christian Immigrant and the American Protestant Churches: A Case Study of the Interaction and Responses. Thesis (D. Min). Dallas, TX: Perkins School of Theology at Southern Methodist University.

18026. Assad, Maurice. (1987) "The Coptic Family and Social Change in Egypt," pp. 31-57 in Masamba ma Mpolo and Cecile Sweemer, eds. Families in Transition. Geneva, Switzerland: World Council of Churches Publications. Bibliography.

18027. Atherton, Richard. (1987) Summons to Serve: The Christian Call to Prison Ministry. London: Geoffrey Chapman.

18028. Atherton, Richard. (1987) "AIDS and the Prison Apostolate," pp. 121-126 in Vicky Cosstick, ed. AIDS: Meeting the Community Challenge. Middlegreen, Slough, England: St. Paul Publications.

18029. Azzi, Riolando. (1987) A igreja e os migrantes. São Paulo, Brazil: Edições Paulinas. Re: church work with migrants in Brazil.

18030. Bachelder, Robert S. (1987) "Have Ethics Disappeared from Wall Street?" Christian Century. Vol. 104, No. 21 (July 15-22), pp. 628-630. Bachelder blames churches for moral decline in the nation's financial establishments.

18031. Bagwell, Philip S. (1987) Outcast London, A Christian Response: The West London Mission of the Methodist Church. London: Epworth Press. Bagwell, a historian of British transportation, labor, and industry, writes a centennial history of the Methodist West London Mission. Among the leaders who have been superintendents of the Mission are Hugh Price Hughes, J. Ernest Rattenbury, and Donald Soper. The Mission spearheaded the "Forward Movement" and emphasized social ministry to the poor of central London at a time when Methodism seemed primarily concerned with the salvation of the individual.

18032. Bairati, Piero. (1987) "Cultura salesiana e societa industriale," pp. 331-357 in Francesco Traniello, ed. Don Bosco nella storia della cultura popolare. Torino, Italy: Società editrice internazionale. Re: church and industry in Italy. St. John Bosco founded the Salesians (Society of St. Francis de Sales) in 1859 to befriend orphans and child laborers in Turin, Italy.

18033. Bakke, Raymond J. (1987) "Take Another Look at the City: Interview with R. Bakke," Decision. Vol. 28, No. 1 (January), pp. 23-24+.

18034. Bakke, Raymond J. and Jim Hart. (1987) The Urban Christian: Effective Ministry in Today's Urban World. Downers Grove, IL: InterVarsity Press. Bakke emphasizes the trend that many of the rapidly growing large cities throughout the world are becoming less Christian. This he interprets as an evangelical challenge. Many of his suggestions for strategy, which he lists throughout the book, derive from his own experience in city ministry. Bakke has an unusual view regarding refugees. He interprets God as sending them into the cities so that they might advance His kingdom! See page 78.

18035. Baldovin, John Francis. (1987) The Urban Character of Christian Worship: The Origins, Development and Meaning of Stational Liturgy. Rome, Italy: Pont. Institutum Studiorum Orientalium. [Based on 1982 Ph. D. thesis at Yale of the same title].

18036. Ballard, Paul. (1987) In and Out of Work, a Pastoral Perspective. Edinburgh, Scotland: Saint Andrew Press.

18037. Barbanti, Maria Lucia. (1987) "Colégios Americanos de confissão Protestante na Província de SP: sua aceitação das elites progressistas da época," Comunicacões do ISER [Brazil]. Vol. 24, pp. 44-54. Re: Protestantism's acceptance by urban progressive elites.

18038. Barnes, Trevor. (1987) The Wounded City: Hope and Healing in Belfast. London: Collins. Personal stories of persons caught in Belfast's religious wars reflect courage, humor, and vision of a better world notwithstanding unrelenting violence and tragedy.

18039. Barton, Carol. (1987) "Drawing the Connections in St. Louis Inside-Out," Engage/Social Action. Vol. 15, No. 1 (January), pp. 12-15.

18040. Bauernschmitt, Kathryn Eloise. (1987) A Description of the Patterns of Resource Utilization by Urban Homeless Men to Meet Their Physical, Mental, and Spiritual Needs. Thesis (MSN). Tulsa, OK: Oral Roberts University.

18041. Bellah, Robert N. and Frederick E. Greenspan. (1987) Uncivil Religion: Interreligious Hostility in America. New York: Crossroad.

18042. Beng, Timothy N. (1987) "Landflucht aus einem Kameruner Dorf und was degegen getan wird," Zeitschrift für Mission. Vol. 13, No. 3, pp. 137-141. Measures against rural flight in a village of Cameroon.

18043. Bennett, G. Willis. (1987) "An Urban Church Model: Allen Temple Baptist Church," Urban Mission. Vol. 5, No. 1 (September), pp. 30-37.

18044. Bibby, Reginald Wayne. (1987) Fragmented Gods: The Poverty of Potential of Religion in Canada. Toronto, Canada: Irwin Publishers.

18045. Billings, Alan. (1987) An Urban Parish in Transition. Thesis (D. Min.). New York: New York Theological Seminary, Urban Theology Unit Program, Sheffield, England. Conducted through the Urban Theology Unit under the auspices of the New York Theological Seminary, this study of St. Mary's Church in Walkley Parish of Sheffield, 1984-87, was written by a leader in the Church of England in the area of urban education for clergy.

18046. Black, Neville. (1987?) "Evangelical Spirituality in the Inner City," pp. 92-100 in Jill Robson and David Lonsdale, eds. Can Spirituality Be Taught? England: Association of Centers of Adult Theological Association [i.e., Education].

18047. Blakeborough, Eric. (1987) Called to be Giants: The Faith Which Inspired a City Mission. Basingstoke, England: Marshall Pickering.

18048. Bleakley, David. (1987) "Belfast--London--Dublin: Eternal Triangle or Three-Fold Cord?" Crucible. [Vol. 26, No. 2] (April-June), pp. 61-65.

18049. Bledsoe, Anita G. (1987) "Two Churches That Dared," The Interpreter [United Methodist]. Vol. 31, No. 4 (May), pp. 12-13.

18050. Bledsoe, Ben W. (1987) "The Church in the World: Ecumenism and Prison Chaplaincy," Theology Today. Vol. 44, No. 3 (October), pp. 365-370.

18051. Bloom, Davis C. (1987) "An Ecumenical Approach to Urban Ministry," Church and Society. Vol. 78, No. 1 (September), pp. 13-15.

18052. Bloom, Dorothy B. (1987) Church Doors Open Outward: A Practical Guide to Beginning Community Ministry. Valley Forge, PA: Judson. A primer for local churches interested in starting community outreach ministries.

18053. Bowen, Roger. (1987) "Theological Education after 'Faith in the City,'" British Journal of Theological Education. Vol. 1, No. 3 (Summer), pp. 32-43.

18054. Boyer, Paul S. (1987) Mission on Taylor Street: The Founding and Early Years of the Dayton [OH] Brethren in Christ Mission. Grantham, PA: Brethren in Christ Historical Society. Nappanee, IN: Evangel Press.

18055. Brakelmann, Günter. (1987) Ruhrgebiets-Protestantismus. Bielefeld, West Germany: Luther-Verlag. Protestantism and trade unions in the Ruhr area of Germany. Bibliography.

18056. Brinkerhoff, Merlin B. and Jeffrey C. Jacob. (1987) "Quasi-Religious Meaning Systems, Official Religion, and Quality of Life in an Alternative Lifestyle: Survey, Back-to-the-Land Movement," Journal for the Scientific Study of Religion. Vol. 26, No. 1 (March), pp.

63-80. A study of the resurgence of back-to-the-land emphases in the 1970s. Bibliography.

18057. Brown, C. G. (1987) "The Cost of Pew-Renting: Church Management, Church Going and Social Class in Nineteenth Century Glasgow," Journal of Ecclesiastical History. Vol. 38, No. 3 (July), pp. 347-361.

18058. Brown, Mary Elizabeth. (1987) "The Making of Italian-American Catholics," Catholic Historical Review. Vol. 73, pp. 195-210. Reprinted: Dolores A. Liptak, ed. A Church of Many Cultures. New York: Garland, 1988.

18059. Brown, Mary Elizabeth. (1987) Italian Immigrants and the Catholic Church in the Archdiocese of New York, 1880-1950. Thesis (Ph. D.). New York: Columbia University.

18060. Brown, Robert. (1987) "The Significance of Local Church Audits," Crucible. [Vol. 26, No. 1] (January-March), pp. 6-12. Brown describes the audits recommended in the report of the Archbishop of Centerbury's Commission on Urban Priorities. See: Church of England, Commission on Urban Priorities (1985).

18061. Browne, Lynn. (1987) Faith in Leeds: Searching for God in Our City--One Year Later. Leeds, England: Leeds Churches Community Involvement Project.

18062. Brunson, Ronnie L. (1987) The San Luis Plan: A Guide to Contextualized Church Planting in the Latin American Urban Context. Thesis (D. Min.). Chestnut Hill, PA: Westminster Theological Seminary.

18063. Buckwalter, Paul W. (1987) "Engaging the Powers in a Southwestern City," Alban Institute Action Information. Vol. 13, No. 3 (May), pp. 10-13. The rector of an Episcopal church writes about a one-day "Urban Plunge" with his parishioners and about the ministry that evolved from it. Most of the article is concerned with getting ready to do something (e.g., computerizing a list of volunteers) rather than with what they actually did.

18064. Buekwass, Henry. (1987) "Building a Church: Things to Remember," AFER: African Ecclesial Review (Gaba). Vol. 29, No. 6 (December), pp. 326-338.

18065. Bukowczyk, John J. (1987) And My Children Did Not

Know Me: A History of the Polish Americans. Bloomington, IN: Indiana University Press.

18066. Bukowczyk, John J. (1987) "The Church in the Immigrant City," Journal of Urban History. Vol. 13 No. 2 (February), pp. 207-217. A review article assesses O'Connor (1984), Orton (1981), Parot (1981), Kantowicz (1983), and Shanabruch (1981), all of which focus on the Roman Catholic Church and its accommodation to successive waves of immigrants in the United States. Bukowczyk offers suggestions for further study of the effects of the immigrant groups on the church and its conservative hierarchy.

18067. Burks, Paul. (1987) "Putting Values--and People--to Work," Christianity and Crisis. Vol. 47, No. 1, (Feb 2), pp. 11-14.

18068. Burks, Paul. (1987) "Homeless Women: Priorities," Christianity and Crisis. Vol. 47, No. 4 (March 16), pp. 94-96.

18069. Burnett, James C. (1987) A Critical Examination of Mainline Protestant Churches Existing in Blue-Collar Communities, with Implications for New Church Development by the Episcopal Church in the United States. Thesis (D. Min.). San Francisco, CA: San Anselmo, CA: San Francisco Theological Seminary.

18070. Burstin, Barbara Stern. (1987) "The Early Experience of Polish Jewish and Christian Immigrants in Pittsburgh after World War II," Western Pennsylvania Historical Magazine. Vol. 70, No. 4 (October), pp. 359-381.

18071. Byrne, Patrick H. and Richard C. Keeley. (1987) "LeCorbusier's Finger and Jacob's Thought: The Loss and Recovery of the Subject in the City," pp. 62-108 in Fred Lawrence, ed. Communicating a Dangerous Memory. Atlanta, GA: Scholars Press.

18072. Campbell, Scott. (1987) "Handing Out Without Being Taken In," Leadership: A Practical Journal for Church Leaders. Vol. 8, No. 1 (Winter), p. 129.

18073. Caplan, Lionel. (1987) Class and Culture in Urban India: Fundamentalism in a Christian Community. Oxford, England: Clarendon Press.

18074. Carver, Dave. (1987) "Report from the Front Lines: The Open Door: Opening a Door for Inner-City Youth," Youthworker. Vol. 4, No. 1 (Spring), pp. 106-109.

18075. Cassette Tapes: Models for Metropolitan Ministry Conferences, 1984-1987, Urban Training Cooperative. (1987?) Richmond, VA: Edens Tapes Service. A bibliography listing 60 cassette recordings, mostly about Southern Baptist urban ministries, collected from addresses made at the Metropolitan Ministry Conferences sponsored by the Home Mission Board of the Southern Baptist Convention. The Board lists 17 such regional conferences for the years 1988-1990, hence additional cassettes beyond those listed in this bibliography exist.

18076. Castro, Emilio. (1987) "Mission and Evangelism in Urban Rural Mission," International Review of Mission. Vol. 74, No. 303 (July), pp. 324-330. Castro defends the Urban Rural Mission (URM) movement in the WCC as a new form of evangelism.

18077. Catholic Church, National Conference of Catholic Bishops, Committee on Migration and Tourism. (1987) Together a new People: Pastoral Statement on Migrants and Refugees, November 8, 1986. Washington, DC: Office of Publishing and Promotion Services, United States Catholic Conference.

18078. Center for Church and Community Ministries. (beginning in 1987) [Miscellaneous reports, periodicals, and documents]. Chicago, IL: the Center. A project funded by the Lilly Endowment.

18079. Christiano, Kevin J. (1987) Religious Diversity and Social Change: American Cities, 1890-1906. New York: Cambridge University Press. A discussion of urbanization and religious pluralism in the 19th century based on author's 1983 Ph. D. dissertation at Princeton University. Christiano observes that the degree of religious diversity is associated with the presence of racial and ethnic subcultures more than with city size.

18080. Clanton, Jann Aldredge. (1987) "Being a Family to Disadvantaged Children," Christian Ministry. Vol. 18, No. 6 (November), pp. 26-28. Re: church work with children in Waco, TX.

18081. Cohen, Susan M. (1987) Antisemitism: An Annotated Bibliography. New York: Garland. Annotated and multilingual, with a section on modern antisemitism.

18082. Coleman, Willie. (1987) "The Children of Lazarus: The Homeless in the Urban Context and Presbyterian Responses to Them," Church and Society [Thematic issue: Homelessness]. Vol. 78, No. 1

(September), pp. 31-37.

18083. Committee for Ministerial Formation of the Bishop's Conference of England and Wales. (1987) "Ministry and Mission: Proposals for a National Policy for Lifelong Priestly Formation," Briefing. Vol. 17, No. 17 (September 4). A working paper.

18084. Conn, Harvie M. (1987) A Clarified Vision for Urban Mission: Dispelling the Urban Stereotypes. Grand Rapids, MI: Zondervan Publishing House. Rural and suburban people have, according to Conn, a misinformed conception of the city which extends even to some people who live in cities. He challenges seven mythic assumptions about the city: 1) the rural/urban myth, 2) the depersonalization misunderstanding, 3) the crime generalization, 4) the secularization myth, 5) the privatization myth, 6) the power misunderstanding, and 7) the monoclass (i.e., the poor are omnipresent) generalization. Bibliography.

18085. Conroy, John. (1987) Belfast Diary: War as a Way of Life. Boston, MA: Beacon. A Chicago journalist lives in Northern Ireland on the front lines of conflict in order to understand the motivations, strengths and personal struggles of people caught up in the Belfast tragedy. His frequent comments about religious leaders are not encouraging. Instead of helping the people to understand the conflict and to resolve it, clergy are deeply divided within and between Protestant and Catholic camps. Some speak only in detached spiritualized terms while others actually become deeply involved in the strife.

18086. Cortes, Ernesto, Jr. (1987) "Changing the Locus of Political Decision Making," Christianity and Crisis. Vol. 47, No. 1 (February 2), pp. 18-20.

18087. Cortes, Ernesto, Jr. (1987) "The 'Organizer's Organizer' on Organizing," Christianity and Crisis. Vol. 47, No. 1 (February 2), pp. 20-22.

18088. Council of Churches of Greater Seattle. (1987) State of the City, the Growing Crisis: Action Guide. Seattle, WA: the Council.

18089. Countryman, Louis William. (1987) "The AIDS Crisis: Theological and Ethical Reflections," Anglican Theological Review. Vol. 69, No. 2 (April), pp. 125-134. Refutes theologically the notion of AIDS as punishment.

18090. Courtney, Thomas J. (1987) A Church Planting Strategy for the Urban Poor. Thesis (D. Min.). Chestnut Hill, PA: Westminster Theological Seminary.

18091. Crews, Clyde F. (1987) An American Holy Land: A History of the Archdiocese of Louisville. Wilmington, DE: Glazier.

18092. Crichton, Iain. (1987) "Case Study: The Center for Urban Theological Studies--Philadelphia," Urban Mission. Vol. 5, No. 2 (November), pp. 33-42.

18093. Curtis, David D. C. (1987) Suburbia through the Looking Glass. Thesis (D. Min.). New York: New York Theological Seminary. A dissertation completed at the Urban Theology Unit of Sheffield under the auspices of the New York Theological Seminary.

18094. David, Edward G. (1987) Urban Ministry Activity Report, March, 1987. Madras, India: World Vision India.

18095. David, Kenith A. (1987) "An Introduction to Urban-Rural Mission," International Review of Mission [Thematic issue: Urban-Rural Mission]. Vol. 76, No. 303 (July), pp. 319-323.

18096. de la Torre, Edicio. (1987) "Social Action: Its Relation to Socio-Political Change," International Review of Mission. Vol. 76, No. 303 (July), pp. 332-347. A defense of the Urban Rural Mission programs of the World Council of Churches.

18097. Decker, Robert Owen. (1987) Hartford Immigrants: A History of the Christian Activities Council (Congregational), 1850-1980. New York: Published for the Christian Activities Council by United Church Press. A detailed history of Congregational city missionary societies in Hartford, CT, beginning at mid-19th century, based on extant documents produced by the societies. Bibliography.

18098. de George, Richard T. (1987) "Business, Responsibility, and the Common Good," pp. 304-327 in Oliver Williams and John Houck, eds. The Common Good and US Capitalism. Lanham, MD: University Press of America.

18099. Delacoste, Frédérique and Priscilla Alexander, eds. (1987) Sex Work: Writings by Women in the Sex Industry. Pittsburgh, PA: Cleis.

18100. Delgado, Gary. (1987) Activists' Guide to Religious Funders: Leveraging God's Funds from Her Representatives on Earth, a Working Model. Oakland, CA: Center for Third World Organizing.

18101. Dellheim, Charles. (1987) "The Creation of a Company Culture: Cadburys, 1861-1931," The American Historical Review. Vol. 92, No. 1 (February), pp. 13-44. Quaker ethics serve as a cornerstone for corporate policy.

18102. De Swarte, Carolyn, ed. (1987) The American Deaconess Movement in the Early Twentieth Century. New York: Garland. Reprints, among other documents, Horton's 1904 work titled: The Burden of the City.

18103. Diehl, William E. (1987) "To Expand Our Ministry," Word and World: Theology for Christian Ministry. Vol. 7, No. 4 (Fall), pp. 345-352.

18104. Dill, Ellen Renee. (1987) "Sharing the Load in Small Churches," Christian Ministry. Vol. 18, No. 2 (March), pp. 16-17. In seeking to find solutions to persistent problems of small church administration, Dill advocates need identification techniques, surveys of local resources, proposals seeking the possibility of denominational assistance, and ecumenical ventures. A local church can join forces with other small churches for such purposes as advocacy, hiring a business manager, legal advice, etc. Most suggestions have an urban orientation.

18105. Divida, James J. (1987) "The Indiana Churches and the Italian Immigrants, 1890-1935," US Catholic Historian. Vol. 6, pp. 325-350. Reprinted: Dolores A. Liptak, ed. A Church of Many Cultures. New York: Garland, 1988.

18106. Dolan, Jay P., ed. (1987) The American Catholic Parish: A History from 1850 to the Present. New York: Paulist Press. This book consists of a series of regional histories of the Catholic Church, with chapters given to the local church, parish life, and ethnic groups.

18107. Donahue, Thomas R. (1987) "The Crisis Facing Labor," pp. 27-35 in Alan B. Anderson, ed. Annual of the Society of Christian Ethics, 1986. Knoxville, TN: Society of Christian Ethics.

18108. Donahue, Thomas R. and Rudolph A. Oswald. (1987) "Labor Views of the Pastoral Letter on the Economy," pp. 228-245 Thomas M. Gannon, ed. The Catholic Challenge to the American Economy: Reflections on the US Bishops' Pastoral Letter on Catholic Social Teaching and the US Economy. New York: Macmillan.

18109. Downing, David C. (1987) A Design for Enabling Urban Congregations to Cope with Their Fear of Displacement when Faced with Communities in Transition. Thesis (D. Min.). San Anselmo, CA: San Francisco Theological Seminary. City congregations fail to adapt to changing neighborhoods because of their leaders' fears of being displaced from their churches and neighborhoods, Downing concludes, resulting in their sensing a loss of power, control, and leadership prestige. A manual for helping churches cope with social transition is included, as are case studies of congregations in Kansas City. Bibliography. Questionnaire.

18110. Dyrness, Grace R. (1987) "Urbanization in the Two-Thirds World," Urban Mission. Vol. 4, No. 4 (March), pp. 6-11. Same title: Radix. Vol. 15, No. 3 (November, 1983), pp. 11-14.

18111. Eastman, Michael. (1987) "Faith in the City: A Review Article," Urban Mission. Vol. 4, No. 3 (January), pp. 6-15. Eastman, who at the time of writing had served 27 years on the staff of London's Scripture Union and 19 years as Secretary and Director for Frontier Youth Trust, is a founding partner of the Evangelical Coalition for Urban Mission. A Baptist layman, he served as adviser for the Archbishop of Canterbury's Commission of Urban Priority Areas which produced the Faith in the City report. Here Eastman reflects on the process that led to the Commission's report and comments on its substance.

18112. Echlin, Edward P. (1987) "The City Comes to Thirsk," Crucible. Vol. 26, No. 3] (July-September), pp. 107-112. Re: ethical aspects of investments.

18113. Edrington, Roger B. (1987) Everyday Men: Living in a Climate of Unbelief. New York: P. Lang.

18114. Elliott, Michael. (1987) The Society of Salty Saints: Story and Prayer from the Street. Oak Park, IL: Meyer Stone Books. Glimpses of the worship and spiritual life of city residents at Jefferson Street Baptist Church, Louisville, KY.

18115. Ellis, Marc H. (1987) Toward a Jewish Theology of Liberation. Maryknoll, NY: Orbis Books.

18116. Ellison, Craig W. (1987) "Addressing Felt Needs of Urban Dwellers," Urban Mission. Vol. 4, No. 4 (March), pp. 26-41.

18117. Ensman, Richard G., Jr. (1987) "The Thriving Urban Parish," Today's Parish. Vol. 19, No. 4 (April-May), pp. 9-11.

18118. Erharter, Helmut and Rudolf Schwarzenberger, eds. (1987) Der Mensch in der Arbeitswelt: unserer Verantwortung als Kirche heute. Vienna, Austria: Herder. Proceeding of Österreichische Pastoralinstitut. Bibliography.

18119. Erickson, Art. (1987) "Soul Liberation Festival: A Soul-Winning Block Party," Youthworker. Vol. 4, No. 3 (Fall), pp. 62-67.

18120. Evans, Alice Frazer, Robert A. Evans, and William Bean Kennedy. (1987) Pedagogies for the Non-Poor. Maryknoll, NY: Orbis Books. Evans provides eight illustrations of how wealthy North Americans have tried to become involved in peacemaking, fighting injustice, stopping plant closings, ameliorating hunger, and eradicating sexism and racism without making things worse than they already are.

18121. Evans, Anthony T. (1987) "Christian Broadcasting and the Urban Crisis," Religious Broadcasting. Vol. 19, No. 2 (February), pp. 80+.

18122. Evans, Clay. (1987) "Clay Evans: Preacher of Hope for the City," [Interview with Clay Evans by Doug Brendel] Religious Broadcasting. Vol. 19, No. 4 (April), pp. 16-18.

18123. Fagan, Ronald W. (1987) "Skid-Row Rescue Missions: A Religious Approach to Alcoholism," Journal of Religion and Health. Vol. 26, No. 2 (Summer), pp. 153-171. Thirty-seven worship services in skid-row missions are analyzed for their content, and Fagan conjectures about the effects of the worship services as deterrence from alcoholism.

18124. Fassin, Didier. (1987) "Rituels villageois, rituels urbains: La reproduction sociale chez les femmes joola du Sénégal," L'Homme. No. 104, No. 4, pp. 54-75. A discussion of what happens to village rituals when people migrate to the city, based on a study of the Joola right for preserving women's fertility, shows that residence in cities tends to weaken ritual constraints, to simplify the rites, and eventually to reduce efficacy.

18125. Faupel, Charles E., Gregory S. Kowalski, and Paul D. Star. (1987) "Sociology's One Law: Religion and Suicide in the Urban Context," Journal for the Scientific Study of Religion. Vol. 26, No. 4 (December), pp. 523-534. A test of Durkheim's theories on suicide using data collected in US cities. Bibliography.

18126. Fenn, Richard K. (1987) The Dream of the Perfect Act: An Inquiry into the Fate of Religion in a Secular World. New York: Tavistock Publications. For a comparison of Fenn's views on secularization with those of other theorists, see Oliver Tschannen (1991) "The Secularization Paradigm: A Systemization," Journal for the Scientific Study of Religion. Vol. 30, No. 4 (December), pp. 395-415.

18127. Fiorenza, Elizabeth Schussler and Anne Carr. (1987) Women, Work and Poverty. Edinburgh, Scotland: T. and T. Clark, Concilium Issue No. 194.

18128. Fishburn, Janet F. (1987) "Seminary, Ministry and Social Responsibility," The Christian Century. Vol. 104, No. 4 (February 4-11), pp. 100-102. Reports on a conference on Theological Education for Socially Responsible Ministry held in Washington, D.C., January 8-10, 1987.

18129. Fortunato, John. (1987) AIDS: The Spiritual Dilemma. San Francisco, CA: Harper and Row. Written from the perspective of a gay man who is a lay theologian and psychologist.

18130. Frame, Randall L. (1987) "Churches Band Together to Help Register Undocumented Aliens," Christianity Today. Vol. 31, No. 9 (July 10), pp. 34-35.

18131. Freebairn, Harry A. (1987) "There Is Life after Burnout," Alban Institute Action Information. Vol. 13, No. 2 (March), pp. 15-17. Presbyterian pastor in Easton, PA, talks about his own burnout and suggests that "burnout pastors" are attracted to "burnout churches."

18132. Fruhauf, Henry. (1987) "Responding to Threats with the Wisdom of Solomon," Security Management. Vol. 31 (March), pp. 47-50. Re: security systems and protective measures for synagogues and churches.

18133. Fulton, Brent. (1987) "Seminary of the Field: A Model for Mission among the Skyscrapers," Urban Mission. Vol. 4, No. 4 (March), pp. 52-54.

18134. Furr, James Harold. (1987) A Critical Analysis of Selected Urban Church and Community Classifications. Thesis (Ph. D.). Louisville, KY: Southern Baptist Theological Seminary. Furr reviews the literature on typologies of city communities and city churches, recommending a new typology based on four variables: type of city community (inner city, transitional, stable, suburban, fringe), size of congregation (small, medium, large, and extra-large), neighborhood orientation (one neighborhood or multi neighborhoods), and whether or not the church's program is focused internally on the members or has an external focus on the city. He suggests that the 80 theoretical types generated by this conceptualization do not all exist empirically. No empirical test is undertaken.

18135. Gallup, George, Jr. (1987) The American Catholic People, Their Beliefs, Practices, and Values. Garden City, NY: Doubleday. Questionnaire.

18136. Gannon, Thomas M., ed. (1987) The Catholic Challenge to the American Economy. New York: Macmillan.

18137. Garvin, Alexander. (1987) "The City of Tomorrow," World Order. Vol. 21 (Spring-Summer), pp. 25-44. Re: Le Corbusier, urban renewal and city planning.

18138. Gesualdi, Louis John. (1987) The Religious Acculturation of the Italian-American Catholics: Cultural and Socio-Economic Factors. Thesis (Ph. D.). New York: Fordham University.

18139. Giles, Philip L. (1987) "A Millennium Denied: Northern Methodists and Workers, 1865-1886," Methodist History. Vol. 26, No. 1 (October), pp. 27-43.

18140. Gittings, James A. (1987) "Churches in Communities: A Place to Stand," Christianity and Crisis. Vol. 47, No. 1 (February 2), pp. 5-11.

18141. Gittings, James A. (1987) Breach of Promise. New York: Friendship Press. By telling the stories of homeless people, a journalist outlines empathic strategies for local churches. Most but not all vignettes are drawn from cities. This slender volume is an expansion of Gittings' Christianity and Crisis article of February 2, 1987.

18142. Goodell, Michael. (1987) "Housing and Hope for Census Tract 5130," The Christian Century. Vol. 104, No. 7 (March 4), pp. 213-215. Goodell reports on a self-help housing project in inner city Detroit, advocating "sweat equity" as a way of helping people find a way out of their poverty. He draws parallels between the Detroit group's experiences and circumstances in other large cities which have area where over 70 percent of the people live in poverty. Strategies for big cities are not necessarily fitting for smaller cities, he observes. Goodell's group managed to renovate only four houses, then experienced debilitating conflict in the staff and board. Goodell says the approach followed is noteworthy, however.

18143. Goodell, Michael. (1987) "Renovation at the Roots: PIFU [People in Faith United] Builds a Model of Neighborhood Development," Other Side. Vol. 23, No. 7 (September), pp. 8-9.

18144. Granvogl, Heinz. (1987) Adolph Kolping und die christlich-soziale Bewegung: eine regionalgeschichtliche Untersuchung zum Verhaltnis zwischen Kirche und Arbeitnehmer in den Jahren 1830-1866. Augsburg, Germany: AV-Verlag.

18145. Green, Laurie. (1987) Power to the Powerless: Theology Brought to Life. Basingstoke, England: Marshall Pickering. Green writes grass-roots theology based on the his experiences in St. Chad's church, a working class parish in inner city Birmingham, England -- a revision of a D. Min. dissertation submitted to a program jointly operated by the Urban Theology Unit, Sheffield, and New York Theological Seminary.

18146. Greenway, Roger S. (1987) "The Importance of Missionary Research," Urban Mission. Vol. 4, No. 3 (January), pp. 3-5.

18147. Grigg, Viv. (1987) "The Urban Poor: Prime Missionary Target," Evangelical Review of Theology. Vol. 11, No. 3 (July), pp. 263-265.

18148. Grigg, Viv. (1987) "Urban Perspectives: The Poor Wise Man of Calcutta," Urban Mission. Vol. 5, No. 2 (November), pp. 43-44.

18149. Grigg, Viv. (1987) "Sorry! The Frontier Moved," Urban Mission. Vol. 4, No. 4 (March), pp. 12-25. Grigg offers a scheme for involving middle and elite classes in ministry to the poor based on incarnational theology and pastoral leadership.

18150. Grigg, Viv. (1987) "God's War on Poverty: Taking the Good News to a Bad Neighborhood," World Christian. Vol. 6, No. 3 (May-June), pp. 9-12. The poor, even in the worst areas, can still be a blessing.

18151. Guest, Avery M. and Barrett A. Lee. (1987) "Metropolitan Residential Environments and Church Organizational Activities," Sociological Analysis: A Journal in the Sociology of Religion. Vol. 47, No. 4 (Winter), pp. 335-354. Using 1981 data collected by questionnaires mailed to clergy in Nashville and Seattle, the authors find support for hypotheses traced back to Park's Chicago school and to H. Paul Douglass (1926). Specifically, they hypothesize that a church's surrounding environment influences its activities. They measured three kinds of activities in local churches -- community programs, counseling services, and internal programs for the members. Although their data are admittedly few, they use multiple regression analysis to show community programming is greater in churches which have been located in the community for more years, in churches physically closer to the central business district, in larger churches but with proportionately fewer children, and, as expected, in liberal churches. Churches with more internal programs tend to have more attenders from the immediate neighborhood, smaller attendance but with proportionately more children, and more people with conservative attitudes. Questionnaire.

18152. Gupta, Shiv Prakash. (1987) "Comparative Study of Religiosity among the Rural and the Urban Poor," The Journal of Sociological Studies. Vol. 6 (January), pp. 173-178. In India, the urban poor are more likely than rural poor to go on pilgrimages. In both groups, there is high incidence of belief in God and reincarnation, but belief in spirits of the dead is rare. Sample size: urban (250), rural (150).

18153. Gurock, Jeffrey S. (1987) "Jewish Communal Divisiveness in Response to Christian Influences on the Lower East Side, 1900-1910," pp. 255-271 in Todd M. Endelman, ed. Jewish Apostasy in the Modern World. New York: Holmes and Meier. A scholarly Jewish point of view. Bibliography.

18154. Hadaway, C. Kirk, Francis M. Dubose, and Stuart A. Wright. (1987) Home Cell Groups and House Churches. Nashville, TN: Broadman.

18155. Hadden, Jeffrey K. (1987) "Toward Desacralizing Secularization Theory," Social Forces. Vol. 65, No. 4 (June), pp. 587-611. Hadden contributes to the emerging notion that secularization theory is ideologically inspired and poorly conceived as a social scientific concept. Perhaps there never was a more religious era from which present society became secularized. For a comparison of Hadden's views on secularization with those of other theorists, see Oliver Tschannen (1991) "The Secularization Paradigm: A Systemization," Journal for the Scientific Study of Religion. Vol. 30, No. 4 (December), pp. 395-415.

18156. Haines, Robin and Holly Folger. (1987) "Raising His Children: Reaching the World's 100 Million Street Kids," World Christian. Vol. 6, No. 3 (May-June), pp. 16-24.

18157. Handy, Robert T. (1987) A History of Union Theological Seminary in New York. New York: Columbia University Press.

18158. Harahap, Basyral Hamidy. (1987) "Islam and Adat among South Tapanuli Migrants in Three Indonesian Cities," pp. 221-237 in Rita Smith Kipp and Susan Rodgers, eds. Indonesian Religion in Transition. Tucson, AZ: University of Arizona Press.

18159. Harrington, Michael. (1987?) Who Are the Poor? Washington, DC: Justice for All, National Office. A brief summary of what all Americans should know about the poor, but do not. A pamphlet.

18160. Harris, Alex. (1987) "The Challenge of Being a Black Women in America," Urban Mission. Vol. 5, No. 2 (November), pp. 25-32.

18161. Harris, James Henry. (1987) Black Ministers and Laity in the Urban Church: An Analysis of Political and Social Expectations. Lanham, MD: University Press of America. Harris reports the results of a questionnaire completed by 338 members of ten Black urban congregations affiliated with seven denominations. The data illuminate the nature of lay expectations of clergy in the areas of social and political involvement. Conclusions are cast in terms of liberation theology. Bibliography.

18162. Harris, John F. (1987) "Seeking the Faithful in DC Suburbs: Door-to-Door Missionaries Scour Subdivisions to Build Congregations," The Washington Post. Vol. 110 (February 2), p. A1.

18163. Harrison, Barbara. (1987) "Escaping the Work Ethic," Crucible. Vol. 26, No. 4 (October-December), pp. 146-152.

18164. Harrison, Gordon W. (1987) Voicing the Gospel Experience in Gorton [England]. Thesis (D. Min.). New York: New York Theological Seminary.

18165. Hart, Jim and Neville Black. (1987) "Housing Tenure and the Gospel," Crucible. [Vol. 26, No. 4 (October-December), Pt. 1, pp. 167-172; [Vol 27, No. 1] (January-March, 1988), Pt. 2, pp. 15-19; [No. 3] (July-September), Pt. 3, pp. 173-181.

18166. Harvey, John. (1987) Bridging the Gap: Has the Church Failed the Poor? Edinburgh, Scotland: St. Andrew Press. A Glasgow pastor contends that the Church of Scotland has failed the poor, assesses the reasons why the poor are not associated at all with the church, and declares the church's failure to be disobedience and leading to disaster. Positive examples of churches reaching the poor are offered. The Gorbals Group of Glasgow, an assemblage of radical middle class teachers, social workers, youth workers, and clergy who pooled incomes and became politically active, is assessed. Bibliography.

18167. Hastings, Adrian. (1987) "Cities and Gods," New Blackfriars. Vol. 68, No. 808 (September), pp. 372-379.

18168. Hazelden Foundation. (1987) The Twelve Steps of Alcoholics Anonymous, Interpreted by the Hazelden Foundation. San Francisco, CA: Harper.

18169. Hedlund, Roger E. (1987) "Urbanization and Evangelization in South Asia," Urban Mission. Vol. 4, No. 3 (January), pp. 16-30.

18170. Hempel, Joel R. (1987) "What It Takes to Stay Downtown," Leadership: A Practical Journal for Church Leaders. Vol. 8, No. 1 (Winter), pp. 124-128. Hempel tells the story of what was once a suburban church close to Cincinnati, OH, but now changing into an inner city neighborhood church. Dying downtown churches can survive if they are willing to embrace the inner city.

18171. Hewitt, W. E. (1987) "The Influence of Social Class on Activity Preferences of Comunidades Eclesiais de Base," Journal of Latin American Studies. Vol. 19 (May), pp. 141-156.

18172. Hiebert, Paul G. (1987) "Window Shopping the Gospel," Urban Mission. Vol. 4, No. 5 (May), pp. 5-12.

18173. Hill, Edward V. (1987) "Poverty and Prejudice in the Church: Interview with Edward V. Hill by Steven Lawson," Charisma. Vol. 13, No. 4 (November), pp. 93-96.

18174. Hirschfield, Robert. (1987) "Rebuilding the City: East Brooklyn's Churches Build the Nehemiah Plan," The Other Side. Vol. 23 (December), pp. 6-7.

18175. História da ACO: fidelidade e compromisso na classe operária. (1987) Rio de Janeiro, RJ, Brazil: Ação Católica Operária. Re: history of the Ação Católica Operária, a labor union, and its efforts in behalf of the working class.

18176. Hock, Douglas A. (1987) "Neglected by Mission: The

Homosexual Person," Urban Mission. Vol. 4, No. 5 (May), pp. 13-20.

18177. Hollister, J. Elliott. (1987) "Ethnocentrism among Free Methodist Leaders and Students," Journal of Psychology and Theology. Vol. 15, No. 1 (Winter), pp. 57-67. Based on a national sample of Free Methodist students, clergy, and lay leaders, Hollister concludes that respondents demonstrating the least degree of ethnocentricity were clergy, college graduates, judicatory officials, professionals, and members of inner city churches. Seniors at college were less enthnocentric than freshmen. Questionnaire.

18178. Holman, Bob. (1987) "George Landsbury: Labour's Forgotten Christian Leader," Crucible. [Vol. 26, No. 4] (October-December), pp. 173-181.

18179. Holthaus, H. Lee. (1987) Configuration of the Large Metropolitan Mission in an Age of Urban Renewal. Thesis (Ph. D.). s.l., CA: California Coast University.

18180. "Homeless Deaths Triple, March Remembers: Permanent Service Demanded by Clergy." (1987) Sequoia: The Church at Work [Published by the Northern California Ecumenical Council]. Vol. 7, No. 4 (January), pp. 1-3. A group of San Francisco clergy process in solemn observance of the homeless who died in the streets.

18181. Hope, Glenda. (1987) "Why Fast for Lent--or Anytime?" The Witness [Ambler, PA]. Vol. 70, No. 3 (March), pp. 12-14.

18182. Hope, Glenda. (1987) "A Cooperative Ministry Model," Church and Society [Thematic issue: Urban ministry]. Vol. 78, No. 1 (September), pp. 23-25. A declining Presbyterian church in San Francisco finds strength to minister with the poor.

18183. Hopewell, James F. (1987) Congregation: Stories and Structures. Philadelphia, PA: Fortress. Published posthumously, Hopewell's analysis of congregations derives from his interests in ethnographic methods and literary analysis. Chapter 2, which has excellent footnotes, provides a novel approach to categorizing the ever expanding and largely formless literature about congregations. Hopewell uses powerful metaphors (are they more than that?) drawn mostly from secular sources to describe types of congregations and types of studies of congregations. The central notion of the book is that congregations are not deeply understood until their "story" is understood. Theoretical underpinnings for this thesis are drawn from the works of anthropologists Clifford Geertz and Claude Lévi-Strauss and the literary analyses of Victor Turner and Northrop Frye. Methodology for obtaining congregational stories is more fully developed in Carroll, et. al., (1986). Hopewell's approach to study of congregations offers an alternative to the more traditional social scientific church studies. Case studies include Trinity United Methodist Church, Atlanta. Bibliography.

18184. Howe, Leroy T. (1987) "Theological Foundations for Crisis Intervention," The Modern Churchman. n.s. Vol. 29, No. 4, pp. 20-22.

18185. Howell, Leon. (1987) "The Churches: Prime Ingredient for Change," Christianity and Crisis. Vol. 47, No. 1 (February 2), pp. 3-4. Editorial.

18186. Howell, Leon. (1987) "Minority Coalitions: A Place in the Sun," Christianity and Crisis. Vol. 47, No. 1 (February 2), pp. 15-18.

18187. Hullum, Everett, Kathy Choy, and Sherri Brown. (1987) "Special Supplement: The Cities," Missions USA. Vol. 58, No. 4 (July-August), 32 pages. Reprinted: Home Mission Board, Southern Baptist Convention. Intended as a call for Southern Baptists to return to the urban ministries they have "forgotten" or "abandoned."

18188. Hummell, Gert. (1987) "Morality and Beyond: Anthropology and New Ethics in Tomorrow's Information Society," pp. 125-154 in John J. Carey, ed. Being and Doing: Paul Tillich as Ethicist. Macon, GA: Mercer.

18189. Humphrey, Michael. (1987) "Community, Mosque and Ethnic Politics," The Australian and New Zealand Journal of Sociology. Vol. 23, No. 2 (July), pp. 233-245.

18190. Hunt, Angela Elwell. (1987) "First Urban Summit Held at LU," Fundamentalist Journal. Vol. 6 No. 1 (January), pp. 61-62.

18191. Hunt, Angela Elwell. (1987) "Lemuel S. Tucker: Building Bridges to the Inner City," Fundamentalist Journal. Vol. 6, No. 2 (February), pp. 17-19. Lem Tucker is a Black who presides over the Voice of Calvary Ministries in Jackson, Mississippi. Tries to combine justice and evangelism. Programs of the ministry include: health care, housing, Christian social services, cooperative economic development, international training for missionaries, and youth leadership development. Tucker appeals to suburban churches to "help in the battle for the soul of the city.

18192. Hunter, James Davison. (1987) "Religious Elites in Advanced Industrial Society," Comparative Studies in Society and History. Vol. 29, No. 2, pp. 360-374. Religious elites are becoming fewer and less influential. Left-liberal clergy, a position held by the largest number of elites, differ significantly from the laity and appear detached or excluded from society in general. Data are drawn from North America, Western Europe, and Japan.

18193. Hütter, Gottfried and Joachim Keden. (1987) Kirche für die City: Wenn die Kirche auf den Markt geht. Neukirchen-Vluyn, West Germany: Schriftenmissions-Verlag. In Bonn, the church has established a center, "Kirchenpavillon," into which persons disenchanted with the church are invited to receive coffee and current information about churches and activities. Counseling and referrals services for persons in need are also available. Bibliography.

18194. Hyman, Paula E. (1987) "From City to Suburb: Temple Mishkan Tefila of Boston," pp. 185-205 in Jack Wertheimer, ed. The American Synagogue: A Sanctuary Transformed. New York: Cambridge University Press. Bibliography.

18195. Jablonowski, Harry W., ed. (1987) Kirche und Gewerkschaften im Dialog. Bochum, West Germany: SWI-Verlag. Re: the church and trade unions in dialog, a report prepared by Sozialwissenschaftliches Institut of the Evangelische Kirche in Deutschland. Multiple volumes. Bibliography.

18196. Jackson, Bruce W., ed. (1987-1988) CUME: Center for Urban Ministerial Education, Catalog. Hamilton, MA: Gordon-Conwell Theological Seminary. A pamphlet.

18197. Jackson, Dave and Neta Jackson. (1987) Glimpses of Glory: Thirty Years of Community, the Story of Reba Place Fellowship. Elgin, IL: Brethren Press. Reba Place in Evanston, IL, bases its vision of a church in the city on Acts 4. A history in story form of the church's origins in 1951 and its subsequent development, the Jacksons' book describes outreach ministries in evangelism, social justice, mental health, and inner healing in the Anabaptist tradition.

18198. Jennings, George. (1987) "Mission among Metropolitan Muslims," Urban Mission. Vol. 5, No. 2 (November), pp. 12-18.

18199. "Jesus Lives in Florida City." (1987) Latin America Evangelist. Vol. 67, No. 2 (April), pp. 12-13.

18200. Johnson, Douglas W. (1987) Racial/Ethnic Minority Membership in the United Methodist Church. New York: National Program Division, General Board of Global Ministries, United Methodist Church.

18201. Johnson, Sherman E. (1987) Paul the Apostle and His Cities. Wilmington, DE: Michael Glazier.

18202. Johnson, Suzan D. (1987) "The Church That Didn't Die," Leadership. Vol. 8, No. 4 (Fall), pp. 24-30. Re: Mariners' Baptist Temple (New York).

18203. Jones, Buck. (1987) The Role of the Black Church as Facilitator of Political Participation in Metropolitan St. Louis. Thesis (MA). St. Louis, MO: University of Missouri.

18204. Jones, William Clossen, ed. (1987) AIDS in Religious Perspective. Kingston, Ontario, Canada: Queens Theological College. Academic essays on the church's response to AIDS, homophobia and the AIDS panic.

18205. Juguet, E. (1987) "Japan: The World of Work," Pro Mundi Vita Dossiers: Asia and Australia. Dossier No. 50, pp. 3-24.

18206. Juhl, Paulgeorg. (1987) "Wie können wir politische und soziale Mitverantwortung praktizieren?" Zeitschrift für Evangelische Ethik, Vol. 31, No. 4 (October-December), pp. 448-456. A discussion of political and social responsibility of laborers, and of church work with the unemployed.

18207. Kaellis, Eugene and Rhoda Kaellis, eds. (1987) Toward a Jewish America. Lewiston, NY: Mellen. Judaism is seen as the most fitting religion for America. Mass conversions to it are recommended.

18208. Kahn, Masood Ali. (1987) "Intergenerational Mobility among Muslims in Aurangabad: A South Indian City," Journal, Institute of Muslim Minority Affairs. Vol. 8 (January), pp. 88-108.

18209. Karp, Abraham J. (1987) "Overview: The Synagogue in America--A Historical Typology," pp. 1-34 in Jack Wertheimer, ed. The American Synagogue: A Sanctuary Transformed. New York: Cambridge University Press.

18210. Kauffman, John Timothy. (1987) The Use of Surveys to Promote Home Bible Studies in the German Urban Context. Thesis

(Th. M.). Pasadena, CA: Fuller Theological Seminary.

18211. Kelly, Tom. (1987) "A Room Without A View," Christianity and Crisis. Vol. 47, No. 4 (March 16), pp. 90-94.

18212. Kemper, Vicki and Cathleen Morris. (1987) "Steelworkers Pray for Justice," Sojourners. Vol. 16, No. 5 (May), pp. 10-11.

18213. Kenel, Sally A. (1987) "Urban Psychology and Spirituality," Journal of Psychology and Theology. Vol. 15, No. 4 (Fall), pp. 300-307. Kenel, of St. John's University on Staten Island, NY, advances the proposition that environmental psychology provides appropriate methodologies and theory for the study of Christian spirituality. She examines the ability of urban environment to support such spirituality, drawing on the models of the human being as a territorial animal, a passive sensor, and a preference holder. Each model is explored for implications for spirituality and in terms of the kind of commitment warranted, especially for the practice of compassion.

18214. Killinger, John. (1987) "The Preacher and the Panhandlers," The Christian Century. Vol. 104, No. 10 (April 1), pp. 301-302. An urban pastor reflects on turning away a beggar requesting money for food.

18215. Kim, Shin Kuk. (1987) Urbanization and Pastoral Ministry, with Special Reference to Karakdong Church Ministry. Thesis (D. Min.). Pasadena, CA: Fuller Theological Seminary. Text in Korean with English summary.

18216. Kirtland, Stephany. (1987) "Clearinghouse for Ministry: ESA/Fresno Connects the City and the Church," World Christian. Vol. 6, No. 3 (May), pp. 13-14.

18217. Kollar, Rene. (1987) "Anglican Brotherhoods and Urban Social Work," Churchman: Journal of Anglical Theology. Vol. 101, No. 2, pp. 140-145.

18218. Kowalski, Gregory S., Charles E. Faupel and Paul D. Starr. (1987) "Urbanism and Suicide: A Study of American Counties," Social Forces. Vol. 66, No. 1 (September), pp. 85-101. Re: hypotheses about increased suicide in urban areas.

18219. Kroll, Una. (1987) "God in Handicapped People," Crucible. [Vol. 26, No. 2] (April-June), pp. 66-71.

18220. Kromkowski, John A. (1987) "Elderly Urban Catholic Ethnics: Their Churches and Neighborhoods," Journal of Religion and Aging. Vol. 3, Nos. 3-4 (Spring), pp. 61-81.

18221. Lamar, Robert C. (1987) "The Changing Face of Public Ministry: Trusting the Spirit for Social Mission," Christian Ministry. Vol. 18, No. 3 (May), pp. 7-9.

18222. Landau, Yeshaiahu. (1987) Yega' u-ma'a's be-fi . hakhamim: osef amarot u-fitgamim 'al 'avodah ... mi-pi .hakhme Yi'sra'el .veha-'olam. Jerusalem, Israel: Re'uven Mas.

18223. Larson, Craig Brian. (1987) "The Unmalleable in Me," Leadership: A Practical Journal for Christian Leaders. Vol. 8, No. 4 (Fall), p. 23.

18224. Lass, Herb. (1987) "Church Repairs Impossible," Engineering News-Record. Vol. 218 (February 5), p. 13. Re: Trinity Church, Boston.

18225. Laurinkari, Juhani and Pauli Niemela. (1987) Aspects of Differences in Urban and Rural Church Activities. Kuopio, Finland: Department of Social Sciences, University of Kuopio.

18226. Lee, Sang Hyun, ed. (1987) Korean American Ministry: A Resource Book. [s.l.: Consulting Committee on Korean American Ministry, The Program Agency, Presbyterian Church in the USA. [Location: General Theological Seminary, New York].

18227. Lee, Sang-Woon. (1987) A Study of Urban Pastoral Ministry: With Reference to Dangsan Dong Presbyterian Church. Thesis (D. Min.). Pasadena, CA: Fuller Theological Seminary. Text in Korean with an English summary.

18228. Lees, Andrew. (1987) "The Civic Pride of the Middle Classes in Wilhelmian Germany," Thought. Vol. 62, No. 246 (September), pp. 251-267.

18229. Lewin, Hugh, comp. (1987) A Community of Clowns: Testimonies of People in Urban Rural Mission. Geneva: World Council of Churches. Stories related to the World Council of Churches supported movement called Urban Rural Mission, formerly called Urban Industrial Mission, collected over a 25-year period. For additional materials on Urban Rural Mission, see Abstract Service (1970-1981) and the ICUIS collection [Location: see note 2].

18230. Lewis, Gregg. (1987) "Smalltown, USA," Campus Life. Vol. 45, No. 8 (March), pp. 71-73. [See note 3].

18231. Linthicum, Robert C., comp. (1987) Into All the City: The Urban Mission Strategy of World Vision International. [Pasadena, CA]: Technical Services, World Vision International.

18232. Linthicum, Robert C. (1987) "The Urban World and World Vision," Urban Mission. Vol. 5, No. 1 (September), pp. 5-15.

18233. Long, Larry Simeon. (1987) Helping a Suburban Congregation to Grow Consciously in Its Ministry of Caring. Thesis (D. Min.). Madison, NJ: Drew University.

18234. Lorenz, Eckehart. (1987) Kirchliche Reaktionen auf die Arbeiterbewegung in Mannheim 1890-1933: ein Beitrag zur Sozialgeschichte der evangelischen Landeskirche in Baden. Sigmaringen, West Germany: J. Thorbecke. A history of church (Evangelische Landeskirche in Baden) reactions to the trade union movement in Baden and Mannheim, Germany.

18235. Loux, Gordon D. (1987) Uncommon Courage: The Story of Prison Fellowship International. Ann Arbor, MI: Servant Publications.

18236. Luecke, Richard Henry. (1987) "Gospel Confession and Arts of Ministry in the Late Industrial City," Currents in Theology and Mission. Vol. 14, No. 2 (April), pp. 94-104. Luecke, of the Community Renewal Society in Chicago, interprets the city in escatological terms -- the world is headed toward the city transformed, not back to Eden. He argues that Jesus gave preferential treatment to the poor not because of any inherent merit in poverty, but because they were more receptive to him, they having nothing to lose, so to speak.

18237. Lutz, Charles P. (1987) Public Voice: Social Policy Development in the American Lutheran Church, 1960-1987. Minneapolis, MN: Office of Church in Society.

18238. Mabry, Hunter P. (1987) "Technology and Human Values," Engage/Social Action. Vol. 15, No. 6 (June), pp. 5-8+. Social problems lie not so much in the tensions between technology and human values as between the rich and the poor.

18239. Machor, James L. (1987) Pastoral Cities: Urban Ideas and the Symbolic Landscape of America. Madison, WI: University of Wisconsin Press.

18240. MacInnes, George R. (1987) "Site and Service Housing Without Informal Sector Economics: Dandora Project, Phase II," AFER: African Ecclesial Review (Gaba). Vol. 29, No. 4 (August), pp. 236-241.

18241. Mackey, Lloyd. (1987) "Ethnic Chinese Churches Prepare for Influx of Hong Kong Immigrants," Christianity Today. Vol. 31, No. 5 (March 20), pp. 54-55.

18242. MacLennan, Anne. (1987) "Charity and Change: Montreal English Protestant Charity Faces the Crisis of Depression," Urban History Review (Revue d'histoire urbaine). Vol. 16, No. 1 (June), pp. 1-16. Depression in the 1930s forced private and public charities across Canada to adapt. The crisis was particularly acute for the Montreal Council of Social Agencies, a minority Protestant organization in a city reluctant to accept any responsibility for public service.

18243. Malkin, Irad. (1987) "La place des dieux dans la cité des hommes: le découpage des aires sacrées dans les colonies grecques," Revue de l'Histoire des Religions. Vol. 204 (October), pp. 331-352.

18244. Maritain, Jacques. (1987) "The Spiritual Mission of the City," Communio: International Catholic Review. Vol. 14, No. 2, pp. 193-202. Maritain, a French theologian and Catholic thinker, in a 1965 memo to Pope Paul VI, expresses concern about the mission and ministry of lay people. He opposes the appendage-to-clergy approach to understanding laity-clergy relations.

18245. Marty, Martin E. (1987) "Porchless," Christian Century. Vol. 104, No. 24 (August 26-September 2), p. 735. Marty reflects on the lost importance of porches on houses.

18246. Maurer, Imelda and Bernie Galvin. (1987) "A Circle of Solidarity: Women in Ministry, Women in the Factory," Journal of Women and Religion. Vol. 6 (Winter), pp. 18-25

18247. McCoy, Dulci. (1987) "Lafayette Park: Rebirth of a Neighborhood Church," New World Outlook. n.s. Vol. 47, No. 4 (February), pp. 16-20. Re: the renewal of a United Methodist congregation's struggle to minister in the city and measured success against urban blight in St. Louis, MO.

18248. McDonnell, Claudia. (1987) "St. Augustine: Hope Comes to the Inner City," St. Anthony Messenger. Vol. 94, No. 8 (January), pp. 14-20. Re: a South Bronx parish that emphasizes community ministries.

18249. Meacham, Standish. (1987) Toynbee Hall and Social Reform, 1880-1914. New Haven, CT: Yale University Press.

18250. Mendoza Sadaba, Andrés. (1987) "Comunidad y trabajo en el discurso social de la iglesia," Informes de Pro Mundi Vita América Latina. Vol. 49, pp. 1-32.

18251. Middleton, Robert G. (1987) "The Church Academy Training the Jobless," The Christian Ministry. Vol. 18, No. 3 (May), pp. 16-18. Re: Central Baptist Church, Hartford, CT.

18252. Miller, Mike. (1987) "Organizing: A Map for Explorers," Christianity and Crisis. Vol. 47, No. 1 (February 2), pp. 22-30. Bibliography.

18253. Million, Linda Penrod. (1987) Revision of the Church's Mission and Ministry in Our World: Business Chaplaincy in Re-Invented Corporate America. Thesis (D. Min.). Louisville, KY: Louisville Presbyterian Theological Seminary.

18254. Mills, J. (1987) "Diviners as Social Healers within an Urban Township Context," South African Journal of Sociology. Vol. 18, No. 1, pp. 7-13. [See Note 3].

18255. Mills, John Orme, ed. (1987) "Class and Church after Ghetto Catholicism," New Blackfriars [Thematic issue: Catholic sociology]. Vol. 68, No. 802 (February), pp. 54-108. Reviews, comments and discussion about Anthony Archer's book titled: The Two Catholic Churches (1986).

18256. Moffatt, Jessica and Ruby Galloway Parish. (1987) "Helping the Unemployed," Leadership: A Practical Journal for Church Leaders. Vol. 8, No. 1 (Winter), pp. 121-122.

18257. Montoya, Alex D. (1987) Hispanic Ministry in North America. Grand Rapids, MI: Zondervan.

18258. Mooney, Bernice Maher. (1987) Salt of the Earth: The History of the Catholic Diocese of Salt Lake City, 1776-1987. Salt Lake City, UT: the Diocese.

18259. Mt. Auburn Baptist Church. (beginning in 1987) UMN: Urban Ministry Newsletter. Cincinnati, OH: the Church. A periodical produced by a local church.

18260. Mullins, Mark R. (1987) "The Life-Cycle of Ethnic Churches in Sociological Perspective," Japanese Journal of Religious Studies. Vol. 14 (December), pp. 321-334.

18261. Munif, Abdelrahman. (1987) Cities of Salt. New York: Random House. A novel set in an unnamed middle-eastern kingdom depicts the consequences of Americans discovering oil for a poor oasis community. Industrialization, urbanization, disruption, and diaspora result. Part of a trilogy.

18262. Murray, Charles K. (1987?) Church and Labor: A Reflective Hiistory of the Cleveland Catholic Diocese and the Cleveland AFL-CIO Federation of Labor. Cleveland, OH: the Diocese. A paper.

18263. Muthalaly, Alexander Koshy. (1987) The Application of Ludwig von Bertalanffy's General Systems Theory as a Basis for Pastoral Assessment of Urban South Indian Christian Families. Thesis (Ph. D.). Louisville, KY: Southern Baptist Theological Seminary.

18264. Neddens, Martin C. and Waldemar Wucher, eds. (1987) Die Wiederkehr des genius Loci: die Kirche im Stadtraum, die Stadt im Kirchenraum: Okologie, Geschichte, Liturgie. Wiesbaden, Germany: Bauverlag.

18265. Neighbour, Ralph Webster, Jr. and Lorna Jenkins. (1987) No Room in the Inn--Brisbane, Resilient or Neglected? An Urban Strategy Study of Australia's Third Largest City. Ferny Hills, Queensland, Australia: Touch International Ministries. Columbia, SC: Columbia Biblical Seminary.

18266. Neitzel, Sarah Cain. (1987) Priests and Journeymen: The German Catholic Gesellenverein and the Christian Social Movement in the Nineteenth Century. Bonn, West Germany: Röhrscheid. Bibliography.

18267. Nelson, G. Edward. (1987) The Church in the City. Springfield, MO: Division of Foreign Missions, Assemblies of God.

18268. Nelson, Gary Vincent. (1987) The Pre-Conditions Necessary for Evangelism in the Urban Context: A Study of Toronto Baptist

Churches (Canada). Thesis (D. Min.). Pasadena, CA: Fuller Theological Seminary.

18269. Nelson, Mary. (1987) "Rebuilding on the Ruins," Christian Ministry. Vol. 18, No. 3 (May), pp. 10-12. Re: Bethel New Life, Inc., a Lutheran program concerned with housing and community organization in Chicago, IL.

18270. Newbigin, Leslie. (1987) "The Pastor's Opportunities VI: Evangelism in the City," The Expository Times. Vol. 98, No. 12 (September), pp. 355-358. Same title: Reformed Review. Vol. 41 (Autumn, 1987), pp. 3-8. A British evangelist from Birmingham describes the "Urban Priority Areas" as being characterized by a minority of older people who think of the world in categories formed in earlier times and a majority who are caught up in "pagan" society. Churches that think of the Christian story as mere fairy-tale miss their evangelical opportunity. Newbigin calls Christians to hope in a radical otherworldly vision, but a vision that is neither privatized nor anti-social. Evangelism means proselytism.

18271. Newby, Donald O. (1987) "Urban Migration and the Christian Council of Metropolitan Atlanta," Ecumenical Trends. Vol. 16 (May), pp. 93-94.

18272. Newenhuyse, Frederick. (1987) "White-Collar Pastor in a Blue-Collar World," Leadership: A Practical Journal for Church Leaders. Vol. 8, No. 2 (Spring), pp. 126-127.

18273. Nichols, Alan, Joan Clarke, and Trevor Hogan. (1987) Transforming Families and Communities: Christian Hope in a World of Change. London: Anglican Consultative Council, International Project on Family and Community.

18274. Norman, Edward. (1987) The Victorian Christian Socialists. Cambridge, England: Cambridge University Press. A succinct description of the philosophy of 19th century Christian socialists, with particular attention to the contributions of nine leaders: Maurice, Kingsley, Ludlow, Thomas Hughes, Headlam, Ruskin, Hugh Price Hughes, and Westcott. Bibliography.

18275. Nurnberger, Klaus. (1987) "Industrial Conflicts and Pastoral Concern," Theologia Evangelica. Vol. 20 (September), pp. 64-73.

18276. O'Connor, Elizabeth. (1987) Cry Pain, Cry Hope. Waco, TX: Word Books.

18277. Ogle, George. (1987) "Victory for Corporations, Defeat for Unions, Challenge for Churches," Engage/Social Action. Vol. 15, No. 11 (November), pp. 10-31.

18278. Oh, Heisik. (1987) Marriage Enrichment in the Korean Immigrant Church. Thesis (D. Min.). Claremont, CA: School of Theology at Claremont.

18279. Olzak, Susan. (1987) "Causes of Ethnic Conflict and Protest in Urban America, 1877-1889," Social Science Research. Vol. 16, No. 2 (June), pp. 185-210.

18280. Oswald, Roy M. and Speed B. Leas. (1987) The Inviting Church: A Study of New Member Assimilation. [Washington, DC]: Alban Institute.

18281. Pacek, Walter. (1987) Campaign Leadership Guide for Smaller Cities. Alexandria, VA: United Way of America. A pamphlet.

18282. Pasquariello, Ronald D. (1987) "The Skewing of America: Disparities in Wealth and Income," The Christian Century. Vol. 104, No. 5 (February 18), pp. 164-166. Poverty results from the maldistribution of the nation's wealth and the lack of a sense of the common good.

18283. Pazzaglia, Luciano. (1987) "Apprendistato e istruzione degli artigiani a Valdocco (1846-1886)," pp. 13-80 in Francesco Traniello, ed. Don Bosco nella storia della cultura popolare. Torino, Italy: Società editrice internazionale. Re: church work with laboring classes and children. St. John Bosco founded the Salesians (Society of St. Francis de Sales) in 1859 to befriend orphans and child laborers in Turin, Italy.

18284. Pearce, John and Angela Pearce. (1987) Inner-City Spirituality. Grove Spirituality Series No. 21. Bramcote, England: Grove. The Pearces write their insights from their perspective as a pastoral couple in East London about how to discern God at work in the inner city. They emphasize the strengths inner city people bring to their spiritual quest as well as the problems they encounter. A pamphlet. Bibliography.

18285. Penny, David. (1987) "New Age Travelling People: Personal Reflections in Light of Experience," Crucible. [Vol. 26, No. 2] (April-June), pp. 72-78. A description of people who have rejected culture or who are rejected by it in Great Britain.

18286. Perrot, Daniel. (1987) Les fondations de la Mission de France. Paris: Cerf. Re: church and labor and worker priests in France.

18287. Pile, William. (1987) "To Live and Cry in LA," Christian Herald. Vol. 110, No. 1 (January), pp. 18-22. Christian work with people caught in the cocaine culture of Los Angeles, CA.

18288. Power, Anne. (1987) Property before People: The Management of Twentieth-Century Council Housing. London: Allen and Unwin. Power traces the complicated history of the decay and abandonment of many of Britain's Council Estates. She examines how successive governments have tried to combat slum conditions and homelessness, and asks why some Council Houses are rejected by housing applicants. Bibliography.

18289. "Practicing Ecumenism in Urban Priority Areas." (1987) One in Christ: A Catholic Ecumenical Review. Vol. 23, No. 3, pp. 273-280.

18290. Prange, Amy. (1987) "One Typical Town: Glimpses into the Closet," World Christian. Vol. 6, No. 2 (March), pp. 16-20.

18291. Prentice, William Edward. (1987) Folk Religion, the Suburban Church, and Sacramental Ecclesiology: A Report on a Project in Ministry. Thesis (D. Min). Toronto, Canada: Trinity College of the University of Toronto.

18292. Preston, Ronald H. (1987) "Theology and the Economy: Roman Catholic Bishops in the USA," Crucible. [Vol. 26, No. 3] (July-September), pp. 98-106. Commentary from a British perspective on the 1986 document produced by the National Conference of Catholic Bishops titled: Economic Justice for All: Pastoral Letter on Catholic Social Teaching and the US Economy.

18293. Pretiz, Paul E. (1987) "Case Study: Medellin, Colombia: Research Can Be Motivational," Urban Mission. Vol. 4, No. 3 (January), p. 52.

18294. Price, Clay. (1987) The Largest United States Metropolitan Areas by the Year 2000: Selected Data on Mega Focus Cities. Atlanta, GA: Research Division, Home Mission Board of the Southern Baptist Convention.

18295. Rendle, Gilbert R., Jr. (1987) "Data-Guided Ministry: Evidence to Grow On," The Christian Ministry. Vol. 18, No. 5 (September), pp. 29-30. Rendle suggests the sort of data churches need for planning their ministries and how to get them. Questionnaire.

18296. Rendle, Gilbert R., Jr. and Frank H. Sanders, III. (1987) "'Third Class' Ministry: Urban Ministry in the Smaller City," Quarterly Review. Vol. 7, No. 2 (Summer), pp. 24-37. Rendle and Sanders compare ministry in large and medium-sized cities in one of the few articles that deal with ministry in middle-sized cities. Based on their personal experience, the authors find that churches in middle-sized cities: 1) depend more on volunteers, 2) are less likely to have a pastoral staff, 3) have more members who commute from the suburbs, 4) can be controlled longer by ethnic Whites who have fled to the suburbs, 5) have greater mixing of rich and poor members, 6) depend more on ecumenical cooperation, 7) depend less on city-wide denominational strategies, 8) have more difficulty getting denominational funding for service programs, 9) require clergy to pastor to more status levels in the congregation, 10) produce greater clergy burnout, 11) find social problems appear more solvable, 12) are more likely to seek systemic solutions to social problems, 13) assume their clergy have more power in the city, and 14) hold more traditional values. The authors served churches in Philadelphia, Reading, and Allentown, PA.

18297. Richesin, L. Dale. (1987) Atlanta Religious Profile. [ICUIS Urban Profile Series]. Chicago, IL: Institute on the Church in Urban-Industrial Society.

18298. Richesin, L. Dale, Dick Simpson, and Clinton Stockwell, eds. (1987) Fighting against Hunger, Homelessness, and Joblessness (Justice Ministries Series, Winter 1987). Chicago, IL: Institute on the Church in Urban Industrial Society (ICUIS). A revision of an earlier workbook that compiles materials from journals, newspapers, and other occasional bulletins that the editors assembled for use in church and community educational groups as well as in college and seminary classes.

18299. Roberts, Lewis. (1987) "The Nuclear Industry after Chernobyl," Crucible. [Vol. 27, No. 2] (April-June), pp. 53-60.

18300. Rodgers-Melnick, Ann. (1987) "Resurrection: Mill-Town Churches Making Comeback" [Title refers to the first of three articles], The Pittsburgh Press. Vol. 105, Nos. 155-157 (November 27-29), pp. 1+.

18301. Roof, Wade Clark and William McKinney. (1987) American Mainline Religion: Its Changing Shape and Future. New Brunswick, NJ: Rutgers University Press. A description of problems internal to Protestantism, particularly in regard to membership decline. Reviewed: Journal for the Scientific Study of Religion. (September, 1988), p. 442.

18302. Rosoli, Gianfausto. (1987) "Impegno missionario e assistenza religiosa agli emigranti nella visione e nell'opera di don Bosco e dei Salesiani," pp. 189-329 in Francesco Traniello, ed. Don Bosco nella storia della cultura popolare. Torino, Italy: Società editrice internazionale.

18303. Rubingh, Eugene. (1987) "Mission in an Urban World," Reformed Ecumenical Synod Mission Bulletin. Vol. 7, No. 1, pp. 1-10. Repirnted in: Evangelical Review of Theology. Vol. 11, No. 4 (October, 1987), pp. 369-379.

18304. Rubingh, George. (1987) "The City in the Mission of God," Urban Mission. Vol. 5, No. 2 (November), pp. 5-11.

18305. Rybeck, Walter and Ronald D. Pasquariello. (1987) "Combating Modern-Day Feudalism: Land as God's Gift," The Christian Century. Vol. 104, No. 16 (May 13), pp. 470-472. Wealth flows into the hands of fewer and fewer people in the USA. Cities are crowded with poor people while urban land values provide a gold mine for the rich.

18306. Rykwert, Joseph and Michael Milojeviá. (1987) "Cities," pp. 513-524 in Mircea Eliade, ed. The Encyclopedia of Religion. New York: Macmillan. An essay on the origins and development of urban forms and importance of religious factors. Bibliography. See further by Rykwert: The Idea of a Town: The Anthropology of Urban Form in Rome, Italy, and the Ancient World. London: Farber and Farber, 1976.

18307. Salsgiver, Thomas L. (1987) A Process for Developing a Relationship between Inner-City Youth and Adults. Thesis (D. Min.). Dayton, OH: United Theological Seminary. Lay people engage in training to discover the needs of inner city youth, then are paired with a particular youth in order to develop a relationship. Salsgiver's study was conducted in Harrisburg, PA.

18308. Salzgeber, Robert L. (1987) Christian Community, Individualism and Work in Butler, Pennsylvania. Thesis (D. Min.). Pittsburgh, PA: Pittsburgh Theological Seminary.

18309. Sanford, David. (1987) "Christian Soldier: An Ex-Guerrilla Fights a War of Another Kind," World Christian. Vol. 6, No. 1

(January), pp. 14-17.

18310. Sarna, Jonathan D. (1987) "The Impact of Nineteenth-Century Christian Mission on American Jews," pp. 232-254 in Todd M. Endelman, ed. Jewish Apostasy in the Modern World. New York: Holmes and Meier. A scholarly Jewish point of view. Bibliography.

18311. Satre, Gary and Doug Nichols. (1987) "Case Study: Christ for Greater Manila," Urban Mission. Vol. 4, No. 5 (May), pp. 36-37.

18312. Schaer, Hans Rudolf. (1987) "Migration: Fakten und Folgerungen," Zeitschrift für Mission. Vol. 13, No. 3, pp. 132-136.

18313. Schaper, Richard L. (1987) "Pastoral Care for Persons with AIDS and for Their Families," Christian Century. Vol. 104, No. 23 (August 12-19), pp. 691-694. Schaper is associate pastor of the Lutheran Church of the Redeemer, Atlanta, GA.

18314. Schare, Hans Rudolf. (1987) "Migration: Theologische und ethische Überlegungen," Zeitschrift für Evangelische Ethik. Vol. 31, No. 4 (October-December), pp. 456-466. Ethical and theological considerations regarding migration and immigration.

18315. Scheets, Francis Kelly, OCS. (1987) "Another Neighborhood Parish Abandoned?" Priest. Vol. 43, No. 1 (January), pp. 35-42. Recommendations for church survival in central cities.

18316. Scheuermeier, Robert. (1987) "Die Heimkehr der Mission," Zeitschrift für Mission [Thematic issue: Church work with immigrants and migrants]. Vol. 13, No. 3, pp. 168-171. Re: home missions in regard to church work with immigrants.

18317. Schlegel, Jean-Louis. (1987) "Immigration, morale et politique," Lumière et Vie. Vol. 34, No. 181 (March), pp. 19-36. Questions of xenophobia and racism are posed by immigration and increasing pluralism in France, especially concerning the Islamic community.

18318. Schreck, Harley and David Barrett, eds. (1987) Unreached Peoples: Clarifying the Task. Monrovia, CA: MARC.

18319. Schreck, Harley Carl, Jr. (1987) "African Urban People Groups," Urban Mission. Vol. 4, No. 4 (1987), pp. 42-51. Anthropologist Schreck describes social relations in urban Africa in terms of social class, residence and ethnicity. At the time of writing, Schreck was employed by World Vision.

18320. Schumacher, Christian. (1987) To Live and Work: A Theological Interpretation. Bromley, Kent: MARC Europe.

18321. Sedgwick, Peter. (1987) "Health and Deprivation in Easington, Co. Durham:--A Comment on 'Faith in the City," Crucible. [Vol. 26, No. 3] (July-September), pp. 116-125. De-industrialization has effects on people's health and well-being.

18322. Shelley, Mark. (1987) "Toward an Urban Strategy for Mindanao, Philippines," Urban Mission. Vol. 4, No. 5 (May), pp. 21-31.

18323. Shelp, Earl E. and Ronald H. Sunderland. (1987) AIDS and the Church. Philadelphia, PA: Westminster. An introduction to strategies. See further by Shelp: 1) AIDS: A Manual for Pastoral Care. Philadelphia, PA: Westminster, 1987. 2) AIDS: Personal Stories and Pastoral Perspectives. New York: Pilgrim, 1986.

18324. Shor, Ira and Paulo Freire. (1987) A Pedagogy for Liberation: Dialogues on Transforming Education. South Hadley, MA: Bergin and Garvey Publishers.

18325. Sidey, Ken. (1987) "Missing: Minorities in Ministry," Moody Monthly. Vol. 87, No. 11 (July-August), pp. 60-63. Sidey discusses reasons why minorities are unattracted to and unsuccessful in gaining funding for evangelical parachurch ministries such as Inter-Varsity. He refers to a program in Chicago called The Navigator's, directed by a Bob Price.

18326. Simpson, Dick and Clinton Stockwell, eds. (1987) Congregations and Community Organization. Chicago, IL: Institute on the Church in Urban-Industrial Society [Justice Ministries series]. Bibliography.

18327. Simpson-Clement, Jan, ed. (1987) "Metro-Urban Ministry," Church and Society [Thematic issue]. Vol. 78, No. 1 (September), pp. 3-62. The theological section identifies two biblical perspectives on the city: the city is, on the one hand, an expression of human arrogance and pride where we create the illusion that we are the masters of our own destiny. At the same time, the city is, on the other hand, a symbol of God's mercy and of hope--the image of the redeemed city. One article suggests that Luke 16:19ff, the story of Lazarus and the rich man, may be a biblical warrant for reciprocity in mission. [Cf: Luke 17: 21f]. Bloom's article on janitors in Seattle is quotable, as is the article by Coleman on the homeless. Much of the material has a regrettable "mission to" orientation. Bibliography.

18328. Smarto, Donald. (1987) Justice and Mercy. Wheaton, IL: Tyndale House.

18329. Smith, Austin. (1987) "Ministry in the Inner City," New Blackfriars. Vol. 68, No. 810 (November), pp. 516-528.

18330. Smith, Bardwell L. and Holly Baker Reynolds, eds. (1987) The City as Sacred Center: Essays on Six Asian Contexts. Leiden: E. J. Brill.

18331. Smith, Donald C. (1987) Passive Obedience and Prophetic Protest: Social Criticism in the Scottish Church, 1830-1970. New York: P. Lang.

18332. Smith, Eric Michael. (1987) The Saving Possibilities of Video Technology. Thesis (D. Min.). Claremont, CA: School of Theology at Claremont.

18333. Smith, Harry H. (1987) "Remaining People of Faith in the Life of the World," Engage/Social Action. Vol. 15, No. 1 (January), pp. 16-19. An interview with Smith, the director of the Methodist Metro Ministry of St. Louis, MO.

18334. Smith, Jonathan Z. (1987) To Take Place: Toward Theory in Ritual. Chicago, IL: University of Chicago. Re: religious life and customs in Jerusalem. Bibliography.

18335. Smith, Sandy. (1987) "Chester's Troubled Youth: An In-Depth Study of Young People in an Old American City," Urban Mission. Vol. 5, No. 1 (September), pp. 20-29.

18336. Soden, Dale E. (1987) "In Quest of the 'City on a Hill': Seattle Minister Mark Mathews and the Moral Leadership of the Middle Class," pp. 355-373 in Carl Guarneri and David Alvarez, eds. Religion and Society in the American West: Historical Essays. Lanham, MD: University Press of America.

18337. South, Scott J. (1987) "Metropolitan Migration and Social Problems," Social Science Quarterly. Vol. 68, No. 1 (March), pp. 3-18.

18338. Sowel, Robert M. (1987) "Personal Evangelism in the Inner City," Urban Mission. Vol. 5, No. 2 (November), pp. 19-24.

18339. Speer, Pat. (1987) "Beginning with Alinsky," Christianity and Crisis. Vol. 47, No. 1 (February 2), pp. 30-32.

18340. Sponseller, Michael P. (1987) "In-Wall Bracing Bolsters Church Against Quakes," Engineering News-Record. Vol. 218 (January 8), pp. 16.

18341. Stark, Rodney. (1987) "Correcting Church Membership Rates: 1971 and 1980," Review of Religious Research. Vol. 29, No. 1 (September), pp. 69-77. Data reported by Douglas Johnson, et al. (1974) and Bernard Quinn, et al. (1982) on church membership need to be corrected for omission of Blacks and Jews in order to serve as an ecumenical measure of church membership.

18342. Stein, Jock. (1987) Ministry and Mission in the City. Edinburgh, Scotland: Handsel.

18343. Steinhouer, Paul. (1987) "Unbabbling Pentecost: A Case for Multi-Ethnic Church Planting," Urban Mission. Vol. 4, No. 5 (May), pp. 32-35.

18344. Stockwell, Clinton E. (1987) Richmond Profile [ICUIS Urban Profile Series]. Chicago, IL: Institute on the Church in Urban Society. Statistics for church planning in Richmond, Virginia.

18345. Stockwell, Clinton E. (1987) "A Basic Bibliography for Metropolitan Ministry," Church and Society. Vol. 78, No. 1 (September-October), pp. 59-62.

18346. Stockwell, Eugene L. (1987) "Celebration and Challenge: Urban-Rural Mission," International Review of Mission [Thematic issue: Urban-Rural Mission]. Vol. 76, No. 303 (July), pp. 315-318. A thematic issue given to Urban-Rural Mission (URM) describes URM as being focused on the poor, oppressed victims of social systems. It promotes local action at community levels to resist injustice. Stockwell raises the question of how systemic approaches could be made for redressing injustice. See further the articles in this issue by Emilio Castro and Edicio de la Torre.

18347. Stott, John R. W. (1987) "Strategy for Cities," Beacon [The Evangelical Beacon Association, Minneapolis, MN]. Vol. 60, No. 13 (June 22), pp. 8-10.

18348. Stow, Peter and Mike Fearon. (1987) Youth in the City: The Church's Response to the Challenge of Youth Work. London:

Hodder and Stoughton. Stow and Fearon describe the lives of inner city youth for Christians who think their churches have nothing to offer such young people, or who simply are unaware of inner city life. They draw from their experience in East London where they find that the love and compassion of Christ has transforming effects on youth.

18349. Sullivan, Patrick J. (1987) Blue Collar, Roman Collar, White Collar: US Catholic Involvement in Labor Management Controversies, 1960-1980. Lanham, MD: University Press of America. Bibliography.

18350. Swatos, William H., Jr. (1987) "Clinical Pastoral Sociology," pp. 153-164 in William H. Swatos, Jr. Religious Sociology: Interfaces and Boundaries. New York: Greenwood Press. Re: the application of sociology to ministry.

18351. Sweetser, Thomas P. and Carol Wisniewski Holden. (1987) Leadership in a Successful Parish. San Francisco, CA: Harper and Row.

18352. Szto, Paul C. H. (1987) A Model of Covenential Church Renewal and Inter-Church Relation: The Development of Multi-Racial, Multi-Cultural Reformed Urban Ministry in New York City. Thesis (D. Min.). Chestnut Hill, PA: Westminster Theological Seminary.

18353. Tabb, William K. (1987) "Jobs: A Matter of Commitment," Christianity and Crisis. Vol. 47, No. 8 (May 18), pp. 194-197.

18354. Taran, Patrick A., ed. (1987) Fulfilling the Promise: Church Orientation Guide to the New Immigration Law. New York: Church World Service, Immigration and Refugee Program.

18355. Tilford, N. Allen. (1987) "Team Ministry in a Prison," Ecumenism. No. 86 (June), pp. 25-27.

18356. Todd, Norman, et al. (1987) A Thing Called Aston: An Experiment in Reflective Learning. London: Church House Publishing. An approach to pre-theological training that is profoundly theological, emphasizing education by interaction with people.

18357. Tollefson, Kenneth. (1987) "The Nehemiah Model for Christian Missions," Missiology. Vol. 15, No. 1 (January), pp. 31-55.

18358. Tomasi, Silvano M. (1987) A Lesson from History: The Integration of Immigrants in the Pastoral Practice of the Church of the United States. New York: Center for Migration Studies. Reprinted: Dolores Liptak, ed. A Church of Many Cultures. New York: Garland, 1988.

18359. Tomasik, Kristine. (1987) "The Salvation of the Lord: Hattie Williams, One of God's Gifts to Chicago," The Other Side. Vol. 23, No. 1 (January), pp. 6-8.

18360. Torres, Alcides. (1987) Reparando la brecha entre la iglesia y la comunidad. Thesis (D. Min.). New York: New York Theological Seminary. Re: community organization and Hispanic American Presbyterians.

18361. Trolander, Judith Ann. (1987) Professionalism and Social Change: From the Settlement House Movement to Neighborhood Center, 1886 to the Present. New York: Columbia University Press.

18362. Turner, Christopher B. (1987) "Revivalism and Welsh Society in the Ninteenth Century," pp. 311-323 in Jim Obelkevich, et al, eds. Disciplines of Faith. London: Routledge and Kegan Paul.

18363. Updike, John. (1987) Roger's Version. New York: Ballantine. A novel. In Boston, a theological seminary professor and a new age computer whiz test one another's views of God, justice, and the human condition. Social conditions in Boston are vividly portrayed.

18364. Vaquero, Quintín Aldea, Joaquín García Granda, and Jesús Martín Tejedor. (1987) Iglesia y sociedad en la España del siglo XX: Catolicismo social, 1909-1940. Madrid, Spain: Consejo Superior de Investigaciones Científicas, Centro de Estudios Históricos, Departamento Enrique Flórez. Re: the Catholic Church and social issues in Spain.

18365. Vaughan, Patrick. (1987) "Bibliography: Non-Stipendiary Ministry," The Modern Churchman. n.s. Vol. 22, No. 2, pp. 45-53.

18366. von Dreele, James D. (1987) "Wielding the Sharp Edge of the Gospel: Pittsburgh Prophetic Ministry," Engage/Social Action. Vol. 15, No. 10 (October), pp. 12-17.

18367. Wagner, C. Peter. (1987) Strategies for Church Growth: Tools for Effective Mission and Evangelism. Ventura, CA: Regal.

18368. Wald, Kenneth D. (1987) Religion and Politics in the United States. New York: St. Martin's Press.

18369. Wall, James M. (1987) "Harold Washington: Protest and Politics," Christian Century. Vol. 104, No. 38 (December 16), pp. 1131-1132. Editorial comment on the sudden death of Chicago's popular mayor.

18370. Wallace, Martin. (1987) Healing Encounters in the City: Insights from an Urban Perspective. Grove Pastoral Series No. 30. Bramcote, England: Grove. Spiritual healing in a city parish.

18371. Waters, Brent. (1987) "Technology as a Problem for Christian Ministry," Word and World: Theology for Christian Ministry. Vol. 7, No. 4 (Fall), pp. 385-393.

18372. Webber, Helen and George Webber. (1987) "Christian Witness in the City of Philadelphia." Consultant's report to the Pew Charitable Trusts. Philadelphia, PA: Pew Charitable Trusts [draft report]. The Webbers wrote this report to help the Pew Trust develop its strategy for funding of religious groups in Philadelphia. It reflects much of the Webbers' accumulated wisdom, given a temporary focus by their 21 day data collection marathon on Philadelphia. The sections on how to evaluate a request for funding and on clergy education are especially helpful. They support, among other strategies, the Urban Academy model. Also, they urge new partnerships between urban and suburban churches, based on solidarity rather than guilt. The Webbers have a long standing interest in helping congregations respond to the needs of the disadvantaged.

18373. Weiss, Ellen. (1987) City in the Woods: The Life and Design of an American Camp Meeting on Martha's Vineyard. New York: Oxford University Press. A history of the camp meeting as an alternative to and escape from urban life. The architecture of the cottages and design of the communities with their gardens, dappled shade, and picturesque irregularities, Weiss concludes, represent an ideal city lost in the uncontrolled expansion of cities. The camp meetings are predecessors of the American suburbs. Martha's Vineyard was begun by Methodists. Bibliography.

18374. Wertheimer, Jack. (1987) "The Conservative Synagogue," pp. 111-149 in Jack Wertheimer, ed. The American Synagogue: A Sanctuary Transformed. New York: Cambridge University Press.

18375. West, Melvin E. (1987) "Social Issues in the City of Busch and McDonald," Engage/Social Action. Vol. 15, No. 1 (January), pp. 4-11. Two large corporations in St. Louis employ many people and frequently make important contributions to civic and social concerns, yet their products (alcohol and weapons) and activities are opposed by Christians.

18376. White, Charles Edward. (1987) "The Beauty of Holiness: The Career of Phoebe Palmer," Methodist History. Vol. 25, No. 2 (January), pp. 76-90. Palmer (1807-1874) was a revivalist, feminist, theologian, and humanist who conducted evangelistic efforts in 19th century US cities. Her contribution began the Methodist mission at Five Points, New York City.

18377. White, James F. (1987) "Moving Christian Worship toward Social Justice," The Christian Century. Vol. 104, No. 19 (June 17-24), pp. 558-560. A critical assessment of worship in terms of how it contributes either toward justice or injustice.

18378. Whiteside, Barbara Jeanne Taylor. (1987) A Study of the Structure, Norms and Folkways of the Educational Institutions of the Nation of Islam in the United States from 1932 to 1975. Thesis (Ed. D.). Detroit, MI: Wayne State University.

18379. Wickremeratne, Ananda. (1987) "Shifting Metaphors of Sacrality: The Mythic Dimension of Anuradhapura," pp. 45-59 in Bardwell L. Smith and Holly Baker Reynolds, eds. The City as Sacred Center: Essays on Six Asian Contexts. Leiden: E. J. Brill.

18380. Wilson, Anne. (1987) "Enough to Go Around: Sister Dolly Be Here Rain or Shine," The Other Side. Vol. 23, No. 9 (November), pp. 6-7. City ministry in Albuquerque, NM, by a caring woman on whom the poor have learned to depend.

18381. Wilson, William Julius. (1987) The Truly Disadvantaged: The Inner City, the Underclass, and Public Policy. Chicago, IL: University of Chicago Press. Social isolation entraps poor city dwellers and gives rise to a permanent underclass. Reviewed: Christianity and Crisis (May 16, 1988), pp. 183-186.

18382. Woofenden, Louise D. (1987) "The Building of an Architect," Chrysalis, Journal of the Swedenborg Foundation. Vol. 2, No. 2 (Summer), pp. 118-129. Daniel Hudson Burnham, architect and builder of the Chicago World's Columbia Exposition, was influenced by the thought of Emanuel Swedenborg.

18383. World Council of Churches, Commission on World Mission and Evangelism. (1987) Celebration and Challenge: Urban-Rural Mission, April 1-6, 1987. Geneva, Switzerland: World Council of

Churches, Commission on World Mission and Evangelism, Urban-Rural Mission.

18384. Yancey, Philip. (1987) "The Shape of God's Body," Leadership: A Practical Journal for Church Leaders. Vol. 8, No. 3 (Summer), pp. 88-94.

18385. Younger, George D. (1987) From New Creation to Urban Crisis: A History of Action Training Ministries, 1962-1975. Chicago, IL: Center for the Scientific Study of Religion. A study of urban action-training centers, organized between 1962 and 1975 by a variety of groups concerned about the education of clergy for ministry in changing society, traces their origination in the ecumenical spirit of the 1960s, through their rise to challenge the relevancy of training in theological seminaries, to their demise in the late 1970s and 1980s. Chronology. Bibliography.

18386. Yuen, Bessie Kawaguchi. (1987) "Urban Poor-ology: A Theology of Ministry to the World's Urban Poor," Urban Mission. Vol. 5, No. 1 (September), pp. 13-19.

18387. Zagano, Phyllis. (1987) Religion and Public Affairs, A Directory of Organizations and People. Rockford, IL: Rockford Institute. A pamphlet.

18388. Zalent, Kim. (1987) Economic Home Cookin': An Action Guide for Churches and Community Economic Development. Chicago, IL: Community Workshop on Economic Development. A manual for churches seeking involvement in local economic development with lists of ideas and resources.

18389. Addy, Tony [Anthony J.]. (1988) Ministry towards 2000: Context and Strategy. Manchester, England: William Temple Foundation. Re: diakonial ministry with the poor in Great Britain in the context of the rise of "new right" political policies.

18390. Addy, Tony [Anthony J.] and Roger Clarke, eds. (1988) Poverty and Polarization, the Report of the West European Network on Work, Unemployment and the Churches Consultation. Manchester, England: the William Temple Foundation. Papers and findings from a European consultation examining the nature and extent of poverty in Europe and the churches' response.

18391. Addy, Tony [Anthony J.] and Duncan Scott. (1988) Fatal Impacts? The MSC [Manpower Service Commission] and Voluntary

Action. Manchester, England: William Temple Foundation. The director of the William Temple Foundation and a lecturer at the University of Manchester, England, illustrate ways in which a government program might result in undermining the volunteer organizations it was designed to help. Bibliography.

18392. Adornato, Giselda. (1988) Giovanni Battista Montini: religione e lavoro nella Milano degli anni '50. Brecia, Italy: Morcelliana. Re: Pope Paul VI (1897-1978) and labor issues in Italy. Bibliography.

18393. Advisory Council for the Church's Ministry. (1988) Theology in Practice: The Proposals of the ACCM Working Party on Urban Studies Centres for Colleges. [London?]: Advisory Council for the Church's Ministry, Occasional Paper No. 29. Guidelines for establishing urban study centers.

18394. Agócs, Sándor. (1988) The Troubled Origins of the Italian Catholic Labor Movement, 1878-1914. Detroit, MI: Wayne State University Press. Bibliography.

18395. Akbar, Jamel. (1988) Crisis in the Built Environment: The Case of the Muslim City. Singapore: Concept Media. Akbar investigates Islamic principles for constructing and managing the "built environment." Reviewed: American Journal of Islamic Social Studies. Vol. 5, No. 2 (December, 1988), pp. 279-281.

18396. Alexander, Robert S. (1988) Albany's First Church and Its Role in the Growth of the City. Albany, NY: First Church, Reformed Church in America. A detailed history of a local church. Bibliography.

18397. Alicea, Benjamín. (1988) Christian Colonizers: A History of the East Harlem Protestant Parish in New York City, 1948-68. Thesis (Ph. D.). New York: Union Theological Seminary. Based on a study of the documents about the East Harlem Protestant Parish in Union Theological Seminary archives. Extensive bibliography.

18398. Allen, Frank W. (1988) "Kamuning, Philippines--An Urban Church-Planting Model," Urban Mission. Vol. 6, No. 2 (November), pp. 56-60.

18399. American Society of Interior Designers. (1988) Design of the Times: The Homeless Living on Hope, A Guide for Local Chapters of the ASID [a seminar held at the ASID National Conference and Expo, Washington, DC, August 4, 1988]. San Francisco, CA: Independent Housing Services for ASID. Produced by a professional society for interior designers, this booklet resulted from the Society's concern for the homeless. Design professionals "can become agents of hope" for the homeless, affirms the introductory letter. The booklet publishes the ASID's position paper on homelessness, reports instances of housing built or retrofitted for the homeless (some of which are church sponsored), identifies funding sources, lists state agencies and local coalitions for the homeless (200 in all), offers ideas for projects, identifies resources, gives advice for starting a shelter, and promotes a "Scavenger Hotline" for getting needed supplies to the place where they can be used. Bibliography.

18400. Amerson, Philip A. (1988) "Miracle on 29th Street," The Other Side [Thematic issue: Urban ministry]. Vol. 24, No. 4 (May), pp. 32-35. Compelling stories are told by the poor.

18401. Amerson, Philip A. (1988) Tell Me City Stories. Chicago, IL: SCUPE Urban Church Resources. Amerson, a United Methodist pastor in Indianapolis, IN, relates church stories and reflects on storytelling as a tool for planning in city churches. Planning with authentic stories obviates some of the excessive dependence on social surveys and systems analysis strategies in church planning. Chapter 3 was distributed as advanced preparation for participants in the 1988 Urban Ministries Congress (SCUPE).

18402. Amos, William E., Jr. (1988) When AIDS Comes to Church. Philadelphia, PA: Westminster Press. An introduction to AIDS ministry written by a Baptist pastor in Florida.

18403. Anderson, David E. (1988) "Counting Heads," Christianity and Crisis. Vol. 48, No. 3 (March 7), pp. 60-62.

18404. Anderson, Gary M. (1988) "Mr. Smith and the Preachers: The Economics of Religion and the Wealth of Nations," Journal of Political Economy. Vol. 96 (October), pp. 1066-1088. Economic theory advanced by religious leaders compared with that of Adam Smith, 1723-1790.

18405. Andrews, David. (1988) "The Notre Dame Study of Catholic Parish Life: Reflections on the Church in Small Towns and Rural America," Living Light. Vol. 24, No. 2 (January), pp. 111-122.

18406. "Annotated Bibliography." (1988) Social Action [India]. Vol. 38 (January), pp. 95-103. A bibliography regarding development policies and the people's struggle for economic survival.

18407. Apthorp, Stephen P. (1988) "Drug Abuse and the Church: Are the Blind Leading the Blind?" The Christian Century. Vol. 105, No. 33 (November 9), pp. 1010-1013. Church effectiveness is undercut because of church leaders who are among the afflicted and addicted.

18408. Armacost, Robert L. (1988) "Productivity and the Economic Pastoral: Implications for Growth," Journal of Business Ethics. Vol. 7 (June), pp. 467-473.

18409. Atherton, John. (1988) Faith in the Nation: A Christian Vision for Britain. London: SPCK. Atherton, Canon Theologian of Manchester Cathedral, played a role in the research undertaken for the Archbishop of Canterbury's Commission on Urban Priority Areas and its report titled: Faith in the City (1985). He criticizes and develops parts of that report herein from the perspectives of theology and worship.

18410. Bachelder, Robert S. (1988) "Blinded by Metaphor: Churches and Welfare Reform," Christian Century. Vol. 105, No. 38 (December 14), pp. 1147-1149. Bachelder, minister of the Worcester, MA, City Missionary Society, seeks rediscovery of the God-as-governor metaphor.

18411. Baer, Hans A. (1988) "Bibliography of Social Science Literature on Afro-American Religion in the United States," Review of Religious Research. Vol. 29, No. 4 (June), pp. 413-430. A highly selective bibliography prepared by an anthropologist who served as guest editor of this edition of the Review of Religious Research.

18412. Baer, Hans A. (1988) Recreating Utopia in the Desert: A Sectarian Challenge to Modern Mormonism. Albany, NY: State University of New York Press.

18413. Baranowski, Arthur R. (1988) Creating Small Communities of Faith: A Plea for Restructuring the Parish and Renewing Catholic Life. Cincinnati, OH: St. Anthony Messenger Press.

18414. Barrett, John M. (1988) It's Hard Not to Worry: Stories for Children about Poverty. New York: Friendship Press. Accompanying teacher's guide. Barrett, a New York City school teacher, provides an introduction to poverty for children, ages 6 to 12.

18415. Bender, Thomas, ed. (1988) The University and the City, from Medieval Origins to the Present. New York: Oxford.

18416. Berger, Peter L. (1988) "American Lutheranism at the Crossroads," Dialog. Vol. 27, No. 2 (Spring), pp. 90-96. [A series of negative replies follow in subsequent issues].

18417. Berry, Kathy and Stanley Leary. (1988) "Where's the Steeple?" Missions USA. Vol. 59, No. 5 (September-October), pp. 22-26.

18418. Billings, Alan and Richard Atkinson. (1988) "Responding to 'Faith in the City,'" British Journal of Theological Education. Vol. 1, No. 3 (Spring), pp. 3-10.

18419. Birkey, Del. (1988) The House Church: A Model for Renewing the Church. Scottdale, PA: Herald. Birkey, who comes from a mid-western rural Mennonite background, established a house church in his suburban Chicago home. This volume defends house churches as a strategy for church renewal and traces biblical and historical rootage for the house church. Bibliography.

18420. Blackwood, Vernon L. (1988) "Toward a Biblical Theology for the Urban Context." [Graduate Student Paper]. Lombard, IL: Northern Baptist Theological Seminary.

18421. Blackwood, Vernon L. (1988) Self-Directed Learning Projects of Selected Urban Minority Church Leaders for Spiritual Growth and Professional Ministry Competency. Thesis (Ed. D.). Deerfield, IL: Trinity Evangelical Divinity School.

18422. Bockmuehl, Klaus, ed. (1988) [Thematic issue: Work]. Crux: A Quarterly Journal of Christian Thought and Opinion. Vol. 24, (June), pp. 2-31.

18423. Boff, Leonardo. (1988) When Theology Listens to the Poor. San Francisco, CA: Harper. A translation of: Do lugar do pobre. Petrópolis, Brazil: Vozes, 1984. Bibliography.

18424. Boogaart, Thomas. (1988) "Meeting God in the City," Church Herald [Thematic issue: Urban ministry]. Vol. 45, No. 20 (November 18), pp. 6-7. Theology of the city based on the Old Testament.

18425. Bos, A. David. (1988) "Community Ministries: The Wild Card in Ecumenical Relations and Social Ministry," Journal of Ecumenical Studies. Vol. 25, No. 4 (Fall), pp. 592-598.

18426. Branch, Taylor. (1988) Parting the Waters: America in the King Years, 1954-1963. New York: Simon and Shuster. Re: Martin Luther King, Jr. Reviewed: Robert Westbrook, "In the Churches, in the Streets: Taylor Branch on 'The King Years,'" The Christian Century. Vol. 106, No. 11 (April 5, 1989), pp. 351-354.

18427. Breitman, George, Homer Porter and Baxter Smith. (1988) The Assassination of Malcolm X. New York: Pathfinder Press.

18428. Brereton, Virginia. (1988) The Early History of New York Theological Seminary, 1901-1960. [Typed manuscript]. New York: New York Theological Seminary. A pamphlet.

18429. Brooks, Evelyn. (1988) "Religion, Politics, and Gender: The Leadership of Nannie Helen Burroughs," Journal of Religious Thought. Vol. 44, No. 2 (Winter, Spring), pp. 7-22. Burroughs was a prominent Black social reformer during the first half of the 20th century.

18430. Brown, Clayton. (1988) "Beyond the Bottom Line," United Evangelical Action [Thematic issue: Christian Business Ethics]. Vol. 47, No. 3 (May-June), pp. 4-5.

18431. Brown, Sherri and Mark Sandlin. (1988) "Million Dollar Missions," Missions USA. Vol. 59, No. 5 (September-October), pp. 6-13.

18432. Brown, Truman, Jr. (1988) "Shaping the Future of the Urban Fringe Church," Church Administration. Vol. 30, No. 8 (May), pp. 6-8.

18433. Buhofer, Ines. (1988) "Option für die Arbeitwelt," Reformatio. Vol. 37 (December), pp. 428-434. Re: clergy involvement with social problems in the work world.

18434. Burkhartzmeyer, Brad. (1988) "Making the Connections: From Detroit to Central America and Back," The Other Side [Thematic issue: Urban ministry]. Vol. 24, No. 4 (May), pp. 30-31. As in Central America with its many displaced refugees, Detroit has many people evicted from homes. Parallels are drawn.

18435. Buttry, Daniel L. (1988) Bringing Your Church Back to Life: Beyond Survival Mentality. Valley Forge, PA: Judson. A pastor of the Dorchester Temple Baptist Church, Boston, describes his church's success at renewal, with the intention of helping other churches. He names the "survival mentality" as enemy.

18436. Butz, Geneva M. (1988) Christmas Comes Alive. New York: Pilgrim Press. Vivid vignettes of urban ministry in a historic Philadelphia United Church of Christ congregation with a rediscovered social conscience.

18437. Catholic Church, Archdiocese of New York, Office of Pastoral Research. (1988) One Faith--One Lord--One Baptism: The Hopes and Experiences of the Black Community in the Archdiocese of New York. New York: the Archdiocese.

18438. Catholic Church, Archdiocese of Newark, Office of Research and Planning. (1988) Presencia nueva: Conocimiento para servicio y esperanza unsestudio sobre los hispanos en la Arquidiocesis de Newark. Newark, NJ: the Archdiocese. An English version of this report was issued under the title: Presencia nueva: Knowledge for Service and Hope, a Study of Hispanics in the Archdiocese of Newark. Bibliography.

18439. Chalmers, Glenn. (1988) "A Ministry of Hope in the Inner City," Christian Ministry. Vol. 19, No. 1 (January-February), pp. 18-19. Chalmers emphasizes ministry with, rather than for, the poor.

18440. Chan, Frederick C. C. (1988) How to Develop a Strong Family Ministry in North American Chinese Churches--Scriptural Principles for Family Living. Thesis (D. Min.). Portland, OR: Western Conservative Baptist Seminary.

18441. Cherry, Kittredge and James Mitulski. (1988) "We Are the Church Alive: The Church with AIDS," Christian Century. Vol. 105, No. 3 (January 27), pp. 85-88. Cherry, a student minister in a Metropolitan Community Church in San Francisco, comments on the AIDS crisis.

18442. Christensen, Michael J. (1988) City Streets, City People: A Call for Compassion. Nashville, TN: Abingdon. Case studies portray ministry among street people, AIDS victims, and the homeless. Christensen works for a conservative Wesleyan theology.

18443. Christiano, Kevin J. (1988) "Religion and Radical Labor Unionism: American States in the 1920s," Journal for the Scientific Study of Religion. Vol. 27, No. 3 (September), pp. 378-388. Using 1920's data from the International Worker's of the World (IWW), Christiano questions the hypothesis advanced by Coser (1954), Lipset (1981, p. 97ff), and O'Toole (1977) and others that there is a positive association between radical political groups and religious sects. Data reported in this article show a negative association between religious participation and radical unionism. Christiano is professor of sociology at Notre Dame in 1988. Bibliography.

18444. Chupungco, Anscar J. (1988) Cultural Adaptation of the Liturgy. New York: Paulist.

18445. Church of England, Board for Social Responsibility, Industrial and Economic Affairs Committee. (1988) Industrial Mission, an Appraisal. London: the Board.

18446. "City Mission of Salvation Includes Rescue of Neighborhood." (1988) New York Times. (February 10), p. 19. Re: St. Nicholas Roman Catholic Church in Brooklyn, NY.

18447. Claassen, Oliver J. (1988) A Course for Launching Prospective Church Planters. Thesis (D. Min.). Chestnut Hill, PA: Westminster Theological Seminary.

18448. Clucas, Joan Groff. (1988) Mother Teresa. New York: Chelsea House.

18449. Conn, Harvie M. (1988) "Looking to the Future: Evangelical Missions from North America in the Years Ahead," Urban Mission. Vol. 5, No. 3 (January), pp. 18-31.

18450. Conn, Harvie M. (1988) "The Secularization Myth," Evangelical Review of Theology. Vol. 12, No. 1 (January), pp. 78-92.

18451. Connor, James A. (1988) "Homeless (A Short Story)," New Catholic World. Vol. 231, No. 1383 (May-June), pp. 109-113.

18452. Cook, Bonnie. (1988?) Helping the Homeless: God's Word in Action. Chicago, IL: Interfaith Council for the Homeless. A pamphlet.

18453. Cort, John C. (1988) Christian Socialism: An Informal History. New York: Orbis Books. Cort surveys socialism from the beginnings of Christianity forward. He argues that socialism is basically Christian. Particular attention is given the roles of the 19th century leaders: Maurice, Ludlow, and Noel. Bibliography.

18454. Council of Churches of Greater Seattle. (1988) State of the City: Rich/Poor. Seattle, WA: the Council. Re: theological aspects of economic issues, including a section on recent reformulations of the Christian vision of economic justice. Church efforts for economic justice are described.

18455. Cox, Donna McNeil. (1988) "Contemporary Trends in the Music Ministry of the Church of God in Christ," Journal of Black Sacred Music. Vol. 2 (Fall), pp. 96-101.

18456. Coy, Patrick G., ed. (1988) A Revolution of the Heart: Essays on the Catholic Worker. Philadelphia, PA: Temple University Press. A collection of articles regarding Peter Maurin, Dorothy Day and the Catholic Worker Movement. Bibliography.

18457. Cram, Ronald H. (1988) "AIDS: A Note from the Review Editor," Religious Education [Thematic issue: AIDS]. Vol. 83, No. 1 (Winter), pp. 133-137; No. 2 (Spring), pp. 291-299. A bibliographic essay on organizations and materials available for ministry with AIDS victims is accompanied by articles which deal with AIDS from a variety of perspectives. Particularly notable is Charles McCarthy's plea, as a physician, for church involvement.

18458. Crittenden, Ann. (1988) Sanctuary: A Story of American Conscience and the Law. New York: Weidenfeld and Nicholson. Bibliography.

18459. Cryderman, Lyn. (1988) "Harder to Ignore?" Christianity Today. Vol. 32, No. 18 (November 15), pp. 52-54. Re: the urban homeless.

18460. Dale, Robert D. (1988) Keeping the Dream Alive. Nashville, TN: Broadman. Re: church renewal. A sequel to Dale's: To Dream Again (1981). Bibliography.

18461. Davidson, Miriam. (1988) Convictions of the Heart: Jim Corbett and the Sanctuary Movement. Tucson, AZ: University of Arizona Press.

18462. DeBoer, John C. (1988) JSAC's First Twenty Years. New York: Joint Strategy and Action Committee (JSAC). [Location: JSAC Archives, Drew University Library, Madison, NJ].

18463. DeCosse, David E. (1988) "Politics and the Promise of God," America. Vol. 158, No. 14 (April 9), pp. 382-385.

18464. Deegan, Mary Jo. (1988) Jane Addams and the Men of the Chicago School, 1892-1930. New Brunswick, NJ: Transaction Books.

Re: Addams and the sociology faculty of the University of Chicago.

18465. Delloff, Linda-Marie. (1988) "Old St. Patrick's New Art," Christian Century. Vol. 105, No. 18 (June 1), pp. 534-535. Fine art programs sponsored by Chicago's oldest church.

18466. De Wolfe, Mark Mosher. (1988) "Love and Let Love," Christianity and Crisis [Thematic issue: AIDS]. Vol. 48, No. 10 (July 4), pp. 221-223. Congregations confront the AIDS crisis.

18467. Dierks, Sheila Durkin and Patricia Powers Ladley. (1988) Catholic Worker Houses: Ordinary Miracles. Kansas City, MO: Sheed and Ward.

18468. Discovering Faith in the City. (1988) London: Church House Publishing. A pamphlet describing ways to implement the report of the Archbishop of Canterbury's Commission on Urban Priority Areas, Faith in the City: A Call for Action by Church and Nation (1985). Included are suggestions for experience in urban areas, self evaluation, fund raising for urban charity, influencing public opinion, and prayer.

18469. Dolan, Jay P. (1988) "Immigration and American Christianity: A History of Their Histories," in Henry W. Bowden, ed. A Century of Church History: The Legacy of Philip Schaff. Carbondale, IL: Southern Illinois University Press. Dolan critiques historians' treatment of the impact of immigration on the American church.

18470. Domosh, Mona. (1988) "The Symbolism of the Skyscraper: Case Studies of New York's First Tall Buildings," Journal of Urban History. Vol. 14, No. 3 (May), pp. 320-345. In seeking to answer the question raised in 1966 by Jean Gottmann -- "Why the skyscraper?" -- Domosh moves beyond traditional economic explanations to the symbolic. She suggests that New York's elite class was less cohesive than was the case in other 19th century cities, and the skyscrapers became the status expression and basis for legitimacy for the increasingly wealthy. Skyscrapers are, among other things, monuments of individual prestige, symbols of corporate power, and announcements of speculative money making ventures. Domosh encourages further inquiry.

18471. Driedger, Leo. (1988) "Post-War Canadian Mennonites: From Rural to Urban Dominance," Journal of Mennonite Studies. Vol. 6, pp. 70-88.

18472. Dudley, Carl S. and Douglas Alan Walrath. (1988) Developing Your Small Church's Potential. Valley Forge, PA: Judson Press. Although mostly about urban fringe, ex-urban, and rural churches, this book does give some examples of churches in changing communities in Chapter 4.

18473. Duncombe, David C. (1988) "Street Ministry CPE: An Experiment in the Haight-Ashbury," The Journal of Pastoral Care. Vol. 42, No. 4 (Winter), pp. 339-348.

18474. Eades, Robert E. (1988) "National Institute of Business and Industrial Chaplains, Inc." Journal of Pastoral Care. Vol. 42, No. 3 (Fall), pp. 245-251.

18475. Early, Tracy. (1988) "Corporate Responsibility: Challenge, Confrontation, and 15 Years of ICCR," Christianity and Crisis. Vol. 48, No. 4 (March 14), pp. 86-90.

18476. Eastman, Michael, ed. (1988) Ten Inner City Churches. Eastbourne, England: MARC. Eastman's volume collects British case studies from London, Skelmersdale, Sheffield, Birmingham, Cardiff, Belfast, and Nottingham; all reflect hope in the city. An advisor to the Archbishop's Commission on Urban Priority Areas, Eastman is a Baptist and the Secretary to the Evangelical Coalition for Urban Mission and the Frontier Youth Trust.

18477. Edelman, Marian Wright. (1988) "Children: Our Poorest Americans," New Catholic World. Vol. 231, No. 1383 (May-June), pp. 100-104. Edelman is founder and president of the Children's Defense Fund.

18478. Egan, James P. (1988) "Sin and the Economic Analysis of the Pastoral: A Class Act?" Journal of Business Ethics. Vol. 7 (June), pp. 425-431.

18479. Ejerfeldt, Lennart. (1988) "La fréquentation des offices religieux dans le grand Stokholm: Vingt-cinq ans de recensement au cours du développement de l'agglomération," Social Compass. Vol. 35, No. 1 (March), pp. 33-43. Reports the status of various religious groups in Stockholm: Lutherans, Pentecostals, and various sects.

18480. Elshtain, Jean Bethke. (1988) "A Return to Hull House: Reflections on Jane Addams," Cross Currents. Vol. 38, No. 3 (Fall), pp. 257-276.

18481. Faith in the City of Birmingham: An Examination of

Problems and Opportunities Facing the City. (1988) Exeter, Devon, England: Paternoster Press. Report of a city commission set up by the Bishop of Birmingham in response to the work of the Church of England's Commission on Urban Priority Areas. Recommendations are made for church and public policy.

18482. Faramelli, Norman J. (1988) "White Racism Still Victimizes Minorities," Witness [Thematic issue: Racism]. Vol. 71, No. 5 (May), pp. 6-8+.

18483. Fearon, Mike. (1988) With God on the Frontiers. London: Scripture Union. Nine stories about ministry with inner city youth in England, Ireland, and Scotland are intended to correct some of the "bad press" that depicts them as violent, lazy, arrogant and selfish.

18484. Feldman, Linda. (1988) "St. Benedict's Offers Food, Solace, and Stability," Food and Nutrition. Vol. 18 (Fall), pp. 8-11. Re: ministry among the homeless in Holmdel, NJ.

18485. Feldmeier, Russell, et al. (1988) "The Church in the Defense of Workers' Rights in the Republic of Korea," Pro Mundi Vita Studies. No. 3 (May), pp. 12-20.

18486. Fichter, Joseph H. (1988) A Sociologist Looks at Religion. Wilmington, DE: N. Glasier.

18487. Figge, Robert J., Jr. (1988) Responsive Urban Bible Education Formulating Objectives for Manna Bible Institute. Thesis (D. Min.). Philadelphia, PA: Eastern Baptist Theological Seminary.

18488. Finke, Roger and Rodney Stark. (1988) "Religious Economies and Sacred Canopies: Religious Mobilization in American Cities," American Sociological Review. Vol. 53, No. 1 (February), pp. 41-49. Finke and Stark report results that differ from most research on the association between religious adherence and urban pluralism. Most researchers have found a negative association, but Finke and Stark argue that the association may be positive. For criticism, see Breault (1990).

18489. Fisher, Irving D. (1988) "An Iconology of City Planning--The Plan of Chicago," pp. 449-467 in Erland J. Brock, et al., eds. Swedenborg and His Influence. Bryn Athyn, PA: The Academy of the New Church. Fisher traces the roots of Daniel H. Burnham's plan for Chicago to the Heavenly City described in Emanuel Swedenborg's: Heaven and Its Wonders and Hell. Some of Burnham's drawings of Chicago, which were in part adopted, are reproduced in the article.

Burnham also developed city plans for Washington, DC, Manila, and San Francisco. Bibliography.

18490. Fitzpatrick, Joseph P. (1988) "The Hispanic Poor in a Middle Class Church," America. Vol. 159, No. 1 (June 25), pp. 11-13. Fitzpatrick observes that the church is not as immersed in the lives of recent immigrants to the USA as it was with the earlier European immigrants. The Catholic church, a middle class institution, has not found an effective way of ministering to the poor.

18491. Fones-Wolf, Kenneth Alan. (1988) "Religion and Trade Union Politics in the US, 1880-1920," International Labor and Working Class History [Thematic issue: Religion and labor]. No. 34 (Fall), pp. 39-55.

18492. Forward, Martin H. F. (1988) "The Pastor's Opportunities, Part 12: Christian Relationships with People of Other Faiths," The Expository Times. Vol. 99, No. 6 (March), pp. 164-168. A pastor in Leicester, England, comments on living in a neighborhood with Muslims, Hindus, and Sikhs, discussing implications for pastoral ministry.

18493. Fotia, Ralph. (1988) "Inner-City Ministry in a Small Church," Christian Ministry. Vol. 19, No. 5 (September-October), pp. 11-12. Church and community programs at Shaffer Memorial United Methodist Church, Cleveland, OH.

18494. Franz, Delton. (1988) "Planting a Church in a Changing City [Interview by R. Kreider; Woodlawn Mennonite Church, Chicago, IL, 1951-1968]," Mennonite Life. Vol. 43, No. 1 (March), pp. 23-27.

18495. Freeman, John F. and Roger L. Williams. (1988) How Modernity Came to a Provençal Town. Lewiston, NY: Mellen. History of Grasse, France, and the relations between church and municipal authorities from the 12th century to the formal separation of church and state in 1905. Modernity stems, according to the authors, from laicization, not dechristianization.

18496. Fritz, Paul J. (1988) "Summer Urban Church-Planting Internships for Seminary Students: Nigeria," Urban Mission. Vol. 5, No. 5 (May), pp. 38-42.

18497. Geering, Lloyd George. (1988) In the World Today: Essays. Wellington, New Zealand: Allen and Unwin. One essay deals with cities and towns.

18498. Gibbs, Nancy R. (1988) "Begging: To Give or Not to Give," Time. Vol. 132 (September 5), pp. 68-74.

18499. Gieniec, Nancy, et al. (1988) Accreditation Manual: The Official Evaluation Instrument for the Triennial Accreditation of Local CONTACT Centers. Harrisburg, PA: CONTACT Teleministries. Standards and evaluation procedures for telephone ministries.

18500. Gill, Robin. (1988) Beyond Decline. London: SCM. Gill interprets Faith in the City (1985), the report of the Archbishop of Canterbury's Commission on Urban Priority Areas, to call for an urban approach basically similar to the church growth strategies recommended by Donald McGavran, although differing in language and theological presuppositions.

18501. Glaser, Chris. (1988) Uncommon Calling: A Gay Man's Struggle to Serve the Church. San Francisco, CA: Harper and Row.

18502. González, Justo L. (1988) The Theological Education of Hispanics. New York: Fund for Theological Education. Demographic and historical background and a survey of five different approaches to theological education serve as a basis for recommending approaches for the support of theological education among Hispanics.

18503. Goodman, Julie, ed. (1988) "Sheltering the Homeless: The St. Vincent de Paul--Joan Kroc Center," Designers West. Vol. 35, No. 14 (November), pp. 136-138. An interior decorating magazine editor describes briefly the architectural design and decorating plan of the temporary shelter for the homeless in San Diego which won a 1987 United Nations award.

18504. Goodwin, John C. (1988) "The United Methodist City Society of New York," New World Outlook. n.s. Vol. 48, No. 3 (January), pp. 23-29. Current programs of a society founded in 1820.

18505. Gorrell, Donald K. (1988) "The Great Mutation of the Social Creed, 1928-1944," pp. 10-35 in Jan Kindwoman. Journey toward Justice: Commemorating the 80th Anniversary of the Social Creed of the People Called the Methodists. Staten Island, NY: Methodist Federation for Social Action. A historical analysis of the continuing significance of the Methodist Social creed of 1908.

18506. Gorrell, Donald K. (1988) The Age of Social Responsibility: The Social Gospel in the Progressive Era, 1900-1920. Macon, GA:

Mercer University Press.

18507. Graham, W. Ralph and Bryn A. Carson. (1988) "American Protestant Correctional Chaplains Association, Inc.," Journal of Pastoral Care. Vol. 42, No. 3 (Fall), pp. 220-227.

18508. Gray, Charlotte. (1988) Mother Teresa: The Nun Whose "Mission of Love" Has Helped Millions of the World's People. Dublin, Ireland: Wolfhound Press. Also published elsewhere. Inspiration for juveniles.

18509. Greeley, Andrew M. (1988) God in Popular Culture. Chicago, IL: The Thomas More Press. Greeley searches for contemporary parables and finds them in the modern romances and escapist entertainment of mass media.

18510. Griffin, Benjamin. (1988?) New Life in Central City Churches. [New York: United Church Board for Homeland Ministries]. A pamphlet.

18511. Gunderson, Gary. (1988) "Who's Hungry?" Missions USA. Vol. 59, No. 5 (September-October), pp. 28-35.

18512. Hadaway, Robin Dale. (1988) A Church Planting and Discipleship Training Project for Mwanze, Tanzania, East Africa. Thesis (D. Min.). Mill Valley, CA: Golden Gate Baptist Theological Seminary.

18513. Hagedorn, John M. and Perry Macon. (1988) People and Folks: Gangs, Crime and the Underclass in a Rust-Belt City. Chicago, IL: Lake View Press.

18514. Hall, Douglas. (1988) "Theological Education in the Urban Context," in Ruy O. Costa, ed. One Faith, Many Cultures. The Boston Theological Institute Annual, Volume 2. Maryknoll, NY: Orbis Books. Hall, the director of Emmanuel Gospel Center in Boston, describes the impact of urban theological education on the poor and observes that it can be destructive. A lot of "humble unlearning" is necessary if people are going to learn to be effective in urban ministry. The article promotes a systemic approach and a research orientation. Hall says persons who minister need to be aware of their own brokenness. The article provides a corrective for the "schoolish" assumptions reflected in much currently being written about education in the city, i.e., that "real" education occurs on the campus and that students go to the city to apply what they've learned there.

18515. Hall, Douglas. (1988) "De-Evangelism: Exploring the Mystery of the Deserted Urban Church," Urban Mission. Vol. 6, No. 1 (September), pp. 6-12.

18516. Hammersley, John. (1988) "Christianity and Metrocenter Do Not Mix ...?" Crucible. [Vol. 27, No. 2] (April-June), pp. 57-61.

18517. Härle, Wilfried. (1988) "Theologische Vorüberlegungen für eine Theorie kirchlichen Handelns in Gefängnissen," Zeitschrift für Evangelische Ethik. Vol. 32, No. 3 (July-September), pp. 199-209. Re: theological bases for church work with prisoners.

18518. Harrell, Rob. (1988) "Report from the Front Lines: Walk Your Talk: An Authentic Dose of Inner-city Ministry," Youthworker. Vol. 5, No. 1 (Spring), pp. 90-92.

18519. Harrison, M. E. (1988) "Urban Perspectives: Too Much Separatism?" Urban Mission. Vol. 5, No. 4 (March), pp. 40-41.

18520. Hart, Jim. (1988) "Adult Learning Adventures with EUTP," British Journal of Theological Education. Vol. 1, No. 3 (Spring), pp. 32-43.

18521. Hawkins, M. Elizabeth. (1988) New Life Behind Steel Bars. Washington, DC: Middle Atlantic Regional Press. Re: prison work and the United Outreach for Christ Mission Team.

18522. Hawkins, Richard T. (1988) "AIDS Ministry: Curing the Sickness of Homophobia," Witness [Ambler, PA]. Vol. 71, No. 3 (March), pp. 19-21.

18523. "Health Care: Ethical and Religious Issues." (1988) Chicago Studies [Thematic issue]. Vol. 27, No. 3 (November).

18524. "Heartside: A Storefront Congregation." (1988) Church Herald. Vol. 45, No. 1 (January 1), pp. 28-29. Dedication of a storefront worship facility in Grand Rapids, MI.

18525. Heinemeier, John. (1988) "Faces of Faith: Hope Blooming in the Urban Desert," The Other Side [Thematic issue: Urban Ministry]. Vol. 24, No. 4 (May), pp. 14-19. An interview with Heinemeier, a Lutheran involved in parish-based community organizing in Brooklyn and South Bronx.

18526. Hessel, Dieter T., ed. (1988) Theological Education for Social Ministry. New York: Pilgrim Press. Papers commissioned for a symposium on Theological Education for Socially Responsible Ministry, 1987, Washington, DC.

18527. Hibbert, Christopher. (1988) London's Churches. London: Macdonald. An elaborately illustrated history of London church architecture and historical landmarks.

18528. Hirschfield, Robert. (1988) "For Life at the Edge of Life," Christianity and Crisis [Thematic issue: AIDS]. Vol. 48, No. 10 (July 4), pp. 223-225.

18529. Hoekstra, Wim. (1988) "Migrants, the Church and the Bible," pp. 114-128 in Margaret Press and Neil Brown, eds, Faith and Culture. Manly, Australia: Catholic Institute of Sydney.

18530. Hoffman, Pam. (1988) "Keeping the Down and Out Afloat," Christianity Today. Vol. 32, No. 13 (September 16), pp. 12-13.

18531. Holden, Tony. (1988) Keeping Faith: Sharing God's Mission: Ten Years of Inner City Ministry. London: Methodist Church, Home Mission Division. Re: Stratford Methodist Church, London.

18532. Hollinger, Denis and Joseph Modica. (1988) "The Feminization of Poverty," Urban Mission. Vol. 5, No. 5 (May), pp. 14-22. Hollinger describes the economic, political, and social factors underlying the rapid increase in the number of poor women in the United States.

18533. Hollyday, Joyce. (1988) "Rest for the Weary," Sojourners. Vol. 17, No. 1 (January), pp. 14-20.

18534. Hoover, Stewart M. (1988) Mass Media Religion. Newbury Park, CA: Sage. A historical analysis of religious broadcasting.

18535. Horton, Anne L. and Judith A. Williamson, eds. (1988) Abuse and Religion: When Praying Isn't Enough. Indianapolis, IN: Lexington Books. This book addresses the issue of domestic and sexual abuse, relating it to the complexity of counseling victims regarding the resulting spiritual and psychological problems. It describes a dilemma that victims encounter when seeking help from the church: 1) going to clergy for counseling and limiting themselves to theological perspectives, or 2) going for secular counseling and finding that their spiritual damage is not being addressed.

18536. Hsu, Ming Chau. (1988) Toward a Ministry of Passionate Compassion: Call for Congregational Involvement with Taiwanese Immigrants. Thesis (D. Min). San Anselmo, CA: San Francisco Theological Seminary.

18537. Hullum, Everett and Jim Wright. (1988) "A Parable of Church Growth," Missions USA. Vol. 59, No. 5 (September), pp. 14-21.

18538. Hunt, Angela Elwell and Kay Raysor. (1988) "Reconciling the Forgotten: Three Ministries Rebuild Lives," Fundamentalist Journal. Vol. 7, No. 3 (March), pp. 23-28.

18539. Hunter, Lea Anne. (1988) "The Learning Club: Empowering Poor Youth," New Catholic World. Vol. 231, No. 1383 (May-June), pp. 129-132.

18540. I. M. -- An Appraisal: The Church's Response to the Changing Industrial and Economic Order: The Report of a Working Party Commissioned By the Industrial and Economic Affairs Committee of the Church of England's Board for Social Responsibility. (1988) London: Board for Social Responsibility. [Location: General Theological Seminary, New York, NY]. Re: industrial mission sponsored by the Church of England.

18541. Isasi-Píaz, Ada María and Yolanda Tarango. (1988) Hispanic Women Prophetic Voice in the Church: Toward a Hispanic Women's Liberation Theology. San Francisco, CA: Harper and Row. Isasi-Píaz, a Cuban by birth, is a theologian, feminist, and activist. Text is in Spanish and English. Bibliography.

18542. Jackson, K. Logan. (1988) "Victimization and Community Violence within Metropolitan Washington: A Theological Perspective," AME Zion Quarterly Review. Vol. 99, No. 4 (January), pp. 8-17. Theological methods for interpreting city problems.

18543. Jackson, Michael E. (1988) "Fighting AIDS in the Streets," Christianity and Crisis [Thematic issue: AIDS]. Vol. 48, No. 10 (July 4), pp. 238-240. Jackson is associated with ADAPT, a volunteer organization in Brooklyn, NY, dedicated to preventing the spread of AIDS.

18544. Jackson, Patrick. (1988) "Understanding Alienation through Social Factors: Which Cause or Shape It?" Journal of Pastoral Counseling. Vol. 23, No. 1, pp. 89-107.

18545. Jefferson, Kinmoth W. and William Ramsden. (1988) Metro: Channel for Urban Mission--Metropolitan Mission Agencies in the United Methodist Church. New York: National Program Division, General Board of Global Ministries, The United Methodist Church. A survey of 77 United Methodist cooperative ministries in US cities.

18546. Jenkins, Karen. (1988) "When No Place Is Home: Refugees Flee to a World that Waits with Folded Arms," World Christian. Vol. 7, No. 3 (September-October), pp. 14-17.

18547. Jeremy, David J., ed. (1988) Business and Religion in Britain. Aldershot, England: Gower.

18548. John Paul II, Pope [Karol Wojtyla]. (1988) "Address to Participants in a Meeting of the World Federation of Towns and Cities Saying Their Peace Is an Objective to Pursue and Realize Concretely." October 28, 1988.

18549. Johnson, Lyn. (1988) "Hope for the Homeless," Fundamentalist Journal. Vol. 7, No. 9 (October), pp. 14-17.

18550. Johnson, Peter. (1988) "One Boy against the Chill," Christian Herald. Vol. 111, No. 11 (December), pp. 30-33. A youth helps Philadelphia, PA, homeless.

18551. Kane, Margaret. (1988) "Community Church," Modern Churchman. n.s. Vol. 30, No. 2, pp. 1-6.

18552. Kang, Dong Soo. (1988) A Small Group Study Curriculum for Korean-American Churches in the Presbyterian Church, USA. Thesis (D. Min.). San Anselmo, CA: San Francisco Theological Seminary.

18553. Keene, Michael. (1988) "Theology and Unemployment in the Dearne Valley," Crucible. Vol. 27, No. 4 (October-December). Keene, at the time of writing, was Sheffield's first Diocesan Unemployment Officer.

18554. Keil, Harmut and John Jentz. (1988) German Workers in Chicago: A Documentary History of Working Class Culture from 1850 to World War I. Urbana, IL: University of Illinois. See especially Chapters 5 and 6.

18555. Kemp, Jim. (1988) "'Normalizing' an Epidemic," Christianity and Crisis [Thematic issue: AIDS]. Vol. 48, No. 10 (July 4), pp. 227-229.

18556. Kempf, Denise M. (1988) "Phoenix South Finds Jobs for the Homeless," The Other Side. Vol. 24, No. 6 (July-August), p. 19.

18557. Khalil, Victor and Deborah Khalil. (1988) "The Mars Hill Collection: When Christians Meet Muslims," Christian Herald. Vol. 111, No. 7 (July-August), pp. 42-44. Christian witness to Muslims.

18558. Kimura, Noritaugu. (1988) "Folk Religion in the Ise-Shima Region: The Takemairi Custom at Mount Asama," Japan Journal of Religious Studies. Vol. 15, Nos. 2-3 (June 8), pp. 103-119. Folk religion does not necessarily decline with urbanization, and in some instances appears to give rise to a plethora of magical rites. This article deals with the Buddhist sect of Rinzai and the Bon Festival in Japan.

18559. Kindwoman, Jan and Ron Ozier, eds. (1988) Journey toward Justice: Commemorating the 80th Anniversary of the Social Creed of the People Called the Methodists. Staten Island, NY: Methodist Federation for Social Action.

18560. Kirkpatrick, Bill. (1988) AIDS: Sharing the Pain: Pastoral Guidelines. London: Darton, Longman, and Todd. Reprinted: New York: Pilgrim Press, 1990. Kirkpatrick is a priest in the Church of England, pioneer in London AIDS ministry, and cofounder of Reaching Out, a center for HIV sufferers. Bibliography.

18561. Kozol, Jonathan. (1988) Rachel and her Children: Homeless Families in America. New York: Crown. An education expert, who often addresses issues of adult illiteracy and education of poor people, describes the rise of homelessness in the USA.

18562. Krass, Alfred C. (1988) "Beyond 'Ecumenical Dialogue': A 'Floating Shelter' Brings Churches to Life," The Other Side [Thematic issue: Homelessness]. Vol. 24, No. 3 (April), pp. 43-45.

18563. Krover, Harold. (1988) "A Mission in the City," Church Herald [Thematic issue: Urban ministry]. Vol. 45, No. 20 (November 18), pp. 12-14. Church adaptations to city changes.

18564. Kunzel, Regina G. (1988) "The Professionalization of Benevolences: Evangelicals and Social Workers in the Florence Crittenton Homes, 1915-1945," Journal of Social History. Vol. 22 (Fall), pp.

21-43. An assessment of evangelical Christianity's effect on social work.

18565. Kyle, John E., ed. (1988) Urban Mission, God's Concern for the City: Papers Presented at the 15th InterVarsity Student Missions Convocation, December 27-31, 1987 at the University of Illinois, Urbana-Champaign. Downers Grove, IL: InterVarsity. This conference was sponsored by the InterVarsity Christian Fellowship.

18566. Lambeth Conference. (1988) The Resolutions of the Lambeth Conferences, 1867-1978. London: Anglican Consultative Council. A source for study of the Church of England's social teaching.

18567. LeBlanc, Doug. (1988) "The Fight Goes On: 25 Years in the NBEA," Eternity. Vol. 39, No. 15 (May), pp. 26-27.

18568. Lee, Sang-Taek. (1988) Exploring an Appropriate Church Structure for Korean Speaking Congregations which Are Members of the Uniting Church in Australia. Thesis (D. Min.). San Anselmo, CA: San Francisco Theological Seminary.

18569. Leslie, Bill. (1988) "What It Costs to Reach the Community," Leadership: A Practical Journal for Church Leaders. Vol. 9, No. 3 (Summer), pp. 12-19. Re: LaSalle Street Church, Chicago, IL.

18570. Liebman, Robert, John R. Sutton, and Robert Wuthnow. (1988) "Exploring the Social Sources of Denominationalism: Schisms in American Protestant Denominations, 1890-1980," American Sociological Review. Vol. 52, No. 3 (June), pp. 343-352.

18571. Lightstone, Jack W. (1988) "Ritual, Reality, and Contemporary Society: The Case of a Reconstructionist Synagogue," Journal of Ritual Studies. Vol. 2 (Summer), pp. 35-56.

18572. Lim, David S. (1988) "The City in the Bible," Evangelical Review of Theology. Vol. 12, No. 2 (April), pp. 138-156.

18573. Lingenfelter, Judith. (1988) "Public Transportation and Urban Witness," Urban Mission. Vol. 5, No. 4 (March), pp. 5-10.

18574. Lingle, Virginia A. (1988) How to Find Information about AIDS. New York: Harrington Park Press. A bibliography.

18575. Linthicum, Robert C. (1988) "Doing Effective Ministry in the City," Together. (April-June). [See note 3].

18576. Linthicum, Robert C. (1988) "Towards a Biblical Urban Theology," Together. (April-June). [See note 3].

18577. Lippel, Israel. (1988) "Jerusalem--City of Religions: The Universality of Jerusalem," Christian Jewish Relations. Vol. 21, No. 2 (Summer), pp. 6-16. Despite all difficulties, Jerusalem does have coexistence of people with divergent religious preferences. It also has relatively good security of places of worship, thanks to the majority of residents -- Jews, Christians and Muslims alike -- who are moderate and constructive.

18578. Lippy, Charles H. (1988) "Social Christianity," pp. 917-931 in Charles H. Lippey and Peter W. Williams, eds. Encyclopedia of the American Religious Experience. New York: Charles Scribner's Sons.

18579. Liptak, Dolores A., ed. (1988) A Church of Many Cultures: Selected Historical Essays on Ethnic American Catholicism. New York: Garland. A series of articles on religion and ethnicity, all published elsewhere.

18580. Livingston, Debra and Judy Kittleson. (1988) Voter Registration, Education and Get Out the Vote. Washington, DC: Churches' Committee for Voter Registration/Education (CCVR/E). Step-by-step plans for church involvement in an election campaign. Bibliography of resources.

18581. Lloyd, Larry Bishop. (1988) Urban Ministry: A Partnership Model for the White Suburban Church in the South. Thesis (D. Min.). Pasadena, CA: Fuller Theological Seminary.

18582. Loewenberg, Frank M. (1988) Religion and Social Work Practice in Contemporary American Society. New York: Columbia University Press. Loewenberg identifies the religious aspects of modern scientific social work. Bibliography.

18583. Lord, Richard. (1988) "Digging Out in Rio," New World Outlook. n.s. Vol. 48, No. 10 [i.e., Vol. 49, No. 1], (October), pp. 18-21. United Methodist aid is provided after a flood devastated some of Rio de Janeiro's poorest slums.

18584. Louw, Daniel J. (1988) "Spirituality in South Africa: An Existential and Theological Approach," Journal of Theology for South Africa. No. 65 (December), pp. 47-59.

18585. Lowndes, Marian. (1988) A Mission in the City: The Sheffield Inner City Ecumenical Mission. New City Special, No. 5. Sheffield, England: Urban Theology Unit. Small urban congregations find new mission and direction in Sheffield through their cooperation with one another and with the Urban Theology Unit. Strategies include sharing buildings with groups of radically different traditions, joint projects, and other practices which give the congregations a sense of worth. The Urban Theology Unit was, at the time of this writing, directed by John Vincent. A pamphlet.

18586. Macarewa, Fredy Lowell. (1988) An Evangelistic Program in the Indonesian-American Seventh Day Adventist Church. Thesis (D. Min). Claremont, CA: School of Theology at Claremont.

18587. Macke, Paul B. (1988) Stress and Burnout in Jesuit Priests: A Comparison between Those in Rural Cross-Cultural and Those in Urban Non-Cross-Cultural Ministry. Thesis (D. Min.). Evanston, IL: Garrett-Evangelical Theological Seminary.

18588. Majka, Theo J. and Patrick D. Donnelly. (1988) "Cohesiveness within a Heterogeneous Urban Neighborhood: Implications for Community in a Diverse Setting," Journal of Urban Affairs. Vol. 10, No. 2, pp. 141-159. A study in Dayton, OH, advances theory about urban networks.

18589. Mak, Arthur F. (1988) "Case Study: The Case of a Threatened Church: A Study of the Hong Kong Christian Confession in View of the 1997 Communist Takeover," Urban Mission. Vol. 5, No. 3 (January), pp. 32-39.

18590. Mallon, Elias D. (1988) "Why the Christian-Muslim Dialogue Is Important," New Catholic World [Thematic issue: Muslim-Christian Dialogue]. Vol. 231, No. 1386 (November-December), pp. 244-247.

18591. Mamiya, Lawrence H. (1988) "The Black Muslims as a New Religious Movement: Their Evolution and Implications for the Study of Religion in a Pluralistic Society," in Chuo Academic Research Group. Conflict and Cooperation between Contemporary Religious Groups. Tokyo: Nakamura.

18592. Marshall, Mary Ruth, et al., compilers [Sara Little, project director]. (1988) Youth and Youth Ministry: Professors' Bibliography. Richmond, VA: Youth Ministry and Theological Schools Project, Union Theological Seminary in Virginia. Professors interested in youth and youth ministries from twenty-two theological schools met and exchanged course syllabi and bibliographies. This annotated bibliography of books published mostly since 1975, including some items of interest to urban studies, represents the combined bibliographies of the participating professors.

18593. Marty, Martin E. (1988) "When My Virtue Doesn't Match Your Virtue," The Christian Century. Vol. 105, No. 36 (November 30), pp. 1094-1098. Re: conflict and ethnic pluralism.

18594. McClelland, Albert. (1988) "Solomon Franklin Dowis: Cooperative Missions Administrator," Baptist History and Heritage. Vol. 23, No. 1 (January), pp. 32-41.

18595. McCoy, Marjorie Casebier and Charles S. McCoy. (1988) Frederick Buechner: Novelist/Theologian of the Lost and Found. San Francisco, CA: Harper and Row. Buechner's novels often deal with urban social issues from the perspective of Christian theology.

18596. McGuire, Meredith B. (1988) Ritual Healing in Suburban America. New Brunswick, NJ: Rutgers University Press. An analysis of non-medical healing in middle-class America includes chapters on healing in Christian groups, metaphysical movements, human potential groups, and psychic and occult groups. Ritualistic and symbolic aspects of healing are considered.

18597. Meagher, Timothy J., ed. (1988) Urban American Catholicism: The Culture and Identity of the American Catholic People. New York: Garland.

18598. Menning, Bruce. (1988) "Building Bridges with the City," Church Herald [Thematic issue: Urban ministry]. Vol. 45, No. 20 (November 18), pp. 15-16. Although cooperation between inner city and suburban churches is rare, it's worth striving for. Menning provides examples.

18599. Menninga, Arland D. (1988) "Seek Peace in the Workplace," Military Chaplains' Review. (Summer), pp. 37-42.

18600. Meyere, Michael A. (1988) Response to Modernity: A History of the Reformed Movement in Judaism. New York: Oxford Univcersity Press.

18601. Michael, Colette V. (1988) Negritude: An Annotated Bibliography. West Cornwall, CT: Locust Hill Press.

18602. Miller, Calvin. (1988) "Rethinking Suburban Evangelism," Leadership: A Journal for Church Leaders. Vol. 9, No. 4 (Fall), pp. 64-68.

18603. Millet-Gérard, Dominique. (1988) "Thomson, James, 'BV': 'La cité de terrifiante ténèbre' 1874," [Introduction and French translation], Foi et Vie. Vol. 87, No. 2 (April), pp. 31-61.

18604. Miranda, Juan Carlos. (1988) "Needed: 20,000 Hispanic Churches," United Evangelical Action [Thematic issue: Los Hispanos]. Vol. 47, No. 4 (July-August), pp. 4-5.

18605. Mitchell, Brian, ed. (1988) Building the American Catholic City: P rishes and Institutions. New York: Garland. A collection of articles on Catholic growth in American cities, all published elsewhere.

18606. Mitchell, Kenneth R. (1988) Multiple Staff Ministries. Philadelphia, PA: Westminster. Mitchell provides examples of successful group ministries, lists problems that often arise, and identifies ways to increase effectiveness. Bibliography.

18607. Mitchell, Rudy. (1988) Boston: A Socio-Economic and Religious Profile. Boston, MA: Emmanuel Gospel Center. A brief secondary summary of information about Boston assembled for the purpose of supporting ministry at the Emmanuel Gospel Center, offered as an example of how such data can be assembled relatively quickly by persons involved in urban ministries elsewhere.

18608. Miyoshi, Hiromu. (1988) "Auf der Suche nach dem Bild des arbeitenden Menschen," pp. 136-141 in Yoshiki Terazono, ed. Brennpunkte in Kirche und Theologie Japans. Neukirchen-Vluyn, Germany: Neukirchener Verlag. Bibliography.

18609. Mohr, Richard D. (1988) Gays/Justice: A Study of Ethics, Society and Law. New York: Columbia University Press.

18610. Mollner, Terry. (1988) "Is There an Alternative to Capitalism and Socialism?" New Catholic World. Vol. 231, No. 1383 (May-June), pp. 114-119.

18611. Monsma, Timothy. (1988) "Homogeneous Networks--A Babel that Promotes Good Urban Strategy," Urban Mission. Vol. 5, No. 3 (January), pp. 11-17.

18612. Moore, Jerome A. (1988) Mini Bible Institutes for Maxi Church Development. Thesis (D. Min.). Chestnut Hill, PA: Westminster Theological Seminary.

18613. Morgan, Thomas. (1988) "Muslim Patrol Reduces Crime in Brooklyn Area," New York Times. (February 25).

18614. Morton, Marian J. (1988) "Fallen Women, Federated Charities, and Maternity Homes: 1913-1973," Social Service Review. Vol. 62 (March), pp. 61-82.

18615. Mottesi, Alberto. (1988) "Cultural Considerations," United Evangelical Action [Thematic issue: Los Hispanos]. Vol. 47, No. 4 (July-August), pp. 6-7. Mottesi is an evangelist in Latin America.

18616. Mullins, Mark R. (1988) "The Organizational Dilemmas of Ethnic Churches: A Case Study of Japanese Buddhism in Canada," Sociological Analysis. Vol. 49, No. 3 (Fall), pp. 217-233.

18617. Murphy, Joseph M. (1988) Santería: An African Religion in America. Boston, MA: Beacon. A participant observation study of the Santería community in the Bronx, NY. Murphy traces this African/Cuban group to West African Yoruba origins and from there to its presence in American urban centers. Bibliography.

18618. Myrick, Judith. (1988) "Ministry to the Banned," The Witness [Thematic issue: Urban Mission]. Vol. 71, No. 5 (May), pp. 13-15.

18619. National Conference of Catholic Bishops. (1988) National Pastoral Plan for Hispanic Ministry. Washington, DC: United States Catholic Conference.

18620. Navarro, Nelson. (1988) "Why Singapore Is Different," New World Outlook. n.s. Vol. 48, No. 5 (March), pp. 14-19. Religious tolerance contributes to social harmony in a busy Asian city-state.

18621. Navarro, Peter. (1988) "Why Do Corporations Give to Charity?" Journal of Business. Vol. 61 (January), pp. 65-93.

18622. Nees, Tom. (1988) "Neighbors Without Shelter: The Trauma of Homeless Families," Sojourners. Vol. 17, No. 6 (June), pp. 34-35.

18623. Nelsen, Hart M. (1988) "Unchurched Black Americans: Patterns of Religiosity and Affiliation," Review of Religious Research. Vol. 29, No. 4 (June), pp. 398-412. Using data from the Gallup Unchurched American Study, Nelsen finds that the highest incidence of Blacks being unchurched occurs among those residing in metropolitan places outside the Southern states, followed by those in the metropolitan South and finally by those in the non-metropolitan South, which had the lowest rate of being unchurched. Occupation, education, and income were not found to be related to being churched. Nelson interprets these results to reflect differences in Black religiosity in urban locations, especially in the non-South. Urbanization brings differentiation, except for those migrants who hold persistently to a rural world-view.

18624. Nelson, Bruce C. (1988) Beyond the Martyrs: A Social History of Chicago's Anarchists. New Brunswick, NJ: Rutgers University Press. Re: anarchism and radical free thought in mid and late 19th century.

18625. Ng, Don, ed. (1988) Asian Pacific American Youth Ministry: Planning, Helps, and Programs. Valley Forge, PA: Judson.

18626. Ngai, David and Katherine Lo, eds. (1988) Mission in Urban Hong Kong. Kowloon, Hong Kong: Chinese Coordinating Center of World Evangelism. Text in Chinese. Bibliography.

18627. Nieves, Alvaro L. (1988) "Minority Issues in the Justice System," Urban Mission. Vol. 5, No. 4 (March), pp. 27-34.

18628. Nikkel, Steven. (1988) "Case Study: Holistic Ministry in Freetown, Sierra Leone," Urban Mission. Vol. 5, No. 4 (March), pp. 35-39.

18629. Novak, Michael. (1988) The Joy of Sport: End Zones, Bases, Baskets, Balls and the Consecration of the American Spirit. Lanham, MD: University Press of America.

18630. Nucciarone, Albert P. (1988) A Handbook for Church Growth in Italy. Thesis (D. Min.). Chestnut Hill, PA: Westminster Theological Seminary.

18631. O'Brien, David J. (1988) Public Catholicism. New York: Macmillan. O'Brien offers a summary history of different ways in which the American Catholic church has dealt with social and political realities across the history of its development. Three types are identified: immigrant Catholicism, republican Catholicism and prophetic Catholicism. This is one of a series of volumes commissioned for the bicentennial celebration of the Catholic Church in the USA.

18632. Oglesbee, Clay. (1988) "Closing Detroit Churches: A Strategic Retreat?" The Christian Century. Vol. 105, No. 38 (December 14), pp. 1143-1144. Reflection on the closing of 46 Roman Catholic churches in Detroit by Cardinal Edmund Szoda. See further: "Detroit Verdict," Christian Century. Vol. 106, No. 4 (February 1-8), p. 105.

18633. Oh, Mark Edward. (1988) Cultural Pluralism and Multi-Ethnic Congregation as a Ministry Model in an Urban Society. Thesis (D. Min.). Pasadena, CA: Fuller Theological Seminary.

18634. Oldham, Edward L. (1988) "Volunteers Minister to Inmates," Corrections Today. Vol. 50 (August), pp. 203+.

18635. Olson, Lynn M., Janet Reis, and Larry Murphy. (1988) "The Religious Community as a Partner in Health Care," Journal of Community Health. Vol. 13 (Winter), pp. 249-257.

18636. Olson, Mark, ed. (1988) "God in Metropolis: Ministering to the Urban Soul," The Other Side [Thematic issue]. Vol. 24, No. 4 (May), pp. 20-47.

18637. Open Door Community. (1988?) The Open Door Community. Atlanta, GA: the Community. [Location: United Theological Seminary, Dayton, OH]. A description of a Christian residential community in Atlanta with inspirational articles.

18638. Ortiz, Manuel. (1988) "The Rise of Spiritism in North America," Urban Mission. Vol. 5, No. 4 (March), pp. 11-17.

18639. Overbea, Luix Virgil. (1988) "Homeless in America," New World Outlook. n.s. Vol. 48, No. 8 (June), pp. 18-23. A new breed of homeless people include whole families. Government is slow to act, and private organizations barely make a dent in the problem. Health care issues are critical.

18640. Parker, Christian. (1988) "Popular Religion in Latin America," Pro Mundi Vita Studies. No. 6 (November), pp. 18-28.

18641. Pasquariello, Ronald D., ed. (1988) "Shalom: The Promise of the City," A Shalom Paper, No. 18. Washington, DC: Urban Policy

Panel of the Churches' Center for Theology and Public Policy. Often people writing about the city and city ministry focus only on urban pathologies. Pasquariello finds the positive image of "shalom" reflected in the ways the city enriches life and opens new possibilities, even for people who live beyond the city. He offers policy recommendations for cities and for religious communities. A pamphlet.

18642. "The Pastor's Opportunity, XIV, Thoughts on Twinning from the Inner City." (1988) Expository Times. Vol. 99, No. 8 (May), pp. 228-230. A pastor's wife reflects on the value of linking inner city and suburban churches from the perspective of older women in the inner city church.

18643. Pazmiño, Robert William. (1988) The Seminary in the City: A Study of New York Theological Seminary. New York: University Press of America. A study of theological education in general and NYTS in particular during the post World War II years, with emphasis on the transformation of the school under the leadership of George Williams Webber. Bibliography of Webber's works, works on NYTS, and philosophy of theological education.

18644. Pedigo, Marlene Morrison. (1988) New Church in the City: The Work of the Chicago Fellowship of Friends. Richmond, IN: Friends United Press.

18645. Perrin, Jacques. (1988) "Marseille: une ville pour demain," Etudes. Vol. 369 (December), pp. 613-623. Re: social conditions in Marseille, France.

18646. Perry, Leroy Odinda. (1988) No Place to Call Home: Hospitality as Missions. Thesis (D. Min.). New York: New York Theological Seminary.

18647. Peterson, Wallace C. (1988) "Economic Imperatives of the American Bishops' Pastoral Letter," Journal of Economic Issues. Vol. 22 (December), pp. 1023-1033.

18648. Petras, Harri. (1988) 100 Jahre Evangelische Arbeiter-Bewegung in Hattingen, 1886-1986. Hattingen, Germany: Stadtarchiv. Anniversary of the Evangelische Arbeiter-Bewegung in Hattingen, Germany. Bibliography.

18649. Peuquet, Steven W. and Pamela J. Leland. (1988) Homelessness in Delaware. [Newark, DE]: The Urban Agent Division, College of Urban Affairs and Public Policy, University of Delaware in Cooperation with the Salvation Army. Several church groups participated in conducting this inquiry.

18650. Peyton, Rosemary. (1988) "Assir DaSilva: A Quick Mind, a Caring Heart," Adventist Review. Vol. 165, No. 39 (September 29), pp. 8-9. Ministry among Chicago's Hispanic population.

18651. Phillips, Jennifer M. (1988) "The Future of AIDS: Parishes Can Help," Christian Century. Vol. 105, No. 18 (June 1), pp. 548-551. Practical suggestions from a Boston, MA, hospital chaplain in the areas of education, home care, housing, prayer and counseling.

18652. Pierce, Susan E. (1988) "Union-Busting at 'St. Elsewhere,'" The Witness. Vol. 71, No. 6 (June), pp. 10-11+.

18653. Pratt, Hugh. (1988) "They Move About Like Ghosts of the Grapes of Wrath" Christian Social Action. Vol. 1, No. 2 (February), pp. 18-19. Pratt, a pastor, reflects on the conditions of the poor and homeless.

18654. Pretiz, Paul. (1988) "Church Planters Needed--Mexico City Directory Reveals Few Evangelicals," Urban Mission. Vol. 5, No. 3 (January), pp. 6-10.

18655. Privett, Stephen A. (1988) The US Catholic Church and Its Hispanic Members: The Pastoral Vision of Archbishop Robert E. Lucey. San Antonio, TX: Trinity University Press.

18656. Purdy, Martin. (1988) "An English Strategy for Church Restoration." Faith and Form. Vol. 21 (Spring), pp. 16-19. Even the financial benefit of a church tax cannot mitigate the growing need for restoration of deteriorating buildings.

18657. Purvis, James D. (1988) Jerusalem, the Holy City (ATLA Bibliography Series, No. 20) Metuchen, NJ: Scarecrow Press. This volume consists of 5,827 bibliographic entries about Jerusalem from all disciplines, arranged according to historical eras from pre-587 BCE to post-1967 CE, without annotation. The entries represent largely 19th and 20th century scholarship, most of which are in English, although some entries are in French, German, Italian, Spanish, and modern Hebrew (with English translations of the Hebrew titles).

18658. Rees, David John. (1988) Making It Multicultural. Thesis (D. Min.). New York: New York Theological Seminary.

18659. Reeves, James M. (1988) Program to Introduce Cell Group Ministry into an Urban Southern Baptist Church. Thesis (D. Min.). Fort Worth, TX: Southwestern Baptist Theological Seminary.

18660. Resener, Carl R. (1988) Crisis in the Streets. Nashville, TN: Broadman. An analysis of homelessness and theological mandates for the church's response. Bibliography.

18661. Richardson, James T., ed. (1988) Money and Power in the New Religions. Lewiston, NY: Mellen. Essays examine views of wealth in Mormonism, the Unification Church, Hare Krishna, the Love Family, and other groups.

18662. Ritter, Bruce. (1988) Sometimes God Has a Kid's Face: The Story of America's Exploited Street Kids. [New York]: Covenant House. Franciscan priest, Bruce Ritter, heads the Covenant House for homeless children on the Lower East Side of New York City. His pained first person account of those whom Covenant House has helped -- and even more devastating, those it could not reach -- portrays the lives of children sold into prostitution and seduced into drug culture. The book is written for two audiences, for those who might participate in the rescue of children and for the children themselves, and their parents. For further information on Covenant House and Father Ritter, see New York Times. Vol. 139, No. 48,317 (August 4, 1990), pp. 25-26. Ritter himself was accused of "unacceptable poor judgment" in sexual relations with Covenant House residents. A special inquiry conducted by Kroll Associates reported that the accumulated evidence regarding Ritter's sexual activities with male residents is extensive. Ritter denied all allegations, but resigned as director.

18663. Ro, Bong Rin. (1988) "Urban Missions: A Historical Perspective," Evangelical Review of Theology. Vol. 12, No. 2 (April), pp. 157-173.

18664. Roberts, Ronald T. (1988) "Stages in the Life of Our Urban Congregation," Alban Institute Action Information. Vol. 14, No. 5 (September), pp. 12-14.

18665. Rodriguez, Cecilia. (1988) Empowerment and Marginalized Women Workers," Church and Society. Vol. 79, No. 2 (November-December), pp. 36-38.

18666. Rosado, Caleb. (1988) "The Nature of Society and the Challenge to the Mission of the Church," International Review of Mission. Vol. 77, No. 305 (January), pp. 22-37.

18667. Rosche, Jan-Dirk. (1988) Katholische Soziallehre und Unternehmensordnung. Paderborn, Germany: F. Schoningh. Re: Catholic social teaching and labor issues. Bibliography.

18668. Rush, Ralph Roger. (1988) Developing an Awareness for Community Ministry in the Curtis Avenue Baptist Church, Joliet, Illinois. Thesis (D. Min.). Lousiville, KY: Southern Baptist Theological Seminary.

18669. Russell, Letty M. (1988) "The City as Battered Woman," The Other Side [Thematic Issue: Urban ministry]. Vol. 24, No. 4 (May), pp. 20-21. The city is victim, abused by the economic forces that have been the source of her strength.

18670. Russell, Letty M. (1988) "Partnership in Models in Renewed Community," Ecumenical Review. Vol. 40, No. 1 (January), pp. 16-26.

18671. Rutayisire, Paul. (1988) "Kenya and Zaire," Pro Mundi Vita Forum. No. 1 (January), pp. 11-12.

18672. Rutledge, Paul. (1988) "Traditional Patterns and Belief Orientations: The Prognosis for Vietnamese Acculturation and Assimilation in the US," Asia Journal of Theology. Vol. 2, No. 2 (October), pp. 516-545. Bibliography.

18673. Ryan, Paul-David. (1988) Enhancing the Sense of Belonging and Ownership in a Church Community. Thesis (D. Min.), Dayton, OH: United Theological Seminary. Re: Holy Angels Catholic Church, Dayton, OH.

18674. Saunders, John Edward. (1988) The Role of the Director of Religious Education in a Metropolitan Baptist Association. Thesis (Ed. D.). Lousiville, KY: Southern Baptist Theological Seminary.

18675. Schaller, Lyle E. (1988) The Senior Minister. Nashville, TN: Abingdon. Bibliographical notes.

18676. Schmidt, Ron. (1988) "Moving to the Larger Church," Youthworker. Vol. 5, No. 1 (Spring), pp. 36-37.

18677. Schmool, Marlena. (1988) "Register of Social Research on the Anglo-Jewish Community: 1987-1988," Jewish Journal of Sociology. Vol. 30, No. 1 (June), pp. 37-50. A list of works in progress.

18678. Schreck, Harley Carl, Jr. (1988) "Mexico City: A Church-Based Model of Community Service," Urban Mission. Vol. 6, No. 2 (November), pp. 43-55.

18679. Schwartz, David C., Richard C. Ferlauto, and Daniel N. Hoffman. (1988) A New Housing Policy for America. Philadelphia, PA: Temple University Press.

18680. Scott, Waldron. (1988) "Man at His Best and Worst: A Biblical View of Urban Life," World Christian. (January-February), pp. 27-29.

18681. Seoka, Johannes Thomas. (1988) Worker Education: An Approach to Social Justice Ministry. Chicago, IL: [manuscript]. [Location: Chicago Theological Seminary].

18682. Sheppard, David and Derek Worlock. (1988) Better Together. London: Hodder and Stoughton. Two bishops, one Catholic and the other Church of England, present a courageous symbol of unity in a potentially explosive city, Liverpool. Liverpool has many of the same social dynamics and conflicts as Northern Ireland.

18683. Shorter, Aylward. (1988) Toward a Theology of Inculturation. London: G. Chapman. Bibliography.

18684. Showstack, Gerald Lee. (1988) Suburban Communities: The Jewishness of American Reform Jews. Atlanta, GA: Scholars Press.

18685. Shriver, Donald N. [i.e., Donald W.], Jr. (1988) "Give Generously--the Poor Do," Christian Century. Vol. 105, No. 38 (December 14), pp. 1140-1141. Poor people give away a large part of their resources to help other poor people. They are more generous than other Americans.

18686. Sigmon, Vivkie. (1988) "Hunger USA," New World Outlook. Vol. 49, No. 4 (July-August), pp. 20-21. Re: poverty in Washington, DC.

18687. Simmons, Henry. (1988) "Expanding Invitations: New Life in Central City Churches, Based on Research by the Rev. Dr. Benjamin Griffin," Growingplans, An Occasional Resource Magazine. United Church Board for Homeland Ministries, Division of Evangelism and Local Church Development. Simmons summarizes Griffin's findings that some central city churches are growing at unexpectedly large rates.

18688. Sinnott, Thomas G. (1988) Mission Training. Thesis (D. Min.). New York: New York Theological Seminary.

18689. Smith, Christine. (1988) St. Bartholomew's Church in the City of New York. New York: Oxford University Press.

18690. Smith, Dennis. (1988) "In Pursuit of the Urban Variable," Journal of Urban History. Vol. 14, No. 3 (May), pp. 399-405. A review article: Derek Fraser and Anthony Sutcliff, eds. (1983). Smith urges even broader cross-disciplinary strategies than envisioned by Fraser and Sutcliff. Bibliography.

18691. Smith, Edward D. (1988) Climbing Jacob's Ladder: The Rise of Black Churches in Eastern American Cities, 1740-1877. Washington, DC: The Smithsonian Institution. A popular history with attractive illustrations. A large bibliography is arranged by denomination and city sub-categories.

18692. Smith, Eunice and Cecil Smith. (1988) "A 'David' Church in a 'Goliath' City," The Alliance Witness. Vol. 122, No. 4 (February 18), pp. 16-17.

18693. Smith, Glenn, ed. (1988) Evangelizing Blacks. Wheaton, IL: Tyndale House. Papers on the history and mission of Black churches, especially Roman Catholic churches.

18694. Smith, Greg. (1988) Christianity in the Inner City: Some Sociological Issues. London: MARC Europe. Smith, at the time of writing, was associated with the Evangelical Coalition for Urban Mission (ECUM). Bibliography.

18695. Smith, Walter J. (1988) AIDS: Living and Dying with Hope--Issues in Pastoral Care. New York: Paulist Press. Re: pastoral work in urban churches and the urgency of the AIDS crisis.

18696. Snyder, T. Richard. (1988) Once You Were No People: The Church and the Transformation of Society. Bloomington, IN: Meyer-Stone Books. Snyder attacks the root causes of alienation, suffering, and classism, i.e., the bondage of White, male, first world perspectives. Liberation dictates an agenda for the oppressors as well as for the oppressed. Snyder, himself a White first world male, at the time of writing was professor at New York Theological Seminary.

18697. Sontag, Susan. (1988) AIDS and Its Metaphors. New York: Farrar, Straus, Giroux. A bibliographic study of the AIDS crisis with some attention to church-relateced efforts.

18698. Stackhouse, Max L. (1988) Apologia: Contextualization, Globalization, and Mission in Theological Education. Grand Rapids, MI: Eerdmans. Theological education related to the church's mission. At the time of writing, Stackhouse was a professor at Andover-Newton Theological School.

18699. [Tim Stair, compiler]. (1988) Urban Task Force Report: Surveys and Profiles of Urban Mennonite Congregations. Elkhart, IN: Mennonite Board of Missions. A survey of Anabaptist congregations located in cities which are in some way addressing urban issues. Mimeographed.

18700. Stepp, Laura Sessions. (1988) "Black Church Losing Historic Role: Drug Use, Teen pregnancies Seen as Consequence," Washington Post. (August 20), p. A-1.

18701. Stevens, William K. (1988) "Lama Who Grew in Brooklyn," New York Times. Vol. 138 (October 16), pp. 1, 8. Catharine Burroughs described as a tulku.

18702. Steward, David S. and Rebecca Slough. (1988) "Theological Schooling for Ministry with the Marginalized: Supervision as a Context for Learning," Religious Education. Vol. 83, No. 3 (Summer), pp. 412-422.

18703. Stobaugh, James P. (1988) "Major Ministry on Modest Means," Leadership. Vol. 9, No. 3 (Summer), pp. 70-76. Re: Fourth Presbyterian Church, Pittsburgh, PA, and its efforts to address urban issues with its limited resources.

18704. Stockwell, Clinton E. (1988) "Resources for Urban Mission," The Other Side [Thematic issue: Urban ministry]. Vol. 24, No. 4 (May), pp. 36-47.

18705. Stone, Ronald H. (1988) "The Urban Ethos of Seminary Education," pp. 45-65 in Dieter T. Hessel, ed. Theological Education for Social Ministry. New York: Pilgrim Press. Implications of the Pittsburgh, PA, environment for a Presbyterian theological seminary.

18706. Sumiya, Mikio. (1988) "Urban Mission in Japan," Japan Christian Quarterly. Vol. 54, No. 4 (Fall), pp. 197-203.

18707. Swing, William Edwin. (1988) "Silence in the Sanctuaries," Christianity and Crisis [Thematic issue: AIDS]. Vol. 48, No. 10 (July 4), pp. 225-227. Congregations confront the AIDS crisis.

18708. Syracuse, Ross M. (1988) "Alienation and the Church," Journal of Pastoral Counseling. Vol. 23, No. 1, pp. 75-88.

18709. Tamney, Joseph B., Ronald Burton and Stephen D. Johnson. (1988) "Christianity, Social Class, and the Catholic Bishops' Economic Policy," Sociological Analysis. Vol. 49, Supplement (December), pp. s79-s96. Catholic and liberal Protestants call for change in the economic order while fundamentalists defend it. The authors analyze data which reflect the degree to which people are persuaded by the positions of religious bodies on the economy.

18710. Tamoush, Vivki. (1988) "A New Anti-Semitism," The Other Side. Vol. 12 No. 1 (January-February), pp. 24-25. Anti-Arab prejudices in the United States.

18711. Taylor, Barbara Brown. (1988) "Cities 1988: The New Wilderness," The Witness [Ambler, PA]. Vol. 71, No. 1 (January), pp. 14-17.

18712. Taylor, Barbara Brown. (1988) "Keeping Our Feet on the Ground," The Witness [Ambler, PA]. Vol. 71, No. 2 (February), pp. 14-17.

18713. Taylor, Gavin M. (1988) Mutual Strangers. Thesis (D. Min.). New York: New York Theological Seminary.

18714. Taylor, Robert J. (1988) "Correlates of Religious Non-Involvement among Black Americans," Review of Religious Research. Vol. 30, No. 3 (December), pp. 126-139.

18715. Tillapaugh, Frank R. (1988) Unleashing Your Potential: Discovering Your God Given Opportunities for Ministry. Ventura, CA: Regal Books.

18716. Trotman, C. James. (1988) "Mathew Anderson: Black Pastor, Churchman, and Social Reformer," American Presbyterians. Vol. 66, No. 1 (Spring), pp. 11-21. Matthew Anderson, in 1880 the founder and pastor of Berean Church (Presbyterian), started a bank and a vocational training school, all bearing the name Berean. This article provides a brief biography and a listing of primary documents. At a time when Philadelphia's Blacks were experiencing an undeniably anti-Black and feverishly racist social order, Berean Church became the platform from which Anderson launched his programs of social reform and social service . He therefore becomes an early prototype for 20th century urban Black church ministries.

18717. Turner, Richard B. (1988) "The Ahmadiyya Mission to Blacks in the United States in the 1920s," Journal of Religious Thought. Vol. 44 (Winter-Spring), pp. 50-66.

18718. Turrentine, Jan. (1988) Always a Friend: The Story of Mildred McWhorter. Birmingham, AL: New Hope. Biography of a missionary serving in the inner city of Houston, Texas.

18719. Van, Byung Sub. (1988) Guidelines for Korean Ministry in the United Church of Canada. Thesis (D. Min.). San Anselmo, CA: San Francisco Theological Seminary.

18720. Van Anda, Jackie. (1988) "A New Role for Labor: Texas Workers Try Self-Determination," Christianity and Crisis. Vol. 48, No. 2 (February 15), pp. 39-42. Re: the Amalgamated Clothing and Textile Workers' Union.

18721. Van Eyl, Chris. (1988) "Big Work in the City," Church Herald [Thematic issue: Urban ministry]. Vol. 45, No. 20 (November 18), pp. 8-11. Van Eyl describes urban ministries of the Reformed Church in America. For additional information on urban ministries in the RCA, see the periodical titled: The City Gate, published by the denomination's Office of Social Witness, beginning 1986.

18722. Van Houten, Mark. (1988) God's Inner-City Address: Crossing the Boundaries. Grand Rapids, MI: Ministry Resources Library, Zondervan. A minister to street people in Northside Chicago discerns God's presence in cities.

18723. Walch, Timothy, general ed. (1988) The Heritage of American Catholicism. New York: Garland. A 28 volume series documenting the history of the Catholic Church in the USA contains on ethnic groups, urban characteristics of Catholicism, and parochial schools, among many other topics.

18724. Wald, Kenneth D., Dennis E. Ewen and Samuel S. Hill, Jr. (1988) "Churches as Political Communities," American Political Science Review. Vol. 82, No. 2 (June), pp. 531-548.

18725. Waldecker, Gary. (1988) "The City--The Eschatological Garden," Urban Mission. Vol. 5, No. 4 (March), pp. 18-26.

18726. Walker, Andrew. (1988) Restoring the Kingdom: the Radical Christianity of the House Church Movement. London: Hodder and Stoughton.

18727. Washington, Joseph R., Jr. (1988) Race and Religion in Early Nineteenth Century America, 1800-1850, Constitution, Conscience, and Calvinist Compromise. [Two volumes]. Lewiston, NY: Edwin Mellon Press. In spite of the author's heavy writing style -- alliteration and the interminably long sentences -- this book represents an important effort to tell the history of religion and race from the perspective of African Americans. Much in these two volumes relates to cities.

18728. Washington, Joseph R., Jr. (1988) Race and Religion in Mid-Nineteenth Century America, 1850-1877, Protestant Parochial Philanthropists. [Two volumes]. Lewiston, NY: Edwin Mellon Press.

18729. Washington, Preston R. (1988) God's Transforming Spirit: Black Church Renewal. Valley Forge, PA: Judson Press. Re: church renewal in Memorial Baptist Church, Harlem, New York City.

18730. Watt, William Montgomery. (1988) Islamic Fundamentalism and Modernity. London: Routledge.

18731. Webber, George Williams. (1988) "The Center for Urban Ministerial Education." [Location: Photocopy report, CUME, Gordon Conwell Theological Seminary, Hamilton, MA].

18732. Welch, Elizabeth. (1988) "Living in a United Church in the Continuing Search for Unity," pp. 39-48 in Thomas F. Best, ed. Living Today towards Visible Unity. Geneva, Switzerland: World Council of Churches.

18733. Whyte, William Hollingsworth. (1988) City: Rediscovering the Center. New York: Doubleday. Much of city planing is wrongheaded and ignores the needs of people. Whyte questions whether or not decentralization has progressed to such an extent that the "center" will collapse. With industries, shopping areas, offices, and apartment buildings all moving to suburbs, what new meaning will the center have? Bibliography.

18734. Wilkerson, Isabel. (1988) "Detroit Citizens Join with

Church to Rid Community of Drugs," New York Times. (June 14), pp. c-1, c-14.

18735. Williams, Cecil. (1988) Spirituality and Social Responsibility [videorecording]. Berkeley, CA: Conference Recording Service. Recorded October, 1988, at the International Transpersonal Conference in Santa Rosa, CA.

18736. Willimon, William H. (1988) "Millard Fuller's Theology of the Hammer," Christian Century. Vol. 105, No. 28 (October 5), pp. 862-863. Re: Habitat for Humanity.

18737. Wilson, Basil and Charles Green. (1988) The Black Church and the Struggle for Community Empowerment in New York City," Afro-Americans in New York Life and History. Vol. 12, No. 1 (January), pp. 51-80.

18738. Wilson, Pip. (1988) Games without Frontiers: Growth and Development Games for Group Workers. Basingstoke, England: Marshalls.

18739. Wilson, Samuel. (1988) "Why Love the City?: How Do We Get Over Our Urban Fears?" World Christian. Vol. 7, No. 1 (January), pp. 16-19+.

18740. Wimberly, Anne Streaty. (1988) "Spiritual Care for the Homeless," Explor: A Journal of Theology [Garrett-Evangelical Theological Seminary]. Vol. 9 (Spring), pp. 83-107.

18741. Wimberly, Anne Streaty and Edward Powell Wimberly. (1988) One Household, One Hope: Building Ethnic Minority Clergy Family Support Networks. Nashville, TN: Division of Ordained Ministry, Board of Higher Education and Ministry, The United Methodist Church.

18742. Windsor, Pat. (1988) "Detroiters Vow to Defy Closing of City Churches," National Catholic Reporter. Vol. 24 (October 14), pp. 1+.

18743. Wolterstorff, Nicholas. (1988) "Liturgy, Justice, and Tears," Worship. Vol. 62, No. 5 (September), pp. 386-403.

18744. Wood, Ralph C. (1988) "British Churches Encounter the Challenge of Pluralism," The Christian Century. Vol. 105, No. 30 (October 19), pp. 923-926. Comment on the vitality of the church in

Britain.

18745. Wood, Stephanie. (1988) "The Red Lights of Chicago: A Case Study in Urban Ministry," World Christian. Vol. 7, No. 1 (January), pp. 20-21. Re: the evangelistic work of Robert Linthicum with prostitutes.

18746. Zabaneh, Ibranim K. (1988) Training a Task Force of Selected Church Members to Plant and Pastor Indigenous Satellite Units in Apartments. Thesis (D. Min.). Fort Worth, TX: Southwestern Baptist Theological Seminary.

18747. Zanotelli, Alex. (1988) "Facing Problems of Rapid Urbanization," AFER: African Ecclesial Review (Gaba). Vol. 30, No. 5 (October), pp. 277-284.

18748. Zubatsky, David S. (1988) Jewish Autobiographies and Biographies: An International Bibliography of Books and Dissertations in English. New York: Garland. Covers the 19th century through 1988.

18749. Aageson, James W. (1989) "City-Building and the Benefit of Babel," Christian Century. Vol. 106, No. 17 (May 17), pp. 517-518. Aageson reflects on the human aspiration to build and the metaphor of Babel. If a city speaks any sort of theological language, it's time for God again to confuse our tongues and scatter us abroad.

18750. Abernathy, Ralph David. (1989) And the Walls Came Tumbling Down. New York: Harper and Row. Abernathy debunks some of the myths about Martin Luther King, Jr. Editorially reviewed: James M. Wall. "Abernathy Takes a Cheap Shot," Christian Century. Vol. 106, No. 32 (November 1, 1989), p. 971.

18751. Addy, Tony [Anthony J.]. (1989) "Community Work in the Inner City Church," pp. 71-84 in British Council of Churches. Changing the Agenda. London: the Council.

18752. [Addy, Tony [Anthony J.]], et al. (1989) Community Work in the New Context: Addresses to the 1989 Church and Community Work Conference. Manchester, England: The William Temple Foundation for the Conference. Includes papers dealing with the church and social change on three levels in Great Britain: Tony Addy (national level), Carol Burns (city level), and Barbara Hancock (community level).

18753. Ahern, Dennis M. (1989) "Modernity: Scaffolding or

Stumbling Block for a Chinese Gospel," Missiology. Vol. 17, No. 3 (July), pp. 321-333. Missionary thinking in China has yet to make the shift from the rural rice fields to the modern cities. Views of modernity and missionary training are discussed. Bibliography.

18754. Alliance for Detroit Churches. (n. d., 1989?) The Rest of the Story. [Detroit, MI: the Alliance]. A collection of letters, documents, rebuttals, and news clippings amassed for the purpose of protesting Cardinal Szoka's announced closing of city parishes in Detroit.

18755. Antonides, Harry. (1989) A Christian Perspective on Work and Labour Relations. Potchefstroom, South Africa: Institute for Reformational Studies. A pamphlet.

18756. Arango, Luz Gabriela. (1989) Mujer, religion e industria: Fabricato, 1923-1982. Medellin, Colombia: Editorial Universidad de Antioguia, Universidad Externado de Colombia. Re: the church and women textile workers in Medellin, Colombia. Bibliography.

18757. Arthur, Thomas. (1989) "Urban Ministry as Exodus," The Christian Ministry [Thematic issue: Urban Ministry Today]. Vol. 20, No. 2 (March-April), pp. 8-9. A Chicago native migrates to Wales to serve as pastor in a "council estate," i.e., a government housing project for the poor near Cardiff.

18758. Ateshin, Hussein Mehmet. (1989) "Urbanization and the Environment: An Islamic Perspective," pp. 163-194 in Ziauddin Sarder, ed. An Early Cresent. London: Mansell.

18759. Austin, John. (1989) "Some Challenges to the Church Arising from Community Development," pp. 57-70 in British Council of Churches. Changing the Agenda. London: the Council.

18760. Badiee, Julie. (1989) "Mark Tobey's City Paintings: Meditations on an Age of Transition," The Journal of Baha'i Studies. Vol. 1, No. 4, pp. 21-39. A study of Tobey's paintings from the 1930s to the 1950s shows they may be interpreted as a reiteration of traditional themes of apocalypse, Hell, judgment day, and the New Jerusalem. This varies from the usual interpretation of the paintings as being merely exuberant expressions of city life, but takes into account Tobey's connections to the Baha'i Faith.

18761. Bakke, Raymond J. (1989) "A Theology as Big as the City," Urban Mission. Vol. 6, No. 5 (May), pp. 8-19.

18762. Ballard, Paul. (1989) "Employment and Contemporary Living," Crucible. [Vol. 18, No. 3] (July-September), pp. 126-131. Ballard identifies and describes five varieties of work ethics: adversarial, instrumental, service, humanistic and corporative.

18763. Barry, Patrick. (1989) Rebuilding the Walls: A Nuts and Bolts Guide to the Community Development Methods of Bethel New Life, Inc. in Chicago. Chicago, IL: Bethel New Life. Re: church-based community development projects in Chicago. Bibliography.

18764. Barton, Carol and Barbara Weaver. (1989) The Global Debt Crisis: A Question of Justice. Washington, DC: Interfaith Foundation; Interfaith Action for Economic Justice. A study guide with suggestions for action and worship. Bibliography.

18765. Beames, Barry. (1989) "Ministry in the Shadows of the City," Church Administration. Vol. 31, No. 12 (September), pp. 6-8. Re: ministry to suburban commuters.

18766. Beaulieu, Don. (1989) "Not another Shelter: A Community of the Poor in Roanoke," Other Side [Thematic issue: Housing]. Vol. 25, No. 6 (November), pp. 12-14.

18767. Bemont, Marc. (1989) "A Special Ministry," One World. No. 143 (March), pp. 14-16.

18768. Berg, Kay Kupper. (1989) "Christian Literacy, the Core Curriculum, and the Urban Church," pp. 50-59 in Donald B. Rogers, ed. Urban Church Education. Birmingham, AL: Religious Education Press.

18769. Billings, Alan. (1989) "From Dreaming Spires to Minarets," Crucible. [Vol. 28, No. 2] (April-June), pp. 60-64. Re: multicultural aspects of British cities.

18770. Bloomquist, Karen L. (1989) The Dream Betrayed: Religious Challenge of the Working Class. Minneapolis, MN: Fortress. In her analysis of social class in America, Bloomquist concludes the American dream is entrapped by individualizing, victimizing, and privatizing. She calls the church to be midwife for a new community of justice, people who help people to become upwardly mobile and to succeed in fulfilling the American dream. An edition of the author's dissertation. Bibliography.

18771. Bobsin, Oneide. (1989) "Lutheranos: migracao, urbanizacao e proletarizacao: observavoes introdutorias," Estudos Teologicos. Vol. 29, No. 2, pp. 207-227. Lutherans: migration, urbanization, and the proletariat.

18772. Boerma, Coenraad. (1989) The Poor Side of Europe: The Church and the (New) Poor of Western Europe. Geneva, Switzerland: World Council of Churches.

18773. Boint, Steve. (1989) "The Blue-Collar Worker and the Church," Urban Mission. Vol. 6, No. 4 (March), pp. 6-17.

18774. Bolton, Robert J. (1989) "Your Urban Church Ministry: A 'Waterloo' or a 'Wellington?'" Urban Mission. Vol. 6, No. 3 (January), pp. 24-36.

18775. Boomershine, Tom. (1989) "Biblical Story Telling in the City," pp. 142-151 in Donald B. Rogers, ed. Urban Church Education. Birmingham, AL: Religious Education Press.

18776. Boyte, Harry C. (1989) Moving into Power: Reenvigorating Public Life for the 1990s. Chicago, IL: Community Renewal Society. Bibliography.

18777. Bradbury, Nicholas. (1989) City of God? Pastoral Care in the Inner City. London: SPCK. Bradbury, vicar of Holy Trinity, Totenham, London, claims that the Archbishop of Canterbury's Commission on Urban Priority Areas insufficiently takes into account the importance of pastoral care as an inner city strategy. He outlines theology and recommends strategies for pastoral care. Reviewed: City Cries. No. 21 (Spring, 1990), p. 20.

18778. Breault, Kevin D. (1989) "New Evidence on Religious Pluralism, Urbanism and Religious Participation," American Sociological Review. Vol. 54, No. 6 (December), pp. 1048-1053. Breault questions the findings of Finke and Stark (1988) that religious adherence is positively associated with pluralism and urbanization. Finke and Stark offer a reply, and Breault submits a rejoinder.

18779. Brichett, Colleen. (1989) "A History of Religious Education in the Black Church," pp. 71-83 in Donald B. Rogers, ed. Urban Church Education. Birmingham, AL: Religious Education Press.

18780. Briggs, John H., ed. (1989) "Baptists in the City," [London] Baptist Quarterly [Thematic issue]. Vol. 33 (January), pp. 2-50.

18781. Brockman, James R. (1989) Romero: A Life. Maryknoll, NY: Orbis. Oscar Romero, Archbishop of San Salvador, was assassinated while saying mass March 24, 1980. This biography describes him as a champion of the poor and a symbol of the power of truth over oppression. The assassination was a major event in the war in El Slavador, and the focus of serveral inquiries.

18782. Brown, Robert McAfee and Sydney T. Brown. (1989) A Cry for Justice. New York: Paulist. Reflections on the statements issued by religious groups -- Protestant, Catholic and Jewish -- about economic justice. A directory of documents is included.

18783. Bryant, David. (1989) "How Do You Pray for a City?" Latin American Evangelist. Vol. 69, No. 1 (January-March). [See note 3].

18784. Budde, Heiner. (1989) Man nannte sie "rote" Kaplane: Priester an der Seite der Arbeiter: Skizzen zur christlichen Sozialtradition. Köln, Germany: Ketteler. Re: church and labor in Germany. Bibliography.

18785. Bunting, Ian D. (1989) Claiming the Urban Village. Bramcote, Nottinghamshire, England: Grove Booklets on Evangelism, No. 6. A pamphlet.

18786. Burgess, David S. (1989) "Struggling for Christian Unity in a Divided City," pp. 278-289 in F. Littell, ed. The Growth of Interreligious Dialogue, 1939-1989. s.l.: Mellen, Toronto Studies in Theology.

18787. Burks, Janet. (1989) "Seminary in the Streets: The Network Center for the Study of Christian Ministry," Christianity and Crisis. Vol. 49, Nos. 5-6 (April 3), pp. 117-121. Network Ministries in San Francisco offers opportunities for students to study theology in the city environment. The program's greatest effects, according to director Glenda Hope, are on the faculty members who come from the seminaries to teach there. Some have torn up their prepared notes and started all over again when they find their old materials ill suited to city circumstances. All students receive spiritual guidance from a city mentor whose faith has been street tested.

18788. Burstin, Barbara Stern. (1989) After the Holocaust: The Migration of Polish Jews and Christians to Pittsburgh. Pittsburgh, PA: University of Pittsburgh Press.

18789. Camacho, Eduardo and Ben Joravsky. (1989) Against the Tide: The Middle Class in Chicago. Chicago, IL: Community Renewal Society. Dwindling numbers of middle class people in Chicago threaten the efficiency of the city government, and may portend the death of the city. Based on neighborhood profiles and interviews with Chicago middle class and affluent residents, this book records the insights of the respondents with little comment from the authors. Efforts to keep the middle class from leaving the city are advocated.

18790. Cascia, Philip J. (1989) Human Services in the Church's Urban Evangelization. Thesis (D. Min.). Hartford, CT: Hartford Seminary. Evangelism effected by means of soup kitchens and shelters for the homeless.

18791. Cetina, Judith G. (1989) "In Times of Immigration," pp. 86-117 in Ursula Stepsis and Dolores Liptak, eds. Pioneer Healers. New York: Crossroads. Bibliography.

18792. Chee, Winfred See-Hing. (1989) A Strategy for Training Members of Chinese Churches in Sydney to Implement a Program for the Evangelization of Chinese-Speaking Vietnamese. Thesis (D. Min.). San Anselmo, CA: San Francisco Theological Seminary.

18793. Church of England, Board for Social Responsibility, Industrial and Economic Affairs Committee. (1989) Church and Economy: Effective Industrial Mission for the 1990s. London: the Board. A follow-up to an earlier study titled: Industrial Mission, an Appraisal (1988).

18794. Churches' Center for Theology and Public Policy. (beginning in 1989) Theology and Public Policy. Washington, DC: the Center. A periodical.

18795. Clapp, Rodney. (1989) "The Church Picnic Goes to Jail," Christianity Today. Vol. 33, No. 9 (June 16), pp. 14-15.

18796. Cockerell, David. (1989) Beginning Where We Are. London: SCM. Re: labor and laboring classes in Great Britain.

18797. Coco, Jean-Pierre and Joseph Debs. (1989) 1937, l'elan jociste: le dixième anniversaire de la JOC, Paris, Juillet 1937. Paris: Editions Ouvrières. Re: Jeunesse ouvrière chrétienne in France and the church in relation to the employment of youth.

18798. Coffey, Ian, et al. (1989) No Stranger in the City: God's Concern for Urban People. Leicester, England: InterVarsity. A volume of evangelical protestant perspectives on the city includes essays by Raymond Bakke and Harvie Conn, among others.

18799. Cohn-Sherbok, Dan. (1989) "Faith in the City: A Jewish Response," pp. 114-132 in Anthony Harvey, ed. Theology in the City: A Theological Response to Faith in the City. London: SPCK.

18800. Coleman, Peter. (1989) "Occupied Territory?" Theology. Vol. 92, No. 749 (September), pp. 361-363. Comment regarding urban whites moving to rural areas in England.

18801. Colon, John E. (1989) "Reaching Out: A City Boy Goes to Camp: A Look at a Christian Herald Ministry," Christian Herald. Vol. 112, No. 8 (September), pp. 29-30. Colon, an officer for the Episcopal Church Center, New York City, describes the Christian Herald's summer camping program which attracts 1000 city children.

18802. Conn, Harvie M. (1989) "Urbanization and Its Implications," pp. 62-83 in J. Dudley Woodberry, ed. Muslims and Christians on the Emmaus Road. Monrovia, CA: MARC Publications.

18803. Conn, Harvie M. (1989) "A Few Tested Ways to Keep an Urban Church from Growing," Urban Mission. Vol. 7, No. 1 (September), pp. 3-6.

18804. Costas, Orlando E. (1989) Liberating News: A Theology of Contextual Evangelization. Grand Rapids, MI: Eerdmans. Costas promotes radical social concern as an expression of evangelical commitment.

18805. Council of Churches of Greater Seattle. (1989) State of the City: Children and Youth at Risk. Seattle, WA: the Council.

18806. Crichton, Iain. (1989) Ghostwriting: A Tool for Getting Oral Urban Church Leaders in Print. Thesis (D. Min). Chestnut Hill, PA: Westminster Theological Seminary.

18807. Cronin, Deborah Kay. (1989) Worship in the "Post-Industrial"/"Rust Belt" Urban Church. Thesis (D. Min.) Washington, DC: Wesley Theological Seminary.

18808. Cross, Dale W. (1989) An Evaluation of Approaches for Urban Mission: Discovering Indicators of Effectiveness. Thesis (D.

Min). Chestnut Hill, PA: Westminster Theological Seminary.

18809. Cuneo, Michael W. (1989) Catholics Against the Church: Anti-Abortion Protest in Toronto, 1969-1985. Toronto, Canada: University of Toronto Press. A study of pro-life movements in Anglo-Canada, based on interviews. Reviewed: Review of Religious Research. Vol. 32, No. 4 (June, 1991), pp. 371-372.

18810. Dawson, John. (1989) Taking Our Cities for God: How to Break Spiritual Strongholds. Lake Mary, FL: Creation House. Dawson, leader in a nondenominational organization named Youth with a Mission, offers hands-on strategies for evangelical Protestant warfare for Christ in urban settings. Every city has staggering problems and is beset by cosmic spirits, Dawson contends. The city and its history can be redeemed through the concerted battle of Christians who evangelize their city for God. Reviewed positively: Urban Connections. Vol. 7, No. 4 (Winter, 1991), p. 7.

18811. Deck, Allan Figueroa. (1989) The Second Wave: Hispanic Ministry and the Evangelization of Culture. New York: Paulist. Re: Ministry with Mexicans in southwestern USA following World War II through the 1980s. Deck has had experience in community organization, parish work, diocesan ministries, and immigrant work. Demographic, cultural, and social characteristics of Mexican American immigrants are described with appreciation, emphasizing their contribution to Anglo culture.

18812. Delooz, Pierre. (1989) "Does Development Lead to Secularization?" Pro Mundi Vita Studies. No. 11 (September), pp. 2-35. Contains articles on Latin American, African, Islamic, Chinese, Buddhist, and Jewish perspectives on cultural space. Bibliography.

18813. De Smet, Kate. (1989) "Hard Times in the Archdiocese of Detroit," The Critic. (Summer), pp. 3-17. Cardinal Szoka closed 30 parishes in Detroit that, in his judgment, could not become self supporting. Other parishes must prove their viability.

18814. Doane, Jeffrey. (1989) "Renewed Possibilities for Urban Ministry," The Christian Ministry [Thematic issue: Urban Ministry Today]. Vol. 20, No. 2 (March-April), pp. 28-30.

18815. Dolan, Jay P. (1989) "Religion and Social Change in the American Catholic Community," pp. 42-60 in David W. Lotz, Donald W. Shriver, Jr., and John F. Wilson, eds. Altered Landscapes: Christianity in America, 1935-1985. Grand Rapids, MI: William B. Eerdmans.

Dolan stresses the importance of social change and the civil rights movement for Black and Hispanic Catholics.

18816. Donovan, Vincent J. (1989) The Church in the Midst of Creation. Maryknoll, NY: Orbis. Re: Catholic church renewal. Bibliography.

18817. Downes, Stan, Robert Oehrig, and John Shane, et al. (1989) Summary of the Nairobi Church Survey. Nairobi, Kenya: Daystar University College. Survey research on membership and program characteristics of Nairobi's 800 city churches. This volume summarizes a larger report titled: Nairobi: Christian Outreach in a World-Class City.

18818. Dudley, Carl S. and Sally A. Johnson. (1989) "Saints, Crises, and Other Memories that Energize the Church," Alban Institute Action Information. Vol. 15, No. 1 (January-February), No. 2 (March-April).

18819. Dudley, Carl S. and Sally A. Johnson. (1989) "Mobilizing Congregations for Community Ministry," The Christian Ministry [Thematic issue: Urban Ministry Today]. Vol. 20, No. 2 (March-April), pp. 31-33. The authors report results of a project involving 40 midwestern congregations in efforts to plan and organize their parishes--the Church and Community Project.

18820. Duin, Julie. (1989) "Aliquippa's Star Attraction," Christianity Today. Vol. 33, No. 1 (January 13), pp. 14-16. Re: community support for unemployed steel workers in Pennsylvania.

18821. Dumper, Tony. (1989) "Community Organization in America," Crucible. [Vol. 28, No. 4] (October-December), pp. 172-174. Dumper comments on the Industrial Areas Foundation's interest in church-based community organization.

18822. Duncan, Michael. (1989) "Serving Christ in the Slums: An Interview with Owen Salter," Evangelical Missions Quarterly. Vol. 25 (January), pp. 6-19.

18823. Eck, Diana L. (1989) My Neighbor's Faith: Ordinary Christians and the Challenge of Religious Pluralism. [Sound cassette, 50 minutes]. Denver, CO: Iliff School of Theology.

18824. Eelwanger, William. (1989) Proposed Curriculum for a Bible Training School for Urban Ministry, an Extension of Olivet

Nazarene University in Chicago. Thesis (D. Miss.). Deerfield, IL: Trinity Evangelical Divinity School.

18825. Ellison, Craig W. (1989) "Understanding Current Urban Realities," United Urban Action [Thematic issue: Reading the city]. Vol. 48, No. 3 (May-June), pp. 4-6.

18826. Estes, Sue. (1989) "On the Frontline of Urban Ministry," New World Outlook. Vol. 49, No. 3 (March-April), pp. 12-15. Re: the United Methodist center in Topeka, Kansas.

18827. Everett, William Johnson. (1989) "Transformation at Work," pp. 153-176 in Allen J. Moore, ed. Religious education as Social Transformation. Birmingham, AL: Religious Education Press.

18828. Falk, Lawrence L. (1989) "Doing Your Own Urban Church Research," pp. 114-126 in Donald B. Rogers, ed. Urban Church Education. Birmingham, AL: Religious Education Press.

18829. Farrell, Edward J. (1989) Free to Be Nothing. Collegeville, MN: Liturgical Press. A case study of St. Agnes Catholic Church, Detroit, MI, and its work with the poor.

18830. Faulkner, James R. (1989) An Innovative Approach to Branch Church Ministry: A Study of Three Baptist Churches. Thesis (D. Min.). Deerfield, IL: Trinity Evangelical Divinity School.

18831. Federation for Industrial Retention and Renewal [FIRR]. (beginning in 1989) News. Chicago, IL: the Federation. This quarterly newsletter is produced by a federation of action groups which address the problems of plant closing and industrial renewal. The membership of the constituent groups is largely made up of local churches and judicatories, ecumenical organizations, community organizations and labor unions. Issues of the newsletter deal with economic policy, organizational techniques, lists of corporations that are notoriously involved in plant closings, and news of the FIRR affiliates.

18832. Felder, Cain H. (1989) Troubling Biblical Waters: Race, Class, and Families. Maryknoll, NY: Orbis. Bibliography.

18833. Finkel, David. (1989) "One Point of Light," Esquire. Vol. 112, No. 4 (October), pp. 123-128+.

18834. Fish, John H. and John Kretzmann. (1989) "Reviving Mexico City: Neighborhood by Neighborhood," Christian Century.

Vol. 106, No. 36 (November 29), pp. 1116-1118. Church based people's movements make progress in communities considered hopelessly impoverished and disorganized.

18835. Fisher, James C. (1989) The Catholic Counter Culture in America, 1933-1962. Chapel Hill, NC: University of North Carolina Press. Fisher describes the contributions of several Catholic literary and social movement authors, including Peter Maurin, Dorothy Day, Thomas Merton, and Jack Kerouac.

18836. Fones-Wolf, Kenneth Alan. (1989) Trade Union Gospel: Christianity and Labor in Industrial Philadelphia, 1865-1915. Philadelphia, PA: Temple University Press. Fones-Wolf, in the process of his inquiry into the significance of the Labor Forward Movement, compares Catholic and Protestant views on labor and desribes labor's views on the church. The Labor Forward Movement was an attempt on the part of the American Federation of Labor to use evangelicalism to organize workers. Fones-Wolf challenges the widely held view that evangelical Protestantism consistently served to help employers maintain control over workers. Extensive bibiographical references, including many citations from labor periodicals. Fones-Wolf draws on materials preserved in the Urban Archive Center, Temple University.

18837. Forbes, James. (1989) The Holy Spirit and Preaching. Nashville, TN: Abingdon. Forbes, first African American pastor of New York City's Riverside Church, explains his philosophy of preaching. Forbes's heritage is in the United Holy Church of America. Bibliography.

18838. Foster, Charles I. and Grant S. Shockley, eds. (1989) Working with Black Youth: Opportunities for Christian Ministry. Nashville, TN: Abingdon. Articles intended for both urban and rural youth ministry.

18839. Franklin, Robert Michael. (1989) "Church and City: Black Christianity's Ministry," The Christian Ministry [Thematic issue: Urban Ministry Today]. Vol. 20, No. 2 (March-April), pp. 17-19. The Church of God in Christ, a rapidly growing Holiness group, seeks to humanize the city through its worship styles.

18840. Fuechtmann, Thomas Gerhard. (1989) Steeples and Stacks: Religion and Steel Crisis in Youngstown. New York: Cambridge University Press. Feuchtmann traces the history of the relationship between religion and industry in Youngstown, OH, from 1900 to the crisis of plant closings in the 1970s. Particular attention is given to the Ecumenical Coalition that fought the plant closings. The volume is based on Feuchtmann's 1982 dissertation at the University of Chicago. Bibliography.

18841. Gafke, Arthur and Bruce McSpadden. (1989) Pastor-as-Organizer: A Model for Pastoral Ministry [Second draft]. s.l.: the authors. Two United Methodist clergy in California advocate a model of pastoral ministry based on concepts of community organization, especially the criteria of relationships, organization, and empowerment. Both of the authors have experience in urban ministry and work with poor people. Their preparation of the written description of the model was supported by the Fund for Theological Education.

18842. Gallagher, Eric. (1989) At Points of Need: The Story of the Belfast Central Mission, Grosvenor Hall, 1889-1989. St. Paul, MN: Blackstaff Press.

18843. Gambrell, Bill. (1989) "Urban Church Growth through Adult Religious Education," pp. 135-141 in Donald B. Rogers, ed. Urban Church Education. Birmingham, AL: Religious Education Press.

18844. Gannon, Ann Ida. (1989) "Perspectives on Women in Business," Chicago Studies. Vol. 28, No. 1 (April), pp. 47-64.

18845. Giamatti, A. Bartlett. (1989) Take Time for Paradise: Americans and Their Games. New York: Summit Books, Simon and Schuster. Giamatti, a university professor turned baseball commissioner, rejects the notion that sport has its origin in religion but contends that sport has ritual functions akin to religious activity. Sport is a form of Aristotelian leisure, not a remnant of primitive religions. Leisure, as defined in Giamatti's subtle line of argument, has qualities similar to religion, and even generates its own version of paradise, but may ultimately be subversive of religion as consequences. Giamatti is relentlessly pro-city and sport is the quintessential urban activity of will and imagination. Sports, like cities, are political, willful, and artificial -- qualities Giamatti admires because they require human choices. He rejects the theory advanced in some sociological and anthropological circles that sport is desacralized religion.

18846. Gilkey, Bertha. (1989?) Come See What I'm Say'n. Chicago, IL: Community Renewal Society. A pamphlet.

18847. Glaves, Brenda. (1989) "Change Is Coming in Our Churches," pp. 23-31 in British Council of Churches. Changing the Agenda. London: the Council.

18848. Gokalp, Altan. (1989) "Mirage "alla turca:" la tradition sera-t-elle de la noce?" Archives de Sciences Sociales des Religions. Vol. 34 (July-September), pp. 51-63. Bibliography.

18849. Goldingay, John. (1989) "The Bible in the City," Theology. Vol. 92, No. 745 (January), pp. 5-15. A study of biblical sources for a theology of the city, as mandated by the Archbishop's Commission in its report: Faith in the City.

18850. Goldman, Ari L. (1989) "Mainstream Islam Rapidly Embraced by Black Americans," New York Times. (February 21), pp. 1, B-4.

18851. Gorday, Peter. (1989) "Raimundo Panikkar: Pluralism without Relativism," Christian Century. Vol. 106, No. 37 (December 6), pp. 1147-1149. Reviews Panikkar's work on cultural and religious diversity.

18852. Grady, Duane. (1989) Helping the Homeless. Elgin, IL: Brethren Press. Stories and sermons about homeless people and the church's response. Bibliography.

18853. Gratton, Thomas A. (1989) Strategizing an Effective Ministry in an Urban, Evangelical, and Racially Integrated Southern Baptist Church. Thesis (D. Min.). Philadelphia, PA: Eastern Baptist Theological Seminary.

18854. Greenway, Roger S. and Timothy M. Monsma. (1989) Cities: Mission's New Frontier. Grand Rapids, MI: Baker. An introduction to urban ministry, this book presents evangelical, missionary perspectives on the city and the church's task in it. Examples and models are collected from the United States, Asia, South America, and Africa. The authors advocate urban programs aimed toward converting individuals to Christ, making new church starts, ministering to meet human need, and reclaiming the world from Satan's control. Beyond their instructional objectives, they want to make urban ministries more palatable among middle class evangelicals who have traditionally been anti-urban, offering, within the strictures of evangelical theology, a rationale for support of urban missions. The authors, who have missionary experience in Asia, Africa, and Latin America, write in an urgent, crisis oriented, no-time-to-lose style. Bibliography.

18855. Gronefeld, Maria. (1989) Arbeiterbildung als politische Praxis: ein Beitrag zu ihrer Konzeption innerhalb der Katholischen Arbeitnehmerbewegung. Köln, Germany: Ketteler-Verlag. Re:

Catholic Worker Movement in Germany. Bibliography.

18856. Guest, Avery M. (1989) "Community Context and Metropolitan Church Growth," Urban Affairs Quarterly. Vol. 24 (March), pp. 435-459. Guest's study of church growth and decline in Seattle, WA, provides support for the contention that the surrounding environment has great effect on the church. The positive and negative effects of a local church's urban surroundings has almost as much impact on its growth rate as do the internal characteristics of the congregation.

18857. Gulick, John. (1989) The Humanity of Cities: An Introduction to Urban Societies. Granby, MA: Bergin and Garvey. Is inhumanity intrinsic to cities? Gulick says, "No." While inhumanity does occur in cities, the notion of "intrinsic inhumanity" is fundamentally unsound given the accumulation of social scientific evidence and given the fact that such a notion both the product and generator of destructive illusions about the city. The concept of the humanity of cities is advanced in this textbook as a constructive and realistic theoretical basis for analyzing urban phenomena. Bibliography.

18858. Hahn, Judith. (1989) "Loving a Prostitute," The Christian Century. Vol. 106, No. 13 (April 19), pp. 415-416. Hahn, a counselor working with prostitutes, argues for their human rights to respect and life opportunities. She is affiliated with the Genesis House in Chicago, a halfway house for prostitutes.

18859. Hake, Andrew. (1989) "Theological Reflections on 'Community,'" pp. 47-67 in Anthony Harvey, ed. Theology in the City: A Theological Response to Faith in the City. London: SPCK.

18860. Hall, John W., Jr. (1989) "Mission in the Cities of Latin America," Urban Mission. Vol. 7, No. 1 (September), pp. 25-34.

18861. Hannaford, William P. (1989) An Organizational Self-Assessment and Goal Setting Experience for Edgewater Baptist Church: An Urban Congregation of the Baptist General Conference. Thesis (D. Min). Deerfield, IL: Trinity Evangelical Divinity School. Based on the leadership theory of Norman Shawchuck.

18862. Hartley, Loyde H. (1989) Ministry in Middle Sized Cities: Results of an Inquiry. Lancaster, PA: Lancaster Theological Seminary. A survey report on churches and church leadership in Lancaster, PA, Harrisburg, PA, York, PA, Reading, PA, and Wilmington, DE. The inquiry was funded by the Pew Charitable Trusts. Bibliography. Questionnaire.

18863. Harvey, Anthony, ed. (1989) Theology in the City: A Theological Response to Faith in the City. London: SPCK. Six articles in response to the Archbishop of Canterbury's Commission on Urban Priority Areas, Faith in the City: A Call for Action by Church and Nation (1985), including one from a Jewish perspective and one on Black theology in England.

18864. Hauerwas, Stanley and Willimon, William H. (1989) Resident Aliens: Life in the Christian Colony. Nashville, TN: Abingdon. Reviewed: Anthony R. Robinson, Christian Century, Vol. 107, No. 23 (August 8, 1990), pp. 739-741.

18865. Hay, Donald A. (1989) Economics Today: A Christian Critique. Leicester, England: Apollos, InterVarsity Press. Hay derives nine biblical principles, mostly from a theology of creation perspective using stewardship language, and applies them to contemporary economic philosophy. Largely missing are biblical principles regarding poverty and justice.

18866. Heck, Terry and Nellie Metz. (1989) "Two Weekday Alternatives in Urban Religious Education," pp. 152-161 in Donald B. Rogers, ed. Urban Church Education. Birmingham, AL: Religious Education Press.

18867. Heidebrecht, Paul Henry. (1989) Faith and Economic Practice: Protestant Businessmen in Chicago, 1900-1920. New York: Garland. Describes the Chicago Sunday Evening Club. Originally the author's doctoral thesis at the University of Illinois, Urbana-Champaign.

18868. Hertzler, Laurel Schmidt. (1989) "A Church on the Move in Philadelphia," Gospel Herald. Vol. 82, No. 47 (November 21), pp. 817-820. Re: Diamond Street Mennonite Church, Philadelphia, PA, and their work with the urban poor.

18869. Hill, Wendy. (1989) "Working with Unwed Teen Mothers: An Interview," Urban Mission. Vol. 7, No. 2 (November), pp. 29-34.

18870. Hitchcock, Lucy V. (1989) "Tables, Windows and Doors: Models of Organizational Structure for Church-Community Cooperative Action," pp. 31-44 in John C. Montgomery, ed. The Urban Church as Community Builder: Proceedings of the 1989 ICUIS Urban/Metropolitan Leadership Workshop. Chicago, IL: Institute on the Church in Urban-Industrial Society. Practical suggestions offered by the New Congregations Program Director of the Unitarian Universalist Association.

18871. Hoge, Dean R. (1989) "Five Differences between Black and White Protestant Youth," Affirmation [Union Theological Seminary in Virginia]. Vol. 2, No. 1 (Spring), pp. 65-74. Whites receive more support from parents. Blacks are more cautious about marriage. Blacks are more cautious about trusting people. Religion is more important to Blacks. Blacks have more concern about the poor.

18872. Hooker, Roger H. (1989) "Ministry in Multi-Faith Britain," International Bulletin of Missionary Research. Vol. 13 (July), pp. 128-130.

18873. Hope, Glenda. (1989) "Revisioning Seminary as Ministry-Centered," The Christian Century. Vol. 106, No. 4 (February 1-8), pp. 107-111. Urban churches require pastoral leadership that is not being anticipated in current seminary curriculums or by seminary faculty. Hope, associated at the time of writing with San Francisco Network Ministries, reports on conversations with other urban theological educators. See further Citation Number: 19352.

18874. Hopler, Marcia. (1989) "Hanging Out," Urban Mission. Vol. 7, No. 2 (November), pp. 23-28.

18875. Horwitt, Sanford D. (1989) Let Them Call Me Rebel: Saul Alinsky: His Life and Legacy. New York: Knopf. Reviewed: Richard Luecke. "Saul Alinsky: Homo Ludens for Urban Democracy," Christian Century. Vol. 106, No. 34 (November 15), pp. 1050-1053.

18876. Hovda, Robert W. (1989) "The Amen Corner," Worship. Vol. 63, No. 6 (November), pp. 535-540. Commentary on drama and art in New York by a priest who retired there because of interest in drama and art.

18877. Huber, Lois V. (1989) Songs of the Street. s.l.: Peace Institute Press.

18878. Hutchinson, William R., ed (1989) Between the Times: The Travail of the Protestant Establishment in America, 1900-1960. New York: Cambridge University Press. Re: articles on the history of mainline Protestant churches' accommodation to social diversity and growing secularism. Bibliography.

18879. Iles, Robert H. (1989) The Gospel Imperative in the Midst of AIDS: Towards a Prophetic Pastoral Theology. Wilton, CT: Morehouse. Episcopalians and others meeting at the Church Divinity School of the Pacific, Berkeley, CA, consider the implications of sexual identities and circumstances for contracting the AIDS virus for the pastoral care of afflicted persons. Consideration is given to the notions of cleanliness and uncleanliness, sexual ethics, healing ministry, death and bereavement, and public theology perspectives on the AIDS crisis.

18880. Interfaith Hunger Coalition of Southern California. (beginning in 1989) Bread and Justice. Los Angeles, CA: Interfaith Hunger Coalition of Southern California. A periodical.

18881. International Union of Gospel Missions. (beginning in 1989) Rescue Happenings. Kansas City, MO: the Union. A periodical. Preceded by a similar periodical titled International Voice.

18882. Jefferson, Kinmoth W., coordinator. (1989) Bishop's Special Assignment: A Response to the National Substance Abuse Crisis. [New York]: General Board of Global Ministries, the United Methodist Church, at the request of Bishop Felton May for the Council of Bishops. Two volumes: Part 1. National Survey, Urban Mission Directors and Mission Personnel; Part 2. National Survey of Health and Welfare Conference-Related Institutions. This data collection project was designed to describe the extent of United Methodist institutional involvement in programs related to drug and alcohol abuse. A variety of strategies is identified. Bishop May, at the time of making this request, was beginning a year's work in an area of Washington, DC, which had severe problems with drugs.

18883. Johnson, Mary Ann, ed. (1989) The Many Faces of Hull House: The Photographs of Wallace Kirkland. Urbana, IL: University of Illinois Press.

18884. Jones, Angela. (1989) "The Christ Room: Hospitality as Revolution," Other Side [Thematic issue: Housing]. Vol. 25, No. 6 (November), pp. 16-17.

18885. Jones, Kirk Byron. (1989) "The Activism of Interpretation: Black Pastors and Public Life," Christian Century. Vol. 106, No. 26 (September 13-20), pp. 817-818. Re: US Representative William Gray and other urban Black clergy who have used their churches as a base for political office. Jones emphasizes the importance of J. Pius Barbour, mentor of Martin Luther King, Jr.

18886. Jones, Robert E. (1989) "Learning to Face Diversity in Urban Churches," pp. 84-101 in Donald B. Rogers, ed. Urban Church Education. Birmingham, AL: Religious Education Press.

18887. Jones, Vaughan. (1989) "A Future in Community," pp. 47-56 in British Council of Churches. Changing the Agenda. London: the Council.

18888. Kaiser, Walter C. (1989) "A Biblical Theology of the City," Urban Mission. Vol. 7, No. 1 (September), pp. 6-18.

18889. Kellerman, Bill. (1989) "The Angel of Detroit: The Spirit and Powers at Work in One City: A Parable for Our Time," Sojourners [Thematic issue: The Soul of the City]. Vol. 18, No. 9 (October), pp. 16-21. Re: theology and spirituality in a post-manufacturing city (Detroit, MI).

18890. Kim, Chung-Sook Chung. (1989) Korean Attitudes towards Women: The Problems Created By It in the Family. Thesis (D. Min.) Chestnut Hill, PA: Westminster Theological Seminary.

18891. Kincheloe, Samuel C. (1989) The Church in the City: Samuel C. Kincheloe and the Sociology of the City Church. Edited and introduced by Yoshio Fukuyama. Chicago, IL: Explorations Press.

18892. Kirk, Andrew. (1989) "A Different Task: Liberation Theology and Local Theology," pp. 15-31 in Anthony Harvey, ed. Theology in the City: A Theological Response to Faith in the City. London: SPCK.

18893. Klein, Christa Ressmeyer and Christian D. Dehsen. (1989) Politics and Policy: The Genesis and Theology of Social Statements in the Lutheran Church in America. Minneapolis, MN: Fortress.

18894. Lechner, Frank L. (1989) "Catholicism and Social Change in the Netherlands: A Case of Radical Secularization?" Journal for the Scientific Study of Religion. Vol. 28, No. 2 (June), pp. 136-147. Drawing on John Coleman's (1978) version of secularization theory, Lechner explores reasons for decline in Dutch Catholicism and offers alternative interpretations. Bibliography.

18895. Lenz, Robert. (1989) "How to Grow Churches in Manila," Urban Mission. Vol. 7, No. 1 (September), pp. 42-47.

18896. Leprieur, François. (1989) Quand Rome condamne: dominicains et prêtres-ouvriers. [Paris]: Plon/Cerf. Re: history of priest workers and opposition to their movement from Rome.

18897. Levi, Werner. (1989) From Alms to Liberation: The Catholic Church, the Theologians, Poverty, and Politics. New York: Praeger.

18898. Linthicum, Robert C. (1989) "Seduced by the City," World Vision. (June-July). [See note 3].

18899. Lissak, Rivka Shpak. (1989) Pluralism and the Progressives: Hull House and the New Immigrants, 1890-1919. Chicago, IL: University of Chicago Press. Lissak assesses the role of Hull-House in the nation-wide debate on immigrants.

18900. Logan, Patrick. (1989) Life to Be Lived: Homelessness and Pastoral Care. London: Darton, Longman, and Todd. This book, written at the request of the organization named Ecumenical Action on Single Homelessness (UNLEASH), challenges the assumption that parish churches should deal with the settled community while specialized churches should reach out to the homeless people. Homelessness must be a priority of all local churches. Strategy recommendations for effective pastoral care are offered. Resources in London are listed.

18901. Luecke, Richard Henry, ed. (1989) We the People of the City: US Constitution and American Cities. Chicago, IL: Community Renewal Society. The collected papers of a conference on the Constitution and city life held at the Newbury Library.

18902. Luecke, Richard Henry. (1989) "The City as Context for Biblical Faith," The Christian Ministry [Thematic issue: Urban Ministry Today]. Vol. 20, No. 2 (March-April), pp. 10-12. Biblical theology for modern cities.

18903. Luecke, Richard Henry. (1989) "Saul Alinsky: Homo Ludens for Urban Democracy," Christian Century. Vol. 106, No. 34 (November 15), pp. 1050-1053. A review of Sanford D. Horwitt's biography of Alinsky titled: Let Them Call Me Rebel: Saul Alinsky: His Life and Legacy.

18904. Lupton, Robert D. (1989) Theirs Is the Kingdom: Celebrating the Gospel in Urban America. San Francisco, CA: Harper and Row. Vignettes taken from the author's ministry in Atlanta, GA, trace how his middle class assumptions about poverty, mission, and urban ministry changed as he worked with the poor. He came to realize his mission dealt as much with his own salvation as with the salvation of the urban poor.

18905. Mackley, Margaret. (1989) Events, Ideas, Courses, People, Students in the Life of the Sheffield Urban Theology Unit, 1978-1989. New City Journal, No. 19. Sheffield, England: Urban Theology Unit. A pamphlet.

18906. Maclin, Stan, Sr. (1989) "Nurturing Families in the Projects," Urban Mission. Vol. 7, No. 2 (November), pp. 51-52.

18907. "Malaysia: Holding on to God's Gift May Be a Political Issue." (1989) One World [World Council of Churches]. No. 142 (January-February), pp. 22-23.

18908. Malik, Ayyub. (1989) "Muslim Cities: Recent History and Possible Future," pp. 195-220 in Ziauddin Sarder, ed. An Early Cresent. London: Mansell.

18909. Marchak, Mark. (1989) "Nibbling the Big Apple," Urban Mission. Vol. 7, No. 1 (September), pp. 35-41. Marchak writes regarding church extension efforts of the Conservative Baptist Home Mission Society in New York City.

18910. Marchant, Olivia. (1989) "Turks in Brussels: Immigrant Laborers Trapped and Unchurched," World Christian. Vol. 8, No. 5 (May), pp. 20-28.

18911. Martin, Steele W. (1989) Blue Collar Ministry: Problems and Opportunities for Mainline "Middle" Congregations. Washington, DC: Alban Institute. A pamphlet.

18912. Matheny, Judy C. (1989) Resources on Small Membership Churches: A Bibliography. Berea, KY: Appalachian Ministries Educational Resource Center. Although mostly about rural churches, some entries of this annotated bibliography consider small urban churches.

18913. Maton, Kenneth I. (1989) "Community Settings as Buffers of Life Stress: Highly Supportive Churches, Mutual Help Groups, and Senior Centers," American Journal of Community Psychology. Vol. 17 (April), pp. 203-232.

18914. McCloskey, Liz Leibold. (1989) "Hearing and Healing Hedda Nussbaum: A Reflection on Mark 5:21-43," Christian Century.

Vol. 106, No. 5 (February 15), pp. 178-179. A battered woman in New York City seeks help for her fatally injured daughter from the man who committed the crime.

18915. McDaniel, James A. (1989) Homelessness and Affordable Housing: A Resource Book for Churches. New York: United Church Board for Homeland Ministries. Bibliography.

18916. McGeever, Patrick J. (1989) Rev. Charles Ogden Rice: Apostle of Contradiction. Pittsburgh, PA: Duquesne University Press. Biography of a priest involved with labor causes. Bibliography.

18917. McMahon, Thomas F. (1989) "Religion and Business, Concepts and Data," Chicago Studies. Vol. 28, No. 1 (April), pp. 3-16. Reports a survey of business executives on the role of religion in business decision making.

18918. Medema, Ken. (1989) "Singing Forth a New Vision," Sojourners. Vol. 18, No. 9 (October), pp. 26-29. A blind popluar musician sings original songs of justice, hope and the city.

18919. Michael, Christine. (1989) "Glimpses of the Kingdom in the Urban Church," pp. 41-49 in Donald B. Rogers, ed. Urban Church Education. Birmingham, AL: Religious Education Press.

18920. Milligan, Fred, guest ed. (1989) "The Church and City in Transition," The Christian Ministry [Thematic issue: Urban Ministry Today]. Vol. 20, No. 2 (March-April), pp. 3-34.

18921. "Ministries Come to Aid of Quake Victims." (1989) Christianity Today. Vol. 33, No. 17 (November 17), pp. 74-75. Re: earthquake in San Francisco, CA.

18922. Miranda-Feliciano, Evelyn. (1989) "Nobody's Child," The Other Side. Vol. 25, No. 1 (January-February), pp. 34-36.

18923. Mohabir, Philip. (1989) "Community Work and Black Experience," pp. 33-46 in British Council of Churches. Changing the Agenda. London: the Council.

18924. Momeni, Jamshid A., ed. (1989) Homelessness in the United States. Westport, CT: Greenwood Press. Describes the nature and extent of homelessness, emphasizing state and local studies.

18925. Montgomery, John C., ed. (1989) The Urban Church as

Community Builder: Proceedings of the 1989 ICUIS Urban/Metropolitan Leadership Workshop. Chicago, IL: Institute on the Church in Urban-Industrial Society. Seven articles on models for church and community cooperative action, including Bible studies by John Auer.

18926. Moore, Lydia C. (1989) The Development of a Self-Study for an Urban Black United Methodist Church in the Philadelphia Area Relating to Ministry. Thesis (D. Min). Philadelphia, PA: Eastern Baptist Theological Seminary.

18927. Moore, R. Laurence. (1989) "Religion, Secularization, and the Shaping of the Culture Industry in Antebellum America," American Quarterly. Vol. 41 (June), pp. 216-242.

18928. Mott, Stephen Charles. (1989) "Because Jesus Was Homeless for Us: A Biblical Study on Our Responsibility to the Homeless," Christian Social Action. Vol. 2, No. 2 (February), pp. 4-15.

18929. Murnion, Philip Joseph and Ann Wenzel. (1989) Crisis of the Church in the Inner City: Pastoral Options for Inner City Parishes. New York: Pastoral Life Center. Research conducted by Wenzel under the supervision of Murnion and funded by the Lilly Endowment points to the need for new strategies for inner city churches. Small congregations in large, deteriorating buildings cannot survive indefinitely. Remedies include such options as: programs of parish renewal, ways to increase revenue and reduce costs, alternative use of buildings, sharing finances and programs and priests with other parishes, closings and mergers, and related comprehensive planning. Case studies are provided.

18930. Myers, Kenneth A. (1989) All God's Children and Blue Suede Shoes: Christians and Pop Culture. Westchester, IL: Crossway Books. An attack on evangelical Protestant accommodation to the ethics of popular culture regarding, for example, divorce, business ethics, abuse, and sexuality.

18931. Myers, William R. (1989) "Models for Urban Youth Ministry: Goals, Styles, and Contexts," pp. 127-134 in Donald B. Rogers, ed. Urban Church Education. Birmingham, AL: Religious Education Press.

18932. Needleman, Ruth. (1989) "The Feminization of Unions," Witness. Vol. 72, No. 2 (February), pp. 10-11, 22-23.

18933. "Newark Ministry to Homeless Is Losing Its Home." (1989) New York Times. (January 8), Section 1, p. 36.

18934. Newbern, Captolia D. (1989) "Making the Dream Come True: Discipleship for All God's People in the Urban Church," pp. 102-113 in Donald B. Rogers, ed. Urban Church Education. Birmingham, AL: Religious Education Press.

18935. Newbigin, Leslie. (1989) The Gospel in a Pluralist Society. Grand Rapids, MI: Eerdmans and the World Council of Churches. Reviewed: Christian Century. Vol. 107, No. 4 (January 31, 1990), pp. 103-108.

18936. Northcott, Michael S. (1989) The Church and Secularization: Urban Industrial Mission in North East England. Frankfurt am Main, Germany: Lang. Bibliography.

18937. O'Brien, William. (1989) "Seeds of Hope: A Land Trust in the Inner City," Other Side [Thematic issue: Housing]. Vol. 25, No. 6 (November), pp. 22-23.

18938. O'Grady, Ron. (1989) "Asian Domestic Maids," One World. Vol. 143 (March), pp. 7-8.

18939. Oglesbee, Clay. (1989) "The Kemp Plan for Rebuilding the City," Christian Century. Vol. 106, No. 11 (August 5), pp. 340-341. Doubts and hopes regarding Kemp's plans for urban housing. Kemp is secretary of the US government's office of Housing and Urban Development (HUD).

18940. Ortiz, Manuel. (1989) Leadership Training Text for Second Generation Hispanic Church Planting. Thesis (D. Min.). Chestnut Hill, PA: Westminster Theolgical Seminary.

18941. Ortiz, Manuel and Blanca Ortiz. (1989) "The Family in the City," Urban Mission. Vol. 7, No. 2 (November), pp. 46-50.

18942. Ostling, Richard N. (1989) "Those Mainline Blues: Old Guard Protestant Churches Confront an Unprecedented Decline," Time. Vol. 133, No. 21 (May 22), pp. 94-96. Time reports opinions about why mainline Protestant churches have lost membership since 1965.

18943. Pannenberg, Wolfhart. (1989) Christianity in a Secularized World. New York: Crossraod. Pannenberg reviews the secularization debates and describes his interpretation of the task of theology in secular culture.

18944. Park, Sun Ai. (1989) "Asian Women's Experience of Injustice: Some Reflections," Mid-Stream: An Ecumenical Journal. Vol. 28 (January), pp. 12-26.

18945. Parker, Matthew. (1989) "Envisioning Success in the Black Christian Community," United Evangelical Action [Thematic issue: Reading the city]. Vol. 48, No. 3 (May-June), p. 7.

18946. Patton, Bill. (1989) "Reaching American Baby Boomers," Urban Mission. Vol. 7, No. 2 (November), pp. 15-22.

18947. Peerman, Dean. (1989) "Romero: Evolution of a Martyr," Christian Century. Vol. 106, No. 28 (October 4), pp. 870-872. Conditions have not improved in El Salvador in the nine and a half years since the Archbishop's assassination.

18948. Penwell, Lanny. (1989) "Church Planting in Inner City Denver," United Urban Action [Thematic issue: Reading the city]. Vol. 48, No. 3 (May-June), pp. 8-9.

18949. Perry, Robert L. (1989) Models of Multi-Family Housing Ministry. Atlanta, GA: Home Mission Board, Southern Baptist Convention.

18950. Peters, Harold. (1989) "Reaching Bamako, Mali," Urban Mission. Vol. 7, No. 1 (September), pp. 48-51.

18951. Peters, Ted. (1989) "Not in My Backyard! The Waste Disposal Crisis," The Christian Century. Vol. 106, No. 5 (February 15), pp. 175-177. Peters reflects theologically on movements to stop the dumping of toxic wastes. He lists ethical criteria for disposal site selection, including: 1) safety and permanence, 2) the availability of technical ability to preserve safety, 3) compensation for anyone suffering adverse effects, 4) the saving of profits for use in the event of unexpected developments, 5) the avoidance of efforts to extort and bribe, and 6) the employment of the most effective technologies.

18952. Pierce, Gregory F. Augustine. (1989) "How Community Organization Can Benefit the Congregation," The Christian Ministry [Thematic issue: Urban Ministry Today]. Vol. 20, No. 2 (March-April), pp. 22-24. Although churches and community organizations have often been at odds, their combined efforts can produce important results.

18953. Pityana, Barney. (1989) "Towards a Black Theology for Britain," pp. 98-113 in Anthony Harvey, ed. Theology in the City: A Theological Response to Faith in the City. London: SPCK.

18954. Plant, Raymond, et al. (1989) "Conservative Capitalism: Theological and Moral Challenges," pp. 68-97 in Anthony Harvey, ed. Theology in the City: A Theological Response to Faith in the City. London: SPCK.

18955. Playthell, Benjamin. (1989) "The Attitude Is the Message: Louis Farrakhan Pursues the Middle Class," The Village Voice. Vol. 33, No. 33 (August 15), pp. 23-31. Farrakhan compared to Elijah Muhammed, Malcolm X, and Marcus Garvey.

18956. Polachek, Hilda Scott. (1989) I Came a Stanger: The Story of a Hull-House Girl. Urbana, IL: University of Illinois Press. Personal recollections and stories of a Polish Jewish immigrant.

18957. Poorman, Roberta S. (1989) Training for Threapeutic Relationships with Dysfuctional Women with Children in an Urban Mission Setting. Thesis (D. Min.). Boston, MA: Gordon-Conwell Theological Seminary.

18958. Pritchett, Harry H. (1989) Morning Run: Sabbatical Reflections on the Church and the City. Atlanta, GA: S. Hunter.

18959. Purves, Andre. (1989) The Search for Compassion: Spirituality and Ministry. Lousiville, KY: Westminster/John Knox. Bibliography.

18960. Raboteau, Albert J. (1989) "The Black Church: Continuity and Change," pp. 77-91 in David W. Lotz, Donald W. Shriver, Jr., and John F. Wilson, eds. Altered Landscapes: Christianity in America, 1935-1985. Grand Rapids, MI: William B. Eerdmans.

18961. "A Raisin in the Sun: The Uncut Version." (1989) Christian Century. Vol. 106, No. 3 (January 25), pp. 71-73. Editorial reflection on the continuing relevance of the 1959 play by Lorraine Hansberry depicting a Chicago Black family's struggle, subsequently adapted for a film starring Sydney Poitier.

18962. Ramsden, William E. and Clinton Stockwell. (1989) Metropolitan Ministry Agencies: Profiles of Twenty Agencies Across the United States. New York: National Program Division, General Board of Global Ministries, the United Methodist Church. Case studies of metropolitan ministry organizations selected from across the US, half are programs sponsored solely by the United Methodist Church and half are ecumenically funded with some United Methodist support. In all, the United Methodists support 77 such organizations, 20 of which were chosen for study. Examples of organizations included in this group of case studies: Houston Metropolitan Ministries, Church Council of Greater Seattle, and Toledo Metropolitan Mission (all ecumenically sponsored); and Denver Urban Ministries, Columbus United Methodist Urban Ministry, and United Methodist Urban Metro Ministries [in] Philadelphia (all United Methodist organizations). Part of a two volume series.

18963. Recinos, Harold Joseph. (1989) Hear the Cry! A Latino Pastor Challenges the Church. Philadelphia, PA: Westminster Press. Recinos recounts the story of the Church of All Nations, Lower East Side, New York City, a Methodist Puerto Rican congregation where he served as pastor. The congregation is a adaptation of the Latin American base communities and committed to social justice. Recinos' volume provides an example of applied liberation theology. For another persective from mainline Protestant denominations, see a pamphlet by Edwin O. Ayala titled "Evangelism and Church Development in UCC Hispanic Churches. New York: United Church Board for Homeland Ministries, 1991.

18964. Reece, William S. (1989) "Why Is the Bishops' Letter on the US Economy So Unconvincing?" Journal of Business Ethics. Vol. 8 (July), pp. 553-560.

18965. Richardson, Nancy D. (1989) "The Women's Theological Center: Learning and Acting for Justice," Christian Century. Vol. 106, No. 4 (February 1-8), pp. 130-135. Richardson is co-director of the Women's Theological Center in Boston, MA.

18966. "Risk Management at Work: Churches" [Special report]. (1989) National Underwriter (Property/Risk and Benefits Management Edition). Vol. 93 (January), pp. 7+.

18967. Ro, Bong Rin. (1989) "Urban Cities and the Gospel in Asia," Urban Mission. Vol. 6, No. 5 (May), pp. 20-30.

18968. Ro, Bong Rin. (1989) Urban Ministry in Asia: Cities, the Exploding Mission Field. Taichung, Taiwan: Asia Theological Association. Ro, at the time of writing, is Executive of the Asian Theological

Association. Bibliography.

18969. Roehlkepartain, Eugene C. (1989) Youth Ministry in City Churches. Loveland, CO: Group Publishers. Roehlkepartain has authored several books on youth ministry. Bibliography.

18970. Rogers, Donald B. (1989) "From Setting to Theory: Principles of Urban Church Education," Religious Education. Vol. 84, No. 2 (Spring), pp. 249-261. Rogers, using inductive methods, outlines a theory of education that takes into account the urban environment and promotes the development of an indigenous theology. Urban church members must be allowed to develop their own understandings of the church and to extrapolate the implications for ministry. The theory is presented as an alternative to the activist approach to urban ministry which places heavy directives on church members and often omits educational ministry altogether.

18971. Rogers, Donald B., ed. (1989) Urban Church Education. Birmingham, AL: Religious Education Press. Offered as a series of practical discussions about dealing with the complexities of urban church education.

18972. Roozen, David A. and Jackson W. Carroll. (1989) "Methodological Issues in Denominational Surveys of Congregations," Review of Religious Research. Vol. 31, No. 2 (December), pp. 115-131. Research methodology for the study of congregations has shifted from the census type surveys of the church federation era (1920s through 1965) to the "multi-layered" approach of more recent times. Examples of pivotal studies are Kleotzli's The City Church -- Death or Renewal (1961) and Glock and Ringer's "Church Policy and Attitudes of Ministers and Parishioners on Social Issues" (1956). The authors list and discuss persistent methodological problems. Bibliography.

18973. Rosado, Caleb. (1989) "The Church, the City, and the Compassionate Christ," Apuntes: Reflexiones Teologicas desde el Margen Hispano. Vol. 9 (Summer), pp, 27-35.

18974. Rouse, James. (1989) "Housing--For Everyone," Other Side [Thematic issue: Housing]. Vol. 25, No. 6 (November), pp. 18-21. A developer describes his strategy for making housing available to the poor.

18975. Russell, Letty M. (1989) "Christian Education in the Inner City," pp. 27-40 in Donald B. Rogers, ed. Urban Church Education. Birmingham, AL: Religious Education Press.

18976. Rust, C. Renee. (1989) "Spiritual Formation in Urban Church Education," pp. 60-70 in Donald B. Rogers, ed. Urban Church Education. Birmingham, AL: Religious Education Press.

18977. Ryan, Phyllis, Ira Goldstein and David Bartlet. (1989) Homelessness in Pennsylvania: How Can This Be? [Philadelphia, PA]: Coalition on Homelessness in Pennsylvania. Sponsored by a coalition of funding sources including the Federal Government, businesses, and the Episcopal, Lutheran and Baptist church judicatories, this study describes the systemic causes of homelessness as well as the crushing effects of homelessness on persons. Quotations of the homeless spread throughout the report give an immediacy often lacking in studies of social issues. Questionnaire.

18978. Samuel, Vinay Kumar and Christopher Sugden. (1989) Lambeth: A View from the Two-Thirds World. London: SPCK.

18979. Scheele, Christine. (1989) "Mile High Hope," Christian Herald. Vol. 112, No. 5 (May), pp. 10-15. Scheele describes a Denver, CO, ministry for the homeless.

18980. Schreiner, Sally. (1989) "Swapping Skills to Enrich the City Church," The Christian Ministry [Thematic issue: Urban Ministry Today]. Vol. 20, No. 2 (March-April), pp. 34-35. Re: the Urban Church Resource Exchange Center in Chicago, IL.

18981. Shane, John J. (1989) "Distinctives of African Urban Ministry," Urban Mission. Vol. 6, No. 5 (May), pp. 31-40.

18982. Shopshire, James M. (1989) "Regentrification and the Black Church in the Cities," The AME Zion Quarterly Review. Vol. 101 (April), pp. 6-15. Re: the impact of upper middle class people settling in areas formerly occupied by the poor.

18983. Sills, Horace S. (1989) Possibilities in Relocation: Building a New Church for New Times. New York: United Church Board for Homeland Ministries. A rational for church relocation and suggestions on how to go about it.

18984. Simpson, Dick. (1989) The Politics of Compassion and Transformation. Athens, OH: Swallow Press. Simpson, a United Church of Christ minister and professor at the University of Illinois, writes with prophetic urgency about global problems that portend irreversible declines in the quality of life. His solutions are activist in nature -- people banding together to fight for peace, food, clothing, shelter, non-exploitative technology, good works, and responsive government. Simpson acknowledges a debt to Matthew Fox (1971, 1979, etc.).

18985. Sinnott, Thomas G., comp. (1989) Mission and Ministry: A Training Manual. Northfield, MN: Editorial Advance Lutherano. A reader on various ethnic practices, e.g., West Indian engagement parties and Puerto Rican family rites. The volume is intended to assist pastors and laity achieve some level of sensitvity and sensibility with people with ethnic heritages different from their own. It is based on the author's D. Min. dissertation at New York Theological Seminary, 1988.

18986. Smith, David. (1989?) Saving Sacred Space. Chicago, IL: Community Renewal Society. Remarks addressed to the Landmark Preservation Council of Illinois on a tour of Chicago's historic churches and neighborhoods.

18987. Smith, Greg. (1989) "Community Development and Christian Mission," pp. 7-22 in British Council of Churches. Changing the Agenda. London: the Council.

18988. Smith, J. Alfred. (1989) "What Do We Do Next? A View from the Pew," pp. 143-151 in Robert McAfee Brown and Sydney T. Brown, eds. A Cry for Justice. New York: Paulist. A Baptist lay person's view of church planning and social action.

18989. Smith, Michael Hornsby. (1989) The Changing Parish: A Study of Parishes, Priests and Parishioners after Vatican II. London: Routledge.

18990. Spencer, Jon Michael. (1989) "Hymns of the Social Awakening: Walter Rauschenbusch," The Hymn. Vol. 40, No. 2 (April), pp. 18-23. A description of Rauschenbusch's use of hymns in worship. to promote Social Gospel causes.

18991. Spring, Beth, Stefan Ulstein and Dave Jackson. (1989) "Home, Street Home," Christianity Today. Vol. 33, No. 7 (April 21), pp. 15-20. Rescue missions respond to the plight of the homeless, overwhelmed but persistent in their efforts. Often the poor have noplace else to turn.

18992. Stackpole, Richard L. and Ron Robotham. (1989) "Out of the City/Into the City: Two Competing Models for the Urban Church," pp. 162-181 in Donald B. Rogers, ed. Urban Church Education. Birmingham, AL: Religious Education Press.

18993. Stivers, Robert L., ed. (1989) Reformed Faith and Economics. Lanham, MD: University Press of America. Presbyterian views on the relationships of Reformed faith and economic justice.

18994. Stockwell, Clinton E. (1989) "The New Urban Reality: Hope for a Remnant," The Christian Ministry [Thematic issue: Urban Ministry Today]. Vol. 20, No. 2 (March-April), pp. 13-16. Cities have become filled with the poor., but the presence of the poor is not necessarily a cause for despair. The poor can offer hope to the city.

18995. Sullivan, Joseph P. and Thomas F. McMahon. (1989) "Faith that Mandates Justice," Chicago Studies. Vol. 28, No. 1 (April), pp. 17-32. A survey of the role of religion in business decision making leads the authors to conclude that social responsibility goes beyond the legal and ethical dimension to the realm of religious obligation.

18996. Sweet, Leonard I. (1989) "The Modernization of Protestant Religion in America," pp. 19-41 in David W. Lotz, Donald W. Shriver, Jr., and John F. Wilson, eds. Altered Landscapes: Christianity in America, 1935-1985. Grand Rapids, MI: William B. Eerdmans. Sweet traces the mercurial course of Protestant modernism.

18997. Szoka, Edmund, Cardinal. (1989) Dying and Rising Together with Christ. Detroit, MI: the Archdiocese of Detroit. City churches must establish their viability, or face closing. About half of Detroit's 108 Catholic churches are candidates for closing. Bibliography.

18998. Taylor, Laura. (1989) "Journey into the Brain of an Urban Minister," pp. 124-136 in James B. Ashbrook, ed. Faith and Ministry in Light of the Double Brain. Bristol, IN: Wyndham Hall Press.

18999. Thomas, George B. (1989) "Gerontology in Urban and Rural Congregations and Communities," Journal of Religion and Aging. Vol. 6, Nos. 3-4 (Spring), pp. 141-151.

19000. Thorogood, Bernard. (1989) No Abiding City: Change and Changelessness in the Church. London: SCM.

19001. Tolbert, Alice B. (1989) "The Crisis of Single Parent Families," Urban Mission. Vol. 7, No. 2 (November), pp. 9-14.

19002. "Trinity Church Braces Itself against the Winds of

Change." (1989) Engineering News-Record. Vol. 223 (September), p. 18. Trinity Church, New York City, encounters problems in maintaining its church building.

19003. United Methodist Church, Northeast Jurisdiction, Multi-Ethnic Center for Ministry. (beginning in 1989) Multi-Ethnic Center for Ministry News. Madison, NJ: the Center. A tabloid newsletter reporting news of Korean, Hispanic, Haitian, and Black ministries in the United Methodist Church.

19004. Vander Klay, Stan and Barbara Vander Klay. (1989) "Raising Children in the City: The Responsibility and the Glory," Urban Mission. Vol. 7, No. 2 (November), pp. 35-43.

19005. Van Houten, Mark. (1989) "Inner-City Street Ministry: A Christology," Urban Mission. Vol. 7, No. 1 (September), pp. 52-54.

19006. Van Houten, Mark. (1989) Profane Evangelism: Taking the Gospel into "Unholy Places." Grand Rapids, MI: Ministry Resources Library, Zondervan. Evangelism is profane when it goes into the world of people who are indifferent to the church, such as that of the street people the author ministers to under the auspices of the Northside [Chicago] Ecumenical Night Ministry. A local church evangelizes profanely only if it reaches those for whom God is dead, departed, or disinterested.

19007. Vásquez, Edmundo E. (1989) "Hispanic Urban Ministry Comes of Age," The Christian Ministry [Thematic issue: Urban Ministry Today]. Vol. 20, No. 2 (March-April), pp. 20-21.

19008. Villafañe, Eldin. (1989) Toward an Hispanic American Pentecostal Social Ethic, with Special Reference to North Eastern United States. Thesis (Ph. D.). Boston, MA: Boston University.

19009. Vincent, John J., ed. (1989) Hymns of the City. Sheffield, England: Urban Theology Unit. Words like "pain, sorrow, grime, rage, injustice and struggle" are intermingled with the words of faith in the 31 hymns (with suggested tunes) written by Vincent and others associated with the Urban Theology Unit. Clive Scott is the most frequent contributor.

19010. Vincent, John J. (1989) Britain in the 90s: A Call to the Nation, a Handbook for Pioneers. Peterborough, England: Methodist Publishing House. Vincent, who at the time of writing was President of the Methodist Church in Great Britain, calls the church to radical discipleship and to service in the cities. This 72-page volume outlines his programs for the term of his presidency.

19011. Vincent, John J. (1989) A Campaigning Workbook for Dr. Vincent's Year as President of the Methodist Conference, 1989-1990. [London?]: Methodist Publishing House.

19012. Wangerin, Walter, Jr. (1989) The Manger Is Empty. San Francisco, CA: Harper. Inspiration for Wangerin's stories derives from his experience as a Lutheran inner city pastor.

19013. Warren, Donald I. (1989) Helping Networks of the Aging and Retired. Lewiston, NY: Edwin Mellen Press.

19014. Warren, Jon. (1989) "Gospel in the Ghetto," Moody Monthly. Vol. 89, No. 6 (February), pp. 14-25. A photographic essay about Chicago's West Side.

19015. Warren, Rick. (1989) Contemporary Approaches to Ministry, Evangelism and Organization. Atlanta, GA: Metropolitan Missions Department, Board of Home Mission, the Southern Baptist Convention, Occasional Paper No. 14. Strategy suggestions for reaching "baby boomers" includes recommendations for a high-tech approach to evangelism and church administration.

19016. Westbrook, Robert. (1989) "In the Churches, in the Streets: Taylor Branch on 'The King Years,'" The Christian Century. Vol. 106, No. 11 (April 5), pp. 351-354. Westbrook reviews Branch's book (1988) on the history of the civil rights movement, finding it the most adequate available.

19017. White, James F. (1989) Protestant Worship: Traditions in Transition. Louisville, KY: Westminster/John Knox. Bibliography.

19018. Whiten, Bennie, Jr. (1989) "The Urban Church in the 1990's," pp. 1-11 in John C. Montgomery, ed. The Urban Church as Community Builder: Proceedings of the 1989 ICUIS Urban/Metropolitan Leadership Workshop. Chicago, IL: Institute on the Church in Urban-Industrial Society. Whiten, the Director of Metro Mission for Chicago's Community Renewal Society, discusses the ethnic character of urban ministry and the historic roots of the Community Renewal Society.

19019. Willmer, Haddon. (1989) "Images of the City and the Shaping of Humanity," pp. 32-46 in Anthony Harvey, ed. Theology in the City: A Theological Response to Faith in the City. London: SPCK.

19020. Wind, James P. (1989) "The Church's Challenge in Health Care," Christian Century. Vol. 106, No. 39 (December 20-27), pp. 1201-1204. A conference in Atlanta, GA, discusses alternative approaches for health care.

19021. Winter, Gibson. (1989) Community Spiritual Transformation: Religion and Politics in a Communal Age. New York: Crossroads.

19022. Yancey, Philip. (1989) "Squalor in the 'City of God,'" Christianity Today. Vol. 33, No. 3 (February 17), pp. 12-13.

19023. Yi, Yong Kol. (1989). Elder Training in a Korean-American Church. Thesis (D. Min.) Chestnut Hill, PA: Westminster Theological Seminary.

19024. Young, Charles E. (1989) A Contextualized Methodology for Crisis Evangelism among the Poor. Thesis (D. Min.). Chestnut Hill, PA: Westminster Theological Seminary.

19025. Zalent, Kim. (1989) "Taking Charge of the Community Economy," The Christian Ministry [Thematic issue: Urban Ministry Today]. Vol. 20, No. 2 (March-April), pp. 25-27. A discussion of local churches involved in economic development.

19026. Zepp, Ira G. (1989) The Social Vision of Martin Luther King, Jr. Brooklyn, NY: Carlson.

19027. Zopf, Paul E. (1989) American Women in Poverty. Westport, CT: Greenwood Press. Zopf documents the "Feminization" of poverty in the United States, combining demographic and sociological analysis with humanistic insight. He suggests new strategies.

19028. Addy, Tony [Anthony J.] and Roger Clarke, eds. (1990) The Other Side of 1992, the Report of the West European Network on Work, Unemployment and the Churches Consultation. Manchester, England: the William Temple Foundation. Papers and findings from a European consultation examining the impact of the European economy on those most vulnerable to economic change--ethnic and racial minorities, women, young people, unqualified workers, migrant workers.

19029. Amerson, Philip A. (1990) "The Urban Church: Flight Time or Staying Power?" Circuit Rider [Thematic issue: City ministry and drug abuse]. Vol. 14, No. 10 (December), pp. 4-5. Stories of inner city ministry call the church to reclaim its rich heritage in cities.

19030. Aristide, Jean-Bertrand. (1990) In the Parish of the Poor: Writings from Haiti. Maryknoll, NY: Orbis. Sermons regarding church work among the poor in Haiti and conflict with the conservative church hierarchy and repressive government.

19031. Bachelder, Robert S. (1990) "Solving the Housing Crisis Pragmatically," Christian Century. Vol. 107, No. 13 (April 18), pp. 398-400. Both liberal and conservative approaches to housing problems have failed. Bachelder proposes a public-private partnership.

19032. Bailey, Richard P. (1990) "The Muslims Are Here," United Evangelical Action. Vol. 49, No. 4 (July-August), pp. 4-7. Re: evangelical Protestant alarm over the growing numbers of Muslims in the USA.

19033. Baker, Susan and Debra Ortiz-Vasquez. (1990) "Christian Education towards Community Development," Urban Mission. Vol. 7, No. 5 (May), pp. 20-27.

19034. Bakke, Raymond J. (1990) "The City as Mission Field," Christianity Today. Vol. 34, No. 8 (May 14), pp. 53-54. An interview.

19035. Baptista, Cynder. (1990) "Highway City Is Our Jerusalem," Urban Mission. Vol. 7, No. 5 (May), pp. 36-44. A suburban church establishes ministries in a poorer section of Fresno, Ca.

19036. Barna Research Group. (1990) We have Seen the Future: The Demise of Christianity in Los Angeles County. Glendale, CA: Barna Research Group. A description of the state of religion in Los Angeles, with an overstated title.

19037. Beck, Carolyn S. (1990) "Entrepreneurs in God's Economy: Christian Stronghold Baptist Church," Urban Mission. Vol. 7, No. 5 (May), pp. 7-19.

19038. Bettelheim, Bruno. (1990) Freud's Vienna and Other Essays. New York: Knopf.

19039. Billings, Alan. (1990) "Keeping Chaos at Bay: The Place of Ritual and Community in the Events of Hillsborough," Crucible.

[Vol. 29, No. 1] (January-March), pp. 4-10. Re: events associatied with several people being crushed to death while attending a football game.

19040. Birchett, Coleen. (1990) How to Help Hurting People. Chicago, IL: Urban Ministries, Inc. Re: African Americans who look to the church for redress of their problems. Bibliography.

19041. Blasi, Anthony J. and Michael Cuneo, compilers. (1990) The Sociology of Religion: An Organizational Bibliography. New York: Garland. A partly annotated catalog of literature from 1984 to 1989 continues the work of the author's 1985 bibliography.

19042. Bradbee, Cheryl. (1990) "Ministry at Harbourfront," Urban Mission. Vol. 7, No. 3 (January), pp. 51-56.

19043. Brecher, Jeremy. (1990) "If All the People Are Banded Together," pp. 93-105 in Jeremy Brecher and Tim Costello, eds. Building Bridges: the Emergency Grassroots Coalition of Labor and Community. New York: Monthly Review Press. Re: the Naugatuck Valley Project, a coalition of churches and labor unions aimed at preventing job losses, plant closings, and a community deterioration in south central Connecticut.

19044. Brink, Paul. (1990) "Las Acacias Evangelical Pentecostal Church, Caracas, Venezuela," Urban Mission. Vol. 7, No. 3 (January), pp. 46-50.

19045. Brown, Chris. (1990) "The 'Year' at UTU," The New City [Urban Theology Union, Sheffield, England]. No. 18 (Spring), p. 5. Perspectives on training for urban ministry. Accompanied by related articles and course descriptions.

19046. Bryan, Mary Lynn McCree and Allen F. Davis. (1990) One Hundred Years at Hull House. Indianapolis, IN: Indiana University Press. An update of the authors' earlier title: Eighty Years at Hull House (1969).

19047. Cardwell, Brenda M. and William K. Fox. (1990) Journey toward Wholeness: A History of Black Disciples of Christ in the Mission of the Christian Church. [Nashville, TN]: National Convocation of the Christian Church (Disciples of Christ). Bibliography.

19048. Carson, Mina. (1990) Settlement Folk: Social Thought and the American Settlement Movement, 1885-1930. Chicago, IL: University of Chicago Press. Carson overview examines ideals and practices of leading settlement workers in the USA.

19049. Chang, Robert Tsai-Chin. (1990) Biblically Helping the New Immigrant Chinese Elderly in North America. Thesis (D. Min.). Chestnut Hill, PA: Westminster Theological Seminary.

19050. Chareonwongska, Kriengska. (1990) "Hope of Bangkok: A Visionary Model of Church Growth and Church Planting," Urban Mission. Vol. 7, No. 3 (January), pp. 25-35.

19051. Chen, Peter F. (1990) "A Learning from Japanese American Church Development," pp. 18-30 in United Methodist Church, General Board of Global Ministries, National Program Division. The Burning Heart: Vision for Asian American Missional Congregations. New York: the Division.

19052. Church of England, Commission on Urban Priority Areas. (1990) Living Faith in the City: A Progress Report. London: Church House Publishing for the Commission. Theological reflection stimulated by the Commission's report titled Faith in the City (1985) is summarized in this volume.

19053. Clammer, John. (1990) "Singapore: Urbanism, Culture, and the Church," Urban Mission. Vol. 7, No. 4 (March), pp. 6-20.

19054. Coleman, John A. (1990) "The Secular: A Sociological View," The Way: Contemporary Christian Spirituality. Vol. 30, No. 1 (January), pp. 16-25. Coleman considers the question of whether religion is in decline or is a sociological universal, briefly reviewing relevant literature. Does secularization generate countervailing sacralization? Bryan Wilson, Peter Berger and Thomas Luckmann say,"No." Robert Bellah and Andrew Greeley say, "Yes."

19055. Conn, Harvie M. (1990) "Never Say 'Never' in the City," Urban Mission. Vol. 7, No. 4 (March), pp. 3-6.

19056. Corson, Ben, et al. (1990) Shopping for a Better World: A Quick and Easy Guide to Social Responsible Supermarket Shopping. New York: Ballentine.

19057. Cox, Harvey G. (1990) "We Are One in the Lord: Christians and Muslims," New World Outlook. Vol. 50, No. 4 (March-April), pp. 18-19. Cox asks, "Why the rivalry?"

19058. Cox, Harvey G. (1990) "The Secular City 25 Years Later,"

Christian Century. Vol. 107, No. 32 (November 7), pp. 1025-1029. Cox reviews the possibility for theistic understandings of the city, stressing the importance of ambiguity, pragmatism, provisionality, suspicion of grand schemes, and readiness to risk disorder. He includes an analysis of liberation theologies.

19059. Crijns, Hub and Henk Koetsier, eds. (1990) Tussen arbeid en kapitaal: een eeuw katholiek en protestants sociaal denken. Aalsmeer, The Netherlands: Luyten. Bibliography.

19060. Cryderman, Lyn. (1990) "Two Stupid Moves," Christianity Today. Vol. 34, No. 18 (December 17), p. 15. The Salvation Army and the Sisters of Charity have become victims of excessive federal and local government bureaucracy, hampering their effectiveness with the homeless.

19061. Davidman, Lynn. (1990) "Accommodation and Resistance to Modernity: A Comparison of Two Contemporary Orthodox Jewish Groups," Sociological Analysis. Vol. 51, No. 1 (Spring), pp. 35-51. Two congregations in a Northeastern USA city -- one Orthodox and the other Lubavitch Chassidic -- are studies by means of participant observation. Davidman collects information about how the two communities orient new members, using her information to comment on secularization hypotheses. Much of her data is collected from women's groups in the congregations.

19062. Davidson, Jack. (1990) "The Birth of a Downtown Tokyo Church," Urban Mission. Vol. 8, No. 1 (September), pp. 37-44.

19063. Deck, Allan Figueroa. (1990) "The Crisis of Hispanic Ministry: Multiculturalism as an Ideology," America [Thematic issue: The church in the cities]. Vol. 163, No. 2 (July 14), pp. 33-36. The National Parish strategy, successful in the past century, won't work today for a variety of reasons, but the new multicultural approach runs risks of "putting down" Hispanics, co-opting them in trivializing ways, and leaving them without a church in which to feel at home.

19064. DeParle, Jason. (1990) "Residents of Covenant House Split on Its Future and Ritter," New York Times. Vol. 139 (March 1), p. 86. Re: Bruce Ritter's resignation following accusations of child abuse.

19065. Diehl, Astor Antonio. (1990) Circulos operarios no Rio Grande do Sulo: um projeto social-politico. Pôrto Alegre, Brazil: EDIPUCRS. Re: Catholic trade unions in Brazil. Bibliography.

19066. Dolan, Jay P., R. Scott Appleby, Patricia Byrne, and Debra Campbell. (1990) Transforming Parish Ministry: The Changing Roles of Catholic Clergy, Laity and Women Religious. New York: Crossroads.

19067. Dolin, David. (1990) Locked Doors: Facing the Inner City Challenge. Schaumsburg, IL: Regular Baptist Press.

19068. Dorsett, Lyle W. (1990) "Billy Sunday: Evangelist to Urban America," Urban Mission. Vol. 8, No. 1 (September), pp. 6-13. Dorsett reviews briefly Sunday's career, noting that at the peak of his urban success the evangelist fell prey to the enormous wealth his crusades generated. A loss of effectiveness resulted. Only after Sunday repented, according to Dorsett, did his preaching return to its earlier vigor.

19069. Driedger, Leo. (1990) Mennonites in Winnipeg. Winnipeg, Manitoba: Kindred Press. Winnipeg is the world's largest Mennonite urban center, with 19,000 adherents and 47 congregations. Photographs. Reviewed: Journal for the Scientific Study of Religion. Vol. 30, No. 3 (September, 1991), pp. 326-327.

19070. Duce, Alan. (1990) "Prison Chaplaincy in Poland," Crucible. [Vol. 29, No. 1] (January-March), pp. 29-35.

19071. Duggan, Thomas J., et al. (1990?) Baseline Study of Detroit Catholic Church Closings: Final Report. [Detroit, MI: Wayne State University, Dean of the College of Urban, Labor and Metropolitan Affairs]. A social scientific study of the impact of closing 30 Catholic churches in Detroit.

19072. Eastman, Michael, Jay Gary, Al Hatch, Howard Peskett and Ronald Sider. (1990) "Some Impressions of Lausanne II," Urban Mission. Vol. 7, No. 3 (January), pp. 8-15.

19073. Edgar, John W. (1990) Reconnecting the Urban Neighborhood Church [prepublication copy]. Columbus, OH: Columbus United Methodist Office of Urban Ministry. Many congregations have either lost or seriously diminished their connections with the neighborhoods in which they are located as well as other communities with which they were formerly linked. Edgar's handbook offers corrective measures: an analysis of disconnectedness and a strategy for reconnection. A case study of St. Paul Methodist Church, Dayton, OH, introduces the book. Other case studies are included.

19074. Edgar, Robert E., ed. (1990) Sanctioning Apartheid. Trenton, NJ: Africa World Press.

19075. Edwards, Robert E. (1990) "Church Growth Using Small Home Worship Groups," Urban Mission. Vol. 7, No. 3 (January), pp. 43-45.

19076. Egan, John J., ed. (1990) Space Commerce: Proceedings of the Third International Conference and Exhibition on the Commerical and Industrial Uses of Outer Space. New York: Gordon and Breach Science Publishers, for the Conference

19077. Eickelman, Dale F. and James Piscatori, eds. (1990) Muslim Travellers: Pilgrims, Migration, and the Religious Imagination. London: Routledge.

19078. Elm, Kaspar and Hans Dietrich Loock, eds. (1990) Seelsorge und Diakonie in Berlin: Beiträge zum Verhältnis von Kirche und Großstadt im 19. und beginnenden 20. Jahrhundert. Berlin: W. de Gruyter. Articles about Protestant and Catholic pastoral work in Berlin during the 19th and early 20th centuries. Bibliography.

19079. Escobar, Samuel. (1990) "From Lausanne 1974 to Manila 1989: The Pilgrimage of Urban Mission," Urban Mission. Vol. 7, No. 4 (March), pp. 21-29.

19080. Farnell, Richard. (1990) "Through Powerlessness: Engaging Christian Commitment with Urban Reality," Urban Mission. Vol. 7, No. 3 (January), pp. 15-24.

19081. Fernandez, Arturo. (1990) Sindicalismo e Iglesia (1976-1987). Buenos Aires, Argentina: Centro Editor de America Latina. Re: church relationships to trade unions and labor conditions in Argentina. Bibliography.

19082. Fitzpatrick, Joseph P. (1990) "No Place to Grieve: A Honduran Tragedy," America [Thematic issue: The church in the cities]. Vol. 163, No. 2 (July 14), pp. 37-38. Re: difficulties of Honduran immigrants finding a place to be "at home" in the church.

19083. Fitzpatrick, Joseph P. (1990) Paul: Saint of the Inner City. New York: Paulist.

19084. Franklin, Robert Michael. (1990) Liberating Visions:

Human Fulfillment and Social Justice in African-American Thought. Minneapolis, MN: Fortress. Biographical descriptions of Booker T. Washington, W. E. B. Du Bois, and Martin Luther King, Jr., followed by discussion of African American leaders' ideas about the nature of human fulfillment.

19085. Furnham, Adrian. (1990) The Protestant Work Ethic: The Psychology of Work-Related Beliefs and Behaviors. London: Routledge. An overview of psychological research related to Max Weber's hypothesis. Bibliography. Reviewed negatively: Journal for the Scientific Study of Religion. Vol. 30, No. 3 (September, 1991), pp. 342-343

19086. Garrity, Paul F. (1990) A Theology of the Small Urban Church. Thesis (D. Min.). Chicago, IL: Lutheran School of Theology at Chicago. Written at a time when formerly large churches had become quite small and some perennially small churches showed remarkable survival abilities.

19087. Gill, Robin. (1990) "More Pews Than Parishioners," Church Times. Vol. 275, No. 6638 (May 4), p. 6. Gill contends, based on his analysis of historical statistics, that the spate of urban church extension efforts following the 1851 religious census in England did not reverse losses in church membership. In a perverse way, the new buildings may have actually contributed to a decline in membership. Many urban churches which were disbanded in the 20th century were never heavily used because their development was misconceived from the start. Hence, the number of church closings is not a reliable indicator of religious decline.

19088. Graham, W. Fred, et al. (1990) Reforming Economics: Calvinist Studies on Methods and Institutions. Lewistown, NY: Mellon.

19089. Green, Louise. (1990) "Life in Limbo," World--Journal of the Unitarian Universalist Association. Vol. 4, No. 3 (May-June), pp. 12-14. Conditions of immigrants in the Immigration and Naturalization Service's detention center in Boston are problematic. Life is especially difficult for political refugees who came to the USA seeking freedom, but find themselves once again jailed, the very condition they sought to escape by coming to the USA.

19090. Gregory, Diana. (1990) "Church and Parish," Crucible. [Vol. 29, No. 2] (April-June), pp. 59-65. Gregory reports a sociological study of two parishes in Cardiff, Wales, one near the inner city, the other in an outlying area.

19091. Greiser, David. (1990) A Manual for Planting Urban Mennonite Churches. Thesis (D. Min.). Chestnut Hill, PA: Westminster Theological Seminary. Mennonite urban church extension strategies.

19092. Hadaway, C. Kirk. (1990) "The Impact of New Church Development on Southern Baptist Growth," Review of Religious Research. Vol. 31. No. 4 (June), pp. 370-379. New churches are found to grow faster than older churches, even in similar social and demographic settings. Bibliography.

19093. Hamnett, Ian, ed. (1990) Religious Pluralism and Unbelief. London: Routledge. A multi-disciplinary analysis, including perspectives from anthropology, law, sociology, history, theology, religious studies, and philosophy.

19094. Harris, James Henry. (1990) "Practicing Liberation in the Black Church," Christian Century. Vol. 107, No. 19 (June 13-20), pp. 559-601. Harris calls Black theologians and Black churches to strengthen ties and to implement programs of liberation. A response by Gayraud Wilmore is attached.

19095. Harris, Sidney. (1990) "Urban Life: The View from the Street," The Critic. Vol. 44, No. 4 (Summer), pp. 18-28. Harris' cartoons are pointed about city conditions.

19096. Hedges, Chris. (1990) "Mainline Protestant Ministers Turning from the Inner City," New York Times. Vol. 139, No. 48,252 (May 31), pp. 1+. Few seminarians plan to serve in the inner city. Twenty years ago, unlike today, city ministry was seen as the cutting edge. Those who have attempted inner city ministry in recent years often fail, becoming discouraged because of the lack of financial and moral support they receive from the tiny parishes they serve.

19097. Hertzler, Laurel Schmidt. (1990) "Ministry Goes Forth from a $1 Building: Diamond Street Mennonite Church at Work," The Mennonite. Vol. 105, No. 1 (January 9), pp. 4-6.

19098. Hillam, Corbin. (1990) Jennifer of the City. St. Louis, MO: Concordia. Children's literature. A missionary's daughter explains how her family tells city people about Jesus.

19099. Hollowell, Martha. (1990) "Evangelizing the Homeless,"

Urban Mission. Vol. 7, No. 3 (January), pp. 36-42.

19100. Houghtby, Natalie. (1990) "Los Angeles and the Church in the Year 2000," Impact: Disciples of Christ on the Pacific Slope [Claremont]. No. 24, pp. 29-34. Re: First United Methodist Church, Los Angeles, CA.

19101. Howe, Marvin. (1990) "Mysterious Fall Kills a Minister," New York Times. Vol. 140 (December 20), p. A20. Noah Lewis, a minister who worked with homeless youth in the Bronx, dies under questionable circumstances.

19102. Hunt, Angela Elwell. (1990) "Manhattan's Model Ministry," Christianity Today. Vol. 34, No. 15 (October 22), pp. 17-18. Fashion models are recruited to work with the homeless.

19103. Hwang, Andrew and Richard Ng. (1990) "Singapore: Uniting Social Concern and Evangelism," Urban Mission. Vol. 7, No. 4 (March), pp. 36-44.

19104. Hyre, Meg, Jane Elizabeth Sammon, and Katherine Temple. (1990) "The Scholars Must become Workers So the Workers May become Scholars," Religion and Intellectual Life [Thematic issue: Cities--Boon or Bane to the Life of the Spirit]. Vol. 7, No. 2 (Winter), pp. 12-25. Three participants in the Catholic Worker Movement reflect on the teachings of Dorothy Day and their current experiences in city living.

19105. Jackson, Dave and Neta Jackson. (1990) "Discipleship in the 90s: Taking It to the Sreets," Discipleship Journal. Vol. 10 (January), pp. 16-17. [See Note 3].

19106. Joselit, Jenna Weissman. (1990) New York's Jewish Jews: The Orthodox Community in the Inter-War Years. Bloomington, IN: Indiana University Press.

19107. Kafka, Du^san J. (1990) "Unitarian Prague," The World: Journal of the Unitarian Universalist Association. Vol. 4, No. 3 (May-June), pp. 8-11. A Unitarian minister comments on the long-term effects of church repression in Prague, Czechsolovakia.

19108. Kamel, Rachael. (1990) The Global Factory: Analysis and Action for a New Economic Era. [Philadelphia, PA]: American Friends Service Committee. Discussions about plant closings in the USA and slave wages paid workers in new factories in Mexico and the Philippines.

19109. Katz, Michael. (1990) The Undeserving Poor: From the War on Poverty to the War on Welfare. New York: Pantheon. An examination of intellectual understandings of the poor from the time of Lyndon Johnson to Ronald Reagan.

19110. Kelley, Dean M. (1990) "Dealing with Innovation and Government Regulation: The Zone of Perpetual Turbulence," Social Compass. Vol. 37, No. 1 (March), pp. 137-143. Government has interfered with new religious groups, sometimes acting to suppress them, as in the case of Scientology. Kelley argues that the government needs to maintain a true and just neutrality regarding such groups.

19111. Klieman, Aaron S. and Adrian L Klieman. (1990) American Zionism. New York: Garland. A 17 volume series of documents and source materials of American Jewish and Zionist history for the 19th century to 1968.

19112. Krueger, David A. (1990) "Connecting Ministry and Corporate Life," Christian Century. Vol. 107, No. 10 (May 30-June 6), pp. 572-574. Krueger, at the time of writing, served as Director of the Center for Ethics and Corporate Policy.

19113. Lincoln, C. Eric and Lawrence H. Mamiya. (1990) The Black Church in the African American Experience. Durham, NC: Duke University Press. Contains a chapter on the urban church titled "In the Streets of Black Metropolis: A Profile of Black Urban Clergy and Churches."

19114. Lloyd, George L. (1990) "Ministry in a Diverse Church," The Moravian [Thematic issue: West Indian/Caribbean Churches]. Vol. 21, No. 3 (April), pp. 3-4.

19115. Logan, William S. (1990) "Wayne State University: Ministry on an Escalator," Religion and Intellectual Life [Thematic issue: Cities--Boon or Bane to the Life of the Spirit]. Vol. 7, No. 2 (Winter), pp. 47-51. Logan directed the college work of the Episcopal Diocese of Michigan and, at the time of writing, was president of the Michigan Commission for United Ministries in Higher Education.

19116. Loudon, John B. (1990) Developing a New Self Concept and Staff for a Church in Transition from Understanding Itself as a Small Church to a Large Church. Thesis (D. Min). Chicago, IL: McCormick Theological Seminary.

19117. Luecke, Richard Henry. (1990) "The Oral, the Local and the Timely," Christian Century. Vol. 107, No. 27 (October 3), pp. 875-878. A review of Stephen Edelston Toulmin's Cosmopolis: the Hidden Agenda of Modernity (New York: Macmillan, 1990). Toulmin explores the philosophical meaning of modernity and its probable demise, finding hopeful prospect in reinterpreting 17th century history. Luecke uses the review to anticipate the shape of ministry in the post modern era.

19118. Malone, Nancy M., ed. (1990) "Cities: Boon or Bane of the Life of the Spirit," Religion and Intellectual Life [Thematic issue]. Vol. 7, No. 2 (Winter), pp. 3-74. Eight articles and a poem debate the question of whether or not cities are losing viability as intellectual and spiritual centers.

19119. Marty, Martin E. (1990) "Historic Church Preservation: Clues from the Almost Incommunicable Past," Christian Century. Vol. 107, No. 10 (March 21-28), pp. 303-305. Old houses of worship are valuable not only as beautiful antiques, but also for humanistic and spiritual values as well. Churches are fortunate when their building is well integrated with its profane surroundings.

19120. Meehan, John T. (1990) "In the Midst of Our Chaos, We Can Rejoice," Religion and Intellectual Life [Thematic issue: Cities--Boon or Bane to the Life of the Spirit]. Vol. 7, No. 2 (Winter), pp. 6-11. Meehan, a White Catholic priest serving at All Saints Church, Harlem, New York City, identifies the principles that have guided his ministry in the center of an African American community. Among his list are: listen a lot, discover order in chaos, preach sermons with clear messages, talk big, emphasize community pride, choose music that matters and moves. Meehan gives credit for the principles to Fr. Albert J. McKnight of Opelousas, LA.

19121. Melton, J. Gordon, ed. (1990) Cults and New Religions: Sources for the Study of Nonconventional Religious Groups in Nineteenth- and Twentieth-Century America. New York: Garland. This 24-volume series reproduces 150 rare pamphlets, books, and other fugitive documents produced by non-traditional religious groups. Materials distributed by the Jehovah's Witnesses, Unification Church, Hare Krishna, People's Temple (Jonestown), Spiritualism, Theosophy, as well as others and anti-cult literature are included.

19122. Miller, Lori. (1990) "Methodist Bishop [Felton E. May] Confronts Drug Abuse in the Region," The Washington Post. (June 2), p. B7. May, the United Methodist bishop of Harrisburg, PA, is spending a year working with 14 congregations in a troubled part of Washington, DC, on drug abuse and violence. Tent ministries are to be opened for 24 hours a day during the summer.

19123. Miller, Robert Moats. (1990) Bishop G. Bromley Oxnam: Paladin of Liberal Protestantism. Nashville, TN: Abingdon.

19124. Monsma, Timothy. (1990) "Understanding Urban Poverty: Perspectives from the Social Sciences," City Watch: A Research Bulletin of the Institute of Global Urban Studies [Pasadena, CA]. Vol. 5, No. 1 (February), pp. 1-2+.

19125. Montgomery, John C. (1990) Congregations, Faith and Economics: Selected Resources, an Annotated Bibliography. Chicago, IL: The Institute on the Church in Urban-Industrial Society. Resources for churches seeking involvement in local economic development.

19126. Moody, Kim. (1990) "What's Good for General Motors...," Christianity and Crisis. Vol. 50 (February 19), pp. 42-45. A Review of Jeanie Wylie's: Poletown: A Community Betrayed. Champaign, IL: University of Illinois, 1989.

19127. Moribe, Yoshimasa and Steve Hoke. (1990) "Reaching the World Changers: Understanding Japanese Youth," World Christian. Vol. 9, No. 2 (February), pp. 8-16.

19128. Morikawa, Hazel. (1990) Footprints: One Man's Pilgrimage: A Biography of Jitsuo Morikawa. Berkeley, CA: Jennings Associates for the Jitsuo Morikawa Memorial. Morikawa was highly influential in American Baptist policy toward cities during the 1960s.

19129. Murnion, Philip Joseph. (1990) "The Future of the Church in the Inner City," America. Vol. 163, No. 19 (December 15), pp. 478-485. Murnion searches for goals in inner city churches.

19130. Newton, Michael and Judy Ann Newton. (1990) The Ku Klux Klan: An Encyclopedia. New York: Garland. Begun shortly after the US Civil War, the Klan reached its apex in 1924 with over 4 million members, including President Harding. The Newtons trace the changing fortunes of the Klan and its terrorist activities.

19131. Newton, Michael and Judy Ann Newton. (1990) Racial and Religious Violence: A Chronology. New York: Garland. A chronological listing of 8800 events.

19132. Niemeyer, Larry L. (1990) "Church Growth in Nairobi, Kenya," Urban Mission. Vol. 8, No. 1 (September), pp. 45-54.

19133. Northcott, Michael S. (1990) "Urban Theology, 1960-1990," Crucible. [Vol. 29, No. 4] (October-December), pp. 161-170; Vol. 30, No. 1 (January-March), pp. 17-24. A comprehensive survey of British urban theology in regard to political and economic changes, includes strategy recommendations. Footnotes.

19134. Olley, John W. (1990) "God's Agenda for the City: Some Biblical Perspectives," Urban Mission. Vol. 8, No. 1 (September), pp. 14-23.

19135. Ortiz, Manuel. (1990) "Development Ministries," Urban Mission [Thematic issue: Urban development ministries]. Vol. 7, No. 5 (May), pp. 3-6. Ortiz introduces a thematic issue on community development, emphasizing the importance of an approach which values indigenousness, redemption, compassion, justice, progress, and Biblical obedience.

19136. Ousley, J. Douglas. (1990) "Being a Neighbor to Street People," The Christian Century. Vol. 107, No. 1 (January 3), pp. 6-7.

19137. Palmer, Parker. (1990) Scarcity, Abundance, and the Gift of Community. Chicago, IL: Community Renewal Society. Bibliography.

19138. Perry, Cynthia. (1990) Organizing for Change: IAF 50 Years -- Power, Action, Justice. New York: Industrial Areas Foundation. A celebratory history of the IAF's efforts to organize the poor, with emphasis on the church's involvement in organizing efforts.

19139. Pinnock, Wesley. (1990) Training Youth Leaders in the Urban Church. Thesis (D. Min). Chestnut Hill, PA: Westminster Theological Seminary.

19140. Plelan, Thomas. (1990) "Building the World: Thoughts on the University and the City," Religion and Intellectual Life [Thematic issue: Cities--Boon or Bane to the Life of the Spirit]. Vol. 7, No. 2 (Winter), pp. 52-59. Plelan, a Catholic priest, recounts his experiences in several university-related roles and summarizes his conclusions on the service of the university to the city.

19141. Pohorski, Susan. (1990) "Students in Urban Ministry,"

World Christian. Vol. 9, No. 5 (May), pp. 32+.

19142. Pozzetta, George E., ed. (1990) The Immigrant Religious Experience. New York: Garland. A series of studies of the popular piety of immigrants as well as their involvement in the national churches.

19143. Prell, Riv-Ellen. (1990) "Leaving the Suburbs: Reformulating American Judaism in the 1970s," Religion and Intellectual Life [Thematic issue: Cities--Boon or Bane to the Life of the Spirit]. Vol. 7, No. 2 (Winter), pp. 26-39. Prell reports participant observation of innovative Jewish communities, the Havurah, in Los Angeles, CA. Bibliography.

19144. Ramsden, William E. and John C. Montgomery. (1990) Biblical Integrity and People Power: A New Look at Church-Based Community Organizing in the 1990s. Chicago, IL: Institute on the Church in Urban-Industrial Society (ICUIS). Ramsden and Montgomery assess the practice of the community organizing techniques developed by the Industrial Areas Foundation and similar organizations being used as a part of local churches' community ministry strategy. Church-based organizing is differentiated from other varieties. The former builds community organization around churches as the primary members. It starts the organizing process by ascertaining and acting on perceived concerns of church members, then proceeds to address concerns identified by the wider community.

19145. Recinos, Harold Joseph. (1990) "God's Sacred Place: the City," Circuit Rider [Thematic issue: City ministry and drug abuse]. Vol. 14, No. 10 (December), pp. 28-30.

19146. Renewing Old Friendships: Religion and Organized Labor. (1990) [Three 60 to 90 minute audio tapes]. Chicago, IL: ACTA Publications for the Department of Urban Affairs. Edited presentations from a conference on the history and state of present relationships between religion and labor, organized by John Egan. Topics include continuing education, health and health care, plant closings, salaries and benefits, alternatives to the strike, and worker organization.

19147. Richardson, Lynda. (1990) "Lesbian Couple Wed in District Church," The Washington Post. (June 2), p. B7. Holy union ceremonies for a lesbian couple were moved from a United Methodist congregation to a Presbyterian church when Bishop Joseph H. Yeakle warned that such a ceremony was incompatible with church law.

19148. Rogers, Mary Beth. (1990) Cold Anger: The Story of

Faith and Politics. Denton, TX: University of North Texas Press.

19149. Rubenson, Birgitta. (1990) "What the World Council of Churches Is Doing about AIDS," Contact [Thematic issue: AIDS]. No. 117 (December), pp. 7-18.

19150. Russell, Letty M., ed. (1990) The Church with AIDS: Renewal in the Midst of Crisis. Louisville, KY: Westminster, John Knox. Experiences of persons ministering with AIDS victims and theological reflection on the AIDS crisis.

19151. Ruud, Marie. (1990) Women and Judaism: A Select Annotated Bibliography. New York: Garland.

19152. Salem, Dorothy. (1990) To Better Our World: Black Women in Organized Reform 1890-1920. Brooklyn, NY: Carlson. A history of Black women's involvement in social reform traces their support in the emergence of the NAACP and the National Urban League.

19153. Saliba, John A. (1990) Social Science and the Cults: An Annotated Bibliography. New York: Garland. Saliba lists social scientific literature on cults and sects in Western culture.

19154. Sawyer, Joy Roulier. (1990) "Where Only the Brave and the Addicted Dare Tread," Christianity Today. Vol. 34, No. 11 (August 20), pp. 12-13. Re: Upper Room outreach ministries to the poor and downtrodden in New York City.

19155. Schaper, Donna. (1990) "Urban Ministry: The Bricks without Straw Syndrom," Other Side. Vol. 26, No. 4 (July), pp. 49-52. Re: church work with the poor from a "Christ against culture" perspective.

19156. Senior, Donald. (1990) "Urban-Based Formation," SEDOS. Vol. 22 (May 15), pp. 152-155. Re: biblical teaching on the city in light of the world trend toward urbanization.

19157. Sennett, Richard. (1990) Conscience of the Eye: The Design and Social Life of Cities. New York: Knopf.

19158. Shorter, Aylward. (1990) "Urbanization: Today's Missionary Reality in Africa," AFER: African Ecclesial Review. Vol. 32, No. 5 (October), pp. 290-300. Shorter describes anti-urbanism and the urban bias. He comments on urban pollution, poverty, disorganization and secularization. Pastoral strategies are listed.

19159. Smith, Glenn. (1990) "Reaching Canada's Cities for Christ," Urban Mission. Vol. 8, No. 1 (September), pp. 27-36.

19160. Steinfels, Peter. (1990) "New York City Clergy Hope Neighborliness Will Help Race Relations," New York Times. (January 14), p. 25.

19161. Stephens, Carol Brethour. (1990) Neighbour to Neighbour. Ontario, Canada: Interfaith Social Assistance Reform Coalition on Poverty in Ontario. A historical summary of ISARC's work is followed by analysis of the causes of poverty. Housing problems, health issues and employment issues are described. Policy recommendations for faith community and governments are included.

19162. Strom, Stephanie. (1990) "Ministers in Some Poor Areas of New York Are Arming Themselves," New York Times. Vol. 139 (April 23), p. 17.

19163. Symanowski, Horst. (1990) "Das Konzept der Industriearbeit in Mainz-Kastel," Zeitschrift für evangelische Ethik. Vol. 34, No. 2 (April-June), pp. 122-127. Symanowski reviews developments since his earlier writing on industrial mission.

19164. Thomas, Stanley F. (1990) "The Emergence of West Indian Congregations," The Moravian [Thematic issue: West Indian/Caribbean Churches]. Vol. 21, No. 3 (April), pp. 6-7.

19165. Thornburg, John D. and Elizabeth Thornberg. (1990) "East Dallas Cooperative Parish: Born to Serve, Grown to Redeem," Circuit Rider [Thematic issue: City ministry and drug abuse]. Vol. 14, No. 10 (December), pp. 6-7.

19166. Thung, Mady A. (1990) "Dealing with Problems of Pluralism," Social Compass. Vol. 37, No. 1 (March), pp. 153-160. Thung responds to Dean M. Kelley and other contributors to this issue of Social Compass on the sociology of religious pluralism.

19167. Tink, Fletcher L. (1990) "The Strand Hotel: A Case Study in Faith or Failure," Urban Mission. Vol. 7, No. 5 (May), pp. 28-36. Tink is director of the Bresee Institute, Los Angeles, CA, which is affiliated with the First Church of the Nazarene in that city. The urban ministries supported by the institute are described. The church has multiple language groups.

19168. Toh, Serene S. (1990) "Home Cell Groups in St. John's-St. Margaret's Church," Urban Mission. Vol. 7, No. 4 (March), pp. 45-52.

19169. United Methodist Church, General Board of Global Ministries, National Program Division. (1990) The Burning Heart: Vision for Asian American Missional Congregations. New York: the Division. A report of a conference on Asian American United Methodist church work. Ethnic groups included are: Chinese, Filipino, Formosan, Indochinese, Japanese, Korean, and South Asian.

19170. Updike, John. (1990) Rabbit at Rest. New York: Knopf. Presumably the last of four novels in a series, in this installment a prematurely aged Rabbit dies. This volume won the Pultizer Prize for Literature. For other novels in the Rabbit series, see Updike (1960, 1971, 1981).

19171. Urban Ministry in Indonesia. (1990?) Jakarta, Indonesia: World Vision International, Indonesia Office. A description of World Vision's ministry in Jakarta, including recommendations. A pamphlet.

19172. Vickrey, Raymond. (1990) "Dallas: City with Many Souls," Religion and Intellectual Life [Thematic issue: Cities--Boon or Bane to the Life of the Spirit]. Vol. 7, No. 2 (Winter), pp. 40-46. Dallas has not decided what its identity is, and therefore tries to be everything. The result is a crisis in the religious and intellectual life of the city. Vickrey, pastor of Royal Lane Baptist Church, analyzes the various religious elements present in the city.

19173. Vilankulu, Sarah J. (1990) "Churches Uniting Against Drugs," Christian Century. Vol. 107, No. 33 (November 14), pp. 1052-1053. Vilankulu reviews church involvement in Washington, Los Angeles, and Houston. Approaches of Blacks and Whites are compared.

19174. We Share in God's Great Help: Four Weeks of Prayer for Congregations. (1990) Nashville, TN: The Upper Room. Prayer recommendations for congregations associated with Methodist Bishop Felton E. May's year-long work among the people of the drug culture in Washington, DC.

19175. Webber, George Williams. (1990) Led by the Spirit: The Story of New York Theological Seminary. New York: Pilgrim Press.

19176. Westberg, Granger E. (1990) Parish Nurse: Providing a Minister of Health for Your Congregation. Minneapolis, MN: Augsburg.

19177. Weyer, Adam and Stephan Wippermann. (1990) Kirche im Industriegebeit am Beispiel das westlichen Ruhrgebeites. Duisburg, Germany: Gilles und Fracke. Re: church and labor. Bibliography.

19178. Wichira, Haron. (1990) "Ghettos of Nairobi," World Christian. Vol. 9, No. 1 (January), pp. 10-19.

19179. Wilkerson, Isabel. (1990) "Catholic Parish Closings Bring Tears in Chicago," New York Times. Vol. 139 (July 9), National pages A10, col. 1. Chicago's Archdiocese closes 28 churches. See further a related article: New York Times. Vol. 139 (January 22, 1990), p. 8.

19180. Wilkerson, Isabel. (1990) "Students Deplore Plan to Shut Chicago Seminary," New York Times. Vol. 139 (February 25), p. 17.

19181. Williams, Cecil. (1990) Redefining the Drug Crisis. [Spoken recording: Southwestern Lectures]. Georgetown, TX: Southwestern University. Williams, pastor at Glide Memorial Methodist Church, San Francisco, CA, made the drug problem a major part of his ministry.

19182. Williams, Norma. (1990) The Mexican American Family: Tradition and Change. New York: General Hall. Williams describes the role of religious beliefs and rituals in Mexican American family life. Reviewed: Journal for the Scientific Study of Religion. Vol. 30, No. 3 (September, 1991), p. 325.

19183. Williams, Preston N. (1990) "A More Perfect Union: The Silence of the Church," America. Vol. 162, No. 12 (March 31), pp. 315-318. Williams believes the church has failed to support and understand African Americans.

19184. Winter, Gibson. (1990) "Urbanization in the Great City," Religion and Intellectual Life [Thematic issue: Cities--Boon or Bane to the Life of the Spirit]. Vol. 7, No. 2 (Winter), pp. 65-73. Winter reflects on the symbolic aspects of the contemporary city and on the fact that society has been enfolded in a single city -- the Great City -- with all its pathologies and potential for improvement.

19185. Wogaman, J. Philip. (1990) "Socialism's Obituary Is Premature," Christian Century. Vol. 107, No. 13 (April 18), pp. 398-400. Written shortly after eastern European countries began moving toward becoming more like western capitalist economies.

19186. Wolcott, Roger T. and Dorita F. Bolger. (1990) Church and Social Action: A Critical Assessment and Bibliographical Survey. New York: Greenwood. A bibliographic retracing of debates about religious social movements and the church's role in promoting social action, principally in the United States during the 1960s and following. Also included is a wide range of comparative studies drawn from the literature of other nations.

19187. Wolff, Robert C. (1990) Sister Henrietta of Hough--She Reclaimed a Cleveland Slum. Chicago, IL: Loyola University Press.

19188. Addy, Tony [Anthony J.]. (1991) Changing Europe--Changing Urban-Industrial and Rural Mission. Manchester, England: the William Temple Foundation for The European Contact Group on UIRM. Re: local and regional strategies for Urban-Industrial Mission in Europe.

19189. Adriance, Madeleine. (1991) "Agents of Change: The Roles of Priests, Sisters, and lay Workers in the Grassroots Catholic Church in Brazil," Journal for the Scientific Study of Religion. Vol. 30, No. 3 (Spetember), pp. 292-305. Adriance contends that much of the research on basic Christian communities has suffered from an urban bias. Bibliography.

19190. Balmer, Randall. (1991) "Churchgoing: First Community Church, Columbus, Ohio," Christian Century. Vol. 108, No. 27 (October 2), pp. 876-881. Balmer revisits one of the congregations chosen as a "great American church" by the Christian Century in 1950 [Vol. 67, No. 51 (December 20), pp. 1513-1520]. First in a series of articles.

19191. Barnes, Howard A. (1991) Horace Bushnell and the Virtuous Republic. Metuchen, NJ: Sacrecrow, ATLA Monograph Series, No. 27. Barnes provides an introduction to Bushnell's vision of the ideal society and its dependence on nurturing institutions. Bibliography.

19192. Breton, Denese and Christopher Largent. (1991) The Gospel of Economics: Spiritual Evolution Goes to the Marketplace. Wilmington, DE: Idea House. Bibliographical notes.

19193. Campo, Juan Eduardo. (1991) The Other Sides of Paradise: Explorations into the Meanings of Domestice Space in Islam. Columbia, SC: University of South Carolina Press. Re: family life and housing in Cairo, Egypt. Bibliography.

19194. Center for Church and Community Ministries. (1991) Saints and Neighbors. Chicago, IL: the Center. Stories from people in churches participating in the Center's projects.

19195. Center for Church and Community Ministries. (beginning in 1991) Church and Community Forum. Chicago, IL: the Center. A newsletter on planning justice oriented community ministries, renewal of congregational life, and parish outreach. Carl S. Dudley is director of the ecumenical center. Substantive articles are included along with information about developments in the field and news items.

19196. Champion, A. G. (1991) Counterurbanization: The Changing Pace and Nature of Population Decentralization. New York: Edward Arnold. A description of population decentralization in the USA, Australia, Japan, and Great Britain.

19197. Choron-Baix, Catherine. (1991) "De forêts en banlieues: La transplantation du bouddhisme lao en France," Archives de Sciences Sociales des Religions [Thematic issue: Anthropologie urbaine religieuse]. Vol. 36, No. 73 (January-March), pp. 17-34. Re: Lao Buddhists who have taken refuge in France transplant their religious rites. Abstract in English. Bibliography.

19198. Coalter, Milton J., John M. Mulder, and Louis B. Weeks, eds. (1991) The Diversity of Discipleship: Presbyterians and the Twentieth Century Christian Witness. Lousiville, KY: Westminster/John Knox. Part of a series of studies on Presbyterianism funded by the Lilly Endowment, this volume evaluates the ethnic ministries within that denomination. Bibliography. See further a volume edited by the same authors: The Mainline Protestant "Decline:" The Presbyterian Pattern. Louisville, KY: Westminster/John Knox, 1990.

19199. Danker, William J. (1991) "Vertical Thinking Revived a Downtown Church," Christian Ministry [Thematic issue: City Ministry]. Vol. 22, no. 4 (September-October), pp. 19-22. A United Methodist Church in Denver, CO, sells some of its land and air rights to support its budget.

19200. Dill, Ellen Renee. (1991) "A Multipoint Approach to Urban Community Ministry," Christian Ministry [Thematic issue: City Ministry]. Vol. 22, no. 4 (September-October), pp. 12-13.

19201. Dorsett, Lyle W. (1991) Billy Sunday and the Redemption of Urban America. Grand Rapids, MI: Eerdmans. A biography of Sunday and an assessment of his urban revivals.

19202. Dudley, Carl S. (1991) Basic Steps toward Community Ministry. New York: Alban Institute. A guide for congregation-based social ministry.

19203. Dudley, Carl S., Jackson W. Carroll, and James D. Wind. (1991) Carriers of Faith: Lessons from Congregational Studies. Louisville, KY: Westminster/John Knox. Includes an article on the development of the Church and Community Ministries program, Chicago, IL.

19204. Ellison, Craig W. and Edward S. Maynard. (1991) Healing for the City: Counseling for the Urban Setting. Grand Rapids, MI: Zondervan. Ellison proposes models for psycho-spiritual counseling from an evangelical Protestant perspective. Chapters address the counseling issues most often confronted by urban pastors, e.g., AIDS, addiction, victimization. Bibliography.

19205. Fahey, David M. (1991) "Elites, Evangelicals, and the London Poor," Journal of Urban History. Vol. 17, No. 3 (May), pp. 293-295. A review of recent monographs on religion and London's poor.

19206. Fenn, Richard K. (1991) The Secularization of Sin: An Investigation of the Daedalus Complex. Louisville, KY: Westminster/John Knox. Bibliography.

19207. Fischel, Jack and Sanford Pinsker. (1991) Jewish-American History and Culture: An Encyclopedia. New York: Garland. A reference work on Jewish religious bodies, communal organizations, secular activities, biography, and notable contributions.

19208. Fonseca, Claudia. (1991) "La religion dans la vie quotidienne d'un groupe populaire brésilien," Archives de Sciences Sociales des Religions [Thematic issue: Anthropologie urbaine religieuse]. Vol. 36, No. 73 (January-March), pp. 125-139. Abstract in English. Bibliography.

19209. Frangipane, Francis. (1991) The House of the Lord: God's Plan to Liberate Your City from Darkness. Lake Mary, FL: Creation House. Frangipane, a pastor in Cedar Rapids, IA, offers a plan for city evangelization and issues a call to Christians to lay aside individual doctrinal differences in favor of unity in common cause for worship of God and warfare with city evil. Salvation of the city is dependent on the salvation of individuals.

19210. Fribourg, Jeanine. (1991) "Les rues de la ville: Scéne du Religieux," Archives de Sciences Sociales des Religions [Thematic issue: Anthropologie urbaine religieuse]. Vol. 36, No. 73 (January-March), pp. 51-62. Some Spanish city streets become grandiose religious groundplays. Photographs. Abstract in English. Bibliography.

19211. Gibbal, Jean-Marie. (1991) "La Pomba Gira reçoit ce soir: Urbanité et religiosité à Porto Alegre," Archives de Sciences Sociales des Religions [Thematic issue: Anthropologie urbaine religieuse]. Vol. 36, No. 73 (January-March), pp. 115-124. Abstract in English. Bibliography.

19212. Gutwirth, Jacques. (1991) "Anthropologie urbaine religieuse: une introduction," Archives de Sciences Sociales des Religions [Thematic issue: Anthropologie urbaine religieuse]. Vol. 36, No. 73 (January-March), pp. 5-17. An introduction to the articles in this thematic issues and comment on the status of the anthropology of urban religion. Bibliography.

19213. Gutwirth, Jacques. (1991) "Pentecôtisme national et audiovisuel à Porto Alegre, Brésil," Archives de Sciences Sociales des Religions [Thematic issue: Anthropologie urbaine religieuse]. Vol. 36, No. 73 (January-March), pp. 99-114. Gutwirth, an anthropologist, describes the uses of radio and television by Pentecostal churches in Brazil. Abstract in English. Bibliography.

19214. Halker, Clark. (1991) "Jesus Was a Carpenter: Labor Song-Poems, Labor Protest, and True Religion in Gilded Age America," Labor History. Vol. 32, No. 2 (Spring), pp. 273-289. Halker interprets the poetry and popular hymns of the working class, several of which condemn the church and offer reasons for workers to leaving it. Reference is made to a forthcoming monograph by the author titled: For Democracy, Workers and God: Labor Song-Poems and Labor Protest. Urbana, IL (1991).

19215. Henslin, James M. (1991) Homelessness: An Annotated Bibliography. New York: Garland. Henslin bibliography covers both scholarly and popular press materials, including the Wall Street Journal and the New York Times. Some church-related citations and materials are included.

19216. Hoover, Dwight W. (1991) "Middletown: A Case Study

of Religious Development, 1827-1892," Social Compass. Vol. 38, No. 3 (September), pp. 273-284. Hoover tests Alexis de Tocqueville's and the Lynns' ideas about religious development using data from Muncie, IN, the quintessential middle-American city.

19217. Kavanaugh, John F. and Mev Puleo. (1991) Faces of Poverty, Faces of Christ. Maryknoll, NY: Orbis. Moving vignettes of poor people. Includes photographs.

19218. Leman, Nicholas. (1991) The Promised Land: The Great Black Migration and How it Changed America. New York: Knopf. The history and consequences of the northward migration of African Americans in the 20th century.

19219. Linthicum, Robert C. (1991) City of God, City of Satan: A Biblical Theology of the Urban Church. Grand Rapids, MI: Zondervan. Linthicum, an executive of World Vision International, offers an evangelical perspective on the church's mission based on biblical references about cities. Bibliography.

19220. Linthicum, Robert C. (1991) Empowering the Poor: Community Organizing among the City's Ragtag and Bobtail. Monrovia, CA: MARC. Bibliography.

19221. Littler, June D. (1991) The Church of Scientology: A Bibliography. New York: Garland. Littler lists writings of L. Ron Hubbard and the Scientology movement, including audio-visual materials.

19222. Lorentzen, Robin. (1991) Women in the Sanctuary Movement. Philadelphia, PA: Temple University Press. Re: women leaders in the sanctuary movement in Chicago, IL. Bibliography.

19223. Lovett, S. C. Campbell. (1991) The Local Church and Community Organizing. Thesis (D. Min.). Hartford, CT: Hartford Seminary Foundation.

19224. MacKeith, John. (1991) "Health in the City," Crucible. [Vol 30, No. 1] (January-March), pp. 36-41. Re: ecumenical follow-up to the health policy section of the report titled Faith in the City prepared by the Church of England's Commission on Urban Priority Areas (1985).

19225. McClung, Floyd. (1991) Seeing Cities with the Eyes of God. Tarrytown, NY: Chosen Books. Originally published in Britain under the title: Spirits of the City.

19226. McFadden, Robert D. (1991) "New York Hears Words of Hope from Billy Graham," New York Times. Vol. 141, No. 48,732 (September 23), pp. B1+. A one day campaign conducted by Graham in New York City's Central Park attracted 250,000 people, the largest gathering ever to hear Graham in North America. Mayor Dinkins welcomed Graham, who spoke of New York's prominence as a "world capital" and of its social problems and desperate spiritual needs. Graham spoke appreciation for Roman Catholic support of the event. His text was John 3:16 and he preached personal salvation. Promotional materials were distributed at the event and a video prepared for syndication on television.

19227. Milligan, Fred D., Jr. (1991) "Perservering and Preserving: An Inspired Partnership," Christian Ministry [Thematic issue: City Ministry]. Vol. 22, no. 4 (September-October), pp. 15-18. Re: a Lilly Endowment funded project for preserving deteriorating inner city church buildings.

19228. Mueller, Samuel A. (1991) "General and Organizational Religious Elites: The Case of Lutherans in Indiana," Sociological Focus. Vol. 24, No. 3 (August), pp. 197-210. Indiana has had an unusually high number of Lutheran politicians (six governors and senators since World War II). The Lutheran politicians were drawn exclusively from areas of "thin scatter" while the state-wide denominational leadership has been drawn disproportionately from the few areas of heavy Lutheran concentration. This pattern is explained in terms of the existence of a "thick" network of Lutheran organizations and institutions in the concentrated areas, which requires the expenditure of time and energy on the part of Lutheran potential members of the elite, creating for these people a social ladder into the church's leadership positions. Potential Lutheran leaders in areas of thin scatter, conversely, lack such a denominational network and are forced onto the social ladders of general society. Mueller, at the time of writing, was a professor at the University of Akron.

19229. O'Connor, June. (1991) The Moral Vision of Dorothy Day: A Feminist Perspective. New York: Crossroads. A biography of the founder of the Catholic Worker Movement. Bibliography.

19230. Pannell, William E. (1991) Evangelism from the Bottom Up. Grand Rapids, MI: Zondervan.

19231. Perez y Mena, Andres Isidoro. (1991) Speaking with the

Dead: Development of Afro-Latin Religion among Puerto Ricans in the United States: A Study into the Interpretation of Civilizations in the New World. New York: AMS Press. Re: spiritualism and the Santeria cult in the Bronx, New York City. Bibliography.

19232. Pettersson, Thorleif. (1991) "Religion and Criminality: Structural Relationships between Church Involvement and Crime Rates in Contemporary Sweden," Journal for the Scientific Study of Religion. Vol. 30, No. 3 (September), pp. 279-291. Swedish data support the notion of a negative association between religious involvement and criminal behavior. Bibliography.

19233. Pierrard, Pierre. (1991) L'Eglise et les ouvriers en France: 1940-1990. [Paris]: Hachette littérature. Re: church and labor relations in France.

19234. Radner, Ephraim. (1991) "Knowing God, Committing to Ministry," Christian Ministry [Thematic issue: City Ministry]. Vol. 22, no. 4 (September-October), pp. 8-11. Radner describes the importance of volunteers in inner city ministries and laments the abandonment of poorer areas of inner cities by mainline churches.

19235. Raphael, Pierre. (1991) Inside Rikers Island. Maryknoll, NY: Orbis. A former French worker priest relates experiences and insights stemming from his 10 years chaplaincy in a New York City prison colony.

19236. Raulin, Anne. (1991) "The Aesthetic and Sacred Dimension of Urban Ecology: Paris' Little Asia," Archives de Sciences Sociales des Religions [Thematic issue: Anthropologie urbaine religieuse]. Vol. 36, No. 73 (January-March), pp. 35-51. Re: anthropology of urban Asian religions in Paris.

19237. Rico, Christine. (1991) Religious Support for Community-Based Development. Washington, DC: Council for Community Based Development and Interfaith Center on Corporate Responsibility. A study of denominational contributions to the finances of community organization efforts.

19238. Scheie, David M., et al. (1991) Religious Institutions as Partners in Community Based Development: Findings from Year One of the Lilly Endowment Program. Minneapolis, MN: Rainbow Research. A description of the variety of partnerships existing between churches and community organization agencies: single organizers with religious connections, single congregations affiliated with a community based organization, groups of congregations similarly affiliated, hybrid agencies, etc. Examples are described.

19239. Shannon, Thomas A. (1991) "Rerum Novarum: A Century of Social Thinking," Theology and Public Policy. Vol. 3, No. 1 (Summer), pp. 11-25.

19240. Shorter, Aylward. (1991) The Church in the African City. London: Geoffrey Chapman. Shorter, at the time of writing, was a Catholic priest and President of the Missionary Institute, London. This volume, which reports his years of experience as a missionary in sub-Sahara Africa, describes cultural and religious conflicts, desperate poverty, the AIDS crisis, the conditions of street children, the lack of employment opportunities and job training, and the churches' efforts to cope with burgeoning urbanization. Shorter frequently writes on African urban churches. Bibliography.

19241. Spohn, Willfried. (1991) "Religion and Working-Class Formation in Imperial Germany 1871-1914," Politics and Society. Vol.19 (March), pp. 109-132.

19242. Stumme, Wayne, ed. (1991) The Experience of Hope: Mission and Ministry in Changing Urban Communities. Minneapolis, MN: Augsburg. A collection of articles about Lutheran urban ministries and goals. Includes "The Parish as Place: Principles of Parish Minsitry," a document adopted by three Lutheran bodies: LCA, ALC and ELCA.

19243. Trolander, Judith Ann. (1991) "Hull-House and the Settlement Movement," Journal of Urban History. Vol. 17, No. 4 (August), pp. 410-420. A review of recent histories of Hull-House and the settlement movement in the late 19th and early 20th centuries.

19244. Watt, William Montgomery. (1991) Muslim-Christian Encounters. London: Routledge. Re: the mythology that surrounds Muslim-Christian relations. Suggestions for more accurate understandings are offered.

19245. Wheeler, Barbara G. and Edward Forley, eds. (1991) Shifting Boundaries: Contextual Approaches to the Structure of Theological Education. Louisville, KY: Westminster/John Knox. A assessment of theological education which takes into account implications of mainline Protestant membership decline in urban areas.

19246. Ziegenhals, Gretchen E. (1991) "Black Values, Families and Churches," Christian Century. Vol. 108, No. 16 (May 8), p. 509. An editorial on a conference regarding problems faced by Black families and churches.

19247. Zotti, Mary Irene. (1991) A Time of Awakening: The Young Christian Worker Story in the United States, 1938-1970. Chicago, IL: Loyola University Press. Bibliography.

Addendum

The following citations were collected after identifying numbers were assigned to the preceding citations. The Addendum is organized by date with the authors listed alphabetically within each year. Citations listed in the Addendum have been indexed.

19248. Sombart, Werner. (1913) The Jews and Modern Capitalism. New York: E. P. Dutton. Bibliography.

19249. Drachsler, Julius. (1920) Intermarriage in New York City. New York: Columbia University Press. Re: Jewish marriage rites and practices.

19250. Yoffie, Leah Rachel. (1920) "Yiddish Proverbs, Sayings ... etc. in St. Louis, MO," Journal of American Folklore. Vol. 33, No. 128 (April), pp. 134-165.

19251. Bercovici, Konrad. (1923) "The Greatest Jewish City in the World," Nation. Vol. 117, No. 3036 (September 12), pp. 259-261. Re: New York City.

19252. Gardiner, Alfred George. (1923?) The Life of George Cadbury. London: Cassell. A history of Cadbury's vision of Christian capitalism based on his Quaker heritage and of the development of Selly Oaks, England.

19253. Bloch, Chajim. (1925) The Golem: Legends of the Ghettos of Prague. Vienna, Austria: The Golem.

19254. Newman, Lewis I. (1925) Jewish Influences on Christian Reform Movements. New York: Columbia University Press. Based on the author's dissertation at Columbia. Bibliography.

19255. Jones, Richard G. (1926) God of Concrete. [A hymn in the Hymnal of the United Church of Christ, among others]. A hymn asserts the power of God over concrete, steel, piston, wheel, pylon, steam, girder, beam, atom and mine.

19256. Bosner, Edna M. (1927) The Golden Rule City: A Course in Religious Education Based on Activities. Boston, MA: Pilgrim Press. A teacher's guide to Sunday School work with children, this volume recommends building a pretend city inspired by the story of the Pilgrim's efforts toward a Golden Rule City.

19257. Tibbits, Clark. (1927) "A Study of Chicago Settlements and Their Districts," Social Forces. Vol. 6, No. 3 (March), pp. 430-437.

19258. Jacquet, Constant H., ed. [and others]. (beginning in 1933) Yearbook of American and Canadian Churches. [Title varies]. New York: Federal Council of Churches [after 1950: National Council of Churches of Christ in the USA]. Among other useful data, the addresses of city church organizations are often listed.

19259. Scudder, Vida Dutton. (1939) "Challenge to the Church," pp. 245-264 in Vida Dutton Scudder. Privilege of Age: Essays Secular and Spiritual. London: Dent. Re: church and labor issues.

19260. Borders, William Holmes. (1947?) Men Must Live as Brothers. [Atlanta, GA?]: s.n. Twenty sermons delivered by the pastor of Wheat Street Baptist Church, Atlanta, GA.

19261. Fremantle, Anne. (1950) "The Work of Dorothy Day in the Slums," Catholic World. Vol. 170, No. 1019 (February), pp. 333-337.

19262. McConnell, Francis John, bp. (1952) By the Way: An Autobiography. New York: Abingdon-Cokesbury. McConnell, a

Methodist bishop, was active in urban affairs and a liberal crusader for labor reform. See especially the chapter titled "The Steel Strike."

19263. Stewart, Betty, ed. (1952) How ... Home Missions Works for Human Rights. New York: Friendship Press. A collection of articles about the right to belong, to health, to education, to work, and to worship. A photo essay on East Harlem Protestant Parish is included.

19264. McCann, Richard V. (1957) Delinquency: Sickness or Sin? New York: Harper. Bibliography.

19265. Greene, Shirley E. (1960) Ferment on the Fringe: Studies of Rural Churches in Transition. Philadelphia, PA: Christian Education Press. Case studies of rural communities located close to major metropolitan areas.

19266. Crean, Robert. (1963?) The People Next Door. New York: National Conference of Christians and Jews. A drama intended to promote discussion about human relations.

19267. Heise, Kenan. (1965) They Speak for Themselves: Interviews with the Destitute in Chicago. [Chicago, IL?]: Young Christian Workers.

19268. Witt, Raymond H. (1965) It Ain't Been Easy, Charlie. New York: Pageant Press. The story of St. Stephen's Lutheran Church, Chicago, IL.

19269. English, James W. (1967) Handyman of the Lord: Life and Ministry of the Rev. William Holmes Borders. New York: Meredith. Borders served as pastor of the Wheat Street Baptist Church, Atlanta, GA, which is situated a short distance from Ebeneser Baptist Church which was served by the King family. Borders' church built high rise apartments for the elderly, erected low cost housing, established a credit union, installed a shopping center and provided a wide range of services to the community.

19270. Kaan, Frederick Herman. (1968) Sing We of the Modern City. [A hymn in the Hymnal of the United Church of Christ, among others]. A hymn celebrating God's immanence among endless rows of houses, nameless people, and urban wildernesses.

19271. West, Richard F. (1968) Christian Decision and Action: A Resource and Discussion Book for Youth. Boston, MA: United Church Press.

19272. Paul VI, Pope. (1969) Pastoralis Migratorum [An Apostolic Letter]. Vatican City: The Vatican. English edition: On the Care of Migrants. Washington, DC: National Catholic Conference, 1969. Instruction on the pastoral care of migrating people.

19273. Toren, Marian A., ed. (1969) Being the Good News: Twelve Contemporary Worship / Programs with Suggestions for Discussion, Study, and Action. New York: Council for Lay Life and Work, United Church of Christ. Worship suggestions filled with urban imagery.

19274. McConahay, John B. (1970) "Attitudes of Negroes toward the Church Following the Los Angeles Riots," Sociological Analysis. Vol. 31, No. 1 (Spring), pp. 12-22.

19275. Streyffeler, Alan. (1971) Prophets, Priests, and Politicians. Valley Forge, PA: Judson. An essay on secularization. Bibliography.

19276. Jackson, Dave and Neta Jackson. (1974) Living Together in a World Fallen Apart. Carol Stream, IL: Creation House. Re: Christian community life and Reba Place Fellowship, Evanston, IL.

19277. Novitsky, Anthony. (1975) "Peter Maurin's Green Revolution: The Radical Implications of Reactionary Social Catholicism," Review of Politics. Vol. 37, No. 1 (January), pp. 83-103. Based on the author's doctoral dissertation.

19278. Ludwig, Charles. (1976) Cities and New Testament Times. Denver, CO: Accent Books.

19279. Scott, Nathan A., Jr. (1976) The Poetry of Civic Virtue: Eliot, Malraux, and Auden. Philadelphia, PA: Fortress. An analysis of the city (polis) as a poetic and moral theme in the writings of three poets.

19280. Wallis, Jim and Wes Michaelson. (1976) "Dorothy Day: Exalting Those of Low Degree," Sojourners. Vol. 5, No. 10 (December), pp. 16-19. An interview with Dorothy Day. Other articles about the Catholic Worker Movement are published in Sojourners.

19281. Hayden, Edwin V. (1978) "Concern for Lost Cities," Christian Standard. Vol. 113, No. 22 (May 28), pp. 497-499. Christian

Churches and Churches of Christ should follow St. Paul's example in evangelizing cities.

19282. Jackson, Dave. (1978) Coming Together. Minneapolis, MN: Bethany Fellowship. Re: Christian community life and Reba Place Fellowship, Evanston, IL.

19283. New Brunswick Theological Seminary. (1978-1980) Urban Studies Bulletin. New Brunswick, NJ: Department of Urban Studies, the Seminary.

19284. Paris, Peter J. (1978) Black Leaders in Conflict: Joseph H. Jackson, Martin Luther King, Jr., Malcolm X, and Adam Clayton Powell. New York: Pilgrim Press.

19285. Phillips, Calvin L. (1979) "Cloning--Chicago Style: Mourhous and Sloniger Plant Churches," Christian Standard. Vol. 114, No. 30 (July 29), pp. 684-685. Re: church extension of the Christian Churches and Churches of Christ denomination in Chicago, IL.

19286. Cort, John C. (1980) "My Life at the Catholic Worker," Commonweal. Vol. 107, No. 10 (December), pp. 361-367.

19287. Grant, Carl A., Marilynne Boyle, Christine E. Sleeter. (1980) The Public School and the Challenge of Ethnic Pluralism. New York: Pilgrim Press. A pamphlet.

19288. Jackson, Joseph Harrison. (1980) A Story of Christian Activism: The Story of the National Baptist Convention, USA, Inc. Nashville, TN: Townsend. A denominational history written by its president.

19289. Koenig, Harry C., ed. (1980) A History of the Parishes of the Archdiocese of Chicago. [Two volumes]. Chicago, IL: the Archdiocese.

19290. Boatman, Roger. (1981) "Reaching Ethnic America," Christian Standard. Vol. 116, No. 22 (May 31), pp. 492-494. Re: urban evangelism strategies for Christian Churches and Churches of Christ.

19291. Dahm, Charles W. (1981) Power and Authority in the Catholic Church: Cardinal Cody in Chicago. Notre Dame, IN: University of Notre Dame.

19292. Borders, William Holmes, et al. (1982) 45th Pastoral Anniversary: Rev. William Holmes Borders, 1937-1982, Wheat Street Baptist Church, Atlanta, GA. s.l.: Josten's American Yearbook Company.

19293. McCarthy, Kathleen. (1982) Noblesse Oblige: Charity and Cultural Philanthropy in Chicago, 1849-1929. Chicago, IL: University of Chicago.

19294. Scott, Eddie. (1982) "A Challenge for New Church Planting," Christian Standard. Vol. 117, No. 49 (December 5), pp. 1121-1122. Re: suburban church extension.

19295. Heald, Ben F. (1983) "Riches in the Midst of Recession," Christian Standard. Vol. 118, No. 4 (January 23), pp. 74-75. Economic hardship can be a blessing in disguise for the spiritually-minded.

19296. Palin, Michael. (1983) The Missionary [Film, color, 82 min.]. London: Methuen. In a comedy of sexual misadventure set in Edwardian England, Palin plays the role of Rev. Fortescue, a returned missionary who is assigned by the Bishop of London to minister among prostitutes in the East End. The prostitutes succeed in converting Fortescue. Rated "R."

19297. Arnold, John. (1984) Give Me Your Hungry: A Food Pantry Operation Handbook. St. Louis, MO: The Salvation Army.

19298. Burdick, Bruce. (1984) "Can an All White Church Reach Out to a Black Community?" Christian Standard. Vol. 119, No. 16 (April 15), pp. 350-351. Re: strategy of a Christian Church in a racially changing community of Kansas City, Mo.

19299. Lane, Thomas. (1984) "The Challenge of the City," Christian Standard. Vol. 119, No. 32 (August 5), pp. 702-704. Part 2: No. 33 (August 12), pp. 735-736. Lane calls Christian Churches and Churches of Christ to greater involvement in cities.

19300. Wade, John W. (1984) "Atlanta--'A City Too Busy to Hate,'" Christian Standard. Vol. 119, No. 9 (February 26), pp. 187-190. Re: work of the Christian Churches and Churches of Christ in Atlanta, GA.

19301. Johnson, Paul G. (1985) Grace: God's Work Ethic, Making Connections between the Gospel and Weekday Work. Valley Forge, PA: Judson. A Lutheran pastor comments on the relationship of work and worship. Bibliography.

19302. Lane, Thomas. (1985) "Hope for the Inner City," Christian Standard. Vol. 120, No. 1 (January 6), pp. 6-9. Re: evangelism strategies for the inner city.

19303. Dawes, Gil. (1986) "Working People and the Church: Profile of a Liberated Church in Reactionary Territory," pp. 223-239 in William K. Tabb, ed. Churches in Struggle. New York: Monthly Review Press. Re: a United Methodist Church in Iowa.

19304. Fong, Norman. (1986) "Chinatown: Theology Emerging Out of Community," pp. 240-253 in William K. Tabb, ed. Churches in Struggle. New York: Monthly Review Press.

19305. Lilly, Elizabeth and Michael E. Maloney. (1986) A Layperson's Manual for Social Ministry Planning and Implementation. Cincinnati, OH: The Appalachian People's Service Organization, Urban Ministries Unit. A description of how to do church planning using needs assessments, networks, workshops, and fund raising efforts with foundations. Questionnaire. Glossary. Bibliography.

19306. Reformed Church in America, Office of Social Witness. (beginning in 1986) The City Gate. New York: the Office. [Location: New Brunswick Theological Seminary, New Brunswick, NJ]. A periodical.

19307. Washington, James Melvin. (1986) Frustrated Fellowship: The Black Baptist Quest for Social Power. Macon, GA: Mercer. Black Baptist history to the end of the 19th century. Bibliographical essay.

19308. Winger, Sam J. (1986) "The Church in Urban America: Excerpts from a Paper Delivered at the Urban Forum, 1985," Christian Standard. Vol. 121, No. 2 (January 12), pp. 33-34.

19309. Anderson, James Desmond. (1987) Taking Heart: Empowering Older Adults for Community Ministry: A Handbook. Washington, DC: Cathedral College for the Laity. A plan for training adults as "service givers."

19310. Baird, Harry R. (1987) "The Challenge of the Ethnic Mosaic," Christian Standard. Vol. 122, No. 4 (January 25), pp. 71-72. Re: evangelism among urban ethnic populations.

19311. Brethren House Ministries. (1987) Homelessness: Activities about People Who Are Homeless. St. Petersburg, FL: Mission in Christian Education, Brethren House Ministries. A course of study with a teacher's guide.

19312. Brunsman, Deborah Sue. (1987) "When the World Arrives at Your Doorstep," Christian Standard. Vol. 112, No. 10 (March 8), pp. 209+. Re: church work with immigrants.

19313. Hostetter, Richard. (1987) "Some Absolutes for Achieving 'Double Vision,'" Christian Standard. Vol. 122, No. 19 (May 10), pp. 417-418. Church extension goals for the Christian Churches and Churches of Christ will require starting many new urban churches. The Christian Standard, a denominational periodical, frequently publishes articles about urban churches in the Christian Churches and Churches of Christ.

19314. Netting, Park H. (1987) "An Inner-City Multi-Ethnic Church," Christian Standard. Vol. 122, No. 40 (October 4), pp. 897, 900-901. Re: a Christian Church in Los Angeles, CA, which has included various ethnic groups.

19315. Smith, John and Malcolm Doney. (1987) On the Side of the Angels. Oxford, England: Lion Publications. [See Note 3]. Re: street ministry with motorcycle riders in Melbourne, Australia.

19316. May, Gerald G. (1988) Addiction and Grace: Love and Spirituality in the Healing of Addictions. San Francisco, CA: Harper.

19317. Moorhous, Carl W. (1988) "Reaching Our Cities for Christ," Christian Standard. Vol. 123, No. 31 (July 31), pp. 700-701. The Gospel message is not being made clear in many cities.

19318. Norris, Judy. (1988) "Come Ye Blessed ... ," Christian Standard. Vol. 123, No. 18 (May 1), pp. 406-408. Re: attempts of a multi-ethnic church to help the homeless and poor in Johnson City, TN.

19319. Gaslin, William D. (1989) "New Church Planting in Louisville," Christian Standard. Vol. 123, No. 12 (March 19), pp. 259-261. One Louisville, KY, church starts several others.

19320. Gilmore, Robert M., Sr. (1989) The Development of an Urban Ministry Program and Model [for the Independent Missionary Baptist General Association of Texas]. Thesis (M. Div.). Houston, TX: Houston Graduate School of Theology.

19321. Johnson, Sherman E. (1989) Jesus and His Towns. Wilmington, DE: Michael Glazier. Descriptions of the towns in which Jesus conducted his ministry.

19322. Gill, Athol. (1990?) The Fringes of Freedom: Following Jesus, Living Together, Working for Justice. Homebush West, Australia: Lancer. Re: radical discipleship and Christian community in Australia, including The House of the Gentle Bunyip in Melbourne.

19323. Brown, Callum G. (1990) "Faith in the City?" History Today. Vol. 40, No. 5 (May), pp. 41-47. Re: Thomas Chalmers and the religion of working classes in 19th century Glasgow, Scotland.

19324. Dallard, Shyrlee. (1990) Ella Baker: A Leader behind the Scenes. Englewood Cliffs, NJ: Silver Burdett Press, Simon and Schuster. Baker was a worker in the civil rights movement of the 1960s and an associate of Martin Luther King, Jr.

19325. Ecumenical Great Lakes / Appalachian Network (GLAN). (1990s) [Miscellaneous materials, bible studies, etc]. Springfield, IL: the Network. A network of people and organizations interested in church-based economic development. One of their publications is titled: Building Justice in Communities: An Adult Religious Education Process.

19326. Entwhistle, Basil. (1990) Making Cities Work: How Two People Mobilized a Community to Meet Its Needs. Pasadena, CA: Hope Publishing Co. Two Episcopalians marshall their church's and community's resources to address drug problems, unemployment, and other social concerns.

19327. Gateley, Edwina. (1990) I Hear a Seed Growing: God of the Forest, God of the Streets. Trabuco Canyon, CA: Source Books. Poetry, art, and prayers fill this volume intended to bridge the gap between forests and Chicago's sidewalks and brothels. Gateley seeks God among the victims of alcoholism and prostitution.

19328. Gilmore, Robert M., Sr. (1990) Hope after Dope: True Story of How a Drug Addict Became a Doctor. Houston, TX: the author [Real Publishing]. A story of the author's personal conversion and the resulting ministry in Houston, TX.

19329. Interreligious Economic Crisis Organization Network (I/ECON). (beginning in the 1990s) I/ECON. New York: the Network. A journal that documents church efforts to mitigate the effects of plant closings and other community economic problems.

19330. Kingdomworks. (beginning in the 1990s) [Miscellaneous materials, programs, and brochures related to urban youth ministry]. Philadelphia, PA: Kingdomworks. An organization dedicated to urban youth conferences and leadership training for work with inner city youth. Bart Campolo is director. Kingdomworks anticipates starting a periodical titled: Urban Youth Leader.

19331. Lang, J. David. (1990) "Oakley: A Small Church with a Big Heart," Christian Standard. Vol. 125, No. 6 (February 11), pp. 117-118. A Christian Church, begun in 1972, ministers in a multi-ethnic neighborhood near downtown Cincinnati, OH.

19332. Mortensen, Phyllis. (1990) "A Visit to Nonos de Mexico," Christian Standard. Vol. 125, No. 15 (April 15), pp. 326-327. Re: work of the church in Mexico City, especially among homeless and abandoned children.

19333. Partners for Sacred Places. (beginning in 1990) [Miscellaneous materials, reports, newsletters. Philadelphia, PA: PSP. An interfaith organization dedicated to preserving religious buildings.

19334. Regele, Michael B., Mark S. Schulz, and David K. Bleeker. (1990) Exploring Your Ministry Area Study Guide: A Guide to Understanding and Interpreting Your Ministry Area Profile. Costa Mesa, CA: Church Information and Development Services [CIDS]. CIDS provides a demographic data interpretation service for churches. This manual helps subscribers to the service derive insights from the data assembled for them. Several reports prepared by CIDS for specific urban areas exist.

19335. "Urban Suburban Partnerships Model Positive Change." (1990) Christianity Today. Vol. 34, No. 11 (August 20), pp. 50-51. Re: volunteers working in urban ministries.

19336. Woolfolk, Robert E. (1990) "Agape Christian Church Reaches Urban Area for Christ," Christian Standard. Vol. 125, No. 33 (August 19), pp. 740-741. Re: the establishment of an Afro-American Christian Church in 1968 in Denver, CO.

19337. Ayala, Edwin O. (1991) Evangelism and Church Development in UCC Hispanic Churches. New York: United Church Board for Homeland Ministries. A report of a study on Hispanic UCCs. A pamphlet.

19338. Baldovin, John Francis. (1991) Worship -- City, Church and Renewal. Washington, DC: Pastoral Press. Re: the Catholic liturgy and the impact of public worship and liturgy on city life.

19339. Batey, Richard A. (1991) Jesus and the Forgotten City: New Light on Sepphoris and the Urban World of Jesus. Grand Rapids, MI: Baker. Batey argues that Jesus' youth was spent in an urban environment.

19340. Bellah, Robert N., Richard Madsen, William M. Sullivan, Ann Swidler, and Steven M. Tipton. (1991) The Good Society. New York: Knopf. Pro-society and democracy; anti-privatism. See especially the chapter on the Public Church.

19341. Brown, Karen. (1991) Mama Lola: A Vodou Priestess in Brooklyn. Berkeley, CA: University of California Press.

19342. Dale, Eric Steven. (1991) Bringing Heaven Down to Earth: A Practical Spirituality of Work. New York: Lang.

19343. Drews, Rainer. (1991) Zur Krise katholischer Jungendverbandsarbeit: Eine Lokalstudie von Strukturen kirchlicher Jungendarbeit in Berlin (West). Frankfurt, Germany: Peter Lang. Re: Catholic church work with youth in Berlin, Germany. Based on the author's doctoral thesis.

19344. Frisbie, Margery. (1991) An Alley in Chicago: The Ministry of a City Priest. Kansas City, MO: Sheed and Ward. A biography of John J. Egan, a leader of the urban Catholic movement and community organization efforts in Chicago, IL.

19345. Garreua, Joel. (1991) Edge City: Life on the New Frontier. New York: Doubleday. A writer for the Washington Post describes the emergence of burgeoning new cities and suburbs that function as cities. A small section of this large volume deals with the church.

19346. Gerloff, Roswith. (1991?) A Plea for Black Theologies: The Black Church Movement in Britain in Its Transatlantic Cultural Theological Interaction with Special Reference to the Pentecostal Oneness (Apostolic) and Sabbatarian Movements. Thesis (Ph. D.). Birmingham, England: University of Birmingham. A study of a thousand Black independent congregations in Britain, with particular attention to theology and cultural traditions.

19347. Hayghe, Howard V. (1991) "Volunteers in the US: Who Donates Time?" Monthly Labor Review. Vol. 114, No. 2 (February), pp. 17-23. Hayghe describes social characteristics of volunteers. Churches receive larger amounts of donated time than do charities, civic organizations, schools, political parties, etc.

19348. John Paul II, Pope. (1991) Centesimus Annus. Città del Vaticano: The Vatican. English edition: On the Hundredth Anniversary of Rerum Novarum. Washington, DC: United States Catholic Conference, 1991. A review of Catholic social teaching.

19349. Jones, Dean C. (1991) Face to Face with Society's Lepers: Downtown Night Ministry. Lima, OH: Fairway Press. Jones is director of a night ministry in Tacoma, WA, which reaches out to alcoholics, drug abusers, the mentally ill, and the suicidal.

19350. Luker, Ralph E. (1991) The Social Gospel in Black and White: American Racial Reform, 1885-1912. Chapel Hill, NC: University of North Carolina Press.

19351. McConnaughhay, J. D. (1991) "Jobless but Not Hopeless," Christian Standard. Vol. 126, No. 35 (September 1), pp. 4-5. A Christian Church in St Louis, MO, helps the jobless among their membership.

19352. Rhodes, Lynn Nell and Nancy D. Richardson. (1991) Mending Severed Connections: Theological Education for Communal Transformation. San Francisco, CA: San Francisco Network Ministries. A critique of establishment-oriented theological education which argues that the marginalized people of society have a great deal to say about theology.

19353. Russell, Bob. (1991) "Make Christianity Attractive in the Marketplace," Christian Standard. Vol. 126, No. 15 (April 14), pp. 308-310. Christians can evangelize work-place friends.

19354. Rutherford, Elizabeth. (1991) "Twelve Ways the Church Can Help the Homeless," Christian Standard. Vol. 126, No. 31 (August 4), pp. 12-13.

19355. Resener, Carl R. and Judy Hall. (1992) Kids on the Street. Nashville, TN: Broadman.

19356. Stockwell, Clinton E. (1992) "A Better Class of People:" Protestants in the Shaping of Early Chicago, 1833-1873. Thesis (Ph. D.). Chicago, IL: University of Illinois at Chicago.

19357. Watts, Jill. (1992) God, Harlem USA: The Father Divine Story. Berkeley, CA: University of California Press. A biography of a charismatic and controversial African American religious leader, based on scarce and previously unknown sources.

19358. Costello, Tim, ed. (1991) Ministry in an Urban World: Responding to the City. Canberra, Australia: Acorn Press. A series of articles about urban ministry in Australia (by Costello, Michael Riddell, Athol Gill, Alan Nichols, John U'Ren, Michael Duncan, and Peter Corney) deals with such problems as urban poverty, city clergy burnout, public policy and the church, rural-urban migration, and the pursuit of Christian community.

Author Index

Included in this index are the names of individual authors, corporate authors, and the titles of works without authors listed. Publication dates of the works indexed can be inferred from the the citation number, the smaller the number the earlier the date. Numbers between 1 and 7745 are located in Volume I; between 7746 and 15330 in Volume II; and between 15331 and 19247 in Volume III.

1940 Outlook Regarding Child Labor 4889
37500 Weddings in 25 Years: Protestant Episcopal Church of the Transfiguration, Known as Little Church Around the Corner 4998
Aageson, James W. 18749
Aaron, Appadural 3866
Aaseng, Rolf E. 14898
Abatso, George 15332
Abatso, Yvonne 15332
Abbott, Ernest Hamlin 1832
Abbott, Lyman 1105, 1267, 1446, 1447, 1789, 2002, 2681, 2852
Abbott, Lyman, Mrs. 1347
Abbott, Martina 6261
Abel, Steven 443
Abel, Theodore Fred 4259
Abell, Aaron Ignatius 4692, 5138, 5334, 5745, 6120, 6812, 7746, 10670
Abels, Paul 14107
Abercrombie, Nicholas 11637
Abernathy, Ralph David 11163, 11164, 18750
Abner, Maud M. 5237
Abonyi, Malvina Hauk 18010
Abrahams, Amere 12738
Abrams, Charles 9287
Abramson, Harold J. 9719, 11165, 11638, 12739, 14899
Abramtsov, David F. 5432, 5433
Abrecht, Paul 7747, 8067, 10609,

13420, 14900, 17601
Absolom, Peter 12740
Abts, Dorothy M. 5335
Abts, Emerson 8068
Abu-Lughod, Janet L. 11166, 12039, 18011
Abuse of Police Power 11639
Abyssinian Baptist Church 1833
Acción Social Patronal 8344
Achievement of Dr. Rainsford 2059
Ackerman, S. E. 15527
Ackerman, Todd 16480
Acland, Richard 5139
Acosta, Samuel 14901
Acquaviva, Sabino Samele 7748, 8069, 8642
Action catholique ouvrière 12040
Action catholique ouvrière: Session nationale des aumôniers 10192
Action Training Coalition [ATC] 10193
Action Training Network of Ohio 11167
Adair, James R. 9720, 9721, 18012
Adam, Tom 17214
Adams, Albert S. 8643
Adams, Charles G. 12041
Adams, Fred Winslow 3046, 3477, 4019
Adams, Frederick J. 5746
Adams, Gordon 16960
Adams, Helen 10194
Adams, Henry C. 1348
Adams, Herbert Baxter 1106, 1730
Adams, J. 10195
Adams, James L. 11640
Adams, James Luther 5731
Adams, James R. 13421
Adams, Jennifer A. 16084
Adams, Joseph H. 2003
Adams, Kenneth 14498, 15333
Adams, Mathew 17215
Adams, Oscar Fay 774
Adams, Pat 10194
Adams, Robert M. 7749
Adams, William W. 775
Addams, Jane 1107, 1108, 1192, 1193, 1194, 1349, 1679, 1834, 2060, 2116, 2117, 2193, 2194, 2287, 2288, 2289, 2373, 2374, 2478, 2562, 2765, 3867, 4058, 4200, 4407, 4452, 4462, 4465, 4496, 9526, 9527, 11249, 12221, 12813, 18464, 18480 >> See further: Subject Index: Hull House
Adderley, James Granville 1036, 2079, 2919
Addicks, G. B. 1889
Addison, Howard A. 17216
Addleshaw, George William Outram 5642
Addy, Tony [Anthony J.] 13787, 14902, 16481, 16802, 18389, 18390, 18391, 18751, 18752, 19028, 19188
Adendorff, R. Desmond 12741
Aderhold, J. Don 17217
Adornato, Giselda 18392
Adorno, T. W. 5850
Adriance, Madeleine 19189
Advisory Council for the Church's Ministry 18393
African Union Methodist Protestant Church 15713
Against the Community Church 3109
Agape, Eros P. 12384
Agarwal, Anil 16085
Agnew, John A. 16803
Agus, Jacob 6412
Agócs, Carol 15714
Agócs, Sándor 12742, 18394
Ahern, Dennis M. 18753
Ahern, Geoffrey 18013
Ahern, Patrick V. 13422

Ahlheim, Klaus 14903
Ahlstrom, Sydney 12385
Ahmann, Mathew 8644, 10196
Ahn, Yoo Kwang 17602
Aiken, John R. 10197, 11641
Ainger, Geoffrey 10472
Ainsworth, A. 14108
Ainsworth, Catherine Harris 12743, 13099
Airport Interfaith Ministry 12042
Ajaegbu, Hyacinth I. 12386
Akbar, Jamel 18395
Akers, Lilialyce Sink 7492
Akpem, Yosev Yina 16086
Albany City Mission, City Tract and Mission Society 546
Albeda, W. 7022
Alberione, Giacomo Giuseppe 8345
Albert, Charles S. 820
Alberts, William Edward 8346
Albertyn, J. R. 5540
Albregts, A. H. M. 5851
Alcoholics Anonymous 12744
Alcoholics Anonymous Publishing, Inc 6604
Alden, Edmund K. 1037, 1109, 1110, 1268
Alden, Joseph 602
Aldon, Edmund K. 1195
Aldred, Guy Alfred 4352
Aldrich, Howard 13752, 14904
Aldrich, Sandra P 18014
Aldridge, David 17218
Aldridge, John M. 10671
Aldwinkle, Russell 12387
Aleman, Louis T. 16804
Aleshire, Daniel 13212
Aletti, Arturo 5064
Alevizopoulos, Antonios 13100
Alexander Research and Communications 16482
Alexander, David 15715
Alexander, Fred A. 12043
Alexander, Gross 872
Alexander, James Waddel 264, 329, 330, 331
Alexander, Jessica 13101
Alexander, June Granatir 16805, 18015
Alexander, Priscilla 18099
Alexander, Robert S. 18396
Alexander, Vernon P. 18016
Alexander, Walter R. 5541
Alexander, Will Winton 4890, 5434
Alford, Bradley H. 2061
Alger, Horatio 444
Alger, William Rounseville 312, 323
Alicea, Benjamín 18397
Alienation of Working Men from the Church 2062
Alinsky, Saul David 5435, 7023, 7383, 7628, 7948, 8347, 8462, 8645, 8991, 9044, 9052, 9288, 9387, 9412, 9623, 9728, 10028, 10098, 10198, 10303, 10385, 10553, 10554, 10645, 10672, 10830, 11168, 11410, 11520, 11656, 11799, 12044, 12045, 12295, 12388, 12418, 12472, 12526, 12578, 12851, 13096, 13117, 13661, 16211, 16934, 18339, 18875, 18903 >> See further: Subject Index: Community organization
All Africa Christian Conference 8348, 8349, 11642
All Africa Conference of Churches, Urban Industrial and Rural Mission Department, Southern Africa Contact Group 12745
All-Africa Christian Conference 7750
Allan, Maurice 10673
Allan, Tom 6413
Allario, Mario 12389

Alleluia, A Hymnbook for Inner City Parishes 7751
Allen, Annie Winsor 2563
Allen, Archibald J. 2564
Allen, Donald R. 12390
Allen, E. H., Mrs. 2853
Allen, Frank W. 17603, 17604, 18017, 18398
Allen, H. David 13316
Allen, Irving Lewis 13102
Allen, Ivan, Jr. 11169
Allen, Jere 15334, 15716, 16087, 16243, 16483, 17219, 17605, 18018
Allen, Jimmy R. 11643, 13103
Allen, Joseph Henry 671
Allen, Kerry Kenn 14905
Allen, Kring 7024
Allen, Margaret 2375
Allen, Michael 12046
Allen, Ralph 8070
Allen, Richard 58, 2922, 12047, 13423
Allen, Robert 9722
Allen, Robert Raymond 18019
Allen, Roland 2565, 3814
Allen, Tom 6605
Allen, William H. 528, 2118, 2566, 2567
Allen-Baley, C. 16484
Allender, Howard F. 7234
Allerton, Thomas Duane 13104
Alley, Henry Clarence 2854
Allgood, B. Dexter 16806
Alliance for Detroit Churches 18754
Allibone, Samuel Austin 284
Allinsmith, Beverly 5643
Allinsmith, Wesley 5643
Allis, Andrew P. B. 17606
Allison, Clyde 8289
Allport, Gordon W. 5644
Almy, Frederic 1448, 1602, 1790, 2479
Alnor, William 17607
Alperovitz, Gar 14499
Alpert, David B. 14109
Alsne, Sten 11644
Alston, Jon P. 10345, 12048, 14906, 15927
Alston, Letitia T. 12048
Alston, Percel O. 9289
Alt, Herschel 4810
Alter, James P. 7235, 8071
Altheimer, Rosenwald Delano 15335
Althouse, Lawrence W. 9723
Altmix, Tip 14500
Altruist Interchange 1196
Alvarez, David J. 12746, 14907
Alves, Rubem Azevedo 12049
Amadei, Roberto 14908
Ambacher, Harry 14909
Amberson, Talmadge R. 13753, 15336
Ambler, Rex 15337
Ambrose, Kenneth Paul 14501, 16147
Amelink, H. 5852, 5853
Ament, Ernest Paul 4504
America's Bright New Cities 9724
American Academy of Political and Social Science 3380
American Association for Organizing Family Social Work 3740
American Baptist Convention, Council on Christian Social Progress 6262, 6606
American Baptist Convention, General Board 17608
American Baptist Convention, Social Service Committee 3303
American Baptist Home Mission Societies 586, 7025, 7752
American Baptist Home Mission Societies, Department of Cities, Field Staff of the Juvenile Protection Program 6607

American Baptist Home Mission Societies, Division of Church Extension and Edifice Funds 7236
American Baptist Home Mission Societies, Division of Church Missions 10199
American Baptist Home Mission Societies, Division of Church Missions, Church Strategy Program 5854
American Baptist Home Mission Societies, Juvenile Protection Staff 6414
American Baptist Home Mission Society; Women's American Baptist Home Mission Society 12391
American Baptist Mariners' Society 324
American Bible Society 40
American Catholic Historical Researches 736
American Christian Commission 425
American Federation of Labor and Congress of Industrial Organizations 7026
American Federation of Teachers 5238
American Friends Service Committee 4811, 8072
American Friends Service Committee and the National Committee against Discrimination in Housing 8973
American Home Missionary Society 94, 185
American Industry States Its Case 4891
American Institute of Social Service 2195
American Jewish Committee 2063
American Jewish Committee, Institute of Human Relations 11170, 13754
American Jewish Committee, Research Institute on Peace and Post-War Problems 5140
American Jewish Congress 7027
American Lutheran Church 6121, 7753
American Lutheran Church, Board of Christian Social Action 9290
American Lutheran Church, Social Concerns Coordinating Committee 14910
American Missionary Association 5747, 13105
American Seamen's Friend Society 95, 529
American Social Hygiene Association and the Church 4408
American Society for Meliorating the Condition of the Jews 77
American Society of Interior Designers 18399
American Society of Planning Officials 7237
American Sunday School Union 82, 83, 313
American Tract Society 84, 192, 384
American Unitarian Association 65
American Unitarian Association, Department of Adult Education 5645
Ameringer, Oscar 2682
Amerson, Philip A. 13468, 13755, 14911, 14912, 14913, 15338, 16088, 16485, 16486, 16807, 16808, 17220, 17609, 18400, 18401, 19029
Amerson, William A. 10674
Amidei, Nancy 18020

Amirtham, Samuel 17610, 17611
Ammerdown Group 14914
Ammering, Josef 16089
Ammerman, Nancy T. 15339
Ammon, Charles George 2568, 3381
Ammons, Edsel A. 8646, 13756, 14915
Amorim Pimentel, Belardin de 15340
Amos, A. 1928
Amos, William E., Jr. 18402
Amsel, Abraham 8350
Amundson, Robert H. 7028
Ancel, Alfred 6813, 7754, 8073, 8647, 10675, 12747, 13106, 16264, 16809
Anders, Sarah Frances 6608, 17612
Anderson, Afraim 10676
Anderson, Alan B. 8351, 17613
Anderson, Arthur L. 14502
Anderson, Charles 10677, 11645
Anderson, Clyde 15341
Anderson, David E. 18021, 18403
Anderson, Digby 16810
Anderson, Elin L. 4577
Anderson, Frank L. 3586
Anderson, Fred R. 18022
Anderson, Gary M. 18404
Anderson, George M. 14916
Anderson, Gerald H. 10678
Anderson, Harrison Ray 7755
Anderson, James D. 14503, 17614, 19309
Anderson, John Q. 7756
Anderson, Ken 14110
Anderson, L. Vann 12392
Anderson, Lorna 15342
Anderson, Martin 5239, 7493, 8974, 9291
Anderson, Matthew 1513, 18716
Anderson, Nels 3478
Anderson, Paul B. 10679
Anderson, Paul L. 13424
Anderson, Philip 11646, 13425
Anderson, Phoebe 13425
Anderson, Richard James 13107
Anderson, Richard William 9725
Anderson, Robert Gordon 5646
Anderson, Ruth Diana 14917
Anderson, Sidney R. 5855
Anderson, Stuart Leroy 4505
Anderson, T. Lee 15343
Anderson, Tim 15984
Anderson, Wayne 15650
Anderson, William F., II 6129
Anderton, Douglas L. 17615
Andover Review 711
André-Gallego, José 14918, 16811
Andrea, Miguel de 4999
Andreae, Johan Valentin 2920
Andreu, Pierre 6609, 7757
Andrews Charles Freer 3587
Andrews, Charles Freer 3382, 4578
Andrews, David 18405
Andrews, Dee 16812
Andrews, Edward G. 910
Andrews, F. Emerson 6263
Andrews, Richard T., Jr. 8742
Andrews, Theodore 6264
Andrieux, F. 12393
Angel, Stephen W. 14111
Angelade, Jean 7238
Angell, James W. 11647
Angell, Robert Cooley 5748, 6006, 8352, 13108
Angus, David L. 15344
Ankeny, Edwin Alonzo 15717
Annotated Bibliography 18406
Annotated Bibliography on the Church in the Urban Community 9726
Ansari, Hamied N. 16813
Anstice, Henry 2480
Anthes, Philip E. 6265
Anthony, Dick 15997
Anthony, Everett 16814

Anthony, Robert W. 3304
Anthony, Tom 12394
Anti-Catholic Riots in Philadelphia in 1844 1449
Anti-Defamation League of B'nai B'rith 8648
Anti-Mormon Mass Meeting 2766
Anti-Social Religion 3680
Antonides, Harry 13757, 18755
Antrim, Doron K. 7029
Antweiler, Anton 4579
Anzenbacher, Arno 16815
Apartment Dwellers in Nation's Capital Unreached by Churches 9727
Apartment House Ministry 12050
Apol, Isaac J. 11171
Aponte, Harry J. 7494
Appleby, R. Scott 19066
Appleyard, Robert B. 15718
Aproximación: Religiosidad popular urbana 14919
Aptheker, Herbert 10680
Apthorp, Stephen P. 17221, 18407
Arango, Jorge 11648
Arango, Luz Gabriela 18756
Araujo, Djaalma 17222
Arbeitskonflikte und Arbeitskampf: Auswirkungen u. Berechtigungen von Arbeitskonflikten 12748
Archambault, Joseph-Papin 3110
Archer, Anthony 17616
Archer, C. W. 13426
Archer, Kieth 16090
Archibald, Helen Allen 6266, 7758, 8975, 9292
Arden, Eugene 6415
Ardoin, Paul 4506
Are the Cities Exploiting Town and Country Life 6814
Arellano, Estuardo 12395
Arena 911
Arès, Richard 13109
Aretz, Jürgen 14504
Argast, Charles 11172
Ariarajah, S. Wesley 17610
Arias, Esther 15345
Arias, Mortimer 15345, 16816, 16817
Aristide, Jean-Bertrand 19030
Arjomand, Saïd Amir 17617
Arker, Hadley 12051
Armacost, Robert L. 18408
Armendáriz, Rubén P. 16487
Armitage, John 5377
Armitage, Michael 17618
Armitstead, Austin H. 9293, 11649
Armour Mission [Chicago, Illinois] 776
Armstrong, Anthony 12749
Armstrong, Donald 8353
Armstrong, Floris Barry 17619
Armstrong, J. C. 2196
Armstrong, James 8976, 9294, 12052, 12053, 15719, 17223
Armstrong, James Stanley 13110
Armstrong, Richard Stoll 12054, 14920, 16818
Armstrong, William Howard 7030
Arnal, Oscar L. 17620, 18023
Arndt, Elmer J. F. 5000, 6815
Arnhem, Carol van 10681
Arnold, Franz X. 5647, 5749, 6610, 8977
Arnold, George B. 125
Arnold, Gregg 10682
Arnold, John 19297
Arnot, William 265
Arnou, André 4260
Arnow, Harriet 6416
Arnquist, James 10683
Arns, Paulo E. 17224
Aron, Cliff 15428
Aronica, Michele Teresa 17225,

18024
Aronovici, Carol 2569, 2921, 3111, 3170
Arrighi, Antonio 912
Arrunategui, Herbert 17226
Arter, Rhetta M. 6267, 14112
Arthur, Joseph 13111
Arthur, Thomas 18757
Artino, Carmen V. 7759
Artis, Wayne 8074, 8354, 8355, 8649, 8650
Asaf, Menahem 17227
Asbury, Herbert 5856
Asch, Sholom 3171
Ash, Ann 7495
Ash, Maurice 11173
Ash, Robert J. 7239, 7760, 8356
Ash, Roberta 10189
Ashby, LeRoy 16819
Asher, Robert E. 4201
Ashley, Percy 2481
Ashley, William 1350, 3681
Ashton, Elwyn T. 7021
Ashton, John 2197
Asian Conference on Industrial Evangelism, 1st, June 2-13, 1958, Manila 7240
Asimpi, Kofi 18025
Asirvatham, Eddy 6611
Askew, Rebecca Ann 15346
Askin, Steve 15347
Askola, Irja 14280
Asmuth, Robert C. 12055
Asociacion Nacional de Jovenes Empresarios (Dominican Republic) 17621
Assad, Maurice 18026
Association for Christian Training and Service [ACTS] 10200, 11174, 14505
Association for the Relief of Jewish Widows and Orphans, New Orleans 2064
Association for the Relief of Respectable, Aged, Indigent Females 20
Association for the Study of Negro Life 2922
Association of Catholic Trade Unionists 4580, 4581, 4892, 5065
Association of Members of the Episcopal Conferences of East Africa [AMECEA] and the All Africa Conference of Churches 13427
Associaxioni cristiane lavoratori italiani 7241
Aswad, Barbara C. 13112, 13113
Ata, A. W. 16820
Ateshin, Hussein Mehmet 18758
Athearn, Walter Scott 2855, 2856, 3047, 3172, 3173, 3305, 3479, 3741
Athens Center of Ekistics 12396
Atherton, John 15720, 16488, 18409
Atherton, Richard 18027, 18028
Atkins, Julia Mason 11477
Atkinson, A. G. B. 1450
Atkinson, Clifford 14921
Atkinson, Henry A. 2683, 2758, 2767, 2857, 2987, 3048, 3174
Atkinson, John 574
Atkinson, M. H. 11175
Atkinson, Michael 8978, 12750, 13114, 14498
Atkinson, Richard 18418
Atlanta Interfaith Taskforce on Metro Ministry 14506
Attack on Catholic Charities in New York 1269
Atterbury, Anson P. 1514
Attwood, David 14922
Atwater, W. O. 1515
Atwood, J. Howell 5436
Auchenbaum, W. Andrew 13115
Audet, Lucille 5857
Auffenberg, Thomas L. 14923

Augustana Evangelical Lutheran Church, Board of American Missions, Committee on Urban Church Planning 5858
Augustana Lutheran Church 14113
Augustine, Brother D. 6612
Aumot, Michael 6816
Austin, Anne 5859
Austin, John 18759
Austin, Michael 14924
Austin, Richard Cartwright 9728
Austin, Tom 15721
Aveling, T. W. 530
Avesing, Frank B. 7067, 11650
Avrunin, William 8357, 8651
Awalt, William J. 7031
Awe, B. 10454
Axelrod, Morris 6817
Aylal, Edwin O. 19337
Ayalon, Hannah 17946
Ayer, William Ward 5931
Ayers, Thomas G. 9295
Ayres, Ann 623
Ayres, William 14283
Azpiazu y Zulaica, José Joaquín 4261, 4693, 4893
Azzi, Riolando 18029
Baas, H. 6818
Babbie, Earl R. 10346
Babson, Roger Ward 2684, 2768, 3175, 3176, 3383, 3384, 3936, 4020, 4262, 5066
Bachelard, Gaston 8979
Bachelder, Robert S. 16821, 18030, 18410, 19031
Bachelor, A. H. 10201
Bachmann, E. Theodore 6613, 6819
Bachmann, Ernst F. 2923
Bacigalupo, Leonard 13428, 14114
Backer, James 12056, 13429
Backhaus, Gunther 7496
Backlund, Oscar Theodore 4409
Backstrom, Philip N., Jr. 8652, 13116
Backstrom, William K. 13360
Bacon, Albion Fellows 2570
Bacon, Alexander Samuel 3049
Bacon, Leonard 358
Bacon, Margaret Hope 14507
Badcock, Blair 16822
Badiee, Julie 18760
Baer, Hans A. 15348, 15722, 16823, 17228, 18411, 18412
Baerg, Ben 12397
Bagby, Grover C. 11176
Bagdikian, Ben H. 8980
Bagdon, Philip 15349
Bagge, Carl E. 7242
Baggs, Albert Edward 9729
Bagnell, Ken 8653
Bagwell, Philip S. 18031
Baharian, Bedros 5067
Bahr, Howard M. 10684, 11651, 12057, 12751, 13758, 14925, 16091, 16518
Bailey, Faith Coxe 8358
Bailey, J. Martin 9730
Bailey, Richard P. 19032
Bailey, Robert W. 14926
Bailey, Robert, Jr. 13117
Bailey, Ron 12398, 12752, 14115
Bailey, Ronald 8654
Bailey, Samuel W. 314
Bailey, Stephen K. 9296
Bailey, Wilfred M. 11652
Bailey, Wilma A. 16489
Bainbridge, Lucy Seaman 2988
Bainbridge, William 17541
Bair, Fred 6820
Bairati, Piero 18032
Baird, H. M. 1270
Baird, Harry R. 19310
Baird, Robert 197
Baird, William 8981
Baizerman, Michael 13759
Baker, A. E. 5437
Baker, Benjamin S. 16490

Baker, Clarence Garfield 2769
Baker, Derek 13430
Baker, George 4529, 6326, 8672, 16779
Baker, Helen E. 9297
Baker, James T. 14116
Baker, Lance Richard 13760
Baker, Oliver E. 5336
Baker, Oren H. 6268
Baker, Paul J. 8982, 10202, 11177
Baker, Ray Stannard 2290, 2291, 2292, 2293, 2376
Baker, Susan 19033
Baker, Vaughn Willard 16092
Bakke, Corean 17229
Bakke, Dennis 14927
Bakke, Raymond J. 13431, 14117, 14928, 14929, 14930, 14931, 15350, 15723, 16808, 16824, 16825, 16826, 17230, 17231, 17622, 17623, 17624, 18033, 18034, 18761, 19034
Balaam's Ass Joins Campus Coffee Houses 9298
Balanoff, Elizabeth 17232
Balasuriya, Tissa 11178, 15724
Balcerak, C. A. 11179
Balch, William Monroe 2571
Baldassare, Mark 13761
Baldock, N. 16827
Baldovin, John Francis 16491, 18035, 19338
Baldwin, Charles Sears 2294
Baldwin, Charles W. 2198
Baldwin, James 6614, 8075
Baldwin, Leland Dewitt 13762, 15725
Baldwin, Stephen, Mrs. 2482
Baldwin, William 1451
Balk, Alfred 10203
Ballard, Adela J. 4126
Ballard, F. W. 409
Ballard, JoeAnn 17625
Ballard, Joseph 445
Ballard, Monroe 17625
Ballard, Paul 14932, 17233, 17234, 17626, 18036, 18762
Ballou, Earle H. 7243
Ballweg, ohn A. 12117
Balm in Gilead 8655
Balmer, Randall 19190
Baltimore Church Home and Infirmary 2858
Baltimore City Mission 304
Baltzell, E. Digby 7244, 9731, 14933
Baltzell, John 17192
Bampton, Joseph M. 3480
Banana, Canaan 13118, 16093
Banfield, Edward C. 8656, 8839, 10685, 11738, 13119
Banks, Louis Albert 1038, 1835, 1890, 2989
Banks, Melvin E. 11653
Banner, Lois W. 12753
Bannerman, J. Yedu 13120
Banton, Michael 11180
Baptist Congress for the Discussions of Current Questions 672
Baptist Domestic Mission Society of the City of New York 186
Baptist Goal: City Dwellers 7245
Baptist World Alliance, Fourth Congress 3868
Baptist World Alliance, Second Congress 2483
Baptista, Cynder 19035
Baranowski, Arthur R. 18413
Barbanti, Maria Lucia 18037
Barbat, Gustav 15443
Barber, Jesse Belmont 4507
Barbour, Claude Marie 16828
Barbour, June 12399
Barbour, Russell B. 10204
Barchewitz, Gustav 2572
Bardaglio, Peter W. 13432
Bare, Paul W. 4127
Barker, Edwin 12754
Barker, John Marshall 2004, 3112

Barker, Michael Kenneth 16094
Barker, Reginald J. 4508
Barkevicius, Jocelyn 15886
Barlow, Ralph 10686, 13433
Barlow, T. Ed 14508
Barna Research Group 19036
Barna, George 16829
Barnard, Charles F. 128
Barndt, Joseph R. 10687, 12400
Barnes, Albert 175, 176, 410
Barnes, Bill 13763
Barnes, Calvin Rankin 4202, 4509
Barnes, Charles Wesley 1929, 2859
Barnes, G. N 3113
Barnes, Howard A. 19191
Barnes, Joseph W. 13121
Barnes, Lemuel Call 2686
Barnes, Mary Clark 2573, 2685, 2686
Barnes, Roswell P. 6269, 8076
Barnes, Sandra T. 14118
Barnes, Trevor 18038
Barneson, June Rothe 13764
Barnet, Richard 14119
Barnett, Henrietta Octavia 1271, 2296, 3306
Barnett, Samuel Augustus 712, 1111, 1197, 1271, 1351, 1930, 2079, 2295, 2296, 2574, 2761, 3177, 3306 >> See further: Subject Index: Toynbee Hall
Barnette, Henlee H. 5648, 6270, 6821, 7032
Barney, Jane L. 10688
Barnfather, William C. 3411
Barnhart, Kenneth Edwin 3588
Barnhart, Phil 12401
Barns, Helen 7246
Baroni, Geno Charles 9299, 9732, 11654, 11655, 12402, 12722, 13122, 13765, 14120, 14509, 14510, 14511, 14512, 14934
Barr, Browne 12403, 13766
Barr, William E. 6615
Barrau, Paul 8077, 10689
Barreira, I. A. F. 16095
Barreiro, Alvaro 15351, 16096
Barrett, David B. 8657, 10690, 12058, 16097, 16492, 17627, 17628, 18318
Barrett, E. R. 1516
Barrett, Francis Dermot 6271
Barrett, John M. 18414
Barrett, Joseph P. 13434
Barrett, Kate Harwood Waller 1377, 1731, 1891
Barrett, Lois 17629
Barrett, Patricia 9733
Barros Couto Rosado, Joao de 5438
Barroso, Gustavo 4582
Barry, Colman J. 6272, 7247
Barry, David W. 4812, 5068, 5240, 5241, 5242, 5243, 5337, 5338, 5339, 5439, 5440, 5441, 5442, 5443, 5542, 5543, 5544, 5545, 5546, 5603, 5604, 5750, 5947, 6007, 6122, 6273, 6274, 6275, 6417, 6616, 6617, 6618, 6751, 6822, 6823, 7033, 7248, 7497, 7498, 7761, 7762, 8359, 9300, 11181
Barry, F. R. 9734
Barry, Frank T. 5444
Barry, Patrick 18763
Barry, Robert M. 9301
Barry, William 247
Barstow, David 11656
Bartel, Louis Franz 12057
Bartelt, Michael 14121, 16098
Barth, Karl 5001, 17656
Barth, Marcus 9302
Barth, Robert 15726
Barthold, Mary 16830
Barthold, Stan 16830
Bartles-Smith, Douglass 13767
Bartlet, David 18977

Bartlett, Dana Webster 2119
Bartlett, N. Warren 12404
Bartocci, Enzo 17235
Barton, Bruce 2770, 3682
Barton, Carol 18039, 18764
Barton, George 1352
Barton, Josef J. 14122
Bascom, John 343, 426, 492, 713, 821, 1353
Bass, Joseph O. 12755
Bassand, Michel 13768
Bastenier, Albert 14994
Bastian, Hans-Dieter 15727
Bastin, Dan E. 12059
Batchelder, Robert C. 8658, 9696
Batchelor, Alex R. 6276
Batchelor, George 822
Batchelor, John C. 12405
Bates, H. Roswell 2801
Bates, M. Searle 10691
Bates, William M. 7763
Batey, Richard A. 19339
Batigne, Émile 14935
Batistella, Renzo 6619
Batt, Harriet 5649
Batten, Mollie 12060
Batten, Samuel Zane 2199, 2377, 2484, 2575, 2576, 2771, 2860, 3385
Battle of Detroit 3742
Bau, Ignatius 17236
Bauberot, Jean 13435, 14513
Baudelaire, Charles 154
Bauen mit Geschichte 15352
Bauer, Edwin Theodore 4410
Bauer, Gerhard 11182, 12061
Bauer, Richard W. 9303
Bauernschmitt, Kathryn Eloise 18040
Baugh, C. Don [Willard M. Wickizer?] 6824
Baugher, Norman J. 8983
Baum, Gregory 13436, 14936, 15353, 16099, 16100, 17630, 17631
Baum, Vernon Herbert 12062
Bäumler, Christof 12756, 14514
Baunach, Phyllis J. 13437
Bavarei, Michael 15354
Bavinck, J. H. 16101
Bay, Eugene C. 14515, 14937
Bayard, Ralph 865
Baybrook, George W. 13769
Bayley, Henry 657
Bayod y Serrat, Ramón 11183
Bayor, Ronald H. 14516
Beach, David Nelson 1198
Beach, Waldo 7499, 11184, 14938
Beal, John David 15355, 15728, 16102
Beale, Robert 16103
Beali, Jewel Chancey 9304
Beames, Barry 18765
Bean, Kevin 15356
Beard, Mary 2861
Beard, W. L. 2990
Beardsley, Waite 2485, 2486, 2487
Beasley, Ronald 12406
Beatley, Clara Bancroft 2577, 2862
Beaulieu, Don 18766
Beauman, C. B. B. 13123
Beaupin, Eugène 5860
Beaven, A. W. 3869
Bebbington, D. W. 1836
Bechler, LeRoy 17632
Bechtold, G. H. 4694
Bechtolsheimer, Heinrich 2120
Beck, Bertram M. 6620
Beck, Carl C. 12063
Beck, Carolyn S. 19037
Becker, Dorothy G. 7764, 8078
Becker, Howard Paul 7034
Becker, Howard S. 8659
Becker, Walter 7500
Beckett, Colin 5650
Beckford, James A. 12757, 16831, 17633
Beckley, Robert E. 15758

Beckstrom, J. M. 3589
Bédarida, François 8360, 13438
Bedell, bp. 624
Bedfore, Scott E. W. 3815
Bednorz, Herbert 13770
Beebe, Frederick J. 12064
Beebe, Wally 11657
Beebee, James A. 3307
Beecham, Noel Oscar 16832
Beecher, Henry Ward 385, 386, 429, 454, 493, 526, 827, 10285, 11891, 17766
Beecher, Lyman 277, 8079
Beers, George Pitt 6418, 7035
Beeson, Trevor 8660, 9305, 12065, 12407, 12408, 16104
Beetham, Thomas Allen 10205
Beffa, P. 14517
Begbie, Harold 2297, 3178
Béguin, Albert 6419
Beher, Linda 11658, 11659
Behle, A. H. 6277
Behrends, Adolphus Julius Frederick 777
Behrens, William W., III 12594
Beijbom, Anders 16105
Beisswenger, Donald 12758
Belaûnde, César H. 8984
Belcher, F. J. 1603
Belcher, Joseph 344
Belden, E. Porter 248
Belew, M. Wendell 12066, 12067, 13124
Belfrage, Cedric 4894
Belgum, Harold J. 8985
Belknap, Charles 15729, 15730, 16106
Bell, Bernard 4695
Bell, Daniel 12759, 13771, 14123
Bell, Ernest A. 2578
Bell, George Kennedy Allen 3743
Bell, Marion L. 14124
Bell, Stephen 4583
Bell, Steve 10206
Bell, Wendell 6825
Bellah, Robert N. 7036, 7249, 9306, 10207, 11660, 13439, 15357, 17237, 17238, 18041, 19340
Bellaire, Henry Walford 278
Bellamy, Edward 873
Bellanger, Jacques 5141
Bellevue Baptist [Memphis, Tennessee] 5861
Bellows, Henry C. 737
Bellows, Henry W. 169, 226, 238, 325, 367, 368, 603, 823, 13441
Belser, Julius H. 7250, 7501
Belth, Nathan C. 7251, 15731
Belury, William R. 16833
Bemis, Edward W. 967
Bemont, Marc 18767
Bemporad, Jack 13440
Ben-Rafael, Eliezer 17946
Benckiser, Nikolaus 6123
Bender, Eugene I. 10692
Bender, Margaret 5862
Bender, Thomas 13441, 18415
Bendtz, Nils Arne 8361
Benedict Center for Criminal Justice 14518
Benedict XV, Pope 17664
Benedict, Donald L. 5651, 5751, 7765, 8362, 8363, 8765, 8986, 10071, 13442, 14519, 15358, 16107
Benedict, H. J. 13125
Benedict, Ivan Howland 2488
Bener, F. 8661
Benes, Louis H. 9735
Benet, F. 8987
Benevolent Christian Society in the City of New York 28
Benevolent Fraternity of Unitarian Churches of Boston 143
Benfield, Knolan 12760
Beng, Timothy N. 18042
Benham, DeWitt M. 1892
Benington, John 12761

Benjamin, Barbara 14520, 15732, 15733
Benjamin, Don C. 16493
Benjamin, Philip S. 11661, 13772
Benjamin, Walter W. 8662
Benkart, Paula Kaye 12068, 13443, 16108
Benne, Robert 11185
Bennet, R. J., Mrs. 575
Bennett, Caroline Barker 16109
Bennett, Charles 11500
Bennett, D. S. 10693
Bennett, E. Lansing 6124
Bennett, Edmonds 3937
Bennett, Edward H. 2303
Bennett, F. Russell 10694, 11662, 11663, 11664, 12069
Bennett, G. Willis 9736, 9737, 9738, 10208, 10695, 10696, 11186, 11187, 11665, 11666, 13444, 16110, 16111, 16112, 16494, 16495, 17239, 18043
Bennett, Harold C. 8663, 8988, 10209
Bennett, J. O. 2772
Bennett, John Coleman 4411, 4510, 5002, 5445, 6420, 6421, 6621, 8364, 9739, 11667
Bennett, M. Katherine 3050
Bensin, Basil M. 5340
Benson, Dennis C. 11188
Benson, J. Kenneth 15074
Benson, Louis F. 2924
Benson, W. H. 824
Bentall, J. O. 2121
Bentham, John 17634
Bentley, John Eduard 3179
Bentley, Ruth Lewis 14521
Bentley, William 12762, 13445
Benton, John 10697, 17240
Bentz, Thomas Orrin 13446
Benvinisti, J. L. 4813
Benyon, E. D. 4696
Benz, Ernst 9740
Benz, Franz 7252, 8080, 10210
Berckman, Edward M. 14939, 15359, 16113, 16834
Berdiaev, Nicholai 4263
Berdyaev, Nicholas 4159
Bercovici, Konrad 19251
Berenbaum, May 13447
Berg, Barbara 14522
Berg, Harold E. 10131, 10211
Berg, Kay Kupper 18768
Berge, Mark Vanden 17241
Bergel, Egon Ernest 6622
Bergendoff, R. N. 8081
Berger, Alan S. 14523
Berger, Brigitte 12763
Berger, Horst 13448
Berger, Peter L. 5863, 5864, 6422, 7253, 7254, 7766, 8082, 8083, 8521, 8522, 8664, 10212, 10213, 10214, 10215, 11189, 11668, 12763, 13773, 14125, 14126, 14940, 16874, 17311, 17635, 17777, 18416
Bergland, Jim 14127
Bergonzoni, Luciano 12070
Bergquist, James A. 14406
Bergs, Manfred 16114
Bergsma, Paul 16835
Bergstraesser, Edward W. 12409, 12764, 14128
Berkeley Center for Human Interaction [BCHI] 9741
Berkhof, Hendricks 7037
Berkowitz, Bill 16836
Berkowitz, Henry 874, 2378
Berkowitz, Leonard 11882
Berkowitz, Morris I. 10216, 11190
Berkson, Isaac B. 3180
Berlack, Freeman Roosevelt 4895
Berle, Beatrice Bishop 7255
Berlin City Mission 547, 14129
Bernard, Frederick A. P. 130
Bernard, Jessie 5142, 5752
Bernard, Luther Lee 5142
Bernhard, Leopold 9307

Bernhardt, William H. 5244
Bernheimer, Charles Seligman 2005, 2298, 2379, 2773, 5652
Bernstein, Scott 15070
Berrian, William 223
Berrigan, Daniel 9742, 10698, 11669, 11670, 12071, 12072, 12410, 12765
Berrigan, Philip 12669
Berry, Brian Joe Lobley 12766
Berry, Edwin C. 11256
Berry, Fred 1199
Berry, Henry Havelock 1354
Berry, John W. 6423, 6623
Berry, Kathy 18417
Berry, Raymond 10217
Berry, Shirley 10217
Bers, Günter 14941
Berson, Lenora E. 9743
Berthoff, Rowland 9308, 12073
Berton, Pierre 9309
Bervine, Junius W. 11191
Besant, Walter 673, 1452
Besecker, H. M. 9744
Besecker, I. G. 9744
Bess, C. W. 12767, 13126
Best, Ernest E. 16115
Best, Walter L. 2122
Bestard, Joan 16837
Bethany Theological Seminary, Church of the Brethren Symposium on Urban Ministry 14942
Bethel, Elizabeth Rauh 15734
Bethell, Laura 2774
Bettany, Frederick George 3744
Bettelheim, Bruno 19038
Betten, Neil Bernard 10699, 11192, 13774, 13775, 17881
Betts, Lillian Williams 1837, 1893
Beukema, George G. 11193, 15360, 16116
Bevan, Llewelyn D. 625
Bevan, R. J. W. 12411
Beveridge, W. E. 7038
Bevins, Peggy 6624
Beyreuther, Erich 8365
Bharati, Agehananda 12074
Bianchi, Giovanni 13776
Bianchi, Luisito 12412
Bianchi, Raymond 10434
Bibby, Reginald Wayne 13127, 18044
Bible and Fruit Mission to the Public Hospitals of New York City, Coffee House 626
Bicknell, Catherine 16496
Bicknell, W. M. 968
Biddle, Elizabeth N. 778
Biddle, William W. 6278, 8989, 9310, 9311
Bideaux, Rene O. 17488
Bidegain de Uran, Ana Maria 17242
Bidwai, Praful 17243
Biederlack, Joseph 2380
Biederwolf, W. E. 2579
Biemen, Adrianus van 5865
Bienstock, Marvin 14943
Biéler, André 14526, 16117
Bierbower, Austin 738, 969
Bierman, A. K. 12768
Bierne, Joseph A. 12413
Biersdorf, John E. 13449, 13777
Big Cities USA 7039
Bigelow, E. Victor 3181
Bigelow, Herbert S. 1732
Biger, Gideon 17636
Biggar, Nigel 17637
Biggins, Maria Goretti 17638
Bigman, Stanley K. 7040
Bigordá, José 8826
Bilhartz, Terry D. 14944, 17639
Bilheimer, Robert S. 6826
Billings, Alan 18045, 18418, 18769, 19039
Billings, Peggy 11194
Billingsley, Andrew 10700, 13128
Billington, Allen 8990

Billington, David P. 16497
Billington, Louis 14945
Billington, Ray A. 4697
Billington, Raymond J. 12075
Binder, Rudolph M. 2925, 2926
Binfield, Clyde 12769
Bing, John H. 9745
Bingham, June 8084
Binkley, Olin Trivette 5653
Binyon, G. C. 4412
Binyon, Gilbert Clive 4128
Binzen, Peter 11671
Birch, Bruce 14524, 17244
Birchard, Roy 14130
Birchett, Coleen 19040
Bird, Arthur Henry 6125
Bird, Richard S. 4814
Bird, Warren 16838, 17245
Birkey, Del 18419
Birmingham Council of Christian Churches 8085
Birmingham, Stephen 10218
Birmingham, Walter 9746
Birnbaum, Lucille B. 9312
Birnbaum, Norman 7502
Bisbee, Robert E. 1604
Bisceglia, John B. 5654
Bishop of the Bowery 7503
Bishop, Bryan 16839, 16852, 17246
Bishop, Claire Huchet 5547, 6126
Bishop, Jim 12076
Bishop, Samuel H. 1838, 2580
Bishop's Conference on Capital and Labor 5341
Bishop's Program of Social Reconstruction 3114
Bismarck, K. von 8366
Bits and Pieces on the Church and Housing 12414
Bitser, Donald R. 14946
Bittar, Helen 14947
Bjerring, Nicholas 600, 1680, 5432
Bjork, Don 17247
Blachly, Clarence Dan 3182
Black Churchmen's Ecumenical Institute [BCHI] 10219
Black Experience and the Church 12770
Black Manifesto 11195
Black, Hillel 8991
Black, Ira D. 6127
Black, Linda Perlis 14525
Black, Neville 18046, 18165
Black, Peter 8992
Black, Samuel Charles 2489
Blackburn, Tom 15735
Blacklidge, John Hathaway 5143
Blackman, Edward B. 10220
Blackmore, John 369
Blackwell, Gordon W. 5446, 5753
Blackwell, James E. 13450, 16118
Blackwood, Larry 14948
Blackwood, Vernon L. 18420, 18421
Blaikie, W. G. 411, 427, 476
Blair, Bertha 7504
Blair, H. W., Mrs. 825
Blake, Peter 6424
Blake, Richard A. 16119
Blakeborough, Eric 17640, 18047
Blakeley, Ulysses B. 8367
Blakelock, Mildred P. 4203
Blakely, Paul L. 2863
Blakey, C. Robert 6625
Blanc, Henri 8086
Bland, Thomas Albert 10221, 10701, 13129, 13451, 14131
Blankenhorn, Heber 4584
Blanpied, Charles W. 3183, 3308
Blanshard, Paul 3481
Blanton, Wyndham B. 5342
Blantz, Thomas E. 10702, 11672
Blardone, Gilbert 14526
Blasi, Anthony J. 17248, 19041
Blast, Robert L. 11196
Blaustein Library 9313, 9747, 9748, 9749

Bleakley, David 18048
Bledsaw, Jim 15736
Bledsoe, Anita G. 18049
Bledsoe, Ben W. 18050
Bledstein, Burton J. 13778
Bleeker, David K. 19334
Blejwas, Stanislaus A. 14132, 14527
Blessing on Labor 3745
Blessing, Joseph Marx 4129
Blieweis, Theodor 6279
Bliss, P. P. 559
Bliss, William Dwight Porter 779, 875, 986, 970, 1272, 1273, 1355, 1517, 2065, 2123, 2200, 7730
Blissard, William 2991
Blizzard, Samuel W. 6128, 6129, 6130, 6280, 6281, 6282, 6425, 6426, 6427, 6428, 6827, 6828, 7256, 7257, 17249
Bloch, Chajim 19253
Bloch, Richard 12973
Blöchlinger, Alex 8368
Block, W 16120
Bloede, Louis William 9314
Blomfield, Charles James 96, 144, 187, 193
Bloom, Davis C. 18051
Bloom, Dorothy B. 18052
Bloomquist, Karen L. 16840, 17250, 18770
Bloy, Philip 7767, 7768, 11673, 11674
Bluestone, Barry 16121
Blum, Fred H. 6283, 8665, 11675
Blum, Sam 10222
Blumberg, Janice Rothschild 9750, 16498, 17251
Blumberg, L. 12771
Blumenfeld, Hans 10223
Blumenreich, John 390
Blumhardt, Christoph 17656
Blumhorst, Roy 10224, 14725
Blumin, Stuart M. 13452
Blyton, W. J. 4130
Boal, Arnold S. 6008
Boal, F. W. 13009
Boan, Rudee Devon 16499, 17252
Board for Urban Ministry 10703
Boardman, David W. 14949
Boatman, Roger 19290
Bobbrow, J. 12772
Bobick, Michael W. 17253
Bobo, Kimberley A. 17641
Bobo, Lawrence 17514
Bobsin, Oneide 18771
Boche, Beverly 14133
Bock, Paul 13130, 13453
Bockelman, W. 9751
Bockmuehl, Klaus 18422
Bocock, Kemper 1839
Bocock, Robert 13131
Bode, Jerry George 10225
Bodein, Vernon Parker 4585, 5245
Bodeker, Sherri 14528
Bodelschwingh, Friedrich von 17409
Bodnar, John E. 17254
Bodner, John E. 13454, 16122, 16123, 16841
Bodo, John R. 6429, 8993
Bodzenta, Erich 6829, 6830, 7041, 7042, 7258, 7769, 7770, 8369, 9315
Boerma, Coenraad 14529, 18772
Boff, Clodovis 17642
Boff, Leonardo 16842, 17643, 18423
Bogen, Boris D. 2992
Boggs, Beverly 14134
Boggs, William 17222
Bogue, Donald 8666, 10247, 11197
Bohn, Anitar 10704
Bohr, David 14135
Bohran, Rudolf 14136
Bohrer, Richard 11198
Boid, C. T. 13455

Boint, Steve 18773
Boisard, Louis 5799
Boisen, Anton T. 4815, 4816
Boiten, Rolf G. H. 11199, 12415
Bójnowski, Lucyan 13141
Bok, C. Soule 1931
Bok, Edward 3590
Boland, John P. 4965
Boles, Robert 10705
Bolger, Dorita F. 19186
Boling, T. Edwin 10706, 12416, 12773, 13456, 13457
Bolle, Pierre 7259
Bollen, John Daniel 12417
Bolte, K. M. 8059
Boltniew, George 17644
Bolton, George 7503
Bolton, Robert H. 8994, 12077
Bolton, Robert J. 13779, 18774
Bomar, W. Melmoth 4586
Bombay Urban-Industrial League for Development 11676, 14530
Bonar, Horatius 604, 627
Bond, Charles H. 1518
Bond, Earl Danford 4587
Bond, Thomas S. 1932
Bonhoeffer, Dietrich 5754, 6430
Bonicelli, Gaetano 10226
Bonkowsky, Elizabeth Leitch 12774
Bonner, Arthur 10227
Bonner, Daniel E. 13780, 16124
Bonner, David Findley 2581
Bonney, C. C. 780
Bonthius, Robert H. 10228, 10229, 10707, 11200, 11201, 11202, 11203, 11204, 11205, 11677, 11678, 11679, 12078
Bontrager, Francis M. 11206
Boogaart, Thomas 18424
Bookchin, Murray 11680
Bookser Feister, John 17255
Boole, Ella Alexander 3938
Boom Time 7771
Boomershine, Tom 18775
Boone, James Shergold 198
Boone, Rudolph F. 11681
Boone, William J. 9316
Boonstra, John 15737
Boos-Nünning, Ursula 13132
Booth, Alan 12835
Booth, Ballington 1039, 1040
Booth, Bramwell 1356, 2079, 2201, 3683, 3939, 3998
Booth, Catherine 1112
Booth, Charles 913
Booth, Evangeline Cory 1933, 3115, 5742
Booth, Heather 17648
Booth, Henry Kendall 4511
Booth, Maud Ballington 914, 1040, 1357, 1519, 1733, 1791, 1894, 8329
Booth, William 859, 971, 1072, 1335, 1606, 2006, 2646, 3178, 4432, 5452, 9367, 10504, 12016, 17888 >> See further: Subject Index: Salvation Army
Booth, William, Mrs. 1778
Booth-Tucker, Frederick St. George de Latour 1041, 1112, 1520, 1605, 1606, 1681, 1734, 1735, 1895
Borchard, Toti 15361
Borchert, James 15362
Bordelon, Marvin 10230
Borders, Cline W. 16814
Borders, William Holmes 19260, 19269, 19292
Borei, Maj Ellen 9752
Borgeault, Guy 16125
Borgetto, Romano 12775
Borggrefe, Friedhelm 12776, 13781
Borgmann, Florence 6284
Borhek, James T. 7772, 11682, 13458
Bormann, Günther 12079
Bormann-Heischkeil, Sigrid 12079

Borne, Étienne 4588
Bornstein, Jerry 13782
Borovoj, Vitaly 9753
Borrowdale, Anne 17256
Börsch, Ekkehard 10231
Bos, A. David 18425
Bos, Robert 12418
Bosanquet, Bernard 1042, 1072, 1200, 1358
Bosch, Austin L. P. 6431
Boschini, Aurelio 5866, 13459
Bose, Ashish 13783, 16126
Bosi, Alessandro 15363
Boskoff, Alvin 8370
Bosley, Harold A. 6418
Bosner, Edna M. 19256
Bosser, Pierre 11683
Bosserman, Vern 17257
Bossman, Norma 14725
Bostnagel, Clement 5144
Boston Church Home for Orphan and Destitute Children 345
Boston Episcopal City Mission, Act of Incorporation and By-Laws 206
Boston Missionary and Church Extension Society of the Methodist Episcopal Church 428
Boston Port and Seamen's Aid Society 1934
Boston Seamen's Friend Society 98
Boston Society for the Moral and Religious Instruction of the Poor 31, 48
Boston Society for the Religious and Moral Improvement of Seamen 21
Boswell, Charles M. 2381
Bosworth, Bill 17370
Botero Salazar, Tulio 10232
Botnick, Irving 10233
Botswana Christian Council, Urban-Industrial Division 12080
Botts, Bud 10234
Boudon, Raymon 16127
Bouillane de Lacoste, J. N. 6831, 7043
Boulard, Fernand 5867, 6432, 7773, 10708, 10709, 12081
Boulding, Kenneth E. 6285, 9754
Boulter, Robert O. 16128
Bouman, Stephen Paul 17645
Bounsall, Ted 13133
Bourdilon, A. F. C. 5343
Bourg, Carroll J. 16843
Bourne, Theodore 714
Bourner, H. L. 2687
Bouvier, Leon F. 13134
Bouvier, Émile 6009, 6010
Bowden, Charles 15738
Bowden, James H. 11684
Bowden, Raymond 8371, 8667
Bowen, Don R. 10710
Bowen, Francis 315
Bowen, Howard 6286, 6421
Bowen, Roger 18053
Bowens, Marx G. 6535
Bower, Leslie 1201
Bower, William Clayton 3940, 4413
Bowers, George Palmer 7260
Bowery Young Men's Institute 1792
Bowie, Vaughan 17258, 17391
Bowie, Walter Russell 2382, 3568
Bowker, Lee H. 16129, 17646
Bowles, Paul Wilson 6011
Bowman, James R. 15118
Bowman, James S. 15364, 16500
Bowman, O. J. 3386
Bowman, W. T. 7505
Bowne, Borden P. 1113
Boyd, Beverley M. 5655
Boyd, Leonard T. 14531
Boyd, Malcolm 7044, 8995, 8996, 9317, 9755, 9930, 10711, 10712,

11207, 11685, 13135, 13784, 17647
Boyd, R. E. 2864
Boyer, Arthur 5246
Boyer, James W. 3684
Boyer, John W. 15739
Boyer, Paul S. 10713, 14532, 18054
Boyer, Richard 17259
Boyesen, Hjalmar Hjorth 826
Boylan, Anne Mary 12777
Boylan, Marguerite T. 5003, 8087
Boyle, George 6287
Boyle, Marilynne 19287
Boyle, Sarah Patton 10714
Boynton, Ernest 11208
Boynton, Morrison Russell 2857
Boynton, Nehemiah 972
Boynton, Percy H. 4021
Boynton, Thomas 9638
Boyte, Harry C. 15365, 16844, 17648, 17649, 18776
Boyum, Arnold E. 6186
Brabham, Mouzon William 3870
Brabner-Smity, Joyce 5868
Bracamonte, Jose A. 15366
Brace, Charles Loring 346, 412, 458, 504, 562, 605, 674, 1106, 1274, 1275
Brace, Emma 1275
Bracken, Walter H. 6832
Brackenridge, R. Douglas 13136
Brackett, Jeffrey R. 1840, 2299, 3482, 3483
Bradbee, Cheryl 19042
Bradbury, Nicholas 18777
Braden, Charles S. 5247, 5755, 7506
Bradford, Amory Howe 739, 740, 876, 973, 1359, 1607, 1841
Bradford, Gamaliel 3816
Bradley, Dwight J. 4698
Bradley, J. C. 16845, 16846
Bradshaw, Kenneth A. 8372
Bradshaw, Thornton F. 15740
Bradshaw, York W. 17260
Brady, E. B. 1043
Brady, William O. 5656
Bragg, George Freeman 3387
Braidfoot, Larry 16501
Brakelmann, Günter 12419, 14137, 14533, 15741, 16847, 17650, 17651, 18055
Branch, Harold T. 15742
Branch, Taylor 18426
Brand, M. Vivian 8668
Brandaur, Frederick P. 11190
Brandenburg, Walter F. 11686
Brandon, David 12778, 13137, 13785
Brandt, LeRoy C. 4589
Brandão, Carlos 15367
Branley, Brendan R. 9756
Branner, John Ky 16502
Brantley, Clovis A. 5447
Brathwaite, Joan 13460
Bratton, Mary J. 14950
Brauer, Jerald C. 8997
Brauer, Theodor 3484
Braumbaugh, Lewis Henry 5344
Braun, Theodore A. 10715
Brauns, Heinrich 13786
Bray, Charles 177
Bray, Reginald Arthur 2582
Brayan, Robert Lawson 17261
Brazier, Arthur M. 11209
Bread for All 4896
Bready, J. Wesley 3746, 4699
Breault, Kevin D. 18778
Brecher, Jeremy 19043
Breckinridge, Peter 12474
Bredkenfield, Gurney 7383
Breed, David M. 14138
Breen, Jay 5869
Bregstone, Philip P. 4264
Brehmer, Robert George, Jr. 4512
Breidenstein, Gerhard 12082
Breines, Andrew R. 6131
Breitman, George 9318, 9757,

10235, 18427
Brekke, Milo 14951, 15635
Bremer, Hendric 8998
Bremner, Robert Hamlett 6833, 7774, 9319, 12083
Brenkus, Milan C. 9758
Brenneman, Michael 14534
Brent, Charles H. 2927, 3309, 3685
Brereton, Virginia 18428
Bressan, V. 8088, 8373
Brethren House Ministries 19311
Breton, Denese 19192
Brett, Paul 14535, 17262
Brewbaker, Charles W. 1935
Brewer, Earl D. C. 6132, 6433, 6434, 6512, 6834, 8089, 8374, 8375, 8999, 9320, 9759, 9760, 10236, 10237, 10238, 10716, 10717, 11687, 11688, 14035, 16130
Brewer, Kathleen 16131
Brewer, Richard L. 15368
Brewster, Chauncey B. 2583
Brewster, David 9321
Brewster, Edward Eldridge 6133
Breyer, Karl 14139
Brezzi, Paulo 11689
Brichett, Colleen 18779
Brickman, W. W. 8090
Bridge Street African Wesleyan Methodist Episcopal Church 15369
Bridge, Anthony Ciprian 10239
Bridgehead in East Harlem 7507
Bridgeman, Charles T. 3485, 6835
Bridgeman, Howard Allen 1114
Bridgeman, R. L. 1360
Bridgeman, Thornley 3310
Bridges, Amy 14445
Bridges, George B. 9322
Bridges, Jesse Eugene, Jr. 11210
Bridgman, Howard A. 2007
Bridston, Keith R. 6012, 13138
Brief History of the Movement to Abolish the Slums of Philadelphia and Provide Decent Homes for the Poor 1202
Brief Record of One Year's Preventive and rescue Work, in Connection with St. Giles Christian Mission 715
Brief Sketch of the Revival of Religion in Boston 5
Briefs, Henry 17652
Briggs, Charles A. 1203, 1276
Briggs, John H. 18780
Briggs, Kenneth 14140
Briggs, William 10240
Bright, Howard Hugh, Jr. 8376
Bright, Laurence 9323
Brill, Earl H. 9761
Brink, Carol Ryrie 4817
Brink, Paul 19044
Brinkerhoff, Merlin B. 18056
Briscoe, Margaret Sutton 1115
Brister, C. W. 10241, 11690
British Committee of the French Protestant Industrial Mission 11691
British Council of Churches 11692, 13787, 15743
British Council of Churches, Social Responsibility Department 7261
British Council of Churches, Working Party on Britain as a Multi-Racial Society 13788
British Council of Churches, Youth Department, Industrial Research Group 5870
Britt, David T. 15370, 16112, 17263
Britt, Kevin M. 13139
Britt, Steuart Henderson 5093
Britton, Margaret 16132
Bro, Margueritte Harmon 4513, 4590, 4700, 4701

Broadbent, Charles D. 14536
Broadbent, Pete 16550
Broady, Maurice 10242
Broch, Ernst-Detlef 14141
Brock, Charles 15744
Brockman, Francis L. 9324
Brockman, James R. 18781
Brockmann, Gerard 13461
Brockmöller, Klemens 6288, 9000
Brockway, Allan R. 11211, 11693, 12084
Broderick, Francis L. 8669, 11212
Broderick, John 5548
Brodie, Sarah Eddleston 5248
Brodsky, Harold 16848
Brogan, Dick 14537
Broholm, Richard R. 9001, 11213
Brokering, Herbert Frederick 11694
Bronkema, Fred 16849
Bronnecke, Jack 9325
Bronson, Louise 11443
Bronstein, David 6435
Brooke, Henry 10243
Brooke, Stepford Augustus 505
Brookins, Jimmy L. 13462
Brooklyn Assistant Society, for Relieving and Advising Sick and Poor Persons 22
Brooklyn Church and Mission Federation, Greater New York Federation of Churches, Queens Federation of Churches, and the Federation of 4514
Brooklyn City Mission and the Goodwill Industries of Brooklyn 3051
Brooklyn City Mission and Tract Society 628
Brooklyn Message on Fair Housing 9762
Brooks, A. A. 4591
Brooks, Arthur Thomas 4022
Brooks, Charles Alvin 3052, 3116, 3117, 3388
Brooks, Evelyn 18429
Brooks, James A. 16133
Brooks, John Graham 3686
Brooks, Lee M. 5448, 5753
Brooks, Melaine 16738
Brooks, Phillips 576, 606, 781, 1044, 1204, 1361, 1842, 1936
Brooks, Robert C. 1793
Brose, Eric Dorn 17264
Brotherhood Movement 3184, 3185
Brothers, Joan 9002
Brotz, Howard 6134, 7045, 9003
Brougham, H. Bruce 3883
Broughton, Leonard Gaston 2300
Brouwers, Louis 13463
Browder, Earl R. 4702
Brower, Elizabeth 14952
Brown, A. Theodore 10343
Brown, Barbara 14953
Brown, Bertram S. 11695
Brown, Bob W. 9767, 10718
Brown, C. G. 14538, 18057, 19323
Brown, C. Richard 8670
Brown, Carl R. 9763
Brown, Charles 12779
Brown, Charles Oliver 782, 1362
Brown, Charles R. 2066, 4023
Brown, Chris 19045
Brown, Claude 9326
Brown, Clayton 18430
Brown, David 10719
Brown, David O. 14954
Brown, Diane R. 16134
Brown, Donald S. 14539
Brown, Earl R. 4818
Brown, Edwin A. 5345
Brown, Edwin R. 3871
Brown, Elizabeth Read 10720
Brown, Elmer E. 2124
Brown, Emory J. 6282

Brown, Forrest R. 5069
Brown, Frank Llewellyn 2067
Brown, Fred 7775
Brown, Frederick Kenyon 2540, 2645
Brown, Harold O. J. 12420
Brown, Harsh J. 9327
Brown, Henry Seymour 4024
Brown, Hubert 16135
Brown, Hubert L. 13789
Brown, James S. 12310
Brown, Jeanette Perkins 6436
Brown, John T. 1937
Brown, Jon K. 12078
Brown, Joseph 16503
Brown, Karen 19341
Brown, L. P. 9328
Brown, Leo C. 9764
Brown, M. Terese Avila 9765
Brown, Mary Elizabeth 18058, 18059
Brown, O. C. 13464
Brown, Oril 4515
Brown, Raymond Kay 14955
Brown, Robert 18060
Brown, Robert McAfee 7046, 9329, 12780, 12781, 14540, 15745, 16850, 18782
Brown, Robert R. 7262
Brown, Ronald A. 15746
Brown, Sherri 18431
Brown, Sydney T. 15371, 18782
Brown, Theodore E. 5145
Brown, Thomas 16504
Brown, Thomas Edwin 783
Brown, Truman 17605
Brown, Truman, Jr. 18432
Brown, William A., Jr. 6421
Brown, William Adams 3118, 3389, 5146
Brown, William F. 3390
Brown, William Henry 3591
Browne, Alice 4025
Browne, Henry Joseph 5346, 5449, 5756, 6135, 12085
Browne, J. T. 1159
Browne, Lynn 18061
Brownell, Blaine A. 14142, 15949
Browning, Neil 16505
Browning, Ron 17653
Brownson, Henry F. 1608
Brownson, Orestes A. 178, 188, 207, 1608, 4824, 6455, 6468
Brubaker, Ethel 4819
Brubaker, Paul 14541
Bruce, Alexander B. 1045
Bruce, James M. 1609
Bruce, Joe Wayne 15747
Bruce, Steve 17654
Brückbauer, Fred 3119
Bruckmann, H. 11214
Brueggemann, Walter 14143, 16136
Bruehl, Charles P. 4820
Brugarola, Martin 5549, 5657, 7508
Bruggink, Donald J. 13790
Brumbaugh, T. T. 5147, 5871
Brumm, Anne Marie 16851
Brun, Henri 3687
Brundage, David 17655
Bruner, F. Dale 7776
Brungs, Robert A. 14144
Brunini, J. G. 4265
Brunk, G. 10244
Brunner, August 14145
Brunner, Edmund de Schweinitz 2993, 4026, 4131, 4429, 5004, 5384, 6626, 7509
Brunner, Emil 5347, 6136
Bruno, Frank J. 4266
Brunsman, Deborah Sue 19312
Brunson, Ronnie L. 18062
Bruse, Tom 14542
Bruyn, Severyn T. 12782
Bruyn, W. Van Oosterwyk 446
Bryan, Dawson C. 5348, 6137
Bryan, Mary Lynn McCree 19046
Bryant, David 18783

Bryant, Drayton S. 6836
Bryant, Marcus D. 14146
Bryant, Robert H. 9766
Bryant, William Cullen 495
Bryce, Herrington J. 14147, 14956
Bryman, Alan 13465
Brys, A. 8377
Bryson, Gladys 4204
Bucci, Victor 8091
Bucey, Harry Richard 16137
Buchanan, Bill 13140
Buchanan, Colin 11215
Buchanan, Henry A. 9767
Buchanan, P. R. 1116
Buchanan, Susan H. 14957, 17265
Buck, Roy C. 9330
Bucklee, Sally 16204, 16317, 16448
Buckleiter, Anne 15748
Buckley, Anne 15372
Buckley, George W. 1610
Buckley, James Monroe 2301
Buckley, Louis F. 10245
Buckwalter, Paul W. 18063
Buczek, Daniel S. 13141, 13791
Buczkowski, Claudia 14148
Budd, Susan 14149
Budde, Heiner 18784
Buddha on 94th Street 5550
Budenz, Louis Francis 5551
Buechner, Frederick 18595
Buehrer, Edwin T. 4414, 4703, 4897
Buekwass, Henry 18064
Buel, Clarence 658
Buenker, John D. 12783, 15749
Bueno Losada, Jose 10246
Buess, Eduard 17656
Bühlmann, Walbert 14150, 14543, 14958, 17657
Buhofer, Ines 18433
Building and Urban Strategy 17658
Building A Moral Reserve: or, The Civic Responsibility of the Christian Citizen 4027
Built as a City 15750
Bukowczyk, John J. 18065, 18066
Buksbazen, Lydia Sitenhof 6627
Bull, Geoffery T. 12421
Bull, Paul B. 3817
Bullard, George W. 13792, 15334, 15373, 15716, 16243, 16506, 16507, 16508
Bullen, Frank Thomas 1794
Bullock, James R. 6837
Bultena, Louis 5249, 5349, 5757
Bundervoet, Albert 12784
Bunting, Ian D. 18785
Burbach, Jack L. 9768
Burchard, John E. 7047
Burchard, Waldo W. 8671
Burdick, Bruce 19298
Burdick, Jeanne Helen 14151
Burdick, Thelma 4415, 6437
Bureau of Jewish Social Research 3391
Burgalassi, Silvano 7048
Burgess, David S. 18786
Burgess, Ernest Watson 3688, 3717, 10247
Burgess, Thomas 2688, 3186, 3310
Bürgel, Rainer 13142, 15374
Bürgler, J. C. 915
Burgman, Hans 16138
Burke, Cyril C. 16139
Burke, Helen 5450
Burke, John C. 13143
Burke, Shane Robinson 17266
Burkett, Randall K. 13793, 14544, 14545, 14546
Burkhart, Roy A. 5451
Burkhartzmeyer, Brad 18434
Burkholder, J. Richard 9004
Burks, Janet 18787
Burks, Paul 18067, 18068
Burleigh, Betty 5148, 5758, 6013

Burlingame, George E. 2302
Burma, John H. 6438
Burnap, George 170
Burnett, James C. 18069
Burnett, Richard George 4132, 4205
Burnett, Scott 16852
Burnham, Chilo 10248
Burnham, Daniel H. 2303, 18382, 18489
Burnham, George 7049
Burnham, Kenneth E. 8672, 14959
Burns, Alfred Warren 8092
Burns, Carol 18752
Burns, Charles D. 12086
Burns, Charles Wesley 4267
Burns, Gail 16140
Burns, Islay 494
Burns, James Aloysius 2202, 4592
Burns, Melvin P. 3053, 3187, 3188, 3189, 3311, 3486, 3592, 3689
Burns, Terry 16140
Burns, Thomas A. 14547
Burr, Agnes Rush 2994
Burr, Angela 16853
Burr, Everett D. 1521
Burr, Nelson R. 8093
Burr, Walter 3818
Burrell, Curtis 10721
Burrell, David James 2125, 2203
Burrough, Paul 11216
Burroughs, Nannie Helen 1795, 3190, 3191, 4028, 4206, 4898, 18429
Burroughs, Prince Emmanuel 3487, 4704
Burrows, William R. 15375
Bursk, Edward C. 7510
Burson-Marsteller, Public Affairs 16141
Burstin, Barbara Stern 17659, 18070, 18788
Burt, Guy L. 13466
Burt, Robert 9769
Burtis, David 12087
Burton, George 9331
Burton, Joe Wright 10722
Burton, Lewis 13467
Burton, Richard F. 375
Burton, Ronald 18709
Büscher, Hans 11217
Bush, Hamilton Brinsley 6289
Bush, John C. 14960
Bushee, Frederick Alexander 1896, 5149
Bushnell, Horace 166, 194, 293, 316, 332, 413, 459, 506, 659, 5805, 19191
Busia, Kofi Abrefa 6117, 9770
Bussell, Frederick W. 2126, 3054
Bustanobey, Andre 11696
Butcher, G. F. 10249
Buteyn, Donald P. 11218
Butler, Angela 14152
Butler, John R. 12088
Butler, Jonathan 11697
Buttenheim, Harold S. 3488
Butterfield, Erston M. 5872
Butterworth, Eric 11219
Büttner, Manfred 17660
Buttrey, A. J. 3941
Buttry, Daniel L. 17661, 18435
Butts, Calvin Otis, III 16142
Butyn, Donald P. 10723, 11220
Butz, Geneva M. 17662, 18436
Buzard, Clifford 7654
Byar, Norman Gerald 6439
Byars, Larry L. 17663
Byers, David M. 17267
Byfield, Richard 7511
Byford, E. C. 16509
Byler, Ron 14548
Byles, Holden 1522, 1523
Byrd, Cameron Wells 9332
Byrne, Barry 3489
Byrne, Katherine 8094
Byrne, Kevin 16854
Byrne, Patricia 19066

Byrne, Patrick H. 18071
Byrt, A. W. 1736
Cabot, Ella Lyman 2689
Cadbury, George 19252
Cadigan, George L. 9333
Cadman, H. W. 877
Cadman, Samuel Parkes 1524, 1525, 1938
Cady, George L. 3392
Cafferty, Pastora San Juan 14549, 15751, 16510, 16511
Cahnman, Werner J. 7520, 8673
Cahoon, M. Janelle 8674
Cain, Richard W. 9334
Cairns, Earle Edwin 7777
Calahan, H. A. 4705
Calcutta Urban Service 12089, 15376
Caldwell, Gilbert H. 11221
Caldwell, J. C. 1277
Caldwell, Mary French 4899
Calfee, John E. 3050
Calhoun, John A. 9335
Calhoun, Robert L. 4416, 5150, 6138
Calian, Carnegie Samuel 10724, 16855
Caliandro, Arthur 10725
Caliaro, Marco 14153
Calkins, Raymond 1796
Call for National Emergency Coalition on Economic Crisis 16143
Callahan, Daniel 9771, 9772, 10250, 15753
Callahan, John D. 4516
Callahan, Kennon L. 16512
Calley, Malcolm J. C. 9336
Calthorpe, Peter 15752
Calvez, Jean-Yves 8095
Calzavarini, Giuseppe 14862
Camacho, Eduardo 18789
Cameron, Alexa Grace 12785
Cameron, C. E. 11951
Cameron, Catherine 10251
Cameron, Colin 10726
Cameron, Donaldina 4353
Cameron, Richard Morgan 8096
Cammann, Henry J. 447
Camp Morals and Self Rule 5005
Camp, Hugh N. 447
Camp, Richard L. 11222, 17664
Campaigning with the Men and Religion Teams 2490
Campbell, Alexander E. 14497
Campbell, Colin 12090
Campbell, Debra 19066
Campbell, Ernest Queener 7263, 7264, 7512, 7513, 7674
Campbell, George Duncan 14154
Campbell, Harvey 4593
Campbell, Helen 675, 741, 916, 1117
Campbell, James 1118, 1205, 8097, 12422, 12786, 14961
Campbell, Joan B. 14550
Campbell, John 199
Campbell, Kathleen 16513
Campbell, Reginald John 2127, 2204, 8898
Campbell, Robert D. 11698
Campbell, Scott 18072
Campbell, T. G. 4268
Campbell, Thomas C. 11699, 12091
Campbell, Will D. 8378, 8675
Campbell, William J. 16514
Campeau, C. E. 6139
Campiche, Roland J. 10727
Campion, Donald R. 6838, 9773
Campling, Andrew 15377
Campo, Juan Eduardo 19193
Campolo, Anthony 14962, 14963, 16515, 16516, 16517
Campolo, Bart 19330
Camus, Albert 5552
Can Four Women Ministers Start a Co-op Taxicab Company 15378
Can the Church Take It 4706

Canadian Information Sharing Service 13794
Canadian Urban Training [CUT] 9774
Canby, Henry Seidel 4354
Cancik, Hubert 17665
Candee, Marjorie Dent 4269
Canitrot M., Fernando 10439
Cantril, Hadley 4707, 5151
Cantwell, John J. 13080
Canty, Donald 16856
Capek, Thomas 3192
Capellades, Jean 12092
Capenerhurst, Ralph 12423
Capitman, William 9337
Caplan, Arthur L. 15753
Caplan, Lionel 13795, 14155, 15379, 15754, 16857, 18073
Caplow, Theodore 16518
Caprile, G. 17268
Caraballo, José A. 16519
Carburg, Warren 7514
Cardenal, Ernesto 14156
Carder, Kenneth 15755
Cardijn, Joseph 7285, 7778
Cardin, Jean Réal 7050
Cardwell, Brenda M. 19047
Caresché, Edward F. 3942
Carey, Clifford M. 5250, 6014
Carey, George 16858
Carey, Kenneth M. 4417
Carey, Patrick 14964
Carig, Yvonne 14965
Carleton, Will 2068
Carlin, Paige 10252, 11223
Carling, Vivienne 12424
Carlisle, Wilson 2008, 2009, 17888
Carlos, Serge 11700
Carlson, Arthur B. 16144
Carlson, C. Emanuel 11701
Carlson, Martin E. 5070
Carlson, Ronald W. 17666
Carlton, Alford 8599
Carmen, Arlene 17269
Carmines, Al 10194
Carnahan, Roy E. 15756
Carnegie, Andrew 917
Carnegie, Dale 5452
Carnegie, David 3193
Carner, Lucy Perkins 9005
Carney, Glandion 16859, 16860, 17270
Carney, M. K. 11702
Caro, Robert A. 13144
Carothers, J. Edward 5759, 7265, 8379, 8676, 9006, 9775, 9776, 10253, 10728, 10729, 11224, 11703, 12093, 12425
Carothers, Samuel McCord 2491
Carpenter, David B. 6371
Carpenter, George Wayland 10254
Carpenter, Horace Thompson 2584
Carpenter, James A. 9007, 16145
Carpenter, Julius Henry 4594
Carpenter, Niles 3819, 3820, 3943, 4029, 4030, 4031, 4133, 4355, 4595, 4708, 4821
Carpenter, Spence Cecil 5760
Carpenter, Thomas Phelps 3872
Carper, Eugene G. 11225
Carr, Alan 16146
Carr, Anne 18127
Carr, Jack Ladd 10730
Carranza, Salvador 7779
Carré, A. M. 6290
Carretto, Carlo 14966
Carrier, Hervé 7780, 9008
Carroll, Charles Eden 2865
Carroll, Edward G. 9338
Carroll, G. A. 7781
Carroll, Gene 9339
Carroll, Henry King 587, 1206
Carroll, Jackson W. 13468, 14157, 14681, 14913, 14967, 15380, 16326, 17127, 17667, 17751, 18972, 19203
Carrow, David J. 17668

Carson, Bryn A. 18507
Carson, Clayborne, Jr. 16861
Carson, John Roy 5152
Carson, Mina 19048
Carstens, C. C. 2128
Carter, Harold A. 13796
Carter, Lawrence 11226
Carter, Luther C., Jr. 6628
Carter, Michael V. 16147
Carter, Nancy A. 17669
Carter, Paul Allen 6839, 8677, 12094
Carter, Paul C. 10255
Carter, Robert L. 9777, 17670
Carter, Ronald L. 14968
Carter, Stephan J. 17361
Carter, Thomas 676
Carter, Weptanomah W. 13797
Carter, William 171
Cartmell, Constance W. 4858
Cartwright, James V., Jr. 11704
Carver, Dave 18074
Carver, Humphrey 13469
Carwardine, Richard 12426
Carwardine, William H. 1278
Casartelli, L. C. 2010
Casasco, Juan A. 11227
Cascia, Philip J. 18790
Case, Carl Delos 2775
Case, Edwin Max 11705
Casey, William Van Etten 12095
Cashmore, Ernest E. 16520
Cashmore, Gwen 17671
Casper, Dale E. 16521, 17271, 17272, 17672
Cassady, Maynard L. 5071
Cassel, John 12427
Cassell, Frank H. 8678
Casselman, Arthur V. 4032
Casserley, J. V. Langmead 6629
Cassette Tapes: Models for Metropolitan Ministry Conferences 18075
Cassler, Henry H. 6440
Casson, Herbert N. 974, 975, 976, 1363, 1611
Casson, Lloyd 16148
Castano Colomer, Jose. 14551
Castells, Manuel 16522
Casterline, Gail Farr 16862
Castillo, Metosalem Q. 16149, 16150
Castle, David 9340
Castle, Robert W. 10731
Castro, Emilio 10732, 13145, 13798, 14158, 15381, 18076
Catechesis in a Technical World 7266
Cater, Douglas G. 9341, 9778, 9779
Cater, S. Douglass 6442
Cathedral of St. John the Divine 1119
Catherwood, Henry Fredrick R. 9780
Catholic Charities Inc. of Portland, Oregon 7782
Catholic Church Extension Society of Canada 16151
Catholic Church, Archdiocese of Boston, Institute of Industrial Relations 11706
Catholic Church, Archdiocese of Detroit 17673
Catholic Church, Archdiocese of New York, Office of Pastoral Research 16152
Catholic Church, Archdiocese of New York, Office of Pastoral Research. 18437, 18438
Catholic Church, Archdiocese of Philadelphia, the Committee on Research and Development of the Urban Ministry [CORDUM] 13470
Catholic Church, Archdiocese of San Francisco, Catholic Social Services, Parish Outreach 14552
Catholic Church, Archdiocese of

St. Louis 16523
Catholic Church, Diocese of Brooklyn, Catholic Charities 3194
Catholic Church, National Conference of Catholic Bishops, Committee on Migration 18077
Catholic Church, The Commission for Catholic Missions among the Colored People and the Indians 5761
Catholic Committee on Urban Ministry 13146, 13147, 13471
Catholic Council on Working Life 5553, 8380
Catholic Digest 5453
Catholic Interracial Council of New York City 7051
Catholic Progress in London 401
Catholic Seminary Foundation of Indianapolis, St. Maur Seminary [Catholic Seminary of Indianapolis] 10733
Catholic Social Guild 1737
Catholic Worker Movement 4270
Catholics and Urban Problems 9781
Catlista, Frank J. 7783
Catton, Ione 6441
Católicos Hispanos en los Estados Unidos 15757
Cavan, Ruth Shonle 3873, 3944, 3945, 5658, 8381, 8806
Cavanaugh, John 16863
Cave, Clarence L. 9782
Cave, Dave 17273
Cavenaugh, Gerald E. 16864
Cavenaugh, Thomas E. 16865
Cavendish-Bentinck, Henry, Lord 3747
Cavert, Inez M. 5072, 5073
Cavert, Samuel McCrea 3312, 3748, 11707
Cavileer, Jesse 5251
Cavin, Susan 13472
Caylor, John 6015
Cayton, Horace R. 4900, 5367, 6630, 6631
Cheshire, Christopher 4207
Cecic, Vinko 7052
Cedotal, Arthur Edward 10734
Celebrating 10 Years ... 14553
Celebration in Experimentation 11708
Center for Church and Community Ministries 18078, 19194, 19195
Center for Human Action, Research, and Training [CHART] 10735
Center for Migration Studies 12787
Center for Parish Development 14159
Center for the Study of the Christian World Mission 7515
Center for Urban Education [CUE-P] 10736, 13148
Center for Urban Encounter [CUE-M] 10737
Center of Metropolitan Mission In-Service Training [COMMIT] 9783
Centre de recherches socio-religieuses [CDRSR] 7784, 7785, 7786
Centre for Christian Studies 14554
Centro Brasileiro de Analise e Planejamento 14555
Century-Old Church Saved 16524
Certificate Program in Christian Ministry 12788
Cesarz, Kathleen M. 17674
Cetina, Judith G. 18791
Chadwick, Bruce A. 12057, 14925, 16518

Chaffee, Edmund B. 3490, 3874, 4208, 4271, 4272
Chafin, Kenneth L. 9342, 9784, 9785, 10738
Chai, S. 12789
Chakerian, Charles G. 6632
Chalasinsky, Joseph 4418
Chaldean Catholics: Refugees from Assyria and Mesopotamia in Chicago 4517
Chalfant, H. Paul 15758
Challenge of the City 6840
Challenge of the Inner City: Service or Survival 13473, 13474
Challenge of Urban Ministry: Diocese of Oakland 17274
Chalmers, Glenn 18439
Chalmers, Thomas 41, 59, 66, 67, 120, 255, 287, 288, 1541, 17416, 19323
Chamber of Commerce of the United States 5873
Chamberlain, Audrey 13063
Chamberlain, David Barnes 7267
Chamberlain, H. R. 2304
Chamberlain, John 4209
Chamberlain, Montague 1526
Chamberlain, Neil W. 12790
Chamberlain, Neville 14160
Chamberlain, Theadore J. 12096, 12097, 12791
Chambers, Clarke A. 8679
Chambers, Curtis A. 10256
Chambers, J. Allen 6291
Chambers, Mary Jane 12792, 13475, 17675
Chambers, Talbot Wilson 249, 333
Chambers, William N. 6960
Champion, A. G. 19196
Chan, Frederick C. C. 18440
Chance, Jerry 10739
Chandler, C. W. 8098
Chandler, Larnie I. 11228
Chaney, Charles L. 14161, 16153
Chang, Donald Mark 8099
Chang, Peter 17676
Chang, Robert Tsai-Chin 19049
Chang, Yoon Sung 17275
Changing the World 17677
Channing, William Ellery 131, 189, 448
Channing, William Henry 227
Chanson, Paul 6633
Chapin, Aaron L. 629
Chapin, Dorothy W. 7053
Chapin, Edwin Hubbell 179, 200, 285, 294, 295
Chapin, F. Stuart 4419, 7054
Chapman, Ernest Eugene 10257
Chapman, Ian 17276
Chapman, John Wilbur 1046, 2069
Chapman, Peter 13799
Chapman, Robert C. 11709
Chapman, S. H. 5350
Chapman, Terry S. 16866
Chapman, Tom 8680, 9009
Chappel, Arthur H. 5874
Chappell, Winifred 3055
Characteristics of American Jews 9343
Charaux, Claud Charles 1364
Chareonwongska, Kriengska 19050
Charity Organization Society of the City of New York 1527
Charles F. Longino, Jr. 13216
Charles, Daniel E. 14969
Charleston Port Society for Promoting the Gospel Among Seamen 85
Charley, Julian W. 16867
Charlton, William 17678
Charpentier, Alfred 5454
Charpin, Fernand 9010
Chartier, Ricardo A. 9344, 10740
Chase, Edward T. 7055
Chase, Stewart 3821

Chastain, C. R., Jr. 15759
Chatfield, Charles 13800
Chatterji, Saral 14970
Chaudhury, Rafiqul Huda 16154
Chauncey, George A. 10258, 10259, 11229
Chavez, Josias V. 11230
Chavez, Tomas 14162
Chavy, Jacques 5120
Cheathamm, Carl Wade 16155
Check List of Works Relating to the Churches and Ecclesiastical History of the City of New York in the New York Public Library 1797
Chee, Winfred See-Hing 18792
Cheer, Pat 7878
Cheesewright, Arthur 827
Cheesman, G. W. 2205
Cheever, George B. 17766
Chein, Isador 6879
Chélini, Jean 6292, 6634, 7268
Chen, Peter F. 13801, 13802, 19051
Chen, Wen-Hui C. 6016
Cheng, David Te-Chao 5659
Chenu, Marie Dominique 6140, 6293
Cherouny, Henry 677, 742
Cherry, Gordon E. 13803, 15328
Cherry, Kittredge 18441
Chesebro, Scott Elliot 16156
Chesham, Mrs. H. 10260
Chesham, Sallie 9345, 12428
Cheshire, Ashley 13149
Chesnut, R. A. 11231
Cheswick Center and the Boston Municipal Research Bureau 12793
Cheswick Center and the National Endowment for the Arts, Conference on the Challenge of Underused Church Property and the Search for Alternatives, First International 13476
Chetkow, B. H. 7056
Cheuiche, Antônio do Carmo 16525
Chevallier, Dominique 16157
Chicago 4033
Chicago Baptist Association 507, 1365
Chicago Christian Missionary Society 1738
Chicago City Missionary Society 9786
Chicago Commission on Race Relations 3393
Chicago Congregational Union 678
Chicago Gospel Mission 14556
Chicago Hebrew Mission 2585
Chicago Home Missionary and Church Extension Society of the M. E. Church 743
Chicago West Side Christian Parish 5875
Chicago's Union Chinese Church 2690
Child, Irvin 5153
Children of the City Streets 9011
Childs, John Brown 13477, 15382
Childs, Loyd 17277
Childs, Marquis W. 6442
Chilton, Charles A. 15383
Chisholm, Shirley 15762
Chiyo, Takeshi 12794
Cho, Paul Yonggi 15760, 16868, 16869
Cho, Sung-Whan 16870
Choquette, Robert 13478
Chorley, Edward Clowes 3491, 4420, 5554
Choron-Baix, Catherine 12098, 17679, 19197
Choy, Kathy 18187
Choy, Wilbur W. 6635, 7057
Christ and Labour: Speeches

Made at Browning Hall During Labour Week 2492
Christ-Janer, Albert 8382, 14971
Christensen, Gordon A. 10261
Christensen, James L. 8100
Christensen, M. 16158
Christensen, Michael J. 16526, 18442
Christensen, Torben 8383
Christensen, Winnie 11710
Christenson, James A. 15086
Christenson, Reo M. 12099
Christian and Civic Economy of Large Towns 67
Christian and Missionary Alliance 2493
Christian Activities Council [Hartford, CT] 250
Christian Almsgiving: A Dialogue 744
Christian Care for Seafarers in Port 12100
Christian Century 6017
Christian Century Foundation 517, 6018
Christian Church of Thailand, Urban-Industrial Life Division 14163
Christian Church [Disciples of Christ] 3875
Christian Coffee House Is Smash Hit in St. Louis 9346
Christian Commission for Camp and Defense Communities 5154, 5155
Christian Conference of Asia 12795
Christian Conference of Asia, Urban Rural Mission 15761
Christian Conference of Asia, Urban Rural Mission Office 14164, 14972, 15384
Christian Cooperation in Buffalo: A Study of a Successful Council of Churches 6019
Christian Council of Ghana 6636
Christian Council of Nigeria, Institute of Church and Society 10262
Christian Ethics and Pittsburg Employers 3120
Christian Herald 32, 577
Christian in a Secularized World 10741
Christian Labor Union 531, 578
Christian Philanthropy 449
Christian Reformed Church, Board of Home Missions 12429
Christian Service to Industrial Society 13150
Christian Social Union 1279, 1366, 1367, 2928
Christian Social Union, Oxford University Branch 1047
Christian Socialist 692, 1897
Christian Socialist Movement 7787, 8681
Christian Socialist: A Journal of Association 251
Christian Union 477
Christian Worker and Cry of the Children 1207
Christian Workers at New Haven 1368
Christian Workers Fellowship 7269
Christian, Henry A. 16527
Christian, Portia 11711
Christian's Magazine 7
Christianity and Industry Series 3313
Christianity and the Economic Order 5455, 5456, 5457, 5458
Christianization of Politics 1369
Christiano, Kevin J. 15321, 16528, 18079, 18443
Christians for Socialism'

Movement: Documentation 13804
Christians for Urban Justice 14973
Christianson, Wayne 9787
Christie, Bruce D. 10240
Christlich Sozialer Pressedienst 3195
Christman, Jesse 8097, 9347, 12101, 12102, 12103, 12430
Christoff, Nicholas B. 14557
Christopher, Louise 13805
Chrysostom, Philipose Mar 7516
Chuck, James 17680
Chudacoff, Howard P 17278
Chun, Sung C. 12431
Chung, Hong Kwon 17279
Chung, Si Woo 15385
Chung, Tai Ki 16529
Chung, Young Kwan 16530
Chupungco, Anscar J. 18444
Church and Industry Institute 10742
Church and Poverty 9348
Church and Reform 3749
Church and Social Action 3946
Church and Social Classes 716
Church and the Changing Urban Parish: Five Vignettes 10743
Church and the City: Signs of Despair, Signs of Hope 15762
Church and the Dynamic of Social Change 12104
Church and Urban Renewal 9349
Church and Women in the Armed Forces 5156
Church Abandons Inner City, Aids Genocide 13479
Church Activism and Corporate America 17280
Church as Landlord 2586
Church Association for the Advancement of the Interests of Labor 1120
Church Building Society [London] 376, 5555
Church Club of New York 828
Church Community Ministries 12796
Church Conference of Social Work 4518
Church Extension 9012
Church Extension Association of London 588
Church Extension in Houston 5876
Church Federation of Greater Chicago 6294, 9013, 9350
Church Federation of Greater Chicago, Bureau of Church Planning and Religious Research, Chicago Urban Research and Development Project 7788
Church Federation of Greater Chicago, Department of Social Welfare 9014
Church Federation of Los Angeles 4901
Church Goes Where the People Are 9351
Church Help for Unemployment 2866
Church in a Changing World 4709
Church in City Politics. 1682
Church in Economic Affairs: The Policies of the Presbyterian Church, USA, 1930-1980 16871
Church in Industrial India 9352
Church in Middle America 11712
Church in the American City 6443
Church in the Changing City 9788
Church in the Ghetto 10744
Church Labor Letter 5877

Church League for Industrial Democracy 3196
Church Mission of Help, New York. 2494
Church Money for the Slums 10745
Church of All Nations and Neighborhood House 13151
Church of All Nations [Los Angeles, CA] 3394
Church of England 3197
Church of England, Archbishop of York's Committee of Industrialists and Economists with Theologians to Consider the Findings of the Malvern Conference 5074
Church of England, Archbishops' Committees of Inquiry 3121
Church of England, Board for Social Responsibility 8384, 18445, 18793
Church of England, Commission on Urban Priority Areas 17281, 19052
Church of England, Diocese of Sheffield Social Responsibility Committee 16872
Church of England, General Synod 17681
Church of England, General Synod, Working Party on the Pastoral Measure, 1968 13480
Church of England, Prison Chaplaincies Council 10263
Church of England, Social and Industrial Council 7517
Church of England, Social Policy Committee of the Board for Social Responsibility 17682
Church of Scotland 15386
Church of the Brethren 7789
Church of the Brethren, General Brotherhood Board, Brethren Service Commission 6020
Church of the Brethren, Ministry and Home Missions Commission 6444
Church of the Savior 8101
Church Penetrates the High-Rise World 9789
Church Review 228
Church Social Union 1370, 1453
Church Social Work 4356
Church Socialist League 2776
Church Socialist League (London) 2587
Church Speaks in a Riot-Torn City 10264
Church That Isn't Like Church 10746
Church That Stays Down-Town 2588
Church under Fire: Taiwan National Report 15387
Church Union Housing Association 4357
Church Ushers' Association of New York 6021
Church without a Theology: Community Church of New York 3122
Church Women United 14558, 14974
Church Work in Cities 918
Church Work in Large Cities 402
Church, the City and the Poor: A Challenge 17282
Church, The Community and the Child 5157
Church: Symposium on Church and Social Work 3492
Church's Duty in Relation to Industry 3395
Church's Growing Edge, Single Adults: A Planning Guide 15388
Church's Ministry to the Family among War Workers 5351
Churches and Charities 1843

Churches and Corporate Responsibility -- 1975 13481
Churches Committee on Migrant Workers in Western Europe 13482
Churches for the Cities 17683
Churches Help Low-Income Families Purchase Homes 10747
Churches in Megalopolis 9353
Churches in Racial or Ethnic Transition 14975
Churches Main Committee to the War Damages Commission 5252
Churches Merge in Baltimore's Inner City 7518
Churches Speak to Business: Studies Made Under Auspices of Federal Council of Churches 5660
Churches' Center for Theology and Public Policy 18794
Churches' Influence on Secular Society 10265
Churchmen Help Beat 'Right to Work' Laws 7270
Churchmen's Missionary Association for Seamen of the Port of Philadelphia 229
Cicala, Antonio 12797
Ciesluk, Joseph E. 5253
Cigich, Patrick Matthew 14165
Cimíc, Esad 12105
Cinisello Community [Milan, Italy] 15389
Cinnéide, Séamus 12432
Cipolla, Costantino 15763
Cipriani, Roberto 14559, 15390
Cirillo, R. 6841
CISL: 1948-1957: Ispirazione cattolica, scelta de classe, nuovo sindacato 15764
Cities of Destruction 5762
Cities of Tomorrow: The Church in the Modern City 3947
Cities: Challenges and Dreams 15765
Citron, Pierre 8102
City and Country Churches Together 9354
City and Its Suburbs 1371
City Affairs--Necessity of a General Application of the Local System 68
City Church: First Methodist Episcopal Church, Gary, Indiana 3750
City Evangelization 829
City Lutherans in Action 15391
City Mission and Coffee House [Youngstown, OH] 630
City Mission of Salvation Includes Rescue of Neighborhood 18446
City Mission Sketch 548
City Mission Society [Hartford, CT] 359
City Missionary Association [New Haven, CT] 252
City Missionary Society of Boston 42, 55, 60, 69
City Missionary Society [Columbus, OH] 253
City Missions 305
City of Churches Illustrated Church Annual 977
City of London Churches Commission 3123
City Reformation, Prescribed and Demanded by the Holy Bible 78
City Temperance Society, Providence [RI] 180
City Temple [London], Church Council 3396
City Tract Society [Hartford, CT] 347
City Venture Corporation 14976
City Vigilance League 1280

City: Frustration or Fulfillment 9355
Ciucci, Giorgio 14977
Civardi, Luigi 5254, 7058, 8103, 8682
Civil Liberties in Industrial Disputes 4902
Claassen, Oliver J. 18447
Claerbaut, David 13483, 14166, 14560, 16531
Claiming Turf in Hispanic Chicago 16873
Clair, William H. 6445
Clammer, John 19053
Clancey, Jack 16532, 16612
Clanton, Jann Aldredge 18080
Clapham, William Edward 4710
Clapp, Rodney 17283, 18795
Clapp, Theodore 13680
Clar, Reva 14307
Clarebaut, David 15392
Clark, Alexander 495
Clark, Carl A. 9015
Clark, Charles W. 9356
Clark, D. 7790
Clark, David 14167
Clark, David B. 8104, 9357, 11713, 12106
Clark, David L. 14561, 15766
Clark, Dennis 6141, 6637, 6838, 7791, 7792, 8105, 8385, 8683, 8684, 9016, 9790, 10748, 11714, 12107, 13152, 14168, 14562, 16159
Clark, Ellen 12433, 12798, 13484, 13806, 13807, 14169, 14170
Clark, Elmer T. 3593, 3948, 5763
Clark, Francis E. 978, 1454, 1612
Clark, Fred 9791
Clark, Harriet Woodward 2206
Clark, Henry 9017, 9358, 9359, 9792, 9793, 9794, 10266, 10267, 11232, 12108
Clark, Izeyl 5158
Clark, John Bates 5470
Clark, Joseph B. 1898
Clark, Kenneth B. 9018, 9360
Clark, M. Edward 10268
Clark, Merlin 6142
Clark, Roger 13153
Clark, Rufus Wheelwright 549
Clark, Samuel M. 9361
Clark, Stephen B. 12434
Clark, Thomas Curtis 4134
Clark, Tony 15393
Clark, William 5878, 8386
Clarke, C. P. S. 2777
Clarke, David 14563
Clarke, Dorus 145
Clarke, Henry William 1613
Clarke, J. F. 460
Clarke, Joan 18273
Clarke, Merrill F. 4273
Clarke, Peter B. 14564
Clarke, Richard, II 1614
Clarke, Roger 18390, 19028
Clarke, Sarah D. 2778
Clarke, Sundar 12799
Clarke, T. Erskine 13485
Clarke, Tina 15394
Clarke, W. Norris 7519
Clarke, William 1121
Clarkson, Kathy 15395
Clasper, Paul 16874
Classen, Allen 13486
Claus, Kenneth Edward 13808
Clausen, Bernard C. 5556
Claver, Donald A. 14171
Claver, Francisco F. 13809
Clavier, Henri 5159
Clay-Tor, Francois 15767
Clayton, Joseph 1844
Clayton, Louisa 589
Clayton, Paul Clark 16875
Cleage, Albert B., Jr. 10749, 10750, 10751, 12109, 12435
Cleal, C. H. 5352, 6638
Clear, Valorous Bernard 5459, 6295, 7271, 14172

Cleary, John Martin 8106
Cleary, William H. 11233, 12110
Cleaver, Eldridge 10752, 16585
Clebsch, William A. 10269
Clechet, Bernard 10753
Cleckner, Patricia 14565
Clelland, Donald A. 13154
Clemens, Eugene Philip 12111
Clemens, Jakob 5764
Clément, Marcel 8387
Clemens, Samuel Langhorn 508
Clements, Simon 9323
Clemes, William 5765
Clemmer, Myrtle M. 8563
Clergy and Laity Concerned 12436
Clergyman's Study of the 'Stranded 1845
Cleveland Baptist Association 461
Cleveland Christian Endeavor Union 1208
Cleveland Church Federation 6296, 6842
Cleveland Church Federation, Social Welfare Department 7272
Cleveland Church Gives Its Property to Blacks 11234
Cleveland Covenant 15396
Clever, C. 1455
Clews, Rosemary A. 12257
Clifford, James S. 13155
Clifford, John 1528, 2207
Clifford, Paul Rowntree 5879
Clifford, Richard Lorenzo 15768
Clifford, Virginia I. 9019
Clinard, Marshall B. 7273, 9020
Clinebell, Howard J. 11715
Clinebell, Howard J., Jr. 11534, 12437
Clingenpeel, Michael James 14978
Clippinger, A. R. 3751
Cliquet, Maurice 16876
Close, Sandy 15245
Cloud, Fred 12112
Clouse, Robert G. 16877
Clow, William M. 2691, 3314, 3594
Cloward, Richard 9795, 12274, 13156, 14391
Clowney, Edmund P. 7274
Club of Rome 12594
Clucas, Joan Groff 18448
Clune, Robert M. 9796
Clyde, Nathana Lore 2692
Coady, M. M. 4822, 5160, 5255, 5353
Coakley, Jay J. 11399
Coale, James J. 3198, 3315, 3595
Coalter, Milton J. 1739, 19198
Coates, Bryan Ellis 14173
Coates, Charles H. 9362
Cobb, Alice 8107
Cobb, John B. 13157, 14566
Cobb, William H. 1683
Coblentz, H. S. 7793
Coburn, Martha G. 11334
Cochran, John R. 13487, 15397
Cochran, Joseph Wilson 2129
Cochran, Robert Dennis 16878
Cochran, Thomas Childs 17284
Cochrane, James 17285
Cockerell, David 18796
Cocklin, Paul 17684
Cockran, Clay L. 13488
Cocks, Orrin G. 2589
Coco, Jean-Pierre 18797
Coddington, Herbert G. 2011
Coe, George A. 1740, 2929, 2995, 3397, 3876, 4274, 4903
Coe, Shoki 12800
Coen, James A. 9119
Coffee and... 9363
Coffee House Theology in a Small Town 9364
Coffee Houses 9365
Coffey, Ian 18798
Coffin, Brent 14979

Coffin, Henry Sloane 3056, 3199
Coffin, Paulina 14979
Coggin, James E. 12113
Coggins, Ross 9366
Coggle, P. J. 6843
Cogswell, James A. 16533
Cohen, Abner 11235, 13158
Cohen, Chapman 3124, 4135
Cohen, Erik 11716
Cohen, Henry 6297, 6844
Cohen, J. X. 4596, 4711
Cohen, Jacob M. 2773
Cohen, Paul A. 13159
Cohen, Stanley 12438
Cohen, Steven Martin 16534
Cohen, Susan M. 18081
Cohn, J. 15398
Cohn, James 17685
Cohn-Sherbok, Dan 17686, 18799
Coit, Stanton 1122
Colaw, E. 10754
Colbaugh, Lloyd N. 14980
Cole, Charles C., Jr. 6298, 6446
Cole, Larry 10270, 11717, 11718
Cole, Mary 10271
Cole, Raymond E. 3596
Cole, William I. 1529, 1615, 2208
Coleman, B. I. 10755
Coleman, Benjamin I. 6584
Coleman, Bonnie 17687
Coleman, George Williams 2383
Coleman, James 6845, 7059
Coleman, John A. 14567, 14568, 16160, 19054
Coleman, Michael 5006
Coleman, Peter 18800
Coleman, Robert E. 11236
Coleman, Willie 18082
Coler, Bird S. 1684
Coles, Robert 11719, 12801
Colford, Paul D. 16568
Colins, Frédéric-Louis-De-Gonzague 462
Coll, Blanche D. 6639
Collegiate Methodist, Ames, Iowa 5880
Collens, T. Wharton 563
Collier, Richard 9367
Collin, G. L. 2070
Collins, Dean S. 7794
Collins, Gary R. 13810
Collins, Joan. A. 14569
Collins, John 8685, 14174, 14570
Collins, John C. 607, 1123
Collins, Rebecca 16161
Collins, Ruth Philpott 8388
Collins, Sheila 15399, 17286, 17688
Collins, Trudy B. 17689
Collins, William B. 10756
Collum, Danny 17287
Collyer, Robert 2071
Colman, George D. 13160
Colombo, Vittorino 16535
Colon, John E. 18801
Colony, David Carl 4823
Colson, Charles 17288
Colton, Calvin 230
Colton, Chauncey 190
Columbia Cooperative Ministry 10272
Columbia Maryland Mission Development Committee 9368
Columbus Action Training Associates [CATA] 10757
Colvin, David Leigh 3752
Colwell, Stephen 266, 279, 296
Comblin, Joseph 10758
Combs, George Hamilton 2631
Come, Arnold B. 7795, 9369
Comer, Harry 7796
Comhaire, Jean Louis Léopold 6299, 7520
Comité National des Constructions d'Eglises, Colloque sur l'implantation de lieux de culte dans l'aménagement du territoire

9797
Commemorating the 50th Anniversary of the Pacific Garden Mission 3822
Committee for Ministerial Formation of the Bishop's Conference of England and Wales 18083
Committee on the War and the Religious Outlook 3200, 3201
Common Christian Responsibility Towards Areas of Rapid Social Change 7275
Commons, John R. 1124, 1125, 1209, 1281, 1616, 1617, 1618, 2012, 2130, 4358, 8099
Community Action Training Services [CATS] 9798
Community Analysis 15769
Community Chest and Councils of America 5661
Community Church: A Dilemma 3949
Community Churches Go Forward 3950
Community for Creative Nonviolence 14571
Community Organization 14175
Community Progress, Inc. 10273
Community Renewal Society 10759, 11237, 14572, 14981
Community Tension Center 7521
Community Work in the Inner City 15770
Compa, Lance 16879
Comstock, Oliver E. 14665
Conant, James B. 8108
Concept, A Pamphlet Series for Questions of Christian Renewal 7276
Concerned Citizens for Freedom and Justice 13811
Concetta, sr. 5881
Concrete Vineyard 6640
Condit, Ira Miller 1741
Cone, James H. 11238, 11720, 11721, 12802, 13489, 13490, 15311, 16880
Cone, Roger Daniel 15771
Confederation of Canadian Catholic Workers 5161
Conference on Christian Politics, Economics and Citizenship -- Commission on In 3597
Conference on Christians in the Inner City 12803
Conferences Face Urban Tasks 10760
Conferencia--"La Enseñanza Social de la Iglesia y el mundo del trabajo en la América Latina de los 80 17289
Confraternity of Christian Doctrine, Religious Education Office 13812
Confédération Internationale des Syndicats Chrétiens 3753
Conférence d'Eglises de toute l'Afrique 8686
Congregation Finds Opportunity Next Door 11239
Congregation for Reconciliation 11722
Congregational Association of Detroit 717
Congregational Christian Churches, Board of Home Missions 4359
Congregational Christian Churches, General Council 5662
Congregational Christian Churches, the Council for Social Action 7277
Congregational Church-Building Society 679
Congregational Churches 33
Congregational Churches,

Council for Social Action 4360
Congregational Home Missionary Society 718
Congregational Renewal 13161
Congregational Union [Chicago] 5766
Congress of Industrial Organizations [CIO] 6641
Congress of Industrial Organizations, Department of Education and Research 5256
Congresso Batista Latino Americano de evangelismo urbano e missôes 16162
Congresso Nacional de Jovens Trabalhadores 17290
Conklin, George H. 13813
Conklin, James 14573, 14982
Conklin, R. 14574
Conley, J. 14176
Conley, John J. 13162
Conn, Harvie M. 14983, 14984, 16163, 16536, 16881, 16882, 16883, 16884, 16885, 16886, 16887, 16888, 16889, 16890, 17291, 17292, 17293, 17294, 17295, 17690, 17691, 17692, 17693, 18084, 18449, 18450, 18802, 18803, 19055
Conn, Howard 6642
Connecticut Bible Society 919
Connecticut Evangelical Magazine 1
Connell, Francis J. 5257, 5354, 5460, 5461, 5557
Connell, John 15772
Connelly, James F. 13814
Conner, Bill 14177
Conner, J. E. 4275
Conners, Kenneth W. 10274
Conning, John Stuart 3823
Connolly, G. P. 16164
Connor, Brian Nichols 14178
Connor, James A. 18451
Connor, John Harold 17694
Conover, Elbert Moore 3202, 3877, 5355, 5462, 5663, 5767
Conover, Patrick W. 11723
Conrad, Ann Patrick 15504
Conrad, R. L. 9370
Conroy, John 18085
Conroy, Thomas M. 3598
Consecration of St. Patrick's Cathedral 2384
Consejo Episcopal Latinoamericano 15773, 16165
Consejo General de la Pontificia Comisión para América Latina 16166
Considine, Michael J. 1282
Constant, Alphonse Louis 231
Consultation in the Urban Community and the Urban Church 7060
Consultation on Community Ministries, October 31-November 2, 1983, Lousiville, KY 16537
Consultation on Industrial Urban Missions and Laymen Abroad, Bankok 10761
Consultation on Migrant Workers in Western Europe 10762
Convegno nazionale assistenti ecclesiastici delle ACLI 7278
Convengo nazionale assistenti ecclesiastici delle ACLI 7061
Conversation with a Rank and File Worker 14985
Converted Catholic 693
Convocation on the City Church 5882
Conwell, Russell H. 1126, 1195, 1456, 1530, 2867, 2994, 10987
Conwell, William H. 1447
Conwill, Giles A. 15400
Conzemius, Victor 16167
Coogan, John E. 7797
Cook, Bonnie 18452

Cook, Charles Thomas 6447
Cook, Clair M. 5258, 5463, 5768, 5883, 6300, 6448, 6643, 6846, 7178, 7279, 7280, 7522, 7798, 8389, 9021
Cook, J. 1127
Cook, J. Keith 16538
Cook, James 10475
Cook, Joseph 496, 590, 631, 632, 878
Cook, Laurence D. 11240
Cook, Paul 17695
Cook, R. Franklin 15736, 15774, 16168
Cook, Tim 14986
Cook, William [Guillermo] 16169, 16539
Cooke, George Willis 1457, 1846
Cooke, Gerald 13163
Cooke, Leslie Edward 7062
Cooley, Charles Horton 2305
Cooley, Gilbert E. 14179
Coons, Irene Mae 5075
Cooper, Anthony Ashley 334, 727, 840, 2245, 3510, 3746
Cooper, Daniel 707
Cooper, Howard 15401
Cooper, James Fenimore 391
Cooper, John 14152
Cooper, John Montgomery 4421
Cooper, Lee R. 13164
Cooper, Mattie Lula 6449, 8687
Cooperation in Planned Cities: A Sticky Issue for Baptists 10275
Coote, Robert T. 16891
Cope, Gilbert 11241, 11724, 12439
Cope, Henry Frederick 3125
Copeland, E. Luther 10221, 10763, 14180
Copeland, S. Bruce 10276
Coppens, Betty 6143
Copsey, Katheryn 15775
Copus, J. E. 2013
Corcoran, Sanford W. 4276, 4422
Corcoran, Theresa 13491, 14987, 16170
Cordasco, Francesco 10764
Cordes, Valorie 16171
Cordner, John 317, 463
Corince, R. P. de 6450
Cork, Delores Freeman 15402
Cormack, Margaret L. 7281
Corneck, Graham 15403
Cornehls, James 17296
Cornelius, Gollapalli 12114
Cornelius, John C. 6847
Cornelius, Wayne A. 13492, 13493, 13815, 14575
Cornell, George 12534
Cornish, F. Joseph 6644
Corporate Responsibility: An Update 12804
Corresion, Vittorio 6022
Correu, Larry M. 9799
Corrigan, John 6759, 15445
Corrigan, M. Felicia 4824
Corruption in Labor and Management 7282
Corsi, Edward 6301
Corson, Ben 19056
Cort, John C. 5558, 6023, 6144, 7283, 18453, 19286
Cortes, Ernesto, Jr. 18086, 18087
Cortese, Anthony Joseph Paul 15404
Corwin, Charles 15776
Cory, E. S. 1939
Cosby, Gordon 8688
Coser, Lewis 6451
Cossette, Jean Paul 6145
Costantino, Frank 15777
Costas, Orlando E. 12805, 13165, 13166, 14988, 16172, 16173, 16892, 18804
Coste, René 11725
Costello, George 16893
Costello, Tim 19358
Costello, Vincent Francis 13816, 14181
Cotham, Perry C. 13817

Cottier, M. Martin 8811
Coughlin, Bernard J. 9022
Coughlin, Charles E. 4277, 4315, 4361, 4423, 4495, 4980, 5152, 7437, 9673
Coulson, Charles Alfred 6302, 6645, 10765
Council of Church Women of Parkersburg [WV] 6646
Council of Churches of Greater Cleveland, Commission on Ecumenical Education 9371
Council of Churches of Greater Seattle 18088, 18454, 18805
Council of Women for Home Missions 2803, 4060, 4623
Country Girl in the City Church 2693
Countryman, Louis William 18089
Cours de formation: Ministère de l'église dans les zones de changement rapide social 12115
Courtes-Lapeyrat, Jean 15778
Courtney, Paul 6024
Courtney, Thomas 16540, 16894, 18090
Cousineau, Jacques 15779
Cousins, Peter 14182
Coutts, Frederick 5621
Covell, Ralph 17297
Covello, Leonard 5259, 5758
Covenant House Always Overwhelmed 15405
Coventry Industrial Mission 11242, 12806
Cowan, Michael H. 10277
Cowan, W. H. 10278
Cowgill, Donald 7799
Cowhig, James D. 8390
Cowles, S. Macon 10766
Cox, Alistair 14183
Cox, David F. 6647, 7063, 8391, 13167
Cox, Donald William 12440
Cox, Donna McNeil 18455
Cox, Gabrielle 14183, 17696
Cox, George Barnsdale 10965
Cox, Harvey G. 8689, 9372, 9373, 9800, 9801, 10279, 10280, 10281, 10497, 10767, 10768, 10769, 10770, 11726, 12116, 12807, 15551, 16895, 16896, 16897, 17013, 17033, 19057, 19058 >> See further: Subject Index: Secular City Debate
Cox, Jean 12441
Cox, Jeffrey 14576, 16174
Cox, Kevin B. 16175
Cox, Sydney H. 2014
Coy, Patrick G. 18456
Coyle, Albert F. 3493, 3494
Coyle, John P. 1128, 1129
Coyle, Robert F. 1899
Cozzens, James Gould 4519
Crabites, Pierre 4278
Crabot, abbé 478
Cracknell, Kenneth 17697
Craddock, Fred B. 14577
Crafts, Wilbur Fisk 694, 719, 745, 830, 1283, 1372, 1531, 2385
Craig, A. E. 3203, 3599
Craig, Earl 14989
Craig, Gordon Neville, Jr. 14578
Craig, Maxwell 11504
Craig, Robert 8690
Craig, Robert Hedborg 13494
Craig, Samuel B., Jr. 7800, 9374, 9375, 10282
Craighill, Peyton G. 16176
Crain, James A. 5884
Cram, Leo L. 17698
Cram, Ralph Adams 1798, 2131, 2996, 3057
Cram, Ronald H. 18457
Cram, Ronald Hugh 17298
Cramblet, T. E. 1940
Cramer, John W. 608
Cramer-Heuerman, Jean 14990

Cramp, A. B. 16541
Crane, Caroline B. 1742, 2015, 2072, 2386, 2387, 2495, 2496
Crane, Frank 3316
Crane, Stephen 1210, 1458
Cranston, Earl, Mrs. 6512
Cranwell, Brian 13818
Crawford, Alphonso 14184
Crawford, Clarence W. 9376
Crawford, Evans Edgar, Jr. 6648, 7064
Crawford, Hanford 1743, 2497
Crawford, James W. 16542
Crawford, M. D'C 920
Crawford, William Henry 2209
Crawley, Winston 16898
Crean, Robert 19266
Creasey, Graham 16543
Crecelius, Daniel 15406
Cremer, Marlies 10283
Crepu, Michel 16545
Cressey, F. G. 1941
Cressey, Paul Frederick 4034
Cressy, Earl Herbert 6649, 6848, 6849, 6850, 7065, 7523, 7801, 7802
Crews, Clyde F. 12808, 14185, 18091
Crichton, Iain 16899, 17689, 17699, 18092, 18806
Crijns, Hub 19059
Criminal Justice 13819
Crimmins, Timothy 16736
Crimmins, W. F. 14579
Crisis: The Gift of Judgement -- Three Statements on Revolt in Our Cities 10284
Crissey, Orlo Lee 4136
Crist, John F. 12442
Criswell, W. A. 19172
Crite, Allan Rohan 5664
Criticism and Endorsement 3317
Crittenden, Ann 18458
Crittenden, Harriett 6326
Crittenton, Charles Nelson 2388
Crocker, David 8392
Croll, Marty 17299
Croly, H. D. 3600
Cromwell, John W. 3398
Cromwell, Ronald E. 14301
Cronin, Deborah Kay 18807
Cronin, J. C. 1211
Cronin, John Francis 5356, 5665, 5885, 6650, 7524, 7803, 8691, 9377, 9378, 17700
Cronon, E. David 6651
Cropper, W. V. 5162
Crosby, Beverly 8109
Crosby, Fred A. 2694
Crosby, Michael H. 13168
Cross, Dale W. 18808
Cross, Robert Dougherty 7284, 7525, 8393, 10285
Crossland, Weldon 5666
Crossley, John P., Jr. 14186
Crossman, Richard C. 13820
Crouthamel, Luther A. 17701
Crow, Richard 10771
Crowder, Felix 9379
Crowder, Roy B. 15407
Crowe, Charles M. 5886
Crowell, George H. 10772
Crowell, James 410
Crowley, James W. 12117
Crowley, Ronald W. 12809
Cruickshank, Mary 14991
Cruikschank, Nelson H. 9380
Crume, Harold 8692
Crunden, Robert M. 16900
Cruz, Rogelio El 17300
Cry of Need 8693
Cryderman, Lyn 18459, 19060
Cryer, Neville Barker 10773
Cryer, Newman 9802
Crysdale, Stewart 8110, 9381, 9803, 10774, 12443, 13169, 13821, 15780
Cuban Home Training School 1744
Cuber, John Frank 5559, 5769

Cuckson, John 979
Cuddy, Edward 13822
Cudney, A. J. 13625
Culber, Lowell W. 14992
Cullen, James Bernard 921
Cullinan, Thomas 12810
Cullis, Charles 747
Cully, Iris V. 8394
Cully, Kendig B. 11243
Culver, Dwight W. 6303
Culverhouse, Patricia 11727
Cumbie, William J. 10286
Cumming, John 497
Cummings, Oliver deW. 10287
Cummings, Scott 10775, 14993, 16544
Cummins, Ralph 4424, 4425
Cuneo, Michael 17248, 18809, 19041
Cunliffe-Jones, Huber 8111
Cunningham, A. 10776
Cunningham, Barry K. 15781
Cunningham, Earl Harold 8395
Cunningham, James V. 8112, 9382, 9383
Cunningham, Patrick 13170, 13823
Cunningham, W. J. 15408
Cunningham, William 680, 746, 831, 1048, 1373, 1374, 1459, 1532, 1847, 1942, 2210, 2306, 2307, 2389, 2590, 2591, 2779, 2930, 3126, 3204
Cunningham, William T. 16177
Cunstance, J. Harry and, Ponsford, Arthur 4597
Cupples, William Ralph 14580
Curnock, Nehemiah 2390
Curran, Charles E. 16178
Curran, Robert Emmett 14581
Curran, Ronald J. 9804
Curran, Thomas J. 13495, 15409
Currie, Raymond 16559
Currie, Thomas White 6452
Curry, Daniel 832
Curry, James E. 9023
Curry, Leonard P. 15782
Curry, Thomas J. 14187
Cursler, Will 9384
Curti, Merle 8694
Curtis, Charles J. 7066, 9024
Curtis, David D. C. 18093
Curtis, E. W. 1460
Curtis, Frederick 12811
Curtis, H. S. 2695
Curtis, J. H. 7067
Curtis, Mitchell 5667
Curtis, Olga 5667
Curtis, Pierson 2931
Curtis, Richard F. 13458
Curtis, Richard K. 8396, 8397
Cushing, Caleb 167
Cushing, Richard J. 5560, 9805, 11728
Cussiánovich, Alejandro 13824
Cuthbert, Father 1943, 3399
Cutler, Benjamin 113
Cutler, John Henry 11728
Cutler, Wolcott 6146
Cutolo, Eugenio 16179
Cuttell, Colin 8398
Cutting, Robert Fulton 922, 1130, 2592
Cutting, Tom 12444
Cuyler, John Potter 4362, 9025
Cuyler, Theodore L. 297, 1848
Cyrus, John Willoughby 4904
Dabbs, James McBride 4598, 5260
Dade, Malcolm G. 16180
D'Agostino, Carlo Francesco 5561
Dahl, Curtis 14188
Dahm, Charles W. 19291
Dahrendorf, Ralf 7526
Dailey, Charles A. 11244
Daille, R. 6711
Dale, Eric Steven 19342
Dale, Robert D. 15410, 15783, 16901, 16902, 17702, 17703, 18460

Dale, Robert William 16391
Dallard, Shyrlee 19324
Daloz, Lucien 9026
Daly, Gabriel 15411
Dalzell, H. A. 3951
Damboriena, Prudencio 11245
Damm, Henry J. 8695
Damonte, Roy 10777
Damrell, Joseph David 12445
Dana, Ethel Nathalie 8399, 8696
Danforth, James R. 784
Danforth, W. E. 2868
Daniel, H. 10778
Daniel, John 5562, 7068
Daniel, Vattel Elbert 4905, 5076
Daniel, Yvan 6147, 7069, 7070
Daniels, Bill 16181
Daniels, H. F. J. 9668
Daniels, Harriet McDoval 2780
Daniels, John 3205
Daniels, William Haven 591, 747
Dankenbring, Ray 9806
Danker, William J. 19199
Dannenbaum, Jed 14582, 16903
Dannowski, H. W. 16904
Dansette, Adrien 7071
Danzig, David 10779
Danziger, Sheldon 14104
Darby, James E. 3400
Dargan, Edwin Charles 1745, 2132
Darling, Edward M. 6851, 7072
Darnell, Susanne B. 15271
Dart, John 10780, 11246, 12118
Darwen, Robert, S. J. 17704
Dassetto, Felice 14994
Daub, Edward E. 6852
David, Anne 9807
David, Edward G. 18094
David, Kenith A. 18095
David, Ozora Stearns 2308
Davidman, Lynn 19061
Davidoff, Linda 11729
Davidoff, Paul 11729
Davidson, Essie Mae 2781
Davidson, Jack 19062
Davidson, James D. 11247, 11248, 13825, 14189, 14995, 17301, 17705
Davidson, John Morrison 1212
Davidson, John Thain 785
Davidson, Miriam 18461
Davidson, R. B. 9385
Davidson, Robert 9386, 9387, 12812
Davidson, W. T. 2593
Davie, Grace 18013
Davie, Maurice R. 5563
Davies, D. C. 5887
Davies, Ebenezer Thomas 8400, 13826
Davies, Graham 16546
Davies, Helen E. 5464
Davies, Henry 3058
Davies, Horton 7527
Davies, J. G. 12119, 12446, 14996
Davies, J. Kenneth 7804, 14190
Davies, James 9388
Davies, John Gordon 10781
Davies, Jon Gower 12447
Davies, Michael J. 16547
Davies, Mostyn D. 10782, 14191, 14583, 14584
Davies, Ronald 7350
Davies, Stanley 6453
Davis, Allen F. 10288, 11249, 11730, 12813, 12814, 19046
Davis, Allison 4906
Davis, Arnor S. 11731
Davis, C. Anne 16548
Davis, Cameron J. 1799
Davis, Creath 12815
Davis, Cyprian 14997
Davis, David 17706
Davis, Dewitt 15412
Davis, Donald M. 8697
Davis, Donald R. 10783
Davis, Dora W. 2869
Davis, Harold McGill 1375
Davis, Horton 6454

Davis, Howard 17302
Davis, J. Merle 4712, 5163
Davis, James Hill 8218, 8401, 8698, 9027, 9028, 9389, 9390, 9706, 9808, 9809, 9810, 10176, 10289, 10784, 10785, 11250, 11251, 11732, 12120, 12816, 13171, 13827, 14585, 15413, 15784, 16182
Davis, Jennifer 13828
Davis, Jerome 3754, 3755, 3824, 3878, 3952, 4035, 4036, 4279, 4426, 6853
Davis, John 15414, 17303
Davis, John Merle 10290
Davis, Kenneth 13829
Davis, King E. 13496, 16183
Davis, Lawrence Bennion 10786, 12817
Davis, Lyman Edwin 1284
Davis, Moshe 8699
Davis, Ozora Stearns 1213, 3401
Davis, Russell G. 11438
Davis, Samuel 70
Davis, Thurston N. 10787
Davis, Winston 15415
Dawes, Gil 15416, 19324
Dawes, S., Jr. 12448
Dawkins, O. C. 5668
Dawley, Alan 13830
Dawson, Alan 10291
Dawson, Albert 2016
Dawson, Christopher 3953, 4427, 4825, 5669, 7805, 7806
Dawson, John 18810
Dawson, Rosemary 17707
Day, Dorothy 4270, 4655, 4826, 5670, 5888, 6023, 6148, 8700, 12231, 12974, 14917, 15192, 15785, 16068, 16178, 16336, 16370, 16385, 16746, 16772, 16905, 17124, 17225, 17390, 17745, 17825, 18024, 18456, 18835, 19104, 19229, 19261, 19280 >> See further: Subject Index: Catholic Worker Movement
Day, Duane L. 9997, 9998, 10292, 10293
Day, Edward 6455
Day, Frank Edward 2782
Day, James Roscoe 3206
Day, LeRoy J. 7807
Day-Lower, Donna C. 17915
Dayton, Donald 14586
Dayton, Donald W. 13172, 13497
Dayton, Edward 16184, 16549
Dayton, Edward R. 15417, 16185
Dayton, Lucille 13348
de la Bedoyere, Michael 7285
de la Torre, Edicio 17708, 18096
de Lange, H. M. 7219
Deakin, N. D. 9391
Dean, Beverly W. 6149, 6304
Dean, George B. 3059, 3207, 3318
Dearden, John F. 10294
Deardorff, Neva R. 6652
Dearman, Marion V. 14274
Dearmer, Percy 1533, 2133, 2391, 2594
Dearnley, Pat 16550, 16906, 17710
De'Ath, Erica 17709
Deats, Paul, Jr. 8590
Deats, Richard 13498
DeBardeleben, Mary 3601
DeBenedetti, Charles 13800
Debès, Joseph 16186, 17711, 18797
DeBethune, Ade 4827
DeBilio, Francis D. 5770
DeBlank, Joost 6456, 7808
DeBoer, Cecil 7073
DeBoer, John C. 11252, 11733, 12449, 12450, 12451, 12452, 12818, 13173, 14587, 15418, 16551, 18462
DeBreffny, Brian 14588
DeBroen, Josephine 589

Debs, Eugene V. 1278, 1390, 4241
Deck, Allan Figueroa 14589, 16187, 18811, 19063
Decker, Robert Owen 18097
DeCosse, David E. 18463
DeCosta, Benjamin F. 923
Deedy, John 15786
Deegan, Mary Jo 18464
Deeks, Frank 12453
Deelen, Godofredo J. 8113
Deems, Charles Force 695, 833, 1534
Dees, Jesse Walter 5671
DeFolo, Keith 6305
DeFoore, John Norris 6025
DeForest, Robert W. 1131
Defoy, Henri B. 1132
deGaspar, Diogo 12819
Degen, Johannes 13499
deGeorge, Richard T. 14590, 18098
DeGruchy, John W. 11734
Dehn, Ulrich 16907
Dehoney, Wayne 12121
Dehsen, Christian D. 18893
Deiman, Harry 2696
Deitz, Purd Eugene 11253
deJong, Dennis 14998
DeKadt, Emanuel J. 11735
Delacoste, Frédérique 18099
Delahaye, Karl 10295
Delamarter, Walter R. 9811, 11736, 12122
Delaney, John J. 1535, 1619
DeLaney, Moses Nathaniel 7528, 7529, 7809
DeLange, H. M. 7810
Delekat, Friedrich 7286
Delespesse, Max 12123
Delgado, Gary 17712, 18100
Delgado, Hilda 14591
Deliat, Roger 12820
Delk, Edwin Heyl 2309
Delk, Yvonne Virginia 8701
Dellepoort, Johannes Joseph 8114
Dellheim, Charles 18101
Delloff, Linda Marie 14999, 18465
Delon, Pierre 8115
DeLong, William F. 5215
Delooz, Pierre 16908, 16909, 18812
Demant, Vigo Auguste 4280, 6150
Demarchi, Franco 11254
Demerath, Nicholas Jay, III 8116, 8402, 9392, 10788
DeMestral, Claude 5564
DeMille, George Edmed 5889, 6854, 7287, 10296, 10297, 14192
Dempsey, Jan 15419
Dempsey, Timothy 5298
Dempsey, William J. 10298
Dempster, George Fyfe 4428, 4599, 4828, 5465, 6855
DeMuth, Jerry 12454, 14193
Deniel, Raymond 10789, 11737, 13500, 13501, 15000, 16188
Denisoff, R. Serge 12124, 12455
Denison, John Hopkins 2783
Denk, Hans Dieter 15420
Denning, Walter 13174
Dennison, Henry S. 4137
Denny, Collins 1285
Denny, Norwyn 10472
Denson, John Lane 9393
Dentler, Robert A. 8286, 9029, 9812, 10790, 11738
Denton, Patrica 8969
Denver Inner City Protestant Parish 7811
DeParle, Jason 19064
DeRidder, Richard R. 15001
Derochers, John 14194
Deroo, André 15421
Derr, Thomas S. 14526
Derrick, Paul 9394
Descriptive Study of Baltimore Baptist Association 10791

Descriptive Study of Greenville Baptist Association 11255
Desegregation 13502
DeSilva, Ranjit 15422, 17304
DeSmet, Kate 18813
Desmettre, Henri 10299
Desmond, H. J. 1746
Desmonde, William H. 8403
DeSouza Martins, Helosia Helena T. 17713
DeSouza, Luis Alberto Gomez 16189
DesPortes, Elisa L. 11739, 12125, 12592, 12821
Destler, Chester M. 13931
DeSwarte, Carolyn 18102
Detroit Baptist Union 592, 3060
Detroit Industrial Mission [DIM] 7288, 13175
Detroit Industrial Mission: Its Place and Purpose [a brochure] 7812
Detroit, Newark and the Church 10300
Detwiler, George H. 2392
Detwiler, Marilyn 10792
Detwyler, Thomas R. 12456
Deutsch, Martin 7355
Deutsch, Wilhelm Otto 16910
Deutsche Bischofskonferenz 16190
Deutschmann, William M. 15002
Devasundaram, Alexander 13503, 15003
Developing to Preserve 16911
Devine, Edward T. 1800, 2211, 2310, 2595, 2697, 3208
Devine, Michael T. 8391
Devins, John Bancroft 1376, 1685, 2649
deVise, Pierre 11256, 11740
DeVries, Egbert 8117
DeVries, Peter 7289
Dew, Bob 16552
Dew, Randle 9395
Dewey, A. G. 11741
Dewey, Harry P. 2393
Dewey, John 1747, 3825
Dewey, M. 12126
Dewey, Orville 146, 147, 157, 208
Dewey, Roger L. 13176, 13504, 15004
Dewitt, Robert L. 13831, 14195, 15005, 15787, 15788
DeWolf, Harold L. 14111
DeWolf, L. Harold 6306, 9396
DeWolfe, Mark Mosher 18466
Dexter, N. B. 4600
Dexter, William M. 232
Deyling, Rosemary Jean 5771
DeYoung, Donald 7813, 9397, 9813, 9814
Diack, Walter T. 2311
Diaz Ramirez, Ana Maria 16553
Diaz, Ana Maria 13505
Dibelius, Otto 2394, 8118
Dick, John 12822
Dick, Lois Hoadley 11742, 12457
Dick, Malcolm 15789
Dickens, Charles 158, 280, 298, 392, 1286
Dickerman, D. L. 12458
Dickinson, Charles A. 924
Dickinson, Charles Henry 2698, 3495, 4037
Dickinson, Cyril Loren 11257
Dickinson, Harry 12459
Dickinson, Joan Younger 9815
Dickinson, Richard D. N. 13506, 16554
Dickson, Elaine 8404
Dickson, Lynda 12615
Did We Endorse the Black Manifesto 11258
DiDonato, Pietro 4601
Diehl, Astor Antonio 19065
Diehl, C. G. 9398
Diehl, Richard Clinton 17714
Diehl, William E. 17305, 17306,

17307, 18103
Dienel, Peter 8405
Dierks, Sheila Durkin 18467
Dietrich, Glenn M. 17308
Dietrich, Jeff 15790
Dietrich, Joachim 1620
Dietrich, Suzanne de 7290
Dietterich, Paul 13832
Dietz, Peter 6316, 8737
Diez-Alegria, J. M. 10301
Diffendorfer, Ralph Eugene 3209
Digan, Parig 16912
Dijsselbloem, W. J. J. 4602
Dill, Ellen Renee 18104, 19200
Dilling, Yvonne 16913
Dillingham, Manuel Lamont 17309
Dillon, David 16914
Dilworth, Joan 10793
Dimock, Alice 8331, 11259
Dimock, Herb 10794
Dimock, Marshall E. 4965
Dimond, Jean Ann 17310
Dingemans, L. 9030
Dinin, Samuel 4281
Dinnerstein, Leonard 12127, 13507, 15006
Dinwiddie, Emily Wayland 2395, 2396
Dippel, Christian 2212
Directives for the Building of a Church 5772
Directory of Congregational Studies 16555
Dirks, Lee E. 9399
Disciples of Christ 3210
Discovering Faith in the City 18468
Discrimination and National Welfare: Addresses and Discussion 5773
Discrimination without Prejudice 9031
Dismissal Compensation for Employees 4713
Dissington, Paul W. 10302
District of Columbia Baptist Convention, Department of Missions and Evangelism and Department of Research and Planning, Council of Churches, National Capital Area 9400
Dittes, James E. 11260, 12823
Divida, James J. 18105
Division of Urban Life of the Department of Social Development, USCC 11261
Dix, Dorothea Lynde 121
Dix, Morgan 980, 1801
Dixon, Dorothy A. 9032
Dixon, Robert 15007
Dixon, Thomas 1461
Djait, Hichem 17715
Do Labor and the Church Have Anything to Say to Each Other 8119
Doane, Jeffrey 18814
Dobbelaere, Karel 12824, 15791, 16915, 17311
Dobkin de Rios, Marlene 12825
Dobra, Al 17716
Dobriner, William 8702
Dodd, Charles Harold 6582
Dodd, Peter 13508
Dodd, Peter C. 10795
Dodds, Elizabeth 17737
Dodge, John W. 450
Dodge, William E. 1002
Dodson, Dan W. 4520, 4907, 5774, 6151, 6856, 7530, 7814, 8120, 8703, 8704, 9033, 9401, 9816, 9817, 10303, 11262
Dodson, Linden Seymour 4210
Doe, Evelyn 4714
Doepke, Dale K. 12826
Doering, David, Jr. 11743, 12460
Doescher, W. O. 6307
Dogberry, Obediah 13121

Doggenweiler, S. René 13833
Doggett, Laurence Locke 1462, 1802, 1849
Dohen, Dorothy M. 11744
Doherty, Jack 16027
Doherty, John Frances 8705
Doherty, Robert W. 14196
Dohrs, Fred E. 15263
Doig, Carol M. 9402, 9818, 9819, 9820
Doig, Desmond 13834, 15423
Dolan, Jay P. 12461, 13509, 14197, 17312, 18106, 18469, 18815, 19066
Dolbey, Dorothy N. 6457
Dole, Charles Fletcher 720, 1287, 2312
Dolezal, Arnold 8121
Dolin, David 19067
Doling, J. 14592
Dollar, Truman 17717
Dollard, John 4603, 4906
Dolley, James P. 12462
Dolling, Robert William Radcliffe 1463, 1844, 1914
Dolloff, Eugene Dinsmore 5466
Dom, Kuri 15008
Dombrowski, James 4521
Domenach, Jean-Marie 7815
Dominch, Mark 'I' Akovlevich 13835
Domínguez, Javier 9403, 17313
Domini, May L. 16916
Dominich, Mark I. 13836
Domosh, Mona 17314, 18470
Donahower, Elise Linder 9404
Donahue, Mary 12463
Donahue, Thomas R. 17718, 18107, 18108
Donaldson, F. L. 3127
Donaldson, Peter J. 16191
Donaldson, Robert S. 3319
Donaldson, Thomas 16192, 16556
Donatus, Mary 9034
Doney, Malcolm 15009, 19315
Donnelley, Benignus 10796
Donnelly, Dody 14198
Donnelly, Joseph F. 5357, 5467, 13177
Donnelly, Patrick D. 18588
Donnison, David 15424, 17898
Donovan, John D. 5890
Donovan, Vincent J. 18816
Donus, Robert B. 13178
Doody, Henry 6458
Doomed Churches of London City 3211
Doot, Peter 11745
Dorchester, Daniel 660, 834, 879
Dorey, Frank David 5891
Dorff, Nina 16557
Dorfman, Joseph 5468
Dorion, Eustache Charles Edouard 2870
Dorman, A. 12464
Dorn, Jacob Henry 10304, 17719
Dornbusch, Sanford M. 7433
Dorr, Rheta Childe 2397
Dorsett, Lyle W. 10797, 16558, 19068, 19201
Doster, Philip 7291
Doten, Dana 5077
Dotson, Floyd 6026
Dotts, Franklin 10798
Dotts, Maryann 10798
Dougherty, James 15425
Dougherty, John J. 10799
Dougherty, Katherine 8406
Dougherty, Mary A. 15792
Dougherty, Paul V. 14593
Douglas, Earl W. 5892
Douglas, J. D. 10800
Douglas, Mary 16193
Douglas, Paul H. 4282, 4522
Douglas, R. Bruce 17720
Douglas, William 12128
Douglass, Harlan Paul 2398, 2596, 2784, 3128, 3320, 3602, 3690, 3756, 3757, 3826, 3879,

3954, 3955, 4038, 4039, 4040, 4041, 4211, 4363, 4429, 4523, 4604, 4715, 4908, 5007, 5078, 5079, 5080, 5081, 5164, 5165, 5166, 5167, 5168, 5169, 5170, 5171, 5261, 5262, 5263, 5264, 5265, 5266, 5358, 5359, 5360, 5361, 5362, 5363, 5364, 5365, 5366, 5469, 5565, 5566, 5567, 5568, 5569, 5672, 5775, 5776, 5893, 5894, 6387, 7509, 11688, 14051, 15476
Douglass, Truman B. 6027, 6459, 6460, 7074, 7292, 7293, 7294, 7816, 8122, 8407, 9035, 9405, 9821
Dourmap, Médand 7149
Doutreloux, Victor Joseph 2017
Dow, Robert Arthur 14199
Dowd, Jerome 1850, 3758
Dowdy, R. Edward. 10305
Dowis, Solomon 5082, 5172, 6028, 6029, 18594
Dowley, Roger 16917
Downes, Stan 18817
Downey, Glanville 7817, 8408, 9036
Downing, David C. 18109
Downing, William Henry 3759
Downs, David William 16918
Downtown Church Focuses on Evangelism 7818
Downtown Neighbors 10801
Downtown Niagara Falls: Guide Lines for the Church 9037
Doxiades, Konstantinos Apostolou 9405, 9822, 10072, 10306, 10802, 10803, 10804, 11263, 12396, 12906, 13179
Doyle, B. W. 5673
Doyo, Ceres 17721
Draak, J. den 8123
Drachsler, Julius 19249
Dragastin, S. 10307
Drake, Robert 15010
Drake, St. Clair 4909, 4910, 5367
Drane, James F. 12827, 13837
Draper, Edgar 10162
Dreirer, Hartmunt A. 9038
Dreis, David 14528
Dreiser, Theodore 1803, 2785, 3496, 4138
Drescher, Tim 15793
Drews, Rainer 19343
Dreyfus, François G. 7531
Driedger, Leo 10805, 12465, 13510, 14200, 14594, 15426, 16194, 16559, 16560, 18471, 19069
Driggers, B. Carlisle 13838, 14201, 15011
Drimmelen, Rob van 15794
Dring, Lincoln 17870
Dripps, Philip M. 8409
Driskill, J. Lawrence 12466
Droege, D. 10308
Droel, William 16919, 16920
Droulers, Paul 13511
Drucker, Peter F. 8706
Drummon, Andrew L. 4139
Drummon, Henry 1133, 1288
Drummond, Clarence Everett 13180
Drummond, L. 11264
Drummond, Terry 17032
Drury, Clifford M. 6152
Dryer, Daniel A. 15012
Dubalen, Marie Thérèse 6653
Dubb, A. A. 8124
DuBois, Paul 3497
DuBois, Wilbur L. 5173
DuBois, William Edward Burghardt 1464, 1686, 1900, 1901, 3498, 19084
DuBose, Francis M. 9823, 10309, 10310, 10311, 10312, 10806, 10807, 10808, 11265, 11746, 14595, 15795, 16561, 16921, 16922, 18154
DuBose, Joseph Palmer 13512

Duce, Alan 16923, 19070
Ducey, John M. 9406
Ducey, Michael H. 14202
Duchrow, Ulrich 15427
Ducos, Marcel 7532
Dudde, William A. 6308
Dudley, Carl 18078
Dudley, Carl S. 14203, 14596, 14597, 14598, 15013, 15014, 15015, 16562, 17667, 18472, 18818, 18819, 19195, 19202, 19203
Duff, E. S., Mrs. 2018
Duff, Edward 6857
Duff, Frank 8125
Duffield, Howard 2533
Duffy, R. 13181
Dufour, Charles L. 7295
Duggan, Dan 16195
Duggan, Thomas J. 19071
Duhl, Leonard J. 9039
Duin, Julie 18820
Duke, C. W. 1851
Duke, Keith Eugene 9407
Dulles, Avery Robert 10313, 13182, 14204, 16196, 17315
Dumas, André 12467, 13183, 14599
Dumas, Lloyd J. 15428
Dummett, Ann 16197
Dumont, F. 7819
DuMont, Herbert 10314, 10809
Dumont, Patricia 13768
Dumper, Tony 18821
Dunamis: Pastor-Prophet to People in Power 12828
Dunbar, Patricia 10315
Duncan, Beverly 6858
Duncan, Clarence E. 13513
Duncan, David 15016, 15730
Duncan, Denis 14205
Duncan, Dick 13839, 14206, 15017
Duncan, Graham 17316
Duncan, Malcolm Graeme 6309
Duncan, Michael 18822
Duncan, Otis Dudley 6858, 7533, 12829
Duncan, W. Wofford T. 3603
Duncan, William J. 10810
Duncombe, David C. 18473
Dunham, Arthur 7587
Dunlap, George Arthur 4364, 8410
Dunn, C. V. 3760
Dunn, Charles E. 5674
Dunn, David 6859
Dunn, Ethel 14207
Dunn, Frederick Roger 4911, 5267
Dunn, James D. G. 17722
Dunn, Stephen P. 14207
Dunne, George H. 5570, 10316
Dunnell, Terry 17317
Dunstan, John Leslie 4716, 9824
Duntze, Klaus 11266, 12468, 13840, 13841, 15796
Duocastella, Rogelio 5895, 7534, 7820, 8126
duPlessis, J. 3129
Dupree, A. Hunter 12830
Durden, Lewis M., Jr. 5083
Duren, James 16563
Durgin, Lawrence L. 9408
Durham, Jacqueline 9825
Durham, James Edward 15429
Durham, Lewis E. 9826
Durkheim, Emile 1214, 1536, 2597, 12714, 18125
Durkin, Mary G. 13514
Durston, Rhondda 16564
Duryee, J. R. 1621
Dushkin, Alexander M. 3061
Dusmet, Giuseppe Benedetto 12797
Duties of the Rich in Christian Society 509
duToit, Brian M. 12129, 12130, 15430
Dutton, Charles J. 4605

Dutton, Elwood Herbert 4042
Dutton, W. C., Jr. 8127
Duval, William 303
Duyckinck, Henry 479
Dwan, Peter 15431
Dwight, Henry E. 748
Dwight, Henry Otis 1944
Dwyer, Philip 1072
Dwyer, William 13515
Dybdahl, Tom 13304
Dye, Richard 17723
Dyer, Gustavus Walker 2699
Dykstra, D. Ivan 6654
Dykstra, Robert 13184
Dynes, Russell R. 6461, 6750, 6860, 6937, 7535, 9409
Dyrness, Grace R. 18110
Dyrud, Keith P. 14600
Dyson, David 16924
E., D. H. 335
Eades, Robert E. 18474
Eagan, John J. 3212
Eager, George Boardman 2997
Eagle, Julian 17318
Eagleson, John 13516, 16447
Eakin, Mary 12403
Eames, Edwin 12831, 14208
Earle, John R. 13842
Early, H. C. 3604
Early, Ruth 8128
Early, T. 11747
Early, Tracy 12469, 12832, 12833, 13843, 13844, 16565, 18475
Earp, Edwin L. 2213, 2498, 2998
Eash, A. M. 2932
East Asia Christian Conference, Asian Conference on Church and Society 10317
East Asia Christian Conference, Committee on Society, Development and Peace [SODEPAX] 11748
East Asia Christian Conference, Committee on Urban-Industrial Mission 7821
East Asia Christian Conference, Urban-Industrial Mission Committee 10318, 10811
East Harlem Protestant Parish 5675, 6153
Easter, Maud 14601
Eastman, A. Theodore 17724
Eastman, Elaine Goodale 4283
Eastman, Fred 5368
Eastman, Michael 13845, 18111, 18476, 19072
Eaton, Allan 4043
Eaton, Charles Aubrey 1687
Eaton, David H. 9827
Eaves, James F. 16198, 16199
Eberdt, Mary Lois 6154
Eberhard, Paul 7536
Eberhardt, Herbert E. 4717, 6155
Eberl, Friedrich 414
Ebersole, Charles David 4912
Ebersole, Eleanor 9040
Ebersole, Jay Franklin 9410
Ebner, Michael 12131
Eby, Kermit 5008, 5268, 5571, 6156, 7075, 7296, 7537, 8129
Ecclestone, A. 11267
Echlin, Edward P. 18112
Eck, Diana L. 16566, 18823
Eckardt, Ralph W. 13185
Eckbald, Eric 16925
Eckerstrom, Peggy 9828
Eckman, George Peck 2214
Economic Justice within Environmental Limits: The Need for a New Economic Ethic 13846
Economic Value of Fresh Air 1465
Ecumenical Coalition of the Mahoning Valley 14602
Ecumenical Commission for Urban Mission 14209
Ecumenical Great Lakes/Appalachian Network (GLAN) 19325

Ecumenical Institute, Chicago, Illinois 8411
Ecumenical Material on 'The Missionary Structure of the Congregation 8707
Ecumenical Metropolitan Ministry [EMM] 11749, 12470
Eddington, Neil A. 12894
Eddy, Elizabeth M. 10812
Eddy, George Sherwood 3313, 3499, 3761, 3827, 4430, 4606, 5009
Eddy, Norman 7297, 7538, 8708, 9041, 9411, 10319, 10320
Ede, William Moore 1466, 2313
Edele, Andrew 14210, 14603, 14604
Edelman, Marian Wright 18477
Eden, Lynn 12471
Edgar, Irving I. 12834
Edgar, John W. 19073
Edgar, Richard 10321
Edgar, Robert E. 19074
Edge, Clifford 13186
Edge, Findley B. 8709, 10322, 12132
Edgewater Presbyterian Church 11750
Edholm, Charlton 1215
Edidin, Ben M. 5572
Ediger, Peter 9042, 12133
Edinburgh City Mission, Friends of 181
Editorial 1945
Editors of Fortune Magazine 7298
Edmonds, Edwin Richardson 5777
Edmonds, Franklin Spencer 3691
Edmonds, Patty 16200
Edrington, Roger B. 18113
Edson, Theodore 14377
Edwards, Adrian 12134
Edwards, Arthur Trystan 5084
Edwards, Clifford 12135
Edwards, Dan W. 16201
Edwards, David L. 8130, 11268, 11751
Edwards, Franklin G. 7539
Edwards, Fred E. 12136
Edwards, George 10813
Edwards, John 12835
Edwards, Maldwyn 5778
Edwards, Mary M. 8710
Edwards, Nymphas R. 17725
Edwards, Philip C. 7299, 8131, 8412, 8711, 9829, 10044
Edwards, Richard Henry 3042
Edwards, Rick 13187
Edwards, Robert E. 19075
Edwards, Rowland Alexander 4829, 6310
Edwards, Tilden H., Jr. 12152
Eells, Edwin 3062
Eells, Richard 10814
Eelwanger, William 18824
Egan, Eileen 15432
Egan, Gerard 13517
Egan, James P. 18478
Egan, John J. 8132, 8413, 8712, 9043, 9044, 9412, 9830, 9831, 12472, 13188, 13518, 13847, 15018, 15144, 16567, 16568, 19076, 19344
Egan, Leta 6462
Egerton, Hakluyt 2215
Eggleston, Nathaniel H. 209, 318
Eggold, Henry J. 9413
Eglise dans la ville 7300
Ehara, Jun 9414, 15433
Ehle, John 7822
Ehrenström, Nils 8713
Ehrlich, M. 12137
Ehrman, Albert 12138
Eichenberger, Alan J. 9832
Eichholz, Georg 8414
Eichhorn, David Max 14605
Eichhorn, Garth L. 17726
Eichner, David N. 12836
Eickelman, Dale F. 13189, 19077

Eighmy, John Lee 11269, 12473
Eipper, Chris 17727
Eisenstadt, S. N. 6655, 9833, 10323, 17728
Eister, Allen W. 7076
Ejerfeldt, Lennart 18479
Ekland-Olson, Sheldon 15646
Ekollo, Thomas 9415
El Banna, Gamel 17729
Elazar, Daniel 13848
Elder, Harris J. 14211
Eldredge, Lucy M. 5369, 6463, 8714
Eliade, Mircea 5779, 13849
Elias, C. E. 9045
Elicker, Elaine 10815
Elifson, Kirk W. 13850, 14212
Eliot, Charles William 1622, 2314, 2399, 2598
Eliot, Christopher Rhodes 4044, 4431
Eliot, T. S. 3402, 4159, 4308, 4830, 4913, 19279
Elizabeth, Charlotte 11082
Elizondo, Virgil 16842
Elizondo, Virgilio P. 13519
Ellena, Aldo 11254
Ellens, J. Harold 13520
Eller, Jim 16926
Eller, Vernard 15434
Ellerman, David P. 15797
Ellerton, Jacynth 10816
Ellett, Charles A. 9046, 11270
Ellington, George 609
Elliott, Charles 12139
Elliott, George 2073
Elliott, John H. 15798
Elliott, John Y. 15435
Elliott, Michael 18114
Elliott, Odessa Southern 16202
Elliott, Ralph 15799
Elliott, W. Winston 17730
Elliott, Willis E. 10817
Ellis, Bryan 15436
Ellis, D. T. 4914
Ellis, John Tracy 6157, 6861, 8415
Ellis, Marc H. 13851, 14606, 15800, 18115
Ellis, Norman 13190, 15437
Ellis, Sarah Stickney 132
Ellis, Walter E. 14213
Ellis, Wayne 10324, 11271
Ellis, William T. 1537, 1623, 2786
Ellison, Craig W. 12837, 13191, 14607, 14608, 15438, 16569, 17319, 18116, 18825, 19204
Ellison, Frederick A. 16570
Ellison, Jerome 7077, 9047, 9048
Ellul, Jacque 16316
Ellul, Jacques 6158, 9049, 9739, 11272, 11752, 11901, 12116, 14335, 17354, 18889
Ellwood, Charles Abram 3403, 3500, 3828, 13719
Ellwood, Robert S., Jr. 12838
Elm, Kaspar 19078
Elmore, Ralph Monroe 15801
Elrod, John W. 15802
Elsas, Christoph 16203
Elsbree, Oliver W. 3880
Else, Anne 14609
Elshtain, Jean Bethke 18480
Elsing, W. T. 925, 1289, 1467, 1538, 2134
Elwood, Douglas J. 15439
Elwyn, Thornton 15440
Ely, Ezra Stiles 14, 17, 99
Ely, Richard Theodore 786, 787, 788, 880, 926, 981, 1290, 1291, 1388, 1852, 4718, 5470, 9887, 10053
Ely, Robert E. 1468
Emerson, Lynn Arthur 4212
Emerson, Ralph Waldo 1902
Emerson, Tilly Jo 16204
Emery, George N. 14214
Emery, Joseph 835
Emhardt, William Chauncey

3881
Enaka, Maseo 14215
Encíclica Laborem Excercens y América Latina 16205
Encuentro Latinoamericano de Pastoral Urbana (Barueri, Brazil) 9416, 10325
End of the Promotional Church? 9417
Ende, W. M. I. van den 8715
Endres, William D. 2216
Engel, James F. 14216, 14217, 15019
Engelman, Gerson S. 6311
Engelman, Uriah Z. 5972
Engelmann, Wilhelm 4831
England, Edward O. 7078
England, John 12839, 14218
Engle, M. H. 11991
English, H. D. W. 2700
English, James W. 19269
English, Theodore 5174
Engstrom, George 6656
Enlow, David R. 17731
Enright, Vincent L. 14610
Enright, William G. 14611
Enroth, Ronald M. 12474, 13192
Ensman, Richard G., Jr. 18117
Entering Opportunity 7079
Entwhistle, Basil 19326
Episcopal City Mission 210
Episcopal City Mission and Archdeaconry of Boston 100, 1049
Episcopal City Mission Society, St. Barnabas Multi Service Senior Center 15441
Episcopal Committee to Inquire into the Expediency of Forming a Mission Church 122
Episcopal Fellowship of Urban Workers 5676
Episcopal Theological Seminary of the South, Research Center 7301
Episcopalians Recently Established a Church Structure for Ministry to the Cities 15442
Episcopalians Shape a Response in Ministering to AIDS Victims 17732
Epp, Frank H. 10818
Epp, Margaret A. 14612
Eppinga, Jacob Dirk 6464
Eppley, Martha A. 9834
Epps, Dwain C. 11753
Erb, Alta Mae 3213, 4607
Erdman, W. J. 2787
Erdmann, August 2074, 2315, 2701
Erdmann, Judith Klein 16927
Erharter, Helmut 18118
Erickson, Art 18119
Erickson, Dale E. 10326
Erickson, Eugene P. 15323
Erickson, Theodore H. 9418, 9835, 11273
Erickson, Thomas A. 11274
Erickson, Vincent W. 9419
Erickson, William 12840
Ericson, C. George 12841
Ericson, Edward E. 12474
Ernsberger, David 9420
Ernst, Eldon G. 11754
Ernst, Robert 5780
Erskine, W. H. 3130, 3404
Ervine, St. John Greer 4432
Erwin, John Robert 14613
Escamilla, Roberto 11755
Esch, Maurice J. 11756
Escobar, Samuel 16206, 19079
Escoffier, Anne Marie 12140
Eshelman, Byron E. 8416
Espenshade, Kevin R. 14969
Espy, R. H. Edwin 6657
Essien-Udom, E. U. 8417
Estep, William R. 11275
Estes, Ludwell H. 4915
Estes, Robert Lee 9836

Estes, Sue 18826
Estévez, Filipe J. 16571
Estivill, Jordi 15443
Estoesta, Consorcio 11757
Estus, Charles 7823, 7824, 8047, 8331
Etchells, D. R. 17320
Etchells, Frederick 5642
Ethnicity in the Church: Symposium 13852
Etling, Mark G. 16928
Etz, Donald V. 11758
Etzioni, Amitai W. 12141
Etzioni-Halevy, Eva 17321
Eubank, Earle Edward 4433
Eugene, Toinette 15020
Evangel Temple Inner City Pastors Conference 16929
Evangelical and Reformed Church, Board of National Missions, City Church and Urban Strategy 6658
Evangelical and Reformed Church, Board of National Missions, Office of City Church and Urban Strategy 7302
Evangelical and Reformed Church, Commission on Christian Social Action 5573, 5896
Evangelical and Reformed Church, Commission on Christian Social Action and Churchmen's Brotherhood 6465
Evangelical and Reformed Church, General Synod 5085
Evangelical Alliance for the United States 836, 982, 1292
Evangelical Alliance, New Town Study Group 12142
Evangelical Coalition for Urban Mission 11759, 16572, 17733
Evangelical Committee for Urban Ministries in Boston 10819
Evangelical Lutheran Church in New York City, Inner Mission Society 2499
Evangelical Lutheran Church of Finland 12143
Evangelical Lutheran Church, Inner Mission Society 2871
Evangelical United Brethren Church, General Council of Administration 10820
Evangelische Kirche in Deutschland 16930
Evangelische-Sozial 3214
Evangelization in Urban Ministry 15021
Evangelization Portraits: Hispanic Communities 15803
Evans, Alice Frazer 18120
Evans, Anthony T. 18121
Evans, Bernard F. 15022
Evans, Clay 18122
Evans, Colleen Townsend 17749
Evans, D. Edward 3605
Evans, Daniel 2135
Evans, J. Claude 10327, 12475
Evans, Richard Philip 17734
Evans, Robert A. 16573, 18120
Evans, Sarah Elizabeth 5010, 5370
Evans, Stanley George 8418
Evans, Thomas S. 2136
Evanston Ecumenical Action Council, Hunger Coalition 13521
Everard, K. B. 14219
Everett, Gail 9421
Everett, Harvey A. 6862, 6883, 7080, 7540, 9050
Everett, John Rutherford 5470
Everett, O. C. 319
Everett, Robert F. 13985
Everett, William Johnson 18827
Everist, Norma J. 16574

Everitt, Julia 9051, 9422
Evers, Ernst 1853
Eversole, Finley 8133
Everts, William Wallace 267, 268
Every, George 11760
Evjen, John Oluf 4719
Evjen, Victor Harold 4045
Ewen, Dennis E. 18724
Ewer, Phyllis A. 11292
Ewers, John Ray 4213
Ewing, S. E. 2788
Examining Our Church 7825
Executive Council of the Episcopal Church, Asian American Episcopalians National Conference 14220
Exploiting Urban Decay 9052
Eyster, Walter C. 6312
Ezekiel, Raphael S. 16931
Ezell, Paul 13853
Faber, Heije 15444
Face of the Future 7826
Fackre, Dorothy 7081
Fackre, Gabriel J. 7081, 7541, 8134, 8716, 9053, 9054, 9423, 10328, 10821, 11276, 11277, 12476
Fagan, Harry 15023
Fagan, Ronald W. 17735, 18123
Fager, Charles 12144
Fagley, Richard M. 7827
Faherty, William B. 11761
Fahey, David M. 19205
Fahey, Frank J. 13729
Fahlbusch, Wilhelm 16932
Fainstein, Norman I. 12145, 13193
Fainstein, Susan S. 12145, 13193
Fairbairn, Andrew Martin 696, 1293
Fairbairn, Robert B. 789
Fairchild, Henry Pratt 3692, 3829
Fairchild, Roy W. 7082, 8135
Fairfield, James 10329, 10822
Faison, Thermond L. 12477
Faith in the City of Birmingham 18481
Falardeau, Jean C. 6030
Falcón, Rafael 17736
Faler, Paul 12146
Faling, Richard 17322
Falk, Lawrence L. 18828
Falk, Nicholas 13522
Falk, Peter 15024
Falkner, Clyde W., Jr. 10716
Fallding, Harold 13194
Falwell, Jerry 12147, 12842
Fanfani, Amintore 6659
Fann, Bridget E. 17737
Fanning, Charles 15445
Fant, David J. 5677, 9424
Fantino, Eileen 6660
Fappani, Antonio 11886
Faramelli, Norman J. 11762, 12148, 12478, 12782, 12843, 12844, 12845, 13195, 13196, 13197, 13200, 13523, 13854, 13855, 14221, 18482
Farber, Bernard 15025
Farley, Gary 11763, 16207, 16208
Farmer, Gladys 15402
Farnam, William Warren 3063
Farnell, Richard 19080
Farquhar-Nicol, Glenn 17391
Farra, Kathryn 4458
Farrakhan, Louis 13198, 15030, 16661, 18955
Farrar, F. W. 1050
Farrell, Carolyn 17323
Farrell, Edward J. 18829
Farrer, Austin 17354
Farwell, Parris 2137
Fasol, Al 16209
Fass, Moshe 13856
Fasset, Thom M. 15026
Fassin, Didier 18124
Father George 6661
Father Pollock and His Brother: Mission Priests of St. Alban's, Birmingham 2500

Faue, Jeffrey 12901
Faughnan, Pauline 12479
Faulkner, Arthur 13048, 15027
Faulkner, Brooks R. 10823
Faulkner, H. U. 2933
Faulkner, James R. 18830
Faulkner, Joseph Edward, Sr. 8419
Faulkner, William John 4524
Faunce, W. H. P. 2217
Faupel, Charles E. 18125, 18218
Fauset, Arthur Huff 5269
Fauset, Jessie 3762
Faust, Herman Paul 1748
Faux, Jeff 14499
Fava, Sylvia F. 6863, 10824, 13524
Favero, Luigi 15028, 17552
Feagin, Joe R. 10825, 13525, 14614
Fearon, Mike 18348, 18483
Federal Council of the Churches of Christ in America 2218, 2219, 3064, 3131, 3215, 3216, 3217, 3218, 3219, 3321, 3405, 3501, 5086, 5471, 5897
Federal Council of the Churches of Christ in America, Christian Commission for Camp and Defense Communities 5087, 5088
Federal Council of the Churches of Christ in America, Commission on the Church and Social Service 2220, 2599
Federal Council of the Churches of Christ in America, Department of Race Relations 4046, 5270
Federal Council of the Churches of Christ in America, Department of Research and Development 3693, 3882, 4214, 4720, 5574
Federal Council of the Churches of Christ in America, Department of the Church and Social Service 2501, 2702, 2789, 3220, 3322, 4215, 5575, 5678
Federal Council of the Churches of Christ in America, Executive Committee 5781
Federal Council of the Churches on Christ in America, Commission of the Church and Social Service 4047
Federated Churches of Cleveland, Comity Committee 2934, 3221, 3323
Federated Work among Aliens 2600
Fédération des Eglises et Missions Evangéliques du Cameroun 12846
Federation for Industrial Retention and Renewal 18831
Federation of Jewish Philanthropies of New York 6864
Federation of Protestant Welfare Agencies [New York] 3222, 4434, 6159
Federation of Social Agencies of Pittsburgh and Allegheny County, Bureau of Social Research 5679
Federbusch, Simon 6865
Fedewa, Thomas Cyril 13526
Feeley, S. V. 5011
Feldberg, Michael 13527
Felder, Cain H. 11764, 13857, 18832
Feldman, Abraham J. 7828
Feldman, Egal 11278
Feldman, Eugene 13858
Feldman, Linda 18484
Feldmeier, Russell 18485
Feldon, Victoria Beatrice 13859
Feldstein, Stanley 14615
Fell, Gilbert S. 7542

Fellowship of Christian Socialists 4916
Fells, Ian 14616
Felmeth, William F. 12847
Felsenthal, Bernhard 1294
Felter, Eunice 5012
Felton, Carroll M, Jr. 15446
Felton, Paul 15403
Felton, Ralph A. 3223, 5576, 6466
Female Bible Society of Philadelphia 25
Female Domestic Missionary Society of Philadelphia 43
Female Missionary Society for the Poor of the City of New York 34
Female Society of Boston and Vicinity for Promoting Christianity among the Jews 35
Femminella, Francis X. 8136
Fenn, Eric 5782
Fenn, Richard K. 18126, 19206
Fenn, Steve 11765
Fenton, Joseph Clifford 5783
Ferguson, Francis L. 1539
Ferguson, Gene M. 15447
Ferguson, John 12848, 14222
Ferguson, Ron 15029
Ferkiss, Victor C. 7829
Ferlauto, Richard C. 18679
Ferm, Deane William 16575
Ferm, Martin E. 8420
Fermaud, Charles 633
Fernandez, Arturo 19081
Fernandez, Vivian Eloise 17738
Ferree, William 6662
Ferrell, Gilbert 13528
Ferrin, Allen Conant 2790
Ferrin, Augustin William 2400
Ferry, John G. 7543
Fetsch, Cornelius 16210
Feuer, Lewis S. 9837
Fey, Harold E. 4608, 5271, 5272, 5273, 6031, 8137, 8717
Fey, Thomas M. 17739
Fiawoo, Dzigbodi K. 7544
Fichman, David 3224
Fichter, Joseph H. 4609, 5898, 6032, 6160, 6313, 6314, 6467, 7303, 7304, 8138, 9055, 9425, 9426, 9427, 13199, 18486
Fichtner, Horst 5784
Fiederling, M. Irmturdis 5013
Field, Frank 14223
Field, John 10779
Fields, Dan 12149
Fife, Eric S. 8155
Fiftieth Anniversary Yearbook, 1895-1945: Commemoration of Half a Century of Organized Jewish Philanthropy in Boston 5371
Figart, Thomas O. 12849
Figge, Robert J., Jr. 18487
Figgis, John Neville 10020
Figueroa, Jose E. 15804
File, Edgar 14617, 15448
Filippini, Mable de 14618
Filler, Darrell Charles 14619
Filpot, Dave 10826
Final Call 15030
Findji, Marie Terese 11766
Findlay, James Franklin 8139, 8421, 11279
Findley, Cecil 12150
Findley, J. G. 2075
Fine, Howard D. 13529
Fineberg, S. Andhil 9838
Finestead, David Ray 16933
Finger, Bill 14873, 14874
Finger, Tom 15031
Fink, George Washington 3606
Finke, Roger 18488
Finkel, David 18833
Finkelstein, Louis 7305
Finks, P. David 11767, 13530, 13860, 14620, 16211, 16934
Finley, James Bradley 306

Finley, John H. 1295
Finley, Woodward 8140
Finn, Peter 15032
Finnell, David 16935, 17049, 17740
Finney, Charles G. 133, 564, 565, 7648, 12426, 13351
Finney, Ross Lee 2703, 3406
Fiorenza, Elizabeth Schussler 18127
Firebaugh, Glenn 15805
First Annual Report of the Society for the Reformation of Juvenile Offenders in New York 89
First Community Church, Columbus Ohio 5899
First Methodist, Orlando, FL 5900
First Presbyterian, Hollywood, CA 5901
First Presbyterian, Topeka, Kansas 5902
Fischel, Jack 19207
Fischel, Walter J. 6866
Fischer, Alfons 8141
Fischer, Clare B. 16936
Fischer, Claude F. 13761
Fischer, Claude S. 12480, 12850, 13531, 13532, 13533, 13861, 13862, 15449, 15806, 16212
Fischer, Marie 1296
Fish, Aloys M. 2138
Fish, Calvert, Mrs. 2139
Fish, Carl Russell 3830
Fish, Henry C. 532
Fish, John Hall 10330, 10827, 12851, 14621, 17324, 18834
Fish, Lydia Marie 13863
Fish, Merle Edison 7545
Fishberg, Maurice 2502
Fishburn, Janet F 18128
Fisher, Galen 5089, 5274
Fisher, Harriet 195
Fisher, Humphrey J. 17741
Fisher, Irving 3763, 3883
Fisher, Irving D. 18489
Fisher, James C. 13534, 18835
Fisher, Lee 7049
Fisher, Miles Mark 3407
Fisher, Minnie 13864
Fisher, Neal F. 13200, 13535, 16213, 16214
Fisher, Paul 15807
Fisher, Peter 15428
Fisher, Robert Moore 6663
Fisher, Wallace E. 9428, 9429, 9839, 10828, 12481
Fisher, William H. 14224
Fishman, Joshua A. 7355, 7830, 8718
Fishman, Robert 14225
Fiske, Amos Kidder 2791
Fitch, Bob 10829
Fitch, John A. 6867, 7083
Fitch, R. F. 3225
Fitzgerald, Robert 7831
Fitzpatrick, Franklin E. 14226
Fitzpatrick, John Bernard 17092
Fitzpatrick, Joseph P. 6662, 6664, 6665, 8422, 9840, 12151, 14227, 15033, 18490, 19082, 19083
Fitzpatrick, Mallary, Jr. 5372
Fitzroy Ecumenical Center 11768
Fitzsimmons, M. A. 6468
Five Churches That Didn't Run 6666
Five Points House of Industry 336
Five Points Mission >> See further: Subject Index
Five Points Mission 254
Flanagan, Denis 9841
Flanagan, William G. 14661
Flanderin, Paul Hippolyte 1946
Flannery, Harry W. 9377
Flatbush, Adda M. 1688
Fleeting Talk with Saul Alinsky 10830

Fleischer, Hermann Paul 2503
Fleming, C. James 10831
Fleming, Daniel J. 5785
Fleming, Kenneth C. 17742
Fletcher, James E. 13206
Fletcher, John C. 11769, 12152
Fletcher, Joseph F. 4074, 4365, 4366, 4384, 4721, 5577, 5578, 7832
Fletcher, Verne H. 7833
Fleuriot, Gerard de 15034
Fliegende Blätter aus dem Rauhen Hause zu Horn 239
Flier, G. van der. 10832
Flint, Cort R. 11299
Floating Church of Our Savior, for Seamen 201
Flora, Cornelia Butler 13865
Floreen, Harold 5680, 6161
Florence Crittenton Missions, [National and local affiliates] 1377
Floridi, Alexis U. 12852
Floristán Samones, Casiaio 8719, 16576
Florovsky, Georges 6033
Flower, Benjamin Orange 1216, 2221
Floyd, Arva Colbert 5472
Floyd, Roger W. 9842, 9843
Fluent, Mike 17743
Flynn, Elizabeth B. 13201
Flynt, J. Wayne 14228, 15808
Fogarty, Gerald P. 17325
Fogarty, James W. 9844
Fogarty, Joan 13866, 13867, 13868
Fogarty, Michael 5090, 5473, 5579, 6667, 7084, 8423, 8720
Fogle, Joe E. 11770
Foley, Ann 6162
Foley, Judy M. 11280
Foley, Mary Mix 8382
Foley, Timothy 13398
Folger, Holly 18156
Folliet, Joseph 6668
Folsom, C. M. 1624
Folsom, Harry G. 15450
Folsom, William Harrison 13424
Foner, Lorraine 9845
Foner, Philip 13536
Foner, Philip S. 16577
Fones-Wolf, Elizabeth 16578
Fones-Wolf, Kenneth Alan 16215, 16578, 17326, 17327, 18491, 18836
Fong, Norman 14622, 19304
Fonseca, Claudia 19208
Foote, Catherine Jeanne 16216
Forbes, Anne 17744
Forbes, Avary H. 1378
Forbes, Cheryl A. 12482
Forbes, Elmer Severance 2401, 2601, 2602
Forbes, James 18837
Forbush, William Byron 1804, 2402, 2872
Force, Maryanne T. 6825
Ford, Austin 16477
Ford, George A. 1625
Ford, Henry 3797
Ford, Larry Royden 11771
Forde, Walter 12483
Fordham, Monroe 13537
Foreign Missions Industrial Association 1903
Forell, George W. 15035, 15451
Foreman, James 12484
Foreman, Tim 15403
Forest, James E. 17328
Forest, James H. 17745
Forley, Edward 19245
Forman, Charles 6163
Forman, Robert E. 12153
Forrest, Thomas Robert 10833
Forrester, Duncan 17898
Forrester, W. R. 6315
Forsberg, Robert 11772
Forshaw, Eric 14160, 17746
Forshey, Gerald E. 9430

Forster, Greg 17747
Forster, Harvey G. 5091, 9846
Forsyth, Anne 2504
Forsyth, David D. 3065
Fortunato, John 16217, 18129
Forty Years at Hull House: The Story of Jane Addams 3956
Forward, Martin H. F. 18492
Fosdick, Harry Emerson 3324, 3502, 6868
Foshoe, Howard B. 10834
Fosselman, D. Harold 6034, 6164
Fossum, Paul R. 5275
Foster, Alice 15809
Foster, Arthur L. 11773
Foster, Charles I. 6035, 7834, 18838
Foster, D. B. 4048
Foster, Howell S. 9056
Foster, Lorn S. 16865
Foster, Virgil E. 6869, 8142
Foster, William W. 1540
Foth, Elizabeth 4456
Fotia, Ralph 18493
Fourteen Southern Ministers: The Stevens-Union Struggle 14229
Fourth Congregational Society of Lowell [MA] 299
Foust, John J. 1626
Fowell, Myron F. 7546
Fowke, Edith 7835
Fowler, C. H. 610, 2019
Fowler, Dorothy Granfield 15810
Fowler, Henry G. 12154
Fowler, James 12853, 15811
Fox, James H. 6601
Fox, Mary Harrita 6316
Fox, Matthew 12155, 15036, 18984
Fox, Paul 16108
Fox, Robert 10271, 15037, 15038
Fox, Walter 11774
Fox, William K. 19047
Foy, Peter L. 721
Frady, Marshall 15039
Frakes, Margaret 6870, 7085, 7306
Frame, John Davidson 6036
Frame, Randall L. 18130
França, Maria Cecilia 15040
Frances, Mary 14926
Francesconi, Mario 14153, 17329
Franch, M. S. 13869
Francis, John J. 1134, 1135
Francis, Russell E. 5474
Francis, Samuel 3517
Franciscans, Province of the Immaculate Conception 3694
Frangipane, Francis 19209
Frank, Jennings 6037
Frankenberg, Ellen 15041
Franklin, Doris 17748
Franklin, J. E. 2792
Franklin, John Hope 13202
Franklin, R. W. 16579
Franklin, Robert Michael 18839, 19084
Frantz, Earl M. 3503
Franz, Delton 18494
Franzen, Janice Gosnell 17749
Franzen, Lyle 13870
Frase, Ronald 13538
Fraser, David A. 15417
Fraser, Derek 16580
Fraser, Ian M. 7547, 13539
Fraser, J. G. 1947
Fraser, James 842
Fray, Harold R. 8143, 10026, 11281, 12485
Frazier, E. Franklin 4216, 4832, 4917, 7086, 9057, 10331
Frazier, Vernon F. 9058
Freas, William 2935
Frederick, Arthur Lester 6165, 7836
Frederick, Peter J. 13871
Fredsell, Harold F. 9847
Free and Open Church Association 550

Freebairn, Harry A. 18131
Freedom Reborn in Los Angeles 8424
Freeman, Edward Barnes, Jr. 12854, 13540, 16581
Freeman, Harry 16937
Freeman, James M. 15452
Freeman, John F. 18495
Freeman, Moses 3957
Freeman, Richard B. 17750
Freeman, Ronald 12383
Freiderichs, Hulda 2222
Freire, Paulo 11775, 16998
Frellick, Francis I. 9431
Fremantle, Anne 19261
Fremantle, William Henry 551, 749, 1805
French Bishops' Commission on the Workers' World 12855
French Protestant Industrial Mission 12486
French, Dwight L. 9059
French, James Wilford 13541
French, Maurice 13542
French, William H. 9535
Frenchak, David 15042, 15043, 16938
Frenkel-Brunswick, Else 5850
Fresno Metropolitan Ministry 15453
Frett, Calvin F. 12156
Fretz, F. K. 2316, 2317
Fretz, J. Winfred 14594
Frey, Donald S. 8721
Freytag, Justus 7548, 11776
Freytag, Walter 6166
Fribourg, Jeanine 19210
Frick, Frank S. 14230
Frick, Hans H. 15044, 15308
Frickstad, Taral T. 1297
Fried, Marc 12856
Friedberger, Walter 14623
Frieden, Bernard J. 13543
Friedlander, Eva 17383
Friedli, Markus 14231
Friedman, Georges 6038
Friedman, Murray 13848
Friedman, Oliver A. 4435, 4833
Friedman, Theodore 6669
Friedrichs, David W. 10835
Friere, Paulo 18324
Friese, Philip C. 983
Friesen, Jim 9250
Friesen, Vernon 12857
Friffioen, Donald J. 16939
Frindte, Matthias 15454
Frisbie, Margery 19344
Frisch, Ephraim 3607
Frisque, J. 8425
Fritschel, Herman L. 2936
Fritz, Paul J. 18496
Fritzsching, Günter 14624
Frohman, Roderic Paul 15045, 16582
From Anarchy to Tyranny 10332
From Church to Press: Dr. Parkhurst's Church Transformed into a Newspaper Office 3226
Fromer, Paul 16583
Fromm, Erich 6670, 6871
Frost, Linda Gail 16218
Frostin, Per 17330
Frothingham, Octavius B. 518
Froyd, Milton C. 6648
Fruhauf, Henry 18132
Fry, C. George. 11777
Fry, Charles Luther 1379, 3884, 4049, 4367
Fry, John 8144, 8722, 9060, 9432, 10836, 12157, 13544
Fryman, Jeleta 16940
Fuechtmann, Thomas Gerhard 16219, 18840
Fuerst, J. S. 9433
Fueter, Paul D. 8449
Fuga, Francis J. 14418
Fugmann, Gernot 11282
Fujihira, Toge 12487
Fujii, Masao 11778

Fukada, Robert M. 9434, 10333
Fukuyama, Yoshio 6671, 6672, 6673, 6872, 6873, 7307, 7549, 8145, 8426, 8723, 9848, 11699, 12488, 17331, 17751, 18891
Fulcher, Gwyneth Mary 3408
Fulkerson, William Miller 13203
Full Employment -- A National Priority 13872
Fuller, George C. 16941
Fuller, Howard S. 9061
Fuller, John 17752
Fuller, Millard 15455, 15812, 17753
Fuller, R. M. 697
Fuller, Reginald H. 9849
Fullilove, Robert E., III. 11283
Fulton, Brent 18133
Fulwood, Charles 14625
Funchion, Michael M. 15813
Fung, Raymond 12158, 12858, 12859, 13204, 13545, 13873, 13874, 14232, 15046, 15047, 15048
Fuoss, Robert 12860
Furfey, Paul 4436, 4610, 5681, 6167, 14626, 14627
Furlow, Elaine 12861
Furlow, F. 9062
Furlow, Frances 8724, 11284
Furness, Charles Y. 9850, 9851, 12489, 14628
Furnham, Adrian 19085
Furr, James Harold 18134
Fürstenberg, Friedrich 8725
Fusfeld, Daniel R. 9063
Fustel de Coulanges, Numa Denis 415
Fustero, Steven 16942
Fütterer, Klaus 16943
Gable, Dennis R. 15814, 16584, 16944
Gabriel, R. H. 4918
Gaebelein, A. C. 1217
Gaffey, James Patrick 12862, 13875
Gafke, Arthur 18841
Gager, John G. 13546
Gagne, David W. 16220
Gaillard, Frye 12159, 12863
Gaither, Gloria 17754
Galbraith, John Kenneth 15049
Galbraith, Les 12184
Gale, Horace 12811
Galilea, Segundo 10334, 14233, 15815
Galin, Amira 16221
Gallagher, Eric 18842
Gallagher, John P. 10837
Gallagher, Robert 12490, 15816
Gallagher, Sharon 16585, 17332
Galland, Daniel 9064
Galli, Carlos 17755
Galli, Giascarlo 11285
Galli, Luigi M. 10335
Gallis, Marion 12864
Galloway, Russell 11410
Gallup, George, Jr. 14629, 15456, 16222, 16945, 17681, 18135
Galtier, Denis 9852
Galush, William 16946
Galush, William J. 14234
Galvan, Elísas Gabriel 11286
Galvin, Bernie 18246
Galvin, John T. 14235
Gambrell, Bill 18843
Gammon, Roland 8146
Gandasegui, Larrauri, Jose Manuel 4919
Gandhi, Mohandas 5960
Gannes, Abraham P. 6674
Gannett, W. C. 579
Gannon, Ann Ida 18844
Gannon, Thomas M. 13876, 14630, 18136
Gans, Herbert J. 7087, 7308, 8427, 8428, 8429, 9435, 10336, 12491
Gant, Edwin P. 17333
Gappert, Gary 16223

Garbett, Cyril Forster 2505, 2873, 4140, 4284, 5682, 6168
Garbutt, J. D. 12303
Garcia, Ana de 17756
García, Epifanio 7837
Garcia, Rafael 7309
Garcia, Richard A. 14236
Garcia, S. 15817
Garcia, Xavier 14237
García-Nieto París, Juan N. 7838
García-Treto, Francisco O. 13136
Gard, Wayne 4437
Gardet, Louis 14631
Gardiner, Alfred George 19252
Gardiner, John A. 13205
Gardner, Charles Spurgeon 2793, 2937, 3066
Gardner, E. Clinton 12160
Gardner, Ian 17334
Gardner, John 2938
Garesche, Edward F. 4217
Garíepy, Wilfrid 6317
Garland, S. G. 3958
Garman, Harold W. 9436, 9853, 10838
Garmon, William S. 9437, 10839, 10840, 11779
Garner, Howard G. 14632
Garraghan, Gilbert J. 3325
Garrett, Roberta 10337
Garrett, Shirley Stone 9854
Garrett, Wilfred 6469
Garrett, William 12865
Garreua, Joel 19345
Garrigan, Kathleen 13547
Garrison, Elton P. 6874
Garrison, Winfred E. 4285, 5683
Garrity, Paul F. 19086
Garrott, E. P. J 2020
Gartner, Alan 16224
Gartner, Lloyd P. 7839, 8909, 9065, 10841, 12010, 14633, 15818, 16947
Gartrell, Leland E. 7310, 7311, 7550, 7551, 7552, 7553, 7554, 7555, 7840, 7841, 7842, 8147, 8148, 8430, 8431, 8432, 8433, 8434, 9051, 9066, 9067, 9068, 9855, 10338, 10339, 10842, 11287
Garvey, Amy Jacques 8726
Garvey, Marcus 3498, 3527, 6651, 12606, 14544, 14545, 16610, 18955
Garvey, Michael 14634, 16385
Garvie, Alfred Ernest 3227, 4050, 4286
Garvin, Alexander 16225, 18137
Garvin, John C. 10340
Garvin, Tom 14238
Garwood, John 286
Gary, Jay 19072
Gaskell, Elizabeth 233
Gaskell, Elizabeth Cleghorn 12330
Gaslin, William D. 19319
Gast, Rudolf 7088
Gaston, Maria Luisa 15457
Gastwirt, Harold Philip 12161
Gateley, Edwina 19327
Gates, C. W. 12492
Gates, George A. 1136
Gates, Herbert W. 2506, 2874
Gates, John Palmer 5684
Gates, Merrill E. 1218
Gaucher, Guy 15050
Gauder, Winston 16586
Gaudreau, William L. 11288
Gaulke, M. 11289
Gaume, Jean Joseph 234
Gauthier, Paul 9438, 9856
Gauvin, Marshall J. 2999
Gaventa, John 13877
Gavigan, Kathleen 13548
Gavit, John P. 1689
Gawith, A. 16802
Gay Men's Liberation 12493
Gay, John D. 12162
Geaney, Dennis J. 7556
Gearty, Patrick 6318

Geck, Ludwig Heinrich Adolph 10341
Gee, Kenneth 6705
Geering, Lloyd George 18497
Geertz, Clifford 15458
Geffen, Elizabeth M. 8149, 8727
Gehret, Kenneth S. 7557
Geier, M. A. 14635, 14636
Geier, Woodrow A. 7843
Geiser, Floramae 14239
Gelfant, Blanche Housman 6470
Gell, Philip Lyttelton 945
Gelles, Roberta 10843
Gemeinschaft der Katholischen Männer Deutschlands 8150
Gemmer, H. Robert 9439
General Booth's Plan: Can It Be Applied to the Outcasts of New York? 984
General Conference Mennonite Church, Board of Missions, Committee on City Churches 7844
General Council of the Assemblies of God 14637
Genet, Harry 15819
Gensel, John 10475, 11136
Genska, Depaul A. 15459
Georg-Eckert-Institut für Internationale Schulbuchforschumg 14240
George, Alan 17757
George, Bryant 9440
George, Floyd E. 10844
George, Gordon 9857
George, Henry 611, 661, 750, 1051, 2450, 3067, 17468
George, Joseph, Jr. 14638, 15051
George, Lyman F. 1690
Gepford, William George 12866
Gephart, Jerry C. 13206
Gérando, Joseph Marie de, baron 114
Gerard, Emmanuel 15820
Gerard, Karen 16948
Gerber, Leslie E. 13549
Gerber, Virgil 13878
Gerberding, G. H. 2076, 2939
Geremia, Peter 17721
Gérin, Paul 7312
Gerlach, Gary G. 11290
Gerlach, Luther P. 11780
Gerloff, Roswith 19346
German, John S. 4287
Gerrand, David 13767
Gerrard, Ginny 14639
Gersh, Harry 6471
Gessell, John M. 10342
Gesualdi, Louis John 18138
Gettell, Marilyn 11291
Gettleman, Marvin E. 8728
Gettman, Seymour 15460
Geyer, Alan 16363
Gheddo, Piero 12867
Ghirelli, Tommaso 15821
Giamatti, A. Bartlett 18845
Gibbal, Jean-Marie 19211
Gibbins, Ronald C. 13879
Gibbons, James 3471, 6157
Gibbs, David R. 12868
Gibbs, Eddie 14241
Gibbs, Jack P. 8151
Gibbs, James O. 11292
Gibbs, Mark 7845, 15822, 16949
Gibbs, Nancy R. 18498
Gibson, Donald 11293
Gibson, Jo 16950
Gibson, John E. 7558
Giddens, Anthony 12163
Giddings, Lynn 17335
Gidney, William Thomas 2223
Gieniec, Nancy 18499
Giersbach, Walter C. 4368, 4525
Giese, Vincent J. 8152, 8435, 15461
Gieseler, Carl A. 3831
Giesen, Heinrich 8436
Gifford, O. P. 986
Gift for the Neighborhood: Church to do Urban

Developing of Their Own 11781
Gilbert, Alan 13880, 15462, 16226
Gilbert, Charles Kendall 3310, 3326
Gilbert, Levi 1627
Gilbert, Richard R. 9441
Gilbert, William M. 3409, 3885, 4051
Gilder, George 15823
Giles, Dorothy 3608
Giles, Philip L. 18139
Gilhooley, James 9069, 13881, 14640
Gilkes, Cheryl Townsend 17758
Gilkey, Bertha 18846
Gilkey, C. W. 2794
Gilkey, James Gordon 7313, 8153, 8437
Gilkey, Langdon 9070, 13207
Gill, Athol 19322
Gill, Corrington 4834
Gill, David 11294
Gill, Eric 4920, 5014
Gill, Neville David 8154
Gill, Robin 18500, 19087
Gillander, Alexander Charles Ewen 4722
Gillard, John Thomas 4052, 5015, 7559
Gillespie, David E. 14242
Gillett, G. S. 3504
Gillett, Richard W. 9442, 12869, 15463, 15824, 16227, 16587, 16951, 17336, 17759
Gilley, S. W. 11295, 12164
Gillies, James 9045
Gillingham, David 12870
Gilman, Elizabeth 1541
Gilmore, J. Herbert 12494
Gilmore, Robert M. 19320, 19328
Gilson, Etienne 6472
Ginsberg, Yona 13208
Gipey, Gomi J. 15073
Giraud, Pierre, Cardinal 211
Girdlestone, G. D. 837
Girgis, Sami Said 15825
Girouard, Mark 17337
Girs, Gabriel B. 15052
Gish, Arthur G. 11782
Gist, Noel P. 4288
Gitelman, Howard M. 13209
Gittings, James A. 9858, 12165, 14641, 18140, 18141
Gizelis, Gregory 13210
Glaab, Charles N. 8729, 10343
Gladden, Washington 566, 612, 751, 752, 753, 790, 838, 881, 1066, 1137, 1138, 1219, 1220, 1221, 1380, 1381, 1382, 1388, 1542, 1628, 1629, 1691, 1854, 1975, 2021, 2022, 2023, 2024, 2025, 2140, 2224, 2318, 2403, 2507, 2508, 2509, 2510, 2795, 2875, 2940, 4238, 5709, 9887, 10304, 11390, 12166, 14764, 17984
Gladwin, John 15053, 17760
Glanville, Lewis K. 11296
Glaser, Chris 18501
Glaser, Mitch 17338
Glasner, Peter 12167, 14243
Glasner, Samuel 5903
Glass, Bill 13882
Glass, Esther Eby 9859
Glass, Ian 10344
Glasse, James D. 10845, 12495
Glasser, Arthur F. 8155, 13883
Glassman, Bess 2979
Glaves, Brenda 18847
Glazer, Joe 7835
Glazer, Nathan 7560, 8730, 9071, 16952
Glazer, Simon 16723
Glazier, Robert 8731
Glazier, Willard 698
Gleason, Arthur Huntington 2141
Gleason, Philip 10846, 11297,

14642
Gleason, William F. 9860
Gleig, G. R. 370
Glen, John Stanley 15054
Glenn, Charles L. 17761
Glenn, John M. 2704
Glenn, Norval 10345, 11783
Glide Foundation 16228
Glide Urban Center 9443
Glock, Charles Y. 6559, 6875, 6876, 6879, 8156, 9444, 9861, 10346, 11298, 11550, 12329, 13550, 14643, 15207
Gloyn, Cyril Kennard 5092
Glynn, Thomas P. 14934
Gmeiner, John 1052
Gneuhs, Geoffrey B. 15055
Goad, J. Newcombe 3695
Goba, Bonganjalo 16229
Goblovensky, David I. 7314
Goddard, Burton L. 10347
Goddard, Carrie Lou 8157, 8732
Goddard, John 2225
Goddard, Oscar Elmo 3132
Goddijn, Johannes Jacobus Oscar 7089
Goddijn, Walter 7561
Godfrey, Aaron 11784
Godfrey, Wendy 17339
Gods Must Be Crazy 16953
Godwin, C. J. 12496
Godwin, Roy E. 10348, 12497, 16588
Goebel, Hans 14644
Goedecke, Raymond M. 14645
Goetschius, George W. 10349
Goetz, Ronald 10847
Goheen, Peter 12871
Göhre, Paul 1383, 1630
Goist, Park Dixon 14244
Gokalp, Altan 18848
Golab, Caroline 12872
Golbeck, Kay 14646
Gold, Bertram H. 10848
Gold, Martin 8158
Gold, Neil 11729
Goldberg, A. 13551
Goldberg, David 7090
Golden, J. D. 11785
Golden, Renny 17762
Golder, Christian 2226
Goldfarb, Nathan 7315
Goldfield, David R. 14142
Goldingay, John 18849
Goldman, Ari L. 18850
Goldman, Julia 6362
Goldman, Peter 9445
Goldscheider, Calvin 10849
Goldsen, Rose Kohn 5948
Goldsmith, Malcolm 14160, 14245
Goldstein, Ira 18977
Goldstein, Israel 6473
Goldstein, Sidney E. 3410, 3505, 6675, 10849
Goldstone, Roberta 12498
Gollin, Gillian Lindt 10350
Gollobin, Ira 12557
Golomb, Egon 8733, 8734
Goltz, Eduard Freiherr von der 2941
Golzio, Karl H. 17340
Gomes, David 15464
Gompers, Samuel 2603, 7883, 7899
Gondolf, Edward 15826
Gonzalez Nieves, Roberto Octavio 16954
Gonzalez, Justo L. 17341, 18502
Gonzáles, Roberto O. 14227
González-Balado, José Luis 15465
Goo, Choi Seung 13211
Good Housing for America 4611
Good News to the Poor: The Church and City Problems 15466
Good, Homer L 11299
Good, James I. 2404
Good, Particia 13552
Good, Robert W. 16955

Goodall, Nan 4921
Goodall, Norman 10351
Goodchild, Frank M. 1469
Goode, Erich 9862, 10850, 11300, 11786
Goode, James E. 15467
Goode, Judith Granich 12831, 14208
Goode, R. 15056
Goode, Richard 8159
Goodell, Michael 18142, 18143
Gooden, George 14246
Gooden, Robert B. 5580
Goodenough, Cecelia 7846
Goodhue, Bertram Grosvenor 18689
Goodin, Robert E. 17342
Goodluck, Jack 14247
Goodman, C. 14647
Goodman, Edward 8735
Goodman, Grace Ann 9446, 9447, 9448, 9449, 9450, 9451, 9863, 10352, 10353, 10354, 10355, 10851, 11301, 11302, 11303, 11787, 11788, 12873
Goodman, Julie 18503
Goodrich, Howard, Jr. 10356
Goodridge, R. Martin 11304
Goodspeed, Edgar Johnson 580
Goodwill Industries of America 3228, 5373
Goodwin, John Albert Reed 16230
Goodwin, John C. 18504
Goossen, Rachel Waltner 17763
Göpfert, Michael 15827
Gorday, Peter 18851
Gorden, Albert I. 5786
Gordis, Robert 6669
Gordon, Albert I. 5787, 7562
Gordon, Arthur 12499
Gordon, C. 7411
Gordon, David F. 16956
Gordon, James 8736
Gordon, Leland 6676
Gordon, Mark W. 17343
Gordon, Milton M. 9072
Gordon, Oliver Brown 3959
Gordon, Paul 17764
Gore, Charles 927, 1139, 1631, 2227, 2942, 3229, 3764, 3886, 4486, 9007, 10020
Gorman, Charles D. 15828
Gorman, M. Adele Francis 8737
Gornick, Mark R. 17765
Gornitzka, A. Reuben 10357
Gorrell, Donald K. 13553, 18505, 18506
Gorreux, René 7563
Gorsuch, Richard L. 13212
Gortner, W. A. 12168
Goslin, Thomas S. 16957
Gosling, David 17302
Gosnell, L. W. 3000
Gospel of Labour 2604
Goss, Mary Lathrop 2511
Gossard, Edgar A. 8438
Gossard, John Harvey 17766
Gossett, Thomas 12169
Gossner Mission 13554
Gossner Mission in der DDR und Oekumenischmissionarisches Zentrum 15057
Gostelow, Ray 12500
Gott, John 882
Gottleib, David 11305
Gottman, Jean 8160, 8439
Gotts, Larry 14648, 16768
Goudzwaard, Bob 12170, 15058
Gould, E. M. Lawrence 2943
Gould, E. R. L. 1470
Gould, Frederick A. 3697
Gould, George H. 1384
Gouyon, Paul 7091, 7092
Gowan, Richard 8440, 9864
Gowdy, Kenneth 16231
Gowell, Elaine Childs 13884
Gowing, John 6474
Gowland, William 6475, 7543
Goyder, George 9073

Grace, William R. 9452, 9865, 10358
Gracie, David 14248
Gracie, Marjory 4141
Grady, Duane 18852
Graeber, Isacque 5093
Graebner, Theodore Conrad 5175
Grafton, Warren 7316
Graham and King as Ghetto-Mates 9866
Graham Taylor: 1851-1938 4723
Graham, Billy 5874, 6165, 6447, 6476, 6532, 6805, 6939, 7049, 7078, 7169, 7260, 7648, 7725, 7738, 8409, 9573, 9866, 9918, 9991, 10800, 11257, 11306, 13005, 13053, 13101, 13541, 13631, 15039, 15203, 15805, 16626, 17004, 19226
Graham, Jerry 14249
Graham, W. Fred 12874, 15468, 19088
Graham, W. Ralph 18507
Gram, Harold 11307
Grandi, Achille 13885
Granfield, Patrick 12875, 17315
Granger, Marshall Allen 2796
Grant, Carl A. 19287
Grant, E. Milton 5374
Grant, Frederick C. 3765
Grant, Geraldine S. 15829
Grant, James 16589
Grant, Percy Stickney 2405, 3068, 3506, 3507
Grants of Land and Gifts of Money to Catholic and Non-Catholic Institutions in New York Compared 613
Granville, Austyn 1298
Granvogl, Heinz 18144
Gratton, Thomas A. 18853
Gratz, Rebecca 7423
Graubard, Stephen R. 10852
Graves, James F. 14649
Gray, Arthur E. 1632
Gray, Charlotte 18508
Gray, Clifton D. 2228
Gray, David Lawther 14650
Gray, Donald B. 8441
Gray, Elmer L. 9453
Gray, Francine du Plessix 11308
Gray, Frederick T. 128
Gray, Helen T. 16232
Gray, Henry David 15830
Gray, John Henry 3508
Gray, Joseph M. M. 3230
Gray, Rhea 14651
Gray, Richard 16233
Greater Kampala Project 10853
Greater Lawrence Ecumenical Area Ministry 7847
Greater New York Federation of Churches 985, 1471, 1633, 1855, 4053
Greathouse, Gordon 14652, 14653, 16958
Greeley, Andrew M. 7317, 7564, 7565, 7566, 7567, 7568, 7848, 7849, 8442, 8443, 8444, 10359, 10854, 11309, 11310, 11789, 12171, 12172, 12501, 12502, 13213, 13214, 14250, 14251, 14252, 14253, 15059, 18509
Green, Alfred 15831
Green, Alice Stevenson 5176
Green, Barbara 6690
Green, Beriah 115
Green, Charles 18737
Green, Clifford 17767
Green, Garey 16234
Green, Gerson 14120
Green, Hollis L. 12503
Green, Judith 8694
Green, Laurie 18145
Green, Louise 19089
Green, Mark 15469
Green, Norman M. 8738, 9074, 9867, 9868, 10360, 10361, 10855, 10856, 11311, 11312

Green, Peter 3133
Green, R. H. 17344
Green, Shirley E. 4438, 9454
Green, William 3696, 3771, 7883, 7899, 17905
Greenblum, Joseph 10580, 11541
Greenburg, Harold 11790
Greene, Amy Blanche 3697
Greene, Carol 16590
Greene, Graham 4724
Greene, Shirley E. 9075, 10362, 17719, 19265
Greene, Thomas R. 16959
Greene, Victor 13555
Greene, W. L. 9511
Greenfield, Edward W. 7318
Greenfield, Gerald Michael 15749
Greenleaf, Jonathan 219
Greenleaf, Robert K. 14254, 16235
Greenlee, Sam 11313
Greenoe, John Covert 2797
Greensdale, Alexander 13173
Greenspan, Frederick E. 18041
Greenstein, Robert 16960
Greenway, John 6319
Greenway, Roger S. 11791, 11792, 12504, 12505, 12876, 12877, 13556, 13557, 13886, 14654, 15060, 16591, 16592, 16593, 16961, 16962, 16963, 17345, 17346, 17347, 17768, 17769, 17770, 18146, 18854
Greenwood, Elma L. 10363
Greenwood, L. B. 1135
Greer, Colin 16224
Greer, David Hummell 3368
Greer, Loyal 6574
Greer, Scott 8445, 10857, 11147, 15470
Greer, Thomas H. 5788
Gregg, Albert Sidney 1948
Gregg, Howard D. 15471
Gregory, A. 8739
Gregory, Alfred 581
Gregory, Benjamin 1299
Gregory, Diana 19090
Gregory, Dick 11314
Gregory, H. William 10364
Gregory, Joel 17348
Gregory, W. Edgar 5581
Greinacher, Norbert 7569, 8114, 9315, 9869, 14255
Greiser, David 19091
Gremillion, Joseph B. 7570, 8161
Gremmels, Christian 15832
Gresham, LeRoy 1949
Gresham, Perry E. 7850
Gressle, Francis A. 3231
Greth, Morris S. 6039
Grey, Lennox Bouton 4439
Grichting, Wolfgang L. 11315
Grider, Edgar M. 11316, 14655
Grier, Eunice 7851
Grier, George 7851
Grier, Louis 10035
Grier, William H. 11317
Grierson, Denham 12173
Griess, Helmut 11318
Griffen, Clyde 7852, 10365, 14656
Griffen, Sally 14656
Griffin, Benjamin 18510
Griffin, Clifford S. 7093, 7853, 10366
Griffin, John Howard 8162, 10714, 11319
Griffin, Martin I. J. 1385
Griffin, Maude K. 2026
Griffin, Nicholas J. 14657
Griffis, William Eliot 1053
Griffith, David Wark 2876
Griffith, Ernest S. 4725, 4726, 4727, 4728
Griffith, Gertrude 2705
Griffith, Lee 14658
Griffiths, Brian 16236, 16594, 16964
Griffiths, Carl Warren 5094,

5095
Grifone, Francis V. 6169
Grigg, Charles M. 8483
Grigg, Viv 16965, 18147, 18148, 18149, 18150
Grimes, Leonard 543
Grimes, Seamus 15472
Grimley, John B. 9870
Grindal, B. T. 12878
Grinstein, Hyman Bogomolny 5276
Griscom, John Hoskins 212
Gritter, Joseph 5475, 6320
Grivas, Theodore 9455
Grizzard, Nigel 15473
Grodka, Sonia 7854
Groen van Prinsterer, Guillaume 360
Grond, Linus 6040, 9315
Gronefeld, Maria 18855
Gronlund, Lawrence 1054
Gros, Lucien 6477
Grosch, Robert J. 14659
Grose, Howard Benjamin 2077, 2078, 2944
Gross, Alfred A. 8446
Gross, Bertram 15474
Gross, Robert 16966, 16967
Grossley, R. S. 3509
Grote, Jim 17071
Grove, P. Richard 12879
Groves, Reginald 10367
Grubbs, Bruce 15061
Grubbs, Larry J. 17771
Gruehn, Werner 3609
Gruenberg, B. 11957
Grugel, Lee E. 15062
Grumbach, Doris 11320
Grünberg, D. Paul. 2406
Grundy, Malcolm 17772
Grundy, Michael 14660
Gruner, LeRoy 16968
Grunier, Robert 14256
Gruson, Claude 12880
Gruver, Kate Ellen 8740
Guenther, Richard 7571
Guerre, René 6877
Guerry, Emile 8163
Guest, Avery M. 16969, 17031, 18151, 18856
Gugler, Josef 14661
Guglielmi, Francesco 2605
Guidarelli, Ena 10858
Guide for Establishing Ethnic Congregations 15833
Guide to the Churches and Missions in the City of New York 662
Guild, Lewis Thurber 3960
Guild, Roy Bergen 3069, 3134, 3232
Guilfoyle, George H. 7094
Guinan, Michael D. 15834
Gulick, John 8741, 10368, 12881, 18857
Gulick, Luther H. 2606, 8447
Gulick, Sidney Lewis 2798, 2799, 2945, 2946, 3070, 3233, 3234
Gumrukcu, Pat 9456
Gums, Reuben H. 9871
Gunderson, Gary 18511
Gunn, James 3411
Gunnemann, Jon P. 12675
Gunnerson, Bruce 11321
Günther, Heinz 6878
Guntrip, Henry James Samuel 5277
Gupta, Shiv Prakash 18152
Gurak, Douglas T. 15033
Gurock, Jeffrey S. 15063, 18153
Gurteen, S. Humphreys 681
Gusfield, Joseph R. 6677, 9872
Gustafson, James H. 6935
Gustafson, James M. 6478, 7095, 7572, 8164, 9873, 11793
Gustafsson, Berndt 6321
Gustafsson, Goran 17349
Gusweller, James A. 7573, 7822
Guthrie, Ernest Graham 4054, 4729

Guthrie, Thomas 348, 498
Gutiérrez, Gustavo 7855, 12882, 15064, 16237
Gutiérrez-Cortés, Rolando 16238
Gutkind, Erwin Anton 8448
Gutkind, Peter 13215
Gutman, Herbert 9874, 13887, 16970
Gutmann, Reinhart B. 9457, 9875, 9876
Gutstein, Morris Aaron 6322, 7856
Guttmann, David 12883
Gutwirth, Jacques 12506, 12884, 16595, 19212, 19213
Guynes, H. Don 10475
Guyot, Jean 14662
Haack, Friedrich W. 14663
Haan, T. 12885
Haas, Francis J. 3832, 3887, 4289, 4440, 4612, 4613, 5016, 10702, 11672
Habgood, John 14664
Hackett, Allen 8742, 9076
Hackett, David G. 16972
Hackett, Dorothy S. 9077, 9877
Hadaway, C. Kirk 13444, 15835, 16239, 16240, 16400, 16596, 16971, 16972, 17128, 17350, 17773, 18154, 19092
Hadaway, Robin Dale 18512
Haddad, Juliette 16241
Haddad, Yvonne Y. 15065
Hadden, Jeffrey K. 9878, 10369, 11322, 12174, 13216, 13217, 15475, 15476, 15836, 18155
Hadley, Henry Harrison 1222, 1386, 1856
Hadley, Samuel H. 1300, 1387, 1634, 1806, 1807, 1857, 1950, 2069, 4576
Haebler, Peter 15066
Hagan, John Wesley 1543
Hagedorn, John M. 18513
Hageman, Howard G. 7574, 10859, 11323, 11324, 11794
Hager, Don J. 6879
Hager, Gerhard 7575
Hager, John H. 7857, 8165, 9028
Haggard, Henry Rider, Sir 2027, 2407
Haggerty, Louis 2877
Hagman, Donald G. 10860
Hague, William 269, 403
Hahn, Celia A. 13218, 13219, 13421, 14257
Hahn, Judith 18858
Hahn, Wilhelm 7576
Haider, Gulzar 16973
Haines, John F. 16974
Haines, Robin 18156
Hake, Andrew 8449, 12175, 14258, 18859
Halbert, L. A. 4288
Halbrook, Marion 11795
Haldane, Donna 12176
Haldane, Jean 12886
Hale, Edward Everett 464, 533, 534, 593, 634, 883, 986, 1055, 1056, 1301
Hale, Russell 15477
Hale, Viola Sabia 6479
Hale, William Harlan 6678
Hales, Peter B. 16975
Halevy, Elie 12177
Haley, Alex 9283
Haley, William D. 307
Halfmann, Wilhelm 5904
Halker, Clark 19214
Halko, John 5365, 5685, 5905, 5906, 6041, 8450
Hall, A. 10861
Hall, Arthur C. A. 987
Hall, Arthur R. 9879
Hall, Bob 13888
Hall, Cameron P. 5278, 5582, 5686, 5789, 6042, 6170, 7096, 7858, 8451, 9078, 9880, 10370
Hall, Charles Cuthbert 988, 1692
Hall, Charlotte Chambers 1544

Hall, Clarence W. 5375
Hall, Dick 14665
Hall, Douglas 10187, 12887, 15478, 15837, 16597, 17774, 18514, 18515
Hall, Frank Oliver 2512
Hall, George B. 9458
Hall, John 928, 1635
Hall, John W., Jr. 18860
Hall, Judy 19355
Hall, Lawrence W. 8743
Hall, Leda McIntyre 16976
Hall, Mary Penelope 9459
Hall, Maxwell 3235
Hall, Newton M. 929, 2800
Hall, Peter Geoffrey 15838
Hall, Robert King 8744
Hall, Robert L. 15067
Hall, Thomas C. 1749, 1951, 2408
Halladay, Anne M. 6480
Hallenbeck, Wilbur Chapman 3961, 4055, 4056, 4142, 4143, 4369, 4730, 6043, 6626
Hallenweger, Walter 12507
Haller, Mark H. 12814
Hallett, Stanley J. 8745, 8746, 9079, 9080, 9460, 9461, 9462, 9881, 9882, 9883, 10371, 11796, 13889, 14666, 15068, 15069, 15070, 15479, 15480, 15481, 16977
Halley, Rudolph 6171
Halliday, Samuel Byram 349, 519
Halligan, John Martin 13558
Hallimond, John G. 2947, 3698
Hallstrom, J. H. 3699
Halper, Jeff 16978
Halsey, Abram Woodruff 3071
Halsey, Peggy 16598
Halstead, William Riley 1636
Halvarson, Loren E. 9884
Halvorson, Lawrence W. 9081
Ham, Clifford Carmichael, Jr. 6679, 7577, 7859, 8166, 8167, 8168, 8452, 8747, 8748, 9082, 9885, 10372
Hamakonda, Koiki Gikoe 17775
Hamao, F. 12888
Hamblen, Frank R. 5687
Hamblett, Beatrice 15839
Hambrick, Charles H. 13220
Hamer, Jérôme 9083, 9084
Hames, Constant 15071
Hamill, Patricia Beall 7578
Hamilton, C. M. 15482
Hamilton, Charles V. 12508
Hamilton, Dale 6172, 6680
Hamilton, Dorthy 13559
Hamilton, John W. 3072
Hamlin, Julian D. 4290
Hamlin, Richard E. 7579
Hamlin, Teunis S. 1545
Hamm, Heinrich 13890
Hammer, Don E. 14667, 15483, 16242, 16243, 16599, 17776
Hammersley, John 10862, 15840, 18516
Hammerton, H. J. 6173
Hammond Tooke, W. D. 11797
Hammond, Barbara 3510
Hammond, J. L. 3510
Hammond, John D., Mrs. 1858, 1952
Hammond, Mason 12509
Hammond, Peter 7860
Hammond, Phillip E. 9886, 11798, 17351, 17777
Hamnett, Ian 19093
Han, Sang En 12889
Hancock, Barbara 18752
Hand, Irving 7580
Hand, James Edward 1693
Handcock, Thomas andNoel, Conrad le Despencer Roden 11033
Handlin, Mary F. 5688
Handlin, Oscar 5017, 5688, 6044, 6481, 7319, 7581
Handspicker, Meredith B. 12178,

14055
Handy, Robert T. 6174, 6323, 7097, 7582, 9887, 11325, 11876, 12179, 17352, 18157
Haney, David 13221
Hanley, Carl 7320
Hanley, Thomas O. 6324
Hanna, Judith L. 15841
Hanna, William 255, 287, 288
Hanna, William J. 15841
Hannaford, William P. 18861
Hannan, Jerome D. 4218
Hannerz, Ulf 11326, 15484
Hansberry, Lorraine 7583
Hansell, George H. 1694
Hansen, Marcus L. 4731
Hansen, Marcus Lee 4922, 6175
Hansen, William G. 9888
Hanson, Allen 16600, 17353
Hanson, Herbert 6325
Hanson, Howland 2607
Hanson, P. J. 17354
Hapgood, Hutchins 1859
Hapke, William R. 7584
Harahap, Basyral Hamidy 18158
Harbour, J. L. 1140
Harbrecht, John J. 3962
Harder, Leland 6176, 9085, 9086, 9889
Harding, Vincent 9087, 10373, 16601
Hardisty, Margaret 10374
Hardoy, Jorge E. 12180
Hardwick, Robert Sterling 13222
Hardy, Edward R. 4923
Hardy, Keir 3236
Hare, R. M. 8453
Hare, Richard 11327
Hargleroad, Bobbi Wells 11799, 12890, 13560, 13891, 14668, 15485
Hargraves, J. Archie 5790, 6304, 7098, 7321, 7585, 8169, 8170, 8454, 8749, 8750, 9088, 9890, 10863, 10864, 11328
Hargreaves, J. Robert 4057
Hargrove, Barbara Watts 16602, 16603
Hargrove, Beverly Milton 16244
Häring, Bernhard 7586
Harkness, Georgia 3327, 7099, 9089
Harlan, Howard H. 4526
Härle, Wilfried 18517
Harlow, Ralph Volney 4835
Harlow, Samuel Ralph 2801
Harman, Jim 16245
Harman, Robert 15072
Harmel, Léon 4527
Harmon, John J. 8751, 9090, 9091, 9891, 9892, 10865
Harmon, Richard 10866, 13223
Harms, John W. 6681
Harmsel, Henrietta 16979
Harnack, Adolph 2142
Harney, Andy Leon 13561
Harp, H. Richard 12181
Harper, Charles 9893
Harper, Ernest Bouldin 4086, 7587
Harper, Eugenia 989
Harper, F. Nile 7861, 11243
Harper, L. Alexander 11329
Harper, Michael 12891
Harper, William A. 10375
Harrell, Irene Burk 14646
Harrell, Rob 18518
Harrelson, Walter 7100
Harriet Fisher: or, The Missionary at Home 195
Harrington, Charles W. 5376
Harrington, Edward T. 5293
Harrington, Janette T. 6482, 9463, 9894, 9895
Harrington, Jeremiah C. 3766, 3767
Harrington, Michael 7862, 7863, 8455, 15762, 18159
Harrington, W. Frank 13224
Harris, Alex 18160

Harris, Barbara C. 17778
Harris, C. C. 9896
Harris, Catherine R. 10867
Harris, Ethel Ramsey 4614
Harris, Frank J. 13892
Harris, G. T. 15073
Harris, George 1472
Harris, Hugh H. 2802
Harris, James Henry 17355, 18161, 19094
Harris, James R. 11330
Harris, Jamie 15842
Harris, Jeffrey 13562, 14669, 15843
Harris, John 152, 153
Harris, John F. 18162
Harris, M. A. 10868
Harris, Richard Earl 6483
Harris, Samuel 300
Harris, Samuel Smith 699, 700, 754
Harris, Sara 6326
Harris, Sidney 19095
Harris, Sydney 12510
Harrison, Barbara 18163
Harrison, Bennett 16121
Harrison, Beverly W. 17779
Harrison, D. Tommy 16980
Harrison, Ernest W. 9897
Harrison, Gordon W. 18164
Harrison, Ira E. 8456, 9464, 9898, 10376, 10377, 10378
Harrison, Jonathan Baxter 635, 636, 791
Harrison, M. E. 18519
Harrison, Paul 7864, 17356
Harrison, Paul M. 7588, 10379
Harrison, Peter 13029
Harrison, R. K. 9465
Harrison, Shelby M. 4043
Harrison, William Pope 930
Harrod, H. 9899
Harrod, Howard L. 10869
Harrold, Howard 11331
Harrower, Charles S. 1302
Hart, Henry Martin 12282
Hart, Jim 17357, 18034, 18165, 18520
Hart, Mary F. B. 13893
Hart, Philip S. 16118
Hart, William Coolidge 7589
Harte, Thomas J. 5279, 6045, 6074
Hartigan, Richard Shelly 10870
Hartley, Ben 10380
Hartley, Isaac Smithson 682
Hartley, Loyde H. 16604, 16981, 18862
Hartley, Richard 931
Hartley, Robert Milham 682
Hartman, Edward Randolph 2319
Hartman, Orval C. 8457
Hartmann, Edward George 5689
Hartshorne, Hugh 4219, 4220
Hartt, Mary Bronson 1637
Hartt, Rollin Lynde 2143
Hartzell, J. C. 614
Hartzell, Wesley 11332
Harvard University, Divinity School 9092
Harvey, Anthony 18863
Harvey, David 12892, 17358
Harvey, J. D. 10381
Harvey, John 18166
Harvey, Nick 11800
Harvey, Pharis 10871, 14259
Harvey, Van A. 10382
Harwell, Jack V. 8752
Haselden, Kyle 7590, 8753
Haskell, S. N. 722
Haskin, Frederic Jennings 2706
Haslam, David 15337
Hassan, Riaz 10872, 11801
Hasse, John 14260
Hassinger, Edward W. 13392, 15074
Hastings, Adrian 13894, 18167
Hastings, Thomas 480
Hatch, Al 19072

Hatcher, Harold O. 4615
Hatcher, William E. 2229
Hatt, Paul K. 7101
Hatton, George 1057
Hauck, Friedrich 3328
Hauerwas, Stanley 17780, 18864
Haughey, John C. 14261, 15075
Hauglin, Otto 11802
Haunca, Hilario 17359
Hauser, Philip M. 7591
Hauser, Richard 11333
Hausknecht, Murray 8458
Hausknecht, Phil 12511
Haven, Gilbert 510
Haven, Joseph 350
Haven, William I. 1388
Haverlandt, Ronald Otto 11803
Haw, George 2079
Hawes, Jospeh M. 12182
Hawke, Gwendolyn 13225
Hawkins, M. Elizabeth 18521
Hawkins, Peter S. 17781
Hawkins, Richard T. 18522
Hawley, Amos H. 5018, 5907, 7743, 7744, 10873
Haworth, Lawrence 8754
Hawthorne, Marion O. 3511
Hawthorne, Nathaniel 154
Hay, Donald A. 18865
Hay, H. Clinton 2230
Hay, John 701
Hayden, Edwin V. 19281
Hayes, Frank L. 4058
Hayes, John 16246
Hayes, John M. 5019, 6327, 8755
Hayes, Patrick 10094
Hayes, Ronald C. 10874
Hayes, Ruth 15873
Hayes, Sylda 14262
Hayghe, Howard V. 19347
Hayne, Coe 4059
Hayne, Emory J. 839
Haynes, George Edmund 3700
Haynes, Mary Stoors 1058
Haynes, Nathaniel Smith 2878
Haynes, Titus 14670
Hays, Jane 15076
Hays, John B. 6705
Hays, Samuel P. 9093
Hazard, David M. 15486
Hazelden Foundation 18168
Hazelrigg, Lawrence 11804
He Couldn't Say No 9900
Heacock, Jack D. 16247
Head, Edward D. 7102
Headlam, Arthur Cayley 3135, 3833
Headlam, Stewart Duckworth 552, 1141, 2144, 2231, 8899, 11033, 15178
Heald, Ben F. 19295
Heald, Morrell 11805
Heale, M. J. 10875, 12183, 12893, 13895
Healey, John 7322
Healey, Joseph G. 16605
Health Care: Ethical 18523
Healy, James 9901
Hear the Cry of Jerusalem: A National Urban Pastoral Statement 14671
Heartside: A Storefront Congregation 18524
Heasman, Kathleen 8459, 9466, 9902
Heath, Susan 17360
Heaton, George D. 6484
Heavens Above 8756
Hecht, James L. 12512
Heck, Earl C. 3610
Heck, Terry 18866
Heckman, Leon 7103
Hedges, Chris 19096
Hedges, Marion Hawthorne 3888
Hedgley, David Rice 4441
Hedley, George P. 4370, 5476
Hedlund, Roger E. 14263, 18169
Heehan, Edward F. 12513
Heeney, Brian 10876

Heer, Friedrich 6682
Heermance, Edgar L. 3768
Hefley, James C. 10877, 10878, 13896
Hefley, Marti 13896
Hefner, Hugh 8766
Hefner, Philip J. 9903, 10879, 10880, 14264
Hegeman, J. Winthrop 1638
Hegy, Pierre 16982
Heidebrecht, Paul Henry 18867
Heideman, Eugene P. 10383
Heider, David A. 11334
Heifetz, Julie Ann 16983
Heilfurth, Gerhard 6485
Heilman, Samuel C. 13563, 13897
Heim, David 17782, 17783
Heimsath, Charles N. 4836
Heine, Karl 8305
Heinecken, Martin J. 16984
Heinemeier, John 18525
Heise, Kenan 10881, 19267
Heiskell, Andrew 11335
Heitmann, Ludwig 2707
Heitzer, Horstwalter 16606
Heitzman, Anthony E. 11806
Helen F. Clark Mission 1750
Helfgot, Joseph 13226
Hell is a City 7323
Heller, Mildred O. 11807
Hellman, Ellen 5690
Hellweg, H. 4291
Hellwig, Randolph B. 9095
Helly, Walter 13564
Helmer, John 12894
Helmreich, Theodore 6880
Helms, Edgar James 1303, 1695, 2409, 3136, 3237, 3834, 3963, 4442
Helms, Pauline 2952
Hemenway, Joan 9467
Hemmeter, H. B. 5583
Hempel, Joel R. 18170
Hemphill, Martha Locke 12895
Hemstreet, Charles 1996
Henderson, Arthur 2708
Henderson, Charles Richmond 723, 1223, 1473, 1546, 1547, 1639, 1696, 1697, 1953, 2320, 2321, 2322, 2608, 2879
Henderson, Frank Martin 14265
Henderson, John 8757
Henderson, Mary 7112
Hendrick, John R. 11336
Hendrick, Polly S. 12371
Hendricks, Charles E. 16985
Hendricks, Robert J. 4292
Hendrickse, Clarry 16607
Hendrik, Kraemer 6881
Hengel, Martin 13227
Hengsbach, Friedhelm 15487, 16248, 16249
Henkelman, Ervin F. 17361
Hennes, Gerhard 7495, 7854
Hennig, Martin 1887, 2028, 2609
Hennock, E. P. 15844
Henretta, James 15077
Henrici, Peter 16608
Henricksen, Glenn Irving 14672
Henriot, Peter 12514, 15488
Henry Ward Beecher's Church 429
Henry, Antonin Marcel 8758
Henry, Caleb Sprague 371
Henry, Carl F. H. 5096
Henry, David B. 16986
Henry, Edward L. 11808
Henry, François 4588
Henry, H. T. 3611
Henry, Helga Bender 6683
Henry, John R. 1954, 2610, 3001, 9904
Henry, Pierre 4527
Henry, W. E. 2880
Henslin, James M. 19215
Henson, Herbert Hensley 1904
Henthorne, Mary Evangela 4221
Hentsch, Robert 6328

Herb, Carol Marie 11337
Herberg, Will 5908, 5909, 6177, 6178, 6684, 7104, 7865, 12250
Herbers, John 17784
Herbert, A. G. 4443
Herbert, Jerry Scott 14673
Herbert, Marjorie M. 9468
Herbst, Jurgen 8171
Hercher, Uri D. 13898
Herder-Korrespondenz 5477
Herman, Nancy J. 16987
Hermann, Franz 4616
Hermann, Mildred M. 9469, 9905
Hermanowicz, Ryszard 12896
Hernandez, Joseph 7592
Herndon, Emily 1142
Herntrich, Volkmar 10882
Heron, T. M. 3238, 5097, 5177, 5377, 7324
Héroux, Omer 3137
Herrick, Robert P. 1955
Herring, Hubert C. 2881, 3769, 3770, 3771
Herrmann, Wilhelm 2142
Herron, George D. 1059, 1060, 1143, 1144, 1224, 1304, 1389, 1698
Hersey, April 11338
Hershberger, Guy Franklin 7325
Herskovits, Melville J. 3889, 4444, 4617, 4732, 5020, 5691
Hertell, E. Sinclair 4924
Hertz, Karl H. 7105, 8172, 8460, 10384, 10385, 11809, 13228
Hertzberg, Steven 14674
Hertzler, J. O. 4445, 5478
Hertzler, Laurel Schmidt 18868, 19097
Herzog, F. 10883
Hess, John Daniel 14266
Hessel, Dieter T. 11810, 12184, 12515, 13565, 14675, 15078, 15489, 16250, 16609, 18526
Hesselgrave, David J. 14676, 15490
Hessler, Hans W. 14677
Hester, John 11811
Hetico, Robert P. 12516
Heutgren, Arland J. 16988
Hevia Cangas, Fernando 8173
Hewat, Elizabeth G. K. 6685
Hewitt, Abram Stevens 594
Hewitt, John H. 17785
Hewitt, W. E. 18171
Hey, God, Hooray! 11812
Heyhoe, Albert 1808
Heymann, Michel 1548
Heywood, Jean S. 9094
Hibbert, Christopher 18527
Hibbs, Mary Ellen 6882, 6883, 7326
Hickey, John V. 7866, 10386
Hickman, M. 9906
Hiebert, Paul G. 16989, 18172
Hiemstra, John 17786
Higgins, George 16893
Higgins, George G. 6661, 6884, 7327, 8759, 11813, 17787, 17788
Higgins, Katherine 12290
High Cost of Housing 14267
High, David Gilbert 17362
Higham, John 6686, 7106, 7328
Highmore, Anthony 15, 72
Hilfiker, Warren 4925
Hill, Clifford S. 7329, 8760, 11339, 12185, 12186, 12187, 13899, 15491
Hill, David Jayne 884
Hill, Edgar P. 2611
Hill, Edward V. 13229, 15845, 18173
Hill, Hamilton Andrews 990
Hill, John Clark 1640
Hill, Joseph 13230
Hill, Kim Q. 14968
Hill, Marvin S. 13900
Hill, Micaiah 308, 351
Hill, Michael 11340

Hill, Octavia 553, 582
Hill, Robert A. 16610
Hill, Ronald 17049
Hill, Samuel S., Jr. 9907, 11341, 18724
Hill, Walter H. 595
Hill, Wendy 18869
Hillam, Corbin 19098
Hillis, Newell Dwight 1956
Hillman, Arthur 5910, 7107, 7348, 7867, 8174, 8461, 10387
Hillquit, Morris 14891
Hillquitt, Morris 2323
Hiltner, Seward 5707, 7108, 7593, 9470, 9908
Hilton, Bruce 8761
Hilton, J. D. 1549
Hilton, Marie 1549
Hinckley, Frederic A. 2612
Hindman, Tom 16611
Hindus, Milton 11342
Hine, Leland D. 9096, 9909
Hine, Robert V. 6486
Hine, Virginia H. 11780
Hines, John E. 10388
Hines, Samuel George 15492
Hinman, George W. 2709, 3890
Hinrichs, Donald W. 13231
Hinrichsen, Carl C. 8762
Hinsberg, Thomas F. 14268
Hinshaw, George R. 5280
Hinson, E. Glenn 10389, 11814, 13901, 14678
Hinton, Keith 17363
Hinton, Leonard O. 16251
Hints Designed to Aid Christians in Their Efforts to Convert Men to God 116
Hirota, Filo 16532, 16612
Hirsch, Richard 8175, 9471
Hirschfield, Robert 16613, 16990, 17789, 18174, 18528
Hirschon, Renée B. 16614
Hirschson, Louis M. 6487
Hirshfield, Ruth Bacon 13232
Hispanic-Americans: the "New People 12897
História da ACO: fidelidade e compromisso na classe operária 18175
Historical Records Survey, California 4926, 4927, 5021
Historical Records Survey, District of Columbia 4837
Historical Records Survey, Illinois 5098
Historical Records Survey, Louisiana 5022, 5023
Historical Records Survey, Michigan 4928, 4929, 4930, 4931, 5024, 5025, 5099
Historical Records Survey, New Jersey 4932, 4933, 4934, 5026, 5027, 5028
Historical Records Survey, New York City 4838, 4935, 4936, 4937, 4938, 4939, 4940, 5029, 5100
Historical Records Survey, Virginia 4941
History 2922
Hitchcock, James 14269
Hitchcock, Lucy V. 18870
Hitchcock, Roswell D. 615
Hitt, Russell T. 14270
Hitti, Philip Khuri 12898
Ho, Esther Mohler 9910
Hoadley, James A. 885
Hoadley, Walter E. 12188
Hobart, C. W. 8763
Hobart, George H. 4144, 4145, 4618, 4619, 4733
Hobart, John Henry 29, 49, 61
Hobbing, U. G. 2232
Hobbs, S. H., Jr. 5753
Hobden, Sheila M. 12899
Hoben, Allan 2613, 2614, 2879, 3239
Hobsbawm, Eric J. 9097
Hobson, John Atkinson 3412,

4146
Hochbaum, Jerry 11343
Hock, Douglas A 18176
Hocking, Michael 7868, 14271
Hocking, William John 1751
Hodder, Edwin 840
Hodgen, Margaret 3240
Hodges, Frank 3772
Hodges, George 1145, 1146, 1305, 1474, 1475, 1476, 1641, 1975, 2080, 2513, 2514, 2882, 13929
Hodges, Jubal 281
Hodges, Leroy 2615
Hodgin, W. 10390
Hodgkin, J. E. 3073
Hodson, Alice Lucy 2324
Hodzi, C. 16998
Hoeben, Henry C. 15079
Hoefnagels, Harry 9098
Hoehl, Lockwood 15493
Hoehler, Judith L. 10391
Hoehn, Richard A. 16615
Hoekendijk, J. C. 9099
Hoekendijk, Johannes C. 5911, 5912, 15080
Hoekstra, Wim 18529
Hoellein, Ronald R. 15846
Hoenig, Sidney B. 14679
Hoffecker, Carol E. 12900
Hoffer, Eric 6046
Hoffman, Alfred 5178
Hoffman, Conrad, Jr. 5030
Hoffman, Daniel N. 18679
Hoffman, Dick 8764
Hoffman, Douglas R. 15081
Hoffman, Gerhard 13902, 14680
Hoffman, Harold 9472
Hoffman, J. W. 9911
Hoffman, James W. 6885, 8176, 9473, 12189
Hoffman, Nicholas von 8462, 8765
Hoffman, Pam 18530
Hoffman, R. W. 10884
Hoffmann, Ingeborg 16991
Höffner, Joseph 5584, 8177
Hoffsis, Larry A. 17790
Hofstader, Richard 6687
Hofstaetter, Peter 6179
Hogan, David John 17364
Hogan, J. Philip 13903
Hogan, John P. 14272
Hogan, Trevor 18273
Hoge, Dean R. 12901, 13904, 14681, 14682, 15007, 15082, 16665, 18871
Hoggart, Richard 7109
Hoglund, Gunnar 8463
Hogrefe, Russell 6535
Hogren, Chuck 14560
Hogue, R. W. 3002, 3612
Hoguet, Henry L. 886
Hohenberg, P. M. 17365
Hoisington, R. Michael 17366
Hoke, Steve 19127
Holaind, René 841, 1061, 1752
Holbrook, Z. Swift 1390
Holcombe, Steve P. 872
Holden, Arthur C. 3413, 9474
Holden, Carol Wisniewski 18351
Holden, Tony 15083, 16992, 18531
Hole, Samuel Reynolds 1306
Holifield, E. B. 16616
Holladay, J. Douglas 16252
Holland, Clifton L. 13233
Holland, Darrell 11344
Holland, Henry Scott 3127, 3354
Holland, James S. 2616
Holland, Joe 15488, 16993, 17649
Hollenbach, David 16994
Hollenwenger, Walter J. 10885
Holler, S. 15847
Holli, Melvin G. 11345, 14293, 15858
Holliday, Carl 3773
Hollifield, Jeannie 16444
Hollinger, Denis 18532

Hollinghead, August B. 8284
Hollingshead, George G. 3613
Hollingsworth, William G. 17367
Hollis, Christopher 8178
Hollis, Harry 13234
Hollister, J. Elliott 18177
Hollister, Robert M. 17125
Hollister, William H. 8179, 9475
Holloway, Louise 10886
Hollowell, Martha 19099
Hollyday, Joyce 15084, 15494, 18533
Holman, Bob 15848, 18178
Holman, C. T. 4147
Holman, Robert 14683
Holmes, A. B. 3614
Holmes, Ann 12902
Holmes, Douglas Reginald 15849
Holmes, J. A. 4620
Holmes, John Haynes 2325, 2410, 2710, 3414, 3512, 4371
Holmes, Thomas 2145
Holmes, Urban T. 13905, 14684
Holmes, William A. 10887
Holstead, Roland Edward 16253
Holt, Anne 4446, 4528
Holt, Arthur E. 3415, 3513, 3514, 3615, 3617, 3835, 3891, 3964, 4148, 4149, 4222, 4293, 4372, 4447, 4621, 4622, 4734, 4735, 4839, 17719
Holt, Bill 16444
Holt, Harold 3892, 4736
Holt, John Bradshaw 4942
Holt, Raymond V. 6180
Holt, William 8464
Holthaus, H. Lee 16995, 16996, 18179
Holton, Susan 17368
Homan, Roger 17791
Hombs, Mary Ellen 16617
Home Field 240
Home Missionary Society of the City of Philadelphia 4448
Home Missions Council 2803, 3416, 4060, 4294, 4623, 4840, 5913
Homeless 16997
Homeless Deaths Triple, March Remembers: Permanent Service Demanded By Clergy 18180
Homer, Marion 6488, 6489
Homewood, Hugh W. 8465
Homiletic Review 567
Homrichhausen, Christian 13566
Honan, Park 8766
Honeycutt, Roy L. 16618
Honeywell, Charles L. 17792
Hong Kong Christian Industrial Committee 11815
Hong, Chi-young 14273, 14685
Hong, Edna H. 10392
Hong, Howard V. 10392
Hong, Lawrence K. 14274
Honorio, Cirilo S. 3701
Honsby-Smith, Michael P. 15085
Hood, Elizabeth 9476
Hood, Thomas C. 13154
Hoogewind, Allen Jay 14686
Hook, H. Phillip. 11816
Hooker, Elizabeth R. 3893
Hooker, Roger 17793, 18872
Hoover, Dwight W. 19216
Hoover, J. Edgar 9100, 10393
Hoover, Robert C. 6688, 7869, 8180
Hoover, S. L. 1905
Hoover, Stewart M. 18534
Hope, Anne 16998
Hope, Glenda 17794, 18181, 18182, 18787, 18873
Hope, Marjorie 16999, 17369
Hopewell, James F. 9912, 16254, 16619, 17000, 17001, 18183
Hopkins, C. H. G. 5914
Hopkins, Charles Howard 4737, 4943, 5101, 6047, 6886, 14088

Hopkins, Stephen 17370
Hopkinson, Alfred Stephan 8466
Hopler, Marcia 18874
Hopler, Thomas 13567, 15850
Hore, Kathleen 3003
Horlick, Allan Stanley 13568
Horn, Frank S. 6689
Horne, Charles Silvester 2081
Horne, Raymond Wright 13906
Horowitz, Helen Lefkowitz 13907
Horsman, O. C. 2617
Horton, Anne L. 18535
Horton, Isabella 1957, 2082
Horton, Loren N. 14275
Horton, Robert F. 1391
Horvath, William J. 11817
Horwich, Bernard 4841
Horwill, Herbert W. 3074
Horwitt, Sanford D. 18875, 18903
Hoshor, John 4529
Hostetler, Harriet 6690
Hostetler, Hugh 5791, 6048
Hostetler, Virginia 16620
Hostetter, Donald A. 14687
Hostetter, Richard 13908, 19313
Hotchkiss, Wesley Akin 5692, 5915, 5926, 6329
Hott, J. W. 1147
Houck, John W. 16467, 16621, 17002, 17371
Houdijk, Krien 12903
Hough, Joseph C. 10888, 12190, 12517, 14276
Hough, Lynn Harold 3417
Hough, Robert L. 5916
Hough, Rolf 14725
Hough, W. W. 1928
Houghtby, Natalie 19100
Houghton, Amory 10889
Houghton, Graham 16255, 16256
Houghton, Louise Seymour 1062, 1307, 1809
Hougland, James G. 13235, 15086, 15495
Hoult, Thomas Ford 5917, 7330
Hourani, A. H. 11818
House Church 11819
House of Refuge 430
House, Jay Wesley 16622
House, Loren G., Jr. 12518
Houser, George M. 14688
Houser, Susie A. 3702
Houses and People 6887
Houseworth-Findlay, J. 17795
Housing for the Aged an Urgent Need 7594
Housing Projects and Protestant Churches 6691
Housing: Rehabilitating the Rainbow 16257
Housley, Kathleen 17796
Houston Metropolitan Ministries, Interfaith Refugee Settlement Committtee 16623
Houston Ordered to Integrate Schools 7595
Houtart, François 6490, 6692, 6693, 6694, 6695, 6696, 6697, 6698, 6888, 6889, 7110, 7111, 7331, 7332, 7333, 7596, 7597, 7598, 7870, 8181, 8182, 8767, 9030, 9101, 9477, 9478, 9479, 9480, 10400, 10890, 10891, 10892, 11346, 12191, 13236
Hovda, Robert W. 11347, 13569, 18876
Hovell, Mark 3075
Hovinen, Elizabeth 13909
How Far Scientific Management Can Be Applied to Religion 2515
How New York's Subways Affect Her Churches 2618
How, Gordon C. 15087
Howard, Ebenezer 1642, 4303, 14225
Howard, Francis W. 1477

Howard, James Merrian 3329
Howard, John R. 9913
Howard, John W. 8768
Howard, Robert W. 11649
Howard, Thomas 11348
Howe, Elizabeth 15851, 15852
Howe, Frederic Clemson 2029, 2619, 2883, 3703
Howe, Irving 13910
Howe, John W 9600
Howe, Leroy T. 18184
Howe, Louise Kapp 14277
Howe, Marvin 19101
Howe, Reuel L. 7599, 8183, 9102
Howe, William 182
Howell, Barbara 16258
Howell, Hazel Wanner 9914
Howell, Leon 12519, 12520, 12904, 14689, 14690, 15496, 15853, 16258, 18185, 18186
Howells, William Dean 724, 755, 932, 1308, 2146
Howerton, James Robert 2711
Howes, Ismene V. 9459
Howes, Robert G. 7600, 7601, 7871, 8184, 8185, 8769, 8770, 9481, 9915, 9916, 10394, 10893, 11349, 11350, 11820
Howitson, Betty 14961
Howlett, Floyd 12521
Hoyer, H. Conrad 7602, 8186, 8187, 9482, 12192
Hoyes, Herbert 7603
Hoyles, J. Arthur 9483
Hoyt, C. J. 2030
Hoyt, Michael 17003, 17372
Hronek, Mary Linda 6699
Hsieh, Tien-Chiao 12522
Hsu, Ming Chau 18536
Hualde, A. C. 17373
Huang, Edward 10395
Hubbard, George H. 887
Hubbard, Thomas F. 7334
Hubble, Beverley 12523
Huber, Lois V. 9484, 18877
Huber, Milton John, Jr. 5792
Huber, Roger 12193
Huck, Gabe 11347
Huck, V. 10396
Huckstep, Mary 17797
Huddleston, Trevor 12524
Hudnut, Robert K. 12905
Hudson, Cyril E. 4295
Hudson, Norman S. 15497
Hudson, Winthrop S. 6330, 6700, 9485
Huebner, Grover G. 2083
Huegel, John 8836
Huenefeld, John 11821
Huenemann, Edward 15088, 15089
Huey, Don 9917
Huff, E. Eugene 9440
Huffman, D. L. 16624
Huffman, Donald Waldo 12906
Huffman, Jasper Abraham 3965
Huggins, Nathan Irvin 12194
Hughes, Agnes Lockhart 3004
Hughes, Allan J. 12195
Hughes, Dorothea Price 2031
Hughes, Edwin Holt 3515, 3894
Hughes, Fred 3138
Hughes, Hugh Price 906, 933, 991, 1063, 1148, 1309, 1392, 2031, 2166, 9942, 16391, 17019
Hughes, John E. 7335
Hughes, Katherine Price 5378
Hughes, Philip 5281
Hughes, R. 15090
Hughes, Thomas 372, 616, 842
Hughes, W. A. C. 4061, 4449
Hughes, William 1810
Hughley, J. Neal 5693
Hugo, Victor 377
Huldschiner, Robert E. 9486, 9487, 9488, 10397, 10894
Hull, Jerry 15854
Hull, Roger, Jr. 10895, 11822
Hull, Thomas Patrick 15091
Hull, William 568, 1257

Hullum, Everett 18187, 18537
Hulse, Erroll 9918
Hult, Kathryn A. 12525
Hultman, Tami 12548
Human Factor in Industry 4296
Human Values in Planning 9919
Humane Society of the City of New York 26
Hummel, Margaret G. 9103
Hummell, Gert 8771, 18188
Humphrey, Hubert H. 9920
Humphrey, Michael 18189
Humphrey, Norman D. 5191, 5585
Humphrey, W. E. 3616
Hunger 11823
Hunger in America 17374
Hungerford, Edward 431
Hunsicker, Ronald 16625
Hunt, Angela Elwell 18190, 18191, 18538, 19102
Hunt, Chester K. 7604
Hunt, Janet G. 13570, 13911, 14278, 14279, 14691
Hunt, Larry L. 13570, 13911, 14278, 14279, 14691
Hunt, Terrence 12526
Hunt, William Henry 2084, 2233
Hunter, Albert, Jr. 13237
Hunter, Allan Armstrong 4373
Hunter, Floyd 6331
Hunter, James Davison 18192
Hunter, Jim Ernest, Jr. 17798
Hunter, Lea Anne 18539
Hunter, R. V. 1225
Hunter, Robert 3139
Hunting, Eunice 4738
Huntington, Frederic Dan 320, 361, 511, 554, 992, 1064, 4470
Huntington, George 499
Huntington, William Reed 843, 1643
Huntong, Harold Bruce 4738
Huntzinger, Robert 8991
Huotari, Voitto 14280
Hurh, Won Moo 13912
Hurley, Cornelius P. 6701
Hurley, Neil P. 7336, 7337, 7605
Hurley, Timothy 1550
Hurlin, William 535
Hurn, R. W. 13238
Hurst, Antony 17799
Hurst, Charles V. 14281
Hurst, Sam T. 8467
Hurston, Zora 4150
Huskey, Richard 13239
Hussey, Edith 7112
Hussey, M. Edmund 14692
Husslein, Joseph 3076, 3140, 3275, 3330, 4151, 4152, 4944, 5179
Husted, Harold R. 3966
Huston, Sterling W. 16626, 17004
Hutcheson, Maud MacDonald 4739
Hutcheson, Richard G., Jr. 15092
Hutchinson, C. R. 4450
Hutchinson, Edward W. 9489, 9490
Hutchinson, Paul 4223, 7113
Hutchinson, William R. 13571, 13913, 18878
Hutchison, John A. 5031, 6332
Huttenlocker, K. 10896
Hütter, Gottfried 18193
Huxhold, Harry N. 10897
Hwang, Andrew 19103
Hwang, Bernard 14282
Hwang, C. H. 9921
Hyde, C. B. 5102
Hyde, Hal Edward 6181, 6365
Hyde, Mary K. 2147, 2234
Hyde, William DeWitt 1393, 1753
Hyer, Marjorie 13240, 17005
Hyman, Paula E. 18194
Hynes, Michael J. 6333
Hynes, P. W. 2326
Hyre, Meg 19104

Hyslop, J. H. 1065
Hyung-Kyu, Park 17800
I T V 17375
I. M. -- An Appraisal: The Church's Response to the Changing Industrial and Economic Order: The Report of a Working Party Commissioned By the Industrial and Economic Affairs Committee of the Church of England's Board for Social Responsibility 18540
Ichniowski, Thomas 14283
Ide, George B. 213
Idea of Christian Vocation 5918
Idle, Christopher 17801
Idleman, Finis 2948
IDOC, North America, Inc. 11824
Idowu, E. Bolaji 9491
Igarashi, Isaac 8188, 9922
Ihmels, Ludwig 2235
Ikado, Fujio 9923, 10898, 12907
Iles, Robert H. 18879
Iliff School of Theology, Iliff Town and Country Survey 5919
Illich, Ivan 6662, 7338, 10398, 10899, 11825, 12908, 13914
Illinois Committee for Responsible Investment 13572
Ilyin, V. N. 4297
Imes, William Lloyd 4533
Immanuel Woman's Home 4624
Immigration and Missions: A Bird's-Eye View 2411
Immigration Restriction League 1310, 1311
Immigration: Year of Decision 15855
Impact of the American City on the World Scene 7606
In Defense of Violence: Churchmen Willing to Endorse Violence as Means of Achieving Social Justice 10900
In Mathare Valley with the Poorest of the Poor, the Acts of the Council of Youth 15093
In the Beginning 8772
In the Heart of Haight 10399
In the Inner City 7114
In, Myung-Jin 17802
Inagaki, Yoichiro 3516
Incarnation and the Inner City 9924
Incense of Cities 11351
Inchausti, Robert 17376
Independent 235
Individual Work for the Immigrants 2804
Indonesian Committee on Community Organization 12527
Industrial and Social Problems 3241
Industrial Christian Alliance 1644
Industrial Christian Fellowship 3242, 3243, 3244, 3836, 4451, 4740, 4945, 5032, 5180, 5282, 5379, 5479, 17377, 17803
Industrial Christian Fellowship: A Reply to Some Criticism by the Bishop 3245
Industrial Evangelism 4946
Industrial Mission Association 11826, 11827
Industrial Mission Association, Theology Development Group 15498, 16259
Industrial Mission in Hertfordshire and Bedfordshire 11828
Industrial Missionary Association 1754, 2412
Industrial Missionary Record 1755
Industrial Missions Aid Society

1906
Industrial Relations Seventy Years after Rerum Novarum 8189, 8468
Industrial Team Service 9492
Infiltrating City Hall 9493
Inge, W. R. 3774, 4062, 4063
Inglis, Kenneth Stanley 7339, 8773
Ingram, Kenneth 4530
Ingram, Mary 9104
Inman, Lee Bertram 5793
Inner City 9925
Inner City Mission Church 10901
Inner City Protestant Parish 6491
Inner City Protestant Parish [Cleveland, Ohio] 8469
Inner City: A Newsletter for Lutherans 9105
Inner Mission Society of Brooklyn and Vicinity 3331
Inner Mission Work 4298
Inner-City Church Planning 8190
Innerchurch Social Mission: Forming Interreligious Committee Against Poverty 9926
Innere Mission im evangelischen Deutschland 2148
Inside City Church 2236
Insko, C. Arthur 11265
Institut für Kirchliche Sozialforschung (Austria) 13241, 13915
Institute for the Study of Contemporary Problems in the Social Order 9106
Institute for Theological Encounter with Science and Technology [ITEST] 13242
Institute for Urban Ministries 12196
Institute of Global Urban Studies 17804
Institute of Industrial and Commercial Ministries, Inc. 11829
Institute of Social and Religious Research 4374
Institute on the Church in Urban-Industrial Society [ICUIS] 9927, 11830, 12909, 13243, 13244, 13573, 13916, 13917, 13918, 13919, 13920, 14284, 14285, 17378, 17805
Institutional Church in New York 1478
Instituto Fe y Secularidad 13574
Inter-Denominational Congress, Cincinnati 792
Inter-Met 11831
Inter-Religious Center for Urban Affairs [ICUA] 9928
Inter-Religious Committee for the Los Angeles Region Goals Project 7607
Inter-Religious Task Force for Social Analysis 15094
Inter-Seminary Urban-Industrial Institute 12197
Interchurch Conference of City Workers 3141
Interchurch Federation of Philadelphia 2805
Interchurch Trade and Industry Mission in Australia and New Zealand 8470, 11352, 12910, 13575, 13576
Interchurch World Movement of North America, Commission of Inquiry 3246, 3332
Interchurch World Movement of North America, Home Missions Department, Survey Department 3247
Interdenominational Committee for Industrial Mission on the

Witwatersrand 12911
Interdenominational Conference on Work with New Americans 4531
Interfaith Action for Economic Justice 15499
Interfaith Center on Corporate Responsibility [ICCR] 13577, 13921, 16260
Interfaith Coalition on Energy 16261
Interfaith Committee on Social Responsibility in Investments 12912
Interfaith Economic Crisis Organization Network (I/ECON) 19329
Interfaith Hunger Coalition of Southern California 18880
Interfaith Mission Service, Inc., a Coalition of the Religious Community in Huntsville, AL. 12528
International Church Conference of Urban Pastors, Manila, 1962 8774
International Conference of Settlements 3418
International Congregational Council 1066
International Congress on Religion, Architecture and Visual Arts 10400
International Corporate Responsibility and the Church - - Selected Abstracts 12913
International Council of Religious Education 4532, 4842, 5033, 5103
International Council of Religious Education, Conference on Religious Research, Sub Committee II 5283
International Federation of Protestant Workers' Associations 6182
International Missionary Council, the Jerusalem Conference, March 24 - April 8, 1928 3895
International Movement of Catholic Students, Asian Secretariat 15095
International Social Institute, Geneva 4064
International Union of Gospel Missions 11832, 17806, 18881
Internship for Clergymen in Urban Ministry [CIP] 9929
Interreligious Foundation for Community Organization 12198
Interview with Chief Rocky Pomerana, Miami Beach, Florida, Police Department 12914
Investing Church Funds for Maximum Social Impact 11833
Investment Policy Guidelines 12199
Ipema, William 15096
Ireland, John 793
Iremonger, F. A. 5694
Ironsides, H. A. 4741
Irvine, Gordon P. 16262
Irvine, Ingram N. W. 2884, 5433
Irwin, Joseph 14212
Irwin, Leonard G. 9107, 10401, 10902, 10903, 11353, 11354, 11355, 11356
Is Christ in the Rented Pew 2806
Is Your Church Burning 10904
Isambert, François André 6334, 7340, 8191
Isasi-Píaz, Ada María 18541
Ishii, Kenji 17807
Ishimaru, Minoru 7341, 13578
Islamic City 16627

Israel, C. Wesley 8192
It Still Takes the Gospel 9930
Ito, Karen Lee 14693
Iverson, William 10475, 15097
Ives, Connie L. 5034
Iwao, Munakata 13922
Iyer, R. 16263
Izarny, R. d' 7342, 8471
Jable, J. Thomas 13245
Jablonowski, Harry W. 18195
Jack, Homer 5920, 12529
Jackson, Alice 2267
Jackson, Bruce W. 18196
Jackson, Dave 15856, 18197, 18991, 19105, 19276, 19282
Jackson, Douglas 7343
Jackson, George 3517
Jackson, Jesse 10421, 10631, 10905, 16865, 17286, 17918
Jackson, John L. 2237
Jackson, Joseph Harrison 19284, 19288
Jackson, K. Logan 18542
Jackson, Kenneth T. 10402, 17379
Jackson, Lewis Evans 596
Jackson, Luther P. 4625
Jackson, M. J. 8193, 9494
Jackson, Mance 11834
Jackson, Maurice 16472
Jackson, Michael 9116
Jackson, Michael E. 18543
Jackson, Neta 18197, 19105, 19276
Jackson, P. 17006
Jackson, Patrick 18544
Jackson, R. M. 13862
Jackson, Samuel M. 1312
Jackson, Thomas 3994
Jacob, Edgar 993
Jacob, Ernest 5181
Jacob, Jeffrey C. 18056
Jacobi, Peter F. 9495
Jacobs, Clarence 13246
Jacobs, Clarence C. 12200
Jacobs, Claude 15863
Jacobs, Jane 8194, 11357, 17007, 17982, 18071
Jacobs, Leo 3419
Jacobs, Robert P. 13923
Jacobs-Wessels, W. 7872
Jacobson, Elden 8320, 12201, 12266
Jacobson, Philip 7873
Jacoby, George Paul 5035
Jacquart, Joanne 17008
Jacques, André 17808
Jacquet, Constant H., Jr. 7125, 8775, 19258
Jacquet, Joseph 16264
Jaech, Richard E. 16265
Jaekel, Blaire 2620
Jaekle, Charles A. 10269
Jahn, Christoph 17380
Jahrbuch der Berliner Stadtmission 934
Jakobovits, Immanuel 13247
James, Charles Thomas 134
James, Eric 10906, 17009, 17381
James, F. J. 2085
James, Gilbert 9931, 10403, 10907
James, Henry, Sr. 256
James, J. W. 4224, 4225
James, M. Stephen 3420
James, P. 8776
James, Paul S. 9496, 10404
James, Samuel M. 17010
James, Stanley Bloomfield 4843
James, William 1699, 1860, 2149, 4482
Jameson, Anna, Mrs. 309
Jameson, Frank 17930
Jameson, Kenneth P. 16783
Jameson, Samuel Haig 4153
Jameson, Vic 11358
Jamieson, Edward 9108
Jamieson, Robert G. 13579, 13924
Jamison, Gerald E. 13192

Jamison, Leland 8195
Jane Addams 4452
Janeway, John L 11359
Janik, Allan 12915
Janis, Ralph 12530, 14694
Janowitz, Morris 6183, 15268
Janowsky, Oscar 5104, 5695, 6702, 9109
Jansen, Anton 11360
Jansen, William 6335
Janssen, Henk 17382
Janssen, Lawrence H. 6492, 6703, 6882, 6890, 8196, 8472, 8473, 8777, 8778, 8779, 9110, 10908
Jaramillo, Esteban 8780
Jarrell, Charles C. 3518
Jarvis, Peter 14669
Jarvis, Sally Melcher 10909
Jasper, John 728, 2229, 4526, 14950
Jayakar, Samuel 6184
Jeanneret, Charles Edward 3621
Jefferson, Charles E. 2032, 2413
Jefferson, Kinmoth W. 13580, 13581, 13925, 14695, 15098, 15099, 15100, 15101, 15102, 17488, 18545, 18882
Jefferson, Thomas 3967, 4372, 8618, 9151, 11927, 13441
Jeffersonian View of Cities 3967
Jefferys, William Hamilton 3421
Jeffrey, E. M. C. 12531
Jeffrey, Kirk 12532
Jehu-Appiah, Jerisdan 16266
Jenkins, David E. 15103
Jenkins, J. Craig 14286, 16628
Jenkins, Karen 18546
Jenkins, Keith 17011
Jenkins, Lorna 18265
Jenkins, Robin 11361
Jenkins, Shirley 17383
Jenkins, T. J. 1226
Jenkinson, Charles 6173
Jenks, Jeremiah Whipple 2238
Jenne, Ulrich 13926
Jenner, Brian 17809
Jenness, Mary 4533
Jennings, Alvin Ray 17384
Jennings, Frank Leonard 6336
Jennings, George 18198
Jennings, James R. 16267
Jennings, William H. 12533
Jensen, Billie Barners 9111
Jensen, Richard J. 12202
Jentz, John 18554
Jentz, John Barkley 14287
Jeremy, David J. 18547
Jeske, R. 10405
Jesuits of the United States and Canada 2327
Jesus Lives in Florida City 18199
Jetter, Hartmut 9497, 11835
Jewett, E. Melvin 8474, 9498
Jewett, Paul N. 8197
Jewish Agricultural and Industrial Aid Society 1756
Jewish Labor Committee and the Anti-Defamation League of B'nai B'rith 6049
Jewish Welfare Board 3519
Jewish Work 5105
Jick, Leon 10406, 12916
Jiménez Carvajal, Jorge 16629
Jimenez Suarez, Jesus Maria 9112
Jimmerson, Robin Leroy 16630
Jitodai, Ted T. 9113
Johannes, Harald 11362
Johansen-Berg, John 16268
John Paul II, Pope 15857, 16100, 16179, 16210, 16237, 16269, 16359, 16453, 16621, 16657, 16681, 16815, 17012, 17631, 18548, 19348
John Swinton's Paper 683
John XXIII, Pope 8198, 8759, 9378, 9692, 9978, 16249
John, A. J. 17385
John, Alexander D. 16270
John, Macklin E. 6130
Johns, John 4446

Johns, R. Elizabeth 9499
Johnson, Ben Campbell 16631
Johnson, Benton 8199, 11798, 17013
Johnson, Beverly 10449
Johnson, Bruce D. 8200
Johnson, C. Oscar 5956
Johnson, Charles S. 4534, 5284, 5594
Johnson, Darlington Gyeladi 17810
Johnson, David James 17386
Johnson, Douglas W. 9114, 9500, 9501, 9502, 9932, 11363, 11688, 12534, 13248, 13582, 14696, 14967, 15500, 16271, 16632, 18200
Johnson, Eric D. 14697
Johnson, F. Ernest 3077, 3102, 3142, 3422, 3423, 3617, 3704, 4065, 4375, 4453, 4947, 6337, 7115
Johnson, George S. 17756
Johnson, Harmon A. 15614
Johnson, Harold L. 7116
Johnson, Harry M. 14698
Johnson, Herrick 500
Johnson, J. Edward 10216
Johnson, James K. 11364
Johnson, James M. 10910
Johnson, James W. 11365
Johnson, John Edgar 935, 2328
Johnson, Joseph K. 4626
Johnson, Lyn 18549
Johnson, Lynn G. 10407
Johnson, Mary Ann 18883
Johnson, Mary Mangum 3248
Johnson, Paul E. 14699
Johnson, Paul G. 19301
Johnson, Paul L. 17387
Johnson, Peter 18550
Johnson, Philip A. 9503
Johnson, Ray E. 17811
Johnson, Reginald A. 8781
Johnson, Ronald 9933, 16633
Johnson, Roy H. 3968, 4154
Johnson, Ruby F. 6493
Johnson, Sally A. 18818, 18819
Johnson, Sherman E. 18201, 19321
Johnson, Stephen D. 16754, 17812, 18709
Johnson, Suzan D. 18202
Johnson, Timothy V. 17813
Johnson, Warren 12535
Johnson, William Eugene 1926
Johnsson, J. W. 5586
Johnston, Arthur P. 17388
Johnston, Earl W. 15501
Johnston, John Wesley 1645
Johnston, R. J. 14173
Johnston, Robert K. 15104
Johnston, Ruby Funchess 6891
Johnstone, Ronald 11366
Joice, Lois M. 11367, 11368, 11369, 11836, 11837, 11838, 11839
Joint Office for Urban Minsitry [JOUM] 10911
Joint Strategy and Action Committee [JSAC] 9115, 11370, 11371, 12536, 13249, 13250, 13251, 16272
Joint Strategy and Action Committee [JSAC], Strategy/Screening Task Force for Church Development 13252
Jones, A. Jase 11372
Jones, Absalom 9, 2922, 17131
Jones, Angela 18884
Jones, Beatrice 14288
Jones, Buck 18203
Jones, Carmel 14700
Jones, Charles C. 191
Jones, Charles E. 13253
Jones, Chris 17014
Jones, David C. 14289
Jones, David L. 17368
Jones, Dean C. 19349

Jones, Dionne J. 14290
Jones, Donald G. 14291, 16273
Jones, E. Stanley 4627, 5285
Jones, Edgar DeWitt 3249
Jones, Emrys 7874, 9504
Jones, Ezra Earl 10912, 12537, 13254, 13583, 13927, 13928, 14292, 14503, 17614
Jones, George Curtis 12917
Jones, Grace 5284
Jones, Henry 2414, 4454, 6050, 7344, 7875
Jones, Jacqueline 16274
Jones, James G. 8475
Jones, Jenkin Lloyd 1149, 1313
Jones, Jesse H. 501, 520, 531, 578, 637, 2150
Jones, Kathleen 9934
Jones, Kirk Byron 18885
Jones, L. A. 13349
Jones, Lawrence N. 15105, 16275
Jones, Lloyd 433
Jones, Major J. 12203
Jones, Maldwyn Lee 7876
Jones, Marcus E. 15502
Jones, Margot 16413
Jones, Nathan 15106, 15503, 16276
Jones, Percy 12204
Jones, Peter d'A. 10913, 14293, 15858
Jones, Phillip B. 17814
Jones, R. Francis 6185
Jones, Raymond Julius 4844
Jones, Richard G. 11840, 19255
Jones, Robert C. 4155
Jones, Robert E. 18886
Jones, Ronald W. 13929
Jones, Rufus 9935
Jones, Samuel Milton 1700
Jones, Vaughan 18887
Jones, W. Paul 11373, 11374, 11375
Jones, William A., Jr. 13796, 15107
Jones, William Clossen 18204
Jones, William R. 12918
Jonghe, Eugeen de 15820
Jonker, J. 7117
Jonsson, John N. 17389
Joos, Josef 6051
Joravsky, Ben 18789
Jordan, David Morris, Sr. 7118
Jordan, M. 13255
Jordan, Orvis F. 2621, 3896
Jordan, Patrick 17390
Jordan, Philip D. 14701
Jordan, Robert H. 6704
Jørgensen, Anton Marius 6052
Jorgensen, Richard 9068
Joselit, Jenna Weissman 15859, 16634, 16635, 19106
Joseph, James A. 14294, 15108
Joseph, M. Vincentia 15504
Joseph, P. C. 8782
Joseph, Samuel 2807, 4455
Joshi, R. D. 13584
Joslin, Roy 16277
Journal of Urban History 13256
Jowett, Alfred 9116
Joyce, John T. 17815
Joyce, Jon L. 12205
Joyce, Patrick 15505
Jud, Gerald 10408
Judah, J. Stillson 13257
Judd, Sylvester 214, 257, 258
Judson Memorial Church, New York City 994
Judson, Edward 794, 1227, 1479, 1701, 2151, 3033
Judy, Marvin T. 6705, 8783, 11376, 12538, 12919
Juguet, E. 18205
Juhl, Paulgeorg 17816, 18206
Jukic, Jakov 12920
Jules-Rosette, Bennetta 15860
Juliani, Richard J. 13258, 17817
Jump, Herbert Atchinson 3424
Jung, Loyle Shannon 12921
Junge, Hildegard 5182

Juppenlatz, Morris 11841
Jures, Ernest August 10409
Jurgensen, Barbara 17818
Justice and Beyond Justice: United Church's Council for Christian Social Action 9505
Justice Ministries: Resource for Urban Mission 14702
Justice, John 8201
Juventud Obrero Catolica 13585
Kaan, Frederick Herman 19270
Kaebnick, Herman W. 6053
Kaellis, Eugene 18207
Kaellis, Rhoda 18207
Kafka, Du^san J. 19107
Kaganoff, Nathan M. 7877, 9936, 13930, 13931, 17819
Kagawa, Toyohiko 4535
Kagerer, Paul 2949
Kagiwada, George 10692
Kahn, Alfred J. 9117
Kahn, Hilda R. 10410
Kahn, Masood Ali 18208
Kahn, Si 11842, 16278
Kaiser, Clyde Vernon 4226
Kaiser, Jochen-Christoph 15861
Kaiser, Walter C. 17820, 18888
Kaiser, Ward 8789
Kaldor, Peter 17015, 17391
Kalif, George T. 5921
Kallas, Endel 17392
Kallen, Horace M. 6494
Kaller, Max 3520
Kalshoven, Thomas Nicholas 6495, 8476, 8477, 9506, 9937, 10914, 11377
Kamel, Rachael 19108
Kamp, Henry 14211
Kamphuis, Marie 6706
Kamstra, J. H. 15506
Kane, John J. 5922, 6707
Kane, Margaret 9938, 10411, 12206, 13586, 15507, 18551
Kane, Matt 16279
Kanellos, Nicolás 13932
Kang, Dong Soo 18552
Kang, Wi Jo 17016
Kantor, Harvey 13938
Kantowicz, Edward R. 15508, 16636
Kao, Chun-Ming 15509
Kaplan, Abraham 8784
Kaplan, Harold 8785
Kaplan, Howard M. 11378
Kaplan, Marshall 13543
Kappeler, Edward R. 9507
Kares, Olavi 10412
Karim, David 10915
Karp, Abraham J. 18209
Karpf, Maurice J. 4742
Karrenberg, Friedrich 7345, 11379
Karris, Robert J. 14703
Karsch, Carl G. 10413
Karson, Marc 6054, 13259
Kasdorf, Hans 15510
Kashima, Tetsuden 14295
Kaslow, Andrew J. 15862, 15863, 17393
Kaslow, George W. 8478, 8479, 9508, 9509, 9939, 10916, 11380, 11381, 11382, 11383
Kasson, Frank H. 1551
Kate, Jacob 10414
Kateri 16280
Katlin, Fay 16557
Kato, Hidetoshi 13260
Katz, Daniel 3943
Katz, L. 9940
Katz, Michael 19109
Katz, Shlomo 10415
Katz, William L. 11384
Katznelson, Ira 15864
Kauffman, J. Howard 14296, 16194
Kauffman, John Timothy 18210
Kauffman, Nelson 9118
Kauffman, Russell E. 4456
Kaufman, Jay 8480
Kaufman, Jerome 15851, 15852,

15865
Kaufmann, Moritz 888, 1150
Kavanaugh, James J. 12539
Kavanaugh, John 15866
Kavanaugh, John F. 19217
Kawano, Roland. M. 16281
Kay, Joseph 337
Kayal, Philip M. 13261
Kayser, Conrad 995
Kazemi, Farhad 15511
Kazin, Alfred 6055, 16637
Kdubia, G. K. 12303
Keach, Richard L. 12207
Kean, Charles D. 5380, 8786
Keane, John J. 1067
Kear, Donald L. 13933
Kearns, Francis E. 4845
Kearns, Robert M. 14036
Keating, Barry 8047, 8331
Keats, Ezra Jack 7878
Keats, John 6338
Keck, Leander E. 9510
Keden, Joachim 18193
Kee, Howard Clark 7608
Kee, Ralph 12922, 13587
Keeble, Samuel Edward 1480, 2086, 2239, 2329, 3005, 3425, 5778
Keeler, Ralph W. 2152, 3065, 3250, 3333
Keeley, Richard C. 18071
Keely, Charles B. 13934
Keenan, Boyd 12923
Keenan, Marjorie 16282
Keene, Michael 18553
Kehl, Timothy H. 12924
Kehm, George H. 9941
Kehr, Otto 15109
Kehrer, Günter 10416
Keidel, Levi 10917, 10918
Keighley, Allen 12540
Keighley, Leonard 8787, 10035, 11843
Keightly, D. N. 12925
Keil, Gunter 13935
Keil, Harmut 18554
Keim, Norman 7119
Keir, Harold B. 8788
Keiser, Julian J. 10417
Keiser, Victor Hugo 3521
Kellar, Jeanne 5696
Keller, David A. 13262
Keller, Edward A. 6339
Keller, Hansfried 12763
Keller, Robert 10418
Keller, Rosemary Skinner 15110
Keller, Suzanne 10919
Kellerman, Bill 18889
Kelley, Allen 17017
Kelley, Arleon L. 9511, 10190
Kelley, Dean M. 12541, 14297, 19110
Kelley, Francis Clement 2033
Kelley, John 13263, 14298, 14704
Kelley, Joseph B. 6892
Kelley, M. V. 2885, 4156
Kelley, Richard M. 5923
Kelley, William J. 6496
Kellogg, Arthur P. 2622
Kellogg, John Harvey 11530
Kellogg, Paul 4457
Kelly, George A. 5587
Kelly, James R. 15111
Kelly, Mary Gilbert 4846
Kelly, Michael Francis 7609
Kelly, Pete 15867
Kelly, Tom 17821, 18211
Kelsey, George D. 5480, 9512, 12926
Kelsey, Henry H. 1552
Kelsey, Morton T. 14299
Kemendo, Robert B. 15868
Kemp, Charles F. 7879, 12542, 14146
Kemp, Jim 18555
Kemper, Donald J. 14705
Kemper, Robert V. 14575
Kemper, Vicki 18212
Kempf, Denise M. 18556
Kendall, Guy 4847, 5697

Kenel, Sally A. 18213
Kenhoe, Mary 17394
Kenkelen, B. 14706
Kennedy, Albert J. 2330, 2560, 2762, 3474, 4458, 8631
Kennedy, Estella 14300
Kennedy, John C. 2623
Kennedy, Michael 16638
Kennedy, R. 5183
Kennedy, Roger C. 16283
Kennedy, Thomas F. 6901
Kennedy, William Bean 18120
Kennell, Joseph Eugene 17822
Kenney, Bradford P. 14301
Kennion, John W 638
Kenny, Michael 3251
Kenrick, Bruce 8481
Kent, Charles Foster 3006
Kent, George 8482
Kent, John 9942, 14707
Kenyon, John 16284
Kenyon, Ruth 4157, 4948
Keogh, J. G. 11844
Kerby, William J. 2153, 2712, 3334, 3522, 3523
Kerins, James F. 9119
Kerr, Annie B. 5184
Kerr, Ian 11385
Kerr, John Stevens 11845
Kerr, Robert M. 3775
Kerr, William N. 13264
Kerschner, Harold Benner 3335
Kersey, Robert J. 16285
Kershaw, Walter 1151
Kessler, Edward 13265
Kessler, J. B. A. 10419
Kessner, Thomas 14302
Kestler, Lloyd K. 3336
Ketcherside, W. Carl 11846
Ketteler, Ludwig 2415
Ketteler, Wilhelm Emmanuel 1152, 2634
Kevren, Floyd Van 3524
Keyes, Sharrel 15043
Keyser, Harriet A. 2416
Khalil, Deborah 18557
Khalil, Victor 18557
Khodorkovskii, Leonid Dmitrievich 14708
Khodr, Georges 12208
Kibble, David G. 15869
Kidd, Beth 17395
Kidder, B. F. 1394
Kidder, Maurice A. 10420
Kiefel, Gerhard 14709
Kiely, John M. 1481
Kierkegaard, Søren 220, 10392, 15802
Kiernan, J. P. 17018
Kiester, Edwin, Jr. 10493
Kietzell, Dieter von 16114
Kikuchi, Toshio 12927
Kilbourn, William 9943
Kildare, Owen Frawley 1958, 1959, 2034, 2087
Kilgore, L. Wilson 7610
Kilian, Thomas Randolph 5924, 6186
Killian, David 15112
Killian, Lewis 5925, 8483, 11847
Killing Flies with a Hammer 12209
Killinger, John 18214
Kilpatrick, Harold C. 7611
Kilson, Marion 13266
Kim, Byong-suh 15512
Kim, Chung-Sook Chung 18890
Kim, Dae Gee 17396
Kim, Ick Won 16639
Kim, Kyong-Dong 15086
Kim, Kyung-Suk 16286
Kim, Paul Shu 15513
Kim, Sangho Joseph 13588
Kim, Shin Kuk 18215
Kim, Stephen, Cardinal 14710
Kim, Won Kie 16640
Kim, Woong-min 15870
Kim, Young-Ir 15871
Kim, Young-suk 17397
Kimani, David 13590

Kimball, John C. 465
Kimball, Sylvester 1960
Kimmel, Ted 8789
Kimura, Noritaugu 18558
Kinast, Robert L. 17937
Kincheloe, Samuel C. 3891, 3897, 3898, 3969, 4066, 4459, 4628, 4743, 4949, 5068, 5481, 5926, 6056, 6340, 9513, 9514, 18891
Kindwoman, Jan 18559
King, Charles H. 10421
King, Clarence 9515
King, Coretta Scott 11848, 17251
King, David S. 7346, 15514
King, George Wales 3970
King, Henry Churchill 1811, 1861, 1862, 2417, 2516, 2713
King, James M. 936, 937, 1702
King, Joan 14965
King, Martin Luther, Jr. 5927, 7120, 7121, 7347, 8790, 8791, 9120, 9866, 10421, 10422, 10423, 11848, 11864, 11866, 12076, 13414, 14224, 14852, 16356, 17668, 18750, 19016, 19026, 19084, 19284
King, Martin Luther, Sr. 15515
King, T. Starr 352
King, Terry Johnson 8792
King, W. L. Mackenzie 1646
King, William M. 15872, 17019
King, William Peter 4158
King, William Richard 4067
Kingdomworks 19330
Kingma, Stuart J. 14303
Kingsbury, Mary M. 1647
Kingsdale, Jon M. 12928
Kingsley, Charles 259, 270, 639, 1150, 1992, 2840, 3591
Kingston, Temple 13267
Kinney, Terry D. 17020
Kinsler, F. Ross 16641
Kinsolving, Lester 10424
Kipling, Rudyard 1703
Kirby, Ermal 15113
Kirche in der Stadt: Bd. I: Grundlagen und Analysen 10425
Kirche inmitten der Welt und gegenüber einer neuen Zivilisation 6497
Kirche und Raumordnung 9944
Kirckus, Richard J. 11386
Kirk, Andrew 18892
Kirk, David 11387
Kirk, Edward Norris 13351
Kirk, Paul Thomas Radford-Rowe 3252, 3618, 4950, 5036, 5381
Kirkeby, Oliver Murle 15516
Kirkland, James H. 2240
Kirkland, Wallace 18883
Kirkpatrick, A. M. 9516
Kirkpatrick, Bill 18560
Kirlin, Joseph L. J. 2331
Kirtland, Stephany 18216
Kirtley, James A. 4376
Kiryluk, Nicholas T. 5382
Kistler, Robert C. 9362, 17021
Kitagawa, Diasuke 10426, 10427
Kitagawa, Joseph M. 10428
Kitchen, William B 12210
Kitson Clark, George Sidney Roberts 12929
Kittlaus, Paul 12941
Kittleson, Judy 18580
Klassen, Jacob P. 17398
Klassen, William 11388
Klausner, Carla L. 16723
Klausner, Samuel Z. 12543
Kleba, Gerald J. 17399, 17823
Kleiman, Carol 9517
Kleiman, Jeffery D. 17824
Klein, Christa Ressmeyer 13936, 18893
Klein, Gerhard 13937
Klein, James H. 15517
Klein, Malcolm W. 12211
Klein, Maury 13938
Klein, Norbert Hans 8793

Kleinschmidt, Sarah 3619
Klejment, Alice 17825
Klejment, Anne 17825
Klemme, Huber F. 6341, 7122
Klever, Gerald L. 14682
Klieman, Aaron S. 19111
Klieman, Adrian L. 19111
Klingbeil, Kurt A. 14304
Klink, Thomas W. 11849
Kloetzli, Walter 6708, 6709, 7348, 7880, 7881, 8202, 8203, 8204, 8205, 8484, 8485, 8486, 8794, 9121, 9518, 9519
Klopfenstein, Gordon 17022
Kloppenburg, Bonaventure 14711
Klopsch, Louis 2435
Klose, Alfred 16287
Klose, L. V. 4951
Klose, Robert 9922
Klosek, I. 7067
Kloss, Charles L. 2035
Klosterman, Charles 5485
Klostermann, Ferdinand 9520
Kluckhohn, Clyde 12930
Knapp, Jacob 13351
Knapp, John M. 1395
Knapp, Shepard 2332
Knight, Barry 15873
Knight, Frances G. 4299
Knight, Frank H. 5383
Knight, H. T. 1757
Knight, J. Robert 5698
Knight, John E. N. 17023
Knight, Richard V. 16223
Knight, Walker L. 9521, 9945, 10429, 10920, 10921, 11389, 11850, 12544
Knights, J. J. 5106
Knock, Stanley F. 7578
Knoerle, Jeanne 12931
Knoke, David 15663, 16288
Knoll, Jorg 13589
Knopp, Fay Honey 14111
Knott, William Wilson 1298
Knowles, Daniel Clark 536
Knowles, James 844
Knox, John 4068
Knox, Marv 16289
Knox, Paul L. 14173
Knox, Robert 537
Knoxville United Ministries 15518
Knubel, Frederick H. 8206
Knubel, Frederick Hermann 3143
Knudsen, Dean D. 13842, 14189
Knudsen, Raymond B. 13268, 14712
Knudten, Richard D. 11390
Koberg, Josef 8207
Kobiah, Samuel 13590, 13939
Koch, Felix J. 3971
Kochman, Thomas 12545, 15874
Koelling, Donald F. 8487, 9122
Koenig, Harry C. 19289
Koetsier, C. Henk 17826
Koetsier, Henk 19059
Kogan, Michael S. 13591
Koh, Jae Sik 12932
Kohlbrenner, Bernard J. 4592
Kohlstedt, E. D. 5107
Kohn, Solomon Joshua 7612
Kohnstamm, Ph. 3078
Kohs, Samuels Calmin 9946
Kohut, Rebekah Bettelheim 3972
Kolb, Charles B. 2418
Kolbe, Edward H. 15519
Kollar, Nathan 11851
Kollar, Rene 18217
Kolm, Gerrit Jan van der 13940, 13941
Kolodney, Nathan 11391
Kolping, Adolf 996, 2741, 3337, 3484, 3713, 4806, 5013, 5623, 16167, 18144
Kolsti, Arthur H. 7613
Komarovsky, Mirra 4379, 5482
Koning, Gerry 17400

Konophka, Gisela 10922
Konovitch, Barry 14305
Kontz, Emil 4460
Koontz, Donald H. 9947
Koopman, LeRoy 13942
Koops, Hugh A. 9948, 12546
Koos, Earl Lomon 5384
Koosmann, Konrad 6342
Kopp, Georg 16606
Koppe, William A. 7123
Korea Student Christian Federation 12212
Korean Church Industrial Mission 17024
Kortekangas, Paavo 9522, 10430
Kortrey, Walter A. 15114
Kortright, Jackie 15115
Kortright, Michael 15115
Kortzfleisch, Siegfried von 8795
Kory, William B. 12547
Köster, Reinhard 7614
Kostyu, Frank A. 9523
Kothen, Robert 5385, 5483, 5699, 5794, 6498
Kotler, Milton 15116
Kotz, Mary Lynn 14306
Kotz, Nick 14306
Kowalski, Gregory S. 18125, 18218
Koyama, Kosuke 13269
Kozol, Jonathan 10431, 13592, 18561
Kracht, Hans Joachim 13593
Kraemer, Hendrik 5588, 7349
Kraemer, Paul E. 8796, 8797, 10923
Kräling, Emil 2517
Kramer, Alfred S. 6187, 6710
Kramer, Hannes 13174
Kramer, Paul 11852
Kramer, Reed 12548
Krämer, Werner 17401
Kramer, William M. 13270, 14307
Kranich, Wilmer L. 6499
Krapf-Askari, Eva 11392
Krasner, Barbara 11393
Krass, Alfred C. 12933, 13271, 14713, 15875, 15876, 15877, 16290, 16291, 16292, 16642, 16643, 17025, 18562
Krätzig, Guillermo 13594, 17827
Kraus, Ingrid Marianne 15878
Kraus, Norman C 15520
Krause, Larry 13272
Krause, Pat 13595
Krauskopf, Joseph 1228
Krauß-Siemann, Jutta 14714, 16644
Krawczyk, Joseph 15879
Kraybill, Donald B. 14715, 14969
Kraybill, J. Nelson 17402
Kreider, Robert 5037
Kreinberg, Lew 15738
Kremm, Thomas W. 13596
Kresge, Elijah Everett 3426
Kretzmann, John 18834
Krickus, Richard J. 11853
Krietemeyer, Ronald T. 16645
Kristol, Irving 12549
Kritzinger, J. J. 17026
Kroehler, Armin 10035
Kroeze, Jan 11854
Kroll, Una 18219
Kromer, Helen 6057, 6500, 12934, 13597, 14308, 15117, 15118, 15521
Kromkowski, John A. 18220
Krooth, David L. 5589
Krout, John Allen 3705
Krover, Harold 18563
Krueger, David A. 19112
Krug, Mark M. 6893
Kruizenga, H. A. 10924
Krumwiede, Hans W. 10432
Krumwiede, Walter 2950
Krupavicius, Mykolas 16646
Krusche, Günter 10433
Kruuse, Elsa 6501, 6502
Kubiak, Hieronim 12550

Kubler-Ross, Elizabeth 14597
Kucharsky, David 11855
Kuckuk, John W. 9123
Kuehn, Barbara H. 11394
Kuehn, Erich 9524
Kuenning, Larry 14716
Kuenster, J. 10434
Kugelmass, J. Alvin 6188, 6343, 6894
Kugelmass, Jack 17403, 17828
Kuhn, Donald 9124, 9826, 11395
Kuhn, Hannah R. 14309, 14310
Kuhn, Harold B. 10925
Kuhn, James 8208, 11856, 12551
Kuhn, Margaret E. 6503, 10926
Kuizenga, Henry B. 8798
Kulski, Julian Eugene 10435
Kumagai, Sonoko 10001
Kuman, Alexander 8488
Kumazawa, Yoshinobu 10927
Kunkelman, Gary A. 17829
Kunzel, Regina G. 18564
Kunzman, J. C. 1482
Kuper, Leo 7350, 9525
Kurts, Theodore L. 6344
Kurtz, Ernest 15119
Kurtz, Russell H. 3973
Kurucz, Jenö 10507
Kutcher, Stan 13943
Kuttner, Karen Parker 13944
Kutzik, Alred J. 7615
Kuykendall, John W. 12552
Kuyper, Abraham 5928
Kuznicki, Ellen Marie 14717
Kuzniewski, Anthony J. 14718
Kwant, Kees 17404
Kyewalyanga, Francis X. 16293
Kyle, John E. 18565
La Cossitt, Henry 6189
La Farge, John 13402, 13403, 13733
La Fontaine, Charles V. 14719
La Noue, George R. 7882
La pastorale missionaria nel mondo del lavoro 10436
La Roe, Wilbur, Jr. 5185
Labaree, Benjamin W., Mrs. 2624
Labbens, Jean 6504, 6711, 7351, 7352, 7616, 7617, 9125
Labor and the Church--An Exploratory Study 13598
Labor Day in the Church 3620
Labor History 17830
Labor Priests 5795
Labor Temple, Presbyterian 2419
Labor Windows in the Washington Cathedral 7883
Labor, Livio 5929
Labor's Case against the Church 2951
Labor-Management Relations Act, 1947 5590
Labrador, Stenio 12264
Lacambre, Felix 13599
Lachaga, José María de 14720
Lachmann, Werner 17027
Lacinak, Michael 16294, 16295
Lackland, George S. 5386
Lackritz, Marc E. 10928
Lacoste, N. 6698
Lacount, Helen 2952
Lacquement, C. H. 11396
Lacroix, Paul 11397
Lacrosse, J. M. 14311
Lacy, Creighton 10437
Ladd, Everett C. 9949
Ladd, William Palmer 3525
Laden, Norman 7618
Ladies of the Mission 301
Ladley, Patricia Powers 18467
Laetsch, Th. 4952
LaFarge, John 4629, 4848, 5186, 5187, 5591, 5592, 5796, 6895, 7051, 7353, 7559
Lago, Mary M. 6505
Lahalle, Dominique 8489
Lai, Mary L. 16866
Laidlaw, Walter 1471, 1648, 1649, 1650, 1961, 2518
Laidler, Harry W. 4300

Laity Bulletin 6896
Laity Commission Working Party 11857
Lalive d'Epinay, Christian 11398, 12213, 13768, 14312, 15880, 15881
Lally, Francis Joseph 9126
Lam, George Chung Yon 14313
Lam, Peter 16647
Lamanna, Richard A. 11399
Lamar, Robert C. 18221
Lamb, Christopher 17697, 17793
Lamb, Edwin G. 2333
Lamb, James A. 10929
Lambert, Irving C. 10930
Lambert, Louise Mary 7124
Lambert, Richard D. 7884
Lambeth Conference 2241, 18566
Lambrinides, John S. 9950
Lammers, Ann Conrad 16296
Lamont, Robert J. 9951
Lampe, Philip E. 13600, 13945, 14314
Lampley, Lewis C. 14649
Lamson, C. M. 2886
Lancaster Theological Seminary, Faculty 15120
Land, Kurt 7885
Landau, Yeshaiahu 18222
Landes, Ruth 10438
Landesman, Alter F. 11400
Landfear, N. Maria 583
Landgraff, John R. 16297
Landis, Benson Young 3706, 3776, 4536, 4537, 4538, 4630, 4744, 4953, 4954, 4955, 5188, 5189, 5286, 5484, 6897, 7125, 7619, 7620, 8209, 8490
Landrey, J. Paul 16648
Landsberger, Henry A 10439
Landsbury, George 18178
Lane, Francis E. 4227
Lane, George A. 15882
Lane, Martha A. 10931
Lane, Thomas 13946, 19299, 19302
Lane, W. D. 3079
Lang, Engel 7885
Lang, Gladys E. 10440
Lang, Gordon 4228
Lang, J. David 19331
Lang, Kurt 10440
Langan, John 17831
Langford, Charles C. 13273
Langsam, Miriam Z. 9127
Lannes, S. 9952
Lanpher, B. W. 11401
Lansbury, George 3007
Lanser, J. 13947
Lapidus, Ira M. 11858, 12935
Lapierre, Dominique 17405
Lapointe, Eugène 14776
Lapping, Mark B. 13274
Laqueur, Thomas Walter 13948
Large Metros Becoming More Racially Polarized 17832
Largent, Christopher 19192
Larkin, Emmet 9128
Larkins, John 8210
Larkio, Mauri 10441
Larson, Calvin J. 10369, 11402
Larson, Craig Brian 18223
Larson, G. R. 4745
Larson, Melvin 5930, 5931, 6712
Larson, Peter A. 12936
Larson, R. 10442
Larson, Robert C. 10443
Larson, Robert E., Jr. 15814, 16584, 17406, 17833
Larson, Ross H. 12553
Larsson, Tage 12554
Lasch, Christopher 9526, 9527
Laska, Shirley Bradway 15522
Lass, Herb 18224
Lassen, Christen 13949
Late Awakening: Jonathan's Wake: Counter-Proposal Mission in the '70's 11403
Latham, Henry J. 938

Latham, Robert 17834
Lathrop, Charles N. 3326, 3427
Lathrop, Charles Newton 3253
Lathrop, Edward 271
Lathuihamallo, Peter D. 16298
Latourette, Kenneth Scott 4746, 5190
Latta, Maurice C. 4539
Lau, Lawson 16299, 17028
Laubenstein, Paul F. 3707
Laue, James H. 9129
Lauer, Robert H. 13601
Laumann, Edward O. 11404, 12214, 12937
Laurie, Thomas 1068
Laurinkari, Juhani 18225
Lausanne Commitee for World Evangelization 15523
Lausanne Commitee for World Evangelization, Consultation on World Evangelism, Mini-Consultation on Reaching the Urban Poor, Pattaya, Thailand 15524
Lausanne Commitee for World Evangelization, Consultation on World Evangelization, Mini-Consultation on Reaching Large Cities 15525
Lavelle, Robert 16383
Lavipour, Farid 12087
Lawler, Loretto Ross 6058
Lawrence, Charles 2036
Lawrence, F. 8491
Lawrence, J. B. 5108
Lawrence, Nancy 6713
Lawrence, W. Appleton 4747
Lawrence, William 2519
Lawson, Albert G. 794
Lawson, Lowell F. 12938
Lawton, J. Kenneth 10444
Lax, William Henry 3837, 3974, 4301, 4631
Layman, Emma M. 13950
Laymen in the Urban Church 7886
Layne, Norman R 12939
Lazareth, William H. 15035, 15451
Lazerow, Jama 17835
Lazerson, Marvin 14315
Lazerwitz, Bernard 8211, 8212, 9130, 12314, 12940, 14316
Le Bras, Gabriel 8576
Leach, Keith A. 10445
Leach, Richard H. 7887, 7888, 9131
Leach, Wilbur C. 7354
Leach, William H. 3428, 3777
Leacock, Eleanor 7355
Leading Your Church in Long Range Planning 13602
League of the Kingdom of God 4159
Leak, A. S. 16649
Leals, Daniel J. 16300
Learn to Say No: or, The City Apprentice 321
Learnings from GCSP, A Report on Five Years' Experience with the Episcopal Church's Most Controversial Mission Program 12555
Leary, Stanley 18417
Leas, Speed 12941, 15121, 15122, 17029, 17030, 17407, 18280
Leask, George Alfred 2334
Leavell, L. P. 2420
Leaven for the City 8799
Leaver, Lawrence 2242
Leber, Charles T., Jr. 8367
LeBlanc, Doug 18567
LeBras, Gabriel 5109, 6432, 6714, 7356, 8492
Lechner, Frank L. 18894
Lecky, Robert S. 11405, 11406
Leclercq, Jacques 7621, 11407
LeCorbusier 3621, 14225, 18071, 18137
Lecordier, Gaston 5387

Lecornu, Clifton 8540
Ledit, Joseph Henry 4956
Lee, Alfred McClung 5191, 5700
Lee, Amy 7126, 7889, 8800, 8801, 10446, 11408, 11409, 11859, 12215
Lee, Barrett A. 17031, 18151
Lee, Betsy 15883
Lee, Carleton Lafayette 12556
Lee, Chang Soon 14721, 17222
Lee, Dallas M. 9953, 10447, 10932, 11860
Lee, David S. 11861
Lee, Edwar 4377
Lee, Edward 939
Lee, Ernest George 5593
Lee, Eun Soo 15526
Lee, George Alan 7622, 8213
Lee, In Ha 12216
Lee, J. Oscar 7890
Lee, James M. 12942
Lee, Joseph 2953
Lee, Kit-chung 11862
Lee, Maryat 6059
Lee, Raymond L. M. 15527
Lee, Robert 3838, 3839, 4632, 6190, 6345, 6506, 6507, 6508, 6509, 7127, 7357, 7623, 7891, 7892, 7893, 8214, 8493, 8494, 8802, 9132, 9133, 9528, 9529, 10448, 11410
Lee, Rose Hum 6715, 7894
Lee, Roswell 13385
Lee, Sang Hyun 15512, 18226
Lee, Sang-Taek 18568
Lee, Sang-Woon 18227
Leech, Kenneth 15528, 15529, 15884, 16650, 17032, 17836
Leent, J. A. A. van 8215
Lees, Andrew 17408, 18228
Lees, L. H. 17365
Leete, Frederick de Land 2887
Leeuwen, A, Th. van 10933
LeFeber, Larry A. 13603, 15530
Lefebvre, Pierre 15531
Lefever, Harry G. 11411, 12217, 12943, 14317, 16301
Lefèvre, Luc J. 6898
Lefringhausen, Klaus 9134, 11412
LeGates, Richard T. 15978
Lehman, Edward C., Jr. 17837
Lehman, Warren 8803
Lehmann, Dorothea 8315
Lehmann, E. G. 555
Lehmann, Hartmut 17409
Lehmann, Paul 9530, 12557, 17033
Lehn, Cornelia 11863
Lehrer, E. 8090
Leibling, Leonard 5797
Leichliter, G. A. 3778
Leiffer, Murray Howard 4229, 4461, 4748, 4849, 4850, 5485, 5798, 6510, 6511, 6512, 6899, 6900, 6901, 6902, 7128, 7358, 7359, 7360, 7624, 8216, 8217, 8218, 9531, 9954, 10449
Leigh, Vanora 17410
Leighbody, G. W. 4633
Leighton, Barry 15305
Leighton, Sally 8804
Leinberger, Hugo 6716
Leininger, Madeleine 12944
Leith, Dorothy M. 10934
Lejeunesse, Marcel 13604
LeJoly, Edward 14318, 17411
Lekachman, Robert 9955, 16302
Leland, Pamela J. 18649
Leland, Thomas Elgon 15885
Leman, Johan 15123
Leman, Nicholas 19218
Lembugusala, Pierre C. 16366
LeMouel, Gilbert 6717
LeMouël, Gabriel 7070
Lenardi, Barbara 15886
Lend A Hand 795
Lenhart, Thomas Emerson 15887
Lenin, Vladmir Ilích 4069
Lennan, John J. 13951

Lennon, Brad 17370
Lennon, Joseph L. 6718
Lenroot, Katharine 4462
Lens, Sidney 7625
Lenski, Gerhard E., Jr. 7626, 8219, 8495
Lentz, Harold Herbert 5192
Lenz, Frank B. 2888
Lenz, Robert 18895
Leo XIII, Pope 1061, 1067, 1069, 1080, 1417, 4152, 4944, 5334, 6472, 10150, 12241, 16249, 16342, 16674, 17235, 17468, 17664
Leonard of Taizé, Brother 17412, 17413, 17838
Leonard, Charles 16651
Leonard, H. Robinson 5932
Leonard, Harriet Virginia 14722
Leonard, Henry B. 13952, 17414
Leonard, Joseph T. 8805
Leonard, Norman H., Jr. 7895
Leoni, Aldo 6191
LePlay, Frédéric 416, 481, 502, 569
Leprieur, François 18896
Lercaro, Giacomo 9956
Lercaro, Jacques 12218
LeRoy, Albert 4634
LeRoy, Michael G. 16652
Lerrigo, Charles 12558, 13953, 14319
Lesage, Germain 12559
Lesbaupin, Ivo 15532
Lesbian / Feminist Issues 12560
Lesemann, L. F. W. 3254
Leslie, Annie Ruth Johnson 16653
Leslie, Bill 12945, 18569
Leslie, W. Bruce 14320
Leslie, William 14321, 15124, 17839
LeSourd, G. 7129
LeSourd, Len 5933
Lestchinsky, J. 5486
Lester, Andrew D. 17415
Lester, Muriel 4463
Lestra, Antoine 5799
Letman, Sloan T. 16201
Letts, Harold C. 5934, 6346, 7130, 13605
Leung, P. L 13954
Leuwers, Jean-Marie 11413, 12219, 13275
Levan, Charles W. 2421
Levander, Mary 7361
Levard, Georges 6719
Levens, Helene 12220
Lever, Oscar William 5038
Levering, Johnson 8806
Levesque, George A. 13606
Levi, Werner 18897
Levi-Strauss, Claude 15766
Levin, Harry 7362
Levin, Lester I. 17593
Levine, Daniel 12221, 17840
Levine, Edward M. 9957, 10935
Levine, Irving M. 11414
Levinson, Daniel J. 5850
Levinson, Harry 12561
Levinthal, Louis E. 4540
Levit, Maurice E. 3429
Levtzion, Hehemia 17841
Levy, Charles S. 7627, 8807, 9532
Levy, Edgar Mortimer 466
Levy, Walter J. 7131
Lewcock, R. 16726
Lewin, Hugh 18229
Lewins, Frank William 14723, 16303
Lewis, A. William 2243
Lewis, Charles W. 14724
Lewis, Christopher 15888
Lewis, David L. 11864
Lewis, Donald M. 17416, 17842
Lewis, G. Douglass 12222, 14322, 15889
Lewis, Gregg 18230
Lewis, H. S. 1774
Lewis, Jacob 10915

Lewis, John 4464
Lewis, John Fulton 14323
Lewis, John Henry 2808
Lewis, L. David 11865
Lewis, Oscar 6192, 8056, 8220, 9135, 9533, 9958, 11415
Lewis, Robert 2335
Lewis, Ron S. 14161
Lewis, Sinclair 3840
Lewis, Theodore 13607
Lews, James N., Jr. 17843
Lewter, Nicholas Cooper 17880
Ley, David 13276
Leys, Wayne A. R. 7628
Libro bianco sulle Officine Galileo 7629, 7630
Lichtenberger, James P. 2336
Licorish, David Nathaniel 6903
Liddall, Marton Gloria 15890
Lieberson, Stanley 7533, 8808
Liebman, Robert 18570
Liebow, Elliot 10450
Liechti, Steve 14725
Liedel, Ann 12562
Liefde, E. de. 10936
Lieff, Pearl J. 4957
Lieurance, Tom 10937
Life of Duncan Macpherson: the Story of 2809
Light, Paul W. 17844
Lightbody, C. Stuart 17034, 17845, 17846
Lightstone, Jack W. 18571
Lilly, Eli 7132
Lilly, Elizabeth 19305
Lim, David S. 18572
Limbert, Paul M. 5487, 9136
Linberg, Edwin C. 16304
Lincoln, C. Eric 7896, 8221, 10451, 10452, 11866, 12563, 13277, 13278, 13608, 15533, 16654, 19113
Lincoln, C. Eric, 2nd 12563
Lincoln, William F. 12258
Lind, Millard C. 16305
Lindamood, Robert Lee 13609
Lindars, Barnabas 10938
Lindberg, Carter 15891
Lindberg, Milton B. 6513
Lindberg, Tod 17847
Lindblad, Gunnar 11867
Lindeboom, C. 3622
Lindeman, Edward Christian 3975
Linden, Rick 16559
Linder, John Thomas 15892
Lindevall, G. 5528
Lindholm, Sara 14445
Lindley, Susan 16655
Lindner, Reinhold 13955
Lindquist, Gustavus Elmer Emanuel 5701
Lindqvist, M. 12223
Lindsay, Alexander Dunlop 4378
Lindsay, John V. 11868, 11869
Lindsey, Dorothea M. 9959
Lindsey, Harold E. 10453
Lindt, Andreas 12946
Linen, James A. 11335
Lingeman, Richard 15534
Lingenfelter, Judith 18573
Lingle, Virginia A. 18574
Link, Eugene P. 16656
Linkh, Richard M. 13610
Linn, James Weber 4465
Linowes, David F. 13279
Linsley, Stanley F. 7133
Linthicum, Robert C. 12564, 17848, 18231, 18232, 18575, 18576, 18745, 18898, 19219, 19220
Linton, Thomas Dwight 17849
Linz, Juan J. 15535
Linzer, Norman 15536
Lipman, Eugene J. 7363, 8496
Lipman, V. D. 9137
Lippel, Israel 18577
Lippy, Charles H. 18578
Lipset, Seymour Martin 7679, 15893

Lipsey, C. M. 13154
Liptak, Dolores A 16306
Liptak, Dolores A. 17417, 18579
Lipton, Michael 14324
Lishman, W. E. 3338
Liskofsky, Sidney 9960
Lissak, Rivka Shpak 18899
Littell, Franklin H. 8222, 8497, 8498, 8809, 9138, 9534, 9961, 10939, 11416
Little, Bryce 12224
Little, Daniel 8289, 9139
Little, David 9962
Little, Kenneth 9963, 13280
Little, Sarah 18592
Little Mother Grows Up: Work Done by the Church of All Nations 3144
Littlefield, Charles 1758
Littlejohns, Donald G. 15125
Littler, June D. 19221
Littlewood, John 11870
Liu, Chiang 4466
Liu, William Thomas 11871
Liv, William T. 9964
Lively, Anne O. 6630, 6720, 6904, 7504, 8047, 8331
Lively, Charles E. 7364
Lively, Robert D. 17418
Liveright, A. A. 7631
Livermore, Charles P. 9965
Living Church 597
Living Issues for Pulpit Treatment: Discrimination Against the Chinese 1229
Living Issues for Pulpit Treatment: Dr. Parkhurst's Crusade 1396
Living Issues for Pulpit Treatment: Immigration 1230
Living Issues for Pulpit Treatment: Immigration and Naturalization 1070
Living Issues for Pulpit Treatment: Municipal Misgovernment 997
Living Issues for Pulpit Treatment: The Immigration Question 889
Living Issues for Pulpit Treatment: To Debar Illiterate Immigrants 1553
Livingston, Debra 18580
Livingston, Paul L. 17035
Lloyd Webber, Andrew 11417
Lloyd, Anthony Frazier 17419
Lloyd, George L. 19114
Lloyd, Henry Demarest 2088
Lloyd, Larry Bishop 18581
Lloyd, Peter Cutt 10454, 15126
Lloyd, Roger 6193, 6721, 7632
Lloyd, W. F. 2244
Lo, Katherine 18626
Loach, Judi 15127
Local Church and Local Community Organization 8810
Local Church and Unemployment -- A Record of Performance 4302
Loch, Charles Stewart 998, 999, 1071, 1072, 1153, 2422
Lochridge, Patricia 5006
Lockard, W. David 17850
Locke, Hubert G. 11872
Lockhart, William S. 2245
Lockridge, Ruby G. 13281
Lockwood, George Frank 15894
Lockwood, Lee 12565
Loder, Ted 17851
Loescher, Frank S. 5702, 6905
Loetscher, Lefferts A. 5287, 5288
Loew, Jacques 5800, 5935, 7633, 7897, 8811
Loewenberg, Frank M. 18582
Loewenstein, F. von 6722
Loewenstein, Susan Fleiss 11873
Löffler, Paul 10940, 10941, 12225
Lofton, Fred C. 14726

Logan, Patrick 18900
Logan, Richard A. 9535
Logan, William S. 10455, 10456, 19115
Logue, Edward J. 11874
Logue, Frank 11875
Loh, I-to 12566
Lohse, Jens Marten 10457
Lomax, Louis E. 8812
London City Mission 221
London City Temple 3623
London, Herbert I. 15895
Lonely Crowd at Prayer 6906
Lonergan, Connie 17420
Lonergan, T. S. 1651
Long, Daniel M. 17421
Long, Edward Leroy, Jr. 11876
Long, George 2714
Long, Grace Cumming 17036
Long, Herman H. 5284, 5594, 8813
Long, Jacob Avery 4958, 5193, 5194, 5289, 5290, 5291, 5388, 5595
Long, Larry Simeon 18233
Long, Loran Dean 16307
Long, Mason 684
Long, Norton E. 15896
Long, Robert W. 9966
Long, Russell 16633
Longemann, J. H. A. 6907
Longino, Charles F. 13217
Longinotti, Giovanni Maria 11886
Loock, Hans-Dietrich 19078
Loomis, Mildred Jensen 5292
Loomis, Samuel Lane 845, 846, 847, 848, 950, 1231
Loosley, Elizabeth W. 6979
Lopata, H. Z. 10458
Loper, Joseph Norris 6194
Lopez, Bernardo 15897
Lopez, Robert 15898
Lopez, Rudy Villalobos 15128
Loraux, Nicole 17852
Lord, Richard 18583
Lord, Robert H. 5293
Lorentzen, Robin 19222
Lorenz, Eckehart 18234
Lorimer, George Claude 663, 796, 1154, 1652
Loritts, Crawford W., Jr. 17037
Lorwin, Val R. 13611
Loss, Kenneth D. 13282
Loth, Paul Edward 7898
Lothrop, William Henry 5110
Lottman, Herbert R. 13956
Lotz, Jim 13612
Loudon, John B. 19116
Loury, Glenn C. 17853
Louw, Daniel J. 18584
Loux, Gordon D. 17038, 18235
Love, Edgar 4851
Love, Gervase N. 7899
Love, James Franklin 2625
Love, Maria M. 1448
Lovejoy, Derek 9967
Lovejoy, Owen R. 2626, 2627
Loveless, Frances B. 3430, 3431
Lovell, George 12226, 12227, 12567, 14727, 15537, 16308
Lovett, Leonard 17422
Lovett, Robert Morss 4467
Lovett, S. C. Campbell 19223
Low, A. Ritchie 5294
Lowder, C. F. 432
Lowder, Stella 17854
Lowder, Virgil E. 7365
Lowe, Jeanne R. 7900, 10459
Lowe, Pardee 5195
Lowell Mission Society 215
Lowell, C. R., Mrs. 1554
Lowell, E. J. 14728
Lowell, Josephine Shaw 2551
Lowenstein, Solomon 2246
Lowery, James L. 12947, 13957
Lowi, Theodore J. 11418
Lowndes, Marian 18585
Lübbe, Hermann 9536
Lubove, Roy 7634, 7635, 8499,

9537
Lucas, Isidro 15899
Lucas, Keith 8223
Lucas, Paul R. 13283
Lucas, Rex A. 13958
Lucas, Robert 12948
Luccock, Halford Edward 2954, 4541, 5801
Lucey, Michael Henry 2337
Luchs, Susan M 15129
Luck, James Russell 17039
Luckhardt, Ken 15900
Luckman, Thomas 14559
Luckmann, Thomas 7636, 8814, 8815, 10214, 10215, 10460, 14092, 15881, 17311
Ludlow, John Malcolm Forbes 260, 261, 272, 433, 8830, 15901
Ludwig, Charles 19278
Ludwig, Heiner 17040
Ludwig, Heinrich 15902
Ludwig, Heinz-Georg 15902
Luebke, Frederick C. 13959
Luecke, Richard Henry 9140, 9538, 9968, 10461, 10942, 10943, 11419, 11877, 12228, 12568, 12949, 13284, 13960, 15035, 15130, 15131, 15538, 15539, 17041, 17423, 18236, 18901, 18902, 18903, 19117
Lueking, F. Dean 9141
Luker, Ralph E. 13961, 14325, 19350
Lukonic, Joseph Lee 15132
Lumerman, Juan Pedro 16657
Lumkin, Paul 15133
Lumley, John Barry 17042
Lummis, Adair T. 11999
Luna, David 17855
Lund, Marjorie Lee 14729
Lundberg, George A. 4379
Lunger, Harold Lehman 4542
Lupfer, Michael B. 16773
Lupton, Robert D. 17043, 17044, 17856, 18904
Lurie, Ellen 9142
Lutheran Center for Church Renewal 15540
Lutheran Church in America, Board of American Missions 11878
Lutheran Church in America, Board of Parish Education 12569, 12950
Lutheran Church in America, Board of Social Ministry 9143, 10462, 12570, 12571
Lutheran Church in America, Commission on the Nature 9969
Lutheran Church in America, Division for Mission in North America 14326, 14327
Lutheran Church in America, Division for Parish Services 11879, 12951
Lutheran Church of Finland, Church and Society Committee 11420, 11880
Lutheran Church of Finland, Industrial Committee 9539
Lutheran Council in the United States of America 15903
Lutheran Council in the USA, Division of Mission and Ministry, Lutheran Immigration and Refugee Service 12572
Lutheran Inner City Ministry 11421
Lutheran Inner Mission Society in New York City 4635
Lutheran Metropolitan Ministry Association 14328
Lutheran School of Theology, Task Force on Banking Alternatives 15904
Lutheran Seaman's Center 5936
Lutheran Social Welfare Conference 8224

Lutheran Theological Seminary at Philadelphia 12952
Lutheran World Federation, Department of Studies 14329
Luton Industrial College 15905
Lutz, Charles P. 18237
Luzbetak, Louis J. 8816, 9970
Luzi, Gerolamo 5295
Lybarger, Lee H. 9971
Lydall, H. G. 3339
Lyke, James 15541
Lyles, James V. 9540
Lyles, Jean Caffey 13285, 14730, 14731, 16309
Lynch, Frederick Harry 3976
Lynch, Kevin 7901, 15906, 17045
Lynch, William F. 9541, 11881
Lynd, Helen M. 3977, 4636
Lynd, Robert Staughton 3977, 4636
Lynn, Edwin Charles 12573
Lynn, Robert C. 9542
Lynn, Robert W. 7198, 8817, 9144, 12229
Lyon, David 13613, 15907
Lyon, Ruth A. 12230
Lyon, William 14330
M. Gertrude 6060
Mabee, Frank C. 12953
Mabie, Janet 4637, 4749
Mabogunje, A. L. 9972, 10454
Mabry, Don F. 10401, 12954, 12955, 13286, 13287
Mabry, Hunter P. 18238
MacAdam, George 3708
MacAfee, Cleland B. 4072
MacAirt, Julian 15134, 15135
Macarewa, Fredy Lowell 18586
MacArthur, Ellen A. 1459
MacArthur, Robert Stuart 940, 1962, 2247
Macaulay, Jacqueline 11882
MacCallum, Donald J. 10944
MacCunn, John 1653
MacDonald, A. 9973
MacDonald, A. J. 469
Macdonald, Amy 17834
MacDonald, Angus 4543
MacDonald, Frederic William 3145
MacDonald, James Ramsay 2628
Macdonald, John Wilkie 3779
MacDonald, Margaret Ethel 2628
MacDonald, Robert 2338
MacDonald, Rod 13288, 13289, 13290, 13291
Macdonald, Stephen 13614
MacDonell, Tochie Williams 2955, 2956, 3526
MacElvaney, William K. 11652
Macfadyen, Dugald 4303
MacFarland, Charles S. 1555, 1963, 2339, 2629, 2630, 2715, 2810, 2889, 2957, 3008, 3009
MacFarlane, P. C. 2631
MacGowan, R. A. 3364
MacGregor, Malcolm 1397
MacGregor, Robert W. 9543
MacGréil, Mícheál 13292
Machalek, Richard 13962
Machar, Agnes Maule 1155
Macharia, D. 12303
Machor, James L. 15542, 18239
MacInnes, George R. 18240
MacInorny, Mary Alice 4379
Macintosh, Douglas Clyde 4852
MacIntosh, William Alex 14906
Macisco, John J. 7637
MacIver, R. M. 5296, 7366, 9544
MacKay, Donald M. 11422
Mackay-Smith, archdeacon 941
Macke, Paul B. 18587
MacKean, Kip 17442
MacKee, Thomas 16664
MacKeith, John 19224
MacKenzie, Murdoch 10945, 14732
MacKenzie, Thompson 15136
Mackey, Lloyd 18241

Mackey, Virginia 17424
Mackie, Steven 11883
Mackley, Margaret 18905
Macklin, G. P. 1863
MacLaren, A. Allan 13293
Maclean, Donald 3624
MacLennan, Anne 18242
Macleod, David I. 16658
Macleod, Donald 1232
MacLeod, George F. 5389, 6908, 6909, 12956
Maclin, Stan, Sr. 18906
MacMahon, Thomas F. 18995
MacManus, James 10915
MacMullen, Wallace 1964
Macmurray, John 4544
Macnab, John B. 14331
MacNair, Van, Jr. 8818
MacNeill, Ian 9145
Macoll, Dugald 434
Macon, Perry 18513
MacPherson, Annie 512
Macpherson, Duncan 2809
Macquarrie, John 10463
MacQueen, David A. 6514, 8819
MacVean, B. 14332
Madany, Bassam M. 17046
Maddox, John Lee 3978
Madeiros, Humberto Sousa 12574
Mader, Donald 15543, 16310, 16659
Madigan, Kathleen E. 15544
Madigen, Kevin V. 16311
Madison Square Presbyterian Church, New York City 1000
Madörin, Ernst 7638
Madron, Thomas W. 12254, 12986
Madsen, Paul O. 6515, 10946
Madsen, Richard 17238, 19340
Maduro, Otto 16660
Maduro, Renaldo J. 13615
Maesen, William A. 11884
Magalis, Elaine 12231, 12575, 12957, 12958, 12959, 14333, 17425
Magano, Paul M. 5937
Magee, Wilber R. 7367
Magee, William Connor 16391
Magidson, Judith 11423
Maginnio, Charles D. 2520
Maglaya, Filipe E. 14733
Magnuson, Norris 14334
Magoun, George F. 378
Magri, Francesco 7134
Magri, Francis Joseph 2089
Magruder, J. W. 2340, 2716
Maguire, J. D. 9146
Maguire, J. W. R. 3080
Mahairas, T. 17047
Mahan, Mary Brian 8820
Maher, Edward I. 7902
Maher, Tom 15545
Maher, Trafford P. 9974
Mahomed, James 1001
Mahoney, Daniel H. 1398
Mahoney, John Patrick 15137
Mahr, Gustav 3081
Maida, Adam J. 16312
Main, Earl D. 8821, 8822, 9545
Mains, David R. 11424, 12232
Mains, George P. 1314
Mains, Karen 12233
Mainwaring, Scott 17840
Maitron, Jean 13438
Majka, Jazef 7903
Majka, Theo J. 18588
Mak, Arthur F. 18589
Makdisi, Nadim 7640
Making the Cities Livable 12576
Making the Hotel My Parish 17048
Maklin, G. P. 1704
Makulu, Henry F. 7904, 8500
Malaysia: Holding on to God's Gift May Be a Political Issue 18907
Malcomson, William L. 10268
Maldonado, Lionel 17426

Malgeri, Francesco 11112
Malik, Ayyub 18908
Malin, Patrick Murphy 5111
Malitza, Mircea 13294
Malkin, Irad 18243
Mallard, R. Q. 1483, 1556
Mallette, Daniel J. 8823
Malley, F. 6723
Mallon, Elias D. 18590
Mallone, George 16313
Malone, Nancy M. 19118
Maloney, Alice 5719
Maloney, Michael E. 15138, 19305
Malsch, Carl 15908
Malthus, Thomas 39, 105
Malthus, Thomas Robert 4, 30, 62
Mambo, George K. 12963
Mamiya, Lawrence H. 15533, 16314, 16661, 18591, 19113
Mammonism and the Poor 337
Mancini, Janet K 15546
Mand, Ewald 6195
Mandel, Irving A. 5938
Mandell, Lee M. 15698
Mandeville, Kathleen 17857
Maness, William 11425
Mangalam, J. J. 12310
Mangano, Antonio 1907, 3010, 3011, 3340, 13616
Mangold, George B. 2154, 3012
Manheim, Ernest 5196
Manley, Robert S. 8225, 8501
Mann, A. Chester 4750
Mann, Arthur 6516
Mann, Delbert M. 4959
Mann, Gail L. 15547
Mann, Michael 9546
Mann, Richard 11308
Mann, William Edward 6724
Mannheim, Karl 5297
Manning, Henry Edward 73, 3842, 14032
Manning, William T. 3723, 4638
Mano, D. Keith 11426
Manross, William Wilson 5197
Manson, George 1073
Manz, James G. 8824, 9147
Marby, Harold P. 3979
Marcel, Gabriel 6517, 8502, 8689
Marchak, Mark 18909
Marchant, Colin 15548, 17427, 17858
Marchant, Olivia 18910
Marciniak, Edward 6196, 6910, 7368, 9547, 9975, 13617
Marcum, John P. 15909
Marcus Garvey and 'Garveyism' 3527
Marcus, Jacob 5488
Marcus, Melvin G. 12456
Marcuse, Herbert 9148
Marguardt, Werner 17428
Margull, Hans J. 8825, 10947, 12577
Marianski, Janusz 15910, 17429
Mariante, Benjamin R. 15911
Marie Lucita 10464
Mariners 3709
Marins, José 15139
Maritain, Jacques 4468, 14865, 18244
Markiewicz, Stanslaw 17430
Markland, Arne K. 15140
Marks, Stephen 13963
Markus, Thomas A. 12234
Marlin, William 12960
Marney, Carlyle 8226
Marone, Lois 9548
Maroney, Jimmy K. 17049, 17859
Márquez Montiel, Joaquin 4853
Marriott, Victor Edward 4230
Marris, Peter 16315
Marsden, George 15549
Marsh, Clifton E. 17050
Marsh, Daniel L. 3013, 3014, 3255, 3432, 3528, 3625
Marsh, John 6197

Marshall, Arthur F. 890
Marshall, David F. 10465, 10466
Marshall, Harvey 17860
Marshall, Mary Ruth 18592
Marshall, Paul 15912, 16316
Marshall, Ronald 12235
Marshall, Sandy 16317
Marshall, Thomas Chalmers 5703
Marsman, Leon 14017
Marson, Charles L. 11033
Marsot, Afaf Lutfi al-Sayyid 17051
Martí, Casmiro 8826, 17052
Martin R. D. 5039
Martin, Dan 16318
Martin, David 9549, 10467, 10948, 11427, 14734
Martin, Gary 16722
Martin, Hugh 3841
Martin, J. H. 3626
Martin, Joan 17861
Martin, Keith 14335, 14735, 14736, 15913
Martin, Kenneth Mayes 4960
Martin, Larry Kenneth 14737
Martin, Luke 8503
Martin, Merilyn 7905
Martin, Michael 13962
Martin, Ralph P. 15141
Martin, Robert Ray 3980
Martin, Roy Newman 14336
Martin, Steele W. 18911
Martin, Tony 13964
Martin, William C. 10468, 12578
Martindale, C. C. 4070
Martindale, Don 7369
Martinez, Joel 15914
Martínez, Rafael V. 9149
Martini, Carlos María 16319, 17431, 17432
Martino, Cesare 15550
Martinus, Wilhelm 685
Martling, Carl H. 12579
Marty, Martin E. 6911, 7370, 7610, 7641, 7906, 8227, 8504, 8827, 8828, 9133, 9150, 9550, 9864, 10949, 11428, 11429, 11430, 11885, 12580, 13295, 14337, 14338, 14967, 15551, 15915, 15916, 16320, 17053, 17433, 18245, 18593, 19119
Marty, Myron A. 12961
Martyn, Carlos 1002, 1557, 1558
Marvin, Ernest 10469
Marvin, George 4751
Marx, Barbara 7112
Marx, Gary T. 10470
Marx, Karl 202, 236, 435, 7371, 12163
Marx, Leo 9151, 17054
Mary Vincentia 12236
Maryknoll Fathers and Brothers 15142, 15917
Maryland Council of Churches, Department of Research 9976
Marzik, Thomas D. 14357
Masaki, Hiroshi 6725
Mascall, E. L. 9551, 10471
Maser, Frederick E. 14339
Masetti Zannini, Gian Ludovico 11886
Maslow, Will 7907
Maslow-Armand, Laura 17862
Máspero, Emilio 8505, 11431, 17055, 17434
Mason, Charles Harrison 11477
Mason, David 10472, 10950
Mason, John 13618
Mason, Philip 9552, 13619
Masott, Louis H. 10369
Massachusetts Council of Churches, Department of Research and Strategy 5939
Masse, Benjamin L. 7136, 8829, 9152, 9553, 9977, 9978
Masses urbaines et missions 7137
Massey, David 12962
Massey, Floyd, Jr. 13965
Massey, James Earl 10473, 11432

Massie, Robert, Jr. 15469
Masson, J. 14738
Masterman, Charles F. G. 1812, 1972, 2037, 2155
Masterman, H. 891
Masterman, Neville Charles 8830
Masters, D. C. 14739
Masters, Victor Irvine 2632, 2811, 3082, 3341
Maston, Thomas B. 7642, 10951
Mastrude, Roger G. 6061
Mastruko, Lvica 15918
Masure, Roger 17435
Mateo, Jose A. 7372
Matheny, Judy C. 18912
Mather, Thomas Bradley 5112
Mather, William G. 10952
Mathew, David 7908
Mathews, Basil Joseph 4380
Mathews, Joanna H. 1233
Mathews, Mark Stanley 6518
Mathews, Shailer 1559, 1705, 1759, 2156, 2225, 2423, 2424, 2515, 2717, 2718, 2812, 2822, 3384, 3529, 3530, 3531, 3627, 4071, 4545, 13719
Mathews, Thomas 10474
Maton, Kenneth I. 18913
Matson, Theodore E. 6418, 8228
Matsuda, Mizuho 17436
Matsumoto, Toru 5489
Mattai, Giuseppe 15919
Matthes, Joachim 9153, 11433, 13620
Matthews, Joseph 8411
Matthews, Joseph B. 7909
Matthews, Stanley G. 10475
Matthews, William H. 14290
Mattingly, Trueblood 8831
Mattis, Mary 17751
Mattmuller, Markus 17656
Mattson, Alvin Daniel 6347
Matuszeski, Bill 14790
Matza, D 12237
Maugham, W. Somerset 4854
Maureira Lagos, Jorge 10953
Maurer, Beryl Blake 7643
Maurer, Imelda 18246
Maurice, Arthur Bartlett 1813, 2958
Maurice, Frederick 725
Maurice, Frederick Denison 135, 159, 241, 273, 393, 404, 417, 418, 467, 725, 797, 2041, 2061, 2155, 2859, 5517, 5733, 5734, 9248, 10145, 12587, 14538, 16115, 18009 >> See further: Subject Index: Socialism, Christian
Maurin, Peter 4270, 4546, 5802, 5888, 7694, 8229, 15800, 16178, 16370, 18024, 18456, 18835, 19277 >> See further: Subject Index: Catholic Worker Movement
Maury, Philippe 8832
Mauss, Armand L. 12581, 12582, 13127, 13966, 16321
Maust, John 15143, 15920, 17056
Maves, Paul B. 6348
Mavis, W. Curry 7138
Mawson, Richard 9523, 10475
Max, Steve 17648
Maxen, Wilhelm 8634
Maxwell, Farley 11434
Maxwell, Milton A. 17057
May, Ernest V. 8412, 9154, 9155, 9156, 9277, 9829, 12583
May, Gerald G. 19316
May, Henry F. 5803, 7644
May, Malcolm 12238
May, Mark A. 4381
May, Rollo 6349
May, William 6350
May, William Egli 6912
Mayer, Albert 7645
Mayer, H. H. 3083
Mayer, Philip 8833, 8834
Mayers, Marvin K. 10954, 13296

Mayhew, Henry 337
Maynard, Edward S. 19204
Maynard, Herb 10476
Maynard, Kent Arthur 15921
Mayo, Amory D. 353
Mayo, R. A. 14740
Mayor, Stephen 10477
Mays, Benjamin E. 4304, 4752, 5490, 12584
Mays, John Barron 13621
Mazzawi, Musa 10478
Mazzocchi, Anthony 13622
Maître, Jacques 7135, 7639
Mbea, François 12963, 13967
McAfee, Joseph Ernest 2248, 3899
McAll Mission in France 482
McAll, Robert Whitaker 604, 702, 849, 1239, 11115, 16002
McAll, Robert Whitaker, Mrs. 1484
McAnally, Thomas S. 13297
McAndrews, William 2719
McAuley Water Street Mission, New York 483
McAuley, Jeremiah 483, 556, 758, 759, 1300, 1634, 1857, 4576, 10227, 11077, 12633
McAuliffe, Harold J. 5298
McAvoy, Thomas 7910, 11435
McBeth, Leon 15922
McBride, Esther Barnhart 12585, 16662
McBride, Paul 13623
McBride, Thomas Garth 5299
McBrien, Richard D. 17058
McBrien, Richard P. 11436
McBurney, Robert R. 798, 1849
McCabe, Alice R. 5198
McCabe, Joseph 3146
McCabe, Joseph E. 7646
McCabe, Lida Rose 1234, 1485, 2720
McCall, Carl A. 11437
McCall, Emmanuel L. 12586, 15923, 17863
McCandless, Richard L. 17437
McCann, Richard V. 6726, 19264
McCarthy, Eugene R. 5940
McCarthy, Jake 10479
McCarthy, John D. 15329
McCarthy, Kathleen 19293
McCarthy, Peter H. 4160
McCarty, Doran 13624, 14667, 15924
McCash, Isaac Newton 2721
McCawley, James 5596
McClain, Frank M. 12587
McClain, George D. 15552
McClain, M. C. 2249, 2250
McClain, William B. 15925, 17864
McClellan, Albert 7139
McClellan, Graydon E. 10480
McClelland, Albert 18594
McClelland, Alexander 50, 63
McClemens, Mary Ann 15814
McClorey, John A. 4161
McClory, Robert 15144, 15926
McCloskey, Liz Leibold 18914
McCloud, J. Oscar 9979
McCloughry, R. 17865
McClung, Floyd 19225
McClung, Lloyd Grant 17059, 17438, 17866
McClure, Archibald 2959
McClusky, Throp 5941
McColgan, Daniel T. 4961, 6062
McCollough, Charles R. 14340
McCombs, Vernon Monroe 3628
McCommon, Margaret 17867
McConahay, John B. 19274
McConkey, Clarence Marion 11887
McConnaughhay, J. D. 19315
McConnel, C. Douglas 17439
McConnell, Dorothy 5491, 8835
McConnell, Doug 17440
McConnell, Francis John 3147, 3256, 3532, 3533, 3534, 3535,

3536, 3710, 3981, 4231, 4469, 4639, 8662, 19262
McConnell, S. D. 1654
McConnon, Thomas 7911
McCook, Henry C. 1399
McCormack, Arthur 17060
McCormick Theological Seminary, Advisory Group on Latino Theological Studies 13298
McCormick, Bert E. 13968
McCormick, Ira G. 3433, 4305
McCormick, John Newton 2633
McCorry, Vincent P. 10481
McCosh, James 503, 1400
McCoy, Charles S. 17061, 18595
McCoy, Dulci 18247
McCoy, John 17441
McCoy, Marjorie Casebier 18595
McCracken, Daniel D. 12425
McCrackin, Maurice F. 6519
McCready, Charles 1655
McCready, William C. 12502, 13214
McCreary, David Neal 13299
McCreary, E. D. 892, 1315
McCree, Mary Lynn 11249
McCudden, John 8506
McCulloch, Frank W. 4855, 5390
McCulloch, James Edward 2038
McCulloch, Oscar C. 640, 9690, 9691, 11132
McCurry, Dan 11888
McDaniel, James A. 18915
McDermot, George 1401
McDermott, John J. 12588, 13300
McDermott, William F. 5804, 6198, 8507
McDill, Robert 8508
McDill, Wayne 13969
McDonagh, Thomas J. 6063
McDonald, Carol 9554
McDonald, John R. 6913
McDonald, R. W. [Mrs.] 3132
McDonnell, Claudia 18248
McDonnell, James R. 11641
McDonough, James J. 13759
McDowall, John R. 117, 160, 12552
McDowell, Edith 3434
McDowell, John 4072, 4750
McDowell, John Patrick 16322
McDowell, Kenyon L. 15145
McDowell, Mary E. 2425
McDowell, William F. 1486
McDowell, William O. 1156
McEachern, Theodore 10482, 12964, 14341, 14741, 14742, 15146, 16323
McElroy, James L. 14342
McElway, A. J. 1965
McEntee, Georgiana Putnam 3842
McEvoy, Hubert 9157
McFadden, Dwight J. 15553, 17062
McFadden, Robert D. 19226
McFarland, Horace Neill 7912, 10483
McFarland, John R. 9555, 10955
McFarland, M. Carter 7913
McGarrah, Albert Franklin 2890, 2960, 3015, 3148
McGavran, Donald 6727, 11889, 14343, 15147, 16663
McGavran, Donald A. 8836, 11890, 12589, 13970, 17442
McGaw, Douglas 15554
McGee, Clyde 4073
McGeever, Patrick J. 18916
McGehee, Donald Edward 14344
McGehee, H. Coleman 15148
McGiffert, A. C. 5805
McGill, Jacob W. 436
McGinley, A. A. 1656, 1760
McGinley, Laurence J. 9980
McGinn, Noel F. 11438
McGinnis, James B. 15149
McGlamery, Orlene 10956

McGlinchey, Anne 15371
McGlynn, Edward 4583
McGohon, Buddy Clay 15555
McGovern, James R. 9923
McGowan, Julia 4856
McGowan, Neal K. 7373
McGowan, Raymond A. 4306, 4307, 4547
McGraw, James R. 9556, 9557, 10484, 10485, 11439, 12590, 12965
McGreevey, Mary Virginia 9981
McGuckin, Michael 13625
McGuire, Malcolm 17063
McGuire, Meredith B. 12591, 13301, 18596
McGuire, U. M. 3982
McHugh, L. C. 9982
McIlhiney, David Brown 14345
McIlvenna, R. Ted 9826
McIlwraith, Niel 16324
McInerney, T. 14346, 14743
McIntosh, Alex 15927
McIntosh, Jack 15150
McIntyre, Dewitt Thomas 15928
McKee, Elmore M. 4753, 5492, 6728
McKee, Judith 16664
McKelvey, Blake 8837, 10957
McKelway, A. J. 2341
McKenna, David 11440, 11441, 14347
McKenna, Lambert Andrew Joseph 2813
McKenna, Mary J. 1706
McKenney, Theodore Roosevelt 12239
McKeon, Richard 9983
McKernan, Michale 14744
McKervill, Hugh W. 7374
McKibben, Robert A. 4640, 6511, 6520, 7375, 7376, 7647, 14348
McKim, Audrey 8509
McKinley, Edward H. 17868
McKinney, George 14349, 15929, 16325
McKinney, Richard I. 12240
McKinney, Samuel Berry 13965
McKinney, William 15151, 16326, 16665, 17127, 17667, 18301
McKinney, William Ayer 3983
McLanahan, Samuel 1966
McLean, Donald Alexander 3342
McLean, Edward B. 17443
McLean, F. H. 1967
McLean, Robert Craik 3016
McLean, Timothy A. 17869
McLelland, Joseph 10486
McLeod, Hugh 12966, 13302, 15556, 15930, 17064
McLoughlin, Emmett 6521
McLoughlin, G. William 11891
McLoughlin, William G. 6729, 7648, 14745
McLuhan, Marshall 16119
McMahan, C. A. 6103
McMahen, Gene 8354, 8650
McMahon, Joseph H. 3257
McMahon, Thomas F. 12241, 18917
McManis, Lester W. 9984
McManus, James 17444
McMath, Neil C. 15557
McMillan, Henry Hudson 3258
McMillan, Mary 8838
McMurry, Lucile 6199, 6351
McNailly, John Thomas 13478
McNamara, Patrick H. 17445
McNaspy, C. J. 14746
McNeil, Jesse Jai 8230, 9558
McNeill, Donald 15582
McNeill, John J. 13971
McNicholas, John T. 2251, 3984
McNiff, William J. 4962
McPeek, Francis W. 5300, 5597, 5942
McPhail, David P. 8231
McPherson, Simon J. 850
McQuade, Vincent Augustine

4754
McQuaid, J. B. 703
McRory, Peg 17870
McShane, Joseph M. 17871
McSorley, Joseph 2722
McSpadden, Bruce 17872, 18841
McSwain, Harold Warren 12242
McSwain, Horace R. 7914
McSwain, Larry L. 11442, 11892, 12243, 12967, 13303, 13626, 14667, 15931, 15932, 16327, 16328, 16329, 16666, 17065, 17873
McVickar, John 51, 88
McVickar, William Augustus 451
McWhorter, Mildred 18718
McWilliam, John 17446
McWilliams, Carey 5704
Meacham, Standish 10958, 18249
Meacham, Stewart 6200, 6730
Mead, Frank S. 4857, 5199, 5493, 5598
Mead, George Whitefield 1560
Mead, Loren B. 12592
Mead, Margaret 7140, 12425, 12593
Meade, Dave 8510
Meade, Emily Fogg 1968
Meadow, Arnold 11443
Meadowcroft, Ralph S. 5040
Meadows, Dennis L. 12594
Meadows, Donella H. 12594
Meadows, P. 12968
Meagher, Timothy J 18597
Means, F. H. 2157
Means, Richard L. 13627
Mearns, Andrew 704
Mears, John William 326
Medager, Betty 11893
Medearis, Dale W. 6914
Medema, Ken 18918
Medhurst, Kenneth 17066
Meehan, John T. 19120
Meeks, Wayne A. 15558, 16667
Meen, Sharon P. 15559
Meeting the Housing Crisis 13972
Megalopolis--Mess or Miracles 9158
Mehl, Roger 11894
Meister, John W. 8232
Meites, Hyman 3629
Meith, Dietmar 15202
Meland, Bernard Eugene 9985
Melder, Kieth 10487
Melendez, Enedino 14747
Melendy, Royal Loren 1814
Melhuish, Nigel 7915
Melish, John Howard 2521
Mellblom, Niel 8233, 8234
Mellin, John Otto 9159
Melton, Alpha Walters M. 11895
Melton, J. Gordon 14748, 16668, 16669, 19121
Melton, Loyd Dale 14749
Melville, Herman 203, 282, 13024
Melvin, Harold Wesley 11896
Melwick, Ralph 15560
Memoir and Select Remains of the Late Rev. John R. McDowall, the Martyr of the Seventh Commandment 160
Memorial of St. Mark's Church in the Bowery 1707
Memphis Social Service Conference 3900
Men and Religion Forward Movement 1761, 2522, 2723
Men's Clubs and the Churches 1908
Men's Federation of London, Ontario 2724
Ménard, Guy 14750
Mendonca, Robert 13628
Mendoza Sadaba, Andres 18250
Menes, Abraham 6201, 6522
Menezes, Carlos Alberto de 17874
Menezes, Louis 16330

Menges, Walter 8114, 8235
Menking, Stanley J. 10959
Menning, Bruce 14350, 18598
Menninga, Arland D. 18599
Menninger, Karl 15152
Mens, Larry W. 15933
Menter, Florence R. 4308
Menuez, D. Barry 9559, 9876
Menzies, Lucy 5806
Menzies, William W. 12244
Mercer, Blaine E. 6915
Mercer, Edward Clifford Anderson 3901
Mercer, John 16803
Merchant, Joseph W. 6523, 7377, 7649, 9160
Meredith, A. R. 12969
Merker, Margaret 15934
Mermann, Alan C. 11444
Merriam, Alexander R. 1909
Merriam, Eve 11445
Merriam, Thornton W. 5383
Merrick, George Purnell 1074
Merrill, Daniel D. 5943
Merrill, R. N. 3630, 4309, 4641
Merrill, William 1316, 2523
Merrix, A. Roland 5365
Merry, Sally Engle 15935
Merton, Robert King 7141, 7378
Merton, Thomas 5599, 18835
Mervis, Leonard Judah 6064
Mesar, Joe 13304
Messer, Bonnie J. 13305
Messer, Donald 13305, 16331
Mesthene, Emmanuel 9739
Metake, George 2524
Metcalf, George 14751
Metcalf, I. E. 4755
Metcalf, Walter 4548
Metch, Barbara J. 17031
Methodism and Social Services 2252
Methodism Among the Foreigners in New York City 1762
Methodist Church [Canada], Department of Evangelism and Social Service 2725
Methodist Church, Board of Education, Division of the Local Church 9560
Methodist Church, Board of Education, Joint Division of Education and Cultivation 4963
Methodist Church, Board of Home Missions and Church Extension 2426
Methodist Church, Board of Missions, National Division 10488
Methodist Church, Board of Social and Economic Relations, Commission on Chaplains 7142
Methodist Church, Canada, Department of Evangelism and Social Service 3149
Methodist Church, Committee on Urban Mission 10489
Methodist Church, Department of City Work 7650
Methodist Church, General Conference 5705, 9161
Methodist Church, New York Metropolitan Area Planning Commission 8511
Methodist Church, Rock River and Lexington Annual Conferences, Inner City Methodist Ministers' Fellowship 7651
Methodist Committee on Relief 4964
Methodist Episcopal Church 942, 2253
Methodist Episcopal Church at Work in the City 4756
Methodist Episcopal Church Union of Pittsburgh 641

Methodist Episcopal Church, Board of Home Missions and Church Extension 1003
Methodist Episcopal Church, Board of Home Missions and Church Extension, Bureau of Foreign Speaking Work 3150
Methodist Episcopal Church, Board of Home Missions and Church Extension, Department of CIty Work 3631
Methodist Episcopal Church, Board of Temperance, Prohibition and Public Morals 3017
Methodist Episcopal Church, Council of Cities 3018, 3632
Methodist Episcopal Church, Joint Centenary Committee 3084
Methodist Episcopal Church, National City Evangelization Union 1657
Methodist Episcopal Church, New York Church Extension and Missionary Society 1317, 2090, 2254
Methodist Episcopal Social Union 2342
Methodist Federation for Social Action 4310, 13629
Methodist Federation for Social Service 2158, 2525, 2961, 3085, 3780, 3902
Methodist Social Union of Chicago and Vicinity 756
Methodist Social Union, Boston 468
Metlake, George 2634
Metraux, Rhoda 9986
Metro Ministry, Landmark Shopping Center 9561
Metro United Church 15561
Metropolitan Associates of Philadelphia 9562, 12245, 12595
Metropolitan Catholic Almanac 262
Metropolitan Catholic Telephone Guide [21st Edition] 6731
Metropolitan Church 1487
Metropolitan Church Life 3903
Metropolitan Church News 11446
Metropolitan Dayton Mission Strategy Task Force: Final Report 15153
Metropolitan Ecumenical Training Center 9987
Metropolitan Inter-Faith Association 12246
Metropolitan Lutheran Ministry of Greater Kansas City 16332
Metropolitan Pulpit 570
Metropolitan Urban Service Training [MUST] 9563, 11447, 11897
Metropolitan: A Monthly Magazine Devoted to Religion Education, Literature and General Information 289
Metz, Donald L. 10490
Metz, Johannes Baptist 15936
Metz, Judith 15154
Metz, Nellie 18866
Meurer, Siegfried 12970
Mews, Stuart P. 15155
Meyer, Charles 16333
Meyer, Connie 14351
Meyer, Donald B. 7916
Meyer, Frederick Brotherton 3985
Meyer, Jeffrey F. 14752
Meyer, L. 10960
Meyer, Louis 1910
Meyer, Lucy Rider 943
Meyer, Matthew M. 10961
Meyer, Norma 11898

Meyer, Robert 8236
Meyer, Theodor 1402
Meyere, Michael A. 18600
Meyers, Patricia Ann 17067
Meyerson, Martin 7143, 8839
Meynell, Hugo 9988
Meyners, Robert 10491
Meziane, Abdelmajid 14352
Mia, Ahmadullah 11448
Michael, Christine 17068, 17875, 18919
Michael, Colette V. 18601
Michael, Stanley Reginald 17447
Michaelson, Robert 5807
Michaelson, Wes 19280
Michel, Barbara 15937
Michel, Bernard E. 11449
Michel, Fred W. 5944, 6732, 7144, 7145
Michel, J. 14353
Michel, Virgil George 4642, 4757
Michonneau, Georges 5494, 5945, 8512
Mickey, Paul A. 12971, 14354
Micksch, Jürgen 14753, 17069, 17876
Mid-Hudson Ecumenical Council on Criminal Justice 15156
Midcentury Pioneers and Protestants 6524
Middlebrook, Martin 14355
Middleton, Robert G. 11450, 18251
Midwest Training Network [MTN] 10492
Miel, Alice 10493
Miesel, Walter Emanuel 5600
Mieth, Dietmar 16377
Migliore, Daniel L. 15562
Míguez Bonino, Jose 13630, 14356, 15701
Mikesell, Milton L. 17070
Mikhailova, L. V. 15563
Mikva, Abner J. 9162
Milani, A. 7917
Mildon, Ivan 6525
Miles, Delos 15938, 16334, 17703
Miles, Henry A. 222
Milgrom, Jacob 16335
Milio, Nancy 11899
Milkman, Howard Louis, Jr. 15157
Millar, Moorhouse F. X. 4965
Millard, A. Douglas 7379
Millen, Nina 5946
Miller, A. C. 6916
Miller, A. H. 1318
Miller, Alexander 5495
Miller, Allen O. 11900
Miller, Andrew 12596
Miller, Calvin 18602
Miller, Cecil 10962
Miller, David Hunter 3343
Miller, DeWitt L. 6526, 6527
Miller, Donald F. 9989
Miller, Douglas 13631
Miller, Duane Russell 11901
Miller, Edward M. 15939
Miller, Ethel Prince 8513
Miller, George 1864
Miller, Haskell M. 7380, 8237
Miller, Howard A. 14754
Miller, Isaac E. 3435, 3537
Miller, J. Irwin 8238
Miller, J. R. 1561
Miller, James E. 13306
Miller, James Fogle 16972
Miller, Joan B. 12597
Miller, John 108
Miller, John P. 10494
Miller, Joseph I. 6917
Miller, K. 12598
Miller, Keith 15940
Miller, Kenneth D. 3436, 3538, 5200, 5201, 5601, 5602, 5603, 5604, 5947, 6065, 6528, 6733, 6734, 8513
Miller, Kenneth R. 17448
Miller, Lori 19122

Miller, Mike 15158, 15941, 18252
Miller, Patrick 15698
Miller, Quintor J. 4220
Miller, Randall M. 14357
Miller, Raymond Joseph 5605
Miller, Robert Moats 6735, 7381, 19123
Miller, Robert Scott 12972
Miller, Roger 274
Miller, Roy D. 6736
Miller, Samuel 23, 64
Miller, Samuel H. 7918, 10963
Miller, Spencer 3259, 4074, 4311, 4382, 4383, 4384, 4470
Miller, Steven I. 12973
Miller, Stuart C. 11451
Miller, Vern 11902, 15564
Miller, Walter B. 7919
Miller, Wayne 13973
Miller, William D. 12974, 16336
Miller, William L. 6066
Miller, William Robert 10964
Miller, Zane L. 10965, 12975
Millet-Gérard, Dominique 18603
Milligan, Fred 18920, 19227
Milliken, Bill 10966, 11452, 12976, 17877
Millin, George Francis 1763
Milling, Kim 9990
Million, Elmer G. 6737
Million, Linda Penrod 18253
Millis, Harry Alvin 2891
Milloy, Courtland 16670
Mills, B. Fay 1135, 1428
Mills, C. Wright 5948, 6067, 7382, 7652
Mills, Charles S. 1157, 1562, 1969
Mills, Edgar W. 6202, 11148, 12371
Mills, Edward Laird 3781
Mills, J. 18254
Mills, John Orme 18255
Mills, Ralph J. 9163
Mills, V. G. 2526
Millspaugh, Martin 7383
Milner, Alfred 1403
Milojeviá, Michael 18306
Milson, Fred 13307
Milum, J. Parton 2427
Min, Kyoung-bae 13308
Minangkabua! Stories of People vs. TNCs in Asia 15942
Mindolo Ecumenical Centre [Kitwe, Zambia] 13632
Mingione, Enzo 15943
Mininger, Jacob D. 4643
Minister and Industrial Peace 5706
Minister and Social Problems 4162
Minister's Periodical Library 9164
Ministers Social Helper 2159
Ministries Come to Aid of Quake Victims 18921
Ministry in Social Change, Twin Cities Graduate Program [MISC] 11453
Ministry of Urban Concerns [MUC] 10967
Ministry Opportunities in Multifamily Housing 16337
Ministry to International Seamen 15565
Ministry: A Quarterly Theological Review for East and South Africa 9165
Minneapolis Church Federation 4163
Minoru, Sonoda 13633
Miracle on LaSalle Street 12599
Mirak, Robert 14358
Miranda, Juan Carlos 18604
Miranda-Feliciano, Evelyn 18922
Mirek, Franciszek 3904, 6068
Mision Urbana 10968
Mission Advance Research and Communications [MARC]

17878
Mission Church 79
Mission Public Relation Office 5808
Mission to Metropolis 7920
Missionary Review of the World 598
Missionary Structure of the Congregation: An Introduction 8514
Missions in the City 6529
MISUR [Thematic issue: Housing, Squatters, Slums] 11454
Mitcham, Carl 17071
Mitchel, William E. 14755
Mitchell, Brian 18605
Mitchell, Brian C. 17879
Mitchell, Broadus 5496
Mitchell, Curtis 9991
Mitchell, H. G. 1404
Mitchell, Henry H. 10969, 12247, 15159, 17880
Mitchell, J. B. 3260
Mitchell, J. Clyde 6203, 6530, 6918
Mitchell, James Erskine 11903
Mitchell, John 1970
Mitchell, Kenneth R. 9992, 18606
Mitchell, Robert E. 13309
Mitchell, Rudy 17072, 17073, 18607
Mitchell, William S. 3086, 3344, 3437, 3633, 3986
Mitterling, Philip I. 15566
Mitulski, James 18441
Mitzman, Arthur 12977
Mivart, Frederick St. George 851
Mixon, John L. 5707, 8239, 11455
Mixon, Rosalie W. 6919, 7146, 11455
Miyoshi, Hiromu 18608
Mizoguchi, Yasuo 4164
Moakley, Joe 13634
Moberg, David O. 7384, 7921, 8240, 8515, 9564, 10970, 12600, 14756, 16338
Modehn, Christian 15827
Model Working Church 1158
Models of Local Mission 12601
Modica, Joseph 18532
Moeser, Donald H. 9993
Moffatt, Jessica 18256
Moggridge, E. H. 1235
Mogok Kerdja: alat jang terachir. Terbitan pertama dari 6531
Mohabir, Philip 18923
Mohan, Robert Paul 7922
Mohl, Raymond A. 10495, 11904, 12602, 12978, 17881
Mohr, Richard D. 18609
Mohring, Helmut 11905
Mohs, Mayo 14757
Mol, Johannis J. [Hans] 7653, 7923, 8241, 8840, 9565, 9566, 12248, 13974, 15160, 16671
Mole, David 13635, 15161
Moley, R. 7385
Molgren, Gerald 14359
Moll, Peter 14758
Mollner, Terry 18610
Moltmann, Jürgen 9567, 14360, 15162, 17882
Molton, Warren Lane 10268
Momeni, Jamshid A. 18924
Monahan, Sharon 15944
Monatsschrift für Innere Mission 664
Moncada, P. S. 2892
Money Management in Black Families 15567
Mongan, Daniel J. 11906
Monro, Edward 379, 10876
Monroe, Anne Shannon 4312
Monroe, H. A. 944
Monroe, Harriet Earhart 2814
Monroe, Johnnie 15568
Monroe, Paul 1405

Monsma, Timothy 13636, 13975, 14361, 15163, 15945, 16672, 17883, 18611, 18854, 19124
Montage, Francis Charles 945
Montagu, Lily H. 16051, 16763
Monteiro, Anthony A. 6124
Monteith, John 9847
Montêquin, François-Augusta de 16673
Montero García, Feliciano 16674
Monterroso, Victor M. 15614
Montesano, Philip M. 12979
Montgomery, Caroline Williamson 2039
Montgomery, Harry Earl 2527
Montgomery, John C. 18925, 19125, 19144
Montgomery, John K. 6920
Montgomery, Lois 9166
Montgomery, Louise 2528
Montgomery, M. W. 2040
Monthly Letter On Evangelism 6921
Montilus, Guerin C. 15164
Montoya, Alex D. 18257
Moody -- the Consecrated Commoner 4644
Moody, Dwight L. 549, 571, 580, 1764, 2815, 3816, 4644, 4758, 5395, 8139, 8396, 8397, 8421, 8862, 11279, 17971
Moody, Howard 7924, 7925, 8516, 8517, 8518, 8841, 8842, 9568, 10026, 11456, 13976, 17269
Moody, Joseph N. 6352, 7386, 9994
Moody, Kim 19126
Moody, Paul Dwight 4758
Moody, William G. 852
Moody, William R. 1764
Moon, Parker Thomas 3345
Mooney, Bernice Maher 18258
Mooneyham, W. Stanley 13637
Moore, A. C. 6204
Moore, Allen J. 10971
Moore, Arthur J. 9167
Moore, Arthur Newell 4232
Moore, Aubrey S. 4759, 5041
Moore, Barbara 12603
Moore, Barrington, Jr. 12604
Moore, David 15569
Moore, David B. 17884
Moore, David O. 15946
Moore, Deborah Dash 13977
Moore, E. C. 1563
Moore, E. Paul, Jr. 9168, 10496, 10972, 13978, 15165
Moore, Gordon B. 1865
Moore, Jenny 10973
Moore, Jerome A. 18612
Moore, Joan 17426
Moore, John Milton 4165
Moore, Joseph G. 7387, 7654
Moore, L. H. 9995
Moore, Lucy M. 2428
Moore, Lydia C. 18926
Moore, Michael Allen 12605
Moore, Mildred 2893
Moore, Paul 14362
Moore, Philip D. 8519
Moore, R. Laurence 18927
Moore, Ralph 10974
Moore, Richard E. 9996, 9997, 9998, 10293
Moore, Robert Samuel 13310, 13638
Moore, Sidney Harrison 13639
Moore, Trevor Wyatt 11457, 11907
Moore, W. T. 14759
Moore, Watson S. 3634
Moore, William Hoyt 4471, 4760
Moorehead, Lee C. 9569
Moorhous, Carl W. 19317
Morais, Henry S. 1319
Moral Precepts Carved in Stone in the Design of St. Thomas's Church 3346
Moran, Gabriel 10975

Moran, Peter 4761
Moran, Theodore 12980
Morano, Roy William 16339, 17074
Morauta, Louise 15947
Morcillo, Casimiro 7147
More Advertizing against Crime 3711
Morehouse, Frederic Cook 2726
Morey, Charles E. 7655, 8843
Morey, George 9469
Morgan Memorial Goodwill Industries 3261
Morgan, Elaine 14760
Morgan, Everett J. 9169, 11908
Morgan, G. Campbell 2816
Morgan, Kent 13274
Morgan, Margaret 11458
Morgan, Neil 15166
Morgan, Pliny Brett 551
Morgan, Raymond Earl 4233
Morgan, Thomas 9999, 18613
Morgan, William Ferdinand 338
Morgan, William S. 2732
Morgan, Y. Peyton 1564
Moribe, Yoshimasa 19127
Morikawa, Hazel 19128
Morikawa, Jitsuo 6404, 7926, 9570, 10000, 19128
Morioka, Kiyomi 10001, 11909, 13640
Moritz, Hans 17449
Morizono, Michael M. 14363
Morlan, Beth 14761
Morland, John Kenneth 7388
Morley, Charles 2343
Morrell, Charles B. 1135
Morris, Aldon D 17075
Morris, Cathleen 18212
Morris, Dan 14762
Morris, E. D. 538
Morris, Edwin 11459
Morris, George Perry 2041
Morris, J. Kenneth 4472
Morris, Orrin D. 9107, 9170, 16675, 17885
Morris, Philip D. 11910
Morris, Robert 6353
Morris, S. L. 1971
Morrisay, Elizabeth 4645
Morrison, Arthur 1320
Morrison, Charles Clayton 4313, 5497, 5708
Morrison, Henry 15570
Morrison, John Alexander 3262
Morrison, Robert Paterson 11911
Morriss, Mack 6532
Morrow, Sara Sprott 13641
Morse, Herman N. 4385, 4473
Morse, S. M. 946
Morse, Stearns 4646
Morse-Boycott, Desmond Lionel 4075
Mortensen, Phyllis 19332
Morton, Frances H. 7148
Morton, James P. 8844, 9171
Morton, Marian J. 18614
Morton, T. Ralph 6533
Moseley, Fred B. 8242
Mosender, Ursula 15948
Moses, Robert 13144
Moses, Wilson J. 12606, 14763
Moslem Missionaries in America 3782
Moslems Praying for World Unity 4549
Mosley, Marvin Jarvis 13311
Mosotti, Louis 10710
Moss, Len 17886
Mosso, Sabastiano 16340
Mostrom, Donald 8845
Mott, John R. 1565
Mott, Stephen Charles 18928
Motte, Jean-François 7149, 7656, 7927, 7928
Motter, Alton 5809
Mottesi, Alberto 18615
Motts, Bonnie 13642
Mould, D. 10976
Mould, Ralph Norman 4647,

5606
Moulder, Wayne 13312
Moulton, Elizabeth 9172
Moussé, Jean 11460
Mouw, Richard 13979, 15571, 17076
Movido, Jose Salazar, Jr. 13980
Movimiento de Trabajadores Cristianos 17077
Mowrey, George E. 15949
Mowry, Charles E. 10002
Moxom, Philip S. 799, 1321, 1658
Moyes, Gordon Keith M. 17078
Moynagh, James 8243
Moynihan, Daniel P. 8730, 9173, 9174
Moynihan Report 9571
Mpayo, Owdencalm 15572
Mt. Auburn Baptist Church 18259
Mt. Olivet Lutheran, Minneapolis, MN 5949
Muckley, G. W. 3347
Mudd, Rita 12271
Mudge, Lewis S. 11912
Mudie, Robert 148
Mudie-Smith, Richard 1972, 9683
Muelder, Herman R. 5709
Muelder, Walter G. 5391, 5607, 5608, 6354, 6534, 6738, 6922, 7150, 7657, 7929, 7930, 8520, 8713, 12981
Mueller, Beata 5765, 6205
Mueller, E. W. 6206, 10003
Mueller, F. W. 4314
Mueller, Franz 12249
Mueller, Samuel 12250, 14364
Mueller, Samuel A. 10004, 10497, 12868, 13235, 19228
Muggeridge, Malcolm 14365
Mugglebee, Ruth 4315
Muhammad, Elijah 8596
Muhlenberg, William Augustus 136, 263, 305, 394, 452, 623, 1007, 7986, 12319
Muir, William 2429
Mukenge, Ida Faye Rousseau 15573
Mulder, John M. 1739, 14764, 19198
Muldoon, Maureen 15574
Mulkey, James Broughton 17450
Mullen, Thomas J. 10005
Mullenbach Industrial Institute 4966
Mullendore, F. K. 10006
Mullens, Joseph 453
Muller, Carol D. 9572
Muller, Dorothea Rosalie 6923, 7658
Müller, Eberhard 8244, 10977
Muller, L. C. 1236
Müller, Werner 13643, 13644
Mullett, M. B. 3635
Mulligan, Raymond A. 8245
Mullins, Mark R. 18260, 18616
Mulry, Thomas M. 1911
Mulvey, Ann Marie 7659
Mumford, Lewis 3712, 3783, 3784, 4762, 5392, 6739, 6924, 6925, 8246, 9145, 11901
Mumford, Mary 1406
Mumford, Melba M. 4858
Mumford, Stephen 15950
Mumper, Sharon E. 17887
Munby, Denys Lawrence 5393, 6926, 7660, 8247, 8846
Munds, William C. 4763
Munger, Theodore Thornton 705, 853, 1407
Munier, John David 5202
Munif, Abdelrahman 18261
Munro, John Josiah 2042
Muraro, Valmir Francisco 17451
Murayama, Moritada 11913
Murdoch, Norman H. 17452, 17888
Murdock, Clyde 9573

Murdock, Vergil E. 12607
Murin, William J. 15749
Murkland, H. Banta 4550
Murnion, Philip Joseph 12608, 13645, 15018, 15167, 16676, 16677, 18929, 19129
Murphy, Bonneau Pernell 6355, 8248, 8249
Murphy, David John 15168
Murphy, Denis 16532, 16612, 17079
Murphy, Edgar Gardner 1973
Murphy, Edward 12609
Murphy, Frederick V. 4386
Murphy, Harry Williams 4166
Murphy, Humphrey Joseph 16341
Murphy, Jimmy 17453
Murphy, John 1075
Murphy, Joseph M. 18617
Murphy, Kenneth 10475
Murphy, Larry 18635
Murphy, Mable Ansley 3151
Murphy, Raymond E. 10007
Murphy, Ruth Elizabeth 5113
Murphy, Thomas P. 10978, 10979
Murphy, Tom 10980, 11284
Murphy, W. B. 10008
Murphy, William P. 16342
Murray, Charles K. 18262
Murray, Clyde E. 6207, 6535
Murray, Eileen H. 17454
Murray, John B. 10498
Murray, John Clark 16343
Murray, John Courtney 16178
Murray, Michael H. 10499, 10500
Murray, Philip 7883, 7899
Murray, Ralph L. 11914
Murray, Richard C. 9645
Murray, Robert 8847
Murray, Walter I. 9574
Murray, William Henry Harrison 484
Murrieta, Sara Marie 14366
Murry, J. M. 5114
Murthy, B. Srinivasa 16678
Muspratt, Max 3636
Musselman, G. Paul 6208, 6547, 6740, 7931, 7932, 8250
Mussina, Malcolm Vivian 4551
Must for Urban Mission 10009
Muste, Abraham John 2817, 3438, 4552, 4764
Muthalaly, Alexander Koshy 18263
Mwantila, Simalike 17455
My Church Stayed Out of Business 4648
My God! My God! Why Hast Thou Forsaken Me 7389
Myer, Connie 12610, 12982, 13313, 13646, 15169
Myerowitz, Arthur 4474
Myers, Chauncie Kilmer 7151, 7390
Myers, Erskine Roy 3348
Myers, H. W. 3263, 3349
Myers, James 3439, 3637, 3905, 3987, 4076, 4077, 4078, 4167, 4387, 4475, 4649, 4859, 4967, 5203, 5484
Myers, K. 17080
Myers, Kenneth A. 18930
Myers, Kenneth H. 9575
Myers, Richard 8848
Myers, Richard A. 5609, 6356, 6927, 7661, 10981
Myers, William R. 18931
Mylander, Charles 15170
Myra, Harold 17081
Myrick, Judith 18618
NADIR 7933
Nagai, Willie Tsunetaka 13981
Nagano, Paul M. 12983
Naison, Mark 6536
Nakajima, John 14765
Nakamaki, Hirochika 16679
Nakamori, Ikunoshi 10010,

11461
Nallo, Larry T. 12984
Nam, Moon Hee 17082
Nanfelt, Peter N. 14367
Nash, Arthur 3539
Nash, Dennison J. 8521, 8522
Nash, George 11915, 13647
Nash, H. S. 1659
Nash, Joseph 599
Nash, Roderick 8694
Nasmith, David 199, 4124, 17416
Natale, Samuel M. 16680, 17456
Nathe, Patricia A. 13982
National Association of Community Counsel, Community Legal Counsel, Chicago Division 10982
National Association of Ecumenical Staff [NAES] and Churches' Center for Theology and Public Policy 14766
National Association of Manufacturers, Clergy-Industry Relations Department 7152, 7153
National Association of Manufacturers, Committee on Cooperation with Churches 5301
National Capital Semester for Seminarians [brochure, syllabus] 15575
National Cathedral Association 4968
National Catholic Coordinating Committee on Economic Opportunity 9175
National Catholic Education Association 1974
National Catholic Welfare Conference 3152, 3264, 3265, 3540, 4234, 4476, 4860
National Catholic Welfare Conference, Administrative Board 4969
National Catholic Welfare Conference, Department of Social Action 5498, 9176
National Catholic Welfare Conference, Social Action Department 4765
National Christian Council of India, International Mobile Team 9177
National Christian Council of Kenya 13648
National City Evangelization Union 1317
National Conference of Catholic Bishops 17083, 17889, 18619
National Conference of Catholic Charities 2430, 3019, 6741
National Conference of Jewish Social Service 6928
National Conference on Religious Architecture 10011
National Conference on the Christian Way of Life 3638, 3639
National Conference on the Church and Urban America: Book of Reports 10983
National Congress on Pastoral Care 10501
National Council of Churches in Korea 13983
National Council of Churches in New Zealand 5302
National Council of Churches of New Zealand, Conference on Christian Order 5394
National Council of the Churches of Christ in the USA 6537, 6742, 7391, 7662, 10502
National Council of the Churches of Christ in the USA, Broadcasting and Film Commission 6538, 6539, 6540, 7154, 7155, 8251
National Council of the

Churches of Christ in the USA, Bureau of Research and Survey 8523
National Council of the Churches of Christ in the USA, Commission on the Church and Economic Life 9178, 10012, 10503
National Council of the Churches of Christ in the USA, Commission on Urban Life 9179
National Council of the Churches of Christ in the USA, Corporate Information Center 12251, 12252, 12611, 12612
National Council of the Churches of Christ in the USA, Department of Educational Development 10013
National Council of the Churches of Christ in the USA, Department of International Affairs, Immigration Services 8252
National Council of the Churches of Christ in the USA, Department of Ministry, Vocation, and Pastoral Services 9576
National Council of the Churches of Christ in the USA, Department of Pastoral Services, and the Department of Social Welfare 6209
National Council of the Churches of Christ in the USA, Department of Racial and Cultural Relations 6210
National Council of the Churches of Christ in the USA, Department of Social Welfare 6357
National Council of the Churches of Christ in the USA, Department of the Church and Economic Life 5950, 6358, 6743, 6744, 6929, 6930, 7934, 8253, 8524
National Council of the Churches of Christ in the USA, Department of the Urban Church 5951, 6931, 7935, 7936
National Council of the Churches of Christ in the USA, Division of Christian Life and Work, Department of the Church and Economic Life 6745, 6932, 7156, 8525, 8526, 8849, 12985
National Council of the Churches of Christ in the USA, Division of Christian Unity, Department of Youth Ministry 10014
National Council of the Churches of Christ in the USA, Division of Home Mission, Department of the Urban Church 7392, 9577
National Council of the Churches of Christ in the USA, General Board 7157, 8527
National Council of the Churches of Christ in the USA, Joint Commission on Mission Education 15576
National Council of the Churches of Christ in the USA, Joint Commission on the Urban Church, Department of the Urban Church 5952
National Council of the Congregational Churches of the US, Labor Committee 5953

National Federation of Catholic College Students, Social Action Secretariat 8528
National Federation of Settlements and Neighborhood Centers 7393
National Fire Protection Association 3906
National Florence Crittendon Mission 1566
National Hispanic Consultation 17457
National Hispanic Lutheran Assembly 14368
National Industrial Mission 7937
National Lutheran Council 6746
National Lutheran Council, Division of American Missions 6211
National Lutheran Council, Division of American Missions, Urban Church Planning 8529, 9180
National Office for Black Catholics 15577
National Reform Association 437
National Religion and Labor Foundation 4235, 5499, 5500, 5710, 5711
National Right to Work Committee 5954
National Sex and Drug Forum 11916
National Social Welfare Assembly 7394
Natterman, Johannes 3713
Naujoks, Eberhard 4861
Naumann, Dorothy 8850
Navarro, Nelson 18620
Navarro, Peter 18621
Nawyn, Bert 12613
Nawyn, William E. 15951
Naylor, Phyllis Reynolds 10984
Nazario, Ruth 14767
NCCB Committee on Migration and Tourism 17458
Neal, Marie Augusta 9578, 10015
Neale, Eddie 13314
Neale, Edward Vansittart 616, 13116
Nearing, Scott 2431, 2894
Neddens, Martin C. 18264
Nederduits Gereformeerde Kerk 11462
Nederhood, Joel H. 10016
Needham, Barrie 17459
Needham, Philip D. 10504
Needleman, Ruth 18932
Nees, Thomas G. 13984, 16168, 17084, 18622
Neff, David 17890
Neff, Eleanore 5501
Neff, William Howard 1004
Negen, Gordon 10985
Negro in American Life 5303
Neibuhr, Reinhold 5693
Neighbor, Chad 16344
Neighborhood House of Christ Church, Philadelphia: With a Social Survey of Its District 2895
Neighbour, Ralph Webster, Jr. 12253, 12614, 13315, 13649, 15578, 15952, 17085, 17891, 18265
Neill, Charles Patrick 2255
Neitzel, Sarah C. 16345, 18266
Nell-Breuning, Oswald von 4650, 5610, 5810, 6933, 16681
Nellessen-Schumacher, Traute 11463
Nelsen, Anne K. 12255, 13651
Nelsen, Hart M. 10986, 12254, 12255, 12615, 12616, 12986, 13316, 13650, 13651, 13985, 13986, 18623
Nelson, Amirtharaj 13317, 13652
Nelson, Bruce C. 18624
Nelson, Clarence T. 6359

Nelson, Clyde Kenneth 10987
Nelson, Douglas J. 17892
Nelson, E. C. 9181
Nelson, F. Burton 13172, 16346
Nelson, Frank 3843, 4316
Nelson, G. Edward 18267
Nelson, Gary Vincent 18268
Nelson, Geoffrey K. 11464, 12256, 12257, 12617
Nelson, J. Robert 13318, 14768
Nelson, Jack A. 15579
Nelson, James Melvin 5395
Nelson, James W. 14369
Nelson, Joan 15171
Nelson, John O. 5502, 6069, 6541, 6934
Nelson, Mary 10505, 18269
Nelson, N. O. 1700
Nelson, Sarah 14370
Nelson, Wesley W. 10017, 10018, 13987
Nelson, William R. 12258
Neptune, A. Ray 8530
Nesmith, Richard 10506, 10988
Nesti, Arnaldo 14371, 15580
Netting, F. Ellen 17086
Netting, Park H. 19314
Netzer, E 13653
Neubert, E. 17893
Neuhaus, Richard J. 11668, 14126, 14372
Neuhause, Richard J. 8531
Neuloh, Otto 10507
Neumann, A. Lin 15172
Neumeyer, Robert E. 13654
Neussendorfer, Macaria 9579
Neve, Herbert T. 10989
Nevill, Florence 3714
Nevin, Alfred 893
Nevin, Ethan A. 9580
Nevins, Joseph V. 3907
Nevius, John L. 1708
New Advance of the Salvation Army 1005
New Americans for a New America 2727
New Brunswick Theological Seminary 19283
New Church Every Day 6747
New City in the German Democratic Republic 12259
New Departure 1076
New Evangelism Contrasted With the Old 2529
New Jersey Council of Churches 8532
New Kinds of Churches 10990
New Life in the City Series 11917
New McAuley Mission 2635
New Shape of Metropolitan Mission 11465
New Techniquė for the City 6542
New Training for City Ministers 9581
New York Bible and Common Prayer Book Society 11
New York Bible Society 12
New York Charities' Directory 1408
New York Circus, A Center for Social Justice and International Awareness 15173
New York City as a Field for Church Work 395
New York City Evangelization Records of the City Commission 419
New York City Mission 854
New York City Mission and Tract Society 405, 420
New York City Mission Society 3153, 3541
New York City Missions Society 757
New York City Tract Society 161
New York Evangelical Missionary Society of Young Men 44
New York Female Moral Reform

Society 137
New York Female Union Society for the Promotion of Sabbath Schools 36
New York Port Society 406
New York Preachers' Address on Municipal Misrule 1006
New York Protestant Episcopal City Mission Society 104, 126
New York Protestant Episcopal Mission Society 1866, 5042
New York Protestant Episcopal Tract Society 27
New York Public Library 7938, 12618
New York Religious Tract Society 19
New York State Council of Churches, Prison Research Education Action Project 13988
New York Sunday School Union Society 45
New York's Biggest and Oldest Negro Churches 5955
New York's Puerto Ricans 7158
New York's Religious Skyline 3908
New York's Riverside: What Is Happening Today in This Mighty Church in a Great City 6070
Newark Ministry to Homeless Is Losing Its Home 18933
Newbern, Captolia D. 18934
Newbery, Alfred S. 3785
Newbigin, Leslie 10019, 18270, 18935
Newby, Donald O. 13319, 18271
Newell, Barbara Ware 8254
Newell, Fred B. 4862
Newenhuyse, Frederick 18272
Newland, John 13351
Newman, Aubrey 15953, 17460
Newman, David 17894
Newman, Lewis I 19254
Newman, Richard 14546
Newman, William Kincaid 7395
Newman, William M. 12619, 12987, 13989
Newmann, Harvey K. 15174
Newport and Gwent Industrial Mission 13655
Newsinger, John 17895
Newsom, G. E. 3440
Newsom, Reuben J. 9582
Newsome, David 10020
Newton, Jim 16682
Newton, Judy Ann 19130, 19131
Newton, Michael 19130, 19131
Newton, Richard Heber 572, 800, 855
Newton, William Wilberforce 1007
Ng, Don 18625
Ng, John Lai 17461
Ng, Richard 19103
Ng, Wing-Cheung 14486
Ngai, David 18626
Nichelson, F. Patrick 11925
Nichol, John 10991
Nicholas, Tim 12988
Nicholas, William 1237
Nicholl, Grier 9182, 10992
Nicholls, Bruce J. 17896
Nicholls, David 17087
Nichols, Alan 18273
Nichols, Bruce 17462
Nichols, Doug 18311
Nichols, Frank 15954
Nichols, Fred S. 4766
Nichols, James Hastings 6071, 8255
Nichols, Roger L. 13507, 15006
Nicholson, Joseph William 4304
Nicholson, Thomas 2967
Nickel, Herman 15581
Nickels, Frances J. 4651
Nickles, Albert 13990
Niebuhr, H. Richard 3988, 4553,

4652, 5712, 6072, 6935, 12906, 14597
Niebuhr, Reinhold 3441, 3844, 4236, 4317, 4318, 4477, 5304, 6748, 7159, 7396, 8099, 8533, 9172, 9583, 9584, 14621
Nieden, Ernst zur 7663
Niehaus, Juliet Anne 15955
Nielsen, D. A. 13320
Niemela, Pauli 18225
Niemeyer, Larry L. 19132
Nietzsche, Freidrich 5725
Nieves, Alvaro L. 17463, 18627
Nikkel, Steven 18628
Niklaus, Robert 15956, 16347, 16348, 17088, 17089, 17464, 17465
Niles, D. T. 7939, 7940, 8256, 8534
Niles, Edward Samuel 1322
Nimwegen, Holland 7434
Ninde, H. S. 1159
Nishi, Setsuko M. 6631
Nishimoto, George N. 6936
Nissen, Jørgen 8535
Nitti, Francesco Saverio 1409
Njiraini, Ng'ang'a 12989
Nkonge, Julius M. 15957
No Man Is an Island 12990
Nobel, John M. 8536
Nobile, Philip 12095
Noble, David W. 6749
Noble, Franklin 1410
Noel, Conrad le Despencer Roden 2530, 3154, 5396, 10367
Noffs, Ted 11338, 11466
Noland, James R. 6750, 6937
Nolen, John 2636
Noll, C. Edward 9719
Noonan, Dana 13656
Noonan, Edward J. 8537, 8538
Noppel, Constantin 4863
Nordby, Juel Magnar Arnt 10508
Nordhoff, Charles 557
Noreen, Robert G. 9585
Noren, Loren E. 7802, 8539
Norman, B. 17466
Norman, Colin 16349
Norman, Edward 13991, 18274
Norman, John 6073
Norquist, Ernest 9586
Norquist, M. 12260
Norris, Beauford A. 11918
Norris, Judy 19318
North American Lay Conference on the Christian and His Daily Work, Buffalo, NY, February 21-24, 1952 6212, 6213
North, Cecil Clare 4168
North, Frank Mason 1008, 1077, 1078, 1238, 1567, 1709, 1765, 1912, 1913, 2256, 2344, 2345, 2432, 2531, 3989, 5971, 10437
North, Lila Verplanck 1660
North, Louise M. 1239
North, Stanley U. 5115, 5116, 5204, 5205, 5305, 5397, 5398, 5503, 6214, 6360, 6543
Northcott, Cecil 7664, 8851, 10021, 10993
Northcott, Clarence Hunter 7397
Northcott, Michael S. 18936, 19133
Northcott, R. J. 4653
Northern Baptist Convention, Social Service Commission 2433
Northrup, Flora L. 4388
Northrup, R. W. 7523
Norton, H. Wilbert 14217
Norton, Perry L. 7665, 7941, 7942, 7943, 8257, 9183
Norton, Thomas Joseph Aquinas 16683
Norton, Will 16350
Norwood, Ella Friedman 15175
Norwood, Frederick A. 11467
Noser, H. B. 7160
Notre Dame Study of Catholic

Parish Life 17090
Nott, Eliphalet 6
Nouwen, Henri 12620
Novak, Michael 10022, 10994, 12621, 12622, 12991, 12992, 14600, 15958, 15959, 16351, 16352, 17091, 17467, 18629
Novitsky, Anthony 19277
Nowell, Robert 17897
Nowlin, Robert Deen 13321
Noyce, Gaylord B. 9587, 11468, 11919, 11920, 13657
Noyes, Henry Drury 10023, 10509
Noyes, John Humphrey 469
Nucciarone, Albert P. 18630
Nuckols, Clyde 8540
Nuesse, C. Joseph 6074, 10024, 17468
Nugent, Robert 16353
Nuij, Ton 12993
Nunez, Joseph Armando 16187
Nunn, Douglas 11442
Nurnberger, Klaus 18275
Nussbaum, Fred M. 6215
Nutly, Leslie Ellen 14373
Nyce, Ray 12994
Nygaard, Norman E. 5956
Nykamp, R. A. 12995
O'Boyle, Patrick A. 10025
O'Brien, David J. 10510, 10995, 18631
O'Brien, Grace 2434
O'Brien, John A. 4654
O'Brien, John T. 14769
O'Brien, Maureen R. 15582
O'Brien, Richard 17898
O'Brien, William 17469, 18937
O'Cleireacain, Carol 16684
O'Connor, Anthony M. 15960
O'Connor, Denis 14374
O'Connor, Elizabeth 8852, 10026, 10996, 12261, 12623, 13992, 16354, 18276
O'Connor, James 706
O'Connor, James A. 1962
O'Connor, June 19229
O'Connor, Michael Joseph Lalor 5306
O'Connor, Richard Allan 16355
O'Connor, Thomas H. 17092
O'Connor, William R. 4655
O'Dea, Janet Koffler 11921
O'Dea, Thomas F. 6938, 7161, 7162, 7944, 7953
O'Dwyler, Thomas J. 6216
O'Gallagher, Marianna 13993
O'Gara, James 7666, 8259
O'Gligáin, Mícheál 13292
O'Grady, John 3020, 3442, 3990, 3991, 4079
O'Grady, Ron 18938
O'Hara, John 14375
O'Hara, M. 1160
O'Harrow, Dennis 7163
O'Keeffe, Henry E. 1009, 3542
O'Leary, Cornelius 11761
O'Melia, John C., Jr. 7579
O'Neal, Eddie S. 12247
O'Neal, Jack 11265
O'Neill, Charles 17470
O'Neill, Charles A. 7164
O'Neill, Daniel 15176
O'Neill, Patrick Ireland 15583
O'Neill, W. B. 4478
O'Rahilly, Alfred 5713
O'Reilly, F. Patricia 12262
O'Shea, David 7667
O'Toole, James 17548
O'Toole, Roger 14376
Oakley, Jerry 16685
Oastler, Richard 138, 149
Oates, Mary J. 14770
Oates, Stephen B. 16356
Oates, Wayne E. 5611, 6939, 11469, 12263
Obendieck, Hermannus 5957
Obenhaus, Victor 6361, 7165, 7398, 7399, 8541, 8853, 9588, 10511, 13349

Oberle, Joseph F. 5043
Obers, Samuel J. 6362
Obert, J. C. 8542
Obidinski, Eugene 17093
Oblepias-Ramos, Lilia 12264
Obregón, Paul 16070
Odegard, Peter 3909
Odell, Carolyn J. 6767, 6940, 7166, 7400, 7450, 7668, 7669, 7945, 8258, 8433, 8434
Oden, Thomas C. 11922
Odom, William 3021
Odum, Howard 5399
Oehrig, Robert 18817
Oelinger, Josef 10512
Oerter, John Henry 856
Offer, Henry J. 10997
Offerman, Bernard J. 10027
Office of Energy Policy 15584
Office of Triumphs of Faith 665
Offord, Robert M. 758, 759
Ogasapian, John 14377
Ogden, James 10449
Ogden, Jean Carter 5504
Ogden, Jess 5504
Ogden, R. 1323
Ogden, Robert C. 1161
Ogle, Alice 10028
Ogle, George 12265, 15961, 16686, 18277
Oglesbee, Clay 18632, 18939
Oglesby, Stuart Roscoe 7946
Ogletree, Thomas W. 10513, 17471
Oh Lord -- Our City Is in Flames 10998
Oh, Heisik 18278
Oh, Jae Shik 12624
Oh, Mark Edward 18633
Ohl, Jeremiah Franklin 1766, 2532, 2962
Ohsberg, H. Oliver 16357
Oil Conspiracy: An Investigation into How Multinational Oil Companies Provide Rhodesia's Oil Needs 13994
Oines, Joel H. 17094
Oishi, Shuten 9184
Oldham, Edward L. 18634
Oldham, George Ashton 14192
Oldham, John Houldsworth 4479, 4656, 4657, 4658, 5811, 5958
Olds, Marshall 3443
Olguin, John Phillip 13995
Olguin, Mary T. 13995
Olivarez, Graciela [Grace] 17095
Olive Branch 485
Oliveira, Carlos Josaphat Pinto de 8543
Oliveira, Francisco de 15585
Oliver, John 10999
Oliver, Kay 12625
Oliver, Miriam K. 2637
Oliver, William James 1324
Oliviery, Angelo 13658
Olley, John W. 19134
Olmstead, Clifton E. 11923
Olmstead, Frederick Law 486, 1867, 13441
Olsen, Marshall R. 3543
Olson, David 14771, 14772
Olson, David J. 13205
Olson, George Nils 10514
Olson, James Stewart 15177
Olson, Joan 17472
Olson, Karl Edward 5714
Olson, Lynn M. 18635
Olson, Mark 14773, 18636
Olstad, Keith 16358
Olszamovski, Leon Marion 17096
Olthuis, James H. 12626
Olver, Howard L. 14378
Olver, Paul S. 17473
Olzak, Susan 18279
On Human Work: A Resource Book for the Study of Pope John Paul II's Third Encyclical 16359

Ong, Walter J. 7167, 7519, 10515
Oniki, S. Gary 8260
Ontiveros, Suzanne 17899
Oostdyk, Harv 16687
Oosterling, James 4554
Oosterwal, Gottfried 15586
Oosthuizen, Gerhardus Cornelis 13659
Open and Institutional Church League 1325, 1568
Open Church 2533
Open Door Community 18637
Open Housing: A Climate for Progress 10516
Open Letter to Employers and to Labor 3544
Open or Institutional Church 1569
Oppen, Dietrich von 7401, 8261
Oppenheimer, Martin 11470
Oppusunggu, Hotma P. 15962
Orchard, W. E. 3444
Oren, Martin Luther 17900
Orens, John R. 15178, 15963
Organized Labor and Capitol 1975
Organizing for Family and Congregation 14774
Orientaciones cristianas del fuero del trabajo 4864
Oriental Church Magazine: Devoted to Religion, Science, Literature and Art 600
Orlandis, Jose 15587
Orlans, Harold 6574
Orme, George 274
Orna, Mary Virginia 11471
Ornstein, Allan C. 15964
Oropesa, R. S. 16969, 17031
Orphan Asylum Society of the City of New York 8
Orr, C. 6509
Orr, John B. 11924, 11925
Orsi, Robert Anthony 17474
Ortega y Gasset, José 13295
Ortegon, Samuel M. 4237
Orthodox Bubbles: or, A Review of the First Annual Report of the Executive Committee of the Magdalen Society 109
Ortiz, Blanca 18941
Ortiz, Enrique 13996
Ortiz, Hector 17097
Ortiz, Isidro 17098
Ortiz, Manuel 17099, 18638, 18940, 18941, 19135
Ortiz-Vasquez, Debra 19033
Orton, Lawrence D. 15965
Ortquist, Milton R. 8262
Orwell, George 16068
Osborn, Michelle 11000
Osborne, Charles Edward 1914
Osborne, Herbert L. 5400
Osborne, W. A. 11472
Osman, John 7168, 7402, 7670, 8263
Osofsky, Gilbert 9589
Oster, August 13935
Ostermann, Robert 8854
Ostling, Richard N. 18942
Ostrom, Henry 2638
Ostrom, Karl A. 14420
Oswald, Roy M. 18280
Oswald, Rudolph A. 18108
Other Side 9590
Ott, Hugo 14379
Otti, Phyllis Betts 14445
Ouma, Joseph P. M. B. 11926
Our Day 894
Our Mission in the Changing Neighborhood 13322
Oursler, Fulton 5812
Ousley, J. Douglas 19136
Overbea, Luix Virgil 13660, 18639
Overman, J. Andrew 17901
Overstreet, H. A. 5117
Ovitt, George 17902
Owen, David Edward 9185
Owen, James R. 15966

Owen, Margaret R. 7403
Owen, Raymond E. 13661
Owen, Robert 10475
Owen, Robert H. 11065
Owen, Wilfred 7671
Owens, J. A. 8544
Owens, Joseph 13997
Owens, Marie R. 3715
Owens, Owen D. 13998
Owens, Raymond Lee 8545
Owens, Virginia Sten 15588
Owyang, George R. 15180
Oxnam, G. Bromley 3350, 3445, 3640, 4319, 5044, 5401, 5959, 5960, 6421, 6544, 19123
Oyer, Emma 5813
Oyono, Guillaume 9591
Ozier, Ron 18559
Paape, Edward D. 14775
Pace, Charles N. 3641
Pace, Dale K. 13999
Pacek, Walter 18281
Pacey, Lorene M. 5961
Packard, Vance 8264
Paddock, William S. 7654
Paden, John N. 12996
Paden, W. M. 1570
Padilla, Elena 7404
Pagano, Nan 14000
Pagden, Frank 11001
Page, J. E. 7405
Page, Kirby 3313, 3351, 3352, 3353, 3446, 3447, 3448, 3761, 4080, 4081, 4320, 4321, 4389, 4606, 5206, 5402, 5693, 13662, 13800
Pager, Stephen 3354
Pagés, José 5403
Paget-Wilkes, Michael 15967
Paine, Robert Treat 1571
Palau, Gabriel 4480
Palau, Luis 17368
Palin, Michael 19296
Pallás-Vilaltella, Francisco 4865
Pallen, Conde B. 1010, 2963
Pallmeyer, Dwight 15968
Palm, Irving 16360
Palmer, Albert W. 4390, 5207
Palmer, Bernard 10517
Palmer, Craig A. 10029
Palmer, Derek 8855
Palmer, E. Eddie 15758
Palmer, Gerald B. 9186
Palmer, Parker 9468, 12201, 12266, 14380, 15969, 19137
Pancoast, Elinor 8856
Pangborn, Cyrus Ransom 6075
Panhandlers and the Church 6941
Panikkar, Raimundo 9187, 11473, 15181, 18851
Pannell, William 11474, 19230
Pannenberg, Wolfhart 18943
Pannier, Wendy S. 12997
Panorama del sindicalismo mundial, circulo de estudios, 1960-1969 8265
Panton, Kenneth J. 12998
Panunzion, Constantine Maria 3355
Papaioannou, J. G. 13179
Papers, Addresses, and Discussions of the Protestant Episcopal Church Congress 539
Pappani, Antonio 7947
Parachin, Victor M. 15589
Paradise, Frank I. 2728
Paradise, Scott I. 8266, 9592, 11002, 11475, 13323
Parcells, George M. 7672
Pardington, Rayner S. 1572
Paré, George 6076
Parenti, Michael 9188
Paris, Arthur E. 16361
Paris, Peter J. 17475, 19284
Parish of Trinity Church 558
Parish or Perish: New Interest in Local Church Development 15182
Parish, Ruby Galloway 18256

Parisé, Robert 14776
Park, J. Philip. 15183
Park, Jang Kyun 15184
Park, Robert E. 2964, 3716, 3717, 3910, 4555, 5307, 6217
Park, Sun Ai 18944
Parker, Andrew T. 17101, 17476
Parker, C. A. 1976
Parker, Christian 18640
Parker, Everett C. 6751, 7169, 7406, 7948, 11003
Parker, Harold M., Jr. 14381
Parker, Joseph 1815
Parker, Karen Kuttner 13324
Parker, Matthew 18945
Parker, Theodore 224, 242, 387
Parker, Theodore Kwaku 15185
Parker, Thomas D. 16573
Parker, Tony 16688
Parker, Wesley 12267
Parkhurst, Charles Henry 895, 1011, 1396, 1411, 1434, 2091, 3226, 3545
Parkin, Christine 12627
Parks, Haggard 11859
Parod, E. 513
Parodi, Maurice 11004, 11005
Parot, Joseph John 12268, 15970
Parr, Clarence Elmer 4238
Parratt, John K. 13663
Parrinder, Edward G. 6363
Parrott, Sarah S. 6942
Parsons, Anne 9593
Parsons, Edward L. 2639, 4767, 4970
Parsons, Frank 1767
Parsons, Talcott 6077, 8857, 10518, 11476, 13325, 16301
Parsons, Waymon 6943
Partain, Eugene C. 17477
Partners for Sacred Places 19333
Parton, James 454
Partridge, Warren G. 1710
Parvin, Earl 17478
Pascall, S. W. 3718
Pasquariello, Ronald D. 14511, 14512, 15971, 15972, 16362, 16363, 16689, 17479, 17480, 18282, 18305, 18641
Passavant, W. A. 2076
Passi, Michael M. 13664
Pastor in Urban-Industrial Mission Life: Report of the 15th Urban Mission Course, March 29-April 11, 1974 13326
Pastor's Opportunity, XIV, Thoughts on Twinning 18642
Pastoral Constitution on the Church in the Modern World 10030
Pastoral das Migrações 16690
Patch, William L. 17481
Paterson, J. 14001
Patnaik, Theophilus 17102
Paton, Alan 5715
Paton, John Brown 896
Patten, James Alexander 540
Patten, Simon Nelson 2160, 2534, 2535, 5470
Patterson, Bob E. 12269
Patterson, F. W. 2536
Patterson, H. L. 3356
Patterson, Jack 11006
Patterson, James H. 11007
Patterson, James O. 11477, 15590
Patterson, R. S. 14382
Patterson, Robert Mayne 642
Patterson, William B. 2818
Pattison, E. Mansell 12270
Patton, Alan 7350
Patton, Bill 18946
Patton, John W. 15517
Patton, William 92
Paul VI, Pope 9293, 9594, 11478, 18392, 19272
Paul, Rajaiah D. 6944
Paul, William E. 4971, 5505, 5962
Paul, Winston 2729
Paulden, M. D. 3642

Paulist Fathers 354, 7407
Paulson, Belden 7170
Paulson, Ross E. 11008
Pauper Children of a Rich City 1711
Paus, Roma 6545
Pauw, B. A. 8858, 13327
Pawlikowski, John T. 15186, 17903
Payne, Daniel Alexander 1079
Payne, Philip Francis 4391
Paz, Denis G. 15591, 16364
Pazmiño, Robert William 15973, 18643
Pazzaglia, Luciano 18283
p'Bitek., Okot 17100
Peabody, Francis Greenwood 801, 1162, 1412, 1488, 1489, 1768, 1975, 2346, 2640, 2730, 5777, 8171
Peachey, Paul 8859, 9189, 12271, 16365
Peachey, Urban 15592
Peale, Norman Vincent 3643, 12499, 13631
Pearce, Angela 18284
Pearce, John 18284
Pearsall, James W. 1977, 1978
Pearsall, Kenneth H. 11479
Pease, Lewis 74
Peattie, Lisa Redfield 11009
Peck, David G. 5045
Peck, George Clarke 2965
Peck, John P. 9595
Peck, William George 3719, 3845, 4322, 4392, 5118, 5208, 5308, 6546
Pederson, Duane 15187
Pedigo, Marlene Morrison 18644
Peerman, Dean 16691, 18947
Peil, Margaret 14118, 15974, 16366
Peirce, Bradford K. 470
Pekrul, Melvin 11480
Pelham, Joseph 14777
Pellow, John 10519
Peloso, Alex 13665
Pelton, Doby 12999
Peltz, George A. 1490
Pemberton, Prentice L. 9190
Pemberton, Sherman Shipley 17904
Pence, Owen Earle 4866
Pender, Donald Wagner 15975
Penfield, William N. 10520
Penman, John Simpson 2896
Pennewell, Almer M. 5119
Pennick, Paul, Jr. 17482
Pennings, Johannes M. 15593
Pennington, Basil M. 14002
Penny, David 18285
Penny, J. C. 4082
Penny, W. A. 13666, 14383
Pentecost, George F. 760, 802, 857
Penty, Arthur J. 4481
Penwell, Lanny 18948
People's Institute of Applied Religion 4972
Peopling of Michigan Series 14384
Pepper, Almond R. 4768, 6547
Pepper, C. B. 15594
Pepper, Charles M. 2435
Per costruire la Chiesa nel mondo del lavoro 11010
Perani, Cláudio 15976
Percy, Douglas Cecil 14003
Perdue, Robert E. 13000
Perdue, William G. 17103
Pérez, César Moreno 16367
Pérez Leñero, José 7673
Perez y Mena, Andres Isidoro 19231
Perkins, Edgar A. 3644
Perkins, Eugene 13667
Perkins, H. Wesley 16692
Perkins, Harvey 15188
Perkins, J. Newton 2641
Perkins, J. Stanley 2092, 4169

Perkins, James Handasyd 275
Perkins, Jill 15188
Perkins, John 14004, 14005, 15189, 15190, 16350, 16368, 16585, 16693
Perkins, Perry 14778, 14779, 15595
Perman, Dagmar Horna 9596
Perotti, Antonio 12628
Perrin, Henri 5404, 7408
Perrin, Jacques 8095, 18645
Perrine, Mervyn W. 9837
Perrot, Daniel 18286
Perrot, Jean 6218, 7409
Perry, Arthur Latham 407
Perry, Cynthia 19138
Perry, D. A. 11951
Perry, David C. 14385
Perry, E. S. 14780
Perry, Edmund 7410
Perry, Everett L. 5405, 5406, 5407, 5443, 5506, 5507, 5508, 5509, 5510, 5511, 5546, 5716, 5717, 5718, 5719, 5814, 5815, 5816, 5963, 5964, 5965, 6078, 6181, 6219, 6220, 6364, 6365, 6688, 6945, 11810, 12629, 14682, 15596
Perry, H. Francis 1712, 1713
Perry, John D. 9597, 9598, 9599, 9600, 10031
Perry, Jos 16694
Perry, Leroy Odinda 18646
Perry, Ralph Barton 4482
Perry, Robert L. 18949
Perspectives on the Church in Transitional Communities 14386
Peskett, Howard 19072
Peter, Val J. 16695
Peterman, Richard L. 8267
Peters, B. A. M. 11481
Peters, Claude R. 9601
Peters, Harold 18950
Peters, Harvey S., Jr. 14387
Peters, John P. 1491, 2161
Peters, Madison C. 1326
Peters, Ted 18951
Peters, Victor 15977
Petersen, Larry 16696
Petersen, William J. 9602, 10032
Peterson, C. Arvid 11482
Peterson, Jon A. 14006
Peterson, Larry 14781
Peterson, Merrill D. 11927
Peterson, Ralph E. 15191
Peterson, Wallace C. 18647
Peterson, William 9603
Petit, Jacques 6946
Petras, Harri 18648
Petri, W. 10033
Petrie, A. Hunter 13001
Petrie, Robert John 6947
Petrosa, Jason 14782
Pettersson, Thorleif 19232
Pettigrew, Thomas F. 7263, 7264, 7512, 7513, 7674
Peuquet, Steven W. 18649
Peursem, Mel Van 14007
Peursen, C. A. van 11011
Pew, J. Howard 7949
Peyton, Rosemary 18650
Pfautz, Harold Winston 6752, 9191
Pfeffer, Leo 6948
Pflum, H. J. 3911
Phayre, John F. 2043
Phelan, Craig 17905
Phenix, Philip H. 10034
Phibbs, Raymond C. 10521
Philadelphia City Mission of the [Episcopal] Diocese of Pennsylvania 3022
Philadelphia City Mission [Protestant Episcopal] 172
Philadelphia Civic Club 1915
Philadelphia Protestant Episcopal City Mission 1492
Philadelphia Society for Organizing Charity 617

Philadelphia Sunday and Adult School Union 52
Philbrick, Herbert A. 6366
Philbrick, Richard 8510
Philippines for Christ Movement 11928
Philipson, David 2537
Phillips, Benjamin Thomas 302
Phillips, Brian Douglas 17906
Phillips, Calvin L. 19285
Phillips, E. Barbara 15978
Phillips, George S. 421
Phillips, H. D. 2642
Phillips, Harlan B. 6221
Phillips, Harry P. 8546, 8860
Phillips, James 10035
Phillips, Jennifer M. 18651
Phillips, Karl 8861
Phillips, Keith W. 12630, 13668, 14008, 14388
Phillips, McCandush 8547
Phillips, N. Taylor 1573
Phillips, Paul T. 15597
Phillips, Ronald L. 13197
Phillips, Walter 11929
Philpot, David 13590
Philpott, T. L. 14783
Phipps, Joyce 17104
Phipps, Simon Wilton 10036
Phipps, William E. 16369
Photiadis, John 9604
Phraner, Wilson 1868
Piat, Stephane Joseph 5408
Piat, Stéphane-Joseph 15421
Picard, Paul 11012, 13248
Pichaske, Donald R. 10522
Pichler, Joseph A. 14590, 17105, 17106
Pichon, Armand 5120
Picht, Werner Robert Valentin 2731
Pickard, Don 13002
Pickard, Donald A. 14389
Pickard-Cambridge, Arthur 6367
Pickering, John 16697
Pickering, W. S. F. 8268
Pickett, Deets 3357, 3580
Pickett, J. Waskom 4323
Picque, N. D. 11013
Piehl, Mel 15192, 16370
Piekoszewski, Jan 7950
Pielstick, Don F. 5171
Pierce, Edith Lovejoy 6753
Pierce, Gregory F. Augustine 16698, 18952
Pierce, Robert M. 17483
Pierce, Susan E. 15193, 18652
Pierrard, Pierre 14390, 17107, 19233
Pierrel, Gren O. 6079
Pierson, Arthur T. 1327, 1714, 1769
Piet, John H. 11930
Pieterse, Hennie J. C. 16699
Pike, Burton 15979
Pike, Garnet Elmer 12631
Pike, Godfry Holden 487, 514, 521, 726, 727, 761, 1163
Pike, James A. 6080, 6754, 11483
Pildain y Zapiain, Antonio de 5309
Pile, William 18287
Pilgrim, Walter E. 15980
Pilkington, James P. 6949
Pillsbury, Peter 9192
Pimlott, John Alfred Ralph 4483
Pin, Emile J. 6950, 6951, 7951, 8548, 9008, 9479, 9605, 11014, 11484
Pina, Rolando E. 11015
Pingree, Hazen S. 11345
Pinnock, Wesley 19139
Pinsker, Sanford 19207
Pinsky, Mark 14784
Pinson, William M., Jr. 11016, 11931, 12272, 12273, 13003, 13669
Pinyan, Charles 17484
Pinzón, Carlos Ernesto 17916
Pioch, Reinhard 14785

Piper, David R. 3449, 3912
Piper, Otto A. 7171
Pipkin, H. W. 10037
Pippert, Wesley G. 11485
Pirazzini, Francis Xavier 10038
Pisek, Vincent 947
Pistas para una pastoral urbana 15194
Pitcher, Alvin 7952, 10523
Pitcher, W. A. 10039
Pitkin, D. S. 7675
Pitt, Harriett Philmau 10524
Pittman, Clarence O. 16371
Pittman, D. 7411
Pityana, Barney 18953
Pius XI, Pope 4152, 4170, 4171, 4177, 4178, 4218, 4307, 4476, 4642, 4820, 5179, 5202, 5605, 14908, 17700
Pius XII, Pope 5512
Pivar, David J. 9606, 10040, 13004
Piven, Frances Fox 9795, 12274, 13156, 14391, 15195, 16372
Piwowarski, Wladyslaw 12275, 13670, 14009, 17907
Plainfield, J. F. 4867
Planning Notes 6952
Plant Closings Challenge Churches 15981
Plant, Raymond 18954
Plantz, Samuel 2093
Platt, John Vernon 17108
Platte, Ardeth 17485
Play, Frederic Le 8086
Playthell, Benjamin 18955
Pledger, Carolyn Brastow 12632
Plelan, Thomas 19140
Pleuthner, Willard A. 5966
Plinzner, Frida 2897
Ploeg, J. Vander 11017
Plowman, Edward E. 12276, 12633, 13005
Plumptre, Edward Hayes 643
Plumstead, Wayne Jack 15196
Plunge: Urban Training Center for Christian Mission, Chicago 9607
Pluralism 15982
Pluralism -- National Menace 6081
Plyler, Henry Ellis 8269
Pobe, John S. 17611
Poblete, Renato 7953
Podojil, Catherine 16373
Poe, Edgar Allan 3992
Poell, Ivar H. 13006
Poethig, Enice Blanchard 16374
Poethig, Richard P. 7954, 7955, 9608, 10041, 10525, 11486, 11487, 11932, 12264, 12634, 12635, 12636, 13007, 13008, 13098, 13328, 13329, 13560, 13671, 14392, 14786, 14787, 15197, 15198, 15199, 15200, 15201, 15598, 15599, 15600, 15601, 15983, 15984, 16375, 16376 >> See further: Subject Index: Institute on the Church in Urban Industrial Society
Poff, Betty 6548
Pohier, Jacques 15202, 16377
Pohorski, Susan 19141
Pojman, Louis 10526
Pol, Willem H. van de 11018
Polachek, Hilda Scott 18956
Polany, Karl 4464
Polca, Hugo 11488
Polding, M. Fred 17908
Polen, Nehemiah 16700
Polier, Justine Wise 6953
Poling, Daniel A. 8270
Poling, David 15456
Poling, James 10527
Politics for the People 237
Pollard, David A. 16378
Pollock, Horatio Milo 2732
Pollock, James Samuel 2500
Pollock, John Charles 8862, 15203

Polner, M. 9609
Pomeroy, Charles S. 686
Pompian, Lillian 10042
Ponce, Frank 15602, 15603
Ponsonby, Arthur 2436
Pontiac Ecumenical Ministry 13672
Pontifica Commissio de Spirituali Migratorum Atque Itinerantium Cura 14788
Poole, M. A. 13009
Poorman, Roberta S. 18957
Pope, Hugh 3358
Pope, Liston 4360, 5046, 5121, 5612, 5613, 5720, 6368, 7172
Pope's Encyclical 4171 >> See further: Subject Index, Encyclicals, Papal
Popenoe, David 10043, 11489
Poppy, John 16701
Port, Michael Harry 8271
Portaro, Sam A. 17486
Portasik, Richard 10528
Porter, Arlie E. 10456, 10529
Porter, David 17909
Porter, Homer 18427
Porter, Janet W. 15604
Porter, Noah 762
Porter, Thomas W. 12637, 12638
Portes, Alejandro 14010
Portland City Club Foundation, Inc 11490
Portland [ME] Congregational Club: the Record of Over Half a Century 4324
Portlock, Carver A. 11019
Portor, Deborah 17109
Portor, John 17109
Positive Program for the Renewal of Slum Life: Toward Responsible Freedom 10530
Potashinskaia, Nataliia Nikolaevna 15204
Poteat, Edwin McNeill, Jr. 4393, 4484, 4659
Poteat, Edwin McNeill, Sr. 2437, 2438, 3023
Poteat, William Louis 2733, 3993, 4485
Potel, Julien 11020, 11491
Pott, Archdeacon 2643
Potter, Alonzo 173
Potter, Burtt 14011
Potter, Frances S. 6369, 6755
Potter, Henry Codman 438, 479, 644, 858, 1164, 2416, 2882, 13929
Potter, John Hasloch 3846
Potter, Juanita Wright 16702
Potter, Rockwell Harmon 2347
Potter, Truman W. 10044
Potter, William 3994
Pottieger, Cecil P. E. 10045, 10531, 10532, 15605
Poulain, Jean Claude 8272
Poulat, Émile 7676, 8273, 8274, 9610, 11933, 13673, 17711
Poulson, E. N. 11934
Pound, Keith 17910
Poverty Packet: Multi-Media Resources for Informal Groups [Nine items] 12639
Powderly, Terence V. 5346, 5449, 5756
Powell, Adam Clayton, Jr. 5209, 10533, 12277
Powell, Adam Clayton, Sr. 4769, 5409
Powell, Don 11492
Powell, Madelyn 11492
Powell, P. E. 2162
Powell, S. W. 1165
Powell, Sidney 7412
Powell, William D. 7173
Power and Pathos of the Preaching Mission 4556
Power, Anne 18288
Power, David N. 16703
Power, P. B. 471
Powers, Charles W. 12278, 12640,

12674
Pozio, Guilio 10046
Pozzetta, George E. 19142
Practicing Ecumenism in Urban Priority Areas 18289
Prades, J. A 9193
Prall, William 1413
Prange, Amy 18290
Pratt, Henry J. 7677, 8549, 11935
Pratt, Hugh 18653
Pratt, William David 7678
Pre-Conference Position Papers: JSAC National Ecumenical Conference on Churches in Racial/Ethnic Transitional Communities 15205
Preliminary Survey of Social Service Activities of Interdenominational Organizations 4770
Prell, Riv-Ellen 19143
Prentice, William Edward 18291
Prentiss, George L. 948, 1414
Presbyterian Board of Christian Education, Department of Social Education and Action 5410
Presbyterian Church in the US, Board of Church Extension, Department of Urban Church 9611
Presbyterian Church in the US, Board of National Ministries 10047
Presbyterian Church in the US, Division of Corporate and Social Mission, Office of Ethnic Minority Affairs 14393
Presbyterian Church in the US, United Presbyterian Church in the USA 15985
Presbyterian Church in the USA 3155
Presbyterian Church in the USA, Board of Christian Education 4660
Presbyterian Church in the USA, Board of Christian Education, Board of Temperance and Moral Welfare 3266
Presbyterian Church in the USA, Board of Christian Education, Department of Social Education 2257, 5310, 5311, 6549
Presbyterian Church in the USA, Board of Christian Education, Division of Social Education and Action 5721
Presbyterian Church in the USA, Board of Home Missions 2538, 2644, 3267, 3359
Presbyterian Church in the USA, Board of Home Missions, Department of Church and Labor 2439
Presbyterian Church in the USA, Board of Home Missions, Department of Immigration 2440, 2539
Presbyterian Church in the USA, Board of National Missions 3720, 4083, 5513, 6550, 6551, 6756
Presbyterian Church in the USA, Board of National Missions, City, Immigrant, and Industrial Department 3721
Presbyterian Church in the USA, Board of National Missions, Department of Jewish Evangelization 3546
Presbyterian Church in the USA, Board of National Missions, Special Committee on Study of the Inner City 6954
Presbyterian Church in the USA, Board of National Missions, Unit of City 4557
Presbyterian Church in the USA,

General Assembly 4558
Presbyterian Church in the USA, Presbytery of New York 645, 1166, 3024
Presbyterian Church in the USA, Presbytery of New York, Committee on Church Extension and Sustentation 439, 1415
Presbyterian Church in the USA, Presbytery of St. Louis 2966
Presbyterian Church in the USA, Special Committee on Inner City 6955
Presbyterian Church in the USA, the Woman's Board of Home Missions 803
Presbyterian Church of Philadelphia 1979
Presbyterian Institute on Industrial Relations [PIIR] 5411
Presbyterian Labor Temple 2441
Presbyterian Union of Cleveland 472, 2898
Presbyterian Urban Ministry Council [Tulsa, OK] 14789
Presbytery of Chicago 14394
Prescott, Anthony John 13330
Presence in Urban 'Worlds:' Metropolitan Associates of Philadelphia 10048
Present Unemployment and the Future of Work 14395
Presenting Ten Decades, 1862-1962: The History of the Sydney City Mission 8550
Preservation League of New York State 16704
Presler, Henry Hughs 5722
Pressensé, Edmond de 243
Prestige, George Leonard 4486
Preston, D. S. 16379
Preston, James 15452
Preston, John Hyde 3995
Preston, Noel William 12641
Preston, Ronald H. 14396, 15986, 16705, 18292
Preston, Thomas B. 1080
Preston, Thomas Scott 488
Preston, William C. 1081
Pretiz, Paul 18293, 18654
Pretzlaff, Theodore 9612
Prevailing Attitudes to Work: Black Workers 12642
Price, Bob 18325
Price, Clay 16380, 17911, 18294
Price, Derek William 8863
Price, Gwilym A. 6757
Price, M. Cobbs 11317
Price, Orlo J. 2967
Price, Percy S. 3645
Price, S. E. 1328
Price, Thomas 12279
Prickett, Robert S. 11493
Priddy, Al 2540, 2645
Priddy, Benjamin, Jr. 13674
Priest of the Slum 6956
Priest-Workman in England: A Study in Life 6082
Priestman, Alice B. 2044
Priests Who Don't Get Paid for It 9194
Prime, Samuel Irenaeus 174, 355, 515
Prindiville, Kathryn 1661
Pringle, John Christian 4661
Pringle, R. 11021
Prinz, Franz 13331
Pritchard, Colin 14397
Pritchett, Harry H. 18958
Privett, Stephen A. 18655
Pro-Cathedral, New York 1816
Problem der Großstädte des 20. Jahrhunderts 1662
Problem of Japanese Resettlement 5210
Problems of Labor 4559
Problems of the Inner-City Church: a Symposium 8275

Proceedings of the Convention of Christian Workers 804
Procession 7956
Procter, Mary 14790
Proctor, William 13332
Proelss, E. Frederick 7413
Programa de Renovacion y Investigacion Social para Adiestramiento en la Mision [PRISA] 11022
Progress of the Institutional Church 1574
Project Equality Council 10534
Project Works 14791
Prongué, Bernard 11023
Proposal for an Emphasis in the United Church of Christ on the Church and Urbanization 8864
Proposals for the Creation of a Fund to Be Applied to the Buildings and Endowment of Additional Churches in the Metropolis 168
Protestant Church and Welfare Directory of Greater New York Including Nassau and Westchester Counties 5412
Protestant Church Buildings and Equipment 6370
Protestant Church in Buffalo's East Side 8865
Protestant Churches Divided on Their Urban Crisis Programs 11494
Protestant Cooperative Giving in Rochester 5312
Protestant Council of the City of New York 5614, 5967, 6957, 9195
Protestant Council of the City of New York, Department of Church Planning and Research 7957
Protestant Council of the City of New York, Pathfinding Service for the Churches 5615
Protestant Episcopal Association for the Promotion of Christianity Among the Jews 339
Protestant Episcopal Church in the USA 3450, 6222
Protestant Episcopal Church in the USA, American Church Building Fund Commission 646
Protestant Episcopal Church in the USA, Board of Missions, Committee to Consider Means to Reach the More Neglected with Christian Instruction 388
Protestant Episcopal Church in the USA, Church Temperance Society 666
Protestant Episcopal Church in the USA, Department of Christian Social Services, Division of Industrial Relations 3913
Protestant Episcopal Church in the USA, Diocese of Los Angeles, Committee for Urban Studies 16381
Protestant Episcopal Church in the USA, Diocese of New York, Italian Mission 1167
Protestant Episcopal Church in the USA, Executive Council 11495
Protestant Episcopal Church in the USA, Executive Council, Department of Christian Social Relations, Division of Community Services 10049
Protestant Episcopal Church in the USA, Joint Commission on Social Service 2968, 3087, 3088
Protestant Episcopal Church in the USA, National Council

162, 3268, 3646, 3914, 5122, 8276, 8866
Protestant Episcopal Church in the USA, National Council, Department of Christian Social Service 4560, 5968
Protestant Episcopal Church in the USA, National Council, Department of Missions and Church Extension 3451
Protestant Episcopal Church in the USA, National Council, Division of Urban and Industrial Church Work 5969
Protestant Episcopal Church in the USA, National Council, Woman's Auxiliary, Washington [DC] Branch 3915
Protestant Episcopal Church in the USA, New York Diocese 4084
Protestant Episcopal Church in the USA, Office of Hispanic Ministries 17110
Protestant Episcopal Church in the USA, Protestant Episcopal Mission to Public Insitutions of the City of New York 473
Protestant Episcopal Church in the USA, Washington [DC] Diocese 2899
Protestant Master Plan and Strategy for Manhattan 8551
Protestant Methodist Church 12280
Protestant Trade Union Brotherhood 4973
Protestantism and Labor 5817
Protestants Look at Social Welfare 6958
Protestants, Catholics, and Jews in Joint Statement on Unemployment 4172
Providencia, Sister 6656
Prucha, John 4085
Prugh, John 1663
Pryor, Thomas M. 13675
Psalm for the Inner City 15206
Psychologist's Criticism of the Emmanuel Movement 2348
Ptolemy, Kathleen 16382
Public Housing Rent Action Committee 14792
Pucheu, F. R. 6223
Puleo, Mev 19217
Pulker, E. A. 15606
Pulkingham, W. Graham 12643, 13010
Pullen, G. R. 4771
Pulliam, Russ 16383, 17912
Pullman's Testimony -- An Object Lesson 1416
Pullman, James M. 1715
Purcell, John Baptist 14692
Purdy, Fred 12281
Purdy, Martin 18656
Purkey, Donald R. 8552
Purkiser, W. T. 10050, 10051, 10535
Pursiainen, Terho 15607
Purves, Andre 18959
Purvis, Burt 14667
Purvis, James D. 18657
Pury, Pascal de 16706
Pusey, Edward B. 16579
Putting Christ Where the Action Is 11496
Putz, Louis J. 6959, 10536
Pyko, Kimberly 17487
Pyle, John W. 6754
Quandt, Jean B. 11936
Quayle, Vincent P. 16384
Quayle, William A. 3269
Queen, Stuart Alfred 4086, 4868, 6371, 6960
Queffélec, Henri 9196
Quertemont, E. 11937
Quesada, Ernesto 1417
Quest for Truly Human Communities 14012

Quigley, Margaret 16385
Quimby, Karl K. 4325
Quinley, Harold E. 13333, 15207
Quinlivan, Frank 11024, 11025
Quinn, Bernard 13248, 16386
Quinn, Francis X. 10052
Quinn, James Alfred 6758
Quinn, Patrick J. 14013
Quinn, Peter A. 16387
Quintanilla, A. 15208
Quoist, Michel 6224
Raab, Earl 7679
Raban, Jonathan 13334
Rabe, Rudolf M. 7958
Rabey, Steve 17111
Rabinowitz, Benjamin 5211
Rabinowitz, Howard N. 14793
Raborg, Frederick A. 16388
Raboteau, Albert J. 14794, 18960
Raby, William L. 15608
Race Relations 5047
Racetrack Preacher 12644
Racial Cauldron Boils Over 9197
Racial Integrity through Free Choice: Text of Statement by Atlanta Ministers 7174
Racine, Carl 15987
Rackman, Emanuel 13247
Radding, Michael 17112
Radelet, Joseph 14014
Rader, Benjamin G. 10053
Rader, Victoria 17913
Radner, Ephraim 19234
Radosh, Mary 15909
Raeburn, Walter 6552
Ragan, Phyllis 12938
Ragan, Roger Lee 8867
Ragaz, Leonhard 17113, 17656
Ragged Schools 474
Ragon, Michel 10054
Ragsdale, W. B. 11938, 12861
Raguin, Yves 13011, 13012
Rahill, Peter J. 13676
Rahman, Falzur 17914
Rahn, Sheldon 6372
Raikes, Richard 37
Raikes, Robert 344, 581, 4847
Railton, George S. 859, 2646, 12016
Raines, John C. 15209, 15988, 16389, 16707, 17915
Raines, Robert 9198
Raines, Robert A. 8277, 8553, 9199, 10537, 11026
Rainsford, George N. 12282
Rainsford, William S. 1012, 1082, 1131, 1168, 1418, 1980, 2059, 3452
Raisin in the Sun: The Uncut Version 18961
Raisman, Paula 15473
Rajana, Eimi Watanabe 13677
Rall, Harris Franklin 3025, 3453, 4662
Ralph, George 11027
Ralph, J. A. A. 4663
Ralph, James 15210
Ralph, Raymond M. 14795
Ramage, David Jr. 8868
Ramalho, J. P. 15609
Ramer, A. L. 3722
Ramirez, Christine 15989
Ramirez, Ricardo 16708
Ramírez de Jara, María Clemencia 17916
Ramsay, John Gates 5514
Ramsay, John Gates. 4561
Ramsay, William M. 2163
Ramsdell, F. E. 1419
Ramsden, William E. 15610, 15990, 17488, 18545, 18962, 19144
Ramsey, Duane Van Dyke 3996
Ramsey, John 5616
Ramsey, Paul 8278
Ramsey, William H. 4394
Ramseyer, Robert L. 17114
Ranck, James G. 7414
Ranck, Lee 11497, 11498, 15991, 16709, 16710, 17489

Randall, Claire 11028
Randall, Edwin T. 4664
Randall, John S. 5515
Randall, Oscar J. 3997
Randers, Jorgen 12594
Randerson, Richard 13013
Randle, Guiermo 9200
Randolph, A. Benton 9613
Randolph, Craig 6373
Randolph, Edwin A. 728
Rank, Lee 12283
Rankell, Judith Novack 11029
Ranney, David J. 2442
Ransford, Paul 8869
Ranson, Charles Wesley 4772, 5723
Ranyard, Ellen 362, 363
Rao, M. S. A. 13335
Raphael, Marc Lee 13336, 14796, 15211
Raphael, Pierre 19235
Raphaël, Freddy 12284
Rapp, Edward D. 6374, 6883, 7191
Rappe, Louis Amadeus 13952
Rardin, Jared J. 9614
Rascher, Leonard P. 15212
Rashford, Nicholas J. 10538
Raskin, A. H. 9615
Rasmussen, Albert T. 5516, 6961, 9616
Rasmussen, Carl P. 6083, 6084, 6225, 6226, 6375, 6376
Rasmussen, Larry 14524, 16390
Rasmussen, Steen Eiler 4665
Rateree, Bonita 14398
Rath, Robert A. 9330
Ratledge, Wilbert H. 16391
Ratschow, C. H. 9617
Rattenburg, J. E. 2258
Ratus, Leslie J. 14015, 14399
Rauch, Dolores 12285
Rauch, Julia B. 13337
Rauff, Edward A. 15213
Raulin, Anne 19236
Rauschenbusch, Walter 768, 949, 1493, 1575, 2164, 2225, 2443, 2450, 2541, 2647, 2648, 2734, 2819, 2969, 3026, 3790, 4326, 4737, 5125, 5824, 5960, 5970, 6897, 7150, 7175, 7176, 7200, 9887, 10108, 10197, 11030, 11641, 17984, 18990
Raven, Charles Earle 3270
Raven, John 13014
Ravetez, Alison 17115
Ravetz, Alison 15611
Ravitz, Mel Jerome 7680, 8279
Rawles, Warren 11031
Rawlings, Charles W. 8554, 8870
Rawson, Edward Kirk 729
Ray, David R 16392
Ray, Edward Chittenden 2649
Ray, Emit O. 13678
Ray, Gertrude 5413
Rayan, Samule 15612
Raymond, Allen 6759
Raysor, Kay 18538
Rea, Robert J. 10539, 14400
Reaching Out to All People: The Catholic Church 15613
Reactionary Trends in Urban Politics 11499
Read, William 9618, 11500, 15614
Reade, Ben 9619, 10055
Readjustment of City Churches 897
Real Riot Control 11032
Reapsome, James W. 16711, 17116
Reardon, Bernard M. G. 8871
Reason, Will 1664
Reasonover, William 7177
Reccord, Augustus P. 4173
Reccord, Robert Eugene 15214
Recent Acquisitions of ICUIS: Africa 11501
Recent Acquisitions of ICUIS: Asia 11502

Recent Acquisitions of ICUIS: Europe 11503
Recherche de la justice et du shalom dans la ville 17117
Recinos, Harold Joseph 17917, 18963, 19145
Reckitt, Maurice B. 4239, 4666, 5517, 11033
Record of the Society for Promoting the Gospel Among Seamen in the Port of New York 455
Rector, F. E. 6914
Redacción: Pastoral de Barrios 17118
Redefining the City 16393
Redekop, John H. 12645
Redfield, Robert 5048, 5617, 6553
Redford, Jack 14797
Reducing Energy Costs in Religious Buildings 14798
Redwood, William Arthur Hugh 4087, 4240
Reece, William S. 18964
Reeck, Darrell L. 11939, 16513
Reed, Adolph L. 17918
Reed, Bruce 17858
Reed, David Allen 1552
Reed, John 2900
Reed, John H. 11190
Reed, John Shelton 12646
Reed, Millard 15992
Reed, Myer S. 13217, 15993
Reed, Myron W. 1083
Reed, Richard Ernie 15215
Reep, Samuel Nicholas 2444
Rees, D. Ben 15216
Rees, David John 18658
Rees, David W. 15615
Rees, P. S. 14401
Rees, Seth Cook 2045
Reese, W. S. 1665
Reeves, James M. 18659
Reformed Church in America, Board of North American Missions 7959
Reformed Church in America, Office of Social Witness 19306
Reforming City Administration 1666
Refugees at Bay from Miami to Khartoum 15616
Regeher, Ted D. 14402
Regele, Michael B. 19334
Reich, Nathan 6554, 6760
Reichert, John 2080
Reichert, Michael 17119
Reid, Al 8280
Reid, Clyde H. 9201
Reid, David 11504
Reid, John R. 16712
Reid, Malcolm 13338, 13679
Reid, Paul M. 7681
Reid, William Watkins 5971
Reidenbach, Clarence F. 7415
Reidy, W. T. V. 14403
Reilly, Lorraine 17490
Reilly, Timothy F. 13680
Reimer, A. F. 3089
Reimer, David M. 13507, 15006
Reimer, Mavis 16560
Reimers, David M. 9620, 13015
Rein, Charles E. 7960, 7961
Reiner, Walter 15217
Reines, Chaim W. 7682
Reinhold, Hans Ansgar 5313, 5314, 5818
Reinoehl, Waldo Solomon 5212
Reis, Janet 18635
Reisner, Christian F. 2901
Reisner, Christian R. 3151
Reiss, Albert J. 7101, 8281, 13752
Reissig, Herman F. 6555
Reissman, Leonard 9202
Reissner, Anne Campanella 17919
Reissner, Edward A. 9203
Reitz, Rüdiger 11505
Relation of Christian Principles

to Industry 3271
Relation of the Church to the Poor 380
Relayo, Jerry 11940
Religion and Labor Council of America 7178
Religion and Social Service: The Old Faith Still Strong in America 3847
Religion and the J. P. Stevens Campaign 14404
Religion in New York 422
Religion und verstädterte Industriegesellschaft 9621
Religionssociologiska Institutet, Stockholm 8872
Religious Agencies and the Urban Crisis 11506
Religious Education 2094
Religious Facility as Community Center 12286
Religious Issues 18523
Remarkable Growth of the Emmanuel Movement 2259
Remington, Mary E. 1169
Remy, Jean 7962, 7963, 9480, 10056, 10708, 10709, 10892, 11346, 12287, 12647, 15617
Remy, Jules 373
Renascence of London Methodism 763
Rendle, Gilbert R., Jr. 14405, 17120, 18295, 18296
Rendtorff, Trutz 7416, 7683, 8059
Renewal House 15994
Renewal Magazine 7964
Renewing Old Friendships: Religion and Organized Labor 19146
Renkiewicz, Frank 16394
Rennison, Coverdale Smith 2902
Report of Church Conference on Consumers' Cooperatives 4773
Report of St. Ambrose Housing Aid Center 14799
Report of the Interfaith Conference on Unemployment 4974
Report of the Meeting of the Advisory Group on the 'Energy for My Neighborhood' 16395
Report on the Convocation on Industrial Relations 7965
Reps, John W. 17121
Rescue and Rescue Work, Brooklyn, N.Y. 3558
Research Center for Korean Church Affairs 8555
Research Revolution 10540
Resener, Carl R. 18660, 19355
Reshuffled People: The Presbyterian Task in the Urban South 7966
Resnick, Kalman D. 13016
Response to Transients 10057
Restrepo, Luis Alberto 16713
Reuber, Karl 647
Reuman, John 14406
Reus-Smit, Karel 15618
Reuss, Carl F. 6556
Reuteler, James T. 14407
Reuter, Ila 5315
Reuther, Victor G. 7179, 7417
Reuther, Walter 5618, 5897
Review of Religious Research 7684
Reynolds, Alan 14800
Reynolds, Holly Baker 18330
Reynolds, James Bronson 3547
Reynolds, John J. 5619
Reynolds, K. 10058
Reynolds, Keld J. 17920
Reynolds, Marcus T. 1170
Reznikoff, Charles 5972
Rhee, Amos Seung Woon 15995
Rhem, Richard A. 14801
Rhoades, Dan D. 12190
Rhoades, J. Benton 12288
Rhoades, Jacqueline 11229

Rhodes, D. W. 618
Rhodes, Lynn Nell 19352
Rhodesian Urban Church Consultation, 1st, Salisbury 11034
Rhymes, Douglas 10541
Ribeiro, E. F. N. 16396
Ricart Oller, Josep 15218
Riccardi, Andrea 15219
Riccardi, Steven 12087
Rice, Brian K. 9849
Rice, Charles F. 1981
Rice, Charles O. 5518, 5519, 5795, 9204, 18916
Rice, Clayton S. 6557
Rice, Edwin W. 3027
Rice, George 8282
Rice, Howard 14598, 15996
Rice, James 673
Rice, John A. 2735, 2820
Rice, Larry 17491
Rice, Merton S. 4487
Rice, Perry J. 3548, 4975
Rice, T. Richard 11941
Rice, Tim 11417
Rich, Adena Miller 4467
Rich, Arthur 7180, 7685
Rich, David C. 10542
Rich, J. 10543
Rich, Mark 4395, 9205
Rich, William Daniel 15220
Richards, Lawrence O. 11942, 13681
Richards, M. H. 860, 1240
Richards, Michael 17492
Richards, Thomas B. 6761
Richards, William R. 1241, 1494, 2445
Richardson, Alan 6227
Richardson, Channing 4327, 4488, 4667, 5049, 5366
Richardson, Charles 898
Richardson, David 17122
Richardson, Henry Hobson 13403
Richardson, James F. 12978
Richardson, James T. 18661
Richardson, Lincoln 10544, 11035, 12289
Richardson, Lynda 19147
Richardson, Nancy D. 18965, 19352
Richardson, William J. 9622, 10059
Richesin, L. Dale 18297, 18298
Richey, Elinor 10060
Richmond County Society for Charitable and Religious Purposes 46
Richmond County Society for the Education and Protection of Orphans and Destitute Children, and for the Promotion of Virtue and Religion 53
Richmond, J. F. 522
Richmond, Mary Ellen 1716, 2165, 2650
Richmond, Wilfrid 899
Richter, Klaus 17123
Richter, Rainer G. 17921
Rickard, Dorothy 14016
Rico, Christine 19237
Ricœur, Paul 13682
Ridder, Herman J. 7967
Ridgeway, James 9623, 10061
Ridgley, Ronald 11943
Rieder, Jonathan 17493
Riemer, Jerry A. 12290
Riemer, Svend 9045
Rienstra, M. 12648
Riesman, David 5973, 6228, 7181
Riess, J. 12291
Riess, Steven A. 13017
Riessman, Frank 16224, 17649
Riga, Peter 11507, 11944
Riggio, Amedeo 3454
Riggio, Carrado 3455
Riggs, Charles R. 12292
Riggs, Decatur 5520

Right to Work Laws 6762
Rightor, Henry Haskell 15221
Riis, Jacob August 1013, 1084, 1171, 1329, 1667, 1770, 1771, 1772, 1817, 1869, 1916, 2651, 10764
Riley, Frances 6085
Riley, Negail Rudolph 10545, 17494
Riley, William Bell 2446, 12654
Rinden, Gertrude Jenness 6558, 8873, 8874
Rines, Edward Francis 4562
Ring, Roger J. 16397
Ringe, Sharon 13857
Ringer, Benjamin 6559, 6876, 6962, 10346, 10546, 11541
Ringer, Francis E. 9206
Rinvolucri, Mario 10062
Riordan, Patrick 13875
Ripley, Dorothy 2922
Rippin, Bryan 17495
Rischin, Moses 1859, 6560, 8556, 8875, 15222
Rise of Suburban Power 10547
Rishell, Paul W. 10063
Risk Management at Work: Churches 18966
Ritchie, James Ewing 489
Ritter, Bruce 15879, 18662, 19064
Ritual of the Order of the American Protective League of Baltimore City 805
Rivera, Eli S. 14802, 14803, 15223, 15224
Riverside Church Survey Report 6963
Rivkin, Ellis 10064
Ro, Bong Rin 18663, 18967, 18968
Roach, Margaret 10196
Roach, Peggy 15018
Roache, James P. 16398
Roads, Charles 1172
Robbins, Thomas 15997
Roberts, A. L. 5414
Roberts, Bryan R. 11036
Roberts, Colin A. 5415
Roberts, David Worth 6229
Roberts, Doris 7418
Roberts, Florence 2652
Roberts, Guy L. 7419
Roberts, J. Deotis 13339, 15619
Roberts, Lewis 18299
Roberts, Nancy L. 17124
Roberts, Peter 2447, 2653
Roberts, Philip I. 2654, 2903
Roberts, Robert D. 1085
Roberts, Robert E. T. 9624
Roberts, Robert R. 6964
Roberts, Ronald T. 18664
Roberts, Samuel K. 17624, 17922
Roberts, Suzanne F. 14804
Roberts, Ted 13683
Roberts, Thomas D. 1242
Roberts, Ursula W. 6763
Roberts, Vella-Kottarathil 15998
Roberts, William T. 8283
Robertson, Campbell 14408
Robertson, Edwin H. 6965, 7420, 7421, 7686
Robertson, Gretchen 11037
Robertson, Jack 11037
Robertson, James W. 11945
Robertson, John Ross 1982
Robins, John B. 950
Robinson, Allyn P. 7687
Robinson, Clarence C. 2655, 2821
Robinson, E. E. 2448
Robinson, Edwin Bradford 4174
Robinson, Frank A. 3090
Robinson, Gilbert Kelly 4869
Robinson, Gordon E. 9870
Robinson, J. Armitage 2166
Robinson, J. J. 2822
Robinson, James J. 13684
Robinson, John A. T. 7968, 8876, 9625

Robinson, Lawrence B. 9626
Robinson, Lila Wistrand 17923
Robinson, Madeleine 5316
Robinson, Margaret Blake 1773, 1818, 1870
Robinson, Millard L. 3091, 3456, 3549, 3647
Robinson, Ralph S. 11069
Robotham, Ron 18992
Robrahn, Ralph E. 14017
Rochester, Anna 2656
Rochester, Colin 17496
Rochford, E. Burke, Jr. 17497
Rockaway, Robert A. 13340, 13341
Rockefeller, David 10548, 17498
Rockefeller, John D. 2012, 2024
Rockefeller, John D., Jr. 3092, 3648, 3723
Rockefeller, John D., Sr. 1993, 2025
Rockefeller, Rodman C. 10065
Rockey, Alvin 10549, 11038
Rockwell, Joel Edson 396
Rockwell, Lee W. 7422
Rodda, Alan 15999
Rodda, William Francis Benjamin 6377
Rodda, William H. 17924, 17925
Rodehaver, Homer 4563
Rodgers, Daniel T. 14805
Rodgers, Elsie G. 4774
Rodgers-Melnick, Ann 18300
Rodgerson, Phillip E. 13018, 13342
Rodman, Edward W. 15225
Rodney, Stark 12649
Rodrigo, Julian 1173
Rodriguez, Alfonso 9627
Rodriguez, Cecilia 18665
Rodwin, Lloyd 17125
Roe, Jill 11039
Roeder, R. 8059
Roehlkepartain, Eugene C. 17783, 18969
Roessler, D. 9628
Rogan, Eugene Lawrence 17926
Rogan, John 8557, 10550
Rogers, A. Kathryn 4241
Rogers, Cornish 13019, 13020, 13343
Rogers, Donald B. 18970, 18971
Rogers, Donald G. 13021
Rogers, Edward H. 490, 573, 667, 1014, 1086
Rogers, Emma Winner 1668
Rogers, Garth 16399
Rogers, Jean 6624
Rogers, John 23
Rogers, Mary Beth 19148
Rogers, Robert L. 12293
Rogler, Lloyd H. 8284, 12650
Rohrer, Norman B. 9629
Rokeach, Milton 13022
Role of the Church in Urban Renewal 7182
Rolim, Francisco 15620
Rolston, M. A. Z. 9630, 11508
Romeo, Anthony D. 12294
Romero, Emanuel 5974
Romero, Oscar 16025, 18781, 18947
Romig, David W. 14598
Romney, George 11509
Romo, Oscar I. 14806, 17927
Ronald Behm 11949
Roney, T. C. 1576
Roof, Wade Clark 12651, 13344, 14018, 14807, 15226, 15227, 18301
Roohan, James Edmund 14019
Rooke, Patricia 14382
Rooks, Charles Shelby 11510, 11946, 14020, 14808
Rooney, James F. 15621
Roos, Lothar 8558, 17126
Root, Edward Tallmadge 1717, 2046
Root, John 15228, 17499
Root, Robert 6086

Roote, Thomas Stafford, Jr. 10551
Rooy, Sidney H 15229
Roozen, David A. 14809, 15082, 16326, 17127, 18972
Roper, Dave 10066
Rosado, Caleb 18666, 18973
Rosche, Jan-Dirk 18667
Roschke, E. Michael 15230
Rose, Arnold M. 5975
Rose, Larry L. 13444, 16400, 17128
Rose, Lois 10067
Rose, Peter I. 11511
Rose, Philip M. 3028
Rose, Stephen C. 8877, 8878, 9207, 9208, 10067, 10068, 10069, 10070, 10071, 10072, 10552, 10553, 10554, 11040, 11041, 11042, 11512, 11947, 12295, 13345
Roseberry, P. 17500
Rosebush, Judson George 3550
Rosell, Garth 16000
Rosemarie 7969
Rosen, Ben 3360
Rosenbaum, Larry 17928
Rosenberg, Carroll Smith 11043, 12296, 12297
Rosenberg, Monika 13685
Rosenberg, Stuart 6561, 9631, 16714
Rosenberg, Sven Äke 5724
Rosenbloom, Joseph R. 7423
Rosenfeld, Paul 5317
Rosenfeld, Rick 17487
Rosenhause, Sharon 12298
Rosenkranz, D. Gerhard 6966
Rosenstock-Huessy, Eugen 5725
Rosenthal, Erich 7970, 7971
Rosenthal, Steven 16401
Rosner, Henry J. 4242
Rosner, Victor 17501
Rosoli, Gianfausto 18302
Ross, Aileen D. 8285
Ross, D. Reid 7688
Ross, Dorothy 7689
Ross, Edward Alsworth 1819, 2167, 2449, 3848
Ross, Edyth L. 14021
Ross, G. W. C. 6087
Ross, German R. 11477, 15590
Ross, Marc Howard 13023
Ross, Murray G. 7424
Ross, Sherwood 11044, 11513
Ross, Vivian Hudson 14022
Ross, Wilbur T. 14023
Rossi, Peter H. 8286
Roszak, Theodore 11045, 12652, 13686, 14810
Roth, Alice 10073
Roth, G. 5620
Roth, Guenther 14024
Roth, Willard 10073
Rothan, Emmet Herman 5521
Rothauge, Arlin J. 17129
Rothensteiner, John 3916
Rothermel, S. G. 3649
Rothman, David J. 12299
Rothschild, Jacob M. 17251
Rothschild-Whitt, Joyce 14025
Rottenberg, Isaac C. 14811
Rouleau, Jean P. 12300
Rouse, James 18974
Rousseau, Andre 12191
Rousseau, Ann Marie 16001
Roussel, Bernard 16002
Routley, Erik 10074
Rovirosa, Guillermo 14237
Row, W. Harold 4976
Rowan, Ruth Dinkins 14409
Rowe, Albert Prince 16402
Rowe, Henry K. 3029
Rowe, John Goring 9632
Rowe, O. M. E. 687
Rowe, Stephen C. 11514, 13346
Rowell, Don 16403
Rowen, Samuel 16889, 17502, 17503
Rowitz, Louis 9130

Rowland, Beryl 13024
Rowland, Stanley J. Jr 11046
Rowland, Trent 17929, 17930
Rowles, Kathleen 5213
Rowlingson, Donald T. 15622
Rowntree, Benjamin Seebohm 1820, 3361
Rowntree, Maurice 3362
Roy, Andrew 13025
Roy, Martin 12629
Royce, Josiah 2260, 2736, 2970
Royer, Donald M. 7183
Ruane, Eugene 12301
Rubenson, Birgitta 19149
Rubenstein, Judah 8879
Rubenstein, Richard L. 11047, 16715, 17504
Rubenstein, Ron 12539
Rubingh, Eugene 17931, 18303
Rubingh, George 18304
Ruddock, Joan 12398
Rudge, Peter F. 11048
Rudin, Andrew 17158
Rudisill, Alvin 11515
Ruether, Rosemary Radford 12653, 17130
Ruffner, William Henry 290
Rules for Visiting 101
Running Shoes and Big City Blues 15623
Runyon, Theodore 9760
Ruoss, Meryl 6230, 6231, 6378, 6379, 6562, 6764, 6765, 6766, 6767, 6967, 6968, 7184, 7425, 8287, 8288, 8559, 11049
Rupp, J. C. C. 7972, 10075
Ruppert, Ray 12302
Rural and Urban: Conflict or Copperation 4088
Rural Desolation and Congested Cities 1174
Rural-Urban Relations in the Chicago Dairy District 3917
Rush, James P. 17505
Rush, Ralph Roger 18668
Rushby, William F. 14410
Rushmore, Elsie Mitchel 3272, 3363
Ruskin, John 244
Ruslander, Selwyn D. 7690
Russ, Charles Trumbull 9209
Russel, Vera 7973
Russell, Bertrand 6380
Russell, Bob 19353
Russell, C. Allyn 12654
Russell, Charles 1774
Russell, Charles Edward 2261, 2349
Russell, Dora 16716
Russell, Frank 861, 951
Russell, Hilary 17932
Russell, Letty M. 7974, 7975, 8289, 8560, 8561, 9166, 10026, 10076, 10555, 11516, 12655, 15231, 18669, 18670, 18975, 19150
Russell, Michael B. 16003
Russell, Robert V. 4775
Russell, Thomas 510
Russell, Warren D. 9600, 10077, 11050, 11051
Russian Church in New York 2262
Russmann, Josef 7426
Russo, Nicholas John 11517
Rust, C. Renee 18976
Rust, E. Warren 12656, 13687, 13688, 14812
Rustin, John W. 5819
Rutayisire, Paul 18671
Rutgers, J. C. 12303
Rutherford, Elizabeth 19354
Rutledge, Arthur B. 10556, 11518
Rutledge, Paul 18672
Rutman, Darrett B. 9633
Rutter, Michael 15624
Ruud, Marie 19151
Rwehikiza, Felician 15625
Rwoma, Desiderius 17506

Ryan, John A. 1983, 2095, 2263, 2450, 2542, 2737, 2738, 2823, 2971, 3156, 3273, 3274, 3275, 3364, 3457, 3458, 3551, 3552, 3553, 3724, 3786, 3849, 3918, 4089, 4175, 4176, 4177, 4178, 4243, 4489, 4564, 4668, 4977, 5050, 5726, 6318, 8669, 11212, 16178
Ryan, Joseph D. 13026
Ryan, Mary P. 7427, 14813
Ryan, Michael 17507
Ryan, Paul-David 18673
Ryan, Phyllis 18977
Ryan, S. P. 6768
Ryan, Vincent J. 5051
Ryan, William 12304
Rybeck, Walter 18305
Rybnicek, Edward H. 8562
Ryckmans, A. 6232
Rycroft, W. Stanley 8290, 8563
Rykwert, Joseph 18306
Rylance, Joseph Hine 648
Rymer, J. O. 16004
Rymph, Raymond C. 9878
Ryu, Joseph H. 13689
Saarinen, Eliel 5214
Saarinen, Martin F. 17933
Sabanes, Carlos 10078
Sabatier, Maxime 1775
Sacramento First Church Ministers to Inner City 9634
Sadler, Michael Thomas 105, 110
Safford, George B. 1175, 2739
Sage Urban Studies Abstracts 12305
Saggau, Elise 16005
Sain, Raleigh E. 6969
St. Amant, C. Penrose 12683
St. Anthony's Welfare Center 4101
St. Bartholomew's Episcopal Church, New York City 2451
St. Clar, Robert 398
St. Francis Xavier University, Extension Department 6988
St. George's Episcopal Church, New York City 1021
Saint Giles Christian Mission 1087
St. John, Charles J. 4981
St. Joseph's House of Hospitality and Editorial Offices 4782
St. Mark's Church: Ecumenism in the City 11972
Saint Maur Theological Center 15232
Saint Patrick's Parish and Catholic Social Services, Design Co-operative 13690
St. Pierre, Roland H. 17539
St. Stephen's Chapel Report of the Mission to the Poor 225
Saint Thomas Episcopal Church, Philadelphia 17131
St. Vincent de Paul Society .>> See: Society of St. Vincent de Paul
Saint-Pierre, Arthur 2824
Saints among Us: Mother Teresa and Others 13691
Sakai, Kohi 7428
Sala, Ulisese Elisara 15626
Salem Evangelical Church 4669
Salem, Dorothy 19152
Saliba, John A. 19153
Salicrú Puigvert, Carlos 11948
Salisbury, Harrison 7429
Salisbury, William Seward 5976
Salley, Columbus 11949
Sallnow, Theresa 17508
Saloman, Alice 3554
Salsgiver, Thomas L. 18307
Salter, Owen 18822
Salvaterra, David 14642
Salvation Army 491, 523, 619, 1015, 1176, 1577, 1871, 1917, 1984, 1985, 2096, 2740, 3998
Salvation: A New Evangelical Monthly 1718

Salvatore, Nick amd Debs, Eugene V. 16404
Salzer, Wilhelm 8880
Salzgeber, Robert L. 18308
Salzmann, Laurence 12657
Sammon, Jane Elizabeth 19104
Samore, Lee Thomas 16717
Sample, Tex 17132
Samson, Mary E. 3650
Samuel, George 13027, 14814
Samuel, Vinay 15627
Samuel, Vinay Kumar 16006, 16405, 16718, 18978
Samuelson, Clifford 1986
Samuelsson, Kurt 8291
San Francisco and San Mateo Counties Church Extension Society of the Methodist Episcopal Church 730
Sanchez, Daniel 14411, 17934
Sanchez, R. F. 15233
Sandall, Robert 5621
Sandburg, Carl 3850
Sanders, Frank H., III 18296
Sanders, James W. 14412, 15234
Sanders, Ronald 11519
Sanderson, Ross W. 3999, 4244, 4245, 4776, 4794, 5318, 5416, 5417, 5622, 6233, 6381, 6563, 6564, 6565, 6769, 6770, 6771, 6772, 6970, 6971, 8292, 9210
Sandlin, Mark 18431
Sandoval, Moises 16719
Sands, G. 11052
Sands, Herbert S. 4597
Sandsdalen, Lief 11053
Sandstrom, Harry G. 8293
Sandt, George W. 1719, 2972
Sandvik, Marie 14026
Sanford, Arthur Benton 1177
Sanford, David 18309
Sanford, Elias Benjamin 2097, 2973
Sanford, R. Nevitt 5850
Sanger, William W. 340
Sangster, Verley 17133
Sanitary and Moral Condition of the City of New York 456
Sankey, Ira David 559, 2098
Sano, Roy 15235, 15236, 15237, 15238
Sansburn, M. 11950
Santa Ana, Julio de 14413, 14815, 15239
Santomé, Guillermo 14027
Santopolo, Frank A. 6773, 7430
Santorio, Antonio 4490
Santos, Aloysio 16720
Santos, Joao Baptista Pereier dos 8881
Sanua, Victor D. 10557
Saposs, David. 4328
Sapp, Phyllis 6088
Saprykin, Vladimir Aleksandrovich 16007
Sargent, Noel 6566
Sargunam, Ezra 16255, 16256
Sargunam, M. E. 13028, 13347
Sarles, John W. 584
Sarna, Jonathan D. 18310
Sartori, Luís Maria Alves 9635, 15628, 17509
Sartorio, Henry Charles 3093
Sata, L. S. 11951
Satre, Gary 18311
Satterlee, Henry Yates 2927
Satterwhite, John H. 17935
Sauber, Mignon 17383
Saul Alinsky Went To War 11520
Saunders, Edward 8818
Saunders, John Edward 18674
Saurin, Jacques 80
Sauvant, Karl 12087
Savage, John S. 14028
Savage, Minot Judson 806
Savage, Theodore Fisk 5820
Savageau, David 17259
Saving the Cities 9636
Sawatsky, Ben A. 17510
Sawyer, Joy Roulier 19154

Sawyer, Mary R. 17936
Saxon, Eric 10558
Scalabrini, Giovanni Battista 12658, 15240, 17329
Scalabrini, John Baptist 14153, 17172
Scalise, Victor F., Jr. 12659
Scandlin, Horace Winthrop 3030
Scanlon, A. Clark 17134
Scantlan, Sam 6089
Scarlett, William 5821
Scarpati, R. 8294
Schaeffer, Charles E. 2825
Schaeffer, Francis 11521
Schaeffer, William Ashmead 1178, 1669
Schaefle, Ulrich 12306, 14029
Schaer, Hans Rudolf 18312
Schafer, Marvin R. 4000, 4090
Schäfer, Theodor 862, 900, 1016, 1243, 1578
Schaff, Philip 310
Schaffer, Albert 7691
Schaffer, Daniel 16406
Schäffer, Sebastian Georg 2741, 5623
Schaffner, Martin 12660
Schalk, Adolph 6090
Schall, James V. 10079
Schaller, Lyle E. 7976, 7977, 8295, 8296, 8297, 8298, 8299, 8300, 8301, 8564, 8565, 8566, 8567, 8568, 8870, 8882, 8883, 8884, 8885, 8886, 9211, 9212, 9637, 10080, 10081, 10082, 10083, 10084, 10085, 10559, 10560, 10561, 10562, 11054, 11055, 11056, 11522, 11523, 11952, 12307, 12661, 12662, 13692, 14030, 14414, 15241, 15629, 18675
Schaper, Donna 15630, 19155
Schaper, Richard L. 18313
Schare, Hans Rudolf 18314
Scharlemann, Martin H. 7431, 8569, 10086
Schasching, Johann 7978
Schatz, Donald 13348
Schatz, Eunice 13348, 15242
Schatz, Ronald W. 16008, 17135
Schauffler, Adolphus F. 863, 952, 1579, 2099, 2100
Schauffler, H. A. 1872, 1987
Scheele, Christine 18979
Scheets, Francis Kelly 18315
Scheie, David M. 19238
Schell, Edwin 6679
Schellenberg, James 9638
Schelsky, Helmut 7185
Schenck, William Edward 291
Scherer, Ross P. 7432, 11953, 12663
Schermerhorn, James 4091
Scheuer, Joseph F. 6773, 6972
Scheuermeier, Robert 18316
Scheuring, Thomas 11954
Schevill, James 8570
Schibilsky, Michael 16721
Schick, Claude E 5822
Schick, John M. 1580
Schieffelin, Samuel Bradhurst 688
Schildkrout, Enid 14816
Schillebeeckx, Edward 16009
Schiller, John A. 16407
Schindler, Solomon 986, 1088, 1179
Schippers, K. A. 17136
Schissel, Steve M. 17511
Schlachtenhaufen, Ed 11955
Schlegel, Jean-Louis 18317
Schleicher, John David 15243
Schlesinger, Arthur M., Sr. 4092, 4329, 5977
Schless, Nancy Halverson 13029
Schleth, Eckart 7186
Schlitz, Michael E. 9213
Schloegel, Judith M. 17937
Schlueter, Paul J. 6973
Schlundt, Gail 15631

Schmid, Vernon 15244, 15551, 15632, 16408
Schmidt, Henry J. 15633, 17938
Schmidt, Karl T. 9612
Schmidt, Ron 18676
Schmidt, Stephen 14817
Schmidt, Werner G. 12664
Schmieder, Arnold 15634
Schmiedler, Edgar 3851, 4670, 5052
Schmitt-Eglin, Paul 6234
Schmitz, Walter 11524
Schmool, Marlena 18677
Schmucker, B. M. 764
Schneider, Benjamin 12887
Schneider, Herbert Wallace 6235
Schneider, Louis 7433, 9214
Schneider, Michael 16409, 16410
Schneider, Wolf 8887
Schneirov, Richard 17939
Schnell, Hugo 8571
Schnepp, Gerald J. 5123, 6091, 6154, 17512
Schnore, Leo F. 8390
Schobel, Paul 16010
Schodde, George H. 953
Schoenfeld, Eugen 11057
Schomerus, Hans 8302
Schoonenberg, Piet 11525
Schoonmaker, Bruce W. 13693
Schoonmaker, Mary Ellen 17003
Schoonmaker, Paul D. 14818
Schoonover, Melvin E. 10563, 11526, 14819, 17940
Schöpfer, Hans 17513
Schottstädt, Bruno 12665
Schrag, Peter 12666
Schram, P. L. 14820
Schramm, Edward W. 9639
Schramm, John E. 10087, 10564
Schreck, Harley 18318
Schreck, Harley Carl, Jr. 17137, 18319, 18678
Schreckengost, George Earl 17138
Schreiber, Dale 17941
Schreiber, Emanuel 14307
Schreiber, Georg 4330
Schreiner, Sally 18980
Schreuder, Osmund 7434, 8572
Schrock, Dan 16722
Schröder, Ferdinand 7979
Schroeder, P. M. 5053
Schroeder, W. Widick 9215, 10088, 13349
Schroll, Agnes Claire 5319
Schrover, Gilbert 10035
Schuh, J. H. 2350
Schuller, David Simon 7187, 8303, 9216, 10089, 10090, 10565, 11527, 15635
Schulte, Anton 17139
Schultz, Harold Peters 8888
Schultz, John 11528
Schultz, Joseph P. 16723
Schultz, Raymond L. 12667
Schultz, Rima Lumin 17942
Schulz, Florence 8573
Schulz, Larold K. 11058, 11529, 11956
Schulz, Mark S. 19334
Schulze, Andrew 12668
Schumacher, Christian 18320
Schumacher, Ernest Friedrich 13030, 14821
Schuman, A. 11957
Schuman, Howard 12308, 17514
Schurman, Franz 15245
Schurr, Viktor 7188
Schuster, Adolf 11059
Schuster, George Ernest 6092
Schutcler, G. S. 11060
Schutte, A. G. 13350
Schütte, J. 4291
Schuurman, Egbert 17140
Schuyler, George S. 8889
Schuyler, Joseph B. 6773, 6974, 7189, 7435, 7980
Schwantes, Carlos A. 14415
Schwartz, David C. 18679

Schwartz, Gary 11958
Schwartz, Hillel 13351
Schwartz, Richard W. 11530
Schwartz, Stephen 12309
Schwartzman, Sylvan D. 10091
Schwartzweller, Harry K. 12310
Schwarz, Brian 17141, 17515
Schwarzenberger, Rudolf 18118
Schwarztrauber, E. E. 5124
Schweickart, David 16724
Schweiker, William 17637
Schweitzer, Wolfgang 10566
Schwenning, Gustav Theodor 3725
Schwer, Wilhelm 3651
Schwind, Martin 13694
Score, J. N. R. 4870
Scotford, John Ryland 4396
Scott, Allen 11531, 11532, 11560
Scott, Amna M. 1873
Scott, Charles W. H. 11959
Scott, David Wardlaw 341
Scott, Diane 15455
Scott, Duncan 18391
Scott, Eddie 19294
Scott, Frederick George 15606
Scott, James A. 7190, 7191, 7672, 7692, 8890, 9217
Scott, Jamie S. 17637
Scott, Joseph E. 1420
Scott, Manuel L. 13031
Scott, Marshal Logan 5624, 6093, 6382, 6383, 6567, 6975, 10092
Scott, Mel 6976, 11533
Scott, Nathan A., Jr. 7436, 19279
Scott, Raymond D. 9640
Scott, Waldron 15636, 18680
Scott, William D. 11061
Scott, William H. 1442
Scribner, Grace 3050
Scudder, C. E. 3652
Scudder, John J. 1037
Scudder, Vida Dutton 1089, 1421, 1670, 1776, 2351, 2657, 3031, 3032, 3157, 3276, 3365, 4093, 4094, 4397, 4671, 4675, 5320, 13491, 14987, 16170, 16958, 19259 >> See further: Subject Index: Socialism, Christian
Scully, Richard E. 4331
Seaman, William G. 3459
Seamen's Christian Association of the City of New York 2
Search, Pamela 6977
Searle, Mark 17943
Searle, Robert Wycoff 4777, 4871
Sears, Charles Hatch 2543, 2974, 3033, 3555, 3787, 3788, 4001, 4565, 4778
Sears, Earl 15710
Seasholes, Charles Lyon 5418
Seath, William E. 5727, 6568, 6978, 8304, 13352
Seaver, Charles H. 5522, 6094, 6774
Sebba, Anne 16411
Sebold, Charles E. 4179
Seccombe, David P. 16412
Sechrist, Gail L. Schlundt 17944
Secularizacion y "vespino:" La Iglesia del suburbio 13032
Sedgwick, Catharine Maria 106
Sedgwick, Peter 17142, 17143, 18321
Seebach, Margaret Rebecca Hines 3653
Seeger, Theodor 7569
Seeley, John R. 6979
Seelman, Katherine 14822
Seelsorge für morgen 9218
Seelsorge in der industriellen Welt 6980
Segal, David R. 12214
Segal, Samuel Michael 6236
Segbers, Franz 17040
Seger, Imogen 8891
Segerhammar, Ruth 11960
Segregation in Washington 5823
Seguy, Jean 13353

Seifert, Harvey 6237, 7192, 11062, 11534, 14031
Seifert, William 13695, 14823
Selby, D. E. 14032
Seldon, Paul 16413
Selecman, Charles C. 4872
Select Bibliography on Christian Obligation in a Rapidly Changing Secularized Era 9641
Selg, Ottfried 11063, 12311
Seligman, Ben B. 10093
Seligman, Edwin R. A. 1874
Sélim, Monique 16414
Sellers, I. 17516
Sellers, James E. 7193, 17517
Sellin, Thorsten 5728
Selznick, Gertrude J. 11535
Semana Nacional de la Parroquia, 5th Majadahonda (Spain) 13696
Seminario sobre "iglesia y situacion socioeconomica en la Espana de los 80:" materiales: febrero-mayo, 1981 16011
Seminary Consortium for Urban Pastoral Education 15246
Sendler, Hans-Theodor 8305
Sengstock, Mary C. 13354
Senior, Clarence 5948, 6238
Senior, Donald 19156
Senn, Frank C. 16725
Senn, M. 8574
Sennett, Richard 11536, 11564, 11961, 19157
Sentencing in Harrisburg 12669
Seoka, Johannes Thomas 18681
Serjeant, R. B. 15637, 16726
Serrand, A. Zacharie 9642
Servier, Jean 17945
Sethi, S. Prakash 12670, 13073, 15638, 17518
Seton, Robert J. 1244
Settimana di studio sulla pastorale nel mondo del lavoro, 5th., Rome, 1968. 11064
Seutsch, Wilhelm Otto 13697
Sewell, Benjamin T. 356
Sexton, John E. 5293
Seymour, Robert E. 12671
Seymour, Susan 15639
Shachar, A. 17728
Shackford, John Walter 3034
Shaffer, John J. 15247
Shaffer, Robert W. 10567
Shaffer, William P. 13355
Shaffer, William R. 5215
Shaffir, William 13356, 16727
Shame of the Cities 7981
Shanabruch, Charles 13698, 16012
Shanahan, William O. 6569
Shandler, I. 12771
Shands, Alfred Rives 7693, 8575
Shane, John 18817, 18981
Shanfelter, N. 12598
Shannon, David A. 6981
Shannon, Thomas A. 19239
Shannon, William V. 8892
Shannon-Thornberry, Milo 16415
Shao-Yang, Lin 2544
Shaping Tomorrow 16013
Shapir, Joan Hatch 12312
Shapiro, Deanne 13357, 14033
Shapiro, Edward S. 17519
Shapiro, Judah J. 6982
Shapiro, Manheim S. 8306, 8581
Shapiro, Robert D. 17144
Sharot, Stephen 13033, 13034, 14034, 17946
Sharp, Frank A. 11537
Sharp, George 2904
Sharp, Harry 7090
Sharp, John 16728
Sharp, John K. 6570
Sharpe, Dores Robinson 5125, 5824
Sharpton, Delos L. 14649
Shatto, Tom 11940

Shaughnessy, Gerald 3726
Shaull, M. Richard 10568
Shaver, Edwin L. 3460
Shaw, Albert 1495
Shaw, Brian 11065
Shaw, Geoffrey M. 15029
Shaw, George Bernard 2168
Shaw, James P. 7511
Shaw, John 374
Shaw, Mary A. 2905
Shaw, Talbert O. 13035
Shawchuck, Norman 18861
Shea, John Gilmary 620, 807
Shea, Mary Margretta 10094
Shea, Ralph C. 11066
Shear, John Knox 7194
Sheares, Reuben 9643
Shedd, Clarence P. 6775
Sheed, Francis J. 3542
Sheehan, Arthur T. 7694
Sheerin, John B. 5625, 10095, 11538
Sheers, William 2352
Sheffer, George F., Jr. 10096
Sheffield Industrial Mission 5978
Sheffield, Walter R. 16729
Sheldon, Charles Monroe 1017, 1180, 1245, 1496, 2047, 3366, 3727, 4332, 5054
Shelley, Mark 18322
Shelly, Jill 10520
Shelp, Earl E. 17520, 18323
Shelton, Orman Leroy 5523
Shemen, Nachman 8893
Shen, Philip 16416
Shenk, David W. 17947, 17948
Shenk, Dena 15248
Shenk, Paul 16417
Shenton, James 7437
Shepherd, Samuel Claude, Jr. 15640
Sheppard, David 12524, 13358, 16730, 18682
Sheppard, David S. 11067
Sheppard, Dick 4653
Shepperson, G. 8894
Sherard, Robert D. 9219
Sheridan, Wilbur F. 1330, 1422
Sherif, Muzafer 4707
Sherman, C. Bezalel 6384
Sherman, L. Bartine 9644
Sherman, Mitchell 13759
Sherman, Richard J. 11962
Sherrard, Thomas D. 9645
Sherry, Gerard E. 7982
Sherry, Paul H. 14416, 14824
Sherwood, Bill 17145
Sherwood, J. M. 864
Shewmaker, Richard L. 10569, 10570, 10571, 10572, 10573
Shields, Bernard Francis 4566
Shields, Leo W. 5055
Shiffler, Harrold Clarence 6385
Shigeno, Nobuyuki 16418
Shih, Peter 6095
Shik, Oh Jae 17146
Shillito, Edward 3654, 3728
Shim, Steve Sangkwon 13699
Shimeall, Richard Cunningham 397
Shiner, Larry 10574
Shinn, George W. 954, 1671
Shinn, Roger Lincoln 7438, 7695, 9646, 12425, 12672, 13359
Shiozawa, Miyoko 14417
Shipley, David O. 12313
Shipley, T. 12771
Shipman, Andrew J. 2963
Shipp, Glover Harvey 17949
Shippey, Frederick A. 5366, 5419, 5524, 5626, 5627, 5825, 5826, 5827, 5828, 5829, 5979, 5980, 6096, 6097, 6098, 6146, 6239, 6240, 6241, 6386, 6387, 6512, 6776, 6777, 6983, 6984, 7439, 7440, 7441, 7983, 8576, 8895, 9220, 9647, 10575, 11068
Shiraishi, Kiyoshi T. 8577
Shirley, James Michael 17950
Shoaf, Mary Eve 16731

Shock, Dennis 11940
Shockley, Grant S. 14035, 18838
Shoemaker, Denis E. 14825
Shoemaker, Samuel M., Jr. 3852, 4180
Sholl, A. M. 2169
Shonis, Anthony 16732
Shope, John H. 5672, 5981, 6099, 6100, 6101, 6388, 6389, 6390, 6571, 6778, 6985, 6986, 7195, 7196, 7442, 9648
Shopshire, James M. 17147, 18982
Shor, Ira 18324
Shorrock, Helen 13360
Short History of the Slovak Catholics 14418
Shorter, Aylward 13036, 13361, 13362, 14826, 16733, 16734, 18683, 19158, 19240
Shotwell, Louisa R. 6242, 6572, 6573
Should Labor Unions Be Regulated 4672
Shoup, Roger Surrell 14419
Shover, John L. 13037
Showstack, Gerald Lee 18684
Shriver, Donald W., Jr. 9649, 11069, 11963, 12673, 13038, 13842, 14420, 14827, 14828, 15641, 16363, 16735, 17148, 17951, 18685
Shriver, Mark O. 2906
Shriver, Sargent 10097
Shriver, William P. 2742, 3158, 3789, 3919, 3920, 4002, 4095, 4096, 4491, 4567, 4779, 4780, 5321, 5628, 5629, 5630, 5830, 6779
Shuey, Edwin L. 1581
Shultz, Paul 4097
Shumsky, Neil L. 16736
Shupe, Anson D., Jr. 13039
Shurtleff, C. K. 2170
Shuster, George 14036
Shusterman, Donna 16014
Shuttleworth, Frank K. 4381
Siberman, Aviva 13363
Sickels, Frank E. 1875
Sider, Paul S. 14037
Sider, Ronald J. 13364, 14421, 14422, 15642, 16015, 19072
Sidey, Ken 18325
Siebert, Rudolf J. 17521
Siedell, B. 10576
Siedenberg, Frederic 3094, 3277
Siefer, Gregor 7984
Siegel, Adrienne 16016
Siegel, Arthur 6574
Siegel, Michael A. 13206
Siegel, Morris 12314
Siegelman, Ellen 11298
Siegenthaler, Carl 10098
Siegfried, A. H. 955
Siemer, L. 5831
Sigmon, Vivkie 18686
Significance of the Jewish Gathering in New York 1246
Sigrist, Helen 15643
Sikes, Melvin P. 11539
Sikes, W. Walter 9650
Silberman, Charles 8896, 9221, 9222
Silberman, Lou H. 10099
Silcox, Clarence Edwin 4398
Silk, Leonard 14038
Sills, Horace S. 10577, 18983
Sills, Mark R. 14423, 16017
Silva Henríquez, Raúl 13040
Silva, Fred 9638
Silva, Rafael 11070
Silver, Abba Hillel 3853, 4333
Silver, Queen 4181
Silverman, Myrna 14829
Silversides, Mark 17952
Silvoso, Eduardo 14830, 17522
Sim, R. Alexander 6979
Simkhovitch, Mary K. 2171
Simmel, Ernst 5525
Simmel, Georg 1918, 14338

Simmons, Charles 14831
Simmons, Gilbert 1090
Simmons, Henry 18687
Simmons, James Berkley 16419
Simmons, John G. 5832
Simmons, Paul D. 12315, 16737
Simms, Bennett J. 16477
Simms, Florence 3461
Simon, Andrea Judith 14424
Simon, Arthur R. 10100, 10101, 11540, 12316
Simon, Boris 6780
Simon, Deborah 17953
Simon, Edwin 8578
Simon, John 12674, 12674
Simon, John G. 12675
Simon, Maurice D. 16638
Simon, Ralph 7856
Simon, Rita J. 16738
Simonds, Edith 10102
Simons, Emily 5216
Simpkins, Julian A. 10578
Simpson, Dick 17523, 17524, 18298, 18326, 18984
Simpson, George E. 6391, 6411, 7020
Simpson-Clement, Jan 18327
Sims, Edward 11071
Sims, Mary Sophia Steveson 4568, 5982
Sinclair, John F. 3854
Sinclair, Upton 2048, 3462
Sinclair, William 1720
Sinclare, Andrew 8579
Sine, Thomas W., Jr. 16018, 17149, 17954
Singer, Anna M. 3790
Singer, Merrill 16420
Singer, Milton B. 6553
Singer, Steven 17955
Single Person and the Church 14425
Singleton, Gregory H. 13041, 14039, 14040
Sinnott, Thomas G. 17150, 18688, 18985
Sirikwa, Simon 16366
Siromoni, Paul 12317
Sisco, Frederick Allen 4098
Sissel, H. B. 11072
Sittler, Joseph 8580
Sivanandan, A. 16019
Six Million Americanos: A Study Book 9223
Sizer, Sandra S. 15249
Sjoberg, Gideon 7985
Skadra, Gordon H. 12318
Skaggs, Beverly R. 14832
Skapa, Barbara A. 10579
Skardon, Alvin W. 7986, 12319
Skelhorn, Samuel 3791
Skelton, Oscar Douglas 2545
Skerrett, Ellen 15445
Skidmore, Rex A. 5126
Skinner, Elliot Percival 13365
Skinner, Tom 13700
Skipper, Debbie 16020
Skirrow, Paul 15644
Skjelver, Mabel C. 13366
Sklar, Kathryn Kish 17525
Sklare, Marshall 6781, 7197, 7443, 10580, 11541, 12320, 12676, 13367, 13368
Sklba, Richard J. 7987
Skoog, Albert 3655
Sky-Scraper Church for the Chicago Loop 3367
Skymarks: An Analysis and Prognosis of the High-Rise Luxury Apartment as a Context for the Ministry 7988
Skyscraper Church 4003
Slack, Kenneth 17526, 17527, 17956
Slack, Tim 17957
Slattery, Charles L. 3368
Slattery, Margaret 2907
Slaughter, James N. 17958
Slawson, John 7696, 8581, 9651
Slayden, Thelma 10103

Slayton, William L. 8582
Sleeman, John F. 6392
Sleeper, C. Freeman 11542
Sleeter, Christine E. 19287
Slesinger, Zalmen 15250
Slicer, Thomas R. 1777
Sligh, Tom 11940
Sloan, F. 14833
Sloan, William Nichols 1876
Slocum, Stephen Elmer, Jr. 13701
Slough, Rebecca 18702
Slums Are Expensive 7444
Slusher, Steven L. 17528
Slusser, Dorothy M. 12321
Slusser, Gerald H. 9224, 11073, 12321
Sly, Julie 16739
Small, Albion W. 1672, 3159, 3278
Small, H. B. 1582
Small, Sarah Leah 16740
Smaller Churches--Repairers of the Break 12677
Smart, H. T. 1018
Smart, Ninian 11074
Smart, Reginald Keith 9225
Smart, William James 4492, 4978, 5420
Smarto, Donald 18328
Smedt, Emile-Joseph de 7989
Smelser, Neil J. 7697
Smeltzer, Ralph E. 6243
Smeltzer, Wallace G. 7445
Smilde, Hazel M. 3095
Smiley, Francis Edward 1019, 1091
Smith Haven Ministries 12322
Smith, A. R. 10104
Smith, Adam 18404
Smith, Alfredo C. 17151
Smith, Alson J. 5729
Smith, Austin 16741, 17858, 18329
Smith, Bardwell L. 18330
Smith, Baxter 18427
Smith, Bertram 1821, 5277
Smith, Brian H. 17959
Smith, Carl R. 7198
Smith, Cecil 16021, 18692
Smith, Charles Spencer 3463
Smith, Charles Sprague 1988, 2264
Smith, Christine 18689
Smith, Constance 3729
Smith, D. M. 6102
Smith, David 18986
Smith, David Marshall 16022
Smith, Dennis 18690
Smith, Donald C. 9652, 18331
Smith, Donald Eugene 10105, 12323
Smith, Ebbie C. 14041, 17152
Smith, Edward 2975
Smith, Edward D. 18691
Smith, Egbert Watson 2546, 3035
Smith, Elwyn A. 11543
Smith, Eric Michael 18332
Smith, Eugene B. 4399
Smith, Eugene L. 11075
Smith, Eunice 18692
Smith, Famous 17529
Smith, Frances S. 7446, 11964
Smith, Fred 16742
Smith, Geoffrey Boulton 17530
Smith, George 1822
Smith, Gerrit 4835
Smith, Glenn 18693, 19159
Smith, Gordon T. 17960
Smith, Greg 17961, 18694, 18987
Smith, H. Lester 4673
Smith, Harmon L. 10581
Smith, Harry H. 18333
Smith, Hillary 10106
Smith, Homer J. 1423
Smith, J. Alfred 11076, 14426, 16023, 17153, 18988
Smith, J. Brabner 5631
Smith, J. Stephen 14547
Smith, Joanmarie 12678

Smith, Joe E. 17531
Smith, John 19315
Smith, John Chester 8583
Smith, John Robert 9226, 15251
Smith, John Talbot 1331, 2049
Smith, Jonathan Z. 18334
Smith, Luke M. 6393
Smith, Luther E. 16743, 17154
Smith, Matthew Hale 457, 865
Smith, Michael Hornsby 18989
Smith, Norris K. 15252
Smith, Paul Raymond 17155
Smith, Peter 9227
Smith, Philip M. 5217
Smith, Richard C. 6244, 7698, 7699
Smith, Robert Jack 8897
Smith, Rolland F. 11965
Smith, Roy Lemon 3279, 3556, 4246, 4334, 4674, 4781, 5421
Smith, Samuel George 2658
Smith, Sandy 18335
Smith, Sidney 13042, 16024, 17962
Smith, T. Lynn 6103
Smith, Timothy 17532
Smith, Timothy L. 7199, 8584, 10582
Smith, W. Angie 4873
Smith, W. G. 3464
Smith, Wallace Charles 15253, 17533
Smith, Walter J. 18695
Smith, Warren Sylvester 8898, 8899
Smith, Wilbur M. 11077
Smith, William C. 5730
Smith, William Carlson 4874
Smith, William Clyde 3369
Smith, William J. 4875, 5983, 10107
Smithfield Stayed 5322
Smits, P. 6245, 7219
Smolik, Josef 10583
Smucker, Donovan E. 7200, 7700, 10108, 14594
Smucker, John I. 11544, 11966, 17534
Smucker, Joseph 17963
Smylie, James Hutchinson 8900
Smyth, Newman 765, 766, 1181, 1424
Smythe, Charles Hugh E. 6782
Smythe, Dallas W. 6751, 7447
Snider, David J. 15645
Snider, P. M. 5984
Snizek, W. E. 13986
Snow, Albert 2101
Snow, David A. 15646
Snow, Loudell F. 14834
Snowden, Philip 2826
Snyder, Dean 15254
Snyder, Gradon F. 11545
Snyder, Graydon F. 15647
Snyder, Herbert J. 16421
Snyder, Howard A. 10109, 12324, 13702, 15648, 16744, 16808
Snyder, Mitch 16617, 17913
Snyder, T. Richard 18696
Sobel, Mechal 15255
Sobelhoff, Isadore 6987
Sobrinho, João Falcão 14042
Sobrino, Jon 16025, 17156
Social Action: Study Guide Material for Church's Organizations and Related Agencies 12679
Social Concerns Coordinating Committee 15256
Social Evil in Syracuse: Being a Report of an Investigation of the Moral Condition of the City Conducted by a Committee of Eighteen Citizens 2743
Social Service Study Programs 2744
Social Work of the Methodist Church 2265
Social Work under Church

Auspices and Social Work under Community Auspices from the Standpoint of the Urban Community 3557
Society for Preventing of Pauperism in the City of New York 56
Society for the Encouragement of Faithful Domestic Servants 90
Society for the Prevention of Pauperism 54, 86
Society for the Prevention of Pauperism in Boston 123
Society for the Relief of Poor Widows with Small Children 24
Society of Christian Socialists 956
Society of Friends [Hicksite], General Conference, Committee on Unemployment 4493
Society of Inner Mission 3558
Society of Socialist Christians 3280
Society of St. Vincent de Paul, Superior Council of New York 124, 1425
Society of St. Vincent DePaul 124, 3019
Society of Sts. Peter and Paul 3281
Sockman, Ralph W. 3160, 3559, 3656, 4099, 4335, 6489, 6575, 8307
Sodeman, Lowell F. 16422
Soden, Dale E. 18336
Söderberg, Kjell 16026
Söhngen, Oskar 4400
Sojourners 12325
Sokol, Dolly 16027
Sokolski, A. 7990
Sola, José 7991
Soleri, Paolo 12697, 16028
Solomon Community Temple United Methodist Church 11967
Soloway, Richard Allen 11546
Soltero, Conrado G. 15257
Soltes, Mordecai 3657
Solzbacker, Wilhelm 4336
Sombard, Werner 19248
Somers, Sandra L. 8479
Sommers, Charles G. 139
Sommerville, Henry 2976, 3792
Somplatsky-Jarman, Carol 14043
Somplatsky-Jarman, William 14043
Son, Myong Gul 17157
Songs of Anger and Hope 11968
Sontag, Susan 18697
Soon, Cho Wha 10584
Soper, Donald 8585, 12342, 14427
Soper, Judy 14835
Sopher, David E. 16803
Sorenson, Andrew A. 12680
Sorg, Rembert 5833
Sorokin, Pitirim 4004
Soto, Paul 15424
Soto-Fontanez, Santiago 12997, 16423
Soukaros, George James 16745
South Central Ministry 14836
South Leith Parish 14428
South, Scott J. 18337
Southard, Samuel 7701, 14837
Southcott, Ernest William 6576, 7201
Southern Baptist Convention 6577
Southern Baptist Convention, Christian Life Commission 11078, 11547
Southern Baptist Convention, Department of Metropolitan Mission, Home Mission Board, and Church Administration Department, Sunday School Board 11079
Southern Baptist Convention,

Home Mission Board 4100, 6783, 11969, 14838, 16029, 16424
Southern Baptist Convention, Research Division of the Home Mission Board 15258
Southern Baptist Convention, Sunday School Board 5056, 17535
Southern Baptist Theological Seminary 6578
Southern Industrial Conference on Human Relations in Industry 3658
Southern Migrant and the Northern City 9228
Southwest Interparish Ministry 7992
Southwick, William 9653, 10475
Sovik, Edward A. 7993, 13043, 16030
Sowel, Robert M. 18338
Sowell, Thomas 16031
Sozialinstitut des Bistums 9654
Space Age Cathedral 8586
Spae, Joseph J. 10585
Spahr, Charles B. 1247
Spain, Daphne 15522, 17536
Spain, Rufus B. 8308, 10586
Spalding, Henry S. 4182
Spalding, John Lancaster 649, 1092, 1877, 1878, 5319, 8415, 10285, 10670
Spanish Church in New York City 2745
Spann, John Richard 6394
Spann, Ron 15649
Spargo, John 2266, 2353, 2908
Sparks, Malcolm 3855
Spates, James L. 12463
Speakman, Joseph M. 14044
Spear, Alan H. 10587
Special Study of Miami Baptist Association 11548
Speed, Jno. Gilmer 1182
Speer, Pat 18339
Speer, Robert E. 2267
Speers, T. Guthrie 5218
Speight, R. Marston 17537
Spence, Hartzell 4979
Spencer, Jon Michael 18990
Spencer, Ken 15328
Spencer, Malcolm 3921
Spengler, Oswald 3922
Spiazzi, Raimondo M. 14045
Spiegel, Yorik 14429
Spieler, Willy 14046
Spielvogel, Lawrence G. 17158
Spike, Robert W. 5985, 6579, 7202, 7203, 7448, 7994, 8587, 9655, 9656
Spink, Kathryn 16425
Spinka, Matthew 5323
Spitaler, Armin 7995
Spivak, John 4980
Spoelstra, H. H. 6784
Spofford, William B. 4005, 4247, 4675, 16958
Spohn, Willfried 19241
Spong, John Selby 17159
Sponseller, Michael P. 18340
Spooner, Bernard 12113, 17538
Sports Council, Technical Union for Sport 14430
Sprafkin, Benjamin R. 11970
Spragg, Howard 12681
Sprague, Franklin Monroe 1332, 1426
Sprague, Philo Woodruff 1020, 1427, 13929
Spring, Beth 16032, 18991
Spring, Gardiner 18
Springe, Christa 12682
Sprinkle, Henry C. 7449, 7702, 7703
Sproat, John G. 11080
Sproll, Heinz 14431
Sprott, J. H. 6246
Sproul, Robert Charles 15650
Sproull, J. W. 808

Sprouse, Claude Willard 2977
Spurgeon, Charles Haddon 1126, 1154, 1163, 1583, 12969
Squatter Communities: Selected Abstracts 11971
Squires, Enoch 6395
Srole, Leo 5428
Stacey, Gerald F. 16426
Stacey, Nicholas 13369
Stack, John Francis, Jr. 14432
Stack, Kenneth 17964
Stackhouse, Max L. 9657, 11549, 12326, 12327, 12684, 12685, 12686, 13044, 13370, 18698
Stackhouse, Perry J. 4337
Stackpole, Richard L. 18992
Stadler, Martin 15259
Stafford, Russell Henry 6785
Stafford, Ward 47, 75
Stage de pastorale, Sarh, Chad 13371
Stagg, Paul L. 10588
Stahl, William Marvin 14047
Stahura, John 17860
Stair, Tim 18699
Staley, Mary W. 11081
Staley, Ronald 9229
Stall, Sylvanus 731, 866, 1584
Stallings, Earl 9658
Stallings, Gary 10589
Stalvey, Lois Mark 9230
Stambouli, F. 14048
Stamm, Thomas J. 4783
Stammler, Eberhard 7996
Stamp, Josiah Charles Stamp 3793, 4569, 4784
Stanford, John 16, 38, 57, 71, 91, 139
Stang, William 1919, 1989, 2050
Stanley, Anthony 15260
Stanley, Arthur L. 17540
Stanley, Frances 10110
Stanley, John E. 13045
Stanley, Manfred 7450, 7945, 8588
Stano, Marion Joan 7451
Stansfield, Charles 13703
Star, Paul D. 18125
Starbuck, Robert B. 7997
Stark, Beverly 15261
Stark, Rodney 9231, 9444, 9861, 11550, 12328, 12329, 14643, 17541, 18341, 18488
Starkes, M. Thomas 17160
Starkey, Frank F. 14433
Starn, W. Elbert 6580
Starr, Ellen Gates 1497
Starr, Paul D. 18218
Starratt, Alfred B. 7998
State of Education in the City of New York 102
Statement on the Churches' Concern for Housing 6581
Statements, "1969" 11551
Statnick, Roger Andrew 16746
Stauffer, Henry 1428
Stauffer, Milton Theobald 3560
Staunton, William 809
Stave, Bruce M. 13704, 16033
Stave, Sondra A. 16033
Stead, Francis Herbert 2827, 3282, 3659
Stead, William T. 650, 971, 1248, 1298, 1333, 1334, 1335, 1778, 1823, 2051, 12667, 14032
Steady, F. C. 14049
Stean, Robert L. 16427
Stebbins, Katherine 2452
Steeh, Charllotte 17514
Steel, G. M. 1429
Steel, Gerald 6582
Steel, Marshall T. 6583
Steel, William Edward 15262
Steele, Alan 11082, 12330
Steele, George McKendree 957
Steele, Robert E. 14839
Steelman, Albert Judson 2172
Steeman, Theodore 11552
Steere, David A. 12331
Steever, Rolland A. 10590, 11083

Stefaniuk, Myroslava 14434, 15263
Steffens, Lincoln 1990, 4183
Stegall, William H. 12687
Steger, Gerhard 16747
Stegmann, Franz Josef 11553, 17161
Steidl-Mfeier, Paul 7704
Stein, Jock 18342
Stein, Maurice R. 7999
Steinberg, Stephen 11535, 16034
Steinbock, Elmer L. 16866
Steinbruck, John F. 16748, 17965
Steiner, Edward Alfred 2102, 2354, 2547, 2828
Steiner, Frank E. 14840
Steinfels, Peter 19160
Steinhouer, Paul 18343
Steinle, Donald R. 10645
Steinweg, Johannes 3923
Steltser, Theodor 7204
Stelzle, Charles 1673, 1721, 1779, 1879, 1920, 1991, 2052, 2053, 2103, 2173, 2174, 2268, 2269, 2270, 2271, 2272, 2453, 2454, 2455, 2456, 2457, 2458, 2548, 2549, 2550, 2659, 2660, 2661, 2746, 2829, 2830, 2909, 3036, 3096, 3283, 3794, 3795, 3856, 4338, 4785, 11915, 13110, 13565
Stember, Charles Herbert 10111
Stenberg, Odin K. 14050
Stentzel, Cathy 14841
Stenzel, Jim 14435
Stephan, Thomas 13705
Stephens, Bill 13372
Stephens, Carol Brethour 19161
Stephenson, John P. 10591
Stepp, Laura Sessions 18700
Stern, Bernhard Joseph 4184
Stern, Norton B. 10592, 13270
Stern, Samuel M. 11818, 11973
Sternau, Herbert 7452
Stetson, Caleb R. 3730
Stevens, George E. 3796
Stevens, R. S. O. 8901
Stevens, Willard Robert 10593
Stevens, William K. 18701
Stevens-Arroyo, Antonio M. 13373, 15651, 15652, 16035
Stevenson, Andrew 2175
Stevenson, Arthur 8589
Stevenson, David 4786
Stevenson, Foy 15653
Stevenson, J. 10594
Stevenson, John 14436
Stevenson, John J. 1093
Stevenson, William Fleming 381
Steward, David S. 18702
Stewart, Betty 19263
Stewart, Bryce M. 2747, 2748
Stewart, Frank Mann 5986
Stewart, James B. 17966
Stewart, James H. 11554
Stewart, Ollie 10112
Stewart, Ruth A. 17162
Stewart, William Rhinelander 2551, 3660
Stickney, Fred 15689
Stidger, William L. 3465, 3797
Stidley, Leonard Albert 4787, 5324
Stiefbold, Annette E. 12852
Stier, W. Rudolf F. 4982
Stigant, P. 12332
Still, Douglas M. 8902
Stillett, Frederick T. 9232
Stimson, Henry Albert 1921, 2355
Stine, Leo 9638
Stinehelfer, Jeffrey N. 11555
Stith, Joe Ray 11974
Stivers, Robert L. 17779, 18993
Stob, George 7205
Stobaugh, James P. 18703
Stockbridge, Frank Parker 3924
Stockholm Conference 3731
Stockholm's Call to Christianity 3732

Stocking, Jay T. 2662
Stockwell, Clinton E. 15654, 16036, 16163, 16428, 16429, 16430, 16431, 16432, 16433, 16434, 16435, 16749, 16750, 16751, 16808, 16890, 16938, 17163, 17164, 17165, 17523, 17524, 17542, 17967, 17998, 18298, 18326, 18344, 18345, 18704, 18962, 18994, 19356
Stockwell, Eugene L. 18346
Stöd Till Invandrarnas Trossamfund: Rapport 17968
Stoerker, J. Winfred 12688
Stoese, Dennis E. 17543
Stoggers, John 16037
Stokes, Kenneth 13046
Stolarik, M. Mark 14437, 14842
Stoltzfus, Gene 17544
Stone, Daniel Greene 14843
Stone, Edward Durell 9659
Stone, Melville E. 1498
Stone, Michael 11975
Stone, Ronald H. 10645, 17779, 18705
Stone, Sara Margaret 17545
Stone, Sonja H. 17969
Stone, Warren S. 3661
Stonsby, Ella V. 14051
Stoody, Ralph 2978, 7705
Storck, Hans 7706, 10595
Store-Front Church Unlocks Harlem Slum to Protestantism 5834
Store-Front Churches 5835
Storer, Des 13047, 13048, 13374
Storkey, Alan 15264, 17970
Storms, Albert B. 3097
Storrs, Richard S. 399, 732, 17766
Stortz, Gerald J. 14844
Stott, John 13706, 15265, 18347
Stotts, Herbert E. 6247, 6786, 6787, 7453, 8590
Stotts, Jack Leven 9660, 13049
Stout, Harry H. 13707
Stout, Robert Joe 15266
Stoutenburgh, Sara 2831
Stow, Peter 18348
Stowe, Harriet Beecher 524
Stowe, Walter Herbert 5127
Stowell, Jay S. 3662
Straetz, Ralph Arthur 8903
Straley, George 10596
Strategy for Community Change 9661
Straus, Nathan 6248
Strauss, Anselm L. 7485, 8309, 11084
Strauss, James D. 11556
Strauss, Joseph H. 14925
Strayer, Paul Moore 2832
Street, David 14845
Strege, Merle Dennis 16436
Streufert, Victor B. 8591
Streyffeler, Alan 19275
Strharsky, Harry 13831, 14438
Strickland, Phil 11779
Strickland, W. P. 245
Stride, Eddy 12423
Stride, Edgar C. 9662
Strike at Marion, North Carolina 4006
Stringfellow, William 6788, 7206, 7707, 8310, 8311, 8312, 8592, 8593, 8904, 9233, 9234, 9663, 10113, 11976, 13050, 17166
Stritch, Samuel 6396
Stroh, Hans 8244
Stroh, Paul 4494
Strole, W. P. 3663
Stroll, Charles 2979
Strom, Robert 8905, 9235
Strom, Stephanie 19162
Strommen, Merton 14951, 15635
Strommen, Robert T. 14416
Strong, Augustus Hopkins 901
Strong, Donald 4983
Strong, Edgar F. 1430

Strong, Josiah 767, 902, 950, 958, 1022, 1249, 1585, 1586, 1587, 1674, 1780, 1824, 1880, 1996, 2104, 2176, 2177, 2178, 2273, 2356, 2357, 2459, 2749, 2940, 3315, 5709, 6923, 7658, 17984
Strong, Robbins 8906
Stronks, James B. 9236
Strother, Pat 14439
Stroud, Jimmy 5526
Stroup, Herbert Hewitt 5422
Struckel, Omar 9664
Stryker, Peter 423, 440
Stuart, Donald 10475
Stuart, Paul W. 12955
Stubbs, Charles William 601, 1992
Stubley, Peter 15655
Stuckenberg, John Henry W. 651, 1250, 1588, 1589, 1590, 1781, 4719
Studdert-Kennedy, Geoffry Anketell 3284, 3370
Students out in the Marketplace 11557
Study of Social and Economic Factors Relating to Spanish Speaking People in the United States 3857
Stuhr, Walter M., Jr. 11085, 12689
Stumme, Wayne 19242
Sturdivant, Cyrus 689
Sturgis, William C. 3285
Sturhahn, William J. H. 14052
Sturm, Roy A. 6511, 6789, 6989, 6990, 7360, 7454, 7455, 7708, 7709, 7710, 7711, 7712, 8000, 8001, 8002, 8313, 9237
Sturm, Theodore Paul 12333
Sturtevant, Julian Monson 327
Sturzo, Luigi 5527
Styche, Leonard G. 11086
Styles, Lawrie 13708, 14053, 15656
Stylios, Euthymios 14846, 15657
Styron, William 15267
Suburban Field 1094
Suburban Master Plan for Church Extension 9665
Sucherm, Louis, Jr. 15646
Suderman, Dale 14440
Suderman, Elmer F. 8314, 9238
Suelflow, Roy A. 9666, 11977
Sugden, Christopher 16038, 16405, 16718, 17546, 18978
Sugi, Masataka 13051
Sugirtharaj, F. N. 11978
Sugiura, Yoshimichi 2663
Suhard, Emmanuel-Célestin 5836, 8003
Suhor, Mary Lou 13831
Suk, Min Chong 14847
Suk, W. 8004
Sulgit, Julian D. 16039
Sullenger, T. Earl 3664, 5528, 7207
Sullivan, James L. 7713
Sullivan, Joseph P. 18995
Sullivan, Kathryn 14848
Sullivan, Leon 18020
Sullivan, Oona 8594
Sullivan, Patrick J. 17547, 18349
Sullivan, Robert E. 17548
Sullivan, William J. 15544
Sullivan, William M. 17238, 19340
Sully, Charles 261
Sumiya, Mikio 6991, 8005, 18706
Summer, Margaret L. 8907
Summerson, Elizabeth 3037
Sumner, John Bird 39
Sunday, Billy 2786, 2900, 4563, 6729, 13447, 19068, 19201
Sunderland, Ronald H. 17520, 18323
Super, Paul 3286
Surgeon, George P. 14445
Surkehim, Emile 12163
Survey: Social, Charitable, Civic --

A Journal of Constructive Philanthropy 2358
Sussman, Lance J. 17549
Sussman, Sarah 6362
Sutch, E. Leon 8595, 8596, 11087
Sutcliffe, Anthony 16580
Sutherland, Allen 1881
Sutherland, E. A. 5999
Sutherland, John 11730, 13052
Sutherland, Robert L. 4102
Sutherlin, Calvin James 6790
Sutter, Julie 1251, 1825
Suttles, Gerald 11088, 15268
Sutton, John R. 18570
Sutz, Erwin 5423
Suzuki, Lester E. 12690, 15269
Swaffield, Walter J. 986
Swallow, Richard Dawson 3371
Swan, Charles Lundeen 6791
Swan, Eric Philip 3665
Swann, Darius Leander 7208
Swanson, Guy E. 8597, 12334
Swanson, Merwin 14441
Swanstrom, Edward E. 4401
Swantz, L. W. 11979
Swarthout, Marjorie 17550
Swartz, Herman F. 2460, 2664
Swatos, William H., Jr. 18350
Swearer, Donald K. 16040
Swedenborg, Emanuel 18489
Sweeney, Helen M. 1252, 1499
Sweeney, Samuel H. 4676
Sweet, Herman J. 8908
Sweet, Leonard I. 18996
Sweet, William E. 3666
Sweet, William Warren 3667, 4103, 5325, 5632
Sweeting, George 11089, 12335, 12336, 12691, 15658, 17551, 17971
Sweetser, Thomas P. 13349, 13375, 16752, 18351
Swichkow, Louis L. 8909
Swidler, Ann 17238, 19340
Swiecicki, Andrzej 12337
Swift, Arthur L. 3858, 4339, 4788
Swift, Morrison 1023, 1024, 1025, 1095, 1253
Swift, Polemus Hamilton 1782
Swiggett, Ernest 14442
Swing, R. G. 4495
Swing, William Edwin 18707
Swinton, John 733, 1431
Swisher, Okey R. 5837
Swoboda, Heinrich 2359
Swomely, John M., Jr. 11558
Swyngdouw, Jan 14054
Sybesma, A. 10114
Sykes, Tom 4104
Symanowski, Horst 8006, 9239, 11980, 12682, 19163
Symes, Richard A. 15270
Symons, W. G. 5057
Symons, W. T. 4105
Symposium from Rerum Novarum to Laborem Exercens, towards the Year 2000 16437
Symposium: City Church Planning 8007
Symposium: Clergy and Laity in Community Life 8008
Symposium: Religious Education in the Secular City 10115
Symposium: The Metropolitan Church, Its Program 10116
Synan, Vinson 12338
Syracuse, Ross M. 18708
Szabo, D. 6792
Szabo, Marylou Curcio 12692
Szasz, Ferenc M. 12693, 16438
Szoka, Edmund 18754, 18813, 18997, 19071
Szto, Paul C. H. 18352
T., H. W. 3561
Taartakower, Arieh 5987
Tabb, William K. 16439, 18353
Tabor, Margaret Emma 3038
Tafel, Edgar 10597
Taggart, Alice D. 8598
Tahir, Abkul Jalil, al. 6249

Taira, Koji 11559
Taiwan Ecumenical Industrial Ministry 12694
Takayama, K. Peter 15271, 15659, 16696, 16753
Takenaka, Masao 7209, 8009, 8599, 8910, 8911, 9667, 10117, 12339, 12340, 13053, 13376, 14443, 14444, 14849, 14850, 16041, 17972
Talbot, B. J. 11560
Talbot, E. Guy 2980
Tale of Ten Cities: A Series of Authoritative Papers upon Religious and Denominational Conditions in American Cities 2274
Talec, Pierre 10598
Taliaferro, Dale 17973
Tallant, Robert 5529, 6992
Tallon, Mary Teresa 4106
Talmage, Thomas DeWitt 621, 903, 1026, 1096, 1835, 4117
Talmy, Robert 10118
Tamashiro, Sam 10599
Tammen, Margaret 8600
Tamney, Joseph B. 15660, 15661, 16754, 17812, 18709
Tamoush, Vivki 18710
Tamura, Yoshiro 8010
Tanenbaum, Marc H. 9240, 10119
Tanganyika Rapid Social Change Study, Commission "C 9241
Tange, André 12123
Tao Fong Shan Ecumenical Center 16755
Tapp, N. Cleo 11561
Taran, Patrick A. 16131, 18354
Tarango, Yolanda 18541
Tarbell, Ida M. 1993, 3039
Tarr, Joel A. 13054
Tarr, Leslie K. 12695
Tarrant, William George 1432
Tarro, Paul 17974
Tash, M. Joan 10349
Task Force on Gay/Lesbian Issues 16440
Task-Force for Renewal, Urban Strategy and Training [TRUST] 8011, 10600
Tassello, Graziano 15028, 17552
Tate, Francis V. 11981
Tatgenhorst, David 17553
Taub, Richard 14445
Taverne, Dick 13055
Tawney, Richard Henry 2833, 3287, 3288, 3668, 3798, 5530, 15720
Taylor, Alva Wilmot 2552, 4340
Taylor, Barbara Brown 18711, 18712
Taylor, Betty Jo 10601
Taylor, Dick 15272
Taylor, Edward T. 510, 1934, 2071, 14154
Taylor, Gavin M. 18713
Taylor, Graham 867, 959, 1027, 1336, 1337, 1722, 1785, 1922, 2007, 2054, 2105, 2106, 2179, 2180, 2181, 2275, 2360, 2461, 2553, 2554, 2665, 2666, 2750, 2751, 2752, 2753, 4021, 4107, 4496, 4570, 4735, 4839, 5709, 6588, 9209, 13719
Taylor, Graham R., Mrs. 3562
Taylor, Harriet Brown 2182, 2183
Taylor, Jack 8836
Taylor, John V. 8315, 13709, 16042
Taylor, Laura 18998
Taylor, Meg 16043
Taylor, R. P. 11562
Taylor, Raymond P. 14851, 17167
Taylor, Richard 8316
Taylor, Richard K. 10602, 13710
Taylor, Richard S. 11563
Taylor, Richard W. 8912

Taylor, Robert J. 18714
Taylor, Robert P. 8475
Taylor, Ronald L. 11090
Taylor, Torres Eduardo 11982
Taylor, William 322
Taylor, William Craig 17168
Taylor, Winston H 17975
Tcherikower, Elias 6104
Teachers in Harvard University 2462
Teague, Dennis Jay 17169
Technological Future of the Industrialized Nations and the Quality of Life: Report from a North American - European Conference, Pont-à-Mousson, France, May 27 - June 2, 1973 13056
Teel, Charles, Jr. 14852
Teeter, Herman B 10603
Teije, Carel Wilhelm ten 17976
Telfer, David Alden 13711, 16044
Telfer, Walter A. 12178, 14055
Telford, John 810, 2184
Temple to Buddha Is Opened in New York City 4789
Temple, Katherine 19104
Temple, William 2276, 3859, 4677, 4984, 5058, 5128, 5129, 5219, 5308, 5326, 5437, 5517, 5694, 8690, 17087
Templeton, John H. 11359
Ten, E. L. 8012
Tenbruck, F. H. 8013
Tennies, Arthur C. 14446
Tenywa, J. S. 13377
Teplow, Leo 5633
Teresa, Mother 12899, 13691, 13834, 15377, 15423, 15431, 15432, 15465, 15883, 16373, 16411, 16425, 16590, 16678, 17376, 17405, 17410, 17411, 17554, 17584, 17909, 18448, 18508
Tergel, Alf 16045
Terkel, Studs 13378
Terpenning, Peter A. 17555
Terrett, Barbara 7143
Terry, Robert W. 10604, 11091, 11983, 13057
Teske, Robert Thomas 14447
Tesser, Gaston 6993
Thalheimer, Ross 6584
Than, U Kyaw 8599
Thatcher, Joan 11984, 12755, 12983, 12997, 13075
The Bowery Mission and Young Men's Home 2055
Thebaud, Aug. J. 652
Theile, Kenneth 13712
Their Brother's Keeper 5838
Theissen, Gerd 16441
Theobald, Robert 8317, 10120, 11092, 11093, 11094
Theobald, Robin 17556
Theobald, Walter William 1254
Theology Steps into the Industrial Arena: Report on ICWIM Winter 17977
Thernstrom, Stephan 11564, 13058, 15662
They Linked Arms in a Rioting City 10605
They Try to Reach the Church-Shy 10121
Thieme, Richard 15273
Thier, Erich 5988
Third Way 14448
This is Henry Street 8014
Thistlethwaite, Susan Brooks 16756
Tholin, Richard Diener 10606
Thom, John Hamilton 150, 216
Thoma, George A. 4790
Thomas, Allen C. 4108
Thomas, Bettye C. 14056
Thomas, Carl 13649
Thomas, Charles B., Jr. 17557
Thomas, Darwin L. 13401

Thomas, E. 475
Thomas, Esther A. 4402
Thomas, George B. 18999
Thomas, George Finger 4985
Thomas, J. Mark 16757
Thomas, J. S. Ladd 4341
Thomas, J. V. 17978
Thomas, James J. 8015
Thomas, James S. 15274
Thomas, John C. 17979
Thomas, John L. 5839, 10122, 10607
Thomas, Joseph 17558
Thomas, K. M. 14057
Thomas, Latta R. 14058
Thomas, Lewis F. 4868
Thomas, Lizzie M. 17170
Thomas, Madathilparampil M. 8016, 8912, 9242, 9668, 10608, 10609, 14059, 14449
Thomas, Maria H. 17980
Thomas, Marilyn 14450
Thomas, Michael C. 12696
Thomas, Norman 4109, 17232
Thomas, Norman E. 11985, 11986, 13713
Thomas, Piri 10610
Thomas, Stanley F. 19164
Thomas, Stanley Whitaker 8017
Thomas, Wendell Marshall 4110
Thomas, William I. 3860
Thomason, Robert H. 13059
Thompsett, Fredrica Harris 17559
Thompson, Albert Edward 1882
Thompson, Betty 6585, 14853
Thompson, Bryan 12341
Thompson, Cecil 6250
Thompson, Charles L. 1500, 1501, 1994, 3161, 3669
Thompson, Clarence Bertrand 2361
Thompson, Daniel C. 13379
Thompson, Dorothy 10611, 13714
Thompson, Douglas W. 12342
Thompson, E. P. 8913
Thompson, Ernest Trice 5989
Thompson, Frank Victor 3289
Thompson, James J., Jr. 13380
Thompson, John 3040, 3098, 3290, 3291, 3372, 3466, 3563, 4342
Thompson, John A. 6105
Thompson, John Giffin 3861
Thompson, John Rhey 1783
Thompson, Joseph P. 328, 525, 622, 17766
Thompson, Kenneth 8914, 10123
Thompson, Kenneth A. 11987
Thompson, Laura 17298
Thompson, Noyes L. 526
Thompson, Pat 13381
Thompson, Peter 2334
Thompson, Phyllis 17560
Thompson, Ralph Wardlaw 2277
Thompson, Richard Hubert T. 7210
Thompson, Robert Ellis 690, 868, 1097
Thompson, Robert V. 16442
Thompson, Rolland 17981
Thompson, W. I. 12697
Thompson, Warren 4111, 4678
Thompson, William 17888
Thompson, Yancy Samuel 6994
Thompson-McCausland, L. P. 10612
Thoms, Craig Sharp 2834, 3564
Thomson, Randall 15663
Thoreau, Henry David 382
Thorman, Donald J. 8018
Thorn, George E. 4248
Thornberg, Elizabeth 19165
Thornburg, John D. 19165
Thorndike, Edward Lee 4876, 4877, 4986, 4987
Thorne, Charles 6586, 6793, 6995, 6996, 6997, 7211, 7456, 7457, 7458, 7714, 7715, 8019,

8318, 8601, 9669, 9670, 9855, 10124, 10339, 11095, 11287, 11988
Thornton, Barbara 12343
Thorogood, Bernard 19000
Thorpe, Willard B. 2056
Three Mile Island: Diaries of a Near Disaster 16046
Thung, Mady A. 6998, 8915, 9671, 14060, 16758, 17561, 19166
Thurber, Charles S. 5148
Thurman, Howard 7716
Thwing, Charles F. 904, 905
Tibbetts, Orlando 5220, 11565
Tibbits, Clark 19257
Tichenor, George H. 4791, 4988
Tiffany, C. C. 1098
Tilden, Paul L. 6251
Tilford, N. Allen 18355
Tillapaugh, Frank R. 16443, 18715
Tillich, Paul 4571, 5731, 6252, 6397, 8689, 8916, 12344, 13820
Tillman, James A. 8917, 9243, 11566
Tillman, Robert B. 13382
Tilly, Charles 13383
Timasheff, Nicholas Sergeyevitch 6794
Timberlake, James H. 8918
Time for Burning 8020
Timmel, Sally 16998
Timoney, Conan H. 13715
Tinckom-Fernandez, W. G. 4878
Tindley, E. J. 3099
Tink, Fletcher L. 17982, 19167
Tinker, Charles Perley 2185
Tinker, Edward Laroque 4112
Tinney, James S. 14061
Tinsley, Virginia 16444
Tiplady, Thomas 3162, 4497
Tipping, Fred 13716
Tipple, Ezra 1675
Tippy, Worth M. 4572
Tippy, Worth Marion 2107, 2362, 2463, 2835, 3100, 3101, 3102, 3467, 3565, 3566, 3567, 3568, 3581, 3670, 3671, 3799, 3800, 3862, 4343
Tipton, Steven M. 17238, 19340
Tittle, Ernest Fremont 3569, 4879
Titus, Palakunnthu Mathew 4880
Tlapa, Richard J. 14451, 17983
Tlhagale, Buti 17562
To Know Ourselves Loved in the City 10125
To Open a Door: Wanderers in Our Cities 16445
Tobey, Mark 18760
Tocqueville, Alexis de 140, 17392, 19216
Todd, George E. 7212, 7459, 7460, 9244, 10126, 14062
Todd, John 183
Todd, John Murray 8021
Todd, Norman 18356
Todes, David Uriah 6253
Todolf, José 6795
Tödt, Heinz-Eduard 14452
Toffin, Gérard 16446
Toffler, Alvin 11989, 16047
Toh, Serene S. 19168
Tolbert, Alice B. 19001
Toldo, Antonio 6398, 10127
Tolino, John V. 4792, 4881, 4882, 5221
Toll, William 14453
Tollefson, Kenneth 18357
Tolman, William Howe 1255, 1256, 1257, 1338, 1433, 1434, 1784, 1995, 1996, 2363
Tolstoy, Leo 768
Tom, Yuk Sam 3163
Tomandl, Theodor 11990
Tomasi, Silvano M. 10613, 11991, 12698, 12721, 12722, 13060, 13665, 13717, 13718,

13934, 14063, 17171, 17172, 18358
Tomasik, Kristine 18359
Tomassen, Wilhelmus Gerardus Johannes Maria 13384
Tomlinson, B. T. 2754
Tomlinson, Juliette 13385
Tomorrow 8602
Tompkins, Leslie J. 5250
Tonchia, David 8022
Toner, Jerome Leo 5130
Tonn, Milan 16759
Tonna, Benjamin 7870, 8919, 13061, 14854
Tönnies, Ferdinand 869, 3081, 12977
Toogood, Michael 17563
Toole, Margaret M. 5327
Torbet, Robert G. 5328
Toren, Marian A. 19273
Torney, George A. 11992, 11993
Toronto Archdiocesan Office of Social Action 13386
Toronto Area Presbytery and Toronto United Church Council 15664
Torres, Alcides 18360
Torres, Sergis 16447
Torrevillas-Suarez, Domini 12264
Touchton, Ken 13062
Toulmin, Stephen 12915
Tourgee, Albion W. 1028
Tournier, Paul 4249
Toward Common Action 10614
Towe, Emily 5329
Towell, Juli 16448
Tower, Frances Emory 1183
Towes, Paul 14064
Towler, Robert 13063
Towne, Charles Hanson 5059
Towne, Florence H. 4007, 4989
Towns, E. L. 12345
Towns, Elmer 12147
Townsend, Marie 8089, 8375, 10238, 10717, 14035
Townsend, Peter 15275
Towson, Charles R. 3468
Toyhiko, Kagawa 13981
Toynbee, Arnold 734, 945, 1403, 2464
Toynbee, Arnold Joseph 10128, 10615, 11994
Toynbee, Gertrude 2464
Trabert, Michael T. 12346
Trabold, Robert 15665
Tracy, Arthur Linwood 13719
Tradizione cristiana, industrializzazione e pluralismo culturale 16449
Trainin, Isaac N. 13720
Training Clergy and Laity for the Inner City 8920
Training Clergymen in Urban Mental Health 10616
Training Ecumenically to Advance Mission [TEAM] 11567
Tranvouez, Yvon 15666, 16760
Trapp, Shel 14065
Traveller, A. D. 1826
Traverzo-Galarza, David 15276
Travis, Anthony R. 14855
Travis, William George 12699
Trawick, Arcadius McSwain 2755, 2836
Treacy, Gerald C. 2981, 4883
Treadwell, William C., Jr. 15932
Treat, Roger L. 6106
Treese, Patrick L. 10129
Tremaine, D. C. 2837
Tremble, Glen W. 8331, 8603, 8951
Trench, Sally 11096
Trench, William Crowell 17984
Trench, William Robert 1339
Trends of Things 2278
Trenholms, Edward C. 3863
Trese, Thomas 7461
Tress, Arthur 11568, 11569

Tressall, Robert 2838
Trettin, Larry E. 11995
Trevethan, Percy J. 8604
Trevett, Reginald F. 4793
Trevor, John 1435, 1502, 1591
Trexler, Edgar R. 10130, 10131, 10617, 11097, 11098, 11099, 11100, 11101, 11570, 11571, 11996, 12700, 13064
Trial of the Reverend John Roberts McDowall 151
Trickett, Homer L. 7213
Trigo, Pedro 17173
Trimble, Glen W. 5840, 6107, 6399, 7504, 7717, 7824, 8047, 11102
Trimmer, J. Maurice 5634
Trinary Consultation, Chicago, IL 17985
Trinity Church Braces Itself against the Winds of Change 19002
Trinity Church in the City of Boston, Massachusetts 4344
Trinity's Acknowledged Wealth 2667
Tripp, L. A. 4250
Tripp, Thomas Alfred 5131
Tro och gärning: 1853-1928: minnesskrift till Stockholms Stadsmissions sjuttiofemårsjubileum 3925
Troeltsch, Ernst 2668, 2669
Trolander, Judith Ann 11572, 14066, 14454, 18361, 19243
Trombly, Donald Duana 8921
Trotman, C. James 18716
Trott, Norman L. 4794
Trotter, Melvin Earnest 4884, 5793
Trout, John M. 4008
Trout, Nelson W. 11103
Trüb, Adolphe 11573
True, Edmond J. 12746
Trueblood, David Elton 8319, 11997
Trueblood, Felicity M. 13493
Truesdell, C. G. 1184
Trumpet Ready in the West: San Francisco Church Successfully Abolishes the Color Bar in Religious Life 6108
Truth about God's Night Club 9672
Trutza, Peter 6999, 8922
Tsai, Kuo-shan 17564, 17565
Tschetter, Katarina Hofer 5424
Tse, Christina 16048
Tuan, Y. F. 14067
Tucci, Douglass Shand 13387
Tuck, J. Erskine 11574
Tuck, William P. 16049
Tucker, Barbara M. 14455
Tucker, Cynthia Grant 17174
Tucker, Graham 16050
Tucker, Jerry 12701
Tucker, Leon 3672
Tucker, Michael R. 14068, 14856
Tucker, Robert 15667
Tucker, Ruth 17986
Tucker, Sterling 11104, 11575
Tucker, William Jewett 769, 811, 1099, 1100, 1185, 1186, 1503, 1504, 1592, 2465, 2982, 3164
Tuckerman, Joseph 93, 97, 107, 114, 118, 119, 127, 128, 163, 189, 534, 541, 4431, 4961, 13441 >> See further: Subject Index: Ministers at large
Tufari, Paolo 7462
Tuinen, Peter Van 11105
Tull, Charles F. 9673
Tully, Sally 14767
Tunis, John 960, 1505
Tunnard, Christopher 6400
Tunnell, James R. 12347
Tupper, George William 2466, 2839
Turk, Herman 11998
Turkevich, Leontii 2910

Turnbull, Robert 155
Turner, Brian 16761
Turner, Christopher B. 18362
Turner, Donald E. 17987
Turner, Dorothy 13388
Turner, Franklin D. 11999
Turner, Philip William 7000, 11106
Turner, Richard B. 17988, 18717
Turner, Smith 12000
Turner, V. Simpson 15277
Turner, Wesley A. 14857
Turrentine, Jan 18718
Tutterow, Michael 17566
Tuttle, Janet 7214
Tuttle, Penelope T. S. 3801
Two Notable Reports of the Lambeth Conference 1593
Twomey, Louis J. 4795, 4885, 14746
Tyack, David B. 13389
Tyler, Helen E. 5841
Tyler, L. G. 9245
Tyler, Lawrence L. 10132
Tyler, Leonard G. 5990, 6587, 12001, 12702
Tyler, Ransom Hebbard 364
Tyng, Stephen Higginson 365
Tyrell, George 1594
Tyson, Luther E. 13065
Tyson, Reuel 10133
UCC's Covenants for Churches in Change 14456
Udo, Reuben K. 13721
Uehling, Carl T. 13390
Uertz, Rudolf 16762
Ufford, Walter Shephard 1595
Ugandan Christian Moslem Association 14858
Ugo, Pisano 14457
Uhl, Erakine 1159
Uittenbosch, Hans 14686, 17175
Ujvarosy, Helen 16938
Ulrich, Martin 13391
Ulrich, Thomas 12348, 16450
Ulschak, Francis 14458
Ulstein, Stefan 18991
Umansky, Ellen M. 16051, 16763
Umbeck, Sharvy Greiner 4796, 5330
Umberg, Jane 11576
Umbreit, Mark S. 16451, 16452
Unamuno, Miguel de 4185
Under Shadows of Steel 8923
Underhill, Evelyn 3570
Underwood, Earl B. 8023
Underwood, Kenneth 5331, 5531, 7215, 8320, 11577
Underworld Redeeming Itself 2670
Unfinished Business 7216
Union catholique internationale de service social 4498, 5132
Union for Christian Work in the City of Brooklyn 441
Union of American Hebrew Congregations 3373, 4186, 5635
Union of Rescue Missions 2756
Union Theological Seminary 8024
Union Theological Seminary Conference on City Church 3571, 3673
Union Theological Seminary, The Auburn Library, Urban Education Collection 9674
Unions Expand into Church Field 7718
Unique Plan Unfolds 10134
Unitarian Review 542
Unitarian Universalist Association, Black Affairs Council 12703
United Christian Missionary Society, Department of Christian Action and Community Service 4113
United Christian Missionary Society, Department of Social

Welfare 4573, 5991
United Church of Canada, Committee on Investing Church Funds for Social Purposes 13066
United Church of Canada, Division of Mission in Canada, Task Group on the Church in the Metropolitan Core 14859
United Church of Christ in Japan, Occupational Evangelism Committee 8924
United Church of Christ in the Philippines, Committee on Industrial Life and Vocations 7463
United Church of Christ, Council for Christian Social Action 9246
United Church of Christ, General Synod 14069
United Church of Christ, Metropolitan Boston Association, and the City Missionary Society 8025
United Church of Christ, Northern California Conference 9675
United Church of Christ, Office for Audio Visuals 9676
United Church of Christ, United Church Board for Homeland Ministries 8925
United Church of Christ, United Church Board for Homeland Ministries, Department of the Urban Church 8026
United Church of Christ, United Church Board for Homeland Ministries, Economic and Racial Justice Priority Team 14459
United Church of Christ, Urbanization Emphasis Committee 8926
United Church Women 8027
United Domestic Missionary Society 75
United Lutheran Church of America, Executive Board 5532
United Lutheran Church, Board of Social Missions 8605
United Methodist Church, Black Community Developers Program 12704, 13722
United Methodist Church, Board of Christian Social Concerns 11578
United Methodist Church, Board of Discipleship 14070
United Methodist Church, Board of Global Ministries, National Division 14071
United Methodist Church, Board of Global Ministries, National Division, Office of Urban Ministries 15278, 15279
United Methodist Church, Board of Global Ministries, Office of Urban Ministries 12002, 14460, 14461
United Methodist Church, General Board of Discipleship 15668
United Methodist Church, General Board of Global Ministries, National Program Division 19169
United Methodist Church, General Council on Finance and Administration 14860
United Methodist Church, Interagency Coordinating Committee 16052
United Methodist Church, Milwaukee District 14072, 14073
United Methodist Church, Northeast Jurisdiction, Multi-Ethnic Center for Ministry

19003
United Presbyterian Church in the USA 8321, 16053
United Presbyterian Church in the USA, Advisory Committee on Housing Ministries 16054
United Presbyterian Church in the USA, Advisory Council on Church and Society for the General Assembly Mission Council 15280
United Presbyterian Church in the USA, Board of Christian Education 5533, 8028, 10618, 11107
United Presbyterian Church in the USA, Board of Christian Education, Office of Church and Society 10135
United Presbyterian Church in the USA, Board of National Mission, Division of Church and Race 12705
United Presbyterian Church in the USA, Board of National Missions 7464, 8029, 8606, 8927, 10619, 10620
United Presbyterian Church in the USA, Board of National Missions, Committee on the Intermediate Sized City 7719
United Presbyterian Church in the USA, Board of National Missions, Department of Urban Churches 8607
United Presbyterian Church in the USA, Board of National Missions, Division of Church Strategy and Development 8030, 8928
United Presbyterian Church in the USA, Board of National Missions, General Department of Mission Strategy and Development 10136
United Presbyterian Church in the USA, Board of National Missions, Office of Church and Housing 10621
United Presbyterian Church in the USA, Board of National Missions, Office of Field Survey 8031, 8322
United Presbyterian Church in the USA, Chicago Presbytery, Department of Urban Church 8929
United Presbyterian Church in the USA, Joint Office of Urban Industrial Ministries 12706
United Presbyterian Church in the USA, Los Angeles Presbytery 11108
United Presbyterian Church in the USA, Office of Church and Society 10622
United Presbyterian Church in the USA, Office of Study and Research, Board of Christian Education [and] Bureau of Research and Survey, National Council of the Churches of Christ in the USA 8608
United Presbyterian Church in the USA, Presbytery of Chicago, Department of Urban Church Advisory Committee 8930
United Presbyterian Church in the USA, Presbytery of New York City, Office of Missions Development 12349
United Presbyterian Church in the USA, Program Agency, Ministry with Congregations Unit, Congregational Development Program 14074
United Presbyterian Church in the USA, Synod of Ohio, Department of Evangelism and

Social Witness 10623
United Presbyterian Council of the New York Metropolitan Area 9677
United Presbyterian Mission Library 9247
United Presbyterian Missionary Library 8931
United States and Its Aliens 5060
United States Catholic Conference 13723
United States Catholic Conference, Department of Social Development 11109
United States of America, Officer of High Commissioner for Germany, Education and Cultural Relations Division 5842
United States, Office of Economic Opportunity 11579
United Training Organization of Atlanta [UTOA] 10624
Universal Christian Conference on Life and Work 3802, 3803
Universal Christian Council 4114
Universal Fellowship of Metropolitan Community Churches, Board of Institutional Ministry 14462
Universitaire Institut Vormingswerk Bedrijfsleven [UIVB] 8932
University of Missouri, Columbia, Agricultural Experiment Station 13392
University of Wisconsin, Center for the Small City 14075
Updike, John 8032, 12350, 16055, 18363, 19170
Uphaus, Willard 4235, 5534
Upson, William H. 1436
Urbach, Ephraim E. 13247
Urban Anthropology 12707
Urban Church and Urban Problems 7720
Urban Church Center 9678
Urban Church Lending Library 5992, 8933
Urban Church Project 13393
Urban Church Resource Review 15669
Urban Church Strategies, Lutheran and American Baptists Share Their Experiences 17989
Urban Church: Essays and Addresses Delivered at the Third Urban Institute, Held at the Lutheran School for the Deaf, Detroit, MI, Aug 12-14, 1958 7465
Urban Coalition 10625
Urban Comity Principles 6109
Urban Community and the Urban Church 7217
Urban Connection 17567
Urban Crisis 11580
Urban Industrial Mission, Ch'ongju, South Korea 17176
Urban Issues Facing the Churches: Introduction 10137
Urban Life 12708
Urban Ministries 15670
Urban Ministries, Inc. 12003
Urban Ministry 15281, 16764
Urban Ministry for the Church of the Brethren 11110
Urban Ministry in Indonesia 19171
Urban Ministry Special Issue 15282
Urban Mission 16765
Urban Mission for the United Church of Canada 16056
Urban Mission: Entering a New Phase 15283
Urban Renewal and the Church 10138

Uevan Suburban Partnerships Model Positive Change 19335
Urban Training Center 9679
Urban Training Center for Christian Mission 8934, 13067
Urban Update 15671
Urban Young Adult Action [UYAA] 11111
Urbanization and the Small Town: The Church and Change 10139
Urbanman 11581
Urwick, Edward Jones 1883, 1997
US Catholic Conference, Committee on Social Development and World Peace 14861
US Department of Commerce, Bureau of the Census 2467, 3165, 4115, 5061
Use of the Union Label 3292
Utica Christian Repository 76
Vahanian, Gabriel 14463
Vail, Bruce 17568
Vajda, Jaroslav 10626
Valaitis, Egidijus A. 10140
Valdivieso, C. Roberto 14862
Valente, Giambattista 11112
Valentine, Foy Dan 5843, 7001, 10141
Valentine, James C. 17177
Valentine, Milton 408
Vallat, Xavier Joseph 11582
Valle, Flordentino del 5993
Vallier, Ivan 12004
Vallin, Pierre 16766
Valverde, Antônio José 16453
Van e Water, John Ward 5222
Van Vorst, Grace 16448
Van, Byung Sub 18719
VanAckeren, Gerald F. 11583
VanAmringe, Henry Hamlin 217
VanAnda, Jackie 18720
vanAndel, Henk 10142
VanArkel, Gerhard P. 5732
VanArsdol, Ted 7218
VanBoskirk, J. J. 7002
VanBuren, Paul Matthews 8935
vanCleef, E. 7219
Vande Water, John Ward 4116
Vandebroek, Pros 16057
Vanden Blink, A. J. 12005
Vander Klay, Barbara 19004
Vander Klay, Stan 19004
Vander Meulen, Arnold J. 7003
Vander Werf, Nathan H. 14076
VanderHey, E. 10627
Vanderkiste, R. W. 283
Vanderkloet, Edward 14077, 14078, 14863, 15912
Vanderstel, David G. 14864, 16767, 17569
Vandervelde, Émile 1998, 2911
Vandezande, Gerald 12626
Vandiver, Joseph S. 8936
VanDusen, Henry P. 4499, 5223, 6254
VanDyke, Henry 2364
VanDyke, Tertius 4187
VanEvery, Edward 4117
VanEyl, Chris 18721
VanGelder, Craig E. 16454
VanHemert, M. M. J. 15672
VanHouten, Mark 18722, 19005, 19006
VanHouten, Richard L. 17178
VanHoutte, J. 7466
VanHuet, Edmund 11113, 11584
Vanishing Slums 7721
Vanistendael, August 14865
VanKirk, Walter W. 3733, 5133, 5425
VanKleeck, Mary 3293
VanMeter, Mary 15284
VanMeter, W. C. 6401
VanNess, Elizabeth 11585
VanNess, Paul 11585
VanNorden, Warner M. 6402
VanOsdal, N. K. 6255
VanVleck, Joseph 12709

VanVleck, Joseph, Jr. 4188, 4679
VanWyk, Kenneth W. 11586
Vaquero, Quintín Aldea 18364
Varady, David P. 12543
Varbero, Richard A. 13724, 13725
Varga, Laszlo 4990
Vasil'Evskaia, N. S. 13394
Vásquez, Edmundo E 19007
Vázquez, Jesús María 7467, 8609, 10144
Vaughan, Bernard 2671
Vaughan, C. Edwin 14301
Vaughan, D. D. 2186, 3294, 3374, 3734
Vaughan, John 17179
Vaughan, Patrick 17752, 17990, 18365
Vaughan, Robert 196
Vaughn, Ellen Santilli 17570
Vaught, Bonny 16768
Vaux, Kenneth 12710
Vazquez, Art 10143
Veblen, Thorstein 1723
Vecoli, Rudolph J. 11587, 14464, 14600
Vedder, Henry Clay 2672, 2912
Veelenturf, F. 11114
Veiller, Lawrence 2468
Velasquez, Roger 16455
Velichko, Olga I. 17571
Veller, Reinhard 13068
Velten, Georges 11115
Verbunt, Gilles 15673
Verdier, Jean 4886
Verkuyl, Johannes H. 9680, 15285
Vermilye, Elizabeth 2913
Vermilye, Elizabeth B. 2555
Verney, Stephen 11588
Verryn, Trevor D. 12058
Versteeg, John M. 3572
Vethake, Henry 164
Vetter, Charles E. 13726
Vice Commission ... of Chicago 2556
Vicedom, Georg F. 8302, 8323
Vicent, Antonio 1258
Vick, Austin 10475
Vickrey, Raymond 19172
Vidler, Alexander Roper 5733, 5734, 7004, 9248, 10145
Vidyasagara, Vijaya 17572
Vignaux, Paul 4680, 5224, 6403
Vigny, Alfred Victor de 111
Vilankulu, Sarah J. 19173
Villa, James 15674
Villafañe, Eldin 16456, 17073, 19008
Villagrana, Bernardo Castro 11116
Villalba, Angela 16769
Villarreal, Luis 14866
Villaume, William J. 5225, 5636, 5637, 5735, 5844, 6110, 6796
Villot, Jean 11589
Vilmar, Fritz 9239
Vinatier, Jean 17573
Vinay, Tullio 10628
Vincent, Antonio 12711
Vincent, George E. 2757
Vincent, John Heyl 812
Vincent, John J. 11117, 11118, 12006, 12007, 12712, 13069, 13070, 13395, 13727, 13728, 14079, 14080, 15286, 15407, 15675, 15701, 16058, 16059, 16457, 16770, 17180, 17181, 17991, 19009, 19010, 19011 >> See further: Subject Index: Urban Theology Unit
Vincent, Theodore G. 12351
Viollet, Jean 3573
Virton, Pol 8610
Vishnewski, Stanley 15676
Vision Quest Highlights EUC Meet 17992
Visser't Hooft, William Adolph 3926, 4658, 7722, 8937
Visser, H. A. 12352
Vitler, Maureen 15403

Vivian, C. T. 11590, 12008
Vizzard, James L. 8033
Vlamos, James 8938
Voelkel, William R. 9249, 9681, 11591, 12009, 14465
Vogel, David 14867, 15740
Vogelsanger, Peter 13071
Vogt, Karl Heinz 14868
Vogt, Reinhard 9250
Vogt, Roy 16560
Vokkert, Heinrich 13072
Volaitis, Constantine E. 7315
Volksverein 1101
Voll, John A. 3469
Völkl, Richard 9251
Volp, Rainer 17574
Von der Haar, Christine M. 17575
von Dreele, James D. 18366
Von Hoffman, Nicholas 10146
Von Sivers, Peter 17182
Vontobel, Klara 5535
Voorhis, Jerry 5638
Voris, John Ralph 2108
Vorspan, Albert 8496, 11592
Vorspan, Max 12010
Vorster, W. S. 16771
Vos, Nelvin 17183
Vosk, Marc 7197
Voss, Carl Herman 5134
Votaw, Dow 13073
Vrcan, Srdjan 12353, 14466, 15677
Vree, Dale 16772
Vreeman, Jerry 17184
Vrga, Djuro J. 11119, 13729
Vries, Egbert de 8324, 10147
Vrijhof, Pieter Hendrick 8939, 12011, 15287
Vroijlande, K. du Bois de 3674
Vrooman, Frank B. 1437, 11008
Vrooman, Hiram 1340, 11008
Vrooman, Walter 1341, 1342, 6221, 11008
Vulliamy, Colwyn 2840
Waardenburg, Jacques 15287
Wachs, Martin 17576
Wade, Allen 9252
Wade, Elizabeth E. 3804
Wade, John W. 19300
Wade, Louise 6588
Wade, Richard C. 7723, 9253, 9254
Wadsworth, Lincoln Burdette 6404, 6589
Wagner, C. Peter 12354, 13730, 14081, 14467, 15288, 15289, 15290, 16060, 18367
Wagner, Donald O. 4118
Wagner, Geoffrey 6111
Wagner, John 7977, 8325, 9255, 9682, 10629
Wagner, Mabel G. 6256, 6512, 6797
Wagner, Mable G. 5226
Wagner, Murray L. 10148
Wagner, O. Walter 7005
Wagner, Oskar 17185
Wagoner, Harold E. 8034
Wahlberg, Edgar M. 4189, 4500, 4887, 6798
Wahlberg, Rachel Conrad 11593
Wahlstrom, Pera 15678
Wainwright, David 9683
Wakefield, Dan 7468, 7724
Wakefield, Edward Gibbon 112
Wakeford, Peter 11340
Wakeman, Thaddeus B. 1029
Walaskay, Paul William 14082
Walburg, Anton H. 961
Walch, Timothy 14869, 14870, 18723
Wald, Kenneth D. 16773, 18368, 18724
Wald, Lillian D. 2109, 2914, 4403
Waldecker, Gary 18725
Waldorf, E. L. 3295
Waldron, D. W. 2187
Walk without Fear 13731
Walker, Alan 9256, 10149, 15291

Walker, Amasa 129, 424
Walker, Andrew 18726
Walker, Cornelius 303
Walker, David 103
Walker, E. Jerry 7469
Walker, Graham 7725
Walker, Henry 1506
Walker, John Brisben 1102
Walker, John D. 17186
Walker, Joseph Burch 870
Walker, L. 12012
Walker, Lucius 11120
Walker, Orris George, Jr. 15679
Walker, R. H. 8611
Walker, Randolph Meade 15292
Walker, Susan Watts 15293
Walker, W. M. 12713
Walker, Wyatt 15294
Walker, Wyatt T. 13796
Wall Street Ministry 8035
Wall, Brenda 15900
Wall, James M. 8612, 14468, 18369
Wall, Martha 10630
Wall, Steve 12013
Wallace, Anthony F. C. 14871
Wallace, David M. 10631
Wallace, Lee 13074
Wallace, Lillian Parker 10150
Wallace, Martin 18370
Wallace, Samuel E. 9684, 11121, 15680
Wallace, Weldon 12355
Wallant, Edward Lewis 8326
Wallerstein, Edward 9337
Wallis, Frederick A. 3375
Wallis, Jim 14872, 16061, 19280
Wallis, Louis 4681
Walls, William J. 13396
Wallwork, Ernest 12714
Walmsley, Arthur 8940, 9685, 14083
Walrath, Douglas A. 11594, 13397, 14469, 15295, 15296, 16774, 17187, 18472
Walsh, Albeus 6257
Walsh, Bryan O. 16458
Walsh, George Ethelbert 1259
Walsh, Jack 16062
Walsh, James P. 13398
Walsh, John 16459
Walsh, John P. J. 5736
Walsh, Lorne 10151
Walsh, Louis S. 1827
Walsh, Mary Elizabeth 6799
Walsh, William 2279
Walsh, William B. 10152
Walters, Charles Ensor 2110
Walters, E. Walter 4682
Walters, Elizabeth 13075
Walters, Gerald 11122
Walters, Ronald W. 16134
Walters, Thomas Paul 15681
Walters-Bugbee, Christopher 14873, 14874
Walton, Anna Stricklen 1724
Walton, Clarence 10814, 14470
Walton, John 14010
Walton, Norman W. 7006
Walton, Susan 17577
Walton-Lewsey, Ernest W. 11574
Waltz, Alan K. 7128, 8054, 8327, 8626
Walz, Hans Herman 7470
Wand, J. W. C. 5845
Wang, Shis-ch'ing 13399
Wangerin, Walter, Jr. 17188, 17283, 19012
Wanted -- Homes for War Workers 5227
War Against the Poor 8941
Ward, Alfred Dudley 6405, 6800, 10153
Ward, Barbara 10154, 11123, 14084
Ward, Colin 14875
Ward, Conor K. 8328
Ward, Dan 12014
Ward, David 12356
Ward, Edward J. 2673

Ward, Harry Frederick 2158, 2253, 2365, 2469, 2758, 2841, 2842, 2843, 2844, 2915, 2916, 2917, 2983, 3041, 3042, 3103, 3104, 3166, 3167, 3296, 3574, 3575, 3675, 3735, 3805, 3806, 3864, 3927, 3928, 4009, 4010, 4011, 4119, 4190, 4345, 4346, 4991, 5135, 5228, 5693, 5737, 10680, 10867, 15872, 16656 >> See further: Subject Index: Methodist Federation for Social Service
Ward, Hiley H. 8036, 10632, 11124, 11595
Ward, Julius H. 962, 1030
Ward, L. B. 4315
Ward, Leo R. 5426, 5427, 7726, 7727
Ward, Maisie 5846
Ward, Margaret 6590
Ward, Mary Augusta 653
Ward, Richard 7471
Ward, Robin H. 12015
Ward, William 2188
Ward, William Reginald 12715
Ware, Caroline F. 4501
Ware, Lisle Talbot 3929
Wargelin, Raymond W. 14085
Waring, Luther Hess 2189
Waris, Heikki 8942
Warmath, Jerry Shaw 11125
Warne, Colston 4992
Warnecke, Frederick J. 6801
Warner, Amos 963, 1343, 4086
Warner, Sam Bass, Jr. 8613, 11126, 12716, 17189
Warner, W. Lloyd 5428
Warner, Wellman J. 4120
Warren, Donald I. 14471, 16063, 19013
Warren, Edward L. 1507
Warren, Jon 19014
Warren, Rachelle B. 14471
Warren, Rick 19015
Warrick, Emory 12048
Wartgker, H. 10633
Warwick, Jesse Hill 7728
Wasdell, David 14472, 15297, 15298, 15299, 16775
Wasfi, Atif Amin 9257
Washbourn, Penelope 17190
Washburn, E. S. 654
Washburn, Edward H. 560
Washington [DC] Federation of Churches 4993
Washington, Booker T. 2557, 19084
Washington, Forrester B. 4347
Washington, Harold 18369
Washington, James Melvin 19307
Washington, Joseph R., Jr. 9258, 10634, 12717, 18727, 18728
Washington, Preston R. 15682, 17993, 18729
Washington, Walter 11596
Watchorn, John 3105
Waterman, Kenneth S. 9259, 10635
Waterman, Stanley 17578
Waterman, W. P. 13076
Watermulder, David B. 8037, 8943
Waters, Brent 18371
Waterston, Robert Cassie 204, 276
Watkins, Alfred J. 14385
Watkins, Derrel 16460
Watmough, David 6112
Watson, Angus 3297
Watson, Bernard 9260, 12016
Watson, Frank Dekker 3470
Watson, G. Llewellyn 13077
Watson, Goodwin 4683
Watson, Kenneth 8038
Watt, Lewis 4012
Watt, William Montgomery 18730, 19244
Watters, Bob 9686

Watters, Pat 13078
Watts, Gary 17579
Watts, Hilstan 7350, 12718
Watts, Jill 19357
Watts, Joseph T. 2470
Watts, Leon 11597
Wattson, Paul James Francis 14719
Wavrinek, Owen 9261
Way to a Man's Heart 1596
Way, Peggy 8944, 11127
Wayland, Francis 141, 156
Wayman, Lawrence H. 12279
Waynick, Leo Banks 12357
We Share in God's Great Help: Four Weeks of Prayer for Congregations 19174
We the People: Criminals and Victims 15300
Wearmouth, Robert Featherstone 4684, 5738, 6591, 7220, 7729
Weatherford, Willis D. 2471, 7221
Weatherization Ministry Helps People Save 16776
Weaver, Barbara 18764
Weaver, Donald Leroy 15301
Weaver, Fred 14473
Weaver, Galen R. 6802, 7007, 8945
Weaver, Robert C. 9262, 9263
Weaver, Robert Latham 4685
Weaver, Rufus 2674
Weaver, Thomas 12726
Webb, Beatrice 5960
Webb, Edwin B. 770
Webb, Larry Eugene 12358
Webb, Mohammed A. R. 1260
Webb, Muriel 7222
Webb, Pauline 10155
Webb, Robert 7222
Webb, Sidney 5960
Webber, Charles C. 4251, 4686, 5136, 5994, 7472
Webber, Christopher L. 7730
Webber, George Williams 5651, 5739, 5847, 5995, 6406, 7473, 7474, 7731, 8039, 8614, 8615, 8946, 8947, 9264, 9265, 9266, 9687, 9688, 9820, 9959, 10636, 10637, 10638, 11128, 11129, 11598, 11599, 12017, 13079, 13732, 14474, 15302, 15349, 15973, 16064, 16777, 17191, 18372, 18731, 19175 >> See further: Subject Index: East harlem Protestant Parish
Webber, H. C. 4013
Webber, Helen 18372
Webber, Robert E. 15303
Weber, Adna F. 1725
Weber, Carlton N. 7196, 7442
Weber, Francis J. 13080
Weber, Hans-Ruedi 6896, 7223, 7475, 8948, 11600
Weber, Herbert F. 16778
Weber, Herman Carl 4252
Weber, J. Leonard 10639
Weber, Mary Rose 9689
Weber, Max 1999, 3376, 5536, 7476, 7626, 11660, 12163, 17340, 19085
Weber, Susan Anne 8040
Weber, Thomas J. 9267, 10640
Webster, Bradford Gray 6592
Webster, Douglas. D. 15683
Webster, Eugene C. 1785
Webster, George Sidney 1597, 2111, 4253
Wedel, Cynthia 6593, 7732, 12018
Wedel, Leonard E. 10156, 14876
Wedel, Theodore O. 5996
Weeden, William Babcock 691, 1261
Weedman, William Lee 11130
Weekday Work in a City Church 1187
Weekley, W. M. 1188
Weeks, Albert L. 15895

Weeks, Charlotte Bunch 11131
Weeks, Genevieve C. 9690, 9691, 11132
Weeks, Louis 13400, 14475, 14476
Weeks, Louis B. 1739, 19198
Wefer, Marion 4994, 5062
Wefer, William 4994
Wegener, Albert Benjamin 3676
Weib, Robert 11133
Weidman, Robert 17580
Weigel, Gustav 7519
Weigert, Andrew J. 13401
Weigle, Luther Allan 3930
Weil, Simone 16068
Weiler, Conrad 15304
Weimer, David R. 10157
Weinberg, Helene Barbara 13402, 13403, 13733
Weinberg, J. 5740
Weinland, David E. 7224
Weinraub, Bernard 10158
Weinstein, Jacob J. 7477, 8041
Weis, Josef 12019
Weisbrot, Robert 16779
Weisenburger, Francis P. 7733
Weiser, Conrad 12719
Weisman, Celia B. 8042
Weiss, Ellen 18373
Weiss, Nancy J. 14477
Weisshaar, Milton Leon 6258
Weist, Carl S. 4121
Weitjens, Jan 12720
Welch, Claude 7478
Welch, Elizabeth 18732
Welch, Herbert 2000, 2280, 2675
Welch, Kevin W. 16780, 17581
Welch, Michael R. 17192
Weld, Ralph Foster 5537
Weller, Neil Jack 8043
Weller, Robert H. 13134
Wellman, Barry 15305
Wellman, Walter 1828
Wells, Amons R. 1438
Wells, Bobbi 13671
Wells, Carl Douglas 4191, 4192, 4193, 4254, 4404
Wells, Gene 8355
Wells, J. Kenrick 11442
Wells, James L. 1726
Wells, Keith Cameron 7479
Welsh, Alexander 12359
Welshimer, Helen 4687
Welshimer, P. H. 6259
Welty, Antonio R. 13081
Welty, Eberhard 9692
Welty, Susan 8329
Welz Scroeter, Cristina 13082
Wendland, H. D. 7008
Wengenhals, Samuel 1439
Wenger, A. Grace 10641
Wenk, Michael 12721, 12722
Wenke, Karl Ernst 17193
Wenner, George U. 964, 1262, 3106
Wenner, Jerome A. 5215
Wensierski, Peter 16461
Wentholt, G. J. M. 17194
Wentz, Edwin C. 12723
Wenzel, Ann 18929
Wenzel, Kristen 12020
Werhahn, Peter H. 16210
Werhane, Patricia H. 16556
Werneke, Ann L. 11134
Werner, Alfred 5229
Wertheimer, Jack 18374
Wesley, John 2859, 15648
Wesson, Anthony J. 11840, 12360, 15684
West Hartford Congregational, West Hartford, CT 5997
West London Mission 906
West Side Christian Parish 6594
West Side Church and Community Study 10159
West, Arthur Geroge Bainbridge 4888
West, Charles C. 10160
West, Cornel 17994
West, Elmer S. 10161

West, J. W. 3807
West, Martin 12724, 13734, 13735
West, Melvin E. 18375
West, R. Frederick 5998
West, Richard F. 19271
Westberg, Granger E. 10162, 13736, 19176
Westbrook, Robert 19016
Westcott, Brooke Foss 871, 1440, 1829, 1923
Westerhoff, John H. 14086
Westerman, Hans 10163
Westgate, James E. 17582, 17995
Westmeier, Karl Wilhelm 17996
Weston, Frank 3298
Weston, M. Moran 6595
Westrom, Betty 6596, 7009
Wetherill, Francis M. 2918
Weverbergh, Roger 14478, 15685
Weyand, Alfons 8949
Weyer, Adam 12361, 19177
Weyer, Alfred van de 6803
Weygandt, Cornelius 4797
Weylland, John Matthias 668, 707, 735
Whaley, Howard A. 14087
What Churchmen Think of the Invasion of Their Sanctuaries by the Unemployed 2845
What is Action Training 12021
What Kind of Evangelism? 14479
What Labor Thinks of the Church: A Symposium 3576
What the Federal Council Does in Industrial Relations 4014
What the Men and Religion Forward Movement Actually Accomplished 2676
What the Minister Is For 1441
What the Urban Coalition Is 11135
What We Are Learning: A Guide to the Experimental Ministries 11601
What's Ahead for Urban Clergy 15686
Wheale, Gerald 17583
Wheatley, Paul 11602, 12362, 14877, 16781
Wheatley, Richard 771, 1263, 1264
Wheaton, Elizabeth Ryder 2112
Wheaton, William L. C. 8616, 10164
Wheeler, A. S. 813
Wheeler, Barbara G. 19245
Wheeler, David 16065
Wheeler, Edward L. 16462
Wheeler, Edward O. 16066
Wheeler, Everett P. 965
Wheeler, Thomas C. 9268
Wheelock, Lewis Frederick 7010
When Gang Leaders Talk about Religion 9693
When You Feel Lost You Come to the Bowery 16067
Where Are You Going, Father John? 11136
Where Shall the Negro Live 3736
Where Should the National Council Headquarters Locate 6113
Wherry, D. T. 3808
Whichern, Johannes 14820
Whipple, Lee G. 7011, 10642
Whitam, Frederick 8617
White, Andrew J. 9694, 10165, 10643, 11603, 12363
White, Anthony G. 13083, 13404
White, Arthur L. 5999
White, Ben 11604
White, Bouck 2472, 2846
White, Charles Edward 18376
White, Charles L. 4255
White, Clyde R. 6407
White, D. 9695
White, D. Gordon 12725
White, Douglas 12726
White, Edith H. 3577, 4194

White, Edward A. 8044, 10644
White, Eliot 1786
White, Ellen G. 11697
White, Frank 14480
White, Frank J. 4502
White, Gavin D. 15306
White, Gaylord S. 2113, 2366, 2367
White, George Abbott 16068
White, Herbert D. 10645, 12022, 13084
White, Horace A. 4798
White, Hugh C. 7734, 7735, 9696, 12101, 12102, 12103
White, J. R. 10166
White, James 15307
White, James F. 8330, 9269, 18377, 19017
White, James Hale 669
White, Jerry 16782
White, John E. 2190, 2281, 2759
White, Kathleen 17584
White, L. C. 14403
White, Louise 8950
White, Lucia 8618
White, Lynn Townsend 3809, 3810
White, Margaret B. 13084
White, Morton 8618
White, O. Z. 17997
White, R. Clyde 6408
White, Ronald C. 12727, 14088, 14878
White, Stanley 2282
White, William J. 2283, 2558
White, William Prescott 1442
White, Willmon L. 10646, 10647
White, Woodie W. 13827, 15413
Whitehead, Evelyn Eaton 15687, 16463
Whitehead, James D. 15687, 16463
Whitehill, Walter Muir 14089
Whitehurst, James Emerson 15688
Whitely, Oliver Read 11605
Whiteman, Maxwell 7229, 14481
Whiten, Bennie, Jr. 19018
Whitesell, Faris D. 7225
Whiteside, Barbara Jeanne Taylor 18378
Whitham, Richard Robert 8045
Whitin, Ernest Stagg 2677
Whiting, Henry J. 10648, 11137, 11606
Whitlock, Brand 2473
Whitlow, Maurice 4799
Whitman, Howard 6114, 8046
Whitman, Lauris B. 7480, 7824, 8047, 8331, 8951, 9697, 10167
Whitman, Roger C. 6115
Whitney, Alexander Fell 5230
Whitney, Stuart E. 15308
Whiton, J. M. 1508
Whitt, Hugh P. 12616
Whittemore, B. Bruce 6101
Whittemore, Emma 1265, 4195
Whitwell, W. L. 13737
Why Boycott J. P. Stevens Products 14879
Why Did the Auto Workers Strike 4688
Why Labor Dislikes the Church 3578
Why So Much Secrecy? 9698
Whyman, Henry C. 8619
Whyte, Abbie 9270
Whyte, J. A. 12728
Whyte, William Foote 5231
Whyte, William Hollingsworth 7012, 18733
Whyte, William J., Jr. 12023
Wiarda, Howard J. 11607
Wiberg, Sally Johnson 17998
Wichern, Johann Hinrich 218, 246, 292, 342, 389, 708, 1884, 10432 >> See further: Subject Index: Inner Mission
Wichira, Haron 19178
Wichmann, Jürgen 14880

Wick, Reinhold 6597
Wickens, Robert G. 10907
Wicker, Brian 9699
Wickham, Edward R. 5232, 5538, 5978, 7226, 7517, 7736, 8332, 9271, 10168, 10649, 11002, 11608, 13085, 13405, 13738
Wickremeratne, Ananda 18379
Wicksteed, P. M. 1189
Widdicombe, Catherine 14727
Widdrington, P. E. T. 3168, 4159, 5639
Wideman, Bernard 13739
Widenhouse, Philip M. 5233, 5741
Wider City Parish [New Haven, Connecticut] 6000
Widtmann, Heimo 11609
Widyatmadja, Josef 14482
Wiebe, Bernie 16069, 16464
Wiebe, Menno 13086
Wiebe, Robert H. 8620
Wiegers, William C. 15689
Wieman, Reginal Westcott 4689
Wier, L. H. 3737
Wiernik, Peter 2678
Wieser, Thomas 10169, 13902
Wiggin, Arch 5621
Wight, George 184
Wightman, Julia Bainbridge 366
Wilber, Charles K. 16783
Wilbur, Ross T. 13087
Wilcox, Katherine W. 13740
Wilcox, Levy M. 11138
Wilcoxson, Georgeann 12729
Wilde, Margaret D. 17999
Wilder, Charlotte E. 3865, 3931
Wiley, Gary D. 17195
Wiley, George 14306
Wiley, Robert E. 16465, 17196
Wiley, Samuel Wirt 5332
Wilgespruit Fellowship Center, Association of Theological Institutions 12364
Wilhelm, Anthony J. 10650
Wilhelm, Carolyn 12365
Wilk, Stephen W. 14881
Wilke, Harold H. 15690
Wilken, Waldemar 8333
Wilkerson, David 8952, 9700, 10170, 11139, 11610
Wilkerson, Don 11611
Wilkerson, Isabel 18734, 19179, 19180
Wilkerson, Robert Gordon 13741
Wilkie, George 11140, 12024
Wilkinson, David R. 16070
Wilkinson, John 1031
Wilkinson, Juanita Morrill 10651
Wilkinson, T. S. 8953
Wilkinson, William 2057
Will, A. S. 3471
Will, James 14882
Willard, Frances E. 709
Wille, Lois 11612
Willebrandt, M. W. 4015
Willems, Emílio 10652
Willems, Lisa 17197, 17198
Willet, Herbert L. 1830, 4503
Willet, J. 772
William Temple Foundation 10653, 13742, 15691, 16071, 17585, 17586
William Temple Foundation and Ruskin College 17587
William Temple Foundation and the University of Manchester, Department of Extra-Mural Studies 15309
William, John 15692
Williams, Cecil 9456, 9826, 15693, 18735, 19181
Williams, Chancellor 5848
Williams, Charles 7481
Williams, Charles David 3043, 3044, 3579
Williams, Claude 4972
Williams, Claude C. 4894
Williams, Colin W. 8954, 8955, 9272, 9273, 10171, 11141

Williams, Daniel Day 6935
Williams, Doris Marshall 7737
Williams, Dorothy L. 14951
Williams, Eddie N. 11613
Williams, Edward F. 1509
Williams, Ethel Grace 4256
Williams, George 2114, 10654, 12769
Williams, George W. 543
Williams, Hattie 18359
Williams, Henry L. 865
Williams, Hillman T. 5429
Williams, J. E. 2114, 2847
Williams, John A. 14483
Williams, June A. 16466, 17199
Williams, Kathy M. 16072
Williams, Leighton 907, 1032, 1344, 1598, 2848
Williams, Melvin D. 13088, 13406, 16784
Williams, Michael 4405
Williams, Moseley H. 1599
Williams, Norma 19182
Williams, Oliver 15310, 16467, 16621, 17200, 17371
Williams, Peter W. 15694, 15695
Williams, Peter, Jr. 10
Williams, Phyllis H. 4800
Williams, Preston N. 12366, 13089, 19183
Williams, Robin M., Jr. 7013
Williams, Roger L. 18495
Williams, Russell S. 6598
Williams, Sandara 9701
Williams, T. R. 3299
Williams, Talcott 1975
Williams, William Carlos 6116, 9579
Williamson, Jeffrey G. 17017
Williamson, Joseph 8956, 9702
Williamson, Joseph C. 15696
Williamson, Judith A., 18535
Williamson, Margaret 8621
Williamson, S. C. 6117
Willie, Charles V. 8957
Willimon, William H. 16785, 17780, 18736, 18864
Willis, Ron 12367
Willis, W. E. 1727
Willis, Wayne 12025
Willmer, Haddon 18000, 19019
Willock, John 17201, 17588
Willoughby, W. C. 3300
Willoughby, William 11614, 14090
Wills, Theodore 13407
Willy, Joseph 11615
Wilmont, R. 14883
Wilmore, Gayraud S. 7482, 8048, 8049, 8622, 11142, 11616, 15311, 16786, 16787, 18001
Wilmott, Peter 7233
Wilson, Anne 18380
Wilson, Basil 18737
Wilson, Brian R. 17311
Wilson, Bryan R. 8334, 10172, 14091, 14092, 15312, 16468
Wilson, Carol Green 4196
Wilson, Charles 10655
Wilson, Charles Lee 5430
Wilson, Christine T. 3738
Wilson, Clarence True 2474, 3580
Wilson, Elizabeth 2984
Wilson, Frank E. 4257
Wilson, George P. 536
Wilson, Grace H. 4348
Wilson, Herbert Arthur 4574, 4690, 6001
Wilson, J. Christy, Jr. 15313
Wilson, J. Stitt 3472
Wilson, James Hood 383
Wilson, James Q. 8623, 8656, 9703
Wilson, John 11617, 14884
Wilson, John Moran Cochran 3473
Wilson, K. L. 15314
Wilson, Kenneth L. 6259, 7227, 10173

Wilson, Louis R. 4155
Wilson, Mary Elizabeth 17448
Wilson, Maurice E. 1190, 1728
Wilson, Mervyn 14093
Wilson, Michael 10656, 13743
Wilson, Otto 4349
Wilson, P. H. St. John 10174
Wilson, P. W. 2001, 5742
Wilson, Pip 17589, 18738
Wilson, R. Boyce 17590
Wilson, Robert 17591
Wilson, Robert A. 12368
Wilson, Robert Leroy 6902, 7360, 7455, 7483, 7484, 7710, 7711, 7712, 8002, 8050, 8051, 8052, 8053, 8054, 8335, 8336, 8337, 8624, 8625, 8626, 8958, 9274, 9275, 9276, 9277, 9704, 9705, 9706, 9810, 10175, 10176, 10657, 11143, 11144, 11145, 11146, 11618, 11619, 11620, 11621, 11622, 11623, 12026, 12027, 12369, 12730, 12971, 13254, 13744, 14354, 15380, 15697, 15698
Wilson, Rufus Rockwell 1510
Wilson, Russell 13832
Wilson, Samuel 16184, 16549, 17202, 18002, 18739
Wilson, Samuel Paynter 2475
Wilson, Stephen 15699
Wilson, Thomas 15315
Wilson, Thomas C. 17592
Wilson, Warren H. 2559, 2849
Wilson, William D. 1103
Wilson, William Julius 15700, 18381
Wiltsee, Herbert Leon 6409
Wimberly, Anne Streaty 18740, 18741
Wimberly, Edward P. 14094, 15316, 16073, 18741
Wimberly, Ronald 13154
Wimberly, Ware W. 4801
Winch, Robert F. 11147
Wind, James D. 19203
Wind, James P. 19020
Windass, Stanley 10177
Windolph, J. 2368
Windsor, Pat 18742
Wines, E. C. 544
Wingate, Charles F. 773
Winger, Klaus 14429
Winger, Sam J. 19308
Wingert, Vernon L. 11624
Winiarski, Mark 14782
Winninger, Paul 7228
Winnington-Ingram, Arthur F. 1345, 1443, 2985, 4995, 5760
Winpisinger, William 15428
Winslow, David J. 11625
Winslow, Florence E. 1346, 1600
Winslow, Hubbard 142
Winsor, Justin 670
Winston, Charles M. 6960
Winston-Salem [NC] Goodwill Industries Rehabilitation, Inc. 13745
Winstone, Harold 13746
Winter, Derek 15701
Winter, Gibson 6804, 8338, 8627, 8959, 9064, 9096, 9278, 9302, 9707, 9708, 10178, 10179, 10658, 13090, 14885, 15054, 16074, 19021, 19184
Winter, J. Alan 8158, 11148, 11626, 12028, 12029, 12370, 12371, 14484, 17593
Winter, Michael M. 13091, 13092, 15317
Winter, Miriam Therese 17594
Winter, Uwe-Helmut 13747
Winterer, Landelin 908
Winterowd, Kay Beldon 12372
Winters, Donald E. 16075, 17595
Winters, L. Earle. 10659
Wippermann, Stephan 19177
Wirt, Sherwood E. 6805, 7738
Wirth, Louis 3932, 4802, 5431, 7014, 7015

Wisbey, Herbert Andrew, Jr. 6118, 6599, 6806
Wischnitzer, Rachel 6807, 9279
Wise, Stephen M. 17144
Wise, Stephen Samuel 5849
Wiseman, Jacqueline P. 12030
Wiseman, Luke 6105
Wiseman, Neil B. 14095
Wiser, William Henricks 4803, 4804
Wish, Harvey 8628
Wishart, Alfred Wesley 2369, 2370
Wisse, Ruth R. 14096
Wisz, Gerald M 17203
Witheridge, David E. 11149
Witherspoon, Katheryn 9280
Without Fear or Favor: A Dramatic Reading on Immigration and Citizenship 6808
Withrow, Pat B. 5640, 6260
Witnessing to Hippies 11150
Witt, Raymond H. 19268
Wittenberg, Rudolph M. 5641
Wittke, Carl 4996
Woessner, Robert 10180
Wogaman, J. Philip 8055, 11627, 16469, 17204, 18003, 19185
Wohl, Richard 7485
Wölber, Hans Otto 7739
Wolcott, Roger T. 16470, 19186
Wolensky, Robert P. 17205
Wolf, Edmund J. 1033
Wolf, Edwin, 2nd 7229
Wolfe, Ann G. 9709, 12731
Wolfe, Thomas 4016, 4406
Wolff, George Dering 814, 815, 816
Wolff, Miles 12031, 12373
Wolff, Robert C. 19187
Wolfgang, Marvin E. 10181
Wolkovich-Valkavicius, William 14886, 15702
Wolterstorff, Nicholas 14887, 16788, 18743
Wolvington, K. H. 10182
Womack, David A. 13093
Womeldorf, George R., Jr. 6600
Womer, Parley Paul 2760
Wonderly, William L. 8056, 10660, 13094
Wong, James Yui Kok 12374, 13095, 13748
Wong, Joseph 16789
Wong, Paul Yat-Keung 13408
Wong, Wayland 16471
Wongsang, Samrit 14097
Wood, Arthur Skevington 7016
Wood, Britton 14485
Wood, C. W. 3581
Wood, Charles 545
Wood, Cornelius A. 6601
Wood, H. G. 3301
Wood, James L. 14486, 16472
Wood, James R. 10183, 12732, 12868, 13039, 13235, 15495, 16076, 16288
Wood, John Wilson 2115
Wood, Leland Foster 4805
Wood, Marylea 12733
Wood, Patricia A. 14486
Wood, Ralph C. 18744
Wood, Richard R. 13096
Wood, Robert C. 7486, 8629, 14487
Wood, Stephanie 18745
Woodard, G. H. Jack 11628
Woodberry, M. L. 2284
Woodbury, Ida Button 9281
Wooding, Dan 15401
Woodrow, Fred 817
Woodruff, Clinton Rogers 2476, 3302, 3582, 3583, 3677, 3678, 3933, 4197
Woodruff, Lance R. 14488
Woods, Denis J. 16077
Woods, Eleanor H. 4017
Woods, Frances Jerome 7017
Woods, Frank 8630

Woods, Frank Churchill 2371
Woods, Katherine Pearson 966, 1191
Woods, Robert A. 1034, 1104, 1511, 1512, 1676, 1787, 1831, 1885, 1924, 2191, 2560, 2761, 2762, 2850, 3474, 3584, 3585, 3686, 4017, 8631
Woodson, Carter Godwin 3169, 3377
Woodsworth, J. S. 2763
Woodward, Ann 12032
Woodward, Kathleen 15703
Woodward, Margaret 2561
Woodworth, Arthur V. 1925
Woodworth, Ralph 14888
Woofenden, Louise D. 18382
Woofter, T. J., Jr. 3378, 3934
Wooley, John Granville 1926
Woolfolk, Robert E. 19336
Woollard, Anthony 11151
Woolley, Celia Parker 1444
Woolsey, Theodore 655
Worcester, Elwood 2221, 2285, 2372
Worden, R. Clayton 9710
Wordsworth, Christopher 165
Wordsworth, William 3
Work Projects Administration, State of Illinois, Writer's Program 5063
Work: As if People Matter 15318
Worker-Priests: A French Protestant View 7740
Working Church 527, 2851
Working Committee on Church and Society, Nemi, Ital 12375
Working Men and Religious Institutions 442
Working Men's Christian Association 516
Workingman's Distrust of the Church: Its Causes and Remedies 818
Workmen's Advocate 710
World at Your Doorstep: A Consultation on Reaching Ethnics for Christ 16790
World Conference on Church, Community and State [Oxford, England] 4691
World Conference on Problems of International Migration and the Responsibility of the Churches 8339
World Council of Churches 5743, 7487, 8960, 14489, 16791
World Council of Churches, Advisory Group on Urban Industrial Mission 11629, 13097
World Council of Churches, Commission on the Churches' Participation in Development 13409, 16473, 16792
World Council of Churches, Commission on World Mission 15704
World Council of Churches, Commission on World Mission and Evangelism 12734, 18383
World Council of Churches, Communications Department 13410
World Council of Churches, Conference on Migrant Workers in Western Europe 8961
World Council of Churches, Department of Church and Society 7741, 12033
World Council of Churches, Department of Church and Society, Division of Studies 7230
World Council of Churches, Department on Studies in Evangelism 8632
World Council of Churches, Department on Studies in

Evangelism, Western European Working Group 10661
World Council of Churches, Division of World Mission and Evangelism 8633, 11152
World Council of Churches, Division of World Mission and Evangelism, Advisory Group on Urban and Industrial Mission 8057
World Council of Churches, Urban and Industrial Mission Desk 14490
World Council of Churches, Urban Rural Mission 17206
World Council of Churches, World Conference on Faith, Science, and the Future [1979, Massachusetts Institute of Technology, Cambridge, MA] 15705
World Movement of Christian Workers 10184, 15706
World Tomorrow 3107
World Vision International 6002, 7231
World Within 6809
World's Richest Poorhouse 4575
Worley, Robert C. 12376, 14889, 16793
Worlock, Derek 18004, 18682
Worman, E. C. 5333
Wormer, Parley Paul 2764
Worship Songbook: Church in the City 16794
Wortham, Jerry D. 13411
Worthy, James C. 7488, 8962
Worthy, William 14098
Wothe, Franz Josef 4806, 8634, 8963
Wouk, Herman 5744
Would You Believe it? A Statement by the Staid City Club of Chicago 11153
Woycicki, Alexsander 3379
Woznicki, Andrew N. 16474
Wright, C. M. 13412
Wright, Carroll D. 1886
Wright, David E. 11154
Wright, Don 17207
Wright, Edward R. 2986
Wright, Elliott 12229, 15707
Wright, Frank Lloyd 7489, 8618, 14225
Wright, Frederick H. 3045
Wright, G. E. 6602
Wright, H. Elliot 11405, 11406
Wright, J. Robert 13749
Wright, Jeremiah A., Jr. 17208
Wright, Jim 18537
Wright, John J. 6003
Wright, Kenyon 11155, 12377
Wright, L. C. 4122, 4350
Wright, Lawrence 15319
Wright, Mary Olive 3679
Wright, Nathan, Jr. 8964, 10185, 10662, 10663, 11156
Wright, O. A. 1677
Wright, R. R. 2192
Wright, Robert 7018, 17596
Wright, Robert J. 561
Wright, Rose 4807
Wright, Stuart A. 18154
Wright, Tennant C. 16078
Wright, Thomas H. 4351
Wright, William A. 5137
Wright, William Archer, Jr. 6004
Wrigley, Francis 1821, 5277
Wrintmore, Frederick Henry 4123, 4124, 6119, 6410, 8058, 8635, 9282, 9711, 10186, 10664, 10665, 11157, 12034, 12735, 14491
Wristers, J. 12736
Wrobel, Paul 13750, 14099, 15320
Wucher, Waldemar 18264
Wulff, Joan 15708
Wunder, Clinton 3811
Wurster, Paul 1445, 1887

Wurzbacher, Gerhard 8059
Wuthnow, Robert 14100, 14101, 14102, 14890, 15321, 18570
Wyatt, John Will 16475
Wyburn, John 4576
Wyburn, S. May 4576
Wycislo, Aloysius J. 8340
Wyckoff, Amelia 4198
Wylie, Jeanie 19126
Wynn, John Charles 8135
X, Malcolm 9283, 10751, 12035, 17170, 18955, 19284
Xenides, J. P. 3475
Yacoob, May Mirza 15709, 16795, 18005
Yale University Institute of Human Relations 4997
Yamaka, Wes 12355
Yamamori, Tetsuano 12036, 15322, 17209, 17597
Yancey, John M. 9834
Yancey, Philip 18006, 18384, 19022
Yancey, William 15323
Yankauer, Marian Perry 7019
Yankelovich, Daniel 16079
Yankelovich, Skelly, and White, Inc. 18007
Yanker, Henri March 6810
Yap, Kim-Hao 11630
Yard, James M. 4199
Yardeni, Myriam 17598
Yates, Dennis 12782
Yates, Herbert S. 8965
Yates, Walter L. 12378
Yatman, Charles H. 1266
Yeager, Jack C. 15324
Yeames, J. 1035
Yearwood, Lennox 14492
Yeatman, Thomas 819
Yellowitz, Irwin 14891
Yeo, Alfred 17210
Yeo, Eileen 16080
Yeo, Stephen 14103
Yeracaris, Constantine A. 6005
Yergin, Howard Vernon 2679
Yi, Yong Kol 19023
Yinger, J. Milton 5539, 6391, 6411, 7020, 7232, 8060, 8966, 11158, 12379, 14104, 17211
Yingling, L. Carroll, Jr. 17212
Yivo Institute for Jewish Research 8341
Ylvisaker, Paul N. 7143, 8636
Yoder, John Howard 9284, 12737
Yoffie, Leah Rachel 19250
Yoggy, Andrew M. 8967
Yohan, Walter 10666
Yokley, Raytha 12254, 12255, 12986
Yon, William A. 16476, 16477
Yongdongpo Urban Industrial Mission 15325
Yonge, Charlotte 11760
Yordon, Henry K. 15326
York, Lena 5234
Yorke, Peter C. 13398
Young Men's Bible Society of New York City 13
Young Men's Christian Association 205, 357 >> See further: Subject Index
Young Men's Christian Association World Communique 16796
Young Men's Christian Association, Industrial Department 3812
Young Men's Christian Association, National Board, Bureau of Records and Trends 5235
Young Men's Domestic Missionary Society 87
Young People in African Towns: Their Pastoral Care 16797
Young People's Commission of the Chicago Church Federation 3935
Young Woman's Christian

Association 311 >> See further: Subject Index
Young Women with Special Problems Assisted by Sisters in Addis Ababa 14892
Young, Agnes F. 7021
Young, Ann E. 8637
Young, Charles E. 19024
Young, Chester 10187
Young, Clarence Andrew 2680
Young, Frank W. 8061
Young, G. Douglas 11631
Young, Henry 14493
Young, James 16999, 17369
Young, James Mortimer 15327
Young, James T. 1678
Young, John 9712
Young, Jonathan 14494, 15328
Young, Kathy 16081
Young, Kenneth R. 9713
Young, Lois Horton 11159
Young, Michael D. 7233
Young, Owen D. 4125
Young, Whitney M. 9285, 11632
Young, William Field 17835
Younger, George D. 7490, 7742, 8062, 8063, 8638, 8639, 8968, 9714, 9715, 9716, 10667, 10668, 11160, 12371, 12380, 12381, 13098, 13413, 14105, 18385
Younger, Paul A. 9286
Youngstown: Work and the Redemption of Urban America 14893
Yourd, Paul H. 3813
Youth and Religion: A Scientific Inquiry into the Religious Attitudes, Belief and Practice of Urban Youth 7491
Youth and Revolution 10188
Youth Center 14556
Youth Work: Quarterly Review of the World Alliance of Young Men's Christian Associations 3739
Yu, Suk-Chong 16798
Yudell, Clifford 12037
Yuen, Bessie Kawaguchi 18386
Yule, Sandy 16799
Yung, Hak Hyun 11161
Yutzy, Daniel 9409
Yvlgnac, Amédée d' 8064
Zabaneh, Ibranim K. 18746
Zabel, William Leroy 3108
Zabriskie, Francis Nicoll 656, 909
Zacchaeus Collective 14495
Zagano, Phyllis 18387
Zahniser, Charles Reed 4258
Zald, Mayer 8969, 10183, 10189, 10669, 12038, 15329, 16478
Zalent, Kim 18388, 19025
Zander, Leo 6811
Zanotelli, Alex 18747
Zanotti, Gabriel J. 17599
Zdaniewicza, Witolda 17907
Zechariah, Chelliah 17213
Zeckhausen, Harry 1729
Zehr, Howard 15710, 16082
Zeichner, Irving B. 8970, 8971
Zeidler, Frank P. 9717
Zeigler, Earl F. 4808
Zeiler, Judith 17695
Zeisloft, James Howard 14894
Zemans, Eugene S. 8806
Zepp, Ira G. 13414, 18008, 19026
Zetterquist, Håkan 13415
Zewe, Martin Donald 13416
Zezschwitz, Gerhard von 400
Zghal, A. 14048
Ziegenhals, Gretchen E. 19246
Ziegenhals, Walter E. 8640, 11633, 12382, 14106, 14496, 14497, 14895, 14896, 15551, 15711
Ziegert, Richard 15712
Ziegler, Betty Skelton 4809
Ziegler, Jesse H. 13417
Zielhuis, L. 11634
Zill, Stephanie 12383
Zimmer, Basil G. 7743, 7744

Zimmer, Steven L. 13418
Zimmerman, Carle C. 4004, 8342
Zimmerman, Donald E. 8641
Zimmerman, Donald W. 10190
Zimmerman, Joseph Francis 13419
Zimpel, Lloyd 9718, 13751
Zinty, Maurice 6877, 8972
Zion's Herald 81
Ziska, Patrick J. 16479
Znaniecki, Florian 3860
Zoar United Methodist Church, Philadelphia 11635
Zola, Emile 585, 1601
Zoot Suit Riots--Portent of Storm 5236
Zopf, Paul E. 19027
Zoppetti, Leighsa 16800
Zorazim, Josef 16801, 17600
Zorbaugh, Harvey W. 4018
Zotti, Mary Irene 19247
Zubatsky, David S. 18748
Zuber, Robert 18009
Zueblin, Charles 1788, 1888, 1927, 2058, 2286, 2477
Zulehner, Paul Michael 8343, 11636, 16083
Zumbrunnen, Albert Clay 3476
Zunkels, C. Wayne 10191
Zur Männerseelsorge in der modernen Großstadt 7745
Zuurdeeg, J. 6603
Zweig, Franklin M. 11162
Zweigenhaft, Richard L. 15330
Zylstra, Bernard 8066
Zyskowski, B. 14897

Subject Index

The thesaurus for the Subject Index relies on standard terminology used by the Library of Congress and/or the Religion One Index except in those instances where the vocabulary available in these indexes was insufficiently detailed to describe city church phenomena and relationships. Researchers may wish to consult those indexes under the topics listed below for further bibliographic citations. In instances when neither the Library of Congress nor the Religion One Index listed suitable terms, effort was made to employ the terms that were most commonly in usage at the time the work cited was written for the Subject Index heading, e.g, comity, storefront churches. When the Library of Congress and Religion One Index employed different terminology for the same subject, one was chosen and the other cross-referenced.

Publication dates of the works indexed can be inferred from the citation number, the smaller the number the earlier the date. Numbers between 1 and 7745 were published in the years from 1800 to 1959 and are located in Volume I; those between 7746 and 15330 were published in the years from 1960 to 1979 and are found in Volume II; and those between 15331 and 19247 were published in the years from 1980 to 1991 and are found in Volume III.

Aachen (Germany)
--History 14941
Aberdeen (Scotland)
--Religious and ecclesiastical institutions 383
Abidjan (Ivory Coast)

--Religion 13500, 13501
--Religious and ecclesiastical institutions 12280, 14738, 16140, 17716
--Social conditions 10789, 15709, 16188, 16795, 18005
Abortion 14372
--Bibliographies 15574
--History 18809
Academy of Parish Clergy 10845
Acapulco (Mexico)
--Religious and ecclesiastical institutions 17723
Acción Sindical Chilena 10439
Acculturation 1719, 3943, 4732, 4942, 5153, 5659, 6999, 7970, 8199, 9257, 11741, 12250, 12676, 13600, 13951, 17396, 17644, 17963, 18672
--Africa 13266, 16293
--History 5017, 7167, 10350, 11517, 13122, 13159, 13977, 15955, 18138
--Latin America 8897
--South Africa 12130, 17742
Action catholique ouvrière (France) 10192, 12219, 13275
--Congresses 12040
--History 16186
Action reflection training >> See: City clergy, education of
Action research >> See further: City Churches--Research; City Missions--Research; Social sciences--Research; Sociology--Research
Action research 3320, 6107, 7267, 9310, 10540, 10588, 10707, 11203, 11601, 12057, 12245, 12868, 14164, 15488, 16615
--Handbooks 12463
--India 14194
--Methods 15142, 15917
--New Zealand 13575
Action Training Coalition (ACT)
--History 18385
Action Training Coalition (ATC) 10193, 12009
Action Training Network of Ohio (ATN) 11167
Activism >> See: Social action
Addis Ababa (Ethiopia)
--Religious and ecclesiastical institutions 14543
--Social conditions 14892
Adolescence >> See: Youth
Adult education 3042, 3103, 4808, 6383, 7631, 10975, 13104, 13609, 15674, 17063, 17540, 18120, 18843
--Bibliographies 17169
--England 2975, 13614, 15282, 18520
--Germany 14714
--History 14868
Advertising 3711, 6753, 16584
--Churches 1864, 2272, 3151, 3333, 3778, 7705
Advocacy 751, 2060, 10211, 10799, 11058, 13299, 13972, 14560, 15136, 15394, 15399, 15514, 16689, 16914, 17080, 18180
--Bibliographies 13917
--Congresses 15089
--History 13121
Aesthetics 16973
Affirmative action programs
--United States 10534, 11975, 13160
Africa >> See further: [Names of African cities]
Africa
--Bibliographies 10579, 11501, 12386, 13567, 15960
--Church history 10205, 10508, 11939, 13713, 13894, 16366, 19240
--Economic conditions 7230, 10262, 10290, 12745
--History 14048

Africa (cont.)
--Periodicals 7750, 8686, 11642
--Religion 6299, 6363, 8348, 8500, 8894, 9165, 10690, 12058, 12291, 12846, 13036, 13908, 14826, 15024, 17373, 17941, 18683, 18981
--Religious and ecclesiastical institutions 6117, 6636, 8243, 11584, 12115, 13263, 13350, 13377, 14049, 14298, 14603, 16733, 16734, 19240
--Social conditions 7741, 7750, 7904, 8124, 8315, 8349, 8686, 9165, 9525, 9963, 9972, 11180, 11926, 12846, 13280, 13361, 13365, 13371, 14258, 14661, 14892, 15000, 15841, 15960, 16293, 16795, 16797, 17260, 17506, 18319, 18747, 19158
--Social conditions--History 12191
--Social life and customs 11797, 18124, 18254
African American Methodists
--History 11635
African Methodist Episcopal Church
--Case studies 14857
--Case studies--Bibliographies 4929
--History 58, 1079, 3463, 15471
African Methodist Episcopal Zion Church 17147, 18646
--Case studies 923, 18542
--History 13396, 17785
African Union Methodist Protestant Church 15713
African Wesleyan Methodist Episcopal Church 15369
African American Adventists
--History 13304
African American American Baptists 6648, 7064, 9217
African American Baptists 728, 4941, 5083, 5098, 13797, 16985, 17309, 17533, 18729, 18988, 19284, 19292, 19320
--Biography 19269
--History 543, 1833, 2229, 4526, 4625, 13606, 15255, 19288,19307
African American Catholics 4265, 4629, 5144, 5187, 5273, 5279, 5761, 5974, 7051, 7559, 10825, 12048, 12615, 13570, 13765, 13812, 13911, 14036, 14279, 14593, 14691, 14954, 14997, 15335, 15400, 15461, 15467, 15503, 15577, 15604, 15613, 16276, 16523, 18437, 18693, 18815, 19120
--History 4052, 4617, 5015, 13080, 13893, 14705
African American children 9018, 9332, 13667, 14022, 15260, 15332, 15404, 16653
--Education 9292, 13128, 13812, 16276
--Social conditions 4906
African American churches 944, 1686, 1901, 3393, 3700, 4053, 4102, 4127, 4145, 4304, 4676, 4909, 4910, 5098, 5137, 5269, 5367, 6628, 6648, 6872, 7064, 7649, 8190, 8219, 9057, 9217, 9236, 9898, 11319, 11616, 11653, 11731, 11834, 11951, 12255, 12334, 12435, 12762, 12770, 13281, 13339, 13608, 13639, 13796, 13965, 14290, 14426, 14670, 15164, 15291, 15348, 15590, 15928, 16134, 16234, 16670, 17162, 17533, 17625, 17966, 17969, 18693, 18700, 18982, 18988, 19094, 19120, 19246, 19336
--Bibliographies 13793, 16489, 18411
--Bibliography 18691

African American Churches (cont.)
--Case studies 5083, 5905, 12631, 13088, 13406, 13684, 14072, 14288, 14492, 14610, 15573, 15613, 17208, 17309
--Customs and practices 5076, 6673, 11142, 12586
--History 1513, 3248, 3377, 3398, 3407, 4997, 5955, 6891, 7221, 8044, 9254, 12979, 13000, 13277, 13490, 13606, 13651, 14793, 15067, 15105, 15922, 16408, 16880, 17075, 17785, 17936, 18691, 18779, 18960, 19113
--Influence 2192, 4798, 9360, 11149, 18203
--Influence--History 18737
--Mission of 3796, 6523, 12000, 12239, 12240, 12584, 12677, 15107, 15277, 16275, 16856, 16910, 18839
--Mission of--History 18737
--Political activity 10470, 10634, 10831, 13650, 14278
--Social service 2192, 2808, 5145, 6523, 12677, 13684, 13876, 14021
--Social teaching 17475
--Spiritualism 15722, 16823
--Worship 4905, 8615, 9585, 12041, 17545

African American clergy 3498, 4441, 4798, 5409, 5955, 6326, 9057, 9809, 10545, 10749, 10835, 11146, 11164, 11250, 11366, 11595, 12422, 13035, 13477, 13797, 13953, 13965, 14035, 14061, 14212, 14274, 14726, 15274, 15307, 15316, 15573, 16024, 16183, 16234, 16350, 16490, 16503, 16610, 16670, 17138, 17355, 17529, 17918, 18001, 18161, 18191, 18750, 18806, 18837, 18885
--Bibliographies 5927, 14224, 17813
--Biography 58, 728, 2229, 3248, 3527, 4526, 4529, 4533, 4769, 5927, 7347, 8726, 8791, 8812, 9283, 9318, 9445, 10235, 10421, 11592, 11848, 11859, 11864, 11866, 12035, 12076, 12277, 12508, 13414, 14005, 14493, 14546, 14950, 15515, 15693, 16356, 16577, 17170, 17668, 18426, 18716, 18727, 18728, 19084
--History 8075, 15292, 18691, 19113, 19269, 19284, 19357
--Interviews 16585
--Political activity 9949, 15382, 18203

African American clergy, training of 6466, 6648, 7064, 10219, 11510, 11590, 11999, 15274, 15307

African American Congregational Christians 5905
--History 14021

African American Congregationalists 15260

African American Disciples of Christ
--History 19047

African American Episcopalians 9, 10, 11999, 12555, 16139, 16180, 16204
--History 2922, 3387, 17131

African American executives 7539

African American families 4216, 4832, 5047, 9571, 10331, 10700, 13128, 13450, 13639, 15010, 15253, 15515, 15567, 15619, 17533, 17999, 19246
--Fiction 7583, 18961
--History 15362, 16274

African American Jews >> See further: African Americans--

Relations with Jews
African American Jews 5269, 6134, 9003, 10438, 10633, 12138, 13357, 16420
--History 15560
African American Lutherans 6308, 9503
African American men 10450, 12584
African American Mennonites 13789, 16489, 18494
--History 17632
African American Methodists 4851, 6098, 6241, 6303, 6466, 7118, 7483, 8867, 9337, 9809, 11146, 11764, 14035, 14288, 14625, 15274, 15316, 15341, 15413, 15693, 15713, 16371, 17138, 17864, 17935, 18926, 19113
--History 58, 923, 2922, 3463, 11250, 15369, 15471, 16812, 17494
African American music 15294, 16806, 17545, 18019, 18455
--History 19113
African American newspapers 14138
African American Pentecostals >> See further: [Specific Denominations, e.g., Church of God in Christ]
African American Pentecostals 11780, 13406, 16361, 18837, 19113
African American preaching 6628, 9318, 10533, 10749, 13031, 13238, 13246, 14061, 14274, 15159, 16023, 18837, 19260
African American Presbyterians 4812, 5533, 6276, 7482, 8622, 12444, 15311
--History 1513, 4507, 5246, 8044, 15568, 16786, 16787, 18716
African American Protestants 4145, 12615, 14279
--History 6891, 13277, 19113
African American Southern Baptists 12586, 12770, 13031, 14426, 14759, 15011, 15885, 16023, 16024, 16495, 18853
--History 15742, 15922, 15923, 15946, 16066
African American theological seminaries >> See: Theological seminaries, African American
African American Unitarian Universalists 11234
African American United Church of Christ members 12382
African American women >> See further: Black women
African American women 1795, 4028, 4898, 6266, 13797, 15209, 16653, 17758, 18160, 19341
--Biography 18429, 19324
--History 16274, 19113, 19152
African American youth 5294, 7843, 9018, 9332, 9914, 11653, 15461, 16444, 17750, 18838, 18871
--History 19113
--Social conditions 4906
African Americans >> See further: Blacks
African Americans
--Attitudes 9337, 9743, 10545, 10748, 11146, 11208, 11238, 11250, 11575, 11810, 12615, 13483, 13796, 16275, 17994, 19274
--Bibliographies 4941, 7112, 9674, 9749, 18601
--Charities--History 13496, 16408
--Civil rights 4199, 5269, 6090, 7006, 7843, 8278, 8791, 9120, 9217, 10422, 10451, 10470,

10750, 10863, 11060, 11107, 11406, 12008, 13650, 14278, 15225, 16180, 16275, 16861, 17613, 18815
African Americans (cont.)
--Civil rights--History 12979, 17075, 18426, 19016, 19324
--Crimes against 103, 5269, 8162, 11244, 11283, 11317, 17785
--Crimes against--History 11384
--Drama 3190, 7583, 8995, 18961
--Economic conditions 3758, 4206, 4614, 8278, 10245, 10548, 11191, 11209, 11344, 11406, 11551, 11702, 12283, 12704, 13570, 13722, 13876, 14184, 14306, 14691, 15225, 17853
--Education 4441, 5083, 5592, 9914, 10431, 13318, 14022, 15928, 18779, 19328
--Education--History 14021, 14056
--Employment 3762, 4149, 4798, 5047, 5284, 7539, 9718, 11191, 13160, 13244, 13570, 14691, 16577
--Employment--History 16274
--Ethnic relations 10415
--Families 15332
--Fiction 3190, 7583, 18961
--Folklore 11625, 11727, 14834
--Forecasts 15619
--Health and Hygiene 15863
--History 2471, 3889, 4917, 5020, 5209, 8044, 8975, 9292, 9589, 10868, 11365, 13000, 13202, 14763, 14769, 14794, 15782, 15858, 16601
--History--Periodicals 13793
--Housing 3736, 4206, 4900, 5747, 6673, 7019, 8822, 9017, 9285, 9359, 9762, 10081, 10176, 10451, 10641, 12378, 14825, 17862, 18140
--Identity >> See further: Race awareness
--Identity 3191, 3762, 8417, 8730, 8790, 10750, 10752, 10863, 11209, 11542, 12203, 12584, 12615, 13789, 17922
--Identity--History 3889, 5020, 13490, 15922
--Languages 12545
--Legal status, laws, etc. 14609
--Medical care 9285, 11740, 15722, 17419
--Migrants 614, 3500, 3796, 4056, 4061, 4347, 4449, 4832, 4851, 5612, 7128, 8485, 8637, 8896, 9048, 15010
--Migrations--History 19218
--Missions to 1485, 2026, 2596, 2692, 3065, 3509, 3782, 4041, 4052, 4102, 4142, 4265, 4347, 4449, 4733, 4851, 5015, 5144, 5273, 5279, 5533, 5651, 5702, 5761, 6276, 8481, 9843, 10196, 10208, 10739, 11191, 11408, 12378, 12555, 13005, 13238, 14008, 14825, 15065, 15225, 15260, 15461, 15503, 15604, 15781, 16368, 17863, 17962, 18693, 18945
--Missions to--History 4507, 11730, 13015, 18717
--Pastoral counseling of 14094, 14179, 14521, 15185, 15316, 16234, 16490, 19328
--Politics and government 9703, 9949, 15533, 17355, 18161
--Population 6858, 11145, 12755
--Race relations 2190, 8049, 10204, 15874
--Relations with Jews 7830, 7907, 9071, 11393, 13208, 16861, 16952, 16970
--Relations with Jews--Bibliographies 9749
--Relations with Jews--History

14483
African Americans (cont.)
--Religion 1485, 1900, 4226, 4696, 4752, 4844, 6299, 6493, 7297, 7756, 9057, 9258, 9585, 10470, 10750, 10863, 11221, 11727, 12366, 12556, 12717, 13164, 13278, 13457, 13477, 13489, 13615, 13650, 14058, 14260, 14278, 14294, 14301, 14547, 15362, 15533, 15862, 15863, 16610, 16806, 17228, 18019, 18617, 18623, 18714, 18729, 18832, 18850, 19183
--Religion--Bibliographies 18411
--Religion--History 4617, 7221, 12385, 12727, 13537, 15311, 16786, 17988, 18727, 18728, 19113
--Relocation 3099, 4061, 6142, 6673, 7711, 7830, 8870, 9048, 9146, 10081, 12099, 16368
--Relocation--History 16274
--Segregation 3736, 3762, 3820, 4149, 5585, 5702, 5747, 6061, 6303, 7019, 7174, 9620, 9743, 9809, 10081, 10377, 10451, 11088, 11104, 11956, 12153, 12368, 12703, 13318
--Segregation--History 10587, 12979, 13015, 14477
--Social conditions 3758, 3934, 4068, 4603, 4614, 4696, 4732, 4733, 4917, 5047, 5303, 5359, 5450, 5498, 5932, 5975, 6299, 7086, 7172, 7458, 8162, 8870, 8889, 9222, 9240, 9263, 9843, 10123, 10330, 10543, 10687, 10700, 10752, 11105, 11138, 11208, 11314, 11344, 11470, 11474, 11949, 12000, 12008, 12099, 12704, 13379, 13450, 13457, 14260, 14279, 14507, 15209, 15446, 15502, 15734, 16118, 16970, 17084, 17922, 18186, 19040
--Social conditions--History 2471, 3169, 4444, 4997, 5209, 7581, 15174, 19131
--Social life and customs 1464, 12545, 13472, 15567, 16653, 17393, 17699, 17880
--Social life and customs--Bibliographies 9674
--Social life and customs--History 16123
--Statistics 14036
Aged >> See further: Church work with the aged
Aged 5450, 10124, 12657, 15697, 17828, 17900
--Dwellings 6925, 7594, 8883, 13972, 15441, 15697, 15990
--Employment 4834
--Greece 16614
--Switzerland 15880
Ageism >> See: Aged; Church work with the aged
Agnosticism 2323
--History 14891
Agrarianism >> See further: Social values (anti-urban)
Agrarianism 64, 7766, 12535
--History 9151, 11927, 13441, 18373
Agribusiness >> See: Agriculture
Agriculture 1520, 1605, 1756, 3917, 4222, 4293, 4395, 4786, 5180, 13196, 14443, 17972, 18880
--Bibliographies 13243
--Germany 13589
--Nigeria 7767
Ahmadiyya (Muslims) 15709, 16795, 18005, 18717
AIDS (disease) 17520, 17669, 17940, 18089, 18129, 18204, 18323, 18441, 18442, 18522, 18528, 18543, 18555, 18609, 18651, 18707, 18879, 19149,

19150, 19204, 19235
AIDS (disease) (cont.)
--Africa 19240
--Bibliographies 18457, 18574, 18697
--England 18028, 18560
--Patients--Pastoral care of 17732, 18313, 18402, 18466, 18695, 19150
Airport ministry >> See further: Church and Industry; Chaplains, industrial
Airport ministry 9316
--Canada 12042, 13382
Akron (Ohio)
--Religious and ecclesiastical institutions 5370, 6127, 6296, 8295, 8882, 14364
Albany (New York)
--History 19118
--Religious and ecclesiastical institutions 546, 7818, 11302, 11320, 11594, 13397, 13968
--Religious and ecclesiastical institutions--History 10296, 14192, 18396
--Social conditions 6862
Albuquerque (New Mexico)
--Religious and ecclesiastical institutions 7793, 18380
--Social conditions 17663
Alcohol 1945, 2989, 3938
--History 12928
Alcoholics Anonymous 6604, 8491, 12744, 16201, 17057, 18168
--History 15119
Alcoholism 737, 775, 845, 1677, 1856, 3036, 4536, 5173, 5573, 5721, 6260, 6604, 6761, 7411, 7415, 8491, 9860, 9940, 10576, 12030, 12744, 13526, 15155, 16201, 16971, 18123, 19316, 19327, 19349
--England 411
--New Guinea 15008
Alexandria (Egypt)
--Social conditions 16940
Algemeen Christelijk Werkersverbond (Belgium)
--History 15820
Alien labor
--Congresses 8961
--Europe 8961, 10762, 13482, 17069
--France 15673
--Germany 16203, 17123, 17876
Alienation >> See further: Strangers; Individual and society
Alienation 4577, 13758
--Descriptions of 106, 704, 869, 1390, 1918, 3931, 4406, 4802, 5973, 6228, 6486, 8134, 8363, 8678, 8703, 8785, 9080, 9129, 9591, 9957, 10385, 11045, 11184, 11284, 11305, 11317, 12368, 12486, 12657, 12850, 13483, 14130, 14608, 15302, 15618, 15777, 15935, 16118, 17592, 18544
--Descriptions of--History 13206
--England 704, 12399
--Germany--History 12977
--Great Britain 18285
--Religious response to 7203, 11094
--Religious responses to 1203, 2062, 2230, 4942, 6148, 6629, 6906, 7104, 7376, 7566, 7599, 8134, 8183, 8195, 8521, 8761, 8828, 8927, 9931, 10013, 10357, 11184, 11742, 12150, 12294, 12312, 13171, 13436, 14303, 14380, 14946, 15202, 15969, 16067, 17291, 17294, 17589, 17781, 18696, 18708
--Religious responses to--History 18031
--Sociology of 4942, 6670, 6871,

13436
Alienation (from God) 332, 9201, 17781
Alienation (from the church) 427, 516, 660, 725, 739, 745, 790, 817, 818, 836, 1529, 1563, 1712, 1899, 2079, 3987, 8597, 9331, 13880, 14557, 15022, 15746, 16277, 17964
Aliens >> See further: Immigrants; Emigration and immigration; Church work with immigrants
Aliens 1360, 2077, 2600, 2828, 5060, 13050, 18864
--Biblical teaching 14996
--Great Britain 1532
Aliens, illegal 14589, 15366, 15903, 15950, 16265, 17367, 17425, 17688, 18130
All Africa Christian Conference 8348, 8349, 8449, 11642, 11985, 12963, 13427
--Periodicals 7750
Allentown (Pennsylvania)
--Religious and ecclesiastical institutions 18296
--Social conditions 4251, 5493, 14747, 14790
Alliquippa (Pennsylvania)
--Social conditions 12059
Almsgiving >> See: Charity; Wealth
Almshouses 17, 38, 57, 71, 99, 336, 825, 981
--History 2036, 2924
Alternative churches >> See: Christian communities; Para-church; Communal living; Experimental ministries
Amalgamated Clothing and Textile Workers Union 14229, 14873, 15347
Amarillo (Texas)
--Religious and ecclesiastical institutions 11143
AMECEA Documentation Service (Nairobi, Kenya) 14603
American Baptist Convention 6589
--Case studies 994, 1490, 1521, 1623, 1694, 1697, 2247, 3869, 4771, 4836, 5684, 6374, 6579, 6607, 6703, 6870, 6882, 6883, 6890, 6963, 7080, 7119, 7213, 7326, 7450, 7692, 7842, 8196, 8472, 8473, 8564, 8738, 8778, 8779, 9074, 9472, 9867, 9868, 10360, 10570, 10573, 10855, 10856, 11050, 11051, 11061, 11271, 11311, 11312, 11565, 11619, 12207, 12659, 12959, 14213, 14930, 15429, 16985, 17477, 17661, 18202, 18435
--Congresses 7025, 7100
--History 4337
--Periodicals 586, 5854, 10199
--Pronouncements, policies 6262, 9110, 17608, 17805
--Social teaching 6133
American Baptist Home Mission Societies 2974, 3388, 4255, 5854, 6374, 6414, 6492, 6607, 6703, 6862, 6882, 6883, 6890, 7080, 7100, 7191, 7236, 7326, 7672, 7692, 7752, 7818, 7926, 8196, 8472, 8473, 8738, 8778, 8779, 8890, 9050, 9074, 9867, 9868, 10077, 10360, 10361, 10569, 10570, 10571, 10572, 10573, 10855, 10856, 10908, 11050, 11051, 11061, 12391
--Bibliographies 8933
--Congresses 7025
--Periodicals 586, 10199
American Baptist Home Missionary Societies
--History 7035
American Baptist Mariners' Society >> See further:

Merchant Seamen
American Baptist Mariners' Society 324
American Bible Society 12, 40
--History 245, 4551
American Christian Commission 425
American Evangelical Alliance 1674
American Federation of Labor 3696, 3742, 3770, 3771, 5994, 6922, 7026, 7283, 7537, 8017
--History 16578, 18262, 18836
American Federation of Teachers 5238
American Female Guardian Society and Home for the Friendless (New York, NY) 575, 4388
American Friends Service Committee 4811, 5888, 8072, 8973, 14398, 19108
American Home Missionary Society 327, 718, 770
--Periodicals 94
American Indians >> See: Indians of North America
American Jewish Committee 8896, 9071, 9222, 9651, 9743, 9749, 10111
American literature >> See further: Literature; Cities and towns in literature
American literature 8032, 12350, 16055, 18363, 19170
--African American authors 3190, 4752, 11293
American Lutheran Church
--Periodicals 11879
--Pronouncements, policies 17805, 18237
American Lutheran Church, Board of Christian Social Action 7753, 9290
American Missionary Association 2398, 2596, 4041, 5284, 5747, 6061
--History 13105, 15260
American Protective Association 1226
--History 13074
American Protective League (Baltimore, Maryland) 805
American Seaman's Friend Society >> See further: Merchant seamen
American Seaman's Friend Society 4253
American Social Hygiene Association 4408, 4421
American Society of Interior Designers 18399
American Society of Missiology 17297
American Sunday School Union 83, 313
--History 3027
American Tract Society 84, 384, 2442
--History 4551, 13701
--Periodicals 192
American Unitarian Association 2619, 2650, 2832
--History 5645
--Periodicals 65, 542
Americanization >> See further: Church work with immigrants; Emigration and immigration; Acculturation; Assimilation; Christianization
Americanization 767, 1151, 1719, 1724, 1823, 2078, 2083, 2547, 2555, 2625, 2679, 2884, 3052, 3111, 3116, 3170, 3180, 3205, 3279, 3289, 3327, 3434, 3590, 3601, 3608, 3657, 4165, 4473, 4531, 5070, 5689, 5931, 5941, 6760, 7910, 7923, 10846, 13316
--History 4455, 4874, 5382, 6323, 11297, 12693, 13141, 13698,

13952, 14082, 14132, 14269, 14527, 14717, 14886, 15176, 15702, 17414
Ames (Iowa)
--Religious and ecclesiastical institutions 5880
Amman (Jordan)
--Religious and ecclesiastical institutions 17926
Ammerdown Group 14914
Amsterdam (Netherlands)
--Church history 11199
--Religion 12993
--Religious and ecclesiastical institutions 11199, 11481, 12415
--Social conditions 18798
Amusements >> See: Theaters; Sport; Moving pictures; Recreation;
Anabaptists >> See: Mennonites; Church of the Brethren
Anarchism 765, 782, 845, 877, 950, 952, 1258, 10754, 12711, 14571
--History 18624
Ancestor worship 13327, 14282
--Japan 15506
Anchorage (Alaska)
--Social conditions 7177
Andover House Association (Boston, Massachusetts) 1185
Andover Newton Theological School 14055
Anger 8593, 11317, 11968, 15195
Anglican Church >> See: Protestant Episcopal Church in the United States; Episcopal Church; Church of England
Anglican Consultative Council 18273, 18566
Anglo-Catholicism 927, 1670, 3032, 3281, 3365, 3886, 4093, 4094, 4157, 4239, 4290, 4295, 4308, 4322, 4666, 4830, 5045, 5128, 5326, 5393, 5639, 5914, 15844, 16546, 16579
--History 5517
--Periodicals 4159
Angola
--Economic conditions 12103
Ann Arbor (Michigan)
--Ethnic relations--History 13115
Annapolis (Maryland)
--Religious and ecclesiastical institutions 13221
Anomy 1214, 5008, 5045, 5973, 6228, 7378, 7953, 8352, 8483, 11184, 12368, 12990, 13677, 17294
Anthropology >> See further: Ethnology
Anthropology 3889, 5048, 5617, 6553, 7140, 7233, 8220, 9513, 9986, 10336, 10376, 10450, 10812, 11214, 11326, 12726, 12881, 13215, 13639, 13884, 14208, 14693, 14871, 15077, 15484, 17125, 17137, 17298, 17492, 18124, 18306, 18857
--History 15955
--Periodicals 12707
Anthropology and religion 8816, 13088, 13639, 15348, 15430, 15863, 15998, 16806, 16886, 17945, 18019, 18319, 19212
--Case studies 13406
--France 19236
--History 4617
--Latin America 10660
--Spain 19210
Anthropology--Research >> See: Social Sciences--Research; Sociology--Research
Anti-Defamation League of B'nai B'rith 5975
Anti-Saloon League 3909
Anti-urban attitudes >> See: Social values (anti-urban)
Anticatholicism >> See further:

Pluralism; Religious pluralism
Anticatholicism 178, 207, 240, 767, 845, 864, 1226, 1230, 1542, 5708, 14228
--History 1449, 6686, 7247, 7328, 13074, 13822, 14250
--Periodicals 693
Antimormonism 2766
Antiprotestantism >> See further: Pluralism; Religious pluralism
Antiprotestantism 188, 827, 3146, 4885, 17655, 19107
--Europe 14923
Antiquities >> See: Cities and towns--Ancient
Antisemitism >> See further: Pluralism; Religious pluralism
Antisemitism 1182, 2063, 2555, 4361, 4371, 4983, 5093, 5525, 5680, 5688, 5704, 7251, 7679, 9861, 10414, 10415, 10510, 11535, 12328, 13341, 13550, 14228, 15207, 15731, 18710
--Bibliographies 18081
--History 6686, 7106, 12127, 13340, 16893
Apartheid
--South Africa 5715, 7350, 13828, 14688, 15900, 16229, 16771, 17026, 17654, 18020, 19074
Apartment dwellings >> See: Church work with apartment dwellers
Apathy 3441, 4225, 6629, 7023, 9222, 9461, 10406, 11656, 12294, 12894, 14028, 16615
--Great Britain 9231
Appalachian Mountains 4894, 5771, 7320, 8395, 8591, 9469, 10815, 10986, 12310, 14700, 15138, 16147, 19305, 19325
Arab Americans 13113, 13261, 13354, 17537
--Religion 13261
--Social conditions 6249, 13112, 18710
Archaeology 13653, 13853
Archbishop's Commission on Urban Priority Areas >> See: Church of England--Commission on Urban Priority Areas
Architecture >> See further: Church architecture; Church buildings; Steeples and spires; Skyscrapers
Architecture 3057, 5120, 6924, 7168, 7489, 8194, 8537, 9023, 9474, 9659, 9973, 11771, 12468, 12697, 13157, 13956, 14971, 15906, 15962, 16491, 18399, 18503
--Great Britain 5084, 15611
--History 17379, 17549, 18071, 18382
Architecture, Islamic 16973, 17926, 18758
Architecture, Jewish 3712, 5635, 6424, 6807, 9279
Ardmore (Oklahoma)
--Religious and ecclesiastical institutions 4143
Arequipa (Peru)
--Religion 17359
Argentina
--Social conditions 8984, 19081
Arlington (Virginia)
--Religious and ecclesiastical institutions 6041
--Social conditions 11037
Armenian American churches 4938, 14358
Armenian Americans
--Religion 14357
Armenian Church in America
--History 4938
Art 811, 1946, 4920, 5120, 5664, 7047, 7993, 8452, 8839, 9474, 10400, 10599, 10801, 11029,

14704, 15514, 15793, 15839, 16181, 17425, 17890, 18465, 18760, 18876
Art (cont.)
--Asia 14850
--History 12094, 14447, 16731, 17121
Artisans 6193, 14287
Asceticism >> See further: Protestant ethic
Asceticism 4696, 9129, 13395, 14805, 18711
Asheville (North Carolina)
--Religious and ecclesiastical institutions 16419
Asia
--Church history 9608
--History 16781
--Religion 18330
--Social conditions 16612, 17079
Asian American churches
--Congresses 14803, 19169
Asian American Methodists 13802, 14071, 14803, 19169
Asian American youth 18625
Asian Americans >> See further: (Specific nationalities)
Asian Americans 2945, 3890, 16513
--Bibliographies 4390
--Missions to 2709, 4373, 4390, 4391, 14220, 18536, 18625, 19169
--Social conditions 3070, 5472, 7020, 12983, 17016
Asociacion Nacional de Jovenes Empresarios (Dominican Republic) 17621
Assassination 10235, 11864, 11866, 16025, 17813, 18781, 18947
Assemblies of God 8952, 10170, 11139, 13093, 18267
--Case studies 13903, 17213
--History 12244
--Periodicals 14637
Assimilation 3111, 3170, 4281, 5184, 5259, 5659, 6412, 6655, 6665, 6707, 7020, 7533, 7653, 7970, 8128, 9072, 10846, 11682, 12248, 12250, 12621, 13261, 13316, 13945, 14296, 14314, 15288, 16983, 17383, 17644, 18672
--Canada 18616
--Canada--History 14402
--History 4874, 5428, 6684, 7097, 8808, 11297, 11714, 12698, 13115, 13122, 13356, 13507, 13552, 13610, 13977, 14256, 14410, 14784, 15066, 17119
Association for Christian Training and Service (Nashville, Tennessee) 10200, 10671, 10988, 11174, 11341, 14341, 14742
--Periodicals 14505
Association for Evangelical Theological Education in India 16256
Association for the Relief of Respectable, Aged, Indigent Females 20
Association for Training and Christian Service 12964, 14741
Association of Catholic Trade Unionists 4580, 4892, 5518, 5519, 5558, 5795
--History 5043, 7471, 7863, 13774, 13775
--Periodicals 4581, 5065
Association of Theological Schools in the United States and Canada 11204
Associations, institutions, etc. >> See: Citizens' associations
Associazioni cristiane lavoratori italiani (Italy) 13459
Asylums 139, 3680
--History 5035, 12299

Atheism 277, 3928, 8592, 8811, 9309, 12300, 16007, 19093
--Europe 12920
--History 12826, 17939
--Poland 13670, 15910
--Poland--History 14009
Athens (Greece)
--Intellectual life 17852
--Religious life and customs 14846
--Social life and customs--History 6367
Athens (Ohio)
--Religious and ecclesiastical institutions 15631
Atlanta (Georgia)
--Ethnic relations 17251
--Ethnic relations--History 9750, 16498
--Race relations 8753, 13078
--Race relations--History 15174
--Religious and ecclesiastical institutions 2802, 5609, 6256, 7589, 8540, 8999, 9626, 10624, 10666, 11087, 11465, 11686, 12401, 13005, 13224, 13287, 14506, 14655, 14724, 15515, 16477, 18271, 18313, 18637, 18711, 18712, 18904, 19260, 19269, 19292, 19300
--Religious and ecclesiastical institutions--History 9750, 11687, 12943, 14021, 15251
--Religious life and customs 9339, 18297
--Social conditions 2770, 7174, 8753, 10103, 11169, 12217, 14317, 14953, 16301, 17101
--Social conditions--History 14674, 16022
Atlantic City (New Jersey)
--Religious and ecclesiastical institutions 8050, 10657
--Social conditions 14946, 15707, 16709
Atomic energy 5762, 6199, 6573, 6750, 6937, 7218, 12985, 15120, 15493, 16046, 16228
--Canada 15393
--Germany 16287
--Russia 18299
Atonement >> See further: Theology
Attendance >> See: Church attendance
Attitudes >> See further: Public opinion; Ethnic attitudes; (attitudes of various ethnic groups, e.g., Jews--Attitudes); Race relations--Attitudes
Attitudes about churches 955, 2456, 2951, 3103, 3339, 3494, 3576, 3661, 3856, 3952, 7491, 13394, 15007, 19274
--England 10291
--France 9856
Attitudes of church members 1466, 3525, 4376, 4441, 4649, 4958, 5094, 5643, 6063, 6735, 6876, 7480, 8346, 8419, 8705, 8722, 8867, 9320, 9506, 9638, 10545, 10716, 11148, 12020, 12027, 12028, 12096, 12473, 12581, 12791, 13212, 13416, 13796, 14212, 14673, 14969, 15335, 15429, 17319
--Bibliographies 11688
--Canada 9381
--England 15967
--History 5095, 8308, 12068, 13048, 13635, 13991, 15174
Attitudes--Anti-urban >> See: Social values (anti-urban)
Auburn (New York)
--History 16215
Auckland (New Zealand)
--Religious and ecclesiastical institutions 12267
--Religious and ecclesiastical institutions--History 2809

Augustana Evangelical Lutheran Church 5858
Augustana Lutheran Church 14113
Aurangabad (India)
--Social conditions 18208
Aurora (Illinois)
--Religious and ecclesiastical institutions 5407
--Religious and ecclesiastical institutions--History 14832
Australia
--Economic conditions 16822
--History 11039, 11929, 12417, 13542
--Religious and ecclesiastical institutions 8470, 9256, 14053, 17015, 17258, 17391, 17653, 19322 , 19358
--Religious and ecclesiastical institutions--History 16937
--Social conditions 11352, 11532, 12641, 12910, 13047, 13374, 18265, 19196, 19315
Australian Council of Churches 15027
Austria
--Church history 17571
--History 8880, 15739, 16345
--Intellectual life 12915, 19038
--Religious and ecclesiastical institutions 6829, 6830, 10425, 15179
--Religious life and customs 16083
--Social conditions 6012, 7041, 11636
Automation >> See further: Employment problems; Technology; Work--Technical aspects
Automation 5950, 6667, 7324, 7902, 8451, 8519, 8524, 8602, 9047, 9775, 9982, 10027
Automobiles 3595, 3616, 3907, 4351, 4396, 4552, 7671, 12102, 12820, 13968, 16010
Ayre (Massachusetts)
--Religious and ecclesiastical institutions 2486
Ação Católica Operária (Brazil)
--History 18175
Babylon (metaphor) 148, 337, 2282, 2787, 4406, 4695, 8887, 9550, 10392, 11106, 11752, 11976, 12667, 13643, 14514, 14716, 14768, 14811, 15181, 16464, 18611, 18749
Back-to-the-land movements 469, 1465, 1520, 1605, 2058, 4757, 18056
Baden (Germany)
--Social conditions 14431
--Social conditions--History 18234
Baha'i Assemblies
--Bibliographies 4934
Baha'i Faith 16225, 18760
Bakersfield (California)
--Religious and ecclesiastical institutions 9170
Bali Island (Indonesia)
--Politics and government 15458
Baltimore (Maryland)
--History 14944, 17639
--Race relations--History 14056
--Religion 2371, 7998
--Religious and ecclesiastical institutions 304, 1115, 1660, 2605, 2858, 5903, 6679, 6793, 7442, 8205, 9267, 9976, 10394, 10640, 10730, 10791, 10893, 10903, 13797, 13869, 14644, 15291, 15547, 15939, 16384
--Religious and ecclesiastical institutions--History 6157, 12883
--Religious life and customs 11280
--Social conditions 7148, 7451,

8831, 14799
Baltimore (Maryland) (cont.)
--Social conditions--History 14056
Baltimore Society for the Prevention of Pauperism
--History 6639
Baltimore Union for Public Good 1340
Bangalore (India)
--Religious and ecclesiastical institutions 10915, 12799, 15003
--Social conditions 9668, 16126
Bangkok (Thailand)
--Religious and ecclesiastical institutions 14163, 19050
--Social conditions 14097
Bangor (Maine)
--Religious and ecclesiastical institutions 12367
Banks >> See further: Credit unions
Banks 51, 981, 2122, 3854, 4242, 4953, 10135, 12188, 13285, 13634, 14480, 14666, 14767, 15068, 15099, 15904
--Bibliographies 13918
--History 12183, 14844, 18716
Bantu-speaking peoples 13327
Baptism in the Holy Spirit 17996
Baptist churches
--Case studies 543, 1833, 4625, 5083, 5931, 5956, 13797, 14573, 15012, 15277, 16985, 17542, 18861, 19269
--Periodicals 18259
--Sermons 15277
Baptist churches (Brazil) 16162
Baptist churches (Canada) 14646
Baptist churches (England) 17640
Baptist World Alliance 3868
Baptists >> See: American Baptist Convention; National Baptist Convention; Southern Baptist Convention
Baptists, African American >> See: African American Baptists; National Baptist Convention
Barcelona (Spain)
--Religious and ecclesiastical institutions--History 17052
--Social conditions 5993, 7820, 15218, 15443
Barrio >> See: Neighborhoods
Baseball 18845, 19201
--History 13017
Basel (Switzerland)
--History 12660
Basic Christian communities >> See further: Christian communities
Basic Christian communities 14012, 15112, 15351, 15375, 15620, 15936, 16096, 16447, 16605, 16703, 16828, 17515, 18963, 19337
Basic Christian Communities
--Africa 16366, 19240
Basic Christian communities
--Brazil 15976, 18171, 19189
--Canada 15393
--Chile 17959
Basic Christian Communities
--Congresses 15701
Basic Christian communities
--England 14563
Basic Christian Communities
--Great Britain 14167
Basic Christian communities
--Handbooks 15091
--Latin America 13082, 15139, 16169, 17643
--Mexico 18834
Beach ministries 11496, 11557
Beaver Valley (Pennsylvania)
--Social conditions 12059
Begging 695, 1295, 4182, 4503, 6761, 6941, 7613, 7967, 15828, 18072, 18214, 18498

Begging (cont.)
--Fiction 3496
--Korea 9324
Belfast (Northern Ireland)
--Religious and ecclesiastical institutions 9504
--Religious and ecclesiastical institutions--History 18842
--Social conditions 7874, 11361, 13009, 18038, 18085
Belfast Central Mission (Belfast, Northern Ireland)
--Church history 18842
Belgium
--History 15820
--Religion 5887, 6697, 7563, 7785, 7786, 16057
--Religious and ecclesiastical institutions 12824
--Social conditions 7312, 8377, 13463, 13611, 14994, 18910
Belief and doubt >> See further: Secularization
Belief and doubt 1472, 3847, 5887, 5924, 6177, 6645, 7426, 8353, 8876, 9001, 11277, 11476, 12651, 13458, 15746, 17295, 17692, 19093
--Asia 11178
--England 18013, 18113
--Europe 5800, 7815
--Fiction 653
--Great Britain 14149
--History 13510
--Ireland 14238
Benedictines 5833
Benevolent and moral institutions >> See: Charities--Organizations, etc.
Benevolent Fraternity of Unitarian Churches of Boston 143
Bergen County (New Jersey)
--Religious and ecclesiastical institutions 5776, 8532
Berkeley Center for Human Interaction (Berkeley, California) 9741
Berlin (Germany)
--Church history--Congresses 19078
--Religious and ecclesiastical institutions 547, 934, 995, 1853, 8222, 8436, 13566
--Religious and ecclesiastical institutions--History 1620, 14129, 15878, 19078
--Religious life and customs 953
--Social conditions 2897, 6012, 6163, 8222, 10327
--Social conditions--History 19343
Berlin City Mission 547, 953, 995
Bethlehem (Pennsylvania)
--Industries 17305
--Religious and ecclesiastical institutions 5407, 10350
--Social conditions 14747, 14790
Bhopal (India)
--Social conditions 17243, 18238
Bible
--Exposition on churches 1161, 7290, 7511, 13857, 13987, 14378, 14928, 15427, 16305, 16824, 17603, 17769, 17790, 17818, 19144
--Exposition on churches--Bibliographies 16433
--Exposition on cities 627, 2163, 8518, 8981, 9272, 9465, 9529, 10032, 11117, 11388, 11752, 11816, 11873, 12421, 12516, 13370, 13546, 13558, 14180, 14420, 14704, 14749, 14768, 14983, 15425, 15723, 16327, 16493, 16667, 16749, 16824, 16848, 16883, 16891, 17293, 17380, 17480, 17781, 18201, 18420, 18424, 18572, 18576, 18849, 18888, 18902, 19134,

19219
Bible (cont.)
--Exposition on cities--Bibliographies 16434, 18657
--Exposition on social problems 78, 326, 501, 520, 1139, 1212, 3006, 4286, 5038, 5577, 6341, 7547, 7642, 7742, 9073, 9849, 10129, 11556, 12380, 12737, 12849, 13050, 13227, 13372, 13409, 13709, 13979, 14261, 14617, 14715, 15148, 15642, 15647, 15834, 15980, 16412, 16609, 16917, 17150, 17652, 17991, 18440, 18529, 18852, 18993
--Publication and distribution 1, 12, 13, 25, 27, 29, 36, 40, 41, 364, 5677, 9424, 13877
--Publication and distribution--History 245
--Study 13, 36, 362, 626, 909, 2216, 2470, 3430, 3431, 7421, 7974, 8012, 9897, 10180, 11710, 12154, 13482, 15642, 16609, 16850, 17432, 17818, 17965, 18210, 18487, 18552, 18612, 18775, 18824, 18849, 18925
--Theology 6602, 9272, 14143, 14180, 14261, 14529, 14928, 14983, 15647, 16136, 16536, 16881, 16891, 17140, 17820, 18084, 18327, 18420, 18888, 18902
Bible (NT) 6166, 11117, 11816, 12784, 13227, 13395, 13546, 14749, 16441, 16497, 16749, 17769, 19278, 19321, 19339
--Bibliographies 16434
--Epistles 2163, 8981, 16667, 18201, 19083
--Gospels 1139, 14658, 14703, 15427, 15834, 15980, 16412, 17191, 17293, 17991
Bible (OT) 627, 3431, 10032, 10942, 11758, 11873, 12421, 13558, 13811, 14143, 14230, 16136, 16335, 16493, 17244, 17380, 18424
Bibliographies--African American Churches >> See: African American churches--Bibliographies
Bibliographies--African Americans >> See: African Americans--Bibliographies
Bibliographies--Business ethics >> See: Business ethics--Bibliographies
Bibliographies--Church and industry >> See: Church and industry--Bibliographies
Bibliographies--Church and labor >> See: Church and labor--Bibliography
Bibliographies--Church and social problems >> See: Church and social problems--Bibliography
Bibliographies--Emigration and Immigration >> See: Church work with immigrants--Bibliographies
Bibliographies--Emigration and Immigration >> See: Emigration and immigration--Bibliographies
Bibliographies--Ethnicity >> See: Ethnicity--Bibliographies
Bibliographies--Housing >> See: Housing--Bibliographies
Bibliographies--Industrialization >> See: Industrialization--Bibliographies
Bibliographies--Industry--Social Responsibility >> See: Industry--Social responsibility--Bibliography
Bibliographies--Social action >> See: Social action--

Bibliographies
Bibliographies--Social change and church >> See: Social change and church--Bibliographies
Bibliographies--Social problems >> See: Social problems--Bibliography
Bibliographies--Socialism >> See: Socialism--Bibliographies
Bibliographies--Society and Church >> See: Society and church--Bibliography
Bibliographies--Sociology and religion >> See: Sociology and religion--Bibliography
Big churches >> See further: City churches; Downtown churches
Big churches 1881, 3372, 3633, 4252, 6259, 7545, 8214, 8269, 8327, 8437, 8624, 9099, 9294, 12345, 13985, 14757, 15301, 15629, 15668, 17179, 17814, 18676, 19116
--Fiction 12792
--Germany 5904
Binghamton (New York)
--Religious and ecclesiastical institutions--History 14134
Birmingham (Alabama)
--Race relations 17668
--Religion--History 14228
--Religious and ecclesiastical institutions 8001, 9107, 9658, 12459, 12494, 13287, 15117
--Social conditions 8791, 9120
Birmingham (England)
--Church history 13465
--History 13635
--Religion 18113, 18481
--Religious and ecclesiastical institutions 2975, 7210, 9770, 18145, 18713
--Social conditions 8085
Birth control 14212, 15909
Black Churchmen's Ecumenical Institute 10219
Black clergy >> See: African American clergy
Black Jews >> See: African American Jews
Black Manifesto 11164, 11195, 11258, 11406, 11425, 11439, 11494, 11512, 11549, 11592, 11597, 11702
Black Muslims >> See further: Muslim Americans
Black Muslims 4278, 7506, 7896, 8221, 8388, 8417, 8596, 8812, 9129, 9188, 9270, 9283, 9318, 9328, 9445, 9757, 9913, 9914, 10132, 10235, 11378, 11884, 12035, 12563, 13077, 13198, 14022, 15688, 16314, 16654, 16661, 18591, 18613, 18955
--Bibliographies 17813
--Biography 10751, 18427
--History 16899, 17050, 17170, 18427, 18717
--Periodicals 15030
Black nationalism 9129, 10749, 11595, 12109, 12351, 12435, 12606, 13964, 14022, 16610
--History 6651, 14763
Black power 9332, 9755, 10185, 10258, 10373, 10422, 10452, 10663, 10687, 10888, 10905, 10997, 11104, 11107, 11124, 11156, 11238, 11406, 11542, 11575, 11702, 12008, 12351, 12484, 12851, 13489, 13608
--History 15311, 16786, 18737
Black studies 13793
Black theology >> See further: Theology, Liberation theology, African Americans
Black theology 4752, 10373, 10452, 11238, 11542, 11616, 11720, 11721, 12109, 12203, 12802, 12918, 13339, 13489, 13697, 14058, 17475, 17880

Black theology (cont.)
--Great Britain 18953, 19346
--History 13277, 13490, 15311, 16786, 16787, 16880
--South Africa 17562
Black United Fund Movement 15225
Black women >> See: African American women
Blacks >> See further: African Americans
Blacks
--Attitudes 12642
--Economic conditions 15900
--England 10472, 17764, 19346
--Great Britain 7329, 8858, 10653, 11339, 12185, 13788, 14494, 15328, 16992, 18923
--Religion 12185, 12642
--South Africa 7350, 12642, 13327, 13734, 13735, 13828, 15430, 16229, 17026, 17562
--South Africa--Social conditions 13828
Blacks--United States >> See: African Americans
Blackstone Rangers (Chicago, Illinois) 9890, 10836
Bladensburg (Maryland)
--Religious and ecclesiastical institutions 5685
Block clubs >> See: Neighborhoods
Bloomington (Illinois)
--Religious and ecclesiastical institutions 5407
Blue collar workers >> See: Social status and religion; Social classes; Religion and labor; Labor and laboring classes; Church and industry; Church work with skilled labor; Church work with the unemployed
Boblingen (Germany)
--Social conditions 16010
Bogota (Colombia)
--Religious and ecclesiastical institutions 17996
Boise (Idaho)
--Religious and ecclesiastical institutions 8270
Bolivia
--Religious life and customs 14862
Bombay (India)
--Religious and ecclesiastical institutions 6685, 12496, 13584, 14263, 14530, 14814, 17748
--Social conditions 4621, 4622, 14970, 16041, 16396
Bombay Urban Industrial League for Development (Bombay, India) 11676, 13584, 14530, 14970, 15627, 16006
Bonn (Germany)
--Religious and ecclesiastical institutions 18193
Bordeaux (France)
--Religious and ecclesiastical institutions 6831, 7092
Boston (Massachusetts)
--Biography 921
--Buildings, structures, etc. 13225
--Church history 16985
--Economic conditions--History 13658
--Ethnic relations 1885, 1896, 5017, 6095
--Ethnic relations--History 14432
--Fiction 4364
--History 3585, 6516, 9633, 12774
--Moral conditions 242, 1301
--Race relations 9436, 13318, 13345, 13502
--Religion 5, 2228
--Religious and ecclesiastical institutions 31, 35, 42, 55, 97, 98, 100, 119, 127, 143, 163, 182,

206, 210, 225, 312, 387, 445, 468, 541, 543, 794, 921, 924, 1053, 1110, 1127, 1128, 1242, 1303, 1322, 1503, 1521, 1537, 1551, 1656, 1683, 1695, 1924, 2862, 2952, 3136, 3261, 3424, 3561, 3773, 3834, 3963, 5205, 5263, 5625, 5636, 5735, 5840, 5844, 6110, 6265, 6647, 6996, 7063, 7514, 7540, 8025, 8441, 8650, 9482, 10572, 10932, 11409, 12793, 12960, 13176, 13387, 13660, 14089, 15004, 15112, 15242, 15994, 16542, 16745, 16914, 17550, 17557, 17661, 17774, 18194, 18515, 18607

Boston (Mass.) (cont.)
--Religious and ecclesiastical institutions--History 670, 990, 1802, 4344, 5293, 5637, 5770, 6035, 13351, 13403, 13606, 13658, 14355, 14770, 14933, 15234, 15284, 17092, 17548, 17577
--Religious life and customs 12314
--Social conditions 214, 464, 534, 631, 986, 1038, 1216, 1301, 1615, 1676, 1885, 2058, 2167, 2351, 2870, 3584, 5017, 8429, 9092, 10431, 11329, 12844, 13208, 13345, 13892, 15545, 15935, 16611, 18607
--Social conditions--History 8613, 8631, 12194, 14235

Boston Affirmations 13855

Boston Baptist Social Union 794

Boston City Missionary Society 9744
--History 5892

Boston Industrial Mission 11762, 13854, 14221

Boston Missionary and Church Extension Society (Methodist) 3089

Boston Seamen's Friend Society
>> See further: Merchant seamen

Boston Seamen's Friend Society 98

Boston Society for the Moral and Religious Instruction of the Poor 48

Botswana Christian Council 12080

Boulder (Colorado)
--Religious and ecclesiastical institutions 5149

Bowery (New York, NY)
--Religious and ecclesiastical institutions 1707, 1808, 2442, 2947, 3030, 3978, 4714, 6373, 7503, 10476, 11742, 17201
--Religious and ecclesiastical institutions--Fiction 3496
--Religious and ecclesiastical institutions--History 3698, 4981
--Social conditions 1792, 1958, 2034, 2055, 2087, 2783, 4637, 4981, 5520, 5667, 6037, 6172, 6336, 6373, 6680, 8293, 9648, 15395, 16067, 17588

Bowery Young Men's Institute (New York, NY) 1792

Bowling Green (Ohio)
--Religious and ecclesiastical institutions 6312

Boycott 1278, 7120, 7347, 14229, 14404, 14416, 14873, 14879, 15280, 16003
--History 7006, 16871, 17668

Boys 412, 444, 1660, 1721, 1804, 1879, 1991, 1997, 2055, 2162, 2402, 2506, 2602, 2614, 2655, 2687, 2722, 2744, 2773, 2872, 2877, 2906, 2977, 5619, 6362, 6615
--Fiction 1180, 5744

Boys (cont.)
--History 6047, 13936, 16658
--Kenya 15625
Brasilia (Brazil)
--Religion 12504
--Social conditions 10603
Brattleboro (Vermont)
--Religious and ecclesiastical institutions--History 13823
Brazil
--History 4582
--Religion 15367, 19189
--Religious and ecclesiastical institutions 15585, 16162
--Religious life and customs 15620
--Social conditions 9635, 11735, 12053, 15628
Brazzaville (Congo)
--Religious and ecclesiastical institutions 10676
Bresee Institute (Los Angeles, California) 17440, 19167
Brethren in Christ
--History 18054
Bridgeport (Connecticut)
--Religious and ecclesiastical institutions 5622
--Social conditions 14790
Brighton (England)
--Religious and ecclesiastical institutions--History 15844
Brisbane (Australia)
--Social conditions 18265
Bristol (England)
--Social conditions--History 11304
British Columbia (Canada)
--Religious and ecclesiastical institutions 15087
British Council of Churches 5870, 6576, 11692, 12185, 12902, 13787, 13788, 14160, 14902, 14932, 15701, 15743, 15840, 17011, 17339, 17697, 17708, 18847, 18987
British Council of Churches, Social Responsibility Department 7261
Brixton (England)
--Social conditions 17618
Bronx (New York, NY)
--Religion 19231
--Religious and ecclesiastical institutions 5615, 6185, 6940, 7435, 7637, 7980, 8258, 10255, 10339, 11095, 13844, 14346, 14648, 14706, 16272, 16427, 16768, 16927, 17534, 17828, 18248, 18525, 18617
--Religious life and customs 7841
--Social conditions 1726, 4733, 11101, 13422, 15608, 15897
Brooklyn (New York, NY)
--Ethnic relations--History 17493
--Race relations 13059, 15107
--Religion 5229
--Religious and ecclesiastical institutions 74, 429, 441, 454, 628, 697, 698, 977, 1058, 1187, 1938, 1956, 2434, 2851, 2857, 4716, 4982, 5174, 5321, 5441, 5469, 5537, 5629, 6085, 6506, 6708, 6765, 6967, 7552, 8148, 8169, 8531, 8749, 9067, 12991, 13942, 15277, 16659, 18174, 18446
--Religious and ecclesiastical institutions--History 526, 1026, 5544, 6570, 13791, 17162
--Religious and ecclesiastical institutions--Periodicals 3331
--Religious life and customs 19341
--Social conditions 3049, 3194, 5628, 6562, 6766, 8432, 10095, 15804, 18543, 18613
--Social conditions--Fiction 1375
Brooklyn Assistant Society, for Relieving and Advising Sick

and Poor Persons 22
Brooklyn Church and Mission Federation 4514
Brooklyn City Mission 3051
Brotherhood Movement (London, England) 3184, 3185, 4104
Brotherhood of Railroad Trainmen 5230
Brotherhood of the Kingdom
--History 4737
Brownsville (New York, NY)
--Social conditions 11400
Brussels (Belgium)
--History 16057
--Religion 5887
--Religious and ecclesiastical institutions 7785, 7786
--Religious and ecclesiastical institutions--History 6697
--Social conditions 18910
Buddhism 12286, 13011, 16040, 18330, 18379
--Canada 18616
--France 12098, 17679, 19197
--History 14752
--Japan 11778, 13163, 16679, 17340, 18558
--Nepal 16446
--Relations--Christianity 13012
--Sri Lanka 13236
--United States 3004, 4789, 5550, 8128, 10428, 13950, 14295, 16983, 18701
--United States--History 15269
Buenos Aires (Argentina)
--Religious and ecclesiastical institutions 14618
--Social conditions 11337
Buffalo (New York)
--Economic conditions 3820
--History 14148
--Religious and ecclesiastical institutions 1637, 2775, 3672, 3737, 4669, 4776, 5011, 5213, 5567, 6017, 6019, 6219, 7960, 8865, 10159, 13477, 15382
--Religious and ecclesiastical institutions--History 1875, 6096, 10297, 13791, 13863, 14492, 17093
--Religious life and customs 8186, 13099
--Religious life and customs--History 13447, 13863
--Social conditions 1602, 3519, 3943, 10866, 14539
Burkina-Fasso (Upper Volta) 11737
Burlington (Vermont)
--Race relations 5294
--Religious and ecclesiastical institutions 431, 5294, 9837, 10354
--Social conditions 4577
Burnout (psychology) 15553, 18131, 18587, 18711, 19358
Business >> See further: Church work with business people ; Industry; Church and industry; International business enterprises
Business 811, 4020, 4326, 8537, 9174, 11334, 14562
--Great Britain 18547
--History 7244, 18867
--Social aspects 226, 1099, 1145, 1146, 2025, 2728, 3175, 3361, 3448, 3666, 3946, 4137, 4154, 7095, 8238, 8962, 9575, 10040, 10141, 12188, 13279, 13752, 15371, 15959, 18008, 18621, 18917, 19056
--Social aspects--Chile 13833
--Social aspects--England 1763
Business consultants 12561
--United States 15650
Business ethics >> See further: Industry--Social Responsibility
Business ethics 267, 572, 1145, 1886, 2012, 2128, 2167, 2314,

2383, 2791, 3039, 3212, 3533, 3539, 3648, 3718, 3768, 4011, 4082, 4125, 4289, 6131, 6442, 6582, 7282, 7296, 7305, 7662, 9575, 9588, 9616, 10065, 10889, 11069, 11307, 11675, 12102, 12326, 12449, 12551, 12640, 12790, 12804, 13073, 13175, 13332, 13481, 13921, 14038, 14266, 14470, 14495, 14590, 15364, 15451, 15644, 15735, 16141, 16273, 16352, 16439, 16556, 16570, 16810, 17061, 17065, 17204, 17284, 17456, 17518, 17532, 18030, 18098, 18375, 18430, 18930, 18995, 19112

Business ethics (cont.)
--Bibliographies 11711, 12913, 13460, 13918, 14177, 14291, 14438, 16500
--Canada 16050
--England 1480, 4286, 9073
--Fiction 8326
--History 18101

Busses >> See: Church busses

Butler (Pennsylvania)
--Social conditions 18308

Butte (Montana)
--Religious and ecclesiastical institutions 7708

Byzantine Ruthenian Catholic Church in the United States of America 17096

Cairo (Egypt)
--History 12039, 16627
--Social conditions 19193

Cairo (Illinois)
--Race relations 12165

Calcutta (India)
--Religious and ecclesiastical institutions 12520, 14318, 15376, 15377, 16425, 17405
--Social conditions 453, 8782, 11155, 11508, 12089, 12899, 13834, 14488, 15423, 15431, 15432, 15465, 15883, 16126, 16373, 16396, 16411, 16590, 16678, 17376, 17410, 17411, 17554, 17584, 17909, 18448, 18508

Calgary (Canada)
--Church history 13478

Cambridge (Massachusetts)
--Religious and ecclesiastical institutions 4924
--Social conditions 6920

Cambridge University (England) 1928

Camden (New Jersey)
--Religious and ecclesiastical institutions 8053

Cameroon
--Social conditions 18042

Camp meetings >> See further: Revivals

Camp meetings 74, 3561, 18373

Campus Crusade for Christ 12475

Campus ministry >> See: Chaplains, university; Church work with students; Students

Canada
--Religion 18044
--Religious and ecclesiastical institutions 18260, 19258
--Religious life and customs--Bibliographies 13169
--Social conditions 2824, 5454, 10818, 17370

Canadian Conference of Mennonite Brethren 14612

Canadian Information Sharing Service 13794

Canadian Urban Training (Toronto, Canada) 9774

Canberra (Australia)
--Religious and ecclesiastical institutions 16504, 16509, 16564, 16761

Canton (Ohio)
--Religious and ecclesiastical institutions 6259, 6789, 10914
--Social conditions 10378
Cape Cod (Massachusetts)
--Religious and ecclesiastical institutions 9402
Cape Town (South Africa)
--Religious and ecclesiastical institutions 14209
Capitalism 754, 780, 3193, 3550, 4426, 5014, 8992, 9148, 15058, 18954, 19248
Capitalism and Christianity 509, 599, 706, 2682, 3273, 3314, 3587, 3766, 4010, 4081, 4232, 4274, 4277, 4315, 4361, 4365, 4423, 4495, 4980, 5000, 5152, 5660, 6150, 6339, 6659, 7437, 8033, 9673, 9978, 12759, 13629, 13771, 13773, 14252, 16351, 16621, 16707, 16785, 16840, 17504, 17678, 17831, 18003, 18610
--England 2930, 19252
--Great Britain 5139, 18547
--History 3798, 4161, 5530, 12163, 17358, 17835, 18101, 18139, 18867
--Periodicals 3107
Carbondale (Pennsylvania)
--Religious life and customs 6801
Cardiff (Wales)
--Religious and ecclesiastical institutions 19090
Career development >> See further: Work; Vocation; Employment problems
Career development 14939
Caricatures and cartoons 5809, 11581, 19095
--History 13943
Cartoons >> See: Caricatures and cartoons
Case method 11334, 12495, 12597, 13400, 14476, 15687, 16463, 16573, 17714
--Bibliographies 14475, 16000, 16435
Case work (social) >> See: Social service; Social workers; Welfare reform; Charity
Catechism 57, 552, 3364, 15674
Cathedral of St. John the Divine (New York, NY) 3723
Cathedrals 851, 1119, 1164, 2384, 2884, 4793, 4968, 7883, 7899, 8586, 9201, 9278, 11320, 13657, 14757, 16202, 16524, 16649
--Australia 16004
--England 11241
--History 5646, 10296, 10297, 12808, 13385, 13676, 14185, 17942, 18091
--India 12799, 13503, 15003
Catholic action >> See: Social action--Religious aspects--Catholic
Catholic Church
--Case studies 1252, 1385, 1661, 2089, 2720, 5011, 5494, 5764, 5935, 6024, 6032, 6135, 6164, 6167, 6261, 6314, 6467, 6773, 6972, 7067, 7189, 7295, 7337, 7435, 7494, 7564, 7727, 7951, 7980, 8152, 8286, 8328, 8368, 8442, 9069, 9477, 9480, 10730, 10743, 11806, 12085, 12462, 12808, 13182, 13375, 13398, 13434, 13509, 13530, 13690, 13724, 13737, 13746, 14185, 14210, 14346, 14500, 14542, 14706, 14743, 14795, 15335, 15939, 16027, 16196, 16384, 16398, 17090, 17673, 17695, 17943, 18117, 18446, 18673, 18829, 18989
--Case studies--Bibliographies 5025, 5029

Catholic Church (cont.)
--Clergy >> See: City clergy--Catholic sources
--Congresses 908
--Doctrines 3687, 4629, 5187, 10650, 12628, 15034, 15918, 16248, 16568, 16741, 17443, 17552, 18349, 18394, 18683, 18897
--Education 3991, 9034, 9974, 10975, 11650, 15137, 15577, 17638
--History 1398, 2049, 2331, 3325, 3916, 4000, 6076, 6333, 6570, 7659, 8762, 10837, 12658, 12862, 13936, 14355, 15240, 16012, 17512, 18059, 18106, 18258, 18605, 18631, 18816, 19289, 19291, 19338
--History--Periodicals 736
--Liturgy 18035, 19338
--Pastoral theology 1160, 5647, 5749, 5836, 5945, 6722, 7228, 7586, 7597, 9416, 9830, 9869, 10295, 10325, 10436, 11020, 11064, 13036, 13436, 13519, 14399, 14478, 15585, 16677, 17435, 17823, 18351, 18683, 18929, 19272
--Pastoral theology--Congresses 12040
--Pastoral theology--History 15194
--Periodicals 262, 289, 354, 1425, 1737, 2327, 3019, 3194, 4234, 4270, 4782, 5132, 10733, 11109, 11654, 12787, 13147, 15232, 16151
--Pronouncements, policies 9805, 14671, 17083, 17297, 17552, 17889, 18619
--Pronouncements, policies--History 4944, 8674, 17267
--Sermons 1152
--Social teaching >> See further: Encyclicals, papal
--Social teaching 502, 841, 1043, 1069, 1402, 1680, 1943, 2074, 2668, 3114, 3274, 3275, 3330, 3364, 3457, 3766, 3849, 4012, 4089, 4152, 4289, 4405, 4468, 4512, 4610, 4865, 4883, 4969, 5019, 5050, 5055, 5179, 5188, 5281, 5612, 5885, 6352, 6895, 7621, 8095, 8163, 8178, 8198, 9152, 9169, 9176, 9196, 9203, 9229, 9377, 9594, 9901, 11112, 11553, 12742, 13812, 14252, 15857, 16099, 16100, 16179, 16248, 16249, 16269, 16342, 16474, 16720, 16994, 17002, 17091, 17371, 17434, 17467, 17630, 17664, 17718, 17788, 17815, 17889, 18077, 18108, 18250, 18292, 18408, 18456, 18478, 18548, 18647, 18782, 18897, 18964, 19248
--Social teaching--History 5319, 5385, 5745, 6472, 7746, 8387, 9248, 10670, 11222, 11813, 14019, 16178, 16340, 17235, 18667, 18835, 19239
Catholic Church (Africa) 8243, 10753, 11926, 13036, 13361, 13377, 14298, 15079, 15531, 15974, 16366, 16733, 16734, 17373, 17506, 19158, 19240
Catholic Church (Argentina) 5403, 16720, 18302, 19081
Catholic Church (Asia) 14399, 16612
Catholic Church (Australia) 14723, 15472
Catholic Church (Austria) 6279, 6830, 7188, 8343, 11636, 15179, 16083, 16747
--History 16345, 17571
Catholic Church (Belgium) 6888, 7312, 7784, 7785, 7786, 12824
--History 6697, 7563, 16057

Catholic Church (Bolivia) 14862
Catholic Church (Brazil) 8881, 10316, 11735, 14555, 15532, 16189, 16909, 17224, 18171, 19189
--History 4582, 15194, 15585, 17874, 18175
Catholic Church (Canada) 3137, 3958, 4957, 7050, 13194, 13690, 14776, 16125, 16151, 17507, 17630
--Bibliographies 6030
--History 3110, 13478, 13993, 14750, 15779
Catholic Church (Chile) 10439, 13040, 15173, 17959
Catholic Church (Colombia) 10232, 12056, 17066
--History 17242
Catholic Church (Costa Rica) 13429
Catholic Church (El Salvador) 16025, 17156
Catholic Church (England) 401, 8328, 8668, 11857, 13092, 15085, 15317, 17616, 18083
Catholic church (Europe) 2359, 5483, 7597, 8767, 9477
Catholic Church (France) 502, 5109, 5867, 5935, 6293, 6504, 6603, 6609, 6653, 6711, 7071, 7135, 7633, 7740, 7989, 8077, 8273, 8360, 8492, 8719, 10299, 10976, 11004, 11020, 11582, 11933, 12820, 14720, 15421, 15666, 16760, 17107, 18286, 19233
--Congresses 12040
--History 5224, 6947, 10118, 13438, 13673
Catholic Church (Germany) 996, 2074, 2380, 2634, 3520, 4579, 5610, 5647, 5749, 5764, 6597, 6722, 7586, 8114, 8150, 8207, 8977, 9869, 10210, 10295, 11063, 11463, 13331, 13786, 14623, 14880, 15563, 16190, 17123, 17401, 18228, 19343
--History 2524, 2741, 3484, 3713, 4806, 4861, 5623, 11553, 12249, 13593, 13926, 14141, 14504, 14708, 14868, 14941, 15420, 15878, 16167, 16409, 16410, 16606, 17161, 17481, 19078
--Periodicals 1101, 5477
Catholic Church (Great Britain) 9504, 16164, 17678, 18989
--History 10386
Catholic Church (India) 16907
Catholic Church (Ireland) 9128, 9504, 13292, 14238, 14262, 17420
--History 17895
Catholic Church (Italy) 6191, 10127, 11112, 11285, 12628, 12775, 13428, 13776, 14114, 14457, 14908, 16535, 17268, 18394
--History 12797, 13885, 14908, 17329, 18032, 18283
Catholic Church (Ivory Coast) 16188
Catholic Church (Japan) 4291, 16909
Catholic Church (Kenya) 11979, 16138, 18240
Catholic Church (Korea) 14710, 18485
Catholic Church (Latin America) 8505, 9416, 10325, 12004, 12852, 13516, 14233, 14711, 15620, 15773, 16165, 16205, 17055, 17289, 17434, 18250
Catholic Church (Lithuania)
--History 16646
Catholic Church (Mexico) 4853
Catholic Church (Netherlands) 2017, 3674, 6803, 7089, 15672, 18894

--History 14567, 16694, 17194, 17976, 19059
Catholic Church (Niger) 16188
Catholic Church (Poland) 12275, 12896, 16638, 17907
--History 13670, 14009
Catholic Church (Spain) 1258, 4261, 4893, 4919, 7147, 8073, 11183, 15443, 16011, 16811
--History 7838, 14918, 16674, 17313, 18364
Catholic Church (Sweden) 17330
Catholic Church (Switzerland)
--History 11023
Catholic Church (United States) 6490, 7075, 8700, 13177, 14251, 17090, 18135
--Congresses 14357
--History 6861, 7284, 11435, 12249, 13596, 13814, 14870, 14907, 17312, 17547, 18091, 18106, 18723, 18835, 19066, 19247
Catholic Church (Yugoslavia)
--History 7052
Catholic Church (Zaire) 15531, 16909
Catholic Church (Zambia) 14210, 14998
Catholic Church Extension Society of Canada 16151
Catholic Committee on Urban Ministry 13146, 13147, 13471, 14568, 14620
Catholic Council on Working Life (Chicago, Illinois) 5553, 8380
Catholic Housing Aid Society (England) 12810
Catholic Interracial Council of New York City 7051
Catholic Theological Society of America 11910
Catholic Worker Movement 4546, 4580, 4655, 4782, 4826, 4827, 5802, 5888, 6023, 6148, 8229, 8700, 12231, 13201, 13851, 14626, 14634, 15785, 16905, 17289, 19261, 19280
--Archives 4270, 4655
--Bibliographies 17825
--Biography 14606
--Germany 18855
--History 7694, 10683, 12801, 12974, 13774, 14917, 15192, 15676, 15800, 16336, 16370, 16385, 16746, 16772, 17124, 17225, 17390, 17745, 18024, 18456, 18467, 18835, 19104, 19277, 19229, 19286
--Periodicals 4270
Catholics--African American >> See: African American Catholics
Cedar Rapids (Iowa)
--Religious and ecclesiastical institutions 5407
Celebration >> See: Public worship
Censorship 4705
--History 10713
Census
--Statistics 660, 919, 3819, 3991, 5685, 6902, 7550, 7551, 7841, 8051, 8879, 16251, 16348, 16386
--Statistics--England 1972, 9683
--United States 1206, 2467, 3165, 4115, 5061
Center for Applied Research in the Apostolate (Washington, DC) 11315, 16386
Center for Church and Community Ministries (Chicago, Illinois) 19195, 19202
Center for Human Action, Research, and Training (Cincinnati, Ohio) 10735
Center for Intercultural Formation (New York, NY)

8811
Center for Parish Development (Naperville, Illinois) 13832, 14159, 14458
Center for Pastoral and Social Ministry (Notre Dame, Indiana) 15144
Center for Urban Education (Portland, Oregon) 10736
Center for Urban Encounter (Minneapolis, Minnesota) 10737
Center for Urban Ministerial Education (Boston, Massachusetts) 17073, 18196, 18731
Center for Urban Policy, Loyola University (Chicago, Illinois) 15445, 15517, 15964, 16201
Center for Urban Theological Studies (Philadelphia, Pennsylvania) 18092
Center of Metropolitan Mission In-service Training (Los Angeles, California) 9783
Central Conference of American Rabbis 4974
--Congresses 4974
Centre de recherches socio-religieuses (Brussels, Belgium) 7784, 7785, 7786
Centre for Christian Studies 14554
Change (psychology) 16063, 16909, 18109, 18223
Change--Religious aspects >> See: Social change; Social change and church
Chaplains, hospital 17, 99, 2941, 7701, 7856, 15118, 16195, 16625, 18651
Chaplains, industrial >> See further: Church and industry; Merchant seamen--Missions and Charities; Priest workers
Chaplains, industrial 5812, 6328, 6484, 6638, 9316, 9895, 13666
--Africa 12280
--Australia 14053, 15145
--Biography 14154
--Canada 6898, 7374, 12042, 12500, 13382, 16050
--Congresses 7103, 14245
--England 5232, 5376, 6851, 7016, 7226, 8557, 8978, 11861, 11964, 13405, 14245, 15309, 16109, 16552, 17585, 17746, 18445, 18553, 18793, 18936
--Europe 11254, 16089
--France--Congresses 13275
--Great Britain 5352, 10036, 14851, 15440
--History 6448, 13323
--Italy 14457
--Korea 14273, 14685
--New Zealand 14053
--Periodicals 7937
--Scotland 12024
--Training 6382, 6567, 11829, 15309, 15440
--United States 6643, 6798, 6885, 6994, 7096, 7103, 7142, 7179, 8097, 11276, 14686, 16422, 18253, 18474
--United States--Case studies 4924, 6124, 8818, 10397, 11299, 12347, 13806, 16296, 17674
Chaplains, military 14372, 18599
Chaplains, police 7856, 16683
--England 3846
Chaplains, prison >> See further: Church work with prisoners
Chaplains, prison 139, 306, 2138, 6440, 7413, 8416, 11228, 13455, 14518, 14613, 14645, 16333, 16908, 17008, 17214, 17489, 17619, 18050, 18355, 18507, 19235
--England 10263, 16923, 18028

Chaplains, prison (cont.)
--Great Britain 18027
--Poland 19070
Chaplains, recreational 12644
Chaplains, university 9886, 11515, 19118
Charities
--England--History 14103
--Organizations, etc. 46, 447, 498, 617, 640, 795, 825, 998, 1175, 1200, 1408, 1800, 1941, 1953, 2340, 2358, 2422, 2697, 3434, 3470, 3567, 3740, 4086, 5033, 5655, 5679, 6159, 6453, 6624, 6690, 7394, 7688, 7782, 7919, 8223, 8239, 9143, 9376, 13526, 14740, 14923
--Organizations, etc.--Bibliographies 3363
--Organizations, etc.--Great Britain 14103
--Organizations, etc.--Handbooks 681, 3194, 16894
--Organizations, etc.--Lutheran >> See: Inner mission
--Religious--Organizations, etc. 18, 22, 24, 34, 56, 123, 452, 682, 1120, 1269, 1535, 1548, 1619, 1638, 2085, 2644, 2844, 3152, 3911, 4065, 4514, 4810, 5844, 6121, 6593, 6690, 7879, 10094, 10347, 10843, 11506, 12632, 13019, 17086, 17593, 18242, 18545, 18962
Charity
--Canada 17370
--Canada--History 14300, 18242
--England 72, 73, 165, 553, 582, 891, 1153, 3626, 9379, 9902, 13619, 17087
--England--History 15, 840, 913, 1403, 2464, 4661
--Europe--History 234
--Fiction 158
--France 1307
--Germany >> See further: Inner mission
--Germany 664, 1509
--Germany--History 17409
--Great Britain 187, 216, 474, 498, 998, 1358, 2422, 8459, 9934
--Great Britain--History 14923, 16252
--India 14318, 16425, 17405
--Mexico 2172
--Organization, etc.--History 13337
--Organizations, etc. 1492, 12220, 14342
--Periodicals 664, 795, 894, 1207, 1408, 1527, 2358, 3261
--Philippines 16965
--Protestant >> See further: Charity--United States--Protestant
--Protestant 449
--Religious aspects--Catholic 73
--Sermons 14, 38, 61, 96, 115, 224, 267, 506, 1083, 1136, 1220, 1285, 1305, 1407, 2445, 3394, 3843, 4198, 4572, 18214
--United States 156, 204, 275, 447, 640, 681, 723, 744, 822, 839, 917, 963, 1099, 1106, 1175, 1184, 1192, 1194, 1200, 1223, 1267, 1296, 1343, 1412, 1527, 1595, 1696, 1715, 1790, 1799, 1800, 1834, 1838, 1843, 1915, 1953, 2154, 2165, 2299, 2340, 2373, 2418, 2514, 2551, 2567, 2580, 2595, 3470, 3850, 4086, 4201, 4826, 4835, 6263, 8103, 10874, 13526, 13809, 16894, 18007, 18498, 18621, 19347
--United States--Catholic 309, 721, 793, 1269, 1550, 1878, 2283, 2430, 2558, 2712, 3080, 3194, 3334, 3442, 4079, 4227,

6058, 6062, 6120, 7782, 10094, 10398, 12742, 13858, 15154, 15541, 16220, 16378, 17105, 17548, 18897
Charity (cont.)
--United States--Catholic--History 17577
--United States--History 1988, 5940, 6639, 6833, 7634, 8694, 8728, 9537, 9691, 10487, 10495, 11904, 12194, 12893, 13907, 14334, 16252, 17830, 18564, 18614, 19293
--United States--Jewish 2064, 2085, 2246, 2992, 3391, 3519, 3607, 5371, 5652, 6864, 9471, 9936, 12883, 13563, 13858, 14796, 16723, 17593
--United States--Jewish--History 8909
--United States--Protestant 14, 28, 31, 38, 90, 266, 290, 309, 312, 346, 384, 412, 445, 451, 504, 530, 533, 562, 605, 636, 674, 695, 747, 825, 843, 848, 880, 883, 1001, 1060, 1220, 1274, 1275, 1277, 1290, 1433, 1448, 1488, 1546, 1571, 1586, 1602, 1716, 1769, 1949, 2044, 2156, 2199, 2211, 2249, 2437, 2438, 2445, 2755, 2790, 3023, 4084, 4368, 4431, 4434, 4503, 4880, 5324, 5541, 5655, 6121, 6269, 6631, 7613, 8312, 9143, 9419, 9690, 9832, 10227, 12183, 12632, 13858, 14021, 14040, 14999, 15925, 16408, 17086, 17120, 17498, 18072
--United States--Protestant--History 7093, 12753, 13337
Charleston (South Carolina)
--Religion--History 15560
--Religious and ecclesiastical institutions 10175
--Religious and ecclesiastical institutions--History 13485
--Social life and customs--History 5972
Charleston (West Virginia)
--Religious and ecclesiastical institutions 5640, 6260, 9573, 11383, 11618
Charleston Port Society for Promoting the Gospel Among Seamen 85
Charlestown (Massachusetts)
--Religious and ecclesiastical institutions 319
Charlotte (North Carolina)
--Religious and ecclesiastical institutions 5696, 7914, 12863
--Religious and ecclesiastical institutions--History 5829
--Social conditions 15209
Chartist Movement 725, 3075, 3744, 5733, 8899, 10145, 12587, 15901
--History 2933, 7379, 16080, 18274
Chatham (New Jersey)
--Religious and ecclesiastical institutions 6377
Chattanooga (Tennessee)
--Religious and ecclesiastical institutions 8213
Chautauqua Movement 812
Chauvinism and jingoism >> See further: Xenophobia
Chauvinism and jingoism 1147, 1226, 1394, 2077, 2176
Chemnitz (Germany)
--Social conditions 1383
Chester (Pennsylvania)
--Social conditions 18335
Chicago (Illinois)
--Economic conditions 14184, 16375
--Ethnic relations 915, 4034, 4107, 4155, 5925, 6999, 9624, 12268, 15858, 16873

Chicago (Illinois) (cont.)
--Ethnic relations--History 15445, 15508, 15858
--Fiction 4439
--History 8254, 14783, 15813, 15858, 17719, 18867, 19356
--Moral conditions 1333, 1957, 2562, 19006
--Moral conditions--History 15132
--Periodicals 7651, 10759
--Race relations 3393, 4149, 5368, 5594, 6061, 6142, 7066, 7970, 8736, 8986, 9292, 9503, 9547, 10131, 10523, 11244, 12851, 14896, 16374, 17613, 17668
--Race relations--History 10587
--Religion 1205, 2056, 2237, 3290, 3891, 8351, 9463
--Religious and ecclesiastical institutions 421, 756, 1118, 1354, 1505, 1576, 1639, 1661, 1697, 1703, 1738, 2045, 2175, 2588, 2651, 2661, 2690, 2739, 2932, 3095, 3367, 3393, 3543, 3548, 3619, 3800, 3935, 4007, 4102, 4116, 4136, 4233, 4368, 4409, 4418, 4441, 4517, 4525, 4644, 4723, 4734, 4741, 4743, 4796, 4869, 4905, 4909, 4910, 5012, 5041, 5063, 5068, 5076, 5330, 5367, 5411, 5424, 5546, 5692, 5750, 5813, 5875, 6084, 6100, 6256, 6304, 6395, 6404, 6510, 6594, 6648, 6671, 6698, 6870, 6872, 6936, 7009, 7064, 7308, 7359, 7418, 7624, 7700, 7788, 7848, 7881, 7992, 8165, 8200, 8358, 8440, 8507, 8508, 8545, 8591, 8698, 8827, 8848, 8878, 8934, 9013, 9028, 9213, 9236, 9337, 9350, 9389, 9390, 9425, 9447, 9469, 9500, 9501, 9519, 9545, 9585, 9607, 9653, 9679, 9745, 9765, 9769, 9789, 9871, 9878, 9927, 9932, 10004, 10151, 10224, 10252, 10260, 10267, 10449, 10523, 10618, 10669, 10759, 10902, 11065, 11405, 11514, 11624, 11750, 11763, 12003, 12173, 12232, 12293, 12382, 12409, 12599, 12689, 12764, 12816, 13035, 13313, 13375, 13413, 13419, 13445, 13588, 13665, 13896, 14106, 14140, 14159, 14202, 14222, 14281, 14313, 14359, 14451, 14495, 14497, 14556, 14817, 14833, 14888, 14896, 14897, 14901, 14930, 14954, 15144, 15461, 15882, 16027, 16398, 16702, 16828, 17099, 17216, 17472, 17542, 17555, 17836, 18012, 18078, 18269, 18465, 18494, 18569, 18644, 18722, 18745, 18763, 18824, 18986, 19179, 19180, 19194, 19200, 19227, 19268, 19285
--Religious and ecclesiastical institutions--Bibliographies 16163
--Religious and ecclesiastical institutions--History 1294, 2444, 2585, 3325, 3407, 3822, 4000, 4111, 4264, 4337, 4570, 4911, 4975, 5096, 5267, 5736, 6106, 6322, 6409, 6588, 7624, 8421, 9721, 11237, 12862, 13346, 13698, 14412, 14594, 14869, 14870, 15132, 15887, 15970, 16012, 16636, 16986, 17942, 18359, 19289, 19291, 19344, 19356
--Religious life and customs 8510, 8745
--Social conditions 493, 1107, 1211, 1298, 1349, 1365, 1430, 1498, 1689, 1703, 1713, 2013, 2303, 2374, 2475, 2556, 2564,

2765, 3163, 3393, 3872, 3932, 4018, 4033, 4149, 4216, 4407, 4614, 4900, 5008, 5368, 5413, 5671, 5766, 6099, 6435, 6672, 6741, 6858, 7039, 7583, 7882, 7971, 8137, 8286, 8367, 8745, 8764, 8822, 8877, 8925, 8991, 9207, 9222, 9387, 9778, 9860, 9922, 10143, 10234, 10307, 10331, 10631, 10827, 10982, 11035, 11042, 11088, 11153, 11168, 11209, 11296, 11314, 11359, 11612, 11859, 11907, 12418, 12428, 12576, 12870, 13117, 13237, 13348, 13363, 13617, 14386, 14496, 14560, 15069, 15479, 15598, 15738, 16070, 16873, 17544, 18369, 18381, 18489, 18650, 18789, 18846, 18961, 19014, 19222, 19257, 19267, 19327

Chicago (Illinois) (cont.)

--Social conditions--Fiction 2048

--Social conditions--History 4515, 5940, 7010, 8806, 11961, 12822, 13805, 13907, 18382, 18554, 18624, 19293

--Social life and customs 6005

Chicago Christian Industrial League (Chicago, Illinois) 4722, 6568

Chicago Christian Missionary Society 1738

Chicago City Missionary Society 7418, 7964, 9292, 9786

Chicago Commons 1689

--History 4570

Chicago Fellowship of Friends 18644

Chicago Hebrew Mission (Chicago, Illinois) 2585

Chicago Home Missionary and Church Extension Society 9500

Chicago Home Missionary and Church Extension Society of the Methodist Episcopal Church 743, 3290

Chicago Parish Development Project 14322

Chicago Relief and Aid Society 1184

Chicago World's Columbia Exposition

--History 18382

Child abuse 14409, 15879, 19064

Child labor 138, 412, 562, 886, 1113, 1850, 1965, 1973, 2219, 2240, 2341, 2410, 2425, 2506, 2626, 2627, 2655, 2656, 2744, 3785, 4437, 4754, 4889, 5282, 12413

--England 149, 5180

--History 14044

--Kenya 15625

Child rearing 999, 6864, 6953, 9117, 12829, 17241, 17615, 19004

Children >> See further: City children; Church work with children; African American children; Parent and child; Boys; Girls; Orphans and orphanages

Children

--Bibliographies 9313

--Institutional care 6953, 13305

--Institutional care--History 12299

--Institutional care--India 14530

--Philippines 18922

--Social conditions 1973, 3819, 5073, 5157, 10170, 16065

--Sri Lanka 15724

Children, African American >> See: African American children

Children's Aid Society (New York, NY) 346, 504, 605, 1275

--History 1274

Children's Defense Fund 18477
Children's literature 1976, 4738, 4817, 7758, 7878, 7973, 8157, 8406, 8509, 8687, 8710, 11445, 13559, 18414, 19098
Chile
--Social conditions 17959
China
--Religion--History 14752
--Social conditions 17728
--Social conditions--History 10691, 12362
Chinese
--Canada 18241
--Missions to--France 14657
Chinese American churches 2690, 5868, 6564, 6630, 6635, 7894, 16789, 17461
Chinese American Episcopalians 16647
Chinese American families 5195, 18440
Chinese American Methodists 5868, 7057, 12487, 16565
Chinese American youth 6894
Chinese Americans
--Ethnic identity 11800
--Housing 6345
--Missions to 657, 1544, 1724, 1741, 2482, 2544, 3392, 3662, 4196, 4353, 4377, 4402, 5195, 6095, 6564, 7894, 12487, 13843, 14313, 15180, 16565, 16647, 17253, 17461, 18440, 19049
--Religion 17680, 19304
--Social conditions 1229, 5659, 6016, 6894, 11568, 12859, 13782, 14622
--Social life and customs 1140
Chinese Canadians
--Missions to 5857
Christ House (Washington, DC) 18533
Christelijk Nationaal Vakberbond in Nederland 5852, 5853
Christian Action Ministry Academy (Chicago, Illinois) 11756
Christian Activities Council (Hartford, Connecticut) 18097
Christian and Missionary Alliance 14334, 16729, 16838
--Case studies 17245, 18692
--Periodicals 2493
Christian and Missionary Alliance (Zaire) 17908
Christian biography >> See: City clergy--Biography
Christian Century Foundation 517, 6017, 6018
Christian Church of Thailand 14163
Christian Churches and Churches of Christ
--Case studies 19300, 19314, 19331, 19336
--Periodicals 19313
Christian Commission for Camp and Defense Communities 5154
Christian communities >> See further: Basic Christian communities; Church and community; Community
Christian communities 6256, 7951, 10087, 10307, 11565, 12173, 12390, 12434, 12949, 13255, 13449, 13992, 15031, 15084, 15302, 15354, 15856, 16231, 16463, 16784, 17594, 18197, 18397, 18637, 18864, 19276, 19282
--Africa 14603, 17506
--Australia 19322
--England 15407
--Europe 12123
--France 15093, 17413
--Great Britain 13395, 14079, 14167, 15337

Christian communities (cont.)
--Italy 15361, 15389
--Latin America 17432
--New Guinea 17382
--Scotland 15029, 18166
Christian Conciliation Services 17663
Christian Conference of Asia 12795, 13874, 14171, 14215, 14232, 14247, 14443, 14444, 14449, 14482, 14972, 15188, 15384, 15509, 15761, 15942, 17572, 18938
Christian Council of Ghana 6636
Christian Council of Kenya 13023
Christian Council of Nigeria 10262
Christian Council of Rhodesia 11034, 11986
Christian Council of Tanzania 15572
Christian Council of the Gold Coast 6117
Christian councils >> See: (councils for specific nations or area, e.g, All-African Christian Council, British Council of Churches, etc.)
Christian education >> See further: Education and church; Religious education; Sunday schools; Theological education
Christian education
--Administration 2874, 3125, 3940, 3959, 4591, 5767, 6869, 18971
--Case studies 4912, 5758
--Catholic 289, 1974, 5592, 10975, 14165, 14817, 15106, 16276, 17638
--Church of the Brethren 9327
--Congregational 19256
--Curriculum 2689, 3940, 9032, 9077, 9786, 10801, 12719, 12950, 15149, 15670, 15885, 17454, 18768, 18775
--Curriculum--Adult 3103, 3182, 3430, 3431, 3605, 3776, 5934, 6282, 6441, 6482, 8670, 8777, 9484, 12912, 13521, 14340, 14898, 15253, 18552, 18824, 18843, 19325
--Curriculum--Bibliographies 16489
--Curriculum--Children 313, 2929, 5946, 6028, 6436, 6449, 6458, 6480, 6505, 6548, 6558, 6590, 8406, 8560, 8561, 8573, 8687, 8710, 8714, 8732, 8873, 8874, 8950, 9281, 9327, 9859, 11159, 11812, 11917, 12553, 12569, 12951, 15952, 17638, 19256
--Curriculum--Youth 2929, 3885, 3945, 6463, 6479, 6500, 8757, 8761, 8950, 9208, 9723, 9905, 10715, 10777, 10984, 12400, 12729, 15952, 18931, 19271
--England--History 18009
--Episcopal 9984
--History 10395, 18779
--India 17454
--Lutheran 5934, 11812, 11917, 12400, 12553, 12569, 12719, 12950, 12951, 14898, 16574
--Methodist 2152, 3945, 3959, 4325, 4591, 8685, 9723
--Periodicals 289, 2094
--Philosophy 2287, 2478, 2856, 2995, 3422, 3741, 4325, 4716, 5066, 7975, 8394, 8589, 9103, 9144, 9329, 9771, 9801, 9897, 9962, 10022, 10024, 10034, 10091, 10099, 10115, 10555, 10644, 10897, 15276, 16574, 17538, 17776, 17919, 18674, 18843, 18886, 18919, 18934, 18970, 18971, 18976, 18992,

19021, 19033
Christian education (cont.)
--Presbyterian 5946, 6282, 7905, 10555, 10618, 12729
--Protestant 2311, 2856, 3047, 3182, 3422, 4220, 6441, 6458, 6463, 6479, 6480, 6482, 6500, 6505, 6548, 6869, 8670, 8710, 8714, 8732, 8757, 9144, 18975
--Research 3479, 4441, 7309, 7882, 7905, 10618, 10897, 14165, 17298, 18828, 18970
--Southern Baptist 6028, 13906, 15885, 17538, 18674
--United Church of Christ 8573, 9032, 9077, 9499, 9786, 10715, 14340
Christian Endeavor 978, 1208, 1283, 1454, 1612, 1881
Christian ethics >> See: Ethics, Christian
Christian giving 14, 37, 447, 449, 530, 695, 744, 795, 880, 917, 1001, 1060, 1106, 1412, 1546, 1952, 2053, 2154, 2211, 2249, 2358, 2437, 2438, 2514, 2551, 2567, 3023, 3394, 3572, 4503, 4880, 5541, 6263, 7511, 7613, 9832, 10398, 12805, 14999, 15541, 16220, 17120, 17498, 17856, 18072, 18498, 18685
--England 165, 891, 9185
--Great Britain 187
--Great Britain--History 14923
--History 581, 1769, 6833, 7774, 8694, 10487, 11904
Christian Herald 18801
--History 2435, 3698, 3727
Christian Herald Association (New York, NY) 577
Christian Herald Magazine 1835
Christian Industrial League 1552
Christian Labor Association 5475
Christian Labor Union 531, 563, 573, 578, 637, 1086
Christian Labour Association of Canada 13757, 14077, 14863, 15912
Christian Reformed Church 12429, 17931
Christian schools >> See: Private schools
Christian Science 2143, 4626, 9191, 12960, 17174
--History 10285
Christian sects >> See: Sects
Christian Social Union (England) 1279, 1367, 1440, 1751, 2233, 3354
--History 1925, 3127, 8871
--Periodicals 1047
Christian Social Union (United States) 1125, 1350, 1366
Christian socialism >> See: Socialism, Christian
Christian Socialist Fellowship 1786, 1897
Christian Socialist League 1028
Christian Socialist Movement 8585, 9394
--History 8418
--Periodicals 8681
Christian union 1759, 1830, 2986, 3092, 3134, 5007, 5361, 7891, 10353, 12531, 19198
--England 10773
--History 11707
--United States 4363, 4604, 11796, 12816
Christian Workers Fellowship
--Periodicals 7269
Christian Workers' Union 5914
Christianity and culture 18683
Christianity and economics >> See: Economics and Christianity; Economics--Religious aspects
Christianity and justice >> See: Justice--Biblical teaching; Justice--Religious aspects

Christianity and other religions >> See: Religious pluralism
Christianity and other religions--Islam >> See: Islam--Relations--Christianity
Christianity and other religions--Judaism >> See: Jewish Christians; Jews--Relations--Christianity
Christianity and politics >> See: Politics and Christianity
Christianity and socialism >> See: Socialism and Christianity
Christianity in literature >> See: Churches in literature, Protestantism in literature
Christianization >> See further: Americanization
Christianization 1724, 2647, 3042, 3278, 3299, 3439, 3486, 3652, 3781, 4473, 5931, 6917
--History 6323
Christians (Disciples of Christ) >> See: Christian Church (Disciples of Christ)
Christians for Socialism (Latin America) 13804, 14356
Christians for Urban Justice (Boston, Massachusetts) 10819, 16776
Christmas 1131, 1329, 5667, 11314, 16017, 18436
Church >> See further: Mission of the church
Church administration >> See: Church management
Church and community >> See further: Community organization
Church and community 2705, 4114, 4898, 5004, 6282, 7688, 10598, 12286, 14290, 14484, 15826, 15969, 16134, 16139, 18635, 18856
--Africa 11937, 14210, 14604, 16998
--American Baptist sources--(1900 to 1917) 2901, 2998
--American Baptist sources--(1918 to 1944) 4771
--American Baptist sources--(1945 to 1959) 6404, 6607, 6703, 6890, 7326
--American Baptist sources--(1960 to 1969) 8473, 8890, 11061
--American Baptist sources--(1980 to 1991) 17448, 18052, 18202
--Australia 16004
--Austria 13915
--Baptist sources--(1960 to 1969) 19269
--Baptist sources--(1970 to 1979) 13414
--Bibliographies 9726, 12603, 12757, 16163
--Brethren sources--(1970 to 1979) 14146
--Catholic sources--(1918 to 1944) 3094
--Catholic sources--(1945 to 1959) 6034, 6664, 6689, 7161, 7687
--Catholic sources--(1960 to 1969) 7783, 8769, 9382, 9553
--Catholic sources--(1970 to 1979) 12780, 14552, 14630, 14934
--Catholic sources--(1980 to 1991) 15504
--Catholic sources--History 17325
--Church of England sources--(1980 to 1991) 17626, 18273
--Congregational Christian sources--(1945 to 1959) 6291
--Congregational sources--(1900 to 1917) 1947
--Congresses 4479, 4656, 7521, 16537, 18870, 18925
--Disciple of Christ sources--(1918 to 1944) 5143
--Disciples of Christ sources--

(1918 to 1944) 3548, 4755
Church and community (cont.)
--Disciples of Christ sources--(1945 to 1959) 5884, 6943
--England 5479, 13076, 13307, 13787, 14389, 15537, 15691, 17234, 17339
--Episcopal sources--(1918 to 1944) 3087, 3483, 4290, 4721, 4923
--Episcopal sources--(1945 to 1959) 7573, 7693
--Episcopal sources--(1970 to 1979) 11685, 13010
--Episcopal sources--(1980 to 1991) 19021, 19326
--Europe 15427
--Evangelical and Reformed Church sources--(1945 to 1959) 7122
--Evangelical Protestant sources--(1970 to 1979) 15096
--Evangelical Protestant sources--(1980 to 1991) 15769, 16563, 17774, 18569
--Federal Council sources--(1900 to 1917) 2758
--Federal Council sources--(1918 to 1944) 3789, 4730
--France 7430
--Germany 7683, 9520, 12061, 16644
--Great Britain 12567, 16308, 18751, 18752, 18987
--History 13452
--India 14732
--Ireland 14262
--Lutheran sources--(1945 to 1959) 7348
--Lutheran sources--(1960 to 1969) 7766, 8303, 8484, 8495, 8891, 9307, 11085, 11527
--Lutheran sources--(1970 to 1979) 12192
--Lutheran sources--(1980 to 1991) 17020, 18525
--Mennonite sources--(1960 to 1969) 7952
--Methodist sources--(1900 to 1917) 2835, 2952
--Methodist sources--(1918 to 1944) 3100, 3230, 3372, 4229, 4461, 4810
--Methodist sources--(1945 to 1959) 6107, 6256, 7529
--Methodist sources--(1960 to 1969) 7857, 8008, 8239, 8270, 8650, 10236, 11292
--Methodist sources--(1970 to 1979) 11911, 13603, 14802, 14894
--Methodist sources--(1980 to 1991) 17212
--Methodist sources--(1980 to 1991) 16466, 16743, 17168, 17261, 18493, 19073
--Mexico 18678
--NCCCUSA sources--(1960 to 1969) 7879
--NCCCUSA sources--(1970 to 1979) 11859
--Periodicals 5302, 19195
--Philippines 11928, 11968
--Presbyterian sources--(1918 to 1944) 4425, 4994
--Presbyterian sources--(1945 to 1959) 5446, 5718, 5753, 6426, 6435
--Presbyterian sources--(1960 to 1969) 9386
--Presbyterian sources--(1970 to 1979) 12349, 15014
--Presbyterian sources--(1980 to 1991) 17035, 19202
--Protestant sources--(1900 to 1917) 2518, 2559, 2716
--Protestant sources--(1918 to 1944) 3069, 3209, 3223, 3232, 3384, 3414, 3676, 3835, 3898, 4258, 4459, 4763, 5033

Church and community (cont.)
--Protestant sources--(1945 to 1959) 3567, 5655, 6159, 6237, 6294, 6399, 6508, 6632, 6952, 6961, 7224, 7545
--Protestant sources--(1960 to 1969) 8164, 8338, 9300, 11184, 11543
--Protestant sources--(1970 to 1979) 12005, 14086, 14539, 14840, 15125
--Protestant sources--(1980 to 1991) 15888, 16275, 17782, 17993, 18078, 18170, 18388, 18425, 18670, 18818, 18819, 18920, 18925, 19025, 19194, 19203
--Protestant sources--Bibliographies 16435
--Protestant sources--Congresses 6294
--Protestant sources--History 4510, 4746, 13452
--Scotland 7547, 11945, 12998
--Southern Baptist sources--(1918 to 1944) 3258, 3702
--Southern Baptist sources--(1945 to 1959) 5921
--Southern Baptist sources--(1960 to 1969) 9356, 9366, 10322
--Southern Baptist sources--(1970 to 1979) 11704, 12796, 14011
--Southern Baptist sources--(1980 to 1991) 16218, 16537, 16935, 17605, 17884, 18018, 18134
--Unitarian sources--(1960 to 1969) 9596
--United Church of Christ sources--(1945 to 1959) 5751
--United Church of Christ sources--(1960 to 1969) 10138
--United Church of Christ sources--(1980 to 1991) 15514
--Venezuela 17118
--World Council of Churches sources--(1945 to 1959) 5418
--World Council of Churches sources--(1970 to 1979) 14059, 14303
Church and economics >> See: Economics--Religious aspects; Economics and Christianity
Church and industry >> See further: Chaplains, industrial; Industrial relations--Church involvement; Church and labor; Church work with business people
Church and industry 2122, 3120, 3193, 3351, 3395, 5249, 5301, 5583, 6188, 6645, 7152, 7397, 7748, 7918, 8035, 8043, 8857, 9394, 10042, 10550, 10649, 11520, 12170, 12590, 12596, 13940, 14312, 15958, 16260, 16470, 17200, 17280, 17284, 17484, 17487, 17518, 17532, 17969, 19076
--Africa 7180, 7767, 7768, 8315, 8348, 10290, 11674, 12175, 12745, 12963, 13941
--Africa--Bibliographies 11501
--Africa--Congresses 12846
--Africa--Periodicals 7750
--American Baptist sources--(1875 to 1899) 672
--American Baptist sources--(1900 to 1917) 672, 2164, 2437, 2511, 2771, 2894, 3023
--American Baptist sources--(1918 to 1944) 3117, 3303, 3968, 3982, 3983, 4154
--American Baptist sources--(1945 to 1959) 6414
--American Baptist sources--(1960 to 1969) 9714, 11562
--American Baptist sources--(1970 to 1979) 12811, 12984
--American Baptist sources--(1980 to 1991) 17608

Church and industry (cont.)
--Asia 7180, 7240, 7821, 9352, 9667, 10318, 10333, 10761, 10811, 11748, 11932, 12624, 12839, 13708, 13941, 14029, 16612
--Asia--Bibliographies 11502
--Australia 8470, 11352, 11531, 11532, 11560, 13708, 15656
--Austria 7042, 8343, 8369, 11636
--Baptist sources--(1918 to 1944) 3868
--Baptist sources--(1960 to 1969) 11264
--Belgium 7785
--Belgium--History 13463
--Belgium--Liège 7784
--Bibliographies 4074, 4366, 4384, 5289, 5803, 11501, 11502, 11503, 11830, 13671, 14291, 14438, 14490, 14517, 14702, 14882, 15539, 15598, 16919
--Brethren sources--(1918 to 1944) 4976
--Canada 3149, 7072, 8110, 12500, 12645, 13267, 13958
--Catholic sources--(1800 to 1874) 13209
--Catholic sources--(1875 to 1899) 706, 815, 13209
--Catholic sources--(1900 to 1917) 2010, 2130, 13398
--Catholic sources--(1918 to 1944) 3140, 3264, 3274, 3330, 3611, 3724, 3792, 3832, 3849, 3887, 3984, 4089, 4289, 4306, 4440, 4668, 5050, 5052, 11192
--Catholic sources--(1945 to 1959) 5561, 5745, 5983, 6154, 6196, 6841, 7278, 7335
--Catholic sources--(1960 to 1969) 7071, 7784, 7792, 7969, 8077, 8161, 8528, 9108, 9982, 9983, 10027, 10056, 11524, 11589, 11636, 12820
--Catholic sources--(1970 to 1979) 11706, 13168, 14144, 14379, 14710, 15034, 15168, 16219, 18840
--Catholic sources--(1980 to 1991) 17788, 18286, 18647, 18964
--Catholic sources--Archives 2095
--Catholic sources--History 4824, 6812, 12249
--Church of England sources--(1918 to 1944) 3121, 3126, 3268, 4157, 4297, 10999
--Church of England sources--(1945 to 1959) 5538, 6811, 7226, 7517, 7736
--Church of England sources--(1960 to 1969) 8130, 8557, 9116, 9938, 9988, 10168, 10612
--Church of England sources--(1970 to 1979) 12407, 12524, 13508, 13586
--Church of England sources--(1980 to 1991) 15507, 16552, 16810, 16872, 17143, 17752, 17772, 18445, 18540, 18793
--Church of England sources--History 16579
--Colombia 11982, 18756
--Congregational Christian sources--(1918 to 1944) 4855
--Congregational Christian sources--(1945 to 1959) 6757, 6965
--Congregational sources--(1800 to 1874) 247, 299
--Congregational sources--(1875 to 1899) 786, 790, 1249
--Congregational sources--(1900 to 1917) 2025, 2054, 2181, 2275, 2506, 2554
--Congregational sources--(1918 to 1944) 3513
--Congregational sources--

History 9209
Church and industry (cont.)
--Congresses 3597, 3618, 3895, 7240, 10761, 11242, 12745, 13098, 16771, 17621, 17803
--Disciples of Christ sources--(1918 to 1944) 3347
--Dominican Republic 17621
--East Germany 12665, 13448
--Encyclopedias 1995
--England 334, 379, 1754, 1763, 1906, 2277, 2593, 3121, 3135, 3168, 3185, 3238, 3293, 3299, 3618, 3624, 3747, 3836, 3855, 4104, 5036, 5074, 5177, 5639, 5978, 5990, 6289, 6469, 7261, 7543, 8266, 8398, 8978, 10467, 10876, 11074, 11242, 11826, 11828, 11964, 12750, 12806, 15103, 15113, 15309, 16259, 17303, 17320, 17377, 17803
--England--History 727, 3510, 10795, 11154, 13880, 14580, 15655
--England--Periodicals 11827, 15905
--Episcopal sources--(1875 to 1899) 1355, 1593
--Episcopal sources--(1900 to 1917) 1973, 2700
--Episcopal sources--(1918 to 1944) 3292, 3678, 3913, 4074, 4382, 4383
--Episcopal sources--(1945 to 1959) 5341, 5968, 5969, 6547, 6587, 7085, 7735
--Episcopal sources--(1960 to 1969) 8311, 9793
--Episcopal sources--(1970 to 1979) 11762, 12101
--Episcopal sources--(1980 to 1991) 15718, 15824, 16019, 16227, 16834, 16951, 17305, 17437
--Episcopal sources--Bibliographies 4366, 4384
--Episcopal sources--Congresses 5341
--Episcopal sources--History 4074, 14377, 14987, 16958
--Europe 3445, 6633, 6998, 7421, 8332, 9030, 10075, 11254, 11459, 11573, 11634, 13708, 15427, 19188
--Europe--Bibliographies 11503
--Evangelical and Reformed Church sources 5000
--Evangelical Protestant sources--(1960 to 1969) 10141
--Evangelical Protestant sources--(1980 to 1991) 19042
--Evangelical Protestant sources--Periodicals 11759
--Federal Council sources--(1900 to 1917) 2220, 2599, 2789
--Federal Council sources--(1918 to 1944) 3102, 3147, 3174, 3216, 3218, 3219, 3220, 3317, 3322, 3447, 3501, 3637, 3648, 3905, 4014, 4137, 4340
--Federal Council sources--(1945 to 1959) 5455, 5456, 5457, 5660
--Fiction >> See further: Industry--Fiction
--Fiction 1017, 1245, 3462
--Finland 8942, 9539, 12223
--France 502, 5846, 6328, 6609, 10976, 11460, 12467
--France--Periodicals 11691
--Friends sources--Congresses 3073
--Friends sources--History 13772
--Germany 2120, 6980, 7254, 7345, 7706, 7978, 8006, 8244, 8305, 8366, 8861, 9000, 9617, 9621, 9894, 10231, 10341, 10409, 10457, 10595, 11360, 12682, 13554, 13589, 14136, 17882, 19163

Church and industry (cont.)
--Germany--Congresses 14240
--Germany--History 17185
--Germany--Periodicals 5477
--Germany (East) 17816
--Ghana 13120
--Great Britain 3149, 3271, 3297, 3314, 3362, 4105, 8316, 9271, 10765, 12407, 12524, 13655, 14914, 15986, 16090, 17678, 18445, 18547, 18793
--Great Britain--History 3842
--History 7388, 7492, 11336, 12146, 12759, 13771, 14769, 18192
--Hong Kong 10411, 13954
--Hong Kong--Periodicals 12158
--India 7235, 8012, 8912, 8953, 9630, 9668, 10201, 10915, 10945, 11978, 12433, 13150, 16006
--India--Congresses 9177
--India--Periodicals 11676
--Ireland 17420, 17727
--Italy 5561, 17235
--Italy--Congresses 7061, 7278
--Italy--History 18032, 18283
--Japan 3263, 5877, 6852, 6874, 6878, 7344, 7875, 9818, 10117, 12340
--Kenya 11673, 12303, 12989, 13590
--Korea 10584, 12265, 12339, 12932, 13308, 14273, 14444, 14685, 14710, 15325, 17176, 17802
--Latin America 13941, 15463
--Lebanon 1625
--Lutheran sources--(1875 to 1899) 1439
--Lutheran sources--(1945 to 1959) 6211, 7068
--Lutheran sources--(1960 to 1969) 10397, 10617, 11239
--Lutheran sources--(1970 to 1979) 12994, 14985
--Lutheran sources--(1980 to 1991) 17306, 18023, 18103
--Mennonite sources--History 14410
--Methodist sources--(1800 to 1874) 12177
--Methodist sources--(1875 to 1899) 1113, 1581
--Methodist sources--(1900 to 1917) 1858, 2256, 2271, 2469
--Methodist sources--(1918 to 1944) 3034, 3149, 3203, 3294, 3307, 3439, 3518, 3575, 3599, 3675, 4011, 4036, 4099, 4190, 4251, 4326, 4346
--Methodist sources--(1945 to 1959) 6798, 7096, 7103, 7142, 7192
--Methodist sources--(1960 to 1969) 8038, 8379, 8438, 9502, 10584
--Methodist sources--(1970 to 1979) 12638, 13299, 13806, 13888, 14229, 15099, 15324
--Methodist sources--(1980 to 1991) 17223, 18889
--Methodist sources--Congresses 7103, 7142, 7965
--Methodist sources--History 3005, 4120, 5429, 15887
--Methodist sources--Periodicals 2525, 15905
--NCCCUSA sources--(1945 to 1959) 6244, 6285, 6286, 6358, 6442, 6540, 6750, 7154, 7662
--NCCCUSA sources--(1960 to 1969) 7934, 8238, 8474, 9588
--NCCCUSA sources--(1970 to 1979) 12251, 12252, 12425, 12590, 12611, 12985
--NCCCUSA sources--(1980 to 1991) 15638
--Netherlands 6803, 8932, 11854
--New Zealand 5394, 13013,

13575, 13576, 14374
Church and industry (cont.)
--Nigeria 7767, 7768
--Periodicals 3196, 3243, 5877, 7153, 7750, 12251, 18831
--Peru 17034
--Philippines 7463, 8774, 10041, 11230, 11757, 12197
--Poland--History 13670, 14009
--Presbyterian sources--(1918 to 1944) 3071, 3267, 3283, 3324, 3329, 3720, 3795, 4558, 4722, 4750, 4774, 4946, 5310
--Presbyterian sources--(1945 to 1959) 5388, 5410, 5513, 6124, 6383, 6549, 6567, 6909
--Presbyterian sources--(1960 to 1969) 7826, 8097, 8706, 11459
--Presbyterian sources--(1970 to 1979) 12059, 12522, 12860, 14937
--Presbyterian sources--(1980 to 1991) 17802
--Presbyterian sources--Bibliographies 5289
--Presbyterian sources--History 5830, 13565
--Protestant sources--(1800 to 1874) 145, 222, 240, 425, 465, 13209
--Protestant sources--(1875 to 1899) 799, 836, 877, 929, 1172, 1203, 1242, 1636, 1644, 1698, 13209, 15157
--Protestant sources--(1900 to 1917) 1784, 1975, 1993, 2002, 2135, 2156, 2330, 2344, 2472, 2484, 2581, 2630, 2728, 2852, 18867
--Protestant sources--(1918 to 1944) 3118, 3139, 3181, 3182, 3199, 3200, 3212, 3239, 3278, 3300, 3313, 3320, 3352, 3353, 3383, 3384, 3389, 3400, 3461, 3468, 3499, 3508, 3594, 3636, 3658, 3668, 3704, 3748, 3755, 3803, 3810, 3812, 3824, 3946, 4026, 4273, 4505, 4590, 4798, 5057, 5081, 5121, 5154, 5155, 5169, 5284, 6346
--Protestant sources--(1945 to 1959) 5714, 5781, 5886, 6250, 6800, 6994, 7095, 7296, 7421, 7543, 7660, 7698
--Protestant sources--(1960 to 1969) 7812, 7949, 7997, 8266, 8910, 9316, 9494, 9662, 9792, 10583, 10604, 10742, 13057, 13760
--Protestant sources--(1970 to 1979) 11712, 12102, 12245, 12306, 12326, 12377, 12394, 12430, 12551, 12595, 12612, 12670, 12695, 12869, 13073, 13114, 13323, 13481, 13572, 13842, 13874, 13891, 14062, 14232, 14482, 14495, 14791, 14873, 14874, 14961, 15162, 15347, 16219, 16339, 18840
--Protestant sources--(1980 to 1991) 16141, 16680, 16849, 17074, 17320, 17505, 17559, 18475, 18720
--Protestant sources--Bibliographies 13573
--Protestant sources--History 3798, 5803, 6964, 7916, 8084, 8536, 12972, 14805, 15775, 17326, 17950, 18836
--Protestant sources--Periodicals 1755, 4451, 7288, 7937, 17378
--Puerto Rico 12869
--Rhodesia 13994
--Scotland 7420, 7547, 11140
--Singapore 12317, 12994
--South Africa 3129, 11462, 12911, 16771, 17316, 17977, 18275
--Southern Baptist sources--(1900 to 1917) 2438

Church and industry (cont.)
--Southern Baptist sources--(1945 to 1959) 6484
--Southern Baptist sources--(1960 to 1969) 9437
--Spain 4893, 8126, 14027
--Sweden--History 16045
--Taiwan 12522, 17564, 17565
--Taiwan--Periodicals 12694
--Tanzania 15572
--Thailand 14097, 14163
--Unitarian sources--(1800 to 1874) 93, 258
--Unitarian sources--(1875 to 1899) 883
--Unitarian Universalist sources--(1970 to 1979) 12529
--United Church of Christ sources--(1960 to 1969) 8122, 8602, 8799
--United Church of Christ sources--(1970 to 1979) 12059, 13994, 15120
--United Church of Christ sources--(1980 to 1991) 15469
--Wales 13826
--World Council of Churches sources--(1960 to 1969) 8057, 11600, 11629
--World Council of Churches sources--(1970 to 1979) 12225, 12665, 12734, 12819, 12830, 12864, 12880, 13097, 13269, 13294, 13359, 13798, 14444, 14489, 14765
--World Council of Churches sources--(1980 to 1991) 16473, 16792, 17206, 18907
--World Council of Churches sources--Bibliographies 14438
--Yugoslavia 12920
Church and Industry Institute (Winston-Salem, North Carolina) 10742
Church and labor >> See further: Religion and labor; Labor and laboring classes; Church and industry; Church work with skilled labor; Church work with the unemployed; Social status and religion
Church and labor 202, 309, 637, 710, 818, 824, 1014, 1293, 1315, 1563, 1690, 2062, 2129, 2188, 2603, 2645, 2760, 2813, 2846, 2951, 2999, 3058, 3193, 3339, 3380, 3469, 3481, 3525, 3606, 3696, 3878, 3952, 4135, 4181, 4184, 4250, 4566, 4578, 4663, 5230, 5238, 5256, 5499, 5500, 5514, 5556, 5711, 5737, 5994, 6641, 6795, 7133, 7368, 8021, 9780, 9827, 10534, 11675, 13332, 14045, 14376, 14404, 15416, 15600, 15650, 16343, 16470, 17336, 17759, 18246, 18443, 18767, 18827, 19146
--Africa 12175, 12963, 13120, 14858, 15079
--American Baptist sources--(1875 to 1899) 672, 783
--American Baptist sources--(1900 to 1917) 672, 2383, 2457, 2483, 2626, 2672
--American Baptist sources--(1918 to 1944) 4035
--American Baptist sources--(1945 to 1959) 6606
--American Baptist sources--(1970 to 1979) 15221
--American Baptist sources--(1980 to 1991) 17608, 18251
--American Baptist sources--History 11641
--Archives 205, 4561, 16300, 18836
--Argentina 4999, 8984, 11015, 16720, 19081
--Asia 6730, 10010, 10811,

15048, 16532, 16612
Church and labor (cont.)
--Asia--Periodicals 7269
--Australia 8470, 15145, 17015
--Austria 11318, 11362, 11990, 15179, 16747
--Austria--Congresses 18118
--Austria--History 8880, 17571
--Belgium 7312, 8377, 13611, 14311
--Belgium--History 7563, 13463, 15820
--Bibliographies 783, 3103, 5283, 5803, 10867, 11830, 12618, 13008, 13671, 14285, 14668, 14786, 15201, 15598, 15645, 16036, 16919, 17825, 18836
--Bolivia 8780
--Brazil 8543, 8881, 9635, 15628, 17290, 17451, 17509
--Brazil--Congresses 17224
--Brazil--History 4582, 17713, 17874, 18175, 19065
--Brethren sources--(1945 to 1959) 6020
--Canada 317, 462, 1132, 2824, 3137, 3473, 5106, 5161, 5454, 6009, 6010, 6898, 7050, 8066, 9846, 10016, 12626, 12645, 13109, 13133, 13716, 13757, 14077, 14078, 14776, 14863, 15912, 16125, 17394, 17507, 17630
--Canada--History 3110, 8189, 8468, 14213, 14750, 15606, 15779
--Catholic sources--(1800 to 1874) 178, 1152
--Catholic sources--(1875 to 1899) 563, 816, 908, 1009, 1043, 1051, 1069, 1080, 1092, 1244, 1417, 1594, 1680, 5346, 5449, 17468, 18394
--Catholic sources--(1900 to 1917) 1877, 1943, 1983, 2095, 2101, 2634, 2738, 2971, 3020, 6063, 9128, 18394
--Catholic sources--(1918 to 1944) 3076, 3080, 3156, 3273, 3275, 3345, 3364, 3399, 3458, 3480, 3552, 3766, 3767, 3918, 3976, 4151, 4177, 4213, 4277, 4307, 4315, 4328, 4352, 4361, 4423, 4495, 4504, 4516, 4546, 4547, 4580, 4588, 4612, 4613, 4616, 4634, 4642, 4645, 4650, 4654, 4668, 4702, 4795, 4813, 4827, 4865, 4875, 4885, 4886, 4892, 4956, 4965, 4977, 4980, 5013, 5016, 5043, 5050, 5064, 5090, 5130, 5152, 5202, 5272, 5295, 5309, 7437, 9673, 11672, 14908, 16008, 17871
--Catholic sources--(1945 to 1959) 5357, 5453, 5460, 5461, 5467, 5494, 5512, 5518, 5519, 5527, 5551, 5553, 5557, 5560, 5561, 5579, 5670, 5699, 5740, 5740, 5768, 5795, 5802, 5818, 5833, 5851, 5881, 5929, 6144, 6148, 6154, 6224, 6271, 6292, 6316, 6327, 6398, 6472, 6496, 6650, 6661, 6667, 6813, 6910, 6933, 6959, 7058, 7075, 7136, 7147, 7278, 7428, 7556, 7629, 8017, 8700, 8737, 13885
--Catholic sources--(1960 to 1969) 7754, 7778, 7779, 7797, 8161, 8191, 8229, 8265, 8272, 8528, 8829, 9002, 9203, 9377, 9692, 9699, 9764, 9956, 9978, 10025, 10127, 10192, 10226, 10335, 10436, 10479, 10953, 11004, 11010, 11064, 11261, 11478, 11607
--Catholic sources--(1970 to 1979) 12070, 12711, 12855, 13275, 13331, 13598, 13599, 13665, 13934, 14311, 14457, 15034
--Catholic sources--(1980 to 1991)

15366, 15421, 15821, 15857, 15918, 15919, 16100, 16179, 16205, 16210, 16237, 16269, 16312, 16359, 16453, 16535, 16621, 16657, 16681, 16684, 16713, 16760, 16815, 16993, 16994, 17055, 17077, 17106, 17111, 17126, 17135, 17266, 17289, 17394, 17435, 17599, 17616, 17631, 17652, 17700, 17787, 17815, 17831, 18108

Church and labor (cont.)
--Catholic sources--Archives 2095, 4612, 5518
--Catholic sources--Congresses 908, 11064, 16437, 17289
--Catholic sources--History 3842, 4152, 4754, 4944, 5334, 5605, 5650, 5756, 6054, 6318, 6759, 6861, 7285, 7471, 7694, 7863, 8095, 8189, 8387, 8468, 8669, 9901, 10683, 10699, 10702, 10995, 11761, 11886, 12219, 12412, 12722, 12742, 12974, 13774, 13775, 13786, 14746, 14865, 15192, 15353, 15764, 15800, 16178, 16249, 16336, 16340, 16342, 16345, 16370, 16385, 16496, 16746, 16772, 16893, 16905, 16959, 17124, 17235, 17390, 17443, 17547, 17664, 17713, 17718, 17745, 18262, 18266, 18349, 18456, 18896, 18916, 19229, 19239, 19247, 19277, 19286
--Catholic sources--Periodicals 4270, 4581, 4782, 5065, 5553
--Chile 10439, 13040, 13833, 17959
--Church of England sources--(1800 to 1874) 110, 432, 3746, 17842
--Church of England sources--(1875 to 1899) 1345
--Church of England sources--(1900 to 1917) 1829, 2008, 2084, 2276
--Church of England sources--(1918 to 1944) 3054, 3127, 3138, 3764, 5232
--Church of England sources--(1945 to 1959) 5376, 5914, 7226
--Church of England sources--(1960 to 1969) 7868, 8398, 9632, 10174
--Church of England sources--(1970 to 1979) 13405, 13818, 14383, 14535, 15282
--Church of England sources--(1980 to 1991) 15507, 15720, 17142, 17233, 17256, 17262, 17318, 18551, 18553
--Church of England sources--History 3354, 4118, 8466, 8871, 10477
--Colombia 7855, 9112, 12056, 17066, 18756
--Colombia--History 17242
--Congregational Christian sources--(1918 to 1944) 4513, 4548, 4559, 4966
--Congregational Christian sources--(1945 to 1959) 5390, 5674, 5942, 5953, 6350, 6867, 6884
--Congregational sources--(1800 to 1874) 277, 307
--Congregational sources--(1875 to 1899) 566, 740, 751, 752, 765, 784, 1137, 1219, 1249, 1542, 1629
--Congregational sources--(1900 to 1917) 1965, 1970, 2023, 2105, 2507, 2510, 2987
--Congregational sources--(1918 to 1944) 3754, 3769, 3771, 4296
--Congresses 1417, 2412, 3113, 8541, 8961, 9977, 10012,

12486, 12748, 13275, 13482, 14105, 16532
Church and labor (cont.)
--Costa Rica 13429
--Developing countries 5860, 16449
--England 110, 134, 149, 273, 278, 427, 552, 601, 1116, 1189, 1306, 1435, 1466, 1502, 1757, 1821, 2037, 2079, 2101, 2276, 2429, 2492, 2582, 2604, 2708, 2827, 3007, 3282, 3288, 3517, 3695, 4048, 4224, 4225, 5180, 5282, 5377, 6082, 6193, 6475, 7808, 7846, 8268, 8720, 8913, 9097, 9157, 9331, 11857, 12443, 13310, 13638, 14922, 15414, 15498, 17616, 18145, 18178, 18936
--England--Congresses 442
--England--Fiction 2838
--England--History 840, 2061, 3510, 4684, 6591, 7379, 8773, 10477, 12332, 13948, 14103, 15062, 15216, 15505, 15597, 16080, 16705, 17064, 18009
--Episcopal sources--(1800 to 1874) 173, 388
--Episcopal sources--(1875 to 1899) 779, 858, 875, 1120, 1191, 1418, 1554, 1641, 1658, 2416
--Episcopal sources--(1900 to 1917) 2633, 2908, 3043
--Episcopal sources--(1918 to 1944) 3088, 3259, 3450, 3507, 3562, 3677, 4030, 4638, 4924, 19259
--Episcopal sources--(1945 to 1959) 5341, 5580, 6854, 7734
--Episcopal sources--(1960 to 1969) 7883, 7899, 8276, 8938, 9696, 11475
--Episcopal sources--(1970 to 1979) 14731
--Episcopal sources--(1980 to 1991) 15359, 15545, 15570, 15718, 15824, 15898, 15989, 16951, 18069, 18652, 18911, 19326
--Episcopal sources--Biography 4470
--Episcopal sources--Congresses 5341
--Episcopal sources--History 12282, 13491, 15570, 16170, 16958
--Europe 513, 2235, 2911, 4260, 4480, 4616, 5438, 5549, 5657, 5810, 6816, 7238, 7508, 7569, 7754, 7984, 8173, 8558, 8826, 8961, 8972, 9239, 9403, 10046, 10184, 10689, 10762, 11070, 11905, 11980, 12389, 13482, 13836, 18320, 18390, 19028, 19188
--Europe--History 5866, 13835, 15556, 15930
--Evangelical and Reformed Church sources 6465, 9584
--Evangelical Church sources--(1918 to 1944) 4669
--Evangelical Protestant sources--(1900 to 1917) 2900
--Evangelical Protestant sources--(1945 to 1959) 7205
--Evangelical Protestant sources--(1970 to 1979) 12453, 13679, 14435, 15265
--Evangelical Protestant sources--(1980 to 1991) 15869, 17287, 18212, 18773, 18910
--Evangelical Protestant sources--History 17830
--Federal Council sources--(1900 to 1917) 2219, 2341, 2702, 2715
--Federal Council sources--(1918 to 1944) 2219, 3405, 3544, 3693, 4006, 4078, 4302, 4340,

4649, 4889, 5087, 5088, 8017
Church and labor (cont.)
--Federal Council sources--(1945 to 1959) 5458, 5471, 5484, 5590, 5606
--Federal Council sources--Periodicals 2219, 3321
--Fiction 231, 1017, 2838, 10383
--Finland 10412, 10441, 13006, 14085, 15607
--Finland--History 9522, 10430
--France 211, 481, 604, 1775, 4886, 5159, 5387, 5408, 5494, 6223, 6224, 6292, 6328, 6403, 6653, 6719, 6877, 6993, 7071, 7386, 7408, 7532, 7633, 7676, 7757, 8064, 8077, 8115, 8191, 8489, 8647, 9026, 9852, 9856, 10675, 11004, 11005, 11115, 11413, 11460, 11582, 11683, 11725, 12140, 12486, 12820, 12855, 13435, 15421, 15666, 15673, 16264, 16809
--France--Archives 16545
--France--Biography 5141
--France--Congresses 12040, 13275
--France--History 3345, 4506, 4527, 5224, 5799, 7340, 10118, 13438, 13511, 13673, 14390, 14657, 16117, 16186, 16876, 17107, 17711, 18286, 18797, 19233
--Friends sources 3438, 4108, 4493, 4552
--Germany 414, 996, 1383, 1402, 2074, 2315, 2368, 2380, 2415, 2503, 2634, 2701, 3328, 5535, 5842, 6051, 6485, 6933, 6980, 7575, 8150, 8795, 9134, 10409, 10416, 10512, 10595, 11463, 12019, 12361, 12419, 13125, 13331, 13391, 13786, 13890, 13935, 13937, 14379, 14431, 14452, 14623, 14903, 15454, 15487, 15563, 15634, 15832, 15902, 16010, 16098, 16210, 16248, 16450, 16721, 16943, 17027, 17040, 17123, 17193, 17401, 17816, 18055, 18195, 18206, 18855, 19177
--Germany--Bibliographies 14786
--Germany--History 2524, 2741, 3484, 3713, 4806, 4861, 5623, 6569, 13072, 13593, 13926, 14137, 14141, 14504, 14708, 14868, 14941, 15861, 16167, 16410, 16606, 16932, 17161, 17185, 17264, 17409, 17428, 17650, 17651, 18144, 18234, 18266, 18648, 18784, 19241
--Great Britain 433, 1591, 2568, 3381, 3444, 3612, 3791, 3921, 4508, 4843, 5352, 5686, 5870, 6092, 8316, 12090, 12423, 16277, 17707
--Great Britain--History 3370, 8106, 8130, 8400, 14707, 15667
--History 3759, 4161, 4894, 7388, 8419, 12131, 13830, 13887, 14815, 15353, 16068, 16075, 16437, 16766, 17824, 17902, 17905, 18554, 18667, 18836
--Hong Kong 11815, 13545, 13873, 13954, 17676, 18551
--Hungary 4990
--India 2412, 3382, 3587, 6184, 7516
--India--Congresses 9492
--Indonesia. 6531
--Ireland 5713
--Ireland--History 9128, 17895
--Italy 5254, 5561, 6022, 6073, 6619, 7058, 7134, 7241, 7629, 7630, 7947, 8022, 8682, 10127, 10335, 11010, 11112, 11285, 11362, 12775, 13459, 13776, 14371, 15204, 15763, 16535, 18392, 18394

Church and labor (cont.)
--Italy--Congresses 7061, 7278
--Italy--History 11886, 12412, 13885, 15764, 17235, 18032, 18283
--Japan 5877, 6852, 6878, 7209, 7341, 7428, 8236, 8924, 11913, 14849, 18608
--Japan--Congresses 8009
--Japan--History 13578, 13981
--Kenya 11673, 12303, 12989
--Korea 13101, 13230, 14273, 14601, 14685, 14689, 17024, 18485
--Korea--Bibliographies 15201
--Latin America 6050, 8505, 10953, 12852, 13824, 14156, 16166, 16205, 16690, 17055, 17289, 17434, 17642, 18250
--Lithuania--History 16646
--Lutheran sources--(1875 to 1899) 820, 860, 1240, 1588
--Lutheran sources--(1900 to 1917) 1781
--Lutheran sources--(1918 to 1944) 3143
--Lutheran sources--(1945 to 1959) 5532, 5562, 6344, 6880, 7068, 7187
--Lutheran sources--(1960 to 1969) 9612
--Lutheran sources--(1970 to 1979) 12100, 13064, 14085, 14659, 14976, 15035
--Lutheran sources--(1980 to 1991) 17094, 17387, 17701, 18236, 18770, 19301
--Mennonite sources--(1970 to 1979) 14266
--Methodist sources--(1800 to 1874) 178, 495, 4684, 12332
--Methodist sources--(1875 to 1899) 490, 573, 833, 1038, 1077, 1078, 1086, 1278, 14701
--Methodist sources--(1900 to 1917) 1935, 1939, 2253, 2328, 2469, 2571, 2767, 2983, 3041, 13553
--Methodist sources--(1918 to 1944) 3079, 3085, 3166, 3203, 3206, 3246, 3296, 3467, 3490, 3494, 3518, 3532, 3534, 3536, 3574, 3640, 3671, 3799, 4119, 4189, 4584, 4686, 4959, 5135, 5136
--Methodist sources--(1945 to 1959) 5386, 5401, 5491, 5501, 5534, 5608, 6182, 6534, 7179, 7265, 7441, 7472, 7729
--Methodist sources--(1960 to 1969) 9380, 9775, 9796, 9802
--Methodist sources--(1970 to 1979) 12853, 12958, 12981, 13629, 13751, 14229
--Methodist sources--(1980 to 1991) 16371, 17003, 17111, 17132, 17906, 18277, 18366, 19303
--Methodist sources--History 3588, 5069, 5738, 6591, 7220, 8662, 9097, 13065, 13310, 14455, 16656, 18139, 18505, 19262
--Methodist sources--Periodicals 2525
--Mexico 4853
--Mormon sources 7804, 14190
--Nazarene sources--(1970 to 1979) 14095
--NCCCUSA sources--(1945 to 1959) 2219, 5918, 6042, 6138, 6205, 6212, 6213, 6242, 6351, 6465, 6573, 6745, 6762, 6932, 6937, 7083, 7155, 8017
--NCCCUSA sources--(1960 to 1969) 8524, 9078, 9880, 10362, 10503
--NCCCUSA sources--(1970 to 1979) 14023
--NCCCUSA sources--

Periodicals 3321
Church and labor (cont.)
--Netherlands 360, 2017, 3674, 4602, 5851, 5852, 5853, 5865, 6784, 7022, 12720, 13384, 13947
--Netherlands--History 16694, 17194, 17976, 19059
--Nigeria 10262
--Pakistan 12904
--Periodicals 531, 578, 683, 1897, 3243, 3321, 5877, 7178, 15706, 18831, 19329
--Peru 13585
--Philippines 3701, 12264, 13598
--Poland 3379, 16105, 16638, 17430
--Presbyterian sources--(1800 to 1874) 326
--Presbyterian sources--(1875 to 1899) 868, 1181, 1399, 1420
--Presbyterian sources--(1900 to 1917) 1779, 1920, 2052, 2053, 2103, 2173, 2174, 2269, 2270, 2441, 2455, 2456, 2548, 2549, 2660, 2829, 2830, 13110
--Presbyterian sources--(1918 to 1944) 3856, 3874, 4235, 4973, 5178, 5251, 5278, 5290, 5311, 13110
--Presbyterian sources--(1945 to 1959) 5414, 5624, 6382, 6975, 7482
--Presbyterian sources--(1960 to 1969) 9244, 9895, 11604
--Presbyterian sources--(1970 to 1979) 12812, 13244, 14515
--Presbyterian sources--(1980 to 1991) 15608, 15983, 16924
--Presbyterian sources--Congresses 15601
--Presbyterian sources--History 3684, 11915, 15198, 16871
--Protestant sources--(1800 to 1874) 90, 108, 465, 528, 6300
--Protestant sources--(1875 to 1899) 594, 622, 629, 637, 660, 690, 703, 733, 739, 772, 775, 777, 782, 827, 836, 852, 877, 884, 898, 909, 946, 966, 974, 1103, 1129, 1289, 1297, 1328, 1390, 1431, 1455, 1517, 1529, 1644, 1684, 1700, 1712, 4241, 5095, 12924
--Protestant sources--(1900 to 1917) 1899, 2066, 2075, 2088, 2189, 2205, 2216, 2255, 2308, 2326, 2339, 2361, 2364, 2410, 2527, 2555, 2662, 2755, 2796, 2834, 2845, 2847, 2866, 2954, 2980, 12924
--Protestant sources--(1918 to 1944) 3050, 3068, 3103, 3142, 3182, 3198, 3208, 3246, 3332, 3441, 3443, 3493, 3502, 3512, 3560, 3576, 3578, 3617, 3620, 3638, 3644, 3696, 3729, 3731, 3732, 3733, 3745, 3770, 3771, 3786, 3941, 3964, 3987, 4008, 4126, 4167, 4179, 4259, 4272, 4376, 4471, 4590, 4647, 4764, 4859, 5046, 5121, 5175, 5333
--Protestant sources--(1945 to 1959) 4967, 5372, 5463, 5475, 5476, 5496, 5571, 5613, 5616, 5706, 5710, 5768, 5782, 5817, 5908, 6042, 6170, 6200, 6204, 6246, 6485, 6539, 6540, 6917, 7279, 7296, 7306, 7320, 7398, 7522, 7662
--Protestant sources--(1960 to 1969) 7798, 8119, 9778, 10010, 10521, 10578, 11276
--Protestant sources--(1970 to 1979) 11708, 11980, 13305, 13842, 13872, 13937, 14191, 14232, 14416, 14570, 14690, 14873, 14874, 14879, 14939, 15032, 15347
--Protestant sources--(1980 to

1991) 15361, 15389, 15645, 15737, 15797, 15900, 15954, 16143, 16277, 16294, 16442, 16587, 16645, 16785, 16855, 16984, 16988, 17015, 17372, 18016, 18055, 18067, 18195, 18272, 19325
Church and labor (cont.)
Protestant sources--History 3725, 5094, 5803, 6569, 8084, 9874, 11754, 12664, 12943, 12972, 14287, 14652, 14653, 15505, 15726, 16438, 17326, 17327, 17835, 18491, 18836
--Protestant sources--Periodicals 3064, 7288
--Salvation Army sources--(1960 to 1969) 7775
--Scotland 66, 494, 16377, 18036
--Scotland--History 14611, 19323
--Sermons 278, 317, 765, 769, 784, 1038, 1149, 2103, 2548, 3329, 3579, 4072, 7808
--Seventh Day Adventist sources 14415, 17920
--Seventh Day Adventist sources--History 17021
--South Africa 12642, 16771, 17285, 17562, 17977, 18275, 18755
--Southern Baptist sources--(1900 to 1917) 1851, 1865
--Southern Baptist sources--(1918 to 1944) 5082
--Southern Baptist sources--(1945 to 1959) 7479
--Soviet Union 4069
--Spain 1258, 4261, 4693, 4864, 4919, 7372, 7673, 7837, 8073, 8344, 10246, 11183, 11948, 12711, 14237, 15218, 15443, 16811
--Spain--Congresses 16011
--Spain--History 7838, 14551, 14918, 16674, 18364
--Sri Lanka 15853
--Sweden 5724, 6321, 17330
--Sweden--History 12554, 16045, 16360
--Swedenborgian sources 2943
--Switzerland 7638, 14046, 15259
--Switzerland--History 11023, 12660, 13685, 15726, 17656
--Unitarian sources--(1800 to 1874) 107, 233, 317, 448, 533
--Unitarian sources--(1875 to 1899) 636, 691, 979, 1435, 1502, 1591
--Unitarian sources--(1900 to 1917) 1846, 2563, 2677
--United Brethren sources 1704, 2243
--United Church of Christ sources--(1945 to 1959) 7399
--United Church of Christ sources--(1960 to 1969) 8541, 9219, 9418
--United Church of Christ sources--(1970 to 1979) 14069, 14976, 15318
--Wales 18362
--World Council of Churches sources--(1945 to 1959) 5958
--World Council of Churches sources--(1980 to 1991) 16706, 17302, 17344
--Yugoslavia--History 7052
Church and social problems >> See further: Social problems; Judaism and social problems
Church and social problems 967, 1216, 1723, 1839, 2225, 3159, 3316, 4062, 4184, 4657, 6761, 9060, 9399, 10265, 10283, 10594, 10900, 12210, 15475, 15642, 15826, 18017
--Africa 12115, 13023, 14139, 18747
--American Baptist sources--(1900 to 1917) 2164, 2320, 2476,

2541, 2860, 2974
Church and social problems (cont.)
--American Baptist sources--(1960 to 1969) 9510, 11565
--American Baptist sources--(1970 to 1979) 13965
--American Baptist sources--(1980 to 1991) 17448, 17844, 18804
--Argentina 9344, 12936, 19081
--Australia 19358
--Australia--History 12417
--Australia--Periodicals 11768
--Baptist sources--(1800 to1874)155
--Baptist sources--(1900 to 1917) 2151, 2543
--Baptist sources--(1970 to 1979) 12936
--Baptist sources--Periodicals 2433
--Belgium 5794
--Belgium--History 7563
--Bibliographies 266, 5075, 5927, 7199, 7381, 9164, 11016, 13243, 13626, 13794, 15984, 17523, 17524, 18298, 19125, 19215
--Brazil 8543, 16189, 18171
--Brethren sources--(1945 to 1959) 5344
--Brethren sources--(1980 to 1991) 17875
--Canada 3137, 13109, 15393
--Canada--Bibliographies 13794
--Canada--History 13821, 14214, 14739, 14750, 15606, 15779
--Catholic sources--(1800 to 1874) 422, 456, 16164
--Catholic sources--(1875 to 1899) 1417, 5736, 7746, 18394
--Catholic sources--(1900 to 1917) 1989, 2050, 2263, 5736, 7746, 18394
--Catholic sources--(1918 to 1944) 3687, 3984, 4161, 4307, 4436, 4476, 4504, 4642, 4650, 5051, 5187, 5295, 7746, 17871
--Catholic sources--(1945 to 1959) 5498, 5512, 5549, 5665, 5681, 5699, 5794, 6051, 6090, 6154, 6261, 6682, 6741, 7084, 7137, 7524, 7600, 7720
--Catholic sources--(1960 to 1969) 7792, 8272, 8380, 8506, 8831, 9016, 9479, 9481, 9762, 9781, 9978, 10185, 10245, 10271, 10481, 10538, 10731, 10745, 11162
--Catholic sources--(1970 to 1979) 11669, 11990, 12410, 12711, 13109, 13146, 13177, 13331, 13723, 13847, 13852, 13892, 14279, 14311, 14936, 15018, 15034, 15037
--Catholic sources--(1980 to 1991) 15944, 16077, 16099, 16282, 16535, 16612, 16739, 17507, 17599, 17907, 18125, 18408, 18478, 18647, 18747, 18964
--Catholic sources--Congresses 11910
--Catholic sources--History 73, 4754, 5650, 8106, 8387, 9901, 12191, 13774, 14868, 16905, 17552, 18809, 19277
--Catholic sources--Periodicals 1737, 4234, 4581, 5065, 11109
--Chile 13040
--Church of England--History 4118
--Church of England sources--(1800 to 1874) 11546
--Church of England sources--(1875 to 1899) 871, 927, 1036, 1443
--Church of England sources--(1900 to 1917) 2505
--Church of England sources--(1918 to 1944) 3229, 3402, 3719, 3845, 4141, 4239, 4247, 4417, 5129, 10999

Church and social problems (cont.)
--Church of England sources--(1945 to 1959) 5393, 5437
--Church of England sources--(1960 to 1969) 9227
--Church of England sources--(1980 to 1991) 16546, 16730, 16802, 16810, 17281, 17858, 18013, 18217, 19052
--Church of England sources--History 8690
--Church of England sources--Periodicals 4159, 8384
--Church of the Brethren sources--(1980 to 1991) 17022
--Congregational Christian sources--(1918 to 1944) 4900
--Congregational Christian sources--(1945 to 1959) 6057, 6061, 7165
--Congregational sources--(1800 to 1874) 17766
--Congregational sources--(1875 to 1899) 576, 767, 781, 1022, 1044, 1066, 1137, 1204, 1587, 1674, 1936
--Congregational sources--(1900 to 1917) 2021, 2176
--Congregational sources--(1918 to 1944) 3529, 3615, 3754, 4283
--Congregational sources--History 5134, 6923, 13283
--Congresses 982, 6856
--Disciples of Christ sources--(1970 to 1979) 12953
--Disciples of Christ sources--Periodicals 3210, 4573
--Encyclopedias 1995
--England 73, 971, 1751, 2391, 2574, 2593, 3227, 4286, 4492, 5219, 5778, 5878, 8154, 15155, 17722, 18863
--England--History 10906, 12715, 16155, 16174
--Episcopal sources--(1875 to 1899) 875, 954, 992, 1082, 1418, 1491, 1659, 13929, 16364
--Episcopal sources--(1900 to 1917) 2513, 3043, 13929, 16364
--Episcopal sources--(1918 to 1944) 3276, 3302, 3326, 4097
--Episcopal sources--(1945 to 1959) 5821, 6222, 6595, 6754, 6854, 6876
--Episcopal sources--(1960 to 1969) 9309, 10113, 10712, 11483
--Episcopal sources--(1970 to 1979) 11976, 13831, 13855, 14119, 14777
--Episcopal sources--(1980 to 1991) 15787, 15788, 15816, 16148, 17159, 17724, 17732, 19326
--Episcopal sources--History 4322, 5197, 12282, 13491
--Europe 5483, 5810, 7117, 7984, 8610
--Evangelical and Reformed Church sources--(1918 to 1944) 5085, 5896
--Evangelical and Reformed Church sources--(1945 to 1959) 7122
--Evangelical Protestant sources--(1960 to 1969) 10141, 11394
--Evangelical Protestant sources--(1970 to 1979) 12482, 12489, 12600, 13191, 13364, 14166, 14628, 14771, 15230, 15285
--Evangelical Protestant sources--(1980 to 1991) 15683, 16015, 16032, 16060, 16517, 17462, 18930, 19006, 19204, 19226
--Evangelical Protestant sources--History 14334
--Evangelical Protestant sources--Periodicals 12325

Church and social problems (cont.)
--Federal Council sources--(1918 to 1944) 3131, 3427, 3706, 3710, 3955, 4047, 4475, 4777, 4954, 5203
--Fiction 8756
--Finland 10441, 11880, 13006, 14085
--France 5935, 7617, 15778, 16760
--France--History 6947, 9610, 18286
--Friends sources--History 18101
--Germany 218, 1630, 2368, 5535, 6051, 6682, 7186, 7706, 7978, 8150, 8949, 11835, 13068, 13331, 13566, 13786, 14121, 14379, 14785, 16114, 18433, 18648
--Germany--History 6569, 10432, 15741, 17161, 17264
--Germany--Periodicals 3195
--Great Britain 3314, 3390, 4130, 7084, 12567, 14902, 15986, 16858, 17427
--Handbooks 4842
--History 5778, 8674, 17098
--India 13691, 14194, 15594
--Italy 16535
--Japan 12511
--Latin America 9479, 16165
--Lithuania--History 16646
--Lutheran sources--(1875 to 1899) 1588, 1589
--Lutheran sources--(1900 to 1917) 2309, 2350, 2935
--Lutheran sources--(1918 to 1944) 3911, 4952
--Lutheran sources--(1945 to 1959) 5535, 6121, 6347, 7130
--Lutheran sources--(1960 to 1969) 7753, 8424, 8580, 11603
--Lutheran sources--(1970 to 1979) 12316, 12516, 14898, 14910, 15256
--Lutheran sources--Bibliographies 11606
--Lutheran sources--History 4719, 14137
--Melanesia 17515
--Mennonite sources--(1945 to 1959) 7325
--Mennonite sources--(1960 to 1969) 10641, 10721
--Mennonite sources--(1970 to 1979) 11902, 12737, 14715
--Mennonite sources--(1980 to 1991) 16069, 16464, 16559
--Mennonite sources--History 15592
--Methodist sources--(1800 to 1874) 4699, 12749, 14945
--Methodist sources--(1875 to 1899) 614, 933, 950, 1238, 1702
--Methodist sources--(1900 to 1917) 1758, 1782, 1888, 1912, 1969, 2019, 2271, 2345, 2365, 2887, 2917, 13553, 14744
--Methodist sources--(1918 to 1944) 2474, 3099, 3100, 3101, 3132, 3408, 3532, 3536, 3671, 3781, 3800, 3981, 4056, 4061, 4129, 4231, 4347, 4449, 4851, 4887
--Methodist sources--(1945 to 1959) 6053, 6107, 6394, 6512, 6846
--Methodist sources--(1960 to 1969) 10005, 11551, 11596
--Methodist sources--(1970 to 1979) 11703, 13138, 13186, 13313, 13700, 13980
--Methodist sources--(1980 to 1991) 15991, 16247, 16466, 16615, 16686, 17067, 17215, 18531, 19174
--Methodist sources--History 8096, 13235, 14214, 16656
--Methodist sources--Periodicals

4310
Church and social problems (cont.)
--Nazarene sources--(1970 to 1979) 14095
--Nazarene sources--(1980 to 1991) 16168
--NCCCUSA sources--(1945 to 1959) 6007, 6442, 6958, 7148
--NCCCUSA sources--(1960 to 1969) 7879, 7977, 8490, 9080, 9669, 10013, 11092
--Netherlands 2017, 13947, 15794
--Netherlands--History 6245, 19059
--Orthodox Eastern Church sources 6033
--Pentecostal sources 12936
--Periodicals 1370, 4573, 8380, 19329
--Peru 13585
--Philippines 11928, 12636, 12679
--Poland 17907
--Presbyterian sources--(1800 to 1874) 326
--Presbyterian sources--(1875 to 1899) 1539
--Presbyterian sources--(1900 to 1917) 1920, 2659
--Presbyterian sources--(1918 to 1944) 3155
--Presbyterian sources--(1945 to 1959) 5721, 6169, 6282, 6616
--Presbyterian sources--(1960 to 1969) 8049, 8159, 8622, 9543, 10135, 10258, 12189
--Presbyterian sources--(1970 to 1979) 11810, 12184, 12629, 13904, 14336
--Presbyterian sources--(1980 to 1991) 1739, 18327, 18360, 19198, 19202
--Presbyterian sources--History 6385, 6822, 12699
--Presbyterian sources--Periodicals 2257, 3266
--Protestant sources--(1800 to 1874) 78, 142, 167, 217, 284, 402, 403, 425, 449, 7199, 7853, 8990, 10495, 11904, 12774, 15132
--Protestant sources--(1875 to 1899) 606, 625, 713, 733, 766, 775, 834, 850, 856, 878, 884, 982, 1098, 1105, 1218, 1297, 1359, 1376, 1446, 1471, 1558, 1559, 1610, 1615, 7010, 10797, 13497
--Protestant sources--(1900 to 1917) 1740, 1789, 1963, 2093, 2118, 2195, 2214, 2218, 2238, 2389, 2408, 2423, 2473, 2744, 2753, 2755, 2794, 2826, 2852, 2967, 3002, 8209, 10797, 18506
--Protestant sources--(1918 to 1944) 2218, 3000, 3056, 3090, 3182, 3366, 3403, 3596, 3664, 3680, 3742, 3749, 3761, 3774, 3775, 3790, 3802, 3809, 3937, 3964, 3970, 3971, 4001, 4162, 4199, 4236, 4387, 4538, 4658, 4662, 4717, 4801, 4871, 5185, 5285, 6735, 7381, 8209, 13015
--Protestant sources--(1945 to 1959) 5372, 5653, 5673, 5702, 6136, 6237, 6505, 6518, 6690, 7608, 7731, 8209
--Protestant sources--(1960 to 1969) 7864, 7949, 8039, 8237, 8338, 9564, 9583, 9620, 9767, 10043, 10063, 10081, 10211, 10276, 10671, 10827, 10930, 11032, 11066, 11437, 12689
--Protestant sources--(1970 to 1979) 12082, 13019, 13216, 13418, 13453, 14526, 14569, 14757, 14995, 17301
--Protestant sources--(1980 to 1991) 15489, 15632, 16076,

16171, 16408, 16444, 17000, 17422, 17619
Church and social problems (cont.)
--Protestant sources--History 2691, 5693, 7853, 10606, 13127, 13231, 13961, 14287, 17835
--Protestant sources--Periodicals 2195, 2718, 3107, 4916, 7964, 10759, 11722
--Reformed Church in America sources--(1960 to 1969) 10809, 11196
--Salvation Army sources--(1960 to 1969) 7775
--Salvation Army sources--History 12627
--Scotland 9652, 17898
--Seventh Day Adventist sources 17556
--Seventh Day Adventist sources--History 17920
--Southern Baptist sources--(1900 to 1917) 2132, 2733, 2937
--Southern Baptist sources--(1918 to 1944) 3993, 4393, 4485, 4659
--Southern Baptist sources--(1960 to 1969) 9366, 9823, 10310, 10951, 11078, 11547, 11580
--Southern Baptist sources--(1970 to 1979) 11895, 11938, 12132, 13003
--Southern Baptist sources--(1980 to 1991) 16327, 16460, 16548
--Southern Baptist sources--Bibliographies 11016
--Southern Baptist sources--History 8308, 10586, 12926
--Spain 1258, 4261, 4893, 4919, 7372, 7837, 10301, 12711, 15218, 16811, 17431
--Spain--Congresses 16011
--Spain--History 7838, 14918, 17052, 18364
--Sweden 5724, 8872, 17330
--Switzerland 5423
--Switzerland--History 15726
--Unitarian sources--(1875 to 1899) 720, 806
--Unitarian sources--(1900 to 1917) 1768, 2346, 2569, 2640
--Unitarian sources--(1960 to 1969) 8424, 9596
--United Church of Christ sources--(1960 to 1969) 8750, 9265, 9405, 11468, 11529
--United Church of Christ sources--(1970 to 1979) 12471, 12680
--United Church of Christ sources--(1980 to 1991) 15358, 18984
--Universalist sources 285
--World Council of Churches sources--(1980 to 1991) 16791, 19149
Church and society >> See: Society and church Society and religion
Church and state 209, 438, 525, 624, 1643, 4825, 8090, 8883, 8886, 14791, 15575, 19110
--Canada 12559
--Colombia 17066
--Congresses 4479
--England 2574
--Finland 13006
--France--History 13511
--Germany--History 15878, 17481
--Great Britain 6469
--Haiti 19030
--Ireland 17727
--Korea 13053
--Philippines 13498, 13811
--Spain--History 17313
--Taiwan 15387, 15509
Church and the poor >> See further: Church work with the poor; Poor; Poverty; Church

and social problems
Church and the poor 916, 1102, 3316, 4578, 5137, 6941, 7505, 13526, 14255, 14524, 15621, 16603, 19162
--American Baptist sources--(1900 to 1917) 2623
--American Baptist sources--(1980 to 1991) 18804
--Asia 14443, 14850
--Baptist sources--(1970 to 1979) 13165
--Baptist sources--(1980 to 1991) 16173
--Belgium 5887
--Brazil 17643
--Brethren sources 11545
--Canada 13386, 14617
--Catholic sources--(1800 to 1874) 509
--Catholic sources--(1875 to 1899) 773, 890, 1069, 1090, 1680, 14844
--Catholic sources--(1918 to 1944) 3990, 4795
--Catholic sources--(1945 to 1959) 6216, 6780
--Catholic sources--(1960 to 1969) 7871, 8759, 9022, 9175, 9425, 9433, 9438, 9892, 10481, 10799
--Catholic sources--(1970 to 1979) 12574, 14627, 14762, 18781, 18947
--Catholic sources--(1980 to 1991) 15351, 15395, 15541, 15785, 15790, 16096, 17095, 17112, 17156, 17434, 17652, 17831
--Chile 11398
--Christian Churches and Churches of Christ sources 19294, 19313, 19336
--Church of England sources--(1800 to 1874) 39, 16252
--Church of England sources--(1900 to 1917) 2919
--Church of England sources--(1918 to 1944) 3054
--Church of England sources--(1980 to 1991) 16488, 16550, 17682
--Church of England sources--History 10906
--Church of Scotland sources--(1800 to 1874) 120
--Church of Scotland sources--(1980 to 1991) 18166
--Congregational Christian sources--(1945 to 1959) 5766
--Congregational sources--(1800 to 1874) 48, 378, 506
--Congregational sources--(1875 to 1899) 1496
--Congregational sources--(1918 to 1944) 4262
--Congregational sources--History 8079
--Congresses 8364, 17282
--El Salvador 18781, 18947
--England 105, 363, 1749, 1904, 2209, 2574, 3007, 3626, 8154, 12007, 15407, 15548, 15691, 16268, 17888
--England--History 3162, 10958, 11364, 16174, 19205
--Episcopal sources--(1800 to 1874) 305
--Episcopal sources--(1875 to 1899) 608
--Episcopal sources--(1900 to 1917) 2261, 2278, 2290, 2349, 2395, 2586, 2667
--Episcopal sources--(1918 to 1944) 4638
--Episcopal sources--(1945 to 1959) 5664
--Episcopal sources--(1960 to 1969) 9090, 9832, 11359
--Episcopal sources--(1970 to 1979) 12533, 13195, 15225
--Episcopal sources--(1980 to

1991) 16477
Church and the poor (cont.)
--Episcopal sources--History 8696
--Europe 6419, 18772
--Evangelical Protestant sources--(1960 to 1969) 10104, 10403
--Evangelical Protestant sources--(1970 to 1979) 13103, 14422, 14912, 15272
--Evangelical Protestant sources--(1980 to 1991) 15392, 16492, 16531, 16860, 17037, 17856, 18148, 18386, 18798, 19124
--Evangelical Protestant sources--History 14334
--Fiction 270, 669, 3462, 18595
--France 5935, 12140, 12747
--France--History 14390
--Friends sources--History 13337
--Germany 218, 1509, 8799, 12079, 14429, 15796
--Germany--History 14533
--Great Britain 1212, 16071, 17427, 18780
--Guatemala 11036
--History 12131, 14815, 16068, 17668
--Holiness sources 4816
--Hong Kong 8799
--India 14970, 15003, 15376, 15627
--Japan 8799, 11559
--Korea 13053, 13084
--Latin America 14356, 15064, 15948, 17156
--Lutheran sources--(1875 to 1899) 1277
--Lutheran sources--(1960 to 1969) 9507, 10462
--Lutheran sources--(1970 to 1979) 12157
--Lutheran sources--(1980 to 1991) 15571, 16407, 17282, 18236
--Methodist sources--(1800 to 1874) 522
--Methodist sources--(1875 to 1899) 1038
--Methodist sources--(1900 to 1917) 2409, 2916, 3136
--Methodist sources--(1960 to 1969) 8401, 9776, 10253, 11176, 11194
--Methodist sources--(1970 to 1979) 13630, 14356
--Methodist sources--(1980 to 1991) 16039, 18400
--Methodist sources--History 3162, 11364
--NCCCUSA sources--(1945 to 1959) 6617, 7384, 7444, 7717
--NCCCUSA sources--(1960 to 1969) 8525
--NCCCUSA sources--Periodicals 9178
--Orthodox Eastern sources 16788
--Pentecostal churches 10652
--Periodicals 10273, 14448
--Philippines 14007, 16965
--Presbyterian sources--(1800 to 1874) 267, 380
--Presbyterian sources--(1960 to 1969) 9259, 9858
--Presbyterian sources--(1980 to 1991) 16054, 18180, 18685
--Protestant sources--(1800 to 1874) 18, 34, 47, 56, 66, 67, 68, 217, 224, 266, 349, 17416
--Protestant sources--(1875 to 1899) 729, 774, 817, 1114, 1209, 1304, 1582
--Protestant sources--(1918 to 1944) 4147, 4503
--Protestant sources--(1945 to 1959) 6810, 7007
--Protestant sources--(1960 to 1969) 8296, 9252, 9286, 9341, 9422, 10211, 10593, 10930, 11129, 11330

Church and the poor (cont.)
--Protestant sources--(1970 to 1979) 13433, 17301
--Protestant sources--(1980 to 1991) 15557, 15762, 16539, 16850, 16999, 18214
--Protestant sources--History 13127, 13231, 15891
--Reformed Church in America sources--(1960 to 1969) 10859
--Reformed Church in America sources--(1980 to 1991) 15748
--Scotland 348
--South Africa 5715, 17562
--Southern Baptist sources--(1960 to 1969) 8693, 9811
--Southern Baptist sources--(1980 to 1991) 16922
--Spain 15443
--Taiwan 16502
--Turkey 8799
--Unitarian sources--(1800 to 1874) 147, 448, 534, 541
--Unitarian sources--(1875 to 1899) 1412
--Unitarian sources--(1900 to 1917) 2570
--United Church of Christ sources--(1918 to 1944) 5300
--United Church of Christ sources--(1980 to 1991) 16821
--World Council of Churches sources--(1970 to 1979) 15003, 15239
--World Council of Churches sources--(1980 to 1991) 15496, 16554
Church and the world >> See: Society and church; Society and religion
Church architecture >> See further: Sunday School Buildings; Church buildings; Steeples and spires
Church architecture 244, 378, 1119, 1331, 1798, 2131, 2236, 2520, 2996, 3016, 3172, 3346, 3479, 3487, 3489, 3870, 3877, 4003, 4019, 4139, 4600, 4704, 4761, 5239, 5355, 5462, 5663, 5767, 5801, 5915, 5943, 6255, 6309, 6439, 6820, 7054, 7194, 7234, 7493, 7860, 7915, 7993, 8034, 8142, 8330, 8382, 8391, 8452, 8538, 8921, 9269, 9407, 11029, 11240, 11288, 11972, 12168, 12573, 13043, 13387, 14013, 14089, 14292, 15081, 15252, 15482, 15631, 15868, 15882, 15975, 16030, 16283, 16286, 16704, 17672
--Africa 18064
--Congresses 7234, 7395, 8484, 10011, 10400, 11724
--England 2169, 12439, 12446, 12617, 18527
--France 11766, 12092, 12218
--Germany 11609, 18264
--Great Britain 5642
--History 12900, 13029, 13366, 13402, 13403, 13412, 13424, 13674, 13733, 13737, 13853, 14275, 15284, 16731, 17944, 18689
--Periodicals 6370
--Sweden 17349
Church Army (England) 2008, 2009, 15282
Church Army (Massachusetts) 1526
Church Army (Protestant Episcopal) 6215
Church Association for the Advancement of the Interests of Labor (New York, NY) 1120
Church attendance
--Africa 12058, 15974
--Austria 16083
--Canada 11700
--Changes in 3595, 3907, 5123,

8488, 11012, 11250, 15468, 15835, 16091
Church attendance (cont.)
--Correlates 1712, 2326, 2829, 2834, 3441, 3856, 4225, 5151, 5559, 5757, 6710, 6902, 8212, 8390, 8402, 8572, 9027, 9231, 9392, 10706, 11146, 11165, 11248, 11699, 11700, 11786, 12027, 12739, 13134, 13273, 13316, 14157, 14466, 14906, 15082, 15086, 15495, 15672, 15846, 16614, 16972, 17575, 17750, 18488, 18714, 18778
--Encouragement of 326, 753, 2885, 3465, 5466, 7074, 7807, 8100, 9447, 12503, 14028, 14595, 15013, 15213, 15477, 16632, 16980
--England 1972, 4225, 9002
--England--History 9683
--France 7466
--Germany 8572, 10457
--Great Britain 9231
--Greece 16614
--History 7733, 16091
--Ireland 13292
--Laboring classes and 277, 516, 660, 739, 790, 818, 836, 1191, 1529, 1563, 1591, 1712, 1899, 2079, 2834, 3438, 4340, 7868, 9002, 9331, 12486, 16277
--Migration and 5898, 6085, 6175, 6860, 7744, 9113, 9130, 9565, 10692, 11705, 12248, 12254, 12310, 12358, 12550, 12646, 15321, 17192, 17433
--Netherlands 11199, 15672
--Poland 12550
--Scotland--History 14611, 18057
--Sweden 17349
--Typologies 5769, 6313
Church Building Society (London, England) 5555
--Periodicals 376
Church buildings >> See further: Sunday School Buildings; Church architecture; Steeples and spires; Insurance of church buildings
Church buildings 838, 1114, 1227, 1442, 2014, 2384, 2448, 3072, 3172, 3173, 3202, 3870, 3908, 4003, 4314, 5767, 5772, 6820, 7395, 7493, 7678, 9023, 9201, 9269, 10217, 11234, 12253, 15169, 15418, 16084, 16286, 18399
--England 1506, 3211, 11241, 12439, 18656
--England--Periodicals 376
--France 9797, 11766
--France--History 7069
--Germany 17574
--Great Britain 10993
--Handbooks 7145
--History 14275, 15284, 17944
--Hong Kong 11862
--Interdenominational use 1648
--Norway 11053
--Periodicals 679, 6370
--Preservation 3906, 4386, 5220, 6115, 7213, 7354, 12439, 12573, 12793, 13412, 14798, 15081, 15584, 16524, 16704, 16866, 16911, 17148, 17158, 17672, 17739, 17924, 17981, 18132, 18224, 18340, 18986, 19002, 19119, 19227
--Preservation--England 5252, 7664
--Shared facilities >> See further: Churches--Secular use; Secularization (church property)
--Shared facilities 1648, 9460, 10272, 10993, 11288, 11367, 11537, 11972, 12077, 13476, 15191, 16551, 17872
--Shared facilities--Great Britain

12902
Church busses 1123, 11657, 14017, 15920
Church charities >> See further: Charities
Church closings >> See: Church development, merger
Church Club of New York 828
Church clubs 828, 1640, 1721, 1908, 2056, 2113, 2173, 2294, 2504, 2773, 18867
--Catholic 15059, 18539
--History 4324
--Protestant 2651, 4807
Church committees >> See: Church administration
Church controversies >> See further: Social conflict
Church controversies 117, 151, 160, 2376, 2586, 3315, 3998, 6314, 6845, 6879, 7013, 7215, 7227, 7521, 8137, 8202, 8993, 9052, 9133, 9147, 9207, 9601, 9890, 10183, 10346, 10385, 10468, 10490, 10836, 11233, 11322, 11410, 11494, 12049, 12184, 12207, 12329, 12459, 12513, 12578, 12732, 12901, 12941, 12971, 13149, 13530, 13544, 13791, 13904, 14043, 14338, 14682, 15121, 15122, 15659, 15889, 15932, 16076, 16784, 16821, 16987, 17029, 17200, 17387, 17407, 17701, 17792, 18632, 18662, 18742, 18754, 18813, 18818, 18997, 19071
--Asia 16912
--Bibliographies 13007
--Canada--History 14739
--Colombia 17242
--Europe 10177
--France 6603, 11484, 18896
--France--History 9610
--Great Britain 11361, 17897, 18085
--Haiti 19030
--History 12552, 12693, 13676, 13952, 14116, 14377, 14705, 14795, 14923, 16438, 17414, 17573
--Ireland 11361, 18038, 18085
--Malaysia 15527
Church development, merger 961, 5576, 6056, 7624, 8255, 9090, 11144, 18515
--American Baptist Sources--(1970 to 1979) 12659
--Brethren sources 12503
--Canada 16369
--Catholic sources--(1980 to 1991) 17673, 18754, 18813, 18997, 19071
--Germany 2572
--Lutheran sources--(1900 to 1917) 2316
--Lutheran sources--(1960 to 1969) 10577
--Methodist sources--(1945 to 1959) 6098, 7057, 7518
--Methodist sources--(1960 to 1969) 8307, 8375, 8643, 9237
--Methodist sources--(1970 to 1979) 13808, 14288, 14405
--Methodist sources--(1980 to 1991) 16604
--NCCCUSA sources--(1945 to 1959) 6146
--NCCCUSA sources--(1970 to 1979) 14446
--Presbyterian sources--(1960 to 1969) 7976, 11302
--Presbyterian sources--(1970 to 1979) 15308
--Presbyterian sources--(1980 to 1991) 16604
--Protestant sources--(1918 to 1944) 4745
--Protestant sources--(1945 to 1959) 6912

--Protestant sources--(1960 to 1969) 11303
--Protestant sources--(1980 to 1991) 16285, 17441
--Southern Baptist sources--(1970 to 1979) 13462, 14649, 14978
--Southern Baptist sources--(1980 to 1991) 16024
--United Church of Christ sources--(1960 to 1969) 10577
Church development, new >> See further: Comity; Church growth
Church development, new 144, 3814, 6276, 6340, 6673, 7793, 9407, 11240, 11518, 12609, 12877, 13564, 14654, 15457, 15490, 16826, 17252
--Africa 9491, 15291, 15354, 16255, 18512
--American Baptist sources--(1800 to 1874) 461, 507
--American Baptist sources--(1875 to 1899) 592
--American Baptist sources--(1945 to 1959) 7236
--American Baptist sources--(1960 to 1969) 9217
--Asia 15354
--Australia--History 13542
--Brazil 13538
--Brethren sources 7011
--Catholic sources--(1875 to 1899) 1234, 1655
--Catholic sources--(1900 to 1917) 2033
--Catholic sources--(1918 to 1944) 4090
--Catholic sources--(1960 to 1969) 10474, 11350
--Catholic sources--(1970 to 1979) 14603, 15252
--Catholic sources--(1980 to 1991) 15375, 16151, 18413
--Catholic sources--History 4846, 12107
--Catholic sources--Periodicals 16151
--Church of England sources--(1800 to 1874) 168, 8271, 10755
--Church of England sources--(1875 to 1899) 588
--Church of England sources--(1945 to 1959) 5555
--Congregational Christian sources--(1945 to 1959) 6027, 6214, 6873
--Congregational sources--(1875 to 1899) 678, 717
--Congresses 11724
--Disciples of Christ sources--(1918 to 1944) 3356
--Disciples of Christ sources--(1945 to 1959) 5944, 6681
--England--History 8271, 10755, 19087
--England--Periodicals 376
--Episcopal sources--(1800 to 1874) 122
--Episcopal sources--(1875 to 1899) 646, 1597, 14719
--Episcopal sources--(1918 to 1944) 4203
--Episcopal sources--(1980 to 1991) 16833, 18069
--Evangelical Protestant sources--(1970 to 1979) 11791, 11792, 11890, 13886, 14909
--Evangelical Protestant sources--(1980 to 1991) 15633, 16153, 16925, 17438, 17510, 17774, 17995, 18090, 18162, 18343, 18447, 18654, 18830, 18909, 18940, 18948
--Federal Council sources--(1918 to 1944) 4055, 4908, 5086
--France 9797, 12647
--Germany 13142, 15352
--Great Britain 11724, 12142

Church development, new (cont.)
--Great Britain--History 15844
--History 197
--India 6685
--Japan 17114, 19062
--Kenya 14603
--Korea 12431
--Latin America 11791, 15354, 18062
--Lutheran sources--(1875 to 1899) 1482
--Lutheran sources--(1918 to 1944) 5239
--Lutheran sources--(1945 to 1959) 6083, 6084, 6225, 6226, 6325, 6342, 6376, 7009, 7493
--Lutheran sources--(1960 to 1969) 7960
--Lutheran sources--(1980 to 1991) 15352
--Malaysia 17277
--Mennonite sources 18494, 19091
--Methodist sources--(1800 to 1874) 428, 13805
--Methodist sources--(1875 to 1899) 730, 743, 1003, 1236
--Methodist sources--(1900 to 1917) 1765, 1929, 2413
--Methodist sources--(1918 to 1944) 3053, 3086, 3290, 3435, 3631, 3689, 3781, 4914, 4915, 5162
--Methodist sources--(1945 to 1959) 5631, 5696, 5876, 6199, 6355, 6356, 6466, 6747, 7449, 7455, 7514, 11687
--Methodist sources--(1960 to 1969) 8248, 8249, 8313, 8374, 8643, 8650, 9012, 9154, 9220, 9237, 9314, 9509, 9947, 10084, 10238, 10990, 11251, 11380
--Methodist sources--(1970 to 1979) 12816, 13411, 13777, 13927, 13928, 13953, 14479, 15072, 15169
--Methodist sources--(1980 to 1991) 15341, 17473, 19051, 19169
--Methodist sources--History 3084
--Mexico 16307, 18654
--NCCCUSA sources--(1945 to 1959) 6056, 6101, 6109, 6255, 6274, 6311, 6360, 6364, 6379, 6381, 6557, 6969, 7005, 7678, 8603
--NCCCUSA sources--(1960 to 1969) 8583, 9460, 11363
--Netherlands 8939
--New Guinea 15375
--Nigeria 18496
--Philippines 13111, 18398
--Presbyterian sources--(1800 to 1874) 291, 439, 472, 1414
--Presbyterian sources--(1875 to 1899) 642, 645, 928, 1166, 1415, 1708
--Presbyterian sources--(1900 to 1917) 2966, 3024, 3035
--Presbyterian sources--(1918 to 1944) 3920, 4143
--Presbyterian sources--(1945 to 1959) 5407, 5440, 5443, 5546, 5609, 5628, 6220, 6452, 6764, 7715, 7719
--Presbyterian sources--(1960 to 1969) 7946, 8201, 8600, 10490, 10567
--Presbyterian sources--(1970 to 1979) 12318, 12431, 14074
--Presbyterian sources--(1980 to 1991) 17849
--Presbyterian sources--History 1868
--Protestant sources--(1800 to 1874) 68, 185, 190, 15067
--Protestant sources--(1875 to 1899) 960, 1114, 1241, 1400, 1627

Church development, new (cont.)
--Protestant sources--(1900 to 1917) 2033, 2330, 2754
--Protestant sources--(1918 to 1944) 3954, 3961, 4067, 4144, 4233, 4369, 4372, 4523, 5217, 5261, 5263, 5265, 5544
--Protestant sources--(1945 to 1959) 5365, 5576, 5604, 5893, 5913, 6820, 6872, 7555
--Protestant sources--(1960 to 1969) 7760, 8391, 9211, 9511, 10085, 10134, 10562, 11377
--Protestant sources--(1970 to 1979) 12816, 13161, 13251, 13252, 14322, 15182
--Protestant sources--(1980 to 1991) 15914, 16789
--Protestant sources--History 12357, 13209
--Protestant sources--Periodicals 679
--Reformed Church in America sources--(1960 to 1969) 8146
--Reformed Church in the United States sources 2825, 3202
--Singapore 17277
--Southern Baptist sources--(1945 to 1959) 5648
--Southern Baptist sources--(1960 to 1969) 9738, 10902, 11353, 11356
--Southern Baptist sources--(1970 to 1979) 12955, 12962, 13456, 14161, 14426, 14797
--Southern Baptist sources--(1980 to 1991) 15370, 15744, 15833, 16024, 16588, 16745, 16878, 18154, 18746, 19092
--Unitarian Universalist sources--(1980 to 1991) 17834
--United Church of Christ sources--(1960 to 1969) 8426, 9095
--United Church of Christ sources--(1970 to 1979) 12818
--United Church of Christ sources--(1980 to 1991) 16981
Church development, overchurching >> See further: Comity
Church development, overchurching 2486, 2487, 2754, 3035, 4057, 4127, 4369, 4523, 10577
Church development, relocation 1076, 6688, 8603, 17836, 18515, 19029
--Catholic sources 19179, 19180
--Catholic sources--(1970 to 1979) 13479
--Catholic sources--(1980 to 1991) 18315, 18632, 18742
--Church of God sources 10549
--Congregational Christian sources--(1945 to 1959) 5905
--England 13899, 16104
--History 12131
--Methodist sources--(1918 to 1944) 3098
--Methodist sources--(1960 to 1969) 8643
--Methodist sources--(1970 to 1979) 12441
--NCCCUSA sources--(1945 to 1959) 7005
--Orthodox Eastern Church sources 8649
--Presbyterian sources--(1960 to 1969) 8213
--Protestant sources--(1800 to 1874) 13869
--Protestant sources--(1918 to 1944) 4090
--Protestant sources--(1945 to 1959) 6912
--Protestant sources--(1970 to 1979) 15243
--Reformed Church in America

sources--(1970 to 1979) 13942
Church development, relocation (cont.)
--Southern Baptist sources--(1945 to 1959) 7139
--Southern Baptist sources--(1970 to 1979) 13678
--United Church of Christ sources--(1980 to 1991) 18983
Church development, yoked parishes >> See further: Cooperative ministries
Church development, yoked parishes 7700, 15338, 16622
--England 18642
--Methodist sources 15117
Church extension >> See: Church development, new; Home missions (church extension)
Church Federation of Greater Chicago 4812, 6142, 6673, 7788, 8821, 8822, 8848, 9013, 9014, 9350, 9545, 9922, 10267
--Comity Commission 4155
--Congresses 6294
--History 13346
--Pronouncements, policies 8810
Church finances >> See further: Investments, ecclesiastical; Christianity and economics; Economics--Religious aspects
Church finances 305, 525, 550, 613, 702, 866, 1012, 1161, 1227, 1325, 1419, 1545, 1864, 2014, 2025, 2053, 2100, 2293, 2591, 2667, 2960, 3256, 3291, 3572, 3625, 3723, 3979, 4147, 4276, 4372, 4503, 4525, 4648, 5239, 5567, 6720, 6873, 6904, 7493, 7511, 8131, 8196, 10482, 10745, 12392, 12534, 13268, 13470, 13869, 14451, 14506, 15081, 15115, 15413, 15567, 15828, 15925, 15991, 16084, 16232, 16260, 16981, 17120, 17627, 17725, 17856, 18100, 18300, 18661, 19199, 19227, 19305
--Canada 13066
--England--History 10958
--Germany 2572
--History 5722, 8403, 13496, 14869, 18057
--India 4712, 4803, 4804
--Periodicals 16261
Church group work >> See: Group ministries; Group work, social
Church growth >> See further: Church development, new
Church growth
--Africa 10508, 10676, 11981, 17908, 19132
--Africa--Bibliographies 13567
--Africa--History 15024
--Australia 18447
--Brazil 5163, 9618, 12136, 12492, 19213
--Canada--History 14214
--Catholic 1352, 1981, 2885, 8003
--Catholic--History 2331
--Colombia 17996
--Congo 10676
--Congregational 4244
--Developing countries 14263, 17949
--England 14241, 15297, 18500
--Episcopal 2080
--Evangelical Protestant 11889, 13769, 13878, 14081, 14909, 15290, 15633, 15776, 16060, 16868, 16939, 17179, 17384, 17590, 17627, 18830, 18940, 19036
--Great Britain 16042
--History 15082
--Hong Kong 7802, 8539
--India 12114, 13027, 13028,

13317, 13347, 14814, 15147, 16256, 17213
Church growth (cont.)
--Indonesia 17775
--Italy 18630
--Japan 12036
--Kenya 11981, 19132
--Kenya--Bibliographies 13567
--Korea 16530, 16639
--Latin America 11791, 13165, 17151, 17996
--Lutheran 1178, 6206, 11012, 15477, 16651
--Mennonite 15520
--Methodist 7455, 7914, 10508, 11143, 14650, 14754, 15184, 15289, 17177, 17263, 17308
--Methodist sources--(1970 to 1979) 15291
--Mexico 8836, 17723
--Minorities 15801, 16024
--New Guinea 11282
--Nigeria 9870, 13636
--Pentecostal 4816, 7953, 12186, 14343, 17059, 17730, 17996
--Peru 14991, 16742, 17151
--Philippines 5375, 7065, 18895
--Philosophy 5066, 11889, 12541, 12609, 13832, 14081, 14467, 15170, 15646, 15799, 17438, 18367, 18803, 18843, 18856, 19075
--Presbyterian 1442, 7497, 15013, 15227, 15290
--Protestant 5261, 6700, 8821, 9701, 13252, 15468, 17505, 18301, 18942, 19116
--Reformed Church in America 18352
--Scotland 11504
--Singapore 17363
--South America 14241
--Southern Baptist 12066, 12067, 14041, 14161, 14595, 15370, 15383, 15931, 15938, 16024, 16087, 16239, 16240, 16334, 16454, 16483, 16588, 16596, 16878, 17152, 17252, 17263, 17350, 17773, 17814, 18537, 19092
--Southern Baptist--Bibliographies 16198
--Sri Lanka 15422
--Taiwan 13779
--Thailand 19050
--Unitarian 17834
--United Church of Christ 16665, 18687
--Zaire 17908
Church history
--Bibliographies 4838, 4928, 4929, 4930, 4932, 4933, 4934, 4935, 4936, 4937, 4938, 4939, 4940, 5025, 5026, 5027, 5028, 5029, 15591, 17315
--Congresses 13430
Church in transition >> See: Social change and church
Church investments >> See: Investments, ecclesiastical; Christianity and economics
Church League for Industrial Democracy 3293, 3888, 4675, 4767, 4970, 5578, 5580
--History 16958
--Periodicals 3196
Church League of America 7909
Church Life and Work Movement 4658
Church management >> See further: Churches--Security measures
Church management 1168, 1579, 1701, 2080, 2118, 2887, 3788, 4445, 4960, 6559, 7063, 8047, 8733, 13223, 13766, 14151, 17625, 18132
--American Baptist sources--(1875 to 1899) 1623
--American Baptist sources--(1918

to 1944) 3869, 4022, 5066
Church management (cont.)
--American Baptist sources--(1945 to 1959) 7588
--American Baptist sources--(1970 to 1979) 13965
--Baptist sources--(1980 to 1991) 17108
--Canada 13190
--Catholic sources--(1875 to 1899) 1234
--Catholic sources--(1918 to 1944) 3257, 5123
--Catholic sources--(1960 to 1969) 8683, 11315
--Catholic sources--(1970 to 1979) 12085, 12875, 15091
--Catholic sources--History 13548, 18106
--Church of England sources--(1900 to 1917) 2591
--Church of England sources--History 11987, 15890
--Congregational sources--(1875 to 1899) 838, 1628
--Congresses 9432
--Disciples of Christ sources--(1945 to 1959) 5523, 7145
--England 11048, 14727
--Episcopal sources--(1945 to 1959) 7511
--Episcopal sources--(1970 to 1979) 12592
--Evangelical Protestant sources--(1970 to 1979) 15001
--Evangelical Protestant sources--(1980 to 1991) 16185, 18575, 18861
--France 9952
--Germany 5620, 7416, 8261, 8725, 11360, 13781, 13955
--History 18106
--Lutheran sources--(1875 to 1899) 866, 1584
--Lutheran sources--(1918 to 1944) 4694
--Lutheran sources--(1960 to 1969) 8187, 9291, 9518, 10828
--Lutheran sources--(1970 to 1979) 14775
--Methodist sources--(1875 to 1899) 1599
--Methodist sources--(1900 to 1917) 2244
--Methodist sources--(1918 to 1944) 3386, 4246
--Methodist sources--(1945 to 1959) 5626
--Methodist sources--(1960 to 1969) 8166, 8624
--Methodist sources--(1970 to 1979) 12538, 12919, 13889, 14354, 14503, 15289
--Methodist sources--(1980 to 1991) 16933, 17138, 17771, 17872
--NCCCUSA sources--(1945 to 1959) 6755
--NCCCUSA sources--(1960 to 1969) 7824, 8430
--Presbyterian sources--(1900 to 1917) 2489, 2746
--Presbyterian sources--(1970 to 1979) 15092
--Presbyterian sources--(1980 to 1991) 16538, 16793
--Presbyterian sources--History 5722, 18057
--Protestant sources--(1800 to 1874) 527
--Protestant sources--(1875 to 1899) 607, 905, 1560
--Protestant sources--(1900 to 1917) 1864, 1948, 2508, 2515, 2837, 2865, 2890, 2960, 3015
--Protestant sources--(1918 to 1944) 3777, 4648
--Protestant sources--(1960 to 1969) 8214, 8376, 9362, 9694, 10979

Church management (cont.)
--Protestant sources--(1970 to 1979) 12293, 12941, 14596, 14712, 14975
--Protestant sources--(1980 to 1991) 18104, 19116
--Scotland 6413
--Southern Baptist sources--(1960 to 1969) 10834
--Southern Baptist sources--(1970 to 1979) 12253
--Southern Baptist sources--(1980 to 1991) 16506, 16902, 17702, 19015
--United Church of Christ sources--(1970 to 1979) 11733
Church membership
--Africa 12058, 13350
--American Baptist 5066, 6414, 7191, 7807
--Brazil 18171
--Brethren 12503
--Canada 9381
--Catholic 5123, 5757, 6313, 12739, 13316, 13375, 15022, 15613, 18171
--Congregational Churches 4245, 8145
--Congresses 14157
--Descriptive studies 431, 1739, 3969, 4192, 5249, 5434, 5559, 5567, 5643, 5757, 5894, 6026, 6085, 6313, 6860, 6902, 7310, 7620, 7743, 7799, 7983, 8038, 8063, 8145, 8390, 8488, 8521, 8951, 9565, 9848, 9873, 10692, 10706, 11221, 11248, 12248, 12256, 12310, 12358, 12646, 13248, 13601, 13985, 13986, 14376, 14643, 14809, 15151, 15227, 15554, 15909, 16386, 16972, 17192, 18341, 18443, 18623, 18778
--Disciples of Christ 4192
--England 1972
--England--History 9683, 15216, 19087
--Episcopal 18280, 18300
--Ethnic composition 961, 4869, 5941, 6149, 6175, 6378, 6572, 6710, 7146, 7535, 9130, 10692, 11404, 11732, 12214, 12530, 12739, 12758, 12940, 13124, 13316, 13707, 13756, 13801, 13852, 13859, 13980, 14070, 14411, 14573, 14982, 15210, 15508, 15613, 15801, 15833, 16052, 16281, 16789, 16790, 17103, 17298, 18633
--Evangelical Protestant 16980, 17627
--France 7228
--France--History 7069
--Germany 7548, 7614
--Great Britain 9231, 19090
--History 7733, 9837, 11250, 12530, 13596, 15082, 15296, 15742, 16091, 17581, 17639
--India 12520, 14814
--Lutheran 1482, 7881, 8402, 11012, 11100, 15477, 19242
--Methodist 1743, 6776, 6902, 7538, 8327, 8401, 8626, 9320, 9809, 11146, 11687, 13780, 14070, 15668, 16124, 16632, 18200, 19199
--Netherlands 11199
--Netherlands--History 6245
--Presbyterian 1225, 1739, 6229, 6378, 7497, 15227
--Protestant 2291, 5567, 5757, 5894, 6146, 6700, 7272, 7310, 9392, 9701, 10706, 15013, 15468, 17433, 18301, 18942
--Racial composition 5434, 6303, 6308, 6710, 6715, 7057, 7272, 7535, 9320, 9809, 10706, 10716, 11100, 11146, 11221, 13780, 15742, 16582, 16972, 17433, 17844, 18200, 18325,

18623
Church membership (cont.)
--Recruitment 905, 1628, 1743, 1940, 1991, 5066, 5466, 6710, 7548, 8307, 8401, 11663, 14028, 14825, 14982, 15115, 15213, 15477, 15613, 15646, 16392, 16582, 16632, 18280, 18623
--Recruitment Chrysalis 2230
--Scotland 12998
--Social status composition 1225, 2806, 5151, 6026, 6776, 8402, 9231, 9392, 9862, 11786, 12214, 12358, 12520, 13601, 14301, 15086, 15153, 16091
--Southern Baptist 11663, 13286, 14595, 15742, 15835, 16024, 16483, 16588, 16902, 16972, 16980
--Southern Baptist--Bibliographies 16198
--United Church of Christ 8145, 8521, 9848, 15151, 16665
Church merger >> See: Church development, merger
Church music >> See further: Music; Jazz music; African American music; Folk music
Church music 838, 1864, 7029, 8233, 9859, 11417, 11457, 12309, 15894, 16024, 17545, 17594, 18918
Church of All Nations (Boston, Massachusetts) >> See: Morgan Memorial
Church of All Nations (Los Angeles, CA) 5329
Church of All Nations (New York, NY) 3144, 10916, 13151, 13693, 18963
--History 14348
Church of Christ
--History 1937
Church of Christ of Thailand 14097
Church of England
--Bibliographies 13991
--Case studies 2873, 4690, 6001, 6782, 9227, 9357, 10862, 10938, 12119, 12520, 15890, 16607, 17801, 18045, 19090
--Commission on Urban Priority Areas 16802, 17032, 17281, 17681, 17686, 17744, 17747, 17760, 17858, 17865, 17894, 17897, 17898, 17956, 18000, 18004, 18053, 18060, 18061, 18111, 18289, 18321, 18409, 18418, 18468, 18476, 18481, 18500, 18777, 18799, 18849, 18859, 18863, 19052, 19224
--Doctrine 18978
--History 5642, 16579, 17842, 17888
--Pastoral theology 1443, 7517, 10263, 13480, 18777
--Periodicals 1047, 4159, 8384
--Pronouncements, policies 2241, 18566
--Social teaching 1339, 2942, 3121, 3197, 5128, 13738, 17707, 17858, 18000, 18445
--Social teaching--History 10999, 11546
Church of England, Advisory Council for the Church's Ministry 10558, 18393
Church of England, Board for Social Responsibility 8384, 17682, 18445, 18540, 18793
Church of England, Churches Main Committee to the War Damages Commission 5252
Church of England, Prison Chaplaincies Council 10263
Church of England, Social and Industrial Council 7517
Church of God
--Case studies 10549, 11038,

11396, 11785, 12181
Church of God (Anderson, Indiana) 7271, 16436
--History 6295, 14172
--Social teaching 13711, 16044
Church of God and Saints of Christ 17545
Church of God in Christ 17422, 17758, 18455
--Case studies 14134, 14349, 17529, 18839
--Handbooks 15590
--History 3248, 11477, 17892
Church of Scientology
--Bibliographies 19221
Church of Scotland
--Biography 15029
--History 9652, 18331
Church of South India
--Case studies 14015, 15003
Church of the Brethren 16764, 17022
--Case studies 6527, 8128, 9325, 9910, 9961, 10191, 10377, 10642, 11110, 14050, 14942
--Periodicals 7789
--Pronouncements, policies 6020, 17805
--Social teaching 7183, 16966, 16967, 19311
Church of the Brethren, Brethren Service Commission 4976, 6020
Church of the Brethren, Ministry and Home Missions Commission 6444, 11110
Church of the Nazarene 10104, 17084, 18442
--Case studies 13984, 14095, 16158, 16168, 16417, 16526, 16624, 17084, 17440, 17982, 18622, 18824, 19167
--History 8584
Church of the Savior (Washington, DC) 6600, 8101, 8724, 8852, 10996, 12623, 13992, 18276
Church officers >> See: Leadership
Church participation >> See: Church attendance; Church membership
Church planning 3788, 5275, 5798, 6445, 7002, 7088, 7182, 7607, 7836, 8433, 8733, 9092, 9637, 9716, 9768, 10443, 10514, 10766, 12561, 13812, 14825, 15277, 15936, 16240, 16981, 17309, 17667, 18401
--Africa 8348, 10753, 14603, 15163, 16140
--American Baptist sources--(1900 to 1917) 2536, 2848
--American Baptist sources--(1918 to 1944) 3060, 3787
--American Baptist sources--(1945 to 1959) 6492, 6862, 7190, 7672
--American Baptist sources--(1960 to 1969) 7818, 7869, 8735, 8778, 8779, 8890, 9868, 9909, 10077, 10361, 10569, 10667, 10908, 11213, 11619
--American Baptist sources--(1970 to 1979) 12258
--American Baptist sources--(1980 to 1991) 15682, 16985, 17448, 17989, 18052
--Asia 8911
--Australia 18568
--Austria 10425
--Baptist sources--(1960 to 1969) 10571
--Baptist sources--(1980 to 1991) 17108, 17542
--Bibliographies 7935, 16376
--Brethren sources--(1960 to 1969) 9961, 10527
--Brethren sources--(1970 to 1979) 14146

Church planning (cont.)
--Canada 5091, 14881, 15561
--Case studies 15011
--Catholic sources--(1918 to 1944) 4090, 5019
--Catholic sources--(1945 to 1959) 5890, 6972, 7258, 7333
--Catholic sources--(1960 to 1969) 7800, 8023, 9213, 9427, 9732, 9844, 9965, 10015, 10137, 10394, 10893, 10978, 11349, 11457
--Catholic sources--(1970 to 1979) 11650, 11808, 11820, 12462, 12875, 13091, 13656, 14574, 15018, 15112, 15142, 15167, 15917
--Catholic sources--(1980 to 1991) 15972, 16480, 16523, 16698, 16739, 16778, 16854, 17274, 17482, 17641, 17673, 17704, 18632, 18641, 18929, 19129
--Catholic sources--Congresses 13162
--Catholic sources--History 10285, 18358
--Church of England sources--(1875 to 1899) 993, 1516, 1720
--Church of England sources--(1960 to 1969) 8851, 9305, 10862
--Church of England sources--(1970 to 1979) 12407, 12524, 14472, 15297
--Church of England sources--(1980 to 1991) 16872, 17281, 17956, 19052
--Church of England sources--History 11987
--Church participation 7237
--Colombia 16629
--Congregational Christian sources--(1918 to 1944) 5115, 5116, 5131, 5204, 5205, 5305
--Congregational Christian sources--(1945 to 1959) 5872, 6100, 6127, 6873
--Congregational sources--(1918 to 1944) 3615
--Congresses 6772, 7943, 10479, 10655, 15072
--Disciples of Christ sources--(1945 to 1959) 5991, 6824, 7373
--Disciples of Christ sources--(1960 to 1969) 9763
--England 341, 6456, 10351, 11001, 13728, 16399, 18481
--England--Bibliographies 17733
--Episcopal sources--(1918 to 1944) 4597, 4768, 5122
--Episcopal sources--(1945 to 1959) 5906, 6601, 6740, 7387, 7654
--Episcopal sources--(1960 to 1969) 7931, 8844, 11628
--Episcopal sources--(1970 to 1979) 13218, 13219, 13905, 14777, 15016
--Episcopal sources--(1980 to 1991) 15359, 15679, 15687, 15730, 15788, 16463, 17129, 17933, 19305
--Europe 7333, 7409, 7990, 8739, 15827
--Evangelical and Reformed Church sources--(1918 to 1944) 5164, 5167, 5168, 5215
--Evangelical and Reformed Church sources--(1945 to 1959) 5981, 6778, 6815, 6971, 7302, 7442
--Evangelical and Reformed Church sources--Periodicals 6658
--Evangelical Protestant sources--(1960 to 1969) 7776, 8155, 8964
--Evangelical Protestant sources--(1970 to 1979) 12345, 15096

Church planning (cont.)
--Evangelical Protestant sources--(1980 to 1991) 15854, 16116, 16583, 16868, 17139, 17384, 17388, 17580, 17770, 17845, 18575, 18611, 18810, 18861, 19006
--Federal Council sources--(1918 to 1944) 4743, 5469
--Federal Council sources--(1945 to 1959) 5337
--Finland 12143
--France 6232, 7070, 7228, 7258
--Fundamentalist sources--(1970 to 1979) 12354
--Germany 2406, 4863, 7434, 7548, 8734, 8771, 9315, 9654, 11063, 12756, 15374, 16644, 16904
--Great Britain 14079, 14902, 17427
--History 4429, 6107, 6387, 17751
--Hong Kong 17178
--India 4804
--Japan 7523, 7801, 8911, 12340
--Korea 18215
--Lutheran sources--(1875 to 1899) 1178
--Lutheran sources--(1900 to 1917) 2317
--Lutheran sources--(1918 to 1944) 5225, 5239
--Lutheran sources--(1945 to 1959) 5858, 6206, 6359, 6562, 6708, 6709, 7348
--Lutheran sources--(1960 to 1969) 7825, 7881, 7961, 8172, 8187, 8205, 8457, 8484, 8485, 8486, 8529, 9056, 9180, 9267, 9291, 9419, 9486, 9519, 9666, 9993, 10565, 10640, 11095, 11099
--Lutheran sources--(1970 to 1979) 12270, 12363, 12952, 13736, 14375
--Lutheran sources--(1980 to 1991) 16633, 16927, 17361, 17989
--Mennonite sources--(1960 to 1969) 9118
--Mennonite sources--(1980 to 1991) 17629, 19091
--Methodist sources--(1875 to 1899) 1567, 1626
--Methodist sources--(1900 to 1917) 1929, 2043, 2090, 2107, 2463, 2887
--Methodist sources--(1918 to 1944) 3089, 3097, 3188, 3295, 3433, 3572, 4095, 4188, 4287, 4309, 4422, 4488, 4756, 4849
--Methodist sources--(1945 to 1959) 5419, 5826, 5827, 5829, 5919, 5979, 5980, 6096, 6097, 6098, 6132, 6240, 6241, 6247, 6386, 6433, 6434, 6511, 6520, 6623, 6705, 6736, 6777, 6789, 6834, 6900, 6901, 6942, 6983, 6984, 6989, 6990, 7239, 7334, 7343, 7360, 7453, 7454, 7484, 7624, 7647, 7705, 7708, 7709, 7710
--Methodist sources--(1960 to 1969) 7859, 8000, 8001, 8002, 8007, 8050, 8051, 8052, 8053, 8054, 8089, 8131, 8166, 8167, 8168, 8277, 8301, 8313, 8335, 8336, 8351, 8374, 8452, 8479, 8511, 8540, 8590, 8698, 8783, 9028, 9274, 9275, 9276, 9277, 9334, 9389, 9390, 9500, 9508, 9705, 9706, 9808, 9810, 9826, 9932, 10044, 10175, 10202, 10237, 10289, 10302, 10488, 10489, 10657, 10717, 10784, 10785, 10820, 10838, 10912, 11143, 11177, 11380, 11381, 11382, 11383, 11395, 11618, 11621, 11622, 11623, 12120

Church planning (cont.)
--Methodist sources--(1970 to 1979) 11687, 12392, 12537, 13151, 13425, 13580, 13581, 14242, 14341, 14405, 14414, 14423, 14461, 14585, 15072, 15100, 15101, 15278
--Methodist sources--(1980 to 1991) 15341, 15500, 15768, 16323, 16371, 16469, 16485, 17147, 17154, 17488, 17771, 18049, 18295, 18296, 18926, 19144
--Methodist sources--Bibliographies 14460
--Methodist sources--Congresses 6942, 8783
--Moravian Church sources 11259
--NCCCUSA sources--(1945 to 1959) 5894, 6007, 6273, 6727, 6733, 6772, 6919, 7148, 7392, 7425
--NCCCUSA sources--(1960 to 1969) 7823, 7943, 8250, 8583, 11102
--NCCCUSA sources--(1970 to 1979) 14712
--NCCCUSA sources--Bibliographies 7935
--Netherlands 11481
--Nigeria 18496
--Orthodox Eastern sources--History 5382
--Periodicals 7684, 19195
--Philippines 7954, 7955, 18322
--Presbyterian sources--(1875 to 1899) 863
--Presbyterian sources--(1900 to 1917) 2454, 2489, 2661
--Presbyterian sources--(1918 to 1944) 3319, 4002, 4096, 4252, 4779, 4780, 5194, 5240, 5241, 5242, 5243, 5291
--Presbyterian sources--(1945 to 1959) 5338, 5339, 5364, 5405, 5406, 5439, 5440, 5441, 5443, 5448, 5506, 5509, 5510, 5511, 5546, 5569, 5595, 5609, 5628, 5717, 5719, 5816, 5820, 5964, 5965, 6078, 6181, 6219, 6282, 6383, 6425, 6428, 6452, 6495, 6551, 6586, 6647, 6764, 6793, 6954, 6955, 6995, 6996, 6997, 7248, 7456, 7584, 7646, 7714, 7719
--Presbyterian sources--(1960 to 1969) 7794, 7942, 7946, 8031, 8037, 8140, 8318, 8322, 8508, 8600, 8601, 8802, 8943, 9123, 9139, 9226, 9529, 9677, 9879, 9951, 9996, 10031, 10080, 10116, 10126, 10544, 10555, 10618, 10619, 11086, 11181
--Presbyterian sources--(1970 to 1979) 11750, 11988, 12064, 12224, 12349, 12495, 13312, 13870, 14031, 14394, 14400, 14419, 14531, 14789, 15045, 15076, 15153
--Presbyterian sources--(1980 to 1991) 15151, 15386, 15489, 15996, 16250, 16374, 16538, 16562, 17070, 17155, 17606, 17658, 19202
--Presbyterian sources--Congresses 12706
--Protestant sources--(1800 to 1874) 6298
--Protestant sources--(1875 to 1899) 733, 918, 1241, 1268, 1400
--Protestant sources--(1900 to 1917) 1633, 1855, 1864, 2264, 2864, 3037
--Protestant sources--(1918 to 1944) 3383, 3428, 3503, 3561, 3571, 3673, 3971, 4040, 4060, 4085, 4245, 4413, 4623, 4801, 4901, 4993, 5080, 5146, 5170,

5171, 5196, 5261, 5265, 5266, 5544
Church planning (cont.)
--Protestant sources--(1945 to 1959) 5358, 5363, 5366, 5425, 5524, 5543, 5545, 5568, 5581, 5615, 5622, 5636, 5637, 5672, 5685, 5735, 5750, 5814, 5840, 5844, 5926, 6122, 6129, 6369, 6399, 6423, 6506, 6509, 6571, 6765, 6766, 6767, 6786, 6940, 6952, 6967, 6968, 7030, 7054, 7144, 7166, 7203, 7528, 7550, 7551, 7552, 7571, 7668, 7669, 7670
--Protestant sources--(1960 to 1969) 7760, 7788, 7840, 7841, 7941, 8039, 8143, 8147, 8148, 8165, 8295, 8296, 8297, 8298, 8300, 8431, 8432, 8441, 8476, 8551, 8559, 8566, 8568, 8697, 8701, 8744, 8788, 8828, 8848, 8865, 8870, 8882, 9037, 9046, 9066, 9067, 9068, 9115, 9122, 9138, 9211, 9212, 9464, 9482, 9490, 9558, 9644, 9670, 9694, 9715, 9761, 9893, 9922, 9937, 9976, 10159, 10182, 10339, 10378, 10561, 10629, 10693, 10792, 10842, 10914, 11055, 11056, 11203, 11243, 11287
--Protestant sources--(1970 to 1979) 11723, 11753, 11952, 12256, 12661, 12782, 12886, 13019, 13249, 13473, 13692, 14030, 14203, 14420, 14596, 14651, 14735, 14741, 14911, 15197, 15241, 15262, 15283
--Protestant sources--(1980 to 1991) 15434, 15478, 15615, 16376, 16512, 16774, 17187, 17805, 17967, 18088, 18104, 18252, 18344, 18472, 18585, 18818, 18819, 18992, 19018, 19334
--Protestant sources--Congresses 3571, 3673
--Protestant sources--History 7509, 10285, 12357, 14051, 15476, 17331
--Protestant sources--Periodicals 9115, 11370
--Reformed Church in America sources--(1960 to 1969) 10985, 11586, 11594
--Reformed Church in America sources--(1970 to 1979) 13397
--Reformed Church in the United States sources 3202
--Scotland 15386
--Singapore 8217
--South Africa 12741
--Southern Baptist sources--(1960 to 1969) 9107, 9170, 9304, 9736, 9784, 10209, 10286, 10389, 10401, 10447, 10701, 10763, 10791, 10903, 11186, 11316, 11353, 11354, 11355, 11442, 11548
--Southern Baptist sources--(1970 to 1979) 11664, 11666, 11814, 11892, 11931, 11969, 11974, 11992, 11993, 12372, 12416, 12656, 12938, 13003, 13018, 13129, 13180, 13287, 13451, 13602, 13624, 13669, 14737, 15214
--Southern Baptist sources--(1980 to 1991) 15258, 15343, 15373, 15483, 15501, 15783, 16230, 16251, 16424, 16460, 16506, 16596, 16599, 16675, 16737, 16845, 17039, 17128, 17134, 17217, 17239, 17538, 17591, 17702, 17814, 17911, 18043, 18294, 18460, 18659, 18853
--Southern Baptist sources--Periodicals 15258
--Unitarian sources--(1900 to 1917) 2569

Church planning (cont.)
--Unitarian sources--(1980 to 1991) 16926
--United Church of Canada sources--(1970 to 1979) 14859, 14881
--United Church of Canada sources--(1980 to 1991) 15664
--United Church of Christ sources--(1945 to 1959) 7313
--United Church of Christ sources--(1960 to 1969) 8169, 8292, 8749, 8864, 8926, 8947, 9266, 9675, 11252
--United Church of Christ sources--(1970 to 1979) 11733, 12009, 12403, 13534, 14519, 15151
--United Church of Christ sources--(1980 to 1991) 15514, 15690, 16064, 16643, 18510, 18687
--United Church of Christ sources--Congresses 9675
--World Council of Churches sources--(1980 to 1991) 15913
--Zambia 14998
Church planting >> See: Church development, new
Church polity >> See: Church planning; Church management
Church property >> See further: Church buildings
Church property 1622, 1648, 2197, 2376, 3173, 7054, 8391, 8625, 8921, 9407, 10007, 11234, 11490, 12247, 12573, 14853, 15343, 15413, 16030, 16104, 16704, 17739
--England 13683
--Great Britain 12902
--Handbooks 7145
Church renewal 6112, 7198, 7722, 8232, 8277, 8289, 8688, 9199, 9224, 9309, 9420, 9534, 9961, 10068, 10076, 10137, 10274, 10364, 10522, 10544, 10637, 10996, 11236, 11405, 11436, 11516, 11723, 11776, 12240, 12564, 12592, 13832, 14672, 14843, 15397, 15648, 15649, 15674, 15783, 15928, 16476, 16910, 17217, 18417, 18419, 18460, 18510, 18670
--Africa 10690, 11113, 15354
--American Baptist sources--(1960 to 1969) 10305
--American Baptist sources--(1970 to 1979) 11984, 12207, 14930
--American Baptist sources--(1980 to 1991) 18435
--Asia 15354
--Brethren sources 15315
--Canada 10509, 15012, 15437
--Case studies 10026, 10268, 10565, 10828, 10887, 11026, 11226, 11571, 12258, 12269, 12643, 12700, 12891, 13010, 13681, 14050, 16376, 16443, 17208, 17540, 18729
--Catholic sources--(1960 to 1969) 10891
--Catholic sources--(1970 to 1979) 12434, 13092, 14958, 15317
--Catholic Sources--(1980 to 1991) 17695, 18413, 18708, 18816
--Church of England sources--(1875 to 1899) 1631
--Church of England sources--(1945 to 1959) 6721
--Congresses 7943
--England 4830, 12195, 12235, 12360, 13899, 14396, 15291, 18164
--Episcopal sources--(1960 to 1969) 9168, 11207
--Episcopal sources--(1970 to 1979) 11739, 12125, 12643,

12821, 12891, 13010, 14000
Church renewal (cont.)
--Evangelical Protestant sources--(1980 to 1991) 16939, 17795, 19219
--Finland 12223
--France 5494, 7989, 11751
--Germany 5784, 8436, 13620
--Great Britain 15491, 16858
--History 15648
--Latin America 14830, 15354, 17522
--Lutheran sources--(1945 to 1959) 6911
--Lutheran sources--(1960 to 1969) 9428, 9429, 9839, 9966, 10989
--Lutheran sources--(1970 to 1979) 13390
--Methodist sources--(1900 to 1917) 1954
--Methodist sources--(1960 to 1969) 8553, 9198, 10302
--Methodist sources--(1970 to 1979) 11764, 12193, 13780, 13899, 16910
--Methodist sources--(1980 to 1991) 15447, 16124, 17023, 17067, 17614, 17684
--NCCCUSA sources--(1960 to 1969) 8878
--New Guinea 13712
--Norway 15291
--Periodicals 12325, 15540, 15994
--Presbyterian sources--(1960 to 1969) 8989, 11411
--Protestant sources--(1945 to 1959) 6533
--Protestant sources--(1960 to 1969) 8143, 8156, 8183, 8319, 8338, 8378, 8944, 9333, 9556, 9943, 10070, 10071, 10320, 10638
--Protestant sources--(1970 to 1979) 12886, 12905, 13161, 14889
--Protestant sources--(1980 to 1991) 17553
--Protestant sources--Periodicals 10759
--Reformed Church in America 18352
--South Africa 12364
--Southern Baptist sources--(1960 to 1969) 8709, 10921
--Southern Baptist sources--(1970 to 1979) 11850, 12132, 13315
--Southern Baptist sources--(1980 to 1991) 17085, 17528
--United Church of Christ sources--(1945 to 1959) 7053
--United Church of Christ sources--(1960 to 1969) 8407, 11273
--United Church of Christ sources--(1970 to 1979) 12764
Church schools >> See: Sunday Schools; Christian education; Parochial schools
Church Social Union 779, 992, 1348, 1355, 1373, 1374, 1427, 1453, 1468, 1470, 1476, 1491, 1497, 1554, 1593, 1646, 1647, 1658, 1670
--History 2594
--Periodicals 1370
Church Socialist League (England) 2587
Church Socialist League (USA) 2776
--History 13491
Church staffs >> See: Group ministries
Church statements >> See: (Specific denominations)--Pronouncements, policies
Church strategy >> See: Church planning
Church structures >> See: Church administration;

Church buildings
Church tax >> See: Taxation
Church union >> See: Christian union
Church Union Housing Association (London, England) 4357
Church ushers >> See: Ushers and ushering
Church Women United 14558, 14974
Church work
--Bibliographies 9247, 9446, 13288, 13289, 13290, 13291, 13560, 13567, 13626, 13917, 14517, 14722, 15270, 16112, 16428, 17315, 17406, 18075, 18592, 18704
Church work with adults >> See further: Men; Women; Women in church work; Church work with young adults; Adult education; Church work with the aged; Christian education--Curriculum--Adult
Church work with adults
--American Baptist sources--(1918 to 1944) 5066
--Catholic sources--(1980 to 1991) 15674
--England 2975, 18520
--Episcopal sources--(1980 to 1991) 17063, 19309
--Evangelical Protestant sources--(1980 to 1991) 17288
--Germany 14714
--Methodist sources--(1980 to 1991) 15871
--NCCCUSA sources--(1945 to 1959) 6441
--NCCCUSA sources--(1960 to 1969) 8670, 8777
--Presbyterian sources--(1918 to 1944) 4808
--Presbyterian sources--(1945 to 1959) 6383
--Presbyterian sources--(1960 to 1969) 7861
--Protestant sources--(1900 to 1917) 2216
--Protestant sources--(1918 to 1944) 4842
--Protestant sources--(1960 to 1969) 9104
--Protestant sources--(1980 to 1991) 18843
--Southern Baptist sources--(1900 to 1917) 2470
--Southern Baptist sources--(1980 to 1991) 17466
--United Church of Christ sources--(1980 to 1991) 18307
Church work with alcoholics 17221, 17490, 19349
--Church of England sources--(1960 to 1969) 9227
--Presbyterian sources--Periodicals 3266
--Salvation Army sources 17868
--Southern Baptist sources--(1960 to 1969) 11031
Church work with apartment dwellers 9678, 9727, 9735, 10248, 11893, 11898
--American Baptist sources--(1960 to 1969) 9050, 9400
--Baptist sources--(1970 to 1979) 12988
--Belgium 14478
--Bibliographies 13560
--Catholic sources--(1970 to 1979) 14478
--Catholic sources--(1980 to 1991) 17695
--England 6525, 16058, 16688
--Episcopal sources--(1960 to 1969) 8575
--Evangelical Protestant sources--(1970 to 1979) 11934, 12429,

13886
Church work with apartment dwellers (cont.)
--Evangelical Protestant sources--(1980 to 1991) 16963, 17472
--France 14935
--Germany 16991
--Japan 9440, 12405, 12466, 16830
--Lutheran sources--(1960 to 1969) 8188, 9789, 10224, 10910, 11097
--Lutheran sources--(1970 to 1979) 12879, 14387
--Methodist sources--(1945 to 1959) 5627, 6239, 6525
--Methodist sources--(1960 to 1969) 8625, 10045, 10531, 10532, 10542, 10575, 10798, 10931, 11223, 13171
--Methodist sources--(1970 to 1979) 13140, 14242, 14578
--Methodist sources--(1980 to 1991) 15605, 15717, 16058
--NCCCUSA sources--(1945 to 1959) 6379
--NCCCUSA sources--(1960 to 1969) 9024, 9682
--Presbyterian sources--(1960 to 1969) 7988, 8928, 8930, 9440, 9447, 9449, 9450, 9451, 9863, 10352
--Presbyterian sources--Bibliographies 9446
--Protestant sources--(1875 to 1899) 1130
--Protestant sources--(1918 to 1944) 4993
--Protestant sources--(1945 to 1959) 6691
--Protestant sources--(1960 to 1969) 9066, 9374, 9375, 9613, 9997, 10282, 10338, 11505
--Protestant sources--(1970 to 1979) 12312, 13748
--Protestant sources--(1980 to 1991) 15599
--Protestant sources--Bibliographies 13289, 13291
--Protestant sources--Periodicals 9375
--Scotland 6413
--Singapore 11097
--Southern Baptist sources 15336
--Southern Baptist sources--(1960 to 1969) 9496, 9640, 9658
--Southern Baptist sources--(1970 to 1979) 12014, 12050, 12243, 12767, 12967, 13126, 13687, 13906, 14667
--Southern Baptist sources--(1980 to 1991) 15355, 15555, 15728, 16102, 16242, 16337, 16814, 17839, 17867, 18746, 18949
--Southern Baptist sources--Bibliographies 13626
--World Council of Churches sources--(1960 to 1969) 9192
Church work with business people
>> See further: Business
Church work with business people 938, 4082, 7116, 7510, 16680, 18917, 18995
--Canada 16050
--Catholic sources--(1960 to 1969) 9108, 9980
--Catholic sources--(1970 to 1979) 11784, 15168
--Catholic sources--(1980 to 1991) 15959
--Evangelical Protestant sources--(1980 to 1991) 16379
--Methodist sources--(1918 to 1944) 3533, 3666
--Peru 17034
--Protestant sources--(1875 to 1899) 904, 905, 1145, 1146
--Protestant sources--(1900 to 1917) 2012, 2978
--Protestant sources--(1918 to

1944) 3175, 3755, 4020, 4137, 4154, 4904, 5175
Church work with business people (cont.)
--Protestant sources--(1945 to 1959) 7095, 7488
--Protestant sources--(1960 to 1969) 8962, 9604, 9616, 10725, 10889
--Protestant sources--(1970 to 1979) 11658, 12245, 12322, 12449, 15310
--Protestant sources--(1980 to 1991) 15396, 15469, 17973, 18253
--Protestant sources--History 11336
--Scotland 59
--Southern Baptist sources--(1980 to 1991) 19037
Church work with children >> See further: City children; Boys, Girls; Church work with youth
Church work with children 57, 1957, 2139, 6464, 8950, 9117, 12025, 16276, 17415
--American Baptist sources--(1900 to 1917) 2613
--American Baptist sources--(1970 to 1979) 12895
--Catholic sources--(1875 to 1899) 886
--Catholic sources--(1900 to 1917) 2722
--Catholic sources--(1918 to 1944) 4227
--Catholic sources--(1960 to 1969) 7779, 11025, 11179
--Catholic sources--(1980 to 1991) 19064
--Catholic sources--History 5035, 14032
--Church of England sources--(1800 to 1874) 432
--Church of England sources--(1980 to 1991) 17709
--Congregational sources--(1918 to 1944) 4299, 19256
--England 1207, 7868
--England--History 14032
--Episcopal sources--(1800 to 1874) 61
--Episcopal sources--(1900 to 1917) 2070
--Episcopal sources--(1960 to 1969) 11495
--Evangelical Protestant sources--(1980 to 1991) 16586, 17400, 18156, 18957, 19004
--Federal Council sources--(1918 to 1944) 5157
--Germany 389
--History 10395
--Italy--History 18283
--Lutheran sources--(1918 to 1944) 4819
--Lutheran sources--(1960 to 1969) 9421
--Lutheran sources--(1970 to 1979) 11917, 12569, 12951
--Mennonite sources--(1960 to 1969) 9859
--Methodist sources--(1800 to 1874) 254
--Methodist sources--(1960 to 1969) 8561, 9906
--Methodist sources--(1970 to 1979) 14952
--Methodist sources--(1980 to 1991) 15497, 19200
--NCCCUSA sources--(1945 to 1959) 6436, 6449, 6458, 6480, 6548, 6590
--NCCCUSA sources--(1960 to 1969) 8687, 8710, 8714, 8732, 8873, 8874, 10013
--Periodicals 1207
--Presbyterian sources--(1900 to 1917) 1879

Church work with children (cont.)
--Presbyterian sources--(1918 to 1944) 5315
--Presbyterian sources--(1960 to 1969) 7905
--Protestant sources--(1800 to 1874) 313
--Protestant sources--(1875 to 1899) 1540, 1713
--Protestant sources--(1900 to 1917) 2687, 2755, 2856, 2862
--Protestant sources--(1945 to 1959) 6646
--Protestant sources--(1960 to 1969) 8522, 9555, 10103
--Protestant sources--(1980 to 1991) 17810, 18080, 18801, 18805
--Protestant sources--History 5035, 15775, 17364
--Reformed Church in America sources--(1960 to 1969) 10114
--Salvation Army sources 2096, 2201
--Southern Baptist sources--(1960 to 1969) 11210
--United Church of Christ sources--(1960 to 1969) 7758, 8573, 9410, 9476
--United Church of Christ sources--(1980 to 1991) 15514, 17662

Church work with criminals >> See further: Crime and criminals; Chaplains, police; Chaplains, prisons; Church work with prisoners; Justice--Criminal; Rehabilitation of criminals

Church work with criminals 3760, 14111, 15300, 15643, 16451, 17038, 18734
--American Baptist sources--(1875 to 1899) 672
--American Baptist sources--(1900 to 1917) 672
--Brethren sources 17022
--Brethren sources--History 16966
--Canada 9516, 12571
--Catholic sources 6759, 10464
--Catholic sources--(1970 to 1979) 13819, 14861
--Church of England sources--(1800 to 1874) 96
--Church of England sources--(1970 to 1979) 15133
--Congregational sources--(1918 to 1944) 4228
--Congresses 9576
--England 2009, 17910
--Evangelical Protestant sources--(1980 to 1991) 15777
--Lutheran sources--(1970 to 1979) 12571
--Mennonite sources--(1980 to 1991) 15710, 15856, 16082
--Methodist sources--(1918 to 1944) 4129
--Methodist sources--(1945 to 1959) 6306
--Methodist sources--(1970 to 1979) 12279
--Methodist sources--(1980 to 1991) 16452
--NCCCUSA sources--(1945 to 1959) 7919
--Protestant sources--(1800 to 1874) 544
--Protestant sources--(1875 to 1899) 1290
--Protestant sources--(1900 to 1917) 2836
--Protestant sources--(1918 to 1944) 4605
--Protestant sources--(1960 to 1969) 9576
--Protestant sources--(1970 to 1979) 15156
--Protestant sources--(1980 to

1991) 15897, 16333
Church work with criminals (cont.)
--Protestant sources--History 14382
--Salvation Army sources 1733
--Southern Baptist sources--(1960 to 1969) 10839
--Southern Baptist sources--(1970 to 1979) 12055
--Taiwan 15387, 15509
Church work with emigrants >> See : Emigration and immigration--Religious aspects; Church work with immigrants
Church work with employed women >> See: Women--Employment
Church work with families >> See further: Family; Family life
Church work with families 1799, 4689, 14774, 15332, 17602, 18440, 18535
--Africa 15974, 16086
--Catholic sources--(1900 to 1917) 1911
--Catholic sources--(1945 to 1959) 5839
--Catholic sources--(1960 to 1969) 8705, 10607, 11165
--Catholic sources--(1970 to 1979) 13416
--Catholic sources--(1980 to 1991) 19272
--Christian Churches and Churches of Christ sources 19312
--Church of England sources--(1960 to 1969) 8398
--Church of England sources--(1980 to 1991) 18273
--England 17640
--Episcopal sources 6408
--Evangelical Protestant sources--(1980 to 1991) 15837, 17974, 18906, 18941
--History 14813
--India 18263
--Lutheran sources--(1970 to 1979) 11953
--Mennonite sources--(1980 to 1991) 16560
--Methodist sources--(1945 to 1959) 5351
--Methodist sources--(1960 to 1969) 10798
--Methodist sources--(1970 to 1979) 12128, 13140, 14952
--Methodist sources--(1980 to 1991) 15675, 17725
--Nigeria 16086
--Presbyterian sources--(1945 to 1959) 7082
--Presbyterian sources--(1970 to 1979) 14476
--Protestant sources--(1900 to 1917) 2755
--Protestant sources--(1945 to 1959) 5602, 7403
--Protestant sources--(1960 to 1969) 8045, 8135
--Protestant sources--(1970 to 1979) 14344, 14539
--Protestant sources--(1980 to 1991) 17275
--Southern Baptist sources--(1980 to 1991) 15795, 17612, 18263
Church work with foreign students >> See: Church work with students
Church work with foreigners >> See: Church work with immigrants
Church work with homosexuals 9124, 13192, 13971, 18176, 18313, 18501
--Catholic sources--(1980 to 1991) 16353, 16440
Church work with immigrants >> See further: Emigration and

immigration--Religious aspects
Church work with immigrants 3355, 12248, 14357, 18312
--American Baptist sources--(1875 to 1899) 672, 1365, 10786
--American Baptist sources--(1900 to 1917) 672, 2944, 10786, 14082
--American Baptist sources--(1918 to 1944) 3052, 3116, 3340, 3388, 3871, 4255
--American Baptist sources--(1980 to 1991) 17644
--American Baptist sources--History 12817
--Australia 10679, 14723, 15027, 16303, 18529, 18568, 18792
--Baptist sources--(1875 to 1899) 1701
--Baptist sources--(1900 to 1917) 2543
--Baptist sources--(1970 to 1979) 14052
--Brazil 18029
--Canada 3464, 16280, 18719
--Canada--History 14052, 14300
--Catholic sources--(1800 to 1874) 4846, 13509, 14300, 15970
--Catholic sources--(1875 to 1899) 1052, 1499, 3694, 7689, 12461, 12658, 12698, 15066, 15240, 15970
--Catholic sources--(1900 to 1917) 2130, 2251, 2653, 3694, 12698, 15970, 18015
--Catholic sources--(1918 to 1944) 3265, 3715, 4227, 4881
--Catholic sources--(1945 to 1959) 6693, 6707, 6938, 7164, 17659
--Catholic sources--(1960 to 1969) 7759, 7781, 7910, 8136, 10299, 10796, 11246
--Catholic sources--(1970 to 1979) 13106, 13428, 13432, 13600, 13724, 14063, 14114, 14542, 14589, 14600, 14717, 14723, 14788
--Catholic sources--(1980 to 1991) 15950, 16078, 16280, 16282, 16303, 18077, 18302, 18490, 19063
--Catholic sources--History 3726, 5521, 6045, 7167, 7525, 10386, 11297, 11587, 12628, 12721, 13141, 13610, 13623, 13698, 13717, 13718, 13725, 13863, 14153, 14269, 14842, 16306, 16805, 17171, 17172, 17329, 18059, 18066, 18106, 18138, 18358, 18469, 18723, 18791, 19142
--Catholic sources--Periodicals 12787
--Church of God (Anderson, Indiana) 16436
--Congregational sources--(1875 to 1899) 718, 760
--Congregational sources--(1900 to 1917) 2040, 2134, 2157, 2187, 2284, 2356, 2485
--Congregational sources--History 18097
--Congresses 4051, 4531, 8252, 8339
--Disciples of Christ sources--(1918 to 1944) 3875
--England 7329, 8760, 10950, 12015, 12164, 18492
--Episcopal sources--(1875 to 1899) 658, 1167
--Episcopal sources--(1900 to 1917) 2294, 2351
--Episcopal sources--(1918 to 1944) 3186, 3285, 3310, 3451, 3677, 5127
--Episcopal sources--History 8696, 16176
--Europe 17069, 17513, 18314
--Evangelical and Reformed Church sources--History 14211

Church work with immigrants (cont.)
--Evangelical Protestant sources--(1960 to 1969) 11274
--Evangelical Protestant sources--(1980 to 1991) 15732, 15733, 17197, 17247, 17253, 18130
--Federal Council sources--(1900 to 1917) 2888
--Federal Council sources--(1918 to 1944) 4024, 4051, 4373, 5060, 5184, 5200, 5216
--France 9084, 10299
--Germany 7979, 14753, 16203, 17123, 17876, 18316
--Great Britain 10796, 16197, 17793, 18872
--History 5428, 6686
--Japan 15150
--Latin America 12888
--Lutheran sources--(1875 to 1899) 1499
--Lutheran sources--(1900 to 1917) 18015
--Lutheran sources--(1918 to 1944) 4731
--Lutheran sources--(1980 to 1991) 15903, 16265
--Mennonite sources--(1960 to 1969) 10818
--Methodist sources--(1875 to 1899) 942, 14701
--Methodist sources--(1900 to 1917) 1762, 1986, 1987, 2139, 2183, 2185, 2198, 2426, 2605
--Methodist sources--(1918 to 1944) 3001, 3065, 3132, 3150, 3254, 3308, 3348, 3350, 3409, 3434, 3497, 3526, 3538, 3586, 3589, 3593, 3613, 3662, 3665, 3679, 4490, 5329
--Methodist sources--(1960 to 1969) 9156, 10916
--Methodist sources--(1980 to 1991) 15184, 15513, 15626, 15653, 16529, 16640, 17082, 18278, 18864
--Methodist sources--History 14348
--Methodist sources--Periodicals 3394
--NCCCUSA sources--(1945 to 1959) 6094, 6269, 6372, 6564, 6774, 6885, 7125
--NCCCUSA sources--(1960 to 1969) 8252, 8527
--New Zealand 14949
--Orthodox Eastern sources 5340, 5432
--Orthodox Eastern sources--History 2688, 5433
--Pentecostal sources 9593
--Periodicals 8960
--Presbyterian sources--(1800 to 1874) 267
--Presbyterian sources--(1875 to 1899) 12068
--Presbyterian sources--(1900 to 1917) 1971, 2440, 2458, 2539, 2644, 2679, 2742, 3010, 12068
--Presbyterian sources--(1918 to 1944) 3161, 3359, 3369, 3430, 3431, 3721, 3738, 4196, 4454, 4557, 5193
--Presbyterian sources--(1945 to 1959) 6779
--Presbyterian sources--(1970 to 1979) 13689
--Presbyterian sources--(1980 to 1991) 15433, 16426, 17275, 17396, 18536, 18552
--Presbyterian sources--History 1868, 5830, 14331, 15810, 16108
--Protestant sources--(1800 to 1874) 8990
--Protestant sources--(1875 to 1899) 703, 826, 845, 940, 982, 1033, 1070, 1151, 1229, 1231, 1284, 1394, 1580

Church work with immigrants (cont.)
--Protestant sources--(1900 to 1917) 1741, 1872, 1885, 1889, 1966, 2077, 2102, 2130, 2248, 2366, 2367, 2411, 2466, 2573, 2600, 2610, 2615, 2624, 2625, 2649, 2685, 2692, 2721, 2727, 2784, 2804, 2828, 2839, 2881, 2945, 2959, 3011, 3045, 3062, 13616, 14313
--Protestant sources--(1918 to 1944) 3012, 3014, 3320, 3323, 3327, 3389, 3596, 3601, 3605, 3804, 4067, 4259, 4409, 4460, 4491, 4531, 5259, 13616, 15951
--Protestant sources--(1945 to 1959) 5654, 5947, 6110
--Protestant sources--(1960 to 1969) 8241, 11216
--Protestant sources--(1970 to 1979) 15238
--Protestant sources--(1980 to 1991) 15342, 15825, 16471, 17016, 18025, 18241, 18260, 18354
--Protestant sources--Bibliographies 3272, 15984
--Protestant sources--History 7097, 7525, 7923, 9904, 13658, 13719
--Reformed Church in America sources--(1900 to 1917) 2817, 2913, 3028
--Reformed Church in America sources--(1918 to 1944) 3095
--Reformed Church in America sources--(1980 to 1991) 17786
--Salvation Army sources 1508
--Southern Baptist sources--(1918 to 1944) 4867
--Southern Baptist sources--(1960 to 1969) 10315
--Southern Baptist sources--(1980 to 1991) 15833, 16475
--Sweden 17968
--Unitarian Universalist sources--(1980 to 1991) 19089
--United Church of Christ sources--(1945 to 1959) 7243
--United Church of Christ sources--History 18097
--World Council of Churches sources--(1960 to 1969) 8339, 8960
--World Council of Churches sources--(1980 to 1991) 17808
Church work with juvenile delinquents 91, 6102, 7429, 7618, 8952, 9431, 9542, 9700, 10170, 11139, 12709, 14008, 17334
--American Baptist sources--(1945 to 1959) 6515
--American Baptist sources--(1980 to 1991) 17097
--Catholic sources--(1875 to 1899) 1535, 1619
--Catholic sources--(1918 to 1944) 3991
--Catholic sources--(1945 to 1959) 5619, 6615, 7094, 7366, 7461
--Catholic sources--(1960 to 1969) 10464
--Church of England sources--(1970 to 1979) 15166
--Congresses 9576
--Episcopal sources--(1945 to 1959) 7151, 7390
--Evangelical and Reformed Church sources 5573
--History 8158
--Methodist sources--(1945 to 1959) 6585, 7376, 7380
--Methodist sources--(1960 to 1969) 8346
--NCCCUSA sources--(1945 to 1959) 6584, 6885, 7222, 7919
--NCCCUSA sources--(1960 to 1969) 9132

Church work with juvenile delinquents (cont.)
--Presbyterian sources--(1945 to 1959) 7127, 7419, 7459
--Presbyterian sources--(1960 to 1969) 8493
--Protestant sources--(1800 to 1874) 86, 89
--Protestant sources--(1875 to 1899) 1004
--Protestant sources--(1900 to 1917) 2977
--Protestant sources--(1918 to 1944) 3108, 4524
--Protestant sources--(1945 to 1959) 6699, 6726, 6799, 7761, 19264
--Protestant sources--(1960 to 1969) 8251, 10697
--Protestant sources--History 14382
--Southern Baptist sources--(1945 to 1959) 6821, 6916
--Southern Baptist sources--(1960 to 1969) 10651
--United Church of Christ sources--(1945 to 1959) 7321, 7585
--United Church of Christ sources--(1960 to 1969) 9040
Church work with labor and laboring classes >> See: Church and labor
Church work with men 753, 3872, 5671, 9097
--Catholic sources--(1945 to 1959) 5923
--Methodist sources--(1900 to 1917) 2254
--Protestant sources--(1800 to 1874) 205
--Protestant sources--(1900 to 1917) 1856
--Salvation Army sources 9940, 17868
--Salvation Army sources--History 2297
Church work with migrant labor >> See further: Rural-urban migration
Church work with migrant labor 1845, 5088, 6937, 9113
--Catholic sources--(1960 to 1969) 8764
--Catholic sources--(1970 to 1979) 14063
--Catholic sources--(1980 to 1991) 18077, 19272
--Europe 10762, 13482, 17069, 17513, 18314, 19028
--Federal Council sources--(1918 to 1944) 5087
--Germany 14753
--Kenya 11979
--Methodist sources--(1960 to 1969) 8395
--Protestant sources--(1970 to 1979) 14433
Church work with minorities >> See further: (Specific minority groups)
Church work with minorities 10692, 13313, 18421
--American Baptist sources--(1970 to 1979) 13075
--American Baptist sources--(1980 to 1991) 17644, 17844
--Asia 14972
--Baptist sources--(1980 to 1991) 18440
--Baptist sources--History 16423
--Bibliographies 4390
--Canada 18260
--Catholic sources--(1945 to 1959) 6257, 6895
--Catholic sources--(1960 to 1969) 9892
--Catholic sources--(1970 to 1979) 14833, 15128
--Catholic sources--(1980 to 1991)

15803, 16523, 17083, 18220, 18619
Church work with minorities (cont.)
--Catholic sources--Congresses 14357
--Catholic sources--History 961, 13060, 13122, 14412, 16553, 17171, 18066
--Christian Churches and Churches of Christ sources 19290, 19310, 19312, 19314, 19318, 19331
--Church of God sources 13711, 16044
--Congregational sources 4041
--Disciples of Christ sources--(1918 to 1944) 4807
--England 14389, 18658, 18713
--Episcopal sources--(1900 to 1917) 2070
--Episcopal sources--(1918 to 1944) 4257
--Episcopal sources--(1970 to 1979) 12555, 14220
--Episcopal sources--(1980 to 1991) 17110, 17226, 17341, 17457
--Europe 19028
--Evangelical Protestant sources--(1970 to 1979) 12857, 14411, 14676
--Evangelical Protestant sources--(1980 to 1991) 16563, 16592, 16790, 17099, 17209, 17463, 17566, 19204
--Federal Council sources--(1918 to 1944) 4390, 4391, 5030, 5105, 5270
--France 14720
--Great Britain 13158
--Japan 13204
--Lutheran sources--(1945 to 1959) 6359
--Lutheran sources--(1980 to 1991) 18985
--Methodist sources--(1900 to 1917) 1888
--Methodist sources--(1918 to 1944) 3065, 3628, 4520
--Methodist sources--(1960 to 1969) 10449, 11286
--Methodist sources--(1970 to 1979) 11732, 12026, 12982, 13756, 13801, 13802, 13944, 14070, 15098, 15172, 15257
--Methodist sources--(1980 to 1991) 15991, 16052, 16073, 16798, 16992, 17872, 18200, 18741, 18838
--Methodist sources--Periodicals 19003
--Moravian sources 19114, 19164
--NCCCUSA sources--(1945 to 1959) 6095, 6149, 6378, 6538, 6572, 6635
--NCCCUSA sources--(1960 to 1969) 9104, 9149, 10254
--Pentecostal sources--(1980 to 1991) 17730
--Philippines 15172
--Presbyterian sources--(1918 to 1944) 4507, 5193, 5195
--Presbyterian sources--(1945 to 1959) 5941, 6276
--Presbyterian sources--(1960 to 1969) 9627
--Presbyterian sources--(1970 to 1979) 14393
--Presbyterian sources--(1980 to 1991) 15433, 18360, 19198
--Protestant sources--(1918 to 1944) 3697
--Protestant sources--(1945 to 1959) 5891
--Protestant sources--(1970 to 1979) 11712, 12788, 14104, 14433
--Protestant sources--(1980 to 1991) 15801, 16456, 17923,

18633
Church work with minorities (cont.)
--Protestant sources--History 8577, 11935
--Southern Baptist sources--(1960 to 1969) 11130, 11518
--Southern Baptist sources--(1970 to 1979) 14806
--Southern Baptist sources--(1980 to 1991) 17873, 17885
--United Church of Christ sources--(1945 to 1959) 7418
Church work with mobile home dwellers 6351, 6937, 12518
--Bibliographies 13290
--Lutheran sources--(1960 to 1969) 9351
--Methodist sources--(1970 to 1979) 13262, 13282, 14242
--NCCCUSA sources--(1945 to 1959) 6205, 6573
--Southern Baptist sources--(1970 to 1979) 12962, 13687, 13753
--Southern Baptist sources--(1980 to 1991) 15336
--Southern Baptist sources--Bibliographies 13626
Church work with narcotic addicts >> See further: Drug abuse
Church work with narcotic addicts 5476, 6013, 7389, 8708, 9700, 10697, 11610, 11611, 12279, 17490, 18734
Church work with prisoners >> See further: Rehabilitation of criminals; Chaplains (prison); Church work with criminals; Church work with juvenile delinquents; Victim offender reconciliation
Church work with prisoners 1074, 2042, 8731, 13455, 13882, 13999, 14462, 14609, 14613, 15185, 15187, 16234, 17008, 17038, 17214, 18050, 18328, 18355, 18634
--American Baptist sources--(1900 to 1917) 3029
--American Baptist sources--(1970 to 1979) 14818
--Bibliographies 9164
--Brethren sources 17022
--Canada 15393, 17579
--Catholic sources--(1960 to 1969) 10776
--Catholic sources--(1970 to 1979) 14518
--Catholic sources--(1980 to 1991) 15368, 19235
--England 9483, 10263, 16923, 18028
--Episcopal sources--(1945 to 1959) 7413
--Evangelical Protestant sources--(1970 to 1979) 12523, 14658, 14980
--Evangelical Protestant sources--(1980 to 1991) 17195, 17353, 17570, 17689, 17731, 18014, 18521, 18795
--Friends sources 14398
--Fundamentalist sources 18538
--Germany 292, 18517
--Great Britain 18027
--History 18235
--Methodist sources--(1960 to 1969) 9483
--Methodist sources--(1970 to 1979) 11849, 12053, 14579
--Methodist sources--(1980 to 1991) 15368, 16598, 17215, 17489
--Poland 19070
--Presbyterian sources--(1980 to 1991) 17386
--Protestant sources--(1800 to 1874) 115
--Protestant sources--(1875 to 1899) 689, 939, 1004

Church work with prisoners (cont.)
--Protestant sources--(1900 to 1917) 2112, 2138
--Protestant sources--(1918 to 1944) 3824, 4173
--Protestant sources--(1970 to 1979) 12470, 12525, 13437, 13988, 14249, 14528, 15156, 15270
--Protestant sources--(1980 to 1991) 15755, 15897, 16081, 16600, 17619, 17937
--Salvation Army sources 1519, 1733, 1791, 1894
--Salvation Army sources--History 8329
--South Africa 18618
--Southern Baptist sources--(1960 to 1969) 10840
--Southern Baptist sources--(1980 to 1991) 17958
--Sweden 14965
--Unitarian sources--(1900 to 1917) 2677
--Unitarian sources--(1970 to 1979) 14835
--United Church of Christ sources--(1970 to 1979) 15152
Church work with prostitutes 524, 684, 1215, 1688, 1731, 1891, 2045, 4195, 9702, 17269, 18858
--Catholic sources--(1980 to 1991) 15459, 15879, 18662
--Church of England sources--(1970 to 1979) 13799
--Episcopal sources 511
--Episcopal sources--History 12282
--Evangelical Protestant sources--(1980 to 1991) 16961, 17240, 18745
--Fiction 19296
--Germany 14758
--Great Britain 3390
--History 1377, 1566, 2388
--India 8125
--Japan 6725
--Netherlands 14205
--Presbyterian sources--(1800 to 1874) 109, 151, 160, 267
--Presbyterian sources--History 12552
--Presbyterian sources--Periodicals 117
--Protestant sources--(1800 to 1874) 80, 137, 452, 480
--Protestant sources--(1900 to 1917) 2018, 2578, 2589
--Protestant sources--History 2652
Church work with refugees >> See further: Sanctuary movement
Church work with refugees 7950, 8792, 16623, 16983, 17236, 17688, 17762, 17980, 18458, 18461, 19222
--Africa 9297
--Asia 16062
--Australia 18529, 18792
--Brethren sources 8128
--Canada 16382
--Catholic sources--(1918 to 1944) 4275, 4517
--Catholic sources--(1945 to 1959) 7164
--Catholic sources--(1960 to 1969) 10613
--Catholic sources--(1970 to 1979) 14788, 15233
--Catholic sources--(1980 to 1991) 15950, 16458, 18077, 19272
--Congresses 8339
--England 1270
--Episcopal sources--(1945 to 1959) 7062
--Episcopal sources--History 16176
--Evangelical Protestant sources--(1980 to 1991) 16549, 18546

Church work with refugees (cont.)
--Friends sources 4811
--Hong Kong 7099, 8107
--India 12089, 14488
--Korea 6031
--Latin America 16690
--Lutheran sources--(1980 to 1991) 15968, 16265
--Mennonite sources--(1980 to 1991) 16913
--Methodist sources--(1960 to 1969) 8801, 11467
--Methodist sources--(1980 to 1991) 15653, 17851
--NCCCUSA sources--(1945 to 1959) 7216
--NCCCUSA sources--(1960 to 1969) 7854
--Periodicals 12572
--Presbyterian sources--(1960 to 1969) 10110
--Presbyterian sources--(1980 to 1991) 16533
--Protestant sources--(1945 to 1959) 7495
--Protestant sources--(1980 to 1991) 15342, 15616, 16131, 16513, 17598, 18434
--Protestant sources--Bibliographies 17523
--United Church of Christ sources--(1960 to 1969) 9297
--World Council of Churches sources--(1960 to 1969) 8339
--World Council of Churches sources--(1980 to 1991) 17808
Church work with single people 9613, 13810, 14557, 17245, 17366, 17511
--American Baptist sources--(1970 to 1979) 14199
--American Baptist sources--(1980 to 1991) 16271
--Catholic sources--(1980 to 1991) 15583
--England 16132
--Episcopal sources--(1970 to 1979) 14330
--Evangelical Protestant sources--(1980 to 1991) 15940, 19001
--Germany 8244
--Lutheran sources--(1980 to 1991) 16297
--Mennonite sources--(1960 to 1969) 11206
--Methodist sources--(1970 to 1979) 14952
--Methodist sources--(1980 to 1991) 15871
--Presbyterian sources--(1970 to 1979) 14955
--Protestant sources--(1970 to 1979) 12312
--Protestant sources--Bibliographies 14722
--Southern Baptist sources--(1970 to 1979) 13062, 14425, 14485
--Southern Baptist sources--(1980 to 1991) 17466, 17612
--United Church of Christ sources--(1980 to 1991) 15388
Church work with students 3560, 8595, 9886, 14520
--Episcopal sources--(1980 to 1991) 19115
--Evangelical Protestant sources--(1980 to 1991) 17028, 17877, 19141
--Great Britain 11692
--Korea 12212
--Lutheran sources--(1960 to 1969) 11515
--Lutheran sources--(1970 to 1979) 15140
--Presbyterian sources--(1875 to 1899) 1570
--Protestant sources--(1960 to 1969) 9208, 11111
--Protestant sources--(1980 to 1991) 15696

Church work with the aged >> See further: Church work with adults; Christian education--Curriculum--Adult
Church work with the aged 5543, 15248, 17137, 18913, 18999, 19013
--American Baptist sources--(1960 to 1969) 10287
--Canada--History 13993
--Catholic sources--(1945 to 1959) 7720
--Catholic sources--(1960 to 1969) 9981
--Catholic sources--(1980 to 1991) 18220
--England 14271, 18270
--Episcopal sources--(1980 to 1991) 15441, 17063
--Evangelical Protestant sources--(1980 to 1991) 17279, 17900, 19049
--Methodist sources--(1960 to 1969) 9704
--Methodist sources--(1970 to 1979) 15129
--Methodist sources--(1980 to 1991) 16832
--NCCCUSA sources--(1945 to 1959) 6348, 6836
--Protestant sources--(1960 to 1969) 8883, 8886
--Protestant sources--(1980 to 1991) 17997
--Scotland 14428
Church work with the handicapped >> See further: Goodwill Industries
Church work with the handicapped 130, 5373, 12025, 14323, 16030
--Catholic sources 15857
--Church of England sources--(1980 to 1991) 18219
--England 1251
--Ghana 15689
--Great Britain 1930
--Hong Kong 12858
--Mennonite sources 16357
--Methodist sources--(1918 to 1944) 3136, 3228, 3237, 3250, 3610, 3834, 4331, 4435, 4442, 4633, 4833
--Methodist sources--(1960 to 1969) 8604
--United Church of Christ sources--(1980 to 1991) 15514, 15690
Church work with the mentally ill 10616, 11330, 14866, 17419
--Canada 14781
--History 12299
--Protestant sources--(1800 to 1874) 121
--Protestant sources--(1970 to 1979) 11695
Church work with the poor >> See further: Church and the poor; Poor; Poverty; Church and social problems; Charity; Social service--Religious aspects
Church work with the poor 638, 741, 1834, 1843, 6189, 8991, 9287, 10248, 10631, 12288, 18933, 19060
--Africa 12745, 15093, 19240
--American Baptist sources--(1875 to 1899) 672
--American Baptist sources--(1900 to 1917) 672, 2199
--American Baptist sources--(1945 to 1959) 7202
--American Baptist sources--(1980 to 1991) 17477
--Asia 10010, 14449, 15048, 17079
--Australia 19322 , 19358
--Baptist sources--(1980 to 1991) 15548, 17472
--Brethren sources--(1980 to 1991) 17938, 19311

Church work with the poor (cont.)
--Canada 17370, 19161
--Case studies 18442
--Catholic sources--(1800 to 1874) 13893, 15154
--Catholic sources--(1875 to 1899) 721
--Catholic sources--(1900 to 1917) 2558
--Catholic sources--(1918 to 1944) 3522
--Catholic sources--(1945 to 1959) 5783, 5935, 19261
--Catholic sources--(1960 to 1969) 7783, 8700, 9299, 9427, 9926, 11559
--Catholic sources--(1970 to 1979) 12086, 12747, 13691, 13809, 13867, 13881, 14318, 14626
--Catholic sources--(1980 to 1991) 13834, 15431, 15465, 15466, 15883, 15944, 16220, 16568, 16590, 16678, 16703, 16741, 16842, 16990, 17079, 17105, 17410, 17584, 17641, 17823, 18329, 18423, 18484, 18490, 18503, 18508, 18829, 18897, 19120, 19187
--Catholic sources--History 11295, 16496, 18791
--Christian Churches and Churches of Christ sources-- 19294, 19313, 19336, 19354
--Church of England sources--(1800 to 1874) 15
--Church of England sources--(1875 to 1899) 846, 993, 1516
--Church of England sources--(1900 to 1917) 2777
--Church of England sources--(1918 to 1944) 3859, 4284
--Church of England sources--(1980 to 1991) 15848, 15967, 16730, 17218, 18145
--Church of England sources--History 1844, 5760, 9459, 14345
--Congregational sources--(1875 to 1899) 687, 1628
--Congregational sources--History 9690
--Congresses 9977
--Developing countries 16405
--England 150, 216, 474, 521, 891, 1463, 2027, 2873, 11096, 13728, 15466, 15770, 16950, 18900
--England--History 4847, 11295
--Episcopal sources--(1800 to 1874) 225
--Episcopal sources--(1875 to 1899) 1082, 1131, 1418, 14719, 16364
--Episcopal sources--(1900 to 1917) 2070, 16364
--Episcopal sources--(1918 to 1944) 4084
--Episcopal sources--(1945 to 1959) 6215
--Episcopal sources--(1960 to 1969) 9875, 10049, 10865
--Episcopal sources--(1970 to 1979) 14083, 14571, 14730, 15148
--Episcopal sources--(1980 to 1991) 16448, 16701, 16834, 16914
--Evangelical Protestant sources--(1970 to 1979) 12324, 14004, 15004, 15189, 15190
--Evangelical Protestant sources--(1980 to 1991) 15524, 15595, 15721, 16015, 16256, 16540, 16583, 16687, 16859, 17043, 17044, 17198, 17369, 17848, 18090, 18147, 18149, 18150, 18530, 18884, 18904, 18979, 19024, 19102, 19154, 19155, 19220
--Evangelical Protestant sources--

History 10227, 13896
Church work with the poor (cont.)
--Federal Council sources--(1918 to 1944) 4777
--Fiction 1017, 1496, 2168
--Germany 5988, 13499
--Germany--History 17409
--Great Britain 18389, 18391
--Great Britain--History 17416
--Haiti 19030
--History 835, 7093, 8078, 14306, 14413
--India 12899, 13834, 14488, 15377, 15431, 15465, 16041, 16256, 16373, 16590, 16678, 16718, 17411, 17909, 18448, 18508
--Japan 16418
--Kenya 12176, 15093
--Korea 17397
--Latin America 18423
--Lutheran sources--(1960 to 1969) 9143, 9307, 9348, 9413, 9419, 10101, 10747, 11137
--Lutheran sources--(1970 to 1979) 14571
--Lutheran sources--(1980 to 1991) 16748, 16768, 16927, 17756
--Lutheran sources--Congresses 10648
--Mennonite sources--(1960 to 1969) 10962
--Mennonite sources--(1980 to 1991) 18868, 19097
--Methodist sources--(1800 to 1874) 301
--Methodist sources--(1875 to 1899) 1063, 1404, 1515
--Methodist sources--(1900 to 1917) 1952, 2182
--Methodist sources--(1918 to 1944) 3454
--Methodist sources--(1945 to 1959) 5485
--Methodist sources--(1960 to 1969) 8748, 8999, 9361, 9842, 11331
--Methodist sources--(1970 to 1979) 11916, 12215, 13535, 13597, 13844, 15196
--Methodist sources--(1980 to 1991) 15719, 17120, 17725, 17748, 18740, 18841, 19200
--Methodist sources--Congresses 11916
--Methodist sources--History 15792
--Methodist sources--Periodicals 4964
--Nazarene sources--(1980 to 1991) 17084, 17625
--NCCCUSA sources--(1945 to 1959) 6304, 6563
--NCCCUSA sources--(1960 to 1969) 7977, 8364, 8616, 9454, 10363
--NCCCUSA sources--(1980 to 1991) 18141
--Philippines 12519, 18150
--Philippines--Bibliographies 13916
--Presbyterian sources--(1800 to 1874) 545
--Presbyterian sources--(1900 to 1917) 2742
--Presbyterian sources--(1945 to 1959) 7457
--Presbyterian sources--(1960 to 1969) 8223, 8607, 8929, 9447, 9448, 9449, 10621, 11201
--Presbyterian sources--(1970 to 1979) 12639, 14946
--Presbyterian sources--(1980 to 1991) 17848, 18082, 18703
--Protestant sources--(1800 to 1874) 22, 24, 38, 101, 139, 204, 445, 565, 6035, 6639, 7634, 7853, 10495, 11904, 12753
--Protestant sources--(1875 to

1899) 607, 656, 675, 695, 748, 885, 963, 1001, 1295, 1329, 1538, 1716, 13497
Church work with the poor (cont.)
--Protestant sources--(1900 to 1917) 1840, 2045, 2165, 2418, 2592, 2648, 2769, 2879, 2896, 2931, 2988
--Protestant sources--(1918 to 1944) 3014
--Protestant sources--(1945 to 1959) 6691, 6842
--Protestant sources--(1960 to 1969) 9041, 10010, 10153, 10559, 10827, 11058
--Protestant sources--(1970 to 1979) 12312, 13992, 14836, 14841, 14995
--Protestant sources--(1980 to 1991) 16232, 16272, 16617, 18072, 18123, 18439, 18454, 18473, 18533, 18702, 18790, 19136
--Protestant sources--History 9904, 12585, 13041
--Salvation Army sources--(1875 to 1899) 971, 984, 1015, 1034, 1090, 1091, 1122, 1357, 1520, 1605
--Salvation Army sources--(1900 to 1917) 1735, 2006, 2027, 2201, 2222, 2333
--Salvation Army sources--(1918 to 1944) 4087
--Salvation Army sources--(1980 to 1991) 19297
--Salvation Army sources--History 17888
--Scotland 41, 521
--Southern Baptist sources--(1945 to 1959) 5541
--Southern Baptist sources--(1960 to 1969) 10611, 10783
--Southern Baptist sources--(1970 to 1979) 13311
--Southern Baptist sources--(1980 to 1991) 17153, 17850, 18660
--Thailand 14097
--Unitarian sources--(1800 to 1874) 118, 123, 131, 216, 4961
--Unitarian sources--(1875 to 1899) 979, 1055, 1488
--Unitarian sources--(1970 to 1979) 12607
--Unitarian sources--History 4528
--United Church of Christ sources--(1945 to 1959) 7098
--United Church of Christ sources--(1960 to 1969) 9246
--United Church of Christ sources--(1970 to 1979) 14587
--United Church of Christ sources--(1980 to 1991) 16413, 18562, 18915
--World Council of Churches sources--(1970 to 1979) 12890, 12934
--World Council of Churches sources--(1980 to 1991) 17176, 18095, 18346
Church work with the sick >> See further: Medical care; Healing
Church work with the sick 17476, 18466
--Catholic sources--(1875 to 1899) 1160
--Catholic sources--(1980 to 1991) 18695
--Catholic sources--History 16862, 18791
--Congresses 19020
--England 411, 18028, 18560
--Episcopal sources--(1900 to 1917) 2143, 2221, 2259, 2285, 2300, 2301, 2338, 2348, 2372, 2858
--Episcopal sources--(1980 to 1991) 17732, 18522, 18879
--Germany--History 17409

Church work with the sick (cont.)
--Lutheran sources--(1960 to 1969) 10162
--Lutheran sources--(1970 to 1979) 13736
--Lutheran sources--(1980 to 1991) 18313, 19176
--Methodist sources--(1980 to 1991) 17669
--Metropolitan Community Church sources 18441
--Protestant sources--(1875 to 1899) 626
--Protestant sources--(1970 to 1979) 12281
--Protestant sources--(1980 to 1991) 16171, 17520, 18323, 18651
--Southern Baptist sources--(1960 to 1969) 10956
--Southern Baptist sources--(1980 to 1991) 18402
Church work with the unemployed >> See further: Unemployment; Church and labor; poverty; poor
Church work with the unemployed 4250, 9827, 15981, 16397, 16445, 16625, 17524
--American Baptist sources--(1980 to 1991) 18251
--Catholic sources--(1918 to 1944) 4176, 4306, 4783
--Catholic sources--(1970 to 1979) 11975
--Catholic sources--(1980 to 1991) 16800, 16994
--Catholic sources--History 16249
--Church of England sources--(1980 to 1991) 16810
--Congresses 4974
--England 15103, 16867, 17262
--England--Congresses 14245
--Episcopal sources--(1918 to 1944) 3582, 4025
--Episcopal sources--(1980 to 1991) 16834, 17437
--Evangelical Protestant sources--(1918 to 1944) 5316
--Evangelical Protestant sources--(1980 to 1991) 17369, 18012, 18820
--Federal Council sources--(1918 to 1944) 3882, 4172, 4302
--Germany 14452, 16190, 18206
--Great Britain 17167, 18036
--Latin America 18250
--Lutheran sources--(1980 to 1991) 17041, 17387, 17701, 17792, 17811
--Methodist sources--(1918 to 1944) 3456, 4343, 4500
--Methodist sources--(1980 to 1991) 15480, 16686, 16710, 17220, 18256
--NCCCUSA sources--(1945 to 1959) 5950
--NCCCUSA sources--(1970 to 1979) 12425, 14373
--Netherlands 17404
--Presbyterian sources--(1970 to 1979) 14789
--Protestant sources--(1900 to 1917) 2866
--Protestant sources--(1918 to 1944) 4174, 4272
--Protestant sources--(1970 to 1979) 13433, 13872, 14395
--Protestant sources--(1980 to 1991) 15846, 16442, 16840, 16855, 16999, 17104, 18123, 18308, 18556
--Protestant sources--Bibliographies 14285, 18298
--Salvation Army sources--(1900 to 1917) 2006
--Southern Baptist sources--(1980 to 1991) 17153

Church work with the unemployed (cont.)
--United Church of Christ sources--(1960 to 1969) 9219
--World Council of Churches sources--(1980 to 1991) 17344
Church work with the working class >> See: Church and labor
Church work with tourists and travelers >> See: Travel
Church work with women >> See further: Women in church work
Church work with women 684, 2831, 11081
--Africa 14892
--Episcopal sources--(1918 to 1944) 4202
--Evangelical Protestant sources--(1980 to 1991) 18869, 18957
--History 1377, 2388
--Methodist sources--(1980 to 1991) 16598
--Protestant sources--(1900 to 1917) 2781
--Protestant sources--(1918 to 1944) 3240
--Protestant sources--(1970 to 1979) 13437
--Salvation Army sources 2096
Church work with young adults 4716, 9613
--Africa 14892
--American Baptist sources--(1980 to 1991) 15530
--Evangelical Protestant sources--(1980 to 1991) 18946
--Methodist sources--(1918 to 1944) 3532
--Methodist sources--(1960 to 1969) 9051, 9819, 10002
--Methodist sources--(1970 to 1979) 12173
--NCCCUSA sources--(1960 to 1969) 8253
--Protestant sources--(1800 to 1874) 129
--Protestant sources--(1918 to 1944) 4664
--Protestant sources--(1960 to 1969) 9933, 11111
Church work with youth 2695, 5149, 5294, 7429, 7468, 11653, 12709, 13759, 18969
--Africa 17506, 19240
--American Baptist sources--(1945 to 1959) 6492, 6515
--American Baptist sources--(1980 to 1991) 18625
--Brazil 10316
--Canada--History 14300
--Catholic sources--(1900 to 1917) 2877, 2906
--Catholic sources--(1970 to 1979) 12037, 13401
--Catholic sources--(1980 to 1991) 15879, 16187, 18539, 18662
--Catholic sources--History 5013, 5035, 6106, 19343
--China 4430
--Church of England sources--(1918 to 1944) 4141
--Church of England sources--(1980 to 1991) 15848
--Congregational sources--(1900 to 1917) 1824, 2402, 2872
--Congregational sources--(1918 to 1944) 4230
--Disciples of Christ sources--(1918 to 1944) 4755
--Disciples of Christ sources--(1960 to 1969) 10589, 11090
--England 785, 5282, 5379, 7868, 9770, 10469, 11096, 14271, 15569, 17317, 17339, 17589, 18047, 18483
--England--London 18348
--Episcopal sources--(1875 to 1899) 1660
--Episcopal sources--(1945 to

1959) 6809, 7151
Church work with youth (cont.)
--Episcopal sources--(1960 to 1969) 10399, 10424
--Evangelical Protestant sources--(1945 to 1959) 5797
--Evangelical Protestant sources--(1960 to 1969) 9693, 10017, 10096, 10966, 11452
--Evangelical Protestant sources--(1970 to 1979) 12976, 14556
--Evangelical Protestant sources--(1980 to 1991) 16484, 16517, 16729, 16859, 16968, 17133, 17317, 17687, 17765, 17797, 17877, 18074, 18119, 18191, 18335, 18483, 18718, 18810, 18869, 18874, 19139, 19330
--Federal Council sources--(1900 to 1917) 2841
--Federal Council sources--(1918 to 1944) 3999
--Federal Council sources--(1945 to 1959) 5369
--France 6877
--Germany 996, 13125
--Germany--History 2741, 3484, 3713, 4806, 5013, 5623, 16167, 19343
--Great Britain 12226, 12761
--History 6047
--Italy 15361, 15389, 18283
--Japan 4472
--Kenya 15625
--Lutheran sources--(1960 to 1969) 10087, 10130
--Lutheran sources--(1970 to 1979) 11698, 11845, 12400
--Mennonite sources--(1960 to 1969) 10918
--Mennonite sources--(1970 to 1979) 14969
--Methodist sources--(1800 to 1874) 74
--Methodist sources--(1875 to 1899) 1543
--Methodist sources--(1918 to 1944) 3945, 4686
--Methodist sources--(1945 to 1959) 6395
--Methodist sources--(1960 to 1969) 8438, 9051, 9456, 10971, 11087
--Methodist sources--(1970 to 1979) 12150
--Methodist sources--(1980 to 1991) 15990, 15991, 18838
--Moravian sources 11681
--Mormon 13966
--NCCCUSA sources--(1945 to 1959) 6458, 6463, 6479, 6500, 6558
--NCCCUSA sources--(1960 to 1969) 8757, 8761, 9723, 9905, 10013, 10777, 10974, 10984
--Netherlands 17404
--Periodicals 3739
--Presbyterian sources--(1800 to 1874) 264, 321
--Presbyterian sources--(1875 to 1899) 785, 1721
--Presbyterian sources--(1900 to 1917) 1991
--Presbyterian sources--(1918 to 1944) 4958, 5158
--Presbyterian sources--(1960 to 1969) 9890, 10836, 10909, 11284
--Protestant sources--(1800 to 1874) 145, 412, 13351
--Protestant sources--(1875 to 1899) 905, 1555
--Protestant sources--(1900 to 1917) 1792, 1837, 1941, 2108, 2602, 2614, 2689
--Protestant sources--(1918 to 1944) 3416, 3885, 4775
--Protestant sources--(1945 to 1959) 5495
--Protestant sources--(1960 to

1969) 8392, 9208, 9332, 10188, 10494, 11496, 11555
Church work with youth (cont.)
--Protestant sources--(1970 to 1979) 11795, 12204, 12470, 13139, 15254
--Protestant sources--(1980 to 1991) 17796, 18702, 18805, 18931, 18992
--Protestant sources--Bibliographies 18592
--Protestant sources--History 5035, 14382
--Reformed Church in America sources 11837
--Scotland 494, 14428
--Southern Baptist sources--(1960 to 1969) 9945
--Southern Baptist sources--(1980 to 1991) 16971
--Unitarian sources--(1900 to 1917) 2577
--United Church of Christ sources--(1960 to 1969) 9040, 9289, 10980, 19271
--United Church of Christ sources--(1980 to 1991) 15514, 18307
--United Church of Christ sources--History 16986
Church work, social >> See: Charity; Social service--Religious aspects
Church World Service 7495
Churches-in-Transition Project (Chicago, Illinois) 12382, 12409, 12764, 14128, 14496, 14497, 14896, 14901
Churches
--Secular use 1648, 2901, 10781, 12077, 12286, 12793, 13476, 14013, 14592, 16551, 17574
--Secular use--England 12119
--Secular use--Great Britain 12902, 14430
--Secular use--History 15284
Churches in literature >> See: City churches--Fiction; Clergy in literature; Underground literature
Churches in transition >> See: Change--Religious aspects; Social change and church.
Churches' Center for Theology and Public Policy 14766
Churches' Center for Theology and Public Policy (Washington, DC) 16689, 18641
Churches' Committee for Voter Registration/Education (Washington, DC) 18580
Churches' Committee on Migrant Workers in Western Europe 13482
Churches, big >> See: Big churches
Churchmen's Missionary Association for Seamen of the Port of Philadelphia 229
Cicero (Illinois)
--Religious and ecclesiastical institutions 9502, 13839
--Social conditions 14206
Cincinnati (Ohio)
--Ethnic relations--History 14582
--History 16903
--Politics and government 6457
--Politics and government--History 10965
--Religious and ecclesiastical institutions 1134, 1135, 5241, 5566, 5915, 5926, 6519, 6789, 9868, 10735, 11377, 11712, 12873, 13216, 15041, 17684, 18170, 18259, 19331
--Religious and ecclesiastical institutions--History 5826, 13153, 14692, 15154, 15695
--Social conditions 275, 835, 2018, 5809, 7622, 15261

Cities and towns >> See also: Small and middle sized cities
Cities and towns 410, 475, 3376, 3688, 3977, 4802, 4877, 7014, 7369, 8112, 9841, 10100, 10615, 11166, 11388, 11536, 11694, 16465, 16803, 16921, 16948
--Africa 6363, 8449, 9972, 11180, 11937, 13365, 13975, 14048, 14258, 17854, 18319
--Ancient 415, 1068, 1922, 2163, 2787, 5779, 6367, 7749, 7817, 7985, 8408, 8981, 9036, 9465, 9530, 11873, 12362, 12509, 12516, 12925, 13260, 13546, 13558, 14230, 14514, 14811, 14877, 15485, 15558, 16335, 16441, 16493, 16667, 16749, 16781, 17293, 17728, 17781, 18201, 18306, 19278, 19321, 19339
--Asia 16781, 17854
--Austria 10425
--Biblical teaching >> See further: Bible--Exposition on cities
--Biblical teaching 11752, 15425, 16493, 19083, 19219
--Bibliographies 1793, 1888, 2462, 4678, 4762, 5992, 8024, 8246, 8608, 10366, 11602, 12396, 13045, 13102, 13274, 13404, 13626, 14460, 14695, 15398, 16429, 16522, 16736, 16822, 17272, 17666, 18657
--Bolivia 14862
--Brazil 15040, 16909
--Canada 15809
--Canada--History 17121
--China 4502
--China--History 12362
--Civic improvement >> See: Civic improvement
--Developing countries 13061, 17017
--Developing countries--Congresses 13632
--Economic aspects 6814, 15971
--England 196, 16324
--France 1364, 6040
--Germany 2707, 7614, 16930
--Great Britain 1825, 3204, 13334, 18048
--Growth 460, 848, 981, 1254, 1284, 1344, 1539, 1587, 1642, 1663, 1828, 1842, 2058, 2357, 3641, 4026, 4197, 4230, 4595, 4678, 4870, 5214, 5602, 6511, 6520, 7055, 7122, 7298, 7453, 7606, 7641, 7645, 7667, 7681, 8204, 8460, 8477, 8616, 8636, 8885, 8906, 9016, 9079, 9383, 9730, 9766, 10154, 10173, 10343, 10775, 11357, 11500, 12594, 12728, 13761, 14084, 14244, 14385, 14534, 14555, 14921, 15245, 15268, 15752, 15767, 15895, 15956, 16362, 16675, 16909, 17017, 17062, 17231, 17389, 17465, 17503, 17911, 18294, 18739, 19184
--Growth--Africa 11985, 12080
--Growth--Bibliographies 11231
--Growth--England 13738
--Growth--France 7962
--Growth--History 4337, 7520, 8613, 10223, 11936, 12107, 12871, 14871, 15789, 18396
--Growth--India 12114, 16126
--Growth--Japan 12723
--Growth--Latin America 8290, 10758, 13996, 14575
--History 7723, 7985, 8246, 8448, 9145, 11844, 11994, 12978, 14142, 14196, 17121, 17365, 17781
--History--Periodicals 13256
--India 4772, 16839
--Information services 9826,

16648, 17259
Cities and towns (cont.)
--Ireland 13014
--Islamic 6866, 8741, 8987, 10368, 11448, 11858, 11973, 12878, 12898, 12935, 13189, 13816, 14352, 14631, 15406, 15637, 16627, 16673, 16726, 16973, 17715, 17728, 17741, 17841, 17926, 17930, 17945, 18011, 18158, 18802, 18908, 19077, 19193
--Islamic--Congresses 11818
--Islamic--Fiction 18261
--Japan 13694, 14877, 16909
--Latin America 11009, 17854
--Moral and ethical aspects 129, 232, 242, 268, 285, 335, 370, 500, 639, 1221, 1464, 1668, 1819, 2032, 2288, 2556, 2854, 3402, 3716, 4417, 5748, 6006, 7606, 8754, 9521, 9989, 10283, 10852, 11793, 12051, 12691, 12930, 13030, 13108, 13276, 13621, 14380, 14512, 16362, 16522, 18218
--Moral and ethical aspects--History 14532
--Netherlands 6803
--New Zealand 18497
--Nigeria 11392
--Periodicals 911, 14075
--Reform >> See further: Civic improvement; Social reform
--Reform 78, 147, 277, 367, 801, 823, 848, 894, 907, 981, 997, 1006, 1035, 1138, 1162, 1177, 1256, 1264, 1288, 1291, 1292, 1340, 1342, 1344, 1382, 1396, 1406, 1411, 1424, 1434, 1441, 1477, 1486, 1493, 1495, 1517, 1557, 1558, 1588, 1618, 1666, 1684, 1742, 1767, 1852, 1863, 1955, 1990, 1996, 2029, 2035, 2117, 2123, 2176, 2215, 2288, 2299, 2385, 2386, 2387, 2414, 2468, 2495, 2496, 2665, 2711, 2759, 3014, 3101, 3105, 3128, 3226, 3230, 3515, 3545, 3570, 3703, 4183, 4282, 4433, 4438, 4718, 4835, 5331, 5607, 5634, 5777, 5960, 6457, 6502, 6701, 7635, 8299, 8629, 8679, 9854, 10060, 10106, 11529, 12783, 13205, 13956, 15195, 19152
--Reform--Australia 14744
--Reform--Bibliographies 14532
--Reform--England 933, 5473, 7339, 10958
--Reform--History 3746, 3841, 4118, 5197, 5745, 5788, 8499, 8623, 10040, 10366, 10875, 10965, 11008, 11345, 11661, 11936, 12161, 12701, 13041, 13895, 14532, 14638, 14745, 16033, 16401, 17719
--Reform--Periodicals 437, 1280
--Religious aspects 276, 313, 497, 1298, 1494, 1645, 1678, 2729, 2732, 2868, 5999, 6663, 6715, 7168, 10089, 11326, 12334, 13063, 13370, 14294, 15050, 15127, 15209, 15630, 15759, 16028, 16843, 17423, 18035, 18497, 18669, 18680, 18760, 19118, 19225, 19338
--Religious aspects--Africa 13501, 17854
--Religious aspects--American Baptist 4565, 8517, 8518, 8842
--Religious aspects--Asia 18330
--Religious aspects--Bibliographies 13083
--Religious aspects--Catholic 4751, 5314, 7531, 7987, 8018, 8380, 8496, 8506, 8854, 9915, 11349, 14272, 14671, 15425, 15665, 18548
--Religious aspects--Congregational 166, 1504,

1674, 2665, 4230
Cities and towns (cont.)
--Religious aspects--Congresses 11473
--Religious aspects--England 4710, 16572, 17865, 18863
--Religious aspects--Episcopal 3022, 3506, 4133, 14195
--Religious aspects--Europe 7137
--Religious aspects--Evangelical Protestant 7776, 14319, 14347, 14401, 14929, 15492, 15929, 16313, 16393, 16765, 16883, 17357, 17947, 17948, 18084, 18450, 18725, 18810, 19209, 19219
--Religious aspects--France 7531, 15778
--Religious aspects--Germany 9524
--Religious aspects--Great Britain 4130
--Religious aspects--History 9254, 13961, 15725, 16528, 17781, 18079
--Religious aspects--India 7060
--Religious aspects--Jewish 8175, 8496, 11716, 16634
--Religious aspects--Latin America 17854
--Religious aspects--Lutheran 10089, 11421, 11879, 14910
--Religious aspects--Mennonite 7844, 9189, 10704, 11902, 17567
--Religious aspects--Methodist 1314, 1782, 1826, 2184, 3535, 3559, 3631, 4673, 4710, 9369, 19145
--Religious aspects--New Zealand 5302
--Religious aspects--Orthodox Eastern 9036
--Religious aspects--Periodicals 235, 1280, 1317, 1568, 2898, 3022, 3903, 5952, 7789, 7844, 7964, 8026, 8380, 9115, 9590, 9611, 10272, 10733, 10819, 11421, 11446, 11879, 15232, 15518, 16572, 16765, 17378, 17535, 17567
--Religious aspects--Presbyterian 2175, 2898, 4083, 8467, 8903, 10092, 14420
--Religious aspects--Protestant 413, 836, 1211, 3249, 3416, 3440, 4023, 4743, 4759, 4801, 5725, 5952, 6482, 7113, 8091, 8338, 8496, 12990, 17412
--Religious aspects--Southern Baptist 7039, 8242, 9823, 17299, 17535
--Religious aspects--Sweden 16338
--Religious aspects--Unitarian 593
--Religious aspects--United Church of Christ 8026, 9295, 9676, 13044
--Sermons 16, 190, 232, 242, 291, 294, 423, 440, 537, 584, 621, 625, 644, 705, 785, 853, 968, 1100, 1133, 1211, 1305, 1407, 2125, 2519, 3044, 3656, 3813, 4091, 4334, 4335, 4574, 4781, 4873, 5368, 6543, 7998, 8118, 10391, 10423, 10787, 10942, 11432, 11608, 14339, 15045, 15107, 16542, 16735
--Social conditions 2119, 2147, 2883, 2904, 2953, 4736, 4876, 6179, 6217, 6443, 7323, 7752, 7849, 7901, 7999, 8250, 12316, 12539, 17007, 17337
--South Africa 8834
--Switzerland 10727
--Taiwan 13399
--Thailand 16355, 16853
--United States 476, 698, 3488, 8194

Cities and towns (cont.)
--United States--History 1725, 4329, 4725, 4726, 4727, 4728, 5392, 6739, 8729, 10343, 11084, 11564, 11852, 12202, 14977, 15949, 16580
Cities and towns in literature >> See further: Symbolism in literature
Cities and towns in literature 106, 154, 203, 282, 391, 398, 524, 669, 724, 932, 1017, 1155, 1210, 1286, 1308, 1375, 1601, 1803, 1813, 1902, 2048, 2146, 2785, 2958, 3462, 3496, 3714, 3865, 3992, 4016, 4138, 4406, 5715, 7485, 8032, 8326, 8618, 9474, 10157, 10277, 11313, 11445, 12350, 15267, 15425, 15542, 16055, 16527, 17045, 17852, 18363, 18595, 19170, 19279
--England 3, 158, 233, 280, 298, 392, 4724, 11760
--France 111, 154, 377, 585, 4854, 8102
--History 4364, 6415, 6470, 7362, 7436, 7527, 8314, 8410, 8611, 9151, 9163, 9182, 9579, 12359, 14001, 14450, 15979, 16016, 16851, 17054, 17408
--Middle East 18261
Citizen participation >> See: Community Organization
Citizens' associations 6183, 6728, 7743, 8129, 8458, 14098, 14743, 14934, 15365, 16844, 17648, 17649
Citizens' associations--United States >> See further: Cooperative societies
Citizens' organizations >> See: Community organization
Citizenship 152, 1432, 1557, 2286, 2461, 3597, 4027, 5058, 5071, 5721, 6621, 8691, 12118, 13669, 15268, 15663
--Germany 18228
--Great Britain 1693
City (theology) >> See: Theology (of the city); Urbanization--Religious aspects
City and town life 968, 1096, 2068, 2948, 3945, 4133, 4701, 4759, 4777, 4876, 4986, 4987, 5059, 6544, 7489, 7558, 7848, 7893, 7900, 7999, 8083, 8094, 8105, 8183, 8259, 8427, 8542, 8544, 9268, 9865, 9882, 9920, 10311, 10359, 10685, 10801, 11133, 11256, 11263, 11333, 11789, 12234, 12480, 12684, 12760, 12870, 13119, 13533, 13587, 13761, 14253, 14272, 14512, 14760, 15031, 15715, 15738, 15847, 15877, 15935, 15978, 16005, 16070, 16191, 16214, 16295, 16327, 16928, 18172, 18857, 19204
--Africa 16366
--Congresses 5882, 6565, 6856, 11215
--England 1812, 1820, 11327, 14093, 17710
--England--History 913, 15655, 15831
--Fiction 7911
--Finland 11880
--France 15881
--Germany 4330
--Great Britain 374, 5045
--History 11868, 12393, 19157
--Japan 8010
--Periodicals 10273
--Sweden 16338
City Beautiful Movement 486, 873, 1333, 1867, 2303, 3813, 6400
--History 14006, 14225
City children >> See further:

Children; Church work with children; African American children; Parent and child; Boys; Girls
City children 313, 4299, 11445, 18156
--Africa 19240
--Descriptions 504, 605, 775, 1171, 1275, 1711, 4809, 6505, 8040, 8560, 8687, 8710, 8873, 9281, 9421, 9619, 9945, 11024, 11025, 11359, 11717, 12211, 14632, 14875, 15319, 15698, 15837, 16986, 18080
--Education 474, 562, 886, 2152, 3289, 3451, 4348, 5103, 6335, 7905, 8394, 8685, 8703, 8714, 8732, 8873, 8874, 9034, 9103, 9327, 9410, 9812, 9906, 10114, 10431, 11179, 11812, 12262, 12562, 13128, 13592, 14887, 15137, 15497, 15964, 17501, 17638, 17761, 18801
--Education--Fiction 1180
--Education--Great Britain 348
--Education--History 4911, 6236, 15154, 16986, 17364
--England 432, 474, 4070, 4921, 17218, 17709
--Fiction 377, 1772, 1976
--History 1274, 9127, 12182, 15775, 16819
--India 12089, 17501
--Italy--History 18283
--Korea 8509
--Mexico 2172, 19332
--Problems of 346, 412, 464, 748, 1084, 2173, 2528, 2614, 4906, 6437, 6646, 6660, 6864, 8786, 9011, 9555, 10493, 11210, 12025, 13258, 13667, 17241, 18477, 18957, 19004, 19355
City churches >> See further: Cathedrals; Storefront churches; City clergy; City missions; House churches; Rescue missions; Institutional churches; Community churches; Typology (city churches; Coffee House ministries; Cooperative ministries; Night ministries; Big Churches; National churches (Catholic)
City churches
--Africa 6117, 8500, 8686, 10205, 10508, 13427, 13894, 13908, 14298, 14738, 15291, 15531, 15974, 16229, 16366, 17373, 17908, 19240
--Africa--Congresses 8894, 12846, 13371
--Africa--History 8894
--Africa--Periodicals 7750, 8686, 11642
--American Baptist sources--(1800 to 1874) 1694
--American Baptist sources--(1875 to 1899) 672, 1195, 1447, 1490, 1694
--American Baptist sources--(1900 to 1917) 672, 2274, 2848
--American Baptist sources--(1945 to 1959) 7025, 7100, 7191, 7528, 12959
--American Baptist sources--(1960 to 1969) 8922, 10077, 10572, 11526, 12959
--American Baptist sources--(1970 to 1979) 14105
--American Baptist sources--(1980 to 1991) 17680, 18202
--American Baptist sources--History 5328, 10987
--American Baptist sources--Periodicals 5854, 10199
--Argentina 9344, 11488
--Asia 6649, 12566, 14218, 18968
--Assemblies of God sources 18267

City churches (cont.)
--Australia 15291, 16589, 16799, 17258, 17391, 17653, 17726, 18447 , 19358
--Australia--Periodicals 11768
--Austria 6830, 8121, 13915
--Baptist sources--(1800 to 1874) 13606
--Baptist sources--(1875 to 1899) 12654
--Baptist sources--(1918 to 1944) 3407, 3788, 5083
--Baptist sources--(1970 to 1979) 14726, 15107, 15277
--Baptist sources--(1980 to 1991) 15573, 17309, 17640, 18729, 18830, 18861, 18988
--Baptist sources--History 14492
--Baptist sources--Periodicals 18259
--Belgium 6888, 7785, 7786, 14478
--Bibliographies 1793, 3734, 4743, 5138, 5283, 5992, 7268, 7400, 7620, 7936, 8024, 8456, 8608, 8931, 8933, 9008, 9164, 9235, 9446, 9595, 9726, 9864, 10808, 10907, 11079, 11688, 11830, 12618, 13083, 13404, 13747, 14460, 14532, 14812, 15200, 15485, 15654, 16112, 16428, 16432, 16433, 16499, 16555, 16644, 16662, 16750, 16751, 16890, 17163, 17164, 17169, 17272, 17470, 17666, 17693, 18075, 18345, 18704, 18912
--Brazil 8113, 15340, 15464, 15585, 16525
--Brazil--Congresses 10334
--Brazil--History 15194
--Brethren sources--(1945 to 1959) 6444
--Brethren sources--(1960 to 1969) 9961, 10377, 10642, 11110
--Brethren sources--(1970 to 1979) 12427, 14942, 15315
--Brethren sources--(1980 to 1991) 16764, 17938
--Brethren sources--Periodicals 7789
--Canada 3958, 4957, 6317, 8070, 17370
--Canada--Bibliographies 6030
--Case studies 8215, 9752, 12232, 12313, 12561
--Catholic sources--(1800 to 1874) 422, 456, 2049, 6076, 10734, 13509, 14795, 14944
--Catholic sources--(1875 to 1899) 921, 961, 1352, 1614, 1655, 1656, 1661, 2049, 6076
--Catholic sources--1900-1910 2434
--Catholic sources--(1900 to 1917) 2089, 2384, 2434
--Catholic sources--(1918 to 1944) 3860, 3963, 4792, 4882, 5221
--Catholic sources--(1945 to 1959) 5757, 5898, 5974, 6032, 6074, 6160, 6191, 6261, 6314, 6695, 6698, 6718, 6768, 6830, 6974, 7111, 7137, 7189, 7598
--Catholic sources--(1960 to 1969) 7785, 7786, 7791, 7917, 8219, 8380, 9126, 9773, 9869, 10015, 10538, 10733, 10744, 10810, 11320
--Catholic sources--(1970 to 1979) 11789, 11910, 12085, 13147, 13255, 13530, 13561, 13628, 13656, 13765, 13812, 13866, 14226, 14279, 14346, 14451, 14511, 14574, 14593, 14640, 14706, 14743, 14833, 14880, 14897, 15232
--Catholic sources--(1980 to 1991) 15335, 15372, 15457, 15503, 15613, 15849, 15972, 16200,

16341, 16366, 16480, 16568, 16677, 16732, 16827, 16854, 16928, 17012, 17274, 17399, 17444, 17482, 17657, 17704, 18117, 18220, 18248, 18315, 18405, 18632, 18673, 19179, 19240

City churches (cont.)
--Catholic sources--Africa 8243, 11584, 13377
--Catholic sources--Congresses 11910
--Catholic Sources--History 7659, 11587, 11714, 13258, 13316, 13547, 13548, 13623, 13717, 15320, 15508, 15695, 16636, 17817, 18106, 18597, 18605, 18723
--Catholic sources--Periodicals 8380, 10733, 15232
--Chile 10419
--China 5855
--Church of England sources 8423
--Church of England sources--(1800 to 1874) 499
--Church of England sources--(1875 to 1899) 846, 1443
--Church of England sources--(1960 to 1969) 10558, 11588
--Church of England sources--(1970 to 1979) 13330, 13393, 15298
--Church of England sources--(1980 to 1991) 15967, 16042, 16906, 17894, 18060, 18468, 18777
--Church of England sources--History 15890
--Church of God sources 7271, 11396, 13711, 16044
--Collected works 7432, 8494, 9529, 10897, 14677, 18106
--Colombia 10232, 16629
--Congregational Christian sources--(1918 to 1944) 4700, 5205
--Congregational Christian sources--(1945 to 1959) 5516, 6459, 6460, 6502, 6785, 7649
--Congregational Christian sources--History 18891
--Congregational Christian sources--Periodicals 4359
--Congregational sources--(1800 to 1874) 42, 196, 526, 17766
--Congregational sources--(1875 to 1899) 1347
--Congregational sources--(1900 to 1917) 1921, 1924, 1938, 2014, 2046, 2056, 2134, 2178, 2355, 2403, 2851, 2857
--Congregational sources--History 13283, 14536, 14933
--Congresses 792, 3141, 4059, 5882, 6565, 6832, 6856, 6986, 7100, 7446, 7469, 7650, 8029, 10014, 11707
--Developing countries 17049
--Directories 5412, 9195
--Disciples of Christ sources--(1918 to 1944) 3235, 4404
--Disciples of Christ sources--(1945 to 1959) 5523, 6580, 7024
--Disciples of Christ sources--(1960 to 1969) 10937
--Disciples of Christ sources--(1970 to 1979) 12917
--Disciples of Christ sources--Congresses 3141
--England 1523, 1613, 3038, 4888, 5133, 8328, 10291, 10519, 10782, 11067, 12075, 12540, 13727, 13899, 16058, 16547, 17032, 17281, 17634, 17722, 18289, 18694, 18732, 18800, 19052
--England--Bibliographies 17733
--England--Congresses 10726

City churches (cont.)
--England--History 1450, 10958, 12929, 13264, 15161, 16103
--England--London 810, 846, 1506, 3123, 3623, 7664, 8898, 10021, 10656, 11811, 17978
--England--Periodicals 3396, 13393
--Episcopal sources--(1800 to 1874) 27, 49, 223, 539, 2161, 7986, 12319
--Episcopal sources--(1875 to 1899) 597, 954, 1073, 1510, 7852
--Episcopal sources--(1900 to 1917) 1816, 1980, 2059, 2080, 2895, 2927
--Episcopal sources--(1918 to 1944) 3915, 4029, 4708, 4736
--Episcopal sources--(1945 to 1959) 6208, 6487, 7654
--Episcopal sources--(1960 to 1969) 7931, 8751, 8844, 8904, 9168, 10388
--Episcopal sources--(1970 to 1979) 12442, 12592, 12643, 12891, 13010, 13978
--Episcopal sources--(1980 to 1991) 15729, 15816, 16106, 16139, 16180, 16833, 17159, 18958
--Episcopal sources--Congresses 8844
--Episcopal sources--History 1801, 3452, 5554
--Europe 6692, 6889, 7117, 7331, 7332, 7333, 7597, 7639, 7903, 8123, 8715, 8767, 9083, 9477, 10892, 12776, 15827, 17826
--Europe--Bibliographies 9869
--Evangelical and Reformed Church sources--(1918 to 1944) 5164, 5213, 5215
--Evangelical and Reformed Church sources--(1945 to 1959) 6390, 6815, 6823, 6986, 7195
--Evangelical and Reformed Church sources--Periodicals 6658
--Evangelical Protestant sources--(1918 to 1944) 4741
--Evangelical Protestant sources--(1960 to 1969) 8275, 8845, 9342, 9629, 9687, 9769, 9935, 10473, 10718, 10746, 10877, 10896, 10925, 11089, 11332, 11424, 11557
--Evangelical Protestant sources--(1970 to 1979) 9787, 11777, 12233, 12922, 13191, 13431, 13769, 13896, 14087, 14246, 14260, 14321, 14332, 14337, 14548, 14586, 14773, 14962, 15084, 15242, 15281
--Evangelical Protestant sources--(1980 to 1991) 15350, 16037, 16116, 16305, 17469, 17500, 17596, 17607, 18033, 18074, 18121, 18173, 18290, 18325, 18567, 18854, 19204, 19219, 19230
--Evangelical Protestant sources--Bibliographies 17292
--Evangelical Protestant sources--Congresses 12803
--Evangelical Protestant sources--History 13896
--Evangelical Protestant sources--Periodicals 9590, 16765
--Evangelical Synod of North America 4796
--Evangelical United Brethren sources 6736
--Federal Council sources--(1918 to 1944) 3955, 4059, 4066, 4701, 4730, 4743, 5165
--Federal Council sources--(1945 to 1959) 5337, 5834
--Fiction 298, 1210, 1221, 1458, 3190, 4854, 12792, 13024,

14450, 16254
City churches (cont.)
--Finland 14280, 18225
--France 478, 1364, 5494, 6232, 6634, 6714, 6723, 6951, 7043, 7091, 7135, 7149, 7268, 7300, 7342, 7430, 7561, 7616, 7962, 8088, 8273, 8360, 8373, 8471, 8492, 9605, 9952, 10708, 10709, 11020, 11397, 11766, 11933, 12092, 12647, 13353, 15778, 16414, 17558
--France--History 5109, 5547, 7531, 13511
--Friends sources--History 13412, 14933
--Fundamentalist sources--(1980 to 1991) 16503, 17047
--Germany 2406, 2572, 3520, 3651, 4400, 5584, 5764, 5831, 6597, 7008, 7303, 7636, 7663, 8080, 8405, 8734, 9628, 9869, 9944, 10295, 11063, 11217, 11360, 12311, 12756, 13142, 13566, 13840, 14121, 14677, 14880, 15908, 16904, 17574, 18264
--Germany--Congresses 15352
--Germany--History 19078
--Germany--Periodicals 5477
--Germany (East) 9251, 16461, 17893
--Ghana 6636
--Great Britain 8193, 9323, 12185, 13539, 16277
--Great Britain--Periodicals 14448
--Greece 15657
--History 3377, 5138, 5803, 6387, 11325, 14334, 14532, 16528, 18079
--Holiness Church sources--(1980 to 1991) 18839
--Hong Kong 8539
--Hong Kong--Periodicals 16755
--India 4712, 4803, 7060, 10934, 14015, 16256, 16270, 18094
--India--Congresses 7217
--Italy 8294
--Italy--History 12797
--Japan 7246, 19062
--Japan--History 9923
--Kenya 8657
--Korea 8555, 17397, 17800
--Latin America 7110, 7596, 7598, 9200, 9416, 10325, 11753, 13996, 15773, 16165, 17056, 17755
--Lutheran sources--(1875 to 1899) 964, 1379
--Lutheran sources--(1900 to 1917) 2316
--Lutheran sources--(1918 to 1944) 3106
--Lutheran sources--(1945 to 1959) 5858, 6083, 6084, 6211, 6225, 6226, 6308, 6375, 6376, 6911, 7431, 7432, 7465, 7602
--Lutheran sources--(1960 to 1969) 7881, 8116, 8203, 8267, 8485, 8580, 9056, 9105, 9121, 9147, 9150, 9291, 9298, 9488, 9855, 10897, 10922, 11421, 11570, 11603
--Lutheran sources--(1970 to 1979) 11879, 11977, 12205, 12949, 13654, 14326, 14619, 14644
--Lutheran sources--(1980 to 1991) 11879, 16332, 16651, 16759, 17020, 17421, 17818, 19012, 19242
--Lutheran sources--Congresses 7465
--Lutheran sources--Periodicals 9105, 11421, 11879
--Melanesia 17515
--Mennonite sources--(1945 to 1959) 5791
--Mennonite sources--(1960 to

1969) 7844, 8503, 8859, 8998, 9042, 9086, 10704, 10760, 10805, 11544
City churches (cont.)
--Mennonite sources--(1970 to 1979) 11863, 14612
--Mennonite sources--(1980 to 1991) 16156, 16417, 16722, 17567, 17763, 18868, 19091
--Mennonite sources--Bibliographies 16489
--Mennonite sources--Congresses 10805
--Mennonite sources--History 17543
--Mennonite sources--Periodicals 7844, 17567
--Methodist sources--(1800 to 1874) 810, 12426
--Methodist sources--(1875 to 1899) 574, 587, 930, 942, 1317, 1524, 1599
--Methodist sources--(1900 to 1917) 1317, 1736, 1783, 1931, 2038, 2392, 2605, 2782, 2802, 2887, 3261
--Methodist sources--(1918 to 1944) 3053, 3065, 3072, 3144, 3188, 3269, 3367, 3619, 3630, 3960, 3963, 3980, 4056, 4061, 4327, 4347, 4449, 4520, 4620, 4676, 4756, 4833, 4849, 4850, 4851, 4872, 4963, 5010
--Methodist sources--(1945 to 1959) 5798, 6239, 6443, 6510, 6511, 6520, 6565, 7128, 7359, 7439, 7441, 7453, 7484, 7577, 7624, 7650, 7711
--Methodist sources--(1960 to 1969) 7651, 7983, 8074, 8216, 8307, 8354, 8355, 8356, 8540, 8625, 8626, 8895, 8999, 9028, 9082, 9337, 9339, 9389, 9390, 9760, 9885, 10202, 10237, 10377, 10381, 10449, 10771, 10959, 11144, 11145, 11497, 11620
--Methodist sources--(1970 to 1979) 11967, 12002, 12077, 12392, 12537, 12798, 12833, 13581, 13827, 13899, 14072, 14288, 14292, 14339, 15146, 16910
--Methodist sources--(1980 to 1991) 15413, 15991, 16807, 17488, 18164, 18401, 18982, 19029, 19122, 19200
--Methodist sources--Bibliographies 14460
--Methodist sources--Congresses 2000, 3632, 5010, 6511, 6520, 6942, 7453, 7650, 8412, 9829
--Methodist sources--History 17352
--Methodist sources--Periodicals 942, 1317, 3394, 7651
--Nazarene sources--(1970 to 1979) 13984, 14095
--Nazarene sources--(1980 to 1991) 16158, 16168, 16417, 16624, 19167
--NCCCUSA sources--(1945 to 1959) 5542, 5882, 5951, 6122, 6417, 6563, 6688, 6742, 6771, 11688
--NCCCUSA sources--(1960 to 1969) 7824, 7977, 8047, 8523, 9697
--NCCCUSA sources--(1970 to 1979) 12266
--Netherlands 3622, 7219, 11114, 12352, 15685
--New York (NY) 2059
--New Zealand--Periodicals 5302
--Nigeria 8901, 13002
--Pentecostal sources 9593, 13088, 16361, 17730
--Pentecostal sources--History 12631
--Periodicals 7, 3321, 6491, 8686,

9115, 9210, 10819, 19283, 19306
City churches (cont.)
--Peru 8609, 10419, 17151, 18309
--Philippines 6848, 7065, 7954
--Poland 3904, 8963
--Poland--Bibliographies 6068
--Presbyterian sources--(1800 to 1874) 538, 4856
--Presbyterian sources--(1875 to 1899) 645, 893, 1166, 1442, 1501, 1507, 1513, 18716
--Presbyterian sources--(1900 to 1917) 2175, 2452, 2742, 2874, 2898, 14331
--Presbyterian sources--(1918 to 1944) 3226, 4002, 4454, 4780, 4812, 5063, 5079, 5243
--Presbyterian sources--(1945 to 1959) 5339, 5407, 5439, 5441, 5443, 5506, 5546, 5820, 5941, 6229, 6267, 6402, 6413, 6550, 6647, 6793, 6837, 6955, 7077, 7146, 7458, 7528, 7649
--Presbyterian sources--(1960 to 1969) 7755, 8029, 8031, 8144, 8289, 8322, 8607, 8637, 8667, 8768, 8798, 8860, 8943, 8965, 9529, 9611, 10292, 10380, 10539, 10540, 10618, 11142, 11200, 11601, 17035
--Presbyterian sources--(1970 to 1979) 12054, 12956, 13839, 14609, 14687, 14937, 15097
--Presbyterian sources--(1980 to 1991) 18703, 19227
--Presbyterian sources--Bibliographies 8608, 8931
--Presbyterian sources--Congresses 6756, 7464, 12706
--Presbyterian sources--History 844, 5288, 14381, 15568, 15810
--Presbyterian sources--Periodicals 2898, 6550, 9611, 10047
--Protestant sources--(1800 to 1874) 79, 402, 421, 6035, 7834, 12774, 12979, 13869, 14944
--Protestant sources--(1875 to 1899) 792, 809, 836, 864, 905, 910, 918, 924, 1002, 1422, 1461, 1494, 1517, 1568, 1592, 1673, 1686, 15067
--Protestant sources--(1900 to 1917) 1864, 1922, 1957, 2304, 2518, 2543, 2680, 2721, 2774, 2938, 4907
--Protestant sources--(1918 to 1944) 3172, 3393, 3479, 3506, 3602, 3757, 3796, 3879, 3897, 4038, 4053, 4102, 4294, 4305, 4419, 4776, 4788, 4871, 4905, 4907, 4909, 4910, 4949, 5076, 5262, 5330, 5367
--Protestant sources--(1945 to 1959) 5349, 5545, 5603, 5739, 5757, 5815, 5859, 5955, 6018, 6043, 6086, 6142, 6483, 6491, 6594, 6642, 6690, 6796, 6872, 7043, 7101, 7460, 7483, 7528
--Protestant sources--(1960 to 1969) 7811, 8039, 8153, 8219, 8376, 8433, 8440, 8481, 8494, 8671, 8697, 8822, 8946, 8959, 9027, 9064, 9115, 9292, 9360, 9637, 9688, 9768, 10140, 10182, 10307, 10749, 10827, 10981, 11225, 11506, 11628
--Protestant sources--(1970 to 1979) 11817, 12232, 12247, 12990, 13520, 13657, 13825, 14469, 14677, 14963, 14975, 15271, 17301
--Protestant sources--(1980 to 1991) 15518, 15762, 15999, 16113, 16981, 17127, 17355, 17545, 17726, 17783, 18161, 18814, 18862, 18920
--Protestant sources--Congresses 792, 4623, 4982, 6772, 8484

City churches (cont.)
--Protestant sources--Fiction 9238
--Protestant sources--History 4692, 5803, 11852, 12978, 14532, 19113
--Protestant sources--Periodicals 76, 477, 1196, 1568, 3903, 5952, 6000, 6153, 7811, 7964, 7974, 8469, 9115, 10759, 11370, 11446, 12003, 12196, 12528, 14505, 15246, 15453, 15518, 17378
--Reformed Church in America sources--(1960 to 1969) 7959, 9813, 11193
--Reformed Church in America sources--(1970 to 1979) 11745, 12648, 13790
--Reformed Church in America sources--(1980 to 1991) 15360, 18721
--Reformed Church in America sources--Periodicals 19283, 19306
--Scotland 6413, 7547, 11504, 12956, 17898
--Scotland--History 14611
--Seventh Day Adventist sources 4586, 5999, 7772, 12096, 12791, 15586
--Singapore 8217, 17363
--South Africa 9165, 11734, 12718
--South Africa--Congresses 16771
--Southern Baptist sources--(1900 to 1917) 2797, 2880
--Southern Baptist sources--(1918 to 1944) 3258
--Southern Baptist sources--(1945 to 1959) 6270, 7713
--Southern Baptist sources--(1960 to 1969) 8663, 9353, 10166, 10208, 10694, 10738, 10823, 10983, 11079
--Southern Baptist sources--(1970 to 1979) 12239, 13124, 13741, 14439, 15011
--Southern Baptist sources--(1980 to 1991) 15716, 15795, 15835, 16023, 16024, 16070, 16199, 16242, 16318, 16495, 16501, 16561, 16596, 16618, 16666, 16814, 16845, 17535, 17962, 17978, 18043, 18075, 18853
--Southern Baptist sources--Bibliographies 9726, 10808, 14812, 16112, 16499, 17164
--Southern Baptist sources--Congresses 8663, 10983
--Southern Baptist sources--Periodicals 17535
--Spain 16576, 17431
--Spain--Congresses 13696
--Storefronts >> See: Storefront churches
--Sweden 8847
--Sweden--History 16045
--Switzerland 7160, 13071
--Thailand 6849
--Unitarian sources--(1800 to 1874) 352
--Unitarian sources--(1875 to 1899) 1053
--Unitarian sources--(1900 to 1917) 2832
--Unitarian sources--(1945 to 1959) 7063
--United Brethren sources 1460, 1728
--United Church of Christ sources--(1945 to 1959) 7313, 7446, 12959
--United Church of Christ sources--(1960 to 1969) 7816, 7933, 8026, 8169, 8363, 8573, 8749, 8864, 9160, 9295, 10204, 10293, 11468, 11633, 12959
--United Church of Christ

sources--(1970 to 1979) 12382, 14159, 14497, 14896
City churches (cont.)
--United Church of Christ sources--(1980 to 1991) 17555
--United Church of Christ sources--Periodicals 7933, 8025, 8026
--United States (foreign perspectives on) 6695, 7111, 10033
--Venezuela 17118
--World Council of Churches sources--(1960 to 1969) 8615, 8632, 8796
--Yugoslavia 12105
--Zaire 17908
City clergy >> See further: Clergy
City clergy 6761, 7267, 7382, 8269, 8282, 12851, 13392, 17557, 18998, 19162
--Africa 9415, 10753, 14298, 16734
--American Baptist sources--(1875 to 1899) 949
--American Baptist sources--(1945 to 1959) 6648, 7064
--American Baptist sources--(1970 to 1979) 13684
--American Baptist sources--Biography 3033, 3790, 5125, 6401, 10197, 10987, 19128
--Asia 6649
--Australia 16509, 16564, 16712, 16799, 17653, 19358
--Austria 8004
--Baptist sources--(1918 to 1944) 5931
--Baptist sources--(1945 to 1959) 5956
--Baptist sources--Biography 12654
--Bibliographies 9164, 18365
--Biography 638, 670, 1275, 1541, 1714, 1815, 1848, 1962, 2059, 2442, 2809, 2994, 3355, 3452, 3841, 4107, 4358, 4545, 4583, 4961, 5110, 5739, 6868, 7986, 8075, 8084, 9866, 9904, 11033, 12046, 12319, 15973, 16107, 17668, 18427, 19026
--Brazil 8881
--Brethren sources--(1960 to 1969) 9910
--Catholic sources--(1800 to 1874) 17092
--Catholic sources--(1875 to 1899) 649, 4583
--Catholic sources--(1900 to 1917) 2251, 2263, 2722, 3694, 13398
--Catholic sources--(1918 to 1944) 3358, 3542, 3598, 3918, 4176, 4182, 4213, 4306, 5221, 5279, 5298, 13791
--Catholic sources--(1945 to 1959) 5656, 6521, 6694, 6956, 7031, 7071, 7252, 7304, 7745
--Catholic sources--(1960 to 1969) 8077, 8544, 8755, 9426, 9478, 9857, 9975, 10434, 10536, 11524, 11554
--Catholic sources--(1970 to 1979) 12020, 12301, 12887, 13162, 13665, 13715, 14283, 14403, 14568, 14762, 15018
--Catholic sources--(1980 to 1991) 15828, 16341, 16398, 16427, 16676, 16734, 16909, 17268, 17323, 17530, 17539, 17983, 18351, 18587
--Catholic sources--Africa 8243, 11584, 13377
--Catholic sources--Biography 3471, 3484, 3713, 4433, 4806, 5319, 5623, 6157, 6316, 6759, 8415, 8669, 8737, 8881, 11728, 11761, 12095, 13141, 13875, 14746, 15144, 15421, 15461, 16025, 16167, 16636, 16893,

17092, 18781, 18916, 18947, 19344
City clergy (cont.)
--Catholic sources--Fiction 377
--Catholic sources--History 12608, 14269, 14581, 14692, 15176, 15702, 19066
--Church of England sources--(1875 to 1899) 882
--Church of England sources--(1945 to 1959) 5437
--Church of England sources--(1960 to 1969) 10239, 11458
--Church of England sources--(1970 to 1979) 13330, 13369
--Church of England sources--(1980 to 1991) 17583, 17681, 17990
--Church of England sources--Biography 842, 1463, 1844, 2061, 2155, 2859, 3127, 3354, 3744, 4207, 4486, 4995, 5694, 5760, 6173, 8871, 8899
--Congregational Christian sources--(1945 to 1959) 6393, 6785
--Congregational sources--(1800 to 1874) 125, 386, 387, 11891
--Congregational sources--(1875 to 1899) 1027, 1361, 1628
--Congregational sources--Biography 2318, 2459, 2940, 3727, 3867, 4238, 4723, 4735, 4839, 5277, 5709, 6588, 6923, 8079, 9690, 10304, 11390, 12166, 14764
--Congresses 16929
--Disciples of Christ sources--(1945 to 1959) 7316
--Disciples of Christ sources--(1970 to 1979) 12542
--El Salvador 18781
--England 196, 374, 2313, 4075, 5806, 6037, 7845, 8956, 12579, 16547, 17032, 17281, 19052
--England--Biography 1126, 1154, 1163, 1583, 1914, 2031, 2166, 2334, 3145, 3162, 3411, 4446, 4631, 5378, 6763, 12969
--England--Fiction 653
--England--History 913, 12929
--England--London 1815, 3358, 17375
--Episcopal sources--(1800 to 1874) 136, 303, 394, 1007, 7986, 12319
--Episcopal sources--(1875 to 1899) 554, 1082, 1418
--Episcopal sources--(1900 to 1917) 1980, 2059
--Episcopal sources--(1918 to 1944) 3568, 5040
--Episcopal sources--(1945 to 1959) 5676, 6393
--Episcopal sources--(1960 to 1969) 8938, 8996, 10308, 10424, 11065, 11280
--Episcopal sources--(1970 to 1979) 13749, 13957, 14684
--Episcopal sources--(1980 to 1991) 16204, 16296, 17647, 18711, 18958, 19234
--Episcopal sources--Biography 623, 1007, 2416, 2882, 3368, 3452, 3801, 11002, 12282, 14192
--Episcopal sources--Fiction 4519
--Europe 2359, 8182
--Evangelical and Reformed Church sources 5053
--Evangelical and Reformed Church sources--Biography 14211
--Evangelical Protestant sources--(1918 to 1944) 3698
--Evangelical Protestant sources--(1970 to 1979) 15042, 15272
--Evangelical Protestant sources--(1980 to 1991) 17749, 17795, 18122, 18569, 18822, 18904

City clergy (cont.)
--Evangelical Protestant sources--Biography 2435, 9573, 16350, 17912
--Federal Council sources--(1918 to 1944) 4533
--Fiction 1028, 4543, 5054, 6195, 8032, 18363
--France 5836, 5867, 7069, 7656, 15421
--France--Biography 5799
--Germany 996, 2415, 7745, 7927, 8059, 9218, 10231
--Germany--Biography 2741, 3484, 3713, 4806, 5623, 8634, 16167, 17409
--Great Britain 18083, 18217
--Great Britain--History 16164
--History 10992
--Hong Kong 12866
--India 10019, 14015
--Japan 13981
--Jewish 6473, 7314, 7856, 17144, 17251
--Jewish--Biography 14307, 16723
--Jewish--History 6064, 13033
--Kenya 14298
--Latin America 9912, 15773
--Lutheran sources--(1945 to 1959) 5680, 6431
--Lutheran sources--(1960 to 1969) 8824, 9181, 9581, 11085
--Lutheran sources--(1970 to 1979) 13487
--Lutheran sources--(1980 to 1991) 15391, 17283, 17423
--Methodist sources--(1800 to 1874) 443, 2071
--Methodist sources--(1875 to 1899) 832, 930, 1534, 1675
--Methodist sources--(1900 to 1917) 2365
--Methodist sources--(1918 to 1944) 3549
--Methodist sources--(1945 to 1959) 5758, 6583, 7265, 7299
--Methodist sources--(1960 to 1969) 9395, 9932, 10445, 11534
--Methodist sources--(1970 to 1979) 12422, 12662, 13953, 14035, 14461, 14503, 15146, 15279
--Methodist sources--(1980 to 1991) 16110, 16807, 16933, 17609, 18841
--Methodist sources--Biography 1008, 1534, 2859, 5971, 6489, 10437, 12342, 15693, 16656, 19123
--NCCCUSA sources--(1945 to 1959) 6418, 6713, 6737, 6904
--NCCCUSA sources--(1960 to 1969) 7879, 9205
--NCCCUSA sources--(1970 to 1979) 11859
--New Guinea 17382
--New York (NY) 2059
--New Zealand 14403
--Orthodox Eastern sources--Biography 5432, 5433
--Philippines 16149, 17960
--Poland 2394
--Political activity 823
--Presbyterian sources--(1800 to 1874) 23, 443
--Presbyterian sources--(1945 to 1959) 6259
--Presbyterian sources--(1960 to 1969) 9303, 10158, 10772, 11200
--Presbyterian sources--(1980 to 1991) 17310
--Presbyterian sources--Biography 844, 2801, 3545, 3795, 11915, 18336
--Protestant sources--(1800 to 1874) 17, 47, 99, 266, 290, 540, 583, 2994, 6429, 17416

City clergy (cont.)
--Protestant sources--(1875 to 1899) 827, 838, 987, 1001, 1609, 1610
--Protestant sources--(1900 to 1917) 2631
--Protestant sources--(1918 to 1944) 3979, 4107, 4162
--Protestant sources--(1945 to 1959) 6720, 6827, 7613
--Protestant sources--(1960 to 1969) 8039, 8192, 8283, 8545, 8736, 8993, 9362, 10090, 10475, 11366, 11428, 12689
--Protestant sources--(1970 to 1979) 12020, 12028, 12328, 12401, 13035, 13477, 14458, 14951, 15307
--Protestant sources--(1980 to 1991) 15382, 15686, 15756, 16281, 18214, 18223, 18372, 19096, 19101
--Protestant sources--Bibliographies 15654
--Protestant sources--Biography 939, 2681, 11008, 13662, 13800
--Protestant sources--Fiction 1017, 1180, 1496
--Protestant sources--History 6330
--Reformed Church in America sources--(1970 to 1979) 13184
--Reformed Church in America sources--Biography 12499
--Scotland 390, 15029
--Scotland--Biography 199, 255, 287, 288
--Southern Baptist sourccs--(1918 to 1944) 4484
--Southern Baptist sources--(1960 to 1969) 10221
--Southern Baptist sources--(1970 to 1979) 12315, 12497, 13838
--Southern Baptist sources--(1980 to 1991) 15410, 16901, 17276, 17702, 17891
--Sweden 11644
--Unitarian sources--(1800 to 1874) 146, 147, 163, 169, 215, 227, 541
--Unitarian sources--(1875 to 1899) 823, 653
--Unitarian sources--(1980 to 1991) 19107
--Unitarian sources--Biography 189, 1934, 4446, 13680, 17174
--United Church of Christ sources--(1960 to 1969) 8454, 9054, 9061, 9265, 9587, 9601
--United Church of Christ sources--(1970 to 1979) 11946, 14020
--United Church of Christ sources--(1980 to 1991) 16643, 17714
--United Church of Christ sources--Biography 15349
--World Council of Churches sources--(1960 to 1969) 8633
City clergy, training of >> See further: Clergy, training of; Theological education; Theological Seminaries; African American clergy, training of
City clergy, training of 1443, 7316, 10869
--Action orientation 7847, 8011, 8809, 8920, 8934, 9102, 9179, 9395, 9607, 9878, 9974, 10090, 10126, 10229, 10636, 10707, 10864, 10943, 11160, 11203, 11204, 11205, 11373, 11419, 11591, 11626, 11678, 11679, 11756, 11817, 11851, 11877, 12021, 12349, 12371, 12568, 12847, 12859, 13284, 15582
--Action orientation--History 18385
--Africa 7908, 12080, 12115,

13263, 13427, 13967
City clergy, training of (cont.)
--Asia 12635, 14247
--Australia 8470, 16712
--Bibliographies 18643
--Canada 14617
--England 12206, 12228, 12800, 13070, 15309, 16059, 17009, 17180, 18356, 18905, 19045
--Europe 11573
--Evangelical orientation 15229, 15246, 16884, 17010, 17073, 17292, 17439, 17440, 17843, 17859, 17891, 18092, 18940
--Field work 2611, 7593, 8262, 12078, 12378, 17292, 18133, 18702
--France 10675
--Germany 12682
--Great Britain 5045, 15440, 17697, 18053
--History 17548
--Hong Kong 17676
--India 16256
--Industrial orientation 5388, 6382, 7192, 11573, 12024, 12911, 15440
--Industrial orientation--Bibliographies 11503
--Jewish 3505
--Kenya 11673, 13326
--Latin America 9912, 11791
--Melanesia 13924
--Periodicals 15246
--Philippines 10525, 12634
--Schools, programs, etc. 4308, 6567, 7301, 8411, 8748, 9303, 9371, 9442, 9443, 9562, 9563, 9581, 9679, 9741, 9774, 9783, 9798, 9900, 9927, 9928, 9929, 9959, 9987, 10049, 10193, 10403, 10492, 10728, 10735, 10736, 10737, 10757, 10895, 10911, 11167, 11174, 11590, 11749, 11769, 11822, 11829, 11831, 11897, 12152, 12290, 12911, 13104, 13172, 13298, 13451, 13590, 14247, 14257, 14474, 14772, 15002, 15309, 16110, 16455, 16487, 16571, 16597, 16777, 17073, 18196, 18356, 18372, 18421, 18514, 18731, 18787, 18824, 18873, 19352
--Scotland 12024
--Sociology 1125, 1336, 1337, 1505, 2531, 2550, 2879, 3025, 3482, 3485, 3523, 3531, 4587, 6976, 9265, 11665, 14839, 18350
--South Africa 12364, 12911, 17316
City Home Mission Society (New York, NY) 2411, 2538
City housing >> See: Housing
City life >> See: City and town life
City Lutherans in Action (Detroit, Michigan) 15391
City Mission Society (Hartford, Connecticut) 359
City Missionary Society (Chicago, Illinois) 5323
City Missionary Society (Columbus, Ohio) 253
City Missionary Society (Youngstown, Ohio) 630
City Missionary Society of Boston 60, 69
--History 9824
City missions >> See further: Rescue missions; Missions--Biblical teaching
City missions 116, 1596, 2057, 3850, 6189, 14026, 15998
--Africa 8449, 12115, 14298, 14361, 14543, 15163, 16734, 17455, 17716, 18512, 18981, 19240
--Africa--History 15024

City missions (cont)
--American Baptist sources--(1800 to 1874) 461, 507
--American Baptist sources--(1875 to 1899) 592, 931, 1032
--American Baptist sources--(1900 to 1917) 2848
--American Baptist sources--(1918 to 1944) 3555
--American Baptist sources--(1945 to 1959) 6008, 6514, 6589, 7540
--American Baptist sources--(1970 to 1979) 14988
--American Baptist sources--(1980 to 1991) 16423, 19034
--American Baptist sources--History 3033, 6401, 8819
--American Baptist sources--Periodicals 586
--Argentina 10740, 10968, 14618
--Asia 14171, 14399, 18967
--Australia 10149, 11338, 11466, 14053,17078,17258,18447,19358
--Australia--History 8550, 16937, 17207
--Baptist sources--(1800 to 1874) 186, 324, 466
--Baptist sources--(1875 to 1899) 1701
--Baptist sources--(1945 to 1959) 7245
--Baptist sources--(1960 to 1969) 9582
--Baptist sources--(1970 to 1979) 14665
--Baptist sources--(1980 to 1991) 17230, 17231, 18034, 18111, 18476
--Baptist sources--History 5237
--Bibliographies 2962, 6155, 12618, 14334, 15200, 17693
--Brazil 15340, 15464, 16620
--Brethren sources--(1980 to 1991) 17875, 17938
--Brethren sources--History 18054
--Canada 8465, 11311, 14003, 14646
--Canada--History 14256
--Canada--Montréal 5857
--Catholic sources--(1800 to 1874) 12164, 15154
--Catholic sources--(1875 to 1899) 1499
--Catholic sources--(1900 to 1917) 2010
--Catholic sources--(1918 to 1944) 4052, 5015, 5298
--Catholic sources--(1945 to 1959) 7137
--Catholic sources--(1960 to 1969) 8443, 8755, 9204, 9733
--Catholic sources--(1970 to 1979) 13834, 15018, 15461, 17411
--Catholic sources--(1980 to 1991) 12899, 15423, 15431, 15432, 15465, 15883, 15975, 16373, 16411, 16590, 16678, 17297, 17410, 17554, 17584, 17909, 18446, 18448, 18508
--Catholic sources--History 2949, 12608, 16496
--Catholic sources--Periodicals 15232
--Chile 10419
--Church of England sources--(1800 to 1874) 351, 12164, 14345, 16252, 17842
--Church of England sources--(1875 to 1899) 551, 14345
--Church of England sources--(1900 to 1917) 1928, 14345
--Church of England sources--(1918 to 1944) 4428
--Church of England sources--(1980 to 1991) 16546, 17626, 17858, 17956, 18217
--Church of England sources--History 4530

City missions (cont.)
--Colombia 17464
--Congregational Christian sources--(1918 to 1944) 4399
--Congregational Christian sources--(1945 to 1959) 5892, 7170
--Congregational Church sources--(1900 to 1917) 3028
--Congregational sources--(1800 to 1874) 252, 359, 399, 519
--Congregational sources--(1875 to 1899) 678, 717, 718, 802, 867
--Congregational sources--(1900 to 1917) 1808, 2104
--Congregational sources--History 13105
--Congresses 351, 12063, 18565
--Disciples of Christ sources--(1918 to 1944) 4766
--England 132, 351, 374, 1844, 1932, 2975, 4528, 4921, 5248, 6475, 12088, 12164, 12195, 12446, 13314, 13562, 14080, 14389, 15403, 15407, 15436, 15913, 16058, 16572, 17453, 17888, 18531, 18780
--England--Bibliographies 17733
--England--Birmingham 2500
--England--History 1549, 3846, 9683, 13264, 15161, 16103, 17416, 17842
--England--Liverpool 3411, 4268
--England--London 152, 274, 341, 363, 366, 369, 411, 432, 471, 521, 535, 548, 668, 715, 726, 735, 761, 906, 1018, 1019, 1031, 1057, 1081, 1087, 1392, 1506, 1794, 1928, 1972, 2038, 2334, 2352, 3695, 3837, 3939, 3974, 3985, 3994, 4123, 4124, 4132, 4205, 4248, 4301, 4492, 4599, 4631, 4653, 4682, 4710, 4828, 4978, 5378, 5420, 5465, 5845, 5878, 5879, 6105, 6119, 6410, 6855, 8058, 9282, 9711, 10186, 10664, 10665, 11157, 11574, 12735, 13619, 13879, 14345, 14491, 15569, 17368, 17495, 18031, 18047, 18348
--England--Manchester 3517, 3838, 4632
--England--Periodicals 221
--Episcopal sources--(1800 to 1874) 51, 104, 113, 162, 172, 201, 206, 210, 225, 281, 303, 304, 338, 451, 479, 539, 4269
--Episcopal sources--(1875 to 1899) 778, 941, 980, 1049, 1167, 1492, 14719
--Episcopal sources--(1900 to 1917) 1866, 2351, 2494, 3003
--Episcopal sources--(1918 to 1944) 3022, 3421, 3915, 5042
--Episcopal sources--(1945 to 1959) 5968, 6835
--Episcopal sources--(1960 to 1969) 7822, 8818, 9696, 10520, 11065
--Episcopal sources--(1970 to 1979) 12845, 14777, 15225
--Episcopal sources--(1980 to 1991) 15441, 15730, 16106, 16139, 16204, 16381, 16914, 17550, 17724, 18711
--Episcopal sources--History 5703, 15306
--Episcopal sources--Periodicals 162, 3022
--Estonia 3609
--Europe 13949
--Europe--History 14923
--Evangelical and Reformed Church sources 4925, 6529
--Evangelical Protestant sources--(1900 to 1917) 1810, 2475, 2778
--Evangelical Protestant sources--(1918 to 1944) 3672, 3698,

3901, 4194, 4637, 4714, 5316
City missions (cont.)
--Evangelical Protestant sources--(1945 to 1959) 5520, 5793, 5930, 6712, 7503
--Evangelical Protestant sources--(1960 to 1969) 8358, 8547, 9725, 10723, 10954, 11950, 14008
--Evangelical Protestant sources--(1970 to 1979) 12625, 12630, 13176, 13191, 13557, 13886, 13946, 13970, 13987, 14110, 14117, 14176, 14362, 14556, 14647, 14778, 14929, 15001, 15056, 15060, 15143, 15229, 15230, 15272, 15285, 15293, 15314
--Evangelical Protestant sources--(1980 to 1991) 15401, 15405, 15438, 15564, 15589, 15595, 15708, 15723, 15736, 15920, 15934, 16325, 16531, 16593, 16702, 16711, 16728, 16729, 16825, 17084, 17099, 17116, 17198, 17201, 17270, 17395, 17478, 17502, 17603, 17687, 17690, 17861, 17877, 17954, 18006, 18012, 18133, 18146, 18147, 18216, 18303, 18348, 18380, 18431, 18449, 18514, 18518, 18565, 18612, 18636, 18637, 18663, 18718, 18722, 18745, 18761, 18802, 18854, 18957, 18991, 19034
--Evangelical Protestant sources--History 2435
--Evangelical Protestant sources--Periodicals 9590, 11759, 15669, 15671, 16572, 16765
--Federal Council sources--(1918 to 1944) 4738, 4857
--Fiction 3496, 6036
--France 482, 702, 849, 1062, 1235, 1239, 1410, 1484, 1809, 7149, 10628, 16974
--France--History 10118, 16002
--France--Paris 589, 604, 819
--Friends sources 548, 18644
--Fundamentalist sources--(1980 to 1991) 16503, 17743, 18190, 18191, 18549
--Germany 239, 400, 555, 708, 995, 2232, 2949, 4400, 5957, 7252, 14709, 14758, 14785, 15109, 19163
--Germany--Berlin 934, 1853
--Germany--History 1620, 14129
--Germany (East) 15057
--Ghana 11995
--Great Britain 2209, 14902, 16550, 17180, 18217, 18987
--History 1962, 4101
--Hong Kong 7099, 12866, 14909, 18626
--Hong Kong--History 13408
--India 1734, 4712, 8071, 10934, 12785, 14015, 14814
--Ireland--History 18842
--Japan 2663, 11843, 12063, 18706
--Kenya 12175, 14298, 15957, 16138
--Korea 13376, 14215, 15325
--Latin America 16206, 17056, 18860
--Lutheran sources >> See further: Inner mission
--Lutheran sources--(1875 to 1899) 568, 1499, 1669
--Lutheran sources--(1900 to 1917) 2499, 2532, 2814
--Lutheran sources--(1918 to 1944) 3831, 4298
--Lutheran sources--(1945 to 1959) 5586, 6206, 6211
--Lutheran sources--(1960 to 1969) 8794, 9143, 10626, 11603
--Lutheran sources--(1970 to

1979) 11878, 12192, 13654, 14591, 14648
City missions (cont.)
--Lutheran sources--(1980 to 1991) 15892, 17020, 17965, 18525, 19098
--Lutheran sources--History 4635
--Lutheran sources--Periodicals 239
--Melanesia 17515
--Mennonite sources--(1900 to 1917) 2932
--Mennonite sources--(1918 to 1944) 3213, 3965, 4607, 4643
--Mennonite sources--(1945 to 1959) 5424, 5813, 6176
--Mennonite sources--(1960 to 1969) 9859, 10073, 10760
--Mennonite sources--(1970 to 1979) 11966, 12828
--Mennonite sources--(1980 to 1991) 16417, 17534, 19097
--Mennonite sources--History 5400, 16955
--Methodist sources--(1800 to 1874) 254, 301, 336, 356, 428, 524, 1266, 1286, 18376
--Methodist sources--(1875 to 1899) 730, 832, 906, 920, 942, 943, 1003, 1018, 1238, 1266, 1692, 15110
--Methodist sources--(1900 to 1917) 1932, 2073, 2186, 2352, 2392, 2955, 2956
--Methodist sources--(1918 to 1944) 3046, 3183, 3247, 3250, 3628, 3834, 4490, 4710, 4862, 5041, 5112
--Methodist sources--(1960 to 1969) 7889, 7920, 8068, 8197, 9467, 9843, 9853, 9871, 9906, 10256, 11409, 11485
--Methodist sources--(1970 to 1979) 12999, 13562, 13580, 13581, 13700
--Methodist sources--(1980 to 1991) 15991, 16039, 16058, 16092, 16622, 17067, 17147, 17495, 18333, 18531, 18545
--Methodist sources--History 16322
--Methodist sources--Periodicals 942
--Nazarene sources 13246
--Nazarene sources--(1980 to 1991) 16158, 16624
--NCCCUSA sources--(1945 to 1959) 6462, 6463, 6479, 6528, 6720, 6885, 6904, 8359
--NCCCUSA sources--(1960 to 1969) 8251, 10267, 10946, 10984, 11075
--NCCCUSA sources--Periodicals 5952
--Netherlands 11481, 12415, 15704, 17136
--New Guinea 11059, 13663, 14823
--New Zealand 12267
--New Zealand--History 2809
--Nigeria 14361
--Pentecostal sources 14182
--Periodicals 221, 485, 523, 628, 1750, 10733, 10819
--Peru 10419
--Philippines 18322, 18822
--Presbyterian sources--(1800 to 1874) 194, 291, 472
--Presbyterian sources--(1875 to 1899) 662, 686, 952, 1190, 1637
--Presbyterian sources--(1900 to 1917) 1971, 1979, 2742, 2801, 3024, 14256
--Presbyterian sources--(1918 to 1944) 3158, 3161, 3304, 3543, 4083, 4196, 4567, 5321
--Presbyterian sources--(1945 to 1959) 6093, 6779, 6945
--Presbyterian sources--(1960 to

1969) 9917, 10353, 10601, 10901
City missions (cont.)
--Presbyterian sources--(1970 to 1979) 14789, 14828
--Presbyterian sources--(1980 to 1991) 18327
--Presbyterian sources--Congresses 12706
--Presbyterian sources--History 844, 6152, 15198
--Protestant sources--(1800 to 1874) 1, 5, 14, 17, 44, 47, 50, 71, 75, 99, 139, 182, 195, 212, 242, 253, 297, 312, 319, 322, 349, 362, 395, 397, 409, 441, 445, 457, 482, 483, 536, 537, 583, 596, 628, 1549, 4697, 7834, 11043, 12296, 12297, 12602
--Protestant sources--(1875 to 1899) 556, 610, 626, 630, 657, 673, 689, 697, 747, 748, 758, 759, 830, 845, 895, 925, 936, 939, 960, 988, 989, 1115, 1118, 1242, 1284, 1296, 1354, 1397, 1467, 1538, 1551, 1576, 1634, 1644, 1676, 1857, 2069, 10227, 11077, 13658
--Protestant sources--(1900 to 1917) 1741, 1748, 1944, 2099, 2100, 2267, 2418, 2442, 2611, 2652, 2931, 2988, 3011, 3045, 14313
--Protestant sources--(1918 to 1944) 3779, 3804, 3811, 4116, 4132, 4153, 4259, 4409, 4456, 4491, 5182
--Protestant sources--(1945 to 1959) 5913, 6065, 6110, 6336, 6475, 6761
--Protestant sources--(1960 to 1969) 7957, 8039, 8101, 8481, 8946, 9255, 9322, 9430, 9498, 9679, 9881, 10061, 10190, 10347, 10475, 10927, 11011, 11149, 11270, 11403, 11505, 11629
--Protestant sources--(1970 to 1979) 11763, 11796, 12371, 13520, 14827, 14841, 14961, 14995, 15197, 15271, 15283
--Protestant sources--(1980 to 1991) 16113, 16135, 16376, 17146, 17560, 17588, 17810, 18123, 18179, 18221, 18236, 18425, 18459, 18646, 18666
--Protestant sources--Bibliographies 14702
--Protestant sources--History 1769, 1856, 3822, 5770, 8513, 9721, 13107, 13127, 18359
--Protestant sources--Periodicals 1, 32, 546, 577, 776, 1568, 3051, 3903, 7964, 15994
--Reformed Church in America sources--(1800 to 1874) 249, 333
--Reformed Church in America sources--(1875 to 1899) 688
--Reformed Church in America sources--(1900 to 1917) 2831, 2892
--Reformed Church in America sources--(1918 to 1944) 3095
--Reformed Church in America sources--(1945 to 1959) 5630
--Reformed Church in America sources--(1960 to 1969) 11220
--Reformed Church in America sources--(1980 to 1991) 18721
--Reformed Church in the US 2421
--Rhodesia 11034
--Salvation Army >> See further: Salvation Army [Main entry]
--Salvation Army sources--(1970 to 1979) 12428
--Salvation Army sources--History 17452

City missions (cont.)
--Scotland 181, 184, 199, 383, 390, 434, 436, 521, 5389, 12238, 14408, 18342
--Scotland--History 15306
--Seventh Day Adventist sources 722
--Seventh Day Adventist sources--History 11697, 13625
--South Africa 14209, 17742
--Southern Baptist sources--(1900 to 1917) 2788
--Southern Baptist sources--(1918 to 1944) 4896, 5082, 5108
--Southern Baptist sources--(1945 to 1959) 5648, 6029, 6578, 6783, 7079
--Southern Baptist sources--(1960 to 1969) 8923, 8988, 9825, 10057, 10556, 10694, 10739
--Southern Baptist sources--(1970 to 1979) 6088, 6089, 11860, 12273, 12416, 13311, 13408
--Southern Baptist sources--(1980 to 1991) 15402, 15747, 16111, 16133, 16243, 16419, 16462, 16507, 16561, 16921, 17252, 17843, 18808
--Southern Baptist sources--Congresses 8988
--Southern Baptist sources--History 6577, 14665, 18594
--Sweden 5586, 11867, 15678
--Sweden--History 3925
--Taiwan 18774
--Tanzania 11113, 15572
--Unitarian sources--(1800 to 1874) 163
--Unitarian sources--(1900 to 1917) 2832
--United Brethren sources 1460, 1873
--United Church of Canada sources--(1980 to 1991) 15664
--United Church of Christ sources--(1960 to 1969) 8695, 9249
--United Church of Christ sources--(1970 to 1979) 14572, 14895
--United Church of Christ sources--(1980 to 1991) 16292, 17025
--United Church of Christ sources--History 9824
--United Church of Christ sources--Periodicals 8025
--World Council of Churches sources--(1960 to 1969) 8436, 11629
--World Council of Churches sources--(1970 to 1979) 13798
--World Council of Churches sources--(1980 to 1991) 15704, 16769
City of God (metaphor) 696, 2184, 3417, 3892, 4267, 4412, 4829, 6629, 7998, 8132, 10733, 11348, 11872, 12116, 13021, 13157, 13358, 13762, 15232, 17637, 18777, 19022, 19219
--History 15725
City of London Churches Commission 3123
City on a hill (metaphor) 8227, 9633, 12685, 18336, 19256
City planning >> See further: New cities; Urban renewal
City planning 7237, 8380, 8839, 9609, 11680, 12491, 15199, 18137, 19126, 19157
--Asia 16062
--Australia 10163
--Austria 851
--Bibliographies 2462, 4762, 7935, 12343, 13045, 13288, 13747, 13815, 13917, 13919, 14695
--Brazil 15040
--Canada 15962

City planning (cont.)
--Church participation 3787, 5275, 6099, 6101, 6445, 6688, 7088, 7148, 7392, 7577, 7670, 7678, 7793, 7869, 8362, 8452, 8484, 8544, 8735, 9183, 9287, 9698, 10011, 10106, 10418, 10514, 10629, 10926, 11058, 11099, 11253, 11349, 13157, 13803, 15069, 15868, 16375, 18143
--Citizen participation 4638, 8453, 10220, 10982, 11093, 12145, 13492, 13956, 15896
--Congresses 4638, 7395, 9698, 10011, 10655
--Criticism of 3783, 4001, 5368, 7580, 8517, 8842, 9142, 9777, 10054, 10234, 10319, 10597, 11853, 12892, 16822, 17459, 18733, 18749
--Directions, dreams, visions 486, 1867, 1927, 2184, 2303, 2920, 3621, 4267, 5214, 5313, 5314, 7143, 7234, 7489, 7645, 7901, 8081, 8127, 8309, 8517, 8842, 9473, 9822, 9973, 10072, 10306, 10768, 10802, 10803, 10804, 11162, 11173, 11263, 11537, 11781, 11809, 11841, 12454, 13021, 13157, 13179, 13956, 15396, 15479, 15481, 15906, 16973, 16977, 17125, 18489
--England 1642, 4303, 5381, 12447, 13265, 13522, 13963, 14592, 16315
--Ethical aspects 1927, 8180, 8746, 9462, 9919, 10223, 10371, 12451, 12906, 15116, 15851, 15852, 15865, 16822, 17576
--Finland 11880, 12143
--Germany 2619, 6722, 9315, 9944, 12468, 13566, 18264
--Great Britain 5084, 15424, 15611, 16822, 17115
--History 4303, 6400, 10223, 10435, 11533, 12716, 13426, 13441, 14006, 14225, 16335, 16406, 17121, 18071, 18306, 18382, 18489
--India 11508, 16396
--Islamic 9967, 17926, 18011, 18395
--Israel 13653
--Israel--History 17636
--Latin America 9200
--Mormon 4962
--Nepal 16446
--Pakistan 9967
--Philosophy 2636, 3385, 4762, 6924, 7108, 7681, 8168, 8413, 8616, 9724, 11214, 14956
--Public policy 7667, 9804, 10371, 12145, 12576, 14550, 14735, 17685
--South Africa 12741
City societies 7, 21, 71, 75, 253, 441, 630, 748, 6618
--American Baptist 461, 507, 592
--Congregational 42, 55, 69, 250, 252, 359, 678, 717, 2056, 5305, 9824, 12686
--Congregational--History 4111, 5323, 18097
--Episcopal 29, 100, 104, 126, 210, 473, 1866, 5042
--History 3880, 4369, 5323, 7097
--Lutheran 16332
--Methodist 428, 468, 641, 730, 743, 756, 1003, 1236, 2090, 2254, 2342, 2965, 3086, 3255, 3291, 3432, 3528, 3537, 3563, 3603, 3625, 3633, 3647, 4276, 4818, 4915, 18333, 18504, 18545, 18962
--Methodist--History 3634
--Methodist--Periodicals 1317
--Periodicals 546

City societies (cont.)
--Presbyterian 472, 3920, 5321
--Reformed 249
--Unitarian 143
--United Church of Christ 8025, 10759, 16875, 18097
City Temple (London) 3396
City Tract Society (Hartford, Connecticut) 347
City Vigilance League of New York 1255, 1257
--Periodicals 1280
Ciudad Guyana (Venezuela)
--Social conditions 11438
Ciudad Juarez (Mexico)
--Social conditions 13081
Civic improvement 67, 129, 142, 147, 227, 273, 364, 408, 801, 878, 907, 1035, 1248, 1256, 1281, 1375, 1384, 1413, 1424, 1434, 1493, 1517, 1557, 1558, 1777, 1780, 1863, 2123, 2132, 2179, 2213, 2350, 2385, 2414, 2465, 2468, 2673, 2800, 3090, 3105, 3128, 3223, 3230, 3703, 3775, 4027, 4282, 4415, 5565, 6171, 8175, 8769, 9481, 12783, 13226, 17480
--Canada--History 12047, 13943
--Encyclopedias 2200
--England 1642, 2296
--Fiction 1221
--History 2711, 3841, 4209, 6516, 8087, 8806, 9093, 10288, 14088, 14342, 14764, 16033, 17719, 17824
--India 12785
--Turkey--History 16401
Civil disobedience 7843, 10491, 10754, 11308, 11483, 11538, 13333
Civil religion 13796, 14364, 15357, 16491, 17238
--History 14544
--United States 10207, 13439, 18041
Civil rights >> See further: Human rights; Women's rights, African Americans--Civil rights; Right to work; Discrimination; Segregation
Civil rights 4767, 5188, 5927, 7120, 8790, 8970, 8986, 9436, 9795, 10131, 10298, 10346, 10602, 10779, 11066, 11169, 12031, 12373, 12705, 12732, 13333, 13414, 14158, 15339, 17613, 18901, 19324
--Bibliographies 14224
--History 13541, 14391, 16601, 19016, 19026, 19113
--Korea 13983
Civil Rights Act of 1964 12031
Civil War 368, 4856, 10734
Civilization--Islamic >> See: Islam
Clarksburg (West Virginia)
--Religious and ecclesiastical institutions 5407
Class warfare 202, 3159, 3618, 3624, 4263, 5928, 7159, 7526, 9052, 9207, 14487, 15416
Clergy >> See further: City Clergy; African American clergy; Women clergy
Clergy
--Appointment, call and election 3647, 3748, 4410, 5847, 6393, 6406, 6737, 8192, 11233, 11817, 12422, 12637, 12638, 13218, 14924, 15061, 15774, 16538, 17620, 17714, 17752, 18501
--Appointment, call and election--Bibliographies 18365
--Appointment, call and election--Fiction 4543
--Germany 2517, 8114
--Office 838, 4325, 5053, 6478, 6828, 7256, 7257, 7422, 7643,

8230, 8869, 8919, 9362, 10461, 10845, 11148, 11267, 12005, 12947, 13330, 13985, 14672, 15380, 16341, 16933, 17249, 17572, 17983, 18473
Clergy (cont.)
--Political activity >> See further: Politics and Christianity
--Political activity 300, 323, 1323, 2066, 2350, 3780, 4389, 4433, 4952, 5832, 6064, 6171, 7263, 7264, 7512, 7513, 7674, 7909, 7949, 8736, 8765, 8831, 8991, 8993, 9033, 9054, 9384, 9436, 9481, 9493, 9878, 9975, 10211, 10257, 10279, 10468, 10634, 10780, 10831, 10835, 11120, 11301, 11322, 11366, 11416, 11538, 11603, 11640, 11677, 11701, 11943, 12028, 12029, 12108, 12198, 12315, 12514, 12578, 12689, 12865, 12986, 12991, 13228, 13333, 13339, 13715, 14443, 14852, 14908, 15326, 15337, 15339, 15382, 15822, 16331, 16363, 16477, 16976, 17323, 17485, 17539, 17557, 17708, 17812, 18724, 18885
--Political activity--Chile 15173
--Political activity--England 13310, 15569, 17583, 17964
--Political activity--History 6429, 8549, 12742, 13680, 15249, 15292
--Post-ordination training >> See: City clergy, training of; Clergy, training of
--Secular employment >> See further: Priest workers; Ex-clergy; Clergy, part-time
--Secular employment 8633, 9194, 9912, 11233, 12637, 12638, 13085, 13749, 14924, 17990
--Secular employment--England 8130, 9632, 13405, 17746
--Secular employment--Europe 7815
--Secular employment--History 17752
--South Africa 17316
--Training of >> See: Clergy, training of; City clergy, training of
Clergy and laity >> See further: Laity; Women in church work; Church controversies
Clergy and laity 2508, 6876, 8716, 9038, 9053, 9291, 9444, 10276, 11129, 11322, 11534, 11699, 12270, 12538, 12901, 12941, 13039, 13780, 16064, 16124, 16204, 16821, 17355, 17983, 18103, 18161, 18244, 18272
--History 18192
Clergy and social problems >> See further: Clergy--Political activity
Clergy and social problems 4147, 5706, 6171, 6876, 8346, 9384, 9587, 11148, 12028, 12497, 12514, 13744, 15444, 15553
--History 18192
Clergy families 6828, 14926, 18741
Clergy in literature 724, 4519, 4979, 5715, 7289
--England 280
--History 7527, 9238, 10992, 14188
Clergy in secular employment >> See: Clergy--Secular employment; Clergy, part-time, Priest workers
Clergy spouses 10973, 13797
Clergy, part time 8633, 13749, 13953, 13957, 15313
--England 17990

Clergy, training of >> See further: City clergy, training of; Theological education; Theological Seminaries
Clergy, training of 2213, 3795, 4381, 5847, 6406, 9171, 9264, 9548, 10009, 10252, 10356, 10420, 10616, 10637, 11524, 11667, 11769, 11918, 11940, 12017, 12160, 12331, 12372, 12488, 12788, 13046, 13079, 13417, 13778, 14055, 14140, 14827, 14885, 15686, 16603, 16641, 16889, 17001, 17324, 17438, 17780, 17901, 18001, 18502, 18698; 19352
--Congresses 9205, 18526
--History 18428, 18643
--Schools, programs, etc. 3281, 4157, 10564, 10967, 16381
Clergymen's wives >> See: Clergy spouses
Cleveland (Ohio)
--Ethnic relations 8501
--Ethnic relations--History 14633
--Minorities 7272
--Race relations 4142
--Religion 13596
--Religious and ecclesiastical institutions 1208, 1947, 2835, 2934, 2986, 3221, 3323, 4085, 4142, 5164, 5171, 5242, 5305, 5331, 5374, 5444, 5503, 6491, 6789, 6943, 7272, 7320, 7737, 7976, 8300, 8564, 8567, 8568, 9371, 9798, 9863, 9929, 10908, 11051, 11054, 11056, 11193, 11367, 13790, 14308, 18493
--Religious and ecclesiastical institutions--History 5827, 6333, 13952, 17414, 18262
--Social conditions 4056, 5261, 5265, 6842, 8296, 9758, 9832, 10165, 10710, 10928, 15396, 19187
--Social conditions--History 17830
Clinical Pastoral Education 14645, 17316, 18350, 18473
Clinical psychology 17822
Closed churches >> See: Church development, merger
Club of Rome 12594
Coal industry 6244, 17809
--History 9308
Coalitions >> See: Community organization; Networks
Cockeysville (Maryland)
--Religious and ecclesiastical institutions 17695
Coffee house ministry 626, 630, 1596, 7831, 8101, 8716, 8724, 8852, 9053, 9261, 9298, 9317, 9325, 9340, 9346, 9363, 9364, 9365, 9384, 9402, 9417, 9475, 9554, 9572, 9580, 9595, 9597, 9598, 9599, 9600, 9653, 9664, 9689, 9720, 9745, 9828, 9911, 9930, 9998, 10037, 10112, 10121, 10180, 10260, 10375, 10380, 10396, 10524, 10642, 10886, 11041, 11087, 11090, 11188, 11321, 11385, 11528, 11659, 11747, 11839, 12012, 12149, 12230, 12457, 13982
--England 9672
--Germany 18193
--History 10031
Coldwater (Michigan)
--Religious and ecclesiastical institutions--History 14382
Coledale (Alberta, Canada)
--Religious and ecclesiastical institutions--History 14402
Collective bargaining 16312, 17111
--History 12664
Colleges >> See: Universities and colleges
Collingwood (Victoria, Australia)

--Religious and ecclesiastical institutions--History 16937
Cologne (Germany)
--History 14141
Colombia
--Church history 17242
--Religious and ecclesiastical institutions 9112, 17464
Colonialism 13695, 14823, 17335
Colonization of the poor >> See further: Poverty, remedies; Poor
Colonization of the poor 971, 984, 1034, 1520, 1605, 2006, 2027, 2145
Columbia (Maryland)
--Description 9473, 11537
--Religious and ecclesiastical institutions 9368, 9460, 10272, 10540, 11240, 11288, 12355, 13045
Columbia (South Carolina)
--Religious and ecclesiastical institutions 15653
Columbus (Ohio)
--Religious and ecclesiastical institutions 253, 1428, 5243, 5407, 5451, 6789, 7654, 7692, 8895, 9307, 9937, 10757, 12416, 19190
--Religious and ecclesiastical institutions--History 14796, 15211
--Social conditions 2418, 9506, 15521
Columbus Action Training Associates (Columbus, Ohio) 10757
Comity >> See further: Church development, new; Interdenominational cooperation
Comity 1114, 2486, 2487, 2543, 2754, 2857, 2934, 3221, 3323, 3751, 3893, 3954, 3961, 4055, 4057, 4060, 4121, 4155, 4211, 4233, 4523, 4733, 4908, 5086, 5217, 5263, 5365, 5416, 5524, 5622, 5815, 5893, 5926, 5963, 6109, 6214, 6340, 6360, 6507, 6673, 6681, 6872, 7005, 12318
--History 4369, 6613
Commitment 6183, 8852, 13177, 14501, 14766, 16079, 16127, 16288, 17238, 17276, 17412, 18020
Commitment (religion) 6425, 9681, 10674, 12007, 12257, 12649, 12651, 14189, 14466, 16354, 16780, 19080
Commitment to the church 3073, 8082, 8521, 14189, 14681, 14807, 17575
Communal living >> See further: Christian communities
Communal living 12144, 12173, 12840, 16156
--History 15977
Communication >> See further: Information networks
Communication 7267, 7599, 9826, 9840, 11327, 11947, 13241, 13242, 14676, 15454, 16602, 17502
--France 11484
--Methodology 7044, 7109
Communication theory >> See further: Information theory; Communication--Methodology
Communication theory 14216, 15019, 16119, 17423
Communism 227, 561, 648, 714, 1446, 3284, 4292, 4544, 4956, 14746
--History 655
--Hong Kong 18589
Communism and Christianity 236, 2682, 3766, 4149, 4279, 4499, 5682, 5740, 6366, 6536,

7621, 8272, 8811
Communism and Christianity (cont.)
--Asia 14171
--Austria 16747
--England 6546
--Finland 15607
--France--History 16117
--History 234, 10432
--Korea 13101
--Spain 8073
Community 5327
--History 14441
--Theory 12968, 15323
Community (theology) 6426, 6430, 7951, 8338, 8512, 9411, 11184, 12678, 13700, 14012, 14059, 14380, 14566, 15696, 15888, 16666, 16917, 18859, 18973, 19137
Community Action Training Services (Cleveland, Ohio) 9798
Community centers >> See: Social Settlements
Community Chest >> See further: United Way
Community Chest 5655, 5661
Community churches 3109, 3122, 3232, 3476, 3899, 3949, 3950, 3954, 3997, 4897, 4908, 5576, 6557, 7011
--Case studies 5451, 5899
--Handbooks 3449, 3912
Community colleges >> See: Universities and colleges
Community Development >> See further: Community Organization; City planning; Economic development
Community development 7893, 7999, 8279, 8645, 9311, 9698, 10643, 10757, 10766, 11781, 12139, 12982, 14740, 15167, 15199, 15257, 16368, 16780, 16836, 18143, 18763, 19025, 19033, 19135
--Congresses 9577
--England 12227, 13767, 13963, 14727, 16315
--Great Britain 8855, 12567, 16308, 18751, 18759, 18847, 18887, 18923, 18987
--Ireland 17727
Community for Creative Nonviolence (Washington, DC) 14841, 17913
Community health services 2072, 2109, 2858, 3066, 3429, 4098, 5185, 6101, 9456, 10424, 11740, 11899, 12205, 12281, 12610, 13743, 14303, 14866, 17036, 17395, 17419, 18635
--Periodicals 10273
Community life 3042, 3209, 3385, 5752, 5771, 5907, 6331, 6915, 7014, 7059, 7521, 7665, 7766, 7999, 9366, 11265, 11326, 13010, 13140, 13529, 13992, 14201, 14303, 14520, 15323, 16207, 16836, 16844, 17031, 17670, 17963, 18052, 18134, 18776
--Africa 14998
--Bibliographies 12603, 17271
--Canada 9250, 14402
--England 17234
--Great Britain 14167
--Islamic 9257
--Jewish 5276, 5572, 6982, 6987, 7087, 7308, 7319, 7477, 7970, 8245, 8581, 9631, 10849, 11541, 12314, 12506, 13208, 13355, 13356, 13368, 15211, 16723, 16740, 18684
--Religious aspects 10350
Community of Hope (Washington, DC) 17084
Community of Taize (France) >> See: Taize Community (Taize,

France)
Community organization >> See further: Industrial Areas Foundation; Community development; Economic development
Community organization 10623
--Africa 16998
--Agencies, consultants 8462, 9288, 9532, 10830, 10866, 11656, 12472, 15941, 16934, 18339, 18875
--Asia 12388, 12836, 14029, 14733
--Bibliographies 10098, 11799, 12472, 12536, 13747, 13916, 13920, 14509, 14666, 15365, 16163
--Case studies 5504, 7424, 7948, 8367, 9222, 9387, 9623, 10240, 10266, 10278, 10484, 10578, 11209, 11520, 12198, 12283, 12578, 12851, 13313, 13530, 13672, 14175, 14351, 15517, 17098, 17712, 17979, 18174, 18269, 18360
--Church participation 9033, 9425, 9645, 10497, 10505, 11120, 11209, 11434, 11624, 11781, 13250, 13965, 14239, 14774, 17168, 17641, 18100, 18174, 18763, 18821, 19043, 19144, 19223, 19237, 19238
--Church participation--Bibliographies 10098, 18326, 19125, 19186
--Church participation--Catholic 6689, 8137, 8991, 9044, 9412, 9831, 9975, 10978, 12402, 13471, 16211, 16698, 19344
--Church participation--Church of the Brethren 10527
--Church participation--England 17339
--Church participation--Episcopal 9707, 9708, 9876
--Church participation--Evangelical Protestant 17645, 19220
--Church participation--History 19138
--Church participation--Lutheran 8202, 9307, 9518, 10086, 10330, 10384, 10643, 11878, 18269, 18525
--Church participation--Methodist 7857, 9458, 9706, 12704, 13096, 13722, 17872, 18841
--Church participation--NCCCUSA 9432, 9577
--Church participation--Presbyterian 8989, 9310, 9311, 9386, 9728, 10126, 10136, 10866, 11108, 11410, 14539, 15608, 18360
--Church participation--Protestant 4220, 7796, 7952, 8810, 10069, 10303, 10554, 11127, 12295, 15378, 16231, 16279, 17782, 18952
--Church participation--United Church of Christ 5751, 7948, 9505, 14340, 16107
--Church participation--World Council of Churches 13798
--Congresses 9577
--England 1122, 14093, 16481, 17339
--Ghana 13939
--History 12472, 13117, 13661, 18903, 19148
--Hong Kong 13807
--India 14530, 16041
--Indonesia 12527
--Kenya 13648, 13939
--Korea 12022
--Malaysia 18907
--Mexico 18834
--Philippines 12197, 13939

Community organization (cont.)
--Philippines--Bibliographies 13916
--Theory 4742, 5435, 5910, 5920, 6278, 7023, 7587, 8347, 8717, 8902, 8957, 9014, 9033, 9044, 9052, 9207, 9808, 9816, 10083, 10146, 10198, 10385, 10553, 10645, 10672, 10935, 11049, 11168, 11395, 11617, 11821, 11842, 12044, 12045, 12418, 12498, 12526, 13055, 13213, 13237, 13722, 13860, 14065, 14471, 15365, 16278, 16288, 16844, 17648, 17649, 18087
--Training 12022, 12197, 14471, 14655, 15158, 16278, 18252
Community Renewal Society (Chicago, Illinois) 7964, 10759, 14106, 14159, 14395, 14572, 14895, 15130, 15538, 17555, 18236, 18776, 18846, 18901, 19018, 19137
--History 11237, 14981
Community Renewal Society--Churches in Transition Project >> See further: Social change and church
Conduct of life >> See further: Youth--Conduct of life
Conduct of life 264, 2698, 2736, 5973, 5996, 6430, 6684, 8702, 10224, 10282, 10283, 10685, 10707, 10850, 11045, 11205, 12144, 12514, 12891, 13249, 13475, 13624, 14422, 14675, 14691, 15031, 15875, 16058, 16327, 16341, 16415, 16575, 17132, 18056
Confederation of Canadian Catholic Workers 5161
Confederazione italiana sindicatti lavatori
--History 13885
Conference on Christian Politics, Economics and Citizenship (COPEC) 3597, 3654
Conflict (sociology) >> See: Social conflict; Church controversies
Conflict management 1355, 6612, 10955, 11203, 12207, 12578, 13544, 13870, 15889, 16784, 16987, 17029, 17030, 17663
--England 15743
--Handbooks 15121
--Korea 12932
Confédération Française des Travailleurs 10118
Congregational and Christian Churches, Board of Home Missions 6873
Congregational and Christian Churches, Council for Social Action 4744
Congregational Christian Churches
--Case studies 5115, 5174, 5205, 5322, 5374, 5398, 5503, 5741, 5899, 5905, 5997, 6502, 6785
--Case studies--Bibliographies 5026
--History 5101, 6873
--Periodicals 4359, 4360
--Pronouncements, policies 7277
--Social teaching 5662, 6075, 6133
Congregational Christian Churches, Board of Home Missions 5115, 5116, 5131, 5204, 5205, 5305, 5374, 5397, 5398, 5503, 5741, 6955, 7377, 8292
--Periodicals 4359
Congregational Christian Churches, General Council 5662
Congregational Church
--Sermons 705, 853
Congregational Churches

Congregational Churches (cont.)
--Case studies 318, 429, 454, 526, 924, 1058, 1094, 1128, 1187, 1632, 1808, 1947, 2134, 2393, 2851, 3028, 7909, 11132, 13366, 14021, 14536
--Cases studies 5277
--Congresses 1785
--Doctrinal and controversial works 5985
--England 1821, 5277
--History 990
--Periodicals 33, 711
Congregational Home Missionary Society. 2104, 2460
Congregations >> See: Church; City Churches; Church work; (Specific denominations--Case studies)
Congress of Industrial Organizations 4561, 5256, 5514, 5994, 6156, 6641, 6922, 7026, 7537, 8017
--History 13775, 14391, 18262
Congress on Urban Ministry (Chicago, Illinois) 15043, 15246, 16938, 17783
Consejo Episcopal Latinoamericano 15773; 16165
Conservative Baptist Foreign Missions Society 16393, 17683
Conservative Judaism >> See further: Jews; Judaism
Conservative Judaism 18374
--Case studies 12543
--History 6781, 8699, 13206, 18209
Consultation on Church Union 10353, 11743, 11796
Consumers >> See further: Shopping centers
Consumers 2025, 3287, 3706, 4293, 4630, 4670, 4760, 4773, 4992, 5427, 6503, 10042, 10583, 11069, 11507, 12144, 13146, 13486, 13709, 13846, 14495, 14675, 14973, 15866, 17094, 19056
--England 16697
CONTACT Teleministries 15547, 15814, 16584, 16944, 17833
--Bibliographies 17406
Continuing Education >> See: City clergy, training of; Clergy, training of
Contra Costa County (California)
--Religious and ecclesiastical institutions 5581
Convention of Philippine Baptist Churches 7065
Converts >> See further: Missions to Jews
Converts 556, 872, 1265, 1860, 2045, 2652, 2814, 3030, 3782, 3852, 4195, 4278, 6260, 7078, 9424, 12416, 14008, 14830, 15401, 15952, 18280
--Biography 1959, 19328
--Germany 9722
--History 2297, 4824, 14256
Converts, Catholic
--History 1608, 6455
Converts, Protestant 7885, 17589
Converts, to Judaism 18207
--Bibliographies 14310
Cooperation >> See: Interdenominational cooperation; Cooperative ministries; Christian union
Cooperative Council of City Missions (Chicago, Illinois) 2739
Cooperative League of the USA 4538, 4791, 5189, 5255, 5286, 5427, 5638, 7176
Cooperative ministries >> See further: Interdenominational cooperation; Inner city-suburban exchanges

Cooperative ministries 624, 648, 723, 786, 836, 1175, 1327, 1448, 1550, 1598, 1617, 1638, 1648, 1671, 2046, 2097, 2694, 2705, 3134, 3148, 3231, 3232, 3511, 3661, 3723, 3824, 3847, 3893, 3950, 4211, 4342, 4604, 5033, 5172, 5370, 5565, 6017, 6265, 6311, 6389, 6491, 6872, 7311, 7442, 7814, 7847, 8167, 8200, 8255, 8257, 8371, 8496, 8947, 9368, 9486, 9932, 10151, 10153, 10275, 10355, 10361, 10703, 11041, 11367, 11537, 11712, 11918, 11972, 12236, 12460, 12470, 12816, 13250, 13319, 13720, 13769, 13825, 14506, 14729, 14761, 15004, 15111, 15117, 15191, 15271, 15338, 15501, 16113, 16171, 16243, 16604, 16828, 17301, 17872, 17953, 18104, 18182, 19165
--Africa 13713
--Australia 14053
--Canada 10509
--Congresses 18870
--England 10773, 13728, 17640, 17744, 18061, 18289, 18585
--History 7097, 18594
--India 13584
--Malaysia 14407
--Netherlands 11199
--Periodicals 3064, 6000, 8469, 10272, 15453
--Scotland 14428
Cooperative societies >> See further: Citizens' associations
Cooperative societies 616, 3649, 3706, 4076, 4321, 4450, 4535, 4537, 4538, 4627, 4630, 4670, 4683, 4760, 4773, 4791, 4823, 4953, 4955, 4988, 5052, 5189, 5255, 5286, 5353, 5426, 5427, 5638, 6913, 6929, 6988, 7176, 7619, 14973, 15378, 15797
--Canada 4822, 5160, 6287
--Canada--History 13612
--England 15873
Copenhagen (Denmark)
--Social conditions 8535
Coptic Orthodox Church
--Egypt 18026
Corporate Information Center (New York, NY) 12590
Corporate responsibility >> See: Business ethics; Industry--Social responsibility
Corporations >> See: Business; Industry
Corruption in politics 845, 1264, 1411, 1542, 1684, 1852, 1990, 2744, 3545, 3703, 4033, 4183, 4433, 4703, 6262, 13205, 14235
--History 8918, 10965, 12161
Cosmology 18379
Cost and standard of living >> See further: Quality of life
Cost and standard of living 4222, 4395, 4786, 12220, 13196
Council for Community Based Development 19237
Council of Women for Home Missions 2610, 2803, 2853, 3050, 3116, 3209, 3223, 3320, 3416, 3601, 3608, 3653, 3697, 3919, 4001, 4032, 4055, 4060, 4077, 4165, 4294, 4473, 4623, 4840
--Bibliographies 3697
--Congresses 4024, 4066
Council on Religion and International Affairs 12640
Councils of churches
--England 15743
Councils of churches (city) >> See further: Protestant Council of the City of New York
Councils of churches (city) 1650, 2739, 5318, 7623, 14729,

18454, 18962, 19258
Councils of Churches (city) (cont.)
--California 4901, 5365, 5581, 8210
--Canada 15087
--Colorado 6122, 6786
--Connecticut 8788
--Delaware 5963
--England 8085, 15743
--Georgia 18271
--Hong Kong 10411
--Illinois 2739
--Indiana 7144, 8190
--Kentucky 5262
--Massachusetts 6647, 7847
--Michigan 5166, 5191, 6969, 8735
--Missouri 5196
--New Jersey 5358, 9122
--New York (state) 5567, 6019, 7960, 8477, 9439, 10703
--Ohio 5698, 5926, 6273, 7760, 9371
--Oklahoma 12196, 13319
--Oregon 5363, 5366, 6423
--Pennsylvania 3014, 3037, 5815, 7173
--Periodicals 3064, 5614, 12196
--Scotland 12406
--Washington (state) 5080, 18088, 18454, 18805
--Washington, DC 5233, 9046, 9400, 11270, 11787
--West Virginia 6646
Councils of Churches (National) >> See: (name of specific council, e.g., Christian Council of Kenya, British Council of Churches, etc.)
Councils of churches (state)
--California 18180
--Colorado 10967
--Illinois 8821
--Indiana 9511, 10190
--Maryland 9976
--Massachusetts 5263, 5636, 5637, 5735, 5840, 5844, 5939, 6110, 6399, 7224, 8441, 9482, 11225
--New Jersey 5081, 5359, 5776, 8478, 8487, 8532, 9122, 10043
--New York 13988
--Ohio 6750, 6937, 9464, 9506, 10377, 10378, 10914, 11377
--Rhode Island 5775
Counter culture >> See further: Hippies
Counter culture 9312, 10399, 10424, 10630, 10711, 10722, 10767, 11045, 11610, 12071, 12276, 12294, 12474, 12652, 12827, 12838, 12874, 13257, 13686, 14663, 16968, 17211
--England 12438
--Great Britain 12411
--History 18835
Covenant House (New York, NY) 15405, 15879, 18662, 19064
Covenants (theology) 15696
Coventry (England)
--Religious and ecclesiastical institutions 5639, 8586
Coventry Industrial Mission 11964
Credit unions 4953, 6988, 7619, 9596, 13612, 13812, 13965, 17823
Creeds >> See: Social Gospel--Creeds; Social Creed of the Methodist Episcopal Church
Crime and criminals >> See further: Church work with criminals; Justice Criminal; Rehabilitation of criminals; Prisons and prisoners, Victim offender reconciliation; Church work with prisoners
Crime and criminals 544, 562, 845, 1223, 1253, 1302, 1665, 2013, 2475, 2744, 2836, 3655,

3711, 4033, 4117, 4283, 4605, 5658, 6114, 6217, 6552, 6625, 7273, 7282, 7376, 8046, 8338, 9100, 9328, 10181, 10321, 10748, 10839, 11499, 11669, 13731, 13819, 13976, 14111, 14173, 14372, 14523, 14632, 14845, 14968, 15300, 15544, 15856, 15935, 16452, 16948, 16967, 17334, 17739, 17924, 18014, 18513, 18542, 18613
Crime and criminals (cont.)
--England 9483
--Fiction 4724
--History 4501, 8806, 11272, 15449, 15859, 16635
--New York (NY) 16635
--Sweden 19232
Crime prevention
--Citizen participation 3741, 4129, 4228, 6306, 6625, 11522, 13731, 15643, 15777, 15886, 16451, 16452, 17924, 18132
Criminal justice >> See: Justice--Criminal; Crime and Criminals; Church work with prisoners; Church work with criminals
Crisis management >> See further: Disaster; Riots
Crisis management 1830, 3094, 5380, 7792, 8028, 9060, 10109, 10196, 10310, 10332, 10455, 10456, 10488, 10489, 10499, 10500, 10506, 10529, 10625, 10631, 10644, 10721, 10833, 10904, 10998, 11013, 11017, 11037, 11092, 11103, 11343, 11540, 11547, 11744, 11790, 12049, 12954, 13067, 13186, 13232, 13241, 13759, 14113, 14836, 15092, 15547, 15788, 16460, 16944, 17663, 17833, 18184
--England 17587
--Korea 15387
Cross-cultural studies 12831, 14676
Cross culturalism >> See: Inner city-suburban exchanges
Cuba
--Social conditions 8792, 10110, 10344
--Social Conditions--History 12191
Cuban American families 8772
Cuban Americans
--Missions to 8792, 8801
--Social conditions 8772
Cubans
--Missions to 18199
Cults 3453, 4112, 4696, 4832, 4844, 4895, 4951, 5244, 5247, 5269, 5391, 5755, 5763, 6422, 6454, 6486, 7756, 7906, 8672, 9360, 10890, 12544, 12717, 13257, 13472, 13686, 14464, 14663, 14748, 14890, 14959, 15533, 16668, 16831, 16956, 17497, 17738, 18638, 18661, 19221, 19231, 19241
--Bibliographies 17541, 19153
--Canada 6724
--Encyclopedias 16669
--History 14561, 19121
Culture and religion >> See further: Society and Religion
Culture and religion 295, 732, 3078, 5669, 5731, 6072, 6368, 7104, 7281, 7317, 7357, 7370, 7922, 8616, 8816, 9070, 9187, 9214, 9284, 9840, 9985, 10106, 10496, 11798, 11872, 12445, 13094, 13247, 13296, 13519, 17160, 17211, 18571, 18851
--Asia 17972
--Biblical teaching 8981
--Biblical teaching--Bibliographies 16434
--History 4264, 4339, 7806,

13907, 14039, 15549, 17950, 18597, 19293
Culture and religion (cont.)
--India 9398, 18073
--Islamic 12996
--Latin America 10652
--Singapore 19053
--Switzerland 15880
--United States 1832, 3977, 6179, 7695, 7805, 11391, 12155, 12481, 12827, 14464, 15303, 17238, 17880, 18509
--United States--History 18835, 19207
Cumberland Presbyterian Church 4894
Curriculum >> See: Adult education--Curriculum; Christian education--Curriculum; Religious education--Curriculum; Theological seminaries--Curriculum
Cybernetics >> See further; Technology
Cybernetics 9794, 10433, 11471, 12875
Czech American churches 947
Czech Americans
--History 17939
--Religion--History 14122
--Social conditions 3436
--Social life and customs 3192, 5940
Daddy Grace 5848
Daddy Jones 15533
Dallas (Texas)
--Religious and ecclesiastical institutions 4520, 5407, 5506, 6583, 10601, 12953, 13149, 13232, 15497, 16092, 17973, 19165, 19172
--Religious life and customs 4520, 12475
--Social conditions 19118
Damascus (Syria)
--History 16627
Danzig (Poland)
--Religious and ecclesiastical institutions 2394, 8963
Dar es Salaam (Tanzania)
--Religious and ecclesiastical institutions 11113, 11584, 14738
--Social conditions 9297
Day care >> See: City children--Education of
Dayton (Ohio)
--Religious and ecclesiastical institutions 1190, 5169, 5194, 6273, 6789, 6882, 10360, 10401, 11377, 11722, 11940, 13216, 15153, 18673, 19073
--Religious and ecclesiastical institutions--History 18054
--Social conditions 7571, 12204, 18588
Deaconesses 1346, 1957, 2076, 5485, 6542
--History 862, 943, 2226, 15110, 15792, 18102
Dearborn (Michigan)
--Religious and ecclesiastical institutions--History 4930
--Social conditions 13112
Death 464, 10881, 11521, 11844, 12387, 14646, 14916, 18180
--History 16851
Decatur (Georgia)
--Religious and ecclesiastical institutions 11389
Del Rey (California)
--Social conditions 14433
Delémont (Switzerland)
--Social life and customs 13768
Demographic surveys >> See further: Social surveys; Religious surveys
Demographic surveys 919, 1206, 3819, 3991, 5685, 5987, 6574,

6902, 7866, 7882, 8879, 9565, 11650, 15398, 15835, 17060, 17483
Demography 4, 39, 62, 105, 864, 3910, 7298, 7550, 7591, 7622, 8151, 9079, 9954, 10247, 11197, 12594, 13531, 13761, 14084, 14212, 15268, 17017, 17259, 17622, 17623, 17784, 18301, 18318, 18337, 18403, 19334
--History 16091
Denmark
--Social conditions 220, 6052
--Social conditions--History 15802
Denominational priorities >> See: Mission of the Church
Denver (Colorado)
--Religious and ecclesiastical institutions 4597, 5244, 5407, 5919, 6122, 6225, 6786, 7811, 11839, 14952, 15076, 16443, 18948, 19199, 19336
--Religious and ecclesiastical institutions--History 12282, 16558
--Social conditions 11615, 16161, 18979
Denver Inner City Protestant Parish (Denver, Colorado) 7811
Department of Housing and Urban Development, Washington, DC >> See: United States, Department of Housing and Urban Development
Depersonalization 4378, 10672, 16388, 17291, 17294, 18084
Depression (economic) >> See: Great Depression; Economics and Christianity
Des Moines (Iowa)
--Religious and ecclesiastical institutions 2856, 4410, 6083, 10202
--Social conditions 11331
Desegregation >> See: Segregation in education; Discrimination in education
Detroit (Michigan)
--Ethnic relations 13113, 13261, 13354, 13750, 14099
--Ethnic relations--History 14384, 14694, 15965
--History 15210, 15344
--Industries 13760
--Politics and government--History 11345
--Race relations 4199, 5147, 5191, 11124, 16180
--Religion 7626, 12308
--Religious and ecclesiastical institutions 1330, 3060, 4931, 5024, 5166, 5176, 5407, 5443, 5631, 5868, 6208, 6501, 6883, 7080, 7457, 8219, 8336, 8495, 8735, 9123, 9399, 9847, 10289, 10632, 10749, 10785, 11002, 11091, 11355, 11366, 12334, 13139, 13642, 14014, 14246, 14737, 15335, 15494, 15516, 15649, 15679, 15681, 16180, 16200, 16976, 17673, 18434, 18632, 18742, 18754, 18813, 18829, 18997, 19071
--Religious and ecclesiastical institutions--History 4928, 4929, 5025, 5099, 6076, 8084, 12530, 12834, 13760, 16496, 18010
--Religious and ecclesiastical institutions--Periodicals 7288
--Social conditions 3742, 4199, 4696, 5113, 5234, 7681, 8352, 10211, 10264, 10455, 10529, 10605, 10769, 10833, 11899, 12829, 14268, 14831, 16177, 18142, 18734, 18889

Detroit (Michigan) (cont.)
--Social conditions--History 9584, 13340, 15320
--Social life and customs 7090
--Social life and customs--History 13341
Detroit Area Study 7626, 8043, 8219, 8495, 12308, 12334, 12829
Detroit Industrial Mission 7734, 7812, 8266, 8597, 8658, 9399, 9802, 10658, 11091, 11983, 12101, 12102, 12103, 12430, 13175, 13244
--History 10604, 11002, 13057, 13760
--Periodicals 7288
Deutsche Bischofskonferenz 16190
Deutsche Zentrumspartei 2701
Developing countries 12609, 12877, 13061, 15987
--History 17768
--Religion 13165, 14263, 16850, 17049, 17128, 17949
--Religious life and customs 17804
--Social conditions 12065, 12323, 12867, 13939, 15126, 15496, 15719, 16015, 17017, 17389
Developing Countries
--Urbanization 8067, 15987, 17854
Devotional literature >> See further: Spirituality; Hymns
Devotional literature 430, 2821, 3042, 3417, 4695, 5320, 6169, 6678, 7433, 9157, 9742, 10698, 11670, 11914, 12155, 12261, 17838
Dialogue (theology) 7599, 11570, 12108, 18050
Dilemmas of urban church organizations >> See: City churches
Disaster >> See further: Crisis management
Disaster 136, 146, 493, 584, 782, 2115, 3862, 3906, 5006, 5133, 5162, 5252, 5871, 6007, 6499, 9409, 10103, 10194, 10455, 10456, 10488, 10502, 10529, 10998, 11134, 14336, 14916, 14960, 15169, 15493, 15514, 16046, 16144, 16171, 17205, 18583, 18921
--England 19039
--India 17243
--Japan 3504, 3516, 6338
--Periodicals 4964
Disciples of Christ 1738, 3875, 5523, 5944, 6681, 6914
--Case studies 3548, 5143, 6943, 7737, 9059, 10589, 12953, 16304, 17973
--History 2878, 4975, 6580, 19047
--Periodicals 3210, 4113, 4573
--Pronouncements, policies 3141, 5884
--Sermons 12917
Disciples of Christ, Commissions on Church and Society 9650
Discrimination 3818, 4577, 5270, 5472, 5644, 5850, 6391, 6411, 7251, 7272, 7679, 8162, 8226, 8278, 9018, 9782, 10181, 10700, 11250, 11298, 11309, 11441, 11566, 11632, 11709, 11810, 12703, 13026, 13089, 13450, 13502, 14248, 14507, 14925, 15107, 15328, 15804, 15926, 16931, 17758, 17922, 18482
--Bibliographies 9313
--History 7106, 10587, 12979, 13202, 14021, 15174, 16893, 19130, 19131
--Religious aspects 1229, 5796, 6210, 7590, 7642, 8648, 9120,

9512, 11949, 12823, 13212, 14901, 16823
--Syria--History 16157
Discrimination in churches 5434, 5702, 5891, 6303, 6671, 6905, 9620, 9809, 10116, 10348, 10377, 10545, 11406, 11550, 13015, 13042, 13892, 14537, 14913, 15174, 16024, 16239, 16972, 17138, 17705, 18581
--History 15255
Discrimination in education >> See further: Segregation in education
Discrimination in education 1973, 10185, 12779, 13318, 14223
Discrimination in employment >> See further: Employment problems; Justice--Economic
Discrimination in employment 3820, 4596, 9031, 10534, 11006, 15460, 17014
--Asia 17436
--Congresses 10012
--History 12385
Discrimination in housing >> See further: Housing
Discrimination in housing 3736, 3934, 4900, 5594, 5747, 5773, 5823, 5891, 6061, 6190, 6345, 7019, 7121, 7208, 7355, 7533, 7830, 7851, 8260, 8683, 8781, 8866, 8867, 8917, 8945, 8973, 9017, 9146, 9230, 9233, 9243, 9359, 9586, 9743, 9762, 10081, 10176, 10516, 10641, 10705, 11131, 11729, 11875, 11956, 11983, 12099, 12112, 12298, 12454, 12512, 13009, 13059, 13343, 13608, 13723, 13755, 14206, 15226, 16077, 19266
--South Africa 7350
Disinvestment, economic >> See: Investments, foreign; Investments--Moral and ethical aspects
Dissenters, religious
--England 9942
--England--History 15216, 15655, 17019
Divestment >> See: Investments, foreign; Investments--Moral and ethical aspects
Dominican Republic
--Social conditions 17621
Dominicans
--History 18896
Door of Hope Missions 4195
Dorpat (Estonia)
--Religious and ecclesiastical institutions 3609
Doubt >> See: Belief and doubt
Downtown churches >> See further: City churches; Big churches
Downtown churches
--Argentina 14618
--Canada 15012
--Case studies 454, 2772, 2938, 3750, 4362, 5067, 5243, 5322, 5398, 5444, 5537, 5567, 5900, 5901, 5902, 5956, 6135, 6208, 6259, 6434, 6538, 6703, 6890, 6911, 6949, 7077, 7211, 7554, 8375, 8738, 8958, 9429, 9890, 10360, 10572, 10693, 10855, 10856, 11497, 11619, 11621, 12798, 13224, 13896, 13968, 14299, 14937, 15327, 15419, 15810, 17425, 17973, 18022, 19100, 19154
--Characteristics, problems 1422, 1627, 1736, 2177, 2178, 2439, 2454, 2549, 3013, 3437, 3595, 3778, 3924, 3961, 4060, 4788, 5068, 6083, 6487, 6688, 6766, 7139, 7203, 7207, 7343, 7440, 7600, 7713, 7983, 8203, 8218, 9879, 10166, 10694, 10823, 10838, 11079, 12459, 13254,

13390, 13419, 13657, 15828, 16247, 17441, 17591
Downtown churches (cont.)
--Congresses 15448
--England 13879, 17801
--Fiction 4068, 4543
--Great Britain 10993
--History 487, 5063, 5342, 5684, 9472, 13641, 14348, 18396
--Japan 19062
--Korea 16530
--Strategies 1157, 1562, 1817, 2446, 2588, 2680, 2782, 2797, 3230, 3295, 3318, 3372, 3433, 3565, 3642, 4003, 4648, 5421, 5649, 5798, 6164, 6239, 7818, 9037, 9119, 9374, 10536, 10834, 12258, 12289, 12537, 13657, 13927, 13968, 14030, 14825, 15125, 15801, 16419, 17360, 17624, 17662, 18170, 18436, 18510, 18687
Drama 257, 3190, 5062, 6059, 7000, 7208, 7346, 8570, 9495, 10194, 10599, 11019, 11106, 11417, 11685, 12135, 12309, 14133, 18876, 19266
--History 6385, 7609, 13932
--Spain 19210
Drive-in churches 6312, 13968
Drug abuse >> See further: Church work with narcotic addicts
Drug abuse 6048, 8708, 10498, 11916, 17490, 17940, 18700
--Canada 8653
--Europe 16146
--Prevention 6057, 7389, 8475, 8594, 9669, 11031, 11211, 11578, 11779, 11807, 12210, 12215, 12279, 12469, 12680, 15514, 16146, 16971, 17221, 18287, 18407, 18882, 19029, 19122, 19145, 19173, 19174, 19181, 19326, 19328, 19349
--Treatment 6209, 9669, 12404, 12680, 14565, 16968, 19204, 19316
--Treatment--England 17640
Dublin (Ireland)
--Religious life and customs 13292, 14238
Durban (South Africa)
--Religious and ecclesiastical institutions 12718, 13659
--Social conditions 7350
Durham (England)
--Religious and ecclesiastical institutions--History 13310
--Social conditions 13638, 18321
Durham (North Carolina)
--Religious and ecclesiastical institutions 6628
Dutch Americans
--History 17569
Dutch Reformed Church
--Case studies 8939
Dutch Reformed Church in South Africa 5540, 14139, 17285
East Asia Christian Conference 7821, 8599, 10317, 10318, 10333, 10761, 10811, 11932, 12566, 12624, 12839, 13084
East Harlem Interfaith (New York, NY) 15371
East Harlem Protestant Parish >> See further: Interdenominational cooperation
East Harlem Protestant Parish (New York, NY) 5651, 5675, 5739, 5765, 5790, 5808, 5834, 5838, 5859, 5995, 6153, 6284, 6460, 6535, 6640, 6690, 6908, 7361, 7389, 7460, 7536, 7724, 7731, 7751, 7959, 7975, 8039, 8307, 8440, 8481, 8561, 8615, 9411, 10021, 10381, 11516, 15349, 15973, 19263

--History 18397
--Periodicals 7974
East Orange (New Jersey)
--Religious and ecclesiastical institutions 16204
East St. Louis (Illinois)
--Religious and ecclesiastical institutions 8738
Eastern Orthodox Church >> See: Orthodox Eastern Church
Eastman Kodak 9623, 10578, 13530
Easton (Pennsylvania)
--Religious and ecclesiastical institutions 2993
--Social conditions 14747
Ecclesiology >> See: Church; Mission of the church; Theology (of the local church)
Ecological succession >> See further: Social change; Social change and church
Ecological succession 4034, 7816, 13752, 16954
Ecology >> See further: Environmental ethics
Ecology 2964, 3717, 3835, 4555, 5018, 5431, 5907, 6217, 7405, 8151, 8303, 8992, 9404, 9513, 10669, 10873, 11351, 11648, 11680, 12844, 13531, 14845, 14904, 15514, 17860, 17882, 18151, 18856
--Bibliographies 3717
--France 7430
--Germany 16930
--History 10824, 18464
Economic development >> See further: Community development, Plant closings, Work, Church and industry, Church and labor, Trade unions, Economics and Christianity, Wealth, Unemployment, Women--Employment, Youth--Employment, Institutional churches, Social settlements, Technology, Multinational corporations, and Stockholder's meetings.
Economic development 1513, 2684, 5885, 8642, 11116, 11191, 11357, 12283, 12819, 12864, 12908, 13506, 14285, 14324, 14976, 15256, 15876, 16225, 17062, 17176, 17389, 17652, 19043, 19325, 19329
--Africa 7767, 7768, 7904, 16293, 17260
--Asia 16062
--Australia 16822
--Citizen participation 11928, 12139, 13409, 13523, 18388
--Congresses 8541
--Great Britain 16822
--India 14530
--Indonesia 15661
--Japan 8005
--Kenya 12303
--New Guinea 15052, 15073
--Pakistan 11448
--Social aspects 4175, 4489, 13773, 14372, 18812
Economic justice >> See: Justice
Economic policy >> See further: United States--Economic policy
Economic policy 15323, 16099, 16224, 18408, 18478
--England 746
--Germany 17882
Economics >> See further: (Economic conditions, listed under cities and nations); Bible--Economics
Economics 265, 611, 4208, 9148, 14373, 15474, 15978, 16389, 17007, 17125
--England 1942

Economics (cont.)
--Middle East 14181
--Moral and ethical aspects 789, 5356, 6354, 8278, 9650, 10511, 12673, 13523, 14324, 14731, 16120, 16594, 16821, 16847, 18003, 18954
--Religious aspects 435, 786, 4146, 4955, 5135, 6405, 8278, 10511, 15617, 16099, 16236, 16964, 17062, 17726, 17970, 18003, 18408, 18478
--Religious aspects--History 18404, 19088
--Religious aspects--Periodicals 5950
Economics and Christianity >> See further: Economics--Religious aspects; Cooperative societies; Justice--Economic
Economics and Christianity 39, 62, 88, 141, 156, 157, 164, 173, 209, 230, 279, 307, 315, 343, 407, 424, 426, 435, 459, 490, 503, 518, 520, 602, 629, 663, 690, 777, 789, 796, 876, 899, 901, 957, 1261, 1374, 1616, 1723, 2122, 2160, 2220, 2339, 2768, 2779, 2821, 3366, 3400, 3446, 3472, 3508, 3560, 3643, 3681, 3706, 3780, 3793, 3803, 3817, 3894, 3987, 4009, 4011, 4146, 4214, 4262, 4274, 4294, 4345, 4375, 4378, 4541, 4564, 4628, 4691, 4744, 4774, 4784, 4794, 4991, 5111, 5299, 5383, 5402, 5455, 5456, 5457, 5458, 5471, 5536, 5575, 5577, 5678, 5737, 5789, 5821, 5998, 6285, 6346, 6392, 6421, 6442, 6566, 6743, 6744, 6800, 6846, 6926, 6933, 7012, 7367, 7515, 7524, 7803, 7810, 7978, 8035, 8178, 8247, 8291, 8386, 8490, 8524, 8570, 8676, 8856, 9078, 9588, 9692, 9780, 10065, 10323, 12375, 12612, 12649, 12880, 13328, 13523, 13738, 13854, 13901, 14045, 14119, 14397, 14590, 14860, 14882, 15054, 15099, 15149, 15237, 15358, 16143, 16375, 16439, 16684, 16783, 16810, 16877, 17058, 17153, 17244, 17344, 17371, 17467, 17599, 17720, 17788, 17889, 17966, 18136, 18292, 18647, 18709, 18764, 18827, 18865, 18964, 18993, 19025, 19037, 19108, 19192, 19295
--Bibliographies 15539, 19125
--Canada 1132, 16541
--Chile 13833
--Congresses 3597, 3654, 4077, 5582, 5597, 6854, 6929, 6930
--Encyclopedias 1995
--England 680, 746, 831, 2210, 3121, 3281, 4247, 4286, 4950, 5118, 17262, 17318
--Fiction 8756
--France 10192, 11725
--Germany 7345, 11412, 13068, 16762
--Germany--History 3651
--Great Britain 2991, 3833, 18445, 18793
--Great Britain--History 16252
--Handbooks 5934
--History 1999, 2669, 3798, 5306, 5468, 5470, 6318, 8099, 16871, 17267, 19088
--Japan 14259
--Latin America 15064, 17434
--New Zealand 13575
--Periodicals 3196, 5950, 18831
--South Africa 17285, 17562
--Sweden 17330
Economics and Islam 17729, 18908
Economics and Judaism 1647, 1756, 4711, 5773, 7371

--History 13930
Ecuador
--Religious life and customs 15921
Ecumenical Action on Single Homelessness (England) 18900
Ecumenical Institute (Chicago, Illinois) 8411, 10267, 11040, 11185, 11434, 11545, 11624, 12418, 12420, 12671, 14247
Ecumenical Metropolitan Ministry (Seattle, Washington) 11749
Ecumenical ministry >> See: Interdenominational cooperation; Cooperative ministry
Ecumenical movement 982, 6340, 7081, 7891, 8510, 8664, 8713, 9883, 9891, 11751, 14076, 14526, 17767
--Great Britain 18289, 18732
--History 16731
--United States 2220, 4363, 7311, 11796
Edinburgh (Scotland)
--Religious and ecclesiastical institutions 181, 390, 521, 12406, 14428
Education 102, 488, 1255, 2149, 2156, 2191, 2673, 2925, 2929, 5737, 5805, 8090, 10767, 11291, 11772, 11775, 12204, 12562, 13778, 15217, 18324, 18561, 18681
--Africa 13967
--Bibliographies 9019
--Colombia 10232
--Curriculum 13170
--Great Britain 9552
--History 4482, 10197, 15344
--India 12785
--Italy--History 18283
--Research 12262
--Theory 1699, 1747, 1861, 8120, 8703, 10270, 10924
Education and church 1730, 6335, 8817, 9678, 14151, 17869
--History 14187, 14315, 14795, 18106
--New Guinea 17335
Education and urban problems 10790, 12779, 12961, 13647, 14223
Education of adults >> See: Adult education
Education of children >> See: City Children--Education
El Paso (Texas)
--Social conditions 13081
El Salvador
--Social conditions 18781, 18947
Elites 8785, 9731, 11049, 13226, 14673, 15864, 17321, 17705, 18037, 19228
--Developing countries 15171
--Germany 7496
--History 7244, 14871, 15077
Elizabeth City (North Carolina)
--Religious and ecclesiastical institutions--History 14116
Ellis Island (New York, NY) 1986, 2003, 2141, 3692, 6305
Elm Haven (Connecticut)
--Religious and ecclesiastical institutions 9449
Elmira (New York)
--Religious and ecclesiastical institutions 508
Emigration and immigration >> See further: (Specific geographical areas)
Emigration and immigration 2485, 3170, 4532, 4811, 6087, 6655, 8840, 14899, 15160, 16715
--Argentina 18302
--Australia 12641, 13047, 13048, 15472, 16303, 18529, 18568, 18792

Emigration and immigration (cont.)
--Belgium 14994, 18910
--Bibliographies 3272, 3697, 7876, 14434, 15984, 16841, 17271
--Biography 3355
--Brazil 18029
--Burkina Faso 14816
--Canada 10818, 15393, 16382
--Canada--History 14052, 14300
--Congresses 2888
--England 7329, 7839, 8760, 9321, 9385, 9391, 12015, 15085, 16104
--Europe 7979, 8241, 15123
--France 12098, 15071, 15673, 17679, 18243, 18317, 19197
--Ghana 14816
--Great Britain 1532, 7866, 9552, 10653, 10796, 11339, 12187, 12713, 12778, 14662, 15028, 16197, 17011, 18872
--Great Britain--History 10386
--History 14642
--India 12089
--Islamic countries 19077
--Italy 12658, 15240
--Italy--History 12628
--Japan 15150
--New Zealand 14949
--Periodicals 8960, 12787
--Religious aspects--Christianity >> See further: Americanization; Church work with immigrants
--Religious aspects 1147, 2248, 3500, 3608, 4259, 5140, 5184, 6372, 6707, 7979, 8241, 8772, 12248, 12628, 12658, 13106, 15240, 16471, 18314, 19082, 19231
--Religious aspects--Catholic 1052, 3715, 6686, 6693, 6938, 7781, 10613, 12787, 13141, 13428, 14114, 14153, 14589, 14788, 14993, 15950, 16078, 17171, 17329, 18077, 18469
--Religious aspects--History 17552
--Religious aspects--Islamic 19077
--Religious aspects--Jewish 2085, 3180, 14109, 17659
--Religious aspects--Protestant 327, 826, 889, 1033, 1070, 1230, 1365, 2077, 2078, 2212, 2543, 2888, 3340, 3434, 3653, 4259, 5200, 6094, 7125, 7243, 8209, 8527, 8960, 8990, 10786, 12068, 12817, 13719, 14052, 15903, 15984, 17016, 17608, 18354
--Social aspects 1310, 1311, 6243
--Sweden 17968
--Switzerland 15028
--Taiwan 18536
--Tanzania 9297
--United States 302, 620, 767, 775, 826, 1033, 1056, 1088, 1151, 1188, 1226, 1230, 1310, 1311, 1360, 1394, 1885, 1986, 2003, 2102, 2117, 2130, 2141, 2354, 2356, 2447, 2538, 2653, 2686, 2706, 2798, 2828, 2886, 2946, 3070, 3233, 3234, 3279, 3340, 3355, 3375, 3692, 3715, 3818, 3829, 3848, 3948, 4731, 4867, 4996, 5060, 5200, 6094, 6243, 6774, 6808, 6938, 7028, 7243, 7876, 10786, 11274, 11451, 12169, 12557, 14109, 14656, 14957, 14993, 15233, 15829, 15855, 15903, 16078, 16265, 16471, 16511, 16513, 17016, 17367, 17383, 18025, 18130, 18354, 18899
--United States--Demography 3819
--United States--History 4922, 5017, 5780, 6044, 6301, 6686,

8209, 8808, 8990, 9960, 11935, 12530, 13495, 13507, 13719, 13864, 14701, 16026, 17254, 18791
Emmanuel Gospel Center (Boston, Massachusetts) 15669, 15671, 16597, 18514
Emmanuel Movement (Boston, Massachusetts) 2143, 2221, 2259, 2285, 2300, 2301, 2338, 2348, 2372
Emmaus House (New York, NY) 11308
Emory University (Atlanta, Georgia) 8999, 13888
Emotions 9040, 13003, 15015, 16810, 17589, 17592, 17654
--Religious aspects 2950, 4844, 6251, 7330, 19040
Employees' representation in management >> See: Management--Employee participation
Employment >> See: Employment; Unemployment; Church work with the unemployed; Church and industry
Employment problems >> See further: Strikes and lockouts; Right to labor; Unemployment; Church and labor; Church work with the unemployed; Church work with employed women; Management--Employee participation; Wages; Trade unions
Employment problems 782, 816, 1216, 1641, 2379, 2542, 2599, 2660, 3036, 3039, 3068, 3103, 3351, 3405, 3551, 4713, 7327, 7797, 8253, 9532, 13622, 14023, 14780, 15032, 16143, 16312, 17106, 17255
--Canada 14863
--Congresses 6212, 6213, 10012, 14373
--England 5282, 9116, 14383
--Europe 19028
--History 13934
--Italy 7630
--Netherlands 17404
--Spain 4261
Encuentro Latinoamericano de Pastoral Urbana (Barueri, Brazil) 9416, 10325
Encyclicals, Papal 3140, 3275, 3687, 4307, 4820, 4883, 5179, 5202, 5281, 5334, 8780, 15821, 16340, 17434
--History 8095, 8387, 17718
Encyclicals, Papal (Centesimus annus) 19348
Encyclicals, Papal (Laborem exercens) 15857, 15919, 16100, 16179, 16205, 16210, 16237, 16269, 16359, 16437, 16453, 16621, 16657, 16681, 16713, 16815, 17055, 17631
Encyclicals, Papal (Mater et Magistra) 8198, 8759, 9378, 9956, 9978, 9980, 10025, 10052, 10122, 15919
Encyclicals, Papal (Octogesima adveniens) 15919
Encyclicals, Papal (Quadragesimo anno) 4152, 4170, 4171, 4177, 4178, 4218, 4401, 4440, 4476, 4642, 4650, 4813, 5605, 5983, 17700
Encyclicals, Papal (Rerum novarum) 1051, 1061, 1067, 1069, 1258, 1417, 2450, 4152, 5605, 6472, 12241, 15919, 16342, 16674, 17468, 17664
--History 4944, 8189, 8468, 11212, 19239
Encyclopedias 1517, 1944, 10347, 14748, 15662, 16097, 16669,

19130
Energy >> See further: Utilities; Atomic energy
Energy 13197, 13710
Energy conservation 12923, 13223, 14616, 14675, 14798, 14822, 14927, 14989, 15081, 15418, 15584, 15752, 16084, 16395, 16611, 16776, 17158, 18056
--Bibliographies 15070
--Periodicals 16261
England
--Church history 913, 1972, 2079, 2279, 3021, 4446, 4699, 6591, 8271, 8459, 8668, 8690, 8773, 9459, 9683, 10386, 10755, 10958, 11304, 11546, 12177, 12715, 12749, 12929, 13116, 13302, 13310, 13358, 13635, 13880, 13991, 15062, 15161, 15655, 16174, 16579, 17064, 17416, 17616, 17842
--Economic conditions 746, 2930, 3121, 15529
--History 582, 913, 1403, 2464, 4128, 6180, 8913, 9185
--Religion 499, 1774, 1972, 2343, 3814, 4830, 9683, 10291, 12162, 12966, 14576, 15953, 17281, 17681, 17955, 18013, 18289, 18409, 19052
--Religious and ecclesiastical institutions 17722
--Social conditions 286, 366, 553, 704, 1356, 1812, 3177, 5129, 5133, 13293, 14160, 16104, 16488, 16730, 17281, 17618, 18682, 19052
Englewood Ecumenical Ministry (Chicago, Illinois) 8200
Enschede (Netherlands)
--Church history 6245
Environmental ethics >> See further: Ecology
Environmental ethics 11351, 15593, 16084, 17576, 18375, 18951
Environmental protection 16349, 18238
--Citizen participation 11960, 12478
--Germany 17882
Episcopal Church >> See: Protestant Episcopal Church in the United States; Church of England
Episcopal Church in Scotland
--Case studies 15306
Episcopal City Mission (Boston, Massachusetts) 16914
Episcopal City Mission and Archdeaconry of Boston 100
Episcopal Urban Caucus 15359, 15442, 15787, 16148, 16476, 17778, 17992
Equality 14160, 17705
Erie (Pennsylvania)
--Religious and ecclesiastical institutions 5407, 5815, 9906, 10077, 16524
--Social conditions 2387
Erie Chapel Institute (Chicago, Illinois) 4007
Erie Neighborhood House (Erie, Pennsylvania) 4567, 4989
Eschatology 497, 4412, 7608, 9740, 11884, 18725
Ethics >> See: Business ethics; Social ethics; Environmental ethics; Decision making; Situation ethics; Political ethics; Wealth
Ethics, Christian 141, 933, 1181, 2408, 3793, 4062, 4190, 4236, 4286, 4477, 5044, 5299, 5347, 5445, 5712, 7073, 7391, 8526, 8722, 9380, 9660, 9734, 11483, 11542, 12329, 12413, 14882, 16247, 16788

--Congresses 6676, 6748
--England 1148
--History 12664
Ethics, Islamic 17729
Ethics, Jewish 4474, 18222
Ethnic attitudes 4577, 12214, 14993, 18177
--History 7525, 8393, 13122
Ethnic barriers 4577, 7533, 15426, 15714, 16560
--History 6684, 16320
Ethnic groups 10458, 13320, 14301, 14748, 15662, 15663, 15714, 15925, 17383
--England--History 10386
--History 13507
--Political activity 14993
--United States--History 6044
Ethnic identity >> See: Identity--Ethnic; African Americans--Ethnic identity; Race awareness
Ethnic relations 4398, 5472, 11414, 13320, 13980, 15111
--History 18279
Ethnic schools 17869
--History 14412, 18010
Ethnic studies >> See: Minorities--study and teaching; Ethnology--Study and teaching
Ethnicity >> See further: Immigrants; Emigration and immigration; Pluralism--Cultural
Ethnicity 1896, 4107, 4520, 5804, 5941, 6016, 6111, 6391, 6652, 8429, 8702, 8730, 9624, 11088, 11165, 11309, 11310, 11386, 11638, 11645, 11655, 11671, 11853, 12402, 12619, 12937, 12992, 13026, 13037, 13124, 13756, 13782, 13791, 13848, 13859, 14207, 14411, 14523, 14573, 14600, 14806, 15858, 15988, 16034, 16281, 16789, 16790, 17298, 17566, 17597, 17659, 17829, 18186
--Africa 19240
--Asia 13309
--Australia 13374
--Bibliographies 11170, 12341, 13973, 15398, 16429, 16521, 16841, 18081
--Canada 11682, 15426, 18241, 18260, 18616
--Congresses 12271
--Great Britain 13158
--History 7581, 8808, 12473, 12814, 13952, 14315, 14516, 15210, 15955, 17053, 17414, 17881, 18723
--India 15754
--Michigan 14384
--Periodicals 11654
--Religious aspects 4869, 6175, 9072, 9130, 9719, 10692, 11404, 12171, 12739, 13354, 13707, 13852, 14301, 14982, 15651, 16398, 18177
--Religious aspects--Catholic 961, 6272, 6684, 7525, 8393, 10386, 13122, 13316, 13863, 14187, 14642, 14993, 15813, 16474, 16954, 17171, 17417, 18066, 18106, 18579
--Religious aspects--History 13209, 13959, 14207, 15176
--Religious aspects--Islamic 13113
--Religious aspects--Jewish 6684, 12940
--Religious aspects--Protestant 5931, 6684, 11885, 12580, 12940, 13212, 13980, 14694, 15433, 15801, 17103, 17844
--United States 3818, 4577, 7017, 8194, 8659, 10748, 11147, 11885, 12172, 12621, 12622, 13060, 13214, 13320, 14033, 14120, 14293, 14614, 14845, 14925, 14993, 15470, 15662, 15829, 16031, 16201, 17426,

17461, 18633
Ethnicity (cont.)
--United States--History 5428, 7525, 8393, 12356, 12580, 12716, 14855, 15006, 15177, 16123, 16320, 17053, 17254, 18010
Ethnicity in children 6864
--History 14187
Ethnology >> See further: Anthropology
Ethnology 11404, 11654, 12214, 12530, 12825, 13750, 13822, 13884, 14582, 18019, 18220
--Africa 14816
Europe
--Church history--Bibliographies 13574
--Economic conditions 18390, 18772, 19028, 19188
--History 17365
--Religion 4571
--Religion--History 15930
--Religious and ecclesiastical institutions 7473, 17826
--Social conditions 3445, 5483, 7421, 10142, 11346, 11503, 15123, 15556, 17014, 17408, 18314
Evaluation >> See: Experimental ministries--Evaluative studies
Evangelical Academies (Germany) 7253
Evangelical Alliance 446, 449, 528, 530, 537, 633, 654, 1098, 1262
Evangelical Alliance for the United States 804, 826, 834, 836, 850, 861, 863, 982, 1002, 1022, 1292
Evangelical and Reformed Church 6832, 7422
--Board of National Missions 4925
--Case studies 4925, 5167, 5168, 5213, 5215, 6277, 6388, 6545, 6936, 6971, 6973
--History 6859, 9206
--Periodicals 6658
--Pronouncements, policies 5573
--Social teachings 5085
Evangelical and Reformed Church, Board of National Missions 5981, 6388, 6389, 6390, 6529, 6658, 6815, 6832, 6856, 6859, 7302, 7442
Evangelical and Reformed Church, Commission on Christian Social Action 5000, 5085, 5573, 5896, 6465
Evangelical Church in Germany 13461, 13499
Evangelical Coalition for Urban Mission (London, England) 11759, 16572, 16917, 17733
Evangelical Committee for Urban Ministries (Boston, Massachusetts) 10819
Evangelical Lutheran Church
--Case studies 12939, 18688
--Periodicals 2871
Evangelical Protestant churches
--Case studies 12599, 13896, 14068
--Congresses 15524, 15525, 16790, 17768
Evangelical Protestant churches (Peru) 18519
Evangelical Social Movement
--Germany 1630
Evangelical Synod of North America 4796, 5330
--Case studies 4669
--History 8084
Evangelical Union of South America 14991
Evangelical United Brethren Church 3751, 6296, 7920, 9028, 10045, 10820
--Case studies 6736, 8074, 8354,

8355, 9500, 9871, 10256, 10377, 10532, 11497
--Social teaching 6053
Evangelicalism 5931, 13005, 14138, 15104, 15290, 18694
--Canada--History 14739
--England 7868, 8459, 15967
--England--History 840, 17842
--Great Britain 16550
--Great Britain--History 13264
--History 7199, 11043, 12297, 16438
--United States 17635, 18325
Evangelische Kirche in Deutschland 2406, 13142, 14121, 15352, 16098, 16930, 16932, 17876, 18195
--History 17651
Evangelistic sermons 176, 314, 330, 331, 348, 564, 571, 1038, 1890, 3329, 4428, 4556, 5931, 6476, 7501, 10882, 15277
Evangelistic work >> See further: Revivals; Evangelicalism; Witness Bearing (Christianity)
Evangelistic work 116
--Africa 13975, 15163, 15531, 16366, 17122, 17883
--American Baptist sources--(1918 to 1944) 4042, 4836
--American Baptist sources--(1960 to 1969) 7807, 7818, 7926, 10000, 10453, 10588
--American Baptist sources--(1970 to 1979) 13166
--American Baptist sources--(1980 to 1991) 16632, 16892, 17644
--Argentina 17827
--Asia 7240, 10608, 13095, 15048, 17210, 18169
--Australia 7725, 9256, 17726, 18792
--Baptist sources--(1800 to 1874) 271
--Baptist sources--(1900 to 1917) 2543
--Baptist sources--(1918 to 1944) 3788
--Baptist sources--(1970 to 1979) 11657, 14573, 15277
--Baptist sources--(1980 to 1991) 16162, 16173, 16826, 17230, 17231, 17542, 17622, 18034, 18268, 19067
--Belgium 18910
--Biblical teaching 14654, 17756
--Bibliographies 7199, 13671, 14334, 16198, 16808, 17804
--Brazil 8543, 15340, 15585, 15614, 16162, 16347
--Brethren sources--(1970 to 1979) 12503
--Brethren sources--(1980 to 1991) 17300, 17938, 18197
--Canada 14800, 18268, 19159
--Canada--History 14739
--Case studies 12054, 13221, 17896
--Catholic sources--(1800 to 1874) 354
--Catholic sources--(1875 to 1899) 1655
--Catholic sources--(1918 to 1944) 4217, 4792, 4882, 5221
--Catholic sources--(1945 to 1959) 5945, 6696, 7137, 7586
--Catholic sources--(1960 to 1969) 10023, 10127, 10313, 10464, 10528, 10598
--Catholic sources--(1970 to 1979) 11908, 13470, 14144, 14711, 14958
--Catholic sources--(1980 to 1991) 15351, 15503, 15531, 15541, 15602, 15604, 15613, 16096, 16187, 16459, 16703, 17444, 17983, 18286, 18693
--Catholic sources--History 7407, 14135, 15695
--China 2990, 3225

Evangelistic work (cont)
--Christian Churches and Churches of Christ sources 19281, 19290, 19302, 10310, 19317, 19353
--Christian Reformed Church 12429
--Church of England sources--(1800 to 1874) 499, 16252, 17842
--Church of England sources--(1875 to 1899) 1443
--Church of England sources--(1900 to 1917) 2565
--Church of England sources--(1918 to 1944) 3814, 3859, 4428
--Church of England sources--(1945 to 1959) 7038
--Church of England sources--(1970 to 1979) 14241
--Church of England sources--(1980 to 1991) 15967, 17894, 18046
--Colombia 17464
--Congregational Christian sources--(1945 to 1959) 5985, 6459
--Congregational sources--(1800 to 1874) 133, 299, 358, 519
--Congregational sources--(1875 to 1899) 760, 802, 857, 902, 959, 1249, 1562, 1628, 2176
--Congregational sources--(1900 to 1917) 1956, 2907
--Congresses 1368, 15523, 19072, 19079
--Developing countries 16405
--Disciples of Christ sources--(1960 to 1969) 9888
--Ecuador 17398
--England 726, 2038, 2051, 3642, 3836, 3838, 5219, 5874, 6119, 6125, 6447, 6475, 6851, 7016, 7038, 7543, 9770, 11759, 15286, 16572, 17042, 17273, 17368, 18270, 18713, 18785, 18798
--England--History 3746, 16391
--England--London 171, 362, 1019, 2985, 4428, 4710, 4799, 6532, 12034, 17560, 17563, 18348
--Episcopal sources--(1800 to 1874) 27
--Episcopal sources--(1945 to 1959) 6801, 7044, 7085
--Episcopal sources--(1960 to 1969) 9168
--Episcopal sources--(1980 to 1991) 18280
--Europe 6696, 7473, 7984, 17139
--Evangelical and Reformed sources--(1945 to 1959) 7081
--Evangelical Protestant sources--(1875 to 1899) 14334
--Evangelical Protestant sources--(1900 to 1917) 2638, 2900, 14334
--Evangelical Protestant sources--(1945 to 1959) 7049, 7169
--Evangelical Protestant sources--(1960 to 1969) 7885, 8507, 9397, 9931, 10187, 10524, 10590, 10970, 11150, 11198, 11257, 11306
--Evangelical Protestant sources--(1970 to 1979) 11758, 11785, 11794, 11889, 12126, 12336, 12448, 12464, 12475, 12600, 12609, 12625, 12876, 12877, 12885, 12942, 13005, 13093, 13095, 13176, 13229, 13296, 13297, 13515, 13556, 13706, 13878, 13883, 13886, 14004, 14005, 14217, 14411, 14654, 14716, 14830, 15004, 15047, 15060, 15090, 15189, 15322
--Evangelical Protestant sources--

(1980 to 1991) 15401, 15417, 15490, 15524, 15525, 15588, 15769, 15781, 15801, 15819, 15837, 15845, 15850, 15920, 15945, 16018, 16032, 16060, 16061, 16184, 16245, 16277, 16299, 16379, 16517, 16549, 16572, 16593, 16626, 16711, 16729, 16765, 16825, 16860, 16869, 16882, 16884, 16887, 16888, 16989, 17004, 17037, 17042, 17043, 17046, 17047, 17072, 17109, 17116, 17139, 17165, 17209, 17253, 17270, 17288, 17333, 17338, 17345, 17442, 17446, 17462, 17464, 17551, 17563, 17566, 17580, 17597, 17623, 17627, 17734, 17768, 17797, 17804, 17820, 17827, 17887, 17928, 17931, 17949, 17985, 18012, 18084, 18147, 18162, 18199, 18231, 18311, 18318, 18338, 18347, 18367, 18565, 18581, 18722, 18774, 18798, 18810, 18854, 18945, 19006, 19014, 19032, 19079, 19099, 19127, 19209, 19226, 19230

Evangelistic work (cont)
--Evangelical Protestant sources--History 8139, 8421, 13154, 13447
--Evangelical Protestant sources--Periodicals 11759, 12325, 16572, 16765
--Fiction 4068
--France 13435, 14720, 18286
--France--History 16002
--Fundamentalist sources--(1970 to 1979) 12147, 12842
--Germany 7548, 8006, 10882
--Germany--Berlin 953
--Great Britain 5415, 7078, 8396, 9918, 12142, 16277, 17453, 18111, 18476
--Great Britain--History 549, 13264, 17416
--Handbooks 11785, 12503, 16631, 17734
--History 2098, 8139, 8421, 9991, 14116, 14561, 14745, 15549, 17768, 18836
--Honduras 16835
--Hong Kong 13545, 13873, 14169, 14909, 17088
--India 6944, 13347, 14814, 16256, 16718, 17385, 17748
--India--Congresses 9177
--Indonesia 19171
--Italy 10127
--Japan 2663, 3130, 3349, 3404, 6852, 6874, 6878, 7344, 8236, 8924, 9414, 10448, 10800, 16505, 17691, 19127
--Japan--History 13578
--Kenya 11981, 18817
--Korea 12156, 13053, 13101, 17089
--Latin America 12877, 13594, 14042, 14830, 15921, 15987, 16172, 16206, 16238, 16319, 16817, 17056, 17151, 17432, 17522, 18615, 18783
--Lutheran sources--(1945 to 1959) 5680
--Lutheran sources--(1960 to 1969) 7881
--Lutheran sources--(1980 to 1991) 15477, 17421, 17756
--Mali 18950
--Mennonite sources--(1980 to 1991) 15510, 15520
--Methodist sources 15291
--Methodist sources--(1800 to 1874) 70, 74, 12426, 13805, 18376
--Methodist sources--(1875 to 1899) 719, 832, 892, 942, 1404, 1603, 1657, 1692, 1709
--Methodist sources--(1900 to

1917) 1765, 1806, 1890, 1964, 1977, 2107, 2282, 2605, 2870, 2917
Evangelistic work (cont)
--Methodist sources--(1918 to 1944) 3040, 3059, 3207, 3294, 3311, 3318, 3374, 3409, 3455, 3556, 3563, 3652, 4487, 4710
--Methodist sources--(1945 to 1959) 5348, 6125, 6137
--Methodist sources--(1960 to 1969) 8356, 8401, 8530, 9414, 9540, 10121
--Methodist sources--(1970 to 1979) 13282, 13528, 13700, 14169, 14319, 14479, 14577, 15021, 15286
--Methodist sources--(1980 to 1991) 15719, 16088, 16092, 16247, 16632, 17067, 17748
--Methods 2051, 3374, 3404, 4180, 4217, 5348, 5415, 5466, 5666, 6137, 6149, 6605, 8100, 8821, 11785, 12448, 16245, 16626, 17004, 17122, 17139, 17210, 17384, 18774, 19024
--Mexico 12505
--Nazarene sources 10051, 13238, 13246
--NCCCUSA sources--(1945 to 1959) 6149, 6161, 6244, 6970
--NCCCUSA sources--(1960 to 1969) 7939
--New Zealand 14374
--Nigeria 9546, 15163, 16672
--Pentecostal sources 9686, 14182
--Periodicals 6921, 16184, 17804
Peru 13585, 14991, 16742, 17151, 17846, 18519
--Philippines 13111, 18150
--Philosophy 2565, 3814, 4589, 12377, 15525, 15564, 16088, 16515, 16817, 16825, 16882
--Presbyterian sources--(1800 to 1874) 175, 314, 348
--Presbyterian sources--(1900 to 1917) 1892, 1979, 2173, 2679, 14331
--Presbyterian sources--(1918 to 1944) 3329, 3951, 4946
--Presbyterian sources--(1945 to 1959) 6764
--Presbyterian sources--(1960 to 1969) 7826, 8768, 8860, 8927, 8965, 9452, 10555, 10623, 11604
--Presbyterian sources--(1970 to 1979) 12054, 13839, 14920, 15013, 15227
--Presbyterian sources--(1980 to 1991) 16631, 16818, 18327
--Presbyterian sources--History 5287, 6822, 15198
--Protestant sources--(1800 to 1874) 1, 66, 92, 171, 176, 362, 419, 420, 515, 565, 3746, 5474, 6446, 7199, 11043, 12297, 13351, 14124, 15132, 17416
--Protestant sources--(1875 to 1899) 559, 564, 580, 610, 792, 808, 829, 935, 1110, 1123, 1143, 1231, 1289, 1368, 1397, 1423, 1530, 1565, 1616, 1649, 1764, 14124, 15249, 17416
--Protestant sources--(1900 to 1917) 1377, 1940, 1961, 2051, 2057, 2077, 2097, 2112, 2248, 2388, 2529, 2579, 2585, 2621, 2816, 6729, 16578
--Protestant sources--(1918 to 1944) 3424, 3937, 4013, 4180, 4556, 4589, 4981
--Protestant sources--(1945 to 1959) 5466, 5481, 5588, 5911, 5912, 5939, 5966, 6250, 6464, 6881, 6994, 7225, 7698
--Protestant sources--(1960 to 1969) 7795, 7940, 7997, 8821, 8910, 9560, 9597, 9600, 9688, 10927, 11011

Evangelistic work (cont)
--Protestant sources--(1970 to 1979) 11755, 12032, 12933, 13545, 13657, 13748, 13874, 14263, 14982, 15082, 15290
--Protestant sources--(1980 to 1991) 15043, 15636, 15656, 15928, 16938, 17257, 17783, 18076, 18602, 18790
--Protestant sources--Bibliographies 13560
--Protestant sources--Congresses 792
--Protestant sources--History 1714, 1769, 5395, 5654, 6446, 7648, 13127, 16215
--Protestant sources--Periodicals 1
--Reformed Church in America sources--(1960 to 1969) 7967, 11324
--Rhodesia 11986
--Salvation Army sources--History 17452
--Scotland 348, 6413, 6605
--Seventh Day Adventist sources 18586
--Seventh Day Adventist sources--History 13625, 17920
--Singapore 16299, 17740, 19103
--Southern Baptist sources--(1900 to 1917) 1851, 1865, 2470
--Southern Baptist sources--(1918 to 1944) 3341, 13380
--Southern Baptist sources--(1945 to 1959) 6165, 6805, 6939, 7260, 7412, 7738
--Southern Baptist sources--(1960 to 1969) 8409, 9304, 9785, 9825, 9836, 10783, 10991, 11275
--Southern Baptist sources--(1970 to 1979) 11643, 12014, 12066, 12067, 12113, 12121, 12614, 12967, 13031, 13221, 13303, 13444, 13649, 13688, 13969, 14180, 14595
--Southern Baptist sources--(1980 to 1991) 15383, 15402, 15747, 16111, 16199, 16216, 16240, 16400, 16508, 16561, 16626, 16745, 16980, 17004, 17010, 17128, 17152, 17299, 17628, 17703, 17740, 17863, 19015
--Southern Baptist sources--Bibliographies 16198
--Southern Baptist sources--History 17798
--Sri Lanka 15422, 17304
--Sweden 15678
--Taiwan 13779, 17565, 17887, 18774
--Tanzania 15572
--Theology 18804
--Theory 749, 13238, 13246, 13874, 15945, 16199, 16550, 18270
--Unitarian sources 7063
--United Church of Christ sources--(1970 to 1979) 12062, 14713
--United Church of Christ sources--(1980 to 1991) 16290, 19337
--World Council of Churches sources--(1960 to 1969) 8414, 8514, 8632, 8796, 8915, 10661, 11152
--World Council of Churches sources--periodicals 6921, 8632
Evangelistic work, industrial >> See: Church and industry; Chaplains, industrial
Evangelists 13297, 14319
--Biography 580, 1428, 1764, 2051, 2786, 2815, 3816, 4563, 4644, 4758, 6729, 7648, 8139, 8396, 8397, 8421, 8862, 9573, 9918, 9991, 11279, 13541,

13631, 15039, 15203, 15836, 16391, 17691, 17971, 18376, 18615, 19068, 19201, 19285
Evangelists (cont.)
--Fiction 3840
--History 13154, 13447
Evanston (Illinois)
--Religious and ecclesiastical institutions 18006, 18197
--Social conditions 15856, 17477
Everett (Washington)
--Religious and ecclesiastical institutions 7672
Evil >> See: Good and evil
Evolution, social >> See: Social evolution
Experimental ministries >> See further: Para church; Street ministries;
Experimental ministries 3347, 3971, 4897, 7931, 8777, 9562, 9871, 10031, 10354, 10413, 11601, 11708, 12245, 12957, 13289, 13831, 14400, 15031
--Australia 11338, 11466
--Austria 10425
--Church renewal 7198, 8514, 10087, 10364, 10887, 12360, 13832
--Ecumenical 6491, 10773, 11041, 11240, 12224
--Educational 7361, 8595, 9019, 10581, 10618, 11831, 12262, 12440, 12696, 14055, 14257, 18356, 18866, 18873, 19352
--England 8863, 12195, 12235, 12360, 13683, 16950
--Europe 7984, 10177, 15827
--Evaluations, studies 5698, 7698, 10338, 11756, 11897, 12125, 12190, 12290, 12363, 12409, 12821, 12952, 13087, 13312, 13468, 13759, 13825, 14265, 14344, 14531, 14800, 15373, 17226, 18808
--Evangelism 6413, 7038, 8632, 9325, 9540, 9863
--France 7676
--India 10915, 13347
--Netherlands 8939
--Scotland 6413
--Social problems 4524, 5475, 6547, 6699, 7212, 8023, 8174, 9310, 9448, 10126, 10632, 11280, 11505, 11565, 11585, 13216, 13876
--Worship 7460, 7751, 8614, 8615, 11087, 11347, 13569, 13746, 16027, 16421, 16703, 16708, 17229, 18114, 18377, 18444, 19017
--Youth 2689, 4524, 6699, 10494, 10980, 11090, 12173, 15361, 18473
Express highways 3595, 5485, 6924, 7055, 8196, 11290, 11789, 12844, 13054, 13324
Fabian Society 1141, 1528, 2127, 2133, 2207, 2231, 2840, 5473, 13522
Fairfax County (Virginia)
--Social conditions 17675
Fairfield (Connecticut)
--Religious and ecclesiastical institutions 14502
Faith 3627, 9524, 11647
Faith development 4545, 6431, 16092
Family life >> See further: Church work with families
Family life 1406, 1799, 8045, 12458, 15888, 18278
--Africa 6143, 13377, 15974, 16086, 18124
--African American 4216, 7583, 9571, 10331, 10700, 13128, 13639, 15332, 15567, 15619, 16970, 17758, 18961
--African American--History 4832, 15010, 15515, 16274

Family life (cont.)
--Argentina 12936
--Bahamas 17725
--Biblical teaching 1559, 1768, 2424, 18440, 18832, 18930
--Canada 8285
--Changing roles and patterns 2699, 6408, 7082, 7215, 8953, 9643, 11953, 16560, 17615, 17758, 18941
--Egypt 18026, 19193
--England 233, 7233, 8398, 8858, 9002, 18273
--England--History 17130
--Ethnic minority 1893, 5195, 6044, 6656, 7255, 8696, 8772, 8858, 9958, 11147, 11165, 12622, 13443, 13664, 13951, 15320, 15409, 17275, 17602, 18741, 18985, 19182
--Fiction 106, 233, 1496, 6416, 7583, 8157, 13559, 18961
--France 11115
--Germany 8244, 9000
--Great Britain 17682
--History 3851, 8696, 12532, 13664, 14813, 15362
--India 8953, 13813, 16857, 18263
--Indonesia 18158
--Islam 19193
--Islamic 18848
--Japan 12405, 12521, 12723
--Jewish 10218, 10849, 14453, 14755, 15025, 16801, 16970, 17600
--Jewish--History 1319
--Kenya 13648
--Korea 14847
--Korean 17275
--Latin America 10652
--Migrants 5008, 6130, 6416, 6656, 8687, 8772, 8858, 11863, 12310, 12521, 12723, 12936, 13443, 13951, 16086, 18158
--Philippines 16150
--Problems 999, 1834, 1916, 2322, 2537, 2580, 2753, 3740, 3964, 3991, 5573, 5721, 5746, 5839, 5884, 6143, 7403, 7583, 8220, 9117, 10309, 10607, 11698, 13128, 13305, 14398, 14539, 14926, 15332, 15780, 16274, 17195, 17241, 17974, 18535, 18906, 18961
--Problems--History 11961
--Problems, financial 1496, 1799, 1911, 9958, 11856, 15567, 17725
--Problems, housing 106, 5602, 6141, 10747, 12451, 13648, 14799, 15044, 16999, 18561, 18622, 18639
--Problems, medical 4030, 7255, 12944, 15724, 17036
--Religious aspects 1199, 2607, 3042, 3384, 4689, 6556, 6608, 7975, 8045, 8135, 8219, 8522, 8705, 10607, 11165, 13394, 13416, 13475, 13669, 14476, 14774, 15141, 15780, 15795, 15837, 16150
--Religious aspects--England 15675, 17130
--Religious aspects--Hindu 8285
--Residential mobility 5351, 8157, 8772, 9230, 10165, 12073, 12099, 12458, 13624, 16191, 17999
--Residential mobility--Fiction 13559
--Russia 13394
--Single parent >> See further: Church work with young adults; Single people; Single parents
--Single parent 12128, 13140, 14952, 15332, 15599, 17245, 17612, 19001
--Spain 15587

Family life (cont.)
--Sri Lanka 15724
--Turkey 18848
Fascism 4081, 4315, 4361, 4495, 4948, 5152, 15474, 15951
--History 7437, 9673, 14908
--Spain 4693, 4864
Father Divine 4414, 4529, 4707, 4814, 5269, 5848, 6326, 8672, 14959, 15533, 19357
--Biography 16779
Federal Bureau of Investigation 6366, 10393
Federal Council of Churches, Commission on the Church and Social Service 2509
Federal Council of the Churches of Christ in America 2218, 2220, 2341, 2702, 2758, 2789, 2891, 3077, 3131, 3147, 3174, 3208, 3212, 3215, 3216, 3217, 3218, 3219, 3233, 3415, 3427, 3501, 3706, 3710, 3789, 3859, 4014, 4055, 4065, 4076, 4137, 4211, 4294, 4475, 4908, 4955, 5007, 5086, 5167, 5203, 5337, 5455, 5456, 5457, 5458, 5469, 5471, 5566, 5660, 5707, 5811, 5819
--Congresses 2509, 2715, 2888, 3693, 4024, 4039, 4047, 4051, 4059, 4066, 4077, 4198, 4572, 4787, 4805, 4974, 5582, 5897
--History 2973, 3312, 4103, 5031, 8017, 12111
--Periodicals 2219, 3064, 3321
--Pronouncements, policies 2501, 4172, 4215, 5575
Federal Council of the Churches of Christ in America, Christian Commission for Camp and Defense Communities 5087, 5088
Federal Council of the Churches of Christ in America, Commission on the Church and Social Service 2599, 2841, 2844, 3102, 3220, 3322, 3405, 3905, 4953, 5678, 5789
Federal Council of the Churches of Christ in America, Department of Race Relations 4046, 5270
Federal Council of the Churches of Christ in America, Department of Research and Education 3882, 4214, 4720, 5574
Federal Council of the Churches of Christ in America, Department of the Church and Economic Life 5781
Federal Council of the Churches of Christ in America, Industrial Relations Division 4078, 4649, 5484
Federation for Industrial Retention and Renewal
--Periodicals 18831
Federation of Protestant Welfare Agencies (New York, NY) 3222, 5450, 6159
Fellowship of Christian Socialists (New York, NY) 4916
Female Domestic Missionary Society of Philadelphia 43
Female Missionary Society for the Poor (New York, NY) 47, 79
Female Society of Boston and Vicinity for Promoting Christianity among the Jews 35
Feminism >> See further: Women; Women's liberation; Women's rights
Feminism 2628, 12560, 17425, 17758, 18541, 18932, 19229, 19352
--History 14522
Festivals 2068, 6111, 15713, 18119

--Ancient 6367
--Japan 13633
Fifth City Project (Chicago, Illinois) 8411, 11434, 11624, 12418
FIGHT (Rochester, New York) 9623, 10468, 10578, 11520, 12578, 13530
Filipino American Methodists 12487
Filipino American Presbyterians 7146
Filipino Americans
--Missions to 6202, 12487, 17300
Finland
--Religion 18225
--Religious and ecclesiastical institutions 8942, 10441, 12223, 14280
--Religious and ecclesiastical institutions--History 9522, 10430
--Social conditions 6012, 9539, 10412, 11420, 11880, 12143
--Social conditions--History 14085
--Social policy 15607
First churches >> See: Downtown churches; Big churches
Fitzroy Ecumenical Center (Fitzroy, Australia) 13047, 13048, 13374
--Periodicals 11768
Five Points Mission (New York, NY) 74, 254, 301, 336, 1266, 1286, 18376
Florence (Italy)
--Social conditions 7629, 7630
Florida Black Front 11138
Flower Mission (New York, NY) 989
Flushing (New York)
--Religious and ecclesiastical institutions 7315
Folk-urban continuum 5048, 5617, 9533
Folk music and songs 647, 3850, 7368
--History 6319, 7835, 12124, 12455, 13536, 19214
Folk religion 2597, 2765, 4150, 4868, 5048, 8284, 8403, 12743, 13859, 13863, 14100, 14693, 15425, 16035, 19250
--Africa 11797, 12129, 15860, 17018, 18254
--Brazil 19208, 19211
--Canada 18291
--China 11190
--Czechoslovakia 19253
--France--History 15699
--Great Britain 17952
--History 13099, 13210, 14447, 15362, 15694
--Italy 6003
--Japan 13633, 13922, 18558
--Latin America 18640
--Peru 12825, 15208
--South Africa 13734, 15430
--Zambia 15860
Folk songs
--History 16075
Foochow (China)
--Religious and ecclesiastical institutions 4466
Food >> See further: Hunger
Food 1596, 3917, 4222, 4293, 4395, 4786, 4896, 11530, 12220, 13196, 13809, 14037, 14443, 15149, 15196, 16748, 17889, 17965, 17972, 18790, 18880, 18984, 19056, 19297
--Bibliographies 13243
--History 16496
--Sri Lanka 15724
Ford Motors 4351
Forecasts 248, 295, 667, 873, 1127, 1183, 1662, 1852, 1880, 2217, 2432, 2684, 2749, 2768, 3031, 3092, 3315, 3389, 3621, 3891,

3947, 4042, 4190, 4305, 4778, 4793, 5114, 5146, 5214, 5297, 5317, 5326, 5382, 5711, 6692, 6903, 7055, 7143, 7489, 7713, 7840, 7929, 8081, 8127, 8445, 8448, 8518, 8712, 8747, 8887, 8959, 9099, 9138, 9822, 9948, 10128, 10178, 10306, 10442, 10685, 10802, 10803, 10814, 10880, 10887, 11093, 11123, 11173, 11224, 11430, 11459, 11516, 11762, 11808, 11840, 11872, 11988, 11989, 12188, 12684, 12710, 12759, 12768, 13001, 13020, 13056, 13119, 13157, 13179, 13207, 13254, 13696, 13905, 14084, 14086, 14123, 14150, 14420, 14510, 14566, 14616, 14625, 14900, 14931, 14992, 15197, 15478, 15562, 15578, 15615, 15936, 15961, 16013, 16018, 16047, 16223, 16262, 16437, 16675, 16829, 16985, 17007, 17060, 17101, 17128, 17149, 17302, 17321, 17384, 17467, 17521, 17541, 17628, 17657, 17911, 17927, 18137, 18188, 18389, 18449, 18789, 19018, 19036, 19100, 19117, 19129

Forecasts (cont.)
--Bibliographies 14460, 14695, 15304
--England 3371, 8635
--Ireland 13014
--Scotland 497

Foreign missions 453, 1625, 1708, 2565, 3035, 3071, 3300, 5307, 7170, 8290, 8799, 10678, 12020, 12224, 13159, 15490, 16140, 16856, 17859
--China 18753
--Ethiopia 14543
--History 3880, 10691, 15892
--Ivory Coast 17716
--Periodicals 598
--Sierra Leone--History 11939

Foreign Missions Industrial Association 1903

Forgiveness 8353, 10883, 18014

Forgiveness (theology) >> See: Theology

Fort Lauderdale (Florida)
--Social conditions 18186

Fort Wayne (Indiana)
--Religious and ecclesiastical institutions 5400, 6901, 7077, 7728, 8201, 8232, 9511, 13306, 17022
--Religious and ecclesiastical institutions--History 6990

Fort William (Canada)
--Social conditions 2747

Fort Worth (Texas)
--Religious and ecclesiastical institutions 5407, 5507

Forward movements 1330, 2490, 2522, 2529, 2603, 2622, 2659, 2723, 14777
--Archives 1761

Forward Movements
--History 1769, 2676, 12943, 16215, 16578, 18031, 18836

Four Square Gospel Church
--History 14561

France
--Church history 5547, 7069, 11304, 16002, 17107, 19233
--Economic conditions 8489, 11725, 12855
--History 14390
--Literature 8102
--Race relations--History 14657
--Religion 111, 5494, 6477, 7043, 7092, 7135, 7356, 7531, 8360, 10976, 11014, 12081, 13353, 18495
--Religion--History 7340
--Religious and ecclesiastical institutions 604, 6831, 10708,

10709, 11913
France (cont.)
--Social conditions 377, 416, 481, 502, 569, 585, 6040, 6126, 6224, 6780, 7616, 7962, 9084, 11004, 15071, 15673, 18243, 18317, 18645
--Social conditions--History 8086, 12191, 18603
Franciscans 6597, 13428, 17643
--History 3694, 14114, 15421, 16496
Frankfort (Germany)
--Social conditions 3932
Free enterprise
--Moral and ethical aspects 16236, 16594, 16821, 16964, 18003, 18954
Free Methodist Church 14378, 17473, 18177
--Periodicals 485
Free thought 2394
--History 15861, 18624
Freedom 385, 3362, 4468, 4945, 6481, 6981, 7347, 9613, 9655, 9755, 10530, 10658, 12112, 12655, 13175, 13202, 13697, 13757, 15562, 16196, 16743, 16928, 17579
--South Africa 15900
Freedom (theology) >> See further: Liberation theology; Revolution (theology)
Freedom (theology) 10281, 12655
Freedom of religion 705, 7215, 7227
--Colombia 10232
--England 4945
Freetown (Sierra Leone)
--Religious and ecclesiastical institutions 14049, 18628
--Social conditions 11180
Freiburg (Germany)
--Social conditions 14379
French Canadians 12559
--History 15066
Fresh air charities 250, 346, 605, 1433, 1465, 1595, 2183, 2871, 3454, 15319
--History 4227, 9127, 14334, 14382
Fresno (California)
--Religious and ecclesiastical institutions 14528, 15453, 19035
--Social conditions 6892
Friends >> See: Society of Friends
Frontier Fellowship 4916
Ft. Wayne (Indiana)
--Religious and ecclesiastical institutions 8982
Ft. Worth (Texas)
--Religious and ecclesiastical institutions 16833
Fundamentalism 1163, 2446, 14670, 15254, 16245, 16503, 16754, 18191
--Canada--History 14213
--History 12654, 15549, 18336
--India 18073
--Islamic 18730
Future >> See: Forecasts
Futurology >> See: Forecasts
Gambling 183, 872, 2473, 4532, 5573, 8280, 9523, 10063, 11480, 12644, 15707, 16709
Gangs >> See further: Juvenile delinquency; Blackstone Rangers; Young Lords
Gangs 7151, 7468, 9693, 9890, 9945, 10836, 11649, 12071, 12211, 16484, 18513
--History 16986
--New Guinea 17335
Garden cities 1642, 2357, 15542
--History 14225, 16406, 18239
Gardens and gardening 4739, 16284
Gardner (Massachusetts)
--Religious and ecclesiastical

institutions 1419
Gary (Indiana)
--Religion 14260
--Religious and ecclesiastical institutions 3750, 5070, 6901, 7128, 11408
--Social conditions--History 17881
--Social life and customs 13932
Gastonia (North Carolina)
--Religious and ecclesiastical institutions 11068, 13842
--Social conditions 5121
General Conference Mennonite Church
--Periodicals 7844
General Conference Mennonite Church, Board of Missions 7844
General Convention of Regular Baptists 13829
General Motors 12101, 12102, 19126
Geneva (Switzerland)
--Social life and customs 15880
Genocide 13479, 16715
Gentrification 11789, 13956, 14799, 15215, 15244, 15350, 15413, 15522, 15906, 16014, 16175, 16310, 16311, 16387, 16948, 17288, 17536, 17857, 17938, 18982, 19143
Geography 5350, 5915, 8160, 11047, 11054, 11771, 12356, 12456, 13295, 13656, 13761, 14067, 14173, 14754, 16671, 16822, 17125, 19196
Geography and religion 6191, 9407, 10007, 14338
--England 12162, 12966
--Germany 17660
--History 17944
German American Baptists
--History 14410
German American Catholics 6272, 10846, 14197
--History 13509, 14795, 15955
German American churches 964, 4796, 5330
German Americans
--Attitudes 12502
--Ethnic relations--History 12461
--Missions to 1637
--Politics 915
--Religion 10350, 14357
--Social conditions--History 14516
--Social life and customs--History 14582
Germantown (Philadelphia, Pennsylvania)
--Religious and ecclesiastical institutions 8318, 11026
Germany
--Economic conditions 16847
--Economic conditions--History 16410
--History 19241
--Politics 8065
--Politics and government 4861
--Religion 1509, 4330, 9628, 14714
--Religious and ecclesiastical institutions 8080, 9315, 12079, 13499, 18193
--Religious and ecclesiastical institutions--History 14533
--Social conditions 7706, 8065, 10512, 10595, 13937, 14121, 18055, 19163
Ghana
--Ethnic relations 14816
--Religious and ecclesiastical institutions 754
Ghettos >> See further: Inner City; Poverty; Church work with the poor; Church and the poor, Slums
Ghettos 3932, 6055, 8351, 8496, 9404, 9585, 9708, 9782, 9851,

10146, 10314, 10330, 10553, 10635, 10827, 10918, 10930, 11024, 11025, 11083, 11098, 11326, 11719, 12217, 12368, 13668, 14626, 14783, 15189, 15461, 17500
Ghettos (cont.)
--Africa 13118, 19178
--African American 5585, 6614, 9018, 9360, 9589, 10451, 11104, 12153, 13088, 13164, 14008, 14477, 15107, 16910
--African American--History 10587
--Catholic 10744, 16320, 18255
--Catholic--History 17119
--Chinese 11568
--England 13767
--Hispanic 9769
--Irish 16164
--Italian 5231
--Jewish 1706, 1859, 1910, 11511, 12543, 13856, 15772
--Jewish--England 12510, 15473, 15953
--Jewish--History 13898
--Pakistan 12904
--Poland 13856
--South Africa 5690
Girls 1215, 1377, 2070, 2428, 2693, 2780, 4202, 4349, 8820
--England 362
--Fiction 1210, 1803
Giving behavior >> See: Charity; Church finances; Wealth--Religious views on
Glasgow (Scotland)
--Religious and ecclesiastical institutions 199, 434, 6413, 12238, 14408, 15029, 18166
--Religious and ecclesiastical institutions--History 15306
--Social conditions 436
--Social conditions--History 19323
Glastonbury (Connecticut)
--Social conditions 17796
Glide Foundation (San Francisco, California) 9456, 9572
Glide Memorial United Methodist Church (San Francisco, California) 11916, 15693, 18735, 19181
Glide Urban Center (San Francisco, California) 9369, 9443, 9826, 11395, 11800
Gloucester (Massachusetts)
--Religious and ecclesiastical institutions 15786
God >> See further: Image of God; Theology
God
--Activity 357, 4411, 5813, 8912, 10927, 11252, 13855, 14773, 14854, 15231, 15954, 16090, 16185, 17622, 17896, 18284, 18304, 19209
--Attributes 4499, 10036, 10373, 12287, 12918, 14421, 16559, 16730, 17486, 18100, 18236, 19255
--Biblical teaching 7290
--Commands 560, 2710, 3400, 3755, 5402, 6095, 6189, 6260, 6908, 8133, 8709, 9405, 9711, 11793, 15302, 16328, 19134
--Fatherhood 10064
--Hiddenness 1913, 10881, 17781, 17961
--Immanence 465, 2565, 4416, 8039, 8950, 8965, 9103, 9271, 13358, 14443, 15507, 17744, 17961, 17972, 18061, 18424, 18636, 18662, 19145, 19270
--Knowableness 13837, 16090, 19234
--Love of 281, 696, 4599, 5465, 7046, 9168, 12291, 12974, 15777, 17618, 18348
--Mercy 627, 643, 991, 2382,

6592, 7171, 8289, 8321, 8353, 8580, 8841, 9281, 9643, 10104, 12574, 12945, 13305, 13489, 14026, 15107, 15387, 18305, 18327, 18565, 18715, 18798
God (cont.)
--Promises 15231, 18463
--Righteousness 9286, 10074, 14024
--Sovereignty >> See further: Theology (Kingdom)
--Sovereignty 164, 173, 278, 2916, 4652, 4734, 5970, 6854, 7203, 8062, 8466, 8639, 8641, 12877, 14984, 15046, 15053, 15790, 16305, 16343, 16817, 16881, 17320, 18410
--Wrath 10502, 11752
God in literature 4752, 18509
Good and evil 404, 481, 639, 4876, 4877, 4986, 4987, 12768, 13276, 18071, 18497
Goodwill Industries >> See further: Church work with the handicapped
Goodwill Industries 2952, 3228, 3237, 3250, 3261, 3610, 3834, 4331, 4435, 4633, 4833, 4915, 7359, 8604, 13745, 14323, 15689
--History 4442, 5373
--Periodicals 3051
Gorbals Group (Glasgow, Scotland) 15029, 18166
Gossner Mission (West Germany) 10231, 11980, 12911, 13554
Grand Rapids (Michigan)
--Ethnic relations--History 14864
--History 17569
--Religious and ecclesiastical institutions 4884, 5222, 5793, 14017, 18524
--Religious and ecclesiastical institutions--History 7003
--Religious life and customs 16116
--Social conditions--History 16767, 17824
Grasse (France)
--Religion 18495
Great Awakening, second 5, 74, 92, 133, 331, 565, 1428, 6035, 6298, 6429, 6446, 7199, 7853, 8990, 12296, 12426, 12602, 12774, 14124, 14532, 14813, 14944, 14945, 15132, 17639
Great Britain
--Church history 8316, 8400
--Economic conditions 1930, 3833, 12778, 13137, 16858, 18036
--History 1459, 2481, 3204, 15818
--Politics and government 15424
--Religion 4443, 6168, 8334, 11464, 13131, 14149, 15462, 17697, 17793, 17952, 18418, 18744
--Religious and ecclesiastical institutions 2209, 9323, 9770, 11724, 12450, 13539, 14079, 16277, 18083, 18476
--Social conditions 433, 1358, 1532, 1737, 1825, 4240, 6310, 7866, 9231, 9552, 12398, 12752, 13655, 14115, 14183, 14683, 14986, 15275, 15611, 15838, 15848, 15986, 16071, 18085, 18288, 18863, 19196
--Social conditions--History 4699, 7021, 12749, 14436, 14945
--Social life and customs 7109, 13158
Great Britain--Working classes >> See: Labor and laboring classes--Great Britain
Great Depression 4147, 4174, 4176, 4201, 4214, 4223, 4250, 4272, 4274, 4289, 4294, 4302, 4343, 4395, 4425, 4564, 13328,

14391, 14454, 16496
Greater New York Federation of Churches 985, 1471, 1633, 1855, 3903, 4053, 4144, 4514, 4618, 4733, 4777
Greece
--Social conditions--History 415
Greed 265, 618, 1102, 1147, 3171, 3287, 3336, 10398, 14632, 15358, 16302, 18120
--Fiction 932, 1308
Greek American churches 14424
Greek Americans
--History 2688, 15858
--Identity 17829
--Religion 5382, 13178
--Social conditions 3475
--Social life and customs 6005
--Social life and customs--History 13210, 14447
Greek Orthodox Church >> See: Orthodox Eastern Church
Greek Orthodox Church 14424
Green Bay (Wisconsin)
--Religious and ecclesiastical institutions 10180
Greensboro (North Carolina)
--Race relations 12031, 12373
Greenville (South Carolina)
--Religious and ecclesiastical institutions 10912, 11255
Greenwich Village (New York, NY)
--Social conditions--History 4501
Grenoble (France)
--Religious and ecclesiastical institutions 6218, 7259
Gross Lengden (Germany)
--Social conditions 17428
Group ministries 6801, 8947, 12995, 13155, 14198, 14554, 14775, 14801, 15122, 17361, 18674
--Catholic 16341
--England 8863, 10472, 10862, 16042
--Episcopal 14684, 15273
--France 13181
--Lutheran 9291
--Methodist 3305, 3344, 3549, 4122, 4641, 5370, 6679, 8624, 11376, 15629
--Presbyterian 8908, 9992, 18606
--Protestant 15696, 17553, 18355, 18675
--Reformed Church in America 11586
--Southern Baptist 10156, 14876, 16049
--United Church of Christ 8947, 16137
Group work, social 4901, 5370, 6535, 7038, 7198, 8863, 9932, 10885, 11049, 12437, 12639, 13860, 14265, 14697, 15675, 15760, 16092, 17366, 17684, 18154, 18659, 18738, 18913, 19168
--England 10862, 15840
--Germany 7995
Groups >> See: Small groups; Networks
Guaranteed annual income >> See further: Income
Guaranteed annual income 9955, 10093, 10120, 10362, 10511, 10648, 10648, 10874, 11627, 14459
Guatemala
--Social conditions 17492
Guatemala City (Guatemala)
--Religious and ecclesiastical institutions 11036
Guilt >> See: Sin
Gulf Oil Company 12103
Gypsies
--England 10444, 17886
--Missions to 2897
Habitat for Humanity 15455, 15812, 17753, 18736

Haiti
--Social conditions 19030
Haitian Americans
--Identity 14957
--Social conditions 17265
Halifax (Nova Scotia, Canada)
--Social conditions 13690
Halle (Germany)
--Religious and ecclesiastical institutions 2232
Hamburg (Germany)
--Religious and ecclesiastical institutions 9722, 15908
Hamilton (Ontario)
--Religious and ecclesiastical institutions--History 14418
Hamilton (Ontario, Canada)
--Religious and ecclesiastical institutions 14646
Hammond (Indiana)
--Religious and ecclesiastical institutions 11657
Hare Krishna >> See further: Counter Culture; Cults
Hare Krishna 13257, 17497, 19121
Harlem (New York, NY)
--Biography 7214, 8176, 11976
--Economic conditions 6536, 15371
--Ethnic relations 6111, 9322, 10438
--History 8075, 9589, 15063
--Race relations 4226, 5294, 11976
--Religion 4619
--Religious and ecclesiastical institutions 3373, 3700, 4414, 5603, 5651, 5675, 5739, 5758, 5765, 5790, 5808, 5834, 5838, 5859, 5995, 6086, 6153, 6230, 6231, 6284, 6460, 6640, 6690, 7018, 7212, 7361, 7459, 7460, 7507, 7536, 7724, 7731, 8433, 8615, 9003, 9233, 9388, 9688, 9814, 10026, 10381, 11308, 11449, 11526, 11544, 12277, 12833, 14640, 18729, 19120
--Religious and ecclesiastical institutions--History 1833, 17474, 18397, 19357
--Social conditions 2948, 4226, 5409, 6013, 6162, 6614, 6624, 7389, 8312, 8481, 9166, 9197, 9293, 9326, 10610, 11426, 13876, 16142
--Social life and customs 6059, 6111, 6266, 6535
Harrisburg (Pennsylvania)
--Religious and ecclesiastical institutions 11396, 17308, 18307, 18862
--Social conditions 2058, 15493
Harrisonburg (Virginia)
--Religious and ecclesiastical institutions 11411, 12390
Hartford (Connecticut)
--History 19118
--Politics 12746, 15005
--Religious and ecclesiastical institutions 250, 583, 867, 959, 5568, 5997, 6487, 8521, 8788, 10520, 17127, 18251
--Religious and ecclesiastical institutions--History 16306, 17135, 17417, 18097
--Religious life and customs 919
--Social conditions 2622
Harvest (metaphor) 10590, 11785, 14217, 14362
Hasidism 12506, 13355, 13356, 16700
Hattingen (Germany)
--History 18648
Haverhill (Massachusetts)
--Religious and ecclesiastical institutions 6399
Hawaii
--Social conditions 14693
Healers 12620, 13615, 14179,

15430, 15722, 16164
Healing >> See further: Medical care; Mental health; Church work with the sick; Nurses
Healing 10656, 12825, 13884, 18197
--Peru 15208
Healing, spiritual >> See: Spiritual healing
Health Care >> See: Medical Care; Mental health; Church work with the sick
Heidelberg (Germany)
--Religious and ecclesiastical institutions 11063
Hell (metaphor) 3402, 7323, 9145, 18760
Helping behavior 785, 1295, 1433, 2044, 2418, 2458, 2624, 2769, 2866, 2988, 3337, 4126, 4500, 5641, 6515, 6578, 7419, 7856, 7973, 8107, 8293, 9431, 10747, 11882, 13137, 13170, 13228, 13517, 13745, 13785, 14004, 14112, 14628, 14647, 14986, 15221, 15608, 15873, 16063, 16279, 16586, 16691, 16778, 17120, 17137, 17753, 17998, 18130, 18142, 18256, 18452, 18508, 18535, 18685, 18852, 18913, 19013, 19040
--History 5373
--Perverse effects 1883, 10930, 16127, 16810, 18120, 18391
Helsinki (Finland)
--Social Conditions 6012
Henry Street Settlement (New York, NY) 2914, 4403, 8014
Hershey (Pennsylvania)
--Social conditions 4608
High Point (North Carolina)
--Religious and ecclesiastical institutions 11381
High rise apartments >> See: Church work with apartment dwellers
Highland (Illinois)
--Religious and ecclesiastical institutions 10139
Highways >> See: Express Highways; Street ministries
Hillsborough (England)
--Social conditions 19039
Hinduism 9187, 12074, 15452, 15639, 16566
--Nepal 16446
--United States 4110, 4586, 6486
Hippies >> See further: Counter culture
Hippies 10399, 10424, 10630, 10673, 10722, 10829, 10884, 11021, 11045, 11150, 16387
Hiroshima (Japan)
--Social conditions 6338, 8838
Hispanic American Adventists 18650
Hispanic American American Baptists 12997, 16423
Hispanic American Baptists 16455
Hispanic American Catholics 2720, 11246, 11443, 13665, 13951, 14120, 14640, 15128, 15603, 15651, 15757, 15803, 15815, 15899, 16152, 16708, 17083, 18438, 18619, 18655, 18811, 18815
--History 13932
Hispanic American children 7878, 15404
Hispanic American churches 2720, 2745, 5651, 6230, 6231, 6572, 7637, 10449, 11286, 12118, 12982, 13233, 13446, 14227, 14366, 15169, 15899, 15914, 15925, 16892, 18257, 18604, 18940, 19007, 19063
--Bibliographies 9247, 15984
Hispanic American clergy 13953, 14474, 15651, 15897, 16173, 16455, 16487, 16571, 18502,

18963, 19337
Hispanic American Episcopalians 17110, 17341
Hispanic American families 7255, 13951, 18940
Hispanic American Lutherans 14368
Hispanic American Mennonites
--History 17736
Hispanic American Methodists 8619, 8698, 12026, 13802, 13944, 14071, 15169, 15223, 15224
Hispanic American Pentecostals 7953, 8617, 19008
Hispanic American Presbyterians 9627, 18360
--History 13136
Hispanic American Protestants 8617, 11443, 13446, 13951, 14901, 15894
Hispanic American Southern Baptists 17934
Hispanics American UCCs 19337
Hispanic American Women 16265, 18541
Hispanic American youth 10610, 11649, 11649, 16187
Hispanic Americans >> See further: Church work with Hispanic Americans
Hispanic Americans 7504, 12382, 12897
--Attitudes 6574
--Biography 15651
--Economic conditions 15463
--Education 13298, 15276, 15751
Housing 11088, 18140
--Identity 15804
--Migrants 8637
--Missions to 3161, 5651, 6257, 6945, 7592, 7847, 7957, 8481, 8617, 8698, 9104, 9156, 9223, 9277, 9322, 9627, 9769, 10208, 10449, 11286, 11755, 13249, 13446, 14071, 14227, 14368, 14747, 15128, 15223, 15514, 15732, 15803, 15815, 15925, 16398, 16423, 16892, 17110, 17226, 17341, 17421, 17457, 17917, 17934, 18199, 18257, 18360, 18619, 18650, 18811, 18963, 19337
--Missions to--History 1744, 13136
--Pastoral care of 14366
--Religion 5863, 5864, 6230, 6438, 9322, 12444, 13233, 14474, 14640, 14901, 15457, 15651, 15804, 15894, 16487, 16519, 16571, 16708, 17855, 18963, 18973, 19337
--Religious life and customs 7498
--Relocation 9146
--Social conditions 3857, 4619, 5948, 6945, 7724, 7957, 9104, 9149, 9223, 11443, 11649, 12833, 14747, 15224, 16152, 16873, 17083, 18490, 19148
--Social conditions--Bibliographies 9247
--Social conditions--History 7581, 19131
--Social life and customs 15033, 15804, 18086
--Social life and customs--History 13932
Hispanic Manifesto 15762
Hoboken (New Jersey)
--Religious and ecclesiastical institutions 16317, 16476, 16732
--Social conditions 14790
Holiness churches 2045, 4816, 4942, 8199, 13253, 14547
--Case studies 14095, 14134, 14501, 15920, 18622
--History 1769, 7199, 12338
--Social teaching 13984
Hollywood (California)

--Religious and ecclesiastical institutions 5901, 12281, 13944
--Social conditions 5570
Holmdel (New Jersey)
--Social conditions 18484
Holyoke (Massachusetts)
--Religious and ecclesiastical institutions--History 15066
--Social conditions 7215
Home Missionary Society of the City of Philadelphia 748
Home missions 1346, 1397, 2784
--American Baptist sources--(1945 to 1959) 5937
--American Baptist sources--(1970 to 1979) 12391
--American Baptist sources--History 7035
--American Baptist sources--Periodicals 586
--Assemblies of God sources 14637, 18267
--Belgium 14311
--Canada 16151
--Congregational Christian sources--(1945 to 1959) 6873
--Congregational sources--(1800 to 1874) 358
--Congregational sources--(1875 to 1899) 718
--Congregational sources--(1900 to 1917) 1898, 2040, 2147, 2157, 2187, 2284, 2398, 2460
--Congregational sources--History 13105
--Congregational sources--Periodicals 94
--Congresses 4623, 5913
--England 1794, 3695, 13562, 13899, 14669, 16013
--Episcopal sources--(1800 to 1874) 451
--Episcopal sources--(1875 to 1899) 14719
--Episcopal sources--(1918 to 1944) 4448
--Evangelical Protestant sources--(1980 to 1991) 17478, 17690
--Federal Council sources--(1918 to 1944) 4857
--France 589
--Germany 18316
--Great Britain 366, 18780, 18872
--History 4067, 4255
--Italy 10127
--Lutheran sources--(1918 to 1944) 3831
--Mennonite sources--(1918 to 1944) 3213, 4607, 4643
--Mennonite sources--History 5813
--Methodist sources--(1900 to 1917) 2090, 2254, 2381, 2870, 2955
--Methodist sources--(1918 to 1944) 3046, 3132, 3187, 3228, 3650
--Methodist sources--(1945 to 1959) 6797
--Methodist sources--(1970 to 1979) 14669
--Methodist sources--(1980 to 1991) 16013
--Methodist sources--History 3084
--NCCCUSA sources--(1945 to 1959) 6885
--NCCCUSA sources--(1960 to 1969) 7943, 10267
--Periodicals 16151
--Presbyterian sources--(1800 to 1874) 1868
--Presbyterian sources--(1875 to 1899) 1868
--Presbyterian sources--(1900 to 1917) 3024, 3035
--Presbyterian sources--(1918 to 1944) 3158, 3161, 3304, 3669,

4385, 4840
Home missions (cont.)
--Presbyterian sources--(1945 to 1959) 5440
--Presbyterian sources--History 2924, 5830, 6152
--Presbyterian sources--Periodicals 803, 8030
--Protestant sources--(1800 to 1874) 34, 240
--Protestant sources--(1900 to 1917) 1872, 2248, 2803, 2853
--Protestant sources--(1918 to 1944) 3884, 3919, 4032, 4165, 4259, 4385, 4473
--Protestant sources--(1945 to 1959) 5425
--Protestant sources--History 7097
--Reformed Church in America sources 2831, 2905, 2913
--Reformed Church in the United States sources 2825
--Scotland 383
--Southern Baptist sources--(1900 to 1917) 2632, 2811
--Southern Baptist sources--(1918 to 1944) 3082, 5108
--Southern Baptist sources--(1945 to 1959) 6029
--Southern Baptist sources--(1960 to 1969) 8404, 8740, 9453, 9953, 10826
--Southern Baptist sources--(1970 to 1979) 12733, 13381, 13456, 13714
--Southern Baptist sources--(1980 to 1991) 16242, 16682
--Southern Baptist sources--History 18594
--Southern Baptist sources--Periodicals 4100, 16029
Home Missions Council 2803, 3011, 3416, 3857, 3893, 4055, 4060, 4077, 4142, 4143, 4294, 4385, 4460, 4531, 4623, 4840, 5576, 5701
--Congresses 4024, 4066
--History 4067
Homelessness >> See further: Housing; Squatter settlements
Homelessness 6336, 13684, 15514, 17150, 18550, 19101, 19102, 19217, 19318, 19249
--Bibliographies 2462, 11651, 11971, 12398, 13919, 13920, 15070, 15199, 16430, 19215
--Canada 14781
--Descriptions 3478, 5671, 5923, 9135, 10684, 11651, 12398, 12752, 12778, 13137, 13526, 13758, 14875, 15254, 15395, 16001, 16403, 16445, 16533, 16613, 16942, 16997, 16999, 17112, 17675, 17789, 17821, 18068, 18180, 18211, 18288, 18375, 18451, 18459, 18561, 18639, 18649, 18653, 18833, 18924, 18933, 18977, 18994, 19355
--England 11096, 12740, 18900
--Great Britain 12752, 14115, 14986, 17618
--Hong Kong 15095
--Kenya 12176
--Mexico 19332
--Remedies 1958, 2034, 2055, 2087, 2409, 3872, 4126, 4722, 5515, 5862, 6761, 7854, 9953, 10057, 13521, 14115, 14183, 14318, 14571, 14841, 14986, 15455, 15499, 15798, 15957, 16413, 16617, 16691, 16701, 16748, 16962, 16999, 17369, 17477, 17524, 17588, 17706, 17753, 17789, 17913, 18040, 18082, 18141, 18179, 18327, 18399, 18442, 18452, 18473, 18484, 18498, 18503, 18533, 18549, 18556, 18562, 18622,

18646, 18660, 18740, 18766, 18790, 18852, 18915, 18928, 18979, 18991, 19099, 19136, 19311, 19354
Homelessness (cont.)
--Remedies--Bibliographies 18298
--Remedies--History 12633, 16364
--Scotland 12238
--Venezuela 14848
Homosexuality 8446, 10129, 12384, 12493, 12560, 12965, 13192, 13971, 14130, 15104, 15165, 16217, 16353, 16440, 17520, 17647, 17732, 17940, 18176, 18323, 18402, 18501, 18522, 18609, 18651, 18879, 19147, 19150
--Congresses 9124
--New Guinea 16043
Honduran Americans
--Religion 19082
Honduras
--Religious life and customs 16835
Hong Kong
--Religion 11862, 17178
--Religious and ecclesiastical institutions 6850, 13873, 14909, 17676, 18589
--Religious and ecclesiastical institutions--History 15892
--Religious life and customs 16755
--Social conditions 8799, 9964, 11815, 13545, 13873
Hong Kong Christian Council 10411
Hong Kong Christian Industrial Committee 13873
Honolulu (Hawaii)
--Religious and ecclesiastical institutions 6989
--Social conditions 10920
Hope >> See further: Theology
Hope 667, 2029, 2970, 2985, 3765, 4829, 4984, 7353, 7501, 7608, 8612, 9541, 9567, 10261, 10266, 11092, 11262, 11430, 12179, 12203, 12376, 12577, 12595, 12710, 12758, 13044, 13200, 13488, 13844, 13955, 14268, 14335, 14360, 14420, 14488, 14641, 14650, 14811, 14815, 15080, 15126, 15507, 15609, 15842, 16065, 16213, 16295, 16469, 16787, 17084, 17197, 17579, 17747, 18002, 18248, 18327, 18439, 18918, 18937
--History 15725
Hospice 17476
Hospitals 17, 263, 626, 638, 825, 1433, 2858, 4031, 5212, 6395, 7718, 8888, 12558, 13858, 14098, 14665, 15118, 15990, 16144, 16312, 16625, 18652
--Belgium 12824
--Germany 2941
--History 747, 2036, 16862
--Peru 10152
Hotels, taverns, etc. 1489, 1563, 1677, 1796, 1814, 1863, 2004, 2695, 3036, 10324, 10466, 11136, 11770, 12282, 14016, 17048
--Fiction 7911
--History 12928, 13283
House churches 7201, 7223, 7276, 7686, 9099, 10329, 10374, 10822, 10861, 11081, 11198, 11223, 11411, 11563, 11646, 11710, 11765, 11773, 11819, 11846, 12032, 12110, 12126, 12137, 12390, 13425, 14508, 14595, 14773, 15760, 16869, 16957, 17629, 18154, 18419, 19075, 19168
--England 6576

House churches (cont.)
--Great Britain 18726
--Mexico 15291
--Philippines 16150
House of Hospitality (New York, NY) 4826
House of Refuge (New York, NY) 458, 470
--History 11493
Housing >> See further: Homelessness; Housing (tenements); Habitat for Humanity; Public housing; Discrimination in housing; United States, Department of Housing and Urban Development
Housing 212, 741, 1170, 1202, 1228, 1437, 1470, 2357, 2468, 2570, 2586, 2623, 3326, 3859, 4045, 4149, 4206, 4532, 4590, 4611, 5077, 5442, 5515, 5589, 5596, 5862, 6060, 6162, 6207, 6248, 6396, 6741, 7122, 7163, 7444, 7594, 7604, 7688, 8072, 8925, 9406, 9435, 9695, 10153, 10240, 10720, 10962, 11331, 11402, 11482, 11551, 11615, 11870, 12099, 12380, 12381, 12810, 12894, 13146, 13285, 13868, 13933, 13965, 13972, 14480, 14487, 14541, 14569, 14751, 14779, 14799, 14840, 14989, 15055, 15455, 15576, 15842, 16014, 16999, 17150, 18142, 18269, 18679, 18846, 18974, 19031
--Africa 12291
--Africa--Congresses 13632
--Asia 16062
--Bibliographies 2462, 11971, 13560, 13919, 13920, 14666, 15070, 15199, 16430, 19215
--Brazil 16620
--Canada 13690, 15393
--Church involvement 2261, 2278, 2290, 2349, 2376, 2395, 2667, 2818, 5602, 5766, 6141, 6198, 6216, 6262, 6581, 6598, 6672, 6691, 6887, 7007, 7495, 7752, 8027, 8721, 8883, 8886, 8917, 9287, 9361, 9456, 9586, 9705, 10135, 10153, 10211, 10621, 10641, 10647, 10747, 11576, 12414, 12470, 12512, 12607, 12629, 13249, 13466, 13683, 13690, 13723, 14267, 14587, 14669, 14767, 15044, 15371, 15499, 15812, 16054, 16257, 16383, 16384, 16776, 17698, 17753, 17823, 17870, 18140, 18143, 18174, 18736, 18766, 18790, 18884, 18915, 19269
--Church involvement--Periodicals 4357
--Egypt 19193
--England 30, 553, 704, 1466, 1642, 2296, 5393, 6173, 6474, 7329, 9552, 10999, 12740, 13683, 14669, 16688, 17281, 17583, 18165, 19052
--Ethical aspects 8565, 12921, 13723, 14468
--Fiction 106
--France 6780
--Germany 15796, 16114
--Great Britain 12398, 12752, 15611, 17115
--History 10824
--Hong Kong 7099, 13807, 14792, 15095
--India 14530, 16041, 16330
--Ireland 12479
--Islamic 19193
--Japan 6338, 12452
--Kenya 18240
--New Guinea 15008
--Peru 12934
--Relocation 6624, 7790, 7982,

9146, 11071, 12598, 14916, 15199, 15244, 15261, 17168
Housing (cont.)
--Relocation--Congresses 4638
--Venezuela 14848
Housing (tenements) 608, 773, 942, 1013, 1040, 1063, 1117, 1130, 1338, 1433, 1467, 1496, 1525, 1706, 1713, 1869, 1916, 2234, 2261, 2278, 2290, 2349, 2376, 2395, 2396, 2595, 2667, 2765, 4655, 6413, 10170, 11101, 13054, 13881, 15371
--Fiction 1667, 1772, 7911
--History 8499
Houston (Texas)
--Race relations 11593
--Religious and ecclesiastical institutions 5508, 5876, 6837, 7712, 11465, 12347, 12643, 12891, 13010, 13287, 14000, 15975, 16623, 18718, 19320
--Social conditions 7595, 15927, 19328
Howard University (Washington, DC) 14294
Hull House (Chicago, Illinois) 1107, 1108, 1142, 1349, 2374, 3979, 4058, 4407, 4457, 4467, 8461, 9495
--History 3956, 11249, 17174, 17525, 18464, 18480, 18883, 18899, 18956, 19046, 19243
Human rights >> See further: Universal Declaration of Human Rights, 1948; Civil rights; Women's rights, African Americans--Civil rights; Right to work
Human rights 8924, 12325, 19263, 19266
Humane Society of the City of New York 26
Humanism 166, 294, 316, 332, 976, 3495, 4586, 5731, 6670, 6871, 8651, 11456, 12075, 13440
--Great Britain 14149
--History 19191
Humanitarianism >> See: Charity; Christian giving; Social service
Hungarian American families 13443
Hungarian Americans
--Missions to 2905
--Religion 13443
--Relocation 7164
--Social conditions 7216
Hunger >> See further: Poor; Poverty; Church work with the poor; Food
Hunger 1515, 4147, 4222, 4223, 4740, 4786, 9162, 9419, 10552, 11444, 11823, 11907, 13146, 13196, 13464, 13521, 13572, 13637, 13809, 13867, 14422, 14946, 15149, 15642, 15944, 16177, 16258, 17374, 17524, 17850, 18020, 18120, 18511, 18686, 19200, 19297
--Bibliographies 13243, 16431, 17641, 18298
--Canada 13386, 15393
--History 10386
--Japan 14443
--Periodicals 18880
Huntington (West Virginia)
--Religious and ecclesiastical institutions 5569
Hygiene 4408, 4421
Hymns 121, 430, 516, 559, 612, 643, 647, 650, 1222, 1432, 1913, 2308, 2364, 2382, 2523, 2662, 2710, 4134, 5971, 6592, 7751, 10074, 10251, 10620, 12566, 15206, 16794, 18164, 18918, 18990, 19009, 19255, 19270
--History 2098, 3162, 6319, 7835,

11364, 12124, 12455, 13536, 19214
Hypotheses >> See: Tests and measures; Tests and measures in religion
Hämeen Lääni (Finland)
--Religion 10430
Ibidan (Nigeria)
--Social conditions 10454
Identity >> See further: Race awareness; (subheading Identity under ethnic groups); African Americans--Ethnic identity; Hispanic Americans--Identity
Identity
--Catholic 17096, 18597
--Catholic--History 16012
--Ethnic 8417, 11092, 11682, 11800, 13789, 14264, 14957, 15384, 15804, 16436, 16610, 16719, 17402, 17829, 17963
--Ethnic--Africa 14816
--Ethnic--History 18065
--Ethnic--India 15754
--Ethnic--Trinidad 8897
--Jewish 6494, 8578, 9838, 10580, 11541, 11921, 12510, 13754, 13910, 14316, 14829, 15250, 15426, 16534, 17946
Identity, of churches 3548, 6043, 9770, 9932, 10674, 12589, 14595, 15799, 19116
--Latin America 15921
Identity, of cities 7683, 13300, 19172
Identity, of individuals 6397, 7885, 8678, 10154, 10250, 10604, 10658, 12445, 13295, 13974, 14360, 14883, 15353, 16840, 18005
Image of God >> See further: Theology
Image of God 9740, 17517
Imagination 7652, 7932, 8979, 13905, 15425, 18845
Immigrants >> See further: Emigration and immigration; Italian Americans, etc.
Immigrants 845, 1151, 1968, 2078, 2130, 2176, 2447, 3715, 3818, 4731, 4996, 6938, 7017, 11451, 13113, 14562, 14993, 15829, 17383, 17552, 18025, 18066
--African 8858, 9297, 10653, 14389, 14816
--Arab 6249, 9257, 13112, 13113, 13261, 15825
--Armenian 4938, 14357, 14358
--Asian 2945, 4373, 15238, 15626, 15927, 16513, 17793, 18536, 19236
--Bangladesh 12089
--Bibliographies 16841, 17271
--Biography 2828, 3355, 15175
--Buddhist 8128
--Chinese 657, 1229, 1544, 1724, 1741, 3662, 5659, 5857, 6016, 6630, 6635, 7894, 9964, 13782, 17253, 18241, 18792, 19049, 19304
--Chinese--History 14657
--Cuban 8772, 8792, 8801, 10110, 10344, 16458
--Czech 947, 3192, 3436, 14357, 17939
--Czech--History 5940, 14122
--Dutch 9566, 16767, 17569
--Eastern European 2963, 3171, 3662, 10679, 13910, 14481
--Eastern European--History 6104, 6561, 12068
--Economic conditions 3820, 4557, 5691, 16544
--Economic conditions--History 13454
--European 6044
--Fiction 6195
--French Canadian 15066
--German 658, 915, 964, 1719,

4811, 6272, 14197, 14307, 14357, 14516, 14582
Immigrants (cont.)
--German--History 5521, 12461, 12916, 13115, 13509, 14795, 15955, 18554
--Greek 3475, 6005, 14447, 18243
--Greek--History 2688
--Haitian 14957, 17265
--Hindu 18492
--Hispanic 7504, 8617, 12897, 15651, 15732, 16265, 16873, 18490
--History 4501, 4922, 5017, 5780, 6686, 7525, 12356, 13507, 14384, 17171, 17254
--Hungarian 2905, 7164, 13443
--Indian 13659
--Iraqi 13354
--Irish 1827, 1885, 6272, 7866, 12015, 12713, 13823, 14516, 14582, 15085, 15445, 15472, 16164, 17578
--Irish--History 1746, 5922, 7689, 10386, 10748, 11295, 11714, 12461, 13509, 13527, 13552, 14168, 14795, 16159, 17879
--Islamic 8897, 10299, 13112, 15071, 16974, 17014, 18317, 18492, 19077
--Italian 912, 1167, 1907, 1968, 2183, 2251, 2679, 2892, 3010, 3028, 3093, 3285, 3619, 3662, 4107, 4454, 5221, 5231, 9593, 12658, 13428, 13658, 13724, 14357, 14464, 14855, 14994, 15028, 15240, 17172, 17329
--Italian--History 9815, 11517, 11587, 11991, 12628, 12872, 13258, 13432, 13610, 13664, 14114, 14302, 16123, 17817, 18058, 18059, 18105, 18138, 18302
--Japanese 2798, 2799, 2831, 2891, 3233, 3662, 5489, 5937, 10426, 12888, 19051
--Japanese--History 15433
--Jewish 2005, 2298, 3657, 5563, 5689, 6808, 7131, 11519, 12916, 13367, 13910, 14109, 14357, 14516, 14855, 16157, 16557, 16738, 17578, 17659, 18956
--Jewish--History 1319, 2085, 2807, 4455, 6104, 6561, 7612, 7839, 8699, 9960, 10841, 12872, 13336, 13341, 13864, 14096, 14302, 14674, 15951, 18070, 18788
--Korean 2956, 12216, 12889, 13204, 13211, 13699, 13912, 14721, 15150, 15184, 15385, 15512, 15513, 15526, 16529, 16640, 17082, 17275, 17279, 17396, 18278, 18552, 18568, 18719, 18890, 19023
--Laotian 12098, 17679, 19197
--Latin American 3593, 7781, 15732, 16265
--Lithuanian--History 13555, 14886, 15702
--Mexican 3662, 11246, 14314, 14589, 16426, 18811
--New Zealand 14949
--Polish 3860, 3943, 4418, 14357, 17659, 18956
--Polish--History 6264, 12268, 12872, 13099, 13141, 13555, 13610, 14132, 14148, 14234, 14527, 14717, 14718, 15965, 16108, 16123, 16306, 16946, 18065, 18070, 18788
--Polynesian 13013
--Religion 1663, 3355, 3726, 3871, 3988, 4226, 7653, 8840, 8900, 12015, 12248, 14357, 14949, 15160
--Religion--History 17447, 19142
--Roumanian 6999

Immigrants (cont.)
--Russian 1182, 2005, 3285, 4275, 5340, 14402, 14943, 16557, 16738, 17644
--Russian--History 5433, 14207
--Scandinavian 4107, 16436
--Scandinavian--History 16026
--Slavic 1872
--Slovak 2250, 2963, 3436, 3722, 14357
--Slovak--History 14418, 14437, 14842, 16805, 18015
--Swedish--History 12841
--Turkish 18910
--Ukrainian 11682, 15263
--Ukrainian--Bibliographies 14434
--Vietnamese 15653, 16983, 17458, 18672, 18792
--West Indian 7329, 8760, 9336, 10653, 10796, 12015, 12185, 14389, 15228, 18985, 19114, 19164
--West Indian--History 17447
Immigration Restriction League 1310, 1311
Immortality >> See: Death; Theology
Incarnation >> See further: Theology
Incarnation 927, 3473, 5725, 7046, 9393, 9740, 9924, 9998, 10650, 13094, 13200, 14080, 14482, 14854, 16550, 16965, 17671, 18149, 19145
Inclusiveness in churches >> See further: Pluralism--Cultural; Race relations and church; Church work with minorities
Inclusiveness in churches 6187, 6671, 7272, 7375, 7650, 8742, 9320, 9338, 9759, 9809, 9810, 10716, 13756, 15679, 16477, 16798
Income >> See further: Guaranteed annual income; Wages
Income 6720, 6904
India
--Church history 6611
--Economic policy 8016
--Ethnic relations 15754
--Industries 7235
--Politics and government 16907
--Religious and ecclesiastical institutions 4803
--Religious life and customs 9398, 12074, 16857
--Social conditions 1041, 3587, 7235, 8016, 8912, 16041, 16256, 16566, 16907, 18169
--Social conditions--Bibliographies 13783
--Social life and customs 16857
Indianapolis (Indiana)
--Religion 10256
--Religious and ecclesiastical institutions 5524, 6586, 6607, 7123, 7360, 7458, 9340, 10190, 10305, 10356, 10981, 13039, 15118, 17444
--Religious and ecclesiastical institutions--History 7132, 9472, 11132
--Social conditions 8190
--Social conditions--History 9690
Indians of North America 17992
--Canada 14781, 15393, 16852
--Ethnic relations 11391
--History 13995
--Methodist 13802, 14071
--Missions to 5701, 5761, 6242, 7480, 12470, 12798, 13249, 14071, 15212, 15514, 16852, 18587
--Presbyterian 7146
--Public opinion 7480
--Relocation 16161
--Social conditions 6656, 12159, 13075, 15026, 15450, 17418

Indians of North America (cont.)
--Social conditions--History 19131
Individual and society >> See further: Alienation
Individual and society 200, 438, 2612, 2812, 4133, 4236, 5973, 6228, 6408, 6670, 6856, 7232, 8722, 8815, 9033, 9544, 9591, 10215, 12850, 13861, 16212, 17238, 17342, 17979, 18696
Individualism 1168, 2867, 4081, 4321, 6654, 8226, 10987, 12697, 14716, 17238, 17392, 17963, 18308, 18770
Indonesia 14482
--Church history 16298
Indonesian Americans
--Missions to 18586
Industrial Areas Foundation 7023, 7383, 7628, 8137, 8202, 8347, 8462, 8991, 9014, 9044, 9207, 9288, 9387, 9623, 10267, 12418, 12859, 13223, 13661, 14774, 16698, 18821, 19144
--Bibliographies 11799
--History 19138, 19344
Industrial chaplains >> See: Chaplains, industrial
Industrial Christian Alliance (New York, NY) 1644
Industrial Christian Fellowship 3241, 3245, 3252, 3271, 3288, 3298, 3299, 3544, 3618, 4740, 4945, 4948, 4950, 5032, 5084, 5118, 5177, 5180, 5208, 5282, 5376, 5379, 5381, 5479, 5682, 5990, 6289, 7324, 15333, 15414, 15644, 17303, 17320, 17377
--Bibliographies 3244, 12618
--Congresses 5036, 5074, 17803
--History 3242, 3370
--Periodicals 3243, 4451
Industrial development >> See: Industry; Industrialization
Industrial evangelism >> See: Church and industry; Chaplains, industrial
Industrial Mission Association (England) 1754, 15498, 16259
Industrial Missionary Association
--India 2412
Industrial missions >> See: Church and industry
Industrial Missions Aid Society (England) 1906
Industrial relations >> See further: Presbyterian Institute of Industrial Relations (Chicago, Illinois)
Industrial relations 269, 566, 594, 1334, 1355, 1554, 1752, 2744, 2987, 3068, 3338, 3772, 3807, 3812, 4559, 4608, 4615, 4713, 4902, 5562, 5574, 6540, 6582, 7068, 7934, 8528, 9983, 11706, 14191, 15265, 15416, 15650, 15737, 15867, 15898, 16879, 18720
--Canada 2399, 6009, 6010, 14077, 14078
--Church involvement >> See: Church and industry; Church and labor; Trade unions
--Church involvement 790, 868, 3208, 3219, 3246, 3380, 3748, 4014, 4078, 4251, 4606, 5311, 5345, 5818, 6066, 6196, 6549, 16195, 18275
--Congresses 5341
--England 2590, 2593, 3301, 12060
--Europe 6816
--Germany 12019, 12419, 13935, 15487, 16287
--Great Britain 6092, 15986, 16090
--History 4515, 5449, 12664, 16068, 18349

Industrial relations (cont.)
--India 16263
--Italy 5561
--Japan 18205
--Korea 12339
--Netherlands 13384
--Religious aspects >> See further: Church and industry; Church and labor
--Religious aspects 2507, 2764, 2796, 3103, 3147, 3849, 5457, 5781, 5886, 5942, 6262, 6812, 7828, 8208, 9377, 12413, 14077, 15460, 18212
--Religious aspects--History 16342
--South Africa 18275
--Sri Lanka 15853
Industrial Workers of the World
--History 16075, 17595
Industrialization 791, 799, 870, 1784, 2363, 3953, 4062, 4232, 4834, 5522, 7336, 7969, 8069, 8706, 10775, 11648, 12809, 14012, 15428, 15493, 16716
--Africa 7230, 9232, 11674
--Asia 7322, 10678, 16062
--Australia 11532, 11560
--Bibliographies 11182, 12087
--Brazil 12492
--China 3805, 3806
--Congresses 14240
--England 7736, 18321
--England--History 734, 2245, 10795, 11154, 13310, 13880, 14580, 15062, 15505, 15655, 16705
--Europe 6038, 8826
--Fiction 669
--Germany 8177, 10507
--Great Britain 14498
--History 3851, 5803, 7697, 12146, 12871, 13830, 13887, 13938, 14377, 14871, 16394
--India 7516, 17243
--Japan 7036, 13051
--Korea 11161
--Latin America 9479
--People's Republic of China 12725
--Philippines 16062
--Poland 12337, 15910, 17429
--Poland--History 13670, 14009
--Puerto Rico 12985
--Rhodesia 9232
--Singapore 12994
--Social aspects 1788, 1946, 2314, 3239, 3599, 3735, 4026, 5258, 5292, 6324, 6517, 6553, 8815, 9148, 10460, 11600, 12326, 12652, 13098, 14810, 15580, 15843, 16121
--Social aspects--History 6886, 15887
--South Africa 5715, 17285
--Venezuela 11438
Industries--Christian viewpoints >> See: Church and industry
Industry >> See further: Church and industry; Business
Industry 2117, 2191, 3854, 5014, 7526, 15469, 16019, 18008
--Fiction 233, 259, 669, 724, 966, 1017, 1245, 2150, 3462, 11082
--Great Britain--History 1459
--India 16263, 18238
--Moral and ethical aspects 12394, 12590, 12596
--Social aspects >> See further: Welfare work in industry
--Social aspects 1564, 1886, 2791, 3184, 3718, 3876, 4011, 4382, 5260, 6286, 6582, 11357, 12252, 12640, 12908, 14590, 14905, 15638, 15958, 16273, 16467, 16721, 17456
--Social aspects--Canada 9846
--Social aspects--Fiction 2048
--Social responsibility >> See further: Business ethics;

Stockholders' meetings; Interfaith Center on Corporate Responsibility
Industry (cont.)
--Social responsibility 269, 2511, 3039, 3120, 3142, 3648, 3768, 4289, 4340, 4891, 4904, 5097, 5583, 5660, 7026, 7083, 7397, 7850, 7972, 8110, 8658, 8829, 8884, 9780, 10617, 11006, 11307, 11513, 12101, 12103, 12199, 12278, 12436, 12551, 12670, 12782, 12811, 12860, 12869, 12909, 12912, 13168, 13195, 13279, 13572, 13921, 13994, 14038, 14867, 15364, 15428, 15451, 15581, 15740, 16192, 16339, 16352, 16570, 16863, 16879, 17000, 17061, 17074, 17200, 17243, 17280, 17284, 17305, 17484, 17652, 17899, 18020, 18188, 18238, 18277, 18475, 18621, 18951, 19076, 19112
--Social responsibility--Australia 12910
--Social responsibility--Bibliographies 12913, 13573, 14177, 14438, 16500
--Social responsibility--Canada 13066, 17507
--Social responsibility--England 1480, 13123
--Social responsibility--History 8620, 11805
--Spain 15587
Industry and church >> See: Church and industry
Inflation >> See: Economics; Cost and standard of living
Information networks 5625, 9119, 9927, 11422, 13038, 13242, 14112, 15514, 16119, 18188, 18980
Injustice >> See: Justice; Christianity and justice
Inner city >> See further: Ghettos; Poverty; Church work with the poor; Church and the poor, Slums
Inner city
--Description 1771, 3171, 3932, 4018, 7151, 7666, 7956, 7981, 8091, 8108, 8385, 8565, 8589, 8666, 8925, 9602, 9758, 9843, 9851, 9858, 9954, 9990, 10102, 10109, 10165, 10248, 10307, 10378, 10519, 10530, 10654, 10682, 11032, 11071, 11098, 11323, 11326, 11329, 11359, 11368, 11387, 11452, 11569, 11745, 11837, 12030, 12262, 12751, 12771, 12885, 13484, 13668, 13784, 14783, 14883, 15748, 15837, 15847, 15964, 16104, 17189, 17754, 19012, 19067
--Description--Africa 13118
--Description--Asia 15612
--Description--Canada 9925
--Description--Congresses 12086
--Description--England 2919, 3626, 13767, 13799, 14093, 15009, 15967, 16481, 17356, 17381
--Description--Great Britain 6310, 13522, 15407, 15473, 15838, 15873, 17964, 18751, 19090
--Description--History 10764, 13898
--Descriptions--India 16041
--Description--Japan 16418
--Description--Latin America 11227, 13595
--Description--Pakistan 12904
--Description--South Africa 5690
--Description--United States 6931, 6954, 8120, 8607, 9811, 11218, 11274, 12562, 15546,

19204
Inner city (cont.)
--Economic conditions 10930
--Ethnic relations 7121, 11088, 11441, 16931
--Latin America 19022
--Moral conditions 9684, 11121
--Religion 4729, 6189, 7002, 7505, 8289, 8873, 9404, 9468, 9752, 9813, 10314, 10985, 11052, 11171, 11585, 11951, 12025, 12168, 12791, 12945, 13071, 13473, 13705, 14026, 14757, 14866, 15621, 15770, 16547, 17472, 17508, 17822, 17961, 18170, 18694, 19302
--Religion--American Baptist 7124, 8063, 8701
--Religion--Catholic 6956, 8443, 9034, 9733, 9974, 10745, 10810, 11554, 13479, 13628, 14897, 15137, 16005, 16480, 16739, 16741, 17638, 18248, 18329, 18929, 19083, 19129
--Religion--Church of England 15282, 16607, 16906, 18046, 18284, 18777
--Religion--Church of the Brethren 9327, 10148
--Religion--Church of the Nazarene 10051, 10535, 11479
--Religion--Congresses 7248, 9970, 12803, 16929
--Religion--Disciples of Christ 5143, 9763, 9888, 10937
--Religion--England 17453, 18013, 18751
--Religion--Episcopal 8751, 9984, 11280, 11495
--Religion--Evangelical Protestant 9924, 10032, 10096, 10104, 10476, 10674, 10746, 10844, 11083, 11220, 11324, 11394, 11474, 11492, 11794, 12464, 12625, 12922, 12942, 13946, 14670, 15845, 16116, 17084, 17774, 18191, 18338, 18476, 18518, 18948, 19005, 19067, 19330
--Religion--Lutheran 6911, 7431, 8794, 8824, 9105, 9370, 9639, 11007, 11421, 14619, 15206, 16759, 17818, 17965
--Religion--Methodist 7439, 7484, 7518, 7529, 7650, 7651, 8068, 8218, 8336, 8464, 8540, 8685, 8850, 8895, 9154, 9339, 9634, 9705, 9820, 9932, 10021, 10302, 10403, 10445, 10771, 11967, 12084, 12215, 12217, 12369, 13562, 13727, 13899, 14072, 14317, 15286, 16092, 16530, 17067, 17771, 18642
--Religion--NCCCUSA 6563
--Religion--Periodicals 8469
--Religion--Presbyterian 6793, 6954, 7146, 7458, 7464, 7700, 7966, 8037, 10601, 10635, 10901, 11035, 11461, 17035
--Religion--Protestant 1303, 6491, 6985, 7030, 7309, 7320, 7528, 7751, 7811, 7977, 8040, 8190, 8210, 8282, 8353, 8469, 8501, 8744, 8920, 9925, 11367, 11555, 11816, 16103, 17953, 18439, 18585, 18975
--Religion--Reformed Church in America 10859, 11193, 11836
--Religion--Salvation Army 1357
--Religion--Southern Baptist 9784, 9836, 10783, 12292, 12656, 15402, 15501, 16024, 16216
--Religion--Unitarian 9596
--Religion--United Church of Christ 6955, 7737, 8407, 8946, 8947, 9249, 9484, 10293, 10794, 11633, 12062, 18307, 19096
--Religious life and customs

7098, 7974, 8192, 9540, 9799, 14451, 15801, 16860, 16910, 17037, 17589
Inner city (cont.)
--Social conditions 7114, 7579, 8392, 8640, 8850, 9166, 9286, 9684, 9693, 9710, 9713, 9744, 9842, 10029, 10924, 13474, 16481, 17203, 17527, 17757, 18381, 18937
--Social life and customs 8045, 8704
Inner city-suburban exchanges 4729, 7700, 8411, 10959, 13642, 15196, 16375, 18307, 18581, 18642, 19227, 19335
Inner city churches >> See: City churches; Inner city--Religious and ecclesiastical institutions
Inner City Protestant Parish (Cleveland, Ohio) 6491, 9758
--Periodicals 8469
Inner mission 381, 708, 2076, 2499, 2532, 2923, 2936, 2939, 2972, 3143, 4554, 4819, 5600, 6039
--Bibliographies 2532, 2962
--England 1251
Inner Mission
--Estonia 3609
Inner mission
--Germany 218, 246, 342, 389, 400, 685, 900, 1016, 1243, 1445, 1473, 1509, 1578, 1766, 1884, 1887, 2028, 8365, 13499
--Germany--History 896, 1262, 2609, 4831, 10432, 14820
--History 3923, 4624, 4635, 17409
--Periodicals 239, 664, 2148, 2871, 3331, 4298
Inner mission (Lutheran) >> See further: City missions--Lutheran sources
Institut für Kirchliche Sozialforschung (Vienna, Austria) 13241, 13915
Institute for Religious and Social Studies 5613, 5773
Institute for Theological Encounter with Science and Technology (St. Louis, Missouri) 13242
Institute of Ethics and Society (San Anselmo, California) 8802
Institute of Social and Religious Research 3826, 3879, 3884, 3934, 3954, 4304
--History 4038, 4369, 4374, 4429
Institute on the Church in Urban-Industrial Society (Chicago, Illinois) 9927, 11753, 12909, 13244, 13290, 13291, 13323, 13573, 14702, 15983, 16375, 17523, 17805, 17967, 18297, 18326, 19125, 19144
--Bibliographies 11799, 11830, 13007, 13008, 13243, 13560, 13916, 13917, 13918, 13919, 13920, 14284, 14285, 14668, 14786, 15200, 15201, 15598, 15984
--Periodicals 17378
Institutional churches 838, 1002, 1158, 1248, 1316, 1325, 1444, 1457, 1478, 1517, 1522, 1524, 1556, 1560, 1569, 1572, 1574, 1612, 1624, 1627, 1677, 1685, 1710, 1730, 1885, 1892, 1957, 2015, 2081, 2173, 2365, 2397, 2526, 2616, 2680, 2696, 3016, 3062, 3112, 3335, 3804, 4024, 4169
--American Baptist sources 994, 1195, 1447, 1456, 1479, 1490, 1521, 1530, 1701, 2151, 3788, 4685
--American Baptist sources--History 12654
--Bibliographies 16662

Institutional churches (cont.)
--Case studies 2851, 7624
--Congregational sources 508, 924, 1157, 1562, 1585, 1628, 1632, 1780, 1947
--Congregational sources--History 11132
--England 1523, 1821, 5277
--Episcopal sources 550, 954, 1012, 1021, 1168, 1191, 1324, 1418, 1510, 1817, 1980, 2080, 2451, 2927, 2968, 3452, 5492, 9172, 17437
--Episcopal sources--History 18689
--Fiction 4519
--History 2444, 3521, 3996, 5138, 5277, 7624, 7986, 10987, 11132, 12319, 15810, 16662
--Methodist sources 1317, 1524, 1561, 1692, 2082, 2463, 2802, 2870, 2887, 2952, 3261, 3565, 3605, 3670, 3773, 3963, 3986, 4640, 6510, 7624
--Periodicals 1317, 1568
--Presbyterian sources 1000, 1483, 1500, 1501, 1579, 1673, 1892, 1994, 2452, 2746, 2874
--Presbyterian sources--History 15810
--Unitarian 2601
Instituto Pastoral Latinoamericano 9416, 10325
Insurance 2608, 2842, 3906, 5188, 12558, 13577, 14193, 15099, 17394, 18212
Insurance of Church buildings >> See further: Church buildings
Insurance of church buildings 16866, 17924, 17925, 18966
Integration >> See: Segregation; Discrimination
Inter-Met (Washington, DC) 11769, 11831, 12152, 12696, 13046, 14257
Inter-Religious Center for Urban Affairs (St. Louis, Missouri) 9928
Interchurch Federation of Philadelphia 2805
Interchurch Trade and Industry Mission in Australia and New Zealand 8470, 11352, 11531, 11532, 11560, 12910, 13575, 13576, 13708, 14053, 15656
Interchurch World Movement 3172, 3173, 3209, 3223, 3246, 3247, 3332, 3443, 3479
--History 11754
Interdenominational cooperation >> See further: Cooperative ministry; East Harlem Protestant Parish
Interdenominational cooperation 861, 863, 958, 1598, 1650, 2220, 2739, 2754, 2986, 3008, 3009, 3432, 3893, 3954, 3961, 4055, 4211, 4258, 4350, 4363, 4594, 4908, 5007, 5217, 5263, 5312, 5318, 5416, 5417, 5469, 5566, 5567, 5576, 5622, 5963, 6019, 6065, 6214, 6340, 6507, 6772, 6872, 6948, 6968, 6969, 7005, 7218, 7227, 7546, 7623, 7661, 8210, 8300, 8371, 8510, 8567, 8713, 9482, 10134, 10355, 10505, 10696, 10833, 10895, 11576, 11743, 11746, 11751, 11788, 12302, 12732, 12816, 13149, 13167, 13825, 14204, 15117, 15271, 16113, 17553, 17936, 17953, 18050, 18051, 18182, 18296, 18786, 18962
--England 18004, 18682, 18732
--History 3312, 4038, 7097, 11707
--Periodicals 3064, 9115, 12246, 12528
Interdenominational Theological

Center (Atlanta, GA) 7589
Interfaith Action for Economic Justice (Washington, DC) 15394, 15499, 16960, 18764
Interfaith Center on Corporate Responsibility >> See further: Stockholders' meeting; Industry--Social responsibility; Business ethics; National Council of Church, Corporate Information Center; Investments, ecclesiastical
Interfaith Center on Corporate Responsibility 13197, 13577, 13921, 15638, 16260, 17518, 17532, 18475, 19237
Interfaith Council for the Homeless (Chicago, Illinois) 18452
Interfaith Foundation (Washington, DC) 18764
Interfaith Social Assistance Reform Coalition on Poverty in Ontario 19161
International Association of Machinists 6473, 6496, 6534, 7280
International business enterprises 7322, 12782, 13195, 13329, 13554, 13994, 14495, 14688, 15469, 15581, 15794, 16048, 16227, 16439, 16792, 16863
--Bibliographies 12087, 12913, 13460, 14177, 14438
--Moral and ethical aspects 15942; 16473
International Business Machines 12548
International Congress on Religion, Architecture and Visual Arts 10400
International Council of Religious Education 4163, 4532, 4842, 5033, 5103, 5113, 5283, 5767
International Federation of Christian Trade Unions
--History 3753
International Federation of Protestant Workers >> See further: Trade unions--Protestant
International Federation of Protestant Workers 6531
International Foundation Humanum 11524
International Labor Organization 4260, 4634, 5613, 7699
International Missionary Council 3895
International Union of Gospel Missions 6155, 11832, 13352
--History 5505, 12633
--Periodicals 18881
Internship for Clergymen in Urban Ministry (Cleveland, Ohio) 9929
Interreligious Foundation for Community Organization 12198
Interreligious New Communities Coalition 13173
InterVarsity Christian Fellowship 18565
Investments >> See further: Investments, ecclesiastical; Economics--Religious aspects
Investments
--Moral and ethical aspects 10203, 11833, 12199, 12278, 12391, 12436, 12529, 12570, 12640, 12674, 12675, 12804, 12811, 12819, 12860, 12909, 12912, 13123, 13481, 13634, 13921, 14174, 14480, 14569, 14767, 15099, 15581, 15638, 15794, 15904, 15966, 16141, 16260, 16849, 16916, 17200, 17223, 17307, 17518, 17532, 18030, 18112

Investments (cont.)
--Moral and ethical aspects--Bibliographies 11888, 13918, 14666
--South Africa 19074
Investments, ecclesiastical >> See further: Interfaith Center on Corporate Responsibility; Stockholders' meetings; Industry--Social responsibility
Investments, ecclesiastical 2261, 2278, 2290, 2306, 2349, 2376, 2395, 2667, 3256, 10203, 11833, 12199, 12251, 12252, 12430, 12529, 12548, 12611, 12612, 12811, 12860, 12864, 12909, 12912, 13168, 13572, 13577, 14174, 14860, 15099, 15904, 16260, 16981, 17223, 17307, 17484, 17487, 18100, 18366
--Bibliographies 11888
--Canada 13066
Investments, foreign
--South Africa 12101, 12103, 12548, 12612, 14688, 14853, 15904, 15966, 17487, 18020
Iona Community (Scotland) 5389, 6908, 6909, 7420
Iowa City (Iowa)
--Religious and ecclesiastical institutions--History 13366, 14275
Iran
--Social conditions 15511
Iraqi Americans 4517, 13354
Ireland >> See further: Northern Ireland; Irish Americans
Ireland
--Religious and ecclesiastical institutions 13292
--Religious life and customs 14238
--Social conditions 12424, 12432, 15134, 17654
--Migrations 7866
Irish American Catholics 649, 1676, 1885, 6272, 13725, 17869
--History 7689, 13509, 13552, 13724, 13822, 13823, 14168, 14795, 14964, 15409, 15813, 17879
Irish American children 1827
Irish American churches 6768, 13725
Irish American clergy 13398
Irish American families
--History 15409
Irish American Protestants 556
Irish Americans
--Attitudes 10748, 12502
--Biography 921
--Education 17869
--Ethnic relations--History 12461, 13725, 14432
--History 13058, 13152, 15858
--Identity 8730, 17869
--Identity--History 13552
--Missions to 1676
--Politics 9957
--Religion 14357
--Social conditions 11714, 14562
--Social conditions--History 13724
--Social life and customs 5017, 8892
--Social life and customs--History 14168, 14582, 15059
Irish Canadians
--History 13478
Irish Catholic Colonization Association 4221
Islam >> See further: Muslims; Black Muslims
Islam 8661, 8741, 10368, 11818, 11973, 12935, 13189, 14631, 16673, 16820, 17537, 17617, 17637, 19077
--Africa 12878, 12996, 16188, 17182, 17741, 17841, 18005

Islam (cont.)
--Asia 16853
--Egypt 15406
--England 14564
--Europe 16203
--Indonesia 15661, 18158
--Iran 13816
--Ivory Coast 17941
--Jordan 17926
--Middle East 17051
--Relations--Christianity 11737, 17637, 18557, 18590, 18802, 19057, 19244
--Thailand 16853
--United States 1260, 3782, 4278, 4549, 7506, 7640, 12563, 13113, 15065, 18198, 18557, 18850, 19032
--United States--History 17050, 17988, 18378
Islamabad (Pakistan)
--Social conditions 9967
Islamic studies 1260, 6866, 8661, 8741, 11737, 11858, 11973, 12898, 12935, 13113, 13189, 13816, 14352, 15071, 15406, 16673, 16726, 16820, 16853, 16973, 17051, 17617, 17729, 17926, 18208, 18378, 18730
--Congresses 11818, 15637
Istanbul (Turkey)
--Religion 18035
--Social conditions 17929, 17930
--Social conditions--History 16401
Italian American Catholics 3093, 4792, 4881, 4882, 5221, 8136, 11517, 12739, 13428, 13616, 13665, 13717, 14114, 15849
--History 9815, 11587, 11991, 12658, 12698, 13432, 13610, 13718, 13724, 13725, 14331, 15240, 17817, 18058, 18059, 18105, 18138
Italian American children 2139
Italian American churches 912, 3619, 4792, 4881, 4882, 5221, 6265, 8136, 12698, 13717
Italian American Episcopalians 1167
Italian American Methodists 2139, 2605, 3455, 3619, 4490
Italian American Pentecostals 9593
Italian American Presbyterians
--History 14331
Italian American Protestants 4491, 13616, 13658
Italian Americans
--Attitudes 12502
--Economic conditions 18138
--Economic conditions--History 12742, 14302
--Education 2139
--Ethnic relations 14464
--Ethnic relations--History 13725, 14432
--Folklore 4800, 14464
--History 14114, 15858, 17493
--Identity 8730
--Medical care 13258
--Missions to 2183, 2251, 2351, 2605, 2679, 2892, 3010, 3011, 3028, 3045, 3095, 3455, 3662, 4454, 4490, 4491, 5630, 6110, 8481, 9593, 11707, 12698, 13428, 13616, 13623, 13658, 14114
--Missions to--History 3694, 5654, 5770, 12658, 14331, 15240, 17329, 18058, 18059
--Pastoral counseling of--History 12658, 15240
--Religion 3010, 3093, 4881, 11517, 12739, 13658, 13717, 14357, 14464
--Religion--History 13432, 13664, 13718, 17474
--Social conditions 1907, 2183, 3010, 3093, 4107, 4601, 5153,

5231, 8429, 15849
Italian Americans (cont.)
--Social conditions--History 9815, 11991, 12872, 13258, 13724, 14516, 14855
--Social life and customs 4800, 5017, 14464, 18138
--Social life and customs--History 13664, 16123
Italy
--Church history 12658, 15240
--Economic conditions 5929, 7629, 8022, 11010, 18394
--Economic conditions--History 13885
--Religion 14559, 15550, 15763, 17665
--Religious and ecclesiastical institutions 6191, 8294
--Religious life and customs 7048, 11689, 14371, 14559
--Social conditions 7061, 13776, 15550
--Social conditions--History 415
Ithaca (New York)
--Religious and ecclesiastical institutions 9261
Ivory Coast
--Religion 17941
--Social conditions 12280
J. P. Stevens and Company 14229, 14873, 14874, 15347
Jackson (Mississippi)
--Religious and ecclesiastical institutions 12610, 14005, 15408, 16350, 16368, 18191
--Religious and ecclesiastical institutions--History 16454
Jacksonville (Florida)
--Religious and ecclesiastical institutions 7053, 8375
--Social conditions 14409
Jakarta (Indonesia)
--Religious and ecclesiastical institutions 17775, 19171
James Mullenbach Industrial Institute
--History 8536
Jansonists 16026
Japan
--Bibliographies 9923
--Economic conditions 7341, 8005, 9818, 14259, 14417, 18205
--History 6991, 14877
--Periodicals 5877
--Religion 4164, 7036, 7912, 9184, 9414, 10117, 10585, 10898, 11778, 11843, 11909, 12521, 12723, 12907, 13163, 13220, 13633, 13640, 13677, 13694, 13922, 14054, 14849, 15415, 15506, 16679, 17237, 17340, 17807, 18558
--Religious and ecclesiastical institutions 2663, 3130, 3263, 3349, 3404, 3516, 6852, 6874, 6878, 7209, 7246, 7341, 7344, 7428, 7523, 7801, 7875, 8236, 8911, 8924, 9434, 9440, 9756, 10001, 10035, 10448, 10800, 11843, 11913, 12036, 12063, 12216, 12340, 12466, 13981, 15150, 16830, 16909, 17114, 17691, 18706, 19062
--Religious and ecclesiastical institutions--History 9729, 13578
--Religious life and customs 7249, 10483, 10871
--Social conditions 3504, 3645, 4472, 5871, 6338, 6725, 6878, 8010, 8787, 8799, 8838, 11559, 12405, 12452, 12511, 12521, 12723, 12794, 12927, 13051, 13204, 14443, 16020, 16418, 16505, 17728, 18608, 19127, 19196
Japan--Urbanization >> See: Urbanization--Japan

Japanese American Baptists 5937
Japanese American churches 19051
Japanese American clergy 15269
Japanese American Methodists 15269, 19051
Japanese American Presbyterians 7146
Japanese Americans
--Crimes against 5089, 5206, 5207, 5210, 5274, 5489, 10427, 12690, 15269
--Ethnic relations 2799, 3233, 5416
--History 15858
--Missions to 2831, 3662, 5489, 5937, 15433, 19051
--Missions to--History 8577
--Religion 14295, 14363
--Relocation 5089, 5206, 5207, 5210, 5274
--Social conditions 2798, 2891, 10426
Japanese Canadians 18260, 18616
Jazz music 7566, 8233, 8234, 11136, 11417, 12135, 12309, 13472, 14283
Jehovah's Witnesses 11884, 13164, 15123
--History 5422, 10285, 19121
Jersey City (New Jersey)
--Religious and ecclesiastical institutions 1037, 5359, 8197, 10973, 15196, 15825, 16448
--Social conditions 4703, 7592, 8967
Jerusalem (Israel) 8482, 10478, 11631, 18334
--Bibliographies 18657
--History 17636
--Religion 18035, 18577
--Social conditions 13653, 16978
Jerusalem in the Bible 1728, 6783, 8482, 8518, 9272, 14704, 14828, 17781, 18572
--Bibliographies 18657
Jerusalem, New (metaphor) 1133, 2382, 3646, 4412, 4695, 7632, 8517, 8518, 8842, 9633, 9948, 11752, 12784, 13319, 14768, 14811, 15235, 15326, 16979, 18760
Jesuits
--History 13936
Jesus Christ 606, 1531, 1946, 2238, 3886, 7695, 11118, 11496, 11914, 12135, 14983, 16173, 16536, 19321, 19339
--Example 713, 1030, 1963, 2846, 4037, 5044, 8599, 11117, 12007, 14819, 15186, 15427, 15647, 15866, 16058, 17991
--Fiction 231
--Person and offices 2364, 3682, 8122
--Teaching 738, 772, 969, 1059, 1139, 1232, 1389, 1528, 1559, 1768, 1880, 2235, 2423, 2424, 2472, 2568, 2647, 2912, 2969, 3006, 3362, 3366, 3659, 4011, 4048, 4158, 4578, 4759, 5777, 6394, 8985, 18236
Jesus People 12276, 12474, 12838, 16956
Jeunesse ouvrière chrétienne (France) 6877, 8972, 17711
--Archives 16545
--History 16876, 18797
Jewish archives 4931, 5022, 19111
Jewish Child Care Association of New York 6362
Jewish Christians >> See further: Missions to Jews
Jewish Christians 16595
--History 6627
Jewish Community Centers 4742, 8042, 8807
Jewish Community Council 9439
Jewish families 14453, 15025, 16970

--History 1319
Jewish law 13247, 17227, 18222
Jewish literature 5744, 17403
--History 13856, 14096
Jewish orphans 1548, 2064
Jewish religious education 3061, 3180, 3373, 10119, 13754
--History 7612, 13356
Jewish religious schools 3373, 6253, 6674, 6702, 7423, 16740
--History 6236, 6893, 8699
Jewish sects 10557, 12884, 13355, 16700, 16727
--History 13356
Jewish sermons
--History 7877
Jewish Theological Seminary of America 5613, 5773, 5796
Jewish theology 7682
Jewish Welfare Board 3519, 5695, 8042
Jewish women >> See: Women, Jewish
Jewish works
--Bibliographies 4931, 5022, 5276, 6481, 9747, 9748, 9749, 11170, 14309, 14310, 14525, 16521, 18748, 19151
Jews >> See further: Judaism; Orthodox Judaism, Conservative Judaism, Reform Judaism
Jews
--Attitudes 5903, 5938, 7627, 8306, 12502, 15412, 16740
--Bibliographies 7938, 18677
--Canada 9631, 12506, 12884, 13355, 15426, 16727
--Canada--History 13356
--Charities >> See: Charity--Religious aspects--Jewish
--Civil Rights 16861
--Cultural assimilation 6494, 6760, 7319, 8578, 10406, 11541, 13754, 13977, 14316, 15536, 16727, 19061
--Czechoslovakia 19253
--Economic conditions 2298, 2323, 9471, 12731, 13363, 19248
--Economic conditions--History 14302, 14891
--Education 15250
--Employment 7131, 14453
--England 1506, 1774, 7045, 12510, 15473, 17686, 18677, 18799
--England--History 7839, 9137, 13033, 13034, 15772, 15953, 17460, 17955
--Ethnic relations 2502, 6412, 7197, 7371, 10414, 10415, 10440, 11309, 11391, 11423, 11541, 17593
--Ethnic relations--History 13977, 14432, 17493
--Fiction 5744
--Germany--History 3932
--Great Britain 16051, 16763
--Great Britain--History 15818
--History 11921, 16401
--Identity 8730, 11057, 12940
--Intellectual life 1859
--Israel 18577
--Lithuania--History 16646
--Migrations 5140, 7971, 8211, 10557, 13910, 14109, 14302, 14943, 17578, 19143
--Migrations--History 2085, 16947, 18209
--Missions to >> See: Missions to Jews
--New York (NY) 1182, 1217, 1246, 1859, 1910, 3061, 3304, 3373, 5229, 6055, 6522, 6844, 8211, 9003, 9065, 10218, 10438, 10557, 10633, 11342, 11400, 11519, 14755, 16801, 17403, 17600, 19249, 19251
--New York (NY)--History 1573,

5276, 6236, 8556, 9936, 13864, 13910, 14096, 15063, 15859, 16634, 16635, 17819, 18153, 19106
Jews (cont.)
--New York, (NY)--Bibliographies 5276
--Poland 5486
--Poland--History 13856
--Politics and government--History 14891
--Public opinion 10111
--Race relations 5105, 7970
--Relations 3823, 10546, 17828, 17903, 18207, 19254
--Relocation 7830, 8718
--Social conditions 1774, 6201, 8875, 16534, 16970, 17659, 17946
--Social conditions--History 6297, 13206, 13898, 14516, 14855
--Social life and customs 3180, 3519, 4281, 5572, 5786, 6669, 6982, 7040, 7090, 7443, 7562, 8211, 8581, 8673, 9999, 10849, 12314, 12676, 13368, 14200, 14679, 14755, 14829, 15250, 15330, 16714, 18571
--Social life and customs--History 13336
--South Africa 16947
--Syria--History 16157
--United States >> See further: Jews--New York (NY)
--United States 1706, 2298, 2979, 3180, 3360, 5093, 5488, 5787, 5938, 5987, 6412, 6669, 6760, 6807, 6982, 7040, 7087, 7308, 7970, 7971, 8875, 8879, 9343, 9471, 9999, 10546, 12320, 13367, 13368, 14034, 15398, 16738, 19250
--United States--Bibliographies 10592, 14309, 14310, 16521, 19151
--United States--Biography 3972, 4841, 14109
--United States--History 1294, 2085, 2678, 3607, 3629, 3932, 4264, 5104, 5181, 5211, 5972, 6297, 6322, 6384, 6481, 6554, 6560, 6561, 6781, 7229, 7612, 8909, 9109, 9750, 10841, 11511, 12010, 12127, 12834, 12872, 12883, 13143, 13206, 13452, 13551, 13864, 13930, 13931, 14307, 14615, 14633, 14674, 14784, 14796, 15211, 15222, 16498, 17251, 17343, 19111, 19207
Job satisfaction 8021, 10872, 11801, 16341
Johannesburg (South Africa)
--Social conditions--History 5715
John Paul II, Pope 16179, 17630
Johnson City (Tennessee)
--Social conditions 19318
Johnstown (Pennsylvania)
--Religious and ecclesiastical institutions 12547
--Social conditions 17915
Joilet (Illinois)
--Religious and ecclesiastical institutions 4160
Joint Office for Urban Ministry (Rochester, New York) 10911
Joint Strategy and Action Committee (JSAC) 9115, 11371, 12812, 13249, 13250, 13251, 13252, 15418, 16272
--History 18462
--Periodicals 11370
Joliet (Illinois)
--Religious and ecclesiastical institutions 18668
Jones Memorial Community Center (Chicago Heights, Illinois) 6435
Joplin (Missouri)
--Religious and ecclesiastical

institutions 12149
Judaism >> See further: Jews, Orthodox Judaism; Conservative Judaism, Reform Judaism
Judaism and labor 874, 1647, 1756, 2298, 2603, 3410, 3957, 4172, 4596, 4711, 5556, 5849, 6473, 6522, 6760, 6865, 7363, 7682, 8041, 8341, 8875, 8893, 9031, 9532, 13591, 14453, 16221, 17227, 18222
--History 6049, 6178, 6384, 6554, 13930, 14784
Judaism and secularization 12284, 17946
Judaism and social problems 874, 1228, 2063, 2378, 3083, 4380, 4596, 5188, 5563, 5903, 6201, 7355, 8175, 8245, 9022, 9287, 9709, 9743, 10064, 10440, 10534, 10557, 10848, 11343, 11807, 11970, 12294, 12731, 12772, 13208, 13363, 15412, 17637, 17828, 18782, 19254
--History 5371
Judson Memorial Church (New York, NY) 994
--History 6579
Justice 235, 1253, 1700, 1789, 2025, 2373, 4583, 5309, 8067, 8117, 8380, 10405, 11615, 12892, 13089, 13285, 14104, 14158, 14621, 15034, 15261, 15488, 15517, 15609, 16377, 16440, 16554, 16791, 17521, 17761, 18159, 18609, 18770
--Asia 14164
--Biblical teaching 969, 3765, 5347, 6341, 8350, 8893, 12380, 14261, 14996, 15544, 15642, 16917, 17652, 18832
--Bibliographies 11830, 14702, 17523
--Brazil 17290
--Canada 15393
--Chile 13833, 15173
--Criminal >> See further: Victim-offender reconciliation; Church work with criminals
--Criminal 96, 12571, 13249, 13794, 13819, 14248, 14372, 14398, 14518, 14528, 14560, 14609, 14835, 14861, 15156, 15270, 15393, 15544, 15886, 16333, 16452, 16908, 16967, 17022, 17038, 17097, 18014, 18328
--Criminal--Brazil 12053
--Criminal--Canada 9516, 12571
--Criminal--England 17910
--Criminal--History 8806, 16966
--Criminal--Taiwan 15509
--Economic >> See further: Economics and Christianity; Discrimination in employment
--Economic 266, 644, 772, 790, 993, 1020, 1113, 2025, 2240, 2253, 2405, 2834, 2971, 3039, 3080, 3326, 3438, 3469, 3827, 4009, 4154, 4389, 4476, 4615, 4774, 5884, 6405, 7797, 8178, 9401, 10012, 11483, 12220, 12283, 12478, 12810, 13146, 13572, 13846, 13854, 14024, 14173, 14324, 14459, 14590, 14989, 15035, 15070, 15149, 16143, 16362, 16822, 17255, 17342, 17371, 17759, 17889, 18120, 18191, 18292, 18346, 18454
--Europe 502
--France 502, 16876
--History 5055
--Hong Kong 11815, 13545, 13873
--India 16041
--Japan 14259, 14417
--Korea 12082, 12932
--Latin America 12852

Justice (cont.)
--Mexico 16307
--Periodicals 17378
--Racial >> See: Race relations and church; Discrimination; Segregation; African Americans--Crimes against
--Racial 1973, 2784, 4068, 4629, 5186, 5187, 6895, 7353, 9129, 10451, 11975, 13608
--Religious aspects 1608, 4134, 5743, 6455, 6472, 9927, 10623, 13122, 14335, 14517, 15021, 15046, 15239, 16015, 16546, 16791, 18743, 18918, 19009, 19135
--Religious aspects--Bibliographies 14666, 14702
--Religious aspects--Congresses 13146, 15705
--Religious aspects--History 1608, 3927, 6064, 6455, 6468, 6588, 7746, 8095, 12786, 16753, 16966, 18559
--Religious aspects--Periodicals 4360
--Religious aspects (church participation) 2431, 3326, 3853, 3928, 3952, 4340, 4774, 8749, 9387, 9661, 10900, 12514, 13471, 13580, 13811, 14024, 14242, 14766, 14912, 15022, 15023, 15967, 16282, 16486, 16567, 16692, 16967, 17594, 17705, 17759, 18221, 18454
--Religious aspects (organizations) 2784, 14062, 14489, 14490, 15004, 15272, 15393, 16828, 18197, 18681, 18764, 19195
--Religious aspects (theology) 1878, 3296, 3827, 4307, 4476, 4629, 5050, 5186, 5187, 5821, 7051, 7704, 8533, 9229, 13359, 13798, 14004, 14715, 15047, 15064, 15358, 15579, 15636, 15719, 16459, 16568, 16693, 16788, 16888, 17117, 17267, 17371, 17467, 17889, 17917, 18292, 18377, 18627, 18782, 18993, 19084
--South Africa 17562
--Sri Lanka 15724
Juvenile delinquency >> See further: Gangs; Church work with juvenile delinquents
Juvenile delinquency
--History 11493, 12182
Juvenile delinquents 458, 1177, 2289, 6584, 6620, 6894, 7618, 7919, 8046, 8381, 15698
--history 470
Juventude operária Católica (Brazil) 17290, 17451
Kalamazoo (Michigan)
--Religious and ecclesiastical institutions 2015, 6902, 9638
--Social conditions 2072
Kampala (Uganda)
--Religious and ecclesiastical institutions 10853
Kano (Nigeria)
--Social conditions 12996
Kansai Industrial Mission (Japan) 14849
Kansas City (Kansas)
--Religious and ecclesiastical institutions 5407, 8778, 14151, 14165, 18109, 18664
--Religious and ecclesiastical institutions--History 6984
Kansas City (Missouri)
--religious and ecclesiastical institutions 4766, 5112, 5196, 5407, 5440, 6376, 6705, 6890, 9569, 9853, 9917, 10856, 10988, 11090, 11788, 11972, 12084, 12369, 14587, 15308, 16332, 16604, 18109, 19298
--Religious and ecclesiastical

institutions--History 16723
--Social conditions 9990, 14301, 15025, 15044, 16144, 16232
Kashan (Iran)
--Social conditions 13816
Katholischer Verband der Werktätigen 11362
Katmandu (Nepal)
--Religion 16446
Kent (Ohio)
--Religious and ecclesiastical institutions 8297
Kenya
--Church history 12175
--Economic conditions 18240
--Religion 8449
--Religious and ecclesiastical institutions 8657, 11981, 12175, 13567, 13903, 14298, 14603, 16138, 16733, 18817, 19132
--Social conditions 11979, 12176, 12303, 12738, 12989, 13023, 13648, 13939, 15093, 15625, 15957, 18671
Kingdomworks (Philadelphia, Pennsylvania) 19330
Kingsport (Tennessee)
--Religious and ecclesiastical institutions 3356
Kingston (New York)
--Religious and ecclesiastical institutions 12120, 13452
Kingston (Ontario, Canada)
--History 15606
Kinshasa (Zaire)
--Religious and ecclesiastical institutions 14738, 15531, 17908
--Social conditions 16909, 18671
Kisumu (Kenya)
--Church history 16138
Kitwe (Zambia)
--Social conditions 14998
Knights of Columbus
--History 15059
Knights of Labor 818, 875, 11761
--History 5346, 5449, 5756, 13775, 19214
Knoxville (Tennessee)
--Race relations 15010
--Religious and ecclesiastical institutions 5407, 6365, 7702, 10717
--Religious and ecclesiastical institutions--History 13154
--Social conditions 15010
Kolping Society 996, 3337, 5013
Korea
--Church history 13308
--Religious and ecclesiastical institutions 15387
--Social conditions 12082, 17024, 17397
Korean American churches 13588, 13689, 13699, 14721, 15184, 15385, 15513, 15526, 15995, 16798, 16870, 17157, 17279, 17694, 18552, 19023
--History 15870
Korean American clergy 13953
Korean American families 17602, 18890
Korean American Methodists 13944, 14721, 16798, 17157, 17694
Korean American Presbyterians 17396, 18226, 18227, 18552
Korean American women 18890
Korean Americans
--Missions to 2956, 15184, 15513, 16640, 17396, 18226, 18719
--Religion 12889, 15512
--Social conditions 12889, 13689, 17275
Korean Church Industrial Mission 17024
Ku Klux Klan 2876, 3598, 4548
--History 10402, 19130
Kyoto (Japan)

--Religious and ecclesiastical institutions 7523
Labor and church >> See: Church and labor
Labor and laboring classes 156, 212, 496, 528, 590, 594, 622, 631, 632, 635, 661, 714, 754, 780, 782, 800, 813, 817, 858, 883, 887, 1025, 1051, 1092, 1095, 1103, 1156, 1214, 1293, 1360, 1474, 1563, 1690, 1700, 1858, 1877, 1920, 1975, 2117, 2270, 2450, 2453, 2571, 2599, 2655, 2684, 2764, 3036, 3039, 3048, 3096, 3103, 3259, 3313, 3336, 3342, 3343, 3351, 3380, 3467, 3699, 4109, 4126, 4566, 4713, 4902, 4972, 5124, 5173, 5590, 5596, 5613, 5883, 5925, 6026, 6283, 6350, 6661, 6677, 7205, 7327, 7417, 8884, 9615, 9880, 11276, 11671, 12476, 12856, 13332, 13378, 13751, 14277, 14985, 15988, 16389, 16479, 16587, 17060, 17094, 17132, 17255, 18020, 18069, 18665, 18681
--Archives 16300
--Argentina 8984
--Austria--History 8880, 17571
--Bibliographies 783, 13008, 14285
--Brazil 9635, 15628, 17224, 17290, 19208
--Canada 462, 2824, 3137, 6271, 10774
--Canada--History 14750, 15779
--Chile 13040
--Congresses 8541, 16294
--Developing countries 12065
--England 553, 971, 1306, 1345, 2079, 2084, 2429, 2582, 3007, 3640, 7226, 7233, 7868, 8913, 9157, 9331, 18113, 18796
--England--History 913, 3510, 4684, 6591
--Europe 5865, 6038, 15390
--Europe--History 5866, 15930
--Finland 10441
--France 211, 416, 481, 604, 6126, 6328, 7386, 8191, 8647, 9856, 11005, 16809
--France--History 3753, 5224, 16876, 17107, 17711, 19233
--Germany 414, 2315, 5842, 9134, 10416, 10507, 11463, 13391, 13935, 14431, 15454, 15832, 16098, 16190, 16287, 16450, 17027, 17401
--Germany--History 14141, 14941, 16410, 16932, 18234, 18266, 19241
--Great Britain 177, 433, 2568, 3381, 7109, 8316, 9097, 15414
--History 742, 3830, 4612, 5095, 6300, 9584, 16394, 16766, 17135, 17939
--Hungary 4990
--India 3382, 6184, 16263
--Ireland 14370
--Ireland--History 9128
--Italy 5254, 5929, 6619, 8022, 8682
--Japan 12794
--Korea 14710, 14847
--Latin America 17077
--Netherlands 360, 6784
--New Zealand 13576
--Periodicals 710
--Philippines 3701
--Poland 3379
--Religious life 108, 516, 647, 1712, 2173, 2361, 2834, 3287, 3441, 3856, 3952, 6790, 7492, 13638, 15282, 15454, 15780, 18113
--Religious life--History 6319, 7835, 12124, 12455, 13536, 13938, 15667, 17830, 18554, 19214

Labor and laboring classes (cont.)
--Social life and customs--History 13887
--Spain 1258, 4693, 4864, 4919, 7372, 7837, 16011, 16811
--Sweden--History 16360
--Switzerland--History 12660
--United States 490, 787, 1611, 3068, 3182, 4311, 5953, 8875, 10107, 14120, 16544, 17250
--United States--History 6812, 16122, 17595, 18349
--Yugoslavia--History 7052
Labor and laboring classes in literature 524, 585, 701, 1017, 1496, 2838
--England 233
--History 16068
Labor churches 1189, 1435, 1502, 1517, 1591, 1920, 2549, 3534, 3794, 5290, 12812, 13110
--Japan 7341
Labor disputes >> See: Strikes and lockouts
Labor laws and legislation 4504, 4645, 5218, 5461, 5548, 5590, 5732, 6932, 7895
--Colombia 9112
--Spain 4693
Labor mobility 1939, 3380, 5087, 5088, 5771, 6205, 6242, 6351, 6466, 6573, 6750, 6937, 7320, 8395, 10815
--Canada 10774
--Great Britain 14662
Labor reform 459, 496, 2341, 3080, 11192, 14287
--France 569
--France--History 8086
--History 2245, 10995, 11641, 17824, 17835
--Spain 14237
Labor relations >> See: Industrial relations; Right to work
Labor Sunday 2219, 4167
Labor unions >> See: Trade unions
Laboring classes >> See: Labor and laboring classes
Ladies' Society, for the Relief of Distressed Women and Children (Albany, New York) 6
Lafayette (Indiana)
--Religious and ecclesiastical institutions 13825, 16113, 17301
Lafayette Urban Ministry (Lafayette, Indiana) 13825, 16113, 17301
Laity >> See further: Clergy and laity; Lay ministry
Laity 965, 1806, 1978, 3755, 6745, 6791, 6896, 6962, 7074, 7304, 7349, 7864, 8132, 8331, 9136, 9497, 9785, 10274, 11699, 11997, 12401, 13315, 15007, 15121, 15277, 16622, 17000, 17085, 17575, 18063
--Bibliography 8514
--Biography 1002, 10365
--England 15282
--France 5935
--Germany 6610
--History 11336, 13452, 19066
--Spain 10301
Laity, training of 3025, 3089, 3286, 3959, 6278, 7309, 8920, 8948, 10009, 10252, 10267, 10757, 11174, 11897, 11960, 12349, 12358, 12378, 12568, 13655, 14090, 14242, 14577, 14774, 15214, 15272, 15814, 15854, 16106, 16145, 16235, 16292, 16402, 17068, 18307, 18688, 19023, 19139, 19309
--Africa 13263, 13967, 16998
--Australia 18792
--England 13070, 15309, 17009, 17587, 18905, 19045

Laity, training of (cont.)
--History 18385
--Philippines 10525
--Schools, programs, etc. 2420, 2856, 6058, 8411, 8934, 9371, 9562, 9774, 9783, 9798, 9927, 9928, 10564, 10735, 10736, 10737, 10911, 10967, 11111, 11167, 11749, 13321, 14655, 15309, 16381, 16920, 17587, 17776, 19045
Lancashire (England)
--Social conditions 14108
Lancaster (Pennsylvania)
--Religious and ecclesiastical institutions 136, 7196, 8716, 9053, 9428, 10828, 16981, 18862
--Social conditions 9834, 10641, 14790, 14969
Lancaster Theological Seminary, Faculty 15120
Land 613, 661, 7054, 8992, 9023, 10007, 10435, 11047, 11088, 11648, 13146, 13196, 13295, 14067, 16671, 18239, 18937
--Bibliographies 13243, 13919
--Geography 13469
--India 16330
Land (theology) 12381, 14143, 14338, 18056, 18305
Landlords 2586, 9406, 11482
--England 30
Language 2884, 3111, 3170, 7109, 10315, 12542, 12545, 12857, 13676, 14573, 14833, 14957, 17425
Language instruction (English) 2573, 2685, 2831, 3052, 3111, 3170, 3665, 15751
Lansing (Michigan)
--Religious and ecclesiastical institutions 17035
Large churches >> See: Big churches
Large churches 11376
Las Cruces (New Mexico)
--Religious and ecclesiastical institutions 8019
Las Vegas (Nevada)
--Religion 8280, 13597
--Religious and ecclesiastical institutions 9523, 11480
--Social conditions 9399
Latin America
--Church history 13165
--Economic conditions 6050, 8505, 11431, 15463, 15620, 17289, 17642, 18423, 19022
--Religion 17077, 18640
--Religious and ecclesiastical institutions >> See further: Basic Christian Communities
--Religious and ecclesiastical institutions 7596, 7598, 9200, 9912, 10652, 10660, 11791, 12852, 12877, 13082, 14233, 15773, 15948, 16206, 16816, 17434, 17522, 17755, 18250, 18860
--Social conditions 7110, 7741, 8056, 8290, 8563, 9479, 10078, 10953, 11009, 11227, 12004, 12180, 12395, 12852, 12888, 13165, 13493, 13595, 13996, 14010, 14157, 14575, 14711, 15064, 15345, 15455, 16095, 16166, 16226, 16690, 16837, 17056
--Social conditions--History 12191
--Urbanization >> See: Urbanization--Latin America
Lausanne (Switzerland)
--Religion 10727
Lausanne Committee for World Evangelization 15524, 15525, 16825
Law 2473, 6788, 6820, 7206, 7707, 8310, 8312, 13016, 14560

Lawrence (Massachusetts)
--Religious and ecclesiastical institutions 536, 7847
--Social conditions 3220
--Social conditions--History 14987
Lay ministry >> See further: Clergy and laity; Laity; Laity, training of
Lay ministry 1011, 3962, 5641, 6869, 6959, 7309, 7422, 7475, 7795, 7886, 8948, 9419, 9515, 9626, 9835, 10241, 10598, 11200, 12401, 12490, 12595, 13421, 13540, 13605, 14818, 14843, 15041, 15230, 15285, 15571, 16106, 16145, 16234, 16402, 16466, 17000, 17025, 17183, 17614, 18715
--England 16607
Leadership 2175, 2959, 3183, 3549, 3959, 4639, 4679, 5626, 6258, 6791, 7867, 9419, 9949, 11598, 12358, 14014, 14254, 15214, 15307, 15410, 16116, 16124, 16235, 16901, 17440, 17609, 18024, 18351, 18861
--Bibliographies 17169
--Religious 16503
--Taiwan 16502
Lebanese Americans 15248
--History 16717
Leeds (England)
--Ethnic relations 15473
--Religious and ecclesiastical institutions 17744
--Religious life and customs 17744, 18061
--Social conditions 15473
Leisure 745, 2829, 4309, 4379, 9796, 18188
--Finland 11420
--History 13017
--Social aspects 18845
Leo XIII, Pope, 1810-1903. Rerum novarum >> See: Encyclicals, Papal (Rerum novarum)
Levittown (Pennsylvania)
--Religious and ecclesiastical institutions 6309
Liberalism 5383, 5960, 10714, 11104, 11418, 11545, 12593, 12783, 13206, 16051, 16763
--History 4209, 10670, 16438, 17493
Liberalism (religion)
--United States 14807
Liberation theology >> See further: Freedom (theology); Revolution (theology)
Liberation theology 11720, 11721, 12193, 12653, 13165, 13200, 13489, 13506, 13585, 13599, 13722, 13739, 13789, 13824, 14002, 14156, 14413, 14449, 15078, 15106, 15107, 15351, 15562, 16550, 16744, 16842, 16907, 17020, 17156, 17250, 17355, 17362, 17509, 17562, 17630, 17761, 18115, 18161, 18324, 18423, 18541, 18892, 18897, 18963, 19058, 19094, 19337
--Africa 13118
--Bibliographies 11182
--History 12882, 16705, 16786
--Latin America 15345, 17643
--Periodicals 12325
Libourne (France)
--Religious and ecclesiastical institutions 7091
Life style >> See: Conduct of life
Lille (France)
--Religious and ecclesiastical institutions 10299
Lilly Endowment 1739, 14896, 17301, 17331, 18078, 18385, 18819, 19113, 19194, 19198, 19203, 19227, 19238
Lima (Ohio)

--Social conditions 14239
Lima (Peru)
--Religious and ecclesiastical institutions 11455, 17846, 18309
--Religious life and customs 13585
--Social conditions 19022
Limits of growth 12594, 12672, 12728
Lincoln (Nebraska)
--Religious and ecclesiastical institutions--History 13625
--Social conditions 5649
Linguistics 7109, 14957
--History 16717
Linwood United Ministries (Kansas City, Missouri) 14587, 15044, 15308, 16981
Literature >> See further: Cities and towns in literature, Clergy in literature; Religion and literature, Christianity in literature
Literature and religion >> See: Religion and literature
Literature and religion 755, 3496, 3850, 16254, 18183
--England 653
--History 8314, 9182, 10992, 11082, 12094, 13024, 14450
Literature and society >> See further: Labor and laboring classes in literature
Literature and society 1155, 2150
Literature, anti-urban 382, 4406, 17045, 17408
--History 8618, 14532
Literature, anti-urban >> See: Social values (anti-urban)
Lithuania
--History 16646
Lithuanian American clergy
--History 15702
Lithuanian Americans
--History 13555, 15858
Little Rock (Arkansas)
--Race relations 7438
--Social conditions 7263, 7264, 7512, 7513, 7674, 17712
Liturgy 5818, 7860, 8380, 11347, 15191, 16546, 16567, 16708, 18035, 19338
--Europe 7693
Liturgy and culture 18444, 18743
--Great Britain 4443
Liverpool (England)
--Religious and ecclesiastical institutions 2051, 3642, 8328, 11001, 15913, 16607, 18046, 18682
--Religious and ecclesiastical institutions--History 4446, 4528
--Social conditions 15009, 16652, 16741, 17273, 17737, 18329
Liverpool Domestic Mission Society
--History 4528
Liverpool Institute of Socio-Religious Studies (Liverpool, England) 14563
Liège (Belgium)
--Religious and ecclesiastical institutions 7784
--Social conditions 7312
Local-cosmopolitan theory 12651, 14018, 16696
Local church >> See: Church; City Churches; Church work
Local congregation >> See: Church; City Churches; Church work
London (England)
--Moral conditions 148, 362, 1378
--Poetry 3
--Population density 4665
--Religion 489, 2016, 4417, 4574
--Religion--History 13033

London (England) (cont.)
--Religious and ecclesiastical institutions 152, 369, 401, 521, 548, 763, 846, 1018, 1019, 1031, 1081, 1173, 1506, 1613, 1720, 1972, 2169, 2223, 2334, 2343, 3038, 3211, 3371, 3542, 4428, 4492, 4599, 4653, 4690, 4888, 4978, 4995, 5006, 5845, 5874, 6001, 6447, 7038, 7664, 8154, 8851, 10472, 10519, 10773, 11096, 11340, 14345, 14564, 16344, 17416, 17560, 17640, 18284, 18527, 18531
--Religious and ecclesiastical institutions--History 15, 913, 1299, 1450, 2390, 4087, 9683, 10755, 17888
--Social conditions 72, 112, 148, 286, 337, 366, 453, 512, 514, 669, 1356, 1378, 1452, 2557, 2985, 3626, 3939, 3985, 4075, 4132, 4140, 4200, 4463, 4665, 5393, 6474, 7233, 8635, 8858, 10950, 11811, 13767, 14389, 15528, 15648, 15967, 16104, 16650, 17356, 17495, 18348
--Social conditions--Fiction 19296
--Social conditions--History 913, 1512, 4530, 4661, 10906, 17842, 19205
--Social life and customs 7233, 13334
London (Ontario, Canada)
--Religious and ecclesiastical institutions 8465
--Social conditions 2724
London City Mission 152, 221, 283, 535, 3939, 4123, 6119, 6410, 8058, 8635, 9282, 9711, 10186, 10664, 10665, 11157, 12735, 17416, 17560
--History 668, 735, 4124, 14491
London Missionary Society 2277
London Society for Promoting Christianity amongst the Jews
--History 2223
Loneliness >> See: Alienation
Long Island (New York)
--Religious and ecclesiastical institutions 12037
Los Angeles (California)
--Economic conditions 13135
--Ethnic relations--History 12010
--Population 6919
--Race relations 5236, 8867, 13135
--Religion 10629, 19036
--Religion--History 14039
--Religious and ecclesiastical institutions--History 9455
--Religious and ecclesiastical institutions 3350, 3394, 3628, 3905, 4404, 4927, 4951, 5316, 5329, 5416, 6008, 6585, 7024, 7146, 7545, 7607, 8098, 8800, 9407, 9535, 9783, 10287, 10324, 10399, 11100, 11108, 12118, 13233, 13859, 14573, 14729, 15801, 16106, 16381, 16995, 16996, 17222, 17694, 19143, 19167, 19314
--Religious and ecclesiastical institutions--History 5703, 6097, 6683, 13080, 14130, 14307, 14561, 15870
--Social conditions 2119, 3247, 6016, 7146, 10780, 11351, 12630, 13135, 13324, 14008, 15790, 18287, 19100, 19274
--Social conditions--History 17098
--Social life and customs 9058
--Social life and customs--History 13336
Los Angeles Baptist City Mission Society 6008
Los Angeles Regional Goals Project 7607, 10629, 11099

Louisville (Kentucky)
--Religious and ecclesiastical institutions 1507, 2020, 2797, 5262, 6181, 6277, 6388, 6390, 6971, 6973, 7260, 7701, 8140, 10429, 11442, 11806, 11892, 12854, 13104, 13203, 16110, 16218, 16630, 17263, 18114, 19319
--Religious and ecclesiastical institutions--History 5237, 12808, 14185, 18091
--Social conditions 5634
Love 9742, 10405
--Action implications 1278, 8039, 9626, 10674, 13232, 14156, 15455, 16425, 17376, 17411
--Ethical aspects 279, 343, 651, 2189, 2382, 6517, 6854, 7832, 7895, 11184, 12425
Love (of cities) 1504, 2029, 5059, 8517, 9572, 10074, 10361, 11647, 12945, 13619, 14008, 14026, 14095, 14626, 15056, 18739
Love (of people) 880, 7151, 8157, 8183, 8533, 9070, 9251, 10125, 10465, 10466, 10966, 11452, 13175, 14323, 14665, 15368, 15733, 15888, 16353, 17412, 17745, 17793, 18466
Lowell (Massachusetts)
--History 1827, 13441, 17879
--Religious and ecclesiastical institutions 215, 2487
--Religious and ecclesiastical institutions--History 14377
--Social conditions 222, 247, 299
Lower East Side (New York, NY) 1859
--Social conditions 11519
Lusaka (Zambia)
--Religious and ecclesiastical institutions 14210
Luther Place Memorial Church (Washington, DC) 16748
Lutheran Center for Church Renewal (St. Paul, Minnesota) 15540
Lutheran Church in America 10522
--Case studies 9058, 9428, 9487, 13654, 16284
--Missions 14644
--Periodicals 11879
--Pronouncements, policies 14326, 14327, 17805, 18893
Lutheran Church in America, Board of American Missions 8457
Lutheran Church in America, Board of Parish Education 12569, 12950
Lutheran Church in America, Board of Social Ministry 10462, 11137, 12570
Lutheran Church in America, Commission on the Nature and Mission of the Congregation 9969
Lutheran Church in the DDR 17816
Lutheran Church of Finland 9539, 11420, 11880
Lutheran Church, Missouri Synod 6880, 10224
--Case studies 7432, 8531, 9147, 11012
--Congresses 7465
--Home Missions 9141
--Periodicals 11879
--Pronouncements, policies 7431, 11185
Lutheran churches >> See further: National Lutheran Council; City churches--Lutheran sources
Lutheran churches
--Case studies 5949, 6084, 6308, 6911, 7880, 7945, 8020, 8187,

8420, 8891, 9150, 9429, 9489, 9664, 9828, 10087, 10375, 11100, 11239, 11996, 12513, 14265, 14359, 14406, 14619, 14644, 14853, 15191, 15516, 16358, 16768, 17387, 17531, 17818, 18269, 18313, 19268
Lutheran churches (cont.)
--Case studies--Bibliographies 4936
--Case study 9503
--History 764, 19228
--Latin America 18771
--Pastoral theology 9291, 10989, 14775, 16622, 19242
--Periodicals 731, 3331, 5936, 8224, 9105, 11421
--Pronouncements, policies 14326
--Social teaching 5988, 17282, 17790
Lutheran churches (Canada) 18023
Lutheran churches (Germany) >> See further: Inner mission
Lutheran churches (Germany)
--Case studies 7614, 8795
--History 5535, 17409
Lutheran churches (New Guinea) 11059, 13579, 13712
Lutheran churches (Sweden) 17349
Lutheran churches--Social teaching >> See further: Inner mission
Lutheran Council in the USA
--Periodicals 12572
--Pronouncements, policies 11606, 15903
Lutheran Inner City Ministry (Racine, Wisconsin) 11421
Lutheran Inner Mission Society in New York City 4635
Lutheran Social Welfare Conference
--Periodicals 8224
Lutheran World Federation 10989
Luton Industrial College (Luton, England) 7543, 14219, 15684, 15905
Lynn (Massachusetts)
--History 12146
--Religious and ecclesiastical institutions 976, 10570
--Social conditions--History 13830
Lyons (France)
--Religious and ecclesiastical institutions 6504, 6711, 6951
Maastricht (Netherlands)
--History 16694
Madison (Wisconsin)
--Religious and ecclesiastical institutions 318, 5349, 5407, 5757
--Social conditions 5249
Madras (India)
--Religious and ecclesiastical institutions 10934, 13028, 13317, 13347, 13652, 14732
--Religious life and customs 14155
--Social conditions 11978, 16396, 18073
Madrid (Spain)
--Religion 7467
--Religious and ecclesiastical institutions 16576
--Social conditions 16522
Magic 4150, 14179
--Japan 18558
--Peru 15208
Mainz-Kastel (Germany)
--Religious and ecclesiastical institutions 19163
Malaysia
--Religious and ecclesiastical institutions 14407
Malden (Massachusetts)

--Religious and ecclesiastical institutions 17023
Malden Plan (religious education) 3047, 3172, 3173
Mamluk (Syria)
--Social conditions 11858
Management
--Employee participation 3068, 3724, 10977, 12419, 13666, 14191
--Employee participation--Argentina 11015
--Employee participation--Germany 10512, 12019
--Employee participation--Switzerland 14046
--Employee representation--Germany 5842
Manchester (England)
--Religious and ecclesiastical institutions 233, 1932, 3517, 16164, 17583
--Religious and ecclesiastical institutions--History 842, 3838
--Social conditions 12015
Manchester (New Hampshire)
--Religious and ecclesiastical institutions 9867
Manchester City Mission (Manchester, England) 3838
Manhattan (New York, NY)
--Buildings 17314
--History 10868, 11365
--Religious and ecclesiastical institutions 980, 1073, 1748, 1921, 2014, 2100, 2355, 2451, 3452, 3600, 3635, 3660, 3708, 3995, 4053, 5040, 5100, 5199, 5931, 6267, 6509, 6767, 7166, 7668, 7669, 7945, 8431, 8433, 8434, 8551, 9051, 9280, 12959, 13881, 14107, 14757, 15920, 16286
--Religious and ecclesiastical institutions--History 223, 1801, 2091, 3801, 4420, 5225, 6579, 14348, 15810
--Social conditions 7948, 10464, 14751, 14757, 19102
Manila (Philippines)
--Religion 18311
--Religious and ecclesiastical institutions 5375, 9531, 11968, 17960, 18895
--Social conditions 11486, 11487, 12519, 16965, 18150
Mannheim (Germany)
--Social conditions--History 18234
Mansfield (Ohio)
--Religious and ecclesiastical institutions 13390
Mar Thomas Syrian Church
--India 7516, 14530
Marin City (California)
--Religious and ecclesiastical institutions 10567
Marin County (California)
--Religious and ecclesiastical institutions 9276
Marion (North Carolina)
--Social conditions 4005
Marple (England)
--Religious and ecclesiastical institutions 12088
Marriage rites and customs 4998, 5183, 6622, 8045, 8673, 11165, 12829, 13966, 15033, 16560, 18871, 18985, 19147, 19249
--History 13336
--India 16857
--Islamic 18848
Married people >> See: Family life; Church work with families
Marseille (France)
--Religion 6477
--Religious and ecclesiastical institutions 6292
--Religious and ecclesiastical institutions--History 9010

--Social conditions 4506, 18645
--Social conditions--History 11304
Martha's Vineyard
--History 18373
Marxism >> See: Socialism; Socialism and Christianity; Class warfare
Mass media 4720, 7044, 7317, 11093, 11513, 13020, 13260, 14004, 15703, 16368
Mass media in religion 3936, 4361, 5730, 5759, 6751, 7227, 7293, 7406, 7447, 7578, 11046, 11751, 12857, 14283, 14365, 15262, 15492, 15836, 15845, 16209, 17184, 17502, 17627, 18121, 18332, 18509
--Bibliographies 9164
--Brazil 19213
--France 11491
--History 9721, 12841, 14561, 18534
Massachusetts Institute of Technology 8629
Mataro (Spain)
--Social conditions 5895
Maternity homes >> See further: Unmarried mothers
Maternity homes
--History 1566, 2388, 18614
McAll Mission (Paris, France) 482, 604, 702, 849, 1062, 1239, 1307, 1410, 1484, 1809
--History 1944, 11115
McCormick Theological Seminary 13298, 13870
McKeesport (Pennsylvania)
--Religious and ecclesiastical institutions 17155
Medellin (Colombia)
--Religious and ecclesiastical institutions 18293
--Social conditions 18756
Media >> See: Mass media
Medical care >> See further: Healing; Community health services; Nurses and nursing; Mental health; Church work with the sick; Healing
Medical care 368, 1729, 2143, 2221, 2259, 2285, 2300, 2301, 2338, 2348, 2372, 2858, 3429, 3978, 4030, 4031, 4098, 6593, 7255, 9695, 10162, 11443, 11740, 13281, 13622, 13736, 13743, 13914, 14303, 15499, 16144, 16312, 16748, 17036, 17394, 17395, 18523, 18635, 18791, 18914, 19020, 19149, 19176
--Asia 11748
--Canada 6498
--England 432, 17381, 17585, 18321
--Great Britain 19224
--Japan 7246
--New Guinea 17382
--Peru 10152, 15208
--Sri Lanka 15724
Melbourne (Australia)
--Religion--History 11039
--Religious and ecclesiastical institutions 19322
--Social conditions 19358
--Social conditions--History 14744, 19315
Melting pot (metaphor) >> See further: Americanization; Christianization; Pluralism; Ethnicity
Melting pot (metaphor) 5804, 5941, 6684, 7184, 8730, 10677, 12250, 12402, 12621, 12622, 13122, 13316, 13505, 15288, 17566
Melting pot theory >> See: Assimilation; Acculturation
Membership >> See: Church membership
Memphis (Tennessee)

--Race relations 17668, 18581
--Religious and ecclesiastical institutions 5364, 5526, 5861, 5930, 6433, 6434, 6712, 12246, 15271, 16240
--Religious and ecclesiastical institutions--History 13674, 15292
--Social conditions 6198, 10671
Men >> See further: Church work with men
Men 170, 1640, 1644, 1908, 2055, 2113, 2523, 2651, 3937, 7655, 8666, 8766, 13568, 16262
--Social conditions 3478, 5671, 6761, 10610, 11651, 12999, 14099, 16403, 16613, 17588, 18040
Mennonite Board of Missions 16489, 17567, 18699
--Periodicals 17567
Mennonite Board of Missions and Charities 4607, 5813, 10641
Mennonite Brethren Church
--Case studies 5424
Mennonite Brethren in Christ Church
--History 3965
Mennonite Central Committee 16620
Mennonite Central Committee (Canada) 10818
Mennonite churches
--Case studies 2932, 9250, 11544, 14594, 16194, 16417, 16955, 17534, 17763, 18494, 18699, 18868, 19097
--History 5813, 17632
--Pronouncements, policies 15592
--Social teaching 16967
Mennonite churches (Canada) 9250, 10805, 12465, 14200, 16194, 16560, 19069
--Case studies 17543
--History 13510, 14594, 18471
Mennonite House of Fellowship (Bronx, New York) 11966
Mennonites
--Social life and customs 14200
Mental health 1918, 2143, 2221, 2259, 2285, 2300, 2301, 2338, 2348, 2372, 6251, 6828, 9456, 10162, 11715, 12948, 13884, 14186, 14242, 17419, 18197, 19349
--History 17119
Merchant seamen
--Missions and charities 2, 21, 50, 85, 98, 153, 201, 208, 229, 324, 329, 396, 406, 455, 510, 529, 1769, 1934, 3063, 3160, 4064, 4253, 4269, 4399, 4745, 5110, 5148, 10632, 12100, 12260, 12347, 12736, 14178, 14624, 15565, 16296, 17568
--Missions and charities--Canada 7374
--Missions and charities--Fiction 203
--Missions and charities--History 2071, 14154, 14188
--Missions and charities--Periodicals 32, 95, 3709, 5936
Merchant seamen--Missions and charities >> See further: Chaplains, industrial
Merger of denomination >> See: Christian union
Merger of local churches >> See: Church development, merger
Methodist Church >> See further: United Methodist Church; Afro-American Methodists, Hispanic American Methodists
Methodist Church (Africa)
--History 10508
Methodist Church (Argentina) 9344, 14618
Methodist Church (Australia)

--Case studies 17207
--History 16937
Methodist Church (Bahamas)
--Case studies 17725
Methodist Church (Canada) 2724, 2725, 2747, 2748, 2763, 3149
Methodist Church (England) 1749, 3149, 9097, 11001, 12195, 12235, 12360, 15291, 17181, 19010
--Biography 12342
--Case studies 763, 2209, 2390, 3974, 4301, 9357, 11340, 12088, 13467, 13638, 16775, 17906, 18164, 18642, 19011
--History 810, 1299, 2031, 3005, 4699, 6591, 12177, 12332, 12749, 13310, 13880, 15648, 16155, 16391, 17064, 18031
--Home missions 16013
--Social teaching 991, 1148, 1309, 3425, 7729, 16391
--Social teaching--History 7339
Methodist Church (England), Home Mission Department 14669
Methodist Church (Ivory Coast) 12280
Methodist Church (Korea)
--Case studies 16530
Methodist Church (New Zealand)
--Case studies 12267
Methodist Church (Peru) 11455
Methodist Church (Philippines)
--Case studies 9531
Methodist Church (Singapore) 8216
Methodist Church (USA) 8374
--Board of Christian Social Concerns 8856
--Case studies 1954, 5880, 5900, 6041, 6433, 6434, 6510, 6679, 6776, 6870, 7057, 7343, 7358, 7484, 7518, 7702, 7711, 7712, 8053, 8270, 8337, 8375, 8464, 8685, 8800, 8850, 8914, 8958, 8999, 9114, 9155, 9402, 9467, 9500, 9501, 9502, 9569, 9634, 9638, 9760, 9853, 10237, 10274, 10340
--Case studies--Bibliographies 4937
--Congresses 7334, 7469, 8511, 9939
--Creed 9161
--Foreign missions 8216
--History 5119, 5980, 6098, 6241, 7445, 7930
--Periodicals 4964, 7651
--Pronouncements, policies 4915, 9161, 10183
--Social Teaching 4959, 5705, 6133, 16130
--Social teaching--History 9089
--United States >> See further: United Methodist Church
Methodist Church (USA), Board of Education 4963, 8561, 9560
Methodist Church (USA), Board of Evangelism 9540
Methodist Church (USA), Board of Missions and Church Extension 5419, 5627, 5826, 5827, 5828, 5829, 5979, 5980, 6096, 6097, 6098, 6240, 6241
Methodist Church (USA), Board of Missions, National Division 6511, 6512, 6520, 6787, 6789, 6834, 6900, 7299, 7343, 7358, 7441, 7453, 7454, 7455, 7484, 7606, 7708, 7710, 7711, 7712, 7859, 7886, 8000, 8001, 8007, 8008, 8050, 8051, 8052, 8053, 8054, 8089, 8131, 8239, 8249, 8301, 8313, 8335, 8337, 8401, 8412, 8625, 8626, 8643, 8692, 8698, 8982, 9028, 9274, 9275, 9276, 9277, 9334, 9338, 9361, 9389, 9390, 9395, 9396, 9704,

9705, 9706, 9759, 9776, 9796, 9808, 9809, 9810, 9817, 9829, 9939, 9947, 10175, 10202, 10289, 10488, 10657, 10716, 12816
Methodist Church (USA), Board of Social and Economic Relations 7096, 7103, 7179, 7192
Methodist Church (USA), Board of Social and Economic Relations, Commission on Chaplains 7142
Methodist Church (USA), Commission on Ministerial Training 5386, 5421
Methodist church (USA), Council on World Service and Finance 9237
Methodist Church (USA), General Board of Christian Social Concern 9161
Methodist Church (USA), General Board of Christian Social Concerns 7895, 8346, 8676
Methodist Church (USA), General Board of Education 8438
Methodist Church (USA), New York Metropolitan Area Planning Commission 8479, 9508
Methodist Church (USA), New York Metropolitan Planning Commission 9509
Methodist Church, Central Jurisdiction 6466, 7118, 10545
Methodist Church, Home Mission Department (England) 13562, 13899
Methodist Episcopal Church 587
--Case studies 1318, 1451, 1524, 1695, 2605, 2835, 2952, 3046, 3619, 3750, 3773, 3834, 3986, 12900
--History 3084, 3927, 12333, 18559
--Home missions 743
--Missions 2392
--Periodicals 81, 1317, 3018
--Pronouncements, policies 3927, 4422, 18505, 18559
--Social teaching 2253, 2842, 2961, 3518, 3588, 3927, 4845, 5069, 13553, 18505, 18559
--Social teaching--History 5138
Methodist Episcopal Church Union of Pittsburgh (Pittsburgh, Pennsylvania) 641
Methodist Episcopal Church, Board of Home Missions and Church Extension 1003, 2073, 2381, 2426, 3018, 3150, 3187, 3188, 3250, 3279, 3311, 3408, 3494, 3528, 3592, 3628, 3631, 3632, 3689, 4490, 4756
--History 3084
Methodist Episcopal Church, Board of Temperance, Prohibition and Public Morals 3017, 3357
Methodist Episcopal Church, Council of Cities 3018
Methodist Episcopal Church, South
--Case studies 2802
--History 14701, 16322
--Home missions 2955, 2956
--Social teaching 1952, 3132
Methodist Episcopal Church, South, Board of Missions 3526, 3948
Methodist Episcopal Social Union 2342
Methodist Federation for Social Action 13629
--History 5792, 10606, 13187, 15552, 16656
--Periodicals 4310

Methodist Federation for Social Service 2086, 2158, 2365, 2571, 2767, 2961, 3055, 3079, 3085, 3780, 3902, 13553
--History 5729, 15872
--Periodicals 2525
Methodist Social Union 468, 756
Methodists, African American >> See: African American Methodists
Metropolitan >> See: City
Metropolitan Associates of Philadelphia 9418, 9493, 9562, 9570, 9835, 10000, 10048, 10276, 10407, 10588, 12245, 12490, 12595
Metropolitan Community Church >> See: Universal Fellowship of Metropolitan Community Churches
Metropolitan Ecumenical Training Center (Washington, DC) 9987, 15002
Metropolitan Interfaith Association (Memphis, Tennessee) 12246, 15271
Metropolitan Urban Service Training (New York, NY) 9563, 9820, 9959, 10009, 10337, 10728, 10895, 11128, 11447, 11822, 11897
Metropolitan Visiting and Relief Association
--History 4661
Meudon (France)
--Religious and ecclesiastical institutions 11397
Mexican American Catholics 13519
Mexican American children 14314
Mexican American churches 5012, 8907
Mexican American families 8220, 19182
Mexican American Methodists 4478
Mexican American Presbyterians 7146, 13136, 14162
Mexican Americans 6438, 7504, 11286, 15404
--Education 13600, 13945, 14314, 15497
--History 14236, 15858
--Missions to 3350, 3593, 3628, 3662, 4478, 4807, 13081, 14162, 16833, 17590, 18811
--Political activities--History 17098
--Religion 4237, 14301, 16426, 16719
--Social conditions 3247, 4155, 7020, 8220, 10780
Mexico
--Social conditions 4853, 16065
Mexico City (Mexico)
--Religious and ecclesiastical institutions 676, 12505, 12589, 15987, 18678, 18692
--Social conditions 2172, 6192, 8220, 9167, 9533, 16367, 17246, 17296, 18834, 19332
Miami (Florida)
--Religious and ecclesiastical institutions 5407, 6945, 9274, 9277, 11354, 11548, 16318, 18199
--Social conditions 6945, 8772, 8792, 14386, 16458, 17940
Miami Beach (Florida)
--Social conditions 12914
Michigan City (Indiana)
--Social conditions 16451, 16452
Middle classes >> See further: Social status and religion
Middle classes 6067, 7086, 9080, 10004, 11414, 11853, 12045
--England 233, 712, 7226, 7868, 9331, 10958, 17616
--Fiction 233

Middle classes (cont.)
--Germany 18228
--History 8631, 8696, 12777, 14805
--Relations with the poor 233, 681, 712, 3406, 4649, 6617, 8696, 9341, 9467, 10865, 18166, 18490
--Religious life 3441, 3988, 7128, 8116, 9051, 9057, 10958, 13154, 13609, 14202, 18336
--Religious values 13031, 14479, 17780, 18904
--Scotland 15029, 18166
--Social values 6677, 8338, 8442, 8718, 9584, 10406, 11423, 11961, 13778, 16129, 18789, 18854, 18955
Middle East
--Religion 17046
Middlesborough (England)
--History 15655
Middletown (fictitious name) >> See further: Muncie (Indiana)
Middletown (fictitious name) 3977, 4636
--History 16091, 19216
--Religious life 4073, 5271, 16518, 16754, 17812
Middletown (Ohio)
--Religious and ecclesiastical institutions 11177
Midnight Mission (Syracuse, New York) 511
Midwest Training Network (Kansas City, Missouri) 10492
Midwest Urban Studies Program (Chicago, Illinois) 17324
Migrants >> See: Emigration and immigration; Church work with immigrants; Rural-urban migration
Migration >> See: Emigration and immigration; Church work with immigrants; Rural-urban migration
Migration, internal 3910, 4734, 4954, 5913, 6183, 6466, 6511, 6520, 6746, 6750, 7307, 7453, 7591, 9085, 9113, 9228, 9565, 10692, 10815, 15321, 16474, 17192, 18271, 18337
--Argentina 14618
--Bibliographies 13626
--Europe 18314
--Germany 8261
--History 12073, 13934
--India 13795
--Japan 10001
--Kenya 11979
--Latin America 13492, 18771
--Periodicals 12787
Milan (Italy)
--Religious and ecclesiastical institutions 15361, 15389
--Social conditions 18392
Millennial thought >> See further: Seventh Day Adventists
Millennial thought 11697, 13304, 13625, 17556
--History 13887, 13943, 14699, 14944, 16404, 17639, 18139
Mills and millwork 883, 3220, 3941, 4005, 4008, 5046, 5121, 7541, 13842, 14229, 14404, 14416, 14873, 14874, 14879, 16003, 16371, 17505
--Colombia 18756
--England 149, 15597
--France 8489
--History 7388, 14377, 14455, 14987
--Korea 14710, 14847
Milton Keynes (England)
--Religious and ecclesiastical institutions 13076, 18732
Milwaukee (Wisconsin)
--Ethnic relations--History 8909
--Religious and ecclesiastical

institutions 5595, 6596, 8485, 9666, 11087, 11967, 12285, 13534, 14072, 14073, 14518, 17671
--Religious and ecclesiastical institutions--History 14870
--Social conditions 7164, 13087, 13285, 16129
Mindolo Ecumenical Centre (Kitwe, Zambia) 13632
Minister at large 16, 50, 93, 97, 118, 119, 125, 127, 128, 163, 189, 215, 319, 534, 541
Ministry >> See: Church work; Clergy; City Clergy; Laity; Evangelistic work
Ministry in Social Change, Twin Cities Graduate Program (St. Paul, Minnesota) 11453
Ministry of Urban Concerns (Denver, Colorado) 10967
Minneapolis (Minnesota)
--Religious and ecclesiastical institutions 1673, 2393, 3961, 4055, 4163, 5204, 5264, 5407, 5510, 5949, 8218, 10396, 10737, 12798, 14113, 14761, 14836, 14979, 16358
--Religious and ecclesiastical institutions--History 12654, 13283, 14026
--Social conditions 1955, 5787, 9243, 11672, 16990
--Social life and customs 14133
Minorities >> See further: Ethnicity; Church work with minorities; Family life
Minorities 5773, 11593, 12987, 17211
--Asia 14972, 15384
--Bibliographies 13973
--Economic conditions 7146, 10245
--Employment 13160
--Great Britain 7329, 11339, 14494, 15328
--History 19131
--Japan 13204
--Missions to 6895, 11130, 12487, 16651, 17923
--Philippines 14733
--Religion 5796, 6710, 7890, 14301, 14393, 18325
--Social conditions 6391, 6411, 7146, 9757, 11935, 13193, 13313, 13729, 14925, 18186, 18482, 18627
--Social conditions--History 12872
--Social life and customs 10458
--Study and teaching 15404, 17463
--Syria--History 16157
--Turkey 16401
Minority churches 5755, 11732, 13801, 14070, 15385, 15512, 15526, 15833, 15870, 15991, 15995, 16052, 16281, 16398, 16529, 16530, 16640, 16719, 16789, 16798, 16870, 16983, 17082, 17275, 17566, 17694, 18226, 18241, 18421, 18552, 18741
--Australia 18568
--Canada 5564, 18260, 18719
--History 18066
Mission of the church >> See further: Theology (of local church)
Mission of the church 1501, 2325, 6459, 6523, 6559, 8363, 8622, 9770, 10602, 10927, 11141, 11663, 11796, 12239, 12584, 13165, 14593, 15564, 15571, 15830, 18076, 18423
--Africa 8348, 8500, 18981
--American Baptist sources--(1900 to 1917) 2369, 2446, 2734
--American Baptist sources--(1918 to 1944) 3966

Mission of the church (cont.)
--American Baptist sources--(1945 to 1959) 6589, 7448
--American Baptist sources--(1960 to 1969) 7752, 7994, 8062, 8638, 9110, 9800, 10588, 10732
--American Baptist sources--(1970 to 1979) 12805
--American Baptist sources--(1980 to 1991) 17624, 17855
--Argentina 10740
--Asia 18967
--Australia 10149
--Baptist sources--(1960 to 1969) 8516
--Baptist sources--(1970 to 1979) 14931
--Brethren sources--(1918 to 1944) 3663
--Brethren sources--(1945 to 1959) 6526, 6527
--Brethren sources--(1960 to 1969) 10148, 10941, 11605
--Brethren sources--(1980 to 1991) 16365, 17875
--Canada 463, 15393, 15561
--Catholic sources--(1800 to 1874) 188
--Catholic sources--(1960 to 1969) 8105, 8132, 8758, 9427, 9622, 9807, 10023, 10030, 10294, 10313, 10528, 10975
--Catholic sources--(1970 to 1979) 11767, 11944, 12020, 12620, 13092, 13182, 13188, 13770, 14204, 14711, 15007, 15317
--Catholic sources--(1980 to 1991) 15665, 16009, 16196, 16676, 17297, 17445, 17643, 18083, 18244, 18289, 19129
--Catholic sources--Congresses 16282
--Catholic sources--History 8095, 15695
--China 4502
--Christian Churches and Churches of Christ sources 19299
--Church of England sources--(1918 to 1944) 5058
--Church of England sources--(1960 to 1969) 7968, 9625, 11241, 11588
--Church of England sources--(1970 to 1979) 13358
--Church of England sources--(1980 to 1991) 15507, 17897
--Church of England sources--History 11987
--Congregational Christian sources--(1945 to 1959) 6027, 7294
--Congregational sources--(1875 to 1899) 1722
--Congregational sources--(1900 to 1917) 2104, 2460
--Congresses 11034
--Disciples of Christ sources 3249, 19047
--Dutch Reformed Church in South Africa 14139
--England 198, 749, 2110, 7210, 9711, 10351, 12227, 14080, 16038, 17181, 18409, 19010, 19011
--Episcopal sources--(1900 to 1917) 3031
--Episcopal sources--(1918 to 1944) 3157, 3268, 4747, 4753
--Episcopal sources--(1945 to 1959) 6595, 7206, 7735, 8310
--Episcopal sources--(1960 to 1969) 8092, 8311, 8312, 8627, 8940, 8959, 9832, 10388
--Episcopal sources--(1970 to 1979) 12148, 12845, 13905, 13978, 14730, 15193
--Episcopal sources--(1980 to 1991) 17724
--Evangelical and Reformed

Church sources--(1945 to 1959) 6936, 7541
Mission of the church (cont.)
--Evangelical Protestant sources--(1960 to 1969) 7958, 8155, 11401
--Evangelical Protestant sources--(1970 to 1979) 11777, 12335, 12837, 13191, 13364, 13829, 14367, 14388, 14928, 15053, 15104, 15124, 15303
--Evangelical Protestant sources--(1980 to 1991) 15723, 15817, 16018, 16021, 16305, 16443, 16492, 16591, 16941, 17203, 17603, 17677, 17878, 18116, 18172, 18232, 18304, 18860, 18904, 19080, 19134
--Evangelical Protestant sources--Bibliographies 17693
--France 5494, 7129, 8425
--Friends sources--(1980 to 1991) 16365
--Fundamentalist sources--(1900 to 1917) 2446
--Fundamentalist sources--(1970 to 1979) 12147
--Germany 2406, 13142, 13840, 14353
--Great Britain 5001, 17697, 18757, 18987
--Handbooks 11028
--Holiness sources--(1960 to 1969) 10050
--India 15147
--Japan 9434, 18706
--Latin America 18860
--Lutheran churches--(1960 to 1969) 10522
--Lutheran sources--(1875 to 1899) 1250
--Lutheran sources--(1945 to 1959) 5822
--Lutheran sources--(1960 to 1969) 8204, 8484, 8486, 8531, 8569, 9181, 9290, 9429, 9518, 9538, 9713, 9884, 9969, 10894, 10989
--Lutheran sources--(1970 to 1979) 12192, 13605, 14327, 14406, 15114
--Lutheran sources--(1980 to 1991) 19242
--Mennonite sources--(1960 to 1969) 8859, 9085, 10073, 10704
--Mennonite sources--(1970 to 1979) 12133, 14440
--Mennonite sources--(1980 to 1991) 16069, 16365
--Methodist sources--(1875 to 1899) 1451
--Methodist sources--(1900 to 1917) 2497
--Methodist sources--(1918 to 1944) 3189, 3535, 3569, 3592, 3631, 4335, 4488, 4667, 4673, 4674, 4821, 4873
--Methodist sources--(1945 to 1959) 6512, 6575, 6583, 6738
--Methodist sources--(1960 to 1969) 8692, 8976, 9199, 9396, 10149, 10482, 10674, 10729, 10838, 10844, 11375
--Methodist sources--(1970 to 1979) 12052, 12093, 12358, 12712, 13580, 13583, 14292, 14742, 14768, 15101, 15169, 15231
--Methodist sources--(1980 to 1991) 15447, 15610, 16124, 16254, 16457, 17120, 17181, 17425, 17488, 17771, 19010, 19011
--Methodist sources--History 17352
--Nazarene sources--(1960 to 1969) 11479
--Nazarene sources--(1970 to 1979) 12200

Mission of the church (cont.)
--NCCCUSA sources--(1945 to 1959) 6618, 6727, 6969, 6970
--NCCCUSA sources--(1960 to 1969) 8142, 8186, 8362, 8777, 8789, 9080, 9550, 10777, 10974, 11028
--Pentecostal sources 11959, 12477
--Philippines 6202
--Presbyterian sources--(1875 to 1899) 1708
--Presbyterian sources--(1900 to 1917) 1876, 2546, 2664
--Presbyterian sources--(1945 to 1959) 6908, 7248
--Presbyterian sources--(1960 to 1969) 7762, 7795, 8606, 8798, 8903, 9139, 9159, 9224, 9799, 9858, 9996, 10126, 10619
--Presbyterian sources--(1970 to 1979) 12873, 13544, 14393, 14419, 14789, 14828, 15089
--Presbyterian sources--(1980 to 1991) 15596, 15985, 15996, 16250, 17070
--Presbyterian sources--History 5830
--Protestant sources--(1800 to 1874) 92, 276, 463
--Protestant sources--(1875 to 1899) 922, 1144, 1248, 1327, 1472, 1705
--Protestant sources--(1900 to 1917) 1740, 1922, 2526, 2625, 2794, 2849
--Protestant sources--(1918 to 1944) 3000, 3056, 3827, 4032, 4165, 4542, 4600, 4656, 4698, 5150, 5223
--Protestant sources--(1945 to 1959) 5502, 5588, 6935, 6957, 7037, 7076, 7124, 7184, 7370, 7473, 7474
--Protestant sources--(1960 to 1969) 7858, 8338, 8498, 8597, 8828, 8959, 8997, 9070, 9225, 9302, 9370, 9558, 9560, 9602, 10068, 10182, 10280, 10778, 10988, 11202, 11203, 11436
--Protestant sources--(1970 to 1979) 11652, 11753, 12327, 12901, 13145, 13329, 13705, 13902, 14030, 14420, 14558, 14766, 14974, 15105
--Protestant sources--(1980 to 1991) 15557, 15635, 15916, 16275, 16910, 17202, 17244, 18183, 18384, 18526, 18666, 18814, 18919, 18934, 19117
--Protestant sources--Bibliographies 15200
--Protestant sources--History 6323, 10108
--Reformed Church in America sources--(1960 to 1969) 10526, 10659
--Reformed Church in America sources--(1970 to 1979) 12546
--Rhodesia 11034
--Scotland 6908, 18342
--Seventh Day Adventist sources 12097
--South Africa 8124, 12364
--Southern Baptist sources--(1900 to 1917) 2674, 2997
--Southern Baptist sources--(1945 to 1959) 6015, 6028, 6840, 7032
--Southern Baptist sources--(1960 to 1969) 8709, 9736, 9995, 10209, 10556, 10695, 10701, 10807, 10932, 11187
--Southern Baptist sources--(1970 to 1979) 11662, 11938, 11974, 12013, 12069, 12132, 12367, 12683, 13322, 13513, 14011, 14131, 14678
--Southern Baptist sources--(1980 to 1991) 15623, 15765, 16328,

16507, 16685, 16918, 17049, 17196, 17769, 18187
Mission of the church (cont.)
--Unitarian sources--(1800 to 1874) 294
--Unitarian sources--(1875 to 1899) 593
--United Brethren sources 1460
--United Church of Canada sources--(1970 to 1979) 14859
--United Church of Canada sources--(1980 to 1991) 15664
--United Church of Christ sources--(1945 to 1959) 7098
--United Church of Christ sources--(1960 to 1969) 7765, 7925, 8170, 8292, 8749, 8905, 9088, 9266, 9484, 9821, 10125, 10821, 11252, 11281, 11456, 11633
--United Church of Christ sources--(1970 to 1979) 12009, 12601, 15302
--United Church of Christ sources--(1980 to 1991) 15514, 15711, 16875
--United Church of Christ sources--Bibliographies 9235
--World Council of Churches sources--(1960 to 1969) 8348, 8707, 8797, 10661, 10940, 10947
--World Council of Churches sources--(1970 to 1979) 14060, 15046
--World Council of Churches sources--(1980 to 1991) 18095
Missionaries 71, 212, 374, 381, 457, 480, 1467, 1708, 1729, 1808, 2234, 2398, 2532, 2565, 3022, 4041, 6720, 6904, 8251, 10061, 15747, 17395, 17502, 17982, 18162, 19098
--Africa 15967, 16140, 19158
--Africa--History 15024
--Attitudes 7480, 12020
--Australia 16937
--Biography 195, 303, 339, 390, 657, 697, 939, 1169, 2809, 3411, 4456, 5424, 6401, 9722, 14820, 16002, 16937, 18718
--Canada 14646
--Catholic 13061, 16425, 17172
--China 4651
--England 411, 1506, 3411
--Fiction 19296
--France--History 14657
--Germany 246, 1473, 1578, 4831, 7252
--History 3880, 7035, 13105
--Hong Kong 12866
--Muslim 3782, 15065
--Periodicals 94, 598
--Peru 10152
--Political activity 18147
--Political activity--France 14657
--Political activity--History 15249, 17721
--Scotland 390
--Training 2972, 3650, 9558, 15060, 16593, 16884, 17843, 17859, 18753
--Training--History 15792
Missionaries of Charity (India) 12899, 13691, 14318, 15377, 15423, 15431, 16425, 17909, 18508
Missionary Education Movement 2077, 2559, 2742, 2784, 2835, 2849, 2917, 2945, 3008, 3009, 3011, 3012, 3014, 3048, 3103, 3116, 3320, 3601, 3608, 3919, 4001, 4032, 4473
--Bibliographies 3697
Missionary Structure of the Congregation Study (World Council of Churches) 6896, 6921, 7349, 8414, 8514, 8615, 8632, 8707, 8713, 8796, 8797, 8825, 8915, 8946, 8954, 8955,

9273, 9560, 9671, 9896, 9996, 10155, 10169, 10555, 10661, 10885, 10947, 10989, 11822, 12577, 13902
--Asia 8911
--Bibliography 8514
--Periodicals 13393
Missions
--Biblical teaching 8092, 13657, 13987, 14928, 16687, 16824, 17380, 17603, 17818
--Theory 5968, 8256, 8534, 8606, 8955, 9273, 9680, 10059, 11753, 11796, 12733, 12845, 13970, 14117, 14311, 14828, 15046, 15596, 16243, 16828, 17297, 18357, 18449, 18683
Missions to African Americans >> See: African Americans, missions to
Missions to Hispanic Americans >> See: Hispanic Americans--Missions to
Missions to Jews 35, 339, 757, 1217, 1322, 1729, 1882, 1910, 2005, 2100, 3049, 3304, 3546, 3823, 5030, 5105, 5680, 6161, 6513, 11372, 12032, 16595
--Bibliographies 12618
--Canada--History 14256
--England 193, 1031, 2223
--Germany 9722
--History 2585, 6627, 11278, 14605, 18153, 18310
--Periodicals 77, 1718
Missions to seamen >> See: Merchant seamen--Missions and charities
Missions, city >> See: City missions
Missions, foreign >> See: Foreign missions
Missions, home >> See: Home missions
Missions, industrial work >> See: Church and industry
Mobile (Alabama)
--Religious and ecclesiastical institutions 8002
Mobile homes >> See: Church work with mobile home dwellers
Mobility >> See: Migration, internal; Residential mobility; Occupational mobility; Labor mobility
Models of ministry >> See: Church; City Churches--Case Studies; Church work
Modernity 220, 962, 1592, 2982, 3078, 3627, 3947, 5002, 7249, 8010, 8036, 9001, 9271, 9833, 10323, 10408, 10460, 11045, 11660, 12763, 13012, 14125, 14559, 14621, 16193, 16534, 17140, 17351, 17777, 18071, 18600, 18666, 18996
--Africa--History 11939
--Asia 10317
--China 18753
--England 4920
--Fiction 11684
--France 18495
--Germany 8814, 16461
--Great Britain 6168
--History 10392, 13913, 15694, 15802, 19117
--Islamic studies 18730
--Japan 8787, 13163, 13220, 13633, 13922
--Jordan 16241
--Korea 11161
--Latin America 12004
--Singapore 16299
Monastic and religious life >> See further: Priest workers, Nuns
Monastic and religious life 4924, 5404, 5833, 10649, 14114, 14805, 17573
--Germany 8795

--Italy 18283
Money 613, 714, 1048, 2053, 2306, 2438, 4365, 4786, 7511, 7621, 8403, 10745, 15567, 16200, 16232, 18661
--Canada 13066
--Germany 3328
Montclair (New Jersey)
--Religious and ecclesiastical institutions 1094
Montgomery (Alabama)
--History 7006
--Race relations 17668
--Religious and ecclesiastical institutions 15402
--Social conditions 1973, 7120, 7347
Montreal (Quebec, Canada)
--History 13604
--Religious and ecclesiastical institutions 3958, 6233, 10855, 11311, 11312, 11700, 12506, 12884, 13355, 16280, 17175
--Social conditions 4593
Montréal (Canada)
--Religious and ecclesiastical institutions 5857
--Social conditions 2824
Moody Bible Institute 9721, 17551, 17623, 17820
Moonlight Mission (London, England) 369
Moral Majority 16754
Moral reform 1177, 1340, 1343, 1372, 1542, 1834, 2288, 2556, 3167, 6677, 14228
--Bibliographies 1372
--History 6687, 11961
Moravian Church
--Case studies 10350, 11259, 11449, 11681, 19114, 19164
Morgan Memorial Church (Boston, Massachusetts) 1695, 2409, 2870, 2952, 3136, 3228, 3261, 3773, 3834, 3963, 4442
Morgantown (West Virginia)
--Social conditions 6244
Mormonism 18661
Mormons 375, 2555, 2766, 4962, 7162, 7804, 12581, 12582, 13966, 14190, 15482, 17615, 18412
--History 13424, 13900
Mosques 16101, 17926, 18189
Motion pictures >> See: Moving pictures
Moving pictures 3427, 4254, 4283, 4497, 4801
Mullenbach Industrial Institute (Chicago, Illinois) 4966
Multi-national corporations >> See: International business enterprises
Multiple staff ministries >> See: Group ministries
Muncie (Indiana) >> See further: Middletown (fictitious name)
Muncie (Indiana)
--History 16091
--Religion 14700
--Religious and ecclesiastical institutions 16754, 19216
--Social conditions 17812
Munich (Germany)
--Church history 17185
--Religious and ecclesiastical institutions 2949
Municipal government 492, 997, 1006, 1162, 1256, 1287, 1344, 1369, 1384, 1396, 1411, 1413, 1434, 1469, 1618, 1678, 1767, 1777, 1990, 2029, 2060, 2925, 2926, 3699, 3749, 4183, 4433, 4703, 5275, 5331, 5587, 6171, 6457, 7143, 7580, 7635, 8447, 8656, 8785, 9190, 9804, 10060, 10775, 11169, 11418, 12576, 12783, 13193, 14673, 15326, 15786, 15864, 15978, 16291, 16372, 17485, 18369, 18789

Municipal government (cont.)
--Canada--History 13943
--Developing countries 15171
--England 15692
--History 4725, 4726, 4727, 4728, 5986, 8623, 9093, 11345, 12701, 16033, 17098, 17824
--Latin America 14010
--Turkey--History 16401
Municipal reform >> See: Cities and towns--Reform
Music >> See: Jazz music; Church music; African American music; Folk music and songs
Music and religion >> See: Church music
Muskegon Heights (Michigan)
--Religious and ecclesiastical institutions 14350
Muslim Americans >> See further: Islam, Arab Americans; Black Muslims
Muslim Americans 7640, 13112, 15065, 16654, 19057
--Missions to 18198, 18557
Muslims 16101, 16813, 16820, 18395
--Africa 15709, 16795, 17941
--Australia 18189
--Ethnic identity 8897
--Europe 16203, 17014
--Great Britain 9321, 11219
--India 13813, 18208
--Indonesia 15660
--Missions to 16974, 18802
Mwanza (Tanzania)
--Religious and ecclesiastical institutions 18512
Mysticism 4094, 13338
Mythology 2068, 16254, 16387, 18183
--Japanese 7036, 15415, 16679
--United States 2765
Nagasaki (Japan)
--Social conditions 16020
Nairobi (Kenya)
--Religious and ecclesiastical institutions 8449, 11981, 13903, 14603, 14738, 18817
--Social conditions 13023, 14258, 15957, 18240, 18671, 19178
Nanking (China)
--Social conditions 4651
Naples (Italy)
--Religious and ecclesiastical institutions 7170
Narcotic addicts >> See: Church work with narcotic addicts; Drug abuse
Nashville (Tennessee)
--Race relations 7438
--Religious and ecclesiastical institutions 6949, 8001, 13297
--Religious and ecclesiastical institutions--History 13641, 13877, 15255
--Religious life and customs 15348, 18151
--Social conditions 2386, 7580, 7843, 13763, 14212, 14386
Nassau County (New York)
--Religious and ecclesiastical institutions 7550, 9068
National Advisory Commission on Civil Disorders 11135
National Association for the Advancement of Colored People 9285, 11632
--History 19152
National Association of Manufacturers 5301, 7152, 7803, 7828, 7850, 7902, 8033
--Periodicals 7153
National Baptist Convention 4898, 19288
National Catholic Education Association 1974
National Catholic School of Social Service 6058

National Catholic Welfare Conference 3152, 3264, 3273, 3458, 4151, 4476, 4613, 4645, 4670, 4765, 4860, 4969, 5016, 5498, 6316, 8017
--Congresses 4974
--History 8737
--Periodicals 3540, 4234
National Catholic Welfare Council 3275
National Christian Council of India 7217, 7516, 8016, 8071, 10915, 11508, 13584
--Congresses 7060, 9177
National Christian Council of Kenya 12303, 12738, 12989, 13326, 13590, 13648
National Conference of Catholic Bishops
--Pastoral Letter on the Economy 17371, 17467, 17720, 17831, 17889, 18108, 18136, 18292, 18408, 18478, 18647, 18709, 18964
National Conference of Catholic Charities
--Periodicals 3019
National Conference on Religion and Labor 16294
National Conference on Religious Architecture 10011
National Conference on the Christian Way of Life 3638, 3639
National Conference on the Churches and Social Welfare (Cleveland, Ohio) 6770
National Council of Catholic Charities 3442, 4079
National Council of Catholic Men 4089, 4175
National Council of Churches in Korea
--Pronouncements, policies 13983
National Council of Churches in New Zealand
--Periodicals 5302
National Council of Churches in the Philippines 12679
National Council of Churches of New Zealand 5394
National Council of Evangelical Free Churches (England) 2110
National Council of the Churches of Christ in the USA 5882, 6021, 6094, 6113, 6358, 6364, 6378, 6421, 6631, 6720, 6743, 6744, 6745, 6774, 6904, 6937, 7083, 7112, 7222, 7391, 7504, 7619, 7854, 7934, 7942, 7977, 8203, 8238, 8253, 8257, 8490, 8524, 8525, 8772, 8849, 8955, 9273, 9332, 9454, 9460, 9577, 9599, 10013, 10123, 10258, 10267, 10362, 10423, 10503, 10511, 11134, 11363, 12201, 12266, 14023, 14076, 14221, 14550, 14822, 15418, 15576, 15638
--Congresses 6042, 6138, 6170, 6212, 6213, 6635, 6676, 6733, 6748, 6772, 6929, 6930, 7156, 7395, 7732, 7943, 8252, 8364, 8526, 8621, 8775, 8983, 9006, 9063, 9173, 9432, 9576, 10011, 10012, 10014, 10065, 10370, 14373
--Periodicals 5950, 5952, 6357, 9178, 12251
--Pronouncements, policies 6209, 6210, 6581, 6932, 7157, 7662, 8527, 9669, 9880, 10284, 10502, 12732
--Social teaching 6537, 6613, 6819, 12612
National Council of the Churches of Christ in the USA, Broadcasting and Film Commission 6538, 6539, 6540,

6742, 7154, 7155, 8119, 8251
National Council of the Churches of Christ in the USA, Bureau of Research and Survey 6007, 6122, 6273, 6274, 6630, 7125, 7480, 8047, 8331, 8523, 8603, 8608, 8951, 9697
National Council of the Churches of Christ in the USA, Corporate Information Center 12251, 12252, 12548, 12611, 12612, 12985
National Council of the Churches of Christ in the USA, Department of the Urban Church 5542, 5951, 6523, 6563, 6688, 6755, 6771, 6931, 7163, 7392, 7670, 7936, 8288, 9179, 9682
National Council of the Churches of Christ in the USA, Joint Commission on Missionary Education 6449, 6458, 6479, 6480, 6500, 6548, 6590, 15576
National Council of the Churches of Christ in the USA, Joint Commission on the Urban Church 5952
National Federation of Priests' Councils 14671, 15091, 15112
National Federation of Settlements and Neighborhood Centers 7393
National Fire Protection Association 3906
National Florence Crittenton Mission 1215, 1731, 1891
--History 1377, 1566, 2388, 2652, 4349, 18564
National Impact (Washington, DC) 15394
National Industrial Mission (Detroit, Michigan) >> See further: Detroit Industrial Mission
National Industrial Mission (Detroit, Michigan) 12101, 12102, 12103
--Periodicals 7937
National Lutheran Council 5680, 6083, 6084, 6206, 6211, 6225, 6226, 6275, 6325, 6342, 6344, 6359, 6375, 6376, 6709, 7602, 7825, 7880, 7881, 8205, 8485, 8529, 9056, 9180, 9348, 9519, 9993
--Congresses 6746, 8361, 8486
National parishes 961, 3962, 5144, 6074, 16311, 19063
--History 4846, 5253, 6045, 13432, 13509, 13952, 14527, 17414, 17417, 18066, 19142
National Preaching Mission 4556, 4687
National Recovery Administration 4504
National Reform Association (NRA) 2766
--Periodicals 437
National Religion and Labor Foundation 5500, 5711
National Religion and Labor Foundation (New Haven, Connecticut) 4235, 5499
National Sex and Drug Forum 11916
National Urban League 16309
--History 19152
National Vigilance Committee 3547
National Welfare Rights Organization 14306
National Youth Movement (Papua, New Guinea) 17335
Native Americans >> See: Indians of North American
Nativism >> See further: Xenophobia; Anticatholicism; Antisemitism
Nativism 178, 2555

--History 6686, 7328, 7247, 14745
Naugatuck Valley Project (Waterbury, Connecticut) 15356, 19043
Nauvoo (Illinois)
--History 13900
Nederduits Gereformeerde Kerk (South Africa) 11462
Negroes >> See: Blacks; African Americans
Nehemiah Plan (New York, NY) 18174
Neighborhoods 2569, 2850, 3789, 6435, 6825, 9142, 9382, 10919, 12982, 13750, 14120, 14162, 14253, 14934, 15305, 15517, 15738, 16482
--France 6040
--History 17031
--Latin America 11009, 11227, 12888, 13595, 16165, 16169, 16837
--Mexico 18834
Neighborliness 15888, 15937, 19160
Netherlands
--Economic conditions 15794, 17404
--Religion 12011, 15287
--Religious and ecclesiastical institutions 2017, 3622, 3674, 5851, 6803, 7089, 7219, 8932, 8939, 8998, 11114, 11199, 11481, 11854, 12352, 12415, 14205, 15672, 15685, 15704, 16758, 17136, 18894
--Religious and ecclesiastical institutions--History 6245, 14567, 16694, 17194
--Religious life and customs 12993, 16758, 17561
--Social conditions 360, 13384
--Social conditions--History 17976
Network Ministries (San Francisco, California) 18787
Networks >> See further: Information networks
Networks 6203, 10450, 11677, 11998, 12853, 12937, 13177, 13213, 13471, 13639, 13860, 13861, 13862, 13972, 14208, 14380, 14628, 14904, 15305, 15484, 15504, 15646, 15806, 16063, 16073, 16212, 16648, 16828, 16987, 17137, 17192, 17450, 17822, 17848, 17884, 18186, 18588, 18611, 18741, 18913, 19013, 19228, 19305, 19325, 19352
--Bibliographies 17406
--History 17031
New Bedford (Massachusetts)
--Religious and ecclesiastical institutions 5148
--Religious and ecclesiastical institutions--History 14188
New Britain (Connecticut)
--Social conditions--History 14132, 14527
New churches >> See: Church development, new
New cities 2357, 6255, 6309, 6311, 8583, 8684, 9368, 9460, 9473, 9695, 9724, 10336, 10447, 10646, 10766, 11240, 11350, 11537, 11892, 12318, 12355, 12451, 12661, 12760, 12818, 12964, 13021, 13173, 13251, 15752, 19345
--Bibliographies 13045, 13102, 13288, 13626
--Brazil 10603
--Congresses 11724
--England 1642, 5381, 8863, 13076, 18732
--England--History 17516
--Germany 2619, 17660
--Great Britain 5084, 8855,

11724, 12142, 12450
New cities (cont.)
--History 16406
--Japan 12405, 12452
--Netherlands 8939
--Periodicals 10272
New Guinea
--Religious and ecclesiastical institutions 11059
New Haven (Connecticut)
--Ethnic relations 5153
--History 4997
--Religious and ecclesiastical institutions 252, 3028, 5350, 6000, 9508, 15378
--Social conditions 5153, 9048, 11329
New Orleans (Louisiana)
--Religion 4150, 5529, 13472
--Religious and ecclesiastical institutions 5022, 5023, 5407, 6032, 6167, 6256, 6314, 6467, 7295, 9705, 9947, 10835, 11770, 11859, 12367, 15862
--Religious and ecclesiastical institutions--History 4856, 6577, 10551, 10734, 13680, 13893, 14746
--Religious life and customs 4112, 15862
--Social conditions 16070
--Social life and customs 17393
New towns >> See: New Cities
New York (NY) >> See further: (Specific names of New York boroughs and locations: e. g., Harlem, Manhattan, Queens, Bronx, etc.)
New York (NY)
--Benevolent and moral institutions 38, 57, 91
--Correctional institutions 57, 86
--Ethnic relations 1907, 6572, 6652, 7255, 8730, 9065, 11517, 13782
--Ethnic relations--History 7581, 13509, 14516
--Fiction 1813, 2958, 4364
--History 248, 13144, 13895
--Intellectual life 1859
--Moral conditions 27, 397, 1264
--Race relations 5808, 6151, 6308, 6614, 8593, 19160
--Race relations--History 7581
--Religion 1621, 2057, 3304, 12138, 14270, 19226, 19231
--Religious and ecclesiastical institutions 13, 17, 19, 28, 29, 36, 44, 45, 49, 79, 99, 104, 126, 139, 161, 186, 281, 301, 305, 328, 336, 338, 395, 405, 406, 419, 420, 422, 473, 479, 556, 558, 596, 645, 757, 758, 759, 760, 828, 895, 910, 937, 985, 989, 994, 1011, 1021, 1093, 1119, 1166, 1167, 1252, 1266, 1269, 1282, 1289, 1324, 1326, 1331, 1418, 1461, 1478, 1485, 1487, 1491, 1495, 1499, 1501, 1510, 1524, 1538, 1544, 1567, 1600, 1603, 1614, 1633, 1634, 1635, 1638, 1644, 1650, 1651, 1655, 1663, 1816, 1817, 1855, 1950, 2026, 2059, 2069, 2070, 2080, 2090, 2099, 2134, 2236, 2254, 2262, 2267, 2291, 2292, 2337, 2342, 2384, 2499, 2504, 2533, 2720, 2726, 2745, 2801, 2869, 2884, 3024, 3106, 3109, 3119, 3122, 3144, 3151, 3226, 3346, 3545, 3858, 3901, 3908, 3951, 4084, 4098, 4106, 4145, 4188, 4194, 4265, 4269, 4275, 4362, 4454, 4458, 4514, 4586, 4739, 4745, 4771, 4826, 4858, 4938, 4998, 5182, 5412, 5601, 5603, 5614, 5630, 5677, 5741, 5820, 5859, 5943, 5947, 5967, 5974, 6070, 6308, 6374, 6378, 6402, 6489, 6502, 6691, 6731,

6764, 6835, 6957, 6963, 6968, 7049, 7119, 7169, 7203, 7310, 7311, 7338, 7354, 7450, 7553, 7554, 7822, 7842, 7957, 7986, 8015, 8039, 8147, 8454, 8619, 8637, 8685, 9172, 9195, 9316, 9360, 9486, 9665, 9677, 9820, 10009, 10094, 10227, 10320, 10338, 10633, 10842, 10916, 11077, 11086, 11259, 11306, 11446, 11785, 11954, 11996, 12020, 12085, 12319, 12499, 12677, 12698, 12832, 13151, 13603, 13693, 13717, 14227, 14853, 15191, 15314, 16152, 16202, 16284, 16289, 16647, 16806, 17341, 17638, 17890, 17917, 17993, 18019, 18202, 18352, 18437, 18504, 18909, 18963, 19154

New York (NY) (cont.)

--Religious and ecclesiastical institutions--Bibliographies 1797

--Religious and ecclesiastical institutions--Fiction 4519

--Religious and ecclesiastical institutions--History 219, 248, 540, 603, 623, 764, 844, 923, 948, 1694, 1744, 1856, 1857, 1962, 1980, 2049, 2092, 2111, 2161, 2332, 2480, 2641, 3033, 4101, 4212, 4635, 4907, 4935, 4936, 4937, 4940, 5029, 5110, 5554, 5627, 5955, 6035, 6298, 7287, 7659, 7852, 8399, 8513, 8549, 10395, 11043, 12297, 12461, 12602, 12608, 13024, 13402, 13509, 13623, 13733, 13936, 13959, 14331, 14947, 15349, 15369, 17144, 17766, 17785, 18059, 18689, 18737

--Religious and ecclesiastical institutions--Periodicals 854, 1750

--Religious life and customs 5863, 5864, 6652, 7309, 7498, 13316

--Social conditions 17, 34, 47, 99, 102, 174, 212, 238, 263, 346, 353, 367, 384, 391, 405, 409, 444, 456, 457, 504, 605, 608, 626, 638, 675, 823, 865, 936, 937, 952, 984, 1006, 1013, 1040, 1084, 1117, 1171, 1275, 1467, 1471, 1525, 1609, 1633, 1647, 1667, 1771, 1845, 1893, 1996, 2058, 2291, 2293, 2396, 2566, 2780, 2914, 2948, 2988, 3046, 3408, 4117, 4166, 4242, 4403, 4583, 4594, 4618, 4638, 5035, 5450, 5543, 5599, 5602, 6057, 6065, 6171, 6207, 6379, 6810, 6894, 7151, 7158, 7255, 7677, 7724, 7948, 7953, 8481, 9422, 9474, 9619, 9686, 9700, 9958, 10055, 10101, 10124, 10170, 10319, 10438, 10597, 10964, 11329, 11400, 12692, 13784, 13988, 14127, 14957, 15016, 15944, 16191, 16413, 16613, 16635, 16927, 17265, 17269, 17383, 17602, 17789, 17821, 17847, 17857, 17974, 18140, 18646, 18662, 18833, 18876, 18958, 19096, 19249

--Social conditions--Fiction 282, 932, 1773, 3992, 4406, 8410

--Social conditions--History 682, 1274, 6759, 8499, 8556, 8696, 9936, 10495, 11904, 11935, 12161, 13568, 14287, 14638, 15859, 18737

--Social life and customs 609, 3903

New York (NY)--Bronx >> See: Bronx (New York, NY)

New York (NY)--Brooklyn >> See: Brooklyn (New York, NY)

New York (NY)--Five Points

Mission >> See further: Five Points Mission; Church of all Nations
New York (NY)--Harlem >> See: Harlem (New York, NY)
New York (NY)--Manhattan >> See: Manhattan (New York, NY)
New York (NY)--Queens >> See: Queens (New York, NY)
New York (NY)--Staten Island >> See: Staten Island (New York, NY)
New York Association for Improving the Condition of the Poor 2592
--History 682, 7634, 12297
New York Association for the Improvement of the Condition of the Poor
--History 7764
New York Bible and Common Prayer Book Society 11, 51
New York Bible Society 12, 5677, 9424
New York Children's Aid Society
--History 9127
New York City Ladies Home Missionary Society of the Methodist Episcopal Church 301
New York City Mission 854, 925
--History 596, 8513
New York City Mission and Tract Society 405
New York City Mission Society 2988, 3153, 3541, 4619, 5604, 6618, 8359
New York City Tract Society 19, 161
New York Evangelical Missionary Society of Young Men 44
New York Magdalen Society 480
New York Mission Society 6065
New York Missionary Society 63
New York Protestant Episcopal City Mission Society 104, 126
New York Protestant Episcopal Mission Society 1866, 5042
New York Religious Tract Society 19
New York Society for the Prevention of Pauperism
--History 12183
New York Sunday School Union Society 45
New York Theological Seminary 9563, 9900, 12788, 13079, 14474, 16519, 16777, 18643
--History 18428, 19175
New Zealand
--Social conditions 13575, 13576
Newark (Delaware)
--Religious and ecclesiastical institutions 16981
--Social conditions 11239
Newark (New Jersey)
--Ethnic relations--History 14795
--Religious and ecclesiastical institutions 466, 698, 1236, 2030, 3391, 5358, 8478, 8479, 9337, 16476, 18438, 18786
--Religious and ecclesiastical institutions--History 4932, 4933, 4934, 5026, 5027, 5028, 6098, 7809, 8762
--Social conditions 2440, 5358, 8785, 17862, 18933
Newark (Ohio)
--Religious and ecclesiastical institutions 5405
Newcastle-upon-Tyne (England)
--Social conditions 12447
Newport (Rhode Island)
--Ethnic relations--History 13143
--Religious and ecclesiastical institutions--History 13412, 13607
Newport and Gwent Industrial Mission 13655

Newspapers and periodicals >> See further: Religious newspapers and periodicals; African American newspapers and periodicals
Newspapers and periodicals 955, 1990, 3226, 4705, 5700
--Australia--History 11039
--England--History 12667
--History 14638
Newton (Massachusetts)
--Religious and ecclesiastical institutions 1671, 10026, 11281
Niagara Falls (New York)
--Religious and ecclesiastical institutions 9037
Nigeria
--Church history 9491
--Religious and ecclesiastical institutions 9546
--Social conditions 12996
Night ministries 6395, 9058, 9911, 10308, 10324, 10358, 10417, 10465, 10466, 10475, 11038, 11065, 11136, 11369, 11396, 11770, 14283, 14571, 14841, 15514, 17491, 17530, 19349
--England 9672
--History 3822
--India 14488
--Nigeria 13002
Nineveh (metaphor) 11758
Nome (Alaska)
--Social conditions 15247
Non-institutional churches >> See: Underground churches; House churches; Para church; Sects; Cults
Nonconformity
--England 1309, 7339, 16155
--England--History 1836, 12715, 16391
Nonviolence 5037, 7347, 8791, 11294, 11782, 13453, 14841, 15181, 16568, 16791
--History 11272
Norfolk (Virginia)
--Religious and ecclesiastical institutions--History 5979
Normal (Illinois)
--Religious and ecclesiastical institutions 17763
North Side Co-operative Ministry (Chicago, Illinois) 11743
Northern Baptist Convention 2437, 3788
Northern Baptist Convention, Social Service Commission 2383, 2433, 2457, 2476
Northern Rhodesia
--Social conditions 6918
Norwalk (Connecticut)
--Religious and ecclesiastical institutions 15326
Norway
--Social conditions 11802
Norwich (Connecticut)
--Religious and ecclesiastical institutions--History 13551
--Social conditions 14790
Nuclear energy >> See: Atomic energy
Nuns >> See further: Women in Church work
Nuns 9733, 9765, 11179, 16696, 17485, 19060
--Biography 17376, 19187
--Brazil 19189
--History 13893, 14770, 19066
--India 15377, 15431, 15465, 15883, 16411, 16425, 16590, 17584, 18508
Nurses and nursing >> See further: Medical care; Community health services
Nurses and nursing 2072, 2109, 13281, 16195, 17395, 19176
--England 362

Oak Park (Illinois)
--Social conditions 13343
Oakland (California)
--Religious and ecclesiastical institutions 5439, 7211, 9468, 9489, 16023, 16495, 17153, 17274, 18043
--Social conditions 10060, 14386
Occultism >> See further: Witchcraft
Occultism 5529, 6486, 6992, 7756, 11625, 13472, 13615, 13686, 13849, 14100, 14179, 14464, 14834
Occupational mobility 5327, 6746, 7771, 9253, 10872, 12889, 13601, 13848, 13986, 14700
--History 12073, 13058, 14437, 14864
--India 14155
Occupational safety 15032
Office of Economic Opportunity >> See: War on Poverty; United States Government--Office of Economic Opportunity
Okinawa (Japan)
--Social conditions 5871
Oklahoma City (Oklahoma)
--Religious and ecclesiastical institutions 5102, 5291, 5407, 16145
--Religious and ecclesiastical institutions--History 14211
--Social conditions 16070
Old German Baptist Brethren 14410
Olive Branch Mission (Chicago, Illinois) 485, 14888
Omaha (Nebraska)
--Religious and ecclesiastical institutions 5407, 7889, 10517, 10571, 10626, 14609
--Religious and ecclesiastical institutions--History 6240, 14719
--Social conditions 8020, 16364
Ontario (California)
--Social conditions 16227
Open and closed shop 3353, 4561, 7280
Open and Institutional Church League >> See further: Institutional churches
Open and Institutional Church League 1002
--Periodicals 1568
Open churches >> See: Institutional churches
Open Door Community (Atlanta, Georgia) 18637
Orange County (California)
--Social conditions 16070
Orlando (Florida)
--Religious and ecclesiastical institutions 5900, 11382
Orphans and orphanages 8, 53, 61, 345, 346, 504, 605, 807, 1275, 2064, 2201, 3680, 9117
--Canada--History 13993, 14300
--England 999, 1154, 15648
--Fiction 158
--History 747, 1233, 1274, 1769, 5035, 9127, 12299
--Italy--History 18283
--Korea 9324
--Philippines 18922
Orthodox Eastern Church
--Case studies 15657
--Liturgy 18035
Orthodox Eastern Church (Greece) 15657
Orthodox Eastern churches 2910, 4878, 11119, 13729
--Case studies 2884, 5070, 5432, 5433, 6033, 7315, 8649, 10062, 13178, 14846, 17829
--Case studies--Bibliographies 4938

--History 2250, 3881, 5382
--Pastoral theology 13100
--Periodicals 600
--Theology 16788
Orthodox Eastern churches (Australia) 10679
Orthodox Judaism >> See further: Jews; Judaism
Orthodox Judaism 11343, 13563, 17519, 19061
--History 18209
Osaka (Japan)
--Religious and ecclesiastical institutions 12216
Oswego (New York)
--Religious and ecclesiastical institutions 5976
--Social conditions 939
Overchurching >> See: Church development, overchurching
Oxford Conference (1937) 4657
Oxford Movement 4362
--History 4322, 15844, 16579
Pacific basin economic area 15237
Pacific Garden Mission (Chicago, Illinois)
--History 2778, 3822, 5096, 8358, 9721, 18012
Pacific Lutheran Theological School 6976
Paducah (Kentucky)
--Religious and ecclesiastical institutions 6199, 6351, 6834
Pakistan
--Social conditions 12904
Palo Alto (California)
--Religious and ecclesiastical institutions 8337
Palomeras (Spain)
--Religious and ecclesiastical institutions 10144
Papua (New Guinea)
--Economic conditions 15052, 15073
--Religious and ecclesiastical institutions 11282, 13579, 13695, 13712, 17382
--Social conditions 13663, 14823, 15008, 15947, 17141, 17335
Parachurch >> See further: Christian communities
Parachurch 6677, 12372, 12390, 13411, 15920, 16782, 17450, 18325
--England 15407
--Europe 12123
--Great Britain 13395, 14079, 15337
--Scotland 15029, 18166
Parades and processions 6111, 7956, 8627, 19210
Parent and child 999, 3819, 6584, 8522, 8873, 11807, 12128, 13128, 14952, 16586, 17241, 18080, 18561, 18957, 19004
Paris
--Religion 19236
Paris (France)
--History 13604
--Religion 111, 8102, 11014, 17109
--Religion--History 12081
--Religious and ecclesiastical institutions 702, 819, 1062, 1481, 1484, 1809, 5494, 6147, 6946, 13181, 15778
--Religious and ecclesiastical institutions--Fiction 4854
--Religious and ecclesiastical institutions--History 7069, 15699
--Social conditions 478, 585, 6780, 11413, 15778, 16522
Parish of Trinity Church (New York, NY) 61, 558, 980, 1600, 2261, 2278, 2290, 2349, 2376, 2395, 2400, 2494, 2667, 2726, 3660, 3730, 6835, 7354, 17341, 19002
--History 223, 1801, 5554

Park Forest (Illinois)
--Religious and ecclesiastical institutions 6311
Parkersburg (West Virginia)
--Religious and ecclesiastical institutions 5407, 6492
--Social conditions 6646
Parks and playgrounds 367, 486, 1084, 1867, 2124, 2180, 2953, 8831
Parkway Program (Philadelphia, Pennsylvania) 12440
Parochial schools 488, 1075, 1282, 1974, 2202, 2337, 3991, 4418, 5805, 9034, 11179, 11558, 12285, 12562, 12692, 13600, 13945, 14151, 14314, 14719, 15137, 15346, 15681, 17638, 17869
--England 9002
--History 1827, 4592, 13389, 14187, 14315, 14412, 14705, 14717, 14869, 15234, 17093, 17548, 18010, 18106, 18723
Partners for Sacred Places (Philadelphia, Pennsylvania) 19333
Pasadena (California)
--Social conditions 17145
Pastoral care >> See further: Pastoral theology
Pastoral care 5212, 5707, 6251, 6349, 6662, 6980, 7281, 7338, 8284, 9335, 9478, 9480, 9908, 10228, 10241, 10250, 10593, 11127, 11200, 11201, 11266, 11690, 11715, 11736, 11916, 12005, 12542, 12815, 12903, 12944, 13003, 13106, 13311, 13517, 13962, 14063, 14094, 14271, 14344, 14607, 14608, 14645, 14697, 14817, 15435, 15446, 15945, 16129, 16145, 16250, 16529, 16547, 16569, 16909, 16985, 17415, 17448, 17619, 18233, 18323, 18473, 18777, 19272
--Africa 16797, 19240
--England 8154, 15113
--Europe 2359
--Germany 8207
--Great Britain 17167
--History 10269, 16616
--Latin America 7596
Pastoral counseling 4664, 5198, 6251, 6832, 8824, 9431, 10241, 10961, 11585, 12205, 12837, 13140, 14608, 14837, 15643, 15897, 15981, 16129, 16165, 16195, 16397, 16427, 16460, 16625, 16680, 17456, 18116, 18535, 18695, 19040, 19204
--Congresses 10501
--England 12446, 16923
--Great Britain 18036
--History 10269
--New Guinea 17382
Pastoral theology >> See further: Catholic Church--Pastoral Theology
Pastoral theology 6610, 8811, 10230, 10758, 12903, 13188, 13905, 17790, 18103
--Austria 6279, 7188
--Brazil 16525
--Case studies 12971
--Congresses 16929
--England 993, 3133, 17583, 18492
--Europe 2359, 7769
--France 5836, 6450, 7989, 8719
--Germany 7252, 7773, 7927, 8977, 9497, 10210, 14623, 15727
--Latin America 14233, 15773, 16095
--Switzerland 7160
--Taiwan 16502
Paterson (New Jersey)
--Religious and ecclesiastical

institutions 7584, 11838, 11911
--Social conditions 6116
Pathfinding Service (New York, NY) 5604
Paul, the Apostle, Saint 19083
Paulist Fathers 354, 10023
--History 7407
Peabody (Massachusetts)
--Religious and ecclesiastical institutions 8649
Peace 2117, 7183, 10663, 11631, 12326, 12958, 15356, 16020, 16136, 16365, 17124, 17318, 17945 , 19322
--Bibliographies 17523
--India 16041
--Religious aspects 4097, 6341, 11565, 13049, 13662, 14860, 15046, 15592, 15636, 15745, 15856, 15875, 16005, 16015, 16547, 16788, 16828, 16967, 17117, 18120, 18456, 18641, 18984
--Societies 11803, 15272, 16228
Peace (civic) 222, 227, 569, 1642, 12274, 12622, 13049, 14090, 15745, 15875, 16828, 18548
Peace (civil) 14766
Peace (industrial) 426, 644, 790, 1113, 2253, 2399, 2744, 2767, 2842, 2911, 3080, 3301, 3314, 3326, 3594, 3772, 4615, 5570, 5613, 5706, 5818, 6534, 8528, 15265, 16872, 18599
Peace movement >> See: Peace--Societies
Peking (China)
--Religion--History 14752
Pennsylvania
--Social conditions 18977
Pensacola (Florida)
--Religious and ecclesiastical institutions 8002, 8054, 13512
Pentecostal churches 4815, 7953, 9686, 11245, 12931, 13088, 13730, 14343, 16361, 17059
--Case studies 8061, 9593, 13406, 15527, 17730, 19144
--History 10285, 12338, 12631, 17866
--Periodicals 665
Pentecostal churches (Brazil) 16347, 19213
Pentecostal churches (Chile) 11398
Pentecostal churches (Colombia) 13865, 17996
Pentecostal churches (England) 9336, 12507, 15228, 19346
Pentecostal churches (Great Britain) 12186
Pentecostal churches (Guatemala) 11036
Pentecostal churches (Latin America) 10652, 15620, 15948
Pentecostal churches (Malaysia) 15527
Pentecostal churches (South Africa) 13659
Pentecostal churches (Sweden) 18479
Pentecostal churches (Venezuela) 19044
People of God (metaphor) 9336, 9831, 10073, 11473, 15053, 16132, 16206, 16842, 17056
People's Advocacy Service (Schenectady, New York) 15399
People's Christian Coalition 12325
People's Institute in New York City
--History 1988
People's Institute of Applied Religion (Detroit, Michigan) 4972
Peoria (Illinois)
--Religious and ecclesiastical

institutions 5719, 15368
Periodicals >> See: Religious newspapers and periodicals
Peru
--Church history 17151
--Social conditions 17359
Petersburg (Virginia)
--Religious and ecclesiastical institutions 4625
Pew Charitable Trusts (Philadelphia) 18372, 18862
Pew rental 305, 550, 1161, 1325, 1419, 1569, 2038, 2533, 2806
--England--History 10958, 11295
--History 197, 623, 10755, 16662, 18057
--Periodicals 1568
Phelps Settlement (New York, NY) 1514
Phenix City (Alabama)
--Social conditions 6847
Philadelphia (Pennsylvania)
--Ethnic relations 6574, 8128, 14357, 14562
--Ethnic relations--History 9815, 12814, 12872, 13037, 13210, 13724, 14447
--Fiction 4364
--History 1319, 2036, 7492, 8727, 11126, 13052, 13152, 13772
--Race relations 7029, 9743, 11000, 14248, 14507
--Religion 357, 4416, 11625, 13812
--Religious and ecclesiastical institutions 87, 116, 172, 183, 356, 748, 1003, 1046, 1178, 1195, 1352, 1442, 1447, 1490, 1492, 1513, 1518, 1599, 1686, 1724, 1881, 1915, 1979, 2584, 2620, 2670, 2680, 2714, 2805, 2867, 3022, 3421, 4096, 4127, 5079, 5131, 5215, 5269, 6674, 7173, 7714, 7791, 7898, 8601, 8779, 8914, 9337, 9418, 9467, 9562, 9614, 9979, 10048, 10274, 10276, 10407, 10413, 11567, 11623, 11860, 12054, 12245, 12490, 12543, 12879, 12952, 13654, 14197, 14339, 14548, 14975, 15051, 15272, 16421, 16955, 17158, 17279, 17425, 17662, 18372, 18436, 18868, 19097
--Religious and ecclesiastical institutions--History 893, 1385, 1398, 1449, 2331, 2918, 2924, 3691, 4448, 5246, 5287, 5288, 5328, 5474, 5684, 6035, 6777, 8149, 10987, 11635, 13547, 13548, 13725, 13814, 14933, 15568, 16812, 16862, 17131, 17817, 18716
--Religious life and customs--History 14124
--Social conditions 183, 617, 1202, 1228, 1399, 1469, 1686, 2035, 2895, 5659, 6221, 9743, 11000, 12440, 12598, 13526, 14481, 14507, 15254, 15323, 15988, 17080, 17607, 17999, 18550, 18937
--Social conditions--History 5922, 7244, 10040, 11661, 11714, 11730, 13258, 13337, 13527, 16159, 17326, 17327, 18836
--Social life and customs 4797
Philadelphia Baptist Association
--History 5328
Philadelphia Sunday and Adult School Union 52
Philanthropy >> See: Charity; Social Service; Christian giving; Wealth
Philippines
--Church history 17721
--Economic conditions 11230, 12264, 13598
--Religion 13739
--Religious and ecclesiastical

institutions 5375, 6202, 6848, 7065, 7463, 7954, 7955, 8774, 9531, 10041, 11968, 12679, 13111, 16150, 18311, 18398, 18822, 18895
--Social conditions 3701, 11486, 11487, 11928, 12519, 12634, 13498, 13811, 13916, 14007, 14733, 15172, 16965, 17708, 17721, 18150, 18922
Philosophy 220, 350, 901, 1860, 2149, 4482, 4985, 5002, 5552, 5731, 5779, 6046, 7402, 7481, 7489, 8263, 9215, 10128, 10392, 10615, 10814, 12051, 12768, 13334, 13849, 15802, 15888, 17408, 17781, 19058
Philosophy, modern 12915, 13300
Phoenix (Arizona)
--Religious and ecclesiastical institutions 5407, 6521, 17035
Photography 1442, 12383, 12539, 13225, 16975, 17754, 18883, 19014, 19217
Piety >> See further: Folk religion
Piety 1675, 2032, 2612, 2703, 2812, 3423, 6654, 7396, 7542, 8116, 8208, 11483, 12481, 12823, 13962, 15507
--History 14820, 15887, 15977, 17392
Pitman Grove (New Jersey)
--History 13703
Pittsburgh (Pennsylvania)
--Ethnic Relations--History 16123
--Religious and ecclesiastical institutions 70, 641, 808, 3014, 4958, 5115, 5217, 5322, 5407, 5672, 5716, 6261, 7085, 7326, 7710, 7800, 8472, 8473, 8850, 9056, 9155, 9885, 9951, 10282, 10340, 10596, 10792, 13088, 13406, 15143, 16383, 18300, 18703, 18705
--Religious and ecclesiastical institutions--History 5980, 7445, 12333, 13791, 16805
--Social conditions 2250, 2864, 3037, 3120, 4213, 5679, 8772, 9507, 9858, 14829, 16383, 17372, 17659, 17792, 18366
--Social conditions--History 13552, 18015, 18070, 18788
--Social life and customs 9374
Pittsburgh Rationalist Society 2999
Planning >> See: Church planning; City planning
Plant closings 14602, 14641, 14731, 14782, 14882, 14893, 15099, 15324, 15600, 15718, 15824, 15981, 16143, 16219, 16227, 16470, 16724, 17306, 17387, 17437, 17608, 17792, 17915, 18120, 18807, 18840, 19043, 19108, 19146, 19325, 19329
--Bibliographies 14786, 15598
--Germany 15902
--Periodicals 18831
Plunge, urban >> See further: Urban Training Center for Christian Mission (Chicago, Illinois)
Plunge, urban 8934, 9607, 9679, 12371, 12847, 15582, 18063
--History 18385
Pluralism >> See further: Assimilation; Americanization; Religious pluralism; Xenophobia; Ethnicity; Melting pot
Pluralism 1860, 4482, 5117, 7924, 9081, 9242, 16608, 16695
--Cultural 4715, 6080, 6081, 6359, 6469, 6544, 6684, 8361, 9410, 9411, 9474, 10364, 13060, 13519, 13755, 13763,

14467, 14899, 15088, 15092, 15250, 15288, 15497, 15641, 15679, 15776, 15850, 16094, 16124, 16281, 16303, 16421, 16449,16571, 16651, 16918, 17298, 17461, 17661, 17680, 17855, 17951, 18352, 18435, 18886, 19063, 19114, 19164
Pluralism (cont.)
--Cultural--England 18658
--Cultural--History 14211, 18579
--Cultural--India 16270
--Developing countries 16449
--England 14389
--Ethnic 767, 2176, 5644, 5941, 6149, 9071, 11309, 11310, 11386, 11638, 11654, 12172, 12402, 12619, 12621, 12622, 12937, 12987, 12992, 13060, 13214, 15210, 15925, 18633, 19287
--France 18317
--Germany 7496
--History 13115
--Political 13549, 14673
--Racial 6671, 6715, 9230, 9643, 9810, 13711, 13827, 16044, 16582, 18352
--Racial--England 16992
Pluralism, religious >> See: Religious pluralism
Poetry >> See further: Religious poetry; Hymns
Poetry 2068, 4755, 5599, 5984, 6116, 8380, 8979, 9087, 9474, 12765, 15206, 16687, 17604, 19118, 19273, 19279, 19327
--Africa 13118, 17100
--England 3, 3402, 4830
--France 111, 8102
--History 8611, 9163, 14001, 16851, 19214
Poland
--Bibliographies 6068
--Religion 3860, 4418, 5486, 12275, 12337, 12550, 13670, 13856, 14009, 17907
--Religious and ecclesiastical institutions 2394, 3904, 8963, 12896, 16638, 17429, 17430
--Religious life and customs 12275
--Social conditions 15910
Police 1263, 1264, 1302, 2473, 2566, 2595, 2744, 4117, 4332, 5257, 5520, 6343, 6680, 8736, 8970, 8971, 9328, 10060, 10222, 10298, 10332, 10813, 11283, 11301, 11358, 11498, 11539, 11593, 11612, 11639, 12043, 12150, 12365, 12470, 12914, 13360, 13627, 14248, 14609, 15991, 16683, 17424
--Bibliographies 9748
--England 3846, 9245, 10243, 12754, 16104
--Great Britain 12001, 12702, 17526
--History 4515, 8806
--Philippines 13498, 13811
--South Africa 13828
Police Gazette (New York, NY) 4117
Polish American Catholics
--History 13610, 14234, 14718, 15970, 16306, 16394, 16946
Polish American churches
--History 15320
Polish American clergy 14148
--History 13791, 16946
Polish American families
--History 15320
Polish American Presbyterians
--History 16108
Polish Americans
--History 13555, 14148, 15858, 18065
--Identity--History 18065
--Missions to--History 16108

Polish Americans (cont.)
--Religion 4418, 14357
--Religion--History 12268, 13099
--Social conditions 3943, 13750, 14099, 16394, 17659
--Social conditions--History 12872, 14132, 14527, 15965
--Social life 3860
--Social life and customs--History 16123
Polish National Catholic Church
--History 6264
Politics
--Great Britain 19019
Politics and Christianity >> See further: Clergy--Political Activity; Priests--Political Activity
Politics and Christianity 1287, 1369, 2325, 3112, 4677, 6754, 6846, 6884, 8765, 8823, 9190, 10257, 10939, 11640, 12108, 12198, 12481, 13156, 13228, 13250, 13549, 13817, 14126, 14372, 14599, 14673, 15053, 15720, 15822, 16865, 17166, 17286, 17485, 18463, 19148, 19228
--Canada 3137
--Canada--History 14750, 15779
--England 5208
--Great Britain 15337
--History 1836, 13494
--Ireland--History 17895
--Italy 13776
--Italy--History 12797
--Spain 4893
Politics and religion 179, 200, 296, 318, 1389, 1682, 1732, 1777, 3666, 4606, 4785, 5643, 5737, 5752, 6071, 6457, 7791, 7925, 8076, 8691, 8968, 9043, 10039, 10135, 11545, 11701, 11894, 12057, 12214, 12344, 12737, 12829, 12868, 12991, 13213, 13796, 13979, 14427, 14736, 15356, 15893, 16363, 16773, 16976, 17076, 17521, 17637, 17918, 18096, 18368, 19021, 19060
--Asia 10105
--Australia 18189
--Case studies 18724
--Chile 15173
--Congresses 3654, 13430
--Developing countries 12323
--Europe--History 4427
--Finland--History 9522, 10430
--France 8115, 11582
--Germany 6163
--Germany--History 4861, 15741
--Great Britain 15083, 18389
--History 7220, 13606, 14487, 15249, 15344, 15878
--Hong Kong 16416
--Ireland 14238, 17654
--Islamic 12996, 14631, 17914
--Japan 17340
--Latin America 13492, 13820
--Malaysia 18907
--South Africa 17654
--Spain 15535
Politics, city >> See: Municipal government; Cities and towns--Reform
Polity >> See: Church planning; Church management
Pollution 11351, 11569, 12321, 12456, 12478, 18951
--Africa 19158
Pontiac (Michigan)
--Religious and ecclesiastical institutions 5398, 13672
Poona (India)
--Religious and ecclesiastical institutions 12785
Poor >> See further: Church work with the poor; Poverty
Poor 224, 522, 545, 1108, 1223, 1511, 10220, 10298, 10799,

11415, 12731, 13363, 14391, 14617, 14989, 15202, 16510, 17712, 17850, 18381, 18685
--Biography 1959
Poor and the church >> See: Church and the poor; Church work with the poor
Poor People's Campaign 17668
Popular culture 7317, 12445, 13631, 18509, 18930
--Brazil 15367, 15532, 19208, 19211
--England 13069
--France 15881
--Great Britain 13131
--History 15694, 18927
--Italy--History 18032
--Netherlands 15287
--Poland--History 13670, 14009
--Switzerland 15880
Population density 4, 62, 105, 1206, 4049, 5265, 6931, 7827, 8178, 8194, 8925, 9730, 12321, 14212
--Asia 11748
Populism 15365, 16844, 17648, 17649
Port Harcourt (Nigeria)
--Religious and ecclesiastical institutions 9546
Port of Spain (Trinidad and Tobago)
--Ethnic relations 8897
Portland (Maine)
--Religious and ecclesiastical institutions 4324, 5078
Portland (Oregon)
--Religious and ecclesiastical institutions 5339, 5363, 5366, 6423, 6623, 7933, 9275, 10736, 11765, 12441, 14553, 15129, 17531
--Religious and ecclesiastical institutions--History 9582
--Religious life and customs 13148
--Social conditions 14453
Porto Alegre (Brazil)
--Religion 19208, 19211, 19213
Portsea (England)
--Religious and ecclesiastical institutions 2873
Portsmouth (England)
--Religious and ecclesiastical institutions 1914
--Social conditions 1844
Portsmouth (Ohio)
--Social conditions 6750
Post Christian >> See: Secularization
Post industrial >> See: Church and industry; Industrialization (especially works published after 1980)
Post modern >> See: Modernity
Poughkeepsie (New York)
--Social conditions 14656
Poverty
--Africa 16255, 19158
--Argentina 11454
--Asia 17436
--Biblical teaching 520, 969, 1212, 2436, 2916, 8985, 9438, 13489, 14421, 14422, 14529, 14703, 15642, 15798, 15834, 15980, 16730, 16850, 17486, 17756, 18928
--Brazil 8994, 10316, 14555
--Canada 17370, 19161
--Causes and persistence 4, 156, 204, 265, 545, 611, 700, 750, 881, 916, 973, 1834, 1930, 2833, 3336, 4293, 9173, 9252, 9776, 10253, 10511, 10685, 11469, 11566, 11738, 11875, 12304, 12370, 12673, 12729, 13119, 14173, 14324, 14683, 15135, 15353, 15499, 15895, 16071, 16960, 17105, 17586
--Congresses 6676, 6748, 8364,

9246
Poverty (cont.)
--Descriptions 62, 214, 257, 384, 582, 608, 620, 675, 704, 835, 845, 986, 1013, 1170, 1171, 1184, 1216, 1223, 1277, 1437, 1511, 1667, 1706, 1711, 1770, 1820, 1845, 2418, 2557, 2654, 2697, 3067, 3478, 4018, 4274, 4777, 5231, 5393, 6310, 6660, 7675, 7862, 7956, 8108, 8455, 8616, 8631, 8785, 8799, 8877, 8941, 8980, 9135, 9162, 9259, 9406, 9684, 9723, 9834, 9858, 9954, 10029, 10101, 10123, 10298, 10485, 10719, 10881, 11044, 11088, 11121, 11194, 11232, 11305, 11415, 11740, 12153, 12157, 12383, 12432, 12639, 12731, 12751, 12771, 12831, 13128, 13597, 13867, 14104, 14208, 14268, 14289, 14391, 14632, 14883, 14916, 14953, 14989, 15049, 15202, 15209, 15244, 15261, 15395, 15546, 15567, 15658, 15790, 15823, 15891, 16079, 16177, 16352, 16445, 16653, 16877, 16927, 16931, 16948, 17036, 17060, 17189, 17278, 17332, 17675, 18120, 18142, 18159, 18282, 18305, 18381, 18414, 18442, 18532, 18561, 18653, 18924, 18994, 19027, 19109, 19217, 19267
--Descriptions--Africa 19240
--Descriptions--Bibliographies 9747
--Developing countries 12867, 15171, 16405, 16706, 17389
--England 148, 286, 337, 362, 374, 521, 704, 712, 971, 993, 1034, 1320, 1345, 1356, 1914, 2296, 2557, 2833, 3007, 3177, 4132, 4140, 4463, 5393, 13614, 15529, 15548, 15913, 16268, 16488, 16546, 16688, 16741, 17281, 17356, 17585, 17586, 18329, 19052
--England--History 913, 1512, 4528
--England--London 553, 890, 1452
--Europe 18390, 18772, 19188
--Europe--History 234
--Fiction 377, 585, 669, 1210, 1308, 1496, 3496, 4138, 8326, 8756
--France 377, 5935, 6780
--Germany 1383
--Great Britain 1072, 1825, 1930, 2209, 13137, 14115, 14183, 14683, 14986, 15275, 15848, 16071, 17618, 17682, 18418
--Haiti 19030
--History 682, 6639, 7634, 7764, 8631, 9319, 10764, 12194, 12299, 13041, 13058, 16022, 18031
--Hong Kong 7099, 8799
--India 14318, 15377, 15431, 15465, 15883, 16396, 16411, 16425, 16590, 17584, 18152, 18238, 18508
--Ireland 12432, 12479, 15134, 15135
--Japan 8799
--Kenya 13023
--Latin America 9479, 11227, 12805, 13492, 13493, 13595, 15345, 17156
--Mexico 8220, 16307, 17246, 18834
--Pakistan 12904
--Philippines 14007, 17708
--Psychological aspects 9684, 11201, 11330, 12237, 12304, 13525, 13758, 14429, 14883, 15621, 17332, 18532
--Religious aspects 699, 824,

1082, 4532, 7621, 7707, 8103, 8525, 8593, 9259, 9358, 9454, 9663, 10686, 11201, 11579, 12086, 12217, 14301, 14317, 14854, 15618, 15846, 16301, 16492, 17413, 17486, 17725, 18180, 18236

Poverty (cont.)

--Religious aspects--Catholic 178, 620, 890, 6660, 6780, 9175, 9176, 9299, 9406, 9438, 10881, 12086, 13058, 14854, 14916, 15395, 15790, 15883, 16411, 16425, 16741, 16893, 17105, 17156, 17584, 18329

--Religious aspects--Church of England 1345, 1930, 2296, 4140, 5393, 16488, 16546, 16730, 17281, 17618, 17682, 18418, 19052

--Religious aspects--Congregational 1138

--Religious aspects--Episcopal 305, 608, 1082, 2261, 7707, 8593, 9663, 2290, 10049, 10827, 14268, 15195, 15202, 16476,16834

--Religious aspects--Evangelical Protestant 16255, 16492

--Religious aspects--History 15891

--Religious aspects--Judaism 9471, 12731, 13363

--Religious aspects--Lutheran 1277, 1588, 8985, 9348, 9413, 9507, 10101, 10462, 10648, 12157, 15980, 16407, 16927, 17756, 17811, 18236

--Religious aspects--Methodist 1711, 2209, 2916, 3101, 9723, 9776, 9954, 10029, 10253, 11194, 12217, 12383, 13597, 14317, 14872, 15345, 17725, 18031, 18238

--Religious aspects--NCCCUSA 6676, 9454

--Religious aspects--Presbyterian 266, 545, 8428, 9259, 11201, 12639, 12673, 12729, 13846, 14529, 15199, 18685

--Religious aspects--Protestant 120, 346, 504, 1275, 10559, 10719

--Religious aspects--Southern Baptist 9811, 11232, 11469, 14703, 16922, 17389

--Religious aspects--United Church of Christ 7099, 7956, 8877, 9246, 11875, 12451, 14459, 15302, 16821, 18410

--Religious aspects--World Council of Churches 14413, 14517, 15239, 15705, 16706, 18772

--Remedies >> See further: Colonization of the poor

--Remedies, political and governmental >> See further: War on Poverty

--Remedies, political and governmental 9046, 9422, 9507, 10097, 10710, 10720, 10847, 11414, 11444, 11579, 11856, 12274, 12604, 12921, 13016, 13156, 13525, 13543, 14459, 14735, 14778, 14872, 15199, 16224, 17479, 18021, 18410

--Remedies, religious 204, 266, 362, 520, 545, 971, 1034, 1072, 1209, 1241, 1356, 1588, 1959, 2333, 2744, 2755, 2896, 3101, 8190, 8428, 9348, 9471, 9811, 9905, 10013, 10363, 10559, 10648, 10827, 12542, 13231, 13526, 14627, 15135, 16225, 16442, 16476, 16540, 16583, 16611, 16703, 16821, 16834, 16922, 17105, 17625, 17811, 18080, 18141, 18214, 18442

Poverty (cont.)
--Remedies, religious--History 12183, 16893
--Remedies, social 14, 346, 504, 575, 605, 1055, 1138, 1202, 1274, 1275, 1320, 1511, 1771, 1834, 2165, 9544, 9795, 10060, 10342, 10530, 10935, 11775, 12030, 12045, 12288, 12451, 13226, 14306, 14391, 15195, 17342, 18142, 18685
--Remedies, social--Bibliographies 16431
--Scotland 120, 521, 18127, 18166
--South Africa 5690
--Turkey 8799
Power 1819, 4009, 5539, 6331, 6670, 6871, 7588, 8639, 8703, 8829, 8968, 9033, 9401, 10220, 10303, 10547, 11242, 11294, 11358, 11527, 11575, 11965, 12295, 12307, 12957, 13193, 13960, 14126, 14254, 15474, 15618, 16405, 17143, 18145, 18661, 18776, 19080
Power (Christian theology) 9832, 14031, 15023, 19144
Power (philosophy) 9831, 9975, 12045, 12859, 16516
Power (social science) 10672, 11062, 11092, 11131, 11168, 11842
--England 17696
--Korea 13084
Prague (Czechoslovakia)
--Religious and ecclesiastical institutions 19107
--Social life and customs 19253
Prayer 333, 355, 515, 2240, 2443, 2947, 4387, 4659, 5841, 6753, 6906, 8435, 9157, 9742, 10541, 10731, 13901, 13960, 14002, 14726, 14732, 14990, 15050, 15675, 16622, 17004, 17089, 17594, 18022, 18114, 18783, 19174, 19327
Prayer meetings 355, 515
Preaching >> See further: Sermons; Evangelistic sermons; African American preaching; Cities and towns--Sermons; Church and labor--Sermons; Charity--Sermons; Jewish sermons
Preaching 64, 322, 399, 576, 2066, 2578, 3401, 3611, 4346, 4687, 4741, 4749, 4873, 6610, 9839, 10724, 10942, 14274, 14577, 14824, 15326, 15429, 16024, 16622, 16699, 17348
--England 1126, 3542
--Fiction 1017
--Germany 7426
--Scotland--History 14611
Preaching, African American >> See: African American preaching
Prejudices 5472, 5644, 5850, 6391, 6411, 7679, 8226, 8648, 9018, 9031, 9731, 11298, 11550, 11709, 12328, 12823, 13212, 13550, 18173
--Bibliographies 9313
--France 18317
--Japan 5489
Presbyterian Board of Christian Education, Department of Social Education and Action 5410
Presbyterian Board of Publication 321, 396, 642, 868
Presbyterian Church (Canada) 2724, 2747, 2748
Presbyterian Church in the US 2546, 5448, 5989, 10258, 10259
--Case studies 5342, 6949, 10540, 10601, 10666, 11411, 11465, 11601, 13224, 15251, 16604
--Congresses 14393

--History 14400
--Periodicals 10047
--Pronouncements, policies 10622, 11229, 15985, 16053
Presbyterian Church in the US, Board of Church Extension 6276, 6452, 7946, 7966, 9226, 9611
Presbyterian Church in the US, Board of National Ministries 10047, 11411
Presbyterian Church in the US, Home Missions Board 1971
Presbyterian Church in the USA
--Case studies 1046, 2332, 2439, 2533, 2661, 3951, 5063, 5240, 6267, 7146, 7211, 12873
--Case studies--Bibliographies 4928, 4935, 5027
--Pronouncements, policies 439, 3155, 4558, 4660, 6954, 17805
Presbyterian Church in the USA, Board of Christian Education 2257, 3266, 4660, 4774, 4994, 5178, 5185, 5311, 5533, 5721, 6152, 6549
Presbyterian Church in the USA, Board of Home Missions 1779, 2439, 2440, 2458, 2538, 2539, 2644, 2664, 3010, 3155, 3267, 3304, 3319, 3359, 3369
--History 1868, 3161
Presbyterian Church in the USA, Board of National Missions 3546, 3720, 3721, 3738, 3920, 4083, 4096, 4425, 4507, 4557, 4567, 4779, 4780, 5193, 5242, 5243, 5290, 5291, 5338, 5339, 5388, 5406, 5407, 5414, 5442, 5506, 5507, 5508, 5509, 5510, 5511, 5513, 5595, 5716, 5717, 5718, 5719, 5814, 5816, 5964, 5965, 6078, 6093, 6219, 6495, 6503, 6550, 6551, 6586, 6756, 6793
--Bibliographies 5289
Presbyterian Church in the USA, Woman's Board of Home Missions 803
Presbyterian churches
--Case studies 1513, 1635, 2175, 2452, 9535, 9847, 12390, 12444, 18022
--Mexico 11903
--Pastoral theology 11647
--Social teaching 16871, 18993
--Social teaching--History 15198
Presbyterian churches (Canada) 2763
Presbyterian churches (Taiwan) 18536
Presbyterian Institute of Industrial Relations (Chicago, Illinois) 5411, 6382, 6383, 6567
Presbyterian Institute of Industrial Relations (Chicago, Illinois)) 10267
Presbyterian Labor Temple 2441, 2549, 3794, 4272, 4966, 4973, 5251, 5290
--Archives 2419
--History 13110
Preston (England)
--Religious and ecclesiastical institutions 12235
Priest workers >> See further: Chaplains, industrial
Priest workers 5914, 5935, 6112, 6123, 6290, 6419, 7815, 7897, 7984, 8274, 8332, 8633, 9239, 10649, 11233, 12605, 12637, 12638, 13085, 14043, 14231, 14311, 14725, 14924, 15197, 18286
--Bibliographies 7984, 18365
--Biography 7408
--Canada 18023
--England 6082, 12579, 17990
--England--History 8130, 17752
--Europe 11070

Priest workers (cont.)
--Fiction 10383
--France 5799, 5846, 6223, 6328, 6603, 6609, 6653, 6811, 7532, 7633, 7676, 7740, 8077, 9271, 10976, 11913, 12820, 16760, 18286
--France--History 6947, 7071, 7757, 9610, 15712, 17573, 18896
--Germany 5404
--Great Britain 10558
--History 9994, 10177, 12219, 17620, 17752
--Italy 12775
--Italy--History 12412
--Philippines--History 17721
--Spain 10301
Priests, Anglican >> See: City clergy--Church of England
Priests, Catholic >> See: Catholic Church--Clergy; City clergy--Catholic
Priests--Political Activity >> See: Politics and Christianity; Clergy--Political activity
Priorities >> See: Mission of the church
Prison Fellowship International
--History 18235
Prisons and prisoners 60, 1733, 2112, 4173, 4532, 8791, 12565, 12765, 12772, 13455, 14242, 15185, 15266, 16600, 16908, 16966, 19235
--Brazil 12053
--Case studies 16234
--Germany 292
--History 8806
--Sweden 14965
--Women 13437, 13819, 14398, 15777, 16598
Profit 883, 3039, 3042, 3575, 3675, 4010, 4011, 4522, 5228, 5455, 8856, 13629, 14844, 16863
--England--History 10020
Programa de Renovacion y Investigacion Social para Adiestramiento en la Mision (San Juan, Puerto Rico) 11022
Progress 371, 611, 674, 795, 981, 1194, 1254, 1531, 1747, 1805, 1876, 1888, 2126, 2312, 2527, 2793, 2930, 3101, 3953, 4158, 4852, 5960, 6180, 9306, 9378, 9833
--History 2669, 4209, 6749, 7658, 8620, 18336
Progressive Baptist Church 15277
Progressivism 667, 878, 1531, 1696, 1995, 3324
--History 4209, 6749, 7635, 7658, 8499, 8620, 8677, 8918, 9093, 10288, 10965, 11269, 11936, 12179, 12727, 12783, 13938, 16033, 16075, 17144, 17595, 18506
Prohibition >> See further: Temperance
Prohibition 591, 1863, 2281, 2989, 3096, 3357, 3580, 3763, 3883, 3909, 3938, 4015
--History 3705, 3752, 5841, 5856, 6687, 8579, 8918, 9872, 16903
Project Equality 10534, 11975
Project Test-Pattern 11739, 12125, 12592, 12821, 13218, 13219
Property 156, 266, 595, 661, 762, 1069, 1219, 2450, 2842, 3274, 3275, 3315, 3553, 3597, 3636, 3668, 4080, 4397, 5188, 5577, 5594, 5726, 6194, 7128, 8198, 8320, 9663, 9978, 10602, 11290, 13854, 14304, 14517, 14762, 17788, 18288
--England 3281
--History 6964, 8095, 8974, 13227, 13877

Prostitution >> See further: Church work with prostitutes; Social work with prostitutes
Prostitution 78, 137, 183, 480, 511, 1874, 2378, 2473, 2494, 2556, 2562, 2564, 2589, 2780, 4388, 13740, 14565, 17081, 17269, 18099, 18858, 19327
--Asia 17436, 18938, 18944
--Canada 8653
--England 13799, 14152
--Fiction 19296
--Germany 7500
--Great Britain 2204
--History 340, 4349, 12282, 12299, 14032
--Japan 6725
--New Guinea 15008, 16043
--Periodicals 117
Protest >> See further: Conflict (sociology); Social conflict
Protest 647, 8831, 9833, 11094, 11169, 11308, 11440, 11870, 12669, 12986, 13731, 14279, 14705, 15573, 18369
--Asia 15761, 15942, 16912
--Canada 18809
--History 6319, 7835, 12124, 12455, 13536, 14056, 14391, 15667, 16122, 18279, 19214
--Latin America 17840
--Middle East 17051
--Scotland 18331
--South Africa 14688
Protestant churches >> See further: Church; (denominational names)
Protestant churches
--Case studies 1268, 3826, 3969, 5739, 6018, 10068, 10363, 10851, 11883, 13138, 14202, 15295, 15889, 16981, 18183, 18664, 18972
--Case studies--Bibliographies 11688
--Directories 5967
--Education 7882
--France--History 11115
--Germany 2406
--History 4697, 6891, 9731, 16438, 18878, 19356
--Pastoral theology 1560, 1701, 5707, 16171
--Periodicals 517
--Pronouncements, policies 4532, 6337, 6361, 9878, 12804, 15485, 18782
--Social teaching 2218, 2668, 2842, 3200, 3989, 4063, 4215, 4447, 4785, 5188, 5612, 6133, 6337, 6361, 6735, 7019, 7125, 7221, 7381, 12732, 16253
--Social teaching--History 6613, 6819, 8674, 8677, 11379, 12179, 13015, 15725
Protestant churches (Argentina) 12213
Protestant churches (Canada) 463, 5564
Protestant churches (Chile) 10419
Protestant churches (France) 482, 849, 1239, 1307, 1484, 6831, 7043, 7259, 7740, 11751, 12486, 13435, 17598
--History 14513
Protestant churches (Germany) 2368, 6569, 7996, 12079, 13142, 13499, 14677, 17816, 18055, 18195
--History 14533
Protestant churches (India) 13652
Protestant churches (Ireland) 14370
Protestant churches (Italy) 15361, 15389
Protestant churches (Japan) 9923
Protestant churches (Peru) 10419
Protestant churches (Philippines) 5375
Protestant churches (Switzerland)

7638
Protestant Council of the City of New York 5412, 5543, 5601, 5603, 5614, 5615, 5947, 5967, 6369, 6506, 6507, 6508, 6509, 6524, 6562, 6691, 6765, 6766, 6767, 6940, 6957, 6967, 6968, 7166, 7310, 7450, 7498, 7550, 7551, 7552, 7553, 7555, 7668, 7669, 7840, 7841, 7842, 7945, 7957, 8147, 8148, 8258, 8431, 8432, 8433, 8434, 8551, 9051, 9066, 9067, 9068, 9422, 9595, 9669, 9670, 9768, 9855, 10124, 10842, 11095, 11287
--Bibliographies 7400
--Directories 9195
--History 8549
--Periodicals 5614, 11446
Protestant Episcopal Church
--Case studies 223, 558, 980, 1021, 1073, 1082, 1119, 1324, 1487, 1510, 1600, 1801, 1817, 2059, 2070, 2080, 2092, 2261, 2278, 2290, 2349, 2376, 2395, 2451, 2480, 2584, 2588, 2641, 2667, 2726, 3346, 3452, 3483, 3491, 3635, 3660, 3691, 3708, 3730, 3801, 4344, 4362, 4420, 4968, 4998, 5554, 6208, 6740, 6835, 7287, 7354, 7387, 7986, 8399, 9025, 9172, 10296, 10973, 11739, 12125, 12319, 12442, 12555, 12592, 12821, 12900, 13010, 13219, 13385, 13421, 13641, 14018, 14639, 15494, 15649, 15679, 15729, 16180, 16202, 16204, 16317, 16476, 16833, 16987, 17360, 17437, 17550, 18300, 18689, 18712
--Case studies--Bibliographies 4940, 5028, 15591
--Case studies--History 2161, 2918, 7132
--Handbooks 954
--History 5293, 5889
--Pastoral theology 14684
--Periodicals 95, 162, 228, 558, 597, 1049, 2928, 3022, 9115
--Pronouncements, policies 3253, 4097, 6595, 10049, 10284, 17805
--Social teaching 29, 3914, 4093, 15165
--Societies 828, 2504
Protestant Episcopal Church in the USA 473, 1167
Protestant Episcopal Church in the USA, American Church Building Fund Commission 646
Protestant Episcopal Church in the USA, Board of Missions 388
Protestant Episcopal Church in the USA, Joint Commission on Social Service 2968, 3087, 3088
Protestant Episcopal Church, National Council 162, 3259, 3268, 3451, 3562, 3914, 3915, 4366, 4384, 4470, 4509, 4560, 4638, 4721, 4736, 4747, 4753, 4768, 4923, 5341, 5968, 5969, 6222, 6408, 6547, 6788, 6809, 7387, 8276, 8844, 8866, 9876, 10049, 10655, 11495
Protestant ethic 1999, 7012, 8291, 9616, 9660, 10132, 10323, 12023, 14933, 14948, 16098, 17387, 17915, 18163, 18762
--History 16246, 19085
Protestant Trade Union Brotherhood 4973
Providence (Rhode Island)
--History 13432
--Religious and ecclesiastical institutions 2046, 5165, 5397, 6703, 10849, 12154

--Religious and ecclesiastical institutions--History 7213, 13432
Psychoanalysis 19038
Psychological tests 17456
Psychology >> See further: Clinical psychology; Pastoral counseling; Pastoral care, Pastoral Psychology
Psychology 1860, 2417, 4482, 6234, 9039, 9541, 10341, 12304, 12887, 12894, 13295, 14521, 17119, 17738, 18213
--Research 12791
Psychology, industrial 17193
Public housing 5300, 5602, 6099, 6545, 6691, 8023, 8296, 8566, 8929, 9361, 9433, 9447, 9448, 9658, 11153, 12378, 15935, 17168, 17862
--Great Britain 18288
Public ministry 200, 2465, 2495, 4662, 4720, 6429, 8076, 8592, 9054, 11437, 11457, 13063, 13228, 14126, 14999, 15078, 15195, 15630, 15916, 16313, 16326, 17127, 17779, 18221, 18237, 18631, 18885
--England 15913
Public opinion 3832, 4469, 6800, 10345, 11627, 13862, 16482, 16773
Public policy 4375, 4662, 5445, 6248, 6961, 7014, 7143, 8076, 9023, 10179, 10779, 10847, 11013, 11444, 11579, 11613, 11627, 12051, 12921, 13016, 13464, 13488, 13543, 13933, 14126, 14335, 14372, 14510, 14512, 14550, 14590, 14630, 14735, 14736, 14751, 14766, 14778, 15481, 15499, 15630, 15896, 15916, 16142, 16250, 16258, 16302, 16309, 16326, 16346, 16363, 16689, 16960, 17148, 17479, 17576, 18381, 18641, 18679, 18776
--Argentina 8984
--Bibliographies 18387
--Congresses 14549
--England 15913, 17281, 18481, 19052
--Europe 19028
--Great Britain 14902, 15424
--History 6429, 12274, 19109
--Periodicals 18794
Public policy (law) 8784, 12145, 13773, 15075, 15753, 15865, 16976
Public schools >> See further: City children--Education; Church work with students; Education; Segregation in education
Public schools 1290, 1747, 2461, 2719, 2929, 3397, 5598, 6081, 7027, 7521, 7560, 7595, 9812, 10431, 11329, 11772, 12440, 13078, 13600, 13945, 14056, 14221, 14887, 19328
--History 13389, 14412
Public schools and religion 296, 814, 1179, 2875, 5497, 7123, 10440, 11558, 12705, 19287
Public welfare >> See: Social service; Charity; Social workers; Welfare reform
Public worship >> See further: Ritual; Liturgies; Hymns; Prayer; Experimental ministries--Worship
Public worship 838, 3465, 3730, 4046, 4198, 4341, 4572, 4586, 4761, 4905, 4923, 5076, 5369, 6021, 6788, 7046, 7317, 7336, 7460, 7566, 7751, 7915, 7918, 8614, 8615, 9269, 9585, 10620, 11087, 11347, 12041, 12346, 12566, 13470, 13569, 13746, 14134, 14162, 14202, 14274,

14547, 14726, 14990, 15159, 15191, 15397, 15429, 16027, 16250, 16361, 16421, 16491, 16546, 16567, 16582, 16609, 16677, 16699, 16703, 16708, 16725, 16748, 17067, 17228, 17229, 17594, 18114, 18180, 18181, 18377, 18444, 18807, 18839, 19009, 19017, 19273, 19301
Public worship (cont.)
--England 9157, 17377, 17634
--England--History 16579
--Europe 7693, 8767
--Fiction 4854
--France 9010
--Great Britain 4443, 11724, 13131
--History 18035, 19338
Pucallpa (Peru)
--Religion 8609
Puerto Rican Baptists
--History 13932
Puerto Rican Catholics 6074, 6662, 7102, 13951, 15652
--History 16553
Puerto Rican churches 6378, 7637, 18963, 19337
Puerto Rican families 9958
Puerto Rican Lutherans 7960
Puerto Rican Methodists 18963
Puerto Rican Protestants 5601, 6524, 13951
Puerto Ricans 4618, 6438, 6574, 7504, 7592, 15804
--History 12151
--Missions to 2398, 5601, 6572, 6662, 7338, 7418, 7822, 7960, 13847, 14591
--Religion 5863, 5864, 6662, 7953, 8284, 13373, 16035, 17738
--Religion--History 12151
--Religious life and customs 7498, 19231
--Social conditions 4619, 5948, 6238, 6524, 6665, 7020, 7102, 7158, 7255, 7404, 7418, 7822, 9958, 10143, 12650, 14591
--Social life and customs 7452, 18985
Puerto Rico
--Religious and ecclesiastical institutions 7454
--Social conditions 12985
Pullman (Illinois)
--Social conditions 1278, 1390, 4241
Quakers >> See: Society of Friends
Quality of life >> See further: Cost and standard of living
Quality of life 12768, 13056, 14253, 17259, 17483
Quebec (Quebec, Canada)
--Religious and ecclesiastical institutions 5564, 16125
--Religious and ecclesiastical institutions--History 13993
--Social conditions 6139, 14776
Queens (New York, NY)
--Religious and ecclesiastical institutions 1810, 9450, 9855, 11287, 14743
--Social conditions 9609
Questionnaire >> See: Tests and measures; Tests and measures in religion; Religious surveys
Quincey (Florida)
--Religious and ecclesiastical institutions 6608
Race awareness >> See further: African Americans--Ethnic identity; Whites; Hispanic Americans--Identity
Race awareness 2260, 7272, 8742, 8813, 12494, 13042, 14537, 16972
Race relations 8986, 10631, 11729, 19266
--Asia 15183

Race relations (cont.)
--Attitudes 8867, 10545, 11447, 11957, 15174, 15335, 17514
--Bibliographies 9313, 9748
--Canada 13690
--England 5393, 10472, 15113, 15528, 15529, 16104, 17499, 17764
--England--London 8760
--Fiction 5715, 13559
--Great Britain 9552, 11339, 14494, 14996, 15328, 17618
--History 4894, 16022
--Religious aspects 6341, 7521, 8805, 10888, 12849
--Religious aspects--History 18727, 18728
--Religious aspects--Jewish 2502
--South Africa 18618
--United States 2260, 2447, 3378, 3758, 4226, 4629, 5187, 5191, 5236, 5368, 5594, 5773, 5796, 6151, 6614, 7019, 7262, 7355, 7581, 7604, 7679, 7830, 7843, 7907, 8278, 8574, 8666, 8753, 9072, 9129, 9142, 9221, 9240, 10194, 10373, 10493, 10587, 10714, 10905, 10928, 10969, 11000, 11044, 11124, 11163, 11344, 11441, 11566, 11957, 12008, 12031, 12099, 12144, 12153, 12172, 12313, 12373, 12755, 12851, 13020, 13059, 13078, 13089, 13156, 13318, 13343, 13457, 13752, 14386, 14507, 14614, 14973, 15226, 15700, 15874, 16118, 16779, 17557, 17613, 18750
--United States--History 12169, 14793

Race relations and church 8574, 10141, 10376, 11319, 11949, 12459, 12851, 14467, 17557, 19160, 19260
--American Baptist sources--(1945 to 1959) 6262
--American Baptist sources--(1960 to 1969) 8564
--American Baptist sources--(1970 to 1979) 12755
--American Baptist sources--(1980 to 1991) 17844
--American Baptist sources--History 12822
--Asia 15384
--Bibliographies 13925, 19186
--Brethren sources--(1945 to 1959) 6020
--Brethren sources--(1960 to 1969) 10377
--Catholic sources--(1918 to 1944) 4629, 4848, 5186, 5187, 7051, 14705
--Catholic sources--(1945 to 1959) 5591, 5796, 5974, 6045, 6090, 6741, 6892, 6895, 6959, 7353, 7559
--Catholic sources--(1960 to 1969) 8385, 8644, 8683, 8691, 8805, 9547, 10196, 10300, 11399
--Catholic sources--(1970 to 1979) 11975, 13690, 13892, 14120
--Catholic sources--(1980 to 1991) 15335, 16398, 16523, 19183
--Catholic sources--Congresses 10196
--Catholic sources--History 13080, 14746
--Christian Churches and Churches of Christ sources 19298
--Church of England sources--(1918 to 1944) 10999
--Church of God sources 10917
--Congregational Christian sources--(1945 to 1959) 5284, 5294, 5747, 6061, 6757
--Congregational sources--(1900 to 1917) 2770
--Congresses 15384

Race relations and church (cont.)
--Disciples of Christ sources--(1945 to 1959) 5884, 7024
--England 10021, 15113, 16992
--Episcopal sources--(1960 to 1969) 8593, 8866, 8995, 9233, 10346
--Episcopal sources--(1970 to 1979) 11976, 13135, 14248, 15225
--Episcopal sources--(1980 to 1991) 16477, 18482
--Evangelical and Reformed Church sources 6341
--Evangelical Protestant sources--(1960 to 1969) 8675
--Evangelical Protestant sources--(1970 to 1979) 12630, 13502
--Evangelical Protestant sources--(1980 to 1991) 18627
--Evangelical Protestant sources--History 13541
--Federal Council sources--(1918 to 1944) 4046, 4534, 4606, 5047, 5210, 5216, 5270
--Federal Council sources--(1945 to 1959) 5434, 5489, 5490, 5823
--Great Britain 8760, 12186, 13788, 14494, 15083, 15328
--History 14325, 17514, 18727, 18728
--Lutheran sources--(1945 to 1959) 7066
--Lutheran sources--(1960 to 1969) 8020, 8424, 9503, 11100, 11593
--Lutheran sources--(1970 to 1979) 12400, 13487, 14328, 14359
--Lutheran sources--History 12668
--Mennonite sources 10641, 18494
--Methodist sources--(1918 to 1944) 4056, 4068, 4915
--Methodist sources--(1945 to 1959) 5399, 6303, 6544, 6846, 6899, 7057, 7118, 7128, 7375, 7650, 8282
--Methodist sources--(1960 to 1969) 8055, 8625, 8867, 9320, 9338, 9759, 9809, 9810, 10021, 10176, 10183, 10472, 10716, 10888, 11146, 11208, 11250
--Methodist sources--(1970 to 1979) 11764, 12165, 12190, 12454, 12575, 12730, 12863, 13468, 13755, 13780, 13827, 13925, 14107, 14288, 14333, 14724, 14913
--Methodist sources--(1980 to 1991) 15408, 15413, 15784, 16124, 16421, 17138, 17308, 18200, 18926
--NCCCUSA sources--(1945 to 1959) 6185, 6187, 6210, 7172, 7208
--NCCCUSA sources--(1960 to 1969) 7833, 8687, 8761, 10123, 10687
--NCCCUSA sources--(1980 to 1991) 15576
--Presbyterian sources--(1945 to 1959) 5721, 6190, 6519, 6666
--Presbyterian sources--(1960 to 1969) 7861, 8048, 8049, 8378, 9586, 9649, 9782, 10332, 11107, 11169
--Presbyterian sources--(1970 to 1979) 11810, 11963, 12444, 12705, 14206, 14597, 15014, 15183
--Presbyterian sources--(1980 to 1991) 16374, 16582, 17102, 19198
--Presbyterian sources--History 13485, 15198
--Protestant sources--(1875 to 1899) 15174

Race relations and church (cont.)
--Protestant sources--(1900 to 1917) 2692, 2784
--Protestant sources--(1918 to 1944) 3389, 3393, 3736, 3761, 3827, 3964, 4142, 4199, 4532, 5235
--Protestant sources--(1945 to 1959) 5402, 5436, 5891, 6108, 6142, 6149, 6710, 6870, 6905, 7019, 7174, 7263, 7264, 7272, 7499, 7512, 7513, 7590, 7674, 7716
--Protestant sources--(1960 to 1969) 7959, 8260, 8338, 8736, 8791, 8870, 9436, 9731, 9767, 9866, 9878, 10190, 10491, 10499, 10523, 10671, 10905, 10969, 11164, 11244, 11447, 11512, 11550
--Protestant sources--(1970 to 1979) 11924, 12247, 12293, 12401, 12512, 12781, 12823, 13333, 14138, 14852, 15015, 15088
--Protestant sources--(1980 to 1991) 16253, 17779, 18581
--Protestant sources--History 5743, 5927, 15515
--Reformed Church in America sources--(1945 to 1959) 7557
--Reformed Church in America sources--(1980 to 1991) 18352
--South Africa 18584
--Southern Baptist sources--(1900 to 1917) 2190
--Southern Baptist sources--(1945 to 1959) 7642
--Southern Baptist sources--(1960 to 1969) 10208, 11265
--Southern Baptist sources--(1970 to 1979) 12494, 12586, 12854, 13042, 13124, 13180, 13286, 13311, 13669, 14201, 14537, 14838, 16239, 16329, 16972
--Southern Baptist sources--(1980 to 1991) 16087, 17832, 18853
--Southern Baptist sources--Bibliographies 16329
--Southern Baptist sources--History 5843, 15255
--Unitarian Universalist sources--(1960 to 1969) 8424, 11234
--Unitarian Universalist sources--(1970 to 1979) 12703
--United Church of Christ sources--(1945 to 1959) 6802
--United Church of Christ sources--(1960 to 1969) 6671, 8640, 8742, 8781, 8813, 8917, 8945, 8986, 9643, 9646, 10204, 10801
--United Church of Christ sources--(1970 to 1979) 12681, 12382, 14106, 14896
Racine (Wisconsin)
--Religious and ecclesiastical institutions 11421
Racism >> See further: Discrimination; Segregation; Japanese Americans--Crimes against
Racism 5188, 9748, 9782, 10544, 10635, 10663, 10714, 11406, 11566, 11632, 11983, 12703, 13026, 15926, 16931, 17014, 17922, 18120, 18482
--England 17618, 19346
--France 18317
--History 14638, 19350
--Religious aspects 5434, 6905, 9512, 9731, 11142, 12325, 12400, 13755, 14913, 15107, 16823, 16909, 17779, 18581
--South Africa 15900
--Suburban 11709, 13755, 14913, 18581
Radburn (New Jersey)
--History 16406
Radicalism 4546, 5435, 5802,

8229, 10486, 11308, 11374, 11624, 11649, 11668, 11782, 11925, 11943, 12044, 12174, 13117, 13482, 14085, 14279, 15737, 16934, 17390, 18100, 18443
--Austria--History 15739
--Brazil 11735
--England 11840, 12007, 14080, 16038, 17991
--England--History 12332
--Europe 11751
--Finland 14085
--Great Britain 9231
--History 6468, 9527, 10683, 11008, 13680, 14581, 15192, 15552, 15739, 15872, 16370, 16404, 16772, 16786, 17871, 17939
--Latin America 11431
Radio >> See: Mass media
Railroads 815, 1247, 1350, 1542, 2618, 3493, 3502, 3507, 3512, 3534, 3552, 3574, 15254
--Fiction 1180
--History 10392
Raleigh (North Carolina)
--Religious and ecclesiastical institutions 10581, 13451, 17245
Ras Tafari Movement 13997, 16072, 16520
Rationalism 2999
Re-Thinking Chicago Movement 4438
Reading (Pennsylvania)
--Religious and ecclesiastical institutions 8354, 8355, 9993, 17120, 18296, 18862
--Social conditions 14747
Real estate business >> See further: Redlining; Housing
Real estate business 2586, 7005, 7163, 7678, 8320, 8565, 8803, 8886, 9023, 9406, 10720, 10802, 12607, 13059, 14304, 14534, 14541, 14751, 17168, 17862, 18305, 18974
--England 30
Reba Place Fellowship (Evanston, Illinois) 15856, 18197, 19105, 19276, 19282
Reconciliation 3536, 9646, 15710, 16082, 16452, 16967
--Periodicals 11722
Reconciliation (theology) >> See further: Conflict
Reconciliation (theology) 10083, 11485, 11565, 11900, 13089, 16451, 18014, 18914
Recreation 155, 268, 335, 579, 1023, 2116, 2124, 2606, 2637, 2854, 2953, 3101, 3676, 12644
--History 6385, 7609, 13017
Recreation in church work 2694, 2695, 2843, 3420, 3515, 3614, 3737, 3797, 5091, 5126, 5649, 6101
--England 14430, 14592
--Finland 11420
Redemption 392, 1211, 1224, 1854, 2446, 7987, 9168, 9557, 12066, 12877, 14766, 14854, 16363, 19135
Redford (Michigan)
--Religious and ecclesiastical institutions 17717
Redlining >> See further: Banks; Insurance; Real estate business
Redlining 12622, 13285, 13634, 14174, 14193, 14281, 14480, 14569, 14767, 15099
--Bibliographies 13918, 14666
Redundancy .>> .See: Unemployment
Reform >> See: Cities and towns--Reform; Social reform; Moral reform
Reform Judaism >> See further: Jews; Judaism

Reform Judaism 4186, 5849, 16051, 16763, 18684
--History 13206, 17144, 18600
Reform, municipal government >> See: Cities and towns--Reform
Reformatories 91, 470, 1004, 1619, 5619
--History 11493, 12299
Reformed Church (Netherlands) 3622
Reformed Church in America 249, 333, 688, 7574
--Bibliographies 4838
--Case studies 3119, 4858, 5199, 5630, 8015, 11193, 11586, 11594, 11838, 11839, 13397, 13968, 14017, 14350, 16659, 18396, 18721
--Periodicals 19283, 19306
--Social teaching 9948, 12546
Reformed Church in America, Board of North American Missions 7959, 7967
Reformed Church in the United States 3202
Refugees >> See further: Church work with refugees
Refugees 5563, 7495, 7854, 7950, 8339, 11970, 14872, 15342, 15616, 16131, 16176, 16549, 17171, 17688, 18034, 18077, 18546, 19089
--Africa 9297
--Asian 15927, 16062, 16513
--Buddhist 8128
--Canada 16382, 16533
--Cuban 8801, 10110
--England 1270
--German 4811, 15951
--History 11467, 17171
--Hong Kong 8107, 8743
--Hungarian 7164, 7216
--India 8782, 12089, 14488
--Iraqi 4517
--Japanese 5089, 5206, 5207, 5274
--Jewish 5563, 15951
--Laotian 12098, 17679, 19197
--Latin American 15968, 16690, 17236, 17762, 18458, 18461
--Religious life 16533
--Russian 4275
--Vietnamese 16983
Regina (Canada)
--Religious and ecclesiastical institutions 2763
Rehabilitation of criminals >> See further: Crime and Criminals; Church work with criminals
Rehabilitation of criminals 1894, 4173, 4605, 8731, 10840, 11849, 12525, 14528, 14565, 14645, 14835, 15266, 15368, 15897, 16452, 17489, 17619, 17689, 17937, 18538, 18634
--Canada 17579
Rehabilitation of Criminals
--England 15133
Reincarnation 18152
Religion and economics >> See: Economics--Religious aspects; Economics and Christianity
Religion and justice >> See: Justice; Christianity and justice
Religion and labor >> See: Islam and labor; Judaism and labor; Church work with laboring classes; Church and labor
Religion and Labor Council of America 7178, 7798
Religion and literature >> See: Jewish literature; Christianity in literature
Religion and politics >> See: Politics and religion
Religion and social status >> See: Social status and religion
Religion and Sociology >> See: Sociology and religion;

Sociology, Christian
Religion in the public schools >> See: Public schools and religion
Religionssociologiska Institutet (Stockholm, Sweden) 8872
Religiosity 5068, 12254, 12300, 13962, 18778
--Brazil 19211
--France 11014
--Germany 15634
--India 18152
--Italy 7462
--Mexico 14919
--Poland 12275, 12550, 15910, 17907
--Poland--History 13670, 14009
--Russia 13394
--Spain 15535
--Sweden 16338, 19232
--Yugoslavia 12353, 15677
Religious attitudes >> See: Attitudes
Religious communities >> See: Christian communities
Religious controversy
--History 15255
Religious education >> See further: Christian education
Religious education 1165, 2360, 2719, 2929, 4219, 5083, 5176, 5533, 5774, 6664, 10119
--Curriculum 4415, 7361
--Great Britain 17508
--Periodicals 2094
Religious education of children >> See: Church work with children
Religious education, Jewish >> See: Jewish religious education
Religious movements >> See further: Social movements
Religious movements 978, 1454, 1523, 1557, 1558, 1612, 1780, 4363, 7882, 8454, 8705, 9898, 10070, 10367, 16753, 17602
--Africa 10690
--Austria 15739
--Bibliographies 13804
--Canada 13066, 14214
--England 1749, 8268, 16520
--England--History 8668, 10755
--Europe 7693, 7984
--France 11913
--Germany 1630
--Great Britain--History 3842, 4239
--History 2226, 3027, 4442, 5038, 6035, 6352, 13235, 13323, 18102
--India 4323
--Japan 10483, 10898, 12907, 13677, 14363, 16679
--Jewish 7423, 18600
--Jewish--History 6064, 6781
--Mexico 17347
--Sectarian 671, 1134, 3074, 3449, 3498, 3912, 4454, 4491, 4626, 4707, 4814, 5755, 5848, 6994, 8726, 9129, 9191, 11398, 11563, 12351, 12435, 12874, 13077, 13164, 13253, 13301, 14172, 14544, 14545, 14959, 15799, 16314, 16478, 16661, 17059, 17602, 17617, 17633, 17996, 18591
--Sectarian--History 4120, 4322, 4551, 5792, 5889, 6298, 12338, 17556
Religious newspapers and periodicals >> See further: (Specific denominations' periodicals); Newspapers and periodicals; African American newspapers and periodicals
Religious newspapers and periodicals 1604, 3657, 4675, 5700, 9210, 16642, 18806
--Bibliographies 9164
--History 5094, 6297, 9111, 12826, 14886, 15051, 15249

Religious pluralism >> See further: Pluralism; Anticatholicism; Antisemitism; Antiprotestantism
Religious pluralism 4396, 8406, 8518, 10379, 13998, 14202, 14502, 15982, 17903, 18591, 19093, 19190
--Africa 19240
--Asia 16298, 17572
--Canada 12559
--England 10021, 16266, 17499, 18492
--Europe 8302, 15427
--Great Britain 17793, 18744, 18769, 18872
--History 8498, 10670, 15210, 16528, 17392, 17798, 18079, 18878
--Netherlands 16758
Religious pluralism (social science studies) 6684, 7865, 8442, 8966, 10214, 10849, 10952, 12250, 12300, 13990, 14059, 15911, 15997, 16758, 17445, 17777, 18488, 18577, 18778, 19166
Religious pluralism (theological perspectives on) 2555, 3092, 3424, 5785, 6081, 6166, 7410, 7542, 7641, 8227, 8498, 8916, 9076, 9187, 9962, 10024, 10254, 10510, 11275, 12208, 14204, 14264, 14756, 14808, 15181, 15641, 15915, 16491, 16985, 17546, 17610, 17637, 17724, 17793, 18593, 18786, 18823, 18851, 18935, 19057
Religious poetry >> See: Hymns; Poetry
Religious surveys >> See further: Tests and measures in religion; Social surveys; Church planning
Religious surveys 5123, 6828, 11250, 12534, 16615, 17735, 19203
--Africa 18817
--Alabama--Birmingham 9107
--Alabama--Mobile 8002, 13624
--Austria 16083
--Belgium 6697
--Bibliographies 4043
--California 9909
--California--Bakersfield 9170
--California--Los Angeles 6097, 7146, 7607, 8867, 10629
--California--Oakland 5439
--California--San Diego 5417
--California--San Francisco 3319, 5365, 5439, 6078, 6995, 7373, 7456, 7647, 11353
--Canada 2763, 14859, 14881, 15561
--Colorado--Denver 4597, 5919, 6122, 6225, 6786, 15076
--Congo--Brazzaville 10676
--Connecticut--Hartford 5568, 8788
--Connecticut--New Haven 9508
--Delaware--Wilmington 5963, 5965, 13312
--Denominational 4186, 4252, 4748, 4958, 5448, 5680, 6229, 6740, 7105, 7343, 7348, 7484, 7719, 8203, 8336, 8890, 9180, 9320, 10176, 10237, 11144, 11146, 11699, 12027, 12887, 13401, 13850, 14201, 14686, 14726, 15334, 15477, 16329, 16380, 17998, 18135, 18687
--Directories 10681, 11688
--Ecumenical 2522, 3172, 3320, 3479, 3757, 3826, 4131, 5893, 6187, 6631, 6800, 7823, 7824, 9697, 12028, 13333, 14469, 16981, 18161, 18862
--England 9357, 11001, 17281, 18481, 19052
--Europe 15028

Religious surveys (cont.)
--Florida--Jacksonville 8375
--Florida--Miami 6945, 9274, 11354, 11548
--Florida--Orlando 11382
--Florida--Pensacola 8054
--Florida--Tampa 8089
--France 6218, 6432, 6504, 6711, 7135, 7228, 7268, 10708, 10709, 11020, 12300
--France--Paris 6147
--Georgia--Atlanta 5609, 8540, 8999, 11687, 18297
--Great Britain 9770, 18989
--History 4038, 4429, 6107, 17751
--Illinois--Chicago 2661, 5546, 5750, 7359, 7624, 8508, 8698, 8848, 9028, 9213, 9389, 9390, 9500, 10618, 10827, 12689, 16374
--Illinois--Peoria 5719
--Illinois--Washington 9519
--India 4804
--Indiana 3479
--Indiana--Fort Wayne 6990
--Indiana--Gary 7128
--Indiana--Indianapolis 5524, 6586, 7360, 13039
--Iowa--Des Moines 10202
--Italy 14371
--Japan 7523, 10448
--Kansas--Kansas City 6376, 6984, 8778
--Kansas--Topeka 6007, 6787
--Kentucky--Louisville 5262, 6181, 8140, 11442
--Kentucky--Paducah 6834
--Kenya 18817
--Louisiana--New Orleans 6167, 9705
--Maine--Portland 5078
--Maryland 4794
--Maryland--Baltimore 5903, 6793, 8205, 9267, 9976, 10394, 10640, 10791, 10893, 10903
--Massachusetts--Boston 2952, 5636, 5637, 5735, 5840, 6647, 6996, 8441, 8650
--Massachusetts--Springfield 3477, 3756
--Methods 2559, 2569, 2758, 2805, 2921, 2998, 3503, 3756, 3879, 3898, 4040, 4779, 4849, 5240, 5718, 5872, 5890, 5969, 6091, 6129, 6149, 6247, 6824, 7144, 8031, 8172, 8322, 11260, 11704, 11883, 12349, 14341, 14802, 15142, 15483, 15917, 16251, 16596, 16926, 17129, 17331, 17542, 17667, 18295, 18828, 18972
--Michigan--Detroit 3060, 5166, 5176, 5443, 8219, 9123, 10289, 10785, 11355
--Minnesota--Minneapolis 5264
--Minnesota--St. Paul 5511
--Missouri--Kansas City 5196, 5440, 6705
--Missouri--St. Louis 3602, 5167, 5168, 5545, 6241, 6900, 8697, 11650, 17967
--Montana--Butte 7708
--Nebraska--Omaha 6240, 10571
--New Jersey 5081
--New Jersey--Atlantic City 8050, 10657
--New Jersey--Bergen County 5776
--New Jersey--Camden 8053
--New Jersey--Newark 5358, 8479
--New Jersey--Trenton 5406, 8052, 9122
--New York--Albany 6862, 11594, 13397
--New York--Bronx 4145, 4733, 5615, 6940, 7841, 10339, 11095
--New York--Brooklyn 4716, 5441, 5469, 5544, 5628, 6506, 6562, 6708, 6765, 6766, 6967,

7552, 8148, 8432, 9067
Religious surveys (cont.)
--New York--Buffalo 5567, 6096, 6219, 7961, 8865, 10159
--New York--Kingston 12120
--New York--Manhattan 4145, 4619, 6509, 6767, 7668, 7669, 8431, 8433, 8551, 9051
--New York--Queens 4145, 9855, 11287
--New York--Schenectady 11621
--New York--Staten Island 4144, 7840, 9768
--New York--Suffolk County 7551
--New York--Syracuse 6983, 8476
--New York--Troy 7709
--New York--Yonkers 6414, 6997
--New York (NY) 1471, 4188, 4618, 5543, 6508, 6968, 7166, 7498, 8147, 9677, 10338, 10842, 11086
--North Carolina--Charlotte 5829
--North Carolina--Gastonia 5121, 13842
--North Carolina--Greenville 10912
--North Carolina--High Point 11381
--North Carolina--Winston Salem 6386
--Ohio 6750, 6937
--Ohio--Akron 6127, 8295, 8882, 9211, 9212
--Ohio--Canton 10914
--Ohio--Cincinnati 5241, 5566, 5826, 5926, 9868
--Ohio--Cleveland 2934, 2986, 3221, 3323, 4085, 5164, 5171, 5242, 5265, 5305, 5827, 6296, 8568, 8870, 10908, 11056
--Ohio--Columbus 5243, 7654, 9937
--Ohio--Dayton 5194, 6273, 7571, 10401, 15153
--Ohio--Kent 8297
--Ohio--Middletown 11177
--Ohio--Toledo 5419, 5717, 7239, 7760, 11380
--Ohio--Youngstown 5170, 9464
--Oklahoma--Oklahoma City 5291
--Oklahoma--Tulsa 14789
--Oregon--Portland 5363, 5366, 6423, 9275, 13148
--Pennsylvania 18862
--Pennsylvania--Erie 5815
--Pennsylvania--Philadelphia 4096, 5079, 5131, 5215, 5533, 6777, 7714, 8318, 8457, 8601, 8779, 12952
--Pennsylvania--Pittsburgh 2864, 3037, 5115, 5672, 7710, 7800, 9056, 10792
--Pennsylvania--Reading 9993
--Pennsylvania--Scranton 5266
--Pennsylvania--Wilkes-Barre 10693
--Periodicals 7684
--Philippines 7065
--Puerto Rico 7454
--Rhode Island 5775
--Rhode Island--Providence 5165, 10849
--Secular 3847, 14629, 16222, 16945, 18623
--Singapore 8217
--South Carolina--Charleston 10175
--South Dakota 6186
--Sweden 16338
--Taiwan 12522
--Tennessee--Knoxville 10717
--Tennessee--Memphis 5364, 6433, 6434, 16240
--Tennessee--Nashville 8001
--Texas--Amarillo 11143
--Texas--Dallas 5506
--Texas--Fort Worth 5507

Religious surveys (cont.)
--Texas--San Antonio 5509, 8313
--Utah--Salt Lake City 6226
--Vermont--Burlington 431
--Virginia--Norfolk 5979
--Virginia--Richmond 10784, 18344
--Wales--Cardiff 19090
--Washington--Seattle 3980, 5080, 5116, 5337, 5338, 7672, 12224
--Washington--Spokane 5964, 8335
--Washington--Tacoma 5275, 5816, 7672
--Washington (DC) 6601, 9046
--West Virginia--Charleston 11383, 11618
--West Virginia--Parkersburg 6492
--Wisconsin--Madison 5349
--Wisconsin--Milwaukee 5595, 8485, 13534
Relocation >> See: Housing; Whites--Relocation
Renewal >> See: Church Renewal; Urban Renewal
Reno (Nevada)
--Religious and ecclesiastical institutions 15401
Rescue missions >> See further: City missions
Rescue missions 483, 684, 903, 1096, 1115, 1118, 1242, 1265, 1387, 1810, 1870, 2020, 2096, 2112, 2376, 2475, 2620, 2670, 2714, 2756, 3672, 3779, 4116, 4160, 5316, 5727, 6336, 6712, 8358, 9573, 10227, 10576, 11832, 12030, 12999, 16764
--American Baptist sources 7655
--Bibliographies 6155
--Biography 707, 758, 759, 1026, 1835, 2388, 4195, 4563, 4884, 5640, 15402
--Case studies 356, 1215, 1950, 1960, 2045, 3872, 5222, 5447, 5526, 6011, 6260, 10517, 10591, 10632, 14832, 14888, 15401, 16558, 16995, 16996
--Congregational sources 2134
--England 715, 761, 1057, 1087, 1932, 3839, 3863, 8058, 10186, 11574, 13314
--England--History 4124
--England--London 366, 707, 3837, 5845
--Episcopal sources 1222, 1386, 2494
--Fiction 1773, 3496, 6036
--Germany 14758
--History 466, 1727, 1769, 1856, 1857, 2098, 2654, 2778, 3698, 3808, 3822, 4394, 4576, 4981, 5096, 5237, 5280, 5671, 5687, 6683, 7003, 8695, 9721, 12633, 14026
--Japan 2663
--Lutheran sources 2814, 2950, 3558, 10632
--Methodist sources 356, 1300, 1387, 1932, 1950, 2254, 2381, 5280, 5687
--New York (NY) 430, 621, 758, 925, 1074, 1117, 1300, 1386, 1634, 1727, 1856, 1857, 1950, 1958, 1959, 2034, 2042, 2055, 2069, 2087, 2254, 2292, 2494, 2635, 2947, 3030, 3153, 3541, 3558, 3901, 4166, 9648, 11077, 11742, 17588
--New York (NY)--History 854, 2654, 4101, 4576
--New York (NY)--Periodicals 1750
--Periodicals 18881
--Presbyterian sources 621, 903, 1026, 1096, 10591
--Scotland 383
--Southern Baptist sources 2020,

5447, 6025, 15402
Rescue missions (cont.)
--Theory 1688, 1731, 1807, 1818, 1891, 2292, 2814, 2903, 3478, 4971, 5505, 5962, 6025, 6568, 6978, 7655, 8304, 8843, 9648, 11855, 13127, 13231, 13352, 15621, 16321, 17735, 17806, 18123, 18179, 18991
Residential mobility >> See further: Whites--Relocation
Residential mobility 4734, 4954, 5369, 5898, 6085, 6183, 6258, 6746, 7307, 8552, 9253, 9565, 13624, 14120, 14375, 17192
--England 12257
--Fiction 8157
--Japan 10001
Reston (Virginia)
--Description 10646
Revere (Massachusetts)
--Religious and ecclesiastical institutions 15419
Revivalism >> See: Evangelicalism
Revivals >> See further: Evangelistic work
Revivals 1, 5, 74, 133, 175, 330, 331, 355, 559, 565, 571, 1134, 1135, 1428, 1538, 1764, 1864, 1890, 1956, 2603, 2900, 3852, 4687, 4749, 6165, 6532, 6605, 6939, 7049, 7078, 7260, 8409, 11236, 11257, 11306, 15805, 15836, 16187, 16626, 17004, 19226
--Africa 12129
--Argentina 17827
--Asia 17210
--Australia 7725
--Bibliographies 7199
--England 3836, 4758, 5874, 6447
--England--History 4699, 12749
--Europe 17139
--Fiction 4068
--Great Britain 9918, 18362
--Great Britain--History 549
--Handbooks 532
--History 580, 2691, 4539, 5287, 5325, 5474, 6330, 7199, 7648, 11279, 12426, 13107, 13351, 13380, 13447, 13703, 14116, 14124, 14334, 14699, 14745, 14945, 15249, 16215, 17452, 17866, 18376
--Japan 10800
--Korea 13053, 13101
Revolution 3886, 6168, 9333, 9655, 9685, 10022, 10284, 10568, 10943, 10972, 10998, 11116, 11202, 11203, 11470, 11617, 11624, 11668, 11824, 18884
--History 12191
--Religious aspects 9753, 10281
--Religious aspects--History 16786
Revolution (theology) >> See: Liberation theology; Freedom (theology)
Rhodesia
--Church history 13713
--Religious and ecclesiastical institutions 11034, 11986
--Social conditions 9232
Richland (Washington)
--Religious and ecclesiastical institutions 7218
Richmond (Virginia)
--Church history 14950
--Religious and ecclesiastical institutions 728, 2089, 2470, 4895, 4941, 10600, 10784, 14857, 18344
--Religious and ecclesiastical institutions--History 4526, 5342, 14769, 15640
--Religious life and customs--History 14950
Richmond County Society for

Charitable and Religious Purposes 46
Right to work >> See further: Socialism
Right to work 5954, 15035, 19263
Right to work laws 4646, 5873, 6473, 6496, 6534, 6641, 6762, 6932, 7242, 7270, 7280, 7318, 7385, 11990, 15162, 15919, 16377
--Germany 13890
--Great Britain 7547
--History 16249, 17443
Rio de Janeiro (Brazil)
--Religious and ecclesiastical institutions 15464
--social conditions 8994, 13595, 18583
Rio Grande do Sul (Brazil)
--Social conditions 19065
Riots 238, 909, 1733, 2770, 3406, 4593, 5147, 5191, 5236, 5409, 8020, 8028, 8889, 9197, 9557, 9743, 10095, 10195, 10196, 10259, 10264, 10284, 10300, 10332, 10342, 10391, 10393, 10405, 10423, 10455, 10488, 10500, 10502, 10529, 10535, 10537, 10543, 10605, 10625, 10671, 10686, 10724, 10748, 10754, 10769, 10833, 10870, 10883, 10904, 10928, 10955, 11000, 11017, 11032, 11037, 11044, 11060, 11103, 11104, 11134, 11163, 11317, 11506, 11899, 11962, 12428, 12575, 13020, 13135, 14021, 14268, 14831, 16652, 16791, 17999, 18337, 19274
--Bibliographies 9164
--England 432, 15743, 15913, 16104
--Fiction 11313
--France 11413
--History 1449, 3684, 11384, 12191, 12822, 13527, 17785, 19131
--South Africa 13828
Ritual >> See further: Public worship
Ritual 805, 4905, 5076, 7756, 8403, 11741, 13131, 13884, 14202, 17228, 18571, 18596, 19039
--Africa 13327, 15430
--Israel 18334
Riverside Church (New York, NY) 3995, 6070, 6868, 6963, 8437, 14757, 18837
--History 12959
Roadways >> See: Express Highways; Street ministries
Roanoke (Virginia)
--Religious and ecclesiastical institutions--History 13737
--Social conditions 18766
Rochester (Minnesota)
--Religious and ecclesiastical institutions 18049
Rochester (New York)
--History 14342
--Religious and ecclesiastical institutions 2452, 2874, 3869, 8206, 10266, 10703, 10911, 11303, 13530, 15544
--Religious and ecclesiastical institutions--History 14536, 14699
--Social conditions 2496, 5515, 9623, 10468, 10578, 11520, 12578, 13661
--Social conditions--History 13121
--Social life and customs--History 6561
Rockdale (Pennsylvania)
--Social conditions--History 14871, 15077
Rockford (Illinois)
--Social conditions 3699

Rome (Italy)
--Religion 6003, 15219, 16491, 17665, 18035
--Religious life and customs 17268
--Social conditions--History 415
Rotterdam (Netherlands)
--Religious and ecclesiastical institutions 15704
Rouen (France)
--Religious and ecclesiastical institutions 6224
Roumanian Americans
--Social conditions 6999
Runaways
--Adult >> See further: Homelessness
--Adults 16403
--Children >> See further: City children; Boys; Girls; Homelessness
--Children 11717, 15254, 18662
--Youth >> See further: Youth; Church work with youth; Street life; Homelessness
--Youth 10349, 10424, 10829, 10980, 11045, 11284, 11698, 11845, 12294, 12438, 13003, 13139, 13759, 14183, 15405, 15879, 18662, 19064
Rural-urban fringe 5798, 6128, 6129, 6280, 6281, 6427, 7568, 8342, 8372, 8853, 13524, 14369, 15924, 18472, 19265
Rural-urban migration >> See further: Emigration and immigration; Church work with immigrants; Church work with migrant labor
Rural-urban migration 170, 205, 313, 321, 1174, 1214, 1845, 2198, 2203, 2693, 2742, 2926, 3099, 3169, 3249, 3596, 3604, 3796, 3896, 3917, 3934, 3942, 4142, 4678, 4696, 4734, 4815, 4890, 4942, 5008, 5051, 5284, 5344, 5361, 6130, 6378, 6524, 6527, 6656, 6860, 7102, 7118, 7675, 7866, 8301, 8591, 8616, 8687, 9004, 9228, 9469, 9898, 9995, 10008, 10123, 10446, 10872, 11705, 11808, 11841, 11863, 11951, 12159, 12310, 12416, 12616, 12646, 13075, 13184, 13253, 13488, 13637, 13648, 14179, 14296, 14324, 14464, 15010, 15026, 15126, 15138, 15321, 15502, 15589, 16147, 16161, 16970, 17060, 17197, 17418, 17521, 17688, 17963, 18056, 18124, 18271, 18662, 19182, 19196
--Africa 7904, 9415, 10789, 11180, 13266, 13500, 14816, 15974, 16086, 16293, 16795, 17506, 18005
--Africa--Congresses 13632
--Algeria 17182
--Argentina 11337, 12936
--Asia 17436, 18938
--Australia 19358
--Bangladesh 16154
--Brazil 11896
--Cameroon 18042
--Canada 14781, 16852
--Canada--History 13510
--Colombia 17916
--Egypt 16813
--Europe 8182
--Fiction 1803, 1976, 4979, 5715, 6416
--France 7616, 12098, 17679, 19197
--Great Britain 11464
--Greece 14846
--History 3248, 7581, 13456, 13568, 13863, 15808, 16274, 16553, 19218
--Hong Kong 11815
--India 6184, 16839
--Indonesia 18158

Rural-urban migration (cont.)
--Iran 15511
--Japan 12521
--Latin America 18771
--Melanesia 17141
--Mexico 8220
--New Guinea 13579, 13663, 13695, 14823, 15008, 17335
--Nigeria 11235, 13721, 16086
--Northern Rhodesia 6918
--Peru 12825, 15208, 17359
--Philippines 12636
--Poland 12550
--Puerto Rico 6662
--South Africa 8833, 13734, 17742
--Taiwan 12522
--Turkey 17929, 17930
--Venezuela 14848
Rural and urban comparisons 649, 869, 1174, 2540, 2597, 4004, 4088, 4146, 5048, 5249, 5559, 5617, 6553, 6626, 7015, 7893, 8503, 8820, 9020, 9075, 9533, 9657, 9806, 10008, 10345, 12288, 12588, 13669, 14594, 16069, 16665, 18999
--Africa 12846, 13967, 17741, 17841, 18124
--Algeria 17182
--Canada 13194, 16194, 18471
--Church work 1929, 2192, 5051, 5719, 6742, 6827, 17108, 18587
--Churches 1379, 2885, 2902, 4404, 5149, 5656, 5775, 6426, 7183, 7364, 8488, 8671, 9760, 10237, 12242, 13392, 15161, 17814, 18225, 18405
--England 15155
--England--History 15161
--Europe 12105
--Finland 18225
--France 8776, 9605
--Germany 3081
--History 12893, 12977, 13380, 14441, 17556
--India 4148, 18152
--Japan 12723
--Latin America 13493
--Poland 15910
--Religiosity 3866, 6668, 8776, 8815, 9320, 10872, 10986, 12105, 12254, 13222, 13253, 13401, 13986, 15880, 18152
--Russia 4148
--Switzerland 15880
--Thailand 16853
Rural churches 2696, 5162, 5249, 5559, 5656, 6004, 6742, 7691, 8671, 9806, 10237, 10986, 12254, 13392, 15074, 18405, 18587
--Bibliographies 18912
--Europe 12105
--Finland 18225
--France 9605
Rural-Urban Mission (WCC) >> See: World Council of Churches, Rural-Urban Mission
Russian American Catholics 4275
Russian American churches 2884
Russian Americans
--Churches 2262
--History 13822
--Missions to 17644
--Religion 5340
--Religion--History 14207
Saarland (Germany)
--Social conditions--History 17161
Sabbath
--Biblical teaching 13247, 14679
Sabbath legislation, observance 1469
Sabbath observance >> See: Sunday legislation
Sacramento (California)
--Religious and ecclesiastical institutions 7859, 9634

--Social conditions 14249
--Social conditions--History 2652
Sacred places 111, 5779, 8102, 11047, 13849, 14143, 14338, 16671
--Asia 18330
--History 11994, 15699
--India 15639
--Italy 6003, 15219
--Japan 13694
Saginaw (Michigan)
--Religious and ecclesiastical institutions 10465, 10466
--Religious life and customs 11038
--Social conditions 17485
St. Augustine (Florida)
--Religious and ecclesiastical institutions 5407
St. Bartholomew's Church (New York, NY) 2451, 4420
--History 18689
Saint Giles' Christian Mission (London) 715, 761, 1057, 1087
St. Louis (Missouri)
--Industries 18375
--Race relations 5594, 16523
--Race relations--History 14705
--Religion 2196
--Religious and ecclesiastical institutions 721, 1318, 2558, 2966, 3602, 4925, 5167, 5168, 5298, 5545, 5869, 5956, 6900, 7005, 8267, 8371, 8391, 8546, 8667, 8697, 9076, 9346, 9554, 9664, 9928, 11650, 12064, 14585, 15137, 16523, 17823, 18203, 18247, 18333
St. Louis (Missouri) (cont.)
--Religious and ecclesiastical institutions--History 3916, 6241, 8695, 13676, 13923, 14269, 14705, 17512
--Religious life and customs 19250
--Social conditions 340, 3012, 6060, 6505, 6545, 8023, 8888, 17967, 18039, 18203
--Social conditions--History 13929, 19351
St. Paul (Minnesota)
--Religious and ecclesiastical institutions 5407, 5511, 10858, 11453, 14979
--Social conditions 5809
St. Paul's Theological College (Limuru, Kenya) 13326
St. Petersburg (Florida)
--Religious and ecclesiastical institutions 14649, 17020
Salford (England)
--Religious and ecclesiastical institutions--History 16103
Saloons >> See: Hotels, taverns, etc.
Salt Lake City (Utah)
--Religious and ecclesiastical institutions 6226, 8196, 15482
--Religious and ecclesiastical institutions--History 13424, 18258
--Social conditions 13966, 14351
--Social conditions--History 13206
--Social life and customs 373
Salvation Army 914, 1005, 1034, 1122, 1357, 1508, 1517, 1605, 1733, 2027, 2096, 2333, 9940, 19060
--Bibliographies 5621, 14334
--Biography 859, 1112, 1335, 1606, 1778, 1895, 2375, 2646, 3178, 4432, 5742, 8329, 9367, 10504, 12016
--Case studies 9672
--Controversial works 1042, 1072, 2128, 3998
--Fiction 2168
--History 1944, 2222, 2297, 3262, 3683, 5138, 5452, 5621, 8773,

9260, 12627, 12667, 14334, 17452
--Periodicals 523, 619, 1176, 1577, 2740
Salvation Army (England) 491, 971, 1042, 1071, 1072, 1091, 1173, 1335, 1356, 1871, 1984, 1985, 2201, 3178, 7775, 10504
--History 913, 4087, 17888
Salvation Army (Great Britain) 4240
--History 2407
Salvation Army (India) 1041, 1734
Salvation Army (Japan)
--History 9729
Salvation Army (Netherlands) 14205
Salvation Army (United States) 984, 1015, 1039, 1040, 1050, 1109, 1259, 1276, 1520, 1681, 1735, 1933, 3115, 9712, 12428
--Bibliographies 4932
--History 5099, 6118, 6806, 6977, 9345, 17868
Salzburg (Austria)
--Religious and ecclesiastical institutions--History 16345
Samoa 15626
San Angelo (Texas)
--Religious and ecclesiastical institutions 14162
San Antonio (Texas)
--Religious and ecclesiastical institutions 5509, 12444, 13287, 13600, 15501
San Diego (California)
--History 13853
--Religious and ecclesiastical institutions 4926, 5417, 9826, 13764, 14349
--Social conditions 18503
San Francisco (California)
--Ethnic relations 9861
--Ethnic relations--History 14207
--Race relations 5284
--Religion 2302, 6805, 13615, 14100, 14101
--Religious and ecclesiastical institutions 322, 657, 1544, 2115, 3319, 5021, 5365, 5407, 5439, 6078, 6108, 6995, 7373, 7456, 7647, 7715, 7716, 7859, 9443, 9572, 9911, 10424, 11353, 12367, 12957, 13628, 14552, 15115, 15693, 16228, 16526, 16648, 17103, 17794, 18787, 19181
--Religious and ecclesiastical institutions--History 12979, 13270, 13875
--Social conditions 2639, 4196, 4370, 9456, 11076, 13398, 16522, 18067, 18180, 18473, 18921
--Social conditions--History 2652
--Social life and customs 10358
San Francisco Network Ministries 18873, 19352
San Juan (Puerto Rico)
--Religion 13505
--Religious and ecclesiastical institutions 11022
--Social conditions 9958
San Salvador (El Salvador)
--Religious and ecclesiastical institutions 16025, 17156
Sanctuary movement >> See further: Church work with refugees
Sanctuary movement 17236, 17523, 17762, 17851, 17980, 18458, 18461, 19222
Sanitation 212, 368, 1406, 1433, 1742, 2386, 2387, 2495, 2496
Sao Paulo (Brazil)
--Religious and ecclesiastical institutions 18037, 18171
--Social conditions 8881, 10316, 14555, 16909
Sarasota (Florida)

--Religious and ecclesiastical institutions 14305
Savannah (Georgia)
--Religious and ecclesiastical institutions 8958, 12939
--Social conditions 13484
--Social conditions--History 13000
Scandinavian Americans
--Ethnic identity 16436
--Social conditions 4107
Schenectady (New York)
--Religious and ecclesiastical institutions 11621, 15399, 18957
School busing 12687, 12961, 13318
School desegregation >> See: Segregation in education
Schools >> See: Education; Parochial schools; Sunday schools
Scientology 19110
Scioto Valley (Ohio) >> See further: Youngstown (Ohio)
Scioto Valley (Ohio)
--Social conditions 6937
Scotland
--Religion 6605, 12998
--Religious and ecclesiastical institutions 66, 181, 199, 390, 494, 521, 5389, 6413, 6908, 7547, 11140, 11504, 11945, 12024, 12238, 12406, 12956, 14408, 14428, 15029, 17898, 18342
--Religious and ecclesiastical institutions--History 41, 255, 287, 288, 9652, 14611, 15306, 18057, 18331
--Social conditions 59, 66, 120, 348, 434, 7420, 15386, 16377, 18036, 18127, 18166
Scranton (Pennsylvania)
--Religious and ecclesiastical institutions 5266
--Religious and ecclesiastical institutions--History 10837
--Social conditions--History 9308
Seamen >> See: Merchant seamen--Missions and charities
Seamen's Christian Association of the City of New York 2
Seattle (Washington)
--Religious and ecclesiastical institutions 3004, 3980, 5080, 5116, 5337, 5338, 6165, 7672, 11619, 11622, 11749, 12224, 15805, 17441, 18856
--Religious and ecclesiastical institutions--History 13127, 18336
--Religious life and customs 18151
--Social conditions 11619, 12482, 14319, 16969, 17137, 18088, 18454, 18805
--Social conditions--History 17031
Sects 3453, 3988, 4816, 4832, 4895, 4951, 5121, 5269, 5361, 5391, 5755, 5763, 6326, 6422, 6451, 6454, 6790, 6860, 7254, 7906, 7953, 8195, 8199, 8545, 8591, 8966, 10871, 10890, 11119, 11158, 11637, 11894, 11958, 12445, 12474, 12544, 12616, 12717, 12773, 12838, 12874, 13164, 13457, 13905, 14091, 14376, 14748, 14890, 15659, 16097, 16147, 16668, 16831, 16956, 17633, 18443, 19110
--Africa 10690
--Bibliographies 11158, 17541
--Buddhist 13163
--Canada 6724, 13958
--Canada--History 14213
--China 4466
--England 14564

Sects (cont.)
--Germany 8065
--Great Britain 8334, 12185, 12187
--History 5422, 6264, 17798, 18570, 19130
--Japan 7036, 7912, 9184, 10483, 10898, 12907, 13163, 13220, 13677, 17237, 17340, 18558
--Singapore 12374
--South Africa 13734, 13735
--Sweden 18479
Secular city debate 9373, 9441, 9530, 9772, 9857, 9941, 9968, 9989, 10003, 10034, 10079, 10088, 10115, 10133, 10326, 10480, 10513, 10541, 10574, 10639, 10770, 10816, 10878, 10923, 10948, 10994, 11151, 11599, 11908, 11977, 12116, 12387, 12848, 13879, 15551, 16895, 16896, 16897, 16938, 16982, 17013, 17033, 19058
Secularism 554, 1029, 1314, 1981, 2025, 2264, 2389, 3315, 4378, 4830, 5068, 5673, 5708, 5822, 5909, 5913, 5996, 6158, 7113, 7396, 7695, 8622, 8876, 9070, 9242, 9423, 9680, 9734, 9903, 11073, 11430, 11663, 12581, 12832, 13970, 14517, 14809, 15536, 17295, 19206
--England 11427, 16950, 18113
--England--History 14576
--France 8776
--Great Britain 12090
--History 6384
--Italy 14559
--Spain 13032
Secularization 1203, 2885, 4628, 4985, 7033, 7133, 7357, 7996, 8082, 8502, 9800, 9943, 9985, 10280, 10293, 10920, 11429, 12174, 12284, 13012, 13094, 13458, 13879, 14092, 14424, 14810, 15444, 17140, 18084, 18124, 18845, 19006
--Africa 19158
--Austria 16083
--Bibliographies 8069, 9008, 9641, 15791, 17071
--Canada 16369
--England 11427, 14396
--England--History 14576
--France 7386, 9125, 15881, 18495
--France--History 13673
--Germany 2707, 7286, 8013, 8814, 15634
--Great Britain 10036
--Great Britain--History 15462
--History 1225, 6613, 6819, 9536, 14342, 15462, 18243
--Indonesia 15661
--Japan 14054
--Latin America 12395
--Russia 6794
--South Africa 17742
--Spain 13032
--Sri Lanka 18379
--Sweden 19232
Secularization (church property) >> See: Churches--Secular use
Secularization (religion) >> See further: Belief and doubt
Secularization (religion) 3953, 6234, 7073, 7502, 7576, 7735, 7748, 7805, 8846, 8915, 8959, 9136, 9551, 9671, 9801, 9857, 9962, 10022, 10024, 10091, 10099, 10119, 10244, 11018, 11543, 11776, 12193, 12501, 13260, 13401, 14059, 14352, 15550, 17351, 17402, 17504, 17517, 17615, 17617, 17635, 18371, 18450, 18572, 19275
--Bibliographies 17541
--Egypt 18026
--Europe 6692
--France--History 12081

Secularization (religion) (cont.)
--History 14984, 18878, 18927
--India 13813
--Japan 15415
--Netherlands--History 14567
Secularization (sociology) 4156, 5048, 6752, 7034, 7401, 7748, 8069, 8083, 8815, 9202, 9549, 10172, 10212, 10213, 10215, 10460, 10497, 10574, 11189, 11260, 11268, 11300, 12167, 12591, 12651, 12759, 13325, 13682, 13771, 13962, 14024, 14091, 14123, 14125, 14243, 14559, 14698, 14734, 14884, 14940, 15312, 15550, 15573, 15791, 16193, 16468, 16874, 16915, 17311, 17351, 17777, 17946, 18126, 18155, 18623, 18812, 18894, 19054
--Egypt 15406
--England 10467
--Great Britain 12090
--History 15907
--Indonesia 15660
--Japan 17807
--Melanesia 17141
Secularization (theology) >> See further: Belief and doubt
Secularization (theology) 5754, 7274, 7470, 7968, 8069, 8763, 8876, 8935, 9372, 9373, 9423, 9550, 9568, 9625, 9771, 9772, 9891, 9897, 9899, 9968, 10019, 10034, 10088, 10115, 10133, 10171, 10212, 10279, 10463, 10513, 10661, 10686, 10741, 10816, 10832, 10923, 10933, 10936, 10940, 10994, 11118, 11525, 11588, 11881, 11977, 12387, 12807, 12848, 14734, 14924, 15523, 16515, 16895, 16896, 16897, 16982, 17013, 17033, 17692, 18943, 19054, 19058, 19206
--England 10036, 10938, 15462, 18936
SEDOS (Rome, Italy) 12903, 13061
Segregation >> See further: African Americans--Segregation; Discrimination
Segregation 5891, 6303, 10377, 11703, 13009
--Ireland 9504
Segregation in education >> See further: Discrimination in education; Education and urban problems
Segregation in education 6905, 7001, 7027, 7174, 7262, 7263, 7264, 7512, 7513, 7595, 7674, 10348, 10440, 12687, 12705, 12961, 13078, 13318, 13345, 13502, 13892, 14221, 14328, 14705, 17557, 17613
--Congresses 7521
--Fiction 13559
Selly Oaks (England)
--Social conditions 19252
Seminary Consortium for Urban Pastoral Education (Chicago, Illinois) 14772, 15043, 15246, 16163, 16431, 16890, 16938
--Bibliographies 15654, 16036, 16429, 16430, 16431, 16433, 16435, 16751, 17163
Seminary Consortium on Urban Pastoral Education (Chicago, Illinois)
--Bibliographies 16432
Senegal
--Social life and customs 18124
Senior centers >> See: Church work with the aged
Seoul (Korea)
--Religious and ecclesiastical institutions 6031, 8555, 16530, 17800
--Social conditions 8509, 12022,

13053
Sepphoris (ancient city) 19339
Serbian Orthodox Church in America 11119, 13729
Sermons >> See further: Preaching; Evangelistic sermons
Sermons >> See further: Cities and towns--Sermons; Preaching; Church and labor--Sermons; Evangelistic sermons; African American preaching; Charity--Sermons; Jewish sermons
Sermons 18, 113, 136, 152, 249, 293, 320, 385, 386, 393, 410, 479, 484, 500, 505, 658, 705, 766, 770, 781, 853, 871, 988, 1044, 1152, 1204, 1309, 1361, 1610, 1842, 1936, 2867, 2954, 3017, 3160, 3329, 3681, 6204, 6610, 7051, 7755, 10264, 10627, 10754, 12917, 13809, 14364, 14665, 14824, 16023, 16304, 17838, 19030
--England 198, 933, 1279, 2233
--Periodicals 567, 570
Sermons, African American >> See: African American preaching
Serpent handlers 14501, 16147
Servanthood (ministry style) 8798, 9538, 10087, 11843, 13127, 14254, 14568, 14843, 16116, 16124, 16235, 17212, 17609
Settlements >> See: Social settlements
Seventh Day Adventist Church 14415, 18586, 18650
--Case studies 722, 5999, 7772, 11941, 12096, 12097, 12791, 13304, 15586, 18650
--History 11530, 11697, 13625, 17556, 17920
--Social teaching 17021
Sexism >> See: Women; Women in church work; Women; Women's liberation; Women's rights; Feminism
Shalom Ministries (Chicago, Illinois) 16828
Shared facilities >> See: Church buildings--Shared facilities; Churches--Secular use
Sharon (Pennsylvania)
--Religious and ecclesiastical institutions 17437
Sheffield (England)
--History 15831
--Religious and ecclesiastical institutions 13070, 14680, 18045, 18585, 18905
--Religious and ecclesiastical institutions--History 3021
--Social conditions 5180, 7226, 8630, 18553
Sheffield Industrial Mission (Sheffield, England) 5978, 7226, 13085
Sheffield Inner City Ecumenical Mission (Sheffield, England) 18585
Shinto 11909
Shopping centers 9561, 10042, 10082, 10413, 10993, 11658, 11784, 12037, 12289, 12322, 12446, 12537, 12789, 14973, 16624, 18008, 18733
Shreveport (Louisiana)
--Religion 13646
--Religious and ecclesiastical institutions--History 14639
Sierra Leone 18628
--Social life and customs--History 11939
Silver Spring (Maryland)
--Religious and ecclesiastical institutions 7549
Simulation games 9928, 11573, 12729, 12912, 13564, 18738

--Bibliographies 12343
Sin 78, 267, 332, 456, 639, 699, 700, 903, 1117, 3026, 4071, 4117, 4236, 5712, 9663, 13413, 14811, 15247, 16882, 16883, 16885, 17517, 18680, 19206, 19217
Singapore 12836
--Religious and ecclesiastical institutions 8216, 8217, 11097, 11630, 12374, 13095, 16299, 17363, 17740
--Social conditions 16227, 18620
Single parents >> See further: Family life--Single parent
Single parents 12128, 14952, 16800, 18869, 19001
--History 1377, 2388
Single people 6488, 13577, 13758, 16800, 17511
Sioux City (Iowa)
--Religious and ecclesiastical institutions--History 16717
--Social conditions 4979
Sioux Falls (South Dakota)
--Religious and ecclesiastical institutions 6186
Sisters of Charity >> See: Teresa, Mother (in name index)
Sit down strikes 4598, 4609, 7843, 8278, 12031, 12373, 12858
Skepticism >> See: Belief and doubt
Skid-row (metaphor) 5930, 6215, 6336, 7003, 8666, 9684, 9721, 9860, 11121, 11651, 12030, 12751, 12771, 12999, 13127, 13231, 13526, 14883, 15621, 15790, 16321, 17112, 18123
Skyscrapers 3367, 3600, 3621, 4003, 4793, 6379, 11771, 13260, 17189, 17314, 18133
--History 18470
Slavery 323
--History 9254, 19307
Slavery and the church 9, 10, 103, 166, 191, 4135, 4832, 12508, 13485
--History 543, 7221, 9254, 13202, 14287, 14794, 14950, 16786, 17766
Slavic Americans
--Missions to 1872
Slovak American Catholics
--History 14418, 14842, 16805, 18015
Slovak American churches 2250, 2963
Slovak American Lutherans
--History 18015
Slovak Americans
--Missions to 3722
--Social conditions 3436
--Social conditions--History 14437
Slums >> See further: Inner City; Poverty; Church work with the poor; Church and the poor, Ghettos
Slums 1202, 9062, 19261
--Asia 15612
--Belgium 5887
--Brazil 16620
--Description 1427, 1463, 1770, 1808, 1869, 1959, 2173, 2209, 2375, 4018, 4638, 4681, 4809, 5231, 5690, 6310, 6624, 7444, 7567, 7721, 7862, 8108, 9222, 9406, 10530, 10960, 10962, 11088, 11101, 11740, 12153, 12383, 14026, 15126, 17189, 19187
--Description--History 8499, 10764, 13052, 14783
--England 2919, 3626, 4075, 4284, 14345, 16164
--England--Periodicals 4357
--History 6221
--India 14057
--Latin America 11227, 13595,

15948, 19022
Slums (cont.)
--Peru 12825
--Philippines 18822
Small and middle sized cities 861, 1424, 1864, 1909, 2015, 2072, 2486, 2536, 2569, 2636, 3128, 3359, 3433, 3537, 3689, 3756, 3960, 3977, 4073, 4131, 4143, 4567, 4636, 4748, 4801, 4850, 4960, 4986, 5121, 5149, 5271, 5504, 5815, 5816, 5976, 6114, 6492, 6791, 6847, 6862, 7015, 7042, 7196, 7535, 7604, 7719, 8213, 8297, 8322, 8476, 8483, 8525, 9017, 9037, 9122, 9268, 9359, 9364, 9644, 9837, 10077, 10106, 10139, 10328, 10860, 11038, 11051, 11057, 11072, 11225, 11312, 12059, 12165, 12207, 12431, 12442, 12547, 12773, 12809, 13273, 13282, 13457, 13467, 13601, 13669, 13768, 13842, 13956, 14018, 14075, 14147, 14173, 14239, 14316, 14469, 14790, 14943, 14956, 15327, 15493, 15631, 16212, 16465, 16486, 16518, 16664, 16754, 17205, 17308, 17437, 17784, 17812, 17915, 18230, 18281, 18296, 18405, 18807, 18840, 18862
--Ancient 19312
--Bibliographies 11688
--Canada 11682
--England 891
--Fiction 4406
--History 11936, 14784, 15296, 15534, 16091
--Spain 15218
Small churches >> See further: Storefront churches
Small churches 3635, 3708, 4912, 4998, 6146, 6600, 6869, 7138, 8269, 8327, 8852, 10217, 10996, 12110, 12623, 12677, 13992, 14203, 14469, 14596, 14603, 14687, 16233, 16392, 16774, 17684, 18104, 18276, 18413, 18472, 18493, 19086
--Africa 14604
--Bibliographies 18912
--Congresses 14157
--England 14680, 16457
--Germany 8571
Small groups 6362, 6721, 8821, 10851, 11347, 13425, 14596, 14687, 17023, 17684, 18552, 18659, 19075, 19168
Snake handlers >> See: Serpent handlers
Social action 2066, 3026, 4411, 5435, 5504, 6268, 7023, 7867, 7949, 8347, 8645, 9288, 9401, 9461, 10363, 10672, 11066, 11168, 11703, 11821, 11842, 12045, 12437, 12650, 12737, 13407, 13486, 14286, 14340, 14372, 14777, 14778, 15094, 15195, 15365, 15646, 16127, 16288, 16628, 16844, 17351, 17423, 17648, 17649, 17759, 17979, 19340
--Africa 16998
--Asia 12022, 12388, 12795, 12839, 14164, 17079
--Australia 11768
--Biblical teaching 5402, 7742, 12414, 15053, 15186
--Bibliographies 4043, 14177, 19186
--Canada 9803
--Congresses 9246, 11078, 12795, 12839, 17282
--England 1122, 4464, 5001, 6469, 7038, 8459, 10773, 15840, 17339, 17587
--France 5935
--Germany 15363, 18206
--Great Britain 15386

Social action (cont.)
--Great Britain--History 8106
--Handbooks 4842, 5920, 5934, 6518, 6846, 11028, 11468, 12044, 12463, 12515, 12938, 18088
--History 2711, 4510, 8679, 13117, 13774, 16252
--India 4622, 11508, 13584, 14530
--Netherlands 17404
--New Zealand 13575
--Periodicals 4360, 4573, 15391
--Philippines 11928
--Religious aspects 2553, 2753, 3866, 4475, 4544, 4842, 6171, 6332, 6420, 6853, 8049, 8291, 8629, 9387, 9399, 9436, 10206, 10534, 10614, 10879, 11496, 11543, 12057, 12082, 12198, 12868, 13572, 13577, 13603, 13785, 14278, 16076, 16470, 16602, 16976, 17280, 17641, 18100, 18388, 18885, 18988, 19108
--Religious aspects--American Baptist 11160
--Religious aspects--Bibliographies 9574
--Religious aspects--Catholic 4234, 4405, 4583, 5019, 5050, 5385, 5498, 5515, 5665, 6145, 7136, 7746, 8106, 8191, 8705, 9176, 9553, 9831, 9975, 10028, 10192, 11212, 11813, 12810, 13275, 14261, 14934, 15022, 15023, 15037, 16341, 16698
--Religious aspects--Church of England 797, 4830, 9227, 16546, 16810, 16872, 17281, 18321, 19052
--Religious aspects--Church of the Brethren 5344, 10191
--Religious aspects--Congregational Christian Churches 5101, 5662, 6075
--Religious aspects--Disciples of Christ 5884, 5991
--Religious aspects--England 16481, 17234, 17626, 17696
--Religious aspects--Episcopal 3914, 4362, 5320, 6222, 7573, 10346, 10606, 12018, 13831, 13929, 14000, 17159
--Religious aspects--Evangelical and Reformed 5085, 5896
--Religious aspects--Evangelical Protestant 6320, 12489, 16517
--Religious aspects--History 12786, 16364, 16517
--Religious aspects--Jewish 6064, 8807, 9532
--Religious aspects--Lutheran 5192, 5600, 5934, 9290, 9413, 9518, 12290, 12577, 15391, 17282
--Religious aspects--Mennonite 16559
--Religious aspects--Methodist 3472, 4310, 5069, 5370, 5792, 6053, 6237, 7857, 9089, 10606, 11292, 12441, 13069, 14071, 16686, 17532
--Religious aspects--Periodicals 10273
--Religious aspects--Presbyterian 2268, 2550, 2659, 5721, 8028, 8049, 8722, 9463, 12515, 13110, 15386, 16250
--Religious aspects--Protestant 1372, 3320, 3905, 3946, 3987, 4021, 4475, 4477, 4594, 4666, 4689, 4794, 5203, 5304, 5347, 5380, 5578, 5824, 6346, 6358, 6518, 6555, 6884, 7587, 7741, 7941, 9498, 9515, 10090, 10193, 10279, 10468, 10505, 10742, 10757, 10979, 11062, 11092, 11123, 11167, 11174, 11509, 11591, 11626, 11756,

11960, 12021, 12246, 12252, 12371, 12732, 12986, 13019, 13057, 13084, 13216, 13333, 13521, 14995, 15683, 16326, 16615, 18088, 18096, 18221, 18385, 18819
Social action (cont.)
--Religious aspects--Southern Baptist 8404, 10315, 10322, 10611, 10651, 10956, 11031, 11078, 12733, 12938, 13381, 13540, 13669, 13714, 16023, 16737
--Religious aspects--Unitarian 5645
--Religious aspects--United Church of Christ 5751, 8109, 8454, 8587, 8986, 9088, 9246, 9499, 9505, 9574, 9661, 11237, 11277, 11529, 11729, 12009, 16107, 16643, 18984, 19271
--Religious aspects--World Council of Churches 6857
Social action and church >> See: Church and social problems; Justice--Religious aspects (church participation)
Social change 4636, 6183, 6553, 8194, 8445, 8636, 9578, 9766, 9833, 10369, 10423, 10929, 11049, 11256, 11294, 11632, 11989, 12141, 12766, 13001, 13208, 13237, 13532, 13564, 13752, 13773, 14101, 14147, 15323, 15660, 16047, 16079, 16472, 16486, 16836, 17278, 17284, 17957
--Africa 13500, 14661, 16293, 16998
--Africa--History 8894
--Asia 9306, 18330
--Bibliographies 9574, 14904
--Canada 8110
--China 11190
--Developing countries 8324, 12323
--England 16315
--Fiction 16953
--France 16522
--Germany 7496, 9098
--Great Britain 6168
--Handbooks 12463
--History 12356
--India 4772, 15452, 15639
--Japan 10871, 11843, 13640
--Latin America 8056, 17056
--New Guinea 13695
--Religious aspects 8067, 9001, 9306, 9719, 9757, 10788, 11268, 15746, 16193, 16976, 18330, 18379, 18696
--Religious aspects--Hindu 15452
--Religious aspects--Islam 8661, 11448, 12878, 14352, 16820, 17617
--Religious aspects--Jewish 6987, 8245, 15412
--South Africa 17742
--Spain 16522
--Sri Lanka 18379
--Turkey 16401
Social change and church >> See further: Change--Religious aspects
Social change and church 2618, 4709, 5723, 5837, 6175, 6302, 7691, 8225, 8488, 8562, 8628, 9354, 9717, 9753, 9889, 10204, 10214, 10283, 10390, 10688, 11472, 11542, 11614, 11803, 11825, 12379, 12593, 12793, 13344, 14086, 14102, 14125, 14150, 15094, 15210, 15700, 15911, 16518, 16829, 16956, 17521, 17633, 18700, 18827
--Africa 9241, 9963, 11926, 11985, 12115, 13362, 13500, 13501
--Africa--Congresses 7741
--American Baptist sources--(1945

to 1959) 6404, 6414, 6883, 7035, 7080, 7692
Social change and church (cont.)
--American Baptist sources--(1960 to 1969) 8063, 8450, 8518, 8735, 8738, 9001, 9217, 11051
--American Baptist sources--(1980 to 1991) 15429, 16015, 17624, 17661, 18052, 18202
--Asia 10317, 11748
--Asia--Congresses 7741
--Baptist sources--(1800 to 1874) 213
--Baptist sources--(1980 to 1991) 17542
--Bibliographies 5283, 7487, 7936, 8931, 9574, 9641, 11182, 11688, 13626, 13925, 14284, 15304, 17071
--Brazil 11896, 13538, 19189
--Brethren sources--(1945 to 1959) 5344
--Brethren sources--(1960 to 1969) 10961
--Brethren sources--(1970 to 1979) 12503
--Brethren sources--History 14410
--Canada 3958, 4957, 9381, 13190, 18471
--Canada--Bibliographies 6030
--Catholic sources--(1875 to 1899) 1477
--Catholic sources--(1918 to 1944) 3094, 3947, 5011, 5327, 14908
--Catholic sources--(1945 to 1959) 5612, 6164, 6467, 7161
--Catholic sources--(1960 to 1969) 7763, 7870, 7944, 8184, 8185, 8340, 8422, 8444, 8705, 8770, 9055, 9069, 9101, 9106, 9807, 9970, 10230, 10474, 10743, 11172, 11315, 11552
--Catholic sources--(1970 to 1979) 11689, 11871, 11906, 11965, 12004, 12780, 12931, 13665, 14120, 14151, 14261, 14542, 14630, 14854, 14936, 15022
--Catholic sources--(1980 to 1991) 15335, 15411, 15488, 16009, 16267, 16311, 16398, 16523, 16752, 17445, 17695, 18444, 18815, 18894
--Catholic sources--History 13080, 14132, 14527, 19066
--China 11190, 13159
--Christian Churches and Churches of Christ sources 19298
--Church of England sources--(1918 to 1944) 4392, 4913
--Church of England sources--(1945 to 1959) 7736
--Church of England sources--(1960 to 1969) 8851
--Church of England sources--(1970 to 1979) 13358, 15299
--Church of England sources--(1980 to 1991) 18273, 18540
--Church of England sources--History 2279, 11987
--Church of God (Anderson, Indiana) 7271
--Church of the Brethren sources--(1960 to 1969) 9327
--Congregational Christian sources--(1918 to 1944) 5174
--Congregational Christian sources--(1945 to 1959) 6075, 6543, 6769, 7292, 7377
--Congregational sources--(1900 to 1917) 2140, 2224, 2749
--Congresses 6136, 7377, 8541, 9970, 11724, 12063
--Disciples of Christ sources--(1918 to 1944) 4191, 4193, 4404
--Disciples of Christ sources--(1945 to 1959) 6732, 6914, 7737

Social change and church (cont.)
--Disciples of Christ sources--(1970 to 1979) 11686
--Egypt 18026
--England 10566, 11713, 11840, 18045
--England--History 16115, 16579
--Episcopal sources--(1900 to 1917) 2588
--Episcopal sources--(1945 to 1959) 6809, 9444
--Episcopal sources--(1960 to 1969) 7931, 8250, 8627, 9183, 9685, 9984, 9998, 10113, 10455, 10972, 11156, 11226, 11280
--Episcopal sources--(1970 to 1979) 12442, 12821, 13784, 14018
--Episcopal sources--(1980 to 1991) 15494, 15788, 16477, 16833, 18664
--Europe 2359, 8181, 8182, 11346
--Evangelical and Reformed Church sources--(1945 to 1959) 6973
--Evangelical and Reformed Church sources--History 9206
--Evangelical Protestant sources--(1960 to 1969) 9397, 10141, 10970, 14008
--Evangelical Protestant sources--(1970 to 1979) 12448, 12876, 13272, 14068
--Evangelical Protestant sources--(1980 to 1991) 16663, 16702, 16886, 17084, 17319, 17582, 17677, 17690, 18825, 19055
--Evangelical Protestant sources--Periodicals 12325
--Federal Council sources--(1918 to 1944) 5062
--Federal Council sources--(1945 to 1959) 5469, 5819
--Friends sources--(1960 to 1969) 9340, 9580
--Germany 6497, 7345, 7685, 8141, 8177, 8323, 8333, 11217, 12970, 13461, 15727
--Germany (East) 16461
--Great Britain 11074, 18744, 18752, 18759, 18847, 19000
--Greece 9950
--History 3841, 4103, 5038, 16528, 17936, 18079, 19340
--Hong Kong 12866, 13025
--India 7747, 8016, 12496
--Japan 8787, 12063, 12340, 13640
--Jehovah's Witnesses 13164
--Latin America 12004, 13820, 15345, 16816, 16837
--Latin America--Congresses 7741
--Lutheran sources--(1875 to 1899) 1250
--Lutheran sources--(1900 to 1917) 2316
--Lutheran sources--(1918 to 1944) 5225
--Lutheran sources--(1945 to 1959) 6211, 6308, 6375, 6596, 6746, 7066, 7107, 7130, 7431
--Lutheran sources--(1960 to 1969) 8204, 8281, 8361, 8495, 8891, 9181, 9538, 10461, 10922, 11100
--Lutheran sources--(1970 to 1979) 11877, 11996, 12400, 12939, 13487, 14239, 14264, 14328, 14329, 14359, 14644, 18269
--Lutheran sources--(1980 to 1991) 16664, 18416, 19242
--Malta 7870
--Mennonite sources--(1945 to 1959) 5336
--Mennonite sources--(1960 to 1969) 11133

Social change and church (cont.)
--Mennonite sources--(1970 to 1979) 13222, 14200, 14296, 14969
--Mennonite sources--(1980 to 1991) 16560, 17062, 17402, 17948, 17963
--Mennonite sources--History 13510, 14402, 14594, 18471
--Methodist sources--(1900 to 1917) 1736, 1981, 2217, 2497
--methodist sources--(1918 to 1944) 3581, 4190, 4319, 4679, 4748, 4991, 5044, 5119
--Methodist sources--(1945 to 1959) 5485, 5607, 5959, 5980, 6098, 6132, 6268, 7057, 7359, 7414, 7440, 7483, 7624, 7703, 7711
--Methodist sources--(1960 to 1969) 8055, 8301, 8552, 8711, 8747, 8835, 8867, 8982, 8999, 9028, 9079, 9082, 9198, 9338, 9369, 9647, 9759, 9808, 9810, 9817, 9932, 10176, 10202, 10255, 10261, 10382, 10560, 10568, 10716, 10838, 10887, 11026, 11145, 11146, 11250, 11292, 11374, 11534
--Methodist sources--(1970 to 1979) 11715, 12006, 12222, 12358, 12441, 12537, 12583, 12662, 12704, 12730, 12957, 13254, 13306, 13468, 13535, 13582, 13675, 13702, 13722, 13726, 13744, 13755, 13763, 13780, 13827, 13857, 13889, 14072, 14073, 14107, 14222, 14242, 14288, 14341, 14386, 14405, 14414, 14423, 14442, 14724, 14742, 14803, 14843, 14894, 15098, 15223, 15295, 15308, 16910
--Methodist sources--(1980 to 1991) 15408, 15413, 15444, 15480, 15610, 15771, 15784, 16124, 16130, 16182, 16244, 16371, 16816, 16976, 17138, 17222, 17308, 17425, 17921, 18049, 19073
--Methodist sources--Bibliographies 13925, 14460
--Methodist sources--History 7220, 10508
--NCCCUSA sources--(1945 to 1959) 5894, 6056, 6185, 6187, 6417, 6538, 6631, 6771, 6819, 6970, 7163, 7391, 7611
--NCCCUSA sources--(1960 to 1969) 7771, 7939, 8257, 8279, 8437, 8526, 8670, 8775, 8789, 8868, 8955, 9142, 9273, 10904, 10946, 11075
--NCCCUSA sources--(1970 to 1979) 14286
--NCCCUSA sources--History 6613
--Netherlands 8939, 17561, 18894
--Orthodox Eastern Church 13729
--Pentecostal sources 11780
--Pentecostal sources--History 12631
--Poland 15910, 17429
--Presbyterian sources--(1900 to 1917) 2268, 2909
--Presbyterian sources--(1945 to 1959) 5444, 5989, 6169, 6519, 6931, 7082, 7622
--Presbyterian sources--(1960 to 1969) 7976, 8028, 8607, 8706, 8903, 9080, 9224, 9649, 9782, 10006, 10031, 10092, 10116, 10158, 10164, 10228, 10354, 10772, 10851, 11410
--Presbyterian sources--(1970 to 1979) 11876, 12376, 12444, 12655, 14281, 14597, 14598, 15013, 15014, 15076, 15078,

15308
Social change and church (cont.)
--Presbyterian sources--(1980 to 1991) 15996, 17102, 18109
--Presbyterian sources--Bibliographies 8931
--Protestant sources--(1800 to 1874) 79, 501, 6298
--Protestant sources--(1875 to 1899) 897, 962, 1100, 1254, 1654, 1663
--Protestant sources--(1900 to 1917) 2156, 2427, 2516, 2698, 2772, 2902, 15993
--Protestant sources--(1918 to 1944) 3209, 3315, 3500, 3796, 3826, 3891, 3898, 3969, 3970, 3975, 3988, 4060, 4142, 4210, 4244, 4294, 4367, 4411, 4447, 4499, 4532, 4706, 4715, 4716, 4788, 4970, 5039, 5114, 5146, 5263, 5317, 5330
--Protestant sources--(1945 to 1959) 5528, 5612, 5825, 6085, 6657, 6826, 6911, 6912, 7275, 7281, 7364, 7528, 7731, 13346
--Protestant sources--(1960 to 1969) 7858, 7925, 8060, 8067, 8111, 8228, 8338, 8378, 8477, 8515, 8567, 8588, 8646, 8688, 8966, 8969, 9017, 9288, 9292, 9359, 9556, 9559, 9608, 9670, 9739, 9754, 9907, 10071, 10147, 10167, 10523, 10627, 10668, 10756, 11046, 11120, 11202, 11243, 11244, 11322, 11506, 11516, 11522, 11575, 19265
--Protestant sources--(1970 to 1979) 11677, 11695, 11712, 11942, 11955, 12232, 12247, 12307, 12378, 12517, 12616, 12688, 12964, 13349, 13538, 14028, 14392, 14741, 14856, 14975, 15015, 15043, 15074, 15088, 15205, 15296
--Protestant sources--(1980 to 1991) 15551, 15640, 16142, 16253, 16275, 16285, 16298, 16575, 16757, 17103, 17904, 18096, 18140, 18151, 18170, 18185, 18300, 18357, 18633, 18873, 18886, 18920, 18996, 19017, 19334, 19352
--Protestant sources--Congresses 15088
--Protestant sources--History 5743, 6330, 12038, 14483, 14694, 18960
--Reformed Church in America sources--(1970 to 1979) 11836
--Reformed Church in America sources--(1980 to 1991) 15543, 18563
--Seventh Day Adventist sources 17556
--Singapore 16299
--South Africa 12724
--Southern Baptist sources--(1945 to 1959) 5611, 7139
--Southern Baptist sources--(1960 to 1969) 8752, 9015, 9186, 9737, 9788, 10208, 10348, 10404, 10806, 11265, 11580
--Southern Baptist sources--(1970 to 1979) 11895, 12104, 12122, 12263, 12272, 12292, 12497, 12854, 12861, 12954, 13042, 13180, 13286, 13322, 13451, 13624, 13688, 13792, 13838, 14201, 14537, 14838, 15011, 16239, 16329, 16972
--Southern Baptist sources--(1980 to 1991) 15334, 15373, 15716, 15835, 16024, 16066, 16087, 16230, 16240, 16242, 16380, 16465, 16483, 16494, 16548, 16581, 16630, 16682, 17219, 17322, 17328, 17350, 17670, 17927, 17987, 18018

Social change and church (cont.)
--Southern Baptist sources--Bibliographies 16329
--Southern Baptist sources--History 15808
--Southern states 9907
--Spain 4185
--Unitarian sources--(1875 to 1899) 691
--Unitarian Universalist sources--(1960 to 1969) 11234
--Unitarian Universalist sources--(1980 to 1991) 16926
--United Church of Christ sources--(1960 to 1969) 7816, 7956, 8170, 8541, 8742, 8749, 8750, 8813, 8853, 9061, 9076, 9077, 9160, 9401, 9655, 10038, 10139, 10407, 10408, 10456, 10529, 11003, 11252, 11328, 11598
--United Church of Christ sources--(1970 to 1979) 11946, 12017, 12091, 12382, 12409, 12488, 12681, 12758, 12764, 13271, 13534, 14020, 14128, 14159, 14340, 14456, 14465, 14496, 14497, 14519, 14808, 14896, 14901
--United Church of Christ sources--(1980 to 1991) 15419, 17555, 17714, 18984
--United Church of Christ sources--Congresses 14465
--United Church of Christ sources--History 16986
--World Council of Churches sources--(1945 to 1959) 7159, 7487
--World Council of Churches sources--(1960 to 1969) 8117, 8324, 8915, 9650, 10281
--World Council of Churches sources--(1970 to 1979) 12375
--World Council of Churches sources--(1980 to 1991) 18383
Social conflict >> See further: Conflict management; Church controversies
Social conflict
--Africa 19240
--Asia 16912
--Bibliographies 13007
--Church responses to 4088, 4447, 7792, 7861, 8137, 8989, 9436, 9919, 10346, 10385, 10491, 10955, 11156, 11410, 11440, 11494, 11703, 11787, 11804, 11900, 11922, 12018, 12578, 12780, 12901, 12986, 13067, 13530, 13544, 13839, 15064, 15932, 15937, 17792
--Congresses 7521
--Descriptions 3917, 5296, 6331, 6875, 6948, 7059, 7159, 7526, 7919, 8385, 8593, 9045, 9207, 9233, 10083, 11103, 11244, 11575, 11671, 12471, 13318, 13345, 14507, 15195, 15874, 15943
--England 14389, 15884, 18682
--Ethnic aspects 5153, 6272, 6612, 7013, 11309, 11310, 13729, 13822, 14432, 14464, 14516, 14582, 14925, 18279
--Ethnic aspects--History 11119, 13724
--Germany 6163, 14903, 16287
--Germany--History 15741
--Great Britain 11361, 17618, 18085
--Greece 16614
--Guatemala 17492
--History 12202, 13143, 13725, 13822, 13952, 13995, 14056, 14432, 14582, 14694, 15344, 17414, 18279
--Ireland 11361, 18038, 18085
--Italy 11804
--Korea 12932

--Latin America 15064
--Malaysia 15527
--Philippines 17708
--Religious aspects 5062, 6622, 6845, 6879, 7227, 7521, 7865, 8993, 9133, 9444, 10468, 11322, 12513, 12941, 13297, 13904, 15780, 15889, 16660, 16791, 17200, 17407, 17445, 18374
--South Africa 17742, 18275
Social Creed of the Methodist Episcopal Church >> See further: Social Gospel--Creeds
Social Creed of the Methodist Episcopal Church 2253, 2842, 13553
--History 3927, 4959, 5069, 18505, 18559
Social Darwinism 1249, 1426, 16715, 17504
--History 4092
Social ethics 350, 518, 651, 720, 887, 1380, 1653, 2321, 2346, 2730, 3425, 3564, 3718, 4027, 4720, 5304, 5484, 5713, 5777, 5785, 6354, 6405, 6421, 6738, 6843, 6961, 7165, 7657, 7726, 7753, 7777, 7832, 8110, 8180, 8439, 8520, 8746, 8766, 8803, 9263, 9296, 10179, 10511, 10645, 11793, 11948, 12685, 12906, 12908, 13175, 13420, 13621, 13645, 13773, 15078, 15116, 15753, 15865, 16074, 17324, 17471, 17576, 17779, 17951, 18593, 18735, 19008, 19021, 19056
--Bibliographies 9641
--Congresses 6676, 6748
--Germany 12419, 13589, 17882
--History 7200, 8099, 9564, 12926, 16178
Social ethics, Christian >> See: Ethics, Christian; Sociology, Christian
Social Gospel 651, 671, 738, 751, 752, 765, 783, 790, 796, 799, 877, 1038, 1105, 1172, 1181, 1249, 1380, 1382, 1420, 1446, 1493, 1517, 1531, 1542, 1575, 1652, 1698, 1701, 1768, 1780, 1854, 1880, 1994, 2022, 2132, 2142, 2164, 2224, 2365, 2405, 2424, 2443, 2488, 2543, 2583, 2647, 2717, 2734, 2755, 2759, 2793, 2797, 2812, 2819, 2822, 2916, 2917, 2937, 2969, 2997, 3026, 3041, 3103, 3112, 3352, 3385, 3401, 3423, 3446, 3499, 3555, 3675, 3761, 3928, 3993, 4011, 4071, 4093, 4340, 4389, 4393, 4411, 4511, 4606, 4801, 5600, 11030
--Art and hymns 612, 1913, 1946, 2364, 2662, 2710, 3162, 4134, 5971, 18990
--Associations, etc. 1120, 2844, 5792
--Bibliographies 12618, 16662
--Biography 2007, 2416, 2459, 2940, 3452, 3790, 4545, 4585, 5125, 6588, 6897, 8171, 9209, 9690, 10053, 10304, 13662, 17984
--Canada 13821
--Canada--History 12047, 14214
--Catholic parallels 5319
--Collected works 5970, 7175
--Congresses 13423
--Creeds >> See further: Social Creed of the Methodist Episcopal Church
--Creed 2220, 2253, 2264, 2571, 2599, 2842, 3155, 3518, 3648, 3696, 4959, 9161
--Creed--History 3927, 5069, 13553, 18505, 18506, 18559
--Critics 1892, 2546, 2811, 4236, 4285, 4521, 4553, 5445, 5803,

16810
Social gospel (cont.)
--Fiction 966, 1017, 1180, 1496
--Great Britain--History 17019
--History 2318, 3315, 3659, 3926, 4092, 4285, 4313, 4539, 4553, 4652, 4719, 4737, 4918, 4943, 4947, 5009, 5038, 5134, 5138, 5192, 5245, 5803, 6749, 6839, 6886, 6964, 6981, 7150, 7199, 7200, 7658, 7916, 9588, 9887, 9904, 10365, 11269, 11278, 11530, 11641, 12111, 12333, 12473, 12693, 12972, 13110, 13283, 13494, 13565, 13571, 13719, 13800, 13871, 14019, 14064, 14088, 14228, 14325, 14538, 14701, 14764, 14878, 15110, 15552, 15792, 15808, 15872, 15993, 16322, 16364, 16655, 16662, 17232, 17352, 18506, 18578, 19350
--Japan 4164
--Jewish parallels 6064
--Periodicals 2094, 2195, 2718
--Precursors 266, 332, 385, 386, 659, 19191
Social Hygiene Movement 4408, 4421
Social justice >> See : Justice
Social movements >> See further: Religious movements
Social movements 812, 1070, 1186, 1348, 1588, 2106, 2170, 2982, 3470, 4438, 5689, 6046, 6428, 11803, 14306, 14391, 16470, 16522, 17536
--Art, beautification 3813, 4303, 6400, 14006, 15793, 16181
--Brazil 15532
--Canada--History 18809
--Civil rights 10131, 10422, 12031, 15225, 15339, 16861, 17613
--Civil rights--History 13541, 17075
--Encyclopedias 2200
--England 1104, 1942, 2975, 4128, 4303
--England--Fiction 2838
--England--History 13116
--France 15666
--Great Britain 14149
--Great Britain--History 1992
--History 5476, 5517, 17936
--Latin America 13516
--Mexico 18834
--Middle East 17051
--Prohibition 3580
--Prohibition--History 3752, 5856, 8579, 8918, 9872
--Reform 1177, 1255, 1424, 1434, 1486, 1575, 1705, 1742, 1989, 2200, 2628, 3101, 4583, 5788, 7199, 7853, 10288, 10479, 10504, 10867, 11049, 11780, 12785, 14329, 14867, 15365, 17648, 17712
--Reform--History 3419, 5792, 6516, 8620, 8727, 10713, 14441, 17719
--Theory 7652, 10189, 15329, 15646, 16472, 16628, 16956, 17301, 17712
Social movements, cooperative 616, 3649, 4760, 4822, 4992, 5160, 5286, 5353, 6287, 6913
--History 13116, 13612
Social organization >> See: Social structures
Social problems >> See further: Church and social problems
Social problems 310, 496, 518, 590, 635, 1388, 1687, 1888, 1909, 2167, 2449, 2477, 2583, 2904, 3784, 3825, 3828, 4197, 6847, 6960, 7273, 7887, 7888, 8646, 9131, 9543, 10369, 11289, 11556, 11887, 13383, 13956, 14487, 14523, 16063, 16127,

16225, 16948, 16969, 17006
Social problems (cont.)
--Africa 12890, 14543
--Asia 12890
--Austria 13241
--Bangladesh 16154
--Bibliographies 1793, 1888, 2039, 9574, 9747, 11888, 13007, 13917, 14177, 14517, 15574, 16431, 18406, 18457, 18574
--Congresses 10625
--England 1466, 1642
--Great Britain 1358, 1693, 1825, 2991, 14436
--History 12716
--India--Bibliographies 18406
--Latin America 12890
--New Guinea 15008
Social progress >> See: Progress
Social psychology 1918, 6461, 7232, 14926, 16569, 18913
Social reform 137, 147, 227, 273, 364, 408, 437, 459, 492, 801, 822, 878, 894, 907, 926, 936, 1035, 1070, 1177, 1255, 1259, 1281, 1283, 1291, 1341, 1372, 1491, 1493, 1517, 1525, 1531, 1604, 1919, 1955, 1989, 2004, 2035, 2123, 2215, 2286, 2288, 2299, 2323, 2385, 2389, 2414, 2675, 2743, 2850, 3000, 3104, 3105, 3167, 3570, 3703, 3749, 3767, 3886, 4835, 5607, 6677, 7635, 9333, 10846, 11291, 12783, 13226, 14286, 17480
--Australia 10163
--Australia--History 12417, 14744
--Bibliographies 7199, 10366
--Biography 1150, 5960, 6173, 11080, 14764
--Canada--History 12047
--China 9854
--Encyclopedias 2200
--England 418, 1121, 1351, 1466, 1642, 2295, 2296, 4699, 10504
--England--History 7339, 18249
--Europe 569
--Europe--History 1409
--Fiction 1017, 1028, 1180, 1221, 1245
--France 416, 481
--Germany 2634
--History 2711, 3841, 4118, 4209, 5197, 5745, 5788, 5977, 5986, 6221, 6516, 7010, 8499, 8620, 8623, 8679, 8727, 8806, 9093, 9111, 9606, 10040, 10197, 10288, 10365, 10366, 10713, 10995, 11008, 11222, 11661, 11865, 12701, 13004, 13017, 13052, 13606, 13871, 13943, 13961, 14064, 14088, 14325, 14342, 14745, 14783, 14878, 14945, 16819, 16900, 17098, 17751, 18429, 18716, 19152, 19191, 19254
--India 12785
--Japan 17691
--Spain 14237
Social science 426, 7726, 8172, 8486, 12227
--History 4204
--Philosophy 503, 855
--Research 16555
Social service >> See further: Welfare reform, Social workers; Charity
Social service 1192, 1834, 2666, 2675, 4086, 4575, 5018, 5113, 7592, 8786, 9778, 9816, 11856
--Africa 6143
--Austria 11362
--Bibliographies 3077, 3363, 12585
--Congresses 2509, 6958, 7156, 8621
--Denmark 6052, 8535
--England 512, 1985, 4295, 5760,

6474, 9934, 13076
Social service (cont.)
--England--History 913, 4661, 8668
--Germany 218, 400, 5988
--Germany--History 2609
--Germany--Periodicals 239, 664, 3195, 3214
--Great Britain 8085, 10349, 13137, 17682
--Great Britain--History 7021, 8459
--History 8078, 8679, 9537, 10764, 12274, 14306
--Industrial aspects 2511
--Ireland 12424, 14262
--Italy 11362
--Japan 4291
--Mexico 18678
--Periodicals 1527
--Philippines 12679
--Religious aspects 447, 624, 1547, 1715, 1790, 1840, 2118, 2129, 2137, 2211, 2280, 2310, 2576, 2595, 2820, 3044, 3231, 3309, 3408, 3492, 3557, 3843, 3853, 4168, 4333, 5198, 5343, 5679, 5916, 6453, 13185, 13307, 13499, 18582
--Religious aspects--Africa 18817
--Religious aspects--American Baptist 2575, 2795, 4771
--Religious aspects--Baptist 2476, 13684
--Religious aspects--Baptist--Periodicals 2433
--Religious aspects--Bibliographies 2915, 12585
--Religious aspects--Catholic 2153, 2712, 2737, 2976, 3251, 3277, 3573, 3973, 4106, 4218, 4291, 4436, 4498, 5003, 5335, 5354, 5661, 6058, 6145, 6521, 7031, 7494, 8668, 9022, 10464, 10858, 11222, 11362, 12236, 13518, 15504
--Religious aspects--Catholic--History 6120, 8087, 17548, 17577
--Religious aspects--Catholic--Periodicals 1425, 3019, 3540, 5132
--Religious aspects--Church of England 1516, 3197, 4295, 5760, 8085, 9094, 9227, 9459, 18217
--Religious aspects--Congregational 2683, 3529, 14021
--Religious aspects--Congresses 804, 4805, 6770
--Religious aspects--Directories 14473
--Religious aspects--Disciples of Christ 5991
--Religious aspects--England 1251, 2313, 3242
--Religious aspects--Episcopal 1475, 2639, 2968, 3253, 3326, 3483, 3583, 3646, 3892, 3900, 4355, 4509, 4560, 5122, 5703, 6407, 13929, 17724
--Religious aspects--Evangelical Protestant 8459, 9850
--Religious aspects--Friends 2044
--Religious aspects--Germany 13174
--Religious aspects--Great Britain 9466
--Religious aspects--History 4318, 9946
--Religious aspects--Islam 11448
--Religious aspects--Japan 3645
--Religious aspects--Jewish 2064, 3224, 3505, 3973, 4540, 5661, 5695, 6353, 6675, 7056, 7314, 7477, 7615, 7627, 7690, 7696, 7873, 8306, 8350, 8357, 8480, 8651, 8704, 8807, 10843, 11790, 12294, 13720, 16801,

17600
Social service (cont.)
--Religious aspects--Jewish--Periodicals 6928
--Religious aspects--Lutheran 1016, 1590, 2076, 2499, 2532, 2871, 2923, 2936, 2939, 2972, 4554, 4819, 5192, 5988, 8420, 9143, 11137, 13087
--Religious aspects--Lutheran--Periodicals 8224
--Religious aspects--Methodist 1888, 2252, 2265, 2365, 2463, 2531, 2835, 3055, 3973, 4266, 4899, 6542, 6797, 9808, 11176, 11194, 13553, 15990
--Religious aspects--Periodicals 239, 664, 2358, 3195, 3214
--Religious aspects--Presbyterian 2439, 2452, 2550, 4558
--Religious aspects--Protestant 804, 1639, 2135, 2170, 2174, 2192, 2336, 2479, 2491, 2498, 2501, 2509, 2512, 2521, 2552, 2598, 2629, 2704, 2717, 2735, 2751, 2755, 2808, 2810, 2822, 2841, 2844, 2864, 2889, 2957, 3077, 3222, 3260, 3415, 3482, 3485, 3514, 3523, 3524, 3530, 3531, 3554, 3566, 3804, 3911, 3973, 4047, 4065, 4198, 4356, 4434, 4514, 4518, 4572, 4594, 4770, 4787, 4805, 5145, 5324, 5412, 5481, 5542, 5641, 5655, 5661, 6222, 6269, 6358, 6613, 6631, 6632, 6690, 6706, 6819, 6842, 6958, 7115, 7156, 7202, 7879, 8223, 8237, 8497, 8621, 9457, 9690, 10379, 12585, 12632, 13473, 13474, 13618, 13876, 16116, 17199, 18242, 18410
--Religious aspects--Protestant--Periodicals 6357
--Religious aspects--Salvation Army 1735, 1917, 1985, 2027, 2333, 2407, 6977, 17452, 17868
--Religious aspects--Seventh Day Adventist 11941
--Religious aspects--Southern Baptist 9376
--Religious aspects--Unitarian 2401, 2577, 2601, 4044, 8598
--Religious aspects--United Church of Canada 9925
--Religious aspects--United Church of Christ 7422
--South Africa 5540
--United States 3740
Social settlements 673, 2242, 3738, 4007, 15990
--Bibliographies 2039, 2462
--Congresses 3418, 3721, 7393
--Connecticut--New Haven 1169
--England 1104, 1664, 2001, 2027, 2324, 2777, 9746, 14345
--England--London 712, 846, 945, 1271, 1351, 1395, 1928, 2038, 2295, 2731, 2761, 3306, 4200, 4428, 4457, 4483, 18249
--England--Mansfield 1213
--England--Portsmouth 1463
--Europe 14066
--Great Britain 2481
--History 1085, 1831, 2173, 2182, 2208, 2731, 3413, 3418, 3474, 3686, 3996, 5652, 5961, 6797, 6822, 8631, 9527, 10288, 11249, 12221, 12813, 14066, 14454, 18249, 18361, 18464, 18480, 18883, 18899, 18956, 19046, 19048, 19243
--Illinois--Chicago 1107, 1108, 1142, 1349, 1689, 1888, 1957, 2007, 2194, 2289, 2365, 2374, 3163, 3543, 3804, 3867, 3956, 4058, 4407, 4457, 4467, 4496, 4570, 4839, 4880, 5158, 5413, 5459, 6256, 6435, 9495, 18883, 18899, 18956, 19046, 19243,

19257
Social settlements (cont.)
--India--Bombay 4622
--Indiana--Gary 11408
--Italy--Naples 7170
--Louisiana--New Orleans 6256
--Maryland--Baltimore 7451
--Massachusetts--Boston 1185, 1303, 1453, 1497, 1503, 1615, 1676, 1683, 2870, 3585, 4017
--Michigan--Grand Rapids 5485
--New York--Brooklyn 2434, 5629
--New York--Buffalo 1637
--New York--Utica 7126
--New York (NY) 1514, 1837, 1893, 2109, 2914, 2981, 3497, 4403, 4458, 4826, 6267, 8014, 10916, 18662
--Ohio--Cincinnati 2018
--Ohio--Cleveland 5444, 7783, 11572, 14308
--Ohio--Columbus 15521
--Oklahoma--Oklahoma City 5102
--Pennsylvania--Erie 4567, 4989
--Pennsylvania--Philadelphia 2895, 9005
--Pennsylvania--Pittsburgh 9155
--Philosophy 942, 1025, 1108, 1169, 1192, 1193, 1197, 1421, 1474, 1679, 1760, 1776, 1787, 1883, 2106, 2136, 2171, 2176, 2179, 2296, 2560, 2642, 2750, 2752, 2906, 3369, 3824, 4424, 4425, 5201, 5231, 6512, 7393, 7867, 8174, 8461, 9875, 10387, 18877
--Tennessee--Knoxville 10717
--Washington (DC) 6615
Social status 4471, 4614, 6067, 8483, 8702, 8703, 14120, 14845
--Bibliographies 11783
--England--History 8773
--Great Britain 7109
--History 12928
Social status and religion 202, 236, 435, 565, 716, 751, 752, 774, 775, 847, 857, 1111, 1542, 2103, 2879, 3159, 3316, 3428, 3618, 3988, 4263, 4288, 4603, 4903, 4909, 5076, 5151, 5367, 5531, 5612, 5626, 5720, 5757, 5915, 5917, 5928, 6616, 6617, 6791, 7086, 7159, 7253, 7330, 7384, 7441, 7717, 7799, 7921, 8043, 8116, 8363, 8401, 8402, 8442, 9059, 9392, 9447, 9862, 10004, 10132, 10225, 10666, 10669, 10774, 10850, 11248, 11703, 11786, 11870, 11958, 12117, 12214, 12649, 12773, 13467, 13570, 13601, 13986, 14466, 14479, 14683, 14691, 14715, 14829, 14899, 15086, 15330, 15617, 15804, 15869, 15954, 16277, 16531, 16910, 17132, 18255, 18490, 18696, 18709, 18770, 18773, 18832, 18904, 19102
--Australia 15618
--Brazil 15620, 18171
--Canada 13958, 14213
--Canada--History 14213
--England 273, 3624, 7868, 9331, 9632, 10958, 12257, 12966, 13293, 13302, 14160, 15967, 17616
--England--History 8773
--Europe 8548, 15390
--Fiction 13024
--France 6334, 6951
--Germany 8235, 13132, 15563
--Great Britain 9231
--Great Britain--History 17064
--History 1225, 7689, 13041, 13209, 14021, 14855, 14864, 14933, 19356
--India 12520, 14155, 15379, 18073, 18336

Social status and religion (cont.)
--Italy 11804, 14371, 15204
--Japan 8236
--Yugoslavia 15677
Social surveys >> See further: Religious surveys; Demographic surveys
Social surveys 1349, 3858, 4794, 5004, 5543, 6510, 6954, 7620, 9528, 10629, 12027, 15456, 16482, 16555
--Bibliographies 4043
--History 3955, 4429
--Ireland 12479, 14238, 15134
--Methods 2569, 2921
--Periodicals 7684
--Southern states 6032, 6314
Social values 1699, 3975, 3989, 4131, 5924, 6207, 7013, 7017, 7047, 7140, 7625, 7872, 7900, 8199, 8447, 8784, 8820, 9045, 9263, 9411, 9578, 9919, 9964, 10662, 11276, 11418, 12049, 12143, 12145, 12381, 12449, 12476, 12968, 12973, 13022, 13073, 13239, 13504, 13532, 13533, 13627, 13645, 13862, 14067, 14476, 14885, 15075, 15217, 15876, 15937, 16079, 16275, 16301, 16973, 17284, 17459, 17483, 17601, 17963, 18067, 18135
--Europe 9193
--Germany 10507, 16098
--Great Britain 17115
--History 4482, 6684, 11891, 18192
--India 18238
--Jewish 8704
--Korea 11161
--Latin America 9479, 11009
--Switzerland 15880
Social values (anti-urban) 183, 220, 353, 377, 382, 610, 627, 724, 767, 864, 932, 1216, 1226, 1308, 1539, 1674, 1687, 1880, 1902, 1913, 2032, 2146, 2203, 2475, 2674, 2707, 2904, 3784, 3937, 3967, 4001, 4004, 4148, 4757, 5336, 5421, 5656, 5725, 5931, 6617, 6885, 7292, 7323, 7486, 7766, 7908, 8618, 8804, 9039, 9049, 9603, 10154, 10369, 10806, 11738, 11752, 11868, 12535, 12588, 13431, 14067, 14125, 14768, 16848, 16883, 17291, 18084, 18739, 18854, 18898, 19158
--Bibliographies 17408
--History 10392, 10797, 11927, 13380, 15802, 16637, 17054, 17408
Social values (pro-urban) 64, 196, 271, 625, 950, 1197, 1211, 2029, 2382, 3861, 4790, 7901, 7998, 8518, 9373, 11262, 14335, 15877, 18641
Social work >> See: Social service; Case work
Social workers
--Catholic 1425, 2153, 2558, 2712, 2976, 3251, 3277, 3492, 3514, 3740, 5003, 5335, 5354, 5661, 7031, 7494, 8087, 8668, 15504
--Catholic--Periodicals 3019, 3540
--Church of England 1516, 9094, 9459, 9466, 11458, 18217
--Congregational 2683, 3529
--Denmark 8535
--Episcopal 2639, 3326, 4560, 6222, 6407
--Evangelical Protestant 9850, 13185, 14473
--Evangelical Protestant--History 14334
--Germany 218, 5988
--Great Britain 5343, 7021, 8459, 8668, 9459, 9466, 11458, 18217

Social workers (cont.)
--History 8078, 8679, 9537, 9946, 14334, 18564
--Ireland 12424, 14262
--Japan 3645
--Jewish 2064, 3224, 3740, 4540, 5661, 5695, 6353, 6675, 7056, 7314, 7477, 7615, 7627, 7690, 7696, 8350, 8480, 8651, 8704, 8807, 10843, 12294, 13720
--Jewish--Periodicals 6928
--Lutheran 218, 1590, 2076, 2499, 2532, 2871, 2923, 2936, 2939, 2972, 3911, 4554, 4719, 8420, 11137
--Methodist 2252, 2265, 2362, 3566, 4266, 4899, 6542
--Protestant 1639, 1840, 2026, 2135, 2191, 2192, 2280, 2310, 2491, 2501, 2509, 2552, 2808, 2844, 2957, 3222, 3260, 3415, 3492, 3514, 3524, 3530, 3740, 3804, 3905, 4047, 4065, 4355, 4356, 4434, 4514, 4518, 4572, 4594, 4770, 4805, 5145, 5324, 5655, 5661, 6631, 6706, 6770, 7115, 7202, 9457, 9946, 12585
--Protestant--Periodicals 6357
--Religious life 2479, 2675, 3843, 4198, 4318, 4899, 5335, 9850, 18582
--Salvation Army 1735, 1917, 1985, 2027, 2333, 2407, 6977
--Seventh Day Adventist 11941
--Southern Baptist 13203
--Unitarian 2401, 4961, 8598
--United Church of Christ 7422
Social workers, training of 2531, 2550, 2666, 2972, 2976, 3482, 3531
Socialism >> See further: Right to labor; Communism; Class warfare
Socialism 202, 615, 631, 632, 788, 1024, 1261, 1363, 1390, 1998, 2323, 2370, 4109, 4241, 4317, 9148, 13704, 19185
--Bibliographies 783, 8418, 10867, 13804
--Criticism 243, 729, 777, 877, 993, 1291, 1362, 1919, 2093, 2197, 2545, 2583, 3193, 17656
--France--History 16117
--History 469, 655, 6468, 16404, 17939
--Periodicals 710
--Soviet Union 4345
Socialism and Catholic Church 563, 652, 706, 908, 1010, 1092, 1877, 1919, 2050, 2197, 2823, 3156, 3766, 4243, 4352, 4702, 4825, 4956, 12855, 14252, 18610
--Austria--History 16345
--Canada 14776, 17630
--France--History 3345
--Germany--History 4861
--History 1409, 3842, 4161, 4427, 10150, 13259, 16394
--Ireland--History 9128
--Latin America 13516
--Netherlands--History 17976
--Poland 17429
--Spain--History 14918
--Switzerland--History 13685
Socialism and Christianity 326, 648, 654, 674, 677, 740, 1054, 1077, 1078, 1141, 1237, 1323, 1362, 1420, 1528, 1691, 1951, 2093, 2133, 2215, 2231, 2266, 2307, 2555, 2612, 2671, 2682, 2792, 2908, 3159, 3314, 3500, 4081, 4094, 4263, 4320, 10680, 12711, 13276, 13294, 13773, 14278
--Africa 7180, 16093
--Asia 7180
--Austria--History 15739
--Canada 13757
--Congresses 3113

Socialism and Christianity (cont.)
--Europe--History 4427
--Fiction 2150
--Finland 14085
--France 260, 888, 12855
--France--History 14513
--Germany 888, 2315, 6288, 7345, 12946
--Germany--History 14137, 17650
--Great Britain 2568
--History 1846, 2530, 4239, 14108, 14329, 16705, 16880
--Japan 4164
--Latin America 13516, 14356
--Latin America--Bibliographies 13804
--Periodicals 3107
--Poland 15910, 17429
--Switzerland--History 15726, 17656
--Yugoslavia 12353, 14466, 15677
Socialism and Judaism 1647, 2323, 6201, 6522
--History 14891
Socialism, Christian 227, 241, 372, 404, 417, 418, 467, 552, 561, 770, 771, 797, 824, 875, 888, 967, 970, 975, 976, 1020, 1271, 1272, 1278, 1426, 1480, 1533, 1829, 1923, 2047, 2065, 2086, 2121, 2144, 2207, 2227, 2239, 2353, 2391, 3031, 3074, 3138, 3154, 3168, 3229, 4321, 4397, 4666, 5697, 9394
--Associations, etc. 260, 261, 557, 956, 1476, 1786, 1925, 4916, 8383, 8585, 13187, 13407, 13516, 13757, 14356
--Associations, etc.--Bibliographies 8418, 13804
--Biblical or theological defense 256, 393, 501, 520, 837, 950, 1054, 1089, 1183, 1212, 1321, 1332, 1905, 2011, 2022, 2127, 2173, 2188, 2329, 2405, 2612, 2657, 3167, 3365
--Bibliographies 557, 8418, 10680, 10867, 13804
--Biography 251, 725, 1150, 1992, 2041, 2061, 2155, 2840, 3032, 3591, 3744, 4207, 4671, 4675, 4894, 5135, 5396, 5517, 5733, 5734, 6221, 8830, 8899, 9007, 10145, 10367, 11033, 12282, 12587, 13491, 15901, 16170, 16577, 17232, 18009
--Canada 3473
--Criticism 236, 706, 1273, 1405, 1951, 2050, 2215, 2319, 2672, 3124, 4521
--Encyclopedias 1517
--England 259, 272, 273, 433, 1751, 3075, 3236, 4159, 14108, 15178
--Fiction 135, 259, 270, 12330
--History 1405, 1409, 1925, 1992, 2933, 3270, 3370, 3419, 3707, 3842, 4128, 4239, 4292, 5517, 5693, 5729, 6174, 7379, 8383, 8652, 10477, 10913, 13116, 13187, 13494, 13929, 14538, 15963, 16080, 16115, 16958, 18274, 18453
--Periodicals 237, 251, 531, 578, 692, 956, 1897, 2525, 2587, 2776, 2928, 3107, 3280, 4159, 4916, 7787, 8681
--Switzerland--History 17656
Society and church 167, 279, 361, 371, 554, 560, 634, 962, 1059, 1097, 1232, 1248, 1413, 2592, 3466, 4050, 4453, 4571, 4658, 4662, 6066, 6352, 6602, 6704, 6961, 7736, 7884, 8590, 8815, 9650, 10460, 11433, 11923, 12620, 13138, 15264, 18273, 18666, 19340
--Africa 8124, 13036, 13371

Society and church (cont.)
--Brazil 16189
--Congresses 9739, 13430
--England 3719, 3845, 3886, 4569, 8423, 10938, 13480, 14396, 14563
--England--History 5092, 13635, 13991, 16174, 16705
--Europe 4571
--France 12092, 12467
--Germany 1630, 2707, 9153
--Germany--History 11379, 15878
--Germany (East) 16461, 17449
--Great Britain 4443, 5308
--History 2859, 8096, 14116, 17639
--Hong Kong 16416
--Latin America 16166
Society and religion >> See further: Culture and religion
Society and religion 316, 385, 811, 2431, 2713, 3402, 3844, 8846, 9583, 10581
--England--History 13880, 15062
--History 18570, 19191
--Japan 7036, 17237
Society for Promoting the Gospel among Seamen in the Port of New York 406
Society for the Prevention of Pauperism (Boston, Massachusetts) 123, 163, 204
Society for the Prevention of Pauperism (New York, NY) 54, 56
Society of Christian Socialists 1020
--History 7730
Society of Friendly Sons of St. Patrick for the Relief of Emigrants from Ireland 16159
Society of Friends 3074
--Bibliographies 4939
--Canada--History 13909
--Case studies 7029, 9340, 9580, 13412, 18644
--History 4108, 13772
--Social teaching 4493, 16967
Society of Socialist Christians (London) 3236, 3280
Society of St. Francis de Sales
--History 18032, 18283, 18302
Society of St. Vincent de Paul 124, 1234, 2283, 6062, 7763, 18503
--Periodicals 1425, 3019
Socio-economic status >> See: Social class; Labor and laboring classes; Middle classes; poor; wealth
Sociology 821, 1198, 1353, 2305, 5478, 6825, 11433, 12141, 12491, 16127
--Bibliographies 1124, 1257, 1372, 3717, 6103, 9008, 11783, 12714, 14486, 14904
--Europe 12105
--France 6714, 7135
--Germany--History 12977
--History 4204, 5142, 12699
--Japan 7036
--New Guinea 15008
--Research >> See: Religious surveys; Typologies; Tests and Measures; Social surveys; Social Sciences--Research; Anthropology
--Rural 869, 4004
--Theory 1214, 1918, 3376, 5297, 5431, 6067, 6077, 7015, 7141, 7369, 12714
--Urban 869, 1918, 2119, 2964, 3376, 3688, 3717, 3815, 3955, 4004, 4133, 4419, 6043, 6103, 6217, 6371, 6461, 6622, 6626, 6758, 7101, 7369, 7999, 8370, 8448, 10247, 10369, 10919, 11536, 11613, 12480, 12835, 13108, 13531, 13752, 13861, 14523, 15680, 15806, 15896,

16212, 17125, 19157
Sociology (cont.)
--Urban--Bibliographies 14486
--Urban--History 4429, 7520, 7985
--Urban--India 13335
--Urban--Periodicals 12708
Sociology and religion 3988, 4133, 4288, 4942, 6167, 6622, 6915, 7172, 7185, 7232, 7330, 7433, 7434, 7564, 7588, 7626, 7819, 8156, 8219, 8664, 9055, 9057, 10172, 10497, 10952, 11476, 11637, 11744, 12308, 12366, 12556, 13436, 13911, 14278, 14484, 14630, 14940, 15456, 15758, 16301, 16671, 16696, 16780, 17777, 18623, 18778
--Africa 15974, 16229
--Argentina 4999
--Asia 18330
--Australia 16799
--Austria 7041
--Bibliographies 2915, 5992, 7048, 7232, 7268, 7620, 8069, 9008, 10216, 11158, 11688, 12714, 12757, 13169, 13574, 13925, 17248, 17292, 17791, 19041, 19153, 19186
--Canada 13194
--Collected works 2658, 3815, 9214
--Congresses 7258, 12993
--Developing countries 8642
--England 10291, 10467, 12167, 12227, 12617, 15216
--Europe 6888, 7332, 7351, 7639, 7780, 7991, 8069, 8548, 8767, 10075, 11894, 12300, 15580
--France 6147, 6218, 6432, 6714, 6792, 6946, 7356, 7617, 7963, 8193, 8492, 8576, 15881
--France--Bibliographies 7268
--Germany 5764, 7548, 7614, 9098
--Great Britain 12090
--History 6387, 6684, 7509, 8723, 12163, 12946, 13217, 14051, 15476, 15993, 17331, 17751, 18464, 18891
--India 4804
--Indonesia 15660
--Italy 6191, 7048, 14559, 15550
--Japan 10898, 12907, 13677, 17340
--Latin America 13082, 16095
--Netherlands 17561
--Netherlands--Congresses 16758
--New Guinea 14823
--Parish studies 5430, 6034, 8215, 9513, 9514, 12663, 13216, 14060, 14963, 15573, 17127
--Periodicals 7684
--Peru 8609
--Poland 3904, 12275
--Poland--Bibliographies 6068
--Russia 13394
--Spain 8126, 10144, 16811
--Spain--Congresses 13696
--Sweden 17349
--Switzerland 10727
--Taiwan 13399
--Theory 2597, 5539, 6461, 7076, 7476, 8370, 8857, 9057, 9514, 10213, 10215, 10518, 11158, 11189, 12379, 13458, 14884, 16468, 17311, 17351, 18486
Sociology, Buddhist 14295, 16040
Sociology, Christian 898, 1097, 1672, 2813, 19206
--Africa 13371
--American Baptist 2543, 3788
--Bibliographies 11688
--Brazil 4582
--Catholic 1402, 4217, 4512, 4588, 4629, 4999, 5187, 5890, 6024, 6032, 6074, 6167, 6314, 6467, 6773, 6841, 6972, 6974, 7189, 7258, 7342, 7435, 7564, 7617, 7780, 7980, 8345, 9008,

9055, 9478, 9480, 11689, 13199, 14311, 16160, 16811, 17091
Sociology, Christian (cont.)
--Catholic--Congresses 11910, 13696
--Church of England 1047, 1466, 2126, 4308, 4412, 4830
--Congregational 732, 1336, 1337, 1722
--Congregational--History 3867
--England 933, 2429, 13638
--Episcopal 1839, 4316
--Europe 5064
--Evangelical Protestant 13613, 15303
--Germany 2142, 13589, 16721
--History 11923
--Italy 7947
--Lutheran 651, 4719, 6347, 7766, 8172, 8891, 11085, 12270, 17349
--Mennonite 16559
--Methodist 933, 1649, 2213, 2362, 2469, 2841, 2842, 2917, 3042, 3104, 3167, 3486, 4231, 4674, 5798, 6132, 7983, 9759, 11117, 11292, 11375, 13638
--Methodist--Bibliographies 2915
--Methodist--History 15872
--Mexico 4853
--Netherlands 12011
--Periodicals 1047
--Presbyterian 2268, 2659
--Presbyterian--History 12699
--Protestant 714, 926, 1186, 1281, 1304, 1313, 1372, 1393, 1531, 1559, 1652, 1768, 1862, 2066, 2127, 2160, 2258, 2346, 2404, 2498, 2516, 2518, 2534, 2535, 2658, 2730, 2757, 2759, 2764, 2779, 2912, 2982, 3056, 3495, 3776, 3817, 3930, 3955, 4040, 4280, 4429, 4879, 6043, 12227, 14060, 14526, 17667, 18350
--Protestant--History 7150, 12727, 14051
--Southern Baptist 1745, 2793, 16240, 16596, 16971, 16972, 19092
--Southern Baptist--History 13456
--Unitarian 883
Sociology, Jewish 6781, 7197, 7443, 10580, 11541, 12320, 12676, 13367, 13368, 13897, 14034, 17946
Sociology, urban
--Europe 12776
SODEPAX 11182, 11748
Sodom (metaphor) 10032, 11348
South (US) 14242
--History 2471, 4894, 9254, 10586, 11269, 12473, 12646, 13380, 13485, 13680, 14142, 14228, 14784, 14793, 14794, 15640, 16322, 17668
--Race relations 2190, 3378, 7263, 7264, 7512, 7513, 9320, 9649, 11145, 12292, 14386, 15339
--Religion 1971, 2546, 3035, 3082, 5446, 5648, 5753, 6024, 6032, 6270, 6628, 8374, 9226, 9611, 9907, 10080, 10200, 11341, 11963, 12955, 12964, 13418, 13850, 13888, 13962, 14505, 14828, 15501, 16240, 16773, 17255, 18581
--Social conditions 1858, 1968, 1973, 2281, 2699, 3593, 3658, 4906, 5372, 5932, 5989, 6256, 7001, 7966, 7969, 8395, 9228, 9949, 10236, 11847, 14229, 14741, 14873, 14874, 15347, 17251
--Sociology 2759, 4603, 5448, 6167, 14385
South Africa

--Church history 11734
--Economic conditions 12101, 12548, 12642, 14688, 15966, 17285, 17487, 19074
--Fiction 5715
--Race relations 16229
--Religion 12129, 12718, 12724, 13327, 13659, 13734, 13735, 15430, 16947, 17026, 18584
--Religious and ecclesiastical institutions 5540, 12741, 12911, 14139, 16229
--Social conditions 5690, 12548, 13828, 16771, 17654, 18618
South African Council of Churches 11734
South Bend (Indiana)
--Religious and ecclesiastical institutions 6901, 11247, 17780
--Social conditions 16625
South End House (Boston, Massachusetts) 1676, 2870
--History 3585
South Holland (Illinois)
--Religious and ecclesiastical institutions 4210
South London Industrial Mission 7846, 8398
Southampton (England)
--Religious and ecclesiastical institutions 4921, 10242
Southeastern States (US) 6132
Southern Baptist Convention 6270, 16024, 16846
--Case studies 5541, 5861, 9658, 10389, 10551, 11255, 11354, 11355, 11389, 11442, 12494, 12854, 13003, 13203, 13221, 13321, 13512, 13741, 13850, 14369, 14649, 16218, 16289, 16495, 16514, 16630, 17039, 17263, 17528, 17962, 18043, 18114, 18659, 18668, 18808, 18853
--Congresses 10696, 11547, 16537
--History 12473, 15255
--Periodicals 4100, 5056, 15258, 16029
--Pronouncements, policies 17805
--Social teaching 5480, 7642
Southern Baptist Convention, Brotherhood Commission 10739, 10840, 11031, 12243, 13474
Southern Baptist Convention, Christian Life Commission 6821, 6916, 11078, 11547
Southern Baptist Convention, Home Mission Board 2438, 2632, 2811, 3082, 3341, 4867, 4896, 5108, 5172, 5447, 6015, 6028, 6029, 6088, 6783, 6840, 7039, 7079, 7139, 8372, 8663, 8693, 8740, 8923, 8988, 9107, 9170, 9186, 9304, 9995, 10208, 10209, 10401, 10791, 10902, 10903, 11079, 11255, 11275, 11353, 11354, 11355, 11356, 11372, 11548, 11664, 11969, 12014, 12069, 12954, 12955, 13018, 13124, 13286, 13287, 13322, 13342, 13513, 13540, 13624, 13687, 13753, 14131, 14201, 14369, 14426, 14439, 14667, 14759, 14806, 14838, 15334, 15370, 15410, 15483, 15565, 15623, 15716, 15728, 15765, 15833, 15923, 15924, 15931, 16070, 16112, 16207, 16208, 16242, 16251, 16328, 16329, 16334, 16337, 16380, 16422, 16424, 16465, 16508, 16581, 16675, 16682, 17029, 17291, 17769, 17867, 17911, 18018, 18294, 18949, 19015
--Bibliographies 13626, 14812, 17164

--History 10551, 11518, 18594
--Periodicals 4100, 15258, 16029
Southern Baptist Convention, Sunday School Board 5056, 17535, 17773
Southern Christian Leadership Conference 5927, 7120, 7347, 8791, 9120, 10422, 10423, 10631, 11163, 11164
--Bibliographies 14224
--History 11848, 11864, 16356, 17668, 18750, 19026
Southern Sociological Congress 2759
Southern States >> See: South (US)
Southwest (US) 4870, 7365, 18063
--History 13136
Southwest Interparish Ministry (Chicago, Illinois) 7992
Southwood (California)
--Social conditions 6345
Soviet Union
--Economic conditions 4345
--Religion 16007
Soweto (South Africa)
--Religion 13735
Spain
--Economic conditions 4261, 4893
--Religion 19210
--Religious and ecclesiastical institutions 15218, 16811
--Social conditions 4864, 7372
Speyer (Germany)
--Social conditions 15902
Spiritual healing 8284, 14646, 18596
--Africa 15860
--England 18370
--South Africa 18254, 15430
Spiritualism 4112, 8284, 15348, 15722, 15804, 15862, 15863, 16823, 17738, 19231
--Great Britain 11464
--History 19121
Spirituality 876, 1089, 1316, 1963, 1969, 2266, 2629, 2675, 2703, 3237, 3295, 3417, 3459, 4198, 4312, 4338, 4572, 5935, 6324, 6431, 6629, 6668, 7198, 7402, 8263, 8873, 9369, 10044, 12155, 12261, 12614, 12949, 12976, 13201, 14821, 14966, 14988, 14997, 15020, 15036, 15037, 15649, 15736, 15811, 15952, 16061, 16217, 16497, 16680, 16784, 16870, 17166, 17173, 17412, 17413, 17422, 17508, 17794, 17838, 18022, 18046, 18114, 18181, 18213, 18421, 18584, 18735, 18889, 18959, 18976, 19118, 19156, 19295, 19316, 19342
--Africa 14826
--England 14583, 14584, 16543, 17686, 18284, 18370
--History 16170
Spokane (Washington)
--Religious and ecclesiastical institutions 5407, 5964, 8335, 14762
Sport
--England 14430
--History 13245
--Ireland 12483
--Social aspects 4117, 18629, 18845, 19201
Springfield (Illinois)
--Social conditions 9586
Springfield (Massachusetts)
--Religious and ecclesiastical institutions 3477, 3756, 7224, 11225, 16253
--Religious and ecclesiastical institutions--History 13385
Springfield (Missouri)
--Religious life and customs--History 5181
Springfield (Ohio)

--Religious and ecclesiastical institutions 12205, 12773
Squatter settlements >> See further: Homelessness; Rural-urban migration
Squatter settlements
--Argentina 10968, 11454
--Brazil 11870
--Developing countries 11841, 15126
--Developing countries--Bibliographies 11971, 13920
--Egypt 19193
--Ghana 11995, 13939
--Great Britain 12740, 12752, 14115
--Iran 15511
--Kenya 12176, 12738, 12989, 13023, 13648, 13939, 14298, 15093, 15957, 19178
--Latin America 11227, 19022
--Malaysia 12839
--Philippines 11486, 11487, 12519, 12636, 13939, 15172
--Venezuela 14848
--Zambia--Congresses 13632
Sri Lanka
--Religious and ecclesiastical institutions 15422
Standard Oil Company 1993, 2025
Staten Island (New York, NY)
--Religious and ecclesiastical institutions 4144, 6369, 7840, 9768
Steel industry 3181, 3208, 3246, 3332, 3443, 3448, 3501, 4561, 4615, 4647, 5518, 5771, 5883, 6144, 7934, 8379, 14499, 14570, 14731, 15600, 16219, 16470, 17305, 17372, 18820, 18840, 19262
--Bibliographies 15598
--Canada--History 15606
--England 5978, 7226, 8630
--History 11754, 13454
--Korea 12265
Steelton (Pennsylvania)
--History 13454
Steeples and spires >> See further: Church buildings
Steeples and spires 154, 3367, 4003, 4600, 6443, 8437, 8639, 11349, 13260, 18417
--History 17121
Stewardship, Christian >> See: Christian giving; Church finance
Stockholder's meetings 12251, 12612
Stockholders' meetings >> See further: Interfaith Center on Corporate Responsibility; Investments, ecclesiastical
Stockholders' meetings 13921, 15966, 16260
Stockholm (Sweden)
--History 11644, 13415
--Religious and ecclesiastical institutions 8847, 18479
--Religious and ecclesiastical institutions--History 3925
Stockton (California)
--Ethnic relations 7057
--Religious and ecclesiastical institutions 9490
Storefront churches >> See further: East Harlem Protestant Parish
Storefront churches 3393, 4127, 4288, 4304, 4895, 4905, 5083, 5137, 5145, 5349, 5651, 5834, 5835, 5848, 5864, 5933, 5980, 6043, 6086, 6460, 6673, 6715, 7297, 7538, 7637, 9057, 9236, 9585, 9637, 9898, 10312, 10910, 11223, 11614, 11899, 11951, 12677, 13639, 13812, 14670, 14773, 15308, 15323, 16361, 17005, 18524

--Bibliographies 8456
--History 5770, 8075, 14492
Story telling 2573, 12890, 16485, 16619, 17188, 17403, 17809, 17906, 18141, 18775, 19098
Story telling (theology) 11647, 14817, 18183, 18401
Strangers >> See further: Alienation
Strangers 905, 2978, 3150, 3586, 5184, 6238, 6686, 8446, 8670, 8761, 11467, 12557, 15732, 15935, 15969, 16426, 16563, 17157, 17471, 17488, 17786, 17793, 17808, 18713, 18798
--History 15006
Strategy >> See: Church planning
Street life 444, 609, 638, 695, 1320, 2289, 3108, 4738, 5231, 5932, 5984, 9679, 9945, 10130, 10450, 10601, 10610, 11498, 11717, 11742, 12135, 12211, 12294, 12309, 12367, 14565, 15630, 15738, 15879, 16245, 16613, 16942, 16962, 16999, 17042, 17112, 17269, 17491, 18442, 18543, 18660, 18662, 18991, 19136
--Bibliographies 19215
--England 514, 4463
--Fiction 158, 377, 1210, 7911
--France 377
--Great Britain 521
--History 3684, 8696, 15362
--Korea 8509, 9324
Street ministries 322, 638, 1879, 1991, 2112, 2375, 2578, 2931, 3358, 3374, 6003, 7151, 7169, 7822, 8098, 8748, 9384, 9700, 9733, 9910, 10517, 10864, 11496, 11557, 12209, 12211, 12976, 13684, 14274, 14706, 14836, 15459, 15991, 17043, 18114, 18119, 18156, 18473, 18722, 18787, 19005, 19006, 19105, 19327
--Africa 19240
--Australia 19315
--England 3542, 13070
--History 5452, 19016
--India 14488
--Korea 17800
--Spain 19210
Stress (psychology) 6461, 14926, 16569, 18913
Strikes and lockouts >> See further: Trade unions; Church and labor; Church and industry; Wages
Strikes and lockouts 1064, 1278, 1315, 1334, 1350, 1373, 1390, 1399, 1401, 1416, 1436, 2379, 2760, 2789, 3208, 3220, 3246, 3332, 3342, 3443, 3639, 3671, 3764, 3821, 3864, 4006, 4008, 4241, 4351, 4370, 4598, 4647, 4686, 4688, 4902, 4904, 5461, 5518, 5570, 5587, 5618, 5633, 5674, 5740, 6841, 7083, 7155, 7895, 7934, 9778, 10503, 14229, 14404, 14416, 14873, 14874, 14879, 15347, 16003, 17862, 19146, 19262
--Chile 10439
--Congresses 12748
--England 17809
--Fiction 966, 1180
--France 11413
--Germany 15487
--Germany--History 17651
--Great Britain 3833
--History 4515, 5095, 8662, 10702, 11672, 14391, 14987, 17824
--Hong Kong 12858
--Italy 7629
--Sri Lanka 15853
--Sweden--History 12554
Student Christian Movement

2443, 3719, 3855, 4280
--History 3841
Student Christian Movement (London, England) 4479
Student Non-violent Coordinating Committee 12031, 12484
Students
--Foreign 11692, 17028
--Religious life >> See further: Church work with students
--Religious life 1570, 3218, 3560, 11557, 11751, 11872, 12212, 15696, 15847, 17028, 18177, 19141
Students, theological 2611, 10221, 13203, 13590, 14140, 18496, 18565, 18905
Suburban churches 1841, 1967, 2137, 2206, 2448, 2561, 3565, 3690, 4379, 4729, 5567, 7012, 7530, 7603, 7610, 7744, 7836, 8574, 10531, 11450, 13989, 14884, 15321, 16956, 17557, 19345
--American Baptist sources--(1918 to 1944) 4836
--American Baptist sources--(1945 to 1959) 5943
--American Baptist sources--(1970 to 1979) 12207, 14047
--American Baptist sources--(1980 to 1991) 17362
--Australia 16504, 16509, 16761
--Canada 11700, 18291
--Catholic sources--(1875 to 1899) 1234
--Catholic sources--(1900 to 1917) 2520
--Catholic sources--(1945 to 1959) 6570, 6637, 6741, 6838, 7565, 7568, 7570, 13134
--Catholic sources--(1960 to 1969) 7829, 8572, 8683, 8705, 10854
--Catholic sources--(1970 to 1979) 11700, 13375, 13416, 14451, 15007
--Catholic sources--(1980 to 1991) 15681
--Christian Churches and Churches of Christ sources 19294
--Church of England sources--(1960 to 1969) 9305
--Congregational Christian sources--(1945 to 1959) 5872, 5899, 5997, 6100, 6501, 6769
--Congregational sources--(1875 to 1899) 1094
--Disciples of Christ sources--(1970 to 1979) 12542
--England 6456, 8085, 8660, 8855, 11713, 12106, 12446, 17186, 18093
--Episcopal sources--(1900 to 1917) 2643
--Episcopal sources--(1945 to 1959) 6804, 6809
--Episcopal sources--(1970 to 1979) 11739, 13514, 14921
--Episcopal Sources--(1980 to 1991) 17159, 18063
--Evangelical and Reformed Church sources 6985, 7541
--Evangelical Protestant sources--(1960 to 1969) 10066
--Evangelical Protestant sources--(1980 to 1991) 17734, 18191, 18581, 19035
--Federal Council sources--(1918 to 1944) 4039
--Fiction 7289
--France 6292
--Germany 8572, 11835, 17660
--Great Britain 18642
--Great Britain--History 15844
--India 6685, 12496
--Latin America 15987
--Lutheran sources--(1945 to 1959) 6307, 6325, 6342

Suburban churches (cont.)
--Lutheran sources--(1960 to 1969) 7825, 8203, 10004, 10632, 10944
--Lutheran sources--(1970 to 1979) 11698, 12513, 14265
--Lutheran sources--(1980 to 1991) 17790
--Mennonite sources--(1980 to 1991) 18419
--Methodist sources--(1918 to 1944) 3013, 3091, 3435, 3437, 3689, 4334, 4748, 5049, 5162
--Methodist sources--(1945 to 1959) 5696, 5826, 5828, 6239, 6355, 6776, 6787, 7358
--Methodist sources--(1960 to 1969) 7859, 7983, 8249, 9220, 9276, 9467, 9509, 10364, 10959, 11620
--Methodist sources--(1970 to 1979) 12190, 13755, 14913, 15196, 15220, 15301, 16910
--Methodist sources--(1980 to 1991) 15771, 17177, 18233, 18296, 18642
--NCCCUSA sources--(1945 to 1959) 6056, 6275, 6280, 6528, 6688
--NCCCUSA sources--(1960 to 1969) 8092, 8142, 8474
--NCCCUSA sources--(1970 to 1979) 12201
--Norway 11053, 11802
--Pentecostal sources 11561
--Presbyterian sources--(1945 to 1959) 6128, 6428, 6495, 6764, 7700
--Presbyterian sources--(1960 to 1969) 8943, 9038, 9470, 10102, 10352, 10490, 10567, 11465, 14394
--Presbyterian sources--(1970 to 1979) 12289, 14206, 15054
--Protestant sources--(1918 to 1944) 3179, 4060, 4139
--Protestant sources--(1945 to 1959) 5524, 5581, 5685, 5775, 5963, 6129, 6281, 6364, 6377, 6427, 6508, 6716, 6734, 6912, 7198, 7550, 7551, 7555
--Protestant sources--(1960 to 1969) 8179, 8240, 8338, 8487, 8504, 8522, 8567, 9064, 9068, 9075, 9211, 9517, 9665, 11041, 11514, 19265
--Protestant sources--(1970 to 1979) 11652, 11919, 11920, 11955, 12517, 12632, 13349, 13609, 14055, 14469, 14681
--Protestant sources--(1980 to 1991) 18372, 18602
--Protestant sources--Periodicals 6370
--Reformed Church in America sources--(1960 to 1969) 8146, 8869, 10659
--Reformed Church in America sources--(1980 to 1991) 18598
--Southern Baptist sources--(1960 to 1969) 8372, 10161, 11389
--Southern Baptist sources--(1970 to 1979) 11663, 11892, 12013, 12066, 12069, 13342, 14369, 15011
--Southern Baptist sources--(1980 to 1991) 15924, 16495, 16685, 18432, 18765
--Spain 10144, 13032
--Sweden 17349
--United Church of Christ sources--(1960 to 1969) 7816, 8342, 8521, 9095, 9476, 9601, 10328, 11281
--United Church of Christ sources--(1970 to 1979) 12178
--United Church of Christ sources--(1980 to 1991) 15622, 16064, 19190
Suburban life 8094, 9609, 13524

--Bibliographies 14695
--Descriptions 1371, 1607, 3690, 4379, 5384, 6004, 6307, 6471, 6863, 6979, 7486, 7605, 7956, 7971, 8108, 8427, 8578, 8702, 8785, 8870, 9262, 9908, 10165, 10494, 11709, 11924, 11925, 12549, 13054, 13862, 17675, 17784, 17860, 18596, 19345
--England 18093
--Fiction 6380
--History 8613, 17379
--Israel--History 17636
--Japan 11909
--Jewish 7087, 7308, 7355, 7562, 7971, 8578, 8718, 8879, 10580, 10849, 16714, 17519, 19143
--Norway 11802
--Problems 1391, 1438, 4705, 5049, 7181, 7355, 7458, 7818, 9791, 10081, 10493, 10547, 11729, 11874, 11875, 11956, 12298, 12454, 12498, 12607, 13343, 13504, 16118, 17477, 17861
--Religious aspects 4039, 6838, 7829, 9467, 11909, 12973, 13669, 18084
--Spain 10144
Suburban synagogues 7087, 7308, 7562, 8718, 9845, 11541, 16700, 16714, 18194, 18684
--History 17549
Suburban-inner city exchanges >> See: See Inner city-suburban exchanges
Suffering >> See further: Church work with the sick; Justice; Poverty; Church work with the poor
Suffering 93, 1333, 2164, 4176, 4535, 4777, 6251, 6780, 7871, 8506, 9201, 10346, 11238, 11359, 11596, 11740, 12000, 12604, 12620, 12918, 13053, 13137, 13834, 14449, 14482, 14970, 15173, 15345, 15376, 15883, 16020, 16274, 16739, 16741, 17044, 17389, 17411, 17585, 18038, 18276, 18466, 18560, 18873, 18959, 19009, 19040, 19352
Suffolk County (New York)
--Religious and ecclesiastical institutions 7551
Suicide 1536, 3873, 4830, 15547, 17796, 18125, 18218, 19235, 19349
Summer ministry 741, 3561, 9281, 10724, 10950, 15319, 18496
Sunday legislation, observance 745, 833, 1201, 2617, 7542, 8036, 8079, 15460
--Australia--History 11929
--Canada--History 15559
--History 11929, 13017, 13245
Sunday school buildings >> See further: Church architecture; Church buildings
Sunday school buildings 4704, 5767, 10217
Sunday schools >> See further: Christian Education
Sunday schools 47, 49, 121, 183, 313, 1046, 1713, 2020, 2420, 2470, 2577, 3451, 4163, 5567, 5980, 9476, 11917, 17818, 17962
Sunday Schools
--Curriculum 3451, 8714, 8757, 8777, 15925
--England--History 344, 581, 4847, 13948, 15789
--History 365, 3027, 6035, 12229, 12777, 16986, 16986
--India 17454
--Organization and management 37, 838, 1864, 2067, 2855, 2899, 3125, 3179, 4716, 5666,

15928
--Periodicals 82, 102
--Societies, unions, etc. 45, 52, 83, 5056, 15670
Support groups >> See: Networks
Sweden
--Economic conditions 12554
--Economic conditions--History 16360
--History 11644
--Religious and ecclesiastical institutions 3925, 5586, 5724, 8847, 8872, 11867, 15678, 17330, 17349, 17968, 18479
--Religious and ecclesiastical institutions--History 16045
--Religious life and customs 16338
--Social conditions 13415, 19232
Swedenborgianism 2225, 2230, 2303, 2943, 18382, 18489
Swedish American Protestants
--History 12841
Switzerland
--Religion 10727
--Social conditions 14046
Sydney (Australia)
--Religious and ecclesiastical institutions 10149, 11338, 11466, 16509, 16712, 17078, 17391, 18189
--Religious and ecclesiastical institutions--History 8550, 11929, 17207
--Social conditions 15472
Sydney (Nova Scotia, Canada)
--Social conditions 2748
Symbionese Liberation Army 13360
Symbolism 11605, 13859, 16756
--History 14752, 15699
--Japan 16679
Symbolism (urban) 2787, 3865, 3922, 4003, 4600, 5552, 5779, 6400, 7402, 7481, 7485, 7632, 7736, 7901, 7924, 7932, 8263, 8309, 8618, 8766, 8887, 9272, 10173, 10277, 10400, 11084, 11293, 11296, 11348, 11602, 11771, 11789, 11818, 12094, 12234, 12697, 13260, 13849, 14335, 14704, 15236, 15425, 15633, 15766, 15888, 16214, 16316, 16491, 16757, 17045, 17125, 17189, 17314, 17517, 18008, 18167, 18669
--Asia 18330
--Bibliographies 8618, 11602
--Great Britain 19019
--History 7644, 9633, 13762, 14432, 15725, 15979, 17781, 18239, 18373, 18470
Symbolism in literature 8618, 11293, 18183
Synagogue architecture 3712, 5635, 6424, 9279
--Bibliographies 14309, 14525
--History 6807
Synagogues >> See further: Suburban synagogues; Jews; Judaism
Synagogues 4186, 5903, 5909, 6055, 6675, 6982, 7194, 7363, 8219, 9092, 10849, 10981, 12286, 12320, 13452, 13897, 14305, 14588, 15882, 16101, 17216, 17403, 17828, 18132, 18374, 18571
--Bibliographies 4931, 5022, 14309, 14525
--England--History 9137
--History 1294, 1573, 6807, 9750, 12834, 12916, 13029, 13143, 13270, 13607, 16498, 17251, 17343, 18209
--Relocation 12543
Syracuse (New York)
--Ethnic relations--History 14483
--History 16215
--Moral conditions 2743

--Religious and ecclesiastical institutions 6983, 8476, 8477, 9898, 12077
--Social conditions 511, 5145
Syria
--Ethnic relations 16157
--History 16157, 16627
--Social conditions 11858
Syrian Americans 13261
Tacoma (Washington)
--Religious and ecclesiastical institutions 5080, 5275, 5816, 7672
--Social conditions 19349
Taiwan
--History 13399
--Religious and ecclesiastical institutions 12694, 13779, 15387, 16502, 17564, 17565, 17887, 18774
--Social conditions 9921, 12522, 15387, 15509, 18536
Taize Community (Taize, France) 10307, 11751, 15093, 17412, 17413
Tallahassee (Florida)
--Religious and ecclesiastical institutions--History 15067
Tampa (Florida)
--Religious and ecclesiastical institutions 8089, 13287
--Social conditions 4548
Tanzania
--Religious and ecclesiastical institutions 11113, 17455
Tarrasa (Spain)
--Religious and ecclesiastical institutions 15218
Task-Force for Renewal, Urban Strategy and Training (Richmond, Virginia) 10600
Task-Force for Research, Urban Strategy and Training (Richmond, Virginia) 8011
Taxation 661, 1622, 1730, 2450, 11490, 14297, 17479, 18305, 18993
--History 8974
Team ministry >> See: Group ministries
Teamsters' Union 7283
Technocracy 4208, 4271, 4282, 4300
Technology >> See further: Cybernetics
Technology
--Bibliographies 14490
--England 14664
--Fiction 16953
--Germany 15363
--History 6613, 8117, 9151, 14533, 14815, 17902
--Moral and ethical aspects 6397, 8247, 9739, 12148, 13420, 16074, 17243, 17779, 18188, 18497
--Moral and ethical aspects--India 18238
--Religious aspects 2118, 3896, 3953, 4208, 4297, 4481, 6158, 6302, 6517, 6613, 7266, 7519, 7572, 7805, 7922, 8111, 8122, 8247, 8276, 8451, 8502, 8602, 8665, 8689, 8849, 9021, 9047, 9049, 9196, 9271, 9301, 9530, 9660, 9740, 9766, 9794, 9982, 10027, 10160, 10370, 10433, 10471, 10515, 10658, 10698, 10765, 10963, 11074, 11125, 11422, 11428, 11471, 11726, 11881, 11953, 12093, 12148, 12425, 12782, 12843, 12874, 12875, 12880, 13090, 13183, 13207, 13269, 13294, 13359, 13370, 13702, 13837, 14091, 14144, 14145, 14397, 14463, 14938, 15684, 15746, 16074, 16390, 16497, 16716, 17140, 17601, 18371
--Religious aspects--Bibliographies

17071
Technology (cont.)
--Religious aspects--Congresses 8541, 8793, 8983, 9006, 9063, 9173, 9650, 9739, 10609, 11122, 12710, 12795, 13056, 14900, 15705, 17071
--Religious aspects--England 7736, 13069, 15807, 16013
--Religious aspects--History 5743, 12830
--Religious aspects--Islam 11448
--Religious aspects--Japan 11843, 16505
--Religious aspects--Periodicals 12033
--Social aspects 4249, 5292, 6397, 7324, 8379, 8519, 8524, 8826, 9775, 9880, 11045, 11901, 12321, 12375, 12443, 14219, 16085, 16349, 16415, 16479, 16706, 16951, 17302, 17882, 18016, 18238
--Social aspects--Fiction 18261
Technology and civilization 5292, 7922, 8689, 9049, 9173, 12672, 13001, 13294, 14900, 15470, 15703, 15895, 16415, 16716, 17882
--History 17902
Teen Challenge 16968
Telephone in church work 6731, 7193, 10149, 10596, 10909, 11038, 11795, 11845, 13759, 15547, 15814, 16171, 16584, 16944, 17833, 18499
--Australia 9256
--Bibliographies 17406
Television >> See: Mass media
Tema (Ghana)
--Religious and ecclesiastical institutions 13120
Temperance >> See also: Prohibition
Temperance 180, 591, 666, 689, 709, 981, 1489, 1677, 1796, 1814, 1945, 2281, 2377, 2474, 3017, 4485, 4536, 6677
--Canada 2763
--England--History 3746, 3846
--History 1926, 12928, 13153, 13235, 14582, 14945, 16903
--Periodicals 3266
Temples
--Hindu 15452
--Thai Buddhist 16355
Tenements >> See: Housing (tenements)
Tests and measures >> See further: Social surveys
Tests and measures 8352, 8370, 9130, 10669, 13531, 15275, 16079, 16212, 17592, 18977
Tests and measures in religion >> See further: Religious surveys
Tests and measures in religion 6247, 6451, 6750, 6860, 7535, 8219, 8572, 9059, 10323, 10677, 10692, 10850, 11322, 11699, 12248, 12290, 12314, 12371, 12642, 12732, 12739, 13601, 13850, 13904, 14629, 15415, 15660, 15756, 15910, 16076, 16087, 16222, 16301, 16945, 16981, 17127, 17292, 17301, 17308, 17429, 17448, 17542, 17667, 18135, 18151, 18177, 18443, 18828
--Bibliographies 11688
Texarkana (Texas)
--Religious and ecclesiastical institutions 17771
Theaters 183, 268, 325, 335, 2695
Theodicy >> See: Suffering
Theological education 6406, 6935, 11918, 12222, 16641, 16889, 18965
--Asia 12635, 16256
--Bibliographies 16000, 18643
--Case studies 6382, 12488,

14827
Theological education (cont.)
--Congresses 17180, 18128
--England 13070, 18905
--Germany 12682
--Great Britain 17180, 18053, 18393, 18520
--History 18385, 18526
--India--Curriculum 13590
--Melanesia 13924
--Philippines 11757
--South Africa 12364, 17316
--United States--(1960 to 1969) 9265, 11204, 11205, 11373, 11419, 11591, 11626
--United States--(1970 to 1979) 11678, 11679, 11851, 13417, 14474, 14885
--United States--(1980 to 1991) 16487, 16603, 17001, 18001, 18502, 18873, 19352
Theological reflection >> See: Theology
Theological seminaries 2347, 4381, 8809, 13172, 14140, 17346, 19180
--African American 6466, 7589, 11510, 11590
--Curriculum 1336, 1337, 1505, 1745, 1753, 2213, 2404, 2550, 2793, 2967, 3164, 3482, 3485, 3531, 4494, 6935, 6976, 7731, 8262, 9205, 9548, 10221, 10356, 10403, 10637, 10707, 10864, 11204, 11205, 11373, 11419, 11591, 11667, 11851, 11940, 12017, 12078, 12160, 12290, 12331, 12371, 12635, 12696, 13079, 13326, 14257, 14839, 15459, 15575, 15582, 16064, 16487, 16519, 16603, 17001, 17297, 17610, 18001, 18128, 18393, 18698, 18702, 18787, 18873, 19245, 19352
--Curriculum--History 18526
--England 12800
--Field work 2611, 7593, 7813, 11769, 12152, 12696, 14055, 14127, 14257, 17901, 18514, 18702
--Field work--Nigeria 18496
--History 948
--Kenya 13326
--Methodist 7192, 8748
--Periodicals 19283
--Philippines 12634
--Presbyterian 6382, 18705
--Protestant 12870, 14474, 14827, 16777
--Protestant--History 18157
--South Africa 17316
--Southern Baptist 1745, 2793
Theology >> See further: Black theology; Liberation theology; Hope; God; Jesus Christ
Theology 768, 4071, 5916, 6897, 8486, 8580, 8964, 9070, 9512, 9567, 12225, 13114, 13586, 14915, 15235, 15392, 15766, 16573, 16730, 17961, 18184, 18409, 18761
--Africa 8500, 12291
--Asia 7474, 11748, 15439
--Bibliographies 11182, 13574, 16890, 18365
--Case study 14392
--China 16416
--Congresses 15701
--Developing countries 13165, 13630, 15126, 15351, 15496, 15719, 16006, 16018, 16096, 16229, 16405, 16447, 16842, 16850, 17643, 18423, 18978
--Europe 7474
--France 1481
--Methodology 9329
--Spain 4185
Theology (Bible) >> See: Bible; Cities and towns--Biblical teaching

Theology (community) >> See: Community (theology)
Theology (covenant) >> See: Covenants (theology)
Theology (forgiveness) >> See further: Forgiveness
Theology (hope) >> See: Hope
Theology (incarnation) >> See: Incarnation
Theology (Kingdom) >> See further: Kingdom of God
Theology (Kingdom) 159, 227, 393, 501, 573, 699, 700, 811, 983, 1045, 1086, 1172, 2011, 2132, 2177, 2178, 2432, 2583, 2721, 2916, 3297, 3426, 3765, 3817, 3921, 4105, 4128, 4511, 4852, 4879, 5285, 6158, 6237, 7175, 7203, 7481, 8466, 8641, 11030, 12000, 14715, 15046, 15790, 16343, 16507, 16744, 16881, 16965, 17113, 17191, 17618, 17722, 17775, 18034, 18919
--History 5009, 5038, 6174, 14984
Theology (of local church) >> See further: Mission of the church
Theology (of local church) 6617, 7349, 7478, 7574, 7582, 8039, 8231, 8514, 9091, 9159, 9396, 10563, 11930, 13284, 13520, 13583, 13987, 14360, 14650, 14843, 15236, 15768, 16254, 16644, 16756, 16910, 18145, 18183, 19086, 19116, 19219
--England 12407, 12524, 13879
--Germany 5610
Theology (of the city) 1364, 3269, 3687, 4023, 4579, 4801, 5664, 6293, 7924, 7987, 8321, 8494, 8639, 8641, 8832, 9035, 9096, 9189, 9234, 9272, 9355, 9372, 9373, 9656, 10497, 10758, 11027, 11583, 11719, 11752, 11816, 11944, 12116, 12776, 12784, 13442, 13643, 14117, 14195, 14272, 14854, 15038, 15108, 15114, 15131, 15425, 15519, 15595, 15618, 15723, 15954, 15958, 16363, 16387, 16457, 16770, 17150, 17354, 17637, 17810, 17977, 18424, 18576, 18680, 18799, 18810, 18863, 18889, 18898, 18902, 19058, 19156, 19184, 19209, 19219
--Europe 9642
--Great Britain 19133
Theology (redemption) >> See: Redemption
Theology, American Baptist 7490
Theology, Catholic 5745, 5833, 10230, 10650, 11719, 11944, 13106, 14156, 14862, 15038, 18683
Theology, Church of England 696, 5128, 7004, 7632, 7968, 9625, 12206, 13358, 17281
Theology, doctrinal >> See further (Social teaching under specific denominations, e.g., Catholic Church--Social teaching)
Theology, doctrinal 1139, 1717, 2736, 3553, 3914, 4512, 4629, 5187, 5578, 5731, 6227, 6602, 7116, 7183, 7846, 8163, 8916, 10563, 11018, 12868, 15562, 16474
Theology, ecumenical 4829, 6621, 7046, 7349, 7474, 8164, 8599, 8937, 8948, 8959, 9273, 9753, 10927, 12880, 13069, 13200, 13319, 13506, 14140, 14218, 16828, 17611, 18863
--History 6613
Theology, Episcopal 8092, 8592, 13050
Theology, evangelical Protestant

10141, 11521, 11889, 12876, 14117, 14334, 14654, 14928, 15060, 15723, 15967, 16015, 17546, 17551, 17949, 18111, 18722, 18810, 18854, 19209
Theology, Fundamental >> See: Fundamentalism
Theology, Jewish 6177, 11716, 18115
Theology, liberation >> See: Liberation theology
Theology, Lutheran 8569, 9140, 9216, 10089, 10943, 11540, 14372, 18236
Theology, Methodist 10568, 11375, 12007, 15811, 17991
Theology, practical >> See further: Church planning; Mission of the church
Theology, practical 3485, 4464, 4544, 4666, 5001, 5380, 6332, 6420, 10259, 10879, 15101, 15537, 16469, 16721
Theology, Presbyterian 6426, 8049, 9941, 14682
Theology, Protestant 332, 1811, 1862, 3844, 4375, 4411, 4571, 4652, 5731, 5754, 6252, 6302, 6430, 6935, 7474, 8134, 8183, 8494, 9372, 9766, 10067, 10257, 11201, 11876, 12348, 12685, 12807, 13433, 13442, 13528, 13732, 13837, 14540, 14819
--Asia 16298
--History 13913
Theology, radical 10486, 10943, 11374, 11751, 11782, 11840, 12007, 12007, 12712, 14080, 16038, 17991
Theology, Southern Baptist 11763, 11814, 13372
Theology, United Church of Canada 16056
Theology, United Church of Christ 7307, 8832, 9035, 9646, 9821
Theosophy 4586
--History 19121
Third world >> See: Developing countries
Three Mile Island (Pennsylvania) 15120, 16046
Three Rivers (Michigan)
--Religious and ecclesiastical institutions 6791
Times Square Mission (New York, NY) 5182
Tokyo (Japan)
--Religion 17807
--Religious and ecclesiastical institutions 4291, 7523, 7801, 10800
--Social conditions 3504, 3516, 11559, 16418, 16909
Toledo (Ohio)
--Religious and ecclesiastical institutions 5407, 5419, 5698, 5717, 6789, 7239, 7760, 8068, 8356, 11380, 14511
--Social conditions 2473
Topeka (Kansas)
--Religious and ecclesiastical institutions 3727, 5407, 5902, 6007, 6787, 10361, 11061, 12189, 18826
--Social conditions 6007
Toronto (Ontario, Canada)
--Church history 14739
--History 18809
--Religious and ecclesiastical institutions 1982, 9774, 14003, 15561, 16369, 18268
--Religious and ecclesiastical institutions--History 14213, 14256
--Social conditions 6644, 8653
--Social conditions--History 13943, 14844
Torrington (Connecticut)

--Social conditions 10521
Touch International Ministries (Australia) 18265
Toynbee Hall (London, England) 712, 945, 1107, 1197, 1271, 1774, 1883, 1888, 2295, 3177, 4200, 4457, 4483
--History 1503, 2731, 2761, 3306, 3413, 3585, 5961, 18249
Tracts >> See further: American Tract Society
Tracts 1, 7, 19, 27, 84, 161, 267, 347, 372, 379, 457
--England 1749
--Fiction 11760
--History 4551, 7834, 10876, 13701
--Periodicals 546
Trade unions >> See further: Right to work; Church and labor; Wages; Strikes and lockouts; Employment problems
Trade unions 173, 261, 637, 672, 779, 787, 1069, 1095, 1129, 1355, 1399, 1542, 1970, 1983, 2023, 2173, 2270, 2453, 2507, 2603, 2659, 2738, 2744, 3058, 3142, 3353, 3481, 3606, 3638, 3696, 3888, 4030, 4251, 4550, 4561, 4590, 4634, 4654, 4672, 4965, 5037, 5130, 5188, 5345, 5372, 5467, 5496, 5501, 5527, 5557, 5560, 5570, 5954, 6023, 6156, 6283, 6496, 6539, 6641, 6867, 6922, 6932, 7026, 7083, 7155, 7280, 7282, 7283, 7399, 7537, 7625, 7699, 7718, 7797, 7798, 8389, 9347, 9377, 9380, 10107, 10479, 12853, 12958, 13244, 13577, 13665, 14232, 14415, 14435, 14905, 15737, 15857, 15867, 15898, 15961, 15989, 16312, 16879, 17021, 17287, 17729, 18107, 18108, 18277, 18652, 18665, 18720, 18932
--Africa 14858, 15079
--Archives 16300
--Argentina 5403, 19081
--Asia 16612
--Austria 11990
--Austria--History 8880
--Belgium 13611
--Belgium--History 15820, 16057
--Biography 4894
--Brazil 11607
--Brazil--History 17874, 18175, 19065
--Canada 5454, 6271, 7050, 10016, 12645, 14077, 14776, 14863, 17394, 17507
--Canada--History 3110
--Catholic 4580, 4892, 5043, 5558, 6719, 8161, 8265, 10953, 11431, 13593, 17194, 17401, 17547
--Catholic--Europe 11285, 13836
--Catholic--History 6063, 7471, 7863, 10699, 11023, 11192, 13774, 13775, 15820, 19065
--Catholic--Periodicals 4581, 5065
--Colombia 7855, 9112, 12056
--Congresses 12748
--Costa Rica 13429
--England 134, 7729, 8680, 9009, 12443, 13069, 14535, 14583, 14584, 14922
--Europe 4480, 5657, 6633, 7508, 8558, 9403
--Europe--History 4680, 5866, 13835
--Fiction 966, 1017, 5054
--Finland 15607
--France 5387, 6403, 6719, 6993, 8115, 8489, 11683, 15673
--France--History 3753, 4506, 5224, 10118
--Germany 2315, 2368, 2380,

2503, 2701, 4336, 13935, 17401, 18055, 18195
Trade unions (cont)
--Germany--History 4861, 10432, 13593, 14141, 14504, 14868, 14941, 15420, 15861, 15878, 16409, 16410, 16606, 17481, 18266
--Great Britain 3791, 5538, 15720, 16090
--Great Britain--History 3842, 14707
--History 2893, 4612, 4967, 6054, 6063, 6197, 6686, 6759, 7492, 7746, 8017, 8095, 8254, 8419, 9308, 9874, 12742, 13110, 14190, 14865, 16075, 16215, 16342, 16364, 16394, 16438, 16578, 17135, 17264, 17326, 17327, 17443, 17547, 17595, 17718, 17905, 18349, 18491, 18836
--Italy 5929, 6022, 6398, 7134, 7241, 7947, 11285, 15204
--Italy--History 11886, 13885, 15764, 18394
--Japan 7428, 18205
--Jewish membership 6554, 6760, 8875, 13930
--Korea 13230, 14710
--Latin America 8505, 10953, 11431
--Netherlands 3674, 5852, 5853, 6784, 7022
--Netherlands--History 16694, 17194, 17976
--Periodicals 683
--Philippines 13598
--Poland 12896, 16105, 16638, 17430
--Protestant 2441, 4235, 4973, 5914, 6182
--South Africa 15900, 17285
--Spain 7838, 8073, 8344, 11183
--Spain--History 17313, 18364
--Sri Lanka 15853
--Sweden 17330
--Switzerland--History 11023, 13685
Training Ecumenically to Advance Mission (Philadelphia, Pennsylvania) 11567
Transnational corporations >> See: International business enterprises
Transportation 3595, 13054, 17674, 18573
--Canada--History 15559
Transvaal (South Africa)
--Social conditions 12911
Travel 199, 476, 6756, 10444, 12042, 17552
--Guidebooks 1613, 3038
--Islamic 19077
Treble (New York)
--Social conditions 12518
Trenton (New Jersey)
--Religious and ecclesiastical institutions 5406, 8052, 8487, 9122, 17540
--Social conditions 14790
Trois-Rivières (Quebec, Canada)
--Social conditions 6898
Troy (New York)
--Religious and ecclesiastical institutions 7709
--Social conditions 14790
Tucson (Arizona)
--Religious and ecclesiastical institutions 5407
--Religious and ecclesiastical institutions--History 14665
--Social conditions 18063
Tulsa (Oklahoma)
--Race relations 14138
--Religious and ecclesiastical institutions 4896, 5407, 9074, 12196, 13319, 14789, 17810
--Religious and ecclesiastical institutions--History 17798

--Social conditions 14138
Tulsa Metropolitan Ministry (Tulsa, Oklahoma) 13319
Turin (Italy)
--History 14457, 18032, 18283
Turkey
--History 18848
--Religious life and customs 7249
--Social conditions 8799, 17929, 17930
--Social conditions--History 16401
Tuscaloosa (Alabama)
--Race relations 15339
Twinning >> See: Inner city-suburban exchanges; Church development, yoked parishes
Typologies 4748, 5617, 5769, 17231
Typologies (of city churches) 1931, 2742, 3592, 3602, 3613, 3757, 3969, 4743, 4788, 5798, 5894, 6160, 6927, 7207, 7450, 7770, 7945, 8588, 8626, 12873, 13692, 13927, 14469, 14503, 14698, 15296, 15334, 15596, 16208, 16666, 17147, 18134, 18183, 18209
--France 6950
Typologies (psychology) 12508
Typologies (sociology) 2543, 2668, 2742, 3788, 3904, 4217, 5349, 5391, 5798, 6072, 6313, 6371, 6422, 6467, 6825, 7015, 7207, 7254, 7588, 7983, 7985, 9057, 9808, 10574, 11603, 12368, 12773, 13827, 14471, 14698, 14899, 15011, 15413, 15714, 15716, 16207, 16240, 17127, 17365, 18134
Uganda
--Social conditions 14858
Ugandan Christian Moslem Association 14858
Ukrainian Americans
--Histoty 15858
--Social life 15263
Ukrainians
--Canada 11682
Ulster (Northern Ireland)
--Social conditions 12408, 17654
Underdeveloped nations >> See: Developing countries; (Specific city and country names)
Underemployment >> See: Unemployment; Employment problems
Underground churches 9742, 10711, 10712, 10767, 11552, 11696, 11774, 11846, 11922, 12072, 12095, 12134, 12276, 12565, 12591, 12669, 13301
Underground literature 10711
Unemployment >> See further: Employment problems; Church work with the unemployed
Unemployment 3767, 3859, 4493, 4834, 5309, 13608, 13846, 15130, 15538, 17889
--Africa 10262, 19240
--Asia 15188
--Australia 11352, 15188
--Canada 14781, 15393, 17507
--Congresses 3456, 4974, 10012, 14245
--Descriptions of 1930, 2863, 3582, 3933, 3979, 4025, 4109, 4174, 4201, 4513, 4575, 4596, 4664, 4783, 4977, 5268, 7291, 7394, 8524, 8602, 8884, 8925, 9718, 12065, 14112, 14281, 14395, 15545, 15645, 15988, 16397, 16479, 16684, 16800, 16864, 16993, 17524, 17750, 17915, 18308, 18375, 18820
--Descriptions of--Bibliographies 14285
--Developing countries 12065
--England 1466, 2008, 3859,

7324, 10249, 10410, 10999, 13818, 15103, 16552, 17142, 17262, 17932, 18321, 18553
Unemployment (cont.)
--Europe 18390
--Fiction 1017
--Germany 13890, 14452, 16847, 17027, 17193
--Germany--History 17409
--Great Britain 1930, 4508, 5579, 13655, 14914, 17618
--History 8466
--India 14057
--Netherlands 360
--New Guinea 15947
--Philippines 12264
--Puerto Rico 12869
--Religious views on 1466, 3882, 4172, 4250, 4343, 5268, 5390, 5458, 7291, 10582, 15035, 15499, 16645, 16684, 16715, 16815, 16840, 16994, 17220, 17344, 17970, 19326, 19351
--Religious views on--Bibliographies 15598
--Scotland 16377, 18036
--Spain 16011
Unemployment--Religious aspects >> See further: Church work with the unemployed, church and industry
Unification Church 15786
--History 19121
Union >> See: Christian union; Trade unions
Union catholique internationale de service social 5132
--Congresses 4498
Union for Concerted Moral Effort 1341
--History 6221, 11008
Union of American Hebrew Congregations 3373, 4186, 5635, 6424, 8496
Union Theological Seminary (New York, NY) 3199, 6598, 14127, 14791, 14827, 19096
--History 948, 18157
Unitarian Church
--Case studies 603, 1053, 2650, 2832, 4446, 5645, 7063, 9596, 11234
--Case studies--Bibliographies 4933
--History 1846, 8149
--Organizations 143, 16926
--Periodicals 65, 542
Unitarian Church (Czechoslovakia) 19107
Unitarian Church (England) 4446, 6180
Unitarian Universalist Association
--Pronouncements, policies 17805
Unitarian Universalist Association, Urban Church Coalition 16926
United Auto Workers of America 8389, 15416, 17003
United Campus Christian Fellowship 9060
United Christian Missionary Society 4573, 5991
United Church Board for Homeland Ministries 11252, 12450
United Church of Canada 13066, 14859
--Case studies 5091, 6233, 9803, 16369, 18719
--Pronouncements, policies 16056
United Church of Canada, Board of Evangelism and Social Service 9381
United Church of Canada, Board of Home Missions 9925
United Church of Christ >> See further: Congregational churches; Evangelical and

Reformed Church
United Church of Christ
--Case studies 7196, 7549, 8109, 8145, 8716, 8742, 8750, 9053, 9076, 9243, 9246, 9523, 10577, 11281, 11699, 12471, 12485, 12601, 12764, 12959, 13216, 13446, 14106, 14159, 14496, 14896, 15514, 15622, 16542, 16875, 17662, 18436, 18510, 18687, 19190, 19337
--Congresses 7446, 10138
--Periodicals 4360, 7933, 8025, 8026
--Pronouncements, policies 8926, 14069, 14456, 17805
--Social teaching 8864, 9505, 19273
United Church of Christ in Japan 8924
--Case studies 7801
United Church of Christ in the Philippines 7065, 7463, 7954, 7955, 8774, 10041, 11932, 11968
United Church of Christ, Board for Homeland Ministries 7956, 8026, 8426, 8750, 8877, 8925, 9848, 10138, 12451, 12452, 12681, 14459, 16413, 18510, 18687, 18915, 18983
United Church of Christ, Board for World Ministries 8799
United Church of Christ, Board of Homeland Ministries 16875
United Church of Christ, Council for Christian Social Action 8602, 9246, 11468
United Church of Christ, Council for Church and Ministry 12758
United Church of Christ, Council for lay Life and Work 19273
United Church of Christ, Office for Audio Visuals 9676
United Church of Christ, Stewardship Council 7758
United Church Women 5862, 7732, 8027
United Domestic Missionary Society (New York, NY) 75
United Holy Church of America 18837
United Lutheran Church 6431
--Periodicals 4298
United Lutheran Church of America
--Pronouncements, policies 5532, 7130, 8605
United Lutheran Church, Board of Social Missions 5532, 8605
United Lutheran Church, Inner Mission Board 3143, 4298
United Methodist Church 10716, 10717, 10838, 10990, 11224, 11455, 11485, 11732, 11764, 12583, 12637, 13535, 13660, 13726, 13802, 14035, 14073, 14174, 14625, 15308, 15399, 15668, 16182, 16933, 17003, 17138, 17872, 18200, 18504, 18741
--Case studies 7705, 9614, 10728, 10916, 11026, 11068, 11143, 11383, 11395, 11408, 11618, 11620, 11622, 11623, 11635, 11967, 12026, 12077, 12084, 12215, 12369, 12441, 12575, 12610, 12833, 13151, 13240, 13306, 13425, 13693, 13763, 13764, 13801, 13843, 13844, 13944, 14072, 14107, 14170, 14222, 14288, 14333, 14339, 14348, 14351, 14405, 14579, 14721, 14724, 14843, 14952, 15044, 15100, 15129, 15169, 15327, 15408, 16052, 16565, 16604, 16798, 16832, 16976, 17023, 17215, 17222, 17263, 17308, 17425, 17488, 17669,

17684, 17706, 17780, 17921, 17975, 18049, 18247, 18400, 18493, 18807, 18826, 18926, 18963, 19073, 19100, 19199, 19200, 19303
United Methodist Church (cont.)
--Case studies--Bibliographies 14695
--Congresses 11916, 13675, 13827, 13857, 13889, 14461, 14566, 14803, 15072, 15102, 15136, 15279
--Handbooks 15605
--History 11687
--Pastoral theology 16622
--Periodicals 7651, 12002, 16228, 19003
--Pronouncements, policies 11551, 11693, 14860, 17805
United Methodist Church (United States) >> See further: Evangelical United Brethren; Methodist
United Methodist Church, Black Community Developers Program 12704, 13722
United Methodist Church, Board of Christian Social Concerns 11578
United Methodist Church, Board of Discipleship 14070
United Methodist Church, Board of Global Ministries 13889, 13928, 14071, 15072, 15279, 15341, 19169
United Methodist Church, Board of Higher Education 14276, 15274
United Methodist Church, Board of Missions 11619
United Methodist Church, Council of Bishops 13582, 13583, 13675, 13744, 14915, 18882, 19122
United Methodist Church, National Urban Ministries Network 14386, 14461, 14625, 14915, 15100, 15102, 15146, 15224, 15236, 15237, 15257, 15279, 16469
United Methodist Church, Office of Research and Survey 10784, 10785, 10912, 11144, 11146, 11177, 11250, 11251, 11380, 11381, 11382, 11383, 11618, 11620, 11621, 11622, 11623, 12027, 12120, 12537, 12816, 14585
United Methodist Church, Office of Urban Ministries 11374, 11375, 12002, 12392, 13200, 13580, 13581, 13780, 13857, 13925, 14460, 14461, 14695, 14802, 15098, 15099, 15100, 15101, 15223, 15278, 17488, 17494, 18545, 18962
United Nations 7699, 11407
United Presbyterian Church in the USA 8607, 11108
--Case studies 1739, 2091, 5507, 5508, 5511, 5537, 5569, 5716, 5901, 5902, 5963, 6365, 6402, 6945, 6995, 7077, 7457, 7554, 7700, 7809, 7976, 8019, 8213, 8258, 8318, 8434, 8546, 9038, 9451, 9475, 9554, 9653, 9863, 9890, 9951, 9979, 10354, 10851, 10901, 11750, 11912, 12054, 12184, 13110, 14170, 14281, 14609, 15486, 15810, 16604, 17155, 17540, 18300, 18552, 18703
--Congresses 8029
--Periodicals 2257, 6550, 8030
--Pronouncements, policies 2257, 5721, 6551, 7762, 8606, 9139, 9586, 10136, 10284, 10623, 12199, 12705, 12860, 13846, 13870, 14787, 15198, 15280, 15985, 16053, 16871

--Social teaching 6133
--Social teachings 16924
United Presbyterian Church in the USA, Board of Christian Education 7861, 8028, 8049, 10135, 10618, 11107, 11229, 12184
--Bibliographies 8608
United Presbyterian Church in the USA, Board of National Missions 5079, 5240, 5439, 5440, 5441, 5443, 5546, 6282, 6945, 6954, 6995, 6996, 6997, 7146, 7211, 7456, 7457, 7458, 7464, 7584, 7714, 7715, 7719, 7762, 7794, 7905, 7988, 8019, 8029, 8030, 8031, 8062, 8140, 8159, 8201, 8213, 8289, 8318, 8321, 8322, 8589, 8600, 8606, 8607, 8903, 8927, 8928, 9044, 9446, 9447, 9448, 9449, 9450, 9451, 9627, 9863, 9979, 10136, 10354, 10355, 10544, 10619, 10620, 10621, 10623, 10851, 11787, 11788, 12054, 12318, 12705, 12706
United Presbyterian Church in the USA, Commission on Ecumenical Mission and Relations 8290
United Presbyterian Church in the USA, Council for Religion and Race 8048
United Presbyterian Church in the USA, General Council 7826
United Presbyterian Missionary Library 8931
United Reformed Church (England) 13727, 16268
--Case studies 17516
--Clergy 16547
United States
--Church History 197, 879, 3667, 3930, 4103, 4339, 4562, 5138, 5190, 5325, 5632, 5728, 5745, 6235, 7641, 9485, 10949, 11429, 11435, 12385, 14135, 14967, 15635, 15711, 15916, 15977, 17053, 17171, 17172, 17312, 18106
--Church History--Bibliographies 1312, 9864
--Economic conditions 599, 787, 4311, 6800, 6929, 8033, 8455, 8980, 10245, 16121, 16309, 16970, 17058, 18561, 18924, 19109
--Economic conditions--Bibliographies 15539
--Economic policy 14736, 15971, 17267, 17371, 17467, 17720, 17831, 17889, 18292
--Foreign policy 1823, 2742, 2970, 18764
--History 3830, 5009, 7644, 10343, 11927, 12094, 12356, 12716, 12871, 15177, 15949, 16031, 17278, 17392
--History--Bibliographies 13274, 15566, 15749, 16432, 16736
--History--Periodicals 13256
--Intellectual life 129, 1902, 3850, 4288, 6981, 11936, 19048, 19109, 19118
--Intellectual life--Bibliographies 15566
--Intellectual life--History 5142, 5306, 6470, 7644, 7901, 8410, 8618, 8677, 9527, 10157, 13537, 13871, 14532, 15979, 17408, 19084
--Moral conditions 295, 1464, 1674, 5748, 6027, 8791, 9120
--Moral conditions--History 7199, 14532
--Politics 18901
--Politics and government 11013
--Population 1206, 7591, 8160
--Population--Statistics 2467,

3165, 4115, 5061
United States (cont.)
--Religion 3389, 3844, 3977, 5683, 7884, 8828, 10207, 11798, 11885, 12155, 13439, 14251, 14629, 15456, 16222, 16534, 17238, 17635, 18041, 18301
--Religion--Bibliographies 7620, 8093, 10216, 16521
--Religious and ecclesiastical institutions 1901, 4049, 4571, 5763, 8951, 13248, 14748, 16669, 19258
--Religious and ecclesiastical institutions--Bibliographies 4837
--Religious and ecclesiastical institutions--Census 2467, 3165, 4115, 5061
--Social conditions 185, 310, 500, 767, 1388, 1700, 1888, 2659, 3760, 4668, 4876, 5752, 6371, 6626, 6915, 6954, 6960, 7086, 7381, 8162, 8380, 9080, 10007, 10309, 10422, 10423, 10779, 12410, 12604, 16844, 17408, 19027, 19196, 19350
--Social conditions--Bibliographies 17272
--Social conditions--History 8729, 14977, 19131
--Social history 140, 4917, 5788, 5977, 12083
--Social policy 525, 8288, 8784, 9960, 11579, 13016, 14736, 15971, 16363, 16689, 17479, 18368, 18381, 18924
--Social policy--History 11533
United States Catholic Conference 11109, 13723, 14788, 17083, 18077, 18619
--History 17267
United States Government
--Department of Commerce, Bureau of the Census 2467, 3165, 4115, 5061
--Department of Housing and Urban Development 14840, 14872
--Office of Economic Opportunity 10462, 11579, 13016
United Training Organization of Atlanta (Atlanta, Georgia) 10624
United Way of America 18281
Uniting Church in Australia
--Case studies 17391, 17726, 18568
--Missions 17015
Universal Christian Conference on Life and Work (Stockholm, Sweden) 3685, 3693, 3728, 3729, 3731, 3732, 3733, 3743, 3802, 3803
Universal Christian Council 4114
Universal Declaration of Human Rights 11407
Universal Fellowship of Metropolitan Community Churches 13192, 14462
--Case studies 18441
--History 14130
Universal Negro Improvement Association 3527, 8726, 12351, 12606, 13964, 14545, 16610
--History 6651, 14544
Universities and colleges >> See further: Community colleges; Social settlements
Universities and colleges 801, 1025, 1421, 1565, 1664, 1776, 2867, 4174, 8325, 8595, 9790, 9916, 10372, 10787, 11577, 11872, 12201, 12266, 12674, 12675, 13211, 13483, 13647, 13778, 14098, 14276, 14520, 14635, 14636, 14728, 14740, 15140, 15990, 16510, 17266,

17346, 17463, 18824, 19115, 19118, 19140
--England 1395, 1928, 2777
--Great Britain 18393
--History 13936, 14320, 18415
University Settlement Society of New York 2379
University settlements >> See: Social settlements
Unión de Trabajadores de Colombia 17066
Unmarried mothers >> See further: Maternity homes; Single parents
Unmarried mothers 1731, 1891, 15254, 16653, 18700, 18869
--History 1566, 2388, 18564, 18614
Upper Room Outreach Ministries 19154
Upper Volta
--Social conditions 13365
Urban-rural migration 3690, 4039, 5999, 6128, 6280, 6281, 6427, 6428
Urban America, Inc. 10614
Urban Apostolate of the Sisters in Chicago 9765
Urban Church Lending Library (Green Lake, Wisconsin) 5992, 8933
Urban Church Research Center for Asia 6848
Urban Church Resource Exchange Center (Chicago) 18980
Urban churches >> See: City churches
Urban clergy >> See: City clergy
Urban Coalition 10506, 10625
Urban ecology >> See: Ecology; Environmental ethics; Sociology
Urban Industrial Mission (WCC) See: World Council of Churches, Urban and Industrial Mission
Urban League 11632, 14373
Urban Life Center (Chicago, Illinois) 13348, 17544
Urban Missionary Movement 17, 47, 99, 12296
--History 4697, 6035, 7834, 7853, 11043, 12297, 12602
Urban missions >> See: City missions
Urban planning >> See: City planning
Urban reform politics >> See: Municipal government; Citiesa and towns--Reform
Urban renewal 8654, 9062, 9534, 11335, 18137, 18937
--Canada 13690
--Case studies 6207, 6920, 7148, 8286, 8785, 8822, 10319, 11226, 12598, 15935, 16702, 17145, 17607, 17857
--Church participation 6101, 6379, 6598, 6689, 6741, 6952, 7148, 7163, 7182, 7392, 7600, 7601, 7677, 7752, 7859, 7867, 7869, 8203, 8286, 8298, 8301, 8362, 8554, 8735, 8802, 9349, 9545, 9648, 9716, 10153, 10530, 13466, 14541, 14768, 15480, 16225, 16702, 17212, 17607, 18174
--Church participation--Congresses 9092, 10138
--Citizen participation 7383, 8027, 8347, 9029, 9044, 11731, 13112, 13466, 13644, 14098, 14840
--Criticism 4681, 6624, 7233, 7680, 7871, 7913, 7982, 8194, 8518, 8554, 8565, 9052, 9146, 9263, 9435, 9716, 10233, 11071, 11402, 11723, 13112, 14098, 14768, 15199, 15244, 15261, 16388, 17168, 18982

Urban renewal (cont.)
--Criticism--History 8974
--England 7233, 16315
--France 9797
--Germany 13644, 13841, 16930
--Great Britain 15611
--Japan 12927
--Mexico 18834
--Philippines 11487
--Philosophy 5746, 7122, 7681, 7790, 7998, 8413, 8582, 8629, 9043, 9636, 9724, 9822, 10459, 10803, 11042, 13179, 14499, 14534, 15479, 15522, 16735, 17982, 18939
Urban sociology >> See: Sociology
Urban Theology Unit (Sheffield, England) 13070, 13727, 13728, 14079, 14680, 16059, 18905, 19009, 19045
Urban Training Center for Christian Mission (Chicago, Illinois) 8920, 8934, 9329, 9442, 9581, 9607, 9679, 9878, 10018, 10148, 10252, 10267, 10564, 11740, 12028, 12568, 13067
--Bibliographies 10098
Urban Training Organization of Atlanta (Atlanta, Georgia) 14655
Urban training programs >> See further: City clergy, training of; (names of specific training programs, e.g., Seminary Consortium for Urban Pastoral Education)
Urban training programs 5411, 8934, 9371, 9443, 9562, 9774, 9783, 9798, 9927, 9928, 9929, 10600, 10624, 10735, 10736, 10737, 10911, 11022, 11453, 11567, 11749, 13067
--History 18385
Urban Young Adult Action (New York, NY) 11111
Urban-rural migration >> See: Suburban life; Back to the land movements; Whites--Relocation; Rural-urban migration
Urbanization 870, 2322, 7273, 7591, 8853, 9060, 10501, 10857, 12766, 13531, 16975, 18245, 19184
--Africa 7230, 7544, 8349, 8449, 9232, 9963, 9972, 10793, 11392, 11797, 11985, 13280, 14661, 15484, 15841, 17260, 18747, 18812
--Africa--Bibliographies 10579, 12386, 15960
--Africa--History 6299, 8894
--Asia 6907, 6966, 10678, 11178, 17728
--Bangladesh 16154
--Bibliographies 7936, 8802, 8933, 9019, 9235, 9330, 10579, 11231, 11602, 12305, 12386, 13747, 13783, 14486, 14509, 14695, 14812, 14904, 15960, 16736, 17272
--Brazil 8994
--Canada 4957, 10805, 12465, 13510, 16194
--Canada--Quebec 6139
--China 17728
--China--History 13159
--Colombia 17916
--Congresses 10726
--Developing countries 5307, 8117, 11841, 17389, 18110
--Egypt 16813
--England 4913
--England--History 2464
--Europe 6234, 7204, 8181
--Fiction 4406, 11684
--France 10056, 11020, 11397
--France--History 7531, 18603

Urbanization (cont.)
--Germany 2707, 8572, 11412
--Germany (East) 12259
--Great Britain 19019
--Greece 15657
--History 5803, 6330, 7520, 7665, 8837, 10824, 10957, 12975, 13938, 16898, 17358, 17379
--India 13813, 15639, 15933, 16839, 17728
--India--Bibliographies 13783
--India--Congresses 7060, 7217
--Indonesia 6818
--Japan 6991, 9756, 10898, 12723, 12907, 13677, 14877, 16679, 17728, 18558
--Jordan 16241
--Korea 11161, 18215
--Latin America 6192, 7596, 8056, 8563, 9200, 10078, 12180, 12395, 13492, 13493, 13594, 13996, 14010, 14575, 16095, 16226, 17056, 17996, 18812
--Melanesia 17141
--Mexico 17296
--Middle East 14181
--New Guinea 11282, 13579, 13695, 14823, 17382
--Nigeria 11392, 13280, 13721
--Northern Rhodesia 6918
--Pakistan 9971
--People's Republic of China 12725
--Peru 15208
--Peru--Lima 11455
--Philosophy 9659
--Poland 12275, 12337
--Religious aspects 415, 574, 587, 1177, 1203, 1206, 1946, 2152, 2287, 2357, 2665, 2699, 3559, 3604, 3757, 3847, 3861, 4054, 4706, 4715, 4748, 4778, 4868, 5048, 5307, 5336, 5344, 5542, 5593, 5725, 6004, 6270, 6407, 6408, 6461, 6511, 6520, 7012, 7107, 7122, 7157, 7183, 7184, 7271, 7317, 7337, 7365, 7448, 7453, 7462, 7534, 7623, 7744, 7819, 8069, 8082, 8134, 8263, 8287, 8370, 8488, 8628, 8686, 8815, 8906, 8926, 8979, 8987, 9016, 9066, 9075, 9088, 9138, 9158, 9160, 9202, 9208, 9215, 9373, 9405, 9408, 9513, 9514, 9594, 9657, 9717, 9823, 9865, 9877, 10003, 10038, 10058, 10137, 10139, 10153, 10404, 10460, 10627, 10667, 10756, 10882, 10922, 10964, 10986, 11455, 11489, 11523, 11647, 11660, 11666, 11872, 12505, 12593, 12925, 13419, 13440, 13445, 13451, 13682, 13978, 14012, 14117, 14180, 14186, 14200, 14282, 14301, 14338, 14357, 14410, 14532, 14854, 15016, 15060, 15074, 15157, 15458, 15550, 15647, 15709, 15843, 15875, 15962, 16088, 16214, 16229, 16231, 16245, 16305, 16550, 16560, 16824, 16891, 16898, 16909, 17060, 17202, 17230, 17231, 17238, 17270, 17282, 17295, 17521, 17603, 17604, 17615, 17622, 17692, 17767, 17922, 17948, 17965, 18000, 18034, 18169, 18330, 18488, 18515, 18572, 18761, 18778, 18902, 18973, 19118, 19145, 19156, 19308
--Religious aspects--Africa 7767, 7768, 8500, 9525, 12058, 13350, 13362, 13636, 16734, 16795, 17026, 19240
--Religious aspects--Asia 9306, 13309, 16781
--Religious aspects--Australia 16799
--Religious aspects--Australia--

History 13542
Urbanization (cont.)
--Religious aspects--Bibliographies 9164, 16198
--Religious aspects--Buddhist 18379, 18812
--Religious aspects--Canada 12559, 18471
--Religious aspects--Congresses 7741, 9675, 10014, 11341, 11588, 16891
--Religious aspects--England 15297, 15789, 16950, 18516
--Religious aspects--Europe 6717, 7928, 8069, 10892, 17826
--Religious aspects--France 5846, 6634, 7352, 14804, 15699
--Religious aspects--Germany 7636, 9497, 10295
--Religious aspects--Germany (East) 17893
--Religious aspects--History 4092, 4103, 5743, 6886, 11304, 14039, 18079, 18243, 18927
--Religious aspects--History City churches--History 4692
--Religious aspects--India 15452
--Religious aspects--Indonesia 15660
--Religious aspects--Islam 8661, 12878, 12935, 16673, 17945, 18208, 18758, 18802, 18812, 18848, 18908
--Religious aspects--Italy 8069, 11689
--Religious aspects--Japan 7249, 9434, 10035, 11843, 11909, 12063, 12521, 13633, 13922, 15506
--Religious aspects--Jewish 7892, 10064, 18194, 18812
--Religious aspects--Kenya 16138
--Religious aspects--Latin America 18640
--Religious aspects--Lutheran 10089, 18771
--Religious aspects--Singapore 19053
--Religious aspects--Sweden--History 11644
--Religious aspects--Turkey 7249
--Religious aspects--Zambia 15860
--Research 1214, 7012, 7140, 8439, 9039, 9533, 11648, 12456, 12480, 12549, 13295, 13300, 13532, 13956, 16212, 17031, 17592, 18857
--Research--History 18690
--Rhodesia, Northern 6530, 9232
--Russia 6794, 17728
--Scotland--History 14611
--South Africa 8833, 8834, 15430, 16771, 17742, 18584
--Soviet Union 16007
--Spain 7820, 15587
--Switzerland 10727
--Taiwan 9921
--Thailand 16355
--Turkey 18848
--United States 5008, 7107, 7204, 7611, 8160, 8460, 8926, 8936, 9636, 9659, 9724, 12850, 17278
--Venezuela 11438
--Zambia 14998
Uri (Switzerland)
--Social conditions 15259
Ushers and ushering 6021
Utica (New York)
--Religion 9439
--Religious and ecclesiastical institutions 7126
--Religious life and customs--History 14813
--Social life and customs--History 7612
Utilities 13710, 14927
Utopias 469, 501, 563, 873, 1197, 2920, 3813, 11430, 13529, 15906, 16973

--Fiction 2150
--History 10683, 12532, 14225
Utrecht (Netherlands)
--Religious and ecclesiastical institutions 15685
Uttar Pradesh (India)
--Religious and ecclesiastical institutions 4803
Values >> See: Social values
Vancouver (British Columbia, Canada)
--Religious and ecclesiastical institutions 12042, 16852
--Social conditions 2725, 18241
Vatican Council, 2nd, (1962-1965) 10226
Vice 78, 170, 183, 456, 700, 1216, 1333, 1874, 2449, 2556, 2562, 2564, 3101, 3547, 3584
--History 6385, 8918, 10713, 13004
Victim-offender reconciliation 15710, 16082, 16451, 16452
Victim-offender reconciliation >> See further: Justice--Criminal; Church work with criminals; Church work with prisoners
Victims 15047, 15048, 19204
Vienna (Austria)
--Intellectual life 12915
--Religious and ecclesiastical institutions 6829, 8004
--Social conditions 851, 6012, 19038
Vietnam
--Social conditions 12191
Vietnam War 12095, 12669, 16020
Vietnamese American Catholics 17458
Vietnamese Americans
--Missions to 17458
--Social conditions 15653, 16983, 18672
Violence 644, 10195, 10535, 10671, 10682, 11962
--Africa 14858, 15291
--Church responses to 5818, 7513, 8424, 9890, 10332, 10391, 10456, 10836, 10955, 11037, 11301, 11416, 11522, 11703, 15710, 15856, 16082, 16129, 16451, 16452, 18337, 19162
--Descriptions of 2194, 3406, 3821, 3864, 10060, 10342, 10393, 10748, 10899, 11000, 11104, 11163, 11899, 13020, 13345, 13828, 13976, 14248, 14281, 14507, 15017, 15847, 16444, 17424, 17527, 17646, 17999, 18857
--England 15528, 15750, 15884, 16104, 17527, 18682
--Europe--History 14923
--Fiction 11313
--Great Britain 14932, 17526
--History 4515, 10748, 11384, 12822, 15449, 16498, 17785, 19130, 19131
--Ireland 12408, 17654, 18038, 18682
--Religious views on 782, 1302, 8841, 9767, 10259, 10423, 10817, 10900, 11007, 11060, 11092, 11105, 11294, 11540, 11824, 11965, 12781, 12802, 13234, 13453, 13627, 14279, 14609, 16128, 16791, 18542
--Religious views on--History 11272
--South Africa 13828
Virgin Islands of the United States 17447
Visitations 681, 1834, 7764
Visitations (church work) 17, 99, 101, 114, 776, 951, 1716, 1748, 2072, 2165, 2650, 4106, 7973, 8328, 13232, 18162
--Australia 18792

--England 363
--Fiction 1017
--Germany 8244
--History 8078
Vocation >> See further: Work
Vocation 609, 2364, 3748, 4416, 5484, 5807, 5811, 5918, 6069, 6254, 6315, 6541, 6745, 6934, 7427, 8021, 8138, 14939, 15594, 16804, 16949, 18715
--Congresses 6854
--England 3238
Vocational rehabilitation 13745, 15689, 18016
Voice of Calvary Ministries (Jackson, Mississippi) 14005, 16368, 16585, 18191
Volunteers 1791, 1948, 4614, 4715, 5154, 5155, 5343, 5482, 6026, 6518, 6817, 7394, 8329, 8458, 9515, 9744, 9873, 10039, 11733, 11882, 12525, 12632, 12663, 13321, 13540, 14025, 14118, 14445, 14696, 14737, 14905, 14943, 15086, 15329, 15455, 15646, 15663, 15681, 16288, 17038, 17137, 17753, 18063, 18634, 19234, 19335, 19347
--Africa 13908
--England 15873
--Great Britain 18391
--Great Britain--History 14103
--History 8329, 14040, 14770, 14964
--Sweden 14965
Volunteers of America 1039
--History 6599
Voodooism 4150, 4696, 5529, 6992, 7756, 13472, 13615, 14179, 14834, 19341
Voting 1955, 2035, 11057, 12118, 12576, 15499, 15663, 17286, 17323, 18580
Waco (Texas)
--Religious and ecclesiastical institutions 18080
Wages >> See further: Employment problems; Trade unions; Church and labor
Wages 107, 816, 1065, 1349, 1629, 2095, 2542, 2655, 2983, 3039, 3103, 3156, 3208, 3246, 3330, 3405, 3467, 3551, 4119, 4289, 4516, 4613, 4663, 5065, 5660, 9377, 14383, 15857
--Europe 2235, 4616
--History 9901
--Netherlands 4602
--Spain 4261
Wales
--Church history 18362
--History 8400
--Religion 15216
--Religious and ecclesiastical institutions 376, 13826, 14851
--Social conditions 13655, 14914
Waltham (Massachusetts)
--Social conditions--History 13209
War 385, 4389, 4651, 5762, 10870, 11803, 12326, 12611, 15428
War on poverty 8941, 9041, 9175, 9299, 9422, 9454, 9471, 9709, 10049, 10097, 10462, 10559, 10843, 11414, 11579
War on Poverty
--Congresses 9977
War on poverty
--History 19109
--Periodicals 9178
Warfare (metaphor) >> See further: Salvation Army
Warfare (metaphor) 1396, 1526, 1770, 1771, 1869, 2009, 2435, 2723, 4389, 4697, 6057, 6605, 7049, 7822, 8507, 8996, 9062, 9299, 9345, 9454, 9991, 10097, 10559, 11257, 11329, 11579, 12667, 12833, 13004, 13153,

14116, 14124, 15581, 15805, 16626, 16860, 17004, 17524, 18150, 18309, 18810, 19209
Washington (DC)
--Race relations 6090
--Religious and ecclesiastical institutions 2814, 4837, 4968, 4993, 5083, 5233, 5891, 5905, 5906, 6058, 6164, 6601, 7040, 7711, 7883, 7899, 8101, 8575, 8748, 9119, 9337, 9362, 9596, 10087, 10375, 10980, 11270, 11284, 11731, 11787, 11831, 12181, 13240, 13421, 13992, 14288, 14843, 15084, 15486, 15595, 16032, 16354, 16748, 16910, 17212, 17975, 18162, 19122
--Religious and ecclesiastical institutions--History 3398, 3915, 4394
--Social conditions 1867, 2058, 5300, 5823, 6090, 7600, 8786, 9046, 9827, 10153, 11037, 14571, 14778, 14841, 14872, 15362, 17847, 17913, 18533, 18542, 18686, 18882
WASPS >> See further: Whites
WASPS 1823, 5193, 5925, 10865, 11423, 11671, 11847, 11885, 11983, 12666, 12980, 13026, 14206, 17904
--Bibliographies 11170
--Ethnic relations 11645
--History 12580
Water Street Mission (New York, NY) 483, 556, 675, 758, 759, 1300, 1634, 2069, 2292, 2635, 10227, 11077
--History 1857, 2654, 4576
Waterbury (Connecticut)
--Religious and ecclesiastical institutions--History 14886
--Social conditions 14790, 15356, 19043
Waterloo (Iowa)
--Religious and ecclesiastical institutions 14170
Watertown (Wisconsin)
--Social conditions 12471
Wayne (Pennsylvania)
--Religious and ecclesiastical institutions 12207
Wealth 2527, 2937, 3215
--Biblical teaching 1060, 1559, 1717, 1768, 2436, 2437, 2472, 2916, 3682, 7511, 13227, 14524, 14529, 14703
--Descriptions of 694, 1723, 1993, 2088, 2867, 3171, 3176, 3287, 4018, 4345, 6676, 7625, 7660, 7774, 8264, 8317, 8465, 10362, 11232, 11312, 13597, 14632, 15823, 16388, 16554, 16877, 17007, 18282
--England 1048, 1345, 3177, 3281, 3624, 9185, 15333, 15967, 17586
--England--History 913, 10020
--Ethical aspects 187, 265, 509, 518, 611, 839, 843, 884, 917, 932, 1048, 1147, 1345, 1711, 1717, 1822, 2376, 2438, 2551, 2971, 3023, 3336, 3412, 3624, 3675, 4011, 6748, 6929, 8616, 9723, 9905, 10020, 10398, 10511, 10648, 12673, 12805, 13173, 14459, 14675, 15358, 15895, 16302, 16554, 17498, 18100, 18120, 18621, 18789
--Fiction 724, 2838, 3462, 8756, 16055
--Great Britain 187, 14683
--History 4103, 8403, 8694, 10365, 12094, 19293
--Religious views on 14, 178, 424, 479, 618, 774, 843, 898, 1099, 1149, 1304, 1381, 1412, 1429, 1546, 1817, 1940, 1943, 2024, 2025, 2290, 2293, 2744, 3034,

3281, 3578, 3618, 3894, 4154, 4187, 4365, 4532, 7367, 7621, 8103, 8104, 8178, 8247, 8386, 8940, 9751, 9849, 10357, 10617, 11663, 12325, 13901, 14422, 14524, 15721, 16019, 16492, 16821, 16964, 17094, 17362, 17586, 18120, 19137, 19252
Weathermen (gang) 12071
Webster (Massachusetts)
--Religious and ecclesiastical institutions--History 14455
Webster (New York)
--Social conditions 5384
Week-day church schools 2869, 3459, 3460, 5315, 5774, 7123, 7898, 9410, 12569, 12895, 12951, 15682, 18866
--History 7882, 10395
Welfare >> See: Social service; Social workers; Charity
Welfare reform 1138, 9779, 11176, 13618, 18021, 18410, 19109
--History 12274, 14391
Wesley Theological Seminary (Washington, DC) 7577
Wesleyan Methodist Church (England) 308, 2038, 2209
Wesleyan Methodist Union for Social Service (England) 2086, 2329
West Ham Central Mission (London, England) 5879
West Indians
--Social life and customs 7329, 8760, 10796, 12015, 12185, 17447, 18985
West London Mission (London, England)
--History 18031
West Orange (New Jersey)
--Religious and ecclesiastical institutions 17519
West Side Christian Parish (Chicago, Illinois) 5875, 6304, 6594, 6911, 7250, 8440, 8545, 8655
Westchester (Illinois)
--Religious and ecclesiastical institutions 11271
Westchester College Mission (Portsmouth, England) 1463
Westchester County (New York)
--Religious and ecclesiastical institutions 7555
Westinghouse Electric Corporation 12985
Wheeling (West Virginia)
--Religious and ecclesiastical institutions 5407
White flight >> See: Whites--Relocation; Church development, relocation
Whites >> See further: WASPS
Whites 11847, 12845
--Attitudes 3099, 3818, 5591, 5747, 6061, 6308, 6320, 6617, 8020, 8705, 8867, 9240, 9320, 9506, 9620, 9638, 10204, 10258, 10700, 10716, 10888, 11104, 11107, 11276, 11344, 11499, 11671, 11949, 12099, 12247, 12476, 12791, 14507, 14537, 17922
--Attitudes--History 12068, 15174
--Economic conditions 11575, 17250
--Ethnic relations 10716, 11310, 11423, 11655, 12758, 18482
--Housing 9359, 12153
--Identity 11983
--Periodicals 11654
--Race relations 2190, 8049, 10204, 10346, 10905, 11131, 11344, 12313, 13755, 14206, 15874
--Religion 13026, 13457

Whites (cont.)
--Relocation >> See further: Church development, relocation
--Relocation 79, 1465, 1817, 2316, 2454, 2543, 2588, 3098, 3548, 3778, 4090, 5049, 5322, 5360, 5637, 5999, 6043, 6056, 6275, 6280, 6501, 6741, 6809, 6838, 6912, 7019, 7033, 7128, 7355, 7429, 7431, 7458, 7486, 7538, 7574, 7966, 7971, 8092, 8259, 8307, 8338, 8463, 8564, 8637, 8651, 8718, 8785, 8794, 8804, 8828, 9090, 9230, 9559, 10081, 10165, 10674, 10959, 11145, 11323, 11368, 11492, 11522, 11875, 11956, 12232, 12458, 12537, 12543, 13869, 14159, 14288, 14375, 14497, 14825, 15251, 15468, 15649, 15816, 15992, 16277, 16374, 17273, 17433, 17500, 17904, 18170, 18733, 18789
--Relocation--England 18800
--Relocation--History 18373
--Social conditions 11218, 13457
--Social life and customs 12666
--Social problems 11810
Wichita (Kansas)
--Religious and ecclesiastical institutions 5814, 10569, 17629
--Religious life and customs 7799
--Social conditions 12150
Wider City Parish (New Haven, Connecticut) 6000, 11772
Wilkes-Barre (Pennsylvania)
--Religious and ecclesiastical institutions 8000, 8074, 10693
--Social conditions 13466, 17205
--Social conditions--History 9308
William Temple Foundation (Manchester, England) 10653, 15309, 15537, 15691, 16071, 16481, 16802, 17585, 17586, 17587, 18389, 18391, 18752
--Congresses 18390, 19028
--Periodicals 13742
Williamsport (Pennsylvania)
--Religious and ecclesiastical institutions 13282
Wilmington (Delaware)
--History 4354
--Race relations 12575, 12703
--Religion 15713
--Religious and ecclesiastical institutions 5407, 5963, 5965, 9498, 12575, 13312, 15327, 18862
--Religious and ecclesiastical institutions--History 12900
--Social conditions 8474, 12703, 14790, 18649
Wilton (Connecticut)
--Religious and ecclesiastical institutions 11041
Winchester (Massachusetts)
--Religious and ecclesiastical institutions 15622
Winnipeg (Manitoba, Canada)
--Religious and ecclesiastical institutions 7405, 9250, 17543, 19069
--Religious and ecclesiastical institutions--History 14594
--Social condition 13086
--Social conditions 15426
Winston-Salem (North Carolina)
--History 17950
--Religious and ecclesiastical institutions 13745
--Religious and ecclesiastical institutions--History 6386
Witchcraft >> See further: Occultism
Witchcraft 12944, 13849
--Africa 17018
--Zambia 15860
Witness bearing (Christianity) >>

See further: Evangelistic work
Witness bearing (Christianity) 4428, 5723, 5962, 7037, 7104, 7290, 9510, 10715, 10991, 11908, 13228, 13714, 15436, 15523, 16417
--Latin America 14233
Witwatersrand Industrial Mission (South Africa) 12911, 17977
Women >> See further: Single women; African American Women
Women 1179, 2699, 6488, 14693, 16262, 17646, 18890
--Africa 14892, 16795, 17986
--Asia 18938, 18944
--Biography 6266
--Employment >> See further: Church work with employed women
--Employment 107, 362, 459, 916, 972, 1065, 1113, 1646, 1837, 2273, 2425, 2637, 2744, 2762, 2781, 2842, 2861, 2894, 3102, 3118, 3240, 3461, 3562, 3944, 4202, 4312, 4765, 4967, 5156, 5188, 5226, 5234, 5501, 6503, 7732, 10052, 10122, 12027, 12829, 13244, 13305, 13388, 13572, 13577, 14112, 14277, 14662, 15857, 15909, 16740, 16936, 17190, 17707, 18246, 18665, 18844, 18932
--Employment--Asia 15761, 16048
--Employment--Bibliographies 14668
--Employment--England 2145, 11857, 17256, 19028
--Employment--Europe 18390
--Employment--History 2893, 17830
--Employment--Japan 14417
--Employment--Korea 14847
--England 16132
--Great Britain 11857, 17707
--Greece 16614
--Jewish--Bibliographies 19151
--Social and moral questions 2060, 4131
--Social conditions 13137, 13758, 13819, 14398, 14662, 16129, 16403, 18068
Women clergy 15165, 16296, 16603, 17138, 17174, 17837, 18965
Women in charitable work 1107, 2193, 2374, 4407, 8027
--Biography 13834, 15431, 15465, 15883, 16590, 17410, 17411, 18448, 18508
Women in church work >> See further: Church work with women; Nuns; (names of individual women church leaders, e.g, Vida Dutton Scudder, Jane Addams, Mother Teresa, etc.)
Women in church work 6, 25, 34, 301, 575, 1117, 1347, 1742, 1957, 2018, 2077, 2159, 2267, 2284, 2386, 2387, 2495, 2496, 2561, 2853, 2955, 2988, 3055, 3562, 3577, 3653, 4028, 4338, 5670, 5862, 5888, 6148, 6256, 9166, 9733, 11081, 11179, 11960, 12027, 12296, 13148, 13249, 13471, 13514, 13850, 14558, 14974, 15104, 16603, 17310, 17758, 17861, 18541, 19222, 19352
--Africa 14049
--Biography 4671, 12899, 13491, 15423, 15432, 16170, 16373, 16411, 16678, 17554, 17584, 17909
--England 363, 11096
--Germany 342
--Great Britain 10558
--History 862, 943, 4624, 10487,

12297, 13893, 14770, 14813, 15110, 15792, 16322, 16905, 17174, 18376, 19229
--India 17376, 17385
--Scotland 18127
Women in government 6457, 16948, 17323
--History 14235
Women religious >> See: Nuns
Women social reformers 709, 1406, 1742, 1795, 1834, 2060, 2117, 2386, 2387, 2495, 2496, 2562, 2628, 3032, 3039, 4462, 4826, 4898, 5670, 5888, 6148, 8700, 12296, 17174
--Biography 4452, 4465, 4671, 9526, 9527, 12813, 16170, 16336, 16385, 16746, 16772, 17124, 17390, 17745, 18429, 19229
--History 12221, 13153, 14522, 16905, 17525, 19152
Women's Christian Temperance Union 709, 6677
--History 5841, 9872, 16903
Women's liberation >> See further: Feminism
Women's liberation 12295, 18541
Women's rights 2204, 2628, 13577, 16936, 16990, 18535, 18914
Women's Theological Center (Boston, Massachusetts) 18965
Women, black >> See: Black women; African American women
Women, employment
--Colombia 18756
Women, Jewish 16051, 16740, 16763, 18374, 19061
Women, Moslem 16820
Women, poor 24, 916, 2780, 13437, 13482, 13758, 14306, 14565, 16001, 16265, 16598, 16653, 16990, 17332, 17712, 18532, 18833, 18914, 18957, 19027
--Africa 18005
--Argentina 14618
--Asia 17436
--Canada 13086
--Fiction 1210
--History 4624
Woodlawn (Chicago, Illinois) 8367, 9222, 11209, 12851
Woodlawn Organization (Chicago, Illinois) 9207, 11209, 12851
Worcester (Massachusetts)
--Religious and ecclesiastical institutions 1632, 3986, 6329, 6499
Worchester (Massachusetts)
--Race relations 14973
Work >> See further: Vocation; Church and labor; Labor and laboring classes
Work 278, 563, 1847, 5014, 5495, 5807, 5918, 6067, 6069, 6254, 6795, 7427, 7734, 7803, 9592, 12397, 13679, 14780, 14939, 14948, 15217, 16943, 16949, 17599, 18353, 18599
--Asia 15188
--Australia 15145, 15188
--Biblical teaching 4151, 6227, 7171, 15188, 15645
--Canada 9846
--Congresses 6042, 6138, 6212, 6213, 6854
--England 5377, 8720, 14498, 17262
--Ethical aspects 887, 1149, 3412, 5484, 7482, 9078, 9108, 11675, 13798, 15032, 16098, 16993, 17255, 18098, 18188
--Europe 5865, 11905
--Finland 11420
--France 13438
--Germany 5535, 14429, 16287,

18433
Work (cont.)
--Great Britain 5870
--History 14805, 15353
--Psychological aspects 15617, 16680, 19085
--Religious aspects 1069, 2715, 3215, 3217, 3693, 3728, 3729, 3731, 3732, 3733, 4588, 5811, 6042, 6170, 6346, 6465, 6606, 6745, 6934, 7682, 7732, 7837, 7918, 9085, 9895, 10582, 12425, 12745, 14023, 15221, 15857, 16269, 16707, 17094, 17250, 17779, 19342, 19353
--Religious aspects--Congresses 6138, 6170, 6212, 6213
--Social aspects 609, 3501, 5282, 5691, 12642, 13378, 14395, 15895, 15988, 17915
--Technological aspects 7902, 8451, 8519, 8524, 8602, 8665, 8849, 9047, 9775, 9982, 10027, 12425, 14219, 14938, 15470, 15895, 16479, 16706, 16804, 16951, 17302, 18016
Work (theology) 2364, 2380, 2662, 4827, 4885, 5090, 5150, 5159, 5401, 5833, 5958, 6315, 6541, 7171, 7846, 8021, 8103, 8133, 9157, 9699, 9938, 9956, 9988, 10341, 10582, 11125, 11175, 11857, 12023, 12206, 14660, 14821, 15035, 15131, 15162, 15318, 15538, 15645, 15832, 15919, 16248, 16259, 16352, 16453, 16587, 16713, 16815, 17002, 17027, 17041, 17126, 17256, 17302, 17336, 17387, 17434, 17631, 17707, 17799, 18163, 18320, 18422, 18762, 19301
--Bibliographies 13671
--Europe 6140
--History 8387, 8466
--Spain 7673
Work ethic >> See: Protestant ethic
Work Projects Administration (WPA) 4834, 4837, 4909, 4926, 4927, 4928, 4929, 4931, 4932, 4933, 4934, 4935, 4936, 4937, 4938, 4940, 4941, 5021, 5022, 5023, 5024, 5025, 5026, 5027, 5028, 5029, 5063, 5098, 5099
Worker Priests >> See: Priest workers
Working class >> See: Labor and laboring classes; Church and labor; Social classes; Church work with skilled labor
Works Progress Administration (WPA) >> See: Work Projects Administration (WPA)
World Conference on Church, Community and State (Oxford, England) 4691
World Council of Churches 5958, 6818, 6907, 6966, 6991, 7204, 7230, 7322, 7487, 7741, 8005, 8117, 8324, 8514, 8633, 8911, 8915, 9671, 10169, 10281, 10448, 10609, 10661, 10940, 10989, 11152, 13230, 13409, 14413, 14707, 15609, 15704, 15705, 15900, 15948, 16058, 16550, 16791, 17610, 17611, 17808, 17972, 18026, 18096, 18772, 18935
--Bibliographies 11182
--Congresses 8339, 8349, 8961, 14900, 15381, 15705
--Periodicals 6896, 6921, 8632, 8960, 12033, 13393, 13410, 17206
--Pronouncements, policies 5743, 13130
--Pronouncements, policies--Bibliographies 14517
--Social teaching 6857

World Council of Churches, Commission on the Churches' Participation in Development 12819, 12864, 13409, 13506, 15003, 16473, 16554, 16706, 16792, 17344
World Council of Churches, Commission on World Mission and Evangelism 8348, 8449, 10448, 12734, 12890, 13118, 14618, 14765, 15496, 18383
World Council of Churches, Urban-Industrial Mission 8057, 9494, 10318, 10915, 11629, 11708, 12022, 12175, 12306, 12340, 12377, 12433, 12624, 12665, 12734, 12745, 12890, 12963, 13097, 13120, 13554, 13708, 13873, 13941, 13949, 14062, 14184, 14360, 14444, 14482, 14489, 14490, 14618, 14689, 14765, 14996, 15046, 15057, 15201, 15436, 15627, 17176, 17316, 19188
--Bibliographies 11830
--History 13578
World Council of Churches, Urban-Rural Mission 13874, 14164, 14171, 14232, 14449, 14972, 14979, 15381, 15384, 15572, 15761, 15942, 16769, 17146, 17572, 17800, 18076, 18095, 18096, 18229, 18346, 18383
--Periodicals 11676, 17206
World Movement of Christian Workers 10184, 15706
World Union of Progressive Judaism 16051, 16763
World Vision International 6002, 17848, 18232
--Periodicals 7231
World War, 1914-1918 2941, 2970, 13491, 14657, 15155
--Economic aspects 2991
--War Work--Episcopal 3088
--War work--Protestant 3201
World War, 1939-1945 5005, 5006, 5071, 5084, 5133, 5176, 5218, 5252, 5404, 5871, 6005, 10427, 16020, 16959, 17659, 18070
--War work--Church of England 5232
--War work--England 5034
--War work--Methodist 5107, 5226, 5351, 12690, 15269
--War work--Presbyterian 5414
--War work--Protestant 5072, 5073, 5078, 5081, 5087, 5088, 5103, 5154, 5155, 5156, 5210, 5227, 5284, 5362, 5668
Worship >> See: Public worship; Liturgies; Experimental ministries--Worship; Ritual; Hymns
Würtemberg (Germany)
--Social conditions 10416
Xenophobia >> See further: Pluralism; Americanization; Religious pluralism; Nativism; Anticatholicism; Antisemitism
Xenophobia 178, 207, 224, 805, 826, 1147, 1188, 1226, 1230, 1394, 1553, 1968, 2077, 2176, 2212, 2354, 2706, 2742, 3848, 6366, 17014, 17367
--France 18317
--History 7328, 12068, 13495
Yoked parishes >> See: Church development, yoked parishes; Inner city-suburban exchanges
Yokohama (Japan)
--Religious and ecclesiastical institutions 11778
--Social conditions 16418
Yonkers (New York)
--Religious and ecclesiastical institutions 1739, 6414, 6997, 15995

York (Pennsylvania)
--Religious and ecclesiastical institutions 16664, 18862
Yoruba people (Nigeria) 11235
Young Christian Workers
--History 19247
--Spain--History 14551
Young Christian Workers (France) 15666
--History 7285
Young Life 10096
Young Lords (New York, NY) 11649, 12026
Young Men's Christian Association 399
Young Men's Christian Associations 205, 357, 409, 446, 610, 633, 1555, 1769, 2170, 2311, 2335, 2336, 2839, 3215, 3286, 3468, 3658, 3812, 3824, 3858, 3929, 3999, 4045, 4136, 4866, 5235, 5250, 5333, 5418, 5436, 5464, 5487, 6014, 6079, 6657, 7579, 7814, 8559, 8744, 8969, 9136, 9854, 10669, 15689
--Africa 8449
--Archives 205
--Biography 2114
--England 17589
--History 450, 798, 1159, 1462, 1802, 1849, 1875, 3725, 4212, 4911, 5267, 5332, 6047, 6775, 9455, 12038, 12769, 16658
--India--History 6611
--Ireland--History 12483
--Periodicals 3739, 16796
Young Men's Domestic Missionary Society 87
Young Men's Hebrew Association 5211
Young People's Missionary Movement 2005, 2077, 2176
Young Women's Christian Association
--Archives 311
Young Women's Christian Associations 2428, 3118, 3215, 3240, 3272, 3461, 4348, 5284, 7814, 14112
--History 2984, 4256, 4568, 5982, 14947
Youngstown (Ohio)
--Economic conditions 16219, 18840
--Industries 16219
--Religious and ecclesiastical institutions 630, 5170, 6789, 9464, 10573, 14937, 18049
--Social conditions 14499, 14515, 14570, 14602, 14641, 14690, 14731, 14782, 14882, 14893, 15324, 15359, 15598, 15608, 16470
Youth >> See further: Students; Juvenile delinquency; Gangs; Church work with youth; Church work with students
Youth
--Advice to 170, 183, 264, 321, 412, 785, 1824, 2108, 2203, 4230, 4664, 5495, 9431, 9723, 10966, 11718, 11869, 18539
--Africa 10262, 14298, 15000, 16797, 17506
--Attitudes 9914, 14969
--Austria 16747
--Brazil 17290
--Canada 4593
--China 4430
--Conduct of life 145, 1997, 6894, 7491, 8578, 9693, 10130, 10399, 10909, 10971, 10974, 11045, 11845, 12692, 12827, 12973, 13839, 14663, 16444, 18483, 18871, 18874
--Congresses 10494
--Descriptive studies 2289, 2780, 2877, 2906, 5158, 5231, 6102, 7281, 7321, 7429, 7468, 7491, 8381, 8493, 8578, 8703, 8820,

9018, 9914, 9945, 10610, 11305, 11391, 11717, 11807, 12211, 12687, 12827, 12973, 13226, 13345, 13550, 13966, 14663, 15000, 15624, 16971, 17496, 17957, 18335
Youth (cont.)
--Employment 2655, 4472, 4664, 4834, 5950, 8253, 8276, 8972, 12613, 15947, 17404, 17750
--Employment--France 17711
--Employment--History 18797
--England 1997, 12438, 17281, 19052
--Europe 8972, 10142
--Fiction 444
--France 6877, 8064, 11751
--France--History 17711, 18797
--Germany 996, 2741, 4806, 5623, 7739, 13125
--Germany (East) 13448
--Great Britain 10349, 12226, 12761, 12778, 13845, 14183, 15848, 17317, 17640, 18483
--Greece 9950
--Ireland 12483
--Italy 15361, 15389
--Japan 4472, 19127
--Kenya 15625
--Korea 12212
--Netherlands 17404
--New Guinea 15947, 17335
--Organizations 1660, 1721, 1792, 2602, 2773, 8042, 8438, 9456, 9709, 9890, 10096, 10349, 10836, 11284, 11649, 11751, 11949, 12204, 12294, 12445, 12851, 13226, 13845, 15389, 16968, 17133, 17687, 19101, 19330
--Poland 12337
--Religious life 145, 12276, 18871
--Religious life--History 13351
--Scotland 494
Youth in church work 2577, 9723, 9905, 10469, 10974, 11907, 13475, 17028, 18550, 19141, 19330
--France 15093
Youth ministry >> See: Church work with youth
Youth--Runaways >> See: Runaways--Youth
Yugoslavia
--Religion 12105, 12353, 15677
--Religious life and customs 14466
--Social conditions--History 7052
Zacchaeus Collective 14495
Zaire
--Religious and ecclesiastical institutions 15531, 17908
--Social conditions 15455, 16909, 18671
Zambia
--Religion 15860
--Religious and ecclesiastical institutions 14210
--Social conditions 6918, 13632, 14998
Zen Buddhism 13785
Zimbabwe
--Social conditions 13118
Zionism 11716
--History 4264
Zone One Tondo Organization (Manila, Philippines) 12519, 13916
Zulu 12129, 12130, 17018, 17742
Zurich (Switzerland)
--History 15726
--Religious and ecclesiastical institutions 13071

About the Author

Loyde H. Hartley attended Otterbein College, Westerville, OH, from 1958 to 1962, receiving the AB degree. From 1962 to 1965, he pursued theological training at United Seminary, Dayton, OH. His Ph. D. studies were at Emory University, Atlanta, GA, with the degree being awarded in 1968.

He has served pastorates in Newark, DE, Dayton, OH, and Detroit, MI, the latter two being in the inner city. He chaired the Sociology Department at Union College, Barbourville, KY, from 1968 to 1971. From 1971 forward he has taught at Lancaster Theological Seminary, Lancaster, PA, where at various times he has held the positions of Director of Doctoral Studies, Director of the Research Center, and Academic Dean.

He is a member of the American Sociological Association, the Religious Research Association, and the Society for the Scientific Study of Religion. The author of several research reports and articles, he has previously written one book: Understanding Church Finances (Pilgrim Press, 1984).